THE COMPLETE

PINK FLOYD

THIS IS A CARLTON BOOK

First published in Great Britain in 2016 by
Carlton Books Limited
20 Mortimer Street
London W1T 3JW

A CIP catalogue for this book is available from the British Library.

Editorial: Caroline Curtis and Lisa Hughes
Designer: Laurence Bradbury
Art Editor: James Pople
Picture Research: Steve Behan
Production: Rachel Burgess
Project Editor: Matthew Lowing

ISBN 978-1-78097-651-8

Printed in China

10 9 8 7 6 5 4 3 2

THE COMPLETE
PINK FLOYD

GLENN POVEY

CARLTON
BOOKS

CONTENTS

PREFACE

The release of the album the *Endless River* in 2014 marked the culmination of Pink Floyd's hugely successful and unparalleled career, bookended at the outset by the tragic loss of Syd Barrett to mental illness in the first year of their professional career, and 40 years later the loss of Richard Wright, keyboard player and the musical cement that bound the group together. His contribution was memorialised with that release, officially Pink Floyd's last ever original album before David Gilmour and Nick Mason gracefully retired the band.

A year on and I am mindful that Pink Floyd have entered their official 50th anniversary year at time of writing. There is no question that the Pink Floyd story is a well-worn one and, as you might expect from any group that has existed for that length of time, much has been written of their career. This volume draws together details of their performances, recordings and solo careers as a complete reference work that has taken many years to research.

The band may cease to exist in any meaningful form but I doubt the Pink Floyd story will ever truly be complete for their fans as newly discovered archive material emerges, solo albums and tours are pursued. Pink Floyd will continue to enthral new generations and I can only hope that this book finds itself being read and enjoyed by fans old and new.

Glenn Povey,
Hertfordshire, 2015

For Harry and Emily

BELOW: PINK FLOYD, SPRING 1970.

DIARY DATES

Dates for all listed events are as accurate as possible based on available facts.

Much of the information is gleaned from contemporary press reports, the result of many weeks of research, coupled with a slice of good old detective work to help fill in the gaps.

Show set lists from Pink Floyd's earlier years are largely acquired from audience recordings, press reviews or first-hand recollections, the latter two of which may be inaccurate but are included in the absence of any other corroborative evidence and are therefore taken on trust.

Furthermore, it would be impossible to list all of Pink Floyd's, or indeed the precursor bands', earliest gigs with any degree of accuracy as most shows probably weren't publicized beyond the pub chalkboard, which means many more undocumented shows are certain to exist. I welcome any correspondence that helps to fill in the blanks or corrects my research.

RECORDING DATES

Working on the basis that if you don't ask, you don't get, for the first time in print, all of Pink Floyd's Abbey Road studio sessions are now accurately documented inside.

I am therefore extremely grateful to the members of Pink Floyd for granting me permission to research the archives at Abbey Road studios, and to Paul Loasby at One-Fifteen for making this possible. This information gives us a much clearer insight into the recording process.

Negotiations to achieve this took many, many months, and I'd like to thank Ian Pickavance at the Abbey Road tape library for his patience and assistance in helping me with the files and cross-checking facts.

In this volume the abbreviations RS and RM refer to the Abbey Road shorthand for Remix Stereo and Remix Mono respectively. The recording process is better explained elsewhere, but where it is stated a track is "reduced" it generally refers to the process whereby all of the available tracks, say 4-tracks, are used up (drums, vocals, guitar and keyboards for example), and then copied down to one single track, allowing an additional 3 tracks to be used for further overdubs of instruments and/or effects.

THANKS

For a work of this magnitude a huge debt of thanks is owed to a great many people who have generously provided contacts, personal recollections, items of memorabilia, photos and research material, however large or small. Their assistance is gratefully acknowledged, as are the contributors of the now-defunct *Brain Damage* magazine, which I founded in 1985 and which acted as the starting point for my own Pink Floyd odyssey.

A special word of thanks is extended to Warren Dosanjh, Mick Brown, David Parker and Stephen Pyle for their contacts, photos and recollections of the early Cambridge scene; the enthusiastic support of fellow Floyd researchers/ nutcases, including Marc-Olivier Becks, Walter Romanus Donati, Ron Fleischer, Nino Gatti and the rest of the Lunatics, Chris Leith, Chris Moise, Ed Paule, Eugene Reingold, Chris Job, Philip Waters and Elliot Tayman (for their unceasing and enthusiastic assistance, not to mention many hours in libraries on my behalf); Andy Neill for constantly turning up new stuff when he wasn't even looking for it; Johan Ral and Jos Bijnens for their help and contacts in researching Pink Floyd's early European adventures; and Julian Carr at the BBC Written Archives Centre.

Lastly, I am grateful to Carlton Books for their backing and support, especially Roland Hall, Malcolm Croft, Caroline Curtis, Matt Lowing, James Pople and Steve Behan for really getting behind this project and to Laurence at Bradbury & Williams for his design work.

For the most up-to-date news on Pink Floyd please visit: www.brain-damage.co.uk and www.pinkfloydz.com

ABOUT THE AUTHOR

Glenn Povey was the founder of the highly regarded Pink Floyd fan-magazine *Brain Damage*, which he edited between 1985 and 1993. He was responsible for launching the career of the Australian Pink Floyd Show, a band he subsequently managed for two years following their debut UK concert at the first International Pink Floyd Fan Convention, an event he organized at Wembley Stadium Conference Centre in 1993.

Much to his loved-ones' distress, Glenn went on to further moral ruin in the music industry, initially working as a booking agent and promoter for a variety of artists including the Electric Prunes, Caravan, Gong, Hawkwind, Magma, Ozric Tentacles, Porcupine Tree, the Pretty Things and the Seeds. He also promoted the Canterbury Fayre rock festival, headlined in its fourth and final year by Roy Harper and Robert Plant.

In 2002, he successfully re-launched the career of the legendary rock icon Arthur Lee and, acting in a management capacity, toured with the band Love across the world for three years, an experience from which he has never fully recovered. Despite this he still cites *Forever Changes* as one of his all-time favourite albums.

Thereafter Glenn continued to "potter about" in the live music industry working on tours with artists as diverse as Adam Ant, Jon Anderson & Rick Wakeman and Aswad, but after one Alexander O'Neal show too many, and fearful of losing his mind completely, he went into theatre management. There is little evidence to suggest this has made any difference.

Throughout this incredible saga one constant remained in his life, for which the medical profession could prescribe no assistance: Pink Floyd. As an incurable fan he wrote the universally-acclaimed book *Echoes: The Complete History of Pink Floyd* in 2007 and the *Treasures of Pink Floyd* in 2012. He has also written extensively on the band for a variety of music magazines including *Classic Rock*, *Mojo* and *Record Collector*.

He lives in Hertfordshire, England.

1 REMEMBER WHEN YOU WERE YOUNG

1962–67

CAMBRIDGE 1962–67

ABOVE: BARRETT PICTURED AT MORLEY MEMORIAL JUNIOR SCHOOL, CIRCA 1959.

Although Pink Floyd didn't enjoy widespread public recognition until 1967, their roots can be traced as far back as the very early 1960s and an ever-growing circle of interrelated groups and musicians based in and around the cosmopolitan university city of Cambridge located in the east of England.

Cambridge in the 1960s had an incredibly vibrant social scene and many up-and-coming bands flourished on both the university and town circuit. In many ways the university was responsible for a large part of Britain's popular culture, spearheaded by the Footlights Dramatic Club, whose members included the likes of Peter Cook, Eric Idle (of Monty Python) and Tim Brooke-Taylor and Graeme Garden (both of the Goodies). It also gave us a fair share of future presidents, prime ministers, politicians and Soviet spies. But music, as always, was at the core and it produced many internationally renowned musicians from both "town" and "gown".

Among those, post-war, were two of the founder members of Pink Floyd who grew up there: Syd Barrett (born Roger Keith Barrett in Cambridge on Sunday 6 January 1946), and Roger Waters (born George Roger Waters in Great Bookham, Surrey on Monday 6 September 1943). Waters and Barrett were childhood friends, despite the age gap, having been brought together as a result of Waters' mother, Mary, who taught at Morley Memorial Junior School which they both attended.

Both subsequently went on to study at the Cambridgeshire High School For Boys – known as the County – and both were far from model students. Indeed Waters' nemesis and later inspiration for the Teacher character in *The Wall* film was its headmaster Mr Eagling, known to his pupils as "the Beak", or "Beaky". Within his punishment record book canings were recorded for both Waters (for "interfering with boys in the year below", i.e. bullying) and Barrett (for "skiving/lateness").

Barrett was popular among his peer group, and by his mid-teens the family home in Hills Road, Cambridge became host to Sunday afternoon gatherings of his friends. Like so many of their age, they listened avidly to Radio Luxembourg, and played along with makeshift instruments to their latest musical finds – mainly American rock 'n' roll singles – acquired from Millers Music store or indirectly from the hundreds of US Air Force personnel whose bases littered the area. If they were lucky they showed off playing their first acoustic guitars. Barrett, as well as being the youngest in the family, was also the only child still at home, his two sisters and brother having long since moved away. His mother was tolerant and welcomed the company his friends gave him, not only because of this, but also because of his father's recent death.

School friend Albert "Albie" Prior fondly remembered Barrett at that time: "I was at Cambridge High School in the sixties and Syd was a year younger than me at the school. He was artistic, creative and friendly. An incident that sticks in my mind for some reason is a group of us being in the school toilets [bathrooms], of all places, and Syd saying that he wanted to get into a group and asking (as I was already in the Ramblers) what it involved and in particular what sort of haircut was best."[1]

In March of that year Barrett joined his first band, Geoff Mott & the Mottoes, when he was just 16 years old, along with drummer Clive Welham and bassist Tony Sainty. Typical of most teenage groups, they rehearsed in bedrooms and aspired to becoming famous pop stars, without actually performing that much, or not at all.

Band leader Geoff Mott was three years older than Barrett, and something of a minor celebrity on the Cambridge scene, having been expelled from school for his outlandish behaviour. His apparent arrogance and imposing stature made him the natural choice of front man. "Syd wasn't a bad rhythm guitarist," remembered Mott. "It was nice to hear someone who could play as opposed to thumping around."[2]

The Mottoes' only known public performance was at the Friends Meeting House in Cambridge on Sunday 11 March 1962 in support of a demonstration march through the city

LEFT: THE 7TH CAMBRIDGE (COUNTY SCHOOL) SCOUT GROUP PICTURED AT THEIR ANNUAL CAMP AT HOLKHAM NEAR WELLS, NORFOLK IN AUGUST 1958. BARRETT IS THIRD FROM LEFT ON THE BOTTOM ROW.

OPPOSITE: AN EARLY INCARNATION OF PINK FLOYD ON STAGE IN OCTOBER 1965. FROM LEFT: ROGER "SYD" BARRETT, RADOVAN "BOB" KLOSE, CHRIS DENNIS, ROGER WATERS.

by the Cambridge Youth Campaign for Nuclear Disarmament (CYCND). The march itself was widely reported in the Cambridge press, but unfortunately the Mottoes' performance was not, and is therefore based entirely on recollection. Coincidentally, future Pink Floyd member Roger Waters, as an active member of the CYCND, designed the poster, and it is from here that he also began a relationship with his future first wife Judith "Judy" Trim, who was secretary to the organization. (Judy Trim is pictured with Waters on the inner sleeve of Pink Floyd's 1969 album *Ummagumma*.) Although the band aspired to further performances, it was not to be. Geoff Mott went on to form the Boston Crabs, and is remembered by some as the first Cambridge band to get a record deal (with EMI), but shortly after a string of singles, including their May 1965 cover of Leiber and Stoller's 'Mexico Way', they split up. Bass player Fred Friedlein went on to found the bass/guitar amplification company Trace Elliot in 1979.

It was not until the summer of 1964, while in his final few months as a student at Cambridgeshire College of Arts and Technology, that Barrett joined another group: Those Without (named after the Francoise Sagan novel, *Those Without Shadows*). The band was managed by educated drop-out Warren Dosanjh, who worked tirelessly to secure the band bookings across the locality.

In fact, Those Without had been going since June 1963, formed from the ashes of Hollerin' Blues (the band Barrett has incorrectly been described as a member of) and rehearsing at drummer Stephen Pyle's house as well

as the back rooms of the Midland Tavern and Ancient Druids pubs in Cambridge. And, unlike most bands of the era it wasn't strictly covers of the latest chart hits, but American R&B acts such as Chuck Berry, Jimmy Reed, Bo Diddley, John Lee Hooker and the like.

However, Barrett's tenure with the group was patchy at best. He had enrolled into a fine art course at Camberwell School of Arts and Crafts in London, which began in late September 1964, and played only when time permitted or when he was able to return to Cambridge at the weekends.

Following his initial foray with Geoff Mott & the Mottoes, drummer Clive Welham helped form the Ramblers with guitarist Albert "Albie" Prior, John Gordon, Richard Baker and Chris "Jim" Marriot. "In those days we basically played the music of The Shadows and similar groups," recalled Prior. "It was a time when groups had one singer rather than everyone joining in. I recall early Fenders, Vox amps and drum kits that were very basic. I think that just about our first gig was a church hall on Cherry Hinton Road, Cambridge, not far from where Syd eventually lived for some time. This was the first time we publicly used the Watkins Copycat echo chamber, which allowed us to get The Shadows' 'Wonderful Land' just right. Other gigs that I remember were the University May Balls, the Guildhall and Corn Exchange at Cambridge, supporting major acts and also playing at the Town Hall in Newmarket, with jockey's fighting on the dance floor. We and our gear travelled in a little van, owned by our 'manager', Mick Turner."[3]

TOP LEFT: THOSE WITHOUT, SEPTEMBER 1965. FROM LEFT: ROGER "SYD" BARRETT, ROBERT "SMUDGE" SMITH, STEVE PYLE.

BELOW: THE RAMBLERS, PRE-DAVID GILMOUR, SUMMER 1962. FROM LEFT: RICHARD BAKER, MERVYN MARRIOT, CHRIS "JIM" MARRIOT, ALBERT "ALBIE" PRIOR, CLIVE WELHAM, JOHN GORDON, MICK TURNER.

Cambridge was also the hometown of David Gilmour (born David Jon Gilmour in Cambridge on Wednesday 6 March 1946), and it was Welham who first introduced him to Barrett at the Cambridgeshire College of Arts and Technology. Barrett had already done a year of study in Art and Design and Gilmour enrolled in 1963 for one year in order to sit Modern Languages. They became good friends in their year of study: "We spent a lot of time together listening to the same music," recalled Gilmour. "Our influences are probably pretty much the same and I was a couple of streets ahead of him at the time and was teaching him to play Stones riffs."[4] It is surprising therefore that they never formed a band together. The Ramblers' split in early 1964, when Clive Welham and John Gordon joined Gilmour in creating Jokers Wild.

As a consequence of the Ramblers erratic schedule, Gilmour – he never considered himself an actual member, more of a part-time substitute as and when requested – was able to perform simultaneously with the Newcomers, an instrumental jazz band, where his ability soon earned him an excellent reputation on the local scene and which often saw him act as a stand-in for absent band members in many other groups.

THE DOROTHY CAMBRIDGE APPROX 1965
DAVID GILMOUR-GUITAR
2nd-GUITAR
DICK PARRY-SAX
PETER PARKER-BASS

The Newcomers had already been performing some time prior to Gilmour joining in January 1963, with members Dave Thaxter, Chris Ian Culpin, Dave Hurst and singer Susan Hodson, whose father was the manager of the Airport Hotel where rehearsals took place on Sunday afternoons. Their busy schedule ensured Gilmour's place as a fully paid up member of the band, which at that time was performing covers of popular jazz/orchestral standards of the day, including 'Midnight In Moscow', 'Yes, My Darling Daughter' and 'Ain't She Sweet'. Then, under successive managers David Hurst and Nigel Smith, the Newcomers updated their repertoire to include cover versions of Beatles and other Merseybeat numbers while Gilmour also introduced Shadows and Duane Eddy numbers to their set.

Like most bands of the era the line-up was very fluid and could contain any number of musicians depending on who was available that day. By late summer 1963 Chris Ian took over the management and booking duties of the band and the group became known as Chris Ian & the Newcomers, his

BELOW LEFT: JOKERS WILD, SEPTEMBER 1964. FROM LEFT: DAVID GILMOUR, DAVID ALTHAM, JOHN GORDON.

RIGHT: JOKERS WILD, SEPTEMBER 1964. FROM LEFT: DAVID GILMOUR, DAVID ALTHAM, JOHN GORDON, TONY SAINTY.

name writ large on the bass drum.

Vocalist Ken Waterson (stage name Kenny Lennon) recalled, "We used to support a lot of Cambridge bands. We never got any money for it. This guy Chris Ian, any money we got he had, it went on equipment. We'd be up on stage and some bloody great ruck would start in the audience with these American servicemen punching the crap out of each other."[5]

The group effectively ceased toward the end of 1963 when Culpin and Thaxter left the band to form Blues Anonymous. Gilmour left shortly thereafter following an altercation with Waterson.

Some of the rest of the band soldiered on as the Newcomers for a further few weeks, primarily to fulfil existing contractual engagements, and recruited various stand-ins including future Pink Floyd associates Radovan "Bob" Klose, John "Willie" Wilson and Dick Parry (whose other band Soul Committee featured future Floyd road manager Alan Styles).

It was from this large pool of musicians that Jokers Wild was formed, comprising David Altham, Tony Sainty, Clive Welham, John Gordon and David Gilmour. They are regarded as one of the Cambridge scene's most successful semi-pro groups, and they are the one with which Gilmour is most widely associated. They soon gained a loyal following as a result of a series of residencies at the fashionable Dorothy and Victoria ballrooms in the centre of the city, both of which hosted weekly dances, aimed primarily at students attending the University.

"We did R&B, harmony pieces, Beach Boys, Four Seasons, which seemed to appeal to a wide audience," remembered drummer Clive Welham fondly. "We didn't do any of our own material, no one did in those days. People used to write songs and then get bands to do them. We used to do Beatles numbers as well."[6]

Come the New Year the band resumed their residency and, along with other engagements, were enjoying steady work. Taking a break over the University summer holidays, Gilmour joined a group of Cambridge friends in August 1965 – including band-mate David Altham, Roger "Syd" Barrett, Nick Jervis, Frank Hinsley and Mick Lambourn-Brown – on a busking holiday to the south of France, travelling in a beat-up Landrover. Initially they went to St Tropez at the invitation of Claude Picasso, son of the famous artist, who was studying English at Cambridge and an ardent supporter of the band. Apart from devoting time in trying to search out the starlet Brigitte Bardot, the only remarkable event of their activities was a run-in with the local police for busking, as Lambourn-Brown recalled: "Within a few minutes we had a crowd of over 100. Syd and the two Davids played all the latest Beatles numbers while Frank, Nick, and myself sang and collected money. After only 20 minutes the crowd had risen to over 300. But then after 30 minutes the Gendarmes arrived. Frank and myself were arrested while the other four did a runner! Two hours on and Claude came to our rescue."[7]

From there the group found themselves travelling north towards Paris, arriving at a campsite on the outskirts. "We used to drive into the Left Bank most days and busk. After a week or so and the money running dry we decided to head on home back to Cambridge."[8]

Confident the band could succeed, they then headed to the Regent Sounds Studio in London's Denmark Street, to record some of their repertoire, followed by a session for Jonathan

TOP LEFT: GILMOUR MODELLING THE LATEST FASHIONS FOR VARSITY, THE CAMBRIDGE UNIVERSITY NEWSPAPER, JUNE 1966.

BELOW: JOKERS WILD PERFORMING AT THE VICTORIA BALLROOM, 24 FEBRUARY 1965. FROM LEFT: DAVID GILMOUR, DAVID ALTHAM, JOHN GORDON, TONY SAINTY, CLIVE WELHAM.

CHRIS CHENEY

THE JOKERS WILD, one of the town groups, playing at the Victoria Ballroom last Wednesday evening.

King at Decca towards the end of the year where a recording of Sam And Dave's US hit 'You Don't Know Like I Know' was made, but the original was released in the UK in January 1966, thwarting any hope of chart success for Jokers Wild.

This fact sealed their fate overnight and although they continued to perform with the occasional high it was a downhill ride. Tony Sainty left the band in early 1966 and was replaced by Peter Gilmour, David's brother, who had already been a regular stand-in.

The band also began changing its sound. "[We were] getting work at US Air Force bases," recalled John Gordon, "and we introduced more soul, R&B and Tamla Motown numbers into our repertoire by artists including Otis Redding, Wilson Pickett, Chuck Berry, Betty Everett and British band the Spencer Davis Group."[9]

Welham remembers the band briefly progressing to the débutante scene, performing at London society parties and other high–profile gigs: "We drove to London with two coach-loads of fans from Cambridge and did a gig with the Animals at an art college. It was a sizeable audience, about 800 crammed in. We did two 15-minute sets and they did about an hour. We did an Admiralty League at the Dorchester in London, all upper-crust types with Rolls Royces and Bentleys everywhere."[10]

But Welham's departure from the group wasn't far behind Sainty's: he suffered a nervous breakdown trying to hold down a full-time job at the same time as travelling to and from venues. John "Willie" Wilson had been deputizing for him on occasion since April, but with Welham's condition worsening he now took over full time.

However, it wasn't long before Peter Gilmour and John Gordon, another defector to art college, also quit. With Jokers Wild effectively over, Gilmour took the opportunity to leave Cambridge altogether and seek a new life in London. There he met John-Paul Salvatore (brother-in-law of Tony Secunda, infamous manager of the Move), who offered Gilmour and his former band mates John "Willie" Wilson, David Altham and new recruit Richard "Rick" Wills, playing under the moniker Bullit, a run of dates at the newly opened Sybilla's nightclub just off Piccadilly Circus in London. This then led to the offer of a three-month residency at the Los Monteros Hotel in Marbella, Spain, but after a long overland haul by train they were met by a hotel that was half-built and a club that wasn't fully furnished.

"He was always suggesting new things," recalled Gilmour of Salvatore. "He said we had to have a name that was tough and hard, so we became Bullit. Then he said [adopts cockney accent], 'It's all flower power now, so from now on, you're Flowers.' These things are all far more prosaic than you'd like to imagine."[11]

When they returned to the UK after the summer season
Altham quit the band, leaving the trio of Gilmour, Wilson and Wills to continue. They returned to the continent – France

to be precise – possibly because of Gilmour's language skills and worked around the French Riviera as well as a residency at the Jean-Jacques Hotel in St Etienne, France. Somewhere along the way they performed at a ball for a member of the Dutch royal family in the Netherlands and are said to have performed on some demos for French rock 'n' roller Johnny Hallyday. Again, recordings are unlikely to have survived, Hallyday being notorious for recording with just about anyone that happened to be passing through town.

Eventually Flowers settled in Paris, securing a three-month residency at the Bilboquet club in the fashionable St Germain district of Paris. Of the type of material the band performed in their latter period, Gilmour recalled in an interview with *Record Collector*, "We did a lot of soul: Wilson Pickett, the Four Tops and one or two Beach Boys type things. We had some mics stolen in France and I had to zoom back to London to buy some new ones. I went to a club called Blaises in South Kensington and saw Hendrix by chance, jamming with the Brian Auger Trinity [Wednesday 21 December 1966]. It was amazing. So we started to do Hendrix things as well. We did nearly all of *Are You Experienced*."[12]

But living off a pittance in an expensive city was taking its toll. Gilmour's health hit rock-bottom to the point he was forced to seek medical attention for malnutrition. In the early summer of 1967 the band decided to head back home for good. "We were heading for Calais and we didn't have enough money for petrol," Gilmour recalled. "We actually stopped at a building site and siphoned diesel out of a tank into our old Ford Thames van… And at Dover it wouldn't start again so we had to push the van off the ferry. I felt a bit defeated at that point."[13]

Gilmour resisted the temptation of returning to Cambridge, preferring to stay in London, even paying a visit to his old friend Barrett, who was recording 'See Emily Play' with Pink Floyd at Sound Techniques on Thursday 18 May. It wasn't a happy reunion. Barrett was already showing signs of a personality shift and barely spoke to him.

Jokers Wild played one last show in Cambridge on Friday 16 June 1967. This was Gilmour's last known appearance with any band before joining Pink Floyd in early 1968. In later years Wilson would go on to join Sutherland Brothers & Quiver and Wills enjoyed a long career performing with Peter Frampton, Roxy Music and Foreigner to name but a few.

1. Letter from Albert Prior to the author, April 1998.

2. *Crazy Diamond. Syd Barrett & The Dawn of Pink Floyd* by Pete Anderson and Mike Watkinson, Omnibus 1991.

3. Letter from Albert Prior to the author, April 1998.

4. *Mojo*, May 1994.

5. Author interview with Ken Waterson, September 1996.

6. Author interview with Clive Welham, October 1996.

7–9. *I Spy Syd in Cambridge* by Warren Dosanjh.

10. Author interview with Clive Welham, October 1996.

11–13. *Record Collector*, May 2003.

GEOFF MOTT & THE MOTTOES [1962]

Roger "Syd" Barrett (Rhythm Guitar), "Nobby" Clarke (Guitar), Geoff Mott (Vocals), Tony Sainty (Bass Guitar), Clive Welham (Drums).

Little is known of Geoff Mott and the Mottoes but interviewed by *Melody Maker* in October 1967, Syd Barrett recalled that, "At 15 I took a dramatic step forward, becoming the proud possessor of an electric guitar, with a small amplifier that I made myself. And with this kit, which I fitted into a cabinet, I joined my first group – Geoff Mott and the Mottoes – playing at parties and the like around my home town of Cambridge."

SUNDAY 11 MARCH 1962 – PERFORMANCE
Friends Meeting House, Cambridge, England
This is believed to have been the band's only public show.

THE RAMBLERS [1962–1963]

Richard Baker (Bass Guitar), David Gilmour (from November 1962, replacing Albert "Albie" Prior), John Gordon (Rhythm Guitar), Chris "Jim" Marriot (Vocals), Mervyn Marriot (Guitar), Albert "Albie" Prior (Guitar, to November 1963), Clive Welham (Drums).

When Albert Prior left the band in late 1962, to take up employment in London, he was replaced by David Gilmour at the suggestion of Welham, a fellow student at the Perse Preparatory School for Boys, despite being two years his senior. It is believed Gilmour's first show with the band was on Tuesday 13 November 1962.

TUESDAY 13 NOVEMBER 1962 – PERFORMANCE
The King's Head public house, Fen Ditton, near Cambridge, England

The Ramblers were advertised in the local press as performing every Tuesday night from this date, although it is uncertain when their residency ended because no further press adverts appeared for the group.

SATURDAY 24 NOVEMBER 1962 – PERFORMANCE
Youth Club, Free Church Hall, Cambridge, England

SATURDAY 1 DECEMBER 1962 – PERFORMANCE
The Guildhall, Cambridge, England

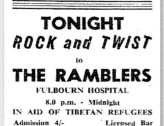

TONIGHT
ROCK and TWIST
to
THE RAMBLERS
FULBOURN HOSPITAL
8.0 p.m. - Midnight
IN AID OF TIBETAN REFUGEES
Admission 4/-   Licensed Bar

SATURDAY 15 DECEMBER 1962 – PERFORMANCE ◄
Staff Social Club, Fulbourn Hospital, Fulbourn, near Cambridge, England
A benefit in aid of Tibetan refugees.

SATURDAY 16 FEBRUARY 1963 – PERFORMANCE
Memorial Hall, Great Shelford, near Cambridge, England

THURSDAY 7 MARCH 1963 – PERFORMANCE
Victoria Ballroom, Cambridge, England
With the Sundowners.

MONDAY 15 APRIL 1963 – PERFORMANCE ►
Free Church Hall, Sawston, near Cambridge, England

THURSDAY 16 MAY 1963 – PERFORMANCE
Victoria Ballroom, Cambridge, England
Supporting the Worryin' Kind.

ROCK TO THE
RAMBLERS
on
EASTER MONDAY
15th April
at
SAWSTON CHURCH HALL
8-11.30 Refreshments Adm. 4/-

FRIDAY 2 AUGUST 1963 – PERFORMANCE
Rex Ballroom, Cambridge, England
With Steve Francis and the London Strollers.

SATURDAY 17 AUGUST 1963 – PERFORMANCE
Rex Ballroom, Cambridge, England
With Rikki & the Caravells.

SATURDAY 21 SEPTEMBER 1963 – PERFORMANCE
Assembly Hall, Melbourn Primary School, Melbourn, near Royston, England

SATURDAY 12 OCTOBER 1963 – PERFORMANCE
Village Hall, Harston, near Cambridge, England
Supporting the Hi-Fis.

SUNDAY 13 OCTOBER 1963 – PERFORMANCE
ABC Regal, Cambridge, England
Opening act for the Billy Fury package tour with Joe Brown & the Bruvvers, the Karl Denver Trio, the Tornados, Marty Wilde & His Wildcats, Daryl Quist, Dickie Pride and Larry Burns.

THE NEWCOMERS [1962–1963]

Johnny Barnes (Rhythm Guitar, from early 1963 replacing Dave Hurst), Roger Bibby (Bass Guitar, from January 1963), Radovan "Bob" Klose (Guitar, Vocals from October 1963), Chris-Ian Culpin (Drums from early 1963 to September 1963), Richard "Dick" Fletcher (Trumpet, to late 1964), David Gilmour (Guitar, Vocals from January to September 1963), Susan Hodson (Vocals, to early 1963), Dave Hurst (Piano, until early 1963), Johnny Philips (Vocals, from July 1963), Dave Thaxter (Saxophone, Clarinet, Vocals, from early 1962 to September 1963), Ken Waterson (aka Kenny Lennon) (Vocals, from July 1963), John "Willie" Wilson (Drums, from October 1963 replacing Chris-Ian Culpin). *Note:* Only shows that are believed to have featured David Gilmour are listed and this is therefore not an exhaustive list of Newcomers engagements. Many of the shows were billed as Chris Ian & the Newcomers.

ABOVE: THE NEWCOMERS PERFORMING AT AN UNKNOWN VALENTINES BALL FEBRUARY 1963. FROM LEFT: DICK FLETCHER, DAVID THAXTER, JOHNNY BARNES, CHRIS-IAN, DAVID GILMOUR, ROGER BIBBY.

SATURDAY 26 JANUARY 1963 – PERFORMANCE
Memorial Hall, Fulbourn, near Cambridge, England

SATURDAY 16 MARCH 1963 – PERFORMANCE
The Guildhall, Cambridge, England
Supporting Mark Arnold & the Dawnbreakers.

SATURDAY 23 MARCH 1963 – PERFORMANCE
Village Hall, Dry Drayton, near Cambridge, England
Band supporter Edward Burman recalled that, "The Beatles LP *Please Please Me* was released on 22 March 1963 and the next day, a Saturday, the band learned all the songs on Side 1 in the TA Drill Hall on Coldham's Lane [Cambridge]. That evening we drove to Dry Drayton and the band played all the songs in the same sequence as on the LP. The local girls were delirious. The Newcomers' line-up that night was Chris-Ian, Johnny Barnes, David Gilmour, Ken Waterson and Roger Bibby."

SATURDAY 4 MAY 1963 – PERFORMANCE
The Guildhall, Cambridge, England
Supporting Johnny Philips & the Swinging Hi-Fis.

SATURDAY 25 MAY 1963 – PERFORMANCE
Village Hall, Trumpington, near Cambridge, England

MONDAY 27 MAY 1963 – PERFORMANCE
Lower Hall, St. Andrew's Street Baptist Church, Cambridge, England

SATURDAY 8 JUNE 1963 – PERFORMANCE
Rex Ballroom, Cambridge, England
Billed as "Chris Ian And The Newcomers with Kenny Lennon vocal", with the Roy Dennis Orchestra Twists.

SATURDAY 3 AUGUST 1963 – PERFORMANCE
Rex Ballroom, Cambridge, England
With the Prowlers.

SATURDAY 24 AUGUST 1963 – PERFORMANCE
Rex Ballroom, Cambridge, England
With Rikki Elwin & the Kobalts.

SATURDAY 5 OCTOBER 1963 – PERFORMANCE ▼
Rex Ballroom, Cambridge, England
With the Johnny Quantrose 5.

Open 7.30 **REX BALLROOM** Sat. 5th Oct.
SATURDAY DOUBLE STAR ATTRACTION
THE JOHNNY QUANTROSE "5"
PLUS
THE NEWCOMERS
Bar and Buffet   Ladies 3/6, Gentlemen 4/6

JOKERS WILD
[1964–1967] ▶

David Altham (Guitar, Saxophone, Keyboards, Vocals), David Gilmour (Guitar, Vocals, Harmonica), Peter Gilmour (Bass Guitar, Vocals, occasional substitute and then replacement for Tony Sainty from early 1966), John Gordon (Rhythm Guitar, Vocals to early 1966), Tony Sainty (Bass Guitar, Vocals, to early 1966), Clive Welham (Drums, Vocals, to early 1966), Jeff Whittaker (Congas, Percussion, from early 1966), John "Willie" Wilson (Drums, replacing Clive Welham from early 1966).

5-PIECE VOCAL HARMONY
Jokers Wild
Bookings: D. J. GILMOUR • Tel. 59510.
109 Grantchester Meadows, Cambridge.

TUESDAY 28, THURSDAY 30, FRIDAY 31 JULY, SATURDAY 1, TUESDAY 4, THURSDAY 6, FRIDAY 7, SATURDAY 8, TUESDAY 11, THURSDAY 13, FRIDAY 14, SATURDAY 15, TUESDAY 18, THURSDAY 20, FRIDAY 21, SATURDAY 22, TUESDAY 25, THURSDAY 27, FRIDAY 28, SATURDAY 29 AUGUST, TUESDAY 2, FRIDAY 4 SEPTEMBER 1964 – PERFORMANCES ▼
Blue Horizon Club, **The Guildhall, Cambridge, England**
Jokers Wild's first known set of engagements was a residency at the Guildhall appearing with the Dawnbreakers.

SATURDAY 5 SEPTEMBER 1964 – PERFORMANCE
Dorothy Ballroom, Cambridge, England
With Bob Kidman & His Orchestra and Eric Squires & His Quartet (*Ballroom*), Squad 5 and the Prestons (*Beat Room*), Jokers Wild and the Beat Syndicate (*Jive Hive*).
Weekly dances at the spacious Dorothy Ballroom often made use of three rooms for different types of bands. The Ballroom was set aside for dance bands and both the "Beat Room" and "Jive Hive" for contemporary bands, the latter of which is where Jokers Wild usually performed.

SATURDAY 19 SEPTEMBER 1964 – PERFORMANCE ▶
Dorothy Ballroom, Cambridge, England
With Bob Kidman & His Orchestra and Eric Squires & His Quartet (*Ballroom*), Squad 5 and Monica & the Vulcans (*Beat Room*), Jokers Wild and Andy & the Paliminos (*Jive Hive*).

COME DANCING **Dorothy** SIDNEY STREET
AT THE   CAMBRIDGE
TONIGHT
★ BOB KIDMAN AND HIS ORCHESTRA
★ SQUAD FIVE
★ THE NIGHTFLIGHTS
THIS SATURDAY
★ BOB KIDMAN AND HIS ORCHESTRA
★ ERIC SQUIRES AND HIS QUARTET
★ SQUAD FIVE
★ JOKERS WILD
★ THE SEMINOLES
★ KEITH POWELL AND THE VALETS

WEDNESDAY 30 SEPTEMBER 1964 – PERFORMANCE
Les Jeux Interdits, Victoria Ballroom, Cambridge, England

Jokers Wild began performing at what would become their longest running residency.

THURSDAY 1 OCTOBER 1964 – AUDITION
London, England

It was reported in the *Cambridge News* that Gilmour had attended a recording session/audition with producer Lionel Bart on this day. Nothing further came from the session and it is uncertain how it was initiated in the first place. It has also been reported that a session took place in this period for Rolling Stones' manager Andrew "Loog" Oldham with future Pretty Things members John Povey and Wally Waller, although no recordings are believed to have survived.

WEDNESDAY 7 OCTOBER 1964 – PERFORMANCE
Les Jeux Interdits, Victoria Ballroom, Cambridge, England

An advert in the local press promoting the club announced "Now resident – the ever popular Jokers Wild – Every Wednesday."

SATURDAY 10 OCTOBER 1964 – PERFORMANCE
Dorothy Ballroom, Cambridge, England

With Bob Kidman & His Orchestra and Eric Squires & His Quartet (*Ballroom*), Squad 5 and Jokers Wild (*Beat Room*), the Seminoles and Keith Powell & the Valets (*Jive Hive*).

WEDNESDAY 14 OCTOBER 1964 – PERFORMANCE
Les Jeux Interdits, Victoria Ballroom, Cambridge, England

Having only just secured their residency, band member David Altham, a second-year student at Trinity College, was suspended (or "rusticated" in University terms) for 12 days and gated until the end of the term, having been found in bed with a girl in his lodgings. It was reported that, "David Altham sings and plays the saxophone for the 'Jokers Wild', a town-university beat group, who have had to cancel their engagements until next term, including a weekly date at the Victoria."

WEDNESDAY 6 JANUARY 1965 – PERFORMANCE
Les Jeux Interdits, Victoria Ballroom, Cambridge, England

This is the first recorded engagement following David Altham's rustication and their appearance was announced as "Resident again, the ever popular Jokers Wild."

WEDNESDAY 13 JANUARY 1965 – PERFORMANCE
Les Jeux Interdits, Victoria Ballroom, Cambridge, England

WEDNESDAY 20 JANUARY 1965 – PERFORMANCE
Les Jeux Interdits, Victoria Ballroom, Cambridge, England

WEDNESDAY 27 JANUARY 1965 – PERFORMANCE
Les Jeux Interdits, Victoria Ballroom, Cambridge, England

SATURDAY 30 JANUARY 1965 – PERFORMANCE
Dorothy Ballroom, Cambridge, England

With Bob Kidman & His Orchestra (*Ballroom*), Mark Arnold & the Dawnbreakers and the Worryin' Kind (*Beat Room*), Jokers Wild and the Blobs (*Jive Hive*).

WEDNESDAY 10 FEBRUARY 1965 – PERFORMANCE
Les Jeux Interdits, Victoria Ballroom, Cambridge, England

SATURDAY 13 FEBRUARY 1965 – PERFORMANCE
Dorothy Ballroom, Cambridge, England

With Bob Kidman & His Orchestra and Eric Squires & His Quartet (*Ballroom*), Larry Bond & The Trojans and Guitars Incorporated (*Beat Room*), Jokers Wild and Johnny Dean & the Deacons (*Jive Hive*).

WEDNESDAY 17 FEBRUARY 1965 – PERFORMANCE
Les Jeux Interdits, Victoria Ballroom, Cambridge, England

FRIDAY 19 FEBRUARY 1965 – PERFORMANCE ▼
The Valentine Ball [Caius College], The Guildhall and Corn Exchange, Cambridge, England

With Tommy Kinsman, Ivan Chin's West Indian Band, cabaret and tombola.

THE VALENTINE BALL

Friday, 19th February, 1965

THREE BANDS   Tommy Kinsman
                             Jokers Wild
                             Ivan Chin's West Indian Band

CABARET
CANDLELIGHT
BAR & BUFFET
TOMBOLA

Guildhall and Corn Exchange

9.30 p.m.   –   2.30 a.m.

TICKETS 3 gns. - Apply: A. WALLS, Caius.

MONDAY 22 FEBRUARY 1965 – PERFORMANCE
The Old English Gentleman public house, Harston, near Cambridge, England

WEDNESDAY 24 FEBRUARY 1965 – PERFORMANCE
Les Jeux Interdits, Victoria Ballroom, Cambridge, England

SATURDAY 27 FEBRUARY 1965 – PERFORMANCE
Dorothy Ballroom, Cambridge, England

With Bob Kidman & His Orchestra and Eric Squires & His Quartet (*Ballroom*), Jokers Wild and The Sonnets (*Beat Room*), the Country Cousins and the Dawnbreakers (*Jive Hive*).

WEDNESDAY 3 MARCH 1965 – PERFORMANCE
Les Jeux Interdits, Victoria Ballroom, Cambridge, England

WEDNESDAY 10 MARCH 1965 – PERFORMANCE
Les Jeux Interdits, Victoria Ballroom, Cambridge, England

WEDNESDAY 17 MARCH 1965 – PERFORMANCE
Les Jeux Interdits, Victoria Ballroom, Cambridge, England

WEDNESDAY 24 MARCH 1965 – PERFORMANCE
Les Jeux Interdits, Victoria Ballroom, Cambridge, England

FRIDAY 26 MARCH 1965 – PERFORMANCE
The Racehorse public house, Cambridge, England

SATURDAY 27 MARCH 1965 – PERFORMANCE
Dorothy Ballroom, Cambridge, England

With Bob Kidman & His Orchestra and the Eric Squires Quartet (*Ballroom*), the Jury Men and Johnny Cullen & The Country Cousins (*Beat Room*), Jokers Wild and the Prowlers (*Jive Hive*).

WEDNESDAY 7 APRIL 1965 – PERFORMANCE
Les Jeux Interdits, Victoria Ballroom, Cambridge, England

SATURDAY 10 APRIL 1965 – PERFORMANCE
Dorothy Ballroom, Cambridge, England

With Bob Kidman & His Orchestra and the Eric Squires Quartet (*Ballroom*), the Country Cousins and the Plebs (*Beat Room*), Jokers Wild and Patrick Dane Club 69 (*Jive Hive*).

WEDNESDAY 14 APRIL 1965 – PERFORMANCE
Les Jeux Interdits, Victoria Ballroom, Cambridge, England

WEDNESDAY 21 APRIL 1965 – PERFORMANCE
Les Jeux Interdits, Victoria Ballroom, Cambridge, England

WEDNESDAY 28 APRIL 1965 – PERFORMANCE
Les Jeux Interdits, Victoria Ballroom, Cambridge, England

WEDNESDAY 5 MAY 1965 – PERFORMANCE
Les Jeux Interdits, Victoria Ballroom, Cambridge, England

SATURDAY 8 MAY 1965 – PERFORMANCE
Dorothy Ballroom, Cambridge, England

With Bob Kidman & His Orchestra (*Ballroom*), the Tykes and the Mamtas (*Beat Room*), Jokers Wild and Fernando & the Hideaways (*Jive Hive*).

TONIGHT AND EVERY WEDNESDAY
LES JEUX INTERDITS
WITH
JOKERS WILD
CAMBRIDGE'S INTERNATIONAL RENDEZVOUS
VICTORIA 8·30 - MIDNIGHT

WEDNESDAY 12 MAY 1965 – PERFORMANCE ▲
Les Jeux Interdits, Victoria Ballroom, Cambridge, England

WEDNESDAY 19 MAY 1965 – PERFORMANCE
Les Jeux Interdits, Victoria Ballroom, Cambridge, England

WEDNESDAY 2 JUNE 1965 – PERFORMANCE
Les Jeux Interdits, Victoria Ballroom, Cambridge, England

SATURDAY 5 JUNE 1965 – PERFORMANCE
Dorothy Ballroom, Cambridge, England

With Bob Kidman & His Orchestra (*Ballroom*), the Prowlers and Bryan & the Brunelles (*Beat Room*), Jokers Wild and Fernando & the Hideaways (*Jive Hive*).

TUESDAY 15 JUNE 1965 – PERFORMANCE
Peterhouse College May Ball, Peterhouse College, Cambridge, England

With Zoot Money's Big Roll Band, the Paramounts (later known as Procol Harum), steel band, dance band and cabaret. Peter Gilmour played with Jokers Wild instead of Tony Sainty.

WEDNESDAY 30 JUNE 1965 – PERFORMANCE
Les Jeux Interdits, Victoria Ballroom, Cambridge, England

SATURDAY 3 JULY 1965 – PERFORMANCE
Dorothy Ballroom, Cambridge, England

With Bob Kidman & His Orchestra (*Ballroom*), the Komodos and Home Grown Blues (*Beat Room*), Jokers Wild and the Druids (*Jive Hive*).

TUESDAY 6 JULY 1965 – PERFORMANCE
Les Jeux Interdits, Victoria Ballroom, Cambridge, England

AUGUST 1965 – PERFORMANCES
France

David Gilmour joined Syd Barrett on a holiday to France where the two only just evaded arrest for busking in St Tropez.

WEDNESDAY 1 SEPTEMBER 1965 – PERFORMANCE ▶
Les Jeux Interdits, Victoria Ballroom, Cambridge, England

TOMORROW   TOMORROW
THE BRITISH ASSOCIATION and
THE INTERNATIONAL CENTRE
DANCE
WITH **JOKERS WILD**
GUILDHALL   8.30 - Midnight

SATURDAY 4 SEPTEMBER 1965 – PERFORMANCE
The British Association & The International Centre Dance, The Guildhall, Cambridge, England

WEDNESDAY 8 SEPTEMBER 1965 – PERFORMANCE
Les Jeux Interdits, Victoria Ballroom, Cambridge, England

OCTOBER 1965 – PERFORMANCE
Great Shelford, near Cambridge, England

With the Tea Set and Paul Simon. (See London 1962–1965 for further information.)

OCTOBER 1965 – PERFORMANCE
The Pitt Club, Cambridge University, Cambridge, England

Supporting George Melly.

OCTOBER 1965 – PERFORMANCE
Byam Shaw School of Art, Kensington, London, England
With Pink Floyd. (See Pink Floyd 1965 for further information.)

SATURDAY 9 OCTOBER 1965 – PERFORMANCE
Dorothy Ballroom, Cambridge, England
With Bob Kidman & The Dorothy Orchestra (*Ballroom*), the Proof and Thee (*Beat Room*) and Fernando's Hideaways and Jokers Wild (*Jive Hive*).

THURSDAY 21 OCTOBER 1965 – PERFORMANCE
Cottage Homes Ball, **The Guildhall & Corn Exchange, Cambridge, England**
With Victor Silvester & His Ballroom Orchestra, Chris Allen & His Band, Eric Donaldson & Edna Barnett and The Cycling Templars.

FRIDAY 30 OCTOBER 1965 – PERFORMANCE
Dorothy Ballroom, Cambridge, England
With the Measels.

MONDAY 2 NOVEMBER 1965 – RECORDING SESSION
Regent Sounds Studio, London, England
Jokers Wild recorded a string of tracks that were pressed up as a 12-inch EP and a 7-inch single to encourage bookings. Most it seems were given away to friends and family. (See Jokers Wild Recordings for further information.)

NOVEMBER 1965 – RECORDING SESSIONS
Decca Studios, West Hampstead, London, England
Jokers Wild recorded a cover of Sam And Dave's US single 'You Don't Know Like I Know' and 'That's How Strong My Love Is' (the B-side to 'Mr. Pitiful', a hit for Otis Redding in January 1965) under the guidance of Jonathan King at Decca studios. (See Jokers Wild Recordings for further information.)

FRIDAY 12 NOVEMBER 1965 – PERFORMANCE
Bassingbourn Area Youth Clubs Dance, **Main Hall, Bassingbourn Village College, Bassingbourn, near Royston, England**
With the Quadrant.

FRIDAY 19 NOVEMBER 1965 – PERFORMANCE ▶
Shadow Ball, **Dorothy Ballroom, Cambridge, England**
With the Riverside Jazz Band and Ballroom Orchestra.

FRIDAY 26 NOVEMBER 1965 – PERFORMANCE
Comberton Village College, Comberton, near Cambridge, England

You don't need to wait for a nurse to ask you to
THE
SHADOW BALL
in the
DOROTHY BALLROOM
Friday, 19th November
9 p.m.–2 a.m.

| Black Tie Double Ticket 30/- | Riverside Jazz Band Jokers Wild Ballroom Orchestra |

(PROCTORIAL PERMISSION).

WEDNESDAY 1 DECEMBER 1965 – PERFORMANCE
Santa Lucia Party, **University Arms Hotel, Cambridge, England**

WEDNESDAY 12 JANUARY 1966 – PERFORMANCE
Les Jeux Interdits, **Victoria Ballroom, Cambridge, England**

WEDNESDAY 30 MARCH 1966 – PERFORMANCE
Les Jeux Interdits, **Victoria Ballroom, Cambridge, England**

FRIDAY 15 APRIL 1966 – PERFORMANCE
Sawtry & District Young Farmers Club Dance, **Sawtry Village College, Sawtry, England**

SATURDAY 16 APRIL 1966 – PERFORMANCE
Victoria Ballroom, Cambridge, England

WEDNESDAY 20 APRIL 1966 – PERFORMANCE
Les Jeux Interdits, **Victoria Ballroom, Cambridge, England**

WEDNESDAY 18 MAY 1966 – PERFORMANCE
Les Jeux Interdits, **Victoria Ballroom, Cambridge, England**
This was the last advertised performance by Jokers Wild in the Cambridge area for 1966.

In addition to the shows listed above, Jokers Wild are said to have performed at dances at the RAF and USAF bases around the Cambridge area, including those at Mildenhall, Lakenheath, Alconbury and Chicksands. Clive Welham recalls, in his last few weeks with the band, performing at various society parties in London as well as an Admiralty dance at the Dorchester Hotel and a support slot for the Animals at Westminster School of Art.

JOKERS WILD / BULLIT / FLOWERS [1966–1967]
David Altham (Bass Guitar, to December 1966), David Gilmour (Guitar, Vocals), Rick Wills (Bass Guitar, replacing David Altham), John "Willie" Wilson (Drums).

JUNE / JULY 1966 – PERFORMANCES
Sybilla's, Swallow Street, London, England

In 1966 Beatle George Harrison invested some of his fortune in a happening new London nightspot named Sybilla's. It was billed as "London's most civilized discotheque",

RIGHT AND OPPOSITE TOP: BULLIT FEATURING DAVID GILMOUR, JOHN "WILLIE" WILSON (DRUMS) AND RICK WILLS (BASS, VOCALS).

and John-Paul Salvatore booked his newfound protégés a series of dates at the club before packing them off to Spain for the summer season.

SUMMER 1966 – SUMMER 1967 – PERFORMANCES
Spain, France & The Netherlands
(See page 13 for locations.)

FRIDAY 16 JUNE 1967 – PERFORMANCE
Cellar Club, Cambridge Union Society, Cambridge, England

A rare return to Cambridge during their continental adventures, this was almost certainly Jokers Wild's last ever UK appearance and the last show to be advertised in the Cambridge press.

Note: A popular eight-piece soul band from London performed under the name Jokers Wild across the south of England throughout 1967 and 1968, but are unrelated.

THOSE WITHOUT [1963–1965]

Alan "Barney" Barnes (Keyboard and Vocals), Roger "Syd" Barrett (Bass Guitar, Guitar, Vocals from 1964), Peter Glass (Harmonica), Stephen Pyle (Drums), Alan Sizer (Lead Guitar, Vocals), Robert "Smudge" Smith (Guitar, Bass Guitar, Vocals).

Historically, Those Without formed from the ashes of Hollerin' Blues, a group that had been performing since 1962 but had folded towards the end of 1963. Under the enthusiastic management of Warren Dosanjh the band reformed and became Those Without. Barrett joined its ranks in mid-1964, despite his claims to the contrary. Interviewed by *Melody Maker* in October 1967, Syd Barrett recalled, "For a couple of years from the age of 16, I was not with any regular group, and during this time I acquired a 12-string guitar and then a bass guitar, which I played with another local group, the Hollering Blues."

Note: Only shows that are believed to feature Roger "Syd" Barrett are listed and it is therefore not an exhaustive list of Those Without engagements. Other undocumented shows include the Sergeants Mess, RAF Lakenheath, England; Masonic Hall, Cambridge, England; The Alley Club, Cambridge, England; The Footlights Club, Cambridge, England; and RAF Wyton, Huntingdon, England (supporting Hedgehopper's Anonymous). In addition, a demo recording session in Northampton was aborted en-route because it was realized no one had the money to pay for it!

SATURDAY 25 JULY 1964 – PERFORMANCE
Blue Horizon Club, The Guildhall, Cambridge, England

Manager Warren Dosanjh recalled Those Without's short-lived residency featured Lionel Barst singing "A gruff version of 'Take This Hammer'", and "A large following of friends who turned up fuelled by alcohol and other substances, which turned the whole evening into one of musical anarchy. I remember that the song 'Hey Bo Diddley' seemed to go on forever, with a non-stop procession of the audience coming on stage to join us. The Council cancelled all further gigs and we were replaced by Jokers Wild."

The line-up at this show was Alan "Barney" Barnes (Harmonica and Vocals), Roger "Syd" Barrett (Bass Guitar, Guitar, Vocals), Stephen Pyle (Drums), Alan Sizer (Lead Guitar, Vocals), Robert "Smudge" Smith (Rhythm Guitar).

ABOVE: THOSE WITHOUT PERFORMING AT THE BLUE HORIZON ON 25 JULY 1964. FROM LEFT: ALAN "BARNEY" BARNES, STEVE PYLE, ROGER "SYD" BARRETT.

SATURDAY 12 SEPTEMBER 1964 – PERFORMANCE ▶
Cheshunt College Lodge, Cambridge, England

This was a farewell party for Barrett, who was heading for Camberwell School of Art in London, and was held in Stephen Pyle's parents' home. The invitation welcomed people to "Bo Siddley's Perverted Bleach Party". As a farewell memento, the band signed and gave Barrett an album entitled *Jimmy Reed Plays 12-String Guitar Blues*.

DECEMBER 1964 – PERFORMANCE
Cellar Club, Cambridge Union Society, Cambridge, England

This was reportedly where Barrett first met girlfriend Jenny Spires.

SATURDAY 2 JANUARY 1965 – PERFORMANCE
Cambridge, England

Those Without performed at the wedding reception of Stephen Pyle's sister Annie, on what was also her 21st birthday. The reception was held at her parents' home.

FRIDAY 5 MARCH 1965 – PERFORMANCE
The Racehorse public house, Cambridge, England

THURSDAY 11 MARCH 1965 – PERFORMANCE
The Racehorse public house, Cambridge, England

SATURDAY 13 MARCH 1965 – PERFORMANCE ▼
Village Hall, Little Gransden, near Cambridge, England
With the Wayfarers.

SATURDAY 24 APRIL 1965 – PERFORMANCE
The Racehorse public house, Cambridge, England

SATURDAY 8 MAY 1965 – PERFORMANCE
Village Hall, Trumpington, near Cambridge, England

SATURDAY 22 MAY 1965 – PERFORMANCE
Youth Club, St John's Church Hall, Cambridge, England

WEDNESDAY 16 JUNE 1965 – PERFORMANCE ▼
Youth Club, Congregational Church Hall, Cambridge, England

SUNDAY 20 JUNE 1965 – PERFORMANCE
The Racehorse public house, Cambridge, England

WEDNESDAY 30 JUNE 1965 – PERFORMANCE
Dorothy Ballroom, Cambridge, England
With Bob Kidman & His Orchestra (*Ballroom*), Those Without and the Washington D.C.'s (*Beat Room*).

THURSDAY 15 JULY 1965 – PERFORMANCE
Victoria Ballroom, Cambridge, England

SATURDAY 17 JULY 1965 – PERFORMANCE
Dorothy Ballroom, Cambridge, England
With Bob Kidman & His Orchestra (*Ballroom*), Those Without and the Hedgehoppers (*Beat Room*), the Seminoles and Bern Elliot & the Klan (*Jive Hive*).

SATURDAY 7 AUGUST 1965 – PERFORMANCE
Gardiner Memorial Hall, Burwell, near Cambridge, England
With DJ Chris Ian.

ABOVE: A PROMOTIONAL FLYER FOR THOSE WITHOUT MADE OF PHOTOS TAKEN AT THE BLUE HORIZON ON 25 JULY 1964.

THURSDAY 2 SEPTEMBER 1965 – PERFORMANCE
Victoria Ballroom, Cambridge, England

SATURDAY 16 OCTOBER 1965 – PERFORMANCE
Dorothy Ballroom, Cambridge, England
With Bob Kidman & His Orchestra (*Ballroom*), Radio Caroline & the Clique and the Pagans (*Beat Room*), Those Without and the Dawnbreakers (*Jive Hive*).

THURSDAY 9 DECEMBER 1965 – PERFORMANCE ▶
Victoria Ballroom, Cambridge, England

SATURDAY 18 DECEMBER 1965 – PERFORMANCE
Dorothy Ballroom, Cambridge, England
With Bob Kidman & the Dorothy Orchestra (*Ballroom*), the Profile and the Dinos (*Beat Room*), Roy Black & the Senators and Those Without (*Jive Hive*).
This was almost certainly the last public appearance of Those Without and the last show to be advertised in the Cambridge press.

JOKERS WILD RECORDINGS

TRACKS

WHY DO FOOLS FALL IN LOVE? (Herman Santiago)
WALK LIKE A MAN (Bob Crewe, Bob Gaudio)
DON'T ASK ME WHAT I SAY (Paul Jones)
BIG GIRLS DON'T CRY (Bob Crewe, Bob Gaudio)
BEAUTIFUL DELILAH (Chuck Berry)
YOU DON'T KNOW LIKE I KNOW (Isaac Hayes, David Porter)
THAT'S HOW STRONG MY LOVE IS (Roosevelt Jamison)

RECORDING DETAILS

On 2 November 1965 Jokers Wild entered Regent Sounds Studio in London's Denmark Street, to record some of their repertoire. This material was pressed on a five–track, 12-inch album and a 7-inch EP single of around 50 copies apiece and these were distributed among family and friend and sold at gigs. Original copies are now highly sought-after collectors' items.

The 12-inch album contained the tracks 'Why Do Fools Fall In Love?' (a cover of the doo-wop classic by the Teenagers featuring Frankie Lymon, released in January 1956), 'Walk Like A Man' (a March 1963 hit for The 4 Seasons), 'Don't Ask Me What I Say' (a track that appeared on the September 1964 album *The Five Faces of Manfred Mann* by Manfred Mann), 'Big Girls Don't Cry' (an earlier hit for the 4 Seasons in October 1962) and 'Beautiful Delilah' (a November 1958 single for Chuck Berry). The 7-inch single comprised of the tracks 'Why Do Fools Fall In Love?' and 'Don't Ask Me What I Say'.

Before the end of the year they were due back in the studio again, this time at Decca, under the guidance of an up-and-coming pop impresario and Cambridge graduate Jonathan King who would go on to enjoy a hit with 'Everyone's Gone To The Moon' in July 1965. Clive Welham recalled that, "He [Jonathan King] went to see us at the Victoria Ballroom, but he went on the wrong night [Saturday 6 March 1965] and saw Hedgehoppers Anonymous and got them to record a single ['It's Good News Week', released Friday 24 September 1965 on Decca]."[1]

King returned to Jokers Wild that November and recorded a cover of Sam and Dave's US single 'You Don't Know Like I Know' and 'That's How Strong My Love Is' (the B-side to 'Mr. Pitiful', a hit for Otis Redding in January 1965).

"It was much better than our first recording effort," remembered Welham. "With Dave singing the lead… Dave Altham and Dave Gilmour produced it. We got it right that time, we were properly prepared. Decca was very pleased with it but Sam And Dave released it here, and that was it."[2] Indeed Sam And Dave recorded the original version at Stax in Memphis in October 1965, and finally released it in the UK on Atlantic on Friday 14 January 1966, even though it failed to chart.

LEFT: REGENT SOUNDS STUDIO IN DENMARK STREET, OR TIN PAN ALLEY AS IT WAS AFFECTIONATELY KNOWN. OVER THE YEARS THE BASEMENT STUDIO ALSO PLAYED HOST TO THE WHO, ROLLING STONES, KINKS, YARDBIRDS, MOTT THE HOOPLE, DONOVAN AND BLACK SABBATH.

ABOVE: DECCA STUDIOS AT BROADHURST GARDENS IN WEST HAMPSTEAD. PINK FLOYD THEMSELVES REHEARSED THERE IN 1971 AHEAD OF COMMENCING THE RECORDING OF *THE DARK SIDE OF THE MOON*. THE STUDIOS CLOSED IN 1980 AND IS PRESENTLY IN USE AS A REHEARSAL SPACE FOR THE ENGLISH NATIONAL OPERA.

1–2. Author interview with Clive Welham, October 1996.

LONDON 1963–65

When Syd Barrett arrived in London, Roger Waters had already been away from Cambridge for over a year. He had never been a part of the Cambridge music scene, but here in London his aspirations to become a musician began; he learned the basics of playing a guitar and formed an acoustic duo, known as the Tailboard Two, with classmate Keith Noble. It was short-lived, and the pair then expanded the line-up to create Sigma 6, a band comprising various students who jammed and rehearsed in the Polytechnic basement common room.

"I was doing architecture at Regent Street Polytechnic," recalled Waters. "I suppose we formed several groups there. It wasn't serious, we didn't play anywhere. We had lots of names, Meggadeaths was a great one. We just sat around talking about how we would spend the money we would make. I invested some of my grant in a Spanish guitar and I went and had two lessons at the Spanish Guitar Centre. But I couldn't do with all that practice. In college there's always a room where people seem to gravitate to with their instruments and bits of things."[1]

The various groups also included future Pink Floyd members Nick Mason and Richard Wright. Mason had flirted with a post-school band called the Hotrods comprising a group of local friends whose career never got beyond the bedroom (or indeed garden, as pictured in his book *Inside Out*, complete with cardboard amp!). Wright had graduated from playing trombone in a long-forgotten trad-jazz band. All three eventually ended up living in a shared house in Highgate, north London, let by live-in landlord Mike Leonard, a part-time lecturer at the Polytechnic.

Sigma 6 even boasted its own manager, a former Poly student called Ken Chapman, who had cards made up of the "Available for Weddings and Parties" variety. "We used to learn his songs and then play them for Gerry Bron [later of the Bronze record label]," recalled Waters. "They were fantastic songs, 'Have You Seen A Morning Rose', to the tune of a Tchaikovsky prelude or something."[2]

By the start of 1964 they became known as the Abdabs (or the Screaming Abdabs) and had the rare distinction of being the only one of the precursor Pink Floyd bands to receive any form of press coverage, in an early edition of *West One*, the Polytechnic's student newspaper. Contrary to popular belief, there never was an "Architectural Abdabs"; this was merely the headline under which the piece appeared. Regarded as the college house band, they performed a fairly solid set that included a cover of John Lee Hooker's 'I'm A Crawling King Snake', various Searchers numbers and, with guest vocals from Richard Wright's girlfriend Juliette Gale, George Gershwin's 'Summertime' and the blues standard 'Careless Love'. The band even made several appearances as the opening act at the Polytechnic dances, including at least one with the Tridents featuring Jeff Beck.

In September 1964 Barrett travelled down to London to take up his studies at Camberwell School of Arts and Crafts with another Cambridge musician, Radovan Klose (who was almost always called Rado, or Bob, by his friends), formerly of Cambridge band Blues Anonymous. Klose was coincidentally enrolled onto the same course, two years below, as Waters, Mason and Wright at the Polytechnic.

So, when Metcalf and Noble decided to leave and form a duo together, Barrett and Klose were immediately recruited to the Abdabs, and after a couple of weeks living in a flat off Tottenham Court Road the pair moved into Leonard's house in Highgate, just as Mason and Wright had decided to vacate their

ARCHITECTURAL ABDABS

By BARBARA WALTERS

AN up-and-coming pop group here at the Poly call themselves "The Abdabs" and hope to establish themselves playing Rhythm and Blues. Most of them are architectural students.

Their names are Nick Mason (drums); Rick Wright (Rhythm guitar); Clive Metcalf (bass); Roger Walters (lead); and finally Keith Noble and Juliette Gale (singers).

Why is it that Rhythm and Blues has suddenly come into its own? Roger was the first to answer.

"It is easier to express yourself rhythmically in Blues-style. It doesn't need practice, just basic understanding."

"I prefer to play it because it is musically more interesting," said Clive. I suppose he was comparing it to Rock. Well, how does it compare? Roger was quite emphatic on this point: "Rock is just beat without expression, though admittedly Rhythm and Blues forms the basis of original rock."

It so happens that they are all modern Jazz enthusiasts.

Was there any similarity? I asked. In Keith's opinion there was. "The Blues is just a primitive form of modern jazz."

ABOVE: LEONARD'S LODGERS PICTURED AT HIGH PINES, OXTED IN OCTOBER 1964.
THE ONLY SURVIVING PHOTOS OF THE PERIOD SHOW A LINE-UP FEATURING CHRIS DENNIS (VOCALS), ROGER
WATERS (GUITAR), RADOVAN "BOB" KLOSE (GUITAR), ROGER "SYD" BARRETT (GUITAR), NICK MASON (DRUMS)
AND MIKE LEONARD (KEYBOARDS).

rooms in order to move back to the more comfortable confines of their respective parents' homes.

Waters recalled that, "With the advent of Bob Close [sic] we actually had someone who could play an instrument. It was really then we did the shuffle job of who played what. I was demoted from lead guitar to rhythm guitar and finally bass. There was always this frightful fear that I could land up as the drummer."[3]

Barrett faced a similar, though not quite so serious dilemma. "I had to buy another guitar," he recalled, "because Roger played bass – a Rickenbacker – and we didn't want a group with two bass players. So I changed guitars and we started doing the pub scene. During that period we kept changing the name of the group."[4]

Fortunately those under the roof of live-in landlord Mike Leonard (a four-story town-house with huge rooms) enjoyed an unusual level of artistic freedom. Leonard was sympathetic to their artistic goals, and apart from being a part-time tutor at the Polytechnic was also a lecturer at the Hornsey College of Art, developing early experiments into sound/light movement.

However, toward the end of the year Wright took a sabbatical, having recognized further education was not best suited to him, and enjoyed an extended holiday in the Greek islands before enrolling at the Royal College of Music for the next term. As a result, Leonard was immediately invited to stand in on organ for the occasional booking, mostly at local pubs, including the Woodman and the Winchester on Archway Road, Highgate, and it wasn't long before the band was calling itself Leonard's Lodgers.

Mason remembers at that time they learned their repertoire from a clutch of albums, "*Authentic R&B Volumes 1–3* and Syd's collection of Bo Diddley."[*] Significantly, it soon became apparent that the band lacked a front-man of substance. Barrett and Klose fumbled through the vocals as best they could, but neither had the confidence or vocal range to carry it off effectively in the style that the band was aiming for. During the autumn break of 1964, Barrett was dispatched to Cambridge to try to convince his former band mate Geoff Mott to join them in London, but there was hardly any incentive for Mott to join a group that had very few gigs, no agency, no manager, and on the face of it, no prospects. In correspondence to his then girlfriend, Barrett talks of unsuccessfully trying to persuade "Fred" to join the band (Fred being the nickname of David Gilmour, who by then was enjoying a semi-pro career with his band Jokers Wild).

Although Barrett couldn't persuade either Gilmour or Mott to join, by extreme good fortune, Klose bumped into a face he vaguely knew from Cambridge: Chris Dennis. "I was in a music shop in Soho looking for a guitar and I saw Bob and he introduced me to Roger Waters," recalled Dennis. "They explained they were looking for a singer for their band and said: 'We'll put you in.' Of course I said yes."[5]

At that time he was a technician serving with the Royal Air Force at its Uxbridge base in West London. "I'd been in bands since I was a 16-year-old lad, playing in various skiffle bands and I knew Bob from the gig circuits in Cambridge when I was posted there. He used to come round and jam with my band."[6]

Dennis rehearsed regularly with the band before becoming the frontman for their first set of gigs as both the Tea Set and the short-lived Spectrum Five, who were booked to appear at a dance at Barrett's college. It's quite likely the band adopted the name for just that one gig.

As Dennis remembered, "At this stage we were like a lot of other bands, doing R&B stuff. Syd did a lot of Bo Diddley numbers on his white Fender guitar. He'd do "No Money Down"[Chuck Berry] and I would sing Jimmy Witherspoon, Muddy Waters and Chuck Berry stuff along with Lazy Lester's 'I'm A Lover Not A Fighter' and 'I Got Love If You Want It' by Slim Harpo.…[7] We would rehearse in the house they shared. At that time we didn't even have a name – and believe me,

it was a dispute. We were rehearsing blues songs for our first gig at a private party in Surrey [October 1964]. It was mostly covers we did back then, we'd practice at the house two or three times a week."[8]

Even in that short time the talents of Leonard were clearly at odds with the image of the group, which a set of surviving photos from that private party in Surrey clearly demonstrates. "Mike thought of himself as one of the band. But we didn't, because he was too old basically. We used to leave the house to play gigs secretly without telling him,"[9] recalled Mason. Over time they started rehearsing away from the house, falling victim to an overwhelming spate of local objection to the volume of their rehearsals, and so operations moved to a function room in the nearby Railway Tavern and the Polytechnic common room.

The Tea Set was a name that drifted in and out of favour, but it was certainly adopted for many bookings in the coming months and indeed right through to early 1966, even after they had found their new and more permanent name of Pink Floyd. Accounts vary considerably but it has been said that the new name was adopted midway through a dance at RAF Uxbridge where, and this does seem highly unlikely, another band was also performing under the name the Tea Set. As improbable as this story may seem, there was indeed another North London band with that name, and they went on to perform across the city throughout the coming year.

The name change to Pink Floyd is credited to Barrett, although its invention has been disputed, at least in Cambridge circles, as being first made up by his Those Without band mate Steve Pyle. Several years earlier, he is said to have concocted the name in conversation with Barrett and others while trying to think of strange band names over ice cream and coffees at the local cafe when they should have been studying at the Tech. However, initially, and according to Keith Noble, they first called themselves "The Pink Floyd Blues Band", although this has never been substantiated elsewhere. From Barrett's perspective, the inspiration is said to have been found in his own record collection from the amalgamation of the first names of two Carolina bluesmen, Pinkney "Pink" Anderson (12 February 1900–12 October 1974), and Floyd "Dipper Boy" Council (2 September 1911–9 May 1976), which Barrett had noticed in the liner notes of the Blind Boy Fuller album *Country Blues 1935–1940* (Philips BBL-7512, released 1962) by Paul Oliver. In it Oliver describes, "Pink Anderson or Floyd Council – these were a few amongst the many blues singers that were to be heard in the rolling hills of the Piedmont, or meandering with the streams through the wooded valleys." As Waters once put it, if they had opted for the other combination, "Anderson Council", it would have sounded like a local authority!

Meanwhile, Dennis was proving to be a comic liability. According to Mason's *Inside Out* he had an unfortunate tendency to make Hitler-like moustaches with his harmonica while saying "Sorry about that folks" and announcing each number as "Looking Through The Knotholes In Granny's Wooden Leg"

---

*There was only ever one *Authentic R&B* album. It was released in 1964 (UK: Stateside SL 10068) and featured tracks by Slim Harpo, Lightnin' Slim, Silas Hogan, Lazy Lester, Jimmy Anderson, Lonesome Sundown, Whispering Smith and Leroy Washington.

(something Waters revived himself during their 1972 tour of West Germany when introducing 'Echoes'). That embarrassing problem was solved when Dennis received a posting to Bahrain at the end of January 1965, leaving Barrett, as the most charismatic member, to take on what was for him the unnatural role of lead singer. Dennis retired from the RAF in 1973, returning to Cambridge to set up a successful recording studio.

Something of an introvert, Klose may have been a far more disciplined musician and indeed of greater ability than Barrett, but he lacked spontaneity and raw talent. As Gilmour reflected, "The thing with Syd was that his guitar playing wasn't his strongest feature. His style was very stiff. I always thought I was the better guitar player. But he was very clever, very intelligent, an artist in every way. And he was a frightening talent when it came to words, and lyrics. They just used to pour out."[10] These changes also gave the band their opportunity to finally nudge Leonard out in favour of Wright, who was invited back on board.

Although the band picked up a short-lived residency at the Countdown in Kensington, where at least one show was performed in an acoustic configuration and included the songs 'Long Tall Texan' (popularized by the Beach Boys on their *Beach Boys Concert* album, released 1964) and 'How High The Moon' (popularized on the 1951 Capitol single by Les Paul and Mary Ford), their career was still slow-going.

However, they remained confident and with what they believed to be a stable line-up the band attempted to record some of their repertoire at Decca in West Hampstead in early 1965. This included the Barrett originals 'Butterfly' and 'Lucy Leave', a cover of 'I'm A King Bee' by Slim Harpo, and 'Double-O-Bo', a group composition. 'Lucy Leave' and 'I'm A King Bee' was even pressed as an acetate single with the intention of sending out to clubs in order to obtain live bookings.

As Klose later recalled, "We recorded a few numbers… I can't remember exactly where we did them… it was some place where a friend of Rick Wright's worked as an engineer. I think they were recorded on two-track. It was definitely a professional set-up. The songs themselves were mainly group compositions, although I think Syd wrote 'Lucy Leave'. 'Double-O-Bo' was a Bo Diddley tribute of sorts, a pun on the James Bond 007 thing. The title was the main lyric! I think we had one verse written out, and then dreamt up a second whilst we were in the studio. I can't remember the title of the last number… it was a shuffle type thing in E as far as I can recall. Nick Mason played them to me during a visit a couple of years after they were recorded. Very embarrassing!"[11]

Klose as it turned out didn't stay much longer and under pressure from both parents and college tutors, maybe even musical differences, he left the band in the summer of 1965. Wright says of Klose's departure, "Before him we used to play the R&B classics, because that's what all groups were supposed to do then. But I never liked R&B very much. I was actually more of a jazz fan. With Syd the direction changed, it became

more improvised around the guitar and keyboards. Roger started playing bass as a lead instrument, and I started to introduce more of my classical feel.'[12]

From this point until the following year Pink Floyd remained a sideline for its members, all still pursuing their studies. Their only notable achievement of the year was to compete in the ninth heat of the *Melody Maker* "National Beat Contest" in June, but after failing to gain a place in the subsequent heats the band slipped back into obscurity.

ABOVE: PINK FLOYD PHOTOGRAPHED IN HIGHGATE, LONDON, IN EARLY 1965 WITH ROGER WATERS, RADOVAN "BOB" KLOSE, ROGER "SYD" BARRETT, NICK MASON AND RICHARD WRIGHT.

1. *Voxpop*, by Michael Wale, George G. Harrap & Co. Ltd., 1972.
2–3. *Zig Zag*, Issue 32, July 1973.
4. *Beat Instrumental*, October 1967.
5–8. *Daily Mail*, 4 December 2012.
9. *Mojo*, May 1994.
10. *Zig Zag*, Issue 32, July 1973.
11–12. *Random Precision*, by David Parker, Cherry Red, 2001.

THE TAILBOARD TWO [AUTUMN 1963]

Keith Noble (Vocals), Roger Waters (Guitar).

In late 1963 Waters teamed up with Regent Street Polytechnic classmate Keith Noble to form his first group, the Tailboard Two. However, it is doubtful they ever performed to an audience.

THE MEGGADEATHS / SIGMA 6 [AUTUMN 1963]

Nick Mason (Drums), Clive Metcalf (Bass Guitar), Keith Noble (Vocals), Sheilagh Noble (Vocals), Vernon Thompson (Rhythm Guitar), Roger Waters (Guitar), Richard Wright (Keyboards, Brass).

With the addition of various fellow students the Waters and Noble duo folded and with it a series of bands were formed before the name Sigma 6 was chosen.

THE ABDABS [SPRING 1964]

Juliette Gale (Vocals), Nick Mason (Drums), Clive Metcalf (Bass Guitar), Keith Noble (Vocals), Roger Waters (Guitar, Vocals), Richard Wright (Rhythm Guitar, Keyboards, Brass).

Essentially a Polytechnic rehearsal band, their only appearance at a proper music venue, according to Keith Noble, was at the Marquee club appearing as extras in an unknown film production. Unfortunately this memory is not shared by any other members. Noble and Metcalf went on to enjoy fleeting success as composers of the minor US hit single 'A Summer Song' for the British folk duo Chad Stuart and Jeremy Clyde. It was released in the UK (United Artists UP-1062) on Friday 31 July 1964, and in the US (World Artists 1027) on Monday 20 July 1964.

LEONARD'S LODGERS [AUTUMN 1964]

Roger "Syd" Barrett (Rhythm Guitar, Vocals), Radovan "Bob" Klose (Guitar, Harmonica, Vocals), Mike Leonard (Keyboards), Nick Mason (Drums), Roger Waters (Bass Guitar, Vocals).

Although no specific dates have been found for Leonard's Lodgers, Mike Leonard recalls that the band performed at the Woodman and Winchester pubs, and Nick Mason recalls the Railway Tavern as a location where they used to rehearse, all of which were local to the house on Stanhope Gardens.

AUTUMN 1964 – PERFORMANCES
The Railway Tavern public house, Crouch End Hill, London, England

AUTUMN 1964 – PERFORMANCES
The Woodman public house, Highgate, London, England

AUTUMN 1964 – PERFORMANCES
The Winchester public house, Highgate, London, England

THE SPECTRUM FIVE [OCTOBER 1964]

Roger "Syd" Barrett (Rhythm Guitar, Vocals), Radovan 'Bob' Klose (Guitar, Harmonica, Vocals), Mike Leonard (Keyboards), Nick Mason (Drums), Roger Waters (Bass Guitar, Vocals).

OCTOBER 1964 – PERFORMANCE
Camberwell School of Arts and Crafts, Camberwell, London, England

Dick Maunders, the promoter of the show, recalled that, "I was attending Camberwell Art School during the mid Sixties at the time Syd Barrett was there (although I seem to remember he was called Roger). He was a couple of years above me. I was the college social secretary and I recall that on one occasion we were stuck for a group to play at a dance. I was told that there was a sort of in-house group who might play on the night in question. This turned out to be Syd Barrett's band, who were called the Spectrum Five, most of whom went on to be Pink Floyd. They played a mixture of blues and rock; I think we paid them about £20 plus booze! We never booked them again, as I think Syd left the college."

LEONARD'S LODGERS / THE TEA SET [OCTOBER – DECEMBER 1964]

Roger "Syd" Barrett (Rhythm Guitar, Vocals), Chris Dennis (Vocals), Radovan "Bob" Klose (Guitar, Harmonica, Vocals), Mike Leonard (occasional appearance on Keyboards), Nick Mason (Drums), Roger Waters (Bass Guitar, Vocals).

OCTOBER 1964 – PERFORMANCE
The Ivy House public house, Nunhead, London, England

It is almost impossible to trace an exact date for the band appearing at this venue, but its close proximity to Camberwell School of Arts and Crafts suggests that Barrett had some influence in obtaining a booking, and rumours persist within the local community to this day that Pink Floyd made an early appearance here. In the early 1970s it was a regular circuit venue and hosted early gigs by the Clash, Elvis Costello and Graham Parker among others.

OCTOBER 1964 – PERFORMANCE
Cambridge, England

Supporting Humphrey Lyttelton at an unknown university ball, as documented in Nick Mason's book *Inside Out*.

OCTOBER 1964 – PERFORMANCE
High Pines, Oxshott, near Leatherhead, England

Sebastian Jenkins captured the only known photographs of the band in this period, recalling "The photos were taken at a private house party organized by some rich school friends of my sister in 1964. It must be amongst the first few gigs that Syd Barrett played with other Floyd members, possibly the first."

OCTOBER 1964 – PERFORMANCE
The Large Hall, Regent Street Polytechnic, London, England

Supporting the Tridents (featuring Jeff Beck on guitar).

PINK FLOYD DEMOS

TRACKS

BUTTERFLY (Barrett)
LUCY LEAVE (Barrett)
I'M A KING BEE (James Moore, aka Slim Harpo)
DOUBLE O-BO (Barrett)
REMEMBER ME (Barrett)
WALK WITH ME SYDNEY (Waters)

RECORDING DETAILS

In early 1965 the fledgling Pink Floyd made their first foray into a recording studio to record some demos in two sessions, at Decca in Broadhurst Gardens, West Hampstead. According to Bob Klose, who was still with the band at that time, the studio was acquired by Richard Wright who knew a junior engineer and was able to secure a couple of sessions during some down time. It's more than likely Wright knew the engineer because he had recently composed the B-side to the Adam, Mike & Tim single 'Little Baby' b/w 'You're The Reason Why' (Decca F12040, released Friday 4 December 1964), which was recorded there.

Considering the band's live repertoire at that time comprised mainly of R&B covers, it's interesting to note the band recorded three Barrett originals, 'Butterfly', 'Lucy Leave' and 'Remember Me' in addition to a cover of Slim Harpo's 'I'm A King Bee', a group composition entitled 'Double-O-Bo' and the Waters' penned 'Walk With Me Sydney', his first ever composition, which curiously even features Juliette Gale vocals.

In early 1965 Barrett wrote twice to his girlfriend Jenny Spires giving a detailed, illustrated account of the sessions. In the first letter he excitedly says, "I'll tell you everything that happened at the recording. We took all the gear into the studio which was lit by horrid white lights, and covered with wires and microphones. Rog had his amp behind a screen and Nicki was also screened off, and after a little bit of chat we tested everything for balance, and then recorded five numbers more or less straight off; but only the guitars and drums. We're going to add all the singing and piano etc, next Wednesday. The tracks sound terrific so far, especially 'King Bee.'"

In a follow up letter he says, "When I sing I have to stand in the middle of the studio with ear phones on, and everyone else watches from the other room, and I can't see them at all but they can all see me. Also I can only just hear what I'm singing."

The tracks 'Lucy Leave' and 'I'm A King Bee' were pressed to acetate to send out to clubs in order to obtain live bookings. No more than a handful of the discs were produced, although one copy found its way onto the collectors' market, an original having been unearthed in the late 1980s during a property clearance in central London. In an interview with *Record Collector* in August 2013, Nick Mason remembered that the acetate was used to audition (unsuccessfully) for TV's *Ready, Steady, Go!* but it did secure their place in the ninth heat of the *Melody Maker* "National Beat Contest" held at Wimbledon Palais on Saturday 27 June 1965, even though they lost out to winners St Louis Union.

On 27 November 2015, in order to retain their copyright in the recordings, a limited edition of 1,050 double 7-inch EPs of the tracks mentioned above was released as *Pink Floyd: Their First Recordings* (UK: Parlophone 0825646018611). The tracks also appeared on the 2016 box set *The Early Years 1965–72*.

ST LOUIS UNION ARE TOPS

THE St Louis Union, a Manchester group, won the ninth heat of the MM National Beat Contest at Wimbledon Palais on Sunday.

Second were Phil Hunter and the Jaguars from Leyton Buzzard, Bedfordshire, and third place was shared by the Ravens, an all girl group from Worcestershire and the Poachers from West Mersea, Essex. All groups go to the semi-final held at the Palais on July 25.

The St Louis Union are Tony Cassidy, vocals, a civil servant aged 17; David Tomlinson, organ, an apprentice TV engineer (18); Keith Millar, guitar, an art student (17); John Nichols, bass guitar, apprentice TV engineer (17); Alex Kirby, tenor sax, insurance clerk (19), and Dave Webb, drums, a clerk (17).

Other groups in the heat were the Memphis Five, from Rolleston, Staffs; the Blue Stars, Berkhampstead, Herts; the Maniacs, from South London; the Pink Floyd, Hampstead; and the Jades, Crawley, Sussex.

PINK FLOYD / THE TEA SET
[JANUARY – OCTOBER 1965]

Roger "Syd" Barrett (Rhythm Guitar, Vocals), Radovan "Bob" Klose (Guitar, Harmonica, Vocals), Nick Mason (Drums), Roger Waters (Bass Guitar, Vocals), Richard Wright (Keyboards).

JANUARY / FEBRUARY 1965 – RECORDING SESSION
Decca Studios, West Hampstead, London, England

(See Pink Floyd Demos for details.)

JANUARY 1965 – PERFORMANCE
RAF Uxbridge, Uxbridge, England

It has been reported that the band changed their name from the Tea Set to Pink Floyd halfway through a show at this west London RAF station due to a double booking with a band of the same name. This seems highly unlikely, and although Chris Dennis was stationed at RAF Uxbridge, further research through RAF Uxbridge archives has failed to reveal anything to corroborate this story.

FEBRUARY 1965 – PERFORMANCE
Count Down, Kensington, London, England ▼

Pink Floyd enjoyed a short-lived residency at this basement coffee house cum wine bar, which was closed down shortly after opening following noise complaints from its neighbours, who occupied residential dwellings above it. In a 2013 interview with *Record Collector*, Nick Mason recalled, "The significant thing about the Count Down club is that it was a proper gig. And we got paid. It felt the closest we'd been to becoming professional. The problem was they had a noise injunction served on them. In our desperation, what we did was we performed as an acoustic band. Not particularly good, but we were desperate. The fond memory was the understanding that people actually wanted to come and see us."

Dance to Blues Group . . .
at
COUNT DOWN
1a PALACE GATE
KENSINGTON W.8.
COFFEE AND WINE BARS.
Every night except Mondays and Tuesdays.

SATURDAY 22 MAY 1965 – PERFORMANCE
Summer Dance, Homerton College, Cambridge, England

Billed as Pink Floyd, with the Boston Crabs and Unit 4 + 2.

SUNDAY 27 JUNE 1965 – PERFORMANCE
Melody Maker National Beat Contest,
Wimbledon Palais, Wimbledon, London, England

Billed as Pink Floyd. The band entered into the ninth heat of this annual contest, organized by *Melody Maker*, but failed to gain a place in any successive heats. Also appearing were St Louis Union (winners of this heat), Phil Hunter & The Jaguars, the Ravens and the Poachers.

SUNDAY 27 JUNE 1965 – PERFORMANCE
Beat Contest, the Country Club,
Belsize Park, London, England

Billed as Pink Floyd. The programme for Pink Floyd's 1974–5 UK/US tour mentions that the group lost both this and the above contest on the same night. The band had already played at this venue on occasion, but no further details could be found.

PINK FLOYD / THE TEA SET
[OCTOBER – DECEMBER 1965]

Roger "Syd" Barrett (Rhythm Guitar, Vocals), Nick Mason (Drums), Roger Waters (Bass Guitar, Vocals), Richard Wright (Keyboards).

OCTOBER 1965 – PERFORMANCE
Great Shelford, near Cambridge, England

Together with Jokers Wild and Paul Simon, Pink Floyd performed at a private party hosted by Douglas January on behalf of his daughter Libby's 21st birthday, who was at the time being courted by designer Storm Thorgerson. Of Paul Simon, Clive Welham recalled that, "He did a set with classics like 'Where Have All The Flowers Gone?' in front of all these rich businessmen. Some songs were quite critical of them, but they had no idea and were applauding wildly. It was in a marquee at the back of this large country house. I sat on and off the drum kit because of my wrist problems. Willie Wilson sat in on drums and I came to the front on tambourine." Four years later the house was used as the location for the cover of Pink Floyd's *Ummagumma* album sleeve.

OCTOBER 1965 – PERFORMANCE
Byam Shaw School of Art, Kensington, London, England

Billed as Pink Floyd. Will Garfitt, the promoter of the show, recalled, "There was a big end-of-term party that had a birdcage theme and we had both Pink Floyd and Jokers Wild play inside this enormous birdcage we had built with bird mobiles hanging up everywhere and all that psychedelic lighting. I think they got paid £10 each for that gig."

SATURDAY 18 DECEMBER 1965 – PERFORMANCE ▼
Village Hall, Old Weston, near Huntingdon, England

Billed as the Tea Set.

OLD WESTON VILLAGE HALL
DANCE
TO THE 'T-SET'
on SATURDAY, 18th DECEMBER
Admission 4/6 - 8.30-11.45 p.m.
HZ16

FRIDAY 31 DECEMBER 1965 – PERFORMANCE
New Years Dance, Youth Centre, Kimbolton,
near Huntingdon, England

Billed as the Tea Set.

2
STREAMING THROUGH THE STARLIT SKIES

1966–67

1966–67

By early 1966 Pink Floyd's fortunes were taking a dramatic turn for the better. The fledgling band had secured a series of gigs at the Marquee club in London's Soho, organized by American film-maker Steve Stollman, younger brother of Bernard and owner of the free-jazz New York record label ESP-Disk. They were essentially an extension of a series of smaller scale performance events that had already been held either side of Christmas at the Goings On club in Soho, hosted by Cream lyricist and poet Pete Brown, where Pink Floyd had apparently already appeared.

The first of these events was held from 4.30pm on Sunday 30 January and was billed in a *Melody Maker* advert as a "Giant Mystery Happening" featuring Donovan and Graham Bond. They ran every Sunday afternoon thereafter with Pink Floyd's first appearance on 13 March, and were advertised on handbills that didn't even mention the band's name, simply bearing the word "Trip".[*]

The audience largely comprised of performers' friends and a handful of freaks who had heard the word on the street or found handbills at select outlets. There were probably never more than fifty or so people at any one of these events although they did prove to be a turning point in the band's emergence as an original talent. No one was there to judge them and their enthusiastic participation brought them to the attention of the people who were beginning to shape "alternative" London.

Coincidentally, and fortuitously, it was at the very last one of these events on 12 June that would-be pop manager Peter Jenner chanced upon the band. Jenner was a lecturer at the London School of Economics and he and his friend John "Hoppy" Hopkins were seeking an easy way of making their fortune in the booming music industry. The pair had already formed a loose partnership with friends Joe Boyd, an ex-pat American who was working as Elektra Records' UK representative, and Ron Atkins in the shape of DNA Productions, and had signed up a group called AMM[**] to a management agreement. Jenner soon realized they would obtain a painfully small financial return for their troubles, and sought to find a more mainstream act as a wiser investment.

So, when Jenner heard Pink Floyd for the first time that afternoon he heard a very conventional blues-rock set, which broadly ticked all the boxes. "At that stage they were a blues band who played things like 'Louie Louie' and then played wacky bits in the middle," he recalled. "I wandered around trying to work out whether the noise was coming from the keyboards or from the guitar and that was what interested me."[1] But, as Waters later said, "We didn't know many songs, so it was a matter of settling on a chord and improvising, if that's the word."[2]

Jenner may have been rejoicing but his initial offer to manage the band was met with complete indifference. They were far more concerned with their impending summer holidays, unsure if they would even bother resuming on their return. It was fortuitous, then, that Mason's travels took him to the States that summer to join his girlfriend, Lindy Rutter, who was studying at the Martha Graham Dance Company in New York. Reading a copy of the underground New York newspaper the *East Village Other,* he was surprised to find an article (written by its UK correspondent Barry Miles) that featured a mention of their performance at the Marquee, thus reinvigorating his interest.

So, when Jenner tried again a few weeks later, in late September, he got a more favourable response. As Hopkins was now concentrating on other things, Jenner decided to draft in a new business partner, Andrew King, an old friend. King had time on his hands to book gigs, having recently quit his job at British European Airways, as well as an inheritance with which to buy the band new equipment (reportedly £1,000 worth of new amplifiers). Jenner relinquished his post at LSE and joined King full-time in their management venture, Blackhill Enterprises, based out of Jenner's Paddington town house with his lodger June Child (the later wife of Marc Bolan) as its secretary. A six-way partnership with Pink Floyd was formalized on 31 October 1966 and with enthusiasm prevailing over experience the pair immediately whisked them away to Hemel Hempstead in leafy Hertfordshire to record a series of demos in order to secure more bookings.

---

*Apart from the first "Happening", the so-called Spontaneous Underground shows were never advertized in the press and even the Marquee's weekly listings advert in *Melody Maker* showed every Sunday as "Closed For Private Hire".

**AMM was already achieving some notoriety. Operating out of Beckenham Arts Lab in south London, they dressed in white lab coats and experimented heavily in infant electronics and unconventional amplification methods, creating a unique sound, which pre-dated "Krautrock" by several years. They too were a regular feature at Sunday's at the Marquee and their album *AMMMusic*, now reissued on CD, must have been an inspiration, in particular to Pink Floyd's more abstract sounds, which were becoming fundamental to their new direction.

When Spontaneous Underground folded that spring, the party moved to Notting Hill in West London. It was a fairly run-down multicultural district at the time: its low rents and the easy availability of drugs from the West Indian community attracted its fair share of students and other young white people keen to live an enlightened bohemian lifestyle. DNA called it a day around this time and Hopkins' interests, after a recent trip to America, now lay in creating a community identity and spirit by setting up an "anti-university" in the form of a night school and Citizens Advice Bureau for the local population. With substantial help from Hopkins' friends, including Peter Jenner, Andrew King and Joe Boyd among others, the London Free School (LFS) began life on Tuesday 8 March.

The LFS was located in a basement flat at 26 Powis Terrace, rented from the notorious British black power activist Michael X (real name Michael de Freitas). For all its good intentions, it was fraught with funding problems from the outset and by the following year had degenerated into a dope-smoking haven and rehearsal space for local bands. If one good thing came from the experiment, it was the fact that it led to the now internationally renowned Notting Hill Carnival, which that July was launched by members of the LFS. Later Boyd recalled above all the "wild-eyed, slightly condescending idealism, bringing the over-educated elite into healthy contact with the working class".[3] However, the core group of organizers were reluctant to let their talents go to waste and sought to raise cash in order to publish a more informed, London-wide newspaper than the LFS's community newsletter, *The Grove*. They decided to do this by holding "social dances" at All Saints Church Hall in nearby Powis Gardens. The vicar was willing to allow the hall to be used for this purpose, because, under the auspices of the LFS, the dances would benefit the whole of the local community.

Thus, on Friday 30 September, Pink Floyd appeared at the inaugural LFS dance accompanied by slide projections to enhance their act, created by Joel and Toni Brown, friends of John Hopkins and visitors to London from Timothy Leary's Millbrook Center in the States. Word spread that something new and exciting was happening in Notting Hill and after only a few appearances by the band the hall was packed to capacity with more than 200 people.

Similar lighting effects to the Browns' had been a common feature at concert dances on the West Coast of America for some time, but it is believed that the couple were responsible for introducing the first psychedelic "light show" to the UK. Before long, however, the phenomenon would be viewed as more sinister than mere visual entertainment. The media linked it to the growing availability of psychedelic drugs such as LSD, and suggested that the purpose of light shows was to intensify the multisensory effects of hallucinogens.

It was also during the latter part of 1966 that their former landlord, Mike Leonard, had been developing what was described as a "sound and light workshop" at Hornsey College of Art. His experiments were based around the control of light by sound. Instead of playing records to his projections, Leonard started to invite the band to perform instead. Waters was particularly enthusiastic in developing the visual aspect of their performances, and as Mason later recalled, "The most important starting point for the light show was Mike Leonard and the Hornsey College of Art. That was the idea that the music could be improvised and the lighting could be improvised to go with it. And that definitely was an influence."[4]

Although far from anything that would later give Pink Floyd its legendary trademark, these rudimentary sessions sowed the seeds for the future and before long many more amateur technicians were busy developing static and moving oil-based slide shows to accompany live music. Pink Floyd's first touring light show was built by Peter Jenner, his wife Sumi and Andrew King using closed-beam spotlights which they mounted on wooden boards and activated by domestic light switches. "The result was these hugely dramatic shadows behind [the band], which I'm sure everyone thought was brilliant," mused Jenner. "Of course, it was a complete fuck-up, and mistake, as all the best things are."[5]

Jack Bracelin was the first to take the light-show business seriously and founded Five Acre Lights, which during the next year was to provide the environmental lighting at many "alternative" venues in London. Over the next few months Pink Floyd used various lighting technicians: Joe Gannon was their first, a former student of the sound-light workshop at Hornsey. He was often regarded in the press of the day as the "fifth Floyd", as he was their first full-time technician on the road. "I design the slides, basing them on my idea of the music," explained Gannon, who had also rebuilt Jenner and King's contraption into something fractionally more sophisticated. "The lights work rhythmically, I just wave my hand over the micro-switches and the different colours flash."[6] Gannon was replaced in the summer of 1967 by Peter Wynne-Wilson and his girlfriend Susie Gawler-Wright, and by Christmas 1967, John Marsh. As with most small-scale operations, they also shared the driving between gigs. Indeed until the arrival of Gannon, it was Richard Wright who had also loaded up the van for each gig in return for some extra cash. Heaven forbid Waters or Mason should lower themselves to that level!

Throughout the early autumn Hopkins was busy organizing the finance and staff to produce his London-wide newspaper and in October the first edition of *International Times*, or *IT* as it came to be known, was published. Issued fortnightly as an information centre and non-political broadsheet dealing with musical, literary, artistic and social issues, as well as the drug culture, it was produced in the basement of co-editor Barry

Miles' influential alternative Indica Bookshop and Gallery[*]. A massive launch party was held for *IT* on Saturday 15 October, not at All Saints Church Hall, but at the vast Roundhouse in Chalk Farm, north London, a very dilapidated Victorian railway turning shed. As Pink Floyd was regarded as the house band, they topped the bill, playing their biggest show to date while securing valuable mainstream media exposure. Indirectly this gig led to a further string of dates at the Roundhouse and by the end of the year they had even appeared at an Oxfam benefit concert at the prestigious Royal Albert Hall.

Pink Floyd were at last making ripples within the alternative music scene and, although they had no record contract yet, they were building a small yet loyal London following. In addition, Barrett was emerging as a prolific songwriter and over a period of time the band's covers of blues standards were giving way to his songs of childlike wonder with frenzied feedback overlaid at an ever-increasing volume.

Unfortunately, things weren't going so well for Hopkins or Boyd. Boyd was fired from Elektra Records and *IT* was suffering major cash-flow problems, mainly because insufficient advertising revenue was being generated. At the same time, although the All Saints Church Hall events were well attended, the LFS still couldn't pay its bills. Its financial burdens were ultimately relieved when Boyd and Hopkins realized that a move away from Notting Hill to a more central London location would attract a wider audience and thereby increase their potential income.

ABOVE: ON STAGE AT THE OPENING NIGHT OF UFO, 23 DECEMBER 1966.

In no time at all they had secured the ideal venue: an Irish basement ballroom, located under the Berkeley Cinema, called the Blarney, conveniently located on Tottenham Court Road in the heart of the West End. The landlord, Mr Gannon, was prepared to hire it out on Friday nights from 10.30pm (when the Irish club closed) until dawn for the grand sum of £15. It was also much larger than All Saints and could therefore cope with the expected increase in attendance.

Initially two dates were booked, one either side of Christmas, and the very last of the combined Hopkins and *IT* money was invested. On 23 and 30 December 1966 "UFO

Presents Night Tripper" was launched at the Blarney. The club's name was a matter of some debate, "Unidentified Flying Object" or "Underground Freak Out", depending on who was asked – either way, the general consensus of opinion was that it was pronounced "You-Foe". Since Boyd elected to manage the venue, it reverted to his preferred title of simply "UFO". "A vacuum waiting to be filled," he remembered. "Hundreds of freaks looking for a central meeting point."[7] As Britain's first, and now legendary, psychedelic club, UFO continued to be held on these premises until the end of July 1967, publicized with large Day-Glo and multicoloured screen-printed posters designed by Michael English and Nigel Waymouth under the moniker Hapshash and the Coloured Coat, and printed and distributed by Osiris Visions, one of Joe Boyd's other small enterprises. As well as showcasing a huge variety of new underground acts and established bands, including Soft Machine, Arthur Brown and Tomorrow, it also promoted the recently converted-to-psychedelia Move and Procol Harum. The future of *IT* was at last secured and indeed it went on to outlive UFO by many years.

The vast amount of coverage the band was now receiving in the music press and the pressure of engagements were compromising their studies. Now, with a good London following, it seemed only logical that if they were to continue seriously they should turn their attention to securing a record deal. Boyd was certain that Elektra would go for the band and played Jac Holzman a tape, but he offered them such a paltry deal that it wasn't pursued. Indeed Blackhill must have been banking heavily on Elektra, or at least got very close to a deal, as some concert adverts in early November 1966 describe Pink Floyd as Elektra recording artists. Boyd even took Island label boss Chris Blackwell to see the band perform. Although Blackwell liked what he saw, his label was still mainly concentrating on Jamaican acts (although they had recorded the VIPs, later renamed Art, as their first "rock" act that same year).

Undeterred Joe Boyd then introduced them to Alan Bates of Polydor Records. He had already seen them perform at All Saints Hall in November 1966, and even went so far as to arrange a rehearsal at their studios in Stratford Place in January, accompanied by Morrison and two of his staff, Tony Howard and one Steve O'Rourke.

But keeping his cards close to his chest the shrewd Morrison had already been courting EMI producer Norman Smith, and was holding out for their decision – after all, that's where the Beatles were and they were the biggest band in the world. Morrison's actions were unbeknown to Boyd, who seeing this as his golden opportunity, rather impetuously formed Witchseason Productions with the intention of producing Pink Floyd and licensing their recordings to Polydor.

---

*Indica was co-owned by Miles, John Dunbar and Peter Asher, one half of pop duo Peter & Gordon, and had the financial support of Paul McCartney, who was dating Asher's sister, Jane, at the time. It also hosted an exhibition of Yoko Ono's work that November and it is here that she first met John Lennon. Jane Asher became an actress and met the illustrator Gerald Scarfe in 1971. They married ten years later.

Not surprisingly Morrison suggested they should hold off on the Polydor deal and get themselves into a studio with the aim of selling a finished master tape to a prospective record company rather than going cap in hand with a rough demo tape. Since the ubiquitous Boyd had at his disposal the facilities of Sound Techniques studios in Chelsea, he offered his services as the band's producer, and with Blackhill barely solvent Morrison shrewdly financed initial recording sessions in return for a percentage of the future publishing. Some initial studio rehearsals were booked and on Sunday 29 January they recorded 'Arnold Layne', selected as the standout song of their repertoire, despite its contentious subject matter, and 'Candy And A Currant Bun' as its B-side. In quick succession, Pink Floyd turned professional on Wednesday 1 February and on Tuesday 28 February they were formally signed to EMI Records. [*]

Curiously, in the middle of all this activity, it was in fact their friend Peter Whitehead who got them into the studio first. A documentary film-maker, Whitehead had made his mark with a short film called *Wholly Communion* which documented the International Poetry Incarnation at the Royal Albert Hall on Friday 11 June 1965. A year later he had begun producing a documentary with its focus on London and the "Swinging Sixties" entitled *Tonite Let's All Make Love in London*, which was funded by the British Film Institute. No doubt egged on by Syd Barrett's girlfriend, Jenny Spires, with whom he was having an illicit affair, Whitehead settled on Pink Floyd to provide a lengthy take of their live favourite, 'Interstellar Overdrive', for part of the soundtrack.

Morrison's master plan had worked, but to Boyd's immense horror EMI weren't so keen on independent producers and insisted on using their own in-house staff and facilities. His days were numbered. "I was choked when Morrison persuaded them to wait," he remembers bitterly. "EMI were very hostile to indie producers at the time."[8] In reality the band had little choice because the man responsible for signing the cheque, Sidney Arthur Beecher-Stevens (who as head of sales at Decca in 1962 was one of many executives to turn down the Beatles), insisted that as part of the deal staff producer Norman Smith should be responsible for watching over, but not interfering with, Pink Floyd's future recording career. This also allayed certain fears within EMI that some of the more undesirable fringe elements associated with the band, including Boyd, would distract them from their professional obligations.

In short, EMI knew they had something unique but, since it was unlike anything else they'd heard before, they more or less took the decision to just let the band get on with it. It was not long before Beecher-Stevens' gamble more than paid off. "I classed them as weird, but good,"[9] he confessed.

Having heard the tracks on offer, EMI set about re-recording them at their own studio at Abbey Road in London's St John's Wood. Although Boyd had been given the nudge, he certainly had the last laugh when his original recordings were used after all. As Norman Smith recalled, "I told the boys I'd like to have

ABOVE: SITTING ON THE STAIRS AT MIKE LEONARD'S HOUSE IN JANUARY 1967.

another go at any rate and in fact we set up this recording to do just that along with other titles. It was an all-night session, and I could see that they weren't too keen to attempt a remake, so in fact we never did have a go at that."[10]

When 'Arnold Layne' came out in March, the band had even made a promo film to back it up. Filmed at Wittering beach on the south coast in the depths of winter, it was a comical tribute to the Beatles' *Help!* movie. Blackhill even paid to have the single hyped in order to ensure that it reached a favourable chart position. As a result the BBC filmed them for *Top of the Pops* (although it was not broadcast) and the single was guaranteed plenty of radio airplay. Bizarrely, although the BBC were happy to oblige on their Light service[**], the more left-field pirate station

---

* Pink Floyd's initial contract was for ten years with a £5,000 advance and an 8 per cent royalty rate but with all studio costs recharged. A little over a year later Pink Floyd renegotiated the deal to have all studio costs paid for, with the caveat of a reduced 5 per cent royalty.

** BBC Radio One began broadcasting at 7.00am on Saturday 30 September 1967 with Tony Blackburn hosting the Daily Disc Delivery show and opening with 'Flowers In The Rain' by the Move. The Light Programme was renamed BBC Radio Two.

ABOVE: PINK FLOYD AT THE PRESS LAUNCH OF 'ARNOLD LAYNE' AT EMI RECORDS, 3 MARCH 1967.

Radio London banned it for being too smutty – in reality a contrived demonstration to display moral standards in their bid for an official government broadcast licence. Even Pete Murray reviewed it on BBC TV's *Juke Box Jury*, on its Friday 11 March edition, but his comments infuriated Waters: "He said we were a con. He thought it was just contrived rubbish to meet some kind of unhealthy demand."[11]

Furthermore, a backlash was brewing in certain media circles. It was suggested that Pink Floyd, then spearheading the "counter-culture", were promoting music sympathetic to certain types of drug abuse. In particular the *News of the World*, then a weekly national broadsheet, set out to alert the general public to the evils of drugs in pop music and set in motion a whole month's worth of investigative reports into this throughout February. The edition of Monday 13 February, in particular, started off with a huge headline that read, "Pop Songs And The Cult Of LSD" above a photo of Pink Floyd with the caption, "The Pink Floyd group specialise in 'psychedelic music' which is designed to illustrate LSD experiences." The two-page article that followed highlighted the London Free School's apparently subversive activities and Pink Floyd's music in particular. This article alone caused the management of the Southampton Guildhall to cancel one of the band's impending shows.

EMI were then forced to issue a statement to the press to effectively deny all knowledge of the drug connections in Pink Floyd's music, which was also exacerbated by the same article slamming their release of the Smoke's single, 'My Friend Jack'. The newspaper allowed some recourse, and Pink Floyd more or less stated that the term "psychedelic", meant, to them, the use of light and sound in performance rather than an excuse to take LSD. Even as late as July the band were hampered by the sideswipes they received, which caused Waters to air his frustrations in the *NME*: "We are simply a pop group. But because we use light and colour in our act a lot of people seem to imagine that we are trying to put across some message with nasty, evil undertones."

Surprisingly, despite all the LSD connotations of their act, the band was a very straight-laced bunch. It was only much later that drugs featured on the agenda: "None of them did drugs when I met them," said Jenner, "except Syd, and we would only smoke dope. Then in the Summer of Love and all that bollocks Syd got very enthusiastic about acid and got into the religious aspect of it. The others were very straight. Rick would take a puff now and again, but Roger and Nick would never go near it."[12]

The reality was that Pink Floyd had barely any interest in psychedelia or the so-called underground other than it offered them a convenient audience. What did interest them was the opportunity to explore the multimedia aspects of live performance which, ultimately, shaped the band it would become.

However, if EMI were worried about the drugs issue, they should have been far more concerned about the band's live performance. Both 'Arnold Layne' and its June follow-up, 'See Emily Play', were as far removed from their stage act as they could possibly be. Their quaint pop songs were ignored completely in favour of high-volume, mind-bending workouts lasting, in some cases, well over ten minutes. While these were acceptable on their home turf of London, provincial audiences were nonplussed, fully expecting to hear their chart hits. Provincial clubs played dance music, soul and pop to an audience who wanted to let their hair down at the weekend. Pink Floyd literally hit the unsuspecting crowd with a wall of sound verging on "white noise".

This reputation had already spread, as *Melody Maker* pointed out: "Are Pink Floyd being quite honest when they make coy and attractive records like 'See Emily Play' then proceed to make the night hideous with a thunderous, incomprehensible, screaming, sonic torture that five American doctors agree could permanently damage the senses?"

When word got around that they rarely played their chart successes, some promoters insisted on making the band sign a pre-performance clause to ensure that they did so, to avoid audience unrest. Many of the out-of-London bookings would often riot when confronted by this vision from hell. Stories of the reception the band received in some parts of the country are near legendary. Beer glasses – and their contents – were thrown at them, fights broke out and torrents of abuse were hurled, as Nick Mason testified: "During that period we were working at Top Rank circuits and they hated it. Hated it. We could clear halls so fast it wasn't true. I mean they were outraged by what came round on the revolving stage and they lost very little time in trying to make this clear."[13] But, he explained, "We were not demoralized. We rejuvenated every time we came back to London and got that fix of finding that there was an audience for us."[14]

Such was the band's determination that not once did they cease trying to win over the masses. There was no way they were going to compromise. It was their way or not at all, and this was summed up in a typically ironic comment by Waters at the time: "We've got the recording side together and not the playing side. So what we've got to do now is get together a stage act that has nothing to do with our records – things like 'Interstellar Overdrive' which is beautiful, and instrumentals that are much easier to play."[15] It's a remark that may also have reflected their ability, or rather lack of ability, at that time.

This approach may have paid off in the long run, but at the time, given their then technical prowess and set list, forcing this material, rather than "the hits", on the public was verging on professional suicide. The industry was a very different beast back in the 1960s – records actually climbed the charts and they had to sell significantly more copies than today. Blackhill had also employed London's most sought-after music PR Tony Brainsby who, remarkably, kept the band name in the weekly music press throughout the year almost without fail.

This, combined with those crucial chart positions, secured more bookings and higher fees. Bands paid their dues by constantly gigging, with endless drives day and night along a network of pre-motorway roads. Structured touring such that we know of today wasn't really heard of, but there was a thriving live music scene and almost every town the length and breadth of Britain had a venue that hosted weekly beat, soul or jazz dances. But the underground psychedelic scene was barely recognized in the provinces and publications such as *IT* and *OZ* had almost no distribution outside of London, leaving only a handful of "freaks" or "heads" in tune with an emerging scene that included Pink Floyd.

With that in mind it wasn't difficult to realize that it was the band's audience in London that held the key and it was this audience which needed to be developed and nurtured first and foremost. Fortunately prominent classical music promoter Christopher Hunt was broad-minded enough to recognize there was great merit in Floyd's performances, assisted no doubt by the fact that Peter Jenner's partner, Sumi, was working for him. Taking the plunge, Hunt produced a show at the Commonwealth Institute on 17 January and, having been well received, again at the stuffy Queen Elizabeth Hall on Friday

ABOVE: PINK FLOYD IN PRE-SHOW REHEARSALS AT THE "GAMES FOR MAY" CONCERT AT THE QUEEN ELIZABETH HALL, 12 MAY 1967.

12 May – the latter was the reserve of the classical elite. Generally regarded as a critical turning point for Pink Floyd, this show included their first public use of an idea developed in the recording studio: additional speakers were placed at the back of the hall to give an effect of "sound in the round". Essentially it was a crude pan-pot device made by Bernard Speight, an Abbey Road engineer, and in technical jargon consisted of four large rheostats, which were converted from 270-degree rotation to 90-degree. Along with the shift stick, these elements were housed in a large box and enabled the panning of quadraphonic sound. The setup was, unfortunately, stolen after the show and didn't resurface again until their 1969 UK tour, when it was dubbed the "Azimuth Co-ordinator". In addition, the Queen Elizabeth Hall show had props that were arranged on stage, bubble machines that let fly and a well-developed light show which incorporated 35mm film slides and movie sequences. New compositions were also written, including the song 'Games For May', which would form the basis of the band's second single, 'See Emily Play'.

It may not have seemed so at the time, because other matters were beginning to concern the band, but 'See Emily Play' also played a decisive part in the band's history, securing them radio play, TV appearances and a healthy chart position. Britain was starting to take note of these rising young stars.

Nevertheless Pink Floyd's meteoric rise to success was having an adverse side effect on Barrett, who was starting to show marked signs of fatigue. The pressure he was under as the band's leader, coupled with the onslaught of constant touring and recording, caused him to withdraw into himself. An increasing use of psychedelics both in private and on stage only made matters worse by filling him with chronic stage fright.

The first hint of something going slightly awry came in July, at the BBC TV Studios, where they were recording 'See Emily Play' for *Top of the Pops*. The single had sold significantly better than their debut, and, as a result of its chart performance, Pink Floyd appeared a remarkable three times on the show. As legend has it, Pink Floyd turned out for their first appearance in their supreme psychedelic King's Road attire. On the second show, Syd's appearance was less immaculate and by the third week he was practically dishevelled, with a careless attitude, uninterested in performing, and insisting that if John Lennon didn't have to appear on the show, then neither did he.

It was the start of Barrett's increasingly erratic behaviour, which caused a catalogue of professional disasters throughout the rest of the year. The first occurred literally the day after their final *Top of the Pops* appearance, at the recording studio for the

BBC Light Programme's *Saturday Club* on Friday 28 July, when Barrett allegedly freaked out and walked out of the session.

For their part, Jenner and King were quick to defuse the situation and ordered the band to have the rest of the month off, cancelling all of their bookings and insisting they take a well-deserved holiday, with Waters, Barrett and friends decamping to Formentera. It is ironic that one major music paper greeted the week of their highly anticipated debut album release date with the headline "Pink Floyd Flake Out". Blackhill spent most of the break trying to convince scoop-hungry music journalists that the band had not actually split

ABOVE: PINK FLOYD PHOTOGRAPHED 1967.

up and that Barrett was merely recuperating from exhaustion on doctor's orders.

Their debut album, *The Piper at the Gates of Dawn*, which took its title from Chapter Seven of the Kenneth Grahame children's novel *The Wind in the Willows*, is still regarded as a psychedelic classic, based largely around Barrett's storytelling and lengthy instrumentals. These ranged from the poppy 'Flaming' and 'Lucifer Sam' through the hippie I-Ching recital of 'Chapter 24' and the whimsical, childlike poetry of 'Gnome' and 'Scarecrow', to the spacey freak-outs of 'Pow R Toc H' and 'Astronomy Domine' (featuring Peter Jenner reeling off names of planets and stars through a megaphone), and of course, the monumentally thunderous 'Interstellar Overdrive'. These last three tracks were possibly the closest representations of their stage act provided you turned your amplifier up to maximum. However, what is striking is Norman Smith's exceptional production. Had Boyd been given the task it is debatable whether he would have reined them in and achieved the same result.

The Piper at the Gates of Dawn also illustrates a band in development and shows Roger Waters' emergence as a composer. He may not have been the most technically gifted member of the band at that stage, that credit goes to Rick Wright, whose talents should never be underestimated – and although this album is largely credited to Barrett, Waters certainly wasn't short of inspiration: 'Pow R Toc H' is an exceptional contribution and a new composition, 'Set The Controls For The Heart Of The Sun', was recorded that August after it had become a staple of their live shows.

While the album lost many of Floyd's hard core UFO followers – at least, those who preferred the cacophonous, freak-out element – it gained many more, garnering rave reviews as a fine achievement that is regarded to this day as one of the greatest UK psychedelic albums of the 1960s.

Returning to active duty, Pink Floyd plunged straight back into a heavy touring schedule, including their first overseas bookings, in Scandinavia and Ireland, in September. With Barrett effectively no longer fronting the band, Waters acted as spokesman in press and radio interviews of this period and for some time afterwards. It may be that this sudden assumption of responsibility was symptomatic of his already strong sense of leadership.

Blackhill, meanwhile, were keen to break into the lucrative US market. EMI's American sister label Capitol Records, based in Hollywood, took them on, assigning them to its subsidiary label Tower, and called for a promotional tour, organized by The General Artists Corporation of Beverly Hills, which would include San Francisco, Los Angeles, New York, Chicago and Boston. The debut album was scheduled for release to coincide with the tour, Tower heralding them "The Light Kings of England".

With the band chaperoned by Andrew King, the tour was due to start in late October at Bill Graham's Fillmore Auditorium in San Francisco. Much to King's distress, and Graham's extreme annoyance, their work permits were delayed and the first set of engagements had to be cancelled. A furious Graham is reported to have even called the US ambassador in London in the middle of the night to hurry the process.

However, the problem was partly exacerbated by the British Musicians Union who, between the late 1930s and 1969, wielded a strong influence over the Ministry of Labour, and discouraged them from granting work permits to any American artists wishing to play in Britain unless a reciprocal

RIGHT: PINK FLOYD PHOTOGRAPHED BY ANDREW WHITTUCK IN HIS BEDROOM AT HIS PARENTS' HOUSE IN JUNE 1967 COMPLETE WITH JOE GANNON LIGHT SHOW.

agreement was in place where a British equivalent could be sent to the US to perform in exchange.

Finally the band took to the stage in support of Big Brother & The Holding Company featuring Janis Joplin. But Pink Floyd's revered light show was far from exceptional. Lighting the Fillmore (a large ballroom) and Winterland – a converted ice rink with a circular gallery – was a daunting task for Peter Wynne-Wilson. Although this was a bearable situation, which resulted in Wynne-Wilson merely augmenting the house lights, Syd's condition was far from normal. "Detuning his guitar all the way through one number, striking the strings," recalled Mason. "He more or less just ceased playing and stood there leaving us to muddle along as best we could."[16]

Several high-profile live TV shows were also scheduled, and were equally catastrophic. On the *Pat Boone in Hollywood* show the band attempted to mime their way through 'The Gnome' and 'Chapter 24', before facing the horrors of an interview in which Barrett responded with total silence to the questions asked of him. On Dick Clark's *American Bandstand,* Waters struggled to mime lead vocals through 'Apples And Oranges', since Barrett's attention seemed to be focused on a gaping void. On their final TV appearance on *Boss City* they once again struggled through 'Apples And Oranges'.

This chain of events was far more than Capitol could handle since they were relying on those important TV plugs to push the album. In a final, somewhat embarrassing meeting with Capitol's MD, King had to witness the man break down before his eyes: "He burst into tears and asked us what he was going to do."[17] It was the last straw and after fulfilling their shows for Bill Graham in San Francisco Pink Floyd were

LEFT: PINK FLOYD AT THE CASA MADRONA HOTEL IN SAUSALITO, 11 NOVEMBER 1967.

recalled to the UK, via an impromptu showcase gig at New York's Cheetah en route.

Remarkably, Blackhill continued to ignore the signs and enthusiastically committed the band to a festival show in the Netherlands followed by a month of intense touring, including a slot on a pop package tour of the UK supporting the Jimi Hendrix Experience. Such tours were normally reserved for lightweight entertainment and rock 'n' roll, but this was the first, and probably the last, to showcase "underground" rock acts. With Hendrix and the Move headlining, and support from Amen Corner, the Nice, the Outer Limits and Eire Apparent, the bands appeared in descending order of importance, with a stage time to match.

Pink Floyd was consequently allocated a 20-minute set, just about long enough for three numbers, which nevertheless caused some bewilderment to the majority of fans, who had turned out for Hendrix. "They got a very mixed reaction,"[18] recalled Noel Redding, Hendrix's bassist.

But at least they were among friends, although Syd's behaviour was still a cause for concern. Often he would sit alone on the tour bus or wander off into town when he should have been on stage. Mitch Mitchell, drummer with the Experience, recalled that: "It was actually good fun, lunacy most of the time. However, Syd Barrett didn't talk to anyone during that time."[19]

Indeed, on at least one occasion the young Davey O'List, guitarist with the Nice, stood in for him. "I used to stand by the side of the stage to watch the Floyd. They only used to play one number in their set and because it was a fairly straightforward guitar thing, I was able to pick it up quite quickly. So when Syd didn't turn up one night, Floyd asked me to go on instead."[20]

Even Barrett's old pal David Gilmour could see little hope: "It was totally impossible for me to understand the way Syd's mind was working at that time. It was also from having been to two or three of their gigs that it was impossible for me to see how they could carry on like that, because Syd was quite obviously not up to being in that group at that time."[21]

Waters later spoke of that first trip to the United States and the *American Bandstand* incident, recalling how the rehearsal takes had gone just fine but, come the final transmission, Barrett just stood there, arms limply hanging by his side. "He knew of course perfectly well what was going on. He was just being crazy."[22]

Additionally there is also the footage from BBC's *Tomorrow's World*, repeated, for the first time, as part of the BBC *Omnibus* documentary on Pink Floyd in November 1994. Filmed in December 1967 and broadcast in January 1968, it shows Barrett in fine fettle. Regardless of this fact, this may merely serve to highlight the extent of Barrett's apparent schizophrenia.

By now it was also very obvious that Barrett was incapable of continuing to produce the catchy pop songs the band had previously relied on to get them into the charts. 'Apples And Oranges', his last single with Pink Floyd, was released in mid-November and failed to even gain a chart placing. This, coupled with a live set that increasingly reflected the emergence of Waters' own brand of science-fiction epics, such as 'Set The Controls For The Heart Of The Sun', was taking them in new directions. This inevitably clashed with Barrett's more recent tortured abstract compositions such as 'Scream Thy Last Scream' (featuring Mason's first ever lead vocal), 'Vegetable Man' and 'Jugband Blues', which were doing nothing to advance Floyd's career. It seemed as if there was a conscious attempt by the rest of the band to radically reinvent themselves, in order to not only survive the collapse of "Flower Power" but Barrett's own strange new directions.

It is likely that Barrett may have sensed this redefinition and, aware of the fact that he was not going to be a part of Floyd's new identity, pre-empted the move.

It wasn't long before word was put out that an "additional" guitarist was being sought, and although Davey O'List and Jeff Beck were initially considered, it was David Gilmour who attracted the band's attention. He was in attendance at their Royal College of Art show that December, and since he wasn't doing anything better, apart from driving a van around London for clothing designers Quorum, he accepted without hesitation.

Whether it was done this way to limit the hurt to Barrett's feelings is also open to speculation; perhaps it was thought that the addition of a friend would help to stabilize him.

1. *Days in the Life* by Jonathan Green, Heinemann, 1988.
2. The *Daily Mail You Magazine*, c. 1990.
3. Author interview with Joe Boyd, 1987.
4. Danish TV interview with Pink Floyd, 1992.
5. *Dancing in the Street*, BBC2 TV, 20 July 1996.
6. *Pink Floyd: A Visual Documentary* by Miles, Omnibus, 1980.
7–8. Author interview with Joe Boyd, 1987.
9. *Pink Floyd* by Rick Sanders, Futura, 1976.
10. *The Pink Floyd Story*, Capital Radio, 17 December 1976.
11. *Zig Zag*, Issue 32, July 1973.

12. *Mojo*, May 1994.
13. *The Pink Floyd Story*, Capital Radio, 17 December 1976.
14. *Mojo*, July 1995.
15. *Melody Maker*, 5 August 1967.
16. *Mojo*, May 1994.
17. *Crazy Diamond* by Pete Anderson and Mike Watkinson, Omnibus, 1991.
18. Author correspondence with Noel Redding, November 1996.
19. *The Hendrix Experience* by Mitch Mitchell, Pyramid, 1990.
20. *Space Daze* by Dave Thompson, Cleopatra, 1994.
21. *The Pink Floyd Story*, Capital Radio, 17 December 1976.
22. *Dancing in the Street*, BBC2 TV, 20 July 1996.

1966

PINK FLOYD, JANUARY 1966 – 25 JANUARY 1968

Roger "Syd" Barrett, Nick Mason, Roger Waters, Richard Wright.

SUNDAY 9 JANUARY – PERFORMANCE
The Goings On, Archer Street, London, England

The Goings On was a short-lived Sunday afternoon club, organised by the beat poets Pete Brown, Johnny Byrne and Spike Hawkins at what was a recently opened bar that reportedly doubled as an infamous illicit gambling den.

FRIDAY 11 MARCH & SATURDAY 12 MARCH – PERFORMANCES
Rag Ball, Concourse Area, University of Essex, Wivenhoe Park, Colchester, England

Appearing on 11 March: Marianne Faithfull, Coletrane Union, the Swinging Blue Jeans and Rick & Us (in the Common Room); the Tea Set (9.00pm–9.30pm) with the Cherrie Pickers and Jimmy Pilgrim & the Classics (in the Concourse Area). Appearing on 12 March: Coletrane Union, Martin Lewis Trad Band and Rick & Us (in the Common Room); the Tea Set (two sets between 2.00am–3.00am and 4.00am–5.00am) with Jimmy Pilgrim & the Classics and the Trends (in the Concourse Area).

The formative Pink Floyd played under the name the Tea Set for the last time at this two-day university rag weekend. It was also their first experience of performing with a projected film show as Roger Waters later recalled in an interview with *Zig Zag* magazine: "Some bright spark down there had done a film with a paraplegic in London, given this paraplegic a film camera and wheeled him round London filming his view. They showed it up on screen behind us as we played."

SUNDAY 13 MARCH – PERFORMANCE
Trip, The Marquee, Wardour Street, London, England

With AMM.

In an article written by *IT* co-founder, for New York's *East Village Other*, Miles wrote: "Every Sunday from about 7.00pm till it's over, the Marquee Club in Soho is happening. Nothing is advertised (there are no advertisements), no one is billed, no tickets, about five phone calls are made. Over two hundred people turn up, sometimes many, many more. When they are there, they do things, meet people, *happen*. Unorganized events have included Donovan, in red Cleopatra makeup, singing to one sitar and five conga drummers, AMM in white coats with electronic tapes, films projected onto dancers. The Pink Floyd, surely London's loudest electronic Beat group."

Despite the possible inaccuracy of the start time, there is some doubt as to the frequency of these events. In his book *Pink Floyd: The Early Years*, Miles goes on to say that, "It is unclear how many times the Pink Floyd played the Spontaneous Underground." Previously published gig lists show them as the house band, but the event was not a regular one: John Hopkins remembered attending only one and can only remember three events taking place in total. In all probability there were less than half a dozen, and it is certain that Pink Floyd did not play them all. Since no adverts and few flyers exist to prove this point, the following list of Marquee dates is therefore debatable.

SUNDAY 27 MARCH – PERFORMANCE
The Marquee, Wardour Street, London, England

SUNDAY 3 APRIL – PERFORMANCE
The Marquee, Wardour Street, London, England

APRIL – TELEVISION AUDITION
Rediffusion TV Studios, Wembley, England

According to Nick Mason, in his book *Inside Out: A Personal History of Pink Floyd*, the band failed a live audition to appear on the London ITV music programme *Ready, Steady, Go!* but were invited back the following week with audience tickets and saw the Lovin' Spoonful perform. This was presumably either their 15 or 22 April appearance.

SUNDAY 17 APRIL – PERFORMANCE
The Marquee, Wardour Street, London, England

SUNDAY 1 MAY – PERFORMANCE
The Marquee, Wardour Street, London, England

SUNDAY 8 MAY – PERFORMANCE
The Marquee, Wardour Street, London, England

SUNDAY 15 MAY – PERFORMANCE
The Marquee, Wardour Street, London, England

SUNDAY 5 JUNE – PERFORMANCE
The Marquee, Wardour Street, London, England

SUNDAY 12 JUNE – PERFORMANCE
The Marquee, Wardour Street, London, England

Set list included 'Roadrunner', 'Louie Louie', 'You Can't Judge A Book By Its Cover', 'Motivating'.

This was also the show at which future Pink Floyd manager Peter Jenner saw the band perform for the first time, and indeed the final Spontaneous Underground show. "At that stage they were a blues band who played things like 'Louie Louie' and then played wacky bits in the middle," recalled Jenner. "I wandered around trying to work out whether the noise was coming from the keyboards or from the guitar and that was what interested me." But, as Waters later said, "We didn't know many songs, so it was a matter of settling on a chord and improvising, if that's the word."

FRIDAY 30 SEPTEMBER – PERFORMANCE
London Free School, **All Saints Church Hall,
Powis Gardens, London, England**

With Soft Machine.
Brian Wilcock, DJ at the popular West Hampstead club called Klooks Kleek, recalled, "One night a well-dressed guy, probably late twenties, came up to me and said he had a new band playing its first show in Ladbroke Grove the next night; would I take the club record console and some records to play in the interval between two sets, for a fiver. I told him I couldn't take the console, but I had a Dansette type deck that plugged into a PA system and he said, 'Fine.' So when I get there, it turns out to be Pink Floyd. I told them I only had soul and R&B records but they said that's what they wanted."

FRIDAY 14 OCTOBER – PERFORMANCE
London Free School, **All Saints Church Hall,
Powis Gardens, London, England**

Set list: 'Pink', 'Let's Roll Another', 'Gimme A Break', 'Stoned Alone', 'I Can Tell', 'The Gnome', 'Interstellar Overdrive', 'Lucy Leave', 'Stethoscope', 'Flapdoodle Dealing', 'Snowing', 'Matilda Mother', 'Pow R Toc H', 'Astronomy Domine'.

As the above set list indicates, Pink Floyd by this time had developed a great deal of original material, some of which was recorded for their debut album. Many other tracks are sadly lost to the mists of time. John Hopkins later wrote in *International Times* that at this time Pink Floyd were playing "mainly instrumentals and numbers that would sometimes last for half an hour."

SATURDAY 15 OCTOBER – PERFORMANCE
International Times First All Night Rave, **The Roundhouse, Chalk Farm, London, England**

With Soft Machine.
Set list included 'Astronomy Domine', 'Interstellar Overdrive'.

Billed in the debut issue of *International Times* as "The Greatest Happening of Them All" and lasting from 11.00pm to dawn, *International Times* described its own launch party thus: "Darkness, only flashing lights, people in masks, girls half naked. Other people standing about wondering what the hell was going on. Pot smoke. Now and then the sound of a bottle breaking. The Pink Floyd, psychedelic pop group did weird things to the feel of the event with their scary feedback sounds, slide projectors playing on their skin – drops of paint run riot on the slides to produce outer space, prehistoric textures – spotlights flashing on them in time with a drum beat.... The Soft Machine, another group with new ideas drove a motorbike into the place…a large car in the middle of it all painted bright pop-art stripes…Simon Postuma and Marijke Koger, the Amsterdam couple, designed an interesting cubicle with coloured screens and nets and within the box one of them, in suitable dress, read palms and told fortunes.... In another part the London Film Co-op gave an all-night film show featuring films like *Scorpio Rising* and *Towers Open Fire*. Famous people turned up: Antonioni and Monica Vitti, Paul McCartney disguised as an Arab, Kenneth Rexroth, Peter Brook, Mickie Most and Tony Secunda…. Of course several things went wrong. There was that narrow entrance for an unpleasant start. That communal toilet that ended up in flood (in fact 2,500 people had to share the two toilets in the building!). A giant jelly made in a bath for the party was unfortunately run over by

a bicycle. How this happened, or what became of the remains of the jelly or the bicycle, no one knows…. To top it all Pink Floyd were the last group to play; [they] made the most melodramatic of climaxes to the evening by blowing out the power in the middle of 'Interstellar Overdrive'. It was a resounding finish to their most important appearance so far."

On the other hand, Kenneth Rexroth, the US beat poet, wrote in the *San Francisco Chronicle* that the music was ear-splitting and he felt as if he were on the *Titanic*. He thought that Pink Floyd had not turned up and that the weird sounds coming from the stage were being made by amateurs, who'd assembled from the audience.

In an article in the *Sunday Times,* joint manager Andrew King said that "We don't call ourselves psychedelic. But we don't deny it. We don't confirm it either. People who want to make up slogans can do it." The group's bass guitarist Roger Waters was a bit less noncommittal. "It's totally anarchistic. But cooperative anarchy if you see what I mean. It's definitely a complete realization of the aims of psychedelia. If you take LSD what you experience depends entirely on who you are. Our music may give you the screaming horrors or throw you into screaming ecstasy. Mostly it's the latter. We find our audiences stop dancing now. We tend to get them standing there totally grooved with their mouths open."

THE
**GRAHAME BOND ORGANISATION
ARTWOODS & PINK FLOYD
TOP RANK SUITE**
WEDNESDAY, 19th OCTOBER
8 p.m.—1 a.m. · Bars · 7/-. Tickets at the door or Art College

WEDNESDAY 19 OCTOBER – PERFORMANCE ▲
Top Rank Suite, Brighton, England

With the Graham Bond Organisation and the Artwoods.

FRIDAY 21 OCTOBER – PERFORMANCE
London Free School, **All Saints Church Hall,
Powis Gardens, London, England**

FRIDAY 28 OCTOBER – PERFORMANCE
London Free School, **All Saints Church Hall,
Powis Gardens, London, England**

MONDAY 31 OCTOBER – RECORDING SESSION
Hemel Hempstead, England

It has been widely documented that on the same day as their management company Blackhill Enterprises was set up, Pink Floyd were whisked away to record a demo tape at "Thompson Private Recording Studios" in Hemel Hempstead to tout around prospective record companies and venues. In fact Thomson (correct spelling) was the family name and the so-called recording studio was not a professional studio by any stretch of the imagination. In fact, no such business is listed in the 1966 telephone directory.

According to Colin Hales of local band Denim Coalition, who also recorded there in 1966, the operation was run by, "the eponymous Richard Thompson [sic], a man who went on to lay down many more memorable tracks – mainly between Bletchley and Leighton Buzzard as an employee of British Rail."

The studio was merely a rudimentary setup comprising a two-track tape recorder, mixer and microphones all set up in the spare room of what is a very large country house situated between Hemel Hempstead and the village of Bovingdon and seemingly operated by the owner's son, Richard Thomson.

Poor quality tapes of 'Let's Roll Another One' and 'I Get Stoned' (also known as 'Stoned Alone') reportedly made at this session, and from an unknown source, began circulating among collectors in the 1980s. The recording facilities would suggest the songs were performed live although there may have been the opportunity to do some basic overdubbing. 'Let's Roll Another One' was adapted much later to become 'Candy And A Currant Bun', the B-side to their debut single 'Arnold Layne'. There is also speculation that a version of 'Interstellar Overdrive' was recorded on this date which was later used on the 1968 film *San Francisco*. This information was allegedly sourced from Nick Mason's diaries, and first appeared in the 1976 paperback *Pink Floyd* by Rick Sanders.

Peter Jenner is understandably vague about the Thomson session: "I don't know why we went there. We just heard about it through someone, and it was cheap. And we went over there and it was really quite nice, it was sort of country-ish and in a nice house.… It was pretty primitive, I would think it was only stereo, I would imagine it was two-track, and then bounced from track to track if anything needed to be bounced. It wouldn't have been four-track, it wasn't that advanced. It might have only been mono with two machines, I don't know. I mean for us then it was lots of wires and microphones and cables and things, it was 'a studio' you know."

Andrew King also recalled, "Going down to this funny little studio, which was sort of in the back bedroom of this guy's house… and he turned out to be rather a nasty piece of work, but at the time it was pretty exciting…. The song I remember was a song called 'I Get Stoned'. 'Sitting here all alone, I get stoned.' I don't know whatever happened to that. I think it was just done with Syd singing with an acoustic guitar, and was then meant to be developed later. I don't know if it ever had a rhythm track on it."

FRIDAY 4 NOVEMBER – PERFORMANCE
London Free School, **All Saints Church Hall, Powis Gardens, London, England**

SATURDAY 5 NOVEMBER – PERFORMANCE
Wilton Hall, Bletchley, England
Supported by the Torments.
The band was billed in local advertising as "Elektra Recording Stars The Pink Freud", which would indicate a premature assumption that Joe Boyd had secured a deal with the label.

SATURDAY 5 NOVEMBER – PERFORMANCE
The Clubhouse, Fiveacres Country Club, Bricket Wood, near Watford, England
Pink Floyd made an impromptu appearance at a private party on their way back from Bletchley, which just so happened to be the site of Britain's oldest naturist club! The caravan park and clubhouse was managed by Jack Bracelin, later proprietor of Five Acre Lights who would go on to supply lighting for the *Free School* and *UFO* club. However, there is little chance the audience would have been naked, not in November anyway!

TUESDAY 8 NOVEMBER – PERFORMANCE
London Free School, **All Saints Church Hall, Powis Gardens, London, England**

FRIDAY 11 NOVEMBER – PERFORMANCE
London Free School, **All Saints Church Hall, Powis Gardens, London, England**

SATURDAY 12 NOVEMBER – PERFORMANCE
Corn Exchange, Bedford, England
Supported by Something Else.

SUNDAY 13 NOVEMBER – PERFORMANCE
Starlite Ballroom, Greenford, England
Supporting the Ram Jam Band featuring Geno Washington.

TUESDAY 15 NOVEMBER – PERFORMANCE
London Free School, **All Saints Church Hall, Powis Gardens, London, England**

FRIDAY 18 NOVEMBER – PERFORMANCE ▼
Psychodilia, **Rooms A & B, Hornsey College of Art, Hornsey, London, England**
With Porrage. Although Pink Floyd had rehearsed here many times

because of their connection with Mike Leonard, who also taught at the Regent Street Polytechnic, this was their first documented gig there. Students of the Advanced Studies Group let fly with an array of lighting equipment they had built as part of their course work. As Mason later recalled, "The most important starting point for the light show was Mike Leonard and the Hornsey College of Art. That was the idea that the music could be improvised and the lighting could be improvised to go with it. And that definitely was an influence."

SATURDAY 19 NOVEMBER – PERFORMANCE
Main Hall, Technical College, Canterbury, England
Supported by the Koalas.
The *Kentish Times* reported that, "Flashing lights, slide-projection, thunderous atmospheric sounds and incense were the essence of the psychedelic Pink Floyd concert held at Canterbury Technical College on Saturday. A purely physical sensation, psychedelic music either

makes your flesh crawl with emotion or leaves you cold. It should be seen and not written about, but it is an experience that should be tried at least once. The Pink Floyd, a London group, comprising two guitars, drums and organ, were super-amplified. Using distortion as a second sound, their music tended to be slow, but not uninteresting, and resembling the sound of a church organ. The opening curtains revealed the group on stage, wearing neutral shirts to reflect the coloured lights, and standing in semi-darkness. Behind was a 15ft-high tinfoil Buddha. On either side, sets of filtered spots sprayed varying colours over the stage, whilst modern art slides were projected behind. This weird conglomeration of sights and sound added up to a strange result. Those watching were a little mystified, but after the first rather frightening discordant notes, began dancing, and gradually relaxed. It was an enjoyable if somewhat odd evening."

TUESDAY 22 NOVEMBER – PERFORMANCE
London Free School, **All Saints Church Hall, Powis Gardens, London, England**

TUESDAY 29 NOVEMBER – PERFORMANCE
London Free School, **All Saints Church Hall, Powis Gardens, London, England**

International Times reported that, "Since I last saw the Pink Floyd they've got hold of bigger amplifiers, new light gear and a rave from Paul McCartney. This time I saw them at Powis Gardens on Tuesday 29th, the last of their regular shows there. Their work is largely improvisation and lead guitarist Sid Barrett shoulders most of the burden of providing continuity and attack in the improvised parts. He was providing a huge range of sounds with the new equipment, from throttled shrieks to mellow feedback roars. Visually the show was less adventurous. Three projectors bathed the group, the walls and sometimes the audience in vivid colour. But the colour was fairly static and there was no searching for the brain alpha rhythms by chopping up the images. The equipment that the group is using now is infant electronics: let's see what they will do with the grown-up electronics that a colour television industry will make available."

SATURDAY 3 DECEMBER – PERFORMANCE ▶
Psychodelphia Versus Ian Smith, **The Roundhouse, Chalk Farm, London, England**

With the Ram Holder Messengers and underground film shows, poets and happenings. This event was promoted by the Majority Rule for Rhodesia Committee and held in protest of Ian Smith, the Governor of Rhodesia (now Zimbabwe), continuing his policy of white minority rule. The show attracted media interest after advertising posters featured Smith made to resemble Hitler.

NME reported that: "Last Friday [29 November] the Pink Floyd, a new London group, embarked upon their first happening – a pop dance incorporating psychedelic effects and mixed media – whatever that is! The slides were excellent – colourful, frightening, grotesque, beautiful and the group's trip into outer-space sounds promised very interesting things to

come. Unfortunately all fell a bit flat in the cold reality of All Saints Church Hall, but on Saturday night at Chalk Farm's Roundhouse things went better when thousands of people turned up to watch the show. The Floyd need to write more of their own material – psychedelic versions of 'Louie Louie' won't come off, but if they can incorporate their electronic prowess with some melodic and lyrical songs – getting away from dated R&B things, they could well score in the near future."

THURSDAY 8 DECEMBER – PERFORMANCE
Chicago Christmas Dance, **Royal College of Art, Kensington, London, England**

With the Graham Bond Organisation, the Convention, the Square 4 and the Minor Birds.
Peter Whitehead, in an interview with *Record Collector* (January 1994), commented this was the first time he ever saw Pink Floyd perform live, which led him to invite them to contribute to his documentary, *Tonite Let's All Make Love in London* the following year.

MONDAY 12 DECEMBER – PERFORMANCE
You're Joking – A Benefit Carnival For Oxfam, **Royal Albert Hall, Kensington, London, England**

This was a marathon four-hour show in aid of Oxfam. Pink Floyd must have felt out of place among a conventional cast that included Peter Cook and Dudley Moore, Paul Jones, Alan Price, Chris Farlowe, Barry Mackenzie, Peter and Gordon and Jackie Trent. Barry Fantoni linked the sets and played clarinet and tenor sax with "The Alberts", a lunacy group, who are said to have contributed some of the best moments of the evening by smashing up a piano on stage. The entire cast joined in a merry chorus finale of 'We All Live On Yellow Margarine' [a parody of the Beatles' 'Yellow Submarine'].

FRIDAY 16 DECEMBER – PERFORMANCE
Annual Prohibition Carnival, **The Architects Association, Bedford Square, London, England**

The annual Christmas dance at the Architects Association was given the theme 'Think Pink', where stewards wore pink suits and the guests ate prawns and drank pink champagne! Pink Floyd was booked only on account of the name association and for no other reason, and it is almost certain the organizers had seen posters of the band appearing at *UFO* which was located only a short distance from here.

TUESDAY 20 DECEMBER – PERFORMANCE
Art School Psychedelic Freak Out, **Life Drawing Studio, Cambridgeshire College of Art and Technology, Cambridge, England**

Set list included 'Arnold Layne'.
Organizer Paul Webb recalled that, "In 1966 after Syd (who had been in the year above me) had moved to London it fell on the more senior students to organize the Art School Christmas party and comic revue. Syd had by now formed Pink Floyd with Cambridge friend Roger Waters and two others, Richard Wright and Nick Mason. They were beginning to make a name for themselves on the

underground music scene in London, playing regularly at the *UFO Club* in Tottenham Court Road, which happened to be near to the grotty flat Syd shared with Roger in Goodge Street. A fellow student friend and myself arranged to meet Syd and Roger at their flat and ask them to do the Christmas party gig. A handsome fee of £20 was agreed and the party was organized. Syd and co. duly turned up with a couple of roadies and set up in the Life Drawing Studio, the biggest in the Art School and it had a stage. They put on their famous psychedelic light show which was simply oils and coloured liquids in slides dancing around to the heat of the projector, and very effective. Apart from anything else the music was the loudest I'd heard or would wish to hear again especially in a small confined space. It was best heard from about two studios away. They played 'Arnold Layne' which they recorded two months later in February 1967 and released in March 1967."

THURSDAY 22 DECEMBER – PERFORMANCE
The Marquee, Wardour Street, London, England
Supported by the Iveys (who later became Apple Records group Badfinger).

FRIDAY 23 DECEMBER – PERFORMANCE
UFO Presents Night Tripper, **The Blarney Club, Tottenham Court Road, London, England**
With Fanta and Ood, the Giant Sun Trolley and Dave Tomlin.

THURSDAY 29 DECEMBER – PERFORMANCE
The Marquee, Wardour Street, London, England
With the Syn (featuring future Yes bassist Chris Squire).

FRIDAY 30 DECEMBER – PERFORMANCE
UFO Presents Night Tripper, **The Blarney Club, Tottenham Court Road, London, England**
With Soft Machine.
Pink Floyd's performance was filmed by Sheldon and Diane Rochlin for a very brief section in their art-house film *Dope*, which was not released until 2009, when it was rediscovered by its producers. There is some speculation that the music is that of Soft Machine dubbed over the images of Pink Floyd. (See Discography for further information.)

SATURDAY 31 DECEMBER – PERFORMANCE
New Year's Eve All Night Rave, **The Roundhouse, Chalk Farm, London, England**
With the Who and the Move.
Set list included 'Pow R Toc H', 'Interstellar Overdrive'.
Melody Maker reported that, "On stage the Pink Floyd, the Who and the Move each attempted to excite the audience into some positive action. The Pink Floyd have a promising sound, and some very groovy picture slides which attract far more attention than the group, as they merge, blossom, burst, grow, divide and die. The Who got on to the stage after an hour wait [and] almost succeeded in winning over the show with an immediate flurry of smoke bombs and sound-barrier smashing. But somebody pulled out the plug and the Who fell quiet as a graveyard. The trouble recurred to cut short two more numbers. After playing most of their new album tracks rather half-heartedly, Pete Townshend wheeled upon a fine pair of speakers and ground them with his shattered guitar into the

stage. It was fair comment. The group had thrice been switched off as well as being constantly being plunged into darkness by a team of lighting men – none of whom seemed to know where, in fact, the stage or the Who were positioned. The Move were more successful. Technically they had no hitches and their act came smoothly to a stage-shaking climax as TV sets with Hitler and Ian Smith pictures were swiped with iron bars, and a car was chopped up. Two girls were incensed enough to strip to the waist and the remaining, shivering crowds surged menacingly towards the stage, the demolished car, and the birds."

1967

PINK FLOYD ROAD CREW – FEBRUARY 1967
Pip Carter (Road Manager).

THURSDAY 5 JANUARY – PERFORMANCE
The Marquee, Wardour Street, London, England
Supported by Eyes of Blue.
Society magazine *Queen* reported, "The Pink Floyd are the most committed psychedelic group I have yet heard in this country. Other groups have been dabbling with light and back projection, but the Floyd have gone into it in some kind of depth and their visuals make a reasonably logical connection with the music. When I caught up with them at the Marquee recently, their apparatus took up more of the club than the audience but the results were quite impressive. There was a giant screen at the back of the stage and the images projected on to it were like something out of *Fantastic Voyage*, great blobs of red and white and purple and blue that diffused and switched and exploded. The effect was like an endless series of action paintings and I found it very enjoyable, although it didn't remotely simulate any drug states that I have ever heard of. Having praised the visuals, I have to say that the actual music wasn't up to much. There was a lot of thumping and crashing and guitar screeching, all of which was presumably meant to signify the intensity and musical explosion. The numbers went on for a long time and they all adopted the same relentless mood. The two guitarists looked moody, the drummer thrashed wildly about and the lights kept flashing. After about twenty minutes it became very boring and after half an hour I left. All in all, I have very mixed feelings about this group. Anyone who can use visuals as well as they do must be talented; anyone who can be so long winded and tedious must need a lot more time before they are ready to break big. The Pink Floyd at this stage are too cerebral by half. I would like to see them produce a better-balanced, more varied act and I would like to see them project a bit more sex. At the moment they look drab on stage, but if they can only loosen themselves a bit, I could imagine them doing well."

FRIDAY 6 JANUARY – PERFORMANCE ▼
Freak Out Ethel, **Seymour Hall, Paddington, London, England**
With Ginger Johnson's African Drum Band, Waygood Ellis & The Zone, Rich St John, Alexander Trocchi, Karma-Sigma, belly dancers, light shows and other happenings.

Having already seen Pink Floyd perform at *UFO*, Pete Townshend skipped an engagement with the Who in Morecambe in order to take Eric Clapton to see Pink Floyd perform.

SUNDAY 8 JANUARY – PERFORMANCE
The Upper Cut, Forest Gate, London, England
Supporting the Mindbenders.

MONDAY 9 & TUESDAY 10 JANUARY – RECORDING REHEARSALS
Polydor Studios, Stratford Place, London, England
On or around these dates, Joe Boyd arranged for Pink Floyd to audition for Polydor Records. In his 2007 autobiography *White Bicycles: Making Music in the Sixties,* Boyd recalled that they went into Polydor studios, "to rehearse the first single. On their second night there, [Peter] Jenner rang me to say they had signed with an agency and the bookers wanted to come down to the studio and meet the band. I retain a vivid memory of the moment Polydor's night-porter buzzed up to announce the visitors: Bryan Morrison, Steve O'Rourke and Tony Howard."

WEDNESDAY 11 JANUARY – RECORDING SESSION
Sound Techniques, Chelsea, London, England
8.00am to 1.30pm: 'Interstellar Overdrive' and 'Nick's Boogie' (which remained unreleased until the 1990 re-release of the soundtrack) were recorded and remixed for the soundtrack to Peter Whitehead's *Tonite Let's All Make Love in London.* The session was produced by Joe Boyd and engineered by John Wood. Peter Whitehead also filmed the recording, which didn't surface until the release of the extended video *Pink Floyd London 1966–67* in 1994. (See Discography for further information).

Whitehead, a film student and friend of the band from Cambridge, was studying at Slade School of Art in London at the time and joked that he invented the Pink Floyd sound. "I was living in this house where the band used to practice in the hall. And their music got louder and louder and my music – lots of Janacek and Bartok – got louder too. Poor old Syd was doing his Chuck Berry and Little Richard and having to compete with my copy of 'Das Rheingold.'"

THURSDAY 12 JANUARY – RECORDING SESSION
Sound Techniques, Chelsea, London, England
4.30pm to 6.00pm: 'Interstellar Overdrive' and 'Nick's Boogie' were remixed for the soundtrack *Tonite Let's All Make Love in London.* The session was produced by Joe Boyd and engineered by John Wood.

FRIDAY 13 JANUARY – PERFORMANCE
UFO, The Blarney, Tottenham Court Road, London, England
With Marilyn Monroe films and Dave Tomlin's the Giant Sun Trolley. Pink Floyd's set was filmed by Peter Whitehead, initially for use in *Tonite Let's All Make Love in London,* but clips taken from this filming was not released until the release of the 1991 video *The Pink Floyd – London 1966–67.* (See Discography for further information.)

SATURDAY 14 JANUARY – PERFORMANCE
Coming-Up Hop, The Great Hall, University of Reading, Whiteknights, Reading, England
The Reading University student newspaper *Shell* published the following letter of complaint about the show: "We would like to express our disgust at the appalling performance given by the Pink Floyd at the 'dance' on Saturday. How could people dance to such an offensive din? The Pink Floyd were so cacophonous that the most cunningly random noise-making machine could hardly have been more oppressive. The only thing we found to console us was that University dances will never be more debased than this; at least we trust not. We very much regret that certain members of the University degraded themselves by applauding such a performance, and we congratulate the element among the few remaining at the end who gave vent to their indignation by booing."

MONDAY 16 JANUARY – PERFORMANCE
The Clubroom, Institute of Contemporary Arts, Mayfair, London, England
This was the first time pop music had been allowed at the ICA and *Record Mirror* reported an informal discussion between the band and audience after the show.

TUESDAY 17 JANUARY – PERFORMANCE ▼
Music in Colour by the Pink Floyd, Commonwealth Institute, Kensington, London
The *Kensington Post* reported that, "The Pink Floyd had been invited to appear at both the ICA and Commonwealth Institute by a young classical music promoter, Christopher Hunt: 'I like what they do', he said to the *Kensington Post.* 'I usually just deal with classical chamber music but I believe that the Pink Floyd are something quite different from normal pop groups'. During the interval between sessions at the Institute there was a performance of *NOIT,* a mime for paper giants. The creation of artist John Latham this work is, I'm told, a three-dimensional representation of Pink Floyd's state of mind."

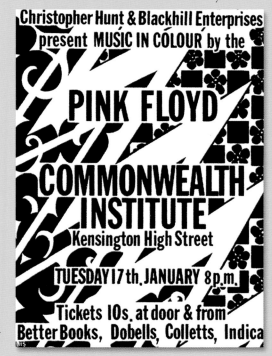

THURSDAY 19 JANUARY – PERFORMANCE
The Marquee, Wardour Street, London

Supported by Marmalade.

FRIDAY 20 JANUARY – PERFORMANCE
UFO, **The Blarney, Tottenham Court Road, London,**

With Spectral Audio Olfactory, Karate, Trip Machine and
Government Propaganda.

SATURDAY 21 JANUARY – PERFORMANCE
The Birdcage, Eastney, Portsmouth, England

PINK FLOYD

announce that their Sole Agents are: **BRYAN MORRISON AGENCY**
142 Charing Cross Road, W.C.2   TEM 0171-2/0606
Sole Management: **BLACKHILL ENTERPRISES**
41 Edbrooke Road, W.9   289-0179

SUNDAY 22 JANUARY – PHOTO SESSION
41 Edbrooke Road, Paddington, London, England

Pink Floyd was photographed by Irene Winsby for *Melody Maker*
at Blackhill's offices on this date. Recollecting the session Winsby
recalled, "Through their manager, Peter Jenner, I arranged to
photograph them [Pink Floyd] on 22nd January 1967, at 8pm,
whilst they were rehearsing at 41 Edbrooke Road, London. I had
been advised by the editor [of *Melody Maker*] not to accept food,
drink, cigarettes etc. from the group for fear of spiking. That was
a misplaced warning – although Syd Barrett was spaced-out, they
were charming, welcoming, polite, and into themselves. When
Peter Jenner was shown the contacts he asked me to photograph
them again two days later, saying the boys would have 'tidied up'
their appearance. We had the second session on 24th January at
6pm. You can see the difference!"

JANUARY 27 FROM 10.30-6PM   & FEBRUARY 3
AMMMUSIC.PINK FLOYD   SOFT MACHINE
FIVE ACRE LIGHT   BROWN'S POETRY
FLIGHT OF THE AEROGENIUS. CHPT 1 CHPT 1
INTERNATIONAL TIMES   BRUCE CONNOR MOVIES
IT GIRL BEAUTY CONTEST.FILM MAKERS CO OP. FOOD
UNDER BERKELY CINEMA. TOT. CT. RD 15/- MEMBERS 10/-

MONDAY 23, TUESDAY 24 & WEDNESDAY 25 JANUARY – RECORDING REHEARSALS
Sound Techniques, Chelsea, London

THURSDAY 26 JANUARY – REHEARSALS
41 Edbrooke Road, Paddington, London, England

FRIDAY 27 JANUARY – PERFORMANCE ◄
UFO, **The Blarney, Tottenham Court Road, London, England**

With AMM, Five Acre Lights, Dave Brown, Plight of the Erogenius
and Chapter 1.

Pink Floyd's first known TV appearance was taken from a
performance at the UFO club in London on this date. Filmed
for the Granada TV magazine arts programme *Scene Special* in an
article subtitled 'It's So Far Out It's Straight Down', based around
"alternative" London, the programme featured clips of 'Interstellar
Overdrive' and 'Matilda Mother' as well as footage of the infamous
Albert Hall poetry reading in 1965, performance art at the
Roundhouse, a "happening" in Piccadilly Circus and interviews with
various luminaries, including Jim Haynes, Barry Miles, John Hopkins
and Paul McCartney. It was broadcast (in black and white) on the
Granada ITV network on Tuesday 7 March 1967 between 10.25pm
and 11.05pm.

SATURDAY 28 JANUARY – PERFORMANCE
Hexagon Restaurant, University of Essex, Wivenhoe Park, Colchester, England

Pink Floyd performed three, one-hour slots during the course of
the evening.

Wyvern, the Essex University student newspaper, reported, "The
psycho-delic dance was a double triumph. The maximum permitted
attendance of 500 was achieved and a profit of about £30 was made.
Never before has a dance at Essex been fully supported or shown
profit. At a social committee meeting on January 30th Mick Gray
(Chairman) reported that the dance was by no means trouble free.
Several outsiders arrived, and when turned away, lingered on the
campus. At about 1am four students from North Essex Technical
College, who had been at the dance, were arrested by a police patrol
whilst attempting to remove the engine from a motor cycle in the
central car park."

SUNDAY 29 JANUARY – RECORDING SESSION
Sound Techniques, Chelsea, London, England

'Arnold Layne' (Takes 1 to 8) and 'Candy And A Currant Bun'
(Takes 1 & 2) were recorded for Pink Floyd's debut 7-inch single. The
session was produced by Joe Boyd and engineered by John Wood.

MONDAY 30 JANUARY – REHEARSALS
41 Edbrooke Road, Paddington, London, England

TUESDAY 31 JANUARY & WEDNESDAY 1 FEBRUARY – RECORDING SESSION
Sound Techniques, Chelsea, London, England

'Arnold Layne' and 'Candy And A Currant Bun' was remixed for the
7-inch single. The session was produced by Joe Boyd and engineered
by John Wood. A surviving acetate from the sessions plays an early
version of 'Candy And A Currant Bun' with the lyrics unchanged
from the 31 October 1966 version, complete with drug references.

WEDNESDAY 1 FEBRUARY – PRESS RELEASE
London, England

It was announced that on this day Pink Floyd officially turned
professional, leaving behind their respective university studies
before formally signing to EMI Records on Tuesday 28 February.

PINK FLOYD ROAD CREW – SEPTEMBER 1967
Pip Carter (Road Manager), Joe Gannon (Lights).

THURSDAY 2 FEBRUARY – PERFORMANCE
Cadenas, Stoke Hotel, Guildford, England

With the Jeremiah Thing.

FRIDAY 3 FEBRUARY 1967 – PERFORMANCE
All Nite Rave, Queen's Hall, Leeds, England

Featuring four stages and 10 hours of nonstop entertainment with 12 groups including Cream plus Go-Go Dancers, a fairground and a barbecue. The rave went on all night and in the morning breakfast was served. The advertisement announced the release of a live gorilla in the crowd at midnight!

MONDAY 6 FEBRUARY – PHOTO SESSION
London, England

Pink Floyd was photographed by *Jackie* magazine and a photo from the session eventually appeared as a full page pin-up in the Saturday 7 October 1967 edition.

TUESDAY 7 FEBRUARY – PHOTO SESSION
London, England

Pink Floyd was photographed by Fiona Adams for *Fabulous 208* magazine and a photo from the session eventually appeared as a full page pin-up in the Saturday 2 September 1967 edition.

WEDNESDAY 8 FEBRUARY – REHEARSALS
41 Edbrooke Road, Paddington, London, England

THURSDAY 9 FEBRUARY – PERFORMANCE
New Addington Hotel, New Addington, Croydon, England

FRIDAY 10 FEBRUARY – PERFORMANCE
Leicester College of Art and Technology, Leicester, England

Pink Floyd was paid £50 for their appearance.

SATURDAY 11 FEBRUARY – PERFORMANCE
Old Refectory, Falmer House, University of Sussex, Falmer, Brighton, England

With the Alan Bown Set, the Wishful Thinking and Russell's Clump.

BELOW: PINK FLOYD PHOTOGRAPHED 6 FEBRUARY 1967 FOR THE TEEN MAGAZINE *JACKIE*.

MONDAY 13 FEBRUARY – PHOTO SESSION
EMI House, 20 Manchester Square, London, England

Pink Floyd was photographed by EMI for the forthcoming press campaign to promote their debut single 'Arnold Layne'. The surviving photos, which also appeared on the cover of the sheet music, show the band lined up against the wall of the Wallace Collection, opposite EMI Records' headquarters.

ABOVE: A PINK FLOYD PHOTO SESSION TO PROMOTE 'ARNOLD LAYNE', 13 FEBRUARY 1967.

THURSDAY 16 FEBRUARY – CANCELLED PERFORMANCE
The Guildhall, Southampton, England

Supported by Soul Trinity.
Following a report in the *News of the World* newspaper on Saturday 11 February that linked Pink Floyd's music to drug usage, the venue management decided to cancel the show. The allegation was denied and the *News of the World* was obliged to publish an apology in the following week's edition.

FRIDAY 17 FEBRUARY – PERFORMANCE
St. Catherine's College Valentine Ball, Dorothy Ballroom, Cambridge, England

With Bob Kidman, Alexis Korner's Blues Incorporated and Pearl Hawaiians.

SATURDAY 18 FEBRUARY – PERFORMANCE
California Ballroom, Dunstable, England

Supported by the Equals and Two of Each.

MONDAY 20 FEBRUARY – PERFORMANCE
Adelphi Ballroom, West Bromwich, England

TUESDAY 21 FEBRUARY – RECORDING SESSION
Studio 3 & Control Room 3, EMI Studios, Abbey Road, London, England

11.00pm to 6.00am: Pink Floyd's first-ever recordings at EMI Studios for the album *The Piper at the Gates of Dawn* commenced late in the evening with an all-night session, apparently with no break in which 'Matilda Mother' was recorded (Take 1 at 3:36; Take 2 False Start, Take 3 at 3:29, Take 4 at 3:27, Take 5 at 3:23 and Take 6 at 3:55 also marked "basic best") for the album *The Piper at the Gates of Dawn*. The session was produced by Norman Smith, engineered by Peter Bown and assisted by Michael Sheady.

THURSDAY 23 FEBRUARY – RECORDING SESSION
Room 53, EMI Studios, Abbey Road, London, England

12.30pm to 1.00pm: Take 6 of 'Matilda's Mother' was remixed and edited (with fade-out, and marked "best") for *The Piper at the Gates of Dawn*. The session was produced by Norman Smith and engineered by Peter Mew.

FRIDAY 24 FEBRUARY – RECORDING SESSION
EMI Studios, Abbey Road, London, England

Cutting 'Candy & A Currant Bun' for the 7-inch single. The session was produced and engineered by Norman Smith. Pink Floyd was not in attendance for this session.

FRIDAY 24 FEBRUARY – CANCELLED PERFORMANCE
Ricky Tick, Thames Hotel, Windsor, England

Rescheduled to Saturday 25 March 1967.

FRIDAY 24 FEBRUARY – PERFORMANCE
UFO, The Blarney, Tottenham Court Road, London, England

With Brothers Grimm and film shows.
Pink Floyd's performance at the UFO club was filmed by Beyerischer Rundfunk [Bavarian Broadcasting], West Germany who featured an excerpt of 'Interstellar Overdrive' along with crowd scenes for inclusion in the documentary arts programme *Die Jungen Nachtwandler* [*The Young Nightwalker*] broadcast on ARD network TV on Monday 3 July 1967 between 9.45pm and 10.35pm.

SATURDAY 25 FEBRUARY – RECORDING SESSION
EMI Studios, Abbey Road, London, England

Cutting 'Arnold Layne' for the 7-inch single. The session was produced and engineered by Norman Smith. Pink Floyd was not in attendance for this session.

SATURDAY 25 FEBRUARY – CANCELLED PERFORMANCE
Ricky Tick, Hounslow, England

Rescheduled to Friday 24 March 1967.

MONDAY 27 FEBRUARY – RECORDING SESSION
Studio 3 & Control Room 3, EMI Studios, Abbey Road, London, England

7.00pm to 2.15am: 'Chapter 24' was recorded (Take 1 at 4:27, Take 2 False Start, Take 3 at 5:10, Take 4 at 4:02 and Take 5 at 4:14 also marked "best"), and 'Interstellar Overdrive' was recorded (Take 1 at 9:24 and Take 2 at 10:20 also marked "best") for *The Piper at the Gates of Dawn*. The session was produced by Norman Smith, engineered by Peter Bown and assisted by Jeff Jarrett.

TUESDAY 28 FEBRUARY – PERFORMANCE
Blaises, Imperial Hotel, Knightsbridge, London, England

Supported by the Majority.

WEDNESDAY 1 MARCH – RECORDING SESSION
Control Room 53, EMI Studios, Abbey Road, London, England

2.30pm to 3.20pm: Take 5 of 'Chapter 24' was remixed (RM1) and Take 2 of 'Interstellar Overdrive' was remixed (RM1) for *The Piper at the Gates of Dawn*. The session was produced by Norman Smith, engineered by Norman Smith and assisted by Jeff Jarrett.

WEDNESDAY 1 MARCH – PERFORMANCE
The Ballroom, Eel Pie Island Hotel, Twickenham, England

Pink Floyd was paid £75 for two 30-minute sets.

THURSDAY 2 MARCH – PERFORMANCE
Assembly Hall, Worthing, England

Supporting Geno Washington & the Ram Jam Band.

FRIDAY 3 MARCH – PRESS RECEPTION
EMI House, 20 Manchester Square, London, England

Pink Floyd attended a 12.30pm press launch and photo session at EMI Records headquarters at which they also mimed a performance of 'Arnold Layne' and 'Candy And A Currant Bun' complete with their lightshow. It was also reported a "surrealistic film" was shown, presumably the West Wittering beach promo for 'Arnold Layne' (see 10 March for further details). The invitations, which were posted to the media with a copy of the 7-inch single in a picture sleeve, invited the holder to a "Special Cocktail Party to meet and hear the most outstanding group of 1967 – the Pink Floyd."

FRIDAY 3 MARCH – PERFORMANCE
Market Hall, St Albans, England

Supported by Tuppence the TV Dancer.

SATURDAY 4 MARCH – PERFORMANCE
Poly Rag Ball, The Large Hall, Regent Street Polytechnic, London, England

With the Minor Birds, the Miss Poly Finals and DJ Ed "Stewpot" Stewart.
A profit of £140 was raised in aid of War on Want and Cancer Research.
West One, the Regent Street Polytechnic student newspaper, reported that, "As usual the Dance posters and tickets were of the very highest standard. Everyone present at the dance appeared to enjoy themselves but in my opinion the Pink Floyd are not at their best as a 'college hop' group. Despite the suggestions of a 'freak-out' implied by the dance tickets, the Rag Ball was a glorified 'hop'. There were more psychedelic effects when the bar flashed the lights on and off to indicate closing time than the rest of the dance put together. The only spontaneous happening I observed was when a young lady who had drunk more than her stomach could bear, had gone out into the cold night air."

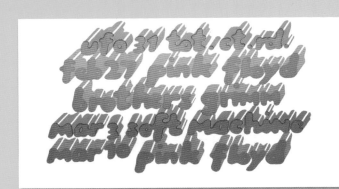

SUNDAY 5 MARCH – PERFORMANCE
Sunday's at the Saville, Saville Theatre,
Shaftesbury Avenue, London, England

With Lee Dorsey (headline) and Summerset.
Melody Maker reported that "Pete Townshend dug Pink Floyd at the Saville."

MONDAY 6 MARCH – TELEVISION RECORDING
The Rave, Granada TV Studios, Manchester, England

Pink Floyd was filmed on this date performing 'Arnold Layne' live for the pilot episode of a new 30-minute Granada TV music programme called *The Rave*. This was a proposed rival replacement for Rediffusion's recently cancelled series *Ready, Steady, Go!*, and hosted by the Move. Unfortunately the series was not commissioned and this pilot was never broadcast.

TUESDAY 7 MARCH – PERFORMANCE
Malvern Big Beat Sessions, Winter Gardens, Malvern, England

The *Malvern Gazette* reported that, "The Malvern Winter Gardens has banned the use of the words 'It's a freak out, it's a psychedelic happening' in advertising for the appearance of London group, The Pink Floyd. Entertainment Manager Mr. J.D. Harrison told us that several hundred pamphlets were distributed at Tuesday night's Big Beat session last week advertising the group's appearance in March. After consulting with the chairman of the Winter Gardens and Publicity Committee, Councillor Ron Holland, decided that the remaining two pamphlets should not be handed out. Also, a poster put up inside the Winter Gardens with similar wording has been taken down. Mr. Harrison said this would be replaced by the London promoters, who do not advertise on billboards in the town. Mr. Harrison said, 'It's a word that should not be used. I think it's a trend to the drug world. It's wrong, completely wrong. I rang up Malvern Public Library to find out the meaning of the word and I was told it related to trances induced by the drug LSD.'"

THURSDAY 9 MARCH – PERFORMANCE
The Marquee, Wardour Street, London, England

With the Thoughts.

FRIDAY 10 MARCH 1967 – SINGLE RELEASE (UK)
'Arnold Layne'

Record Retail and Music Industry News said that, "This is rather way out and this group with its tremendous visual impact have already built a big following. Number is infectious about Arnold's 'strange hobby' with a well-boosted sound behind. Should make the Fifty."

FRIDAY 10 MARCH – PERFORMANCE ◄
UFO, The Blarney,
Tottenham Court Road, London, England

With "Special Guest Robot, films, lights and raids!"
Pink Floyd's regular slot at *UFO* was complimented by a screening of the 'Arnold Layne' promotional film. *Melody Maker* reported Donovan, Peter Cook and Pete Townshend were in attendance to see Pink Floyd perform.

SATURDAY 11 MARCH – PRESS REPORT
London, England

It was reported in the music press that Pink Floyd had prepared a 30-minute television pilot to show to EMI Records in order for the company to decide whether or not to sponsor a series for future broadcast on ITV network television. The project never came to fruition and was described as a 'Monkees-type' TV series.

It is possible the above pilot refers to a piece entitled *Pink Floyd vs IT* by film-maker and writer Stacy Marking. The only known screening of the silent 16mm footage was in January 1968 in Manila, Philippines, as reported by *International Times* (16–29 February 1968 edition) as part of a series of events organized by the Observation Platform, a collective of writers, artists and film-makers. The film has been lost ever since and although Marking made an appeal in the *Guardian* newspaper in September 2009 to help find it, nothing was recovered. Recalling the filming Marking said, "It really involved a lot of them running about in single file, sometimes in silhouette, and the Floyd as good guys taking on some unseen monster/enemy, being chased or fighting back. This was one of the very first films to be tied to a record release. I suppose we thought it would be projected at clubs. The four wore black or at least very dark clothes, and we painted a whole street white. Most of it was filmed in an alley behind Tottenham Court Road where there was a long wall on one side, and I think a derelict site on the other. I wanted it painted white to exaggerate the contrast, so we all – including the Floyd members I think, anyway one or two of them, plus their agent Peter Jenner, Spike Hawkins and me – came along the day before with huge cans of white paint and we whitewashed the whole alley, pavement as well. When challenged by passersby we said it was part of the Keep Britain Clean campaign."

In the same news item it was reported the band would be performing for a whole week in May at the Jeanetta Cochrane Theatre, Long Acre, London, England although evidently this did not come to fruition.

SATURDAY 11 MARCH – TELEVISION BROADCAST
Juke Box Jury, BBC TV Theatre,
Shepherd's Bush, London

'Arnold Layne' was among the selection of discs reviewed by a panel of critics in a live audience recording for BBC1 TV's weekly show broadcast between 5.15pm and 5.40pm. The panel included DJ Pete Murray, Reita Faria (the reigning Miss World) and actress Judy Geeson and was hosted by David Jacobs. Although it is not known what the other panellists thought of the song, Roger Waters has been quoted as saying Murray thought, "we were a con. He thought it was just contrived rubbish to meet some kind of unhealthy demand.'

ARNOLD LAYNE

TRACKS

SIDE A: **ARNOLD LAYNE** (Barrett) 2:55
SIDE B: **CANDY AND A CURRANT BUN** (Barrett) 2:46

RELEASE DATE

UK: Friday 10 March 1967.
US: Monday 24 April 1967.

FORMAT

UK: EMI Columbia DB 8156 (7-inch vinyl single).
US: Capitol Tower 333 (7-inch vinyl single).

HIGHEST CHART POSITION

UK: No.21 (*Melody Maker* 'Pop 30' on Saturday 15 April 1967).

PROMO FILMS

A black-and-white promotional film for the single was filmed at West Wittering beach on the south coast of England by Derek Nice. Very

much a parody of the Beatles film, *Help!*, it has regularly appeared on various global TV shows, and was even shown on-screen by Roger Waters as part of his solo stage shows.

A second film, which was made on 20 March, featured the band larking around Hampstead Heath, Highgate Ponds and outside St. Michael's church, Highgate, London. It appears only to have been shown on the French music programme *Bouton Rouge* broadcast on ORTF2 TV on Sunday 21 May 1967.

TOP LEFT: UK PROMO PICTURE SLEEVE.
TOP RIGHT: US PROMO PICTURE SLEEVE.
ABOVE: INVITATION TO THE PRESS LAUNCH OF 'ARNOLD LAYNE' ON 3 MARCH 1967.
RIGHT: PROMO POSTER FOR THE SINGLE RELEASE.

RECORDING DETAILS

Pink Floyd's first UK single was recorded at Sound Techniques Studios, Chelsea, London and produced by Joe Boyd and engineered by John Wood. Unfortunately no detailed paperwork survived from Sound Techniques, although the recording dates are identified on paperwork held at Abbey Road studios.

ARNOLD LAYNE
Take unknown (RM unknown).
Basic track recorded on 29 January 1967.
Remixed on 31 January and 1 February 1967.

CANDY AND A CURRANT BUN
Take unknown (RM unknown).
Basic track recorded on 29 January 1967.
Remixed on 31 January and 1 February 1967.

"STRAIGHT TO HEAVEN" ON MARCH 11th
AT A STRATOSPHERIC FREAK-OUT!
with the
PINK FLOYD
PLUS
SPECTA QUIN TEAM
8.0 - 11.45 p.m.   6/6
at
CANTERBURY TECH.
Tickets from Marlowe Theatre.
Late Buses to Whitstable and Herne Bay.

SATURDAY 11 MARCH – PERFORMANCE ▲
Main Hall, Canterbury Technical College,
Canterbury, England

Supported by Specta Quinn Team.

SUNDAY 12 MARCH – PERFORMANCE
Agincourt Ballroom, Camberley, England

Supported by Mike Raynor & the Condors.

WEDNESDAY 15 MARCH – RECORDING SESSION
Studio 3 & Control Room 3, EMI Studios,
Abbey Road, London, England

2.30pm to 5.30pm: Bells, Harmonium and Cymbals were
overdubbed onto Take 5 of 'Chapter 24', and 6.30pm to 12.30am:
'Chapter 24' was re-recorded (Take 6 at 3:57 also marked "best")
for *The Piper at the Gates of Dawn*. The session was produced by
Norman Smith, engineered by Peter Bown and assisted by
Jeff Jarrett.

THURSDAY 16 MARCH – RECORDING SESSION
Studio 3 & Control Room 3, EMI Studios, London, England

2.30pm to 5.30pm: A short version of 'Interstellar Overdrive' was
recorded for a French EP release (Takes 1 & 2 False Starts, Take
3 at 5:30, Take 4 False Start, Take 5 at 4:43 and Take 6 at 5:00),
and 7.00pm to 2.00am: 'Flaming' was recorded (Take 1 at 2:43
also marked "best") for *The Piper at the Gates of Dawn*. The session
was produced by Norman Smith, engineered by Peter Bown and
assisted by Jeff Jarrett.

FRIDAY 17 MARCH – PERFORMANCE
Kingston Technical College,
Kingston-upon-Thames, England

Pink Floyd was paid £100 for two 30-minute spots.

SATURDAY 18 MARCH – PERFORMANCE
Enfield College of Technology, Enfield, England

With the Goodtime Losers and the Lymit.
On Tuesday 17 July 2012 a listener to the *Ken Bruce Show* on
BBC Radio 2 called in to say that he was the social secretary of
the college who had booked Pink Floyd for their college dance.
Tickets were printed on pink card and cost 8 shillings. At the
thunderous climax of Pink Floyd's set he recalled a disgusted
janitor pulling the plug on the power, and in a fit of anger at
being interrupted Roger Waters threw his guitar at the wall at
the back of the stage. At a college reunion some 30 years later
the former secretary was amused to note the dent in the wall
was still there.

SUNDAY 19 MARCH – RECORDING SESSION
Studio 3 & Control Room 3, EMI Studios,
Abbey Road, London, England

9.00pm to 1.00am: Celeste, 12-string guitar and vocals were
overdubbed onto Take 6 of 'The Gnome' (Take 6 at 2:12 also
marked "best") for *The Piper at the Gates of Dawn*. As no recording
sheet exists that notes Takes 1 to 5 having been made, it is
likely these were made earlier in the day. The session was
produced by Norman Smith, engineered by Peter Bown and
assisted by Jeff Jarrett.

MONDAY 20 MARCH – FILMING
Hampstead, London

Pink Floyd was reported in *Disc & Music Echo* as having filmed a
black-and-white promotional film for 'Arnold Layne'. This version,
an alternate to the more familiar Wittering Beach promo film,
featured the band larking around Hampstead Heath, Highgate
Ponds and outside St. Michael's Church in Highgate. It appears
only to have been shown on the French music programme *Bouton
Rouge* broadcast on ORTF2 TV on Sunday 21 May 1967 between
7.40pm and 8.30pm.

MONDAY 20 MARCH – RECORDING SESSION
Studio 3 & Control Room 3, EMI Studios,
Abbey Road, London, England

2.30pm to 6.30pm: 'Take Up Thy Stethoscope And Walk' recorded
(Take 1 False Start, Take 2 at 3:32, Take 3 at 3:33, Take 4 at 3:05,
Take 5 at 3:05 also marked "best" and Take 6 at 3:06), and 7.30pm
to 12.00 midnight: Vocals overdubbed onto Take 5 of 'Take Up
Thy Stethoscope And Walk', and 'The Scarecrow' recorded (Take
1 at 2:15 also marked "best") for *The Piper at the Gates of Dawn*. The
session was produced by Norman Smith, engineered by Peter Bown
and assisted by Jeff Jarrett.

TUESDAY 21 MARCH – RECORDING SESSION
Studio 3 & Control Room 3, EMI Studios,
Abbey Road, St. John's Wood, London, England

2.30pm to 7.30pm: 'Pow R Toc H' recorded (Take 1 at 3:28,
Take 2 False Start, Take 3 at 3:41 and Take 4 at 4:14 also marked
"best"), and 8.30pm to 1.30am: Guitar, Tympani's and Organ
overdubbed onto Take 4 of 'Pow R Toc H' for *The Piper at the Gates
of Dawn*. The session was produced by Norman Smith, engineered
by Peter Bown and assisted by Jeff Jarrett.
    Norman Smith took Pink Floyd to see the Beatles at work on
the mixing of 'Lovely Rita' in Studio 2 at around 11pm that night.
Beatles biographer Hunter Davies, present at the session, famously
described the meeting as an exchange of "half-hearted hellos."

WEDNESDAY 22 MARCH – PERFORMANCE
The Canteen, London School of Economics,
London, England

Pink Floyd made an impromptu afternoon appearance along with
Soft Machine and other musicians in support of a week-long sit-in
by students supporting the ideal of an Open University.

WEDNESDAY 22 MARCH – RECORDING SESSION
Studio 3 & Control Room 3, EMI Studios,
Abbey Road, London, England

7.00pm to 2.15am: Organ and Guitar overdubbed onto Take 1 of 'The Scarecrow', for *The Piper at the Gates of Dawn*, and editing the end piece of Take 2 onto Take 1 of 'Interstellar Overdrive' for the French EP release. This edit was used instead of recordings made on Thursday 16 March 1967. The session was produced by Norman Smith, engineered by Peter Bown and assisted by Jeff Jarrett.

THURSDAY 23 MARCH – PERFORMANCE
Rotherham College of Technology Dance, **Clifton Hall, Rotherham, England**

Pink Floyd replaced the advertised Shotgun Express at short notice and was paid £60 for two 30-minute spots.

FRIDAY 24 MARCH – PERFORMANCE ◄
Ricky Tick, **Hounslow, England**

SATURDAY 25 MARCH – PERFORMANCE ▼
Ricky Tick, **Thames Hotel, Windsor, England**

SATURDAY 25 MARCH – PERFORMANCE
The New Yorker Discotheque, Swindon, England

Billed as an "All Niter" with the Outer Limits.

SATURDAY 25 MARCH – PERFORMANCE
Shoreline Club, **Caribbean Hotel, Bognor Regis, England**

Pink Floyd performed in the early hours of 26 March at this Easter weekend all-nighter that also featured the Shame.

TUESDAY 28 MARCH – PERFORMANCE
Chinese R&B Jazz Club, **Corn Exchange, Bristol, England**

WEDNESDAY 29 MARCH – RECORDING SESSION
Control Room 53, EMI Studios,
Abbey Road, London, England

10.00am to 1.15pm: Take 6 of 'The Gnome' remixed (RM1 and RM2 also marked "best"), and 2.30pm to 6.45pm: Take 4 of 'Pow R Toc H' remixed (RM1, RM2, and RM3 also marked "best"), Take 1 of 'The Scarecrow' remixed (RM1 also marked "best"), Take 5 of 'Take Up Thy Stethoscope And Walk' remixed (RM1, and RM2 also marked "best") and "Edit Piece For End" of Take 5 of 'Take

Up Thy Stethoscope And Walk' remixed (RM3) for *The Piper at the Gates of Dawn*. The session was produced by Norman Smith, engineered by Peter Bown and assisted by Jeff Jarrett.

WEDNESDAY 29 MARCH – CANCELLED PERFORMANCE
The Ballroom, Eel Pie Island Hotel, Twickenham, England

Pink Floyd did not appear due to recording commitments.

THURSDAY 30 MARCH – CANCELLED TELEVISION RECORDING
Top of the Pops, **BBC Lime Grove Studios, Shepherd's Bush, London, England**

Pink Floyd was filmed for the UK's most watched pop music show, *Top of the Pops*, miming to 'Arnold Layne' on this date. However, its intended broadcast the following week (Thursday 6 April 1967) on BBC1 was cancelled. A statement was issued by the show's producer, Stanley Dorfman, to *Melody Maker*, (published Saturday 15 April 1967), explaining the omission: "We filmed the Floyd and the Move before last week's show because they were both playing out of town on Thursday night [6 April 1967]. Naturally we wanted the film in the can in case the record entered the chart. In fact, on our combined chart the Floyd dropped three places so it ruled them out of the show."

FRIDAY 31 MARCH – PERFORMANCE
Top Spot Ballroom, Ross-on-Wye, England

Supported by Group 66.

SATURDAY 1 APRIL – PHOTO SESSION
EMI House, 20 Manchester Square, London, England

Pink Floyd was photographed by Dezo Hoffmann for future publicity shots.

SATURDAY 1 APRIL – PERFORMANCE
Birdcage, Eastney, Portsmouth, England

MONDAY 3 APRIL 1967 – RADIO BROADCAST
Monday, Monday!, **BBC Playhouse Theatre, Charing Cross, London, England**

Pink Floyd performed 'Arnold Layne' and 'Candy And A Currant Bun' in a live-to-air broadcast for the BBC Radio Light programme *Monday, Monday!*. Rehearsals were scheduled for a 9.30am start and the show was broadcast between 1.00pm and 2.00pm. Curiously at this time the BBC had a policy of auditioning all bands for appearances by playing the recordings to a committee for approval for transmission. However, in Pink Floyd's case the BBC archives indicate that their tracks were transmitted and considered a 'live audition' in view of the fact the single was already charting.

WEDNESDAY 5 APRIL – PHOTO SESSION
41 Edbrooke Road, Paddington, London, England

Pink Floyd was photographed at Blackhill Enterprises' offices by Alain Dister for the French music magazine *Rock & Folk*.

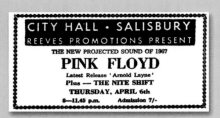

THURSDAY 6 APRIL – PERFORMANCE ◄
City Hall, Salisbury, England

Supported by The Nite Shift. Set list included an untitled instrumental, 'Arnold Layne', 'Interstellar Overdrive', 'Matilda Mother'.

FRIDAY 7 APRIL – PERFORMANCE ◄
Floral Hall, Belfast, Northern Ireland

Supported by the Jimmy Johnston Showband. Richard Wright commented in *Rave* magazine that, "The best reaction so far to the Floyd's lights and sounds was in Belfast. The kind of place where if they don't like you they let you know in no uncertain manner. We were worried about Belfast, but they really rave over there. We were completely knocked out and stunned at the reaction." The show featured an unusual lightshow with 35mm slides of the abstract paintings of local artist Cecil McCartney projected over the band as they performed.

SATURDAY 8 APRIL – PRESS REPORT
London, England

The UK music press reported that Pink Floyd was due to start work on a 30-minute film called *The Life Story of Percy the Ratcatcher*. Although the project never reached fruition the band had been using this as the working title to the song that eventually became 'Lucifer Sam'.

SATURDAY 8 APRIL – PERFORMANCE
Rhodes Centre, Bishops Stortford, England

Supported by the New Generation.

SATURDAY 8 APRIL – PERFORMANCE
The Roundhouse, Chalk Farm, London, England

With the Flies, Earl Fuggle, the Electric Poets [Soft Machine], the Block, Sandy & Narda dancers, Sam Gopal and films and lights by Patrik Trevor.

SUNDAY 9 APRIL – PERFORMANCE
Britannia Rowing Club, Nottingham, England

MONDAY 10 APRIL – PERFORMANCE
The Pavilion, Bath, England

Supported by The Roman Remains.
The *Bath & Wilts Evening Chronicle* reported that, "Three electricians should have taken a bow at the Pavilion last night. Instead four people took the applause – four people who had, apparently haphazardly, thumped out music. The four were the Pink Floyd, one of the most intriguing groups to visit the city. The overall effect created by the noise of those onstage and the lighting from those off-stage was interesting to say the least. Jaundiced blotches ran down mottled multicoloured backgrounds. Flashing

lights transformed the group into ghouls, with giant prancing shadows of distorted beings dwarfing the performers as the lighting changed with the pounding rhythm. The group admits its lighting techniques – which are strictly secret – and sound will and must improve. Roger Waters said, 'We are getting better all the time and our techniques are doing the same.' But the group denies the 'psychedelic' tag it has been branded with. 'If psychedelic is producing LSD feelings then we are not,' said Nick Mason. 'But if psychedelic is light and sound, then we are.'"

TUESDAY 11 APRIL – RECORDING SESSION
Studio 3 & Control Room 3, EMI Studios, Abbey Road, London, England

7.00pm to 2.15am: 'Astronomy Domine' recorded (Take 1 at 4:46; Take 2 at 4:23, Take 3 at 4:25, Take 4 False Start, Take 5 at 4:17, Take 6 False Start, Take 7 at 4:08; Take 8 False Start, Take 9 at 4:20, Take 10 False Start, Take 11 at 4:07, Take 12 at 4:12, Take 13 at 4:10 and Take 14 at 4:07) for *The Piper at the Gates of Dawn*. Takes 13 and 14 were recorded over Takes 1 and 2. The session was produced by Norman Smith, engineered by Peter Bown and assisted by Jeff Jarrett.

WEDNESDAY 12 APRIL – RECORDING SESSION
Studio 3 & Control Room 3, EMI Studios, Abbey Road, London, England

2.30pm to 6.00pm: Vocals overdubbed onto Take 14 of 'Astronomy Domine', and 7.00pm to 2.15am: Guitar and Vocals overdubbed onto Take 14 of 'Astronomy Domine', and 'Percy The Ratcatcher' ['Lucifer Sam'] recorded (Take 1 False Start; Take 2 at 3:02; Take 3 at 3:01; Take 4 False Start; Take 5 at 3:03; Take 6 at 3:04 and Take 7 at 3:03 also marked "best") for *The Piper at the Gates of Dawn*. The session was produced by Norman Smith, engineered by Peter Bown and assisted by Jeff Jarrett.

THURSDAY 13 APRIL – RECORDING SESSION
Studio 3 & Control Room 3, EMI Studios, Abbey Road, London, England

2.30pm to 6.15pm: Maracas, Bowed Bass and Organ overdubbed onto Take 7 of 'Percy The Ratcatcher' ['Lucifer Sam'] for *The Piper at the Gates of Dawn*. The session was produced by Norman Smith, engineered by Peter Bown and assisted by Jeff Jarrett.

THURSDAY 13 APRIL – PERFORMANCE
Tilbury Railway Club, Tilbury, England

FRIDAY 14 APRIL – CANCELLED PERFORMANCE
Club A' Go Go, Newcastle-upon-Tyne, England

Show rescheduled to 19 May 1967.

SATURDAY 15 APRIL – PERFORMANCE
Kinetic Arena – K4 Discoteque, Main Ballroom, West Pier, Brighton, England

With the Hornsey College Light-Sound Workshop and Bruce Lacey & Humanoid Robots.
Set list included 'Candy And A Currant Bun', 'Astronomy Domine', 'Matilda Mother', 'Pow R Toc H', 'Interstellar Overdrive', 'Lucifer Sam'.
Pink Floyd was invited by Hornsey College of Art's Advanced Studies

Group to perform in their "kinetic audio-visual environment" – collectively entitled "K4" – for an event as part of the annual Brighton Festival. They played in front of a 60-foot-wide white projection screen with a PA system suspended from the ceiling. Their performance was also shot for inclusion in the film *Promende* (see Discography for further details)

SUNDAY 16 APRIL – PERFORMANCE
The Brady Club, Stepney, London, England

The *Newham Express* reported that, "Hundreds of youngsters crowded into Stepney's Brady Club on Sunday to hear London's latest rave group, the Pink Floyd. But before the group had finished its second number booing and hissing girls and boys walked out of the club dance hall. 'It's probably because they've never heard anything like us before, they don't really know what to expect,' explained one of the group. 'But we can tell the kids don't like us which is quite disappointing.'"

MONDAY 17 APRIL – RECORDING SESSION
Studio 3 & Control Room 3, EMI Studios, Abbey Road, London, England

2.30pm to 7.00pm: Bass and Organ overdubbed onto Take 7 of 'Percy The Ratcatcher' ['Lucifer Sam'], and 8.15pm to 12.15am: "Wild Vocal Track" recorded for the beginning of 'Astronomy Domine' (Takes 1 and 2 False Starts, Take 3 at 0:55 also marked "best" and Take 4 at 0:56), and then overdubbed onto Take 14 of 'Astronomy Domine' for *The Piper at the Gates of Dawn*. The session was produced by Norman Smith, engineered by Peter Bown and assisted by Jeff Jarrett. Incidentally, it is Peter Jenner's voice that can be heard at the beginning of the track as he shouts the names of various astral bodies through a megaphone.

TUESDAY 18 APRIL – RECORDING SESSION
Studio 3 & Control Room 3, EMI Studios, Abbey Road, London, England

2.30pm to 7.00pm: Vocal introduction ["Wild Vocal Track"] of 'Astronomy Domine' remixed (RM2 also marked "best"), and 8.00pm to 5.00am: 'She Was A Millionaire' [unused outtake] recorded (Take 1 at 4:06, Take 2 False Start and Take 3 at 4:06); Vocals overdubbed onto Take 7 of 'Lucifer Sam' (relabelled Take 8), copy of Take 8 used for Master Vocal overdub onto Take 7 of 'Lucifer Sam' (relabelled Take 9) and Vocals overdubbed onto Take 9 of 'Lucifer Sam' (relabelled Take 10) for *The Piper at the Gates of Dawn*. The session was produced by Norman Smith, engineered by Peter Bown and assisted by Jeff Jarrett.

WEDNESDAY 19 APRIL – PERFORMANCE
Bromel Club, Court Hotel, Downham, Bromley, England

An eyewitness at the show recalled "The Floyd on this occasion boasted their new 200-watt PA system which they had for the first time. The light show consisted of a single overhead projector and a bowl of water whereupon the lighting man dropped various vegetable dyes and oils into the water which were projected onto the most grubby of bed sheets which was pinned to the wall with some small nails. The effect at the time was fantastic, as we pushed ourselves to the front of the crowd to see the band and to be able to take some photos. I found myself pushed up against the PA columns for the entire act, it was just fantastic.

"We met up with the band afterwards for a drink and I was unable to hear a thing and just nodded knowingly as they spoke to us as we sat around whilst they dismantled their equipment. The Bromel Club at the time only served Coca Cola and Fanta, no booze, so it was something of an experience to swig from the same bottle as the band. My hearing came back about three days later."

THURSDAY 20 APRIL – PERFORMANCE ▶
Queen's Hall, Barnstaple, England

Supported by the Gordon Riots.

FRIDAY 21 APRIL – PERFORMANCE
Starlite Ballroom, Greenford, England

FRIDAY 21 APRIL – PERFORMANCE
UFO, The Blarney, Tottenham Court Road, London, England

With the Gas Company.

SATURDAY 22 APRIL – CANCELLED PERFORMANCE
Sixty Nine Club, Royal York Hotel, Ryde, Isle of Wight, England

This show was cancelled in favour of an appearance at Rugby. However, a surviving contract shows the band was contracted for two 45-minute spots for a fee of £150 plus bed and breakfast.

SATURDAY 22 APRIL – PERFORMANCE
Scene 67, Benn Memorial Hall, Rugby, England

Set list included 'Interstellar Overdrive', 'Candy And A Currant Bun', 'Arnold Layne'.
The *Rugby Advertiser* reported that, "Like mad scientists they wielded their instruments treating each guitar string or drum stick with a fanaticism that rivalled the tantrums of the most despotic dictator. On stage at the Benn Memorial Hall on Saturday was the most weird, frighteningly way-out group fans in Rugby had ever seen – The Pink Floyd. Their experiments went far beyond the realms of pop music and backstage the boys explained why. 'We started off as an R&B group, but later decided to adopt our own style', said organist Rick Wright. 'Our music is made to represent hallucinatory effects and this is enhanced by the use of lights'. The boys appeared only once but the 45-minute stint was about all the average onlooker could take. Flipping through their repertoire, which included 'Interstellar Overdrive', 'Candy And A Currant Bun' and their latest, 'Arnold Layne', they displayed a remarkable dedication to a brand of music which may fade into the past, or could be the next progression in the musical annals of the 20th century."

SUNDAY 23 APRIL – PERFORMANCE
Starlight Ballroom, Crawley, England

With, according to local adverts, a "Full Supporting Cast."

MONDAY 24 APRIL – SINGLE RELEASE (US)
'Arnold Layne'

MONDAY 24 APRIL – PERFORMANCE
Blue Opera Club, The Feathers public house,
Ealing Broadway, London, England

Roger Waters recalled in an interview with *Zig Zag* magazine: "The worst thing that ever happened to me was at the Feathers Club, which was a penny, which made a bloody great cut in the middle of my forehead. I bled quite a lot. And I stood at the front of the stage to see if I could see [who threw it]. I was glowering in a real rage, and I was gonna leap out into the audience and get [them]. Happily, there was one freak who turned up who liked us, so the audience spent the whole evening beating the shit out of him, and left us alone."

TUESDAY 25 APRIL – PERFORMANCE
The Stage Club, Clarendon Restaurant, Oxford, England

Supported by the Vibratones.

FRIDAY 28 APRIL – PERFORMANCE
The Tabernacle Club, Hillgate, Stockport, England

SATURDAY 29 APRIL – CANCELLED PERFORMANCE
St. George's Ballroom, Hinckley, England

Show rescheduled to Saturday 13 May 1967.

SATURDAY 29 APRIL – TELEVISION RECORDING
Fan Club, VARA TV Studios, Zaandam, Netherlands

Pink Floyd travelled to the Netherlands for their first overseas engagement to perform 'Arnold Layne' and 'Candy And A Currant Bun' on the *Fan Club* pop music show. It was broadcast on Nederland 1 TV on Friday 5 May between 7.00pm and 7.56pm.

BELOW: PRIOR TO FILMING ON THE *FAN CLUB* TV SHOW IN AMSTERDAM, 29 APRIL 1967.

SATURDAY 29 APRIL – PERFORMANCE ▼
14-Hour Technicolor Dream, Alexandra Palace London,

Presented by *International Times* with 30 other groups, including the Move, the Pretty Things, Soft Machine, Tomorrow, the Flies, the Creation, the Graham Bond Organisation, Crazy World of Arthur Brown, Purple Gang, Champion Jack Dupree, Soft Machine, Savoy Brown Bluesband, Ginger Johnson, Social Deviants, Julie Driscoll, Sam Gopal, Apostolic Intervention, Blossom Toes and a range of light shows and film shows.

Set list included 'Pow R Toc H', 'Interstellar Overdrive'.

This event was billed variously as "The Biggest Party Ever", "A Free Speech Benefit" and a "Giant Benefit Against Fuzz Action" and every act offered to play for free. In addition there were fairground attractions, igloos dispensing banana-peel joints and the usual giant jellies. It is regarded as an historic event in rock history but, predictably, has grown rosier with age. Mick Farren, quoted in Jonathan Green's book *Days in the Life*, gives an account of the Social Deviants' performance that accurately sums up the evening, indicating that it was probably best appreciated by those who were bombed out of their minds: "We were the first band on and we were fuckin' terrible. Nobody had ever played a gig this big. It was a rectangle the size of Paddington station with similar acoustics. Because of the helter-skelter we couldn't see the band playing at the other end of the hall, but we could hear it, like a slightly more melodic version of the 3.15 from Exeter pulling in at the platform."

Pink Floyd turned up at 3.00am (Sunday 30 April) after a breakneck journey by van and ferry from the Netherlands. It is remembered as a magnificent finale to a night of complete madness, the band taking the stage as the dawn sunlight pierced the huge windows of the main hall. The entire event was filmed by three BBC TV camera crews for inclusion in the *Man Alive* documentary series in an edition subtitled *What Is a Happening?* and broadcast on BBC2 TV on Wednesday 17 May at 8.05pm. It included segments of Tomorrow and the Flies performing as well as interviews with various "underground" figures, although sadly nothing of Pink Floyd's set was captured. Filmmaker Peter Whitehead also took cameras to the show, where he spotted John Lennon, among other celebrities, and although he captured the scale of the event as a whole, he failed to pick up Pink Floyd on stage. Segments of Whitehead's work were also featured on the aforementioned video *The Pink Floyd – London 1966–67*.

SUNDAY 30 APRIL – PERFORMANCE
Plaza Teen Club, Thornton Lodge Hall, Huddersfield, England

Supported by the Match Box and DJ Doc Merwin. Pink Floyd's equipment van broke down en route so they borrowed gear from support band the Match Box.

WEDNESDAY 3 MAY – PERFORMANCE
The Moulin Rouge, Ainsdale, Southport, England

Presented by the Southport Technical College and Old Students' Association.

THURSDAY 4 MAY – PERFORMANCE ▶
Locarno Ballroom, Coventry, England

SATURDAY 6 MAY – PERFORMANCE
Rave!, Kitson College, Leeds, England

SUNDAY 7 MAY – PERFORMANCE
Mojo Club, Tollbar, Sheffield, England

Set list included 'Interstellar Overdrive', 'Astronomy Domine', 'Pow R Toc H', 'Lucifer Sam', 'Matilda Mother', 'Arnold Layne'.

TUESDAY 9 MAY – CANCELLED RECORDING SESSION
Studio 3 & Control Room 3, EMI Studios, Abbey Road, London, England

Session cancelled for unknown reasons.

TUESDAY 9 MAY – RADIO BROADCAST
How The Beatles Changed The World, CBC Radio, Canada

Pink Floyd was featured in this documentary about the Fab Four broadcast on CBC network radio in Canada between 8.10pm and 8.40pm. It is also possible that excerpts from an interview with Roger Waters, Syd Barrett and Nick Mason made by freelance journalist Nancy Bacal was used in this, although it is believed that particular interview was made for the one-hour CBC programme *The Action Set*. Unfortunately there are no surviving records to determine the exact broadcast date of this show, but the programme went out on Saturday mornings at 11.00am through the year. The interview itself has become a source of intrigue to collectors because it features a unique recording of 'Interstellar Overdrive' which is heard in the background. The interview was unearthed and broadcast by Capital Radio on Friday 17 December 1976 in Part One of its documentary series *The Pink Floyd Story*, but has been lost to the world ever since.

FRIDAY 12 MAY – RECORDING SESSION
Studio 2 & Control Room 2, EMI Studios, Abbey Road, London, England

10.00am to 11.00am: Take 14 of 'Astronomy Domine' remixed (RS1) for *The Piper at the Gates of Dawn*. The session was produced by Norman Smith, engineered by Peter Bown and assisted by Peter Mew.

FRIDAY 12 MAY – PERFORMANCE ▼
Games For May, Queen Elizabeth Hall, South Bank, London

Set list: 'Dawn' [Tape Recording], 'Matilda Mother', 'Flaming', 'Scarecrow', 'Games For May', 'Bicycle' ['Bike'], 'Arnold Layne', 'Candy And A Currant Bun', 'Pow R Toc H', 'Interstellar Overdrive', 'Bubbles' [Tape Recording] / 'Ending' [Tape Recording] <Encore> 'Lucifer Sam'.

Billed as "Space age relaxation for the climax of spring" this show was generally regarded as a major turning point for the Pink Floyd, and included their first public use of an idea developed in the recording studio: additional speakers were placed at the back of the hall to give an effect of "sound in the round". A joystick was used to pan pre-recorded sound effects and instruments anywhere within the circle formed by the speakers. The setup, which was built by technicians at EMI, was stolen after the show. The idea was resurrected towards the end of 1968 and used on their 1969 tour and dubbed the "Azimuth Co-ordinator". In addition, props were arranged on stage and bubble machines let fly, along with a well developed light show which incorporated 35mm film slides and movie sequences. New compositions were also written, including the song 'Games For May', which would form the basis of Pink Floyd's second single, 'See Emily Play'.

The *Financial Times* reported that, "Pink Floyd have successfully grafted vision on to sound in their performance by the skilful use of projected colours. Last night they emerged from London's underground life, where they have been a cult for six months, to explode with the noisiest and prettiest display ever seen on the South Bank.... Musically the Floyd are not outstanding. There was good organ and drumming but the guitars were rarely allowed to develop a theme. Only on slower numbers was feeling apparent and here the lyrics, which often invoked childhood illusions of unicorns and scarecrows, soothed the mood. In the more strident songs the words were completely lost, and the sound became just an accompaniment to the colours rather than a partnership. A better

ABOVE: "THE PINK FLOYD" FILL OUT A PERFORMING RIGHTS FORM, 12 MAY 1967.

balance was achieved after the interval, when the free flow of the psychedelic mind was given its head. In between some pounding instrumental excursions, which carried the Floyd close to the new dimension in experience they aim for, the group wandered around the stage playing with friction cars, and water, and blowing bubbles against a recorded cacophony. With the sound at full blast and the colours flashing red, blue, green, those who were at all responsive to the performance succumbed to the illusion. By the end of the evening music disappeared and only electronic sounds remained, filling the hall and the head. Unfortunately with the passing of the music went much of the creativity and instead of using a scalpel on the imagination, the Floyd were using an electric drill…. The performance was billed as a salute to spring, but this was far removed from nature. It was instead a triumph of the mechanical and the belligerently avant-garde."

SATURDAY 13 MAY – PERFORMANCE
St George's Ballroom, Hinckley, England

Supported by Deuce Coup, and rescheduled from Saturday 29 April 1967.
Pink Floyd performed two 30-minute sets at 9.00pm and 10.30pm with Deuce Coup performing three sets at the beginning, middle and end of the evening. Deuce Coup band member Malcolm Latham recalled, "It was the period when Pink Floyd's press coverage strongly featured the light show and I can recall this being projected around the stage area and on at least one wall. Sadly, I can also recall that Floyd didn't give a particularly impressive performance but, in fairness, an almost empty ballroom (less than a hundred people) doesn't lend itself to good sound or give inspiration. Basically, one of those gigs a band would gladly forget!"

SUNDAY 14 MAY – TELEVISION BROADCAST
The Look of the Week, Studio C, BBC Lime Grove Studios, Shepherd's Bush, London, England

Pink Floyd performed 'Pow R Toc H' and 'Astronomy Domine' in a live-to-air broadcast on the arts programme *The Look of the Week*. Studio rehearsals commenced at 8.30pm for broadcast on BBC2 TV between 11.05pm and 11.30pm. Barrett and Waters were also interviewed by the classical music critic Professor Hans Keller, who considered their music to be "terribly loud" and a "regression to childhood". This appearance was thankfully archived and has been widely used in Pink Floyd related retrospectives, beginning first with the *Sounds of the Sixties* series broadcast on BBC2 TV between October and December 1991.

THURSDAY 18 MAY – RECORDING SESSION
Sound Techniques Studios, Chelsea, London, England

'See Emily Play' recorded for the 7-inch single. Written records do not survive of this session, so it is uncertain how many takes or overdubs were made, or even if any further mixing took place. The session was produced by Norman Smith, engineered by John Wood and Jeff Jarrett.

Following his return from France, David Gilmour was reported to have dropped in on the session at Barrett's invitation. He recalled in a 2006 interview with *Mojo* magazine that "Syd was very strange. Glassy-eyed. Not really seeming to recognize me. Not terribly friendly."

FRIDAY 19 MAY – PERFORMANCE
Club A' Go Go, Newcastle-upon-Tyne, England

Rescheduled from Friday 14 April 1967.
Set list included 'Interstellar Overdrive', 'Astronomy Domine', 'Pow R Toc H', 'Lucifer Sam', 'Matilda Mother', 'Chapter 24', 'Arnold Layne'.

SATURDAY 20 MAY – PRESS REPORT
NME, London, England

It was reported that Pink Floyd were planning another *Games for May*–type event at Chiswick House, London, England in June and renamed *Games for June*, although this never came to fruition.

SATURDAY 20 MAY – PERFORMANCE
Floral Hall, Southport, England

Supported by Big Sleep.
Set list included 'Interstellar Overdrive', 'Pow R Toc H', 'Arnold Layne'.

SUNDAY 21 MAY – CANCELLED PERFORMANCE
Regent Ballroom, Brighton, England

Show cancelled due to recording commitments.

SUNDAY 21 MAY – RECORDING SESSION
Studio 3 & Control Room 3, EMI Studios, Abbey Road, London, England

2.30pm to 7.00pm: 'The Bike Song' ['Bike'] recorded (Take 1 at 2:57), and 8.00pm to 1.45am: 'The Bike Song' re-recorded (Take 1 at 1:48, Take 2 at 1:51, Takes 3, 4 and 5 False Starts, Take 6 at 1:47, Take 7 at 1:52, Take 8 at 1:49, Take 9 False Start, Take 10 at 1:51, and Take 11 at 1:50 also marked "best") for *The Piper at the Gates of Dawn*. The session was produced by Norman Smith, engineered by Peter Bown and assisted by Jeff Jarrett.

TUESDAY 23 MAY – PERFORMANCE
Town Hall, High Wycombe, England

With Rod Welling and "Top Discs and Prizes".

WEDNESDAY 24 MAY – PERFORMANCE
Bromel Club, Court Hotel, Downham, Bromley, England

The *Kentish Times* said, "Is it music? This is the controversy which has raged about the Pink Floyd, Britain's leading 'Psychedelic' group. Certainly their show is unique. They play eerie, electronic music, while a dazzling spectrum of lights is played on to them. The lights could best be described as an illuminated abstract painting on which the patterns move kaleidoscopically, as one watches. They have a hypnotic effect. Their road manager and light operator was unwilling to explain their technique. He said, 'I do not tell people how it is done because if groups copy each other, there is no room for originality.' The group has two-watt amplifiers with beat frequency oscillators. Percussion is provided by a double-size drum kit. They are Syd Barrett (lead guitar and vocals), Ric Wright (organ), Roger Walter (bass guitar) and Mick Mason (drums)."

ABOVE: NICK MASON PERFORMING AT SPALDING, 29 MAY 1967.

**THURSDAY 25 MAY –
PERFORMANCE ◄**
*Gwent Constabulary ('A' Division)
Spring Holiday Barn Dance,*
**Grosmont Wood Farm, Cross Ash,
near Abergavenny, Wales**

Supported by Volume IV with MC Eddie Tattersall.

**FRIDAY 26 MAY 1967 –
RECORDING SESSION
EMI Studios, Abbey Road,
London, England**

Lacquers were cut for 'See Emily Play' and 'Scarecrow' for the 7-inch single. The session was produced and engineered by Norman Smith. The band was not present at this session.

FRIDAY 26 MAY – PERFORMANCE ◄
*General Post Office North West
Regional Dance,*
**Empress Ballroom, Winter
Gardens, Blackpool, England**

Supported by the Koobas, Johnny Breeze & the Atlantics and the Rest.
David Boderke, a member of support band The Rest, recalled that, "It was through our associations with the Post Office that we got the booking that was to remain the highlight of our brief career. It was at the GPO's (General Post Office) North West Regional Dance at Blackpool's famous Winter Gardens. Topping the bill was the new psychedelic-type band, Pink Floyd. Supporting were the Koobas from Liverpool who had toured with the Beatles [in 1965], Johnny Breeze and the Atlantics, and ourselves (the Rest). After our sound-check we left our guitars and change of clothing in our dressing room and as were leaving we passed the Pink Floyd's road crew coming in with their equipment. Years later they needed a couple of articulated transporters to carry everything, but even in those days it was still impressive. We stayed behind to watch them setting up and felt more than a little envious as their mountain of equipment dwarfed ours to say the least. Of course everything was bigger and better than our modest collection. Following our set we settled down in the balcony to watch the Pink Floyd in action. As they went into their routine, with all the various stage and musical effects, the audience began drifting off the dance floor."

**SATURDAY 27 MAY –
PERFORMANCE ►**
Bank Holiday Beano, **Civic
Hall, Nantwich, England**

Supported by the SOS.

MONDAY 29 MAY – PERFORMANCE
Barbecue '67, **Tulip Bulb Auction Hall, Spalding, England**

With Jimi Hendrix Experience, Cream, Geno Washington & the Ram Jam Band, Zoot Money & His Big Roll Band and Sounds Force Five.
Pink Floyd was the first band on, apparently performing on a smaller side stage at the rear of the hall. About 600 people attended the show but poor organization meant that many fans were still queuing to get in as Pink Floyd was performing.

**THURSDAY 1 JUNE – RECORDING SESSION
Studio 3 & Control Room 3, EMI Studios,
Abbey Road, London, England**

10.00am–1.00pm: Vocals overdubbed onto Take 11 of 'The Bike Song' ['Bike'], and Take 10 of 'Lucifer Sam', and Take 10 of 'Lucifer Sam' remixed (RM1 also marked "best"), and Take 11 of 'The Bike Song' remixed (RM1 also marked "best") for *The Piper at the Gates of Dawn.* The session was produced by Norman Smith, engineered by Malcolm Addey and assisted by Jerry Boyes.

FRIDAY 2 JUNE – PERFORMANCE
UFO, **The Blarney, Tottenham Court Road,
London, England**

With Soft Machine, Suzy Cream Cheese & Mr. Love, the Hydrogen Juke Box and the Sun Trolley.
International Times reported "The Pink Floyd played last week to the largest crowd that UFO has ever held. At times queues stretched for yards up Tottenham Court Road, and twice the box office had to close because the floor was completely packed. The audience included Jimi Hendrix, Chas Chandler, Eric Burdon, Pete Townshend and members of the Yardbirds. Appeals by Suzy Creamcheese and Joe Boyd were made to the rather emotional crowd to prevent them taking any action against John Hopkins' imprisonment, until after his appeal has been heard. It is a pity that with all this happening the Pink Floyd had to play like bums.

The Soft Machine also appeared briefly to perform a poem for John Hopkins. The Tales of Ollin dance group played for about 4 minutes and completely captured the audience imagination, also on the bill was the Hydrogen Jukebox."

MONDAY 5 JUNE – RECORDING SESSION
Studio 3 & Control Room 3, EMI Studios, Abbey Road, London, England

10.00am to 1.45pm: Take 6 of 'Chapter 24' remixed (RM1 also marked "best", and RM2), and 7.00pm to 1.00am: "Wild Noise" for the cross-fade between 'Interstellar Overdrive' and 'Bike' recorded (Take 1 at 0:34 and Take 2 at 1:14), and then overdubbed onto Take 11 of 'The Bike Song' ['Bike'] for *The Piper at the Gates of Dawn*. The session was produced by Norman Smith, engineered by Malcolm Addey and assisted by Jeff Jarrett (morning) and engineered by Geoff Emerick and assisted by Jeff Jarrett (afternoon).

WEDNESDAY 7 JUNE – RECORDING SESSION
Studio 3 & Control Room 3, EMI Studios, Abbey Road, London, England

7.00pm to 10.30pm: Tape reductions and unspecified overdubs onto Take 6 of 'Matilda's Mother' (and relabelled Take 7) for *The Piper at the Gates of Dawn*. The session was produced by Norman Smith, engineered by Malcolm Addey and assisted by Michael Stone.

FRIDAY 9 JUNE – PERFORMANCE
Students' Union, College of Art, Hull, England

With the ABC and the Night Starvation.

SATURDAY 10 JUNE – PERFORMANCE ▼
The Nautilus Club, South Pier, Lowestoft, England

we're having a-happening on saturday night 10th june a psychedelic nite of lite and sounds + the pink floyd the pink floyd the pink floyd the pink floyd the pink floyd the pink floyd the pink floyd d the pink floyd the pink floyd the pink floyd the pink floyd the pink fl oyd the pink floyd the pink floyd the pink floyd the pink floyd the pin

THE NAUTILUS

SOUTH PIER — LOWESTOFT. Telephone 4793

k floyd the pink floyd the pink floyd the pink floyd the pink floyd the p ink floyd the pink floyd the pink floyd the pink floyd the pink floyd the pink floyd the pink floyd the pink floyd the pink floyd the pink floyd th e pink floyd the pink floyd the pink floyd the pink floyd the pink floyd saturday 24th june the graham bond organisation

SUNDAY 11 JUNE – CANCELLED PERFORMANCE
Patronaatsgebouw, Terneuzen, Netherlands

Early show cancelled due to problems with work permits.

SUNDAY 11 JUNE – CANCELLED PERFORMANCE
Concertgebouw, Vlissingen, Netherlands

Late show cancelled due to problems with work permits.

MONDAY 12 JUNE – RECORDING SESSION
Studio 3 & Control Room 3, EMI Studios, Abbey Road, London, England

2.30pm to 6.30pm: Vocals, tympani, guitar and piano overdubbed onto Take 10 of 'Lucifer Sam' for *The Piper at the Gates of Dawn*. The session was produced by Norman Smith, engineered by Malcolm Addey and assisted by Jeff Jarrett.

TUESDAY 13 JUNE – PERFORMANCE
Blue Opera Club, The Feathers public house, Ealing Broadway, London, England

FRIDAY 16 JUNE 1967 – SINGLE RELEASE (UK)
'See Emily Play'

Melody Maker's guest reviewer Gary Brooker wrote, "[It's] The Pink Floyd. I can tell by the horrible organ sound. It's much better than 'Arnold Layne'. They are the only people doing this kind of scene and they have a very distinctive sound. What the hell is a psychedelic record anyway? Is it something with weird sounds on it? The Beatles use weird sounds but I wouldn't call them psychedelic."

FRIDAY 16 JUNE – PERFORMANCE
Tiles, Oxford Street, London, England

Supported by Sugar Simone & The Programme.

SATURDAY 17 JUNE – PERFORMANCE
The Ballroom, Dreamland Amusement Park, Margate, England

Supported by the Tony Merrick Set.

SATURDAY 17 JUNE – PERFORMANCE
Supreme Ballroom, Ramsgate, England

Pink Floyd appeared after their show at Margate at the invitation of the club owner at a benefit for Israeli refugees.

SUNDAY 18 JUNE – APPEARANCE
Radio London Motor Racing & Pop Festival, Brands Hatch Race Track, England

With Dave Dee, Dozy, Beaky, Mick & Tich, David Garrick, the Moody Blues, and Tristram the Seventh Earl of Cricklewood in an open-top car parade in the afternoon. The event was compered by Radio London DJs Mark Roman and Ed Stewart and featured an evening bikini fashion show and pop concert with Chris Farlowe & the Thunderbirds, Episode Six and the Shell Shock. Pink Floyd did not perform.

TUESDAY 20 JUNE – PERFORMANCE
Commemoration Ball, Main Marquee, Magdalen College, Oxford, England

Pink Floyd performed two twenty-minute sets, at 11.00pm and again at 3.15am in the Main Marquee. Also appearing were John Bassett, Georgie Fame, Herbie Goins and comedian Frankie Howerd. Elsewhere on site was the De Quincey Discotheque (in the Old Bursary), the Right Track, Steel Band and the Pooh (in the Cloisters Night Club) and the Spike Wells Trio and film shows (in the Junior Common Room).

SEE EMILY PLAY

TRACKS

SIDE A: **SEE EMILY PLAY** (Barrett) 2:55
SIDE B: **SCARECROW** (Barrett) 2:07

RELEASE DATE

UK: Friday 16 June 1967.
US: Monday 24 July 1967.

FORMAT

UK: Columbia EMI DB 8214 (7-inch vinyl single).
US: Tower 356 (7-inch vinyl single).

HIGHEST CHART POSITION

UK: No.5 (*Melody Maker* 'Pop 30' on Saturday 29 July 1967).
US: No.134 (*Billboard* 'Bubbling Under The Hot 100' on Saturday 16 September 1967).

ARTWORK

The cover sketch of the train on the picture sleeve was drawn by Syd Barrett.

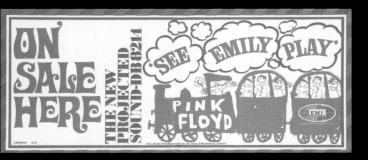

TOP LEFT: UK PROMO PICTURE SLEEVE.
TOP RIGHT: US PROMO PICTURE SLEEVE.
ABOVE: POSTER FOR THE SINGLE RELEASE.
RIGHT: SHEET MUSIC BOOKLET COVER FOR 'SEE EMILY PLAY'.

RECORDING DETAILS

'See Emily Play' was recorded at Sound Techniques, Chelsea, London on 18 May shortly after a version of the track had received its debut performance at the Queen Elizabeth Hall, London on 15 May. 'Scarecrow' was recorded at Abbey Road, London and both tracks were produced by Norman Smith. 'See Emily Play' was engineered by John Wood, and 'Scarecrow' was engineered by Peter Bown. As with 'Arnold Layne' no paperwork remains for sessions recorded at Sound Techniques. The B-side, 'Scarecrow', was taken directly from the album *The Piper at the Gates of Dawn*.

Speaking to *Top Pops*, August 1967 edition, Barrett spoke of his inspiration for writing the song: "I was sleeping in a wood after a gig up north when I saw a girl coming through the trees, shouting and dancing. That's Emily."

Some 32 years later *Mojo* magazine revealed her true identity as sculptor Emily Young, who back in 1966 regularly attended events staged by the London Free School with friends including future actress Anjelica Huston. She recalled that, "I used to go there because there were a lot of Beat philosophers and poets around. There were fundraising concerts with the Pink Floyd Sound, as they were then called. I was more keen on poets than rockers. I was educating myself. I was a seeker. I wanted to meet everyone and take every drug."

SEE EMILY PLAY
Take unknown (RM unknown).
Basic track and overdubs recorded on 18 May 1967.

SCARECROW
Take 1 (RM1).
Basic track recorded on 20 March 1967 (Take 1).
Organ and Guitar overdubbed onto Take 1 on 22 March 1967.
Remixed on 29 March 1967 (RM1).

WEDNESDAY 21 JUNE – CANCELLED RECORDING SESSION
Room 53, EMI Studios, Abbey Road, London

> **BOLTON COLLEGE OF ART MIDSUMMER**
> **BALL**
> # THE PINK FLOYD
> **THE CHASERS, THE NORTHSIDE SIX**
> **AT RIVINGTON BARN**
> **WEDNESDAY, JUNE 21, 1967**
> 8.0 p.m. to 2 a.m.
> Tickets froc College ffice or pay at door.
> Extended bar time. Late night transport

WEDNESDAY 21 JUNE – PERFORMANCE ▲
Bolton College of Art Midsummer Ball,
Rivington Hall Barn, Horwich, Bolton, England

With the Chasers, the Northside Six and Frame of Mind.
Ken Eden of Frame of Mind recalled that, "the high point in that
band was supporting Pink Floyd at Rivington Hall Barn in 1967.
That night left a big impression on us, the loudest thing ever heard,
not by today's standards but unbelievable then, nothing like this
had been heard before, certainly not in Rivi. I'd never seen so many
speaker cabs, it was like Selmer's warehouse. At that time Floyd used
Selmer blue amps, my Goliath blended in perfectly. They had just
charted with 'Arnold Layne' but they were a long way off the mega-
stardom that was to follow."

FRIDAY 23 JUNE – PERFORMANCE
Rolls Royce Apprentices Ball,
Locarno Ballroom, Derby, England

Supported by Paperback Edition and Thorndyke
Mordikai's Imagination.
Ken Cook, a member of support band Thorndyke Mordikai's
Imagination, recalled, "My band appeared with Pink Floyd at the
annual Rolls Royce Apprentices Ball. The majority of the audience
hadn't got a clue what the Pink Floyd were about and the band kept
themselves to themselves. Oil slides were projected onto the dance
floor and they performed in front of a white sheet on one half of
the revolving stage. The other bands on the bill were amazed at
the massive PA they used – it was four watt! The backline (with the
distinguished Farfisa Organ sound) totally drowned
out any vocals that they were trying to get out of the PA,
so I think you can probably imagine what the overall
sound was like. To conclude, 80% of the audience were
totally confused as to the direction of the Floyd whilst
the remainder were possible converts to this new sort of
music never heard before in the likes of Derby."

FRIDAY 23 JUNE – CANCELLED PERFORMANCE
The 8-Hour Psycho-Chromatic Fantasy,
Great & Small Halls, Bradford University,
Bradford, England

Pink Floyd was due to appear with Soft Machine,
Tomorrow, the Children, Cock-A-Hoop and the Roll
Movement, but the event was cancelled.

SATURDAY 24 JUNE – CANCELLED PERFORMANCE
Civic Centre, Corby, England

It was reported in the *Corby Leader*, a month prior to the proposed date,
that Corby Urban Council, owners of the venue, ceased negotiations with
Pink Floyd's management claiming, "The £260 fee was too high for a
group which has no crowd appeal at present." The article was headlined,
"Visit By Drug Music Group Is Off." The show was not rescheduled.

SATURDAY 24 JUNE – CANCELLED PERFORMANCE
César's Club, Bedford, England

The Skatalites replaced Pink Floyd at short notice. Pink Floyd's
appearance was rescheduled to Saturday 14 October 1967.

SUNDAY 25 JUNE – CANCELLED PERFORMANCES
Mister Smiths, Manchester, England

With the Motifs and DJ Dave Lee Travis.
Pink Floyd failed to turn up for their two advertised sets in the Main
Room and Drokiweeny Beach Room for unknown reasons.

MONDAY 26 JUNE – PERFORMANCE
Warwick University, Coventry, England

Melody Maker printed an outraged reader's letter which said, "Having
just seen the Pink Floyd [at Warwick University], I am absolutely
bewildered. Can someone please explain what this psychedelic crap is
about? Their performance bore no connection with music and after
three numbers I walked out in disgust."

TUESDAY 27 JUNE – RECORDING SESSION
Studio 3 & Control Room 3, EMI Studios, Abbey Road, London

7.00pm to 2.30am: Guitar, Organ, Drums and Bass overdubbed onto
Take 2 of 'Interstellar Overdrive', Vocal Harmonies overdubbed onto
Take 1 of 'Flaming' (and relabelled Take 2) and Organ and Guitar
overdubbed onto Take 10 of 'Lucifer Sam' for *The Piper at the Gates of
Dawn*. The session was produced by Norman Smith, engineered by
Peter Bown and assisted by Jeff Jarrett.

WEDNESDAY 28 JUNE – CANCELLED PERFORMANCE
The Ballroom, Eel Pie Island Hotel, Twickenham, England

Show rescheduled to Wednesday 5 July 1967.

BELOW AND RIGHT: RECORDING SESSIONS IN STUDIO 3, ABBEY ROAD, JUNE 1967.

MONDAY 3 JULY – PERFORMANCE
The Pavilion, Bath, England

WEDNESDAY 5 JULY – RECORDING SESSION
Studio 1 & Control Room 1, EMI Studios,
Abbey Road, London, England

10.00am to 1.00pm: Recording the link between 'Astronomy Domine' and 'Lucifer Sam' (Takes 1–2 single links, and Take 3 at 5:00) for *The Piper at the Gates of Dawn*. The session was produced by Norman Smith, engineered by Malcolm Addey and assisted by Michael Stone.

WEDNESDAY 5 JULY – PERFORMANCE
The Ballroom, Eel Pie Island Hotel,
Twickenham, England

Rescheduled from Wednesday 28 June 1967. Pink Floyd was paid £100 for two 30-minute sets.

THURSDAY 6 JULY – TELEVISION BROADCAST
Top of the Pops, **Studio G, BBC Lime Grove Studios,**
Shepherd's Bush, London, England

Pink Floyd mimed to 'See Emily Play' in a live-to-air broadcast for the first of three times on the music programme *Top of the Pops*, hosted by Alan Freeman. It was broadcast (in black and white) on BBC1 TV between 7.30pm and 8.00pm. A rare discovery of previously lost footage from this show, albeit of poor quality, resulted in a screening at the British Film Institute, London, England on Saturday 9 January 2010 in its annual *Missing Believed Wiped* event. It was the first time 'See Emily Play' had been seen in public since its original broadcast and the only one of the three appearances to have been salvaged.

FRIDAY 7 JULY – PERFORMANCE
The Birdcage, Eastney, Portsmouth, England

SATURDAY 8 JULY – PRESS REPORT
London, England

Pink Floyd was reported in *NME* to be making a promotional film of 'Scarecrow' for British Pathé News. The film was syndicated throughout the ABC cinema circuit in the summer of 1967 and featured the band wandering through wheat fields, planting a scarecrow on the edge of an unidentified village pond and having a pretend shoot-out.

SATURDAY 8 JULY – PERFORMANCE
Northwich Memorial Hall, Northwich, England

Supported by the Phoenix Sound.

SUNDAY 9 JULY – PERFORMANCE
Dance, **The Roundhouse, Chalk Farm, London, England**

Supported by the Moody Blues and the Outer Limits.
Promoter Brian Viner recalled that payment for the gig was made not to the bands involved, but to Muscular Dystrophy Research. Pink Floyd's set was scheduled to be 40 minutes. Even then, the stage show was important to them, with a stipulation of a platform,

THURSDAY 29 JUNE – RECORDING SESSION
Room 53, EMI Studios, Abbey Road, London

2.30pm to 9.15pm: "Wild Noise Track" for the cross-fade between 'The Bike Song' ['Bike'] and 'Interstellar Overdrive' remixed (RM1 also marked "best"), Take 11 of 'The Bike Song' remixed (RM2 also marked "best"), Take 2 of 'Flaming' remixed (RM1), Take 2 of 'Flaming' remixed for "Edit Piece For End" (RM2 also marked "best"), Take 7 of 'Matilda Mother' remixed (RM1, RM2, and RM3 also marked "best"), 'Matilda Mother' edit piece with the lyric "Wondering…" remixed (RM4 also marked "best"); Take 7 of 'Matilda Mother' edit piece with the lyric "Sunshine…" remixed (RM5 also marked "best"), RM4 and RM5 of 'Matilda Mother' edited to RM3 and Take 10 of 'Lucifer Sam' remixed (RM2 also marked "best") for *The Piper at the Gates of Dawn*. The session was produced by Norman Smith, engineered by Peter Bown and assisted by Jeff Jarrett.

FRIDAY 30 JUNE – RECORDING SESSION
Studio Control Room 3, EMI Studios,
Abbey Road, London, England

9.30am to 2.00pm: RM1 and RM2 of 'Flaming' reduced and edited (relabelled RM3) and remixed (RM4 and RM5 also marked "best edited") RM2 of 'The Bike Song' ['Bike'] remixed and reduced (RM3 False Start and RM4 also marked "best"), Take 2 of 'Interstellar Overdrive' remixed "from beginning to edit piece" (RM4) and 'Interstellar Overdrive' "Edit Piece" remixed (RM5 and RM6, with RM4 and RM6 also marked "best edited") for *The Piper at the Gates of Dawn*. The session was produced by Norman Smith, engineered by Peter Bown and assisted by Jeff Jarrett.

Nick Mason and Roger Waters took time out from Abbey Road to be interviewed at 11.00am from Studio B15 at BBC Broadcasting House for the BBC World Service programme *Highlight* by its presenter David Griffiths. It was broadcast on Sunday 2 July 1967 between 4.15am and 5.00am.

SATURDAY 1 JULY – PERFORMANCE
The Swan public house, Yardley, Birmingham, England

Supported by Blend 5.

SUNDAY 2 JULY 1967 – PERFORMANCE
Digbeth Institute (Civic Hall), Digbeth,
Birmingham, England

"not less than 8 ft in height and 30 sq ft in surface area to support artistes lighting equipment." The other band for the night was the Moody Blues ("a bargain at £60!") and Brian recalled, "dragging a piano into the Roundhouse that we borrowed from the pub across the road at the request of the Moody Blues."

THURSDAY 13 JULY – RECORDING SESSION
Machine Room 25, EMI Studios, Abbey Road, St. John's Wood, London, England

The mono mix of *The Piper at the Gates of Dawn* was banded and lacquers cut. The session was produced by Norman Smith and engineered by Ken Scott. The band was not present at this session.

THURSDAY 13 JULY – TELEVISION BROADCAST
Top of the Pops, Studio G, BBC Lime Grove Studios, Shepherd's Bush, London, England

Pink Floyd mimed to 'See Emily Play' in a live-to-air broadcast for the second of three times on the music programme *Top of the Pops*, hosted by Pete Murray. It was broadcast (in black and white) on BBC1 TV between 7.30pm and 8.00pm. French magazine *Les Rockers* interviewed the band at the filming in an article that appeared in their September 1967 edition. Asked if he is pleased with 'See Emily Play' Barrett replied, "We didn't like 'Arnold Layne' so much but we are pleased on the whole with 'Emily'. We are trying to get better and better and bring ourselves as near as possible to what we want to do. That's difficult enough, besides which we don't know exactly what we want to do!"

SATURDAY 15 JULY – PRESS REPORT
London, England

NME reported that Pink Floyd would be representing Britain in the June 1968 Olympic Games in Mexico City by performing at an official youth culture festival of music, although this never materialized.

SATURDAY 15 JULY – PERFORMANCE
Stowmarket Carnival, The Cricket Meadow, Stowmarket, England

With the Sullivan James Band, Feel For Soul and Our Generation. DJ John Peel, speaking on *The Pink Floyd Story* broadcast by Capitol Radio, London, England on Friday 17 December 1976, recalled, "I now live in a little town up in East Anglia, which is near Stowmarket. When I first moved up there I was buying a dustbin at the local Woolworths and this fellow came up to me and said, 'It's John Peel, isn't it?' and I said, 'Yes'. He said, 'Having you move into the area is the best thing that's happened since the Pink Floyd played here.' And apparently they did a gig in the cricket grounds at Stowmarket back when they were first starting out, and everybody went along expecting a band playing the top 2 and there were about a dozen people who went there who were knocked out with them – the local freaks and loonies. Everyone else hated them, but it's the biggest thing musically that's ever happened in Stowmarket ever, I think."

SUNDAY 16 JULY – PERFORMANCE
Redcar Jazz Club, The Ballroom, Coatham Hotel, Redcar, England

Supported by the Silverstone Set.

MONDAY 17 JULY – TELEVISION RECORDING
Come Here Often?, Rediffusion TV Studios, Wembley, England

Pink Floyd were filmed for the children's magazine programme *Come Here Often?*, although extensive research has failed to turn up any precise details as the film and archive is now lost. However, it would not be unreasonable to assume they performed 'See Emily Play' given its chart placing and their recent *Top of the Pops* appearances. It was broadcast on the Rediffusion TV network on Tuesday 18 July 1967 at 5.25pm.

TUESDAY 18 JULY 1967 – RECORDING SESSION
Room 53, EMI Studios, Abbey Road, London, England

2.30pm to 5.30pm and 6.30pm–12.30am: Take 14 of 'Astronomy Domine' remixed (RS1 and RS2 also marked "best"), Take 10 of 'Lucifer Sam' remixed (RS1 also marked "best"), Take 7 of 'Matilda Mother' remixed (RS1 also marked "best"), Take 2 of 'Flaming' remixed (RS1 and RS2 edited together and marked "best"), 'Power R Toc H' remixed (RS1 also marked "best"), 'Take Up Thy Stethoscope' remixed (RS1 also marked "best"), 'Interstellar Overdrive' remixed (RS1 also marked "best"); 'The Gnome' remixed (RS1 also marked "best"), 'Chapter 24' remixed (RS1 also marked "best"), 'The Scarecrow' remixed (RS1 also marked "best") and 'Bike' remixed (RS1 also marked "best") for *The Piper at the Gates of Dawn*. The session was produced by Norman Smith, engineered by Norman Smith and assisted by Graham Kirkby (afternoon session), and produced by Norman Smith and engineered by Norman Smith and assisted by Ron Pender (evening session). The band was not present at this session.

TUESDAY 18 JULY – PERFORMANCE
The Palace Ballroom, Douglas, Isle of Man

WEDNESDAY 19 JULY 1967 – RECORDING SESSION
Room 25, EMI Studios, Abbey Road, St. John's Wood, London, England

The stereo mix of *The Piper at the Gates of Dawn* was banded and lacquers cut. The session was produced and engineered by Norman Smith. The band was not present at this session.

WEDNESDAY 19 JULY – PERFORMANCE ▶
Floral Hall, Gorleston, England

Supported by the Alex Wilson Set. The evening was filmed and members of the audience were interviewed by BBC2 TV for inclusion in the series

THE FLORAL HALL
GORLESTON, GT. YARMOUTH
Howard Platt presents
WEDNESDAY, JULY 19th
Your chance to " See Emily play " with
The PINK FLOYD
No 9 in the national record charts
Plus
THE ALEX WILSON SET
From 8 p.m. - Licensed Bars - Admn. 7/6
Rave Sessions every Saturday and Wednesday at East Anglia's own Round House.

Impresarios in an episode entitled 'Transport by Underground', featuring interviews and film of the Social Deviants, Arthur Brown, the Exploding Galaxie Dance Company, Allen Ginsberg, Michael Horowitz and many other contemporary figures of the alternative scene. It was broadcast (in colour) on BBC2 TV on Monday 23 October 1967 between 9.05pm and 9.45pm.

The *Eastern Evening News* reported that, "As the curtains of the stage drew back the Pink Floyd launched themselves into a shuddering opening number, sending the decibels flying round the hall. Flashing green lights, the flashes linked to the rumbles of the guitars, burst around the group from all angles so that at times the different shadows thrown gave the impression that there was a whole crowd of people on the stand. Vocally they were disappointing. This wasn't their fault. Their own amplification had broken down and they had to borrow the Set's PA system. In the middle of that gargantuan instrumental sound they sounded very small – I felt the same way. Visually and sound wise the Pink Floyd are interesting, even exciting, but after the initial effect has worn off, it all seemed a bit thin. As one Floral Hall raver told me, "You've seen one freak-out, you've seen them all." To appreciate this further, I think I needed some other influencing factor, not readily available at the bar. The Floral Hall atmosphere didn't help. Stifled by the heat, my eardrums at perforation point, I dropped out of the Floral Scene."

THURSDAY 20 JULY 1967 – RECORDING SESSION
Machine Room 8, EMI Studios,
Abbey Road, London, England

Side 1 of the mono mix of *The Piper at the Gates of Dawn* was re-cut and the stereo mix of the album was also re-cut. The session was produced by Norman Smith and engineered by Harry Moss. The band was not present at this session.

THURSDAY 20 JULY – PERFORMANCE
Two Red Shoes Ballroom, Elgin, Scotland

Supported by the Copycats.
Set list included 'See Emily Play'.

Roger Waters commented in *Disc & Music Echo*, who had sent a journalist to accompany the first three shows, that, "We've never played on a smaller stage. The audience was very cool to us. Some actually danced while we played. What was that guy saying? 'Do ye ken I could sing better in ma wee bath!'"

FRIDAY 21 JULY – PERFORMANCE
Ballerina Ballroom, Nairn, Scotland

Supported by either the Rebel Sounds or the T-Set, depending on the advert.

SATURDAY 22 JULY – PRESS REPORT
London, England

Disc And Music Echo announced Pink Floyd's follow up single to 'See Emily Play' would be a new Barrett composition entitled 'Old Woman With A Casket' ('Scream Thy Last Scream') or 'Millionaire' released in September. A bizarre promotional film was apparently shot for 'Scream Thy Last Scream' by the poet Spike Hawkins and featuring a stop-motion sequence of an overcoat moving along a side-street to eventually confront a secretary at her place of work, only for her to be rescued by

members of the band. The film unfortunately has not survived (see 11 March for further details).

SATURDAY 22 JULY – PERFORMANCE
Beach Ballroom, Beach Leisure Centre,
Aberdeen, Scotland

Set list included 'See Emily Play', 'Arnold Layne'.

SUNDAY 23 JULY – PERFORMANCE ▼
Cosmopolitan Ballroom, Carlisle, England

Supported by the Lemon Line and the Cobwebs.
Les Leighton, then manager of the Cosmopolitan Ballroom, recalled, "The Pink Floyd arrived late for the show. They were supposed to be on stage at 9.00pm, but didn't arrive until 11.50pm – and my licence was up to 1.00am. The Floyd went on stage at 12.50pm and played until 3.00am and all their stuff was cleared by 4.45am. I risked my licence! I can remember the oil and water slides – they had a huge amount of gear – it was a tremendous night, the Floyd were a bit special. All that night cost me was £15 – the Floyd and their manager were gentlemen, apologising for their late arrival. They were a bit special, not just another band."

MONDAY 24 JULY – SINGLE RELEASE (US)
'See Emily Play'

Cash Box wrote that, "Judging from the reaction in England and first impressions here, the electronic gimmickry and weird goings-on that break up the unusual ballad-rock song it tends toward the hit category."

THURSDAY 27 JULY – TELEVISION BROADCAST
Top of the Pops, Studio G, BBC Lime Grove Studios,
Shepherd's Bush, London, England

Pink Floyd mimed to 'See Emily Play' in a live-to-air broadcast for the third and final time on the music programme *Top of the Pops*, hosted by Alan Freeman. It was broadcast (in black and white) on BBC1 TV between 7.30pm and 8.00pm. Talking to *Cash Box* magazine some years later, the band's studio producer, Norman Smith, recalled that he accompanied the band to the BBC and that, "After a hairdresser had spent many hours making Syd look 'presentable' and after a make-up artist had done the same, Syd looked in the mirror – screamed – and straight away began to mess himself back into his normal self."

FRIDAY 28 JULY – CANCELLED RADIO RECORDING
Saturday Club, BBC Playhouse Theatre,
Charing Cross, London, England

Pink Floyd's session for the BBC Radio Light programme *Saturday Club* commenced at 3.30pm but, according to the engineer's report, Syd just "freaked out" and left the studio during the recording of the first number. He failed to return, so the session was abandoned. Archive paperwork reveals a lengthy correspondence between unimpressed BBC producers and Blackhill over the incident. Pink Floyd's scheduled appearance between 10.00am and 12.00 noon on Saturday 12 August 1967 was replaced by a session from the Spectrum. Any failed takes or recording progress to that point has long since been erased from the archives.

FRIDAY 28 JULY – PERFORMANCE ▼
UFO, The Blarney,
Tottenham Court Road, London, England

With Fairport Convention and Shiva's Children.
Set list included 'Reaction In G', 'Pow R. Toc H.'

Hopes were upheld for a triumphant return performance at *UFO*. Boyd in particular was looking forward to seeing the band after so long. But, when he made eye contact with Barrett the singer just blanked him. "It was like somebody had pulled the blinds, you know, nobody home."

Melody Maker reported, "In a cacophony of sound played to a background of multi-coloured projected lights the Pink Floyd proved they are Britain's top psychedelic group. In two powerful sets they drew nearly every conceivable note from their instruments but ignored their two hit singles. They included 'Pow R Toc H' and a number which received its first hearing called 'Reaction In G', which they say was a reaction against their Scottish tour when they had to do 'See Emily Play'. Bass player Roger Waters gave the group a powerful depth and the lights played on to them to set an impressive scene. Many of the audience found the Floyd's music too much to sit down to and in more subdued parts of the act the sound of jingling bells from their dancing masters joined in. It is clear that the Floyd prefer playing to *UFO* type audiences rather than provincial ones and are at their best in an atmosphere more acceptable to them." Sadly, this was the last time *UFO* opened at these premises. The following Thursday, the landlord gave Joe Boyd notice to quit having seen a lengthy article in the *News of the World* published on 30 July under the heading 'Disturbing World Of The Flower Children', which supposedly revealed the sordid nature of the underground gatherings: "Men danced with men, girls with girls. One girl danced on her own all night," as well as implying drug use, although by today's standards it seems almost laughable it ever went to print. The article even carried a description of Pink Floyd's live performance: "A band crashed on to the stage and somebody's Dalmatian dog padded through the crowd looking for its owner. Discordant music belched from multiple stereo speakers set at full volume. Weirdly dressed men and women jerked to its rhythm. The thumping music was so loud the whole floor vibrated and violent coloured lights flashed in odd sequences." Although Brian Epstein offered Boyd the Champagne Lounge in his Saville Theatre for later shows, the club moved to the larger and far less intimate Roundhouse, where it remained until financial troubles forced its closure in October.

SATURDAY 29 JULY – PERFORMANCE
The Wellington Club, The Dereham Exchange,
East Dereham, England

Supported by the Void.
Roger Waters remembered the show in an interview with *Zig Zag*: "I'll never forget that night. We did a double header that night. First of all we played to a roomful of about five gypsies, hurling abuse and fighting, and then we did Ally Pally. We actually had broken beer mugs smashing into the drum kit."

SATURDAY 29 JULY – PERFORMANCE
Love in Festival, Alexandra Palace,
Muswell Hill, London, England

With Eric Burdon & the Animals, Brian Auger, Julie Driscoll & the Trinity, Crazy World Of Arthur Brown, Creation, Blossom Toes, Sam Gopal's Dream and Apostolic Intervention.
Set list included 'Astronomy Domine', 'Pow R Toc H.'

June Bolan observed the increasingly detached Barrett on stage: "Syd just stood there, his arms hanging down. Suddenly he put his hands on the guitar and we thought he's actually going to do it, but he just stood there, tripping out of his mind."

Go! magazine reported the sudden change in atmosphere from previous events: "What about one fellow who was stabbed and trailed blood in a path outside the Palace early in the morning? Is this a LOVE-IN? No one had planned the tense atmosphere, the robbing, looting and violence. In fact the idea had seemed perfect. Only two groups with top billing got any reaction from the icy crowd. The Pink Floyd got a reaction – a bad one. While the Floyd make ridiculously good records, their music can only be termed boring. When the Animals departed, for thence onwards the music, the people, the atmosphere went abruptly downhill. People floated aimlessly around the hall trying to find where something was at. But 'it' just wasn't there."

MONDAY 31 JULY – CANCELLED PERFORMANCE
Town Hall, Torquay, England

This was the first in a series of cancellations in this period due to Syd Barrett's deteriorating mental health. Andrew King spoke to *NME* who were speculating, in view of the cancellation of the Torquay and West German TV show, on the band having split up. "It is not true Syd has left the group. He is tired and exhausted, and has been advised to rest for two weeks," he said. "We have decided the whole group will holiday for the next fortnight, and any bookings which have to be cancelled will be re-arranged for a later date." Pink Floyd departed for Formentera, Spain, shortly after Wednesday 16 August, returning to the stage on Friday 1 September.

ABOVE: POSING IN RUSKIN PARK, DENMARK HILL, LONDON, JULY 1967.

TUESDAY 1 & WEDNESDAY 2 AUGUST – CANCELLED TELEVISION RECORDING
Hamburg & Bremen, West Germany

It was reported in the music press that Jeff Beck replaced "an ailing Syd Barrett" during a recording session (Tuesday 1 August) for the ZDF network TV programme *Musik Für Junge Leute* [*Music for Young People*] in Hamburg, West Germany. Unfortunately Beck didn't temporarily perform as a member of Pink Floyd as is often tantalizingly assumed – he was engaged in his own promotional duties in West Germany at the time, taking their place on the programme. A further appearance on *Beat Club*, Radio Bremen TV Studios, Bremen, West Germany (Wednesday 2 August) was also cancelled due to Syd Barrett's health.

FRIDAY 4 AUGUST – ALBUM RELEASE (UK)
The Piper at the Gates of Dawn

Record Mirror wrote that, "The psychedelic image of the group really comes to life record-wise on this LP which is a fine showcase for both their talent and the recording technique. Plenty of mind-blowing sound, both blatant and subtle here, and the whole thing is extremely well performed."

SATURDAY 5 AUGUST – CANCELLED PERFORMANCE
Seagull Ballroom, Ryde, Isle of Wight, England

Pink Floyd cancelled this and several further appearances through to the end of the month due to Syd Barrett's ill-health.

MONDAY 7 AUGUST – RECORDING SESSION
Studio 3, EMI Studios, Abbey Road, London, England

7.00pm to 1.30am: Pink Floyd begins work on its next album, *A Saucerful of Secrets*, with the track 'Scream Thy Last Scream' (Takes 1 & 2 False Starts, Take 3 at 4:45 and Take 4 at 4:30 also marked "best"), which remains unreleased. The session was produced by Norman Smith, engineered by Peter Bown and assisted by Jeff Jarrett.

TUESDAY 8 AUGUST – RECORDING SESSION
Studio 3, EMI Studios, Abbey Road, London, England

7.00pm to 1.00am: 'Set The Controls For The Heart Of The Sun' recorded (Take 1 at 4:45 and Take 2 at 5:40 also marked "best") for *A Saucerful of Secrets*. The session was produced by Norman Smith, engineered by Peter Bown and assisted by Jeff Jarrett.

THURSDAY 10 AUGUST – CANCELLED PERFORMANCE
Skyline Ballroom, Hull, England

FRIDAY 11 AUGUST – CANCELLED PERFORMANCE
Top Rank, Doncaster, England

SATURDAY 12 AUGUST – CANCELLED PERFORMANCE
7th National Jazz Federation Pop Ballads & Blues Festival, Balloon Meadow, Royal Windsor Racecourse, Windsor, England

Fans were told of Pink Floyd's no-show by Paul Jones, who bravely made the announcement on stage to much booing and displeasure from the audience.

TUESDAY 15 & WEDNESDAY 16 AUGUST – RECORDING SESSION
Sound Techniques Studios, Chelsea, London, England

7.00pm to 12.00 midnight each day: 'Reaction In G' [an unreleased out-take] recorded for *A Saucerful of Secrets* but the sessions were abandoned after little progress was made. The sessions were engineered by John Wood.

SUNDAY 20 AUGUST – CANCELLED PERFORMANCE
Pavilion Ballroom, Hasting Pier, Hastings, England

FRIDAY 1 SEPTEMBER – CANCELLED PERFORMANCE
Gaiety (Mecca) Ballroom, Grimsby, England

PINK FLOYD ROAD CREW – SATURDAY 16 DECEMBER 1967
Peter Watts (Road Manager / Sound Engineer),
Peter Wynne-Wilson (Lights).

The March 1997 edition of *Sound on Stage* gave some indication of Pink Floyd's PA system at this time, reporting, "Little in terms of purpose-designed PA technology existed before 1967, the only options open to the Floyd being Vox or Selmer columns and 100 Watt amps. Therefore, when Charlie Watkins designed his first WEM single column PA, the Floyd took it to their hearts, and it remained with them for the next four years. The Floyd's system was based around the WEM B and C cabinets. The B cabinet housed four 12-inch Goodmans 301 twin cone speakers, while the C cabinet had four 12-inch Goodmans Audiom 61s. Pinned in between the B and C cabinet was an X32 horn in a narrow column. To drive the system, the Floyd used WEM amplification, and Road Manager/ Sound Engineer Peter Watts mixed with four small five-channel WEM Audiomaster consoles whose comparatively primitive functions

THE PIPER AT THE GATES OF DAWN

SIDE ONE

ASTRONOMY DOMINE (Barrett) 4:12
LUCIFER SAM (Barrett) 3:07
MATILDA MOTHER (Barrett) 3:08
FLAMING (Barrett) 2:46
POW R. TOC H (Barrett, Waters, Wright, Mason) 4:26
TAKE UP THY STETHOSCOPE AND WALK (Barrett) 3:06

SIDE TWO

INTERSTELLAR OVERDRIVE (Barrett, Waters, Wright, Mason) 9:40
THE GNOME (Barrett) 2:13
CHAPTER 24 (Barrett) 3:42
SCARECROW (Barrett) 2:11
BIKE (Barrett) 3:23

RELEASE DATE

UK: Friday 4 August 1967.

FORMAT

UK: Columbia EMI SX 6157 (Mono vinyl album).
UK: Columbia EMI SCX 6157 (Stereo vinyl album).

HIGHEST CHART POSITION

UK: No.3 (*Melody Maker* 'Top 10 LPs' on Saturday 9 September 1967),
Chart re-entry No.44 (*Music Week* 'Top 75 Albums' on Saturday 16
August 1997), Chart re-entry No.22 (*Official UK Album Chart* on
Saturday 15 September 2007).

AWARDS

UK: Certified Silver on Monday 22 July 2013.

ORIGINAL ARTWORK

The front cover image was taken by fashion photographer Vic Singh
and the rear cover illustration was drawn by Syd Barrett outlined
from a group photo of the band taken by Colin Prime in Ruskin Park,
Denmark Hill, London in July 1967.

MUSICIANS

Syd Barrett (Vocals, Guitar).
Roger Waters (Bass Guitar, Vocals).
Richard Wright (Piano, Organ, Farfisa, Hammond, Celeste, Vibraphone,
Cello, Vocals).
Nick Mason (Drums, Percussion).
Peter Jenner (Vocal intro on 'Astronomy Domine').

RECORDING DETAILS

Pink Floyd's debut album was produced by Norman Smith entirely
at EMI Studios, Abbey Road under the working title *Projection*.
Recording commenced on 21 February and continued through to
18 July 1967.

Remarkably the sessions produced just two unreleased outtakes:
a cross-fade link between 'Bike' and 'Interstellar Overdrive', which
indicates a different running order was originally considered, and
the track 'She Was A Millionaire'. This was announced in *Disc & Music
Echo* (22 July 1967) as 'Millionaire' as a possible follow-up single to
'See Emily Play'. The track was also caught on tape by a bootlegger
at a concert in Copenhagen on 13 September – one of only three
surviving concert recordings from that year. Although the track
was abandoned by Pink Floyd, Syd Barrett attempted, but failed, to
revive it during sessions for his second solo album, *Barrett*, although
it is thought some elements of it can be heard on the track 'Opel',
released on the outtakes album of the same name.

A handful of previously unreleased versions of tracks surfaced on
the 40th anniversary CD reissue, notably two versions of 'Interstellar
Overdrive' including the French EP edit. Also included on this set
is the track 'Matilda Mother', another Barrett composition, with
adapted lyrics taken directly from Hilaire Belloc's poem 'Matilda,
Who Told Lies And Burned To Death', published in the 1907 volume
*Cautionary Tales for Children: Designed for the Admonition of Children
Between the Ages of Eight and Fourteen Years: Verses by Hilaire Belloc*.
This was recorded on Tuesday 21 February in anticipation of the
Belloc estate granting permission for its use, which it ultimately
refused, causing Barrett an urgent rewrite (although it is debatable
whether copyright laws would have necessitated permission). The
alternate version eventually surfaced as a bonus track on the album's
CD reissue in 2007.

Astronomy Domine

Take 14 (RM2 / RS2).
Basic track recorded on 11 April 1967 (Take 14).
Guitar and Vocals overdubbed onto Take 14 on
12 April 1967.
Vocal for beginning recorded and overdubbed
onto Take 14 on 17 April 1967.
Link between 'Astronomy Domine' and 'Lucifer
Sam' recorded on 5 July 1967.
Remixed on 18 April 1967 (RM2).
Remixed on 18 July 1967 (RS2).

Lucifer Sam

Take 10 (RM2 / RS1).
Basic track recorded as 'Percy The Ratcatcher' on
12 April 1967 (Take 10).
Maracas, Organ and Bow Bass overdubbed onto
Take 10 on 13 April 1967.
Bass and Organ overdubbed onto Take 10 on
17 April 1967.
Vocal overdubbed onto Take 10 on 18 April 1967.
Vocals, Tympani, Guitar and Piano overdubbed
onto Take 10 on 12 June 1967.
Organ and Guitar overdubbed onto Take 10 on
27 June 1967.
Remixed on 29 June 1967 (RM2).
Remixed on 18 July 1967 (RS1).

Matilda Mother

Take 7 (RM3 / RS1).
Basic track recorded on 21 February 1967 (Take 7).
Unspecified overdubs onto Take 7 on 7 June
1967.
Remixed and edited on 29 June 1967 (RM3).
Remixed on 18 July 1967 (RS1).

ABOVE: PRESS ADVERT FOR THE ALBUM RELEASE.

RIGHT: THIS PHOTO TAKEN AT RUSKIN PARK IN JULY 1967 FORMED
THE OUTLINE OF THE REAR SLEEVE DESIGN DRAWN BY BARRETT.

Flaming

Take 2 (RM5 / RS1&2).
Basic track recorded on 16 March 1967 (Take 2).
Vocal Harmonies overdubbed onto Take 2 on 27
June 1967.
Remixed on 29 June 1967 (RM5).
Remixed on 18 July 1967 (RS1&2).

Pow R. Toc H

Take 4 (RM3 / RS1).
Basic track recorded on 21 March 1967 (Take 4).
Vocals overdubbed onto Take 4 on 21 March
1967.
Remixed on 29 March 1967 (RM3).
Remixed on 18 July 1967 (RS1).

Take Up Thy Stethoscope And Walk

Take 5 (RM2 / RS1).
Basic track recorded on 20 March 1967 (Take 5).
Vocals overdubbed onto Take 5 on 20 March
1967.
Remixed and edited on 29 March 1967 (RM2).
Remixed on 18 July 1967 (RS1).

Interstellar Overdrive

Take 2 (RM6 / RS1).
Basic track recorded on 27 February 1967
(Take 2).
Guitar, Organ, Drums and Bass overdubbed
onto Take 2 on 27 June 1967.
Remixed and edited on 30 June 1967 (RM6).
Remixed on 18 July 1967 (RS1).

The Gnome

Take 6 (RM2 / RS1).
Basic track recorded on 19 March 1967 (Take 6).
Celeste, 12-String Guitar and Vocals overdubbed
onto Take 6 on 19 March 1967.
Remixed on 29 March 1967 (RM2).
Remixed on 18 July 1967 (RS1).

Chapter 24

Take 6 (RM1 / RS1).
Basic track recorded on 15 March 1967 (Take 6).
Remixed on 5 June 1967 (RM1).
Remixed on 18 July 1967 (RS1).

Scarecrow

Take 1 (RM1 / RS1).
Basic track recorded on 20 March 1967 (Take 1).
Organ and Guitar overdubbed onto Take 1 on
22 March 1967.
Remixed on 29 March 1967 (RM1).
Remixed on 18 July 1967 (RS1).

Bike

Take 11 (RM2 / RS1).
Basic track recorded on 21 May 1967 (Take 11).
Vocals overdubbed onto Take 11 on 1 June
1967.
"Wild Noises" recorded and overdubbed onto
Take 11 on 5 June 1967.
Harmonium and Vocals overdubbed onto
Take 11 on 5 June 1967.
Remixed on 29 June 1967 (RM2).
Remixed on 18 July 1967 (RS1).

She Was A Millionaire (Unreleased)

Basic track recorded on 18 April 1967
(Takes 1–3).

included bass, treble, and middle controls, presence and input sensitivity. This was the state of the art back in the late '60s."

FRIDAY 1 SEPTEMBER – PERFORMANCE
UFO Festival, The Roundhouse, Chalk Farm, London, England

With Arthur Brown, Tomorrow, Fairport Convention and the Nack. The *UFO Festival* was originally intended to be held in a circus tent in a park in Paignton, Devon but according to *Melody Maker* was cancelled by the organizers following a dispute with the tent owners who "didn't want the name UFO to appear on their tent and they didn't want *International Times* to be sold in the tent." However, no mention of this proposed event is made in any of the local area newspapers, which leads one to believe it may have been a speculative event or a PR stunt.

SATURDAY 2 SEPTEMBER – PERFORMANCE
UFO Festival, The Roundhouse, Chalk Farm, London, England

With the Move, Soft Machine, Fairport Convention, the Nack and Denny Laine.

MONDAY 4, TUESDAY 5 & WEDNESDAY 6 SEPTEMBER – RECORDING SESSION
Sound Techniques Studios, Chelsea, London, England

Further attempts were made at recording tracks for the album *A Saucerful of Secrets,* but all three sessions were eventually abandoned with no apparent output except an untitled instrumental recorded on Monday 4 September 1967 (Takes 1–6 untimed and Take 7 at 4:32) which was eventually scrapped. It is noted on paperwork that these sessions took place while Norman Smith was on holiday.

FRIDAY 8 SEPTEMBER – CANCELLED PERFORMANCE
The Rolling Stones Benefit Concert, Alexandra Palace, London, England

Following the infamous Redlands arrests of Mick Jagger and Keith Richards in January 1967, manager Andrew "Loog" Oldham announced a benefit concert, but it was shelved after their appeal, which was heard on Monday 31 July 1967, reduced their sentence to a conditional discharge.

SCANDINAVIAN TOUR

Pink Floyd's first tour of mainland Europe saw them perform dates in Scandinavia. Despite the group receiving widespread press coverage in advance, the overall impression of their live performance was one of disappointment.

SATURDAY 9 SEPTEMBER – PERFORMANCE
Boom, Åarhus, Denmark

Supported by Wishful Thinking, Step by Step, Shaking Phantoms, Barnet and His Dandy-Bublers.

Pink Floyd was reported to have left some very strong impressions at their first Danish performance in the Boom dancing centre. More than 1,000 people attended the show, and at least the same number was unable to get in. After the microphones failed, the band was forced to play a mainly instrumental set. The newspaper *Aarhus Stiftstidende* reported, "We heard only three songs from the LP [*The Piper at the Gates of Dawn*] and they were all altered beyond recognition."

SUNDAY 10 SEPTEMBER – PERFORMANCE
Gyllene Cirkeln, Stockholm, Sweden

Supported by the Sleepstones and DJ Errol Devonish.
Set list: 'Reaction In G', 'Matilda Mother', 'Pow R Toc H', 'Scream Thy Last Scream', 'Set The Controls For The Heart Of The Sun', 'See Emily Play', 'Interstellar Overdrive'.

Roger Waters was interviewed after the show for a late night magazine programme broadcast live on Tonarskvall 3 Radio, Stockholm, Sweden. The entire concert was recorded and remained lost until it was rediscovered in 2010 and played back for the very first time at a special commemorative event held at the same venue on Saturday 7 May 2011.

MONDAY 11 SEPTEMBER – PERFORMANCE ◄
Starclub, Copenhagen, Denmark

Supported by the Beefeaters, Peter Belli & B. Brothers, Steppeulvene, the Clan, Hitmakers, Ebonies, the Case and the Defenders.
Set list included 'Set The Controls For The Heart Of The Sun'.

TUESDAY 12 SEPTEMBER – PERFORMANCE
Starclub, Copenhagen, Denmark

Supported by the Beefeaters, Peter Belli & B. Brothers, Steppeulvene, the Clan, Hitmakers, Ebonies, the Case and Melvis.

WEDNESDAY 13 SEPTEMBER – PERFORMANCE
Starclub, Copenhagen, Denmark

Supported by the Beefeaters, Peter Belli & B. Brothers, Steppeulvene, the Clan, Hitmakers, Ebonies, the Case and Melvis.
Set list: 'Reaction In G', 'Arnold Layne', 'One In A Million', 'Matilda Mother', 'Scream Thy Last Scream', 'Astronomy Domine'.

Danish magazine *Borge*, who had enthusiastically previewed Pink Floyd's appearances and had even photographed the band visiting the Tivoli gardens, along with a report of them being thrown out for bad behaviour, reported on their shows as being "a disappointment! You expect a little more musical quality for your money. But the musical surprises were non-existent… they don't play for us. They stand up and play with each other… we won't bother to watch them again. It is too far away from being pop!"

FRIDAY 15 SEPTEMBER – PERFORMANCE
The Starlite Ballroom, Belfast, Northern Ireland
Supported by the Fugitives.

SATURDAY 16 SEPTEMBER – PERFORMANCE
Flamingo Ballroom, Ballymena, Northern Ireland
Supported by the Cousins.

SUNDAY 17 SEPTEMBER – PERFORMANCE
The Arcadia Ballroom, Cork, Ireland
Pink Floyd was widely reported to have flown straight from Cork to Brussels to participate in a "TV Spectacular", but no details exist in the Belgian TV archives. Given the distance and limitations of transport at that time it is unlikely to have been anything more than a publicity stunt.

TUESDAY 19 SEPTEMBER – PERFORMANCE
The Speakeasy, Margaret Street, London, England

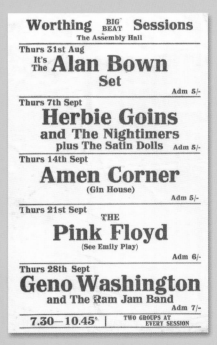

THURSDAY 21 SEPTEMBER – PERFORMANCE ◄
Assembly Hall, Worthing, England
Supported by Love Affair. Set list: 'Scream Thy Last Scream', 'Astronomy Domine', 'Set The Controls For The Heart of The Sun', 'Reaction In G' and 'Interstellar Overdrive'.

Steve Ellis of Love Affair recalled, "We did a gig with Pink Floyd at Worthing Pavilion and completely mullered them. We went on and they got the blown out of the water. That was with Syd Barrett and everything. They got bottled off. They were smoking copious amounts of dope before they went on which wouldn't have helped."

FRIDAY 22 SEPTEMBER – PERFORMANCE
Tiles, Oxford Street, London
Supported by the Roger James Explosion.

SATURDAY 23 SEPTEMBER – PERFORMANCE
Saturday Scene, **Corn Exchange, Chelmsford, England**
With an unnamed support group.

MONDAY 25 SEPTEMBER – RADIO RECORDING
Top Gear, **Studio 1, BBC 201 Piccadilly Studios, London, England**
Pink Floyd recorded a session for the first ever edition of *Top Gear* for BBC Radio 1 at the BBC 201 Piccadilly Studios commencing 2.30pm. Significantly it also marked John Peel's

debut appearance on BBC Radio 1 as a guest presenter with Pete Drummond, and seven tracks were recorded including 'The Gnome' (2:10), 'Scarecrow' (2:05), 'Set The Controls For The Heart Of The Sun' (3:10), 'Matilda Mother' (3:20), 'Reaction In G' (0:34) and 'Flaming' (2:40). 'Reaction In G' was presumably recorded in full, but it was only used as a short fade-out during the show, which was broadcast on Sunday 1 October 1967 between 2.00pm and 5.00pm.

'The Gnome' (2:10), 'Matilda Mother' (3:20), 'Flaming' (2:40) and 'Scarecrow' (2:10) were repeated on *Top Gear* on 5 November 1967 between 2.00pm and 5.00pm.

'Set The Controls For The Heart Of The Sun' was repeated on the *David Symmonds Show* on 13 November 1967 between 5.30pm and 7.30pm, and 'Matilda Mother' was repeated on the *David Symmonds Show* on 17 November 1967 at 5.30pm and 7.30pm.

The original Pink Floyd recordings have long since been erased or lost, but remarkably a complete recording of the original 1 October 1967 broadcast, taped from the radio at the time, was unearthed and played on an edition of *Play it Again* as part of *Keeping it Peel*, a week-long series of John Peel retrospectives broadcast on BBC6 Music on Monday 24 October 2005 between 9.00pm and 10.00pm.

TUESDAY 26 SEPTEMBER – FILM PREMIERE (US)
Tonite Let's All Make Love in London, **5th New York Film Festival, Philharmonic Hall, Lincoln Center, New York, NY, USA**
The *New York Times* said the film was a "random and ricocheting hodgepodge of candidly photographed scenes of people talking or singing at protest meetings; straight-on close-up interviews with prominent motion picture people; sequences of recording sessions of popular rock 'n' roll bands, look-ins and talks with pop artists, and impressionistic shots of people dancing in the street. There is no form or continuity to it."

WEDNESDAY 27 SEPTEMBER – PERFORMANCE
Fifth Dimension, Leicester, England
To celebrate the club's opening they commissioned a specially designed psychedelic poster by Hapshash & the Coloured Coat for their opening week of shows, which included this date.

THURSDAY 28 SEPTEMBER – PERFORMANCE
Top Star Beat Dance, **Skyline Ballroom, Hull, England**
Supported by the Dimples, the Rats [featuring Mick Ronson on guitar], the Disturbance and DJ Rikki Dobbs.

FRIDAY 30 SEPTEMBER – PERFORMANCE
The Imperial Ballroom, Nelson, England
Supported by the Atlantics and the Beatovens.

SUNDAY 1 OCTOBER – PERFORMANCES ▼
Sunday's at the Saville, **Saville Theatre, London, England**
Two evening shows at 6.00pm and 8.30pm, with Tomorrow, the Incredible String Band, Tim Rose and host Joe Boyd.

ABOVE: BACKSTAGE AT THE FIFTH DIMENSION, LEICESTER, ENGLAND, 27 SEPTEMBER 1967.

Set list at the second show: 'Astronomy Domine', 'Flaming', 'Lucifer Sam', 'Matilda Mother', 'Pow R Toc H', 'Scarecrow', 'Candy And A Currant Bun' and 'Interstellar Overdrive'.
NME reported, "The beautiful people and hippies turned up in their shawls, embroidered jackets, Indian headbands and beads to see the Pink Floyd at the Saville on Sunday night. Even the host, Joe Boyd, was from UFO. The Pink Floyd were one of the first groups to experiment with weird effects and they now have it down to a fine art, or rather their lighting man has. The flashing patterns and weaving silhouettes are an integral part of their music, which was very loud and mainly instrumental."

FRIDAY 6 OCTOBER – PERFORMANCE
Miss Teenage Brighton Contest, Top Rank Suite, Brighton, England

Set list included 'Arnold Layne', 'See Emily Play', 'Matilda Mother', 'Astronomy Domine'.

Pink Floyd was paid £300 for two 30-minute spots and provided the musical interlude at the contest, which was compered by Radio Caroline DJ Mike Aherne.

SATURDAY 7 OCTOBER – PRESS REPORT
London, England

The UK music press all reported that Pink Floyd was planning to stage a series of "Spectaculars" in March 1968 with a 100-piece choir and a small chamber orchestra. Provisional dates were even announced: Free Trade Hall, Manchester, England on Saturday 2 March 1968, Philharmonic Hall, Liverpool, England on Saturday 9 March 1968, Royal Albert Hall, London, England on Friday 15 March 1968 and the Town Hall, Birmingham, England on Saturday 16 March 1968, but nothing came of these plans. It was

also reported that Pink Floyd would be recording for television in Germany and Belgium between Tuesday 17 and Friday 20 October, and giving shows in Paris, France between Sunday 22 and Thursday 26 October 1967, and Netherlands between Wednesday 8 and Sunday 12 November 1967. All proposed dates were cancelled to make way for their US tour.

SATURDAY 7 OCTOBER – PERFORMANCE
Victoria Rooms, University of Bristol, Clifton, Bristol, England

MONDAY 9 OCTOBER – STUDIO VISIT
BBC Radiophonic Workshops, Maida Vale, London, England

Pink Floyd made a daytime visit to the Workshops with, according to press reports, a view to co-writing a soundtrack for a new TV series, but this never came to fruition.

MONDAY 9, TUESDAY 10 & WEDNESDAY 11 OCTOBER – RECORDING SESSION
De Lane Lea Studios, Holborn, London, England

7.00pm to 12.00 midnight: 'Remember A Day', 'Jugband Blues' and 'Vegetable Man' [an unreleased track] recorded for the album *A Saucerful of Secrets*. No detailed paperwork exists from these sessions beyond the times the studio was booked. The session was produced by Norman Smith and engineered by Michael Weighell.

THURSDAY 12 OCTOBER – RECORDING SESSION
De Lane Lea Studios, Holborn, London, England

7.00pm to 12.00midnight: 'Remember A Day' and 'Vegetable Man' remixed for *A Saucerful of Secrets*. The session was produced by Norman Smith.

FRIDAY 13 OCTOBER – PERFORMANCE ▼
The Pavilion, Weymouth, England

Presented by the Steering Wheel Clubs with support from Freddy Mack & the Mack Sound and Denise Scott & the Soundsmen. Set list: 'Astronomy Domine', 'Reaction In G', 'Set The Controls For The Heart Of The Sun', 'Matilda Mother', 'Interstellar Overdrive' and 'Pow R Toc H'.

SATURDAY 14 OCTOBER – PERFORMANCE
César's Club, Bedford, England

Supported by the Tecknique. Journalist Steve Peacock recalled in an article he wrote in the 1970s for *Sounds*, "I remember seeing them at Bedford play an aggressive set to a cowed audience. They seemed to take a gloomy kind of pleasure in it: in the dressing-cupboard afterwards, Roger Waters made the grim comment, 'At least we frightened a few people tonight.'"

THURSDAY 19 OCTOBER – RECORDING SESSION
De Lane Lea Studios, Holborn, London, England

7.00pm to 12.00 midnight: Recording 'Jugband Blues' for *A Saucerful of Secrets*. It is noted on the recording booking form that six session musicians, presumably the brass section, were hired for the day at a total cost of £15.00. The session was produced by Norman Smith.

FRIDAY 20 OCTOBER – RECORDING SESSION
De Lane Lea Studios, Holborn, London, England

2.00pm to 5.00pm and 7.00pm to 12.00midnight: Recording 'John Latham', 'Instrumental' (Take 1 at 10:00), and 'In The Beechwoods' (Take 2 breakdown, Take 3 at 2:38, Take 4 at 5:00 and Take 5 at 5:08), all of which remain unreleased. The session was produced by Norman Smith. The track 'John Latham' is believed to have been a commission for a soundtrack for an art installation by the artist of the same name but it is uncertain if it was ever used.

SATURDAY 21 OCTOBER – ALBUM RELEASE (US)
Pink Floyd

Cash Box wrote, "The set is a particularly striking collection of driving, up to date rock ventures. 'The Gnome' is an oft-played track. Among the other outstanding efforts included on the LP are 'See Emily Play', 'Chapter 24' and 'Interstellar Overdrive'."

SATURDAY 21 OCTOBER – PERFORMANCE
Derwent Dining Room, University of York, Heslington, York, England

Supported by Love Sculpture.

MONDAY 23 OCTOBER – RECORDING SESSION
Studio 2 & Control Room 2, EMI Studios, Abbey Road, London, England

10.00am to 6.00pm: 'Paintbox' recorded (Take 1–4 False Starts, Take 5 at 3:55, Take 6 False Start, Take 7 at 3:20 and Take 8 at 3:32 also marked "best"), and 7.00pm to 2.00am: Vibraphone and Voices recorded and overdubbed onto Take 2 of 'Set The Controls For The Heart Of The Sun' and 'Early Morning Henry' recorded (Take 1 marked "Demo Only") for *A Saucerful of Secrets*. The session was produced by Norman Smith, engineered by Ken Scott and assisted by Jeff Jarrett.

'Early Morning Henry' remains an unreleased track and archive paperwork notes that Norman Smith removed the only known tape of this recording.

MONDAY 23 OCTOBER – CANCELLED PERFORMANCE
The Pavilion, Bath, England

Show cancelled due to recording commitments.

TUESDAY 24 OCTOBER – RECORDING SESSION
Studio 2 & Control Room 2, EMI Studios, Abbey Road, London, England

7.00pm to 5.30am: 'Paintbox' recorded (Take 8 breakdown, and Take 9 at 3:22 also marked "best") for the 7-inch single. The session was produced by Norman Smith, engineered by Ken Scott and assisted by Jeff Jarrett.

THURSDAY 26 OCTOBER – RECORDING SESSION
Studio 2 & Control Room 2, EMI Studios, Abbey Road, London, England

7.00pm to 3.30am: 'Paintbox' overdubbed and 'Apples And Oranges' recorded for the 7-inch single. The session was produced by Norman Smith, engineered by Ken Scott and assisted by Jeff Jarrett.

FRIDAY 27 OCTOBER – RECORDING SESSION
Studio 2 & Control Room 2, EMI Studios, Abbey Road, London, England

7.00pm to 7.45am: 'Apples And Oranges' overdubbed for the 7-inch single in a marathon 12 ¾-hour session in order to complete it before their impending US tour. The session was produced by Norman Smith, engineered by Ken Scott and assisted by Jeff Jarrett.

SATURDAY 28 OCTOBER – PERFORMANCE
Dunelm House, University of Durham, Durham, England

FRIDAY 3 NOVEMBER – CANCELLED PERFORMANCE
Caves Club, **Chislehurst Caves, Chislehurst, England**

Show rescheduled to 8 December 1967 due to Pink Floyd's departure to the USA.

FRIDAY 3 NOVEMBER – CANCELLED PERFORMANCE
Royal Festival Hall, South Bank, London England

A proposed show with the Incredible String Band was announced in the music press but was shelved before tickets went on sale.

US TOUR

Pink Floyd's debut US tour was booked by the Premier Talent Agency in New York and was originally set to commence on Monday 23 October in Los Angeles. Plans were altered when the late application for work permits by Blackhill forced the cancellation of many advertised shows.

These included the Whisky a Go Go, West Hollywood, Los Angeles on Monday 23 and Tuesday 24 October; Fillmore Auditorium, San Francisco between Thursday 26 to Saturday 28 October; Whisky a Go Go, Los Angeles between Monday 30 October to Wednesday 1 November; and the KPFA *Radio Benefit Halloween Costume Ball*, Fillmore Auditorium, San Francisco, also on Monday 30 October, where Steve Miller Blues Band took Pink Floyd's place. Several other shows were being explored and a surviving memo from Capitol Records suggests that bookings were being held at the Cheetah, Chicago, on Sunday 5 November and the Cafe Au Go Go, Manhattan, New York City, between Tuesday 7 to Monday 13 November.

After the start date was rescheduled further delays were caused by US Customs and Immigration and shows were cancelled at Winterland Auditorium, San Francisco, on Thursday 2 November, where Richie Havens took Pink Floyd's place and also on Friday 3 November, where Ike & Tina Turner took Pink Floyd's place.

Pink Floyd finally left the UK on Friday 3 November arriving in San Francisco a day later on Friday 4 November at 5.30am, checking into the Casa Madrona Hotel in nearby Sausalito.

PINK FLOYD

SIDE ONE

SEE EMILY PLAY (Barrett) 2:55
POW R. TOC H (Barrett, Waters, Wright, Mason) 4:26
TAKE UP THY STETHOSCOPE AND WALK (Barrett) 3:06
LUCIFER SAM (Barrett) 3:06
MATILDA MOTHER (Barrett) 3:08

SIDE TWO

SCARECROW (Barrett) 2:11
THE GNOME (Barrett) **2:13**
CHAPTER 24 (Barrett) 3:42
INTERSTELLAR OVERDRIVE (Barrett, Waters, Wright, Mason) 9:40

RELEASE DATE

Saturday 21 October 1967.
The US edition of *The Piper at the Gates of Dawn* is notable for its variation of track-listing from the UK release. 'See Emily Play' has been inserted to the album and the tracks 'Astronomy Domine, 'Flaming' and 'Bike' do not appear. Furthermore, the sleeve contains several misspellings: 'Pow R Toc H' is spelt 'Pow R Toch' and 'Take Up Thy Stethoscope And Walk' is spelt 'Take Up My Stethoscope And Walk'.

FORMAT

Tower T5093 (Mono vinyl album).
Tower ST5093 (Stereo vinyl album).

HIGHEST CHART POSITION

No.131 (*Billboard* 'Top LPs' on Saturday 27 January 1968).

ABOVE: ALBUM REVIEW FROM *TEEN SET* MAGAZINE, FEBRUARY 1968.

RIGHT: PRESS ADVERT FROM *L. A. FREE PRESS*, 13 OCTOBER 1967.

Here the band was photographed for *Rolling Stone* magazine by Baron Wolman in anticipation of a feature, but upon seeing the band perform a less than impressive set at Winterland that evening its editor Ralph Gleason immediately cancelled the article.

To appease an already irate Bill Graham, the band was added to the bill of an existing run of shows booked for Procol Harum and HP Lovecraft at the Fillmore and Winterland between Thursday 9 and Saturday 11 November.

A return flight via New York and a one-hour set at the Cheetah in the late afternoon made their show on Sunday 12 November 1967 the last night of the tour.

SATURDAY 4 NOVEMBER – PERFORMANCE
Winterland Auditorium, San Francisco, CA, USA

With Richie Havens and Big Brother & the Holding Company. It is also understood the band made a number of radio interviews in this period, including at least one for KMPX in San Francisco, but exact details could not be found.

Talking of their on-stage visual impact Andrew King exclaimed, "Our lights looked pathetic. The biggest lamp we had was a single kilowatt bulb, but a typical West Coast show had 20. The only things that worked were the more powerful slide projectors."

SUNDAY 5 NOVEMBER – TELEVISION RECORDING
Groovy, Venice Beach, Los Angeles, CA, USA

Prior to their evening engagement Pink Floyd was filmed for an insert on the teenage pop-party show *Groovy*, which was filmed daily on weekdays live from Venice Beach and hosted by Michael Blodgett, although their contribution is unknown. It was broadcast (in colour) on KHJ network TV Channel 9 on Thursday 16 November 1967 between 6.00pm and 6.30pm (PST).

SUNDAY 5 NOVEMBER – PERFORMANCE ▼
Cheetah, Lick Pier, Los Angeles, CA, USA

With Smokestack Lightning and the Candymen. Although press advertising indicated a matinée show, Pink Floyd performed just one set in the evening; the afternoon set was performed by house band the Nazz (forerunners of Alice Cooper).

The *Los Angeles Free Press* reported, "Pink Floyd, another mind-bending group from England, made its only local appearance last weekend at Santa Monica's Cheetah. Even the seaweed was swinging at the end of their first set. The unbelievable sound of Pink Floyd was first heard through a hurricane of color, bringing total sensual involvement of audience and performers, each absorbed in the creation of aural/visual experience. The creation belonged to Pink Floyd, but there was ample room for all of us to share their visions, their feelings. At the end, the audience might have been another creation of the facile, collective mind of Pink Floyd. To quote their press release, 'There can be no barriers, there can be no predictions.'"

"Syd actually went mad on that first American tour," recalled Mason. "He didn't know where he was most of the time. I remember he de-tuned his guitar on stage at Venice, Los Angeles, and just stood there rattling the strings which was a bit weird, even for us. Another time he emptied a can of Brylcreem on his head because he didn't like his curly hair."

After the show Pink Floyd spent the evening in Santa Monica at the house rented by the Nazz. Drummer John Speer later said of that evening, "I remember him [Syd Barrett] at times just staring at this wall and not saying anything to anybody. Many, many, many, many minutes go by, and nobody could talk to him. He was just in his own little world." Talking about the experience in the August 2010 edition of *Rolling Stone*, Alice Cooper recalled, "Pink Floyd basically ran out of money – they didn't have any place to stay. So they stayed with us, in our house in Venice. I remember coming down to breakfast one morning, and there's Syd at the table. He's got purple crushed-velvet pants on, and he is staring at this box of cornflakes – the same way you and I would watch television. He was watching something that we couldn't see." On stage he remembered them as "absolutely the best psychedelic band ever. There was so much stuff coming out of those amps, and they were so organized behind it. And Syd had this appeal – the guy nobody could get to. You could figure out the other guys, talk to them. But Syd was too far away for everybody."

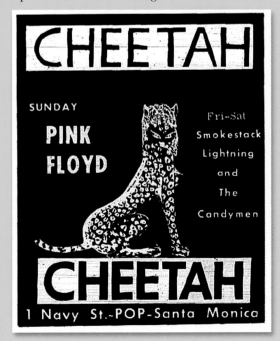

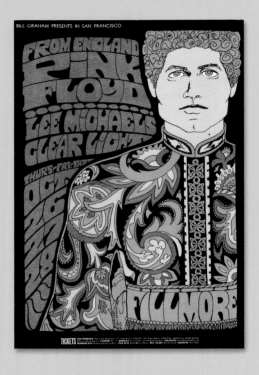

MONDAY 6 NOVEMBER– TELEVISION RECORDING
Pat Boone in Hollywood, NBC–TV Studios,
Los Angeles, CA, USA

Pink Floyd mimed to 'The Gnome' and 'Chapter 24' on the entertainment programme *Pat Boone in Hollywood*. In a brief interview afterwards, Barrett reportedly returned a mute stare. It was broadcast (in colour) on KHJ network TV Channel 9 on Monday 4 December 1967 between 3.30pm and 4.00pm (PST).

TUESDAY 7 NOVEMBER – TELEVISION RECORDING
American Bandstand, ABC TV Center,
Los Angeles, CA, USA

Pink Floyd mimed to 'Apples And Oranges' and 'See Emily Play' on the music programme *American Bandstand*, hosted by Dick Clark. It was broadcast (in colour) on ABC network TV Channel 7 on Saturday 18 November 1967 between 11.30am and 12.00 mid-day (PST). The clip of 'Apples And Oranges' is the only surviving footage from this tour and sees Waters struggling to mime lead vocals, followed by a brief group interview in which Barrett appears vacant.

WEDNESDAY 8 NOVEMBER – TELEVISION RECORDING
Boss City, KHJ TV Studios, Los Angeles, CA, USA

Pink Floyd made their third and final US TV appearance on this tour miming to 'Apples And Oranges' on the teenage magazine programme *Boss City*, hosted by Sam Riddle. It was broadcast (in colour) on KHJ network TV Channel 9 on Saturday 11 November 1967 between 6.00pm and 6.30pm (PST).

THURSDAY 9 NOVEMBER – PERFORMANCE
Fillmore Auditorium, San Francisco, CA, USA

With Procol Harum and HP Lovecraft.

FRIDAY 10 & SATURDAY 11 NOVEMBER – PERFORMANCES
Winterland Auditorium, San Francisco, CA, USA

With Procol Harum and HP Lovecraft.

SUNDAY 12 NOVEMBER – PERFORMANCE
Cheetah, New York, NY, USA

Cash Box and *Variety* magazines reported that Pink Floyd performed a one-hour afternoon set before heading back to London that evening. A long-running source of debate among researchers, this date has always been a difficult one to verify, but recalling the tour for Rob Chapman's Syd Barrett book *A Very Irregular Head*, Andrew King was quoted as saying that, "We should probably never have gone to America. We did pack up and come home in the end after playing at the Cheetah Club in New York."

SUNDAY 12 NOVEMBER – CANCELLED PERFORMANCE
The Public Halls, Harpenden, England

Show cancelled due to the extension of the US tour.

MONDAY 13 NOVEMBER – SINGLE RELEASE (US)
'Flaming'

MONDAY 13 NOVEMBER – PERFORMANCE
Hippy Happy Fair, De Oude Ahoy Hallen,
Rotterdam, Netherlands

With the Jimi Hendrix Experience, the Motions, the Spencer Davis Group, Daddy's Act, the Buffoons, Soft Machine, Golden Earring, Tomorrow, Q65, Armand, the Shoes, Geno Washington & the Ram Jam Band, Rob Hoek's R&B Group, Cuby & the Blizzards and a band talent contest.
Set list: 'Reaction In G', 'Pow R Toc H', 'Scream Thy Last Scream', 'Set The Controls For The Heart Of The Sun', 'Interstellar Overdrive'.

Pink Floyd appeared on the third evening of this four-day festival starting on Friday 10 November 1967, having been rescheduled from the advertised Sunday 12 November 1967 due to a later than anticipated return from the US coupled with cancellations by some of the other advertised bands. Pink Floyd was sandwiched between Group 1850 and the talent contest finals.

TUESDAY 14 NOVEMBER – RECORDING SESSION
Room 53, EMI Studios, Abbey Road, London, England

'Apples And Oranges' and 'Paintbox' remixed for the 7-inch single. The session was produced by Norman Smith and engineered by Ken Scott and assisted by Jeff Jarrett. Pink Floyd was not in attendance at this session.

JIMI HENDRIX UK TOUR

Pink Floyd appeared as second billing on a national package tour presented by Harold Davison and Tito Burns, headlined by the Jimi Hendrix Experience and featuring, in order of appearance, Eire Apparent, Outer Limits, Amen Corner, the Move and the Nice. All dates on the tour, with the exception of the Royal Albert Hall, featured two performances in which Pink Floyd performed a 15- to 20-minute set.

TUESDAY 14 NOVEMBER – PERFORMANCE
The Alchemical Wedding,
Royal Albert Hall, London, England

It was widely reported that Pink Floyd had threatened to walk out of the tour during the afternoon rehearsals at the Royal Albert Hall when they were told they could not use their own lighting gear and projection screen because, being a circular hall, it blocked the view for many in the audience. Accounts suggest that Pink Floyd prevailed on this occasion. It is also worth noting that Mitch Mitchell (drummer with Jimi Hendrix) recalled in his book *The Hendrix Experience* that David Gilmour joined the tour half way through, although there is no other evidence to support this claim.

Disc & Music Echo reported, "Possibly the most interesting act was the Pink Floyd's, fresh from playing hippie emporiums on America's West Coast, with what must be the best light-show yet seen in this country and very inventive music were greeted by silence while most of the audience tried to grasp the 'meaning'

behind their music – although they played hard rock based material with drummer Nick Mason laying down some beautiful rhythms and guitarist Syd Barrett hitting some incredible flights of fantasy.… They won rapturous applause, though from an audience which could have not been in the most part Pink Floyd fans. A very satisfying set."

WEDNESDAY 15 NOVEMBER – PERFORMANCES
Winter Gardens, Bournemouth, England

Two shows at 6.10pm and 8.30pm, with the Jimi Hendrix Experience, the Nice, the Move, Amen Corner, Outer Limits, Eire Apparent and host Pete Drummond.
Set list at the late show included 'Set The Controls For The Heart of The Sun'.

FRIDAY 17 NOVEMBER – PERFORMANCES
City (Oval) Hall, Sheffield, England

Two shows at 6.20pm and 8.50pm, with the Jimi Hendrix Experience, the Nice, the Move, Amen Corner, the Outer Limits, Eire Apparent and host Pete Drummond.

FRIDAY 17 NOVEMBER – SINGLE RELEASE (UK)
'Apples And Oranges'

NME wrote that this was "the most psychedelic single the Pink Floyd have yet come up with. It takes several spins before you get to grips with it, and then you realise that a great deal of thought has gone into it. Although much of the track is way-out, there's a catchy and repetitive chorus, which should prove a reliable sales gimmick."

FRIDAY 17 NOVEMBER – PERFORMANCE
All Night Garden Party, Queen's Hall, Leeds, England

With John Mayall's Bluesbreakers, the Warren Davis Monday Band, Ivan's Jaguars, the JB's, the Peighton Checks, Roger Bloom's Hammer, the Roll Movement, the Screen, the Syndicate and DJ Dave Cash.
An off-tour engagement, Pink Floyd was advertised to appear at this event after their earlier show in Sheffield. However, some eyewitness reports suggest Pink Floyd never showed, and consequently their appearance cannot be confirmed.

SATURDAY 18 NOVEMBER – PERFORMANCES
Empire Theatre, Liverpool, England

Two shows at 6.00pm and 8.35pm, with the Jimi Hendrix Experience, the Nice, the Move, Amen Corner, the Outer Limits, Eire Apparent and host Pete Drummond.
Set list at the late show included 'Interstellar Overdrive' and 'Pow R Toc H'.

LEFT: THE CAST LINEUP OF THE HENDRIX TOUR, NOVEMBER 1967.

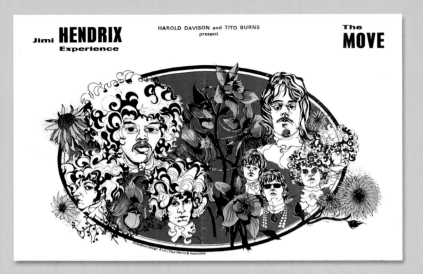

SUNDAY 19 NOVEMBER – PERFORMANCES
Coventry Theatre, Coventry, England

Two shows at 6.00pm and 8.30pm, with the Jimi Hendrix Experience, the Nice, the Move, Amen Corner, the Outer Limits, Eire Apparent and host Pete Drummond.
The *Coventry Evening Telegraph* reported, "Jimi Hendrix fans were unmoved – and I guess somewhat bewildered – by the Pink Floyd, a group of whom the new wave is more of a spring tide. The Floyd's extended instrumental/electronic experiments were fascinating, almost hypnotic, but unappreciated by an audience probably expecting their hit tunes."

WEDNESDAY 22 NOVEMBER – PERFORMANCES
Guildhall, Portsmouth, England

Two shows at 6.30pm and 8.50pm, with the Jimi Hendrix Experience, the Nice, the Move, Amen Corner, the Outer Limits, Eire Apparent and host Pete Drummond.

THURSDAY 23 NOVEMBER – PERFORMANCES
Sophia Gardens Pavilion, Cardiff, Wales

Two shows at 6.15pm and 8.35pm, with the Jimi Hendrix Experience, the Nice, the Move, Amen Corner, the Outer Limits, Eire Apparent and host Pete Drummond.
Set list at the early show included 'Set The Controls For The Heart Of The Sun'.

FRIDAY 24 NOVEMBER – PERFORMANCES
Colston Hall, Bristol, England

Two shows at 6.30pm and 8.45pm, with the Jimi Hendrix Experience, the Nice, the Move, Amen Corner, the Outer Limits, Eire Apparent and host Pete Drummond.
The *Bristol Evening Post* reported, "There was guitar smashing on-stage at the Colston Hall – and glass smashing off-stage last night. Over-boisterous Welsh teenagers were ejected after incidents in the hall bars in the auditorium. Teenagers from over the Severn Bridge came to yell for Welsh group the Amen Corner. Hall officials repeatedly warned the noisier teenagers as they brandished stools and shouted in the bar. In the hall, youths hurled abuse at performers. There was more weird music by the Pink Floyd and the Nice. Between them they beat up an electric organ, shattered a couple of thousand eardrums and lost themselves in a swirling cloud of coloured lights."

SATURDAY 25 NOVEMBER – PERFORMANCES
Opera House, Blackpool, England

Two shows at 6.10pm and 8.20pm, with the Jimi Hendrix Experience, the Nice, the Move, Amen Corner, the Outer Limits, Eire Apparent and compére Pete Drummond.
Set list at the early show: 'Set The Controls For The Heart Of The Sun', 'Interstellar Overdrive', 'Pow R. Toc H'.
Set list at the late show: 'Take Up Thy Stethoscope And Walk', 'Set The Controls For The Heart Of The Sun', 'Interstellar Overdrive'.

SUNDAY 26 NOVEMBER – PERFORMANCES
Palace Theatre, Manchester, England

Two shows at 6.10pm and 8.15pm, with the Jimi Hendrix Experience, the Nice, the Move, Amen Corner, the Outer Limits, Eire Apparent and compére Pete Drummond.

MONDAY 27 NOVEMBER – PERFORMANCES
***Festival '67,* Whitla Hall,**
Queen's College, Belfast, Northern Ireland

Two shows at 7.00pm and 9.15pm, with the Jimi Hendrix Experience, the Nice, the Move, Amen Corner, the Outer Limits, Eire Apparent and compére Pete Drummond.

FRIDAY 1 DECEMBER – PERFORMANCES
Central Hall, Chatham, England

Two shows at 6.15pm and 8.45pm, with the Jimi Hendrix Experience, the Nice, the Move, Amen Corner, the Outer Limits, Eire Apparent and compére Pete Drummond.
The *Chatham Standard* reported, "Chatham Council's first beat promotion on Friday did not have a perfect start. While fans sat listening to the Outer Limits – first on the bill – organisers rushed about in quest of the missing groups – they were at the Town Hall, searching for the audience that had already settled itself at the Central Hall a few hundred yards away. With a few changes to the programme order, the groups all managed to arrive in time to prevent any embarrassingly long gaps during the evening, but the confusion at the start seemed somehow to upset the atmosphere. The Pink Floyd was the biggest disappointment, because I was expecting so much more. They performed in near darkness for most of the time, played some very unrecognisable numbers and were completely overshadowed by the entertaining antics of a young man in a bear skin jacket whose task seemed to be to leap about the stage adjusting amplifiers, twisting knobs and retrieving the odd cymbal or microphone."

SATURDAY 2 DECEMBER –
PERFORMANCES ▶
The Dome, Brighton, England

Two shows at 6.15pm and 8.40pm, with the Jimi Hendrix Experience, the Nice, the Move, Amen Corner, the Outer Limits, Eire Apparent and host Pete Drummond.

APPLES AND ORANGES

TRACKS

SIDE A: APPLES AND ORANGES (Barrett) 3:02
SIDE B: PAINTBOX (Wright) 3:28

RELEASE DATE

UK: Friday 17 November 1967.

FORMAT

UK: Columbia EMI DB 8310 (7-inch vinyl single).

PROMO FILMS

Aside from two rare TV appearances performing 'Apples And Oranges' for *American Bandstand* and *Boss City* during their first US tour, there was no official video for the song.

RECORDING DETAILS

Both tracks were recorded at EMI Studios, Abbey Road and produced by Norman Smith and engineered by Peter Bown. Barrett takes the lead in what would be Pink Floyd's last UK single featuring its original lineup. Unfortunately very little information exists from the sessions, which were hurriedly completed prior to the band's departure for their first US tour.

In one of his last press interviews, published in *Melody Maker* on 9 December 1967, before leaving the band Barrett said that, "It's unlike anything we've done before. It's a new sound. Got a lot of guitar in it. It's a happy song, and it's got a touch of Christmas. It's about a girl I saw just walking round town, in Richmond."

APPLES AND ORANGES

Take unknown (RS1).
Basic track recorded on 26 October 1967.
Unspecified instruments overdubbed on 26 & 27 October 1967.
Remixed on 14 November 1967 (RS1).

PAINTBOX

Take 9 (RS1).
Basic track recorded on 24 October 1967 (Take 9).
Unspecified instruments overdubbed onto Take 9 on 26 & 27 October 1967.
Remixed on 14 November 1967 (RS1).

TOP LEFT: UK PROMO PICTURE SLEEVE.
TOP RIGHT: NETHERLANDS PICTURE SLEEVE.
BOTTOM RIGHT: A PROMO PHOTO FROM THE PERIOD.
LEFT: REVIEW FROM *DISC & MUSIC ECHO,* 18 NOVEMBER 1967.

OUT TOMORROW

PINK FLOYD

APPLES And Oranges (Columbia) —I really find it very hard to review records by the Pink Floyd, mainly because, to be quite honest, I don't really understand what they're trying to do musically—which is my own fault I'll admit. And the other reason is that ever since their manager phoned up to say in a rather pompous way that he and the group hardly considered my reviews worth the paper they were written on, I have never felt exactly drawn with tremendous warmth towards them.

Be that as it may, they have a lot of fans and seem to have worked very hard on this record. It sounds as though the listener has his/her head in a bucket of water and is about a lorry driver talking about a bird (I think, though it IS hard to understand what the hell it's about). There's a few nice things going on and since nobody else will understand what it's about either, it will probably be a hit. I liked the end.
OUT TOMORROW

Set list at the late show: 'Astronomy Domine', 'Set The Controls For The Heart Of The Sun', 'Interstellar Overdrive'.

SUNDAY 3 DECEMBER – PERFORMANCES
Theatre Royal, Nottingham, England

Two shows at 5.30pm and 8.00pm, with the Jimi Hendrix Experience, the Nice, the Move, Amen Corner, the Outer Limits, Eire Apparent and host Pete Drummond.
Set list at the late show included 'Set The Controls For The Heart Of The Sun'.

Tom Croson, a fan in attendance, recalled, "I had the misfortune of going to the first one. Syd Barrett didn't make the first show and David O'List, the lead guitarist with the Nice, who were also on the same bill, stepped in and ad-libbed along with the Floyd! He did the best he could under the circumstances. Some friends of mine went to the second house which he arrived in time for."

MONDAY 4 DECEMBER – PERFORMANCES
City Hall, Newcastle-upon-Tyne, England

Two shows at 6.15pm and 8.30pm, with the Jimi Hendrix Experience, the Nice, the Move, Amen Corner, the Outer Limits, Eire Apparent and host Pete Drummond.

TUESDAY 5 DECEMBER – PERFORMANCES
Green's Playhouse, Glasgow, Scotland

Two shows at 6.15pm and 8.45pm, with the Jimi Hendrix Experience, the Nice, the Move, Amen Corner, the Outer Limits, Eire Apparent and host Pete Drummond.
Set list at the late show: 'Interstellar Overdrive', 'Set The Controls For The Heart Of The Sun'.

WEDNESDAY 6 DECEMBER – PERFORMANCE ◄
Horror Ball, The Hall, Royal College of Art, Kensington, London, England

With the Bonzo Dog Doo-Dah Band, Marmalade, and Blue Rivers & His Maroons.

The *Kensington Post* reported, "When 23-year-old Martin Hayden was refused a grant by his local authority to see him through a two-year course at the Royal College of Art, Kensington, he decided he would have no choice but to leave college. Without the £300 a year grant he could not possibly afford to stay on. But help was on the way from his fellow students. They organised a whip round and decided that the profits from last night's Christmas college dance would be given to Martin."

FRIDAY 8 DECEMBER – PERFORMANCE
Caves Club, Chiselhurst Caves, Chiselhurst, England

SATURDAY 9 DECEMBER – FILM PREMIERE
Tonite Let's All Make Love in London, Academy 2 Cinema, London, England

NME wrote, "Peter Whitehead, intentionally or not, embalms and dispatches almost the whole commercial machine that sets out to sell glamour to the glamourless and youth to the young. Mick Jagger, Andrew Loog Oldham, Julie Christie, Michael Caine, pop singer Genevieve, novelist Edna O'Brien and painters Alan Aldridge and David Hockney, all caught up in and profiting nicely from the machine they are partly to blame for creating, come under Whitehead's cruel camera. The film delves under the superficiality of the whole business and finds yet more superficiality. But perhaps Whitehead's camera is in some cases a little too cruel, cutting at points where you get the feeling that the person concerned might have gone on to say something to give it some meaning."

SATURDAY 9 DECEMBER – PRESS REPORT
London, England

Members of Pink Floyd and their managers were reported in *Melody Maker* to be viewing a colour film clip of the newly recorded 'Jugband Blues' at the Central Office of Information for inclusion in a cultural exchange magazine programme. Widely available on the collectors' market, this film was networked throughout North America and widely reported to be the band's next single. The recording date and location remains unknown.

SUNDAY 10 DECEMBER – PERFORMANCE
Teenagers Sunday Club, The Birdcage, Harlow, England

TUESDAY 12 DECEMBER – TELEVISION RECORDING
Tomorrow's World, Stanhope Gardens, London, England

Pink Floyd was filmed at former landlord Mike Leonard's house for an edition of the *Tomorrow's World* programme that featured his sound and light experiments. To accompany his work the band was seen playing an untitled instrumental piece composed by Waters and Mason. (The soundtrack also included the Floyd jamming a Booker T & the MGs-style of improvisation.)

The programme was broadcast on BBC1 TV on 17 January 1968 between 6.40pm and 7.05pm. It was repeated for the very first time as part of the BBC *Omnibus* special entitled 'Pink Floyd – The Story' and broadcast on BBC1 TV on Tuesday 15 November 1994 between 10.15pm and 10.55pm.

WEDNESDAY 13 DECEMBER – PERFORMANCE
Flamingo Ballroom, Redruth, England

Presented by Cornwall Technical College, with PP Arnold (although Mike Cotton & Lucas and John L. Watson & the Webb were advertised).
Melody Maker continued to receive regular complaints about Pink Floyd's show up to the end of the year, including this little gem: "If any readers are intending to see Pink Floyd, my advice is don't. They played here recently and were so unbelievably bad the supporting group had to be brought back early. It was the opinion of most of the 1,000, students at our dance that they were the worst group ever to appear in Cornwall."

THURSDAY 14 DECEMBER – PERFORMANCE
The Pavilion Ballroom, Bournemouth, England

Presented by Poole College Students Union, with the Clockwork Motion and Caxton.

PINK FLOYD ROAD CREW – JUNE 1968
Peter Watts (Road Manager / Sound Engineer), John Marsh (Lights).

SATURDAY 16 DECEMBER – PERFORMANCE
Ritz Ballroom, King's Heath, Birmingham, England
With Gospel Garden, the Rare Breed and DJ Dave Terry.

SATURDAY 16 DECEMBER – PERFORMANCE ▼
Saturday Spectacular, **The Penthouse,**
Constitution Hill, Birmingham, England
With Gospel Garden, the Rare Breed and DJs Dave Terry & Haig.

8 p.m. —— 8 a.m.   YES, IT'S
SATURDAY   SPECTACULAR
TIME AGAIN
TONIGHT, ALL-NIGHT-LONG at the
P-E-N-T-H-O-U-S-E   CEN. 3524
CONSTITUTION HILL (above Surfside Coffee Bar)
With Britain's Newest Big-time Group.
The Fantastic PINK FLOYD
Supported by GOSPEL GARDEN   Also RARE BREED.
Your D.J.s are DAVE TERRY & HAIG.
Sunday: THE PRETTY THINGS plus THE POWER.
CHRISTMAS LINE-UP:
Thursday, 21st (Look who we've got): LONG JOHN BALDRY.
Saturday, 23rd: THE MARVELETTES. Sunday, 24th: THE TROGGS.
Saturday, 30th: DAVE, DEE, DOZY, BEAKY, MICK & TICH.

WEDNESDAY 20 DECEMBER – RADIO RECORDING
Top Gear, **Studio 4, BBC Maida Vale Studios, London, England**

Pink Floyd recorded a second session for BBC Radio One's *Top Gear*, this time at their Maida Vale studios commencing at 2.30pm. Four tracks were recorded and broadcast including 'Vegetable Man' (3:15), 'Scream Thy Last Scream' (3:40), 'Jugband Blues' (3:50) and 'Pow R Toc H' (4:15). Hosted by John Peel and Tommy Vance, the show was broadcast on Sunday 31 December 1967 between 2.00pm and 5.00pm. In what was one of their stranger radio sessions, and also Syd Barrett's last with the band, 'Vegetable Man' received an extended jam at the end incorporating the *Batman* theme tune!

'Vegetable Man' (3:15), 'Pow R Toc H' (3:00), 'Scream Thy Last Scream' (3:40) and 'Jugband Blues' (3:50) was repeated on *Top Gear*, hosted by John Peel, on Sunday 11 February 1968 between 2.00pm and 4.00pm.

WEDNESDAY 20 DECEMBER – RECORDING SESSION
Studio 2, EMI Studios, Abbey Road, London, England

7.30pm to 1.30pm: Sound Effects overdubbed onto Take 4 of 'Scream Thy Last Scream' for the album *A Saucerful of Secrets*. The session was produced by Norman Smith, engineered by Ken Scott and assisted by Jeff Jarrett. This also marked Syd Barrett's last ever recording session with Pink Floyd.

THURSDAY 21 DECEMBER – PERFORMANCE
The Speakeasy, Margaret Street, London, England

FRIDAY 22 DECEMBER – PERFORMANCE ▶
Christmas on Earth Continued,
Olympia Exhibition Halls, Olympia, London, England

With the Jimi Hendrix Experience, Eric Burdon & the Animals, Traffic, the Move, the Graham Bond Organisation, Soft Machine, Sam Gopal's Dream, Paper Blitz Tissue, Keith West & Tomorrow, DJ John Peel and Jeffrey Shaw & the Plastic Circus and many others. Pink Floyd took to the stage at approximately 5.00am (Saturday 23 December).

The *Kensington Post* reported, "It will be one of the most ambitious pop projects ever undertaken in Britain with an incredible lineup of top groups. By using two large specially erected stages at either end of the Grand Hall it is ensured that their music will continue throughout the night non-stop. A cinema in the National Hall will show top vintage films on one screen while a light show is going on two other screens. In all more than a hundred projectors are being used throughout the building to make up a spectacular display of various lighting effects. In the centre of the hall will be a pool surrounded by sand where one can laze in a tropical atmosphere to watch the film shows. Fun-fair attractions will be assembled around the two halls and there will be an arcade of boutiques and stalls in the West Hall called "Portobello Road, Continued". Here the strolling steel band will provide music. Two three-feet high light towers with three projection levels incorporating a dozen radio-controlled follow spots are the centre feature of the spectacular light show. It is expected that 15,000 young people will be at Olympia tomorrow night."

Unfortunately the show didn't quite live up to the hype, and the promoters lost money on a poorly attended event despite it being a superb bill. They had also arranged for a documentary film to be made, but the crew used old stock film which turned out to be completely useless and only short clips of Hendrix and Traffic appear to have survived.

3 SET THE CONTROLS FOR THE HEART OF THE SUN

1968—69

1968—69

By the first month of 1968, Syd Barrett's role within Pink Floyd was all but over. As a last-ditch attempt to save the situation it was thought they could use him as an off-stage songwriter in the same way the Beach Boys retained Brian Wilson, but almost at once they realized this was an impossibility. Coupled with the announcement that he wanted to add a female vocalist, a banjo player and a saxophonist to the lineup, this left the rest of the band in no doubt as to where this was all leading: he had to go.

Even so, the five-piece Floyd did play a handful of shows together in January. To further complicate matters, Barrett was also sharing a flat with Richard Wright in Richmond. "I had to say things like, 'Syd, I'm going out to get some cigarettes', and go off and do a gig and come back the next day. It was awful; a terrible time."[1]

But polite English reserve prevented them from actually confronting the situation head-on. Instead, and on the sixth show that the band would have played together at Southampton University, Gilmour remembered that someone said, "'Shall we bother to pick up Syd?' and someone said, 'Nah, let's not bother', and that was the end."[2]

Undeterred, or wracked with guilt, Waters even attempted to seek some kind of treatment for Barrett. This came in the shape of anti-psychiatrist R. D. Laing with whom he'd made an appointment for Barrett who refused to get out of the taxi. A short while later Laing was played a tape of Syd Barrett being interviewed. Barrett, he declared, was incurable.

Waters, remarked Gilmour, "was the one who had the courage to drive Syd out, because he realized that as long as Syd was in the band, they wouldn't keep it together. The chaos factor was too great. Roger looked up to Syd and he always felt very guilty about the fact that he'd blown out his mate."[3]

In time Waters would turn those feelings into some of his most powerful lyrics, not least the haunting 'Shine On You Crazy Diamond' from the 1975 album *Wish You Were Here*. In many respects Barrett was destined never to leave the band.

And, just as the remaining members could no longer see a future with him, their managers, Andrew King and Peter Jenner, could no longer see a future in a Pink Floyd without him. Their partnership with Blackhill Enterprises was eventually dissolved in April 1968, but they continued to represent Barrett who, they felt, would fare better as a solo artist.

And Wright very nearly joined him. "Peter and Andrew thought Syd and I were the musical brains of the group, and that we should form a breakaway band, to try to hold Syd together," he recalled. "And believe me, I would have left with him like a shot if I had thought Syd could do it."[4]

"What we underestimated was the power of the band name, the loyalty of the fans," said Jenner. "We thought it was all down to creativity." [5]

As a consequence the Bryan Morrison Agency took over the band management, specifically under Steve O'Rourke, who oversaw the day-to-day management, with Tony Howard taking the bookings.

Gilmour now had some pretty big shoes to fill, and by his own admission took some time to settle in. "I learnt to sing all Syd's parts and all his guitar parts more or less," he recalled. "My guitar style and Syd's weren't even close, so it was very difficult for me to know what to do and it took me a while to settle in… I'd known Syd since I was fourteen; it was hard dealing with replacing one of my close friends. And having to see one of my close friends no longer functioning as a normal human being."[6]

Nevertheless, the band never ceased gigging, and despite having performed very little outside of the UK in their first professional year, now had an established agency able to secure bookings overseas. Their sharp rise in popularity across northern Europe was remarkable to say the least, and 1968 saw Pink Floyd undertake an immense amount of promotional work for European TV channels. France, Netherlands and Belgium, in particular, embraced the band, which enabled them to build up a large and faithful following. Bookings were increasingly focussed on the university and college circuits, and festivals became polarized in their programming of more progressive acts, which complemented a circuit of newly formed alternative music clubs. Pink Floyd was finally able to perform to a captive and receptive audience.

The new lineup was also quick to branch into soundtrack work and composed and recorded some new music for Peter Sykes' avant-garde short film *The Committee*, which starred Paul Jones and featured Arthur Brown. A limited cinematic release in May secured its cult status and the soundtrack, which comprised of a series of improvised instrumental passages, included the earliest known version of 'Careful With That Axe, Eugene'.[*]

Pink Floyd also released a new single called 'It Would Be So Nice' in April, penned by Wright and backed by a new Waters composition, 'Julia Dream'. However, it was soon realized the BBC would never play the A-side, as it contained a lyric that mentioned the London *Evening Standard* newspaper, which constituted product endorsement.[**] The track was re-recorded and the line amended to the fictitious *Daily Standard* for a special run of DJ-only pressings, allegedly at an additional cost of £750 in studio time cutting new acetates. It made little difference, for despite favourable reviews, it failed to generate much airplay. Waters was far more disparaging, claiming that, "Nobody ever heard it because it was such a lousy record!"[7]

December's 'Point Me At The Sky' also failed to chart and so Pink Floyd came to the realization that singles were not their forte, making this the last single they released in the UK for some eleven years.

By the summer of 1968, Blackhill had successfully dragged themselves out of the mire of insolvency by representing, among others, Tyrannosaurus Rex, Roy Harper and the Edgar

---

*The film remained in the archives until the summer of 2005, when it was finally given a DVD release.
**Curiously this didn't seem to affect airplay of the Beatles' May 1966 hit, 'Paperback Writer', which name-checked the *Daily Mail*.

Broughton Band, and announced they were staging the first Hyde Park free concert on 29 June 1968, having been granted a licence by the Royal Parks and Ministry of Works. Relations were still cordial, so naturally they chose Pink Floyd as their headline act and their spellbinding performance was as well received by the press as it was by the assembled crowd. Much of the thanks for Pink Floyd's reassessment in Britain is due to the highly influential BBC broadcaster and journalist John Peel, who, after seeing the show, championed the band over the next few years.

Coincidentally Pink Floyd's second album, *A Saucerful of Secrets,* was released in the same week, with a sleeve designed by their Cambridge friend and graphic designer Storm Thorgerson and his flatmate Aubrey "Po" Powell.[*]

The album fared well in the charts despite some mixed reactions. *International Times,* for example, described the title track as "too long and boring". It was, in reality, an album that was seeing a band in transition; a complete departure from the Barrett-fuelled psychedelic-pop of its predecessor.

In good time, however, Gilmour would introduce his own ideas and unique style. Wright was already regarded as the most talented musician in the band, whereas Waters and Mason were far more concerned with the development of their stage presentation. Fortunately this unique relationship worked exceptionally well and over time it became clear that neither element could work adequately without the other.

Surprisingly, prospects were now looking good in the States. The 1967 tour had been a disaster, but Tower kept pushing out singles, despite limited chart success, at a greater frequency than in Britain. As a result, the band was gaining a cult following and a tour of America, mainly on the West Coast, was rather haphazardly arranged for July and August to tie in with their release of *A Saucerful of Secrets.*

It is a very poorly documented period of the band's history as their US booking agent, Premier Talent, struggled to close the gaps between the key bookings even as they were touring. It was also an expensive exercise and to cut down on hefty freight charges, the band didn't take much of their own equipment, hiring their drums, amps and speakers for each show as they went along. They even borrowed instruments and amplifiers from Jimi Hendrix's Electric Lady studios in New York during their residency at the Scene.

With so many days off and the cost of hotel bills mounting, not to mention increasing boredom, the tour was, not unsurprisingly, cut short.

Nevertheless their profile was bolstered by the flood of rave reviews they received, from the underground press to

*Thorgerson was studying at the Royal College of Art and Powell at the London School of Film Technique, and working under the moniker of Hipgnosis, they provided a unique photomontage of various images culled variously from Marvel Comics and a collection of obscure alchemical illustrations. In time Hipgnosis would become a renowned 70s design team and their distinctive work seen as a trademark of Pink Floyd.

LEFT: BACKSTAGE AT THE MARLOWE THEATRE, CANTERBURY, 25 FEBRUARY 1969.
BOTTOM: PERFORMING AT THE CAMDEN FRINGE FESTIVAL, 9 MAY 1969.

the highly influential industry magazines *Cash Box* and *Billboard*, and this may have temporarily renewed Tower's faith in the band, despite the fact Pink Floyd did not return to the US for another two years.

By the end of the year Pink Floyd's presence in Europe, too, was consolidated by further appearances. They were developing a unique style that advanced their career at an impressive pace.

This was also bolstered by an increasing amount of soundtrack work, their ethereal music capturing the interest of emerging French director Barbet Schroeder among others. In early 1968 he had already commissioned Pink Floyd to score his feature film debut, *More*, which was due to start filming that summer on Ibiza. The soundtrack, which also produced some of the band's most popular live pieces for the next few years, was written, recorded and mixed in five straight days in early February 1969 at Pye Studios in London.

Although the film wasn't screened in Britain until early 1970, the album did reach a healthy No.9 in the UK charts on release, and was well received in America and especially in France, reinforcing their popularity there.

But it was a bleak film demonstrating the worst excesses of heroin abuse, although thanks to the music it has since emerged as a cult classic. More importantly, away from Abbey Road, it allowed Pink Floyd to experience working in a recording studio without the watchful eye of producer Norman Smith, whose role would begin to rapidly diminish.

Back on the road the relentless touring continued, and by early 1969 the Barrett compositions had all but disappeared from the band's repertoire – along with the light shows – as the focus slowly began to shift away from the visual impact that had once masked them from their audience to the gradual refinement of their concert sound.

This was highlighted by a special performance held at the Royal Festival Hall in London on 14 April, which demonstrated Pink Floyd's ability to mix performance, stage and theatrics, made all the more impressive with the unveiling of their "Azimuth Co-ordinator", a brand-new 360-degree surround sound system. The band also presented two suites of music entitled *The Man* and *The Journey*, comprising largely of existing material, and tracks from *More*, all combined to form a concept based around the titles.

Both the music and mainstream press were finally taking notice. Confidence among venue promoters was understandably boosted and remarkably, although there was no new product to promote, the band was booked for their first headline tour of the UK in June, playing large civic halls.

One of the most important shows of the tour was held at the Fairfield Halls in Croydon, an auditorium renowned for its excellent acoustics and atmosphere. The venue even issued its own press release, stating, "As groups go, the Pink Floyd are a strange case. You either love them or hate them. Few past their mid-twenties can tolerate them. For the Pink Floyd were one of Britain's first psychedelic pop groups, placing almost as much importance on their light-show as their musical side. Their concert at Croydon's Fairfield Halls on Friday 30 May, promises to be a sell-out, and if their past concerts are a guide, the Croydon show will include, give or take a song, two numbers. The Floyd – if all goes well – will also be introducing their new concept in audience mind blowing, with a new electronic scheme to fill the concert hall with stereo sound from every angle. And to carry off a show based on 360-degree stereo system, the Floyd have decided to include far more than a mere selection of songs. They plan to assault their unsuspecting audience by hurling music, lights, poetry and melodrama in furious succession. He who leaves the concert on steady feet will be constitutionally superhuman."

The tour culminated in a concert at the prestigious Royal Albert Hall in London that June, with the Royal Philharmonic joining the band to close the show. It was a spectacular moment with such a large and grandiose setting capturing the full splendour of Pink Floyd's theatrics and their remarkable new surround-sound system.

RIGHT: PERFORMING AT THE VAN DYKE CLUB IN PLYMOUTH, 1 AUGUST 1969.

BOTTOM: PINK FLOYD PHOTOGRAPHED IN NOVEMBER 1969.

It was also the band's ability to create an extraterrestrial soundscape that caused the BBC and several other major European TV stations to invite them to compose music for their coverage of the Apollo 11 moon landings. Millions of TV viewers heard their strange and ethereal music accompanying the culmination of NASA's historic mission, not least the BBC who commissioned a live session.

Remarkably there was still time to pursue their personal lives: Mason had married his partner Lindy Rutter at the start of the year and located to Camden, North London and Waters married his partner Judith Trim in August and moved to Islington also in North London, and both Gilmour and Waters assisted in the production of Syd Barrett's debut solo album, *The Madcap Laughs.*

Pink Floyd meanwhile pressed on with the recording of their next album, the official follow-up to *A Saucerful of Secrets.* Entitled *Ummagumma,* it was named after occasional roadie and personal friend of the band Iain "Imo" Moore's personal slang for sex, and was released at the beginning of November as a double album with one disc consisting of live concert recordings and the other of new studio compositions.

For the purposes of the live set, recordings were made during a series of concerts that followed on from the Festival Hall appearance of 14 April and just before the start of the UK tour. These were made at Bromley Technical College, Mothers in Birmingham, a favoured alternative venue of the time, and the College of Commerce in Manchester. The recordings selected were taken from the latter two shows and made up entirely of old audience favourites in the belief that they would soon be dropped from the repertoire. Each track on the finished album was of an almost equal length, allowing two per side. The result was respectable versions of 'Astronomy Domine', 'Careful with That Axe, Eugene', 'Set The Controls For The Heart Of The Sun' and 'A Saucerful Of Secrets'.

The overall impression created by the studio album is one of missed opportunity and self-indulgence. Waters admitted himself, with hindsight, that the album could have been improved with group effort. "It would have been a better album if we'd gone away, done the things, come back together, discussed them and people could have come in and made comments. I don't think it's a good idea to work in total isolation."[8] Mason's summation reinforced this view. "I think what this demonstrates, is that our sum is always better than our parts,"[9] he said.

1–2. *Pink Floyd The Story*, BBC1 TV, 15 November 1994.

3. *The Pink Floyd Story*, Capital Radio, 17 December 1976.

4. *Mojo*, May 1994.

5. *Mojo*, November 2001.

6. *Pink Floyd The Story*, BBC1 TV, 15 November 1994.

7. *Pink Floyd* by Rick Sanders, Futura, 1976.

8. *Disc & Music Echo*, 8 August 1970.

9. *Mojo*, May 1994.

1968

MONDAY 8 & TUESDAY 9 JANUARY – REHEARSALS
**Kensal Rise Primary School,
Brondesbury Park, London, England**

David Gilmour rehearsed with the band for the first time prior to recording and touring commitments. In one particularly well-documented session Barrett wilfully teased the rest of the band with his latest composition, 'Have You Got It Yet?' "[That] was in January '68 at one of my first rehearsals with the five-piece band in a school hall in Chamberlayne Road in Brondesbury Park," recalled Gilmour. "We didn't get it for quite a long time. Amazingly I remember the moment and the song really well. It was really just a twelve-bar, but the responses were always in the wrong places according to Syd. Some parts of his brain were perfectly intact – his sense of humour being one of them."

WEDNESDAY 10 JANUARY – RECORDING SESSION
**Studio 2 & Control Room 2, EMI Studios,
Abbey Road, London, England**

David Gilmour's first recording session with Pink Floyd was booked between 2.30pm to 5.30pm and 7.00pm to 10.00pm. Unfortunately the studio archives are incomplete and only indicate that "unknown titles" were recorded for *A Saucerful of Secrets*. It is quite likely the results were unsatisfactory and the tapes were wiped and reused for a fresh start the following day. The session was produced by Norman Smith, engineered by Ken Scott and assisted by Richard Langham.

THURSDAY 11 JANUARY – RECORDING SESSION
**Studio 2 & Control Room 2, EMI Studios,
Abbey Road, London, England**

2.30pm to 5.30pm: Vocals and Organ overdubbed onto Take 2 of 'Set The Controls For The Heart Of The Sun', and 7.00pm to 10.00pm: Vocals overdubbed onto Take 4 of 'Scream Thy Last Scream' for *A Saucerful of Secrets*. The session was produced by Norman Smith, engineered by Ken Scott and assisted by Richard Langham.

FRIDAY 12 JANUARY – PERFORMANCE
Guild of Students, Aston University, Birmingham, England

Set List included: 'Set The Controls For The Heart Of The Sun', 'Flaming', 'Interstellar Overdrive'.

It is widely accepted that this was the first show that Pink Floyd performed as a five-piece with David Gilmour as a permanent member. Remarkably, there is not one single reliable eyewitness report or press review of the final and fraught performances as a five-piece band. Gilmour's only recollection is that, "Sometimes

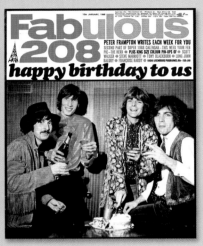

ABOVE: PINK FLOYD CELEBRATE *FAB 208'S* FOURTH BIRTHDAY ON THE COVER OF THEIR JANUARY 1968 EDITION.

Syd sang a bit and sometimes he didn't. It became very obvious that it wasn't going to continue for very long like that."

SATURDAY 13 JANUARY – PERFORMANCE
Saturday Dance Date, **Winter Gardens Pavilion, Weston-super-Mare, England**

Supported by the Ken Birch Band and the 3 Of Spades Plus.

MONDAY 15 & TUESDAY 16 JANUARY – REHEARSALS
**Kensal Rise Primary School,
Brondesbury Park, London, England**

THURSDAY 18 JANUARY – RECORDING SESSION
**Studio 2 & Control Room 2, EMI Studios,
Abbey Road, London, England**

2.30pm to 7.30pm: 'Let There Be More Light' recorded (Take 1 also marked "best"), and 8.30pm to 12.00 midnight: Vocals and Guitar overdubbed onto Take 1 of 'Let There Be More Light', and two untimed recordings of what is labelled "Rhythm" (Takes 1 & 2) which are believed to be for editing onto 'Let There Be More Light' for *A Saucerful of Secrets*. The session was produced by Norman Smith, engineered by Ken Scott and assisted by Richard Langham.

FRIDAY 19 JANUARY – PERFORMANCE ▶
Town Hall, Lewes, England

Presented by Lewes Football Club, supported by Granny's Intentions and Johnny Fine & the Ramblers.

SATURDAY 20 JANUARY – PERFORMANCE
**The Pavilion Ballroom,
Hastings Pier, Hastings, England**

Supported by Beaufords Image and compered by Pete Drummond. This was almost certainly Syd Barrett's final live appearance with Pink Floyd.

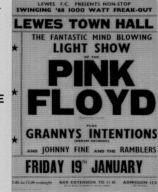

LEWES F.C. PRESENTS NON-STOP
SWINGING '68 1000 WATT FREAK-OUT
LEWES TOWN HALL
THE FANTASTIC MIND BLOWING
LIGHT SHOW
OF THE
**PINK
FLOYD**
PLUS
GRANNYS INTENTIONS
(DERAM RECORDS)
AND JOHNNY FINE AND THE RAMBLERS
FRIDAY 19TH JANUARY
7.45 to 12.00 midnight   BAR EXTENSION TO 11.45   ADMISSION 17/6

MONDAY 22 & TUESDAY 23 JANUARY – REHEARSALS
**Kensal Rise Primary School,
Brondesbury Park, London, England**

WEDNESDAY 24 JANUARY – RECORDING SESSION
**Studio 2 & Control Room 2, EMI Studios,
Abbey Road, London, England**

2.30pm to 8.00pm: Recording rehearsals, and 8.00pm to 12.30am:

'The Most Boring Song I've Ever Heard Bar 2' ['See Saw'] recorded (Takes 1 and 2 False Starts; Take 3 at 4:38 and Take 4 at 4:27) for *A Saucerful of Secrets*. The session was produced by Norman Smith, engineered by Ken Scott and assisted by John Barrett.

THURSDAY 25 JANUARY – RECORDING SESSION
Studio 2 & Control Room 2, EMI Studios, Abbey Road, London, England

2.30pm to 5.45pm and 7.00pm to 12.30am: 'The Most Boring Song I've Ever Heard Bar 2' ['See Saw'] re-recorded (Take 4 at 4:27 also marked "best", Take 5 at 4:34 and Take 6 at 4:32 also marked "best") for *A Saucerful of Secrets*. The session was produced by Norman Smith, engineered by Ken Scott and assisted by John Barrett.

PINK FLOYD
25 JANUARY 1968 – DECEMBER 1979

David Gilmour, Nick Mason, Roger Waters, Richard Wright.

FRIDAY 26 JANUARY – PERFORMANCE
Evolutions, **Student's Union, Southampton University, Highfield, Southampton, England**

With Chicken Shack [featuring Stan Webb and Christine Perfect], Nelson's Column and John Peel in the main room and Tyrannosaurus Rex and the Incredible String Band in the TV room.

SATURDAY 27 JANUARY –
PRESS REPORT ▶
London, England

The UK music press announced that David Gilmour had joined Pink Floyd, increasing its line up to five. A late news report, as most articles stated that he had rehearsed with the band for several weeks, it stated he would join them on their first European tour beginning in February.

SATURDAY 27 JANUARY –
PERFORMANCE
Leicester College of Art and Technology, Leicester, England

MONDAY 29 JANUARY –
REHEARSALS
Kensal Rise Primary School, Brondesbury Park, London, England

The Pink Floyd has become a five-man group with the addition of 21-year-old singer-guitarist DAVID GILMUR (above). The Floyd says it is augmenting "to explore new instruments and add further experimental dimensions" to its sound. Gilmur has been rehearsing with the group for several weeks and is currently recording with them.

WEDNESDAY 31 JANUARY – RECORDING SESSION
Studio 3 & Control Room 3, EMI Studios, Abbey Road, London, England

2.30pm to 6.15pm: Take 6 of 'The Most Boring Song I've Ever Heard

Bar 2' ['See Saw'] overdubbed, and 7.00pm to 12.30am: 'Corporal Clegg' recorded (Take 1 at 3:16, Take 2 at 4:14, Takes 3 & 4 False Starts, Take 5 at 3:00 and Take 6 at 3:45 also marked "best") for *A Saucerful of Secrets*. The session was produced by Norman Smith, engineered by Peter Bown and assisted by John Smith.

FEBRUARY – PRESS REPORT
Beat Instrumental, **London, England**

In its 1967 Gold Star Awards Pink Floyd came in at No.10 as Best Group on Stage; Best Songwriter at No.14 went to Syd Barrett who also picked up No.14 as Best Lead Guitarist and Roger Waters at No.12 for Best Bass Guitarist.

THURSDAY 1 FEBRUARY – RECORDING SESSION
Studio 3 & Control Room 3, EMI Studios, Abbey Road, London, England

2.30pm to 5.30pm: Take 6 of 'Corporal Clegg' overdubbed; 'The Most Boring Song I've Ever Heard, Bar 2' ['See Saw'] overdubbed (and relabelled Take 8), and 8.45pm to 12.30am: Take 6 of 'Corporal Clegg' overdubbed and remixed (RM1 at 3:27 also marked "best") for *A Saucerful of Secrets*. The session was produced by Norman Smith, engineered by Peter Bown and assisted by John Smith.

TUESDAY 6 FEBRUARY – REHEARSALS
Kensal Rise Primary School, Brondesbury Park, London, England

WEDNESDAY 7 FEBRUARY – RECORDING SESSION
Studio 3 & Control Room 3, EMI Studios, Abbey Road, London, England

2.30pm to 7.00pm: Take 6 of 'Corporal Clegg' overdubbed, and 7.30pm to 1.15am: 'Corporal Clegg' recorded (Take 7 breakdown and Take 8 at 3:50 also marked "best" fade) for the album *A Saucerful of Secrets*. The session was produced by Norman Smith and engineered by Ken Scott (afternoon), Peter Bown (evening) and assisted by Michael Sheady.

THURSDAY 8 FEBRUARY – RECORDING SESSION
Studio 3 & Control Room 3, EMI Studios, Abbey Road, London, England

2.30pm to 6.00pm: 'Corporal Clegg' re-recorded (Take 8 at 4:10 also marked "best fade"), and 7.00pm to 10.30pm: 'Corporal Clegg' reductions (RM2 untimed, RM3 at 4:27 and RM4 at 4:07 also marked "best") for *A Saucerful of Secrets*. The session was produced by Norman Smith, engineered by Peter Bown and assisted by Michael Sheady.

SATURDAY 10 FEBRUARY – PERFORMANCE
The Imperial Ballroom, Nelson, England

Supported by the Forth Coming and the Atlantics.

SATURDAY 10 FEBRUARY – PRESS REPORT
London, England

It was reported in the UK music press that Pink Floyd's next single would be 'Corporal Clegg', and would be due for release in four weeks' time. Several European tour dates were also announced, many of which never materialized including:

Hamburg, West Germany (Monday 12 February) Frankfurt, West Germany to record for TV (Tuesday 13 February), Stockholm, Sweden (Wednesday 14 and Thursday 15 February), Netherlands (Saturday 17 February) and Brussels, Belgium (Sunday 18 and Monday 19 February) and to Netherlands (between Thursday 22 and Saturday 24 February) to record for TV shows.

MONDAY 12 FEBRUARY – RECORDING SESSION
Studio 2 & Control Room 2, EMI Studios, Abbey Road, London, England

2.30pm to 8.30pm: 'Corporal Clegg' end section recorded (labelled Take 9 edit piece at 1:50 and Take 10 edit piece at 2:10 and both marked "best when edited"), and 9.30pm to 11.00pm: Overdubbing Orchestra onto 'Corporal Clegg' (Take 9 edit piece and Take 10 edit piece and both marked "edit for best"), for *A Saucerful of Secrets*. The session was produced by Norman Smith, engineered by Peter Bown (afternoon), Ken Scott (evening) and assisted by John Smith. This session also featured the Stanley Myers Orchestra, a six-piece avant-garde outfit who provided the ramshackle horn section for the close of 'Corporal Clegg'. Stanley Myers himself achieved widespread fame in the 70s as a composer of film and TV scores, most notably for the Ivor Novello–award-winning score 'Cavatina', which was performed by John Williams for the film *The Deer Hunter* in 1978.

TUESDAY 13 FEBRUARY – RECORDING SESSION
Studio 2 & Control Room 2, EMI Studios, Abbey Road, London, England

2.30pm to 5.30pm: 'The Boppin' Sound' [an unreleased track] recorded (Take 1 at 3:00 also marked "best"); Take 1 reductions of 'The Boppin' Sound' (RM1 at 2:42 also marked "best" rough); 'It Should Be So Nice' recorded (Take 1 at 3:25 also marked "best"), Take 5 of 'It Should Be So Nice' remixed (RM1 at 3:24 also marked "best rough"); 'Doreen Dream' ['Julia Dream'] recorded (Take 1 at 2:57 also marked "best"), Take 1 reductions of 'Doreen Dream' (RM1 at 2:42 also marked "best"), and 8.00pm to 12.15am: 'Richard's Rave Up' [an unreleased track] recorded (Take 1 at 2:54 also marked "best"); 'Doreen Dream' re-recorded (Take 2 at 2:33 and Take 3 at 2:33 also marked "best") for the 7-inch single. The session was produced by Norman Smith, engineered by Peter Bown and assisted by John Smith.

THURSDAY 15 FEBRUARY – RECORDING SESSION
Control Room 53, EMI Studios, Abbey Road, London, England

3:30pm to 5:45pm: 'Corporal Clegg' reductions (RM1 also marked "best version with lead vocals" and RM2 marked "best version without lead vocals"), and Take 2 of 'Set The Controls For The Heart Of The Sun' remixed (RM1 also marked "best"), for *A Saucerful of Secrets*. The session was produced by Norman Smith, engineered by Ken Scott and assisted by Jeff Jarrett.

It is also noted that copy tapes were also taken of 'Corporal Clegg' (Versions 1 & 2), 'Set The Controls For The Heart Of The Sun', 'Games For Emily' ['See Emily Play'] and 'Chapter 24', for unknown purposes, although there is a possibility some were supplied for use on Pink Floyd's mimed TV recordings in Belgium on 18 and 19 February, which included an early version of 'Corporal Clegg'. (See Television Recording on Sunday 18 and Monday 19 February.)

FRIDAY 16 FEBRUARY – PERFORMANCE
ICI Fibres Club, Pontypool, Wales

EUROPEAN TOUR

Pink Floyd's most extensive tour of Europe saw the band performing to an increasing fanbase in the Netherlands and Belgium boosted by several TV appearances.

SATURDAY 17 FEBRUARY – PERFORMANCE
Patronaatsgebouw, Terneuzen, Netherlands

Early show supported by Dragonfly, Living Kick Formation and the Moods.

SATURDAY 17 FEBRUARY – PERFORMANCE ▼
Concertgegebouw, Vlissingen, Netherlands

Late show supported by Dragonfly, Endatteme Jugband and Living Kick Formation.
Set list included 'Interstellar Overdrive'.

SUNDAY 18 & MONDAY 19 FEBRUARY – TELEVISION RECORDING
***Vibrato* & *Tienerklanken*, BRT TV Studios, Amerikaans Theater & Heysel Exhibition Park, Brussels, Belgium**

David Gilmour made his film debut with Pink Floyd by recording a series of promotional clips for Belgian TV, which included 'Astronomy Domine', 'Set The Controls For The Heart Of The Sun', 'Apples And Oranges', 'Corporal Clegg', 'Paintbox', 'Scarecrow' and 'See Emily Play'.

The first four numbers were shot at the BRT–TV studios based at the Amerikaans Theater with the latter three shot around the Heysel Exhibition Park with the Brussels Atomium visible in the background. All of the tracks were mimed over the original recordings, except for 'Corporal Clegg', which, although mimed, is noticeably different in its earlier incarnation by having a completely different verse ending from that which later appeared on their second album, *A Saucerful of Secrets*. (See Recording Session on Thursday 15 February.)

'Apples And Oranges' was broadcast (in black and white) on the RTB TV pop music programme *Vibrato* on Tuesday 27 February 1968 between 8.30pm and 9.15pm.

'Astronomy Domine', 'Scarecrow', 'Corporal Clegg', 'Paintbox', 'Set The Controls For The Heart Of The Sun' and 'See Emily Play' as well as a photo montage accompanying the album recording of 'Bike' was broadcast (in black and white) in a dedicated Pink Floyd TV special as part of the *Tienerklanken* pop music show on BRT TV on Sunday 31 March 1968 between 3.40pm and 4.05pm.

'See Emily Play' is the only track from these sessions that has ever been semi-officially released, appearing on the 1989 compilation video *Rock & Roll – The Greatest Years – 1967* (UK: Video Collection VC 458).

TUESDAY 20 FEBRUARY – TELEVISION RECORDING ▼
Bouton Rouge, ORTF TV Studios, Buttes Chaumont, Paris, France

Pink Floyd performed 'Astronomy Domine', 'Flaming', 'Set The Controls For The Heart Of The Sun' and 'Let There Be More Light' live for the music programme *Bouton Rouge*. It was broadcast (in colour) on ORFT2 TV on Saturday 24 February 1968 between 6.15pm and 7.00pm.

WEDNESDAY 21 FEBRUARY – TELEVISION RECORDING
Discorama, ORTF TV Studios, Buttes Chaumont, Paris, France

Pink Floyd mimed to 'Paintbox' for the music programme *Discorama*. It was broadcast (in black and white) on ORTF2 TV on 3 March 1968 between 12.30pm and 1.00pm.

THURSDAY 22 FEBRUARY – PERFORMANCE
Rijschool, Leuven, Belgium

As part of the city carnival, students organized an all-night event featuring Pink Floyd (who replaced the Crazy World of Arthur Brown at short notice), Sweet Feeling and the Shake Spears.

However, the show was abandoned just as the band was setting up their gear following the Shake Spears set when a member of the audience poured beer into Richard Wright's organ. Nick Mason spoke of the incident in a February 1972 interview for

Circus magazine recalling that it was the "worst run-in of our career. Flemish on one side and the French on the other. The Flemish are fond of swigging beer and singing all these old drinking songs. That's fine, except that most of the audience was French. Even the seating was divided. Well, they really got into one of their songs and the French kids started yelling and stamping for Pink Floyd. All of a sudden, as if on cue, ALL the Flemish side hurled their beer glasses across the room. It was a beautiful sight, actually. Everything was quiet for a moment while the glasses were in the air. I thought it was some sort of Flemish ritual until I heard the screams when the glasses started landing. Even we decided not to stay around to hear Pink Floyd." According to organizers, the trouble actually began when a long-running feud between left-wing students, who wanted the carnival modernized to include a pop show, and right-wing students, who didn't, finally reached a head. It was only calmed down when police entered the building and broke up the fighting but apparently it was too late to save Pink Floyd from performing. Alan Escombe of the Shake Spears remembered when the fighting started: "It was really frightening as metal tables were being thrown from the upstairs balcony down onto the crowd below. We locked ourselves into a dressing room behind the stage with Pink Floyd and their roadies until the police came. We managed to get out and load the van before people came out of the hall."

FRIDAY 23 FEBRUARY – PERFORMANCE
Pannenhuis, Antwerp, Belgium

Supported by the Mike Stuart Span, replacing the advertised Crazy World of Arthur Brown.

Set list: 'Let There Be More Light', 'Matilda Mother', 'Astronomy Domine', 'Corporal Clegg', 'Set The Controls For The Heart Of The Sun', 'Flaming', 'Lucifer Sam', 'Interstellar Overdive'.

Het Laatste Nieuws reported that "400 youngsters experienced 'the psychedelic thing' at the Pannenhuis which only holds 200 people! This beat-mecca in Antwerp was literally shaking on the very ground it was built on. A mind-expanding experience that lasted for two hours was given by Pink Floyd and the Mike Stuart Span. Everything was perfectly enhanced by a primitive 'sensual laboratory' that provided light and colour explosions all over the stage whilst keeping up with the devilish rhythms of the music, equalling a volcano-like outburst of sight and sound. The whole show was proof of a 'total communication through light and sound', a concept that left a beat-loving teenage audience stunned at first but in the end succeeded in drawing everybody into a whirlpool of music, sounds and multi-coloured light effects."

SATURDAY 24 FEBRUARY – CANCELLED RECORDING SESSION
Studio 3 & Control Room 3, EMI Studios, Abbey Road, London, England

Session cancelled due to performance commitments. It is noted on the studio booking form that previously recorded tapes would be required of 'Julia Dream', 'Set The Controls', 'Mildenhall' ['Let There Be More Light'], 'Demo tapes recorded 13/2/68' and 'Corporal Clegg'.

SATURDAY 24 FEBRUARY – PERFORMANCE
Cheetah Club, Brussels, Belgium

Set list included 'Interstellar Overdrive', 'Corporal Clegg', 'Set The Controls For The Heart Of The Sun'.

SUNDAY 25 FEBRUARY – CANCELLED PERFORMANCES
Netherlands

Pink Floyd's three advertised appearances on this day at T' Smurf, De Engh, Bussum (afternoon show), *Daddle Doofy*, Concertzaal De Jong, Groningen (early evening show) and Jongerencentrum Sopla, Amersfoort (late evening show) were all cancelled due to problems with work permits.

MONDAY 26 FEBRUARY – PERFORMANCE
Domino Club, **Lion Hotel, Cambridge, England**

With the Chequers and the Tykes.
Pink Floyd made an impromptu appearance at the opening night of this club replacing the advertised Wages of Sin.

WEDNESDAY 28 FEBRUARY – TELEVISION BROADCAST
The Gamblers, **Rediffusion TV, London, England**

'Astronomy Domine' featured heavily in an episode of the anthology series *The Gamblers* in an episode called 'Thirty Stretch'. Each episode was linked by the premise of people having to take a chance or risk a gamble on something, sometimes with their lives. It was broadcast on the ITV network between 8.30pm and 9.30pm. The series ran for 20 episodes between Thursday 26 September 1967 and Thursday 18 July 1968.

THURSDAY 29 FEBRUARY – REHEARSALS
London, England

FRIDAY 1 MARCH – PRESS REPORT
London, England

On or around this date Syd Barrett's departure from Pink Floyd was made official, although he had not been appearing on stage with the band since February. Barrett, however, continued to be managed by Blackhill as a solo artist.

MONDAY 4 MARCH – PERFORMANCE
Isleworth Film Studios, Isleworth, London, England

Pink Floyd performed at the invitation of Vanessa Redgrave at the end of filming party for her latest film, *Isadora*.

TUESDAY 5 MARCH – RECORDING SESSION
Studio 3 & Control Room 3, EMI Studios, Abbey Road, London, England

2.30pm to 7.00pm: 'It Would Be So Nice' recorded (Take 1 at 3:50), and 7.00pm to 12.30am: 'It Would Be So Nice' re-recorded (Take 1-6 False Starts, Take 7 and 8 untimed, Takes 9 and 10 False Starts, and Take 11 at 4:06 also marked "best (fade)") for the 7-inch single. The session was produced by Norman Smith, engineered by Peter Bown and assisted by Michael Sheady.

SATURDAY 9 MARCH – PERFORMANCE ▶
Faculty of Technology Union, Manchester Technical College, Manchester, England

WEDNESDAY 13 MARCH – RECORDING SESSION
Studio 3 & Control Room 3, EMI Studios, Abbey Road, London, England

2.30pm to 7.00pm: New Vocals overdubbed onto Take 11 of 'It Would Be So Nice' and faded onto Take 11 (relabelled Take 12) of 'It Would Be So Nice', and 7.30pm to 1.30am: Take 11 of 'It Would Be So Nice' overdubbed (and marked "best (fade)", and relabelled Take 13 untimed, Take 14 false start, Take 15 and 16 untimed, and Take 17 also marked "best") for the 7-inch single. The session was produced by Norman Smith, engineered by Peter Bown and assisted by Michael Sheady.

THURSDAY 14 MARCH – PERFORMANCES
Whitla Hall, Queen's College, Belfast, Northern Ireland

Two shows at 7.00pm and 9.30pm, with the Spencer Davis Group (headline), the Taste (featuring guitarist Rory Gallagher) and the Freshmen.

FRIDAY 15 MARCH – PERFORMANCE
The Stage Club, **Clarendon Restaurant, Oxford, England**

SATURDAY 16 MARCH – PERFORMANCE
Crawdaddy, **The Ballroom, Casino Hotel, Taggs Island, Hampton Court, England**

An early evening appearance, with one eyewitness reporting, "The Casino, having re-opened in July '66 following a fire in the defunct hotel section, was functioning as a dance hall, so the mute, static Pink Floyd, with their slithering oil slides being projected up the ornate walls and ceiling, didn't really gain any acclaim. And they weren't exactly a dance band. The evening was poorly attended."

SATURDAY 16 MARCH – PERFORMANCE ▶
Middle Earth, Covent Garden, London, England

Late show with Juniors Eyes, DJ Jeff Dexter and the Explosive Spectrum Light Show.
David Gilmour recalled in an interview with *Zig Zag* magazine,
"I remember one terrible night when Syd [Barrett] came and stood in front of the stage. He stared at me all night long. Horrible!"

SUNDAY 17 MARCH – PERFORMANCE
Recta (Club '67), Ertvelde, Belgium

Pink Floyd were initially booked on this date to make a return appearance in Leuven, but it was called off fearing a repeat of the events that took place on 22 February, and so the band accepted an invitation to perform at Recta instead. According to eyewitness reports Pink Floyd's music was not well received, emptying the hall faster than it had filled. Support band the Foottappers were invited back on stage to appease the crowd.

WEDNESDAY 20 MARCH – PERFORMANCE ▶
New Grafton Rooms, Liverpool, England

With Ten Years After and Almost Blues. Pink Floyd was paid £200 for one 40-minute spot.

The Pink Floyd
The Ten Years After
The Almost Blues

Admission by ticket only to be paid for at the door 7/6

At the Grafton Rooms West Derby Road

Wednesday March 20th

8pm to 1am. late bars no entrance after 10pm students over 18 only

BELOW: PINK FLOYD APPEARING ON THE DUTCH MAGAZINE *MUZIEK EXPRESS*, MARCH 1968.

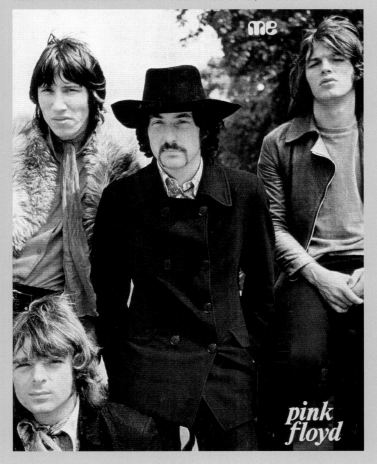

THURSDAY 21 MARCH – RECORDING SESSION
Studio 2 & Control Room 2, EMI Studios, Abbey Road, London, England

2.30pm to 7.00pm: Take 17 of 'It Would be So Nice' overdubbed (and relabelled Take 18 and marked "best"), and 8.00pm to 12.30am: Take 18 of 'It Would Be So Nice' overdubbed (also marked "best"), and 'It Would Be So Nice' remixed (RM1 also marked "best from Take 18", RM2 from Take 17 and RM3 "start edit piece" marked "best from RM1") for the 7-inch single. The session was produced by Norman Smith, engineered by Peter Bown and assisted by Richard Langham.

FRIDAY 22 MARCH – RECORDING SESSION
The Sound of Change, Sound Techniques Studios, Chelsea, London, England

Pink Floyd recorded an untitled instrumental piece (timed at 2:10 and recorded between 1.00pm and 3.00pm, with tape copying between 3.00pm and 3.30pm) at Sound Techniques for use in a one-hour BBC TV film tracing the development of pop music from Vera Lynn to the present day entitled *The Sound of Change*. (See Tuesday 26 March for further details.)

FRIDAY 22 MARCH – PERFORMANCE
Main Hall, Woolwich Polytechnic, Woolwich, London, England

At this poorly publicized all-nighter Pink Floyd took to the stage at 2.00am (Saturday 23 March) reportedly in front of an audience of fewer than fifty.

SUNDAY 24 & MONDAY 25 MARCH – CANCELLED PERFORMANCES
West Germany and Switzerland

Pink Floyd cancelled their appearance at the *11th Deutsches Frankfurt Jazz Festival*, Volksbildungsheim, Frankfurt, West Germany (Sunday 24 March), which featured the Shake Spears, Cuby & the Blizzards, Alexis Korner Blues, the Soul Caravan, and the New York Total Music Company with Don Cherry, and a show in Zurich, Switzerland (Monday 25 March), which was listed in an early fan-club newsletter, due to recording commitments.

MONDAY 25 MARCH – RECORDING SESSION
Studio 3 & Control Room 3, EMI Studios, Abbey Road, London, England

2.30pm to 7.00pm: Vocals overdubbed onto Take 1 of 'Julia Dream' for the 7-inch single, and 8.00pm to 1.05am: Take 11 reductions of 'Corporal Clegg' (edit for end); "Rhythm Tracks" (recorded 18 January) overdubbed onto Take 1 of 'Let There Be More Light', and 'Julia Dream' remixed (RM2 at 2:28) for *A Saucerful of Secrets*. The session was produced by Norman Smith, engineered by Ken Scott and assisted by John Barrett.

TUESDAY 26 MARCH – TELEVISION RECORDING
The Sound Of Change, Barnes Common, Barnes, London, England

Pink Floyd was filmed inside a specially erected 40-foot geodesic dome on Barnes Common in southwest London for sequences in the BBC TV programme *The Sound of Change* (although it had the working title *History of Pop*). Pink Floyd's music was recorded on

Friday 22 March to comply with a "no-noise" enforcement which prevented the band from performing live at this location. The call sheet shows the location time between 4.00pm and 12.00pm at the "open space near graveyard", although correspondence shows the geodesic dome was not erected until 8.00pm, and that filming didn't start until 9.00pm and went on until 12.30am.

Pink Floyd was the only band to be filmed on location as much of the originally proposed programme content was diverted to the BBC Omnibus special *All My Loving*. Pink Floyd's music was also used for flash-back sequences showing the Paris student riots and also over the closing credits. The rest of the programme consisted of records dubbed onto film and interspersed with commentary including contributions from Mick Jagger and Pete Townshend.

It was broadcast in the UK on BBC2 TV on Tuesday 10 September 1968 between 8.00pm and 8.50pm. Extracts of Pink Floyd's contribution was also used on the magazine programme *Late Night Line Up*, as a last-minute replacement in lieu of Sammy Davis Jr who cancelled his appearance, broadcast the same evening on BBC2 between 11.05pm and 11.40pm.

THURSDAY 28 MARCH – TELEVISION RECORDING
All My Loving, Abbey Mills Pumping Station,
East Stratford, London, England

Pink Floyd performed 'Set The Controls For The Heart Of The Sun' live at this location for BBC producer Tony Palmer as part of an Omnibus TV special focusing on the socio-political context of rock music, entitled *All My Loving*. Much of the rest of the documentary, which had various working titles during its production including *Sound and Picture City, My Generation* and simply *Pop Film*, was filmed in the USA and featured live performances by the Who, Donovan, Jimi Hendrix and Cream as well as interviews with Paul McCartney, Eric Burdon, Derek Taylor, Frank Zappa, Anthony Burgess and even George Harrison's mother! In addition to their appearance fee, the BBC also had to compensate Pink Floyd the sum of £90 for damage to their equipment.

Tony Palmer had originally scheduled filming of Pink Floyd to take place on Tuesday 26 March at 7.00pm in a specially erected geodesic dome at Barnes Common, southwest London, but this plan was shelved at short notice and the idea transferred to the previously listed documentary *The Sound of Change*.

All My Loving was previewed at a special screening for cast and crew at the Hanover Grand Film and Arts Theatre, London, England on Friday 1 November at 11.00am, although it is doubtful the band attended having already attended a screening at BBC TV Centre on Tuesday 17 September. The finished programme also included further footage of 'Set The Controls For The Heart Of The Sun' and an audio excerpt from 'A Saucerful Of Secrets' used as background music, which was recorded at the BBC TV Centre on Thursday 11 April.

It was finally broadcast in the UK on BBC1 TV (in black and white) on Sunday 3 November 1968 between 10.40pm and 11.35pm and repeated (in colour) on BBC2 TV on 18 May 1969 between 9.30pm and 10.25pm. It was repeated for the last time as part of the programme *Festival 77*, broadcast on BBC2 TV on Wednesday 17 August 1977 between 10.15pm and 11.15pm.

All My Loving was released on DVD (UK: Voiceprint TPDVD101) on 10 September 2007.

MONDAY 1 APRIL– RECORDING SESSION
Studio 3 & Control Room 3, EMI Studios, Abbey Road,
London, England

2.30pm to 7.00pm: Vocals overdubbed onto Take 17 of 'It Would Be So Nice' for the DJ only 7-inch single, and Vocals overdubbed onto Take 1 of 'Let There Be More Light', and 8.00pm to 11.30pm: Vocals overdubbed onto Take 1 of 'Let There Be More Light' for the album *A Saucerful of Secrets*. The session was produced by Norman Smith, engineered by Ken Scott and assisted by John Barrett (morning) and Peter Mew (afternoon).

MONDAY 1 APRIL – PRESS REPORT
London, England

It is believed that on or around this date the six-way partnership between Pink Floyd members Syd Barrett, Nick Mason, Roger Waters and Richard Wright, and managers Andrew King and Peter Jenner was dissolved.

Wright very nearly departed at the same time saying, "Peter and Andrew thought Syd and I were the musical brains of the group, and that we should form a breakaway band, to try to hold Syd together. And believe me, I would have left with him like a shot if I had thought Syd could do it."

In later years Blackhill could have been accused of making their biggest ever business error, but Jenner takes a philosophical view: "We didn't have the resources to do anything more for them. They needed someone bigger to look after them. I suspect if they'd stayed with us we'd probably have bogged ourselves down in a trough of doom, which was very much in the air at the time."

This had much to do with the fact that the band was also financially drained. Blackhill had even sought an Arts Council grant for about £5,000 to assist a stage production featuring Pink Floyd, but this was clearly a thinly disguised veil to try to pay off the bills. It was at this point, Mason told *Zig Zag* magazine some years later, that their debts reached a peak, Waters adding that, "Cheques were bouncing all the time because there wasn't enough money to pay everybody, so whoever got their cheque first got their money."

TUESDAY 2 APRIL – RECORDING SESSION
Room 25, EMI Studios, Abbey Road, London, England

Lacquers cut of 'It Would Be So Nice' for the DJ-only 7-inch single (timed at 3:10). The session was produced by Norman Smith and engineered by Phil McDonald. Pink Floyd was not in attendance for this session.

WEDNESDAY 3 APRIL – RECORDING SESSION
Room 25, EMI Studios, Abbey Road, London, England

Lacquers cut of 'It Would Be So Nice' for the regular 7-inch single (timed at 3.44) and 'Julia Dream' (untimed) for the 7-inch single. The session was produced by Norman Smith, engineered by Phil McDonald. Pink Floyd was not in attendance for this session.

WEDNESDAY 3 APRIL – RECORDING SESSION
Studio 3 & Control Room 3, EMI Studios,
Abbey Road, London, England

2.30pm to 6.30pm: 'Nick's Boogie' [the First Movement of 'A Saucerful Of Secrets'] recorded (Take 1 at 3:54 also marked "best"), and 7.00pm to 10.00pm: 'Nick's Boogie (Second Movement)' recorded (Take 1 untimed also marked "best") for *A Saucerful of Secrets*. The session was produced by Norman Smith, engineered by Peter Bown and assisted by Peter Mew (afternoon) and Richard Langham (evening).

FRIDAY 5 APRIL – RECORDING SESSION
Studio 3 & Control Room 3, EMI Studios,
Abbey Road, London, England

2.30pm to 6.45pm: 'Nick's Boogie' [First Movement of 'A Saucerful Of Secrets'] re-recorded (Take 2 at 3:40 also marked "best"), and 8.00pm to 12.30am: 'Nick's Boogie (Third Movement)' recorded (Take 1 untimed also marked "best") for *A Saucerful of Secrets*. The session was produced by Norman Smith, engineered by Peter Bown and assisted by John Kurlander (afternoon) and Richard Langham (evening).

SATURDAY 6 – MONDAY 8 APRIL – RECORDING SESSION
3 Belsize Square, Belsize Park, London, England

On or around these dates Pink Floyd recorded the soundtrack to the avant-garde film *The Committee* at a private address in north London, the precise dates of which can only be loosely determined. In his book *Inside Out* Nick Mason states that recording commenced for four consecutive days shortly after Thursday 4 April, noted as being the day of Martin Luther King's assassination. Although the dates given represent only three days, these are the only dates that fit in the period given the band's existing commitments.

Writer Max Steuer recalled in an interview with the website *Spare Bricks* in 2005 that initially Syd Barrett was asked to do the soundtrack: "Syd read the story and said he would do the film. This seemed fine by me. He asked us to book a very expensive studio, and showed up an hour and a half late, and without a guitar. He asked Peter Sykes and me to get lost, which we did. We came back a few hours later to find a trio – drums, bass, and guitar. Syd thought it was a good start. It cost too much money, and would have sunk the film.... Roger Waters heard about these efforts, and suggested the Floyd could do the job. I am so glad he did. It was absolutely wonderful working with them, and the outcome could not be better.... [The recording took place at] 3 Belsize Square, London, the basement flat of the painter Michael Kidner and his wife Marion [both have small parts in the movie]. There was no furniture in the living room, which was large. We started at nine each morning and did twelve hours or so. Roger was always there at 8.30, David Gilmour shortly after, then Nick Mason, and Rick Wright just before nine. It was amazingly professional. The road crew set up the first day by 8 o'clock or so. The van you see on the *Ummagumma* album was parked outside."

The soundtrack was made by improvising music to images of the film projected onto a screen in the front room of the flat. The soundtrack comprised entirely of ethereal instrumental passages but does include the earliest known version of 'Careful With That Axe, Eugene'.

The film opened at the Cameo Poly Cinema, London, England on Thursday 26 September 1968, and was presumed lost for several years before finally being released on DVD in 2005 (UK: Basho DVD 901).

TUESDAY 9 APRIL – RECORDING SESSION
Studio 3 & Control Room 3, EMI Studios,
Abbey Road, London, England

10.00am to 1.00pm: 'Nick's Boogie (Third Movement)' re-recorded (Take 1 at 5:20 also marked "best"), and 2.30pm to 6.35pm: 'Nick's Boogie (Third Movement)' re-recorded (Take 1 at 5:30, also marked "best"), and 'Nick's Boogie (Third Movement)' overdubbed (Take 2 "edit piece" at 0:10) for *A Saucerful of Secrets*. The session was produced by Norman Smith, engineered by Peter Bown and assisted by John Smith.

WEDNESDAY 10 APRIL – TELEVISION BROADCAST
Horoscope, **Granada TV, London, England**

Pink Floyd's 'Astronomy Domine' featured heavily in the documentary programme *Horoscope*, which questioned if astrology really works. It was broadcast on the ITV network between 9.00pm and 10.00pm.

WEDNESDAY 10 APRIL – RECORDING SESSION
Studio 3 & Control Room 3, EMI Studios,
Abbey Road, London, England

10.00am to 1.15pm: Vocals and "Noises" recorded (Take 1, untimed) and overdubbed onto Take 2 of 'Nick's Boogie'; 'Wild Guitar Track' recorded (Take 1, untimed), and 'Wild Guitar Track with Guitar and Piano' recorded (Take 1, untimed) for Take 2 of 'Nick's Boogie', and 2.30pm to 5.30pm: Take 2 of 'Nick's Boogie (First Movement)' remixed (RM1 also marked "best"), and Take 1 of 'Nick's Boogie (Second Movement)' remixed (RM2 also marked "best") for *A Saucerful of Secrets*. The session was produced by Norman Smith, engineered by Peter Bown and assisted by John Barrett.

THURSDAY 11 APRIL – CANCELLED PERFORMANCE
Sjok In, Hilversum, Netherlands

Pink Floyd's show was cancelled due to problems with work permits.

THURSDAY 11 APRIL – TELEVISION RECORDING
All My Loving, **Studio 4, BBC TV Centre,**
London, England

Pink Floyd performed 'Set The Controls For The Heart Of The Sun' for additional footage and recorded 'A Saucerful Of Secrets' as additional soundtrack music for the Omnibus BBC TV special *All My Loving*. (See 28 March entry for further details.)

IT WOULD BE SO NICE

TRACKS

SIDE A: IT WOULD BE SO NICE (Wright) **3:44**
SIDE B: JULIA DREAM (Waters) **2:28**

RELEASE DATE

UK: Friday 19 April 1968.
US: Monday 24 June 1968.

FORMAT

UK: Columbia EMI DB 8410 (7-inch vinyl single).
US: Tower 426 (7-inch vinyl single).

RECORDING DETAILS

Recording of the A-side commenced at EMI Studios, Abbey Road on 13 February 1968, midway through the recording of the album *A Saucerful of Secrets*. However, this particular session was scrubbed and recording recommenced on 5 March with a whopping 11 takes in all, the last of which formed the basic track for the single. Overdubs continued on 13, 21 and 25 March, and on 1 April a new vocal was recorded in order to produce a version of the single for the sole benefit of BBC Radio, replacing the name of the newspaper *Evening Standard* with the fictitious *Daily Standard* in order to satisfy its rules on product placement. Curiously the *Evening Standard* version has, to date, never surfaced, and was most likely only ever issued as a metal acetate.

On the promo version the *Daily Standard* is sung although the central "It would be so nice" chorus is sung only once, and the first lines of the second verse ("Everybody cares about the weather...what a waste of time") are edited.

'Julia Dream', on the other hand, was recorded in just two takes as 'Doreen Dream', also on 13 February 1968, with overdubs added on 25 March.

IT WOULD BE SO NICE
Take 18 (RM1).
Basic track recorded as 'It Should Be So Nice' on 13 February 1968 (Take 1).
Remixed on 13 February 1968 (RM1).
Basic track re-recorded on 5 March 1968 (Take 11).
Edits of Take 11 for 'Fade' made on 13 March 1968 (relabelled Take 12).
Edits of Take 12 for 'Start' made on 13 March 1968 (relabelled Take 17).
Tape reduction and unspecified instruments overdubbed onto Take 17 on 21 March 1968 (relabelled Take 18).
Vocals overdubbed onto Take 18 on 21 March 1968.
Take 18 tape reduced and remixed on 21 March 1968 (RM1).
Take 17 tape reduced and remixed on 21 March 196z8 (RM2).
Take 18 tape reduced and remixed for "Start Edit Piece" (RM3) and edited to RM1 on 21 March 1968.
New vocals overdubbed onto Take 18 on 1 April 1968.

JULIA DREAM
Take 1 (RM2).
Basic track recorded as 'Doreen Dream' on 13 February 1968 (Take 1).
Take 1 tape reduced and remixed on 13 February 1968 (RM1).
Vocals overdubbed onto Take 1 on 25 March 1968.
Remixed on 25 March 1968 (RM2).

ABOVE LEFT: UK PROMO SINGLE.
TOP RIGHT: NETHERLANDS PICTURE SLEEVE SINGLE.
RIGHT: PRESS ADVERT FOR THE UK SINGLE RELEASE.

FRIDAY 12, SATURDAY 13 & SUNDAY 14 APRIL – CANCELLED TELEVISION RECORDING
BRT TV Studios, Amerikaans Theater, Brussels, Belgium

Pink Floyd was reported in the music press to be recording for Belgian TV on these dates, but nothing is recorded in the BRT archives to support this.

FRIDAY 19 APRIL – SINGLE RELEASE (UK)
'It Would Be So Nice'

The *NME* wrote, "My copy bears a message saying that it's a specially edited and shortened version for broadcasting purposes. Despite that, it still runs at 3¾ minutes, so goodness knows how long the ordinary shop-sold copies last! However you get far more than just excess time on this disc! The main body of the performance is a Kinks-like jogging good-time but all manner of other effects are thrown in for good measure – a pulsating and voluminous chorus, tempo changes, crashing cymbals, fuzz guitars. In fact it ends up sounding like a psychedelic "Teenage Opera". But, I'm not being derisive – there's a catchy melody line, an absorbing lyric and a fascinating sound."

Waters later commented that, "Nobody ever heard it because it was such a lousy record!" Of course this was greatly compounded by the fact that the band only ever performed the track live on a handful of occasions, and instead chose the B-side, an arguably superior song, to plug on a BBC session that June.

THURSDAY 18 & FRIDAY 19 APRIL – PERFORMANCES
Piper Club, Rome, Italy

Two shows each night at 5.00pm and 10.00pm, supported by Thane Russal and his Big Bang Band, Mike Liddell's Creation, Studio 6, Boom 67, Fholks and Noise (featuring future Yes and King Crimson band-member Bill Bruford on drums). This was Pink Floyd's first ever appearance in Italy.
Set list at the 5.00pm show on Thursday 18 April included 'Astronomy Domine', 'Set The Controls For The Heart Of The Sun', 'Interstellar Overdrive'.

SATURDAY 20 APRIL – PERFORMANCE ▶
Raven Club, RAF Waddington, Waddington, England

Supported by the Delroy Williams Show (with go-go girls) and the Individual Set.

MONDAY 22 APRIL – RECORDING SESSION
Room 53, EMI Studios, Abbey Road, London, England

2.30pm to 5.30pm: Take 8 of 'The Most Boring Song I've Ever Heard, Bar Two' ['See Saw'] remixed (RM1 and RM2, at 4:33 also marked "best") for *A Saucerful of*

Secrets. The session was produced by Norman Smith, engineered by Martin Benge and assisted by John Barrett.

TUESDAY 23 APRIL – RECORDING SESSION
Room 53, EMI Studios, Abbey Road, London, England

10.00am to 12.30pm: Take 8 of 'The Most Boring Song I've Ever Heard, Bar Two' ['See Saw'] remixed (RM3 at 4:32), and Take 2 of 'Set The Controls For The Heart Of The Sun' remixed (RM2 & RM3 also marked "best to be decided"), and 1.30pm to 5.30pm: Take 2 of 'Set The Controls For The Heart Of The Sun' remixed (RM3 at 5:38 also marked "best"), Take 1 of 'Let There Be More Light' remixed (RM1 at 5:21, and RM2 at 5:26 also marked "best"), and Take 1 of 'Nick's Boogie (Third Movement)' remixed (RM1 at 4:48 also marked "best") for *A Saucerful of Secrets*. The session was produced by Norman Smith, engineered by Martin Benge and assisted by Richard Langham.

WEDNESDAY 24 APRIL – RECORDING SESSION
Room 53, EMI Studios, Abbey Road, London, England

10.00am to 1.00pm: Take 1 of 'Nick's Boogie (Second Movement)' remixed (RM3 untimed also marked "best"), and 'Corporal Clegg' remixed (RM4 untimed and marked "best") for *A Saucerful of Secrets*. The session was produced by Norman Smith, engineered by Martin Benge and assisted by Peter Mew.

FRIDAY 26 APRIL – RECORDING SESSION
Room 53, EMI Studios, Abbey Road, London, England

10.00am to 1.00pm: Take 2 of 'Set The Controls For The Heart Of The Sun' remixed (RS1 and RS2 also marked "best to be decided"), and 2.30pm to 5.30pm: Take 8 of 'See Saw' [previously referred to as 'The Most Boring Song I've Ever Heard, Bar Two'] remixed (RS1 and RS2 untimed also marked "best to be decided"), and Take 1 of 'Let There Be More Light' remixed (RS1 and RS2 at 5:25 also marked "best to be decided") for *A Saucerful of Secrets*. The session was produced by Norman Smith, engineered by Ken Scott and assisted by Richard Langham.

TUESDAY 30 APRIL – RECORDING SESSION
Room 53, EMI Studios, Abbey Road, London, England

10.00am to 2.00pm: 'Corporal Clegg' remixed (RS1-4 also marked "best to be decided") for *A Saucerful of Secrets*. The session was produced by Norman Smith, engineered by Peter Bown and assisted by John Barrett. Pink Floyd was not in attendance for this session.

TUESDAY 30 APRIL – TELEVSION RECORDING
Moef Ga Ga, VARA TV Studios, Zaandam, Netherlands

Pink Floyd performed 'It Would Be So Nice' live in an afternoon recording session for the music programme *Moef Ga Ga*. It was broadcast on Nederland 2 TV on Wednesday 1 May between 7.00pm and 7.35pm.

TUESDAY 30 APRIL – CANCELLED PERFORMANCES
Netherlands

Pink Floyd's two advertised shows on this day at the Whisky a Go Go, RK Verenigingsgebouw, Zaandam (early evening) and the Paradiso, Amsterdam (late evening, despite having set up all their equipment on stage) were both cancelled due to problems with work permits. Both shows were rescheduled to 23 May.

WEDNESDAY 1 MAY – RECORDING SESSION
Room 53, EMI Studios, Abbey Road, London, England

10.00am to 1.00pm: Take 2 of 'Nick's Boogie (First Movement)' remixed (RS1 & RS2, and marked "best to be decided"), and 2.30pm to 5.30pm: Take 2 of 'Nick's Boogie (First Movement)' remixed (RS3 & RS4) and also edited, for *A Saucerful of Secrets*. The session was produced by Norman Smith, engineered by Peter Bown and assisted by John Barrett.

THURSDAY 2 MAY– RECORDING SESSION
Room 53, EMI Studios, Abbey Road, London, England

2.30pm to 6.00pm: Take 1 of 'Let There Be More Light' remixed (RS3 and RS4 untimed also marked "best"), and Take 2 of 'Set The Controls For The Heart Of The Sun' remixed (RS3 and RS4 untimed also marked "best") for *A Saucerful of Secrets*. The session was produced by Norman Smith, engineered by Peter Bown and assisted by John Barrett.

FRIDAY 3 MAY – RECORDING SESSION
Room 53, EMI Studios, Abbey Road, London, England

2.30pm to 5.30pm: Take 6 of 'See Saw' remixed (RS3 and RS4 at 4:30 also marked "best") for *A Saucerful of Secrets*. The session was produced by Norman Smith, engineered by Peter Mew and assisted by John Barrett.

FRIDAY 3 MAY – PERFORMANCE ▶
Westfield College, Hampstead, London, England

With Grand Union.

SATURDAY 4 MAY – CANCELLED PERFORMANCE
Theatre 140, Brussels, Belgium

Pink Floyd's appearance with Dragonfly and Roland and His Blues Workshop was cancelled at the last minute because of a mix-up between the booking agent and management over their travel

plans. Pink Floyd didn't turn up until the Sunday but agreed to two shows by way of compensation.

SUNDAY 5 MAY – PERFORMANCES
Theatre 140, Brussels, Belgium

Two shows at 3.30pm and 8.30pm, supported by Dragonfly and Roland & His Blues Workshop.

MONDAY 6 MAY – PERFORMANCE
First European International Pop Festival, Palazzo Dello Sport, EUR, Rome, Italy

With the Nice, the Move, the Giganti and the Association, Donovan, Hughes Aufray and Julie Driscoll and the Brian Auger Trinity and Captain Beefheart & His Magic Band (Saturday 4 May); Roboti/Five Up, Ten Years After, Fairport Convention, Grapefruit and the Samurai (Sunday 5 May); and Grapefruit, Family and the Byrds (Tuesday 7 May).
Set list included: 'Astronomy Domine', 'Interstellar Overdrive', 'Set The Controls For The Heart Of The Sun', 'Pow R Toc H', 'Remember A Day'.

Pink Floyd's appearance at the ambitious First European International Pop Festival in Rome was first announced as taking place between Monday 19 and Sunday 25 February, and shortly afterwards rescheduled to between Saturday 4 and Friday 10 May. Even then it failed to realize its full potential and was reduced to scattered performances between Saturday 4 to Tuesday 7 May. The main problem was the fact that many of the performers advertised hadn't even agreed to appear. Only 400 people attended Pink Floyd's show in the huge Palazzo Dello Sport on Monday 6 May and many acts were rescheduled to the much smaller Piper Club. Fortunately the entire event was filmed by Bavaria Atelier in Munich, West Germany who captured performances by Donovan, Julie Driscoll & the Brian Auger Trinity, Captain Beefheart & His Magic Band, the Nice, the Association, the Giganti and the Samurai. Their footage was licensed to the BBC for use in the arts magazine programme *Release* in a feature entitled *Rome Goes Pop*, which was broadcast on BBC2 TV (in colour) on Saturday 18 May between 9.55pm and 10.45pm. Curiously, the footage they shot of Pink Floyd was not used in the programme and instead an intriguing insert of Pink Floyd miming to 'It Would Be So Nice' and filmed at the Piper Club in Rome without an audience was used. BBC archives do not indicate the source or recording date of this footage, so it is unclear who made the recordings and if it was shot during the festival period or Pink Floyd's earlier visit to the Piper Club on Thursday 18 and Friday 19 April, which would seem more likely.

In addition to this a short segment of 'Interstellar Overdrive' was featured on the West German programme *Pop '68* broadcast on ZDF2 TV on Wednesday 16 October between 10.00pm and 10.55pm.

Italian RAI radio also recorded parts of the festival and broadcast 'Astronomy Domine', an interview with Roger Waters, 'Set The Controls For The Heart Of The Sun' and 'Interstellar Overdrive', although exact broadcast details could not be traced. This recording also formed the basis of the Dutch VPRO radio programme *Eerste Popfestival te Rome [First Rome Pop Festival]*, with Dutch commentary dubbed over the Italian, and broadcast on Hilversum 1 radio, Netherlands on Friday 7 June between 8.00pm and 9.00pm.

MONDAY 6 MAY – RECORDING SESSION
CBS Studios, Holborn, London, England

2.30pm to 5.30pm: The unused Pink Floyd tracks 'In The Beechwoods' and 'Vegetable Man' previously recorded at EMI Studios for *A Saucerful of Secrets*, were copied for reference for Syd Barrett's first solo album. The session was produced by Norman Smith, engineered by John Wood and assisted by Harry Davies and Mike Weighell. Pink Floyd was not in attendance.

WEDNESDAY 8 MAY 1968 – RECORDING SESSION
De Lane Lea Studios, Holborn, London, England

2.30pm to 5.30pm: 'Jugband Blues' and 'Remember A Day' remixed. It is unclear from archives whether 'Remember A Day' was intended for *A Saucerful of Secrets* or for a proposed single release. The session was produced by Norman Smith. It is unlikely Pink Floyd would have been in attendance.

VOLCANOS — AIR AIDS — MONSTERS and more — all in the
GENTLE SOUND OF LIGHT
Plus PINK FLOYD and SOFT MACHINE :: SATURDAY, 11th MAY, 9 until 1
TICKETS 15/- FROM PORTERS DESK

SATURDAY 11 MAY – PERFORMANCE ▲
Brighton Arts Festival - The Gentle Sound of Light,
Falmer House Courtyard, University of Sussex,
Falmer, Brighton, England

The advertised Soft Machine cancelled, but the event was billed with "volcanos, air raids, monsters and more!"
Set list included: 'Let There Be More Light', 'Set The Controls For The Heart Of The Sun', 'Interstellar Overdrive', 'It Would Be So Nice'.
Wine Press, Sussex University's student newspaper, reported, "Inclement weather, the non-appearance of one group and numerous technical failures turned the University's main contribution to the Brighton Arts Festival into disappointment both for its organisers and the 1,400 people who flooded into Falmer House Courtyard last Saturday night. Technical troubles started almost immediately after the start of the show when one of the giant 35mm projectors burst into flame. Several fuses burned out and very few if any of the mechanical effects worked. When at about 10.15pm the evening first looked like failing it was arranged that the Pink Floyd who were originally to have appeared for two half hour spots were to go on at 10.30pm for an hour. This should have solved some problems since this group had stated that they did not wish the University's lights to operate while they were on stage preferring to use just their own. The light crews therefore had an hour in which to organise the rest of the show starting with the air raid sequence as Pink Floyd finished. This, when it came, could not be described as successful as somehow the volume of the sirens had been turned down and

the two search lights were lost in the glare of the other lights which were left on. Two young girls were mesmerised by the lights and music and had to be treated by the first aid unit."

WEDNESDAY 15 MAY – RECORDING SESSION
EMI Studios, Abbey Road, London, England

Banding the mono edition of *A Saucerful of Secrets*. The session was produced by Norman Smith. Pink Floyd were not in attendance.

FRIDAY 17 MAY – PERFORMANCE
Middle Earth, Covent Garden, London, England

With Alexis Korner, Free, DJ Jeff Dexter and Chakra.

WEDNESDAY 22 MAY – PERFORMANCE
Hotel Billard Palace, Antwerp, Belgium

With Inez & The Racers.
This show was billed as the "Big finale of the competition of Beat Ensembles Pop 68" and sponsored by the city newspaper *Volksgazet*.

THURSDAY 23 MAY – PERFORMANCE
Whisky A Go Go, RK Verenigingsgebouw,
Zaandam, Netherlands

Early evening show, with The Berry Bush Set.
Set list: 'Astronomy Domine', 'Interstellar Overdrive', 'Set The Controls For The Heart Of The Sun', 'Corporal Clegg', 'A Saucerful Of Secrets'.

THURSDAY 23 MAY – PERFORMANCE
Paradiso, Amsterdam, Netherlands

Late evening show.

FRIDAY 24 MAY – CANCELLED PERFORMANCE
The Punch Bowl public house, Lapworth,
Solihull, near Birmingham, England

Pink Floyd was held up at Customs on their return from the Netherlands, forcing the cancellation of their appearance.

SATURDAY 25 MAY – PERFORMANCE
Mayfair Suite, The Belfry Hotel, Wishaw,
Sutton Coldfield, near Birmingham, England

With Young Blood and supported by Pineapple Incident. Admission included supper.

SUNDAY 26 MAY – PERFORMANCE
OZ Magazine Benefit, Middle Earth,
Covent Garden, London, England

One of a series of benefit shows for *OZ* magazine, which was going through its usual round of difficulties with the authorities. Also appearing were the Pretty Things, Social Deviants, Blonde on Blonde, Alexis Korner, Miss Kelly, the Flamingoes, Buzby Lloyd, DJs John Peel and Jeff Dexter, and the Trancendental Aurora Light Show.
Set list included: 'Let There Be More Light', 'Interstellar Overdrive', 'Set The Controls For The Heart Of The Sun'.

MONDAY 27 MAY – RECORDING SESSION
Machine Room 8, EMI Studios,
Abbey Road, London, England

Lacquers were cut for the mono version of the album *A Saucerful of Secrets*. The session was produced by Norman Smith, engineered by Anthony Clarke. Pink Floyd was not in attendance.

TUESDAY 28 MAY – RECORDING SESSION
Machine Room 8, EMI Studios,
Abbey Road, London, England

Lacquers were cut for the stereo version of *A Saucerful of Secrets*. The session was produced by Norman Smith, engineered by Harry Moss. Pink Floyd was not in attendance.

FRIDAY 31 MAY – PERFORMANCE
Paradiso, Amsterdam, Netherlands

Early evening show, supported by Circus.
Set list: 'Let There Be More Light', 'Interstellar Overdrive', 'Set The Controls For The Heart Of The Sun', 'A Saucerful Of Secrets'.

Pink Floyd's performance was also filmed at this show and brief excerpts appeared in the arts programme *Open Oog* [*Open Eye*] in a feature about the Paradiso. It was broadcast (in black and white) on Netherland 2 TV on Saturday 5 July 1968 between 7.25pm and 8.00pm.

FRIDAY 31 MAY – PERFORMANCE
Fantasio, Amsterdam, Netherlands

Late evening show, supported by Circus.
Set list: 'Keep Smiling People' (an unrecorded instrumental similar to 'Careful With That Axe, Eugene'), 'Let There Be More Light', 'Set The Controls For The Heart Of The Sun', 'Flaming', 'A Saucerful Of Secrets'.

SATURDAY 1 JUNE – PERFORMANCE
Lijn 3, Amsterdam, Netherlands

Afternoon show scheduled at very short notice to replace Captain Beefheart & the Magic Band who cancelled their appearance.

Alsmede zaterdagavond 1 juni 8 uur De Engelse Group
PINK FLOYD
+ LIVING KICK FORMATION
Entree f 3.-

SATURDAY 1 JUNE – PERFORMANCE ▲
't Smurf, De Engh, Bussum, Netherlands

Early evening show supported by Living Kick Formation.

SATURDAY 1 JUNE – UNCONFIRMED PERFORMANCE
De Kentering, Rosmalen, Netherlands

Hit Week previewed this show in a gig listing but no further information could be found.

SATURDAY 1 JUNE – PERFORMANCE
Eurobeurs, Apeldoorn, Netherlands

Late evening show, supported by the Mozarts, Les Copains and Outlook. Pink Floyd turned up for this show very late in the evening, and was only able to perform for a few songs before the venue's curfew. When the club owner, Klaas Muller, turned on the house lights to force them to stop playing, the resultant argument with the band was so fierce it had to be broken up by the local police. The incident was even reported in the local newspaper alongside a photo of Klaas Muller and Pink Floyd's lighting technician John Marsh being interviewed by the police.

SUNDAY 2 JUNE – PERFORMANCE
Concertgebouw, Vlissingen, Netherlands

Late evening show supported by Dragonfly.
Set list included 'Let There Be More Light', 'Flaming'.

MONDAY 3 JUNE – PERFORMANCE ▶
De Pas, Heesch, Netherlands

Afternoon show supported by Chockfull, Blaze, the Bubbles and Beauty Fools.

MONDAY 3 JUNE – PERFORMANCE
Parochieel Ontspannings Centrum,
Weesp, Netherlands

Evening show supported by the Motions.

DE PAS HEESCH
TWEEDE PINKSTERDAG:
☆ CHOCKFULL
☆ BLAZE
☆ THE BUBBLES
☆ PSYCHEDELIC SOUND UIT ENGELAND
PINK FLOYD
met knallende ligtsjoo.

SATURDAY 8 JUNE – PERFORMANCE
Market Hall, Haverfordwest, Wales

Supported by the Bond.
The *West Wales Guardian* reported, "From their 'stage door' arrival in a big black Bentley they were the cynosure of all eyes – and ears. Although some misguided joker cut the cable leads and half a dozen coloured bulbs wouldn't function, the group's £1,000 lighting system, which is so much a part of their act, happily it did not affect greatly the overall psychedelic scene. Seldom have I seen a crowd so sharply divided about the merit, or demerit, of the 'near supersonic' emergence from the group's speakers. Quite honestly I've heard too much of this 'sound', to which no one can possibly dance and the sooner it sinks into limbo the better."

WEDNESDAY 12 JUNE – PERFORMANCE
***May Ball*, King's College, Cambridge, England**

Late evening show, with Fairport Convention, Aynsley Dunbar and The King's Choral scholars plus "dance, jazz, folk and classical guitar musicians".
Pink Floyd reportedly made use of a mind-blowing light show supplied by Cambridge band White Unicorn. Soft Machine was also scheduled to appear but cancelled.

FRIDAY 14 JUNE – PERFORMANCE
***Midsummer Ball*, University College London,**
Bloomsbury, London, England

Pi, the UCL student newspaper, reported, "The big surprise to everyone when the Pink Floyd appeared was how little they missed their recently departed leader Syd Barrett. Now led by bass player Roger Waters they are far and away the 'best' psychedelic blues band in the land and frequently play at Middle Earth (this is a cellar opposite Covent Garden Market – a den where you can dance, sit, listen, eat or even attend more pleasing matters. John Peel is often the compére and makes splendid jokes about drugs and ever present police in fluent Scouse which no one can hear, much less understand)."

SATURDAY 15 JUNE – CANCELLED PERFORMANCE
Magic Village, Manchester, England

Pink Floyd was advertised to appear at an all-night event performing two sets at 7.30pm and 11.30pm but cancelled for unknown reasons. Also appearing were Purple Stone and the Alchemist, the Jack Lancaster – Bruce Mitchell Quartet and the Inner Light Show.

FRIDAY 21 JUNE – CANCELLED PERFORMANCE
Corpus Summer Ball, Corpus College, Oxford, England

Pink Floyd was contracted to appear along with Uther, Pendragon, Soft Machine, Wages of Sin and the Shell Steel Band, but by mid-May only 27 out of 250 tickets had been sold, forcing its cancellation. The Oxford University student newspaper *Cherwell* quoted a JGB Williams of the Ball Committee as saying, "The poster was one of our mistakes. It was almost illegible."

FRIDAY 21 JUNE – PERFORMANCE
Middle Earth, Covent Garden, London, England

With Hurdy Gurdy, Easy Moses and DJ Jeff Dexter (billed as Dexasterous).
Set list included 'Let There Be More Light', 'Flaming', 'Set The Controls For The Heart Of The Sun', 'A Saucerful Of Secrets'.

FRIDAY 21 JUNE – PERFORMANCE
The 1st Holiness Kitschgarten For The Liberation of Love & Peace in Colours, Houtrusthallen, Den Haag, Netherlands

With the Small Faces, the Pretty Things, Dirty Underwear, Group 1850, Chemical Explosions Of Death And War, Living Kick and the Trancendental Aurora Lightshow among others.
Originally advertised for Friday 14 and Saturday 15 June, the event was very poorly attended. Pink Floyd appeared at 4.00am on Saturday 22 June, performing only three songs, including 'Interstellar Overdrive', before returning to the UK.

SATURDAY 22 JUNE – PERFORMANCE ▼
Lower Common Room, University of East Anglia, Norwich, England

With Fairport Convention and the Shell.
Set list included 'Interstellar Overdrive'.

MONDAY 24 JUNE – SINGLE RELEASE (US)
'It Would Be So Nice'

Cash Box wrote that, "The English group made some noise with their last outing, and this moving, psychedelic rocker could send them on a long chart trip."

TUESDAY 25 JUNE – RADIO RECORDING
Top Gear, BBC 201 Piccadilly Studios, Piccadilly, London, England

Pink Floyd recorded a live session for BBC Radio One's *Top Gear* show on this day. Confusingly, and according to BBC archives, two complete shows were recorded with exactly the same material, and with the same timings. The first show was logged as being recorded between 2.30pm and 6.00pm and the second show recorded between 6.00pm and 9.00pm. This information does tend to fly in the face of accepted facts, and with no way of verifying if there were two different recorded shows, the reader must decide what they make of this information.

The separate broadcast sheets state that the first show was broadcast on *Top Gear*, hosted by John Peel, on Sunday 11 August between 3.00pm and 5.00pm and included 'Careful With That Axe, Eugene' (announced as 'Murderistic Woman' and listed in BBC archives as 'Murderotic Woman') (3:05), 'A Saucerful Of Secrets' (announced as 'The Massed Gadgets Of Hercules') (6:50), 'Let There Be More Light' (4:15) and 'Julia Dream' (2:35).

The second show was broadcast on *Top Gear*, hosted by John Peel, on Sunday 8 September between 3.00pm and 5.00pm and included 'Julia Dream' (2:35), 'Careful With That Axe, Eugene' (announced as 'Murderistic Woman' and listed in BBC archives as 'Murderotic Woman') (3:05), 'Let There Be More Light' (4:15) and 'A Saucerful Of Secrets' (announced as 'The Massed Gadgets Of Hercules') (6:50).

During the first recording session Roger Waters was also interviewed, and although it was never broadcast at the time, it was unearthed and edited for the series *The Story of Pop Part 26: Transport by Underground* broadcast on BBC Radio One on Tuesday 12 July 1994 between 9.00pm and 10.00pm.

WEDNESDAY 26 JUNE – PERFORMANCE
Sheffield Arts Festival, Lower Refectory, Sheffield University, Sheffield, England

Supported by Jethro Tull.

FRIDAY 28 JUNE – ALBUM RELEASE (UK)
A Saucerful of Secrets

Record Mirror wrote, "Taking 'Let There Be...' as a sampler, this instantly impacts itself as a truly inventive barrier-breaking group performance. The avant-garde writers have already raved about it – and certainly it's way ahead of the singles style of this somewhat under-rated outfit. Particularly on the instrumental side, they launch often savage waves of sound – mostly beautifully constructed and of splendid power. Very highly recommended."

A SAUCERFUL OF SECRETS

SIDE ONE

LET THERE BE MORE LIGHT (Waters) **5:38**
REMEMBER A DAY (Wright) **4:33**
SET THE CONTROLS FOR THE HEART OF THE SUN
(Waters) **5:27**
CORPORAL CLEGG (WATERS) **4:12**

SIDE TWO

A SAUCERFUL OF SECRETS (Waters, Wright, Mason,
Gilmour) **11:59**
SEE-SAW (Wright) **4:36**
JUGBAND BLUES (Barrett) **3:00**

RELEASE DATE

UK: Friday 28 June 1968.
US: Saturday 27 July 1968.

FORMAT

UK: Columbia EMI SCX 6258 (Stereo Vinyl album).
UK: Columbia EMI SX 6258 (Mono Vinyl album).
US: Tower ST 5131 (Stereo vinyl album).

HIGHEST CHART POSITION

UK: No.9 (*Melody Maker* 'Pop 30' on Saturday 17 August 1968).

AWARDS

UK: Certified Silver on Monday 22 July 2013.

ARTWORK

On the front cover is a montage of some fourteen separate
superimpositions including the face of the Living Tribunal in the
upper left corner, Dr Strange on the mid-right side, and the swathe of
planets across the middle – all of which are taken from Marvel Comics'
Strange Tales #158 published in July 1967. In the centre the figure with
arms outstretched and circular chart above is an illustration of the
Rosicrucian Alchemical Cosmology of Inspiration taken from 'Janitor
Pansophus' or 'Figura Anenea Quadriparita' bound into the 1677
edition of *Musaeum Hermeticum*. The various alchemical bottles may
be taken from the *Splendor Solis*, a medieval illuminated alchemical
manuscript. The photo of the band was taken by the bank of Pen
Ponds, Richmond Park, London, England.

MUSICIANS

Syd Barrett (Guitar and Vocals on 'Jugband Blues'. Guitars on 'Set The
Controls For The Heart Of The Sun' and 'Remember A Day').
David Gilmour (Guitar. Vocals on 'Corporal Clegg' and 'Let There Be
More Light'. Vocalization on 'A Saucerful Of Secrets').
Nick Mason (Drums, Percussion. Vocals on 'Corporal Clegg').
Roger Waters (Bass Guitar, Percussion. Vocals on 'Let There Be More
Light' and 'Set The Controls For The Heart Of The Sun').
Richard Wright (Piano, Hammond, Farfisa, Mellotron, Vibraphone,
Xylophone. Vocals on 'Let There Be More Light', 'Remember A Day' and
'See-Saw'. Vocalization on 'A Saucerful Of Secrets').

ADDITIONAL MUSICIANS

Norman Smith (Drums and Backing Vocals on 'Remember A Day').
Members of the Stanley Myers Orchestra (Brass on 'Corporal Clegg').
Members of the Salvation Army International Staff Band comprising
Ray Bowes (Cornet), Terry Camsey (Cornet), Mac Carter (Trombone),
Les Condon (Eb bass), Maurice Cooper (Euphonium), Ian Hankey
(Trombone), George Whittingham (Bb bass) (Brass on 'Jugband Blues').

RECORDING DETAILS

Work commenced on *A Saucerful of Secrets* at Abbey Road on
7 August 1967 with further sessions continuing at De Lane Lea, almost
immediately after the release of their debut album.
    The unreleased track 'Scream Thy Last Scream' was originally
proposed as the follow up single to 'See Emily Play', and coupled with
'Vegetable Man' it is the most widely bootlegged of Pink Floyd out-
takes not to have received an official release at time of writing.
    Further out-takes included an aborted attempt at their live
favourite 'Reaction In G' in August 1967, and the previously

undocumented tracks 'The Boppin' Sound' and 'Richard's Rave Up'.

Three oddities were also recorded at De Lane Lea: 'John Latham', a track that was commissioned for an art installation by the artist himself; an untitled instrumental; and 'In The Beechwoods', which was abandoned but copied for Barrett in May 1968 for his initial solo recordings.

One last outtake, entitled 'Early Morning Henry' was removed from the studio the day it was recorded by producer Norman Smith, and is now vanished forever. What is particularly exceptional is the uncredited contribution of members of the Stanley Myers Orchestra on the track 'Corporal Clegg', which was also announced in the music press on 10 February 1968 as the band's next single due for release in March.

This was followed by *Record Mirror* on 30 March 1968 who reported the album would be called *Corporal Clegg* and would include the track 'Electric, Electric Shock', although this title appears nowhere in the archives.

Barrett's contribution to *A Saucerful of Secrets* is minimal with just one song-writing credit: the sadly prophetic 'Jugband Blues' written just prior to his departure. *Melody Maker* on 9 December 1967 reported they had, "met Barrett and guitarist Roger Waters with managers Jenner and Andrew King at the Central Office of Information in Lambeth. They had been viewing a colour film insert of the group for a magazine programme on Britain networked across America and Canada. The number they filmed was 'Jugband Blues' written by Barrett which manager Jenner said he had wanted to release as their single instead of 'Apples And Oranges'. He said he was pressing for it to be their next single in the New Year. It is almost a poetic recitation by Barrett, with avant-garde sound effects by the group. The centre passage is almost free form pop, with six members of the Salvation Army on the recording session told to 'play what you like.'"

Barrett also plays on 'Set The Controls For The Heart Of The Sun', which is hardly surprising, given the recording process for this track began in August 1967. The only other indication of his contribution comes via a surprisingly coherent response to a reader's letter published in *Melody Maker* on 7 June 1968. In his reply he states that he only played on 'Remember A Day' and added that there had been complications regarding the album. It has been said that his former band mates had made this concession merely to compensate him for the long hours he had spent in the recording studio's reception

area waiting to be invited inside. Incidentally it is also on this track that Norman Smith performed drums in place of Mason, who was struggling with his technique.

Since the album was already in progress when Gilmour joined, his involvement was also minimal and he reportedly received a £300 flat fee for his performance as well as a quarter share in the publishing rights of the title track. "I contributed what I could but I was, quite honestly, a little on the outside through it all. I certainly didn't feel like a full member and I wasn't up front contributing all the way on it."[1]

His suspicions about the band being a pretty weird bunch were confirmed when he saw Waters and Mason "draw out [the track] 'A Saucerful Of Secrets' as an architectural diagram, in dynamic form rather than any sort of musical form, with peaks and troughs."[2] It was an ambitious 12-minute piece, divided into four distinct parts.

This must have been an alienating experience for someone who had just come from a pop-rock covers band, and it's unlikely he was given any clear definition as to the extent he was expected to inject his ideas. While there could be no doubting his ability, his playing style and vocal range were quite removed from Barrett's and it took him some time to find his feet, even more so in the recording studio. "I don't think they, the rest of the band, had fixed ideas of what I should do or how I should do it. I mean I just played rhythm to help it all along. For a good six months, maybe more. I didn't do a single thing. I was pretty paranoid."[3]

On the subject of Gilmour and the management split, Jenner says, "I remember Dave [Gilmour] being auditioned in Abbey Road. Somebody said, 'C'mon, Dave, give us your Hendrix.' And out came this extraordinary sound, quite breathtaking. That was the thing, though; Dave was a great mimic. He could play like Hendrix, and he could also do Syd."[4]

Live, both 'A Saucerful Of Secrets' and 'Set The Controls For The Heart Of The Sun' remained central to their set-list for many years to come, and were frequently performed by Roger Waters during his many solo tours. Nick Mason was even quoted in January 2015 as saying that, "I usually cite 'Set The Controls For The Heart Of The Sun' as my favourite Pink Floyd song. It's fun to play, and has interesting dynamics. I know exactly where it came from in terms of the drum part, which was Chico Hamilton playing in a film called *Jazz on a Summer's Day*. He does a drum solo played with mallets."[5]

1. *The Pink Floyd Story*, Capital Radio, 17 December 1976.
2. *Mojo*, May 1994.
3. *Sounds*, 6 October 1973.
4. *Mojo*, November 2001.
5. *GQ*, February 2015.

A SAUCERFUL OF SECRETS

Let There Be More Light

Take 1 (RM2 / RS4).
Basic track recorded as "Untitled" on 18 January 1968 (Take 1).
Vocals and Guitar overdubbed onto Take 1 on 18 January 1968.
Rhythm Track recorded on 18 January 1968 (Take 2).
Take 2 of "Rhythm Track" overdubbed onto Take 1 on 25 March 1968.
Vocals overdubbed onto Take 1 on 1 April 1968.
Remixed on 23 April 1968 (RM2).
Remixed on 26 April 1968 (RS2) and on 2 May 1968 (RS4).

Remember A Day

Take unknown (RM5 / RS1).
Basic track and all overdubs recorded on 9, 10 & 11 October 1967.
Remixed on 12 October 1967 (RM5 and RS1).

Set The Controls For The Heart Of The Sun

Take 2 (RM3 / RS4).
Basic track recorded on 8 August 1967 (Take 2).
Vibraphone and Voices overdubbed onto Take 2 on 23 October 1967.
Vocals and Organ overdubbed onto Take 2 on 11 January 1968.
Remixed on 23 April 1968 (RM3).
Remixed on 2 May 1968 (RS4).

Corporal Clegg

Take 8 (RM4 / RS4).
Basic track recorded on 31 January 1968 (Take 5).
Unspecified overdubs recorded onto Take 6 on 1 February 1968.
Remixed on 1 February 1968 (RM1).
Unspecified overdubs recorded onto Take 6 on 7 February 1968 (relabelled Take 7).
Unspecified overdubs recorded onto Take 6 on 7 February 1968 (relabelled Take 8 "Best Fade").
Unspecified overdubs recorded onto Take 6 on 7 February 1968.
Remixed on 8 February 1968 (RM4).
Orchestral end section "Edit Piece" [Stanley Myers Orchestra] recorded on 12 February 1968 (labelled Take 9 and Take 10).
Take 9 and Take 10 "Edit Piece" edited into Take 8 on 12 February 1968.
Remixed on 15 February 1968 (RM1 with Lead Vocals).
Remixed on 15 February 1968 (RM1 without Lead Vocals).
"Edit for End Section" made on 25 March 1968 (relabelled Take 11).
Remixed on 24 April 1968 (RM4).
Remixed on 30 April 1968 (RS4).

A Saucerful Of Secrets

Take 1/2 (RM1 / RS5).
Basic track recorded as "Nick's Boogie" on 3 April 1968 (Take 1).
Basic track recorded as "Nick's Boogie, Second Movement" on 3 April 1968 (Take 1).
Basic track re-recorded as "Nick's Boogie" on 5 April 1968 (Take 2).
Basic track recorded as "Nick's Boogie, Third Movement" on 5 April 1968 (Take 2).
Unspecified recordings overdubbed onto Take 2 of "Nick's Boogie, Third Movement" on 9 April 1968.
"Edit Piece" recorded for Take 2 of 'Nick's Boogie, Third Movement' on 9 April 1968.
Vocals and "Noises" overdubbed onto Take 1 of 'Nick's Boogie' on 10 April 1968.
"Wild Guitar Track" recorded for Take 1 of 'Nick's Boogie' on 10 April 1968.
"Wild Guitar Track" with Guitar and Piano recorded for Take 1 of "Nick's Boogie" on 10 April 1968.
"Nick's Boogie, First Movement" remixed on 10 April 1968 (RM1).
"Nick's Boogie, Second Movement" remixed on 10 April 1968 (RM2).
"Nick's Boogie, Third Movement" remixed on 23 April 1968 (RM1).
"Nick's Boogie, Second Movement" remixed on 24 April 1968 (RM3).
"Nick's Boogie, First Movement" remixed on 10 April 1968 (RS1 & RS2 edited together).
"Nick's Boogie" Remixed on 10 April 1968 (RS3 & RS4 edited together and relabelled RS5).

See-Saw

Take 8 (RM3 / RS4).
Basic track recorded as "The Most Boring Song I've Ever Heard, Bar Two" on 25 January 1968 (Take 4).
Basic track re-recorded on 25 January 1968 (Take 6).
Unspecified recordings overdubbed onto Take 6 on 31 January 1968.
Take 6 tape reduction on 31 January 1968 (relabelled Take 8).
Unspecified recordings overdubbed onto Take 8 on 1 February 1968.
Remixed on 22 April 1968 (RM2 and RM3).
Remixed on 26 April 1968 (RS2) and on 3 May 1968 (RS4).

Jugband Blues

Take unknown (RM1 / RS1).
Basic track and all overdubs recorded on 9, 10 & 11 October 1967.
Orchestral section recorded and overdubbed on 19 October 1967.
Remixed on 8 May 1968 (RM1 and RS1).

Scream Thy Last Scream (Unreleased)

Basic track recorded on 7 August 1967 (Take 4).
Unspecified recordings overdubbed onto Take 4 on 20 December 1967.
Vocals overdubbed onto Take 4 on 11 January 1968.

Reaction In G (Unreleased)

Recorded on 15 and 16 August 1967 (Takes unknown).

Vegetable Man (Unreleased)

Recorded on 9, 10 and 11 October 1967 (Takes unknown).

John Latham (Unreleased)

Recorded 20 October 1967 (Takes unknown).

Instrumental (Unreleased)

Recorded 20 October 1967 (Take 1).

In The Beechwoods (Unreleased)

Recorded 20 October 1967 (Takes 2–5).

Early Morning Henry (Unreleased)

Recorded on 23 October 1967 (Take 1).

The Boppin' Sound (Unreleased)

Recorded on 13 February 1968 (Take 1).
Remixed on 13 February 1968 (RM1).

Richard's Rave Up (Unreleased)

Recorded on 13 February 1968 (Take 1).

FRIDAY 28 JUNE – TELEVISION RECORDING
Release, Studio 7, BBC TV Centre,
White City, London, England

Pink Floyd performed 'A Saucerful Of Secrets' live for the magazine programme *Release*. Rehearsals and recording commenced at 10.30am. The 11-minute article was broadcast on BBC2 TV on Saturday 29 June 1968 between 10.10pm and 10.55pm, and included an interview with Roger Waters by the programme presenter Tony Palmer and an excerpt of Pink Floyd's performance of 'Set The Controls For The Heart Of The Sun' taken from the forthcoming Omnibus special *All My Loving*. Parts of the *Release* programme, including 'Set The Controls For The Heart Of The Sun', was repeated on BBC2 TV on Friday 5 July 1968 between 11.15pm and 12.00am as part of the magazine programme *Late Night Line Up*.

**FRIDAY 28 JUNE –
PERFORMANCE ▶**
*Students Celebration
Dance - The End Of It
All Ball*, Music Hall,
Shrewsbury, England

With the Miss Shropshire Student Contest and supporting groups.

**SATURDAY 29 JUNE –
PERFORMANCE**
*Midsummer High
Weekend*, The Cockpit,
Hyde Park, London,
England

FRIDAY, JUNE 28, 1968
MUSIC HALL, SHREWSBURY
STUDENTS CELEBRATION DANCE
The End Of It All Ball
— PRESENTING —
THE PINK FLOYD
and Supporting Groups
plus MISS SHROPSHIRE STUDENT Contest
9-2 a.m. — DRESS (if you want to)
Tickets 10/-. (12 6d. at the door), from:
BERT DANN'S, PRINCESS STREET, OR MUSIC HALL.

Afternoon show, with Tyrannosaurus Rex, Roy Harper and Jethro Tull. Pink Floyd headlined the first ever Hyde Park free concert, organised by Blackhill Enterprises.
Set list: 'Let There Be More Light', 'Set The Controls For The Heart Of The Sun', 'A Saucerful Of Secrets' (with Roy Harper on cymbals), 'Interstellar Overdrive'.

BELOW: ROY HARPER JOINING PINK FLOYD ON STAGE AT HYDE PARK, 29 JUNE 1968.

SATURDAY 29 JUNE – CANCELLED PERFORMANCE
Town Hall, Torquay, England

With Phydeaux Lime and the Phaze.
According to the promoter, Pink Floyd reneged on their contract to appear, preferring to stay in London after their Hyde Park show. Although various excuses were provided, legal action was threatened, and Pink Floyd's management eventually settled out of court.

PINK FLOYD ROAD CREW TO JANUARY 1969
Peter Watts (Road Manager / Sound Engineer).

US TOUR

Pink Floyd's second US tour was also beset by problems concerning their work permits, which again had not been issued in time. This meant a delayed start to the tour and their entry to the USA via New York on Thursday 4 July was on a tourist visa. They reportedly decamped to Canada to square the paperwork immediately after the shows in New York.

Additionally, Nick Mason has stated in his book *Inside Out* that the band performed at the Whisky a Go Go, Los Angeles, USA but venue advertisements in the local press throughout this period do not include Pink Floyd, so this is highly unlikely. However, it is not inconceivable that a press reception may have been held there, at which Pink Floyd may have performed.

Despite some glowing reviews, Pink Floyd's US tour was patchy at best and with too much time spent holed up in motels between shows the band decided to cut their losses and return to the UK. This resulted in the cancellation of their appearance at two festival shows, including the *Sky River Rock Festival and Lighter than Air Fair* at Betty Nelson's Organic Raspberry Farm, Sultan, WA, on Saturday 31 August, which featured appearances by Kaleidoscope, Muddy Waters, Peanut Butter Conspiracy, Santana, Country Joe & the Fish, John Fahey, HP Lovecraft, Steppenwolf and the Youngbloods among others, and the *Oakland Pop Festival* at the Baldwin Pavilion, Oakland University, Rochester, MI, on Sunday 1 September, with Procol Harum, the Rationals, SRC, Thyme, MC5, Jagged Edge, Psychedelic Stooges [later known as the Stooges and featuring Iggy Pop], Frost and the Children. Howlin' Wolf and Chrysalis were also billed but did not appear.

Also reported was a three-night stand at the Electric Theater, Chicago, between Friday 30 August and Sunday 1 September, where Pink Floyd was replaced by Nova and Litter on Friday 30 August and Sunday 1 September, and Nova and the Chicago Transit Authority on Sunday 31 August. The Electric Theatre was renamed Kinetic Playground shortly after the date was advertised.

MONDAY 8 JULY – PERFORMANCE
Kinetic Playground, Chicago, IL, USA

It was reported that one of Gilmour's guitars was stolen en-route to this show. However, there is some doubt as to whether it happened at all because no adverts, press or eyewitness reports could be found for the show. However,

Dancing-Blues-Concert
TUES. &'WED. ONLY
Dir. Fr. Eng.
Only N.Y. Apprce. **PINK FLOYD**

JOHN HAMMOND TRIO
(John Hammond Trio
& Kenny Rankin Thru Sun.)

July 29
Thru Aug 1 **BUDDY GUY**

Steve
Paul **SCENE**   201 W. 46th St.
JU 2-5760

a bizarre reference to this show appeared in an interview given to the *Hollywood Reporter* in September 2013 by legendary manager and agent Shep Gordon following the release of Mike Myers' documentary film *Supermensch: The Legend of Shep Gordon* in which he described managing Pink Floyd for just nine days: "It was very bizarre. We got them a show in Chicago at a place called the Kinetic Playground. And when they got there the place had burned down. They never got paid. The owner had torched the place. They assumed I knew it had happened, and that was it. Nine days later we were fired. We got a letter from Mason Towers – Nick Mason was the drummer. We were like, 'Oh my God, he has his own building?' In fact the timeline is slightly blurred; the Kinetic Playground burned down on Friday 7 November 1969, over a year later, in mysterious circumstances, midway through a King Crimson residency.

TUESDAY 9 JULY – PRESS RECEPTION
Michael Mann's, New York, NY, USA

Tower Records held a press reception for the band at this popular New York nightspot.

FRIDAY 12 JULY – PERFORMANCE
Grande Ballroom, Detroit, MI, USA

Supported by the Thyme and the Jagged Edge.
Set list: 'Interstellar Overdrive', 'A Saucerful Of Secrets', 'Set The Controls For The Heart Of The Sun', 'Astronomy Domine', 'Flaming'.

Reviewing the show underground newspaper *Detroit Fifth Estate* reported, "Pink Floyd is a very weird group. I know that they were

unbelievably bad at the Grande and I'm not about to try and excuse them other than say that in every other performance in this country and in England they ably demonstrated that they are the 'best' psychedelic group in the world. They have never claimed to be the world's 'best' musicians, and they are really at 'best' with their own light show, so unless you have a light show of your own – just close your eyes and turn your amplifier fully on, and your parents fully off by putting *A Saucerful of Secrets* on. Although the album is by no means indicative of what the group is really – oh well, there is absolutely no point in saying this. Either you dig the Floyd or you don't. I do."

MONDAY 15, TUESDAY 16 & WEDNESDAY 17 JULY – PERFORMANCES ◄
Steve Paul's The Scene, New York, NY, USA

Supported by Fleetwood Mac (Monday 15 July) and the John Hammond Trio (Tuesday 16 & Wednesday 17 July).
Set list on Monday 15 July: 'Interstellar Overdrive', 'Let There Be More Light', 'Set The Controls For The Heart Of The Sun', 'Astronomy Domine', 'Flaming', 'A Saucerful Of Secrets'.

Billboard reported, "Pink Floyd overpowered a packed house at the Scene on Monday in a varied programme with a strong emphasis on space and oriental sounds. In the first night of a three-day engagement the quartet was joined by Fleetwood Mac, which made an excellent impression in its initial set. While both British acts were well received, the inventiveness of Tower Records' Pink Floyd was the most remarkable. From opening 'Interstellar Overdrive' to closing 'A Saucerful Of Secrets', the group displayed top-flight musicianship and consistent interest. An act that requires top effort from each member, Pink Floyd drew just that. The selection that made greatest use of church organ effect, however, was 'Astronomy Domine'. Gilmour's 'best' vocal was 'Flaming'. But, it was their inventiveness, musicianship and ability to say something musically, whether playing and vocalising softly or overwhelming with cascades of sound."

TUESDAY 23 JULY – TELEVISION RECORDING
Hy Lit Show, **WKBS–TV Studios, Philadelphia, PA, USA**

Pink Floyd appeared on the *Hy Lit Show*, hosted by Hyman Litsky, although Pink Floyd's contribution is unknown. It was first broadcast on WKBS–TV network Channel 48 on Saturday 12 October 1968 between 6.30pm and 7.00pm (EST).

BELOW: PERFORMING AT STEVE PAUL'S THE SCENE CLUB IN NEW YORK, 15 JULY 1968.

WEDNESDAY 24 JULY – PERFORMANCE
Philadelphia Music Festival,
John F. Kennedy Stadium, Philadelphia, PA, USA

With the Who (headline), the Troggs, the Mandala and Friends of the Family with lights by the Joshua Light Show.
Set list included: 'Let There Be More Light', 'Set The Controls For The Heart Of The Sun', 'A Saucerful Of Secrets'.

Friends of the Family and Pink Floyd (billed as special guests replacing the advertised Procol Harum who cancelled due to problems with work permits) were the only two bands to play at this show in front of approximately 1,000 people in a 100,0000-capacity venue. When the third band on the bill, the Mandala, began their set a lightning strike hit the stage and forced the early closure of the event.

FRIDAY 26 JULY – PERFORMANCE ▼
**Shrine Exposition Hall, Exposition Park,
Los Angeles, CA, USA**

With Blue Cheer (headline) and the Jeff Beck Group [featuring Rod Stewart, Ron Wood and Mickey Waller] (opening) with lights by Single Wing Turquoise Bird.
Set list: 'Interstellar Overdrive', 'Matilda Mother', 'Set The Controls For The Heart Of The Sun', 'A Saucerful Of Secrets'.

The *L.A. Free Press* reported, "The Shrine Hall was so sweltering sticky hot that had you been in some vague bummer frame of mind you might have taken one look at Single Wing Turquoise Bird's light-show, heard Pink Floyd's 'Interstellar Overdrive', and imagined you were in some fundamentalist tent-show evangelist's version of hell. What I hadn't counted on was that the Jeff Beck group, sandwiched between the other two, would put both Pink Floyd AND Blue Cheer to shame. Pink Floyd on record is one thing: live, they're something else. Disappointing. It isn't the overdubbing, the reverses, or the sound effects you particularly miss, but studio control and balance. Clarity. At the Shrine, even the maddening celestial cacophony of 'Overdrive' came off as listless and muddled, sadly lacking in spark and distinction. Maybe it's Rick Wright's organ which saves the Floyd's concerts from disaster. He wanders into some strange things – hypnotic arabesques in 'Matilda Mother', labrynthian flights in 'Set The Controls For The Heart Of The Sun', and mystical mazes in 'A Saucerful Of Secrets'. 'Heart Of The Sun' is an object lesson in the disparity between recorded and live Floyd. On disc, it's a belladonna trip through the inner limits of the listeners' body. Nicky Mason's drums beat out steady rays of sunlight, while Wright's organ evokes the dancing of the rays on waves in a sea of blood. Towards the end, the Floyd ingeniously mixes in the sounds of seagulls and breakers. But in concert much of the ethereality is lost. The organ almost obliterates Syd Barrett's guitar, and Roger Waters, the bassist-vocalist, tries to imitate the gulls and breakers vocally. The result is almost embarrassingly inadequate."

SATURDAY 27 JULY – ALBUM RELEASE (US)
A Saucerful of Secrets

Rolling Stone wrote, "Unfortunately the Pink Floyd's second album, *A Saucerful of Secrets*, is not as interesting as their first, as a matter of fact, it is rather mediocre. With Barrett gone we are left with the work of bassist Roger Waters and organist Rick Wright. Waters is an uninteresting writer, vocalist and bass player. "Let There Be More Light" and "Set The Controls For The Heart Of The Sun" are boring melodically, harmonically and lyrically. The production work is not as glittery as the first album's, and the instrumental work is shoddy and routine; yet both tracks run for some five minutes, two examples of unnecessary length in rock."

SATURDAY 27 JULY – PERFORMANCE
Shrine Exposition Hall, Los Angeles, CA, USA

With Blue Cheer (headline) and the Jeff Beck Group [featuring Rod Stewart, Ron Wood and Mickey Waller] (opening) with lights by Single Wing Turquoise Bird.
Set list included 'Interstellar Overdrive', 'A Saucerful Of Secrets'.

FRIDAY 2, SATURDAY 3 & SUNDAY 4 AUGUST – PERFORMANCES
Avalon Ballroom, San Francisco, CA, USA

Supported by Chrome Syrcus and Holy Modal Rounders with lights by Electro Luminescence.

**FRIDAY 9, SATURDAY 10 & SUNDAY 11 AUGUST –
PERFORMANCES ▶**
Eagles Auditorium, Seattle, WA, USA

Supported by Blue Cheer with lights by the Retina Circus Light Company. The *Seattle Times* reported, "The Pink Floyd, a British rock group on its first visit to Seattle, uses electricity to become complex. Besides organ, drums, guitar and singing, they use vocal hisses, clicks and bird calls that sound as if Marin Denny had joined a rock group. Their amplifiers make science fiction sounds that lift rock into the realm of modern composers like Karlheinz Stockhausen and Pierre Boulez. The group plays music it composes itself. Ninety percent of a performance is improvised – only beginnings and ends of selections are set, they say."

FRIDAY 16 & SATURDAY 17 AUGUST – PERFORMANCES
Sound Factory, Sacramento, CA, USA ▶

Supported by Initial Shock and AB Skhy Blues Band. Members of the band are reported to have seen the Who perform at the Fillmore West, San Francisco, on Thursday 15 August.

MONDAY 26 AUGUST – SINGLE RELEASE (US)
'Let There Be More Light'

Cash Box wrote, "This side from England's psychedelic blues group is a strong contender for chart standing. Kids will dig the outer-space feel."

THURSDAY 22 AUGUST – RECORDING SESSION
Capitol Studios, Capitol Records Building, Hollywood, Los Angeles, CA, USA

An unusual diversion to their US tour saw the band enter Capitol Studios to record two new tracks: 'Instrumental' ['Careful With That Axe, Eugene'] (Take 1 False Start, Take 2 at 3:15, Takes 3 & 4 False Starts, Take 5 at 3:08, and Take 6 at 3:20 also marked "best"), and 'Roger's Boogie' (Take 1 at 4:53, and Take 2 at 4:36 also marked "best"). None of the recordings were developed any further and the tapes remain in the Capitol archive until the 2016 release of the box set *The Early Years 1965–1972* and relaased under the titles 'Song 1 Live, Los Angeles, 1968)' and 'Roger's Boogie (Live Los Angeles, 1968)'.

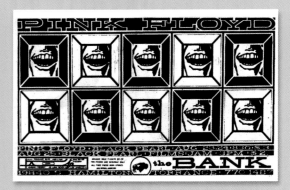

FRIDAY 23 & SATURDAY 24 AUGUST – PERFORMANCES ▲
The Bank, Torrance, Los Angeles, CA, USA

Supported by Black Pearl.
Open City reported, "Top billing this week at the Bank, just off the Harbor Freeway at Torrance, went to the Pink Floyd, a psychedelic progressive rock group from England. The PF led by vocalist and lead guitarist David Gilmore [sic], is a four-man outfit, with Rodger Waters on the bass guitar; Rick Wright, organ and piano; and Nicky

ABOVE: PINK FLOYD PERFORMING AT KASTIVAL, 31 AUGUST, 1968.

Mason, drums. Gilmore's vocals were drowned out at times by a wall of electronic gadgetry, but displayed a worthy lyric sound. Gilmore [sic] also has a touch at solo feedback work. Waters backs up well on his bass and in vocal sections, and Wright's semi atonal organ solos were simple compared to the tight, involved music of the total group. Mason gave instant stability with a beat steadier than most groups·could stand. Lighting design by Bob Stone and Mike Devine is making a tough bid at stealing the show."

FRIDAY 23 AUGUST – CANCELLED PERFORMANCE
Jazz Bilzen Festival, Bilzen, Belgium

Pink Floyd's appearance was cancelled due to the extension of their US tour. Other advertised performers at the three-day event included the Pretty Things (who replaced Pink Floyd), the Action, Tyrannosaurus Rex, the Simon Dupree Big Sound, the Move, the Vipers, Dr. Dereck, Roland and his Blues Workshop, Stable, Brian and the High Five, the Sweet Feeling, the Pebbles, Highway Rescue Group, Living Kick Formation, Dragonfly and Zen and headliners the Small Faces, and an end of night jam with Cuby and the Blizzards, Alexis Korner, Steve Marriot and Chris Farlowe (Saturday 24 August), and the Dexter Gordon Quartet, Archie Shepp and Clark Terry (Sunday 25 August).

SATURDAY 24 AUGUST – CANCELLED PERFORMANCE
The Royal Lido, Central Beach, Prestatyn, Wales

Pink Floyd's appearance was cancelled due to the extension of their US tour.

SATURDAY 31 AUGUST – PERFORMANCE
Kastival '68 Festival, Karekietstraat, Kasterlee, Belgium

With the Martine Bijl, The Cotton City Jazzband, the Dickson Brothers & Derrol Adams, the Milton Buckner Trio, Rita Reys & Pim Jacobs Trio and the Spencer Davis Group, and headliners Dave Pike and Status Quo (1 September).
Set list included 'Astronomy Domine', 'A Saucerful Of Secrets', 'Set The Controls For The Heart Of The Sun'.

Pink Floyd performed a one-hour set in the afternoon on the first day of this two-day festival, having arrived in Belgium directly from the USA on Friday 30 August. The whole event was filmed by BRT TV and highlights, including an interview with Roger Waters and Pink Floyd's performance of 'Astronomy Domine', were broadcast as part of the *Tienerklanken* pop music show in a dedicated 25-minute programme entitled *Kastival 1968* on BRT TV on Tuesday 8 October 1968 between 7.00pm and 7.25pm.

SATURDAY 31 AUGUST – CANCELLED PERFORMANCE
Huis Ter Lucht, Delft, Netherlands

Pink Floyd's early evening show was cancelled due to problems with work permits.

SATURDAY 31 AUGUST – CANCELLED PERFORMANCE
Globe Theatre, Stadsschouwburg, Eindhoven, Netherlands

Pink Floyd's late evening show was cancelled due to problems with work permits. Support bands Dirty Underwear and the New Electric Chamber Music Ensemble had already performed before the venue management made the announcement that Pink Floyd wouldn't be showing, which reportedly caused a near riot among the audience.

SUNDAY 1 SEPTEMBER – CANCELLED PERFORMANCE
Fantasio, Amsterdam, Netherlands

Pink Floyd's evening show was cancelled due to problems with work permits.

WEDNESDAY 4 SEPTEMBER – PERFORMANCE ▼
Middle Earth, **The Club House, Richmond Athletic Club, Richmond, England**

FRIDAY 6 SEPTEMBER – TELEVISION RECORDING
Samedi et Compagnie, **ORTF TV Studios, Buttes Chaumont, Paris, France**

Pink Floyd mimed to 'Let There Be More Light', 'Flaming' and 'Remember A Day' for the magazine programme *Samedi et Compagnie*. It was broadcast (in black and white) on ORTF1 on Saturday 5 October between 4.00pm and 6.20pm.

SUNDAY 8 SEPTEMBER – CANCELLED PERFORMANCE
7th Festival Teenagers, **Parc Communal, Châtelet, Belgium**

Pink Floyd cancelled their headline appearance at this two-day festival because of problems with work permits. Other advertised performers were Opus 23, Marian Maxel, Jean-Marie Merny, Sweet Feeling, Patricia and Serge Lama, the Kinks, Eric Charden, Gilbert Becaud, Micky Day, Nicoletta, Systéme Tony, Jacques Dutronc and the Pebbles (who replaced Pink Floyd), and headliners Inez & the Racers (Saturday 7 September).

MONDAY 9, TUESDAY 10 & WEDNESDAY 11 SEPTEMBER –
CANCELLED RECORDING SESSIONS
Studio 3, EMI Studios, Abbey Road, London, England

Sessions cancelled for unknown reasons and taken instead by the Pretty Things who were recording their album *SF Sorrow*.

FRIDAY 13 SEPTEMBER – PERFORMANCE
Mothers, Erdington, Birmingham, England

Set list included 'Let There Be More Light', 'Set The Controls For The Heart Of The Sun', 'A Saucerful Of Secrets', 'Interstellar Overdrive'.

SATURDAY 14 SEPTEMBER – CANCELLED PERFORMANCE
First Fuq Festivity, **Westerkerk, Leeuwarden, Netherlands**

Pink Floyd's appearance was cancelled due to problems with work permits.

TUESDAY 17 SEPTEMBER – RECORDING SESSION
Studio 3 & Control Room 3, EMI Studios, Abbey Road, London, England

Recording commenced on Pink Floyd's fourth studio album, *Ummagumma*. 2.30pm to 6.00pm: 'Ric's Scene, Part One' ['Sysyphus, Part 1'] recorded (Take 1 untimed and Take 2 at 3:10 also marked "best"), and 7.30pm to 11.30pm: 'Ric's Scene, Part Two' ['Sysyphus, Part 2'] recorded (Takes 3 & 4 untimed and Take 5 at 3:26 also marked "best"). The session was produced by Norman Smith, engineered by Peter Mew and assisted by Jeff Jarrett and Neil Richmond.

TUESDAY 17 SEPTEMBER – FILM SCREENING
All My Loving, **Theatre 4, BBC Lime Grove Studios, Shepherd's Bush, London, England**

Members of Pink Floyd, excluding Richard Wright, and other guests attended a preview screening of the finished BBC TV Omnibus film *All My Loving* in which Pink Floyd was featured. (See Thursday 28 March for further details.)

WEDNESDAY 18 SEPTEMBER – RECORDING SESSION
Studio 3 & Control Room 3, EMI Studios, Abbey Road, London, England

2.30pm to 5.30pm and 7.00pm to 9.30pm: 'Ric's Scene, Part Two' ['Sysyphus, Part 2'] re-recorded (Take 3 at 3:23 also marked "best") for *Ummagumma*. The session was produced by Norman Smith, engineered by Peter Mew and assisted by Jeff Jarrett.

MONDAY 23 SEPTEMBER – RECORDING SESSION
Studio 3 & Control Room 3, EMI Studios, Abbey Road, London, England

2.30pm to 7.00pm: 'Roger's Tune' ['Several Species…'] recorded (Takes 1, 2 & 3 False Starts and Take 4 at 3:30 also marked "best") for *Ummagumma*. The session was produced by Norman Smith, engineered by Peter Mew and assisted by Jeff Jarrett.

TUESDAY 24 SEPTEMBER – RECORDING SESSION
Studio 3 & Control Room 3, EMI Studios, Abbey Road, London, England

2.30pm to 6.15pm: 'Nickey's Tune' ['The Grand Vizier's Garden Party'] recorded (Take 1 at 2:00 and Take 2 at 2:15 also marked "best"), Take 2 of 'Nickey's Tune' overdubbed (and relabelled Take 3 and Take 4 also marked "best"), and 7.30pm to 11.45pm: Take 2 of 'Nickey's Tune' overdubbed (relabelled Take 4 and Take 5 also marked "best") for *Ummagumma*. The session was produced by Norman Smith, engineered by Peter Mew and assisted by Jeff Jarrett (morning) and Neil Richmond (afternoon).

WEDNESDAY 25 SEPTEMBER – RECORDING SESSION
Studio 3 & Control Room 3, EMI Studios,
Abbey Road, London, England

2.30pm to 6.00pm: 'Nicky's Tune (Section 2, Part 2)' ['The Grand Vizier's Garden Party'] recorded (and relabelled Take 6 at 5:11 also marked "best"), and "Rhythm Machine" track recorded (Take 1 at 3.00 also marked "best") and mixed with Take 6 of 'Nicky's Tune (Section 2, Part 2)' for *Ummagumma*. The session was produced by Norman Smith, engineered by Peter Mew and assisted by Jeff Jarrett.

THURSDAY 26 SEPTEMBER – FILM PREMIERE ▼
The Committee, **Cameo Poly Cinema,**
Lower Regent Street, London, England

Peter Sykes' surreal film starring ex-Manfred Mann singer Paul Jones and featuring Pink Floyd's ambient soundtrack opened in London on this date.

International Times said, "Unfortunately, the most dramatic and successful scene, in a conventional sense, occurs at the very opening

of the film and is apt to give the wrong idea of what the film is aiming at. Although *The Committee* is not a complete success it undoubtedly marks a new departure for the British cinema. Arthur Brown makes a suitably apocalyptic appearance with his 'Nightmare' song, and the music for the film is provided by the Pink Floyd. Tom Kempinski makes a superb "victim" in the opening scene, while Paul Jones proves that he can act and is capable of better things than *Privilege*."

THURSDAY 26 SEPTEMBER – PERFORMANCE
Mayfair Ballroom, Newcastle-upon-Tyne, England

With the Nice, the Sect and Coloured Rain.

FRIDAY 27 SEPTEMBER – PERFORMANCE
Queen's Hall, Dunoon, Scotland

Supported by the Poets and DJ Tam Ferrie.
Brian Wilson, promoter of the event, recalled, "Pink Floyd had gone to great lengths to get there, because of the terrible weather. The ferries were off and the band had to hire their own boat from Gourock. It meant they were late and the audience were getting restless. When the audience of 400 heard their futuristic music, the response was less than ecstatic. Although they died on stage, a few people loved it and couldn't believe they were seeing Pink Floyd in Dunoon." Unable to continue their onward journey they did in fact spend the night in a police station, sheltering from the continuing bad weather.

SATURDAY 28 SEPTEMBER – CANCELLED PERFORMANCE
The International Essener Song Tage, **Gruga Halle,**
Essen, West Germany

After the previous evening's fiasco, and being unable to make travel connections, Pink Floyd cancelled their appearance at the

above festival which ran from 25 to 29 September. Other performers scheduled for the same day included Blossom Toes, Tim Buckley, Degenhardt-Beat, Julie Felix , Mothers Of Invention, Olympic, Soul Caravan, Amon Düül, St Giles System and Time Is Now.

TUESDAY 1 OCTOBER – RECORDING SESSION
Studio 3 & Control Room 3, EMI Studios,
Abbey Road, London, England

2.30pm to 6.30pm: Reductions, Sound Effects and Crossfades made for 'Nicky's Tune (Section 1, Part 1)' ['The Grand Vizier's Garden Party'] (Takes 1 & 2 and Take 3 also marked "best"), and 'Nicky's Tune (Section 2, Part 2)' (Take 1, also marked "edited "best""), and 7.30pm to 12.30pm: Reductions, Editing and Crossfades made for 'Nicky's Tune (Sections 1 & 2)' (marked "Edited complete best") for *Ummagumma*. The session was produced by Norman Smith, engineered by Peter Mew and assisted by Nick Webb. It is also noted that a mono copy of the above was made onto a 5-inch spool and taken away by Nick Mason.

WEDNESDAY 2 OCTOBER – RECORDING SESSION
Studio 3 & Control Room 3, EMI Studios,
Abbey Road, London, England

2.30pm to 5.30pm and 6.30pm to 10.00pm: Recording for *Ummagumma*. Paperwork from the archives is missing but this session was most likely used to record further parts of 'Sysyphus'.

THURSDAY 3 OCTOBER – TELEVISION BROADCAST
The Tyrant King, **Thames TV, London, England**

Pink Floyd's music featured heavily in the six-part children's drama, *The Tyrant King*, produced by Thames TV, which began broadcasting on this date on the ITV network between 5.20pm and 5.50pm. It followed the exploits of three hip teenagers as they traversed London's landmark tourist destinations as they slowly uncovered the work of a drug dealer. Aside from a soundtrack that included the music of the Nice, Cream and the Moody Blues, Pink Floyd was heard in the following episodes: Episode 1, *Scarface*, was broadcast on Thursday 3 October 1968 and featured 'A Saucerful Of Secrets'; Episode 2, *Don't Walk, Run!*, was broadcast on Thursday 10 October 1968 and featured 'Astronomy Domine', 'Corporal Clegg', 'Let There Be More Light' and 'Pow R Toc H'; Episode 3, *Nightmare*, was broadcast on Thursday 17 October 1968 and featured 'Pow R Toc H'; Episode 5, *Some Doll!*, was broadcast on Thursday 31 October 1968 and featured 'Interstellar Overdrive'; and Episode 6, *Meet the King*, was broadcast on Thursday 7 November 1968 and featured 'Astronomy Domine'. The series was shot in colour but only ever broadcast once, in black and white. The complete series was eventually released in its colour original on DVD in 2012 (UK: Freemantle / Network 7953519).

FRIDAY 4 OCTOBER – CANCELLED PERFORMANCE
Orford Club, Norwich, England

Following their no-show a news item appeared in the *Eastern Evening News* claiming that Pink Floyd's management knew nothing of this concert, as they were already engaged to perform in Birmingham on that date and that no contract existed with the Orford Club. A rival club immediately seized the opportunity to capitalise on the publicity and successfully booked Pink Floyd for 18 October.

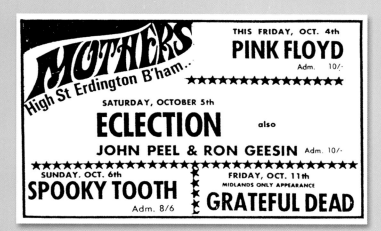

FRIDAY 4 OCTOBER – PERFORMANCE ▲
Mothers, Erdington, Birmingham, England

SUNDAY 6 OCTOBER – PERFORMANCE
The Country Club, Belsize Park, London, England
Supported by Freedom's Children.

TUESDAY 8 OCTOBER – RECORDING SESSION
Studio 3 & Control Room 3, EMI Studios,
Abbey Road, London, England
2.30pm to 5.30pm and 6.30pm to 10.00pm: Recording for the album
Ummagumma. Paperwork from the archives is missing but this session
was most likely used to record further parts of 'Sysyphus'.

WEDNESDAY 9 OCTOBER – RECORDING SESSION
Studio 3 & Control Room 3, EMI Studios,
Abbey Road, London, England
2.30pm to 5.30pm and 6.30pm to 10.00pm: Recording for
Ummagumma. Paperwork from the archives is missing but this session
was most likely used to record further parts of 'Sysyphus'.

WEDNESDAY 16 OCTOBER – PERFORMANCE
Théâtre du Huitième, Lyon, France
With a psychedelic light show by the London Arts Laboratory.
Set list: 'Astronomy Domine', 'A Saucerful Of Secrets', 'Careful With
That Axe, Eugene', 'Interstellar Overdrive', 'It Would Be So Nice',
'Let There be More Light', 'Matilda Mother', 'Set The Controls For The
Heart Of The Sun'.

FRIDAY 18 OCTOBER – PERFORMANCE
Industrial Club, Norwich, England

FRIDAY 18 OCTOBER – CANCELLED PERFORMANCE
Middle Earth, Covent Garden, London, England
Although advertised in the music press, Pink Floyd was
rescheduled to Saturday 26 October.

SATURDAY 19 OCTOBER – CANCELLED PERFORMANCE
Salford University, Salford, Manchester, England
Scaffold replaced the advertised Pink Floyd when they cancelled
this concert in order to play Belgium.

SATURDAY 19 OCTOBER – PERFORMANCE
Theatre 140, Brussels, Belgium

SUNDAY 20 OCTOBER – PERFORMANCE
Theatre 140, Brussels, Belgium
Two shows at 3.30pm and 8.30pm.

MONDAY 21 OCTOBER – CANCELLED RECORDING SESSION
Studio 3 & Control Room 3, EMI Studios,
Abbey Road, London, England
Session cancelled due to a late return from Belgium.

TUESDAY 22 OCTOBER – RECORDING SESSION
Studio 3 & Control Room 3, EMI Studios,
Abbey Road, London, England
2.30pm to 7.00pm: 'Point Me To The Sky' recorded (Takes 1, 2 &
3 Breakdowns, Take 4 False Start and Take 5 at 4:43), and 8.00pm
to 12.30am: 'Point Me To The Sky' recorded (Take 6 at 4:18, also
marked "best") for the 7-inch single. The session was produced
by Norman Smith, engineered by Peter Mew and assisted by Neil
Richmond (afternoon) and Anthony Clarke (evening).

WEDNESDAY 23 OCTOBER – RECORDING SESSION
Studio 3 & Control Room 3, EMI Studios,
Abbey Road, London, England
2.30pm to 6.30pm: 'Point Me To The Sky' re-recorded (Takes 1 &
2 False Starts, Take 3 also marked "best first section", Take 4 False
Start and Take 5 also marked "best second section"), and 7.30pm
to 11.20pm: Guitar and Organ overdubbed onto Take 5 of 'Point
Me To The Sky' for the 7-inch single. The session was produced by
Norman Smith, engineered by Peter Mew and assisted by Graham
Kirkby (afternoon) and Anthony Clarke (evening).

FRIDAY 25 OCTOBER – PERFORMANCE
The Boat House, Kew, London, England

SATURDAY 26 OCTOBER – PERFORMANCE
IC Hop, **Union Hall, Imperial College,**
Kensington, London, England
Early show, with two supporting
groups including the debut show
of Smile, featuring Imperial
College student and future Queen
guitarist Brian May.

SATURDAY 26 OCTOBER –
PERFORMANCE ▶
Middle Earth, **The**
Roundhouse, Chalk Farm,
London, England
Late show with Gary Farr, July and
DJ Jeff Dexter.
Set list included: 'Astronomy Domine',
'Let There Be More Light', 'Interstellar
Overdrive', 'Flaming', 'Set The Controls
For The Heart Of The Sun'.

MONDAY 28 OCTOBER – RECORDING SESSION
Studio 2 & Control Room 2, EMI Studios, Abbey Road, London, England

2.30pm to 7.30pm and 8.30pm to 12.15am: Drums, Guitar, Bass and Organ overdubbed onto Take 5 of 'Point Me To The Sky' (also marked "best") and reductions of Take 5 of 'Point Me To The Sky' (relabelled Take 6 also marked "best") and Vocals overdubbed onto Take 6 of 'Point Me To The Sky' for the 7-inch single. The session was produced by Norman Smith, engineered by Peter Mew and assisted by Neil Richmond.

TUESDAY 29 OCTOBER – RECORDING SESSION
Studio 2 & Control Room 2, EMI Studios, London, England

2.30pm to 5.30pm and 7.00pm to 10.00pm: Cellist, Guitar, Piano, Maracas, Harpsichord and Vocals overdubbed onto Take 6 of 'Point Me To The Sky' for the 7-inch single. The session was produced by Norman Smith, engineered by Peter Mew and assisted by Neil Richmond.

WEDNESDAY 30 OCTOBER – RECORDING SESSION
Studio 2 & Control Room 2, EMI Studios, Abbey Road, London, England

2.30pm to 6.45pm and 8.00pm to 12.15pm: Vocals overdubbed onto Take 6 of 'Point Me To The Sky' for the 7-inch single. The session was produced by Norman Smith, engineered by Peter Mew and assisted by Neil Richmond and Alan Parsons.

THURSDAY 31 OCTOBER – TELEVISION RECORDING
Tous En Scène, L'Antene du Chapiteau du Kremlin-Bicêtre, Val de Marne, Paris, France

Pink Floyd performed 'Let There Be More Light' and 'Flaming' live on the variety programme *Tous en Scéne*. It was broadcast (in colour) on ORTF2 TV on Tuesday 26 November between 8.30pm and 10.00pm.

CANCELLED NORTH AMERICAN TOUR

Pink Floyd had already been reported in the UK music press on Saturday 10 August 1968 to be returning to North America to complete a college tour with Tyrannosaurus Rex through November, but this plan never came to fruition. However, the following shows were advertised and it can only be assumed there was a problem either securing enough dates to make the tour worthwhile or with work permits, as all appearances were cancelled at very short notice: Fillmore East, New York City, on Friday 1 November (two shows at 8.00pm & 11.30pm), with Richie Havens and Quicksilver Messenger Service (Pink Floyd was replaced by the McCoys); Fillmore East, New York City, on Saturday 2 November (two shows at 8.00pm & 11.30pm), with Richie Havens and Quicksilver Messenger Service (Pink Floyd was replaced by the Move); The Electric Factory, Philadelphia, with the Moody Blues on Friday 8 & Saturday 9 November; and the Seattle Arena, Seattle, on Friday 29 November, with the Chicago Transit Authority, supporting Janis Joplin with Big Brother & the Holding Company. This show eventually went ahead with the two remaining acts at the Eagles Auditorium, Seattle, on the same date.

FRIDAY 1 NOVEMBER - TELEVISION RECORDING
Surprise Partie, Le Bilboquet, St Germain des Près, Paris, France

Pink Floyd performed 'Let There Be More Light' live for inclusion in a four-hour TV special entitled *Surprise Partie* that also featured pre-recorded films of the Who, Joe Cocker, the Troggs, Fleetwood Mac, Small Faces, PP Arnold and the Equals among many other artists. It was broadcast (in colour) on ORTF2 TV on Tuesday 31 December between 10.40pm and 2.40am.

FRIDAY 1 NOVEMBER – CANCELLED PERFORMANCE
The Sound of Colours, Highbury Technical College, Portsmouth, England

With the Sonic Invaders and Tangerine Slide.

Sadly Pink Floyd didn't show for their appearance which according to a preview in the *Portsmouth News*, was to include a surround sound system, due to filming commitments in France. In addition to Pink Floyd, the Sonic Invaders also didn't show, leaving Tangerine Slide and another local band, Coconut Mushroom, who were hurriedly engaged, to entertain the students instead.

SATURDAY 2 NOVEMBER – PERFORMANCE
Student Union, London College of Printing, Elephant & Castle, London, England

MONDAY 4 NOVEMBER – RECORDING SESSION
Studio 2 & Control Room 2, EMI Studios, Abbey Road, London, England

2.30pm to 8.00pm: Vocals, Piano, Guitar and Maracas overdubbed onto Take 6 of 'Point Me At The Sky' and Take 6 of 'Point Me At The Sky' remixed (RM1 at 3:44), and 9.00pm to 11.15pm: 'Careful With That Axe, Eugene' recorded (Take 1 at 5:42 also marked "best" and Take 2 at 5:22); Vocals, Guitar and Vibes overdubbed onto Take 1 of 'Careful With That Axe, Eugene' and 'Careful With That Axe, Eugene' remixed (RM1 at 5:43 also marked "best") for the 7-inch single. The session was produced by Norman Smith, engineered by Peter Mew and assisted by Neil Richmond.

TUESDAY 5 NOVEMBER – RECORDING SESSION
Room 70, EMI Studios, Abbey Road, London, England

2.30pm to 4.30pm: 'Point Me At The Sky' remixed (RM2 at 3:27 also marked "best"). The session was produced by Norman Smith, engineered by Peter Mew and assisted by Alan Parsons. It is unlikely Pink Floyd would have been in attendance for this session.

THURSDAY 7 NOVEMBER – PERFORMANCE
Porchester Hall, Queensway, London, England

With Barclay James Harvest and the Edgar Broughton Band. Pink Floyd also reportedly jammed with Alexis Korner and Arthur Brown after their set.

FRIDAY 8 NOVEMBER – PERFORMANCE
Fishmongers Hall, Fishmongers Arms public house, Wood Green, London, England

Supported by Closed Cell Sponge, Stranger Than Yesterday and DJ Jerry Floyd with the Saffron Rainbow Light Show.

Set list included: 'Careful With That Axe, Eugene', 'A Saucerful Of Secrets'.
Record Mirror reported, "The turnout – for what was probably a little-advertised event – was amazing. The hall was absolutely packed – not with the usual sort of kid fans but with a seriously attentive and wildly appreciative crowd. The customers there at a London suburban pub were the most vivid proof of the existence of an increasingly large, new-type audience for intelligent and imaginative pop."

FRIDAY 15 NOVEMBER – PERFORMANCES
Blow Up Club, Munich, West Germany

Two evening shows with the Morgen Soul Star Band and Jackie Edwards. This was Pink Floyd's first ever appearance in West Germany.

SATURDAY 16 NOVEMBER – TELEVISION BROADCAST
A L'Affiche Du Monde, ORTF1, France

Footage of Pink Floyd larking about on the London underground combined with shots of London landmarks was used as a backdrop to the recording of 'Let There Be More Light' taken from the album *A Saucerful of Secrets* and shown on the arts programme *A L'Affiche du Monde* in an article entitled 'Special Angleterre: La Nouvelle Vogue de la Pop Music', broadcast on ORTF1 TV on this day between 9.15pm and 10.45pm.

SATURDAY 16 NOVEMBER – PERFORMANCE ▼
Restaurant Olten-Hammer, Olten, Switzerland

Early evening show with the Black Birds, the Expelled, Adamis Soul Sect and hosted by DJ Tscheisi. Reportedly attended by over 400 fans and marking Pink Floyd's first ever live appearance in Switzerland. During the afternoon Pink Floyd stopped by the Jecklin Disco-Center record store in Zurich for an afternoon signing session.

SATURDAY 16 NOVEMBER – PERFORMANCE
Grosse Tanzparty, Coca-Cola Halle, Abtwil, Switzerland

Late evening show supported by the Blues Club, the Axis, the Wood Chuck and the Ponny's with the Miss Coca-Cola Competition.

SUNDAY 17 NOVEMBER – PERFORMANCE
2nd Pop & Rhythm and Blues Festival, Hazyland, Kongresshaus, Zurich, Switzerland

Afternoon show with Shiver.

SUNDAY 17 NOVEMBER – PERFORMANCE
Spot Bar, Neuchâtel, Switzerland

FRIDAY 22 NOVEMBER – PERFORMANCE
Crawdaddy, The Club House, Richmond Athletic Club, Richmond, England

Supported by Arcadium.

SATURDAY 23 NOVEMBER – PERFORMANCE ▶
The Large Hall, Regent Street Polytechnic, London, England

With Bobby Parker.

SUNDAY 24 NOVEMBER – PERFORMANCE ▶
The Country Club, Belsize Park, London, England

Supported by Andromeda.

TUESDAY 26 NOVEMBER – RECORDING SESSION
Studio 3 & Control Room 3, EMI Studios, Abbey Road, London, England

7.00pm to 12.30am: 'I Am The Embryo' recorded (Take 1 at 5:05) for *Ummagumma*. This track was dropped from the album and remained archived until April 1970 when it was mixed and subsequently released, apparently without the band's approval, on the Harvest label compilation album *Picnic: A Breath of Fresh Air* in May 1970. The session was produced by Norman Smith, engineered by Peter Mew and assisted by Neil Richmond.

WEDNESDAY 27 NOVEMBER – PERFORMANCE
Student Union Building, Keele University, Newcastle-under-Lyme, England

Set list: 'Astronomy Domine', 'Flaming', 'Careful With That Axe, Eugene', 'Interstellar Overdrive', 'Let There Be More Light', 'Set The Controls For The Heart Of The Sun', 'A Saucerful Of Secrets'.

FRIDAY 29 NOVEMBER – PERFORMANCE
Hanover Lodge, Bedford College, Regents Park, London, England

Supported by Blonde on Blonde.
Correspondence in The Royal Holloway College archives noted that: "In protest of students establishing for themselves an annual Christmas Ball, the Social Secretary stated in the minutes of the General Meeting of the college Union on 6 December that,

'Three young ladies had done no academic work for three weeks due to Pink Floyd's dance and the Christmas Ball on account of all the preparations for these events.'"

MONDAY 2 DECEMBER – CANCELLED RECORDING SESSION
**Studio 2 & Control Room 2, EMI Studios,
Abbey Road, London, England**

Pink Floyd cancelled in order to record sessions for BBC Radio One.

MONDAY 2 DECEMBER – RADIO RECORDING
Top Gear, **Studio 4, BBC Maida Vale Studios,
Maida Vale, London, England**

Pink Floyd recorded a live show on this date for BBC Radio One. As with the session on Tuesday 25 June, the BBC archives paperwork is very detailed, and again it is slightly confusing to note that two shows were apparently recorded; the first one was recorded between 2.30pm and 6.00pm and a second show recorded between 6.00pm and 9.30pm. However, the track timings are shown as identical for both sessions, with the exception of 'Interstellar Overdrive' which is slightly longer.

The first show was broadcast on *Top Gear*, hosted by John Peel, on Sunday 15 December 1968 between 3.00pm and 5.00pm and included 'Point Me At The Sky' (4:30), 'The Narrow Way, Part 1' (announced as 'Baby Blue Shuffle In D Major') (4:10), 'Embryo' (3:40) and 'Interstellar Overdrive' (8:15).

The second show was broadcast on *Top Gear*, hosted by John Peel, on Sunday 19 January 1969 at 3.00pm and included 'Point Me To The Sky' (4:30), 'Embryo' (3:40) and 'Interstellar Overdrive' (8:45).

TUESDAY 3 DECEMBER – RECORDING SESSION
**Studio 2 & Control Room 2, EMI Studios,
Abbey Road, London, England**

2.30pm to 6.45pm: 'I Am The Embryo' recorded (Take 1 at 4:36). The previous Take 1 of this track recorded on 26 November was wiped, and 8.00pm to 12.45am: Vocals, Organ and Piano overdubbed onto Take 1 of 'I Am The Embryo' for *Ummagumma*. The session was produced by Norman Smith, engineered by Peter Mew and assisted by Neil Richmond.

WEDNESDAY 4 DECEMBER – RECORDING SESSION
**Studio 2 & Control Room 2, EMI Studios,
Abbey Road, London, England**

2.30pm to 7.00pm and 8.00pm to 2.00am: Vocals, Organ and Piano overdubbed onto Take 1 of 'I Am The Embryo', 'One Night Stand' ['Summer '68'] recorded (Takes 1 & 2 False Starts, Take 3 at 4:51, and Take 4 at 4:57 also marked "best"), Organ, Vocals, Guitar and Piano overdubbed onto Take 4 of 'One Night Stand' and rough remix was made of Take 4 of 'One Night Stand' for *Ummagumma*. The session was produced by Norman Smith, engineered by Peter Mew and assisted by Neil Richmond.

WEDNESDAY 4 DECEMBER – THEATRE PREMIERE
Pawn To King 5, **Jeanetta Cochrane Theatre,
Long Acre, London, England**

Pink Floyd provided some specially recorded music, described by *The Times* as 'fascinating and haunting', for the John Chesworth production of *Pawn To King 5* performed by Ballet Rambert, which premiered on this date and ran through to Saturday 7 December.

The production was repeated several times at the Jeanetta Cochrane Theatre through to the early 1970s.

Reviewing the performance the *Daily Express* reported, "Just as the Floyd group once described their performances as 'co-operative anarchy', so much the same might be said of this exercise in modern dance. It begins and ends with the smallest girl lashing out with fists and feet at the tallest man, which I suppose is where the chess-minded title comes in. The rest has little to do with chess, comprising as it does with a weird succession of incidents including some aggressive beatings-up, discotheque style dancing, and a boy-makes-girl episode leading to a suicide pact. All the while the Pink Floyd and their instruments are moaning, growling or shrieking on the accompanying tapes, with a few seagull cries for good measure and various colour slides are shone on to a suspended mirror, not always quite on cue. I found it difficult to take seriously – possibly because it gave the impression of a mad, inconsequential sort of party viewed strictly from the outside."

THURSDAY 5 DECEMBER – PERFORMANCE ▶
Bournemouth College Students Union Christmas Dance, **Royal Arcade Ballrooms, Boscombe, Bournemouth, England**

With Status Quo and Mouse & the Kats.

FRIDAY 6 DECEMBER – SINGLE RELEASE (UK)
'Point Me At The Sky'

NME wrote, "Apart from the excessive volume I found it quite intriguing and absorbing – quite the 'best' Floyd single to be issued for some long time."

B.C.S.U.

CHRISTMAS DANCE

TONIGHT

**PINK FLOYD
STATUS QUO
MOUSE AND THE KATS**

**ROYAL ARCADE
BALLROOMS**
BOSCOMBE

8 p.m. – 2 a.m.

LICENSED BAR   LATE TRANSPORT

Tickets **NOT AVAILABLE** at the door
Available at STUDENTS UNION OFFICE
(Lansdowne) to 9.30 pm

SATURDAY 7 DECEMBER – PERFORMANCE
Kaleidoscope '68, **Liverpool Stadium, Liverpool, England**

With the Move, Cliff Bennett, the Perfumed Garden, the BJ's, the Reason Why, the Klubs, the Mumbles, the New Mojo Band, the Curiosity Shoppe, the Pattern People, the Chapter Six, Mick Burns and the Humphrey Lyttelton Band. Compéred by BBC Radio One DJ's Dave Symonds, Tony Brandon, Rick Dane and Pete Price. Despite the grandeur of its name, the venue was in fact a large ballroom.

SUNDAY 8 DECEMBER – PERFORMANCE
ABC Cinema, Merthyr Tydfil, Wales

Supporting the Herd [featuring Peter Frampton on guitar] with the Firm.
Set list included 'Set The Controls For The Heart Of The Sun', 'Astronomy Domine'.

The *Merthyr Express* reported, "The Pink Floyd produced an abstract free-form music which was probably too progressive for [a] mainly young audience. The Pink Floyd who closed the first half of the show, used a variety of electronic gadgetry to produce their unusual sound. Their music had a steady compulsive drive to it rather than a foot-tapping beat. Weird and unusual sounds

POINT ME AT THE SKY

TRACKS

SIDE A: POINT ME AT THE SKY (Waters, Gilmour) 3:34
SIDE B: CAREFUL WITH THAT AXE, EUGENE (Waters,
Wright, Gilmour, Mason) 5:43

RELEASE DATE

UK: Friday 6 December 1968.

FORMAT

UK: Columbia EMI DB 8511 (7-inch single).

ADDITIONAL MUSICIAN

Unidentified Cellist on 'Point Me At The Sky'.

PROMO FILM

A unique film was shot for the single at Biggin Hill Aerodrome,
Kent, England showing the band larking around in RAF flying suits
and flying in a 1930s de Havilland DH82A Tiger Moth dual-control
trainer biplane (G-ANKH, which is still flying and in private ownership
today) and an AVRO 504N (G-ADBO) biplane. The film was unlikely to
have been shown in the UK, but was almost certainly broadcast on
European TV channels.

The UK promo 7-inch single also came with a postcard photo of
the band in RAF flying suits standing by the Tiger Moth, and further
shots served as promotional photographs in the period.

RECORDING DETAILS

The basic track for 'Point Me At The Sky' was recorded in five takes on
23 October 1968, with overdubs added at a later date, including an
unidentified session musician on Cello, which was overdubbed on 29
October. Conversely, the B-side was recorded in just one take on
4 November 1968, although curiously the track was first attempted in
a session at Capitol Studios during a break on their second US tour in
August 1968.

'Point Me At The Sky' was not released in the US as a single but
in 1978 it appeared on the mail-order compilation album *A Harvest*
Sampler (Capitol SPRO-8795/6). It was not commercially available
again until 1992 as part of the CD collection *The Early Singles,* which
came in its original mono mix as a bonus CD in the *Shine On* box set
(UK: EMI PFBOX 1 / US: Columbia CXK 53180 S1).

POINT ME AT THE SKY

Take 6 (RM2).
Basic track recorded on 22 October 1968 (Take 6).
Basic track re-recorded on 23 October 1968 (Take 3 for "first section",
Take 5 for "second section").
Guitar and Organ overdubbed onto Take 5 on 23 October 1968.
Drums, Guitar, Bass and Organ overdubbed onto Take 5 on
28 October 1968.
Vocals overdubbed onto Take 5 on 28 October 1968 (relabelled Take 6).
Cello, Guitar, Piano, Maracas, Harpsichord and Vocals overdubbed onto
Take 6 on 29 October 1968.
Vocals overdubbed onto Take 6 on 30 October 1968.
Vocals, Piano, Guitar and Maracas overdubbed onto Take 6 on
4 November 1968.
Remixed on 5 November 1968 (RM2).

CAREFUL WITH THAT AXE, EUGENE

Take 1 (RM1).
Basic track recorded
and Vocals, Guitar and
Vibes overdubbed onto
Take 1 on 4 November
1968 (Take 1).
Remixed on 4 November
1968 (RM1).

TOP LEFT: UK PROMO SINGLE.

TOP RIGHT: POSTCARD ISSUED
WITH THE UK PROMO SINGLE.

RIGHT: PROMOTIONAL PHOTO
FOR THE SINGLE TAKEN AT BIGGIN
HILL AERODROME.

were coaxed from Syd Barrett's [sic] lead guitar and Rick Wright's organ varied from melodic sounds to frantic discords. Their music has a more hypnotic effect when accompanied by the light act they normally use but which was not seen on Sunday."

MONDAY 9 DECEMBER – RECORDING SESSION
Studio 2 & Control Room 2, EMI Studios,
Abbey Road, London, England

2.30pm to 7.00pm and 8.00pm to 2.00am: 'One Night Stand' ['Summer '68'] re-recorded (Take 5 at 4:55, Takes 6 & 7 False Starts and Take 8 at 4:56), and Guitar and Piano overdubbed onto Take 8 of 'One Night Stand' for *Ummagumma*. The session was produced by Norman Smith, engineered by Peter Mew and assisted by Neil Richmond.

TUESDAY 10 DECEMBER – RECORDING SESSION
Studio 2 & Control Room 2, EMI Studios,
Abbey Road, London, England

2.30pm to 6.00pm and 7.30pm to 1.00am: Vocals, Guitars, Drums, Maracas and Piano overdubbed onto Take 8 of 'One Night Stand' ['Summer '68'] for *Ummagumma*. The session was produced by Norman Smith, engineered by Peter Mew and assisted by Neil Richmond.

WEDNESDAY 11 DECEMBER – RECORDING SESSION
Studio 2 & Control Room 2, EMI Studios,
Abbey Road, London, England

2.30pm to 6.15pm and 7.45pm to 1.00am: 'Ricky's Scene (Parts One, Two & Three)' ['Sysyphus'] (Take 1 False Start, Take 2 at 1:24 and Take 3 at 1:20 also marked "best"), for *Ummagumma*. The session was produced by Norman Smith, engineered by Peter Mew and assisted by Neil Richmond.

THURSDAY 12 DECEMBER – PERFORMANCE
Christmas Revels Ball, **Dundee University,**
Dundee, Scotland

With the Sleaz Band and Gethsemane.

FRIDAY 13 DECEMBER – PERFORMANCE ▶
The New Marquee, Leeds, England

With the Rock Machine Record & Light Show.

SATURDAY 14 DECEMBER – PERFORMANCE
College of Technology, Slough,
England

SUNDAY 15 DECEMBER – PERFORMANCE
City Hall, Newcastle-upon-Tyne,
England

Supported by the Pretty Things, Aynsley Dunbar Retaliation, the Deviants and Gordon Snaith.
Pink Floyd arrived late having been delayed on the motorway and were able to perform only two numbers between 10.00pm and the curfew of 10.30pm, at which point the venue management turned off the stage power, sparking off a near riot in the audience.

MONDAY 16 DECEMBER – RECORDING SESSION
Studio 2 & Control Room 2, EMI Studios,
Abbey Road, London, England

2.30pm to 5.30pm and 7.00pm to 1.15am: Recording 'One Night Stand' ['Summer '68'] (Take 9 at 0:18 also marked "best edit piece" and Take 10 at 0:18 also marked "best edit with Take 9"), and Piano, Acoustic Guitar, Mellotron, Harmonium, Brass and Guitar overdubbed onto Take 8 of 'One Night Stand' for *Ummagumma*. The session was produced by Norman Smith, engineered by Peter Mew and assisted by Neil Richmond. Two unidentified session musicians, making up the brass section, are noted as being hired in at a total cost of £18.

TUESDAY 17 DECEMBER – RECORDING SESSION
Studio 2 & Control Room 2, EMI Studios,
Abbey Road, London, England

2.30pm to 6.00pm and 8.00pm to 1.15am: 'Roger's Scene (Parts One and Two)' ['Several Species…'] (Take 1 at 4:17 also marked "best"), and Vibes, Guitar and Mellotron overdubbed onto Take 3 of 'Ricky's Scene' ['Sysyphus'] for *Ummagumma*. The session was produced by Norman Smith, engineered by Peter Mew and assisted by Neil Richmond.

Pink Floyd was also filmed between 2.30pm and 6.00pm on this day for inclusion in the educational BBC TV programme *Science Session* in an edition entitled *Let's Make Pop*. BBC archives describe the footage as "Laying tracks in recording studio with view to using them on an LP. No other details known" with three separate pieces of music timed at 0:20, 4:10 and 0:34 used in the film. It was broadcast (in colour) on BBC1 TV on Wednesday 5 March 1969 between 2.05pm and 2.30pm and repeated on BBC1 TV on Thursday 6 March 1969 between 10.00am and 10.25pm.

WEDNESDAY 18 DECEMBER – RECORDING SESSION
Studio 2 & Control Room 2, EMI Studios,
Abbey Road, London, England

2.30pm to 6.00pm and 7.30pm to 2.00am: Organ, Guitar, Tympani's and Piano overdubbed onto Take 3 of 'Ricky's Scene (Parts Four and Five)' ['Sysyphus'], editing 'Ricky's Scene (Part One)' ['Sysyphus, Part 1'] for *Ummagumma*. The session was produced by Norman Smith, engineered by Peter Mew and assisted by Neil Richmond.

FRIDAY 20 DECEMBER – RADIO RECORDING
Radio One Club, **BBC Paris Cinema, Lower Regent Street, London, England**

Pink Floyd recorded a live-to-air audience show for the *Radio One Club*, presented by David Symonds, on this day for BBC Radio One. They performed 'Let There Be More Light' (3:01), 'Set The Controls For The Heart Of The Sun' (4:45), 'Point Me At The Sky' (3:25) and 'Careful With That Axe, Eugene' (4:20). Rehearsals commenced at 9.30am and the show was broadcast between 12.00midday and 2.00pm.

THE NEW MARQUEE

81, Great George Street, Leeds, 1.   N° 292

presents on DECEMBER 13th,   8 pm – 1 am

live on stage

PINK FLOYD

and

THE ROCK MACHINE RECORD
& LIGHT SHOW

Advance 10/-   Admission at door 12/6   Students 10/-
Late Licensed Bar

FRIDAY 27 DECEMBER – PERFORMANCE
Grote Zaal, De Doelen, Rotterdam, Netherlands

With The Outsiders, Barber Green's Fantastic Collection, the Misfits, R&B Ltd.4, Eye's Blues Formation, the Onlys, Joseph Guy, Heads, Panique, WW Dance Girls and featuring the Provadya Lightshow.

SATURDAY 28 DECEMBER – PERFORMANCE
Flight To Lowlands Paradise II, **Margriethal-Jaarbeurs, Utrecht, Netherlands**

This two-day nonstop event lasting between 4.00pm on Saturday 28 December and 8.00pm on Sunday 29 December featured appearances by the Pretty Things, the Bonzo Dog Doo-Dah Band, the Pebbles, Short 66, the Tykes, Static, the Zipps, Full House, the Living Kick Formation, Set Money, Cuby & the Blizzards, the Outsiders, Inez & the Racers, the New Electric Chamber Orchestra and the Jan Heckert Experience among many other acts and attractions. Jeff Beck Group and Jethro Tull cancelled as did the Jimi Hendrix Experience whom Pink Floyd replaced.
Set list: 'Astronomy Domine', 'Careful With That Axe, Eugene', 'Interstellar Overdrive', 'Set The Controls For The Heart Of The Sun', 'A Saucerful Of Secrets'.

1969

PINK FLOYD ROAD CREW JANUARY – DECEMBER 1969
Alan Styles (Technician / Stage Crew), Peter Watts (Tour Manager / Front of House Sound).

FRIDAY 10 JANUARY – PERFORMANCE
Fishmongers Hall, Fishmongers Arms public house, Wood Green, London, England

Pink Floyd replaced the advertised Jimi Hendrix Experience at short notice.

SATURDAY 11 JANUARY – CANCELLED PERFORMANCE
Provadya Festival, **Zwijndrecht, Netherlands**

Pink Floyd didn't appear at this event due to problems with work permits.

SUNDAY 12 JANUARY – TELEVISION BROADCAST
Pop Uitzending Uit London, **West Germany**

Pink Floyd appeared on the music show *Pop Uitzending Uit London* [*Pop Broadcast from London*], although the recording date and their contribution is unknown. It was broadcast on ZDF2 network TV between 9.00pm and 9.45pm.

SUNDAY 12 JANUARY – PERFORMANCE
Mothers, Erdington, Birmingham, England

With DJ John Peel.

THURSDAY 16 JANUARY – RECORDING SESSION
Studio 2 & Control Room 2, EMI Studios, Abbey Road, London, England

2.30pm to 8.30pm and 9.45pm to 12.00midnight: 'One Night Stand' ['Summer '68'] remixed (RS1 to RS12 untimed, RS13 at 5:11 also marked "best", and RS14 to RS19 untimed) for *Ummagumma*. The session was produced by Norman Smith, engineered by Peter Mew and assisted by Neil Richmond.

THURSDAY 16 JANUARY – RECORDING SESSION
Studio 3 & Control Room 3, EMI Studios, Abbey Road, London, England

7.30pm to 11.30pm: 'Dave's Scene' ['The Narrow Way, Part One'] recorded (Take 1 at 4:00) for *Ummagumma*, followed by a half-hour playback to 12.00midnight. The session was produced by Norman Smith, engineered by Peter Mew and assisted by Neil Richmond.

FRIDAY 17 JANUARY – CANCELLED PERFORMANCE
Brunel University (Uxbridge) Rag Week Ball, **Royal Albert Hall, Kensington, London, England**

With Ten Years After, Family and DJ John Peel. Despite being advertised, Pink Floyd did not appear at this show.

SATURDAY 18 JANUARY – PERFORMANCE
Homerton College, Cambridge, England

Early show with Armageddon, Saffron Knight, discotheque, Southside Jazz Band, Fab-Cab, blues bands and a cabaret.

SATURDAY 18 JANUARY – PERFORMANCE
Middle Earth, **The Roundhouse, Chalk Farm, London, England**

With Arcadium, Jimmy Scott & His Band, DJ Jeff Dexter and the Explosive Spectrum Lightshow. Pink Floyd appeared at 2.15am (Sunday 19 January).
Set list included 'Set The Controls For The Heart Of The Sun', 'A Saucerful Of Secrets'.

Pink Floyd's set was followed by a screening of excerpts from the Tiny Tim film *You Are What You Eat*. The entire band was reported in attendance of the premiere of the film on Wednesday 29 January at the Windmill Theatre, London. Reviewing the event *Time Out* reported, "A large queue began forming outside the Roundhouse from about eleven o'clock at night and by half past one in the morning most of the assembled masses were inside. Under the large central dome there was a large circular floor area. Most of the audience sat on the floor, but latecomers sat on the colonnaded promenade. To brighten things up a bit the back of the stage, the roof of the dome, and a circular strip all the way round under the dome were draped with white sheets, which were used as projection screens for the lights. An hour of recorded music preceded the band's stage entry. At a quarter past two a tentative probing of the immense gong heralded 'Set The Controls For The Heart Of The Sun'. A sixty-five minute set followed which included the breaking of a milk bottle in a rubbish bin and the frying of eggs, and more gong beating."

TUESDAY 21 JANUARY – RECORDING SESSION
Studio 2 & Control Room 2, EMI Studios, Abbey Road, London, England

7.00pm to 11.00pm: "Drum Family Tympanis" recorded (Take 1 at 5:30) for 'Nicky's Tune' ['The Grand Vizier's Garden Party, Part Two – Entertainment'] for *Ummagumma*. The session was produced by Norman Smith, engineered by Peter Mew and assisted by Neil Richmond.

WEDNESDAY 22 JANUARY – TELEVISION RECORDING
Forum Musiques, ORTF Studios,
Buttes Chaumont, Paris, France

Pink Floyd performed 'Point Me At The Sky', 'Set The Controls For The Heart Of The Sun' and 'A Saucerful Of Secrets' live for the music programme *Forum Musiques*. David Gilmour, speaking in fluent French, was also interviewed between tracks. It was broadcast (in black and white) on ORTF1 TV on Saturday 15 February between 10.35pm and 11.35pm.

SATURDAY 25 JANUARY – PERFORMANCE
Sixty Nine Club, Royal York Hotel, Ryde,
Isle of Wight, England

Supported by the Cherokees.
Set list included 'Set The Controls For The Heart Of The Sun'.

MONDAY 27 JANUARY – RECORDING SESSION
Studio 2 & Control Room 2, EMI Studios,
Abbey Road, London, England

2.30pm to 5.30pm and 7.00pm to 12.00 midnight: "Rhythm Machine and Drum Solo" recorded for 'Nicky's Scene' ['The Grand Vizier's Garden Party, Part Two – Entertainment'] (Take 1, untimed) Tympanis and Marimba overdubbed onto Take 1 of 'Nicky's Scene Rhythm Machine and Drum Solo' ['The Grand Vizier's Garden Party, Part Two – Entertainment'] Flute and Marimba recorded for Section 2 part of 'Nicky's Scene' ['The Grand Vizier's Garden Party, Part Two – Entertainment'] (Take 1 at 2:00) for *Ummagumma*, followed by a half-hour playback at 12.30am. The session was produced by Norman Smith, engineered by Peter Mew and assisted by Neil Richmond.

TUESDAY 28 JANUARY – RECORDING SESSION
Studio 2 & Control Room 2, EMI Studios,
Abbey Road, London, England

2.30pm to 6.00pm and 7.30pm to 12.30am: Sound Effects recorded for Section Three of 'Nicky's Tune' ['The Grand Vizier's Garden Party, Part Two – Entertainment'] (Take 1 untimed), Drums and Cymbals overdubbed onto Take 1 of 'Nicky's Tune (Section Three)' ['The Grand Vizier's Garden Party, Part Two – Entertainment'], and a rough stereo mix made of 'Nicky's Scene' (RS1 at 8:22) for *Ummagumma*. The session was produced by Norman Smith, engineered by Peter Mew and assisted by Neil Richmond.

WEDNESDAY 29 JANUARY – RECORDING SESSION
Studio 2 & Control Room 2, EMI Studios,
Abbey Road, London, England

2.30pm to 6.30pm and 7.30pm to 11.30pm: Recording "Spiral Effects and Modulated Vocal Sounds" for 'Dave's Scene (First Movement)' ['The Narrow Way, Part 1'] (Take 1 untimed also marked "best"), recording "Spiral Effects and Stereo Guitar Effects" for 'Dave's Scene (First Movement)' (Take 1 untimed also marked "best"), and recording 'Dave's Scene (Second Movement)' ['The Narrow Way, Part 2'] (Take 1 at 2:50 also marked "best") for *Ummagumma*. The session was produced by Norman Smith, engineered by Peter Mew and assisted by Neil Richmond.

FRIDAY 31 JANUARY – RECORDING
Royal Albert Hall, Kensington, London, England

Richard Wright spent three hours performing on the venue's huge pipe organ, which was recorded by EMI Studios' mobile unit for *Ummagumma*. None of the recordings were used for the album but after their rediscovery a few minutes were later used on Pink Floyd's 2014 album *The Endless River*.

MONDAY 3 – FRIDAY 7 FEBRUARY – RECORDING SESSIONS
Studio One, Pye Recording Studios, ATV House,
Marble Arch, London, England

All-night recording sessions working on the soundtrack to the feature film *More*.

FRIDAY 7 FEBRUARY – CANCELLED PERFORMANCE
West Refectory, University of Hull, Hull, England

This show was cancelled on the night due to heavy snowfalls delaying the arrival of the band and their equipment from London, although in view of the above recording schedule it was likely to have been a convenient excuse.

WEDNESDAY 12 FEBRUARY – PERFORMANCE
Cardiff Inter-College's Charities Appeal,
Top Rank Suite, Cardiff, Wales

With Deep Purple, the Hollies, Geno Washington and DJ Pete Drummond.

FRIDAY 14 FEBRUARY – PERFORMANCE
Valentine's Ball, Edward Herbert Building, University of Loughborough, Loughborough, England

With Free, DJ Emperor Rosco and the Delroy Williams Show. *International Times* had incorrectly listed Pink Floyd as appearing at Warwick University, Coventry on this day.

SATURDAY 15 FEBRUARY – PERFORMANCE
Junior Common Room, University of York, Heslington, York, England

Supported by Love Sculpture.

SUNDAY 16 FEBRUARY – PERFORMANCE
Younger Hall, St Andrew's University,
St Andrew's, Scotland

Billed as "the biggest name and least establishment band that has ever come to St Andrews", the band performed to an audience of 520. Pink Floyd was booked for a cost of £350, but the event ran at a loss of £70 having failed to fill to its capacity of 800.

MONDAY 17 FEBRUARY – PRESS REPORT
Edinburgh, Scotland

The *Edinburgh Evening News* reported, "Pop group Pink Floyd have written the music for a ballet sequence being put on at the Royal Lyceum Theatre [Edinburgh, between Monday 17 and Saturday 22 February]. It is part of a programme being presented by The Ballet Rambert and is a piece of improvisation called 'Pawn To King Five'. The piece will be included in the company's programme, *Number One*, which starts on Monday. The choreography is being handled by John Chesworth."

★ BAY HOTEL THIS MONDAY ★
PRESENTS A GROUP WHO ARE LEADERS IN THEIR
FIELD OF MUSIC
TAKE A TRIP INTO A FANTASY WORLD OF LIGHTS AND
UNIQUE VISUAL EFFECTS. JUST TAKE A "ONE-HOUR TRIP
INTO MUSICLAND"

PINK FLOYD
—— ADMISSION 7/6 ——

**MONDAY 17 FEBRUARY –
PERFORMANCE ◄
The Ballroom, Bay Hotel,
Whitburn, Sunderland,
England**

TUESDAY 18 FEBRUARY – PERFORMANCE
Manchester & Salford Students' Shrove Rag Ball,
Manchester University, Manchester, England

With Fairport Convention (headline) and John Dummer Blues
Band and Bakerloo (in the Open Lounge), Liverpool Scene,
Bridget St John and John Peel (in the Lesser Debating Hall) and
the Foundations and Simon Dupree (at the Burlington Street site).

FRIDAY 21 FEBRUARY – PERFORMANCE
Le Festival Sigma de Bordeaux, **Alhambra Theatre,
Bordeaux, France**

With Roland Kirk. Also appearing at the festival in other venues
were Gunter Hampel (with Barre Phillips), Cannonball Adderley,
Cecil Taylor, Miles Davis, Oscar Peterson, Free Music Group,
Michel Portal and Jean-Pierre Drouet, Duke Ellington with Ronnie
Scott, John Surman, Soft Machine with Tony Oxley and Derek
Bailey, Evan Parker and Kenny Wheeler.

BRIGHTON COMBINATION
presents
Benefit Concert at The Dome
PINK FLOYD
PRETTY THINGS
THIRD EAR BAND
SUPER JAM SESSION !
on
MONDAY, 24th FEBRUARY
at 7.30
TICKETS 7/6 - 10/6 - 12/6
obtainable from **The Dome** (682127) - **Brighton
Combination** (24596) - **Millions of Shirts inc.**
(26589) - **Mike Clayton at Sleeves** (40 Middle
Street).

**MONDAY 24 FEBRUARY –
PERFORMANCE ◄
The Dome, Brighton, England**
With the Pretty Things, Third Ear
Band and a 'Super Jam Session'.
Set list included 'Interstellar
Overdrive', 'Set The Controls For
The Heart Of The Sun', 'A Saucerful
Of Secrets' <Encore> 'Let There Be
More Light'.

The *Wine Press*, Sussex
University's student newspaper,
reported, "On Monday of last
week Jimi Hendrix played his
second concert at London's
Royal Albert Hall. And the Pink Floyd appeared at The Dome.
They did not play their 'Symphony In Sixteen Parts'[*]. It did
not matter. There was no super-jam session. Just who could add
anything to the music of the Floyd? They proved themselves once
more as the most consistently brilliant group in England. The
group are at their best on the two long instrumentals 'Interstellar
Overdrive' and 'A Saucerful Of Secrets'. They probably could
not count the number of times they have performed the first
work; it is an ever-changing tableau of improvisation. At The
Dome they played the finest version of it I have ever heard. It is
a pity that such live performances are not preserved. 'Saucerful'
is the title track of their last album. Their version of this was
simply incredible – superb drumming from Mason leading onto
the centrepiece of polyphonic chaos, news from the quasars.
Waters prowled the stage like a captain on the observation deck

*Note: 'Symphony In Sixteen Parts' is a title that has not appeared in any other
reference to the band's output and consequently it has not been possible to
research this any further.

of a star ship, penetrating ever deeper into the heat of darkness.
At their most brilliant, the group go where no man has gone
before. The beautiful organ solo leading to the conclusion of
the work, showed Rick Wright to be the best organist in Britain.
The group finished with 'More Light' – great speed-freak guitar
from Gilmore [sic], great bass playing from Waters. This number
together with 'Set The Controls' show Roger Waters to be an
even better songwriter than Sid Barrett, whose departure has not
harmed the group, probably helped them. Waters vocal style is
curiously hushed; menacing – too quiet to hear the words, loud
enough to generate the meaning."

**TUESDAY 25 FEBRUARY – PERFORMANCE
Marlowe Theatre, Canterbury, England**
Set list included 'Set The Controls For The Heart Of The Sun',
'Careful With That Axe, Eugene'.

The *Kent Herald* reported, "Pink Floyd began their performance
with impromptu coughs into the microphones, building up into
the opening number. They used electric organ, grand piano,
vibes and two large Chinese gongs as well as guitars and drums,
and the music (or rather sounds) definitely attacked the senses as
advertised. In the second half the musicians wandered about the
stage, playing each other's instruments, and generally seeming
to have a good time. Some brilliant piano and organ work came
from Rick Wright, and the drums were played magnificently by
Nick Mason, who kept the group stable with his good sense of
rhythm. On stage, without the flashing lights for which they are
renowned, they were informal and obviously musically talented.
Perhaps the majority of the audience were flattered, however, to
be allowed to see what looked like the group's rehearsal rather
than a prepared show."

**WEDNESDAY 26 FEBRUARY – PERFORMANCE
New Cavendish Ballroom, Edinburgh, Scotland**
Pink Floyd performed in aid of Shelter, at an event
organized by the University of Edinburgh's charity
campaign. £250 was raised.

THURSDAY 27 FEBRUARY – PERFORMANCE
Glasgow Arts Lab Benefit, **The Maryland,
Glasgow, Scotland**
Supported by the Jimmy Mullen Jazz Group.

FRIDAY 28 FEBRUARY – PERFORMANCE
Commemoration Ball, **Queen
Elizabeth College, Kensington,
London, England**
With the Moody Blues and the Settlers.

**SATURDAY 1 MARCH – PERFORMANCE ►
University College London,
Bloomsbury, London, England**
Set list: 'Astronomy Domine', 'Careful With
That Axe, Eugene', 'Interstellar Overdrive',
'Set The Controls For The Heart of The
Sun', 'Let There Be More Light', 'A Saucerful
Of Secrets'.

THE PINK FLOYD
UNIVERSITY COLLEGE. GOWER ST., WCI
MARCH 1st 10/-

ABOVE: PINK FLOYD PERFORMING AT THE VAN DIKE CLUB, PLYMOUTH, 14 MARCH 1969.

**MONDAY 3 MARCH –
PERFORMANCE ◄**
Vic Rooms Dance, Victoria
Rooms, University of
Bristol, Clifton,
Bristol, England
Supported by East of
Eden and Principal
Edwards Magic Theatre.
Set list: 'Astronomy Domine',
'Interstellar Overdrive', 'Careful
With That Axe, Eugene', 'Set The
Controls For The Heart Of The
Sun', 'Let There Be More Light',
'A Saucerful Of Secrets'.

The *Bristol Evening Post* reported,
"The Pink Floyd played an
extraordinary and very different
show last night. And they even managed to quieten with their music
1,000 students fresh from the Rag torch light procession through
the streets of Bristol. Electronic sounds one usually only hears on
records came through loud and clear at the hall and this remarkable
group played a fascinating set. All the numbers were lengthy, eerie
meanderings through a pop version of science fiction, with loud
guitar and organ interplays creating the strange effects. Throughout
the performance there was a fascinating light-show by Adrian Jones
and Keith Wilkins, who managed to produce a blizzard of colours and
forms to add even more excitement to a remarkable show."

THURSDAY 6 MARCH – RECORDING SESSION
Studio 2 & Control Room 2, EMI Studios,
Abbey Road, London, England
2.30pm to 5.30pm and 7.00pm to 12.00pm: Drums, Guitar Effects
and Jew's Harp overdubbed onto Take 1 of 'Dave's Scene (Second
Movement)' ['The Narrow Way, Part 2'], the link between the
Second and Third Movement of 'Dave's Scene' recorded (Take 1 at
1:24 also marked "best"), 'Dave's
Scene (Third Movement)'
['The Narrow Way, Part 3']
recorded (Take 1 at 4:36, and
marked best) and Guitars and
Bass overdubbed onto Take
1 of 'Dave's Scene (Third
Movement)' for *Ummagumma*.
The Session was produced by
Norman Smith, engineered by
Peter Mew and assisted by Neil
Richmond.

**SATURDAY 8 MARCH –
PERFORMANCE ◄**
Reading University Rag Ball,
New Union, University of
Reading, Reading, England
With the Pretty Things, the
Gods, discotheque, folk singing,
blues, and the Sound Kitchen
light show.

TUESDAY 11 MARCH – PERFORMANCE
Lawns Centre, Cottingham, England
Presented by Huddersfield University, with a disco.

FRIDAY 14 MARCH – PERFORMANCE
Van Dike Club, Devonport, Plymouth, England
Supported by Afterwards.

SATURDAY 15 MARCH – PERFORMANCE
Kee Club, Bridgend, Wales
Set list: 'Astronomy Domine', 'Careful With That Axe, Eugene',
'Interstellar Overdrive', 'Set The Controls For The Heart Of The Sun'
<Encore> 'A Saucerful Of Secrets'.

MONDAY 17 MARCH – RECORDING SESSION
Studio 2 & Control Room 2, EMI Studios,
Abbey Road, London, England
2.30pm to 6.30pm and 8.30pm to 12.15am: Organ overdubbed
onto Take 1 of 'Dave's Movement (Second Movement)' ['The
Narrow Way, Part 2'] and Piano, Guitar and Vocal overdubbed
onto Take 1 of 'Dave's Movement (Third Movement)' ['The
Narrow Way, Part 3'] for *Ummagumma*. The session was produced
by Norman Smith, engineered by Jeff Jarrett and assisted by
Neil Richmond.

TUESDAY 18 MARCH – RECORDING SESSION
Studio 2 & Control Room 2, EMI Studios,
Abbey Road, London, England
2.30pm to 5.00pm and 6.00pm to 11.30pm: Recording 'Rogers
Quarter (First Movement)' ['Several Species…'] (Take 1 False
Start, and Take 2 at 4:58 also marked "best, basic vocal track");
Vocal Effects overdubbed onto Take 2 of 'Rogers Quarter
(First Movement)', and recording sound effects for 'Rogers
Quarter' ['Several Species…'], "to be cut up into loops later"
for *Ummagumma*. The session was produced by Norman Smith,
engineered by Peter Mew and assisted by Neil Richmond.

WEDNESDAY 19 MARCH – PERFORMANCE
Going Down Ball, The Refectory, University College,
Singleton Park, Swansea, Wales
Set list: 'Astronomy Domine', 'Careful With That Axe, Eugene', 'Set The
Controls For The Heart Of The Sun', 'Interstellar Overdrive' <Encore>
'A Saucerful Of Secrets'.

D.T.C. STUDENTS UNION
PRESENTS
the **PINK FLOYD**
also
DOCTOR K's BLUES BAND
THURSDAY MARCH 20th. at
DUNELM HOUSE
8.15 P.M. to 1.30 A.M.
ADMISSION 12'6 LICENSED UNTIL 12:30
TICKETS AVAILABLE FROM THE STUDENTS UNION
TELEPHONE DURHAM 5900

THURSDAY 20 MARCH – PERFORMANCE ◀
Dunelm House, University of Durham, Durham, England

Presented by Durham Technical College Students Union, supported by Doctor K's Blues Band.

FRIDAY 21 MARCH – PERFORMANCE
Arts Ball, **Empress Ballroom, Winter Gardens, Blackpool, England**

Presented by Blackpool Technical College & School of Art and St Anne's College of Further Education, with Love Affair, PP Arnold, Carnaby Square, DJ Gary Wild and a cabaret in the Planet Room.

SATURDAY 22 MARCH – PERFORMANCE ▶
Easter Endsville, **Refectory Hall, University Union, Leeds University, Leeds, England**

With Spooky Tooth and Jan Dukes de Grey.

MONDAY 24 MARCH – RECORDING SESSION
Studio 2 & Control Room 2, EMI Studios, Abbey Road, London, England

2.30pm to 5.30pm and 7.00pm to 12.15am: 'Rogers Quarter (Second Movement)' ['Grantchester Meadows'] recorded (Take 1 at 6:17 also marked "best") and Vocals and Acoustic Guitar overdubbed onto Take 1 of 'Rogers Quarter (Second Movement)' for *Ummagumma*. The session was produced by Norman Smith, engineered by Peter Mew and assisted by Neil Richmond.

TUESDAY 25 MARCH – RECORDING SESSION
Studio 2 & Control Room 2, EMI Studios, Abbey Road, London, England

2.30pm to 7.00pm and 8.30pm to 11.00pm: Guitar, Organ and Vocal overdubbed onto Take 1 of 'Rogers Quarter (First Movement)' ['Several Species…'], and 'Roger's Blues' [an unreleased track] recorded (Take 1 at 4:34 also marked "best") for *Ummagumma*. The session was produced by Norman Smith, engineered by Peter Mew and assisted by Neil Richmond.

WEDNESDAY 26 MARCH – RECORDING SESSION
Studio 2 & Control Room 2, EMI Studios, Abbey Road, London, England

2.30pm to 5.30pm and 8.30pm to 11.30pm: Vocals overdubbed onto Take 1 of 'Dave's Scene (Third Movement)' ['The Narrow Way, Part 3'], and Electric Harpsichord and Vocals overdubbed onto Take 1 of 'Ricky's Scene' ['Sysyphus'] for *Ummagumma*. The session was produced by Norman Smith, engineered by Peter Mew and assisted by Neil Richmond.

" EASTER ENDSVILLE "
PINK FLOYD
PLUS
SPOOKY TOOTH
AND THE MUSIC OF
JAN DUKES DE'GREY
SATURDAY, 22nd MARCH
TICKETS 7/-

THURSDAY 27 MARCH – PERFORMANCE ▶
St James' Church Hall, Chesterfield, England

Supported by Emery Chase and Shape Of The Rain. Set list: 'Astronomy Domine', 'Careful With That Axe, Eugene', 'Interstellar Overdrive', 'Set The Controls For The Heart Of The Sun', 'A Saucerful Of Secrets'.

WEDNESDAY 2 APRIL – RECORDING SESSION
Room 48, EMI Studios, Abbey Road, London, England

10.00pm to 1.00pm and 2.30pm to 6.30pm: Take 1 of 'Nicky's Scene' ['The Grand Vizier's Garden Party, Part 2 – Entertainment'] remixed (RS1 at 7:30 also marked "best") for *Ummagumma*. The session was produced by Norman Smith, engineered by Peter Mew and assisted by Neil Richmond.

WEDNESDAY 9 APRIL – CANCELLED RADIO RECORDING
Radio One Club, **BBC Paris Cinema, Lower Regent Street, London, England**

Pink Floyd was due to record a live show for the BBC Radio One programme *Radio One Club* hosted by John Peel at midday, but the band failed to turn up due to, according to archive sources, Richard Wright having food poisoning. It was rescheduled to Monday 12 May.

MONDAY 14 APRIL – PERFORMANCE ▼
Royal Festival Hall, South Bank, London, England

Set list: 'The Man' suite <Intermission> 'The Journey' suite <Encore> 'Interstellar Overdrive'.

This show saw the introduction of two new suites of music built around existing and new works: *The Man* and *The Journey*.

Waters, in a later interview, explained the band's goal at this time: "We wanted to throw away the old format of the pop show standing on a square stage at one end of a rectangular room and running through a series of numbers. Our idea is to put the sound all around the audience with ourselves in the middle. Then the performance becomes much more theatrical." Indeed in one of his last band interviews for *Melody Maker*, on

ROYAL FESTIVAL HALL
general manager: J. denison c.b.e
THE MASSED GADGETS OF AUXIMENES
MORE FURIOUS MADNESS FROM
PINK FLOYD
INTRODUCING
'THE AZIMUTH CO-ORDINATOR'
On April 14th 1969
At 8·00pm
prices:
BRYAN MORRISON AGENCY
PRESENTATION

9 December 1967, Syd Barrett had accurately predicted that "in the future, groups are going to have to offer much more than just a pop show. They'll have to offer a well-presented theatre show."

The Man told a day-in-the-life story opening with 'Daybreak' (an alternative title for 'Grantchester Meadows' performed here as an acoustic instrumental piece that would later appear on the *Ummagumma* album with lyrics), followed by 'Work' (a Mason-fuelled percussion workout during which the others sawed and nailed pieces of wood to make a table, closing with pre-recorded tapes of tape-recorded machinery clanking away) and then 'Teatime' during which the band's roadies served tea on stage. 'Afternoon' followed, enabling Wright to display his ability on trombone in a piece that was later known as 'Biding My Time' (which appeared as a studio outtake on the May 1971 *Relics* compilation album). This was followed by 'Doing It!' (a crude reference to sex and an instrumental of percussion and taped voices combining elements of the yet to be recorded 'The Grand Vizier's Garden Party', 'Up The Khyber' and 'Heart Beat, Pig Meat'). Next came 'Sleep' (an electronic instrumental of ethereal keyboards, xylophones and slide guitars, reminiscent of 'Quicksilver', a track that would appear on *Music from the Film "More"*) merging into 'Nightmare'. This was an early version of 'Cymbaline', also from *Music from the Film "More"*, which incorporated tapes of heavy breathing, ticking clocks and alarm bells. In the clock sequence on the pre-recorded tapes, Waters' voice yells in a mock Scottish accent, 'If you don't eat your meat, you can't have any pudding', which was to appear on *The Wall* album some ten years later.) A reprise of 'Daybreak' ended the cycle and the first half of the show.

The Journey, however, told of a mythical travelogue opening with 'The Beginning' (later recorded as 'Green Is The Colour' from *Music from the Film "More"*) segueing into 'Beset By Creatures Of The Deep' (a reworking of 'Careful With That Axe, Eugene'), followed by 'The Narrow Way' (which would feature as 'The Narrow Way, Part 3' on *Ummagumma*). As this track faded and the stage lights dimmed, the band came off stage and a long pre-recorded taped sequence of footsteps circling the auditorium with doors opening and closing allowed the audience to appreciate the Azimuth Co-ordinator in all its glory (this particular section would re-emerge as the middle section of live performances of 'Cymbaline'). On their return to the stage, 'The Pink Jungle' (an instrumental) brought the stage back to explosive life, before giving way to the grand finale of the three-part sequence 'The Labyrinths Of Auximenes', 'Behold The Temple Of Light' and 'The End Of The Beginning' (the latter piece taken from the closing section of 'A Saucerful Of Secrets') dramatically displayed by Wright as he took controls of the grand Festival Hall pipe organ.

Film director Anthony Stern attended the afternoon rehearsal prior to soundcheck and was able to film the band working on parts of their set. A recording emerged, filmed in black and white, on the collectors' market in early 2006 and included parts of 'Afternoon' ('Biding My Time'), 'The Beginning' ('Green Is The Colour'), 'Nightmare' ('Cymbaline'), 'Beset By Creatures Of The Deep' ('Careful With That Axe, Eugene'), 'The End of The Beginning' (the closing organ section of 'A Saucerful Of Secrets') and other instrumental passages. Stern had obviously turned up on the off chance, with a view to recording the evening show for posterity. Unfortunately the venue management prevented him from filming in the evening and the ensuing discussion with a venue steward is also caught on tape.

The programme for this concert also gave a listing of Pink Floyd's forthcoming appearances, which included the following shows that were not fulfilled: Sweden (Monday 9 June), France (Monday 16 June) and Netherlands (Wednesday 18 June).

SATURDAY 19 APRIL – TELEVISION BROADCAST
Pink Floyd Mit Einen Neuen Beat Sound, ARD1, West Germany

Pink Floyd appeared on the show *Pink Floyd Mit Einem Neuen Beat Sound* (*Pink Floyd with a New Beat Sound*), although the recording date and their contribution is unknown. It was broadcast on ARD network TV between 10.00pm and 10.30pm.

WEDNESDAY 23 APRIL – RADIO BROADCAST
Psychedelic Sounds, NDR1, West Germany

Pink Floyd appeared on the show *Psychedelic Sounds*, recorded at NDR studios, Hamburg, West Germany, although the recording date and their contribution is unknown. It was broadcast on NDR1 radio between 9.30pm and 10.00pm.

SUNDAY 24 APRIL – CANCELLED PERFORMANCE
Star Club, Hamburg, West Germany

In an article published in *Hamburger Abenblatt* it was reported that Pink Floyd had failed to show for their appearance at the Star Club on this night. In the preceding week the same newspaper also reported that Pink Floyd would be appearing at the Underground, Cologne, West Germany in May.

MONDAY 25 APRIL – RECORDING SESSION
Room 4, EMI Studios, Abbey Road, London, England

10.30am to 12.30pm: Remixing 'Roger's Scene (Second Movement)' ['Grantchester Meadows'] (RS1 at 6:40) for *Ummagumma*. The session was produced by Norman Smith, engineered by Peter Mew and assisted by Neil Richmond.

MONDAY 25 APRIL – RECORDING SESSION
Studio 2 & Control Room 2, EMI Studios, Abbey Road, London, England

12.30pm to 1.15pm: Vocals of Take 1 of 'Roger's Scene (Second Movement)' ['Grantchester Meadows'] remixed for *Ummagumma*. The session was produced by Norman Smith, engineered by Peter Mew and assisted by Neil Richmond.

SATURDAY 26 APRIL – TELEVISION BROADCAST
Beat Club, ARD1, West Germany

An instrumental passage of Pink Floyd's music (reminiscent of the instrumental 'Reaction In G') appeared on the music show *Beat Club* over the news section of the show. *Beat Club* was produced at Radio Bremen studios, Bremen, West Germany and may have been tied in with their earlier dates in Hamburg, West Germany, or may have been supplied as a piece of pre-recorded music. It was broadcast on ARD network TV between 4.15pm and 5.15pm.

SATURDAY 26 APRIL – PERFORMANCE ◄
Light & Sound Concert, Main Hall, Bromley College of Technology, Bromley Common, Bromley, England

With East of Eden, Third Ear Band and lights by Luminiferous Extravaganza and Hippotama in the Refectory Hall.
Set list: 'Astronomy Domine', 'Careful With That Axe, Eugene', 'Interstellar Overdrive', 'Green Is The Colour', 'Pow R Toc H', 'Set The Controls For The Heart Of The Sun', 'A Saucerful Of Secrets'.

Pink Floyd's set was recorded for the *Ummagumma* album but due to technical problems the recording was aborted.

SUNDAY 27 APRIL – PERFORMANCE
Mothers, Erdington, Birmingham, England

Supported by the Flying Hat Band and compered by DJ John Peel.
Set list: 'Astronomy Domine', 'Careful With That Axe, Eugene', 'Interstellar Overdrive', 'Set The Controls For The Heart Of The Sun', 'A Saucerful Of Secrets', 'Let There Be More Light'.

Pink Floyd's set was recorded for the *Ummagumma* album. John Peel wrote an enthusiastic report of the show in his weekly column for *Disc & Music Echo* commenting, "At one moment they are laying surfaces of sound one upon another in symphonic thunder; at another isolated, incredibly melancholy sounds which cross one another sounding like cries of dying galaxies lost in sheer corridors of time and space."

The review also famously earned Peel a mention in the Pseuds Corner column of the satirical magazine *Private Eye*.

MONDAY 28 APRIL – RECORDING SESSION
Studio 2 & Control Room 2, EMI Studios, Abbey Road, London, England

2.30am to 5.30pm: 'Roger's Scene' ['Several Species…'] remixed (RS2 at 6:50), and 'Roger's Scene (Second Movement – Acoustic Guitar Song)' ['Grantchester Meadows'] remixed (RS3 at 7:48) for *Ummagumma*. The session was produced by Norman Smith, engineered by Peter Mew and assisted by Neil Richmond.

TUESDAY 29 APRIL – RECORDING SESSION
Control Room 2, EMI Studios, Abbey Road, London, England

11.00am to 12.30pm: All parts of 'Nicky's Scene' remixed (RS1 untimed also marked "best remix of start and end and edited to master") for *Ummagumma*. The session was produced by Norman Smith, engineered by Peter Mew and assisted by Neil Richmond.

FRIDAY 2 MAY – PERFORMANCE ►
May Ball, Student Union Building, College of Commerce, Manchester, England

With Smokey Rice, White Trash, the Groundhogs, Roy Harper and DJ John Peel with the Nova Express Lightshow in the Main Hall, and the Edgar Broughton Band, Pete Brown & His Battered Ornaments and Principal Edwards Magic Theatre in the Upstairs Bar, and film shows and fairground rides in the grounds.
Set list: 'Astronomy Domine', 'Careful With That Axe, Eugene', 'Interstellar Overdrive', 'Set The Controls For The Heart Of The Sun', 'A Saucerful Of Secrets'.

Pink Floyd's set was recorded for the *Ummagumma* album.

SATURDAY 3 MAY – PERFORMANCE
The Sports Hall, Queen Mary College, Mile End, London, England

Supported by Watch Us Grow.
Set list included 'Astronomy Domine', 'Interstellar Overdrive', 'Set The Controls For The Heart Of The Sun', 'A Saucerful Of Secrets'.

MONDAY 5 MAY – RECORDING SESSION
Room 4, EMI Studios, Abbey Road, London, England

2.30pm to 6.00pm: 'Ricky's Scene' ['Sysyphus'] remixed (RS1 untimed also marked "best") for *Ummagumma*. The session was produced by Norman Smith, engineered by Peter Mew and assisted by Neil Richmond.

WEDNESDAY 7 MAY – RECORDING SESSION
Room 4, EMI Studios, Abbey Road, London, England

10.00am to 1.00pm and 2.30pm to 5.30pm: 'Ricky's Scene' ['Sysyphus'] remixed (RS1, untimed), Crossfades for editing into 'Ricky's Scene' remixed for *Ummagumma*. The session was produced by Norman Smith and engineered by Jeff Jarrett.

FRIDAY 9 MAY – PERFORMANCE
Camden Fringe Festival Free Concert, The Bandstand, Parliament Hill Fields, Hampstead Heath, London, England

With Roy Harper, Jody Grind, Pete Brown's Battered Ornaments and the Pretty Things (headline).
Set list: 'Astronomy Domine', 'Set The Controls For The Heart Of The Sun', 'Careful With That Axe, Eugene', 'A Saucerful Of Secrets'.

The *International Times* reported, "The Floyd took to the stage like they were once more taking part in an all too familiar ritual – they looked tired and dispirited, and were obviously pissed off with the Orange equipment which was making the most unbelievably loud grunts and buzzes. After some rather hesitant beginnings they found where they were going and roared into 'Astronomy Domine' – the crowd yelled its approval. 'Set The Controls' and 'Careful With That Axe, Eugene' were dispensed in hard fashion, though Dave Gilmore [sic] had trouble with his amp, and the band announced that it had a gig to do in Southampton and would finish with a 'quick' version of 'Saucerful'. Roger Waters moved into the dark arena of crashing power in a most mysteriously violent way, and Rick Wright's organ, as ever, swept along fluidly with great sweeps and dives across the rest of the band. Nick Mason managed to drum as succinctly as ever, and by the end of 'Saucerful' the Floyd had created for the evening its colour – the tone and excitement of their playing was not to be lost. They left the stage to huge applause."

FRIDAY 9 MAY – PERFORMANCE
Old Refectory, Student's Union, Southampton University, Highfield, Southampton, England

Supported by Quintessence and Bridget St John.
Set list: 'Astronomy Domine', 'Careful With That Axe, Eugene', 'Interstellar Overdrive', 'The Beginning' ['Green Is The Colour'], 'Beset By Creatures Of The Deep' [an instrumental variation of 'Careful With That Axe, Eugene'], 'A Saucerful Of Secrets'.

SATURDAY 10 MAY – PRESS REPORT
London, England

It was announced in the UK music press that the launch of EMI's new Harvest on Friday 6 June was due to be celebrated with the staging of two free concerts featuring Pink Floyd and the Pretty Things at the Roundhouse, Chalk Farm, London (Friday 30 May), a show in Birmingham (Wednesday 4 June), and a further show in Manchester. Despite ticket applications being invited through EMI records none of the shows reached fruition.

SATURDAY 10 MAY – PERFORMANCE
Nottingham's Pop & Blues Festival, Notts County Football Ground, Nottingham, England

Pink Floyd closed the day's events, performing in the pouring rain, which was headlined by Fleetwood Mac and featured the Tremeloes, Marmalade, Georgie Fame, Love Sculpture, Keef Hartley, Status Quo, Duster Bennett, Dream Police, Van Der Graaf Generator and DJ John Peel.
Set list included 'Interstellar Overdrive'.

MONDAY 12 MAY – RECORDING SESSION
Room 4, EMI Studios, Abbey Road, London, England

2.30pm to 6.00pm: 'Ricky's Scene (Last Part)' ['Sysyphus, Part 4'] remixed (RS1 untimed), 'Ricky's Scene (Crossfades)' remixed (RS1, untimed), and 'Ricky's Scene' ['Sysyphus, Parts 1–4'] remixed (RS1 at 13:17 also marked "best edited") for *Ummagumma*. The session was produced by Norman Smith, engineered by Peter Mew and assisted by Neil Richmond.

MONDAY 12 MAY – RADIO RECORDING
John Peel & *Top Gear*, BBC Paris Cinema, Lower Regent Street, London, England

Pink Floyd recorded a replacement show for the aborted 9 April session for BBC Radio One on this date between 5.30pm and 12.00 midnight. It was broadcast on the *John Peel* programme on 14 May 1969 between 8.15pm and 9.15pm in the following order: 'Daybreak', 'Cymbaline', 'The Narrow Way' and 'Green Is The Colour'; and

repeated on *Top Gear*, hosted by John Peel, on 1 June 1969 between 7.00pm and 9.00pm in the following order: 'Daybreak', 'Cymbaline', 'Green Is The Colour' and 'The Narrow Way'.

THURSDAY 15 MAY – PERFORMANCE
It's A Drag – City of Coventry College of Art May Ball, Locarno Ballroom, Coventry, England

With Spooky Tooth and Free (who replaced the advertised Wellington Kitch at the last moment).

UK TOUR

Pink Floyd's first nationally advertised headline tour began at Leeds Town Hall on Friday 16 May and ended at the Royal Albert Hall, London on Thursday 26 June. It was presented by the Bryan Morrison Agency, complete with generic print and tour programme designed by Hipgnosis, and was interspersed with recording sessions and one-off engagements at both home and abroad.

For the tour Pink Floyd performed material previewed the previous month at the Royal Festival Hall in London. Some fine-tuning resulted in 'Nightmare' ('Cymbaline') now incorporating an additional middle section of a pre-recorded surround-sound sequence of footsteps and doors opening and closing. 'The Pink Jungle' was also extended to include a reworking of 'Pow R Toc H'. As at the Royal Festival Hall show, a costumed "creature" would often lumber around the hall during the set.

FRIDAY 16 MAY – PERFORMANCE
Town Hall, Leeds, England

Set list included 'The Man' suite <Intermission> 'The Journey' suite.

SATURDAY 17 MAY & SUNDAY 18 MAY – CANCELLED PERFORMANCES
Netherlands

Pink Floyd's advertised shows at the Paradiso, Amsterdam (Saturday 17 May) and Concertzaal de Jong, Groningen (Sunday 18 May) were cancelled due to problems with work permits. Although both were rescheduled to Saturday 7 June and Friday 6 June, respectively, those too were cancelled for the same reasons.

THURSDAY 22 MAY – RECORDING SESSION
Room 4, EMI Studios, Abbey Road, London, England

2.30pm to 5.30pm: 'Dave's Scene (1st Movement)' ['The Narrow Way, Part 1'] remixed (RS1 at 4:30, RS2 False Start and RS3 at 3:30 also marked "best") and 'Dave's Scene (2nd Movement)' ['The Narrow Way, Part 2'] (RS1 at 2:50 also marked "rough remix") for *Ummagumma*. The session was produced by Norman Smith, engineered by Peter Mew and assisted by Neil Richmond.

SATURDAY 24 MAY – PRESS REPORT
New York, USA

It was reported in the trade magazine *Billboard* that NEMS Enterprises had taken over the Bryan Morrison Agency, and two of the agency bookers, Tony Howard and Peter Bowyer, would join the staff at NEMS. This now meant that NEMS would now have exclusive booking rights to all of Morrison's acts which included Pink Floyd, Tyrannosaurus Rex, the Incredible String

Band and the Pretty Things. While NEMS continued to book Pink Floyd, personal management was transferred to former Morrison staff member Steve O'Rourke, who later formed his own management company, EMKA (named after his two daughters Emma and Katherine), in a position he retained until his death in October 2003. Tony Howard remained at NEMS and continued to book the band and even occasionally tour managed them through the early 1970s. He remained friends and toured with them between 1987 and 1994. He passed away in 2001 and is remembered on David Gilmour's 2006 album *On an Island*.

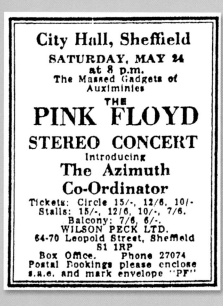

SATURDAY 24 MAY – PERFORMANCE ◄
City (Oval) Hall, Sheffield, England

Set list: 'The Man' suite <Intermission> 'The Journey' suite <Encore> 'Interstellar Overdrive'.

SUNDAY 25 MAY – PERFORMANCE
Benefit for the Fairport Convention, **The Roundhouse, Chalk Farm, London, England**

With Blossom Toes, the Deviants, Eclection, Family, Mick Fleetwood, Mimi & Mouse, Jack Moore, John Peel and the Pretty Things.

This was a hastily arranged benefit show to help pay for the care of members of Fairport Convention, who were injured in a serious accident on the M1 motorway in which drummer Martin Lamble and a female passenger, Gene Franklin, were killed. However, the show was a far from peaceful event, marred by crowd violence.

TUESDAY 27 MAY – RECORDING SESSION
Studio 2 & Control Room 2, EMI Studios, Abbey Road, London, England

7.00pm to 10.00pm: 'Dave's Scene (3rd Movement)' ['The Narrow Way, Part 3'] recorded (Take 1 at 4:36 also marked "best"), Guitar and Organ overdubbed onto Take 1 of 'Dave's Scene (3rd Movement)', and Drums and Bass overdubbed onto Take 1 of 'Dave's Scene (3rd Movement)' for *Ummagumma*. The session was produced by Norman Smith, engineered by Peter Mew and assisted by Michael Sheady.

THURSDAY 29 MAY – TELEVISION BROADCAST
Fusions, **HTV TV studios, Bristol, England**

Pink Floyd appeared live on the music show *Fusions*, although their contribution is unknown. It was broadcast on ITV network TV between 10.30pm and 11.00pm.

FRIDAY 30 MAY – PERFORMANCE
Fairfield Halls, Croydon, England

Set list: 'The Man' suite <Intermission> 'The Journey' suite.

The *Croydon Advertiser* reported, "Before a packed and rapturous audience the Pink Floyd were a brilliant success with a two and a half hour programme of their unique brand of happening music. The first half was called simply 'The Man'. The Floyd took the audience, with music and sound effects, through a day in the life of a man. From 'Daybreak' to 'Daydream' the group went through the whole 24 hours, and in the 24 hours they portrayed and expressed the whole gamut of human experience. 'Work', complete with logs being sawed, the dramatic 'Doing It!', in which the group gave a musical description of the sex act without once going across the borders into poor taste, and the traumatic 'Nightmare' sequence, were all vividly clear. But the real mood-setting half of the programme was Part Two, which described a long and often tortuous journey. And this is where the programme came in useful. With that in front of me, I was able to use it almost as a musical score. Each of the seven sections had a clear and definite division: and it was easy to see the transition from one part to the next. From 'The Beginning' the journey was 'Beset By Creatures Of The Deep', and progressed through the 'Narrow Way' and the 'Pink Jungle' – some magnificently atmospheric organ playing here by Richard Wright. 'The Labyrinths Of Auximenes' featured a special guest appearance by a monster of gargantuan physical proportions who did the most personal things all over the stage…. For me it was the least apposite part of the whole programme. After this the four built up a tremendous climax in 'Behold The Temple Of Light' and 'The End Of The Beginning', with organist Wright moving over to the fine Fairfield organ and creating a breath gasping finale."

SUNDAY 31 MAY – PERFORMANCE ▼
Eights Week Ball, **Main Marquee, Pembroke College, Oxford, England**

With Juniors Eyes (who replaced Van Der Graaf Generator who had split up the previous week) and Dark Blues (in the Main Marquee), Sister Ray Disco with light show (in the Cellar), Proteus Projection Workshop with the Acid Show (in the Junior Common Room), Rmas Band and Tropicanas (in the Hall) and Tropicanas with Limbo dancer, fire eater and Alan Rae (in the North Quad). Pink Floyd was paid £400 for their one-hour set that commenced at 1.30am.

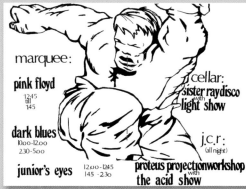

TUESDAY 3 JUNE – RECORDING SESSION
Studio 2 & Control Room 2, EMI Studios, Abbey Road, London, England

2.00pm to 5.15pm: 'Roger's Scene (2nd Movement)' ['Grantchester Meadows'] remixed (RS4 at 7:30 also marked "best") for *Ummagumma*. The session was produced by Norman Smith, engineered by Peter Mew and assisted by Alan Parsons.

FRIDAY 6, SATURDAY 7 & SUNDAY 8 JUNE – CANCELLED PERFORMANCES
Netherlands

Pink Floyd's advertised shows at the Concertzaal de Jong, Groningen (Friday 6 June), Paradiso, Amsterdam (Saturday 7 June) and Meerpaal, Dronten (Sunday 8 June) were all cancelled due to problems with work permits.

SUNDAY 8 JUNE – PERFORMANCE
Rex Ballroom, Cambridge, England

Set list included 'The Man' suite <Intermission> 'The Journey' suite.

TUESDAY 10 JUNE – PERFORMANCE ◄
Ulster Hall, Belfast, Northern Ireland

Set list: 'The Man' suite <Intermission> 'The Journey' suite <Encore> 'Set The Controls For The Heart Of The Sun'.

FRIDAY 13 JUNE – ALBUM RELEASE (UK)
Music from the Film More

Record Song Book wrote, "The music is sometimes purely instrumental, sometimes both instrumental and vocal, always extremely interesting and arresting. Quite weird in parts too. Try the 'Main Theme' on side 2 for example. But it's not all like this. There's a super little Spanish bit that sounds almost traditional, and there are other equally contrasting tracks."

FRIDAY 13 JUNE – CANCELLED PERFORMANCE
Van Dike Club, Devonport, Plymouth, England

This advertised show was postponed to Friday 27 June.

FRIDAY 13 JUNE – PERFORMANCE
Bradninch Dance, Great Hall, Devonshire House, University of Exeter, Exeter, England

Set list included 'Astronomy Domine', 'Set The Controls For The Heart Of The Sun', 'Careful With That Axe, Eugene', 'A Saucerful Of Secrets'.

SATURDAY 14 JUNE – PERFORMANCE
Colston Hall, Bristol, England

Set list included 'The Man' suite <Intermission> 'The Journey' suite.

The *Bristol Evening Post* reported, "The Pink Floyd unleashed the power of modern electronics, modern pop ideas and modern violence at their concert in Bristol. Electronically the show was brilliant. The Floyd played over recorded tapes, which smashed four channel stereo sounds across, around and under the Colston Hall. The ideas were also exciting. A pop concert by a single group with the guts to drop the package tour format, and a concert which followed a musical storyline which wasn't difficult to trace. The concert had its moments. An exciting blues solo by the lead guitarist, which Hendrix would have been proud of, nervous organ solos and some weirdly vicious rock and roll climaxes. But the Floyd pulled the punches and the music played on stage didn't live up to the interesting ideas they have created. The music was only intermittently good. For the Floyd it was a surprise, because they usually play immaculately – and the show had its silly moments. In one weirdo number an unnecessary Caliban staggered on to the stage and went into a music hall lavatory joke routine."

SUNDAY 15 JUNE – PERFORMANCE
Guildhall, Portsmouth, England

Set list included 'The Man' suite <Intermission> 'The Journey' suite.

MONDAY 16 JUNE – PERFORMANCE ►
The Dome, Brighton, England

Set list included 'The Man' suite <Intermission> 'The Journey' suite.

Peter Towner, a fan in attendance, recalled, "There was this small guy dressed up in a grey/green warty skinned costume with a cock that would give a donkey a complex and cause serious damage to a mare. I swear the guy was playing this cock, musically, as he moved, cat-like, around the stage after first stealing around the front and sides of the stalls. My eyes were watering at the sight of this enormous chopper being waved around so my vision could have been impaired."

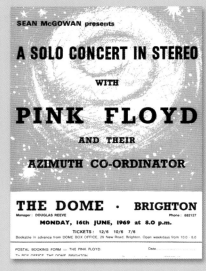

TUESDAY 17 JUNE – RECORDING SESSION
Room 4, EMI Studios, Abbey Road, London, England

10.00am to 1.00pm: 'Dave's Concerto (2nd Movement)' ['The Narrow Way, Part 2'] remixed (RS1 at 3:10 and RS2 at 3:20 also marked "best") for *Ummagumma*. The session was produced by Norman Smith, engineered by Peter Mew and assisted by Michael Sheady.

FRIDAY 20 JUNE – PERFORMANCE
Town Hall, Birmingham, England

Set list included 'The Man' suite <Intermission> 'The Journey' suite.

SATURDAY 21 JUNE – PERFORMANCE ►
Royal Philharmonic, Liverpool, England

Set list: 'The Man' suite <Intermission> 'The Journey' suite <Encore> 'Set The Controls For The Heart Of The Sun'.

SUNDAY 22 JUNE – PERFORMANCE
Free Trade Hall, Manchester, England

Set list: 'The Man' suite <Intermission> 'The Journey' suite <Encore> 'Set The Controls For The Heart Of The Sun'.

MONDAY 23 JUNE – RECORDING SESSION
Room 4, EMI Studios, Abbey Road, London, England

11.15am to 1.00pm: "Scotsman's Voice" recorded (RS1 at 4:00 approx) for 'Roger's Quarter' ['Several Species…'] for *Ummagumma*. The session was produced by Norman Smith, engineered by Phil McDonald and Chris Blair, and assisted by Antony Mone.

TUESDAY 24 JUNE – PERFORMANCE ▶
***Commemoration Ball*, Main Marquee, Front Quad, Queen's College, Oxford, England**

With Ten Years After, who replaced the advertised Procol Harum. Nigel Lewendon, then Steward of Queen's College, recalled, "I remember everyone sitting down on the grass, because it's not the sort of music you could dance to. They had an enormous amount of sound equipment and I was standing by one of the speakers when the drummer hit this huge gong. I don't think I heard another thing for three days!"

THURSDAY 26 JUNE – PERFORMANCE ◀
***The Final Lunacy!*, Royal Albert Hall, Kensington, London, England**

!! TONIGHT !!
THE FINAL LUNACY !!
ROYAL ALBERT HALL
Some more musical callisthenics
PINK FLOYD
with the
AZIMUTH CO-ORDINATOR
(Only 7/6 and 10/6 left)

Set list: 'The Man' suite <Intermission> 'The Journey' suite <Encore> 'Set The Controls For The Heart Of The Sun'.

The final date of the UK tour saw one of Pink Floyd's more experimental performances, featuring Richard Wright playing on the venue's pipe organ, a member of their crew dressed up as a gorilla, and even members of the band sawing wood on stage. The climax to 'The Journey' was especially memorable as the group was joined on stage by a brass section of the Royal Philharmonic Orchestra and members of the Ealing Central Amateur Choir conducted by Norman Smith, and culminating in the firing of two Waterloo cannons and the detonation of a huge pink smoke-bomb at the finale! Pink Floyd was allegedly banned from the venue for life but managed a return visit less than a year later.

FRIDAY 27 JUNE – CANCELLED PERFORMANCE
Van Dike Club, Devonport, Plymouth, England

Although the band arrived at the venue, their equipment van broke down on the way, forcing another cancellation at this venue. The show was successfully rescheduled to Friday 1 August.

SATURDAY 28 JUNE – PERFORMANCE
***Saturday Dance Date*, Winter Gardens Pavilion, Weston-Super-Mare, England**

Supported by the Ken Birch Band and the Mike Slocombe Combo.

MONDAY 30 JUNE – PERFORMANCE
***President's Ball*, Top Rank Suite, Cardiff, Wales**

Presented by the Llandaff Technical College, supported by Stop Watch.
Set list: 'Astronomy Domine', 'Green Is The Colour', 'Careful With That Axe, Eugene', 'Interstellar Overdrive', 'Set The Controls For The Heart Of The Sun' <Encore> 'A Saucerful Of Secrets'.
Pink Floyd was paid £100 for their performance.

FRIDAY 4 JULY – PERFORMANCE
***Selby Festival*, James Street Recreation Ground, Selby, England**

Set list included 'Interstellar Overdrive', 'Green Is The Colour'.

The *Yorkshire Evening Post* reported, "Selby Abbey rocked on its foundations last night and well into Saturday as Pink Floyd, Jon Hiseman's Colosseum and Eire Apparent hammered out the last night of the festival. About 2,000 young people from all over Yorkshire poured into Selby and then into a large marquee to hear music like Selby has never heard before. Pink Floyd produced some lovely sounds, and those crashing supernatural chords could be heard a quarter of a mile away from the marquee. The Floyd didn't have the time or stage space to do some of their recent works such as 'Man', so they concentrated on shorter, more exciting pieces like 'Interstellar Overdrive'. The group can be very gentle too, with things like 'Green is the Colour' and know the art of building up the mood. Add to that a whole roast ox to feed the hungry and a bar until midnight to satisfy the parched. The whole festival marks the 900th anniversary of the Abbey."

SATURDAY 5 JULY – RECORDING SESSION
Room 4, EMI Studios, Abbey Road, London, England

10.00am to 1.00pm: Various existing tapes edited and assembled for 'Daybreak – Roger's Quarter' ['Grantchester Meadows'] for *Ummagumma*. The session was produced by Norman Smith, engineered by Peter Mew and assisted by Richard Langham.

SATURDAY 5 JULY – RECORDING SESSION
Studio 2 & Control Room 2, EMI Studios, Abbey Road, London, England

2.30pm to 8.30pm: All three parts of 'Dave's Scene' ['The Narrow Way, Parts 1–3'] remixed, edited and cross-faded (RS10, RS11 and RS12 also marked "best") for *Ummagumma*. The session was produced by Norman Smith, engineered by Peter Mew and assisted by Richard Langham.

THURSDAY 10 JULY & FRIDAY 11 JULY – CANCELLED PERFORMANCES
Netherlands

Pink Floyd's advertised shows at the Paradiso, Amsterdam (Thursday 10 July) and Popmanifestatie, Veilinggebouw, Groningen (Friday 11 July) were both cancelled due to problems with work permits.

SOUNDTRACK FROM THE FILM *MORE*

SIDE ONE

CIRRUS MINOR (Waters) **5:19**
THE NILE SONG (Waters) **3:27**
CRYING SONG (Waters) **3:33**
UP THE KHYBER (Mason, Wright) **2:13**
GREEN IS THE COLOUR (Waters) **2:59**
CYMABLINE (WATERS) **4:50**
PARTY SEQUENCE (Waters, Wright, Gilmour, Mason) **1:09**

SIDE TWO

MAIN THEME (Waters, Wright, Gilmour, Mason) **5:26**
IBIZA BAR (Waters, Wright, Gilmour, Mason) **3:19**
MORE BLUES (Waters, Wright, Gilmour, Mason) **2:13**
QUICKSILVER (Waters, Wright, Gilmour, Mason) **7:14**
A SPANISH PIECE (Gilmour) **1:05**
DRAMATIC THEME (Waters, Wright, Gilmour, Mason) **2:18**

RELEASE DATE

UK: Friday 13 June 1969.
US: Saturday 9 August 1969.

FORMAT

UK: Columbia EMI SCX 6346 (Vinyl album).
US: Tower ST 5169 (Vinyl album).

HIGHEST CHART POSITION

UK: No.14 (*Melody Maker* 'Top Twenty Albums' on Saturday 19 July 1969).
US: No.153 (*Billboard* 'Top LPs & Tape' (1973 reissue, on 29 September 1973).

ARTWORK

The cover images are taken from stills of the film and feature the 200-year-old windmill in the small town of El Pilar, which is still something of a tourist attraction for Pink Floyd fans.

The original vinyl album in the UK was titled "soundtrack from the film *More* played and composed by the pink floyd" and in the US was titled "original motion picture soundtrack *More* played and composed by the pink floyd". Beginning in 1996, with the remastered re-release of the CD, the album was universally renamed *Music from the film* More.

MUSICIANS

David Gilmour (Vocals, Acoustic Guitar, Electric Guitar, Slide Guitar, Flamenco Guitar, Tape Effects, Bongos).
Nick Mason (Drums, Percussion, Bongos).
Roger Waters (Bass Guitar, Vocals, Tape and Birdsong Effects, Bongos, Gong).
Richard Wright (Hammond, Farfisa, Piano, Vibraphone, Bongos).

ADDITIONAL MUSICIANS

Lindy Mason (Penny Whistle on 'Green Is The Colour', 'Cymbaline' and 'Party Sequence').

RECORDING DETAILS

Pink Floyd's feature film debut was recorded between Monday 3 and Friday 7 February 1969 at Studio One, Pye Recording Studios, ATV House, Marble Arch, London from midnight to eight in the morning each day, working to a rough cut of the film. Director Barbet Schroeder was clear on how he wanted the music to fit the film, preferring the music to be heard as if playing from a stereo in a bar, or at a party, rather than a conventional backing soundtrack.

In order to synch the music to the film, Pink Floyd used Pye instead of Abbey Road, which didn't have a frame counter. Significantly, it was also Pink Floyd's first studio sessions without the attentive eye of producer Norman Smith.

As regards the music itself, in the film it was used as brief excerpts, and in a different sequential order to that of the album. The film features some notable differences to the discerning ear, including early mixes of 'Main Theme', 'Ibiza Bar', 'Party Sequence', 'Quicksilver', 'More Blues' and 'Up The Khyber'. 'Cymbaline' features alternate lyrics and two tracks, 'Hollywood' and 'Seabirds', are only featured in the film. The only official release of 'Seabirds', or rather a version of it, was a cover by Langford & Kerr on the Belgian CD release of *Moving Soundtracks Vol.1* released in 1981. It is also the only album on which all the vocals are handled solely by David Gilmour and it features Nick Mason's then wife, Lindy, on penny whistle. Overall it is an album of extreme contrasts, ranging from the delicate acoustics of 'Green Is The Colour' to the all-out sub-metal thrash of 'The Nile Song'.

Rarely spoken of in contemporary or subsequent interviews, *More* remains a largely undocumented period in the band's recording history. However, in a syndicated interview for *Associated Press* in the

US (April 1971) Waters recalled that "The whole thing was done in a week for $10,000, which is a small budget, and we paid for our own studio time. We didn't have the material for one song when we started. Dave, Nick and Richard put down the backing track in the studio, while I was writing the first verse in the corner."

Speaking to the French magazine *Rock & Folk* (September 1969) Barbet Schroeder said that, "The Pink Floyd made me some absolutely perfect music. I showed them the film and asked them to make music for certain scenes without giving them any guidance. They found an amazing magical element, and especially the sense of space. It really is music, more than just songs. So much so that often I had to turn the volume down because the quality of the music literally destroyed some scenes. Often, music serves to hide some weaknesses, but this is not the case in *More*. For the record, Pink Floyd composed their music in the afternoon, reviewing the film, and recorded in the evening for five consecutive days between midnight and nine o'clock in the morning on a 16-track tape. The studio told me he had never seen musicians so conscientious!"

In the late 1990s two 8-track tape boxes containing material recorded for the soundtrack came up for auction, but were quickly withdrawn. From the poor quality photo and description there were no dates on the boxes but they were labelled Bryan Morrison Agency (Pink Floyd's then management), the engineers' initials BH (Brian Humphries) and AH (unknown). The tapes featured the tracks 'Main Theme', 'Paris Bar', 'Stefan's Tit', 'Ibiza Bar' and 'Theme "Dramatic Version"'. The seller described his acquisition saying that, "I was working as a recording engineer at Pye Studios. I already knew Richard Wright, I had met him at a friend's party and had been round to dinner a few times and had sat in on some of the *Wish You Were Here* sessions at Abbey Road, but I had now lost contact. I was unaware of the *More* tapes

that were sitting, unclaimed, in the Pye Studios tape library until the tape librarian informed me that she had been asked to clear out any tapes that had lain unclaimed for more than ten years. She knew of my Floyd connection and asked if I wanted the tapes. I said yes. There were four tapes in all. Many tapes of other artists were destroyed and I naively didn't salvage any of them. A year or so later I was working in another studio in east London and I tried re-mixing two of the tapes and overnight they were stolen. So I was left with the remaining two tapes that I now own. Each tape is in the one-inch 8 track format and plays at 15ips. The track listing also lists the instrumentation as electric guitar, acoustic guitar, bass, drums, vocals, organ, flute and overdubs."

The current whereabouts of the tape boxes is uncertain. At the Pink Floyd exhibition in Paris in 2003 an original tape box for *More* was exhibited and labelled with the following tracks, revealing a further clutch of likely out-takes: 'Main Theme 1 & 2' / 'Party Sequence 1 & 2' / 'Jukebox (Up The Khyber)' / 'Theme – Beat Version' / 'Spanish Music' / 'Blues – Slow' / 'Hollywood' / 'Seabirds' / 'Crying Song' / 'Waterpipe' / 'Paris Bar'.

THEATRICAL RELEASE

More starred German actor Klaus Grünberg and American actress Mimsy Farmer, and told a sorry tale of love and drug addiction, with some quite explicit scenes, via an obscure sub-plot involving a former Nazi. The film debuted at the International Critics Week, which ran in parallel to the *22nd Festival International du Film at Cannes*, France in May 1969 and received its US premiere at the Plaza Theater, New York on Monday 4 August 1969 and in the UK at the Cameo Victoria, London on Friday 22 February 1970. Director Barbet Schroeder was appointed "Godfather" of Critics Week at the *55th Festival International du Film at Cannes*, France and was honoured by a screening of *More* on Sunday 19 May 2002.

ABOVE: THE WINDMILL AT EL PILAR ON IBIZA.

LEFT: POSTER FOR THE FRENCH FILM RELEASE.

SATURDAY 19 JULY – RECORDING SESSION
Studio 3 & Control Room 3, EMI Studios, Abbey Road, London, England

2.30pm to 7.00pm and 8.00pm to 11.45pm: 'Rest' ['Biding My Time'] recorded (Take 1 False Start, Take 2 at 5:07, Take 3 False Start and Take 4 at 5:15 also marked "best"), and Vocals, Trombones, Piano, Acoustic Guitar and Drums overdubbed onto Take 4 of 'Rest'. The session was produced by Norman Smith. There is no clear reason why this track was recorded, as the final running order for *Ummagumma* was already completed. Whatever the case it remained unreleased until it appeared on the compilation album *Relics* in May 1971. On the original vinyl album sleeve it is incorrectly noted to have been produced on 9 July 1969.

SUNDAY 20 JULY – TELEVISION RECORDING
So What if it's Just Green Cheese?, Studio 5, BBC TV Centre, White City, London, England

Pink Floyd performed a six-minute live-to-air improvisation entitled 'Moonhead' as part of a the BBC's moonlanding coverage in a light-hearted *Omnibus* special entitled *So What if it's Just Green Cheese?* It was broadcast on BBC1 TV between 10.00pm and 11.00pm, and featured appearances by Judi Dench, Ian McKellen, Michael Hordern, Roy Dotrice, Marian Montgomery and Dudley Moore & the Dudley Moore Trio.

TUESDAY 22 JULY – TELEVISION RECORDING
P, SDR TV Studios, Stuttgart, West Germany

Pink Floyd performed 'Corporal Clegg' and 'A Saucerful Of Secrets' live for the children's programme *P*. 'Corporal Clegg' was played over some bizarre footage of the band engaged in a staged restaurant food-fight, while 'A Saucerful Of Secrets' saw the band performing live in the studio. Other acts appearing in what was generally an anarchistic presentation were the Locomotive and the cast of the Munich production of *Hair*. It was broadcast on ARD1 network TV on Sunday 21 September 1969 between 5.15pm and 6.10pm and repeated on ZDF2 network TV on 10 August 1971 between 5.10pm and 5.55pm. 'A Saucerful Of Secrets' was due to have been broadcast on NDR TV's popular music programme *Beat Club* on Sunday 26 December 1971 but the director refused, citing that the footage was not original to his programme.

THURSDAY 24 & FRIDAY 25 JULY – UNCONFIRMED TELEVISION RECORDING
Netherlands

Pink Floyd was reported to have provided music for Nederland 1 TV's coverage of the Apollo 11 moon-landing, but the exact programme and their contribution remains unknown.

FRIDAY 1 AUGUST – PERFORMANCE
Van Dike Club, Devonport, Plymouth, England

MONDAY 4 AUGUST – FILM PREMIERE
7th New York Film Festival, Alice Tulley Hall, Lincoln Center, New York, NY, USA

The *New York Times* said, "*More* [is] a curiously effective dramatisation of the kind of puritan ethic that demands that pleasure be paid for by pain and tragedy. It's a 19th century romance set to a rock tune on a portable cassette recorder."

FRIDAY 8 AUGUST – PERFORMANCE ▼
9th National Jazz Pop Ballads & Blues Festival, Plumpton Race Track, Streat, England

With Soft Machine, East of Eden, Blossom Toes, Keith Tippett Jazz Group, Juniors Eyes and the Village on the same night, and headliners the Who (Saturday 9 August) and the Nice (Sunday 10 August).
Set list: 'Set The Controls For The Heart Of The Sun', 'Cymbaline', 'The Journey' suite <Encore> 'Interstellar Overdrive'.

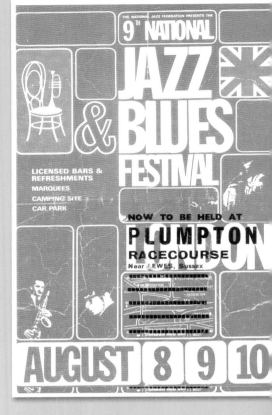

This three-day festival was originally going to be staged on a derelict site on Horton Road, West Drayton, in west London, but the local council refused to grant a license and so the organizers relocated the event to Plumpton. For the bands and the audience in the main arena on the first night, the momentum was lost with power cuts occurring throughout Soft Machine's set. During over an hour of silence the crowd became restless and most had fallen asleep by the time Pink Floyd came on.

SATURDAY 9 AUGUST – ALBUM RELEASE (US)
Music from the Film More

Record World wrote that *More*, "a morality take about immoral people, has been getting marvellous reviews. Pink Floyd's contribution, a searing, wistful score, should not be minimized and won't be when viewers leave the theatre."

SATURDAY 9 AUGUST – PERFORMANCE
Paradiso, Amsterdam, Netherlands

Supported by Dream and Universal Delight.
Set list: 'Interstellar Overdrive', 'Set The Controls For The Heart Of The Sun', 'Careful With That Axe, Eugene' <Encore> 'A Saucerful Of Secrets'.

Hilversum 2 radio recorded this performance for its *Jazz & Pop Live* series for broadcast on Friday 29 August between 8.00pm and 8.45pm, but after a vocal microphone failure early in the show the band was forced to perform an instrumental set and as a result the broadcast was aborted. Recording was rescheduled to their show in Amsterdam on Wednesday 17 September.

SATURDAY 13 SEPTEMBER – PERFORMANCE
The Sam Cutler Stage Show. **Rugby Rag's Blues Festival, Rainsbrook, Rugby, England**

With the Nice, Taste, King Crimson, Free, Edgar Broughton Band, Third Ear Band, Bridget St John, Big Idea and Fagin's Quill, and compered by John Peel and headliners Alexis Korner and His New Church (Friday 12 September) and Eclection (Sunday 14 September).
This three-day open-air festival offered one day of blues, one of pop and one of folk. It was attended by more than 3,000 people despite heavy downpours of cold rain throughout, and was policed peacefully by the Hell's Angels. Pink Floyd appeared on the pop day and, remarkably, given the weather conditions, was said to be accompanied by an impressive light show.

WEDNESDAY 17 SEPTEMBER– PERFORMANCE ▼
Concertgebouw, Amsterdam, Netherlands

Supported by Dream with the Khaphalous Light Show.
Set list: 'The Man' suite <Intermission> 'The Journey' suite.

VPRO's excellent recording of this show has been widely bootlegged from the master tapes, which were leaked in 1997 following their re-discovery during a clear out of the station archives. Various short extracts have been repeated since then, but the full concert was never broadcast following the cancellation of Hilversum 2's *Jazz & Pop Live* series for which the show was recorded.

The original master tape even captures an introductory speech made by a female presenter which roughly translates as "And now a letter which Nicky from the Pink Floyd wrote to us. The concert from Pink Floyd is in two parts. It tells the story of a man and the journey that he makes. Part one is about 24 hours of his life: awakening, working, resting, making love, dreaming and again awakening. The second part tells of the hardships he experiences and the mysterious ending to the story."

FRIDAY 19 SEPTEMBER – PERFORMANCE
Grote Zaal, De Doelen, Rotterdam, Netherlands

Supported by Dream with the Khamphalous Lightshow.

SATURDAY 20 SEPTEMBER – PERFORMANCES
Concertzaal de Jong, Groningen, Netherlands

Two shows at 9.00pm and 12.30am, supported by Dream with the Khamphalous Lightshow and the Happy Heavy Lightshow.
Set list at the second show included 'Astronomy Domine', 'Green Is The Colour', 'Careful With That Axe, Eugene', 'Interstellar Overdrive', 'Set The Controls For The Heart Of The Sun', 'A Saucerful Of Secrets'.

SUNDAY 21 SEPTEMBER – PERFORMANCE
Het Kolpinghuis, Nijmegen, Netherlands

Afternoon show supported by Dream with the Khamphalous Lightshow, rescheduled from Tiel, Netherlands.

MONDAY 22 & TUESDAY 23 SEPTEMBER – UNCONFIRMED TELEVISION RECORDING
BRT TV Studios, Amerikaans Theater, Brussels, Belgium

Pink Floyd was reported to be recording for Belgian TV but no record of their visit is noted in the station archives.

WEDNESDAY 24 SEPTEMBER – PERFORMANCE
Stadtsgehoorzaal, Leiden, Netherlands

Rescheduled from Waarschijnlijk, Nijmegen, Netherlands.

THURSDAY 25 SEPTEMBER – PERFORMANCE
Staargebouw, Maastricht, Netherlands

Rescheduled from Stadsschouwberg, Maastricht, Netherlands.

FRIDAY 26 – SUNDAY 28 SEPTEMBER – PERFORMANCES ▶
Theatre 140, Brussels, Belgium

Set list on 28 September included 'The Man' suite and 'Set The Controls For The Heart Of The Sun'.

FRIDAY 3 OCTOBER – PERFORMANCE
Events, Metallurgy and Production Engineering Dance, **Debating Hall, Birmingham University, Edgbaston, Birmingham, England**

Supported by Pegasus and Barnabas.
Set list included 'Interstellar Overdrive', 'Set The Controls For The Heart Of The Sun', 'A Saucerful Of Secrets'.

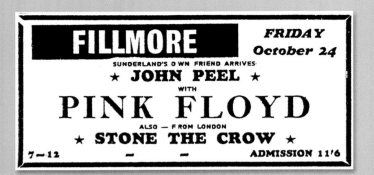

Redbrick, the Birmingham University student newspaper, reported, "Their Floydian majesties did indeed descend on the Union on Friday. They were in a particularly celestial mood, even though the Azimuth was nowhere to be seen. On any occasion the effects of 'Interstellar Overdrive' are likely to be rather disconcerting, but when the sequence extends to 'Set The Controls For The Heart Of The Sun' and the near legendary 'Saucerful Of Secrets' the only wonder is that the floor of the Deb Hall was not littered with the mortal remains of those whose migrant spirits were winging their way to the Heavens. Roger Waters actually attempted to fly, but he was unsuccessful."

SATURDAY 4 OCTOBER – PERFORMANCE
New Union, University of Reading, Whiteknights Park, Reading, England
Supported by Quintessence and Zap Gun Smith.

TUESDAY 7 OCTOBER – PERFORMANCE
Gaiety Lounge Show Bar, South Parade Pier, Southsea, Portsmouth, England

FRIDAY 10 OCTOBER – PERFORMANCE
Edward Herbert Building, University of Loughborough, Loughborough, England
Supported by Jimmy Powell and Arrival.
Set list included 'Astronomy Domine', 'Interstellar Overdrive'.

SATURDAY 11 OCTOBER – PERFORMANCE
***Internationales Essener Pop & Blues Festival '69*, Grugahalle, Essen, West Germany**
With the Nice, Deep Purple, Aynsley Dunbar Retaliation, Taste, Keef Hartley, Hardin And York, Amon Duul II, Cuby's Blues Band, Livin' Blues and Brain Box, and headliners Fleetwood Mac (Thursday 9 October) and Muddy Waters (Friday 10 October).
Set list: 'Astronomy Domine', 'Green Is The Colour', 'Careful With That Axe, Eugene', 'Interstellar Overdrive', 'A Saucerful Of Secrets'.
Edited highlights including footage of Pink Floyd's performance of 'Careful With That Axe, Eugene' and 'A Saucerful Of Secrets' were included as part of the programme *Internationaal Pop en Bluesfestival* in Essen broadcast on ARD1 network TV on Saturday 27 December between 8.15pm and 9.00pm.

SATURDAY 18 OCTOBER – PERFORMANCE
University College London, Bloomsbury, London, England
With the Edgar Broughton Band and Majority.

WEDNESDAY 22 OCTOBER – CANCELLED PERFORMANCE
The Ballroom, University of Nottingham, Beeston, Nottingham, England
Listed in both *Time Out* and *NME*, this show was rescheduled to Saturday 10 January 1970.

FRIDAY 24 OCTOBER – PERFORMANCE ◄
***Fillmore North*, Locarno Ballroom, Sunderland, England**
Supported by Stone The Crows and DJ John Peel.
Set list: 'Astronomy Domine', 'Green Is The Colour', 'Careful With That Axe, Eugene', 'Interstellar Overdrive', 'Set The Controls For The Heart Of The Sun', 'A Saucerful Of Secrets'.

SATURDAY 25 OCTOBER – PERFORMANCE ►
***Actuel Festival*, Kluisbergbos, Amougies, Belgium**

With headliners Ten Years After (Friday 24 October), the Nice (Sunday 26 October), Yes (Monday 27 October) and Soft Machine (Tuesday 28 October).
Set list: 'Astronomy Domine', 'Green Is The Colour', 'Careful With That Axe, Eugene', 'Interstellar Overdrive' (with Frank Zappa), 'Main Theme' from *More*, 'Set The Controls For The Heart Of The Sun', 'A Saucerful Of Secrets'.

This impressive festival was originally advertised to be held at Parc St Cloud, Paris, France as the *First Continental Festival* and then at Bois de Vincennes, Paris, France as the *First Paris Music Festival*, but the French police refused to grant the event a licence. Organizers decided to move the event out of France altogether, to an area just north of the tiny Belgian village of Amougies. Pink Floyd topped the bill on the second night, on a stage which was housed in a massive circus tent and compered by Pierre Lattes and Frank Zappa, who performed with many of the acts, including Pink Floyd, turning in a 20-minute version of 'Interstellar Overdrive'. Although the event packed in over 55 acts and attracted some 20,000 visitors over the five days it suffered huge financial losses.

Melody Maker reported that Pink Floyd was, '[a]t last something to compare with '2001'. They had to battle against a few crackles from the amplifiers, but came over clear and well balanced. Frank Zappa accepted their challenge to join in on 'Interstellar Overdrive' and a few new galaxies were discovered."

Parts of the festival were recorded and broadcast by various networks including RTL radio, Europe 1 radio, ABC TV News, Gaumont Pathe TV and RTB TV, but unbelievably none of them captured anything of Pink Floyd's performance! However, two documentary films were made of the festival, both directed by Jérôme Laperrousaz. The first, entitled *European Music Revolution*, was a documentary of the event as a whole, and *Music Power* which focussed on the actual performances. The latter featured Pink Floyd performing 'Careful With That Axe, Eugene' and 'Green Is The Colour', and both films were released as a double bill on the French cinema circuit in June 1970. Two one-and-a-half minute black-and-white cinema trailers were produced by Gaumont Pathé to advertise the film, one of which included shots of Pink Floyd's to advertise the film, one of which included shots of Pink Floyd's performance. *Music Power* and *European Music Revolution* never saw a theatrical release in the UK or US, but both films were presented as a double bill in France, premiering at the Celtic Plaza and the Pagode, Paris on Thursday 28 May 1970. *Music Power* was shown in its entirety on ORTF2 TV on Sunday 24 September 1972 between 9.20pm and 10.35pm.

Clips from *Music Power* later appeared on French TV including 'Careful With That Axe, Eugene', on the music programme *Samedi et Compagnie* broadcast on ORTF1 TV on Saturday 30 May 1970 between 4.00pm and 5.50pm, and 'Set The Controls For The Heart Of The Sun' broadcast on the music show *Rock en Stock* on ORTF1 TV on Saturday 15 January 1972 between 10.55pm and 11.25pm.

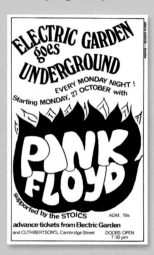

MONDAY 27 OCTOBER – PERFORMANCE ◄
Electric Garden, Glasgow, Scotland

Supported by The Stoics.
Set list included: 'Green Is The Colour', 'Careful With That Axe, Eugene', 'Set The Controls For The Heart Of The Sun'.

FRIDAY 31 OCTOBER – CANCELLED PERFORMANCE
Black Magic & Rock & Roll, Olympia Stadium, Detroit, MI, USA

Because of contractual difficulties many of the advertised performers including Pink Floyd, Arthur Brown, Dr Timothy Leary, MC5, Bonzo Dog Band, Kim Fowley, Alice Cooper, Satan (Himself), Bob Seger, the Frost and Amboy Dukes did not appear. Without many of its star attractions it was a poorly attended festival but several acts including Coven, Peter Hurkos (Mystic), Ralph Adams (Modern Houdini), Plum Wine, Sky, Pluto, Ted Lucas, Frijid Pink, Früt, Teegarden & Van Winkle, All the Lonely People, Pleasure Seekers, Sweetwater, SRC and Savage Grace did make an appearance.

SATURDAY 1 NOVEMBER – PERFORMANCE
Main Debating Hall, Manchester University, Manchester, England

Supported by Stone The Crows with the Nova Express Lightshow.
Set list: 'Astronomy Domine', 'Green Is The Colour', 'Careful With That Axe, Eugene', 'Interstellar Overdrive', 'Cymbaline', 'Set The Controls For The Heart Of The Sun', 'A Saucerful Of Secrets', 'Pow R Toc H'.

Manchester Independent, Manchester University's student newspaper, reported, "It is difficult to imagine the Pink Floyd who played the Free Trade Hall last term fitting their sound into MDH. The Azimuth Co-ordinator should compete fairly strongly with the disco in the open lounge. The Floyd are certainly one of the most technically accomplished groups around, even if flying drumsticks are a feature of their act – their drummer's fingers are notoriously slippery. A packed MDH should prove an interesting animal with creaking doors and ominous footsteps all around it. Their performances are not just musical, but an initiation into the theatre of darkness – a goldmine of sound effects. The removal of the light-show from their act accentuates the sophistication of their sound."

FRIDAY 7 NOVEMBER – ALBUM RELEASE (UK)
Ummagumma

International Times wrote, "These two albums are a really magnificent package. The first disc comprises four pieces from their live repertoire, beautifully played and really well produced by Norman Smith. I think it is probably one of the best live recordings I have ever heard."

FRIDAY 7 NOVEMBER – PERFORMANCE
Main Hall, Waltham Forest Technical College, Walthamstow, London, England

Supported by Jan Dukes de Grey and Mandrake Paddle Steamer. Pink Floyd was paid £450 for their performance.
Set list: 'Astronomy Domine', 'Interstellar Overdrive', 'Green Is The Colour', 'Careful With That Axe, Eugene', 'Set The Controls For The Heart Of The Sun', 'A Saucerful Of Secrets' <Encore> 'Let There Be More Light'.

SATURDAY 8 NOVEMBER – ALBUM RELEASE (US)
Ummagumma

Record World wrote, "The material is all rather ambitious and complex, running to many parts and many bands. The fans will want to get into the music, and way out into it."

SATURDAY 8 NOVEMBER – CANCELLED PERFORMANCE
Refectory Hall, University Union, Leeds University, Leeds, England

Pink Floyd cancelled for unknown reasons and was replaced by Tyrannosaurus Rex, with support from the Idle Race.

SATURDAY 15 – SATURDAY 22 NOVEMBER – RECORDING SESSIONS
International Recording Studios, Rome, Italy

Recording for the soundtrack *Zabriskie Point*. Initial sessions were supervised by the film's director, Michaelangelo Antonioni, and resulted in the recording of 'Heart Beat, Pig Meat', 'Come In Number 51, Your Time Is Up', rough instrumental takes of what would become 'Love Scene' and the unreleased 'Riot Scene'. The latter was more commonly known as 'The Violent Sequence', occasionally performed live in this period and much later formed the basis for the track 'Us And Them' for their album *The Dark Side of the Moon*.

THURSDAY 20 – TUESDAY 25 NOVEMBER – CANCELLED PERFORMANCES
West Germany

NME reported that Pink Floyd would be joining the Pretty Things and Steamhammer on a tour of West Germany, but Pink Floyd pulled out at the last minute due to recording commitments in Italy and were replaced by Fat Mattress, who had just released their eponymous debut album. In some cases fans were not informed of the change until they were inside the venue and violence broke out as a result. The following dates were publicized: Circus Krone, Munich on Thursday 20 November; Messehalle, Nürnburg on Friday 21 November; Volksbildungsheim, Frankfurt (6.00pm and 10.00pm) on Saturday 22 November; Friedrich-Ebert Halle, Hamburg (afternoon show) on Sunday 23 November; Star Club, Hamburg (evening show) on Sunday 23 November; Messe & Kongresshalle 8, Cologne on Monday 24 November; and Stadthalle, Bremen on Tuesday 25 November.

UMMAGUMMA

SIDE ONE

ASTRONOMY DOMINE (Barrett) **8:32**
CAREFUL WITH THAT AXE, EUGENE (Waters, Wright, Gilmour, Mason) **8:49**

SIDE TWO

SET THE CONTROLS FOP THE HEART OF THE SUN (Waters) **9:27**
A SAUCERFUL OF SECRETS (Waters, Wright, Mason, Gilmour) **12:48**

SIDE THREE

SYSYPHUS, PARTS 1–4 (Wright) **12:59**
GRANTCHESTER MEADOWS (Waters) **7:26**
SEVERAL SPECIES OF SMALL FURRY ANIMALS GATHERED TOGETHER IN A CAVE AND GROOVING WITH A PICT (Waters) **4:59**

SIDE FOUR

THE NARROW WAY, PARTS 1–3 (Gilmour) **12:17**
THE GRAND VIZIER'S GARDEN PARTY, PART 1: ENTRANCE; PART 2: ENTERTAINMENT; PART 3: EXIT (Mason) **8:46**

RELEASE DATE

UK: Friday 7 November 1969.
US: Saturday 8 November 1969.

FORMAT

UK: EMI Harvest SHDW 1/2 (Double vinyl album).
US: Harvest STBB 388 (Double vinyl album).

HIGHEST CHART POSITION

UK: No. 6 (*Melody Maker* 'Top Twenty Albums' on Saturday 6 December 1969).
US: No. 74 (*Billboard* 'Top LPs & Tape' on Saturday 7 March 1970).

AWARDS

UK: Certified Silver on Monday 22 July 2013.
US: Certified Gold on 28 February 1974 and Platinum on 11 March 1994.

ARTWORK

The front cover photo was taken at the parental home of Storm Thorgerson's then partner Libby January in Great Shelford, near Cambridge. Both Pink Floyd and Jokers Wild performed at a private party there in late 1965. The rear cover photo – Alan Styles and Peter Watts stand amid a vast array of equipment in front of what would appear to be a Tardis-like van – was taken at Biggin Hill Aerodrome.

The band portraits on the original inner sleeve were shot at various locations in London with Gilmour's having been taken at the Elfin Tree in Hyde Park, London. The original US album sleeve and labels list 'A Saucerful Of Secrets' as being comprised of four parts: 'Something Else', 'Syncopated Pandemonium', 'Storm Signals' and 'Celestial Voices'. This does not appear on the UK version.

The 2011 *Discovery* reissue completely dispensed with the original portraits and instead inexplicably replaced them with a random selection of pictures that do not remotely reflect the period, including studio sequences shot for *Live At Pompeii* in Paris in December 1971, live photos taken at Crystal Palace on Saturday 15 May 1971, a publicity shot taken in London in 1970 and a photo of the band at a sound-check at Radio City Music Hall in New York on 17 March 1973.

MUSICIANS

David Gilmour (Studio compositions: All instruments, Vocals on 'The Narrow Way').
Nick Mason (Studio compositions: All instruments on 'The Grand Vizier's Garden Party', except Flute).
Roger Waters (Studio compositions: All instruments, Vocals, Tape Effects on 'Grantchester Meadows' and 'Several Species Of Small Furry Animals Gathered Together In A Cave And Grooving With A Pict').
Richard Wright (Studio compositions: All instruments, Vocals on 'Sysyphus').

ADDITIONAL MUSICIANS

Lindy Mason (Flute on 'The Grand Vizier's Garden Party, Parts 1 & 3').
Norman Smith (Drums on 'Sysyphus').

RECORDING DETAILS

The studio tracks were recorded at EMI Studios, Abbey Road and produced by Norman Smith and engineered by Peter Mew. The live tracks were recorded at Mother's Club, Birmingham on 27 April 1969 and the College of Commerce, Manchester on 2 May 1969 and produced by Pink Floyd and engineered by Brian Humphries. Further live recordings were intended to have been made at Bromley College of Technology on 26 April 1969, but were aborted due to technical problems.

Talking to *Beat Instrumental* (January 1970) Richard Wright explained, "The live part of the album we had to record twice. The first time, at Mothers in Birmingham, we felt we'd played really well, but the equipment didn't work so we couldn't use nearly all of that one. The second time, at Manchester College of Commerce, was a really bad gig but as the recording equipment was working really well, we had to use it. Parts of 'Saucer' came from the Birmingham gig which we put together with the Manchester stuff but the stuff on the album isn't half as good as we can play."

In any event a large part of the vocals were supposedly overdubbed at a later date at Abbey Road. It is also worth noting that the album sleeve lists incorrect recording dates.

For the studio album each band member was assigned a quarter length of an album to produce a solo piece. Best described as experimental, it was developed from existing, or developing, live performance pieces. Wright nearly makes the grade with his four-part concerto 'Sysyphus', while Waters' 'Grantchester Meadows' had lyrics from its earlier incarnation as a live acoustic instrumental; a nostalgic recollection of his youth and lazy summer days spent by the River Cam. He also penned the ridiculously titled 'Several Species of Small Furry Animals Gathered Together In A Cave And Grooving With A Pict', in which he rants away in a mock-Scottish accent, bridging the two tracks with an amusing sequence involving a fly being swatted, in full stereo!

Mason's contribution is an experimental percussion sequence similar to 'Work', which was incorporated into 'The Man' sequence and, like Wright's piece, it has no lyrics. Gilmour, in enchanting contrast, produced 'The Narrow Way', which was also used as a live piece from early on in the year. Along with 'Grantchester Meadows', it is the strongest material on the studio album.

In fact, in an interview with *Beetle* magazine (May 1973), it was revealed the whole idea of this flawed project came from Gilmour,

who suggested that, "It was down to a lot of paranoia amongst each other, and thinking we would have a good time doing things on our own for a change, just for a laugh."

Although the idea may have been suggested with good intentions, it probably alerted Waters to a weakness he could exploit to his own advantage and thus assert himself, in the long term, as the band's chief lyricist. "I'd never written anything before," asserts Gilmour. "I just went into the studio and started waffling about tacking bits and pieces together. I rang up Roger at one point to ask him to write me some lyrics. He just said 'No.'" Ultimately this highlighted Gilmour's ability to produce worthwhile material under pressure.

There are only a handful of contemporary interviews that talk about the recording process, and of those three are worth mentioning: *Record Mirror* (25 January 1969) reported that Richard Wright had already finished his section, all played by him with the exception of a few percussion bits added by the record's producer Norman Smith. Wright went on to say, "There are no electronic sounds, no juggling with tapes. Theoretically you could do it live – and the only reason I did virtually all of it myself is that it was quicker that way. I didn't write out scores, I drew graphs."

Disc & Music Echo (15 February 1969) talked to Nick Mason who said that, "I've done my quarter twice over. The difficulty is doing something so totally egocentric as this you keep wanting to go back and do something completely different… It's hard to say what's going to come out of it at the moment, because everyone's being incredibly secretive about their bit till they've got it all together."

And finally, in *Beat Instrumental* (January 1970) Wright again gave the first clear indication of how solo pieces were recorded. "We didn't write together; we just went into the studios on our own to record and then we got together to listen to them. We all played alone on our pieces, in fact. Again, we couldn't all agree on this…I thought it was a very valid experiment and it helped me. I think that maybe Roger feels that if we'd all worked together it would have been better. That's something you just don't know, whether it would or not. I think it was a good idea."

The original vinyl release of the album listed 'The Narrow Way' and 'The Grand Vizier's Garden Party' as single tracks. On the remastered CD re-release in 1994, Part 1 of 'Sysyphus' was split into two tracks and labelled 'Part 1' and 'Part 2'. 'Part 2' on vinyl became 'Part 3' on CD, while 'Part 4' of the re-release consists of 'Part 3' and 'Part 4'. Very confusing! During Roger Waters' speech during 'Several Species…' at approx 4:30, you can hear him say into the right channel, "You have to play the song at half speed to hear it properly."

UMMAGUMMA

RECORDING SHEETS

Deciphering the studio recording sheets for the studio album was not made easy as tracks were labelled as either 'Rick's Scene', 'Roger's Scene', 'Roger's Tune', 'Dave's Scene' and 'Nicky's Scene', coupled with various 'Part' numbers, regardless of what part of the track it actually was! After many hours of assembling each track into what I believe to be the correct elements, the major difficulty was identifying the composite parts that made up 'Sysyphus', as several recording sheets were missing from the archives. From what can be pieced together it appears that 'Sysyphus' was broken down into five parts for the recording process: 'Part 1' was an edit piece from the end of 'Part 4' which reflects the song-cycle; 'Part 2' which is predominantly performed on piano has only the basic track information noted; recording sheets for 'Part 3' are completely missing; and 'Part 4' appears to have been recorded as 'Parts 1, 2 and 3', reflecting the three major parts that comprise this one track.

It is also obvious that across all of the solo pieces, the tape loops and effects were recorded "at home" by band members and then brought into the studio and introduced at the mixing and editing stage.

As with previous sessions, only a handful of out-takes remained, including two Roger Waters pieces entitled 'Roger's Tune', which may well have been a backing track, and 'Roger's Blues'. Of great interest, however, is a recording of Richard Wright playing the huge pipe organ at the Royal Albert Hall, London by the Abbey Road mobile unit, of which only a few minutes of the four-hour session made it onto the 2014 album *The Endless River*.

Two out-takes that were later released included the track 'Rest', which formed part of the 'Man' suite performed through 1969 and appeared on the 1971 compilation *Relics* as 'Biding My Time'; and 'Embryo', which was performed live extensively through the early 1970s and appeared on the Harvest sampler album *Picnic: A Breath of Fresh Air*. One further track entitled 'One Night Stand' was abandoned but was later reworked to form the basis of the track 'Summer '68' on *Atom Heart Mother*.

Sysyphus

Take unknown (RS1).
'Ric's Scene, Part 1' ['Sysyphus Part One'] recorded on 17 September 1968 (Take 2).
'Ric's Scene, Part 2' ['Sysyphus Part Two'] recorded on 17 September 1968 (Take 5).
'Ric's Scene, Part 2' [actually 'Sysyphus Part One'] re-recorded on 18 September 1968 (Take 3).
'Ricky's Scene, Parts 1, 2 and 3' ['Sysyphus Part Four'] recorded on 11 December 1968 (Take 3).
Vibes, Guitar and Mellotron overdubbed onto Take 3 of 'Ricky's Scene' ['Sysyphus Part Four'] on 7 December 1968.
Organ, Guitar, Tympanis and Piano overdubbed onto Take 3 of 'Ricky's Scene, Parts 4 and 5' ['Sysyphus Part Four'] on 18 December 1968.

'Ricky's Scene Part 1' ['Sysyphus Part Four'] edited (and relabelled Take 4) and transferred to the end of the track on 18 December 1968.
Electric Harpsichord and Vocals overdubbed onto Take 1 of 'Ricky's Scene' ['Sysyphus Part Three'] on 26 March 1969.
All other recording information is missing from archives.
Remixed on 7 May 1969 (RS1).
Cross-fades edited into Master Tape on 7 May 1969.
'Ricky's Scene (Last Part)' ['Sysyphus Part Four'] remixed on 12 May 1969 (RS1).
Cross-fades remixed on 12 May 1969 (RS1).
All parts remixed and edited on 12 May 1969 (RS1).

Grantchester Meadows

Take 1 (RS4).
Basic track recorded as 'Roger's Scene, Parts 1 and 2' on 17 December 1968 (Take 1).
Basic track re-recorded as 'Roger's Quarter, Second Movement' on 24 March 1969 (Take 1).
Vocal and Acoustic Guitar overdubbed onto Take 1 on 24 March 1969.
Remixed on 25 April 1969 (RS1).
Vocals overdubbed onto Take 1 on 25 April 1969.
Remixed on 3 June 1969 (RS4).

Several Species Of Small Furry Animals Gathered Together In A Cave And Grooving With A Pict

Take 2 (RS1).
Basic track recorded as 'Roger's Quarter, First Movement' on 18 March 1969 (Take 2).
"Vocal Effects" overdubbed onto Take 2 on 18 March 1969.
'Roger's Quarter' "Sound Effects" recorded and cut up for loops on 18 March 1969.
Guitar, Organ and Vocal overdubbed onto Take 2 on 25 March 1969.
"Scotsman's Voice" remixed and overdubbed onto Take 2 on 23 June 1969 (RS1).
Various edits and assembly of tapes made on 5 July 1969.

The Narrow Way, Part 1

Take 1 (RS3 / RS12).
Basic track recorded as 'Dave's Scene' on 16 January 1969 (Take 1).
"Spiral Effects" and "Modulated Vocal Sounds" overdubbed onto Take 1 on 29 January 1969.
"Spiral Effects" and "Stereo Guitar Effects" overdubbed onto Take 1 on 29 January 1969.
Remixed on 22 May 1969 (RS3).

The Narrow Way, Part 2

Take 1 (RS2 / RS12).
Basic track recorded as 'Dave's Scene 2nd Movement' on 29 January 1969 (Take 1).
"Link Track" recorded between Parts 2 & 3 recorded on 6 March 1969 (Take 1).
Drums, Guitar Effects and Jews Harp overdubbed onto Take 1 on 6 March 1969.
Organ overdubbed onto Take 1 on 17 March 1969.
Remixed on 17 June 1969 (RS2).

The Narrow Way, Part 3

Take 1 (RS12).
Basic track recorded as 'Dave's Scene 3rd Movement' on 6 March 1969 (Take 1).
Guitar and Bass overdubbed onto Take 1 on 6 March 1969.
Piano, Guitar and Vocals overdubbed onto Take 1 on 17 March 1969.
Vocals overdubbed onto Take 1 on 26 March 1969.
Guitar, Organ, Drums and Bass overdubbed onto Take 1 on 27 May 1969.
All three parts remixed on 5 July 1969 (RS12).
All three parts of 'The Narrow Way' edited, cross-faded and Remixed on 5 July 1969 (RS12).

The Grand Vizier's Garden Party (Part 1 – Entrance)

Take 5 (RS unknown).
Basic track recorded as 'Nickey's Tune' on 24 September 1968 (Take 4).
Unspecified instruments overdubbed onto Take 4 on 24 September 1968.
Basic track re-recorded as 'Nicky's Tune' on 24 September 1968 (relabelled Take 5).
"Reduction", "SFX", "Edits" and Cross-fades made to 'Nicky's Tune, Section 1, Part 1' of Take 5 on 1 October 1968.
"Drum Family" overdubbed onto Take 5 of 'Nicky's Tune Part 1' on 21 January 1969.

The Grand Vizier's Garden Party (Part 1 – Entertainment)

Take 6 (RS unknown).
Basic track recorded as 'Nicky's Tune, Section 2, Part 2' on 25 September 1968 (Take 6).
Rhythm Machine track recorded for 'Nicky's Tune, Section 2, Part 2' on 25 September 1968 (Take 1).
Reduction, SFX, Edits and Cross-fades made to Take 6 of 'Nicky's Tune, Section 2, Part 2' on 1 October 1968.
Reduction, Cross-fades and Edits made to Take 6 of 'Nicky's Tune, Sections 1 & 2' on 1 October 1968.
'Nicky's Tune Section 2' Take 6 edited on 1 October 1968.
Rhythm Machine and Drum Solo recorded for 'Nicky's Scene' on 27 January 1969.
Tympanis and Marimba overdubbed onto Take 6 of 'Nicky's Scene' on 27 January 1969.
Flute and Marimba overdubbed onto Take 6 of 'Nicky's Scene, Section 2' on 27 January 1969.

The Grand Vizier's Garden Party (Part 3 – Exit)

Take unknown (RS1).
Sound Effects recorded for 'Nicky's Scene, Section 3' on 28 January 1969.
Drums and Cymbals overdubbed onto 'Nicky's Scene, Section 3' on 28 January 1969.
Rough mix of 'Nicky's Scene' (all three parts) made on 28 January 1969 (RS1).
Start and End remixed and edited onto Master Tape on 29 April 1969 (RS1).

Embryo (Released on *Picnic a Breath of Fresh Air*)

Take 1 (RS2).
Basic track recorded as 'I Am The Embryo' on 26 November 1968 (Take 1).
Basic track re-recorded as 'I Am The Embryo' on 26 November 1968 (Take 1).
Vocals, Organ and Piano overdubbed onto Take 1 on 4 December 1968.
Remixed on 13 April 1970 (RS2).

One Night Stand (Reworked and released as Summer '68 on *Atom Heart Mother*)

Basic Track recorded as 'One Night Stand' on 4 December 1968 (Take 8).
Organ, Vocals, Guitar and Piano overdubbed onto Take 8 of 'One Night Stand' 4 December 1968.
Guitar and Piano overdubbed onto Take 8 of 'One Night Stand' on 9 December 1968.
Vocals, Guitar, Drums, Maracas, Piano overdubbed onto Take 8 of 'One Night Stand' on 10 December 1968.
Edited on 16 December (Edit Piece labelled Takes 9 and 10).
Piano, Acoustic Guitar, Mellotron, Harmonium, Bass and Guitar overdubbed onto Take 8 of 'One Night Stand' on 16 December 1968
For all further work see 'Summer '68' on Atom Heart Mother.

Roger's Tune (Unreleased)

Recorded on 23 September 1968 (Take 4).

Untitled (Unreleased)

Recording made by Richard Wright on the pipe organ at the Royal Albert Hall, London on 31 January 1969. Excerpts from this were used in the making of Pink Floyd's 2014 album *The Endless River*.

Roger's Blues (Unreleased)

Recorded on 25 March 1969 (Take 1).

Rest (Released as Biding My Time on *Relics*)

Basic track recorded on 19 July 1969 (Take 4).
Vocals, Trombones, Piano, Acoustic Guitar and Drums overdubbed onto Take 4 on 19 July 1969.

**WEDNESDAY 26 NOVEMBER –
PERFORMANCE ◄**
Friars Club, **Queensway Hall,
Civic Centre, Dunstable, England**

Supported by Mouseproof and DJ Andy Dunkley with Optic Nerve Superlights. Set list: 'Astronomy Domine', 'Green Is The Colour', 'Careful With That Axe, Eugene', 'Interstellar Overdrive', 'Cymbaline', 'Set The Controls For The Heart Of The Sun' <Encore> 'A Saucerful Of Secrets'.

**THURSDAY 27 NOVEMBER – PERFORMANCE
Mountford Hall, Liverpool University, Liverpool, England**

Set list: 'Astronomy Domine', 'Green Is The Colour', 'Careful With That Axe, Eugene', 'The Man' suite, 'Sysyphus', 'Interstellar Overdrive', 'Set The Controls For The Heart Of The Sun' <Encore> 'A Saucerful Of Secrets'.

Guild Gazette, Liverpool University's student newspaper, reported, "The Floyd gave superb renderings of 'A Saucerful Of Secrets' and 'Set The Controls For The Heart Of The Sun', Richard Wright giving an excellent piano solo in 'Sysyphus', and we all enjoyed the chair-breaking and stage-bashing of Roger Waters which did seem to make some sense in the context of the musical violence. It was amazing, too, seeing him making those weird sounds with his mouth, when it might be thought that the Floyd sound is composed of electronic gimmickry. They are an experience of the sixties, and will still lead the way for progressive music into the seventies."

FRIDAY 28 NOVEMBER – PERFORMANCE
Brunel University Arts Festival Weekend,
Refectory Hall, Brunel University, Uxbridge, England

Supported by Gracious with the Explosive Spectrum Lightshow. Set list included 'Astronomy Domine', 'Green Is The Colour', 'Careful With That Axe, Eugene', 'A Saucerful Of Secrets', 'Cymbaline'.

**SUNDAY 30 NOVEMBER – PERFORMANCE
The Lyceum, Strand, London, England**

Supported by Audience, Cuby's Blues Band and DJ Andy Dunkley.

SATURDAY 6 DECEMBER – PERFORMANCE
Afan Festival Of Progressive Music,
Afan Lido Indoor Sports Centre, Port Talbot, Wales

With Pentangle, East of Eden, Sam Apple Pie, Samson, Daddy Long Legs and Solid State. Set list: 'Interstellar Overdrive', 'Green Is The Colour', 'Careful With That Axe, Eugene', 'Set The Controls For The Heart Of The Sun', 'Cymbaline', 'A Saucerful Of Secrets'.

**FRIDAY 12 DECEMBER – RECORDING SESSION
Studio 2 & Control Room 2, EMI Studios,
Abbey Road, London, England**

2.30pm to 5.30: 'Country Song' recorded (Take 1 at 5:43 also marked "best"), and 5.30pm to 7.00pm and 8.30pm to 11.30pm: Guitar, Piano, Bass Guitar and Drums overdubbed onto Take 1 of 'Country Song' for the soundtrack *Zabriskie Point*. The session was produced by Pink Floyd and engineered by Phil MacDonald and Neil Richmond.

**SATURDAY 13 DECEMBER – PRESS REPORT
London, England**

Pink Floyd was reported in the UK music press to have been commissioned to write the score for 17 half-hour cartoons to be shown on US TV from November 1970. The series entitled *Rollo* was being made by Alan Aldridge who edited the illustrated book of the Beatles' songs. Talking to *Melody Maker* (Saturday 1 November 1969), Roger Waters said, "I saw the pilot programme recently – it's rather *Yellow Submarine*-ish, about a little boy in space. We're not going to sit down and take 13 hours of music, of course. What we'll probably do is record a four-hour 'kit' of music, which can be fitted to the film – like there'll be so many take-offs, so many landings, so many impacts and so forth." Unfortunately the project was scrapped without any music being recorded.

**SATURDAY 13 DECEMBER – RECORDING SESSION
Studio 2 & Control Room 2, EMI Studios,
Abbey Road, London, England**

2.30pm to 5.45pm: Piano, Guitar and Drums overdubbed onto Take 1 of 'Country Song'; 7.15pm to 9.00pm: 'Highway Song' recorded (Take 1 at 5:08, Take 2 False Start and Take 3 at 5:07 also marked "best") and 9.00pm to 12.15am: Acoustic Guitar, Electric Guitar, Organ and Piano overdubbed onto Take 3 of 'Highway Song' for the soundtrack *Zabriskie Point*. The session was produced by Pink Floyd, engineered by Phil MacDonald and assisted by Neil Richmond.

**MONDAY 15 DECEMBER – RECORDING SESSION
Studio 2 & Control Room 2, EMI Studios,
Abbey Road, London, England**

2.30pm to 5.30pm and 7.30pm to 11.30pm: Vocals, Tympanis, Bass and Drums overdubbed onto Take 3 of 'Highway Song'. Five tympani drums are noted as being brought in for the session for the soundtrack *Zabriskie Point*. The session was produced by Pink Floyd, engineered by Phil MacDonald and assisted by Neil Richmond.

**TUESDAY 16 DECEMBER – RECORDING SESSION
Studio 2 & Control Room 2, EMI Studios,
Abbey Road, London, England**

2.30pm to 5.30pm: 'Beginning Scene' remixed (RS1 at 3:16, RS2 at 3:17 and RS3 at 3:16); 'Take Off (Version 3)' remixed (RS2 at 1:26 and RS3 at 1:25 also marked "best"); 5.30pm to 7.00pm: Guitar overdubbed onto 'Take Off (Version 2)' and 9.00pm to 12.00midnight: Guitar and Vocals overdubbed onto Take 3 of 'Highway Song' for the soundtrack *Zabriskie Point*. The session was produced by Pink Floyd, engineered by Phil MacDonald and assisted by Neil Richmond.

**WEDNESDAY 17 DECEMBER – RECORDING SESSION
Studio 2 & Control Room 2, EMI Studios,
Abbey Road, London, England**

2.30pm to 5.00pm: Vocals overdubbed onto Take 1 of 'Country Song'; 5.00pm to 6.00pm: 'Alan's Blues' remixed (RS1 at 5:42 also marked "best") and 'Love Scene' remixed (RS1); 7.00pm to 11.00pm: Vocals overdubbed onto Take 1 of 'Country Song'; and 11.00pm to 1.15am: 'Highway Song' remixed (RS1-4) for the soundtrack *Zabriskie Point*. The session was produced by Pink Floyd, engineered by Phil MacDonald and assisted by Neil Richmond.

4 THE SOUND OF MUSIC IN MY EARS

1970—71

1970–71

Early 1970 saw Pink Floyd formulate an extended piece that would form the backbone of their next studio album of the same name: *Atom Heart Mother*. Initiated by Gilmour during a rehearsal session, recording commenced at Abbey Road in early March on this lengthy, and for many months untitled, track that would eventually fill one full side of the album, where it would feature both a choir and orchestra.

In February 1970, Michelangelo Antonioni's movie *Zabriskie Point* – his much anticipated follow-up to the 1966 cult-classic *Blow Up* – was premiered in New York City. Although it was universally panned by the critics and left MGM reeling from its substantial box office losses, it held some attention for its soundtrack that prominently featured a reworking of Pink Floyd's 'Careful With That Axe, Eugene' under the title 'Come On Number 51, Your Time Is Up'.

Originally commissioned to write the entire score, Pink Floyd commenced work in late 1969, first in Rome and then at Abbey Road. Antonioni was a notoriously difficult man to please and although some worthwhile material emerged their efforts were largely wasted, as he chose to fill the remaining soundtrack with a variety of recordings by American artists including the Grateful Dead and some acoustic guitar instrumentals from its guitarist Jerry Garcia, as well as tracks by the Youngbloods, Kaleidoscope, Roscoe Holcomb, John Fahey and Patti Page. However, its lasting effect was to reinforce Pink Floyd's standing in North America, and it was timed perfectly with the advent of their first tour there in two years.

Waters, meanwhile, embarked on his first solo project outside of Pink Floyd, collaborating with the avant-garde performer-composer Ron Geesin on a bizarre experimental documentary film called *The Body*. Introduced by Mason via mutual friend Sam Cutler, they became good friends and golfing partners in a short space of time. It was a natural choice for Geesin to turn to Waters when a lyricist was required for a particular track. "[*The Body*] was intended to be a new style of making a documentary feature," recalled Geesin. "A stimulatory film. The idea in a fundamental way was to get something good with not very much, the ideal was that if you can express everything in a single melody, and variations, that would be very good…. The distributors had had an early sight and said it was too radical for their market, to tame it down, so they added some commentary. Roy Battersby, the director, was forced to get his mate Vanessa Redgrave, who was in the Workers Revolutionary Party, and they did lots of pansy, posey stuff over it, poems and things, that took the whole heat out of it."[1]

Recorded at Island Studios in March, members of Pink Floyd also appeared on one of the tracks, 'Give Birth To A Smile', for which they were paid as session musicians and remain uncredited. Waters and Geesin both wanted a four-piece band, and the others willingly obliged, "You want a big sound?" Geesin remembers them saying, "Well, here we are!"[2]

Likewise, Geesin was then approached by Waters to look at scoring the as yet unnamed title track for their next new album. "Roger proposed to me that I should help Floyd with their next album," remembered Geesin. "He said he would like me to write the brass and choir pieces…Floyd were off to the States then [April and May 1970], and Roger left me with a skeleton tape of rhythm and chords. It was to be a twenty-five minute piece – and that's a hell of a lot of work…. Nobody knew what was wanted, they couldn't read music."[3]

And there were plenty of other distractions besides. Aside from yet more live engagements, Gilmour was busy assisting his former bandmate Syd Barrett with his second solo album, *Barrett*.

LEFT: PINK FLOYD PHOTOGRAPHED IN LONDON, SPRING 1970.

Coast, and another one on the West Coast. So we used three completely different sets of people performing it. We tried to hire musicians from local symphonies, so we'd just get the session musicians. We found our conductor, Peter Philips, by coming over and looking for someone a couple of months before the tour."[5]

Curiously, the track also caught the attention of Stanley Kubrick, who wanted to use the music in his adaptation of Anthony Burgess's novel *A Clockwork Orange*. "He wanted to use 'Atom Heart Mother'," said Waters, "and chop and change it about. He just phoned up and said that he wanted it and we said, 'Well, what do you want to do?' and he didn't know, he just said he wanted to use it, 'How I want – when I want'. And we said right away, 'Right, you can't use it.'"[6] Even so, the director still paid tribute to the album regardless: the sleeve is seen behind the counter of the Korova Milk Bar.

Atom Heart Mother benefitted from an innovative marketing campaign on release, not least adverts that depicted herds of cows clogging up The Mall in the direction of Buckingham Palace. Pink Floyd was finally seeing some recognition for its work and were rewarded with their first UK No. 1 album.

In January 1971 recording commenced on what would become Pink Floyd's most ambitious album to date, *Meddle*. It was also the first time the band entered the recording studio to sketch out ideas rather than elaborate on rough demos they had already worked on either at home, in rehearsal or on stage.

Indeed the initial sessions began with the extension of techniques they had applied on 'Alan's Psychedelic Breakfast' by using found objects – kitchen utensils, bottles, cutlery, glasses, and even sawing up bits of wood – to replicate conventional sounds. It was a complicated process and over the next few weeks 24 pieces of 'music' were produced and labelled 'Nothing, Part One' and so on.

It's hardly surprising the band shelved work on the project (although elements of this process were to resurface again during sessions in late 1973) to pursue a more conventional approach. After recognizing just how long it would take the band to record their new album – not least because of their live commitments, which would see extensive touring not only in the UK, Europe and North America but also debut shows in Australia and Japan – EMI decided to sate the appetite of eager fans by releasing a budget-priced compilation entitled *Relics – A Collection of Bizarre Antiques and Curios*. It contained

Returning to 'Atom Heart Mother', and although Pink Floyd had been performing the piece for some months even as it was still being recorded, the official live premiere didn't take place until the Bath Festival in late June. Here, it featured for the first time on stage a full orchestra and choir. It was one of only a handful of occasions over the next year when a brass and choir section would accompany the band live.

A month later and the band were previewing another performance for a John Peel Radio One session on 16 July, two days before a headline appearance at a Hyde Park concert in London. The title had to be registered for royalties, and although it had been introduced on stage as 'The Amazing Pudding', the band was still looking for something more permanent. Geesin recalled, "We were sitting in the control room and John Peel had his newspaper [the *Evening Standard*] and we were sitting round with Nick, Roger and the others. I think they were all there saying, 'We haven't got a title for this', and I said, 'If you look in there you'll find a title', and then Roger picked up the paper and said, 'Atom Heart Mother' and the others said, 'Yeah, that sounds good.'"[4] The headline appears in the 16 July edition and reads, 'The Atom Heart Mother Is Named' and refers to 56-year-old Mrs. Constance Ladell who received Britain's first plutonium-based pacemaker.

The new composition was well received, but Gilmour also spoke of the problems in taking the new work on the road: "Something on the scale of 'Atom Heart Mother' really takes a lot of getting together. The problem is that we've never done it more than twice with the same people. The choir is usually all right because they're used to working together, but some of the brass people have been really hopeless. We had problems with the sound equipment, getting it mic'd up and balanced and stuff. The trouble was also not having enough rehearsal time everywhere we did it, because we used a different brass and choir group in Europe than the one we used on the East

a collection of works from the band's early years up to *Music from the Film "More"*, early 7-inch single tracks available for the first time since their deletion, and a previously unreleased number, 'Biding My Time'.

The band returned to the studio in March and many of the oddments that had been recorded were then edited and overdubbed into parts of the album's two stand-out tracks 'One Of These Days' and 'Echoes'.

The latter would emerge as a lengthy piece, clocking in at just under 25 minutes and was premiered as a live piece in April. Through further refinement it finally emerged as the track 'Echoes'.

Even so the latter, recorded with the working title 'Return Of The Son Of Nothing', was a lengthy piece at just under 25 minutes and was to prove a live favourite for many years to come. It was also popularized in the cult 1973 Australian surfing film *Crystal Voyager* to accompany spectacular underwater shots and wave tunnels, film of which would later accompany their live performances of 'The Great Gig In The Sky' throughout 1974 and 1975 and be revived for their latter-day tours.

'One Of These Days' would also become another live favourite. This pounding, bass-driven instrumental originally featured a vocal tape loop of the venerable broadcaster Jimmy Young and the BBC Radiophonic Workshop's theme from the TV show *Dr. Who*. The track also features a rare Mason lead vocal: the garbled one-liner "One of these days I'm going to cut you into little pieces."

Broadcaster Jimmy Young, incidentally, was the constant butt of Pink Floyd's warped humour when they chopped up tape recordings of his commentary for his *Family Favourites* BBC2 radio show to make hilarious and nonsensical introductions to their shows throughout the early 1970s.

By comparison, the remaining tracks are subdued and very reminiscent of the acoustic material on *Atom Heart Mother*, none of which were ever performed live and almost all recorded at the new 16-track facilities at Air Studios and Morgan Sound. 'Fearless' is a successful experiment which segues the Liverpool FC "Kop choir" singing their adopted stadium anthem 'You'll Never Walk Alone' into the last few seconds of the song; a reminder of Pink Floyd's collective passion for the sport.

To close side one of the album another throwaway number, typical of the band's sense of humour when it came to improvisation, featured a howling Irish Wolfhound. "Dave was looking after Seamus while Steve Marriott [the dog's owner, who was on tour with Humble Pie] was in

LEFT: PINK FLOYD ON STAGE AT BILL GRAHAM'S FILLMORE EAST, 27 SEPTEMBER 1970.

the States, and he used to bring him into the sessions," explained Waters, "and one day he said, 'There's something I meant to show you – this dog sings', and he got a harmonica out and blew it at the dog, and as soon as the dog hears a harmonica it starts howling. So we all thought we'd do a short 12-bar and stick him on it."[7]

Meddle was released in November and featured another Hipgnosis sleeve design featuring a close-up photograph of an ear submerged in rippling water, designed to suggest the effect of the ear collecting waves of sound. The gatefold inner sleeve also featured a black and white portrait of the band; the last time Pink Floyd would be visually identified on an album for some sixteen years, an absence which increased their mystique with the public.

With *Meddle* only recently completed and their second
North American tour of that year already lined up, the band was persuaded by French TV producer Adrian Maben to be filmed in concert against the spectacular backdrop of the remains of the ancient Roman amphitheatre at Pompeii in Italy.

His interest was sparked when he went to see Pink Floyd perform in London the previous year, recalling that he went "largely out of curiosity. I wanted to understand how on earth they managed to produce those sounds that were so different from the usual rock music that people used to listen to. I was also blown away by the fact that there seemed to be very little publicity: no posters, no press coverage, even less TV. And yet on that evening in London the concert hall was packed, it was a sold out performance. The Floyd were unique in this respect: they became popular by word of mouth, they hated journalists and they promoted themselves by actively avoiding them."[8]

As with most approaches made to the band, he left feeling rather deflated. "I managed to get hold of the telephone number of their manager, Steve O'Rourke, and he (surprisingly) arranged a meeting for me in London. He had a reputation for being tough and I'd been told that he'd turned down dozens of proposals from directors like myself. And yet he came over as a very decent person. I explained to him, and to David Gilmour who also happened to be there, my original idea: it was to combine their music with the work of contemporary artists like Jean Tinguely, Magritte, Delvaux or Nam June Paik. David looked at me and said that they'd think about it and eventually get back. I returned to Paris and waited for six months! At this point I had pretty much given up hope and wanted to forget the embarrassingly bad idea of

mixing Floydian music and Magritte. I decided to go on a holiday to Italy and travelled to Pompeii."[9]

He had found the perfect setting and quite easily convinced the band, who agreed it would be an entirely unique presentation to film them in concert with no audience.

Through tiresome negotiations and good fortune, Maben finally secured all the necessary permits and filming finally took place in October. However, two days was lost due to a failure of the power supply, which in the end had to be run via a very long cable from the nearby cathedral. Maben was also frustrated when his carefully scripted camera shots, angles and positions to link in with the agreed selection of tracks was scuppered the day before filming by Steve O'Rourke clutching a new copy of *Meddle* and suggesting the bulk of the material come from this, their current album.

The set list finally agreed upon, the band set about performing a live set both by day and at night, which included 'Echoes' (which was split into two halves to open and close the film), 'Careful With That Axe, Eugene', 'A Saucerful Of Secrets', 'Set The Controls For The Heart Of The Sun', 'One Of These Days' and 'Mademoiselle Nobs' – a retitled version of 'Seamus'.

Some of the atmospheric shots were filmed at the volcanic crater at Solfatara and the ancient ruins of Pozzuoli whereas various post-production sequences, inserts and interviews were then filmed in Paris in December, including the howls of Nobs, a Russian Wolfhound.

Pink Floyd Live at Pompeii was previewed at the Edinburgh Film Festival in September 1972 to rave reviews, but its official public premiere that November at the Rainbow Theatre in London was cancelled on the night due to a contractual dispute with the distributors, and it didn't see a general theatrical release until the summer of 1974.

As 1971 drew to a close, Pink Floyd's touring schedule was already stretching well into the latter half of 1972. However, they were very aware that their stage material was becoming rather stale – a point that hadn't escaped the music press – and decided to apply themselves to the task of composing an entirely new set of numbers for their imminent UK tour.

1–4. Author interview with Ron Geesin.
5. *Music Now,* 28 November 1970 / *Beetle* May 1973.
6. *Great Lake,* April 1973.
7. *NME,* 11 December 1971.
8–9. *Brain Damage* website (Alfredo Marziano/Mark Worden), 15 April 2014.

1970

PINK FLOYD ROAD CREW JANUARY – SEPTEMBER 1970
Bobby Richardson (Technician, Stage Crew), Brian Scott (Technician, Stage Crew), Alan Styles (Technician, Stage Crew), Peter Watts (Road Manager, Sound Engineer).

THURSDAY 1 JANUARY – RECORDING SESSION
Studio 2, EMI Studios, Abbey Road, London, England
7.00pm to 1.00am: 'Highway Song' remixed (RS5–8, and RS9 at 4:50) and 'Explosions' remixed (RS1 untimed) for the soundtrack *Zabriskie Point*. The session was produced by Pink Floyd and engineered by Phil MacDonald.

THURSDAY 1 JANUARY – RECORDING SESSION
Control Room 4, EMI Studios, Abbey Road, London, England
2.30pm to 5.00pm: Nick Mason spent the afternoon copying sound effects from the EMI tape library for use on the track 'Atom Heart Mother' for their live shows. The session was produced by Pink Floyd and engineered by Phil MacDonald.

MONDAY 5 JANUARY – RECORDING SESSION
Control Room 3, EMI Studios, Abbey Road, London, England
7.15pm to 4.30am: 'Country Song' remixed (RS1–4 untimed, RS5 at 4:25, RS6 False Start and RS7 at 4:36 also marked best); 'Highway Song' remixed (RS10 False Start, RS11 at 4:45, RS12 False Start and RS13 at 5:15 also marked best); 'Explosion' remixed (RS5 False Start and RS6 at 5:00 also marked best); 'Take Off (Version 1)' remixed (RS1 not timed and RS2 at 1:52 also marked best); 'Beginning Scene' remixed (RS4 False Start, RS5 not timed and RS6 at 3:16 also marked best); 'Love Scene' remixed (RS1 at 5:55 and RS2 at 5:10 also marked best), and 'Take Off (Version 2)' remixed (RS1 at 1:05) for the soundtrack *Zabriskie Point*. The session was produced by Pink Floyd and engineered by Phil MacDonald.

SATURDAY 10 JANUARY – PERFORMANCE
The Ballroom, University of Nottingham, Beeston, Nottingham, England
Set list: 'Astronomy Domine', 'Set The Controls For The Heart Of The Sun', 'Green Is The Colour', 'Careful With That Axe, Eugene', 'A Saucerful Of Secrets'.

WEDNESDAY 14 JANUARY – RECORDING SESSION
Room 4, EMI Studios, Abbey Road, London, England
Nick Mason copying sound effects from the EMI tape library for two hours including 'World War II Air Raid', 'Piston Engine, Plane A', 'Piston Engine, Plane B', 'Riot Men Shouting' and 'Motor Racing' for use on the track 'Atom Heart Mother' for their live shows. The session was engineered by Phil MacDonald.

WEDNESDAY 14 JANUARY – RECORDING SESSION
Room 5, EMI Studios, Abbey Road, London, England
Nick Mason copying sound effects from the EMI tape library for 15 minutes including 'Charge Of The Light Brigade', 'Charge Of The Light Brigade, with Bugles', 'Jet Plane' and 'Jet Plane Taking Off' for use on the track 'Atom Heart Mother' for their live shows.

THURSDAY 15 JANUARY – RECORDING SESSION
Control Room 2, EMI Studios, Abbey Road, London, England
3.40pm to 5.40pm: 'Beginning Scene' remixed (rough remix), and 'Love Scene (Final Version)' remixed (RS1 False Start, RS2 & RS3 not timed, RS4 False Start and RS5 at 6:50 also marked best) for the soundtrack *Zabriskie Point*. All tapes were taken away and signed for by David Gilmour. The session was produced by Pink Floyd and engineered by Phil MacDonald.

SATURDAY 17 JANUARY – PERFORMANCE
Lawns Centre, Cottingham, Hull, England
Presented by Hull University.
Set list: 'Astronomy Domine', 'Green Is The Colour', 'Careful With That Axe, Eugene', 'Atom Heart Mother'*, 'Set The Controls For The Heart Of The Sun' <Encore> 'A Saucerful Of Secrets'.
*This is the first known performance of 'Atom Heart Mother'. It has been titled retrospectively for identification purposes, as it was not formally adopted until Thursday 16 July 1970 during the course of a BBC recording session and until that date was introduced at shows as either "a new untitled piece" or 'The Amazing Pudding'.

SUNDAY 18 JANUARY – PERFORMANCE ▼
Fairfield Halls, Croydon, England
Set list: 'Careful With That Axe, Eugene', 'Embryo', 'Main Theme' (from *More*), 'Biding My Time', 'Astronomy Domine', 'The Violent Sequence', 'Set The Controls For The Heart Of The Sun', 'Atom Heart Mother' <Encore> 'A Saucerful Of Secrets'.
The *Croydon Advertiser* reported, "There was a standing ovation, there was an encore. Make no mistake, Pink Floyd are good…. More than that, they are originals,

JOHN & TONY SMITH PRESENT

THE PINK FLOYD
IN CONCERT

APPEARING —
FAIRFIELD HALL, CROYDON
SUNDAY, 18th JAN., at 7.30 p.m.

THE DOME, BRIGHTON
MONDAY, 19th JAN., at 7.45 p.m.

and have been so since earlier days when they practically invented psychedelia. They are individually adept as musicians and command a range of instruments, Rick Wright for instance played organ, piano, trombone and vibraphone at Sunday's concert. Anything can be legitimately used in creating the atmosphere: recourse to heavy timpani, violent assault on cymbal, flogging a gargantuan gong and insistent thumping of fingers on microphones. Pink Floyd are obsessed with the mystery of outer space – 'Set The Controls For The Heart Of The Sun' and 'Interstellar Overdrive' are two titles – and portray it with imagination. Yet the fact remains that their concert on Sunday was marred by repetitive phrasing, by long unmelodic passages, by monotony…. Perhaps with the lighting effects they have abandoned the sterile patches would not have been so noticeable…. Still it was a long concert – nearly three hours – for Messrs. Waters, Wright, Mason and Gilmore [sic] to fill. I liked particularly, the contributions of Wright, including funereal excursions of organ playing in the traumatic 'Saucerful Of Secrets' and his unhurried, halcyon piano in 'Niagara Dellof'[*], which was like a respite from a storm – and which was deservedly applauded. Drummer Nick Mason has said: 'People have the confidence that if we do something extraordinary, it's quite likely not to be a giant con and there's some purpose or meaning behind it.' Certainly not a 'con' – but the end product was lamentably, just lacking."

*Note: 'Niagra Dellof' is a title that has not appeared in any other reference to the band's' output. Although it may have been introduced as such at this concert, this could be a reference to 'The Violent Sequence'.

MONDAY 19 JANUARY – PERFORMANCE
The Dome, Brighton, England
Set list included: 'Careful With That Axe, Eugene', 'Embryo', 'Main Theme' (from *More*), 'Atom Heart Mother', 'Astronomy Domine', 'Set The Controls For The Heart Of The Sun', 'A Saucerful Of Secrets'.

FRIDAY 23 JANUARY – CANCELLED PERFORMANCE
Wolverhampton Polytechnic Annual Ball Polytechnic Melody of 1970!, Civic & Wulfrun Halls, Wolverhampton, England
With Zoot Money, Idle Race, Cliff Bennett and DJ's Andy Arthur & Mr. Max.
Initial posters for this event showed Pink Floyd as headline act but they were replaced by Fairport Convention, only for them to pull out and be replaced by the Bonzo Dog Band.

FRIDAY 23 JANUARY – PERFORMANCE
Théâtre des Champs-Élysées, Champs-Élysée, Paris, France
Set list: 'The Man' suite, 'A Saucerful Of Secrets' <Intermission> 'Astronomy Domine', 'Green Is The Colour', 'Careful With That Axe, Eugene', 'The Violent Sequence', 'Main Theme' (from *More*), 'Set The Controls For The Heart Of The Sun', 'Atom Heart Mother'.

Europe 1 radio broadcast the 'Man' suite live on the programme *Musicorama* between 8.00pm and 10.30pm. In edited repeats 'Work' was broadcast on Europe 1 during an interview with David Gilmour and Nick Mason on *Tout Peut Arriver* on Saturday 1 May 1982, and 'The Violent Sequence' and 'Atom Heart Mother' on Sunday 30 April 1995. Gilmour introduced 'Atom Heart Mother' in fluent French, explaining that the basic track had been written only one week prior to the performance.

SATURDAY 24 JANUARY – PERFORMANCE
Théâtre des Champs-Élysées, Champs-Élysée, Paris, France
Set list included 'The Man' suite, 'Set The Controls For The Heart Of The Sun'.

MONDAY 2 FEBRUARY – PERFORMANCE
Palais des Sports, Lyon, France
Set list included 'The Man' suite <Intermission> 'Astronomy Domine', 'The Violent Sequence', 'Set The Controls For The Heart Of The Sun'.
Europe 1 radio recorded the show but broadcast details could not be found.

THURSDAY 5 FEBRUARY – PERFORMANCE ▶
Cardiff Arts Centre Project Benefit Concert, Sophia Gardens Pavilion, Cardiff, Wales
With Quintessence, Daddy Longlegs, Gary Farr, Heaven, Ron Geesin, Tea & Symphony and Black Sabbath.

CARDIFF ARTS CENTRE PROJECT BENEFIT
Sophia Gardens Pavilion, Cardiff
Thursday February 5th 1970
2.30-5.30pm free concert for ticket-holders
folk.poetry.jazz.mime.& other media
featuring Trader Horne.Tony Crerar
6pm-
2am **pink floyd.quintessence daddylonglegs.garry farr heaven.tea and symphony ron geesin.black sabbath**
late bar.food.late buses:no admission after 10pm

№ 634

SATURDAY 7 FEBRUARY – PERFORMANCE ▼
Royal Albert Hall, Kensington, London, England
Set list: 'Embryo', 'Main Theme' (from *More*), 'Careful With That Axe, Eugene', 'Sysyphus', 'The Violent Sequence', 'Atom Heart Mother', 'Set The Controls For The Heart Of The Sun' <Encore> 'A Saucerful Of Secrets'.

SUNDAY 8 FEBRUARY – PERFORMANCE
Opera House, Manchester, England
Set list: 'Embryo', 'Careful With That Axe, Eugene', 'Main Theme' (from *More*), 'Sysyphus', 'Atom Heart Mother', 'Set The Controls For The Heart Of The Sun', 'Astronomy Domine'.

WEDNESDAY 11 FEBRUARY – PERFORMANCE
Town Hall, Birmingham, England
Set list: 'Embryo', 'Main Theme' (from *More*), 'Careful With That Axe, Eugene', 'Sysyphus', untitled instrumental, 'Set The Controls For The Heart Of The Sun', 'Atom Heart Mother'.

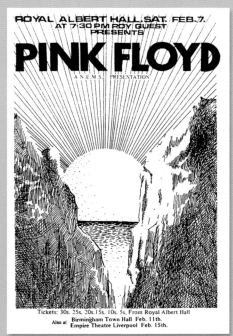

ROYAL ALBERT HALL. SAT. FEB. 7.
AT 7.30 PM ROY GUEST PRESENTS
PINK FLOYD
A N.E.M.S. PRESENTATION
Tickets: 30s. 25s. 20s.15s. 10s. 5s. From Royal Albert Hall
Also at Birmingham Town Hall Feb. 11th.
Empire Theatre Liverpool Feb. 15th.

The untitled instrumental performed at this show was a 25-minute long sequence incorporating elements of 'Heart Beat, Pig Meat', 'Quicksilver, 'Moonhead' and 'The Violent Sequence'.

SATURDAY 14 FEBRUARY – PERFORMANCE
King's Hall, Town Hall, Stoke-on-Trent, England

Presented by North Staffordshire Polytechnic.
Set list: 'Embryo', 'Main Theme' (from *More*), 'Careful With That Axe, Eugene', 'Sysyphus', 'Atom Heart Mother', 'Set The Controls For The Heart Of The Sun', 'A Saucerful Of Secrets', 'Astronomy Domine'.

SUNDAY 15 FEBRUARY – PERFORMANCE
Empire Theatre, Liverpool, England

Set list: 'Embryo', 'Careful With That Axe, Eugene', 'Main Theme' (from *More*), 'Atom Heart Mother', 'Astronomy Domine', 'Interstellar Overdrive', 'Set The Controls For The Heart Of The Sun', 'A Saucerful Of Secrets'.

TUESDAY 17 FEBRUARY – PERFORMANCE
City Hall, Newcastle-upon-Tyne, England

SUNDAY 22 FEBRUARY – PERFORMANCE
Electric Garden, Glasgow, Scotland

Set list included 'A Saucerful Of Secrets', 'Set The Controls For The Heart Of The Sun'.

SATURDAY 28 FEBRUARY – PERFORMANCE
Endsville '70, Refectory Hall, University Union, Leeds University, Leeds, England

Supported by Heavy Jelly.
Set list: 'Embryo', 'Careful With That Axe, Eugene', 'Set The Controls For The Heart Of The Sun', 'Atom Heart Mother', 'A Saucerful Of Secrets' <Encore> 'Interstellar Overdrive'.

MONDAY 2 MARCH – RECORDING SESSION
Studio 2 & Control Room 2, EMI Studios, Abbey Road, London, England

Recording commenced on Pink Floyd's fifth studio album, *Atom Heart Mother*.
7.00pm to 3.00am: 'Untitled 1' ['Atom Heart Mother'] recorded (Take 1 at 18:30, Take 2 False Start and Take 3 at 19:20 marked "best"). The session was produced by Pink Floyd, engineered by Phil MacDonald and assisted by Alan Parsons.

TUESDAY 3 MARCH – RECORDING SESSION
Studio 2 & Control Room 2, EMI Studios, Abbey Road, London, England

7.00pm to 3.15am: Sections of Take 3 of 'Untitled 1' ['Atom Heart Mother'] edited (and marked "best edit sections") and edited into master tape of Take 3, and a rough remix made of the short section of the master take for *Atom Heart Mother*. The session was produced by Pink Floyd, engineered by Phil MacDonald and assisted by Alan Parsons.

WEDNESDAY 4 MARCH – RECORDING SESSION
Studio 2 & Control Room 2, EMI Studios, Abbey Road, London, England

7.00pm to 3.00am: Edit pieces for 'Untitled 1' ['Atom Heart Mother'] recorded (Takes 1 to 5 wiped, Take 6 untimed), and edited into Master Take 2; 'Untitled 2' [the second section of 'Atom Heart Mother'] recorded (Take 2) and Hammond, Guitar, Vocals, Farfisa

and Piano overdubbed onto Take 2 of 'Untitled 2' for *Atom Heart Mother*. A rough remix was made of the compete track ('Untitled 1 and 2'). The session was produced by Pink Floyd, engineered by Phil MacDonald and assisted by Alan Parsons.

THURSDAY 5 MARCH – TELEVISION RECORDING
Line-Up, Studio B, BBC TV Centre, White City, London, England

Pink Floyd recorded some original live music (logged as 'Zabriskie Point' at 4:08 in the BBC archives) for the magazine programme *Line-Up*. It was broadcast in the UK on BBC2 TV on Friday 13 March between 11.10pm and 11.50pm. Pink Floyd's contribution was repeated as part of the year end retrospective, *Line-Up '70*, broadcast on BBC2 TV on Monday 28 December 1970 between 10.40pm and 11.50pm.

FRIDAY 6 MARCH – PERFORMANCE
Great Hall, College Block, Imperial College, Kensington, London, England

Supported by Juicy Lucy with Tom & Jerry cartoons shown between bands.
Set list included 'Atom Heart Mother', 'Set The Controls For The Heart Of The Sun', 'A Saucerful Of Secrets'.

SATURDAY 7 MARCH – PERFORMANCE ▼
University of Bristol Arts Festival Timespace, Colston Hall, Bristol, England

Set list included 'Main Theme' (from *More*), 'Set The Controls For The Heart Of The Sun', 'A Saucerful Of Secrets'.

The *Bristol Evening Post* reported, "The Floyd's Saturday show was something from an underground siesta. Tea time at the weekend isn't exactly the right moment to suffer the violence and intensity of a Floyd concert (it commenced at 3.00pm). Their music's so involving, sometimes overpowering, that the time of day should have been a positive disadvantage. It didn't matter too much however. They somehow generated the right enthusiasm and turned a lazy afternoon into a full, now and again, frightening experience. This show had its faults. The volume on a couple of their disturbing destructive numbers was quite terrifying, enough to make you feel physically ill. Maybe that's what they were after. But in their melancholy numbers – particularly the 'Main Theme' from *More* – they created a sumptuous atmosphere of sadness and regret. The music was effective and it was a thoughtful, worthwhile show."

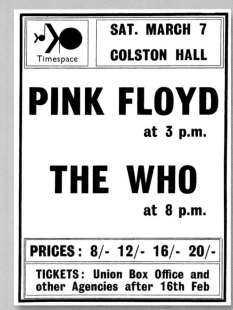

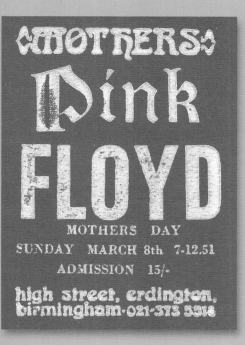

MOTHERS
Pink FLOYD

MOTHERS DAY
SUNDAY MARCH 8th 7-12.51
ADMISSION 15/-

high street, erdington,
birmingham·021-373 3514

SHEFFIELD CITY HALL
Monday, March 9th
"Ummaguma"

An Evening with

PINK FLOYD

IN CONCERT

Commencing at 7-30 p.m.
TICKETS :
7/6   10/6   12/6   15/-   17/6
from WILSON PECK LTD.
64-70, Leopold Street
Sheffield 1 Tel. Sheffield 27074

Please send stamped addressed envelope
with postal bookings

SUNDAY 8 MARCH – PERFORMANCE ◄
Mothers, Erdington, Birmingham, England
Set list: 'Embryo', 'A Saucerful Of Secrets', 'Set The Controls For The Heart Of The Sun', 'Green Is The Colour', 'Careful With That Axe, Eugene', 'Astronomy Domine', 'Atom Heart Mother' <Encore> 'Blues'*.

*Note: Where 'Blues' appears as a track listing from here on it refers to an improvised 12-bar blues instrumental, a common and often impromptu addition to Pink Floyd's set throughout the next few years.

MONDAY 9 MARCH – PERFORMANCE ◄
City (Oval) Hall, Sheffield, England
Set list included: 'Astronomy Domine', 'Green Is The Colour', 'Careful With That Axe, Eugene', 'Cymbaline', 'Interstellar Overdrive', 'Set The Controls For The Heart Of The Sun'.

WEDNESDAY 11 MARCH – PERFORMANCE
Stadthalle, Offenbach, West Germany
Set list: 'Astronomy Domine', 'Green Is The Colour', 'Careful With That Axe, Eugene', 'Cymbaline', 'A Saucerful Of Secrets', <Intermission> 'Interstellar Overdrive', 'Set The Controls For The Heart Of The Sun', 'Atom Heart Mother'.

THURSDAY 12 MARCH – PERFORMANCE
Kleiner Saal, Auditorium Maximum, Hamburg Universität, Hamburg, West Germany
Set list: 'Astronomy Domine', 'Careful With That Axe, Eugene', 'Cymbaline', 'A Saucerful Of Secrets' <Intermission> 'Embryo', 'Interstellar Overdrive', 'Set The Controls For The Heart Of The Sun', 'Atom Heart Mother'.

FRIDAY 13 MARCH – PERFORMANCE
Konzert Saal, Technische Universität, West Berlin, West Germany
Set list: 'Astronomy Domine', 'Careful With That Axe, Eugene', 'Cymbaline', 'A Saucerful Of Secrets' <Intermission> 'Embryo', 'Interstellar Overdrive', 'Set The Controls For The Heart Of The Sun', 'Atom Heart Mother' <Encore> 'Blues'.

SATURDAY 14 MARCH – PERFORMANCE
Grosser Salle, Meistersinger Halle, Nürnberg, West Germany
Set list: 'Astronomy Domine', 'Careful With That Axe, Eugene', 'Cymbaline', 'A Saucerful Of Secrets' <Intermission> 'Embryo', 'Interstellar Overdrive', 'Set The Controls For The Heart Of The Sun', 'Atom Heart Mother'.

SUNDAY 15 MARCH – PERFORMANCE ▼
Niedersachsenhalle, Hannover, West Germany
Set list: 'Astronomy Domine', 'Careful With That Axe, Eugene', 'Cymbaline', 'A Saucerful Of Secrets' <Intermission> 'Embryo', 'Interstellar Overdrive', 'Set The Controls For The Heart Of The Sun', 'Atom Heart Mother' (announced by Roger Waters as 'Consequently').

WEDNESDAY 18 MARCH – FILM PREMIERE (US)
Zabriskie Point, Coronet Theater, New York, NY, USA

THURSDAY 19 MARCH – PERFORMANCE
Stora Salen, Stockholm Konserthus, Stockholm, Sweden
Rescheduled from Gothenberg on Wednesday 18 March.
Set list included 'Interstellar Overdrive', 'Main Theme' (from *More*), 'A Saucerful Of Secrets', 'Atom Heart Mother' <Encore> 'Blues'.

FRIDAY 20 MARCH – PERFORMANCE
Akademiska Föreningens Stora Salen, Lund, Sweden
Set list: 'Astronomy Domine', 'Careful With That Axe, Eugene', 'Cymbaline', 'A Saucerful Of Secrets' <Intermission> 'Embryo', 'Interstellar Overdrive', 'Set The Controls For The Heart Of The Sun', 'Atom Heart Mother'.

SATURDAY 21 MARCH – PERFORMANCE
Tivolis Koncertsal, Copenhagen, Denmark
Set list included 'A Saucerful Of Secrets', 'Interstellar Overdrive', 'Set The Controls For The Heart Of The Sun'.

PETER BRUNE MANAGEMENTS PRESENTS:
PINKFLOYD
IN CONCERT

Sonntag NIEDERSACHSENHALLE HANNOVER
15.3.   Karten ab a.• DM an allen bekannten Vorverkaufsstellen   20Uhr

MONDAY 23 MARCH – CANCELLED RECORDING SESSION
Studio 2 & Control Room 2, EMI Studios,
Abbey Road, London, England

Session cancelled due to "the non-arrival of musicians", presumably due to a delay returning from Denmark.

TUESDAY 24 MARCH – RECORDING SESSION
Studio 2 & Control Room 2, EMI Studios,
Abbey Road, London, England

2.30pm to 7.00pm: Drums and vocals overdubbed onto Take 3 of 'Untitled' ['Atom Heart Mother'] and edited, and 'Untitled' [an edit section for 'Atom Heart Mother'] recorded (Take 1 at 4:00) for *Atom Heart Mother*. A complete rough mix was made of the entire track and handed over to Ron Geesin in order for him to begin work on the score, ready for the return to the studio in June. The session was produced by Pink Floyd, engineered by Phil MacDonald and assisted by John Leckie.

MONDAY 30 MARCH – PERFORMANCE
Le Festival Musique Evolution, **Le Bourget**
(Aéroport de Paris), Siene St Denis, France

With Ginger Baker's Airforce, Pretty Things, Procol Harum, Kevin Ayers and the Whole World, Daddy Longlegs, Keith Relf's Renaissance, Hawkwind, Edgar Broughton Band, Skin Alley, Moving Gelatine Plates and Le Voyage among others.
Set list: 'Astronomy Domine', 'Careful With That Axe, Eugene', 'Cymbaline', 'A Saucerful Of Secrets', 'Embryo', 'Interstellar Overdrive', 'Set The Controls For The Heart Of The Sun'.

This, the first officially sanctioned music festival in France, was staged in an aircraft hangar over the Easter weekend of Friday 27 to Monday 30 March. It promised to be quite an event, with many top name bands, film shows, light shows, cheap food, camping and a "pop village" with market stalls. As it turned out, two adjoining stages accommodated the live entertainment, but little else materialized. Repeatedly, groups were not ready to play, leaving an audience that was far smaller than anticipated listening to impromptu jams by roadies and stray musicians. In addition, food prices were inflated and no authorization was given for camping, so that those who did try to pitch tents were evicted by the police. Cold winds blasted through the hangar, which now doubled as accommodation. Pink Floyd performed to a crowd of some 8,000 fans sandwiched between Kevin Ayers and Edgar Broughton, who closed the show to a fast dwindling audience. Although RTL radio and French TV recorded parts of the festival (two news bulletins broadcast on Sunday 29 March showed a brief glimpse of the Pretty Things performing and on Monday 30 March the group Moving Gelatine Plates), nothing was ever broadcast of Pink Floyd's set.

NORTH AMERICAN TOUR

Pink Floyd's return to North America was organized jointly by New York promoter Jay K Hoffman who handled the East Coast leg of the tour and Chartwell Artists who assumed overall management of the tour while booking the West Coast.

Early drafts of Pink Floyd's tour show the band scheduled to appear at the Electric Factory, Philadelphia, on Sunday 10 and Monday 11 April (rescheduled to Friday 17 and Saturday 18 April), Boston Tea Party, Boston, between Thursday 9 and Saturday 11 April (rescheduled to Sunday 12 April); Kansas City, MO, on Sunday 24 May; Garden Auditorium, Vancouver, BC, Canada, on Sunday 26 April; San Diego on Saturday 9 May; State Fair Music Hall, Dallas, on Thursday 22 May (rescheduled to Friday 23 May and then cancelled as a result of equipment theft); Houston Music Theatre, Houston, on Friday 23 May (rescheduled to Thursday 22 May and then cancelled as a result of equipment theft); HemisFair Arena, San Antonio, on Saturday 24 May (Pink Floyd cancelled supporting Grand Funk Railroad in an early part of the tour scheduling, before tickets were advertised, and not as a result of the aforementioned equipment theft. The entire show was rescheduled to Sunday 31 May with Blood Rock taking Pink Floyd's place and the addition of Lee Michaels to the bill); Freedom Palace, Kansas City, MO, on Saturday 24 May (cancelled as a result of equipment theft); Aragon Ballroom, Chicago, on Friday 29 and Saturday 30 May (rescheduled to Friday 10 April) and Ludlow Garage, Cincinnati, on Friday 17 and Saturday 18 April or Friday 5 and Saturday 6 June.

THURSDAY 9 APRIL – PERFORMANCE
Fillmore East, New York, NY, USA

Set list: 'Grantchester Meadows', 'Astronomy Domine', 'Cymbaline', 'The Violent Sequence', 'A Saucerful Of Secrets' <Intermission> 'Embryo', 'Green Is The Colour', 'Careful With That Axe, Eugene', 'Set The Controls For The Heart Of The Sun', 'Atom Heart Mother' <Encore> 'Interstellar Overdrive'.

Unconvinced of Pink Floyd's potential, the band had to hire the venue from owner and promoter Bill Graham. His concerns were unfounded and a second show was soon added on Thursday 16 April.

FRIDAY 10 APRIL – PERFORMANCE
Aragon Ballroom, Chicago, IL, USA

With Rotary Connection, Mason Proffit and Litter.
Set list included 'Green Is The Colour', 'Careful With That Axe, Eugene', 'A Saucerful Of Secrets'.

SATURDAY 11 APRIL – ALBUM RELEASE (US)
Zabriskie Point

The *Wisconsin Sheboygan Press* wrote, "Floyd's electronics adds hyper-tension to the album (and probably to the movie). They also play on the senses with Moog synthesizers, re-recordings and playbacks. Floyd's best track is "Come in Number 51, Your Time Is Up", which must be designed to be the mood music for destruction. It sounds like the End is at Hand with the electronic screaming and the apocalyptic movement at the beginning."

SATURDAY 11 APRIL – PERFORMANCE
Pritchard Gymnasium, State University of New York,
Stony Brook, NY, USA

Set list: 'Astronomy Domine', 'Careful With That Axe, Eugene', 'Cymbaline', 'Atom Heart Mother', 'Set The Controls For The Heart Of The Sun', 'A Saucerful Of Secrets'.

SUNDAY 12 APRIL – PERFORMANCE
Boston Tea Party, Boston, MA, USA

MONDAY 13 APRIL – RECORDING SESSION
Control Room 2, EMI Studios,
Abbey Road, London, England

7.00pm to 9.10pm: 8-track to stereo reduction of 'I Am The Embryo' ['Embryo'] (RS1 at 4:40 and RS2 at 4:40 marked "best edited") for the Harvest label compilation album *Picnic: A Breath Of Fresh Air*. The session was produced by Norman Smith and engineered by Anthony Clarke and Nick Webb. Pink Floyd was not in attendance at this session.

'Embryo' had first been worked on in the studio during the latter part of 1968 and a version had been recorded for a BBC session in December of that year. The track is surrounded by a certain amount of controversy since it was never officially sanctioned by the band for release, although it is said that this recording was unwittingly authorized by then Harvest label manager Malcolm Jones, for inclusion on the sampler album *Picnic*. Except for its appearance on the 1983 Capitol Records Floyd compilation *Works*, the track has remained unreleased, and *Picnic* is now something of a rarity. Surprisingly, given their reluctance to see it released, the band played the song frequently during the early 1970s, but it was dropped – presumably for bearing too many similarities to 'Echoes'.

THURSDAY 16 APRIL – PERFORMANCE ▼
Fillmore East, New York, NY, USA

Set list: 'Grantchester Meadows', 'Astronomy Domine', 'Cymbaline', 'Atom Heart Mother', 'Set The Controls For The Heart Of The Sun' <Encore> 'A Saucerful Of Secrets'.

Billboard reported, "Pink Floyd, one of the most distinctive British musical groups, gave a lengthy and imaginative show at Fillmore East. The quartet demonstrated its mastery of sound with speakers at the sides and rear of the theatre and a range from opening acoustic guitars to the most amplified of effects, including tape. Richard Wright on organ, grand piano and 'azimuth co-ordinator' was a key to the units' success. The co-ordinator proved an exceptional electronic device with a variety of effects. A gong, a trademark of this quartet, also was much in evidence as played by bass guitarist Roger Waters, who also played cymbals, aiding drummer Nick Mason, whose playing also was exceptional. Lead guitarist David Gilmour also was in top form. In fact, the entire group gave one of its best performances with such material as 'Saucerful Of Secrets' and 'Set The Controls For The Heart Of The Sun'. An untitled number from the next album was also top-notch as were soundtrack numbers from *More* and *Zabriskie Point*, the latter a number cut out from the film."

FRIDAY 17 & SATURDAY 18 APRIL – PERFORMANCES
The Electric Factory, Philadelphia, PA, USA

Two shows at 8.00pm and 11.00pm each night, supported by Insect Trust.

WEDNESDAY 22 APRIL – PERFORMANCE
Capitol Theatre, Port Chester, NY, USA

Set List: 'Grantchester Meadows', 'Astronomy Domine', 'Cymbaline', 'Atom Heart Mother' <Intermission> 'Embryo', 'Green Is The Colour', 'Careful With That Axe, Eugene', 'Set The Controls For The Heart Of The Sun', 'A Saucerful Of Secrets' <Encore> 'Blues'.

FRIDAY 24 & SATURDAY 25 APRIL – PERFORMANCES
East Town Theatre, Detroit, MI, USA

With the Frost and the Up.

WEDNESDAY 29 APRIL – PERFORMANCE
Fillmore West, San Francisco, CA, USA

Set List: 'Grantchester Meadows', 'Astronomy Domine', 'Cymbaline', 'Atom Heart Mother' <Intermission> 'Embryo', 'Green Is The Colour', 'Careful With That Axe, Eugene', 'Set The Controls For The Heart Of The Sun' <Encore> 'A Saucerful Of Secrets'.

THURSDAY 30 APRIL – TELEVISION RECORDING
***An Hour with the Pink Floyd*,**
Fillmore Auditorium, San Francisco, CA, USA

Pink Floyd recorded a one-hour live concert, with no audience, for the PBS TV network at the Fillmore West on this date. The set list comprised 'Atom Heart Mother', 'Cymbaline', 'Grantchester Meadows', 'Green Is The Colour', 'Careful With That Axe, Eugene' and 'Set The Controls For The Heart Of The Sun'. It was first broadcast as *An Hour with the Pink Floyd* on Tuesday 26 January 1971 on the PBS network channel KQED from 8.00pm (PST), and first repeated on the same channel on Monday 12 April 1971 from 8.00pm and Sunday 12 December 1971 from 10.00pm (PST). It appeared on the 2016 box set *The Early Years 1965–1972*.

FRIDAY 1 MAY – PERFORMANCE ▼
Civic Auditorium, Santa Monica, CA, USA

Set list: 'Grantchester Meadows', 'Astronomy Domine', 'Cymbaline', 'Atom Heart Mother', <Intermission> 'Embryo', 'Green Is The Colour', 'Careful With That Axe, Eugene', 'Set The Controls For The Heart Of The Sun', 'Interstellar Overdrive' <Encore> 'A Saucerful Of Secrets'.

THURSDAY 7 MAY – PERFORMANCE
Janss Steps, University of California, Los Angeles, Los Angeles, CA, USA

ZABRISKIE POINT

SIDE ONE (PINK FLOYD TRACK)

HEART BEAT, PIG MEAT (Gilmour, Waters, Wright, Mason) **3:12**

SIDE TWO (PINK FLOYD TRACKS)

CRUMBLING LAND (Gilmour, Waters, Wright, Mason) **4:16**
COME IN NUMBER 51, YOUR TIME IS UP (Gilmour, Waters, Wright, Mason) **5:01**
BONUS TRACKS (1997 Rhino reissue)
COUNTRY SONG (Gilmour, Waters, Wright, Mason) **4:37**
UNKNOWN SONG (Gilmour, Waters, Wright, Mason) **6:01**
LOVE SCENE (VERSION 6) (Gilmour, Waters, Wright, Mason) **7:26**
LOVE SCENE (VERSION 4) (Gilmour, Waters, Wright, Mason) **6:45**

RELEASE DATE

US: Saturday 11 April 1970.
UK: Friday 29 May 1970.

FORMAT

UK: EMI Harvest SHVL 781 (Vinyl album).
US: Harvest SKAO 382 (Vinyl album).

RECORDING DETAILS

Italian director Michelangelo Antonioni's highly anticipated follow-up to the stunning success he achieved with his British feature film debut, *Blow Up*, could not have been a more humiliating disaster. Keen to cash in on the American counter-culture youth market MGM signed Antonioni to a three-year deal and invested an astonishing $7 million into the project, which took nearly two years to make. His search for the perfect soundtrack alone proved to be highly controversial, at first commissioning Pink Floyd to produce the entire score to a film set in California. Panned by critics on release, the film did however garner a huge amount of interest for Pink Floyd's contribution, notably the finale in which a version of 'Careful With That Axe, Eugene' was used and no doubt raised their profile for their tour of that year. However, MGM was less than enthralled: the film took only $900,000 at the box office on its opening weekend.

Bizarrely, Antonioni insisted on using his favoured recording studio in Rome, at first shipping Pink Floyd over to produce the initial clutch of material, and then a succession of other artists. According to Nick Mason director Antonioni was an impossible man to work for. "We'd start work at about nine [in the evening,]" he recalled. "The studio was a few minutes' walk down the road, so we'd stagger down the road. We could have finished the whole thing in about five days because there wasn't too much to do. Antonioni was there and we did some great stuff, but he'd listen and go, and I remember he had this terrible twitch, he'd go, 'Eet's very beauteeful but eet's too sad' or 'Eet's too strong.' It was always wrong consistently. There was always something that stopped it being perfect. You'd still change whatever was wrong and he'd still be unhappy. It was hell. Sheer hell. He'd sit down and fall asleep every so often, and we'd go on working till about seven or eight in the morning."[1]

Mason also recalled in a syndicated article to *Canadian Press* in April 1971 that, "[a]fter seeing the love scene about 15 times a night for a week we were highly depressed."

Much of what was recorded in Rome was either abandoned or developed in a series of further studio sessions held at EMI Studios, Abbey Road in December 1969 and January 1970. Of the combined sessions only three were released on the official soundtrack album: 'Heart Beat, Pig Meat', an acoustic number vaguely reminiscent in style to the material found on *More*; 'Crumbling Land', which was recorded as 'Highway Song', an odd country-rock style number of which only 34 seconds was used in the film from an early mix (the album version features recordings made by Mason of the traffic congestion in Rome); and 'Come In Number 51 Your Time Is Up', a reworking of 'Careful With That Axe, Eugene'.

A bootleg album released in the early 1970s and entitled *Omayyad* revealed a clutch of previously unreleased tracks under the assumed titles 'Rain In Country' (also known as 'Unknown Song') and 'Oenone' (both being alternate versions of 'Love Scene') and 'Fingal's Cave' (recorded as 'Take Off'), and taken from a broadcast on KPPC Radio in Pasadena on Saturday 16 October 1971 in a programme featuring Don Hall, the music director for MGM, who aired the tracks. Also broadcast was 'The Christmas Song', recorded as a gift to Antonioni during the sessions. It is said to have been played on John Peel's annual BBC Radio One Christmas show in the mid-1970s, although this could not be substantiated.

An expanded soundtrack released by Rhino Records in 1997

1. *Disc*, 23 August 1975.

revealed a host of further and previously unreleased titles including 'Country Song', the aforementioned 'Unknown Song' and 'Love Scene (Versions 6 & 4)'.

A further bootleg album which mopped up the remaining tapes submitted to MGM and released around this time featured yet more tracks from the sessions, including the assumed and previously unreleased titles 'Red Queen Theme' (a version of 'Country Song'),

'Blues Scene', 'Riot Scene' and 'Love Scene (Versions 1–6)'.

At the Pink Floyd exhibition in Paris in 2003 an original tape box for *Zabriskie Point* was exhibited, dated 16/17 November 1969, and labelled with the following tracks: 'Love Scene (Version 4)' Take 3 Complete Master, 'Love Scene (Version 5 – Vibes Version)' Take 1 Complete and 'Love Scene (Version 6 – Blues Version)' Take 1 Complete.

Heart Beat, Pig Meat

Take unknown (RS unknown).
Basic track recorded and mixed in Rome, November 1969.

Crumbling Land (Recorded as Highway Song)

Take 3 (RS13).
Basic track recorded on 13 December 1969 (Take 3).
Acoustic Guitar, Electric Guitar, Organ and Piano overdubbed onto Take 3 on 13 December 1969.
Vocals, Tympanis, Bass and Drums overdubbed onto Take 3 on 15 December 1969.
Guitar and Vocals overdubbed onto Take 3 on 16 December 1969.
Mixed on 17 December 1969 (RS1-4).
Mixed on 5 January 1970 (RS13).

Come In Number 51, Your Time Is Up

Take unknown (RS unknown).
Basic track recorded in Rome, November 1969.
"Explosions" for overdubs mixed on 1 January 1970 (RS6).

Country Song
(Released as a bonus track on 1997 Rhino reissue)

Take 1 (RS7).
Basic track recorded on 12 December 1969 (Take 1).
Guitar, Piano, Bass Guitar and Drums overdubbed onto Take 1 on 12 December 1969.
Piano, Guitar and Drums overdubbed onto Take 1 on 13 December 1969.
Vocals overdubbed onto Take 1 of 'Country Song' on 17 December 1969.
Mixed on 5 January 1970 (RS7).

Unknown Song
(Released as a bonus track on 1997 Rhino reissue)

Take unknown (RS unknown).
Basic track recorded in Rome, November 1969.

Love Scene

Take unknown (RS5).
Basic track recorded in Rome, November 1969.
Mixed on 15 January 1970 (RS5).

Love Scene (Version 4)
(Released as a bonus track on 1997 Rhino reissue)

Take 3 (RS unknown).
Basic track recorded in Rome, November 1969.

Love Scene (Version 5 – Vibes Version)
(Unreleased)

Take 1 (RS unknown).
Basic track recorded in Rome, 17 November 1969.

Love Scene (Version 6) (Recorded as Alan's Blues)
(Released as a bonus track on 1997 Rhino reissue)

Take 1 (RS1).
Basic track recorded in Rome, 17 November 1969.
Mixed (RS1).

Beginning Scene
(Unreleased)

Take unknown (RS unknown).
Basic track recorded in Rome, November 1969.
Mixed on 5 January 1970 (RS6).

Take Off (Version 1)
(Unreleased, may have been used for the opening of 'Crumbling Land')

Take unknown (RS2).
Basic track recorded in Rome, November 1969.
Mixed on 5 January 1970 (RS2).

Take Off (Version 2) (Unreleased)

Take unknown (RS1).
Basic track recorded in Rome, November 1969.
Guitar overdubbed on 16 December 1969.
Mixed on 5 January 1970 (RS1).

Take Off (Version 3)
(Unreleased)

Take unknown (RS3).
Basic track recorded in Rome, November 1969.
Mixed on 16 December 1969 (RS3).

LEFT: POSTER FOR THE US FILM RELEASE.

ABOVE: A SAMPLE OF THE EXTENSIVE PRESS COVERAGE THE FILM RECEIVED.

This was a completely unscheduled and unadvertised concert in the wake of a call for a general strike by students at campuses throughout the United States beginning Tuesday 5 May in protest at the killing of four unarmed students by National Guardsmen at Kent State University, Ohio, on Monday 4 May. Eyewitness Paul Cormany remembered that, "I had been in Mexico, had not heard about the student shootings at Kent State, went to class at the then Santa Monica City College and found out classes were cancelled, heard about the PF concert at UCLA and drove over to the campus. I arrived late afternoon and watched the crew set up an outdoor version of the quadraphonic sound system at the top and the bottom of the wide steps [Pink Floyd set up stage at the bottom of the famous steps] and stayed for the concert." *Melody Maker* reported, "Pink Floyd gave a free concert to 10,000 students which even a detachment of National Guardsmen complete with helmets, riot shields and rifles enjoyed."

SATURDAY 9 MAY – PERFORMANCE ▼
Terrace Ballroom, Salt Lake City, UT, USA

Supported by Blue Mountain Eagle.
Set list included 'Cymbaline'.

TUESDAY 12 MAY – PERFORMANCE
Municipal Auditorium, Atlanta, GA, USA

Supporting the Guess Who.
Set list included 'Grantchester Meadows', 'Astronomy Domine', 'Cymbaline', 'A Saucerful Of Secrets'.

The underground newspaper *Great Speckled Bird* reported, "The group uses a 360-degree stereo sound system, meaning that speakers are employed throughout the auditorium, as well as on stage. Pink Floyd's sound system is beyond belief – you can physically feel the music (without good old LSD too!). But it isn't just loudness and volume, like so many concerts, where you leave the place with your ears ringing. They are perhaps one of the few groups that knows how to properly use their sound equipment. And they use a shit-load of it too (three tons worth), most of it conventional amplifiers and speakers but also much sophisticated electronic apparatus. Pink Floyd's music could be best described as the natural merging of electronics and psychedelics. Music of the coming age. Most of their music originates from conventional instruments, but then goes through so many incredible electronic alterations that the final sound is hard to associate with the instruments being played. In addition to the live sounds produced on stage, magnetic tapes are used, especially tape loops of such things as

bird calls to create rhythmic sounds. The concert also includes a stereo tape solo of giant footsteps which appear to walk around the auditorium, as well as doors opening and closing and a fly which finally gets swatted. Doesn't sound very thrilling on paper, but it was very freaky at the time!"

FRIDAY 15 & SATURDAY 16 MAY – PERFORMANCES ▼
Warehouse, New Orleans, LA, USA

With the Allman Brothers Band and Country Funk.
Set list on Thursday 15 May included: 'Grantchester Meadows', 'Astronomy Domine', 'A Saucerful Of Secrets', 'Set The Controls For The Heart Of The Sun'.

Pink Floyd stayed on in New Orleans until their next scheduled show in Houston, but following an early departure on the morning of Thursday 22 May the crew discovered that the band's 30-foot-long U-Haul rental truck containing $40,000 worth of equipment and musical instruments had been stolen from outside the Royal Orleans Hotel in the French Quarter, where they were staying. The list of stolen equipment included four electric guitars, an electric organ and piano, a 4,000-watt sound system with 12 speaker cabinets, five Italian echo units, microphones, two drum kits and 10 miles of cable. The New Orleans *Times-Picayune* reported that the rental truck was found abandoned on Castiglione Street, three miles from the hotel, with its contents intact, save for a couple of guitars which were missing. When the group thought it had lost everything, it cancelled the rest the tour. Nick Mason recalled the event to *Melody Maker* saying that it was, "Nearly a total disaster. We sat down at our hotel thinking – 'Well that's it. It's all over.' We were pouring out our troubles to a girl who worked at the hotel and she said her father worked for the FBI. The police hadn't helped us much, but the FBI got to work and four hours later it was found."

However, even when the stolen truck was found with most of the equipment intact Pink Floyd decided not to reinstate the cancelled gigs and instead returned to England via New York. Gilmour took the opportunity to visit Manny's Music and purchased a new Fender Stratocaster to

BELOW: DAVID GILMOUR AND ROGER WATERS ON STAGE IN NEW ORLEANS, MAY 1970.

replace the one stolen. That guitar became known as the 'Black Strat', a guitar that appeared thereafter on almost all of Pink Floyd's albums, and shows and all of his solo projects.

THURSDAY 22 MAY – CANCELLED PERFORMANCES
Houston Music Theatre, Houston, TX, USA

Pink Floyd cancelled two shows at 7.00pm and 10.00pm supporting Grand Funk Railroad following their vehicle theft on the same day.

FRIDAY 23 MAY – CANCELLED PERFORMANCE
State Fair Music Hall, Dallas, TX, USA

Pink Floyd cancelled supporting Grand Funk Railroad following their vehicle theft on 22 May. Fort Worth band Blood Rock took Pink Floyd's place.

SATURDAY 24 MAY – CANCELLED PERFORMANCE
Freedom Palace, Kansas City, KS, USA

Pink Floyd cancelled supporting Grand Funk Railroad following their vehicle theft on 22 May. Blood Rock took Pink Floyd's place.

FRIDAY 29 MAY – ALBUM RELEASE (UK)
Zabriskie Point

WEDNESDAY 10 JUNE – RECORDING SESSION
Studio 2 & Control Room 2, EMI Studios,
Abbey Road, London, England

2.30pm to 7.00pm: Vocals, Tympani and SFX overdubbed onto Take 3 of 'Untitled Epic' ['Atom Heart Mother'] for *Atom Heart Mother*. The session was produced by Pink Floyd, engineered by Peter Bown and assisted by John Kurlander.

THURSDAY 11 JUNE – RECORDING SESSION
Studio 2 & Control Room 2, EMI Studios,
Abbey Road, London, England

2.30pm to 12.00 midnight: 'Fat Old Sun' recorded (Take 1 at 5:15 and marked "best") for *Atom Heart Mother*. The session was produced by Pink Floyd, engineered by Peter Bown and assisted by Alan Parsons.

FRIDAY 12 JUNE – RECORDING SESSION
Studio 2 & Control Room 2, EMI Studios,
Abbey Road, London, England

2.30pm to 7.00pm and 8.00pm to 11.00pm: Vocals and Flutes overdubbed onto Take 3 of 'Fat Old Sun' and 'Roger's Song' ['If'] recorded (Take 1 False Start and Take 2 at 4:54 also marked "best") for *Atom Heart Mother*. The session was produced by Pink Floyd, engineered by Peter Bown and assisted by Alan Parsons.

SATURDAY 13 JUNE – RECORDING SESSION
Studio 2 & Control Room 2, EMI Studios,
Abbey Road, London, England

2.30pm to 7.00pm and 8.00pm to 12.00 midnight: 'No One Tells Me Anything Around Here' (an unreleased track) recorded (Take 1 at 10:30, Take 2 at 25:00 and Take 3 at 6:45); SFX recorded and Guitar overdubbed onto Take 3 of 'Fat Old Sun', and SFX reductions of Take 3 of 'Fat Old Sun' and remixed (RS1, RS2 and RS3, all

untimed) for *Atom Heart Mother*. The session was produced by Pink Floyd, engineered by Peter Bown and assisted by Alan Parsons. No further work appears to have been done on 'No One Tells Me Anything Around Here' and the track is wiped from the archives.

TUESDAY 16 JUNE – RECORDING SESSION
Studio 2 & Control Room 2, EMI Studios,
Abbey Road, London, England

2.30pm to 7.00pm and 8.00pm to 12.50am: Drums overdubbed onto 'Untitled 1 Epic' ['Atom Heart Mother'], and 'piece for end' of 'Untitled 1 Epic' edited, and Guitar and Bell overdubbed onto 'Untitled 1 Epic' for *Atom Heart Mother*. The session was produced by Pink Floyd, engineered by Peter Bown and assisted by Alan Parsons.

WEDNESDAY 17 JUNE – RECORDING SESSION
Studio 2 & Control Room 2, EMI Studios,
Abbey Road, London, England

2.30pm to 6.30pm and 8.00pm to 12.30am: Click-track, Piano and Guitar overdubbed onto Take 3 of 'Untitled Epic' ['Atom Heart Mother']; various sections of Take 3 of 'Untitled Epic' re-edited, and reductions made of Take 3 of 'Untitled Epic' (relabelled Take 4) for *Atom Heart Mother*. The session was produced by Pink Floyd, engineered by Peter Bown and assisted by Alan Parsons.

THURSDAY 18 JUNE – RECORDING SESSION
Studio 2 & Control Room 2, EMI Studios,
Abbey Road, London, England

2.30pm to 6.00pm and 7.00pm to 12.30am: Various sections remixed for Tape Loops and made up and overdubbed onto Take 4 of 'Untitled Epic' ['Atom Heart Mother']; Hammond, Mellotron, Vocals and Various Special Effects overdubbed and edited onto Take 4 of 'Untitled Epic'; and recording of 'Alan's Story' ['Alan's Psychedelic Breakfast'] (untimed) for *Atom Heart Mother*. The session was produced by Pink Floyd, engineered by Peter Bown and assisted by Alan Parsons.

FRIDAY 19 JUNE – RECORDING SESSION
Studio 2 & Control Room 2, EMI Studios,
Abbey Road, London, England

2.30pm to 7.15pm and 8.15pm to 1.00am: Brass overdubbed onto Take 4 of 'Untitled Epic' ['Atom Heart Mother']; Remixing Tape Loops (Takes 1–6) and Take 6 played backwards and transferred into Take 4 of 'Untitled Epic'; and "Count In for Section After Percussion" edited into Take 4 of 'Untitled Epic' for *Atom Heart Mother*. The session was produced by Pink Floyd, engineered by Peter Bown and assisted by Alan Parsons. It is noted the orchestra comprised 3 Trumpets, 3 Trombones, 3 French Horns and 1 Tuba.

SATURDAY 20 JUNE – RECORDING SESSION
Studio 2 & Control Room 2, EMI Studios,
Abbey Road, London, England

2.30pm to 5.30pm and 7.00pm to 10.45pm: Brass overdubbed onto Take 4 of 'Untitled Epic' ['Atom Heart Mother'] for *Atom Heart Mother*. The session was produced by Pink Floyd, engineered by Peter Bown and assisted by Alan Parsons.

SUNDAY 21 JUNE – RECORDING SESSION
Studio 2 & Control Room 2, EMI Studios,
Abbey Road, London, England

2.30pm to 7.00pm and 8.00pm to 12.15am: Organ and Percussion overdubbed onto Take 4 of 'Untitled Epic' ['Atom Heart Mother']; recording "Experimental percussion section with train sounds" (Take 1 False Start and Take 2 complete) for 'Untitled Epic'; and Choir overdubbed onto Take 4 of 'Untitled Epic' for *Atom Heart Mother*. The session was produced by Pink Floyd, engineered by Peter Bown and assisted by Alan Parsons.

MONDAY 22 JUNE – RECORDING SESSION
Studio 2 & Control Room 2, EMI Studios,
Abbey Road, London, England

2.30pm to 10.30pm: Choir overdubbed onto Take 4 of 'Untitled Epic' ['Atom Heart Mother'] for *Atom Heart Mother*. It is noted that 20 singers were booked for this recording session. The session was produced by Pink Floyd, engineered by Peter Bown and assisted by Alan Parsons.

TUESDAY 23 JUNE – RECORDING SESSION
Studio 2 & Control Room 2, EMI Studios,
Abbey Road, London, England

2.30pm to 12.00midnight: Brass and Cello overdubbed onto Take 4 of 'Untitled Epic' ['Atom Heart Mother'] for *Atom Heart Mother* and a rough stereo remix made. The session was produced by Pink Floyd, engineered by Peter Bown and assisted by Alan Parsons.

WEDNESDAY 24 JUNE – RECORDING SESSION
Studio 2 & Control Room 2, EMI Studios,
Abbey Road, London, England

2.30pm to 12.15am: Guitar, Organ, Piano and Vocals overdubbed onto Take 4 of 'Untitled Epic' ['Atom Heart Mother'] and Backwards Brass Section transferred to percussion section of Take 4 of 'Untitled Epic' for *Atom Heart Mother*. The session was produced by Pink Floyd, engineered by Peter Bown and assisted by Alan Parsons. A band rehearsal is also noted between 12.15pm to 1.00am.

THURSDAY 25 JUNE – RECORDING SESSION
Studio 2 & Control Room 2, EMI Studios,
Abbey Road, London, England

2.30pm to 12.30am: Recording 'If' (Takes 1–4 False Starts, and Take 5 at 4:40 also marked "best") for *Atom Heart Mother*. A special reduction of the percussion section of Take 4 of 'Untitled Epic' and SFX was made specifically as a backing track for the *Bath Festival*. The session was produced by Pink Floyd, engineered by Peter Bown and assisted by Alan Parsons.

SATURDAY 27 JUNE – PERFORMANCE ▶
Bath Festival of Blues & Progressive Music '70,
Bath & West Showgound, Shepton Mallet, England

With Canned Heat, John Mayall, Steppenwolf, Johnny Winter, It's a Beautiful Day, Fairport Convention, Colosseum, Keef Hartley, Maynard Fergusson Big Band and DJs John Peel and Mike Raven, and headliners Led Zeppelin and Jefferson Airplane (Sunday 28 June).

Set list: 'Green Is The Colour', 'Careful With That Axe, Eugene', 'A Saucerful Of Secrets', 'Set The Controls For The Heart Of The Sun', 'Atom Heart Mother' (announced by Roger Waters as 'The Amazing Pudding' with the Philip Jones Brass Ensemble and the John Alldis Choir, conducted by John Alldis).

This huge two-day event, which overran so much it didn't actually finish until the early hours of Monday 29 June, and inspired Michael Eavis to stage the first *Glastonbury Festival*, featured many of the world's top performing artists and was headlined by Led Zeppelin, attracting twice the anticipated audience. A rough estimate put it at 150,000, which put a terrible strain on maintaining food supplies, not to mention the toilets, of which there were often up to 200 people queuing at any one time! The traffic it generated also caused the biggest jams in Somerset's history. Generally speaking it was a very peaceful weekend. The only reported incident occurred when the Hell's Angels, in their customary role of site security, "assisted" in the clearance of the VIP/press area in front of the stage to make way for Pink Floyd's light show projectors to be set up, midway through Steppenwolf's set.

Reviewing the festival *Disc & Music Echo* reported, "We were into the early hours of Sunday morning before Pink Floyd made it on stage. They took a very long time to set up but their act was worth it. People were getting tired but the spectacular close to their set woke everyone up. After laying down some good sounds they were joined by a choir, about 12 strong, and a brass section and went into a 20 minute thing which will be one side of their new album. It was a heavenly sound. The finale saw three flares bursting open the sky with a galaxy of colours – smoke and the light show flooded the stage. It was amazing."

SUNDAY 28 JUNE – PERFORMANCE
The Holland Pop Festival '70, **Kralingse Bos,**
Rotterdam, Netherlands

With Soft Machine, Chicago Art Ensemble, John Surman, Han Bennick, Caravan, Fairport Convention, Fotheringay on the same day, and headliners Jefferson Airplane (Friday 26 June) and the Byrds (Saturday 27 June).
Set list: 'Astronomy Domine', 'Green Is The Colour', 'Careful With That Axe, Eugene', 'Atom Heart Mother', 'Set The Controls For The Heart Of The Sun', 'A Saucerful Of Secrets' <Encore> 'Interstellar Overdrive'.

Sponsored by Coca-Cola, the *Holland Pop Festival* remains the largest event of its kind in the Netherlands with an estimated attendance exceeding 350,000. It ran from Friday 26 to Sunday 28 June and had a reciprocal agreement with the organizers of the *Bath Festival* that enabled many of the same artists to perform at both. The event was in itself so peaceful that the police hardly made any arrests and is said to have led to the Netherlands' relaxed policy on soft drugs. After prolonged delays and overruns Pink Floyd finally took to the stage at 4.00am on Monday 29 June.

The event was captured on film and was officially released to cinema as *Stamping Ground* (and in Germany as *Love and Music*) in order to help offset the huge losses that the festival incurred, and included Pink Floyd's performance of 'Set The Controls For The Heart Of The Sun' and 'A Saucerful Of Secrets'. It premiered at the Cineac in Rotterdam on Wednesday 30 June 1971 and in the US at the Picwood Theatre, Westwood, Los Angeles on Friday 28 April 1972, but received negative reviews for focusing too much on the bands and not the event itself.

The footage has since been released on video under this same title and Pink Floyd's performance has also appeared on many video compilations including *Psychomania*, and more recently a restored version of the *Stamping Ground* entitled the *Dutch Woodstock*.

SATURDAY 4 JULY – RECORDING SESSION
Studio 2 & Control Room 2, EMI Studios, Abbey Road, London, England

2.30pm to 8.00pm and 9.00pm to 1.45am: Recording 'If' (Take 6 at 4:28 also marked "best"), and rough remix of 'If' (RS1 at 4:28) for *Atom Heart Mother*. The session was produced by Pink Floyd, engineered by Peter Bown and assisted by Alan Parsons.

SUNDAY 5 JULY – RECORDING SESSION
Studio 2 & Control Room 2, EMI Studios, Abbey Road, London, England

2.30pm to 7.00pm and 8.00pm to 1.20am: Moog overdubbed onto Take 6 of 'If' and remixed (RS1 at 4.30 and RS2 at 4.30 also marked "best"); 'Fat Old Sun' remixed (RS4 at 5:15 also marked "best" and RS2 at 5:15), and 'Summer '68' recorded (Take 1 at 6:00 also marked "best") for *Atom Heart Mother*. The session was produced by Pink Floyd, engineered by Peter Bown and assisted by Alan Parsons.

WEDNESDAY 8 JULY – RECORDING SESSION
Studio 2 & Control Room 2, EMI Studios, Abbey Road, London, England

7.00pm to 12.15am: Stereo reduction of 'If' and 'Untitled Epic' ['Atom Heart Mother'] remixed with sound effects (RS1 untimed) for *Atom Heart Mother*. The session was produced by Pink Floyd, engineered by Peter Bown and assisted by Alan Parsons.

FRIDAY 10 JULY – RECORDING SESSION
Studio 2 & Control Room 2, EMI Studios, Abbey Road, London, England

2.30pm to 6.30pm and 7.30pm to 12.00 midnight: Various Pink Floyd and EMI tape library sound effects edited for 'Alan's

Psychedelic Breakfast'; 'Alan's Psychedelic Breakfast' recorded (Take 1 untimed also marked "best"); and 'Tape Delays Reel 1' and 'Tape Delays Reel 2' remixed for 'Alan's Psychedelic Breakfast' for *Atom Heart Mother*. The session was produced by Pink Floyd, engineered by Peter Bown and assisted by Alan Parsons.

SUNDAY 12 JULY – PERFORMANCE ▼
1st Open Air Pop Festival, Reiterstadion Soers, Aachen, West Germany

With Fairport Convention, Van Der Gaaf Generator, Hardin and York, Amon Düül II, Tyrannosaurus Rex, Krokodil, Raw Material, Champion Jack Dupree on the same day, and headliners Traffic (Friday 10 July) and Edgar Broughton Band (Saturday 11 July).
Set list: 'Astronomy Domine', 'Green Is The Colour', 'Careful With That Axe, Eugene', 'Atom Heart Mother', 'Set The Controls For The Heart Of The Sun', 'A Saucerful Of Secrets' <Encore> 'Interstellar Overdrive'.

MONDAY 13 JULY – RECORDING SESSION
Studio 2 & Control Room 2, EMI Studios, Abbey Road, London, England

7.00pm to 12.30am: Reduction of 'If'; Organ and Guitar overdubbed onto Take 4 of 'Untitled Epic' ['Atom Heart Mother']; and 'One Night Stand' ['Summer '68'] remixed (RS10, RS11 false start, RS12 and RS13, RS14 False Start, RS15, RS16 False Start and RS17) for *Atom Heart Mother*. The session was produced by Pink Floyd, engineered by Peter Bown and assisted by Alan Parsons.

TUESDAY 14 JULY – RECORDING SESSION
Room 4, EMI Studios, Abbey Road, London, England

2.30pm to 7.00pm and 8.00pm to 12.00midnight: 'One Night Stand' ['Summer '68'] remixed (RS19 to RS31, and editing pieces with RS25 and RS31 and marked "best and edited"); 'Summer '68' remixed (RS32 to RS38 edit pieces, RS38 then edited into master of 'One Night Stand'); 'One Night Stand' remixed (RS39 to RS50, with RS39, 40, 46 and 50 also marked "best and edited into master") for *Atom Heart Mother*. The session was produced by Pink Floyd, engineered by Peter Bown and assisted by Nick Webb.

On Thursday 14, Friday 15, Sunday 17 and Tuesday 21 July Syd Barrett was also recording at Abbey Road with David Gilmour producing.

WEDNESDAY 15 JULY – RECORDING SESSION
Room 4, EMI Studios, Abbey Road, London, England

10.00am to 1.30pm: 'Epic' ['Atom Heart Mother'] remixed (RS2 edit piece, and RS3 and RS4 also marked "basic"), and 2.30pm to 7.00pm: 'Epic' remixed (RS5 Edit Piece and RS6 edit piece also marked "best edited onto RS4"), and 8.00pm to 12.00 midnight: 'Epic' remixed (RS7-RS12, with RS11 edited onto RS9) for *Atom Heart Mother*. The session was produced by Pink Floyd and engineered by Peter Bown and Nick Webb.

THURSDAY 16 JULY – RADIO RECORDING
***Peel Sunday Concert*, BBC Paris Cinema, Lower Regent Street, London, England**

Pink Floyd recorded a live-to-air audience show for the BBC Radio One programme *Peel Sunday Concert*, hosted by John Peel. Rehearsals began at 3.30pm and the show was broadcast in the UK on 19 July between 4.00pm and 5.00pm and repeated on *Sounds of the Seventies* hosted by John Peel on Wednesday 22 July between 6.00pm and 7.00pm.
Set list: 'Embryo', 'Fat Old Sun', 'Green Is The Colour', 'Careful With That Axe, Eugene', 'If', 'Atom Heart Mother' (performed with the 10-piece Philip Jones Brass Ensemble, 20-piece John Alldis Choir and a solo cellist).

It is well documented that 'Atom Heart Mother' was announced at the *Bath Festival* as 'The Amazing Pudding' since they still hadn't figured out a suitable title. When the John Peel session was booked and a title had to be registered for royalties, as well as Peel having something by which to introduce the piece, it was hurriedly renamed. Geesin recalled that, "We were sitting in the control room and John Peel had his newspaper [the *Evening Standard*] and we were sitting round with Nick, Roger and the others. I think they were all there saying, 'We haven't got a title for this', and I said, 'If you look in there you'll find a title', and then Roger picked up the paper and said, "Atom Heart Mother" and the others said, 'Yeah, that sounds good.'" The headline appears on page 9 of the 16 July edition, and reads, 'The Atom Heart Mother Is Named' and refers to 56-year-old Mrs. Constance Ladell who received Britain's first plutonium-based pacemaker.

The show has been heavily syndicated over the years beginning with BBC Transcription Services vinyl albums edited for a one-hour programme, which omitted 'Fat Old Sun' (see Discography). Repeat broadcasts in the UK have been few and far between with its first known repeat being on the *In Concert* series broadcast on BBC Radio One on Saturday 5 August 1972 between 6.30pm and 7.30pm, and again on *Classic Concerts* broadcast on BBC Radio One on Sunday 16 March 1986 between 2.30pm and 3.30pm.

FRIDAY 17 JULY – RECORDING SESSION
Studio 2 & Control Room 2, EMI Studios, Abbey Road, London, England

10.00am to 6.00pm: Tape Echo, Piano and Tape Echo Tones overdubbed onto Take 1 of 'Psychedelic Breakfast', and "Various Takes Random" recorded for 'Psychedelic Breakfast' for *Atom Heart Mother*. The session was produced by Pink Floyd, engineered by Peter Bown and assisted by Nick Webb.

FRIDAY 17 JULY – RECORDING SESSION
Room 4, EMI Studios, Abbey Road, London, England

7.00pm to 1.15pm: Remixing 'Epic' ['Atom Heart Mother'] (RS13 edit piece also marked "best edited last section" and RS14 completed edit piece marked "best edited") and all sections of 'Epic' edited together to make a complete master for *Atom Heart Mother*. The session was produced by Pink Floyd, engineered by Peter Bown and assisted by Nick Webb.

SATURDAY 18 JULY – PERFORMANCE
***Blackhill's Garden Party. Hyde Park Free Concert*, Hyde Park, London, England**

With Formerly Fat Harry (who replaced the advertised Third Ear Band), Kevin Ayers and the Whole World, Edgar Broughton Band and DJ Jeff Dexter.
Set list: 'Blues', 'Embryo', 'Green Is The Colour', 'Careful With That Axe, Eugene', 'Set The Controls For The Heart Of The Sun', 'Atom Heart Mother' (announced by Roger Waters as 'The Atomic Heart Mother' with the Philip Jones Brass Ensemble and the John Alldis Choir, conducted by John Alldis) <Encore> 'Atom Heart Mother' (reprise).

Disc & Music Echo reported, "Over five hours of varied and contrasting music was topped by a performance from the Pink Floyd, who treated the gathering to a preview of their forthcoming album. But most of all, the weather was kind. The

BELOW: PINK FLOYD PERFORMING AT THE FREE CONCERT AT HYDE PARK, LONDON, 18 JULY 1970.

only unusual incident to be witnessed by everybody came just after Edgar Broughton finished his set. A middle-aged father, who had apparently lost his son in the crowd, was handing in a message when he suddenly grabbed the microphone from Jeff Dexter. The bewildered man spluttered into the PA: 'I just want to tell you kids – because that's all you are – that I think this bloody music of yours is a load of rubbish!' The remark was met with uproar, and a shower of empty coke cans rained down on him from the audience.... The Pink Floyd gave an hour of beautifully mature music, soothing and inspiring to listen to. They kept the numbers short, apart from the finale, and carefully restrained. With the sun glinting on Nick Mason's drums and the clouds breaking up overhead, it seemed as if the sounds were dropping from the sky itself. After a quiet and lazy, bluesy, introduction, they went gently into 'Green Is The Colour' and 'Careful With That Axe, Eugene'. Even in the latter the volume was down, and the mood reflective. 'Set The Controls For The Heart Of the Sun' was at its most ethereal, the smooth crescendos flying away over the heads of the captivated audience. To end, a brass section and choir were brought on for the 25-minute finale. The piece began with an arrangement for the brass, and then switched into a lengthy choir pattern, followed by a dash of marvellous Floyd rock-jazz. In came the brass again, pursued by incantations from the choir and swirling special effects in twin-channel stereo."

SUNDAY 19 JULY – RECORDING SESSION
Studio 2 & Control Room 2, EMI Studios, Abbey Road, London, England

2.30pm to 7.30pm and 8.00pm to 1.30am: Hi-Hat, Electric Guitar, Hammond and SFX overdubbed for backwards edit piece on 'Summer '68' (Takes 1 and 2 and Take 3 also marked "best"); 'Alan's Psychedelic Breakfast' recorded (Take 1); 'Alan's Psychedelic Breakfast' re-recorded (Take 1, untimed and marked "to be inserted onto remix tape") and remixed (Takes 1–9 untimed, Take 10 also marked "best") for *Atom Heart Mother*. The session was produced by Pink Floyd, engineered by Peter Bown and assisted by Nick Webb.

MONDAY 20 JULY – RECORDING SESSION
Room 4, EMI Studios, Abbey Road, London, England

2.30pm to 6.15pm and 7.00pm to 3.00am: 'Summer '68' "edit for intro" edited into master tape; 'Alan's Psychedelic Breakfast' edited (RS1 Section 1, RS2 Section 2 and RS3 Section 3), and the complete track remixed (RS1 and RS2 complete with crossfades of sound effects) for *Atom Heart Mother*. The session was produced by Pink Floyd, engineered by Peter Bown and assisted by Nick Webb.

TUESDAY 21 JULY – RECORDING SESSION
Room 4, EMI Studios, Abbey Road, London, England

7.00pm to 12.00midnight: 'Alan's Psychedelic Breakfast' remixed (RS3 and RS4 also marked "best edited onto mastertape") and 'If' remixed (also marked "best editing between EMI mix RS2 and Island mix Take 8"). This refers to Island Studios, where the soundtrack to *The Body* was recorded and where Waters must have re-recorded this track. Side 1 of the album was also banded. The session was produced by Pink

Floyd, engineered by Peter Bown and assisted by Nick Webb.
This was also the last recording session for the album *Atom Heart Mother*.

FRENCH FESTIVAL TOUR

Pink Floyd, members of their family and road crew rented a villa in St Tropez to use as a base for a season of French festival appearances. However, the combined efforts of the police and local authorities saw many of the festivals refused permits and for the most part bands were only allowed to perform as separate day and evening performances rather than continuous multi-artist events with on-site camping. Pink Floyd was also reported to be appearing at the *Festival de Pop Music*, Valbonne (23–25 July), Bandol (August) and Le Barcarès (August), but in the end Pink Floyd appeared at only three events.

SUNDAY 26 JULY – PERFORMANCE
XI Festival International de Jazz, Pinède Gould, Antibes Juan-les-Pins, France

Pink Floyd was added to the programme of the annual jazz festival that ordinarily ran from Friday 17 to Thursday 23 July as a special one-off concert.
Regional French TV are reported to have recorded pre-show interviews with the organizers of the event, but the exact content and broadcast details are not known.

WEDNESDAY 5 AUGUST – CANCELLED PERFORMANCE
Popanalia Festival, Autoroute De L'Esteral, Biot, France

With Joan Baez, Soft Machine, Eric Clapton, Traffic, Balls (featuring ex-members of Plastic Ono Band, the Moody Blues and King Crimson), Spencer Davis, Kevin Ayers, Alan Price, Daevid Allen's Gong, Alice, Ame Son, Alan Jack Civilization, Art Ensemble of Chicago, Archie Shepp, Sonny Scharrock and Don Cherry. Based on the principles of their 1969 *Actuel Festival*, organizers Jean Georgakarakos and Jean Luc Young of Byg Records hoped to stage an event at Plan du Castellets, located between Marseille and Tours, but this soon transformed itself into the RTL radio. sponsored *Popanalia Festival* at Biot. Planned to last 36 hours, with Pink Floyd due to appear on the Thursday 6 August, the event was abandoned soon after it started, and Joan Baez was the only artist to perform. With only 4,000 of the estimated 30,000 audience having paid to get in the promoters couldn't afford to pay the acts, and when Soft Machine were told they wouldn't receive their contracted fee, they refused to perform. As a result disgruntled fans rioted, many of them members of a hippie cult called "Les Compagnons de la Route", egged on by a young left-wing political element, who vandalized the stage and equipment. The extensive damage included a Yamaha grand piano that was pushed off the stage and smashed to pieces and two RTL Radio mobile recording trucks that were set on fire. It was consequently dubbed by the French music press as the *Festival maudit de Biot* (the cursed festival of Biot).
ORFT TV filmed parts of the festival, prior to the rioting, for inclusion in the music programme *Pop 2*, which was broadcast on ORTF2 TV on Thursday 20 August 1970 between 9.50pm and 10.20pm.

SATURDAY 8 AUGUST – CANCELLED PERFORMANCE
Pop Festival Saint Raphael, **Stade Municipal, St Raphaël, France**

This two-day event (Saturday 8 and Sunday 9 August) never even got underway, despite extensive publicity, due to local authority objections. Also due to appear was Family, Edgar Broughton Band, Keef Hartley Blues Band, Frank Zappa, Iron Butterfly, Kevin Ayers and the Whole World, Steamhammer, Geno Washington & the Ram Jam Band, Deep Purple, Hardin and York, Little Free Rock and Ginger Johnson's African Drummers.

SATURDAY 8 AUGUST – PERFORMANCE
Festival de St Tropez, **Route Des Salins, St Tropez, France**

Set list: 'Astronomy Domine', 'Cymbaline', 'Atom Heart Mother', 'Embryo', 'Green Is The Colour', 'Careful With That Axe, Eugene', 'Set The Controls For The Heart Of The Sun'.

Pink Floyd performed in an area of ground, roughly where the current Résidence Moulin Blanc is located, transformed into an all-seated arena for a series of one-off concerts staged through the summer season.

ORTF TV filmed Pink Floyd at soundcheck and during the show for the *Pop 2* music programme in two featured instalments subtitled *Pink Floyd: Premiere Partie*. The first programme was broadcast in Europe on ORTF2 TV on Saturday 10 October 1970 between 6.20pm and 7.00pm, and featured 'Atom Heart Mother' and 'Embryo'. The second programme was broadcast on ORTF2 TV on Saturday 24 October 1970 between 6.20pm and 7.00pm, and featured 'Green Is The Colour', 'Careful With That Axe, Eugene' and 'Set The Controls For The Heart Of The Sun'. Both parts were repeated on *Pop 2* and broadcast on ORTF2 TV on Saturday 4 November 1972 between 5.40pm and 6.00pm.

BELOW: PINK FLOYD PERFORMING IN SAN TROPEZ, FRANCE, 8 AUGUST 1970.

WEDNESDAY 12 AUGUST – PERFORMANCE
Fête de St Raphaël, **L'Amphithéâtre Romain, Fréjus, St Raphaël, France**

The last night of Pink Floyd's festival tour was staged at this preserved Roman arena, although very little publicity surrounded the event and no details of Pink Floyd's performance have emerged.

SATURDAY 15 AUGUST – CANCELLED PERFORMANCE
Yorkshire Folk, Blues & Jazz Festival, **Krumlin, Barkisland, Halifax, England**

With Atomic Rooster, Juicy Lucy, Elton John, the Pretty Things, Alexis Korner, Pentangle, Fairport Convention, Ralph McTell, the Kinks, Taste, Yes and others.

Pink Floyd's headline show on the second day of this three-day festival (Friday 14 to Sunday 16 August) was cancelled due to fog delaying their departure from Paris airport. In the event the entire festival was abandoned by Sunday morning due to torrential rain on the Saturday. A report was later printed in the *Yorkshire Times* of the disappearance of the promoter, who had suffered financial losses in excess of £12,000.

SATURDAY 29 AUGUST – CANCELLED PERFORMANCE
Open Air Festival Heidelberg, **Thingstätte Amphitheatre, Heidelberg, West Germany**

Although extensively advertised, this one-day event was cancelled. Also on the bill was Deep Purple, Xhol, Edgar Broughton Band, Embryo, Quintessence, Tangerine Dream, Guru Guru, Groove, Nosferatu and many other acts. This same weekend saw the staging of the *3rd Isle of Wight Festival*, for which WEM provided the PA and Peter Watts was the front-of-house sound engineer. David Gilmour was also in attendance and reportedly lent a hand at the desk during what would be Jimi Hendrix's final UK performance.

MONDAY 31 AUGUST – PERFORMANCE
Charlton Park, Bishopsbourne, Canterbury, England

With Rod Stewart and the Faces, Mott the Hoople, Edgar

Broughton Band, Stoneground, Silver Meter, Linda Lewis, Shawn Philips, Daddylonglegs and Al Stewart with hosts Wavy Gravy, General Wastemoreland and DJ Jeff Dexter.
Set list included 'Set The Controls For The Heart Of The Sun', 'Cymbaline', 'Careful With That Axe, Eugene', 'Atom Heart Mother'.

For many in attendance this was a post-Isle of Wight party on the Bank Holiday Monday extending from 11.00am until Pink Floyd's headline set finished well after midnight. The event was filmed for inclusion in a film called the *Medicine Ball Caravan*, but none of the footage or Pink Floyd's set was used in the finished film.

The *Kent Herald* reported, "The Great Medicine Ball – a hippie caravan that has trekked across America from San Francisco to take part in a film that sets out to explain the hippie philosophy. A film unit from Warner Brothers had followed the extraordinary journey by the 150 hippies, which started on August 4 and ended up on Bank Holiday Monday with a mammoth pop festival in the beautiful grounds of Charlton Park, home of Lt. Col. and Mrs. Michael Underwood. Hundreds of youngsters made their way to the peaceful village to hear non-stop pop from such groups as Pink Floyd, Small Faces, Mott the Hoople, Edgar Broughton Band and Silver Meter. The hippie hardcore, around whom the film is being made, directed by Frenchman Francois Reichenbach, brought with them multi-coloured tie-dyed tepees which gave the traditionally laid-out English parkland the air of an Indian reservation. As darkness fell on Monday evening Charlton Park was lit by a score or more of small fires started by the audience who by then numbered nearly 1,000."

SATURDAY 12 SEPTEMBER – PERFORMANCE
Féte de L'Humanité, Grand Scene,
Bois de Vincennes, Paris, France

With Les Chalots, Les Enfants Terribles, Les Parisiennes, Fernand Raynaud, Roger Pierre and Jean-Marc Thibault, Marcel Amont, Michel Polnareff and the Voices of East Harlem.
Set list: 'Astronomy Domine', 'Green Is The Colour', 'Careful With That Axe, Eugene', 'Set The Controls For The Heart Of The Sun', 'Atom Heart Mother' (with the Philip Jones Brass Ensemble and the John Alldis Choir, conducted by John Alldis).

Over 500,000 people were reported to have witnessed Pink Floyd headline the first day of this two-day festival, making it their largest single concert attendance, a record that remained unbeaten. French TV covered parts of the event but are believed not to have broadcast any footage of Pink Floyd.

NORTH AMERICAN TOUR

Early drafts of Pink Floyd's tour show the band scheduled to appear at the Memorial Coliseum, Portland on Thursday 1 October (which was cancelled before tickets went on sale); the Gymnasium, Gonzaga University, Spokane, WA, on Friday 2 October (rescheduled to Sunday 4 October); Open House, Seattle, on Sunday 4 October (rescheduled to Moore Theater, Seattle, on Friday 2 & Saturday 3 October); and the Gardens, Edmonton, Canada on Saturday 10 October (rescheduled to the Sales Pavilion Annex, Edmonton, Canada on Friday 9 October).

In a concerted effort to avoid media contact the band was interviewed by Associated Press, who syndicated a ready-made feature article to newspapers in which the band talked about touring in their formative years, their work on the soundtracks for

More and *Zabriskie Point*, and an upcoming ballet project with Roland Petit. Unfortunately the majority of articles didn't appear in newspapers until April 1971, by which time the band had neither a record nor tour to promote.

PINK FLOYD ROAD CREW – DECEMBER 1970
Seth Goldman (Technician, Stage Crew), Bobby Richardson (Technician, Stage Crew), Brian Scott (Technician, Stage Crew), Alan Styles (Technician, Stage Crew), Peter Watts (Road Manager, Sound Engineer).

SATURDAY 26 SEPTEMBER – PERFORMANCE
Electric Factory, Philadelphia, PA, USA

Supporting Savoy Brown.
Set list: 'Astronomy Domine', 'Cymbaline', 'A Saucerful Of Secrets', 'Interstellar Overdrive', 'Fat Old Sun', 'Green Is The Colour', 'Careful With That Axe, Eugene' <Encore> 'Set The Controls For The Heart Of The Sun'.

SUNDAY 27 SEPTEMBER – PERFORMANCES ▼
Fillmore East, New York, NY, USA

Two shows at 6.00pm and 9.00pm.
Set list at both shows: 'Astronomy Domine', 'Green Is The Colour', 'Careful With That Axe, Eugene', 'Fat Old Sun', 'Set The Controls For The Heart Of The Sun', 'A Saucerful Of Secrets' <Encore> 'Atom Heart Mother' (with brass and choir conducted by Peter Phillips).

Billboard reported that, "At one point, Mason played the strings of a grand piano, striking and plucking, while Gilmour aided Wright with tricky electronic effects."

FRIDAY 2 OCTOBER – ALBUM RELEASE (UK)
Atom Heart Mother

Time Out wrote, "'Atom Heart Mother' sees them integrating brass and vocal choirs into their music very successfully. They never fall for the Deep Purple 'bull in a classical china shop' attitude. They excel in quiet things. The striking of a match as an upbeat to a chord in 'Alan's Psychedelic Breakfast' is an unforgettable sound-image."

FRIDAY 2 & SATURDAY 3 OCTOBER – PERFORMANCES
Moore Theater, Seattle, WA, USA

Set list on Friday 2 October included: 'Set The Controls For The Heart Of The Sun', 'A Saucerful Of Secrets'.

The *Seattle Sabot* reported, "If, like me, you'd only heard them on record and went to see them last weekend, the big question was – can they do that live? Yes they can. They produce a sound that at once gives me fantasies of outer-space (as it obviously is supposed to with such titles as 'Set The Controls For The Heart Of The Sun' and 'A Saucerful Of Secrets') and puts me at ease, soothes me. Live, there was also the fascination of watching the actions that help produce these wondrous sounds. At times the guitarist was seated with his back almost directly to the audience, doing things

ATOM HEART MOTHER

SIDE ONE

ATOM HEART MOTHER (Mason, Gilmour, Waters, Wright, Geesin) 23:42

SIDE TWO

IF (Waters) 4:31
SUMMER '68 (Wright) 5:29
FAT OLD SUN (Gilmour) 5:24
ALAN'S PSYCHEDELIC BREAKFAST (Waters, Mason, Gilmour, Wright) 13:01

RELEASE DATE

UK: Friday 2 October 1970.
US: Saturday 10 October 1970.

FORMAT

UK: EMI Harvest SHVL 781 (Vinyl album).
US: Harvest SKAO 382 (Vinyl album).

HIGHEST CHART POSITION

UK: No. 1 (*Melody Maker* "Top 10" on Saturday 24 October 1970).
US: No. 55 (*Billboard* "Top LP's" on Saturday 26 December 1970).

AWARDS

UK: Certified Gold on Monday 22 July 2013.
US: Certified Gold on Wednesday 11 March 1994.

ARTWORK

One of the most instantly recognisable of Pink Floyd's album sleeves, it was probably the cheapest to produce. Storm Thorgerson merely drove out of north London and into Hertfordshire and stumbled upon the first pasture full of cows he met at Potters Bar. The farmer later identified his cow as being Lulubelle III and claimed he should have been paid for his permission and its services, a claim dismissed by manager Steve O'Rourke. Significantly, it also marked a trend of not having the band name or album title printed on the front sleeve.

Publicity for the UK release depicted herds of cattle filling The Mall in London, along with a fictitious story saying it was closed at dawn to create the image, while in the US, what is now a very collectible item, a promotional inflatable udder was produced by Capitol.

The 1994 CD edition included a recipe card, labelled "Breakfast Tips No. 1 and 2" respectively for a "Traditional Bedouin Wedding Feast" and a "Frankish Cow Brain Breakfast".

MUSICIANS

David Gilmour (Vocals, Guitar. Bass, Drums on 'Fat Old Sun' and 'Alan's Psychedelic Breakfast').
Nick Mason (Drums, Percussion. Tape Collage on 'Atom Heart Mother').
Roger Waters (Vocals, Bass Guitar. Acoustic Guitar and Tape Effects on 'If').
Richard Wright (Vocals, Keyboards. Orchestration, Piano on 'Summer '68').

ADDITIONAL MUSICIANS

John Alldis Choir (Vocals on 'Atom Heart Mother'), comprising John Alldis (Conductor), Eleanor Capp (Soprano), Jessica Cash (Soprano), Rosemary Hardy (Soprano), Hazel Holt (Soprano), Margaret Cable (Alto), Peggy Castle (Alto), Meriel Dickinson (Alto), Lynne Hurst (Alto), Geoffrey Mitchell (Alto & Choir Manager), Celia Piercy (Alto), Patricia Sabin (Alto), Roger Covey-Crump (Tenor), Peter Hall (Tenor), John Whitworth (Tenor), Kenneth Woollam (Tenor), John Huw-Davies (Baritone), Brian Etheridge (Baritone), Bryn Evans (Baritone), Brian Kay (Baritone), David Thomas (Bass).
EMI session musicians (Brass on 'Atom Heart Mother').
Haflidi Hallgrimsson (Cello on 'Atom Heart Mother').
Ron Geesin (Orchestration and Co-composition on 'Atom Heart Mother').
Alan Styles (Spoken Word on 'Alan's Psychedelic Breakfast').

RECORDING DETAILS

The basic rhythm track with guitar and organ overdubs for 'Atom Heart Mother' was recorded in March 1970 prior to Pink Floyd's North American tour beginning in April, leaving Ron Geesin to work out the orchestral arrangements which were then added with further overdubs on their return in June.

Talking about the title track on the Capital Radio *Pink Floyd Story* (broadcast 31 December 1976), Gilmour recalled, "That whole main

An Imaginary Western.' It sounded like 'The Magnificent Seven' to me." It is pure coincidence then, that the former Cream bassist Jack Bruce had already released a song called 'Theme For An Imaginary Western' on his August 1969 album *Songs For A Tailor*, popularized by Mountain performing it at the Woodstock festival in the same month and covering it on their March 1970 album *Climbing!*.

As the track was already being performed live before it was recorded, incorporated in its earliest incarnation was a lengthy drum solo and it featured Gilmour and Wright vocalizing on what would develop into the familiar choral section. But recording was difficult due to touring commitments and throughout the whole of March they were able to slot in only three sessions to produce a basic studio track. It was at this stage Ron Geesin was invited to help out with the track.

Talking to this author in 1994 Geesin recalled, "Roger proposed to me that I should help Floyd with their next album. He said he would like me to write the brass and choir pieces.... Floyd were off to the States then [April and May 1970], and Roger left me with a skeleton tape of rhythm and chords. It was to be a twenty-five minute piece, and that's a hell of a lot of work.... Nobody knew what was wanted, they couldn't read music.... Dave proposed strict ideas for melodies, and then we did the choir section together, both at keyboards collaborating with Rick. We all had sleepless nights, worrying about what was going on.... Well, it got done, but then the thing had to be recorded with the brass band, orchestra and choir." [1]

When the band returned from North America the recording process recommenced, but the orchestra and choir proved too much for Geesin to handle, and the cantankerous nature of some of the orchestral musicians was driving him to despair. "I could see the orchestra tuning up and the band playing in all bloody directions, playing different tunes, because I'm not a conductor, simply because I'm self-taught. Conductors are now essential in modern music. I was incapable of telling them what to do. Things were looking terrible, nobody knew what was going to happen. But then John Alldis, who was in charge of the best modern choir in the classical area, came to collect the choir parts and saw our plight. I became advisor and he the conductor." [1]

Even Gilmour couldn't help but notice the problems Geesin was facing with the orchestra. "In the studio they were pretty annoying sometimes; they always used to rush off to the canteen whenever they had the chance, and split right on the dot when the session was over. Towards the end of recording the album it all seemed to get a bit warped. Some of it seems a bit messy, when I listen to it now little things jump out at me and I think, 'Shouldn't have done that.'" [2]

The album *Atom Heart Mother* has contributions from each member of the band except Mason, who is only part-composer of the

title track. There are only four other numbers on the album, three of which have a very summery, bluesy feel to them: Waters''If' (performed rarely at this time, but more frequently on his later solo tours); Wright's 'Summer '68', which was actually a reworking of the track 'One Night Stand' originally recorded in December 1968 and shelved from the *Ummagumma* album and an obvious allusion to their first encounter with groupies on their US tour of that year; and Gilmour's pastoral 'Fat Old Sun', which was performed live throughout the year and again revived for his recent solo tours, and had been written at the time as Waters' 'Grantchester Meadows'.

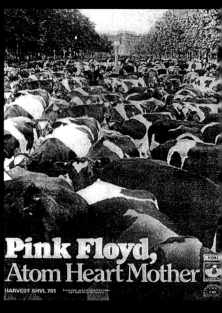

The closing track, 'Alan's Psychedelic Breakfast', is a typical but flawed Floyd experimentation. As Waters explained to *Sounds* on 10 October 1970, "It was the usual thing of an idea coming out of the fact that we'd almost finished an LP but not quite and we needed another so many minutes. We were all frantically trying to write songs, and initially I thought of just doing something on the rhythm of a dripping tap, then it turned into this whole kitchen thing. On the record it's a carefully set up stereo picture of a kitchen with somebody coming in, opening a window, filling a kettle and putting it on the stove. But instead of the gas lighting, there's a chord, so he strikes a match and there's another chord, and so on until it finally goes into a piece of music."

An amusing commentary, by Alan Styles, recorded for the most part in Mason's kitchen, forms the backbone of the piece as he prepares breakfast.

RECORDING SHEETS

There are six distinct parts to the title track, but it was impossible to distinguish from the recording sheets which part of the track was being overdubbed, as the basic track was recorded in its entirety and not in separate sections.

The only curiosities are the unreleased track 'No One Tells Me Anything Around Here' and the song 'If', the latter of which was recorded in part at Island Studios, London because Roger Waters was working on the soundtrack to *The Body* with Ron Geesin at the same time. Unfortunately no records exist from that session.

1. Author interview with Ron Geesin, 16 July 1994.
2. Unknown

RIGHT: COWS LINE THE MALL IN LONDON TO PROMOTE THE ALBUM

Atom Heart Mother

Take 4 (RS14).
Basic track recorded as 'Untitled 1' on 2 March 1970 (Take 3).
Sections of Take 3 copied and edited with a rough remix made on 3 March 1970.
Basic track of second section recorded as 'Untitled 2' on 4 March 1970 (Take 2).
Edit pieces recorded and edited into Take 2 on 4 March 1970.
Hammond, Guitar, Vocals, Farfisa and Piano overdubbed onto Take 2 of 'Untitled 2' on 4 March 1970.
A rough mix made of the complete track ('Untitled 1' and 'Untitled 2' relabelled Take 3) on 4 March 1970.
Drums and vocals overdubbed onto Take 3 on 24 March 1970.
Vocals, Tympani and SFX overdubbed onto Take 3 on 10 June 1970.
Drums overdubbed onto Take 3 on 16 June 1970.
"Edit Piece For End" made on 16 June 1970.
Guitar and Bell overdubbed onto Take 3 on 16 June 1970.
Click-Track, Piano and Guitar overdubbed onto Take 3 on 17 June 1970.
Various sections re-edited on 17 June 1970 (relabelled Take 4).
Various sections mixed for Tape Loops and made up on 18 June 1970.
Hammond, Mellotron, Vocals and "Various SFX" overdubbed onto Take 4 on 18 June 1970.
Take 4 edited on 18 June 1970.
Brass overdubbed onto Take 4 on 19 June 1970.
Loops mixed (RS6), played backwards and overdubbed onto Take 4 on 19 June 1970.
Count-in for section after percussion edited into master Take 4 on 19 June 1970.
Brass overdubbed onto Take 4 on 20 June 1970.
"Blank Section" transferred to master Take 4 for intro on 21 June 1970.
Organ and Percussion overdubbed onto Take 4 on 21 June 1970.
"Experimental percussion section with train sounds" recorded on 21 June 1970 (Take 2).
Choir overdubbed onto Take 4 on 21 June 1970.
Choir overdubbed onto Take 4 on 22 June 1970.
Brass and Cello overdubbed onto Take 4 on 23 June 1970.
Rough mix of Take 4 made on 23 June 1970.
Organ, Piano and Vocals overdubbed onto Take 4 on 24 June 1970.
"Backwards Brass Section" transferred to "Percussion Section" on 24 June 1970.
Sound Effects mixed on 8 July 1970 (RS1).
Organ and Electric Guitar overdubbed onto Take 4 on 13 July 1970.
"Edit Pieces" mixed on 15 July 1970 (RS4 and RS6).

RS6 edited onto RS4 on 15 July 1970 (relabelled RS7).
RS7 mixed on 15 July 1970 (relabelled RS9).
RS10 and RS11 edited onto RS9 on 15 July 1970.
"Last Section" edited and mixed on 17 July 1970 (relabelled RS13).
Complete track edited and mixed on 17 July 1970 (RS14).
All sections edited together to make a complete Master on 17 July 1970.

If

Take 6 (RS2 / RS8).
Basic track recorded as 'Roger's Song' on 12 June 1970 (Take 2).
Basic track re-recorded as 'If' on 25 June 1970 (Take 5).
Basic track re-recorded on 4 July 1970 (Take 6).
Rough mix of Take 6 made on 4 July 1970 (RS1).
Moog overdubbed onto Take 6 on 5 July 1970.
Take 6 mixed on 5 July 1970 (RS2).
Take 6 (RS2) and Island Studios mix of Take 8 edited together on 21 July 1970.
No details exist of the Island Studios sessions for this track.

Summer '68

Take 8 of 'One Night Stand' (RS50) / Take 1 of 'Summer '68' (RS38).
Basic Track recorded as 'One Night Stand' on 4 December 1968 (Take 8).
Organ, Vocals, Guitar and Piano overdubbed onto Take 8 of 'One Night Stand' 4 December 1968.
Guitar and Piano overdubbed onto Take 8 of 'One Night Stand' on 9 December 1968.
Vocals, Guitar, Drums, Maracas and Piano overdubbed onto Take 8 of 'One Night Stand' on 10 December 1968.
'One Night Stand' Take 8 edited for "Edit Pieces" on 16 December (labelled Takes 9 and 10).
Piano, Acoustic Guitar, Mellotron, Harmonium, Brass and Guitar overdubbed onto Take 8 of 'One Night Stand' on 16 December 1968.
Basic Track re-recorded as 'Summer '68' on 5 July 1970 (Take 1).
Take 8 of 'One Night Stand' mixed on 13 July 1970 (RS17).
Take 8 of 'One Night Stand' mixed for "Edit Pieces" and RS25 and RS31 edited together on 13 July 1970.
'Summer '68' mixed for "Edit Pieces" and RS38 edited onto Take 8 of 'One Night Stand' on 14 July 1970.
Take 8 of 'One Night Stand' mixed for "Edit Pieces" on 14 July 1970 (RS39, RS40, RS46 and RS50 edited into Master).
"Backwards Edit Piece" recorded for 'Summer '68' on 19 July 1970 (Take 3).

Hi-Hat, Guitar, Hammond and SFX overdubbed onto "Backwards Edit Piece" for 'Summer '68' on 19 July 1970.
"Edit for Intro" of 'Summer '68' edited into Master on 20 July 1970.

Fat Old Sun

Take 3 (RS4).
Basic Track recorded on 12 June 1970 (Take 3).
Vocals and Flutes overdubbed onto Take 3 on 12 June 1970.
Guitar overdubbed onto Take 3 on 13 June 1970.
SFX recorded on 13 June 1970.
Mixed and SFX Tape Reduction on 13 June 1970 (RS3).
Mixed on 5 July 1970 (RS4).

Alan's Psychedelic Breakfast

Take 1 (RS4).
Basic track recorded on 18 June 1970 (unknown take).
Editing various Pink Floyd and EMI sound effects tapes on 10 July 1970.
Basic track re-recorded on 10 July 1970 (Take 1).
"Tape Delay" Reel 1 and Reel 2 recorded on 10 July 1970.
Basic track re-recorded on 17 July 1970 (Take 1).
"Tape Echo Piano" and "Tape Echo Tones" overdubbed onto Take 1 on 17 July 1970.
Various random takes made on 17 July 1970.
Unknown material recorded (Take 1) on 19 July 1970.
Take 1 of unknown material remixed (RS10) on 19 July 1970.
Edit Piece of "Section 1" mixed on 20 July 1970 (RS1).
Edit Piece of "Section 2" mixed on 20 July 1970 (RS2).
Edit Piece of "Section 3" mixed on 20 July 1970 (RS3).
Complete track mixed with cross-fades and SFX on 20 July 1970 (RS2).
Complete track mixed and edited onto master tape on 20 July 1970 (RS4).

No One Tells Me Anything Around Here (Unreleased)

Recorded on 13 June 1970 (Takes 1-3).

to his instrument in a manner reminiscent of the ape with the bone in *2001*."

SATURDAY 3 OCTOBER – CANCELLED PERFORMANCE
Festival de Musique Pop, Lausanne, Switzerland

Pink Floyd was scheduled to appear at this festival (Friday 2 to Sunday 4 October) but cancelled due to their North American tour, although the entire event was eventually shelved. Other acts scheduled to appear included Traffic, the Wallace Collection, Taste, Free, Ekseption, Golden Earring, Quintessence, Little Free Rock, Krokodil, Mungo Jerry and the Edgar Broughton Band.

SUNDAY 4 OCTOBER – PERFORMANCE
The Gymnasium, Gonzaga University, Spokane, WA, USA

TUESDAY 6 OCTOBER – PERFORMANCE
Central Washington University, Ellensburg, WA, USA

Set list: 'Astronomy Domine', 'Green Is The Colour', 'Careful With That Axe, Eugene', 'Cymbaline', 'Fat Old Sun', 'Atom Heart Mother', 'Embryo', 'Set The Controls For The Heart Of The Sun', 'A Saucerful Of Secrets'.

WEDNESDAY 7 OCTOBER – PERFORMANCE
Garden Auditorium, Vancouver, Canada

Set list: 'Astronomy Domine', 'Fat Old Sun', 'Cymbaline', 'Embryo', 'Atom Heart Mother', 'Green Is The Colour', 'Careful With That Axe, Eugene', 'Set The Controls For The Heart Of The Sun', 'A Saucerful Of Secrets'.

THURSDAY 8 OCTOBER – PERFORMANCE
Jubilee Auditorium, Calgary, Canada

Set list included: 'Astronomy Domine', 'A Saucerful Of Secrets', 'Cymbaline', 'Atom Heart Mother'.

The University of Lethbridge newspaper *Meliorist* reported that the venue was "acoustically near perfect, the auditorium was highly suited for the futuristic sounds of the group. In addition to the thirty-six speakers on stage, there were another half-dozen placed around the auditorium. By rotating the lever on the Azimuth Co-ordinator, the organist was able to direct the sound to any point in the hall. A fantastic innovation, the co-ordinator gave the effects of footsteps across the ceiling, as well as whirling spaceships round and round the auditorium. Calling upon a veritable goldmine of material, the band captivated the entire audience for over two and one half hours."

FRIDAY 9 OCTOBER – PERFORMANCE
Sales Pavilion Annex, Edmonton, Canada

Set list included 'Astronomy Domine', 'Green Is The Colour', 'Careful With That Axe, Eugene', 'Cymbaline', 'Atom Heart Mother', 'Embryo', 'Set The Controls For The Heart Of The Sun'.

SATURDAY 10 OCTOBER – ALBUM RELEASE (US)
Atom Heart Mother

Rolling Stone wrote, "*Atom Heart Mother* is a step headlong into the last century and a dissipation of their collective talents, which are considerable… if Pink Floyd is looking for some new dimensions, they haven't found them here." *Circus* magazine received the album in far more excited tones: "This is a trip. Most of Floyd is a trip. Trip, trip, trip. Tippy top trip."

SATURDAY 10 OCTOBER – PERFORMANCE
Centennial Auditorium, Saskatoon, Canada

SUNDAY 11 OCTOBER – PERFORMANCE
Centre of the Arts, Regina, Canada

Set list included: 'Green Is The Colour', 'Careful With That Axe, Eugene', 'Cymbaline', 'A Saucerful Of Secrets', 'Atom Heart Mother'.

TUESDAY 13 OCTOBER – PERFORMANCE
Centennial Concert Hall, Winnipeg, Canada

Set list included: 'Cymbaline', 'Embryo', 'Atom Heart Mother', 'A Saucerful Of Secrets'.

THURSDAY 15 OCTOBER – PERFORMANCE ◄
Terrace Ballroom, Salt Lake City, UT, USA

Supported by Blue Mountain Eagle. Set list: 'Astronomy Domine', 'Fat Old Sun', 'Cymbaline', 'Atom Heart Mother', 'Embryo', 'Green Is The Colour', 'Careful With That Axe, Eugene', 'Set The Controls For The Heart Of The Sun' <Encore> 'A Saucerful Of Secrets'.

FRIDAY 16 & SATURDAY 17 OCTOBER – PERFORMANCE ►
Pepperland Auditorium, San Rafael, CA, USA

Supported by Kimberley and Osceola with lights by Brotherhood of Light. Set list on Friday 16 October: 'Astronomy Domine' (with several false starts due to power failures), 'Fat Old Sun', 'Cymbaline', 'Atom Heart Mother' <Intermission> 'Embryo', 'Green Is The Colour', 'Careful With That Axe, Eugene', 'Set The Controls For The Heart Of The Sun' <Encore> 'A Saucerful Of Secrets' (with power failures towards the end of the song).

SUNDAY 18 OCTOBER – PERFORMANCE
Intercollegiate Baseball Facility,
University College of San Diego, San Diego, CA, USA

Pink Floyd appeared third on the bill at this open air event that commenced at 12.00 midday with Hot Tuna, Leon Russell, Dry Creek Road and Southwind (replacing the advertised Red Eye). Set list: 'Astronomy Domine', 'Fat Old Sun', 'Cymbaline', 'Embryo', 'Green Is The Colour', 'Careful With That Axe, Eugene', 'Set The Controls For The Heart Of The Sun' <Encore> 'A Saucerful Of Secrets'.

In an interview with Dick Tee in the *San Diego Weekly Reader* in 2007, the one-time concert promoter and member of UCSD's Student Body Council, and one of the people behind the show, recalled, "There was a big marijuana protest on the grounds at the same time. About a hundred people were carrying signs and chanting 'legalize it, legalize it,' and it seemed like there were at least that many cops around too. [The protestors] weren't too organized, though. Before long, most of them were going into the concert instead of protesting…. We used a bunch of their [abandoned] sign poles to prop up a temporary fence that gate-crashers tore down to get into the concert."

WEDNESDAY 21 OCTOBER – PERFORMANCE
Fillmore West, San Francisco, CA, USA

Set list: 'Astronomy Domine', 'Fat Old Sun', 'Green Is The Colour', 'Careful With That Axe, Eugene', 'Cymbaline', 'Set The Controls For The Heart Of The Sun', 'A Saucerful Of Secrets', 'Atom Heart Mother' (with brass and choir conducted by Peter Phillips) <Encore> 'Ave Maria' (choir only).

Rolling Stone reported, "That was Pink Floyd on the Fillmore stage 21 October, along with the Roger Wagner Chorale, three French horns, three trombones, three trumpets, and a tuba. They were performing, for the second time ever on stage, the suite from *Atom Heart Mother*. For an encore the Chorale did an 'Ave Maria' written in 1562. 'Atom Heart Mother' got a standing ovation, and bassist Roger Waters introduced Wagner. But it was too much for some of the more dazed and die-hard Fillmore freaks: as the Chorale neared the 'Amen', scattered give-me-back-my-candy shouts of 'we want Pink Floyd' came through from the sides of the auditorium. If they didn't understand what Pink Floyd's music is all about in the first place, it is a bit puzzling why they spent $3 and four hours to come to see them. The music of Pink Floyd evokes images of cold, clear, far interstellar regions, of black moving water, of the exhilarating bleakness of the moon."

FRIDAY 23 OCTOBER – PERFORMANCE
Civic Auditorium, Santa Monica, CA, USA

Set list: 'Astronomy Domine', 'Green Is The Colour', 'Careful With That Axe, Eugene', 'Fat Old Sun', Set The Controls For The Heart Of The Sun', 'Cymbaline', 'A Saucerful Of Secrets', 'Atom Heart Mother' (with brass and choir conducted by Peter Phillips) <Encore> 'Interstellar Overdrive'.

SUNDAY 25 OCTOBER – PERFORMANCE
The Boston Tea Party, Boston, MA, USA

SATURDAY 31 OCTOBER – CANCELLED PERFORMANCE
Black Magic & Rock & Roll, Cincinnati Gardens, Cincinnati, OH, USA

Promoters Mike Quattro and Russ Gibb attempted to re-stage their ill-fated *Black Magic & Rock & Roll* concert held in Detroit the previous year, and invited Pink Floyd as early as April 1970 to perform at this show. It was reported that the American Musicians Union prevented the band from participating at this event they described as a "voodoo and science fiction convention".

EUROPEAN TOUR

FRIDAY 6 NOVEMBER – PERFORMANCE
Concertgebouw, Amsterdam, Netherlands

Set list: 'Astronomy Domine', 'Fat Old Sun', 'Cymbaline', 'Atom Heart Mother', 'Embryo' <Intermission> 'Green Is The Colour', 'Careful With That Axe, Eugene', 'Set The Controls For The Heart Of The Sun' <Encore> 'A Saucerful Of Secrets'.

SATURDAY 7 NOVEMBER – PERFORMANCE
Grote Zaal, De Doelen, Rotterdam, Netherlands

Set list: 'Astronomy Domine', 'Fat Old Sun', 'Cymbaline', 'Atom Heart Mother', 'Embryo' <Intermission> 'Green Is The Colour', 'Careful With That Axe, Eugene', 'Set The Controls For The Heart Of The Sun', 'A Saucerful Of Secrets' <Encore> 'Blues'.

WEDNESDAY 11 NOVEMBER – PERFORMANCE
Konserthuset, Gothenberg, Sweden

Set list: 'Astronomy Domine', 'Fat Old Sun', 'Cymbaline', 'Atom Heart Mother', untitled improvisations, 'Embryo' <Intermission> 'Green Is The Colour', 'Careful With That Axe, Eugene', 'Set The Controls For The Heart Of The Sun', 'A Saucerful Of Secrets' <Encore> 'Blues'.

The track labelled "untitled improvisation" above is a patchwork of experimental music with elements reminiscent of 'Embryo' and 'Heart Big Pig Meat'. It has also been referred to on bootleg recordings as 'Libest Spacement Monitor'.

THURSDAY 12 NOVEMBER – PERFORMANCE ▼
Falkoner Centret, Copenhagen, Denmark

Two shows at 8.00pm and 10.30pm.
Set list at 8.00pm show: 'Astronomy Domine', 'Fat Old Sun', 'Cymbaline', 'Atom Heart Mother' <Intermission> 'Green Is The Colour', 'Careful With That Axe, Eugene', 'A Saucerful Of Secrets' <Encore> 'Embryo'.
Set list at 10.30pm show: 'Astronomy Domine', 'Fat Old Sun', 'Cymbaline', 'Atom Heart Mother' <Intermission> 'Embryo', 'Green Is The Colour', 'Careful With That Axe, Eugene', 'Set The Controls For The Heart Of The Sun', 'A Saucerful Of Secrets' <Encore> 'Blues'.

FRIDAY 13 NOVEMBER – PERFORMANCE ▼
Vejlby-Risskov Hallen, Åarhus, Denmark

Set list: 'Astronomy Domine', 'Fat Old Sun', 'Cymbaline', 'Atom Heart Mother' <Intermission> 'Embryo', 'Green Is The Colour', 'Careful With That Axe, Eugene', 'Set The Controls For The Heart Of The Sun', 'A Saucerful Of Secrets' <Encore> 'Blues'.

SATURDAY 14 NOVEMBER – PERFORMANCE
Ernst-Merck Halle, Hamburg, West Germany

Set list: 'Astronomy Domine', 'Fat Old Sun', 'Cymbaline', 'Atom Heart Mother' <Intermission> 'Embryo', 'Green Is The Colour', 'Careful With That Axe, Eugene', 'Set The Controls For The Heart Of The Sun', 'A Saucerful Of Secrets' <Encore> 'Blues'.

SATURDAY 14 NOVEMBER – RADIO BROADCAST
Scene And Heard, BBC Broadcasting House, Portland Place, London, England

BBC Radio One broadcast a pre-recorded interview between Nick Mason and programme host Keith Altham on the show *Scene And Heard* broadcast in the UK between 1.30pm and 2.30pm.

SATURDAY 21 NOVEMBER – PERFORMANCE ▼
Montreux Super Pop 70 VII, Casino de Montreux, Montreux, Switzerland

Set list: 'Astronomy Domine', 'Fat Old Sun', 'Cymbaline', 'Atom Heart Mother', 'Embryo' <Intermission> 'Green Is The Colour', 'Careful With That Axe, Eugene', 'Set The Controls For The Heart Of The Sun', 'A Saucerful Of Secrets', 'Just Another 12 Bar' <Encore> 'More Blues'.

The tracks 'Just Another 12 Bar' and 'More Blues' are assumed titles from bootleg recordings, and are both similar tracks based around the blues instrumentals the band performed in this period.

Billboard reported, "EMI invited more than 100 salesgirls and salesmen from all over Switzerland to the event, along with the most important Swiss press and radio people. All expenses were paid including fares, food, hotels and concert tickets. After the concert EMI gave away 2,000 copies of the new 'Handle With Care' sample LP."

SUNDAY 22 NOVEMBER – PERFORMANCE
Montreux Super Pop 70 VII, Casino de Montreux, Montreux, Switzerland

Set list: 'Astronomy Domine', 'Fat Old Sun', 'Cymbaline', 'Atom Heart Mother', 'Embryo' <Intermission> 'Green Is The Colour', 'Careful

With That Axe, Eugene', 'Set The Controls For The Heart Of The Sun', 'A Saucerful Of Secrets' <Encore> 'Interstellar Overdrive'.

Pink Floyd added a second show at short notice due to public demand, performing an afternoon set. After the show David Gilmour was interviewed in French by Eric Lehmann for the programme *Regards* broadcast on Suisse Romande television on Tuesday 15 December 1970 between 9.40pm and 10.30pm.

MONDAY 23 NOVEMBER – CANCELLED PERFORMANCE
Grosser Konzerthaussaal, Wiener Konzerthaus, Vienna, Austria

This show was cancelled due to snow drifts blocking the roads out of Montreux, preventing the band's equipment lorry getting through. A second show was pencilled in for Sunday 29 November, but this too was cancelled in favour of a booking in Munich on the same date.

WEDNESDAY 25 NOVEMBER – PERFORMANCE
Friedrich Ebert Halle, Ebertpark, Ludwigshafen, West Germany

Set list: 'Astronomy Domine', 'Fat Old Sun', 'Cymbaline', 'Atom Heart Mother', 'Embryo' <Intermission> 'Green Is The Colour', 'Careful With That Axe, Eugene', 'Set The Controls For The Heart Of The Sun' <Encore> 'A Saucerful Of Secrets'.

THURSDAY 26 NOVEMBER – PERFORMANCE
Killesberg Halle 14, Stuttgart, West Germany

Set list: 'Astronomy Domine', 'Fat Old Sun', 'Cymbaline', 'Atom Heart Mother', 'Embryo' <Intermission> 'Green Is The Colour', 'Careful With That Axe, Eugene', 'Set The Controls For The Heart Of The Sun' <Encore> 'A Saucerful Of Secrets'.

FRIDAY 27 NOVEMBER – PERFORMANCE
Niedersachsenhalle, Hanover, West Germany

Rescheduled from Cologne, West Germany. Both the Sporthalle and Sartory Saal in Cologne were refused permission to hold the concert by the local authorities following rowdy audiences at previous pop concerts held in the area.
Set list: 'Astronomy Domine', 'Fat Old Sun', 'Cymbaline', untitled improvisations, 'Embryo' <Intermission> 'Atom Heart Mother', 'Green Is The Colour', 'Careful With That Axe, Eugene', 'Set The Controls For The Heart Of The Sun' <Encore> 'A Saucerful Of Secrets'.

The track referred to as 'untitled improvisations' is similar to the track noted on the 11 November show in Gothenberg, except on bootlegs from this show it is often referred to as 'Corrosion'.

SATURDAY 28 NOVEMBER – PERFORMANCE
Saarlandhalle, Saarbrücken, West Germany

Set list: 'Astronomy Domine', 'Fat Old Sun', 'Cymbaline', 'Atom Heart Mother' <Intermission> 'Embryo', 'Green Is The Colour',

'Careful With That Axe, Eugene', 'Set The Controls For The Heart Of The Sun' <Encore> 'A Saucerful Of Secrets'.

SUNDAY 29 NOVEMBER – PERFORMANCE
Circus Krone, Munich, West Germany

Set list: 'Astronomy Domine', 'Fat Old Sun', 'Cymbaline', 'Atom Heart Mother' <Intermission> 'Embryo', 'Green Is The Colour', 'Careful With That Axe, Eugene', 'Set The Controls For The Heart Of The Sun', 'A Saucerful Of Secrets'.

SATURDAY 5 DECEMBER – TELEVISION RECORDING
Volumes, ORTF Studios,
Buttes Chaumont, Paris, France

Pink Floyd performed a lengthy improvised instrumental, which was previewed in Gothenberg on 11 November and Hannover on 27 November, which segues into an equally improvised but wholly instrumental version of 'Embryo'. In recent years this recording for French TV has been commonly referred to as 'Corrosion In The Pink Room' simply because the TV studio was decorated primarily in pink colours.

It was first shown on the documentary programme *Soiree Roland Petit* as part of the ORTF1 TV regional bulletin *Actualités* broadcast between 8.30pm and 10.30pm, and repeated on the arts programme *Volumes* on ORFT1 TV on Thursday 27 May 1971 between 10.35pm and 11.25pm.

ATOM HEART MOTHER IS GOING ON THE ROAD (UK TOUR)

Pink Floyd embarked on a short six-date UK tour performing *Atom Heart Mother* the latter four of which featured brass and choir as well as the experimental 'Alan's Psychedelic Breakfast'. This track was greatly assisted by the roadies, who, to the accompaniment of BBC broadcaster and DJ Jimmy Young's trademark 'Oft we jolly well go', fried eggs and bacon and made tea on stage. To round off the festive spirit, Mason reportedly dressed up as Father Christmas.

FRIDAY 11 DECEMBER – PERFORMANCE
Big Apple, Regent Theatre, Brighton, England

Set list: 'Atom Heart Mother', 'Fat Old Sun', 'Green Is The Colour', 'Careful With That Axe, Eugene', 'Cymbaline', 'Embryo', 'Set The Controls For The Heart Of The Sun', 'A Saucerful Of Secrets' <Encore> 'Astronomy Domine'.

Sounds reported, "The Pink Floyd are brilliant musicians, but it is undoubtedly their technical genius that has made them Britain's No.1 truly progressive pop band. This was proved conclusively at Brighton's Big Apple on Friday night when the Floyd made one of their rare club appearances…. Thankfully the Floyd are one of the few bands who refuse to be governed by sheer volume. They use more than 30 speakers and they are certainly loud. But they obviously go to a lot of trouble to ensure that every sound is clearly audible. At times they were far out, freaky even. For example they made excellent use of tape recorded sounds ranging from crying babies to galloping horses and explosions."

SATURDAY 12 DECEMBER – PERFORMANCE ▼
Village Blues Club, The Roundhouse public house, Dagenham, England

Set list: 'Embryo', 'Set The Controls For The Heart Of The Sun', 'A Saucerful Of Secrets', 'Atom Heart Mother', 'Careful With That Axe, Eugene', 'Blues' <Encore> 'Astronomy Domine'.

VILLAGE, ROUNDHOUSE
LODGE AVENUE, DAGENHAM
SATURDAY, DEC. 12th
PINK FLOYD
Advance tickets 25/-
Only available from: Dagenham Roundhouse on Saturdays, or Romford King's Head on Mondays, or by post (send s.a.e.) to: Asgard Enterprises, 645/7 High Road, Seven Kings, Ilford, Essex. Please send P.O.s (no cheques) crossed and made payable to ASGARD ENTERPRISES. December 19th: DEEP PURPLE.

FRIDAY 18 DECEMBER – PERFORMANCE
Town Hall, Birmingham, England

Set list included 'Alan's Psychedelic Breakfast', 'Fat Old Sun', 'A Saucerful Of Secrets' <Intermission> 'Atom Heart Mother' (with brass and choir conducted by John Alldis) <Encore> 'Atom Heart Mother' (reprise).

Because of its novelty, 'Atom Heart Mother' was rarely performed live with an orchestra and choir, and only a handful of UK shows in the run-up to Christmas featured the track. Waters was anticipating the problems it would cause when he spoke to *Sounds* shortly before the tour: "The logistics of doing it live are quite difficult – we can't obviously take a set of a kitchen round with us and do it all, but we'll have to have some table arrangement to fry eggs on and boil kettles and everything." This was a task eventually left to the roadies, who, to the accompaniment of BBC broadcaster and DJ Jimmy Young's trademark "Oft we jolly well go", fried eggs and bacon and made tea on stage. To round off the festive spirit, Mason often dressed up as Father Christmas.

SUNDAY 20 DECEMBER – PERFORMANCE
Colston Hall, Bristol, England

Set list: 'Alan's Psychedelic Breakfast', 'Fat Old Sun', 'Careful With That Axe, Eugene', 'Set The Controls For The Heart Of The Sun', 'A Saucerful Of Secrets' <Intermission> 'Atom Heart Mother' (with brass and choir conducted by John Alldis) <Encore> 'Atom Heart Mother' (reprise).

The *Bristol Evening Post* reported, "It was one of those 'first time' evenings. For the first time, bacon and eggs sizzled on the Colston Hall stage as the Floyd rippled in the background. And for the first time, a brass section and 18-strong choir came to the city to support the group. The cookery is a bit of a problem. It's obviously nothing more than a stunt – a tedious stunt by the time the smells float up into the balcony. But the augmentation is no problem at all, because it weighs in to produce the magnificent, soaring *Atom Heart Mother*. Core of this work is a proud theme. Its sophistication comes from complex electronic sound effects – and its achievement is that it carries you with it so completely. Before the interval, the Floyd pulled big applause with old and well-known songs. But it was the second half, and this new 35-minute work, that had the crowd on its feet demanding an encore."

MONDAY 21 DECEMBER – PERFORMANCE
Free Trade Hall, Manchester, England

Set list: 'Alan's Psychedelic Breakfast', 'Embryo', 'Fat Old Sun', 'Careful With That Axe, Eugene', 'Set The Controls For The Heart Of The Sun', 'A Saucerful Of Secrets' <Intermission> 'Atom Heart Mother' (with brass and choir conducted by John Alldis) <Encore> 'Atom Heart Mother' (reprise).

TUESDAY 22 DECEMBER –
PERFORMANCE ▶
City (Oval) Hall,
Sheffield, England

Set list: 'Alan's Psychedelic Breakfast', 'Embryo', 'Fat Old Sun', 'Careful With That Axe, Eugene', 'Set The Controls For The Heart Of The Sun', 'A Saucerful Of Secrets' <Intermission> 'Atom Heart Mother' (with brass and choir conducted by John Alldis) <Encore> 'Atom Heart Mother' (reprise).

CITY HALL, SHEFFIELD
TOMORROW, TUESDAY,
22nd Dec. at 7.30 p.m.
"ATOM HEART MOTHER"
HITS THE ROAD !!!
"IN CONCERT"
THE PINK FLOYD
WITH
FULL CHOIR &
BRASS
UNRESERVED PLATFORM
TICKETS 10/-.
Wilson Peck Ltd., 64-70, Leopold
Street, Sheffield, S1 1RP. Box
Office Phone 27074.

1971

SATURDAY 3 JANUARY – TELEVISION BROADCAST
Soiree Roland Petit, **ORTF1 TV, France**

ORTF TV broadcast a documentary on the ballet star Roland Petit in a programme featuring his influences, including the painters Max Ernst, Bernard Buffet, Giorgio de Chirico, the actress Arletty (Léonie Marie Julie Bathiat) and the music of Pink Floyd among others. It was broadcast on the ORTF1 TV regional bulletin *Actualités* between 8.30pm and 10.30pm. Petit, having declared his interest in Pink Floyd, would go on to deliver a ballet production featuring the band performing a live set to his choreographed dancers.

MONDAY 4 JANUARY – RECORDING SESSION
Studio 3 & Control Room 3, EMI Studios,
Abbey Road, London, England

Recording commenced on Pink Floyd's sixth studio album, *Meddle*. 2.30pm to 6.30pm and 7.30pm to 11.00pm: 'Nothing Part 1' recorded (comprising 'Untitled 1' (Take 1 at 8:10), 'Untitled 2' (Take 2 at 0:36) and 'Untitled 3' (Take 3 at 2:25); 'Nothing Part 2' recorded (Take 1 at 9:48) and 'Nothing Part 3' recorded (Take 1 at 3:20). The session was produced by Pink Floyd, engineered by Peter Bown and assisted by John Leckie.

TUESDAY 5 JANUARY – RECORDING SESSION
Studio 3 & Control Room 3, EMI Studios,
Abbey Road, London, England

2.30pm to 6.30pm and 7.30pm to 11.30pm: "Bottles etc." overdubbed onto Take 1 of 'Untitled 1'; 'Nothing Part 4' recorded (Take 1 at 2:10); "Bottles etc. and musical saw" overdubbed onto Take 1 of 'Nothing Part 4'; 'Nothing Part 5' recorded (Take 1 at 2:15); 'Nothing Part 4' remixed (RS1 at 2:15); and 'Nothing Part 6' recorded (Take 1 False Start and erased and new Take 1 at 2:45) for *Meddle*. The session was produced by Pink Floyd, engineered by Peter Bown and assisted by John Leckie.

WEDNESDAY 6 JANUARY – RECORDING SESSION
Studio 3 & Control Room 3, EMI Studios,
Abbey Road, London, England

2.30pm to 6.30pm and 7.30pm to 11.00pm: 'Nothing Part 7' drum loop recorded (Take 1 at 8:50); 'Nothing Part 8' recorded (Take 1 False Start and erased and new Take 1 at 1:55); Guitar overdubbed onto Take 1 of 'Nothing Part 8'; 'Nothing Part 9' recorded (Take 1 at 3:08, Take 2 at 1:30, Take 3 at 2:55); Organ overdubbed onto Take 1, 2 and 3 of 'Nothing Part 9'; 'Nothing Part 10' recorded (Takes 1-4 False Starts and Take 5 at 2:08); and Vocals overdubbed onto Take 5 of 'Nothing Part 10' for *Meddle*. The session was produced by Pink Floyd, engineered by Peter Bown and assisted by John Leckie.

TUESDAY 9 JANUARY – RECORDING SESSION
Studio 3 & Control Room 3, EMI Studios,
Abbey Road, London, England

2.30pm to 7.45pm and 8.45pm to 12.00pm: 'Nothing Part 9' recorded (Take 1 at 7:55); Bass, Organ, Guitar, Drums and Backwards Drums overdubbed onto Take 1 of 'Nothing Part 9'; 'Nothing Part 11' recorded (Take 1 at 4:15); 'Nothing Part 9' re-recorded (Takes 1–3 deleted, Take 4 at 3:00, Take 5 False Start, and Take 6 at 9:55); and rough remix made of Takes 1 and 6 of 'Nothing Part 9' for *Meddle*. The session was produced by Pink Floyd, engineered by Peter Bown and assisted by John Leckie.

WEDNESDAY 10 JANUARY – RECORDING SESSION
Studio 3 & Control Room 3, EMI Studios,
Abbey Road, London, England

3.00pm to 6.15pm and 7.45pm to 12.00 midnight: 'Nothing Part 9' recorded (Take 6 at 10:00); Guitars and Organ overdubbed onto Take 6 of 'Nothing Part 9'; 'Nothing Part 12' recorded (Take 1 at 30:00); "Vocal with long repeat echo on ¼ inch tape" [ie. a pre-recorded tape brought into the studio by the band] overdubbed onto Take 1 of 'Nothing Part 12'; 'Nothing Part 13' recorded (Take 1 at 8:40, Take 2 False Start and further takes not resumed); Bass and Drums overdubbed onto Take 1 of 'Nothing Part 13' for *Meddle*. The session was produced by Pink Floyd, engineered by Peter Bown and assisted by John Leckie.

THURSDAY 11 JANUARY – RECORDING SESSION
Studio 3 & Control Room 3, EMI Studios,
Abbey Road, London, England

2.30pm to 5.30pm and 7.30pm to 11.00pm: 'Nothing Part 13' recorded (Take 3 False Start, and Take 4 at 4:10); 'Nothing Part 1' remixed (RS1 at 4:12); 'Untitled 2' remixed (RS1 at 0:36); 'Nothing Part 2' remixed (RS1 at 2:50); 'Nothing Part 3' remixed

(RS1 at 3:05); 'Nothing Part 4' remixed (RS1 at 1:30); 'Nothing Part 5' remixed (RS1 at 2:10); 'Nothing Part 6' remixed (RS1 at 2:50); 'Nothing Part 7' remixed (RS1 at 1:35); 'Nothing Part 8' remixed (RS1 at 1:55); 'Nothing Part 9' remixed (RS1 at 8:10); 'Nothing Part 9, Take 1 Original' remixed (RS1 at 2:05); 'Nothing Part 9, Take 6 New' remixed (RS1 at 9:50), 'Nothing Part 10' remixed (RS1 at 2:20); 'Nothing Part 11' remixed (RS1 at 2:00); 'Nothing Part 12' remixed (RS1 at 5:00); 'Nothing Part 13' remixed (RS1 at 4:00); and 'Nothing Part 14' recorded (Take 1 at 18:45) for *Meddle*. The session was produced by Pink Floyd, engineered by Peter Bown and assisted by John Leckie.

PINK FLOYD ROAD CREW – DECEMBER 1971
Chris Adamson (Technician, Stage Crew), Seth Goldman (Technician, Stage Crew), Bobby Richardson (Technician, Stage Crew), Brian Scott (Technician, Stage Crew), Alan Styles (Technician, Stage Crew), Peter Watts (Road Manager, Sound Engineer).

SUNDAY 17 JANUARY – PERFORMANCE ▼
Implosion, The Roundhouse, Chalk Farm, London, England

Supported by Quiver, Nico with John Cale and DJ Jeff Dexter.

Set list: 'Embryo', 'Astronomy Domine', 'Fat Old Sun', 'Careful With That Axe, Eugene', 'Cymbaline', 'Set The Controls For The Heart Of The Sun', 'A Saucerful Of Secrets', 'Atom Heart Mother' (with brass and choir conducted by John Aldiss).

WEDNESDAY 20 JANUARY – RECORDING SESSION
Studio 3 & Control Room 3, EMI Studios, Abbey Road, London, England

5.00pm to 6.00pm and 8.00pm to 10.30pm: 'Nothing Part 17' recorded (Take 1 at 3:10); Vocals and "cosmic alien orchestra" overdubbed onto Take 1 of 'Nothing Part 17'; and 'Nothing Part 18' recorded (Take 1 at 18:40) for *Meddle*. The session was produced by Pink Floyd, engineered by Peter Bown and assisted by John Leckie.

THURSDAY 21 JANUARY – RECORDING SESSION
Studio 3 & Control Room 3, EMI Studios, Abbey Road, London, England

2.30pm to 6.30pm and 8.00pm 12.30am: 'Nothing Part 19' recorded (Take 1 at 0:25, Take 2 at 1:15, Take 3 at 1:00, Take 4 at 0:60, Take 5 at 1:00 and Take 6 at 1:06); Loops of 'Nothing Part 19' made and edited; 'Nothing Part 20' recorded (Take 1 at 1:15 and Take 2 at 5:20); Backwards Guitar, Cymbals and Tympani overdubbed onto Take 2 of 'Nothing Part 20'; 'Nothing Part 21' recorded (Take 1 at 5:23); 'Nothing Part 17' remixed (RS1 False Start and RS2 at 4:00); and 'Nothing Part 20' remixed with effects (RS1 at 6:00) for *Meddle*. The session was produced by Pink Floyd, engineered by Peter Bown and assisted by John Leckie.

An 80-minute recording of a band interview with German music magazine *Bravo* was made in the studio canteen between 6.30pm and 8.00pm, which appeared in the 19 April 1971 edition.

SATURDAY 23 JANUARY – PERFORMANCE
Refectory Hall, University Union, Leeds University, Leeds, England

Set list: 'Atom Heart Mother', 'Careful With That Axe, Eugene', 'Cymbaline', 'Set The Controls For The Heart Of The Sun', 'A Saucerful Of Secrets', 'Blues'.

SUNDAY 24 JANUARY – RECORDING SESSION
Studio 3 & Control Room 3, EMI Studios, Abbey Road, London, England

3:00pm to 6.30pm and 8.00pm to 12.00 midnight: 'Nothing Part 22' recorded (Takes 1–6 False Starts, Take 7 at 1:56, Take 8 False Start and Take 9 at 5:56); Bass, Fuzz Bass, Backwards Guitar and Backwards Organ overdubbed onto Take 9 of 'Nothing Part 22'; 'Nothing Part 23' recorded (Take 1 at 5:40); 'Nothing Part 23 Rehearsal' recorded (Take 1 at 20:00); 'Nothing Part 22' remixed with sound effects taken from *Volume 55* and *Volume 56* of sound effects from the EMI tape library (RS1 at 6:45); and 'Nothing Part 23' remixed (RS1 at 6:15) for *Meddle*. The session was produced by Pink Floyd, engineered by Peter Bown and assisted by John Leckie.

WEDNESDAY 3 FEBRUARY – PERFORMANCE
Great Hall, Devonshire House, University of Exeter, Exeter, England

Set list: 'Atom Heart Mother', 'Embryo', 'Astronomy Domine', 'Fat Old Sun', 'Careful With That Axe, Eugene', 'Cymbaline', 'Set The Controls For The Heart Of The Sun', 'A Saucerful Of Secrets'.

WEDNESDAY 10 FEBRUARY – THEATRE PREMIERE
3 à Dancer, La Place, Paris, France

Pink Floyd provided some specially recorded music for the Francoise and Dominique Dupuy production of *3 à Dancer* performed by Ballets Modernes de Paris, featuring an array of props, effects and light show by Pierre Lamaire, which premiered on this date and ran through to Saturday 13 February.

FRIDAY 12 FEBRUARY – PERFORMANCE ▼
Lecture Theatre Block 6 & 7, University of Essex, Wivenhoe Park, Colchester, England

Set list: 'Atom Heart Mother', 'Embryo', 'Careful With That Axe, Eugene', 'Astronomy Domine', 'Cymbaline', 'Set The Controls For The Heart Of The Sun', 'A Saucerful Of Secrets', 'Interstellar Overdrive'.

SATURDAY 13 FEBRUARY – PERFORMANCE
Student Union, Farnborough Technical College, Farnborough, England

Set List: 'Atom Heart Mother', 'Embryo', 'Careful With That Axe, Eugene', 'Cymbaline', 'Astronomy Domine', 'Set The Controls For The Heart Of The Sun', 'A Saucerful Of Secrets', 'Blues'.

SUNDAY 14 FEBRUARY – CANCELLED PERFORMANCE
Palais D'Hiver, Lyon, France

Pink Floyd's show was rescheduled to Théâtre du Huitième, Lyon, France on 22 February, but this was also cancelled because of venue management fears of a repetition of violence by fans attending a recent Rolling Stones show at the nearby Palais des Sports.

SATURDAY 20 FEBRUARY – PERFORMANCE
The Theatre, St Mary's College, Strawberry Hill, Twickenham, England

WEDNESDAY 24 FEBRUARY – PERFORMANCE
Halle Münsterland, Münster, West Germany

Set list: 'Embryo', 'Green Is The Colour', 'Careful With That Axe, Eugene', 'Fat Old Sun', 'Set The Controls For The Heart Of The Sun', 'Cymbaline', 'A Saucerful Of Secrets' <Intermission> 'Atom Heart Mother' (with brass and choir conducted by Geoffrey Mitchell).

ABOVE: PINK FLOYD PHOTOGRAPHED IN EARLY 1971.

The second half of the show very nearly didn't happen when it was realized at about 6.00pm that the score for 'Atom Heart Mother' had been left in London. A courier flew out to Düsseldorf and a police Porsche waiting at the airport raced to the show, arriving at 10.30pm.

THURSDAY 25 FEBRUARY – PERFORMANCE
Grosser Saal, Musikhalle, Hamburg, West Germany

Set list: 'Astronomy Domine', 'Green Is The Colour', 'Careful With That Axe, Eugene', 'Cymbaline', 'Embryo', 'Set The Controls For The Heart Of The Sun', 'A Saucerful Of Secrets' <Intermission> 'Atom Heart Mother' (with brass and choir conducted by Geoffrey Mitchell) <Encore> 'Atom Heart Mother' (reprise).

This show was rescheduled from the Staatsoper, Hamburg, West Germany at a few days notice when the band were told by the venue management they would have less than two hours to set up their equipment. The *Hamburger Abendblatt* commented, "Never before had that many bootleggers and tape recorder microphones been seen in an auditorium." German TV crews filmed this and the following night's show at Offenbach for inclusion in the arts programme *Aspekte* and featured the soundcheck as well as live performance clips of 'Atom Heart Mother', an interview with Geoffrey Mitchell and interviews with the band members on their chartered plane. It was broadcast (in colour) on ZDF2 network TV on Tuesday 2 March 1971 between 9.50pm and 10.35pm.

BELOW: ON STAGE AT MÜNSTER WITH BRASS AND CHOIR.

ABOVE: POST SHOW DRINKS IN HAMBURG.

FRIDAY 26 FEBRUARY – PERFORMANCE
Stadthalle, Offenbach, West Germany

Set list: 'Astronomy Domine', 'Green Is The Colour', 'Careful With That Axe, Eugene', 'Embryo', 'Set The Controls For The Heart Of The Sun', 'Cymbaline', 'A Saucerful Of Secrets' <Intermission> 'Atom Heart Mother' (with brass and choir conducted by Geoffrey Mitchell) <Encore> 'Atom Heart Mother' (reprise), 'Blues'.

This show was rescheduled from Alte Oper, Frankfurt, West Germany for similar reasons as the Hamburg concert.

SATURDAY 27 FEBRUARY – TELEVISION RECORDING
Pop 2, ORTF TV Studios, Paris, France

The end of this European tour culminated in a TV session in which the band performed 'Set The Controls For The Heart Of The Sun' live for the programme *Pop 2*. It was broadcast (in colour) on ORTF2 on Saturday 6 March between 6.20pm and 7.00pm.

SUNDAY 7 MARCH – RECORDING SESSION
Studio 3 & Control Room 3, EMI Studios, Abbey Road, London, England

2:30pm to 7.30pm and 8.30pm to 12.15am: 'Return Of The Son Of Nothing' ['Echoes'] recorded (Take 1 at 6:07, Takes 2 & 3 False Starts, Take 4 at 13:28, Take 5 marked "Bass drum at drum intro up to change to end" at 5:05, Takes 6–10 False Starts, Take 11 at 5:02, Take 12 False Start, Take 13 at 5:30, Take 14 "intro" at 3:34, Take 15 False Start and Take 16 at 23:27 and marked "best") and Guitar, Organ and Super-Weird Bass for crossfade into Drums, Bass, Organ & Guitar overdubbed onto Take 16 of 'Return Of The Son Of Nothing' for *Meddle*. The session was produced by Pink Floyd, engineered by Peter Bown and assisted by John Leckie.

THURSDAY 11 MARCH – RECORDING SESSION
Studio 3 & Control Room 3, EMI Studios, Abbey Road, London, England

2:30pm to 6.30pm and 7.30pm to 11.30pm: Drums, Guitar, Organ and Leslie Piano overdubbed onto Take 16 of 'Return Of The Son Of Nothing' ['Echoes'] and the middle section of Take 16 of 'Return Of The Son Of Nothing' remixed (RS1 at 5:00) for *Meddle*. The session was produced by Pink Floyd, engineered by Peter Bown and assisted by John Leckie.

FRIDAY 12 MARCH – RECORDING SESSION
Studio 3 & Control Room 3, EMI Studios, Abbey Road, London, England

3:00pm to 6.30pm and 7.30pm to 12.00 midnight: "Buzzing Flies" [for 'Echoes'] recorded (Take 1 at 3:03); "Bumble Bee Bass Section" [for 'Echoes'] recorded (Take 1 at 4:00); Organ, Guitar, and "Rooks" from *Volume 7 of Sound Effects*, and "Wind" from *Volume 56 of Sound Effects* overdubbed onto Take 1 of "Bumble Bee Bass Section"; 'Bumble Bee Section' remixed (RS1 at 4:00); and a rough vocal track overdubbed onto Take 16 of 'Return Of The Son Of Nothing' ['Echoes'] for *Meddle*. The session was produced by Pink Floyd, engineered by Peter Bown and assisted by John Leckie.

MONDAY 15 MARCH – RECORDING SESSION
Studio 3 & Control Room 3, EMI Studios, Abbey Road, London, England

2:30pm to 6.15pm and 7.15pm to 12.00midnight: 'One Of These Days' recorded (Take 1 at 5:00. [Previous takes are noted as wiped over with this take]; Backwards Cymbal, Organ, Guitar, Piano and Bass overdubbed onto Take 1 of 'One Of These Days'; "Dialogue 1" [for 'One Of These Days'] recorded (Take 1 at 0:10); "Dialogue 2" [for 'One Of These Days'] recorded (Take 1 at 4:00); and 'One Of These Days' remixed with FX Guitar and overdub of loops (RS1 at 6:00 and RS2 at 6:00) for *Meddle*. The session was produced by Pink Floyd, engineered by Peter Bown and assisted by John Leckie.

FRIDAY 19 MARCH – RECORDING SESSION
Studio 3 & Control Room 3, EMI Studios, Abbey Road, London, England

3.00pm to 6.45pm and 7.45pm to 11.00pm: 'Nothing Part 24' remixed (RS1 at 3:55); Rough Vocal Track overdubbed onto Take 16 of 'The Return Of The Son Of Nothing' ['Echoes'] (Take 2 at 22:15); 'Anything' [an unused out-take] (Take 1 at 2:00) recorded; Guitar on "Train Section" [for 'Echoes'] and Leslie Piano overdubbed onto Take 16 of 'Return Of The Son Of Nothing'; and 'Play The Blues' [an unused out-take] recorded (Take 1 False Start and Take 2 at 12:13) for *Meddle*. The session was produced by Pink Floyd, engineered by Peter Bown and assisted by John Leckie.

SUNDAY 21 MARCH – RECORDING SESSION
Studio 3 & Control Room 3, EMI Studios, Abbey Road, London, England

3.00pm to 6.00pm and 7.00pm to 12.00 midnight: 'Dave's Guitar Thing' ['A Pillow Of Winds'] recorded (Take 1 at 7:00) and Acoustic Guitar, Organ, Bass and Vibes overdubbed onto Take 1 of 'Dave's Guitar Thing' for *Meddle*. The session was produced by Pink Floyd, engineered by Peter Bown and assisted by John Leckie.

THURSDAY 25 MARCH – RECORDING SESSION
Studio 3 & Control Room 3, EMI Studios, Abbey Road, London, England

3.00pm to 6.00pm and 7.00pm to 9.00pm: Vibes and Guitar overdubbed onto Take 1 of 'Dave's Guitar Thing' ['A Pillow Of Winds'] for *Meddle*. The session was produced by Pink Floyd, engineered by Peter Bown and assisted by John Leckie.

TUESDAY 30 MARCH – RECORDING SESSION
Studio 2, Air Studios, Oxford Street, London, England

10.00am to 12.45pm: Take 16 of 'Return Of The Son Of Nothing' ['Echoes'], Take 1 of "Bumble Bee Bass Section" [for 'Echoes'], Take 1 of 'One Of These Days' and Take 1 of 'Dave's Guitar Thing' ['A Pillow Of Winds'] copied to 16-track for *Meddle*. The session was produced by Pink Floyd, engineered by Peter Bown and assisted by John Leckie.

SATURDAY 3 APRIL – PERFORMANCE ▼
Sportpaleis Ahoy, Rotterdam, Netherlands

Set list: 'Astronomy Domine', 'Careful With That Axe, Eugene', 'Fat Old Sun', 'Set The Controls For The Heart Of The Sun', 'Cymbaline', 'Embryo', 'A Saucerful Of Secrets' <Intermission> 'Atom Heart Mother' (with brass and choir conducted by Geoffrey Mitchell).

THURSDAY 8 APRIL – RECORDING SESSION
Studio 2, Air Studios, Oxford Street, London, England

2.30pm to 7.45pm and 8.45pm to 12.30am: Guitar, Drums, Hammond, Vocals, Harmony Vocals and Farfisa overdubbed onto Take 16 of 'Return Of The Son Of Nothing' ['Echoes'] for *Meddle*. The session was produced by Pink Floyd, engineered by Peter Bown and assisted by John Leckie.

FRIDAY 9 APRIL – RECORDING SESSION
Studio 2, Air Studios, Oxford Street, London, England

2.30pm to 7.00pm and 8.00pm to 12.00 midnight: Drums, Cymbals, Leslie Piano, Fuzz Guitar, and Choir Vocal overdubbed onto Take 16 of 'Return Of The Son Of Nothing' ['Echoes']; 'Nothing Part 9' copied from 8-track to 16-track and edited for the start of 'Return Of The Son Of Nothing'; and Steel Guitar and Leslie Piano overdubbed onto Take 16 of 'Return Of The Son Of Nothing' for *Meddle*. The session was produced by Pink Floyd, engineered by Peter Bown and assisted by John Leckie.

SATURDAY 10 APRIL – RECORDING SESSION
Studio 2, Air Studios, Oxford Street, London, England

2.30pm to 7.00pm and 8.00pm to 11.00pm: Slide Guitar and Lead Guitar overdubbed onto Take 16 of 'Return Of The Son Of Nothing' ['Echoes']; Bass and Organ overdubbed onto Take 1 of "Bumble Bee Section" for 'Return Of The Son Of Nothing'; and "Vocal At End" and "Tape Delayed Vocal" overdubbed onto Take 16 of 'Return Of The Son Of Nothing' for *Meddle*. The session was produced by Pink Floyd, engineered by Peter Bown and assisted by John Leckie.

TUESDAY 13 APRIL – RECORDING SESSION
Studio 2, Air Studios, Oxford Street, London, England

2.30pm to 7.00pm and 8.30pm to 12.00 midnight: Guitar, Vocal Start, Leslie Piano, Slide Guitar and Fuzz Guitar overdubbed onto Take 16 of 'Return Of The Son Of Nothing' ['Echoes'] for *Meddle*. The session was produced by Pink Floyd, engineered by Peter Bown and assisted by John Leckie.

WEDNESDAY 14 APRIL – RECORDING SESSION
Studio 2, Air Studios, Oxford Street, London, England

2.30pm to 7.00pm and 8.30pm to 1.45am: Guitar (on beginning section), Hammond, Guitar Strings on end section, Leslie Piano and Chorus Vocals overdubbed onto Take 16 of 'Return Of The Son Of Nothing' ['Echoes']; Rough Mix of Take 16 of 'Return Of The Son Of Nothing' (RS1 at 21:35); and "Bumble Bee Section" ['for 'Echoes'] remixed (RS1 at 3:48) for *Meddle*. The session was produced by Pink Floyd, engineered by Peter Bown and assisted by John Leckie.

FRIDAY 16 APRIL – PERFORMANCE ▶
Top Rank Suite, Doncaster, England

Presented by Doncaster College of Technology, supported by Forevermore, Quiver, America, and DJ Pete Dolin.
Set list: 'Atom Heart Mother', 'A Saucerful Of Secrets', 'Fat Old Sun', 'Embryo', 'Cymbaline', 'Green Is The Colour', 'Careful With That Axe, Eugene', 'Set The Controls For The Heart Of The Sun' <Encore> 'Astronomy Domine'.

THURSDAY 22 APRIL – PERFORMANCE
Norwich Lads Club, Norwich, England

Presented by the University of East Anglia.
Set list: 'Echoes'*, 'Set The Controls For The Heart Of The Sun', 'Cymbaline', 'Atom Heart Mother', 'A Saucerful Of Secrets'.

*'Echoes' has been titled retrospectively for identification purposes only. It was not formally adopted until the commencement of their Japanese tour on Friday 6 August 1971 and was known both in the studio and on stage as 'Return Of The Son Of Nothing'.

MONDAY 26 APRIL – RECORDING SESSION
Studio 2, Air Studios, Oxford Street, London, England

2.30pm to 7.00pm and 8.30pm to 12.00 midnight: Vocals and "Echo Choir" overdubbed onto Take 16 of 'Return Of The Son Of Nothing' ['Echoes']; "Gull Guitar" overdubbed onto Take 1 of "Bumble Bee Section" [for 'Echoes']; 'Wild Thing' [an unused out-take] recorded (Take 1 at 4:00); and Bass overdubbed onto Take 1 of 'Wild Thing' for *Meddle*. The session was produced by Pink Floyd, engineered by Peter Bown and assisted by John Leckie.

TUESDAY 27 APRIL – RECORDING SESSION
Studio 2, Air Studios, Oxford Street, London, England

2.30pm to 7.00pm and 8.30pm to 12.00 midnight: Echo Choir, Vocals, Vocals for last two verses, Guitar, Fuzz Bass on build up and Fuzz Organ overdubbed onto Take 16 of 'Return Of The Son Of Nothing' ['Echoes']; and "End Choir Section" recorded (Take 1 at 2:45) for 'Return Of The Son Of Nothing' for *Meddle*. The session was produced by Pink Floyd, engineered by Peter Bown and assisted by John Leckie.

WEDNESDAY 28 APRIL – RECORDING SESSION
Studio 2, Air Studios, Oxford Street, London, England

2.30pm to 7.00pm and 8.30pm to 2.30am: Guitar, Piano, Farfisa and Feedback Guitar overdubbed for the end section of Take 16 of 'Return Of The Son Of Nothing' ['Echoes']; 16 to 8 track reduction of Take 1 of "Bumble Bee cross fade section" [for 'Echoes']; and Take 16 of 'Return Of The Son Of Nothing' remixed (RS4 False Start, and RS5 at 22:10 also marked "edited best") for *Meddle*. The session was produced by Pink Floyd, engineered by Peter Bown and assisted by John Leckie.

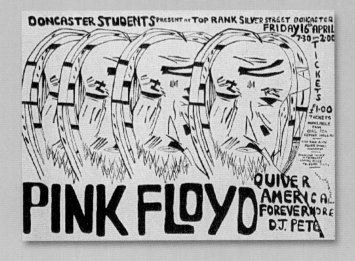

SATURDAY 1 MAY – RECORDING SESSION
Studio 2, Air Studios, Oxford Street, London, England

6.00pm to 7.30pm: Playback of material recorded to date. The session was engineered by Peter Bown and assisted by John Leckie.

WEDNESDAY 5 MAY – REHEARSALS
Granada Cinema, Wandsworth, London, England

Sound on Stage reported in a 1997 feature on Pink Floyd's production that, "Pink Floyd hired the Wandsworth Granada to evaluate a new two-way passive Bill Kelsey system, which initially incorporated seven-foot, 500-lb. RCA "W" cabinets before switching to Martin's 2x15-inch bass bin." Kelsey, who had already built PAs for King Crimson and ELP, recalls: "What happened was indicative of the way the Floyd used to do business in the days when they were more of a cult band. Peter Watts and Steve O'Rourke [Floyd's manager] said they'd like to try a system so I went down with all the gear, and then found there was another PA company there and that it was to be an A/B test. Feeling a bit miffed that I hadn't been told, I set up the gear as did the other company, and they tried it out with the mixing console at the back of the hall. It seemed to be going all right, but Peter said, 'To be quite frank, I'm disappointed…it's rubbish.' And Steve cut in, 'You realize you've wasted my whole day, not to mention the cost of the hall.' Peter continued to push up one fader to produce this horrid, muffled sound, while the second fader produced a nice, clear sound. I just wanted the ground to open up. Suddenly they both burst into laughter and admitted they'd crossed the whole thing over." Despite the elaborate wind-up, Kelsey's system was taken on board at the beginning of the following year."

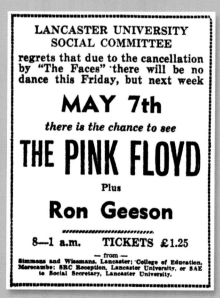

FRIDAY 7 MAY – PERFORMANCE ◄
Central Hall, University of Lancaster, Bailrigg, Lancaster, England

Supported by Ron Geesin. Set list included 'Echoes', 'Set The Controls For The Heart Of The Sun', 'Atom Heart Mother', 'Careful With That Axe, Eugene'.

After the show Roger Waters was interviewed by the University magazine, *Bullsheet*. Asked what it felt like on stage he replied, "I think we all get into what we are playing. I know I do, and I think the others feel the same. As for being bored I think it's inevitable when we play some of our earlier stuff. There is a limit to inventiveness on a worn theme."

SUNDAY 9 MAY – RECORDING SESSION
Studio 2, Air Studios, Oxford Street, London, England

2.30pm to 8.00pm and 9.00pm to 1.30am: 'Bill' ['Fearless'] recorded (Take 1 and 2 False Starts, and Take 3 first part only at 3:00, Takes 4, 5 and 6 False Starts and Take 7 at 5:30) and Double Track Guitar, Fuzz Bass, Bass and Electric Guitar overdubbed onto Take 7 of 'Bill' for *Meddle*. The session was produced by Pink Floyd, engineered by Peter Bown and assisted by John Leckie.

MONDAY 10 MAY – RECORDING SESSION
Studio 2, Air Studios, Oxford Street, London, England

2.30pm to 7.00pm and 8.00pm to 11.15pm: 12-String Guitar, Organ, Drums, Piano, Maracas and Tambourine overdubbed onto Take 7 of 'Bill' ['Fearless'] and 'Knozzee' [an unused out-take] recorded (Take 1 at 7:00) for *Meddle*. The session was produced by Pink Floyd, engineered by Peter Bown and assisted by John Leckie.

FRIDAY 14 MAY – ALBUM RELEASE (UK)
Relics

Record Mirror reviewed *Relics*: "Superb collection of the Floyd's mysterious hit singles and best album tracks at a reasonable price. The fantastic 'See Emily Play', 'Arnold Layne', 'Careful With That Axe, Eugene' and loads more. A definite requirement for all."

SATURDAY 15 MAY – PERFORMANCE ▼
Garden Party, Crystal Palace Bowl, Crystal Palace, London, England

With Quiver, Mountain, the Faces and compère Pete Drummond. Set list: 'Atom Heart Mother', 'Careful With That Axe, Eugene', 'Fat Old Sun', 'Echoes', 'Set The Controls For The Heart Of The Sun', 'Embryo', 'A Saucerful Of Secrets' <Encore> 'Astronomy Domine'.

Reviewing the event the *Croydon Advertiser* reported, "Cold rain coursing down the neck can dampen anyone's ardour for music. But despite the unwanted delivery from the heavens at Crystal Palace Bowl on Saturday, there was no notable exodus before the end of the pop concert, the first of its kind to be put on there. The throng, about 15,000 at a guess, was soaked by the downpour. But everyone stayed to hear the Pink Floyd top the bill at the so-called 'Garden Party'. They were certainly worth waiting for. Imaginative, creative musicians,

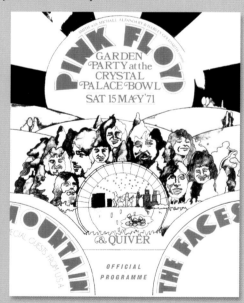

innovators and showmen, the Pink Floyd can rightly claim to being one of the leading rock groups of the day. But soon after the Floyd struck up with 'Atom Heart Mother' the skies opened. The audience huddled under miles of polythene…revellers swam in the muddy pond…and the band played on…. There was also a new work, 'The Return Of The Son Of Nothing', which didn't come across on first hearing as particularly distinguished. Secondly, the absence of the choir and additional orchestration meant that 'Atom Heart' suffered in comparison with the LP and came across

ABOVE: PINK FLOYD PERFORMING AT CRYSTAL PALACE BOWL, 15 MAY 1971.

rather limply. But the performance as a whole underlined the moving, dramatic epic quality of Floyd music, enhanced by the so called quadraphonic sound, achieved by having speakers at different points on the rim of the arena. Visual aids were effective too: orange smoke bombs misting up the pond and the trees at the end, rockets, and for fun, a giant octopus inflated in the water."

TUESDAY 18 MAY – PERFORMANCE
Pathfoot Building Refectory,
University of Stirling, Stirling, Scotland

Supported by Ron Geesin.
Set list: 'Atom Heart Mother', 'Set The Controls For The Heart Of The Sun', 'Fat Old Sun', 'Careful With That Axe, Eugene', 'Echoes' <Encore> 'A Saucerful Of Secrets'.

The surround sound system broke down halfway through the show but continued as a stereo concert. Although it was fixed in time for the show at Glasgow, it broke down again during that show as well. Promoter Paul Martin recalled, "We paid them £1,000 pounds exactly for their performance with two £500 notes which they said [they] were using as pocket money for a golfing holiday in Scotland." Prior to this show the band were interviewed by the Lambert High School magazine and Stirling University newspaper, *Pig*.

WEDNESDAY 19 MAY – PERFORMANCE
Students' Centre Refectory, Edinburgh University,
Edinburgh, Scotland

Supported by Ron Geesin.
Set list included: 'Echoes', 'Atom Heart Mother', 'Set The Controls For The Heart Of The Sun', 'A Saucerful Of Secrets'.

THURSDAY 20 MAY – PERFORMANCE
The Ballroom, University of Strathclyde,
Glasgow, Scotland

Supported by Ron Geesin.

FRIDAY 21 MAY – PERFORMANCE
Student Union, Trent Polytechnic, Nottingham, England

Set list: 'Echoes', 'Set The Controls For The Heart Of The Sun', 'Cymbaline', 'Atom Heart Mother', 'Careful With That Axe, Eugene', 'Fat Old Sun'.

MONDAY 24 MAY – RECORDING SESSION
Studio 2, Air Studios, Oxford Street, London, England

2.30pm to 6.00pm and 7.30pm to 10.30pm: 'Shamus The Dog' ['Seamus'] recorded (Take 1 at 2:50); Singing Dog, Harmonica, Slide Guitar, Piano and Bass overdubbed onto Take 1 of 'Shamus The Dog'; 'Bottles' [an unused out-take] recorded (Take 1 at 3:00); and Click Track, Milk Bottle and Beer Bottle overdubbed onto Take 1 of 'Bottles' for *Meddle*. The session was produced by Pink Floyd, engineered by Peter Bown and assisted by John Leckie.

TUESDAY 25 MAY – RECORDING SESSION
Studio 2, Air Studios, Oxford Street, London, England

2.30pm to 7.00pm and 8.30pm to 12.00 midnight: Cinzano Bottle, Cyder Bottle, Knife Sharpener, Nut Cracker, Popping Bottle, Beer Bottle, ½ Speed Beer Bottle and Lampshade overdubbed onto Take 1 of 'Bottles' [an unused out-take]; Piano overdubbed onto Take 1 of 'Shamus'; and a rough remix made of 'Shamus' (RS1 at 3:00) for *Meddle*. The session was produced by Pink Floyd, engineered by Peter Bown and assisted by John Leckie.

WEDNESDAY 26 MAY – RECORDING SESSION
Studio 2, Air Studios, Oxford Street, London, England

2.30pm to 6.30pm and 8.00pm to 11.30pm: Re-recording 'Bottles' [an unused out-take] (Take 1 at 5:00) and Lampshade, Tuned Bottles; and Bongo Bottles overdubbed onto Take 1 of 'Bottles' for *Meddle*. The session was produced by Pink Floyd, engineered by Peter Bown and assisted by John Leckie.

FRIDAY 28 MAY – RECORDING SESSION
Studio 2, Air Studios, Oxford Street, London, England

2.30pm to 7.00pm and 8.30pm to 9.30pm: Dog, Harmonica and Slide Guitar overdubbed onto Take 1 of 'Shamus'; 'Nothing Part 5' [an unused out-take also known as 'Wine Glass Chords'] transferred to Take 1 of 'Bottles' [an unused out-take]; 'Alien Orchestra' [the middle section of 'One Of These Days'] recorded (Take 1 at 10:00); and Guitar, Piano, Cymbals and Organ overdubbed onto Take 1 of 'Alien Orchestra' for *Meddle*. The session was produced by Pink Floyd, engineered by Peter Bown and assisted by John Leckie.

FRIDAY 4 JUNE – PERFORMANCE
Philipshalle, Düsseldorf, West Germany

Set list: 'Atom Heart Mother', 'Careful With That Axe, Eugene', 'Fat Old Sun', 'Embryo', 'Echoes', 'Set The Controls For The Heart Of The Sun', 'Cymbaline' <Encore> 'A Saucerful Of Secrets'.

SATURDAY 5 JUNE – PERFORMANCE
Berliner Sportpalast, West Berlin, West Germany

Rescheduled from Thursday 27 May.
Set list: 'Careful With That Axe, Eugene', 'Fat Old Sun', 'Embryo', 'Echoes', 'Set The Controls For The Heart Of The Sun', 'Cymbaline', 'A Saucerful Of Secrets' <Encore> 'Astronomy Domine', 'Blues'.

THURSDAY 10 JUNE – CANCELLED PERFORMANCE
Grand Palais, Paris, France

A full page advert appeared in the US record industry trade magazine *Cash Box* advertising the staging of a ballet production featuring Pink Floyd at the 10,000-seat Grand Palais in Paris with a 108-piece orchestra and 60 dancers to be simulcast on TV across Europe.

SATURDAY 12 JUNE – PERFORMANCE
Palais des Sports, Lyon, France

Set list included 'Careful With That Axe, Eugene', 'Set The Controls For The Heart Of The Sun', 'Cymbaline', 'A Saucerful Of Secrets', 'Atom Heart Mother' (with a 20-piece choir, plus three trombones, three trumpets and one tuba, conducted by John Aldiss).

Europe 1 radio recorded this show and broadcast 'Set The Controls For The Heart Of The Sun', 'Cymbaline' and 'Atom Heart Mother' on the programme *Musicorama* on Sunday 13 June 1971 between 1.00pm and 2.00pm.

TUESDAY 15 JUNE – PERFORMANCE
Le Cloître, Abbaye de Royaumont, Asnières-sur-Oise, France

Set list included 'Set The Controls For The Heart Of The Sun', 'Cymbaline', 'Atom Heart Mother'.

Pink Floyd appeared at this unusual location at the request of its owners, who staged a small-scale annual music festival within the grounds of the Abbey, which also featured Jeanne Moreau, Pierre Fresnay, Alexandre Lagoya and Aldo Ciccolini. The event was filmed by ORTF TV, who featured Pink Floyd performing 'Cymbaline' and 'Set The Controls For The Heart Of The Sun' in the arts programme *24 Heures sur la 2 à Royaumont*. It was broadcast (in colour) on ORTF2 on Monday 12 July between 7.30pm and 8.30pm.

SATURDAY 19 JUNE – PERFORMANCE ▼
Palazzo Delle Manifestazioni Artistiche, Brescia, Italy

Set list: 'Atom Heart Mother', 'Careful With That Axe, Eugene', 'Fat Old Sun', 'Embryo', 'Echoes', 'Set The Controls For The Heart Of The Sun', 'Cymbaline' <Encore> 'A Saucerful Of Secrets'.

Pink Floyd's first Italian "tour" was beset by problems from the start. The original plan was to stage a show on Saturday 19 June at the Palazzo Del Ghiaccio in Milan, but there had been rioting at a recent Chicago concert and the authorities

refused to grant permits for the Pink Floyd show. With the Palazzo in Bologna on hold in the event of a change in schedule, it was thought all would be fine, but literally at the point of signing the contracts to hire the venue the authorities declared the concert "an unsuitable event". Eventually, and at short notice, the show was rescheduled to Brescia. EMI Records meanwhile enthusiastically informed the Italian music magazine *CIAO 2001*, sponsors of the two dates, that Syd Barrett would be reunited with the band for these two engagements.

SUNDAY 20 JUNE – PERFORMANCE ►
Palazzo Dello Sport, Rome, Italy

Set list: 'Atom Heart Mother', 'Careful With That Axe, Eugene', 'Fat Old Sun', 'Embryo', 'Echoes', 'Set The Controls For The Heart Of The Sun', 'Cymbaline', 'A Saucerful Of Secrets' <Encore> 'Astronomy Domine'.

MONDAY 21 JUNE – TELEVISION BROADCAST
Unsere Kleine Show, ZDF2 TV, West Germany

An archive clip of Pink Floyd performing 'Interstellar Overdrive' was broadcast on the pop music programme *Unsere Kleine Show* [*Our Small Show*], although the precise details of the source of this track could not be found. It was broadcast on ZDF2 regional network TV between 5.35pm and 6.05pm.

TUESDAY 22 JUNE – CANCELLED PERFORMANCE
Glastonbury Fayre, Worthy Farm, Pilton, England

This was the forerunner to the now enormous annual *Glastonbury Festival*, and Pink Floyd were scheduled to appear at 1.00am on Tuesday 22 June, on the third day of the event scheduled to coincide with the summer solstice. Pink Floyd couldn't make it because their equipment was delayed coming back from Italy but other performers included Traffic, David Bowie, Gong, Marc Bolan and Al Stewart. It was attended by approximately 1,500 people. Admission was £1 and included free milk from the farm.

WEDNESDAY 23 JUNE – PERFORMANCE
Main Hall, Hatfield Polytechnic, Hatfield, England

SATURDAY 26 JUNE – PERFORMANCE ▼
Free Concert, **Amsterdamse Bos, Amsterdam, Netherlands**

With America, Humble Pie, Focus, CCC Inc and Pearls Before Swine.
Set list: 'Careful With That Axe, Eugene', 'Cymbaline', 'Set The Controls
For The Heart Of The Sun', 'A Saucerful Of Secrets', 'Embryo'.

Some 40,000 people attended this free concert, despite enduring heavy downpours throughout. It was heavily criticised in the press for its poor organization and appalling sound. Focus were pulled from the bill prior to the event and CCC Inc and Pearls Before Swine didn't perform at all due to power cuts and delays. Although Pink Floyd was later commended for their excellent performance, it was curtailed by the city authorities due to the event running over six hours beyond its scheduled closing time. At the end of the show the MC thanked all the performers and said Pink Floyd was in a hurry to catch a plane.

MONDAY 28 JUNE – CANCELLED PERFORMANCE
Celebration of Life, **Cypress Pointe Plantation, McCrea, near Baton Rouge, LA, USA**

With the Amboy Dukes, BB King, the Allman Brothers Band, Canned Heat, the Chambers Brothers, Chuck Berry, Country Joe McDonald, the Flying Burrito Brothers, Ike & Tina Turner, It's a Beautiful Day, John Lee Hooker, Richie Havens, Roland Kirk and Taj Mahal among many others.

This ambitious project saw the promoters of the *Toronto Rock & Roll Revival*, *Atlanta Pop* and *New Orleans Pop Festivals* joining forces to stage this huge eight-day festival (Monday 21 to Monday 28 June) on a secluded peninsula off the Atchafalaya River. From the outset it was dogged by problems when the promoters could not obtain a licence to open the festival until Wednesday 23 June. The first live performance was not until the following day and the festival closed down in the early hours of Monday 28 June following an all-night show by some of the billed acts and

an invasion of two motorcycle gangs, members of which were charged with attempted murder, inciting a riot and assaulting a law officer. Two of the promoters also went missing after IRS officials filed tax liens totalling $700,000 on ticket manifestos. *Time* magazine described the festival as an "American nightmare".

WEDNESDAY 30 JUNE – FILM PREMIERE
Stamping Ground, **Cineac, Rotterdam, Netherlands**

De Waarheid wrote, "The film, which shows the great music festival, had an estimated 70,000 to 80,000 visitors young and old. The camera was too focussed on the appearance of the groups such as Santana, Jefferson Airplane, the Byrds, Soft Machine and Pink Floyd. The organizers of the music festival hope the film will yield enough money to reduce its debts."

THURSDAY 1 JULY – PERFORMANCE
Musik-Forum Ossiachersee 1971, **Congress Center, Villach, Austria**

Set list: 'Echoes', 'Careful With That Axe, Eugene', 'Set The Controls For The Heart Of The Sun', 'Atom Heart Mother' (with brass and choir conducted by John Aldiss).

Pink Floyd appeared at this annual music festival, which ran from Friday 25 June to Monday 5 July, on a stage sited underneath a large scale awning erected in front of the Congress Centre, which primarily featured a programme of classical recitals and jazz music. The only other "rock" group to appear was Tangerine Dream on Tuesday 29 June. Over 5,000 fans came to see Pink Floyd's show, which was preceded by a rendition of Mozart's 'Piano concerto KV467' by the Zagreb Philharmonic.

A documentary of the festival, *Ossiach '71*, was broadcast on West German ARD1 network TV on Saturday 13 November 1971 between 3.15pm and 4.00pm, and featured a recording session of 'Atom Heart Mother' played over the introduction to the show and shots of Pink Floyd arriving at nearby Klagenfurt Airport via Austrian Airlines, fans descending on the small town, the band soundchecking and finally performing 'Atom Heart Mother'.

SATURDAY 17 JULY – ALBUM RELEASE (US)
Relics

Billboard wrote, "Before Pink Floyd co-opted for the outer reaches of space-rock in 'Interstellar Overdrive' they were a delightfully British rock band that in 1967 landed their first big single in Europe, 'See Emily Play.' Previously unreleased tracks from the past join 'Cirrus Minor' and 'Nile Song' from the film *More* in this nostalgic and stimulating retrospective into the Pink Floyd, soft and raucous, psychedelic and sophisticated."

MONDAY 19, TUESDAY 20, THURSDAY 22, FRIDAY 23, SATURDAY 24 & SUNDAY 25 JULY – RECORDING SESSIONS
Studio 1, Morgan Sound Studios, London, England

Unknown recording and overdubs for *Meddle*. The session was produced by Pink Floyd, engineered by Peter Bown and assisted by John Leckie.

ABOVE: PINK FLOYD APPEARING AT A PRE-SHOW PRESS CONFRENCE IN JAPAN.

RIGHT: PINK FLOYD IN JAPAN, AUGUST 1971

MONDAY 26 JULY – RECORDING SESSION
Studio 2, Morgan Sound Studios, Willesden, London, England

'Seamus' remixed (RS1 with "Less dog at start" and RS2 with "More dog") and other unknown recording and overdubs for *Meddle*. The session was produced by Pink Floyd, engineered by Peter Bown and assisted by John Leckie.

TUESDAY 27 JULY – RECORDING SESSION
Studio 1, Morgan Sound Studios, Willesden, London, England

'San Tropez' recorded (Take 1 also marked "best" and Takes 2–6) and other unknown recording and overdubs for *Meddle*. The session was produced by Pink Floyd, engineered by Peter Bown and assisted by John Leckie.

WEDNESDAY 28 & THURSDAY 29 JULY – RECORDING SESSIONS
Studio 2, Morgan Sound Studios, Willesden, London, England

Unknown recording and overdubs for *Meddle*. The session was produced by Pink Floyd, engineered by Peter Bown and assisted by John Leckie.

JAPANESE TOUR

Pink Floyd departed for Japan via Hong Kong on Saturday 31 July. This, their first visit to the country, saw them perform twice at an open-air festival and at one indoor show. Extensive publicity surrounded Pink Floyd's debut performances in Japan, which was co-promoted by Universal Orient Promotions, NHK (Nippon Hoso Kyokai – Japan's public radio and TV corporation) and Toshiba Musical Industries. NHK broadcast coverage of the festival including parts of Pink Floyd's set, including 'Atom Heart Mother' and 'Echoes' from one of the open air shows, although the exact broadcast details remain unknown.

In his book, *Inside Out*, Nick Mason recalled, "Of all the overseas tours, our first visit to Japan in August 1971 was a particular success. The record company organized a press conference (something which we generally hate) and presented us with our first gold records. Although these were completely bogus, as they had not been earned through sales, we nonetheless appreciated the gesture."

FRIDAY 6 AUGUST – PERFORMANCE
'71 Hakone Aphrodite, Fuji-Hakone-Izu National Park, Hakone, Kanagawa, Japan

With Buffy Sainte Marie, the 1910 Fruit Gum Company, Mops, Strawberry Path, Happenings Four, Yosuke Yamashita Trio, Masahiko Sato Torio and others.
Set list: 'Atom Heart Mother', 'Green Is The Colour', 'Careful With That Axe, Eugene', 'Echoes', 'Cymbaline' <Encore> 'A Saucerful Of Secrets'.

SATURDAY 7 AUGUST – PERFORMANCE
'71 Hakone Aphrodite, Fuji-Hakone-Izu National Park, Hakone, Kanagawa, Japan

With Buffy Sainte Marie, the 1910 Fruit Gum Company, Mops, Strawberry Path, Happenings Four, Yosuke Yamashita Trio, Masahiko Sato Torio and others.
Set list: 'Atom Heart Mother', 'Green Is The Colour', 'Careful With That Axe, Eugene', 'Echoes', 'Set The Controls For The Heart Of The Sun' <Encore> 'A Saucerful Of Secrets'.

Concert footage exists of 'Atom Heart Mother' and 'Echoes' from this show, which is believed to have been taken from Japanese TV coverage of the event.

MONDAY 9 AUGUST – PERFORMANCE
Festival Hall, Osaka, Japan

Supported by Buffy Sainte Marie and the 1910 Fruit Gum Company.
Set list: 'Green Is The Colour', 'Careful With That Axe, Eugene', 'Fat Old Sun', 'Atom Heart Mother' <Intermission> 'Echoes', 'Set The Controls For The Heart Of The Sun', 'Cymbaline' <Encore> 'A Saucerful Of Secrets'.

Keen-eared listeners to the many bootleg recordings that have been made of this show will note that the lyrics to 'Echoes' still contain an additional verse that was omitted from the final recordeds version as heard on *Meddle*.

AUSTRALIAN TOUR

Pink Floyd's first ever shows in Australia were announced in the Australian music press in June by the International Booking Corporation, to take place at the Dallas Brooks Hall in Melbourne on Saturday 21 and Sunday 22 August. Less than a month later a single show was being advertised for the Festival Hall on Friday 13 August and a single show in Sydney two days later. Both concerts were poorly attended and much of the blame was levelled at the organizers, the Rock Concert Club of Australia, for a lack of effective promotion.

FRIDAY 13 AUGUST – PERFORMANCE ▶
Festival Hall, Melbourne, Australia

Supported by Lindsay Bourke and Pilgrimage.
Set list: 'Atom Heart Mother', 'Green Is The Colour', 'Careful With That Axe, Eugene', 'Set The Controls For The Heart Of The Sun', 'Echoes', 'Cymbaline' <Encore> 'A Saucerful Of Secrets'.

Reviewing the show *Go-Set* magazine reported, "The promoters spent so much time and energy publicising their Rock Concert Club that there was very little mention of the concert actually at hand, the amazing Pink Floyd. The result was a not very full Festival Hall that really didn't do justice to the occasion at all. For a moment, when they first readied themselves on stage before going into 'Atom Heart Mother', I wondered whether all those fascinating electric sounds were really going to come from that stage, from those instruments. As soon as they began playing I realised it was indeed so, rock instruments taken into an adventure of Pink Floyd's. The amazing thing was the quality of their sound, exactly like their records, even at Festival Hall. Pink Floyd are very serious and involved as they play. The only showmanship is that of concentration, listening to one another, waiting for their separate parts, weaving those adventurous, inventive space patterns."

SUNDAY 15 AUGUST – PERFORMANCE
St Leger Stand, Randwick Racecourse,
Sydney, Australia

Supported by Lindsay Bourke and Pirana.
Set list included 'Atom Heart Mother', 'Careful With That Axe, Eugene' and 'Set The Controls For The Heart Of The Sun'.

Pink Floyd was featured on the entertainment show *GTK* [*Get To Know*] which included an interview featuring all four members of the band made before their afternoon appearance, and also part of their performance of 'Careful With That Axe, Eugene' (with music dubbed from the same track from *Ummagumma*). It was broadcast on ABN Channel 2 on 23 August 1971 between 6.30pm and 6.40pm. A further clip featuring Pink Floyd's performance of 'Set The Controls For The Heart Of The Sun' (with music dubbed from 'A Saucerful Of Secrets' from *Ummagumma*) was featured on GTK on Tuesday 17 August 1971 and broadcast on ABN Channel 2 between 6.30pm and 6.40pm

Pink Floyd departed Australia via Hong Kong on the Tuesday 17 August, arriving back in London on Thursday 19 August.

TUESDAY 7 SEPTEMBER – CANCELLED PERFORMANCES
Palermo Pop '71, Parco della Favorita, Palermo, Italy

Pink Floyd withdrew from this three-day festival that featured Colosseum and Jimmy Smith (Sunday 5 September) and the

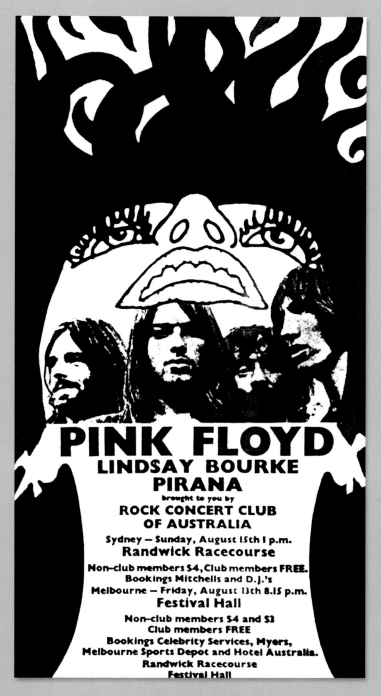

Spontaneous Music Ensemble featuring Julie Driscoll and Mungo Jerry (Monday 6 September). Pink Floyd was replaced by headliners Black Sabbath.

SATURDAY 11 SEPTEMBER – RECORDING SESSION
Studio 2, Air Studios, Oxford Street, London, England

2.30pm to 5.00pm: 'Nozzee' [an unused out-take] recorded (Take 2 and 3 False Starts, Take 4 at 5:20) and Piano and Bass overdubbed onto Take 7 of 'Bill' ['Fearless'] for *Meddle*. The session was produced by Pink Floyd, engineered by Peter Bown and assisted by John Leckie.

SATURDAY 18 SEPTEMBER – PERFORMANCE
Festival De Musique Montreux-Vevey,
Salle de Concert du Pavillon de Montreux, Montreux, Switzerland

Set list: 'Echoes', 'Careful With That Axe, Eugene', 'Set The Controls For The Heart Of The Sun', 'Cymbaline', 'Atom Heart Mother' (with members of the London Philharmonic Orchestra and Choir), 'A Saucerful Of Secrets'.

The entire concert was recorded for the Italian language medium-wave station Monte-Ceneri and highlights were broadcast on Friday 26 November 1971 between 9.00pm and 10.05pm, and repeated at the same time on Friday 3 December 1971.

SUNDAY 19 SEPTEMBER – PERFORMANCE
Festival De Musique Montreux-Vevey,
Salle de Concert du Pavillon de Montreux, Montreux, Switzerland

Set list included: 'Green Is The Colour', 'Careful With That Axe, Eugene', 'Echoes', 'Fat Old Sun' and 'Atom Heart Mother' (with members of the London Philharmonic Orchestra and Choir).

TUESDAY 21 SEPTEMBER – RECORDING SESSION
EMI Studios, Abbey Road, London, England

2.00pm to 5.00pm and 7.00pm to 12.00midnight: Quadraphonic remixing of *Meddle*. Pink Floyd was not in attendance at this session.

WEDNESDAY 22 SEPTEMBER – PERFORMANCE
Kungliga Tennishallen, Stockholm, Sweden

Set list: 'Careful With That Axe, Eugene', 'Fat Old Sun', 'Atom Heart Mother', 'Set The Controls For The Heart Of The Sun', 'Cymbaline', 'Echoes', 'A Saucerful Of Secrets'.

THURSDAY 23 SEPTEMBER – PERFORMANCE
KB Hallen, Copenhagen, Denmark

Set list: 'Careful With That Axe, Eugene', 'Fat Old Sun', 'Set The Controls For The Heart Of The Sun', 'Cymbaline', 'Atom Heart Mother', 'Echoes', 'A Saucerful Of Secrets' <Encore> 'Blues'.

WEDNESDAY 29 & THURSDAY 30 SEPTEMBER – REHEARSALS
Granada Cinema, Wandsworth, London, England

THURSDAY 30 SEPTEMBER – RADIO RECORDING
Sounds Of The Seventies, **BBC Paris Cinema, Lower Regent Street, London, England**

Pink Floyd recorded a live-to-air audience show between 10.00pm and 11.30pm on this day for BBC Radio One in which the band performed 'Fat Old Sun', 'One Of These Days' [its live debut], 'Embryo', 'Echoes' and 'Blues'. It was broadcast in the UK on *Sounds of the Seventies* on Tuesday 12 October 1971 between 10.00pm and 11.00pm.

The track 'Blues' was omitted from broadcast in the UK, including subsequent vinyl pressings of BBC Transcription Services discs, which also omitted 'Embryo', in order to facilitate a one-hour programme presentation. 'Blues' has only ever been broadcast the

one time in a Pink Floyd special on WNEW-FM radio New York, USA hosted by Alison Steele, aired on Wednesday 26 September 1973 between 9.00pm and 10.00pm.

Radio Times commented in a preview of the show, "From their inception, The Pink Floyd have been a pleasantly confusing group. Classic Top 20 hits like "See Emily Play" lured many an unsuspecting pop-picker into range of the harsh feedback of the early Floyd stage act; and their recent Ron Geesin aided "Atom Heart Mother" emphasised the relative feebleness of the songs on the other side of the album. Their fine sense of the dramatic lends itself to sound-pictures painted on a big canvas: hopefully, a new work will be unveiled tonight."

SATURDAY 2 TO THURSDAY 7 OCTOBER – FILMING
Live At Pompeii, **Roman Amphitheatre, Pompeii, Italy**

Pink Floyd was filmed at the preserved Roman arena at Pompeii by Adrian Maben over this period for the film *Live at Pompeii*. However, the first two days of filming was scrapped due to a failure of the power supply, which in the end had to be run via a very long cable from the nearby cathedral. Taking in scenes of the ruined city the film primarily featured the band performing a run-through of their current stage repertoire to an empty auditorium, while some atmospheric shots were filmed at the volcanic crater at Solfatara and the ancient ruins of Pozzuoli. Post-production filming took place in Paris between Monday 13 and Monday 20 December and a first cut was previewed at the *Edinburgh Film Festival*, Edinburgh, Scotland on Saturday 2 September 1972.

SUNDAY 10 OCTOBER – PERFORMANCE
The Great Hall, Bradford University, Bradford, England

Set list: 'Careful With That Axe, Eugene', 'Fat Old Sun', 'Set The Controls For The Heart Of The Sun', 'Atom Heart Mother' <Intermission> 'Echoes', 'Cymbaline', 'One Of These Days', 'A Saucerful Of Secrets' <Encore> 'Blues'.

The audience was kept waiting an hour because of trouble with the group's equipment, followed by the discovery of ticket forgeries. Talking to the *Bradford Telegraph & Argus* Mike Bright, vice-president of the University Union, said, "As far as I know we haven't had any forgeries before, but then we don't usually have a group as big as Pink Floyd. They were reasonably good forgeries." There were also reports of a black market of tickets being sold in the Union bar.

MONDAY 11 OCTOBER – PERFORMANCE
Town Hall, Birmingham, England

Set list: 'Careful With That Axe, Eugene', 'Fat Old Sun', 'Atom Heart Mother', 'Set The Controls For The Heart Of The Sun' <Intermission> 'Echoes', 'Cymbaline', 'One of These Days', 'A Saucerful Of Secrets' <Encore> 'Blues'.

FRIDAY 15 OCTOBER – RECORDING SESSION
Room 4, EMI Studios, Abbey Road, London, England

3.00pm to 4.00pm: Copying *Meddle* in quadraphonic for the press launch of the album on Sunday 17 October. The session was produced by John Kurlander. Pink Floyd was not in attendance at this session.

NORTH AMERICAN TOUR

Pink Floyd's most extensive North American tour to date was booked by Allen Frey of the Ashley Famous Agency based in New York. Frey continued to act as Pink Floyd's booking agent in North America right through to *The Wall* shows in 1980.

Early drafts of Pink Floyd's tour show the band scheduled to appear at Taft Auditorium, Cincinnati, on Saturday 30 October (rescheduled to Saturday 20 November); Music Hall, Boston; on Monday 1 November or Thursday 4 November (rescheduled to Thursday 11 November); Loew's Theatre, Providence, RI; on Friday 5 November (rescheduled to Thursday 4 November); Convention Hall, Asbury Park, NJ; on Saturday 13 November; and Civic Arena, Pittsburgh on Friday 19 November.

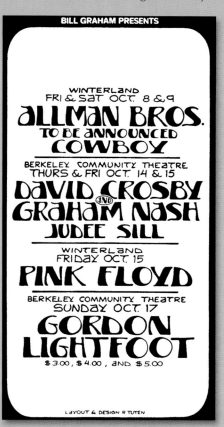

FRIDAY 15 OCTOBER – PERFORMANCE ◄
Winterland Auditorium, San Francisco, CA, USA

Set list: 'Careful With That Axe, Eugene', 'Fat Old Sun', 'Set The Controls For The Heart Of The Sun', 'Atom Heart Mother' <Intermission> 'Embryo', 'One Of These Days', 'Cymbaline', 'Echoes' <Encore> 'A Saucerful Of Secrets'.

SATURDAY 16 OCTOBER – PERFORMANCE
Civic Auditorium, Santa Monica, CA, USA

Set list: 'Careful With That Axe, Eugene', 'Fat Old Sun', 'Set The Controls For The Heart Of The Sun', 'Atom Heart Mother' <Intermission> 'Embryo', 'Cymbaline', 'Blues', 'Echoes', 'A Saucerful Of Secrets'.

Prior to the show, Richard Wright and Nick Mason were interviewed by Ted Alvy (aka "Cosmos Topper") of KPPC-FM radio in Pasadena, in which they discussed the *Meddle* album, their quadraphonic sound system and playing live. During part of the interview it is mentioned that Don Hall, the music director for the film *Zabriskie Point*, had played a series of out-takes on Ted Alvy's show at an earlier date, including the 'Christmas Song', but the broadcast date could not be traced.

SUNDAY 17 OCTOBER – PRESS RECEPTION
The Roundhouse, Chalk Farm, London, England

The press launch for *Meddle* which featured a quadraphonic presentation of the album. Pink Floyd was not in attendance.

SUNDAY 17 OCTOBER – PERFORMANCE ▼
Convention Hall, Community Concourse, San Diego, CA, USA

Supported by Mike Finnigan and Jerry Woods.
Set list: 'Careful With That Axe, Eugene', 'Fat Old Sun', 'Atom Heart Mother', 'Embryo', 'Set The Controls For The Heart Of The Sun' <Intermission> 'Cymbaline', 'One Of These Days', 'Echoes', 'A Saucerful Of Secrets', <Encore> 'Blues'.

Reviewing the show, the *San Diego Union* reported, "The Community Concourse was turned into a space ship for two hours last night by English group Pink Floyd. Their music, as strange as their name, was an odd mixture of electronic effects, whispers, screams and breathy vocal intonations, which created a *2001* effect. The group showed great sensitivity for balance and continuity. Each set Floyd played created an overpowering feeling of weightlessly drifting in space. The music was uncluttered and flowing. Rarely did Floyd sing while they played their instruments. Unique and welcomed by the enthusiastic audience was the special effects they provided. The sounds of seagulls, crashing waves, footsteps, which seemed to come from all corners of the auditorium, and applause. Pink Floyd is unique and totally electric."

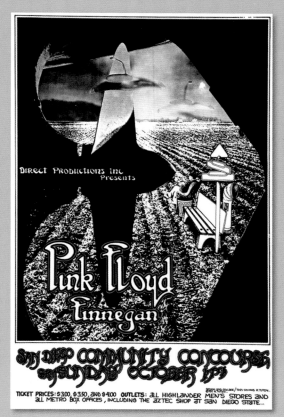

TUESDAY 19 OCTOBER – PERFORMANCE
National Guard Armory, Eugene, OR, USA

Set list: 'Careful With That Axe, Eugene', 'Fat Old Sun', 'Set the Controls For The Heart Of The Sun', 'Atom Heart Mother', 'Embryo', 'Cymbaline', 'Echoes', 'A Saucerful of Secrets' <Encore> 'Blues'.

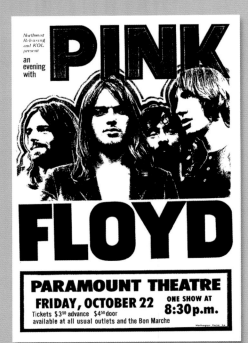

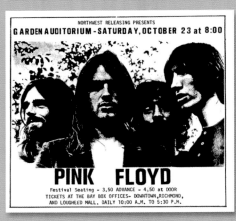

THURSDAY 21 OCTOBER – PERFORMANCE
Willamette University, Salem, OR, USA

FRIDAY 22 OCTOBER – PERFORMANCE ◄
Paramount Theatre, Seattle, WA, USA

Show moved from the Seattle Center Arena, Sunday 17 October 1971. Set list included: 'Atom Heart Mother', 'Set The Controls For The Heart Of The Sun', 'A Saucerful Of Secrets', 'Careful With That Axe, Eugene', 'Cymbaline', 'One Of These Days' <Encore> 'Echoes'.

SATURDAY 23 OCTOBER – PERFORMANCE ◄
Garden Auditorium, Vancouver, Canada

Set list: 'Set The Controls For The Heart Of The Sun', 'Atom Heart Mother', 'Careful With That Axe, Eugene', 'Cymbaline', 'Echoes' <Encore> 'A Saucerful Of Secrets'.

Pink Floyd performed a slightly shorter set than anticipated due to severe technical problems.
Wright, Mason and Waters were interviewed by *Georgia Straight* magazine on the Sunday at their hotel, the Holiday Inn, where they revealed they were already working on material for a new stage show the following year.

TUESDAY 26 OCTOBER – PERFORMANCE
East Town Theater, Detroit, MI, USA

Set list: 'Embryo', 'Fat Old Sun', 'Set The Controls For The Heart Of The Sun', 'Atom Heart Mother' <Intermission> 'One Of These Days', 'Careful With That Axe, Eugene', 'Cymbaline', 'Echoes' <Encore> 'A Saucerful Of Secrets'.

WEDNESDAY 27 OCTOBER – PERFORMANCE
Auditorium Theatre, Chicago, IL, USA

Set list: 'Embryo', 'Fat Old Sun', 'Set The Controls For The Heart Of The Sun', 'Atom Heart Mother' <Intermission> 'One Of These Days', 'Careful With That Axe, Eugene', 'Cymbaline', 'Echoes' <Encore> 'A Saucerful Of Secrets'.

THURSDAY 28 OCTOBER – PERFORMANCE
Hill Auditorium, University of Michigan, Ann Arbor, MI, USA

Supported by Guardian Angel.
Set list: 'Embryo', 'Fat Old Sun', 'Set The Controls For The Heart Of The Sun', 'Atom Heart Mother', 'One Of These Days', 'Careful With That Axe, Eugene', 'Cymbaline', 'Echoes' <Encore> 'Blues'.

SATURDAY 30 OCTOBER – ALBUM RELEASE (US)
Meddle

Rolling Stone wrote, "Their new album *Meddle* not only confirms lead guitarist David Gilmour's emergence as a real shaping force with the group, it states forcefully and accurately that the group is well into the growth track again. *Meddle* is killer Floyd from start to finish."

SUNDAY 31 OCTOBER – PERFORMANCE
Fieldhouse, University of Toledo, Toledo, OH, USA

Set list: 'Embryo', 'Fat Old Sun', 'Set The Controls For The Heart Of The Sun', 'Atom Heart Mother' <Intermission> 'One Of These Days', 'Careful With That Axe, Eugene', 'Cymbaline', 'Echoes' <Encore> 'Blues'.

TUESDAY 2 NOVEMBER – PERFORMANCE
McCarter Theatre, Princeton University, NJ, USA

Set list: 'Embryo', 'Fat Old Sun', 'Set The Controls For The Heart Of The Sun', 'Atom Heart Mother' <Intermission> 'One Of These Days', 'Careful With That Axe, Eugene', 'Cymbaline', 'Echoes'.

Reviewing the show the *Daily Princeton* reported, "The Floyd are something from a different century – rarely smiling, never speaking to their audience except to put down a request with a weary mincingly English, 'We'll never play 'Astronomy Domine' again.' Unreceptive as they may be, the Floyd are undeniably good musicians with a unique style of composition. Their main strength, and their claim to the kingship of psychedelia, is their mastery of electronics – they proved perfectly capable of reproducing the synthetic soundstorms and whispery, sibilant, echoing vocals that characterise their albums in concert. In fact, they actually surpassed their studio work by employing a quadraphonic sound system that, piloted by the organist with a modified joystick control, could seemingly place the group's sound effects anywhere in the theatre. The illusion of movement was sufficiently astonishing that anyone attending the concert drugged must have gotten a far bigger dose of psychedelia than he had bargained for. The magnificent six-ton sound system that accomplished this – the stage was piled ten feet high with amplifiers, while more equipment was set up in the balcony – was also quite sufficient to fill a hall the size of, say, the Spectrum. In McCarter, it was literally painfully loud, and I must admit that sheer volume drove me out halfway through a concert that I was otherwise enjoying very much."

WEDNESDAY 3 NOVEMBER – PERFORMANCE
Central Theatre, Passaic, NJ, USA

Set list: 'Embryo', 'Fat Old Sun', 'Set The Controls For The Heart Of The Sun', 'One Of These Days' <Intermission> 'Atom Heart Mother', 'Careful With That Axe, Eugene', 'Cymbaline', 'Echoes' <Encore> 'Blues'.

THURSDAY 4 NOVEMBER – PERFORMANCE
Loew's Theatre, Providence, RI, USA

FRIDAY 5 NOVEMBER – ALBUM RELEASE (UK)
Meddle

NME wrote, "Pink Floyd have done it again; something I thought would be difficult after the brilliance they showed with the 'Atom Heart Mother Suite', a piece of musical mastery that took great courage to put on record, and even greater courage to perform live – which they did successfully… an exceptionally good album."

COMING SOON
PINK FLOYD
FRIDAY 8 P.M.

TICKETS: $3.50, 4.50, 5.00, 5.50, 6.00
TWO HOURS OF PSYCHEDELIC SOUND.
WARNING: DO NOT HEAD
STRAIGHT TO HUNTER!

FRIDAY 5 NOVEMBER – PERFORMANCE ◄
Assembly Hall, Hunter College, City University of New York, NY, USA
Hosted by Zach of WPLJ Radio.
Set list: 'Embryo', 'Fat Old Sun', 'Set The Controls For The Heart Of The Sun', 'Atom Heart Mother' <Intermission> 'One Of These Days', 'Careful With That Axe, Eugene', 'Cymbaline', 'Echoes' <Encore> 'A Saucerful Of Secrets'.

WKBW AND BUFFALO FESTIVAL present.
PINK FLOYD
TONIGHT, NOV. 8th at 8 P.M.
PEACE BRIDGE CENTER
Porter Avenue at the Peace Bridge (Thruway Exit N-9)
ALL SEATS $5.00
Peace Bridge Center Box Office opens tonight at 6 P.M.

MONDAY 8 NOVEMBER – PERFORMANCE ►
Peace Bridge Exhibition Center, Buffalo, NY, USA
Set list: 'Embryo', 'Fat Old Sun', 'Set The Controls For The Heart Of The Sun', 'One Of These Days' <Intermission> 'Atom Heart Mother', 'Careful With That Axe, Eugene', 'Cymbaline', 'Echoes' <Encore> 'A Saucerful Of Secrets'.

TUESDAY 9 NOVEMBER – PERFORMANCE
Centre Sportif, Université de Montréal, Montréal, Canada
Set list: 'Embryo', 'Fat Old Sun', 'Set The Controls For The Heart Of The Sun', 'Atom Heart Mother' <Intermission> 'One Of These Days', 'Careful With That Axe, Eugene', 'Cymbaline' <Encore> 'Echoes'.

WEDNESDAY 10 NOVEMBER – PERFORMANCE
Pavillon de la Jeunesse, Québec City, Canada
Set list: 'Embryo', 'Fat Old Sun', 'Set The Controls For The Heart Of The Sun', 'One Of These Days' <Intermission> 'Atom Heart Mother', 'Careful With That Axe, Eugene', 'Cymbaline', 'Echoes' <Encore> 'A Saucerful Of Secrets'.

THURSDAY 11 NOVEMBER – PERFORMANCE ▼
Music Hall, Boston, MA, USA
Set list: 'Embryo', 'Fat Old Sun', 'Set The Controls For The Heart Of The Sun', 'Atom Heart Mother' <Intermission> 'One Of These Days', 'Careful With That Axe, Eugene', 'Cymbaline' <Encore> 'Echoes'.

PINK FLOYD
SAT. NOV. 6
8:30 pm
EMERSON GYM
C W R U
$3.50 adv. $4.50 door
All Seats Reserved
On Sale
CRWU Student Union (Mail Order),
Record Revolution (Coventry), Man Talk
(Severance), Man Two (Richmond), Pant
Talk (Great Lakes Mall), Community
Store (Kent), Cheap Thrills AKRON
BROUGHT TO YOU BY
A FRIEND

SATURDAY 6 NOVEMBER – PERFORMANCE ◄
Emerson Gymnasium, Case Western Reserve University, Cleveland, OH, USA
Set list: 'Embryo', 'Fat Old Sun', 'Set The Controls For The Heart Of The Sun', 'Atom Heart Mother' <Intermission> 'One Of These Days', 'Careful With That Axe, Eugene', 'Cymbaline', 'Echoes' <Encore> 'Blues'.

Prior to the show, Pink Floyd was interviewed by Jeff Gelb of WNCR radio Cleveland in which they discussed their music and current tour for the programme *Renaissance Outlook*. It was broadcast on Sunday 14 November 1971 between 11.00pm and 12.00 midnight.

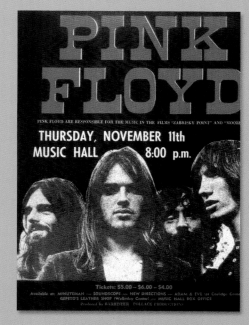

PINK FLOYD
PINK FLOYD ARE RESPONSIBLE FOR THE MUSIC IN THE FILMS "ZABRISKY POINT" AND "MORE"
THURSDAY, NOVEMBER 11th
MUSIC HALL   8:00 p.m.
Tickets: $5.00 – $6.00 – $4.00
Available at: MINUTEMAN – SOUNDSCOPE – NEW DIRECTIONS – ADAM & EVE at Coolidge Corner
GEPETO'S LEATHER SHOP (Wellesley Center) – MUSIC HALL BOX OFFICE
Produced by BARRISTER POLLACK PRODUCTIONS

FRIDAY 12 NOVEMBER – PERFORMANCE
Irvine Auditorium, University of Pennsylvania, Philadelphia, PA, USA
Set list: 'Embryo', 'Fat Old Sun', 'Set The Controls For The Heart Of The Sun', 'Atom Heart Mother' <Intermission> 'One Of These Days', 'Careful With That Axe, Eugene', 'Cymbaline' <Encore> 'Echoes'.

MEDDLE

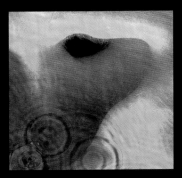

SIDE A

ONE OF THESE DAYS (Waters, Wright, Mason, Gilmour) **5:57**
A PILLOW OF WINDS (Waters, Gilmour) **5:07**
FEARLESS (Waters, Gilmour) **6:05**
SAN TROPEZ (Waters) **3:40**
SEAMUS (Waters, Wright, Mason, Gilmour) **2:13**

SIDE B

ECHOES (Waters, Wright, Mason, Gilmour) **23:31**

RELEASE DATE

US: Saturday 30 October 1971.
UK: Friday 5 November 1971.

FORMAT

UK: EMI Harvest SHVL 795 (Vinyl album).
US: Harvest SMAS 832 (Vinyl album).

HIGHEST CHART POSITION

UK: No. 3 (*Melody Maker* 'Top 10' on Saturday 27 November 1971).
UK: No. 99 (*Official UK Album Chart* on Saturday 8 October 2011).
US: No. 70 (*Billboard* 'Top LPs' on Saturday 27 November 1971).

AWARDS

UK: Certified Gold on Monday July 2013.
US: Certified Gold on 29 October 1973, Platinum on 11 March 1994
and 2 x Multi-Platinum on 11 March 1994.

ARTWORK

By Hipgnosis. The front cover depicts an ear, photographed by Bob
Dowling, collecting waves of sound, represented by the ripples in
the water. The inner sleeve portrait was the last time the band was
depicted on their album sleeves until the release of *A Momentary
Lapse of Reason* in 1987.

MUSICIANS

David Gilmour (Guitars, Vocals, Tape Effects. Bass on 'One Of These
Days. Harmonica on 'Seamus').
Nick Mason (Drums, Percussion, Tape Effects. Vocal on 'One
Of These Days').
Roger Waters (Bass Guitar, Vocals, Tape Effects. Acoustic Guitar on
'St Tropez').
Richard Wright (Piano, Hammond, Farfisa, Vibraphone, Tape Effects,
Vocals).

RECORDING DETAILS

Recorded EMI Studios, Abbey Road, St John's Wood, London,
England; Morgan Sound Studios, Willesden, London, England; and Air
Studios, Oxford Street, London, England. Produced by Pink Floyd and
engineered by Peter Bown and John Leckie (EMI and Air Studios),
and Rob Black and Roger Quested (Morgan Studios).

Perhaps the most complex of Pink Floyd's albums to date, *Meddle*
was an album almost entirely created in the studio from a series of
experiments that led to the creation of its two major tracks, 'Echoes'
and 'One Of These Days', which also became live stalwarts throughout
their career. The sessions also created the infamous 'Wineglass Chords',
which were later used on 1975's 'Shine On You Crazy Diamond' to such
great effect.

There are surprisingly few contemporary interviews that discuss
the recording process behind the album. However, talking to *Sounds* in
its 23 January 1971 edition, Mason revealed, "Ideally we'd like to spend
February sorting out the ideas and March doing the album – and April
and May if necessary. So far we've got down about 14 different ideas
for the album, including one for a piece involving acoustic objects."
Asked what kind of acoustic objects, Mason replied, "Bottles, felling
axes, saws – that sort of thing." It certainly made for intriguing reading.

On 10 April 1971 *Disc* reported, "For the next album they want
to use household objects as a theme – i.e. produce a whole album,
or the whole of one side, entirely made up with sounds from
household implements – wine glasses, knives, a saw. They've already

d and have got some incredibly impressive results down
ing an ordinary garden saw with a bow, arranging glasses
hords and playing them. In places the result sounds
olins." David Gilmour went on to say that, "We did a
he studio in January. And we've got twenty-four things
nder the working title of 'Nothing Parts One to 24.'
l the album *Return of the Son of Nothing* but then we
vhat an album will be called or what it will sound like
the finish."

, in talking to *Sounds* in their 19 February 1972 edition
ed, "In the case of 'San Tropez' Roger came in and the
olutely complete. There was almost no arranging to do
ust a matter of learning the chords. On other songs the
y loose. We may have a bass line and a rough idea for
nd not for the middle eight."

rprisingly 'Echoes' was afforded the greatest amount
studio, although it's almost impossible to tell which
de the final mix, there were so many made. Unfortunately
aper survives of their work at Air and Morgan Studios in
es of overdubbing and mixing the album.

hese Days' would also become another live favourite.
g, bass-driven instrumental originally featured a vocal
he venerable broadcaster Jimmy Young and the BBC
Workshop's theme for the TV show *Dr Who*. The track
a rare Mason lead vocal: the garbled one-liner "One of
h going to cut you into little pieces," before it launches
tar mayhem. Young was the constant butt of Pink

Floyd's warped humour when they chopped up tape recordings of
his commentary for his *Family Favourites* BBC2 radio show to make
hilarious and nonsensical introductions to their shows throughout
early 1970s.

By comparison, the remaining tracks are subdued and very
reminiscent of the acoustic material on *Atom Heart Mother*, none
of which were ever performed live and almost all recorded at the
new 16-track facilities at Air Studios and Morgan Sound. 'Fearless' is
a successful experiment which segues the Liverpool FC "Kop choir"
singing their adopted terrace anthem 'You'll Never Walk Alone' into
the last few seconds of the song; a reminder of Pink Floyd's collectiv
passion for the sport.

To close side one of the album, a howling Irish Wolfhound took
lead vocals. "Dave was looking after Seamus while Steve Marriott [th
dog's owner, who was on tour with Humble Pie] was in the States, a
he used to bring him into the sessions,'" explained Waters in *NME* on
11 December 1971, "and one day he said, 'There's something I mean
to show you – this dog sings', and he got a harmonica out and blew
at the dog, and as soon as the dog hears a harmonica it starts howli
So we all thought we'd do a short 12-bar and stick him on it.'"

Meddle was released in November and featured another Hipgno
sleeve design featuring a close-up photograph of an ear submerged
in rippling water, designed to suggest the effect of the ear collecting
waves of sound. The gatefold inner sleeve also featured a black and
white portrait of the band; the last time Pink Floyd would be visually
identified on an album for some sixteen years, an absence which
increased their mystique with the public.

Days

nown).
orded 15 March 1971 (Take 1).
ecorded (Take 1) and overdubbed
971.
ecorded (Take 1) and overdubbed
971.
with SFX, Guitar and Loops on 15

ra" recorded on 28 May 1971

Cymbals and Organ overdubbed
"Alien Orchestra" on 28 May 1971.
ecorded on 19 July 1971 (Take 1).
ding and mixing information
Sound is missing from archives.

inds

nown).
orded as 'Dave's Guitar Thing' on
(Take 1).
r Organ, Bass, Vibes overdubbed

onto Take 1 on 21 March 1971.
Edited on 21 March 1971.
Vibes and Guitar overdubbed onto Take 1 on 25
March 1971.
All other recording and mixing information
from Morgan Sound is missing from archives.

Fearless

Take 7 (RS unknown).
Basic track recorded as 'Bill' on 9 May 1971 (Take
7).
Guitar, Fuzz Bass and Bass overdubbed onto
Take 7 on 9 May 1971.
12-String Guitar, Organ, Drums, Piano, Maracas
and Tambourine overdubbed onto Take 7 on
10 May 1971.
Piano and Bass overdubbed onto Take 7 on
11 September 1971.
All other recording and mixing information
from Morgan Sound is missing from archives.

San Tropez

Take 1 (RS unknown).
Basic track recorded on 27 July 1971 (Take 1).
All other recording and mixing information
from Morgan Sound is missing from archives.

Seamus

Take 1 (RS unknown).
Basic track recorded as 'Shamus The Dog' on
24 May 1971 (Take 1).
Singing Dog, Harmonica, Slide Guitar, Piano a
Bass overdubbed onto Take 1 on 24 May 197
Piano overdubbed onto Take 1 on 25 May 19
Rough mix of Take 1 made on 25 May 1971
(RS1).
Dog, Harmonica, Slide Guitar and Guitar
overdubbed onto Take 1 on 28 May 1971.
Mixed on 26 July 1971 (RS1 with "Less dog at
start", RS2 with "More dog").
All other recording and remixing information
from Morgan Sound is missing from archives.

oes

e 16 (RS unknown).

ic track recorded as 'Return Of The Son Of
hing' on 7 March 1971 (Take 4).

ic track "Breakdown at drum intro up to
nge to end" recorded on 7 March 1971 (Take

ic track "Intro" recorded on 7 March 1971
ke 14).

ic track re-recorded as 'Return Of The Son Of
hing' on 7 March 1971 (Take 16).

tar, Organ, Weird Bass overdubbed for cross-
e into Drums, Bass, Organ and Guitar onto
e 16 on 7 March 1971.

s, Drums, Leslie Piano overdubbed onto Take
on 11 March 1971.

ddle Section" mixed on 11 March 1971 (RS1).

zzing Flies" recorded for the middle section
12 March 1971 (Take 1).

mble Bee Bass Section" recorded on
March 1971 (Take 1).

an, Guitar, Rooks from Volume 7 Sound
cts and Wind from Volume 56 Sound Effects
rdubbed onto Take 1 of "Bumble Bee Bass
tion" on 12 March 1971.

ugh vocal track recorded on 12 March 1971
ke 1).

ugh vocal track recorded on 19 March 1971
ke 2).

tar on "Train Section" overdubbed onto Take
on 19 March 1971.

tar, Drums and Hammond overdubbed onto
e 16 on 8 April 1971.

als and Harmony Vocals overdubbed onto
e 16 on 8 April 1971.

isa and Drums (for end) overdubbed onto
e 16 on 8 April 1971.

ms, Cymbals, Leslie Piano and Fuzz Guitar
rdubbed onto Take 16 on 9 April 1971.

oir Vocal" overdubbed onto Take 16 on
pril 1971.

thing Part 9' edited onto start of Take 16 of
urn Of The Son Of Nothing' on 9 April 1971.

el Guitar and Leslie Piano overdubbed onto
e 16 on 9 April 1971.

le Guitar and Lead Guitar overdubbed onto
e 16 on 10 April 1971.

s Guitar and Organ overdubbed onto Take 1
Bumble Bee Bass Section" on 10 April 1971.

cal at End" and "Tape Delayed Vocal"
rdubbed onto Take 16 on 10 April 1971.

tar and Vocal for "Beginning Section" of Take
overdubbed on 13 April 1971.

ckwards Echo" drums for "Beginning Section"
ake 16 overdubbed on 13 April 1971.

ie Piano, Slide Guitar and Fuzz Guitar for
ginning Section" of Take 16 overdubbed on
April 1971.

tar for "Beginning Section" of Take 16

overdubbed on 14 April 1971.

Hammond overdubbed onto Take 16 on
14 April 1971.

Guitar and Strings overdubbed onto "End
Section" of Take 16 on 14 April 1971.

Leslie Piano and Vocal Chorus overdubbed onto
Take 16 on 14 April 1971.

Rough mix of Take 16 made on 14 April 1971
(RS1).

Rough mix of "Bumble Bee Bass Section" made
on 14 April 1971 (RS1).

Vocals and Vocals for Verses overdubbed onto
Take 16 on 26 April 1971.

"See You" overdubbed onto "End" of Take 16 on
26 April 1971.

"Echo Choir" overdubbed onto Take 16 on
26 April 1971.

"Gull Guitar" overdubbed onto "Bumble Bee
Section" on 26 April 1971.

"Echo Choir" overdubbed onto Take 16 on
27 April 1971.

Vocal, "See You", "Last Two Verses", Guitar, Fuzz
Bass on "Build Up" and Fuzz Organ overdubbed
onto Take 16 on 27 April 1971.

"End Choir Section" recorded (Take 1) and
overdubbed on 27 April 1971.

Guitar, Piano, Farfisa and Feedback Guitar
overdubbed onto "End Section" on 28 April
1971.

"Bumble Bee Section" Crossfade on 28 April
1971.

'Return Of Son Of Nothing' mixed and edited on
28 April 1971 (RS5).

All other recording and mixing information
from Morgan Sound is missing from archives.

Nothing Part 1 (Untitled 1) (Unreleased)

Basic track comprising "Chopping Wood",
"Knives", "Scissors", "Tape Sprays", "Drips", "Book",
"Wine Glasses" and "Metronome" recorded on
4 January 1971 (Take 1).

"Bottles" overdubbed onto Take 1 on
5 January 1971.

Mixed on 11 January 1971 (RS1).

Nothing Part 2 (Untitled 2) (Unreleased)

Basic track comprising "Glasses 1–8" and
"Musical Saw" recorded on 4 January 1971
(Take 1).

Mixed on 11 January 1971 (RS1).

Nothing Part 1 (Untitled 3) (Unreleased)

Basic track comprising "Glasses, Musical Saw"
recorded on 4 January 1971 (Take 1).

Mixed on 11 January 1971 (RS1).

Nothing Part 2 (Unreleased)

Basic track comprising Bass, Drum.
Piano recorded on 4 January 1971
Mixed on 11 January 1971 (RS1).

Nothing Part 3 (Unreleased)

Basic track comprising Bass, Drum:
Piano (Rick), Piano (Rog) and Click
recorded on 4 January 1971 (Take
Mixed on 11 January 1971 (RS1).

Nothing Part 4 (Unreleased)

Basic track comprising "Milk Bottle
"Ginger Wine Bottle On Wood", "Dr
Metal", "Aerosols", "Drum Stick On V
On Bottle" and "Finger On Beer Bot
recorded on 5 January 1971 (Take
"Bottles" and "Musical Saw" overdu
Take 1 on 5 January 1971.
Mixed on 11 January 1971 (RS1).

Nothing Part 5 [Wine Glass Chor
(Unreleased)

Basic track comprising "Wine Glass
Click Track" recorded on 5 January
Mixed on 5 & 11 January 1971 (RS

Nothing Part 6 (Unreleased)

Basic track comprising "Guitar (Dav
on 5 January 1971 (Take 1).
Mixed on 11 January 1971 (RS1).

Nothing Part 7 (Unreleased)

Basic track comprising "Drum Loop
on 6 January 1971 (Take 1).
Mixed on 11 January 1971 (RS1).

Nothing Part 8 (Unreleased)

Basic track comprising Bass, Drum
Guitar recorded on 6 January 1971
Guitar overdubbed onto Take 1 on
6 January 1971.
Mixed on 11 January 1971 (RS1).

Nothing Part 9 (Unreleased, alth
elements used in Echoes)

Basic track comprising Drums, Bas
Electric Piano recorded on 9 Janua
(Take 6).
Guitars and Organ overdubbed on
10 January 1971.
Mixed on 11 January 1971 (RS1).
Edited for start of 'Return Of The S
Nothing' ['Echoes'] on 9 April 1971

Nothing Part 10 (Unreleased)

Basic track comprising "Nick Drums", "Rog Hi-Hat", "Dave Bass" and "Rick Bass Drum" recorded on 6 January 1971.
Vocals overdubbed on 6 January 1971 (Take 5).
Mixed on 11 January 1971 (RS1).

Nothing Part 11 (Unreleased)

Basic track comprising "Dave Electric Guitar" recorded on 9 January 1971 (Take 1).
Mixed on 11 January 1971 (RS1).

Nothing Part 12 (Unreleased)

Basic track comprising "Voices with Long Repeat Echo" recorded on 10 January 1971 (Take 1).
Mixed on 11 January 1971 (RS1).

Nothing Part 13 (Unreleased)

Basic track comprising Drums, Leslie Piano, Bowed Bass, Ordinary Piano and Electric Piano recorded on 11 January 1971 (Take 4).
Mixed on 11 January 1971 (RS1).

Nothing Part 14 (Unreleased)

Basic track comprising Bass and Drums recorded on 11 January 1971 (Take 1).
Please note it is recognised that the recording sheet does not correspond with the music released on the *Early Years* set and may be a notation error, as Part 13 would seem to be a more accurate description of the instruments used therein. The recording date however is accurate.

Nothing Part 15 (Unreleased, although elements used in Echoes)

Basic track comprising Bass, Cymbals, Piano Leslie, Farfisa and Guitar Click Track. Recording date not known.

Nothing Part 16 (Unreleased, although elements used in Echoes)

Basic track comprising Bass, Guitar 1, Guitar 2 and Drums. Recording date not known.

Nothing Part 17 (Unreleased, although elements used in One Of These Days)

Basic track comprising Electric Piano (Nick), Double Speed Voices, "Alien Musical Sounds" recorded on 20 January 1971 (Take 1).
Vocals and "Cosmic Alien Orchestra" overdubbed onto Take 1 on 20 January 1971.
Mixed on 21 January 1971 (RS2).

Nothing Part 18 (Unreleased, although elements used in One Of These Days)

Basic track composition not known, recorded on 20 January 1971.

Nothing Part 19 (Unreleased, although elements used in One Of These Days)

Basic track comprising Bass, Guitar, Organ recorded on 21 January 1971 (Take 6).
Loops of 'Nothing Part 19' with "Nick recorded at 15ips and replayed at 7½ips" made on 21 January 1971.

Nothing Part 20 (Unreleased, although elements used in One Of These Days)

Basic track comprising "Bass Guitar" recorded on 21 January 1971 (Take 1).
Backwards Guitar, Tympani's, Organ, Forward Cymbal & Tom Tom, Backward Cymbal & Tom Tom overdubbed onto Take 1 on 21 January 1971.
Mixed with "SFX" on 21 January 1971 (RS1).

Nothing Part 21 (Unreleased, although elements used in One Of These Days)

Basic track comprising Bass, Guitar, Organ and Drums recorded on 21 January 1971 (Take 1).

Nothing Part 22 (Unreleased, although elements used in One Of These Days)

Basic track comprising Vocal Loop ('One Of These Days I'm Going To Cut You Into Little Pieces') and "Backwards Farfisa via Leslie"

recorded on 24 January 1971 (Take 9).
Bass, Fuzz Bass, Backwards Guitar, Backwards Organ overdubbed onto Take 9 on 24 January 1971.
Mixed on 24 January 1971 (RS1).

Nothing Part 23 (Unreleased, although elements used in Fearless)

Basic track comprising Bass, Guitar and Organ recorded on 21 January 1971 (Take 1).
Mixed on 24 January 1971 (RS1).

Nothing Part 24 (Unreleased)

Basic track comprising Bass Guitar, Guitar, Vocals, "Peter and Scott", Drums, Dave Fuzz Guitar and Piano (Take 1). Recording date not known.
Mixed on 19 March 1971 (RS1).

Anything (Unreleased)

Chair Squeaking recorded on 19 March 1971 (Take 1).

Play The Blues (Unreleased)

Recorded on 19 March 1971 (Take 2).

Wild Thing (Unreleased)

Basic track recorded on 26 April 1971 (Take 1).
Bass overdubbed onto Take 1 on 26 April 1971.

Knozzee / Nozzee (Unreleased, although reworked on Household Objects 1973)

Basic track recorded on 11 September 1971 (Take 4).

Bottles (Unreleased, although reworked on Household Objects 1973)

Basic track recorded on 24 May 1971 (Take 1).
Milk Bottle, Beer Bottle, Wineglasses overdubbed onto Take 1 on 24 May 1971.
"Cinzano Bottle", "Cyder Bottle", "Knife Sharpener", "Nut Cracker", "Popping Bottle", "Beer Bottle", "½ Speed Milk Bottle" and "Lampshade" overdubbed onto Take 1 on 25 May 1971.
"Lampshade", "Tuned Bottles" and "Bongo Bottles" overdubbed onto Take 1 on 26 May 1971. 'Nothing Part 5' edited onto 'Bottles' on 28 May 1971.

SATURDAY 13 NOVEMBER – PERFORMANCE
Chapin Hall, Williams College, Williamstown, MA, USA

Set list: 'Embryo', 'Fat Old Sun', 'Set The Controls For The Heart Of The Sun', 'Atom Heart Mother' <Intermission> 'One Of These Days', 'Careful With That Axe, Eugene', 'Cymbaline' <Encore> 'Echoes'.

Reviewing the show the *Williams Record* reported, "Pink Floyd was mediocre. With the exception of Nick Mason, the drummer, they played in an uninspiring manner. It would be charitable to say that the vocals were pathetic…. There was no stage presence…. The two songs they are probably most famous for, 'Set The Controls For The Heart Of The Sun' and 'Careful With That Axe, Eugene', were far below the quality that they had achieved for the same songs on the live side of their *Ummagumma* album, yet they were far above any other song that they played. Their last song, 'Echoes', was pure electronic garbage. The music that Pink Floyd made may have served a purpose, but the members of the group exhibited very little musical talent – certainly not talent enough to warrant the price of admission."

SUNDAY 14 NOVEMBER – PERFORMANCE ◄
Pritchard Gymnasium, State University of New York at Stony Brook, NY, USA

Set list: 'Embryo', 'Fat Old Sun', 'Set The Controls For The Heart Of The Sun', 'Atom Heart Mother' <Intermission> 'One Of These Days', 'Careful With That Axe, Eugene', 'Cymbaline', 'Echoes' <Encore> 'Blues'.

MONDAY 15 NOVEMBER – PERFORMANCE
Carnegie Hall, New York, NY, USA

Set list: 'Set The Controls For The Heart Of The Sun', 'Atom Heart Mother', 'One Of These Days', 'Careful With That Axe, Eugene', 'Cymbaline', 'Echoes'.

TUESDAY 16 NOVEMBER – PERFORMANCE ▼
Lisner Auditorium, George Washington University, Washington, DC, USA

Set list: 'Embryo', 'Fat Old Sun', 'Set The Controls For The Heart Of The Sun', 'Atom Heart Mother' <Intermission> 'One Of These Days', 'Careful With That Axe, Eugene', 'Cymbaline' <Encore> 'Echoes'.

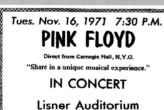

Reviewing the show the *Washington Post* reported, "This was no ordinary rock show – it was the closest thing that rock music has to show in the way of avant-garde music. Even apart from the strange opening – in which a fellow gifted as magician, juggler and fire-eater, breathed forth flame so a white robed lady could light her cigarette – there were other novelties in the Pink Floyd show at Lisner Auditorium last night. This English rock group prepared to satisfy a sold-out house, arrived with electronics in the highest. Echo and reverberation units, time delivery devices, synthesisers and taped sound segments were all part of the act. They played into a 32-channel mixing panel that relayed the joy into a public address system completely encircling the audience. Any given instrument, by these means could be 'placed' at any position in the hall and could be mixed with all kinds of taped wonders such as chirping birds and high volume 'white' noise. They did not worry too much with the usual content of music. When they sang, the vocals were not important as words with meanings but rather as aspects of an exciting tension that you could hear in the process of creation. Form and content were replaced by dynamics. The band sounded sometimes like a screaming saw, sometimes like a fleet of intergalactic jets. A guitar, with this group, became a screeching bird. Drums were explosions. 'Set The Controls' as they sang (and as the audience did) 'For The Heart Of The Sun'".

FRIDAY 19 NOVEMBER – PERFORMANCE
Syria Mosque Theater, Pittsburgh, PA, USA

Supported by Brain Child.

SATURDAY 20 NOVEMBER – PERFORMANCE
Taft Auditorium, Cincinnati, OH, USA

Set list: 'Embryo', 'Fat Old Sun', 'Set The Controls For The Heart Of The Sun', 'Atom Heart Mother' <Intermission> 'Careful With That Axe, Eugene', 'Cymbaline', 'Echoes' <Encore> 'Blues'.

Billboard reported, "Pink Floyd rocked their way to a sell out at 2,500-seat Taft Auditorium on Saturday." This, the last show on their lengthiest North American tour to date, featured a 25-minute version of 'Embryo', which also marked the last time the track was ever performed live. Curiously the band began jamming what was an outline of the track 'Breathe' during a brief technical hitch during the performance of this track.

MONDAY 29 NOVEMBER – SINGLE RELEASE (US)
'One Of These Days'

MONDAY 29 NOVEMBER – FRIDAY 10 DECEMBER – REHEARSALS

Decca Studios, Broadhurst Gardens, West Hampstead, London, England

Pink Floyd spent some time composing, writing and making initial demo recordings for their stage show and album that would eventually become *The Dark Side of the Moon*. This was the same location at which the Beatles failed their Decca Records audition in 1962 and where Jonathan King auditioned Jokers Wild in 1965.

MONDAY 13 – MONDAY 20 DECEMBER – RECORDING SESSION & FILMING
Live at Pompeii, **Studios de Boulogne & Studio Europa-Sonor, Paris, France**

Additional post-production recording and filming for the film *Live At Pompeii* was completed at the Studios de Boulogne in Paris including the tracks 'Careful With That Axe, Eugene', 'Set The Controls For The Heart Of The Sun' and 'Mademoiselle Nobs'.

5 PLAYING DIFFERENT TUNES

1972-73

1972–73

Initial ideas for new material had been discussed towards the end of 1971 at a band meeting in the usual venue of Nick Mason's kitchen, followed by a period of writing at Decca Studios in Broadhurst Gardens, West Hampstead.

Waters, undoubtedly the main source of inspiration, began furiously writing lyrics shortly after the end of their last US tour. An album's worth of material would also be of convenient length for the first half of a new stage show, the second half of which could be given over to established favourites. As Waters explained, "It had to be quick, because we had a tour starting. It might have been only six weeks before we had to have something to perform."[1]

He came up with the specific idea of dealing with all the things that drive people mad, not to mention a link for some unfinished and unused studio pieces. The album would focus on the enormous pressures the band themselves were experiencing on the road: the strains of travelling and the problems of living, often abroad for great stretches of time, and coping with (and without) money. It would also explore violence, social problems and the comforts of religion – this last theme no doubt prompted by their recent tours through middle America.

It all happened in such a short space of time it is almost unbelievable, as Wright confirmed: "At the start we only had vague ideas about madness being a theme. We rehearsed a lot just putting down ideas and then in the next rehearsals we used them. It flowed really well. There was a strong thing in it that made it easier to do."[2]

Lyrically, it was Waters' most profound and focused effort to date, and for the first time he dominated the creative input almost exclusively, conveying a vision all his own. The success of *The Dark Side of the Moon* is probably attributable to the fact that it was kept as deliberately simple and accessible as possible, with strong dynamics and melodies. It was certainly more focussed and down to earth than earlier flights of fancy such as 'Echoes'. Indeed, Waters gave some hint of what to expect on the forthcoming tour when he spoke to *Sounds* that January under the headline, "Pink Floyd Have Gone Mental!" "In concept it's more literal, not as abstract as the things we've done before."[3]

"I think at that time he [Waters] was finding himself as a lyric writer," remembers Gilmour. "He was realizing that he could get to grips with more serious issues, some political and others that involved him personally. His style had developed and improved. I remember him saying that he wanted to write this album absolutely straight, clear and direct, for nothing to be hidden in mysteries, to get away from all the psychedelic warblings and say exactly what he wanted for the first time."[4]

Finally, the new work was given the provisional title of *Dark Side of the Moon*. But, said Gilmour, "At one time it was called *Eclipse* because Medicine Head did an album called *Dark Side*

of the Moon. But that didn't sell well, so what the hell. I was against *Eclipse* and we felt a bit annoyed because we had already thought of the title before Medicine Head came out. Not annoyed at them, but because we wanted to use the title."[5][*]

With their first country-wide UK tour since 1969 about to commence, they were still working out the last few details and intricacies of the piece and booked a few days' rehearsal at a basement studio owned by the Rolling Stones in Bermondsey, south London. Final dress rehearsals would take place at the Rainbow Theatre, where they would return to perform exactly one month later.

To complete the production, the band purchased a brand-new PA system with a 28-channel mixing desk and a four-channel 360-degree quadraphonic sound system. They also had their first complete lighting rig, built to specification by their newly acquired lighting designer, Arthur Max, who had evidently impressed them as house engineer at their Fillmore East show in 1970.[**] In addition, specially recorded backing tapes were created to accompany the music on stage. A total of over nine tons of equipment was put together and transported by three trucks. Wright himself remarked on the scale of the operation: "Sometimes I look at our huge truck and tons of equipment and think, 'Christ, all I'm doing is playing an organ!'"[6]

The tour was generally acclaimed, if not fully comprehended, by the public. This was hardly surprising: performing a couple of new songs would have been difficult enough, but for the whole first half of the show to comprise an entire suite of new music was quite an undertaking for the band and audience alike.

But, proving the value of roadwork, the piece was slowly honed into the piece we all know and love. However, earlier performances were harsh and mechanical. For example, the track 'On The Run' was merely a keyboard and guitar improvisation, sometimes referred to as 'The Travel Sequence', concluding, not in an explosion, but a confused cacophony of very loud sound effects.

'Time' was initially sung as a duet between Gilmour and Wright, with Gilmour singing the line, "Lying supine in the sunshine" instead of "Tired of lying in the sunshine", a habit he couldn't quite shake off, as can be heard on the live concert release from Wembley in November 1974, well after the album's release.

***Dark Side of the Moon* by Medicine Head was released on Dandelion Records on Friday January 14, 1972.

** Max remained with the band through to the end of 1977 and now enjoys a lucrative career as a Hollywood production designer, his credits including *Gladiator, Black Hawk Down, Kingdom of Heaven* and *Prometheus* among others.

'The Great Gig In The Sky', known at the time as 'The Mortality Sequence' or plain 'Religion', was an electric piano solo backed by pre-recorded tapes of readings from the Book of Ephesians, the Lord's Prayer and other biblical discourses, along with recordings of the controversial British broadcaster Malcolm Muggeridge. By the time the group headed out on their second North American tour in September the taped voices had been lowered in the mix and the keyboard was more faithful to the finished album.[*] The band was never shy to recycle worthwhile unused material, and some of the other tracks had been part-written already. 'Us And Them' came out of the aforementioned 'Violent Sequence' from the *Zabriskie Point* sessions, although the 1972 tours lacked a saxophone part. Likewise, the music on 'Brain Damage' had reportedly been written at the time of *Meddle*.

'Eclipse', the climatic finale to the piece, had no lyrics at all, even in its initial performances. Waters came up with the words seven dates into the tour and just in time for their show in Bristol. "The piece felt unfinished to me when we were doing it on the road," he later recalled. "I came in one day and said, 'Here, I've just written the ending and this is it.'"[7]

Undoubtedly the band's pivotal performance of the piece came in mid-February at the Rainbow, where the world's press sat in attendance to witness *The Dark Side of the Moon* in all its seemingly well-rehearsed glory. In a series of presentations, and despite some rather stilted performances, Pink Floyd were heralded as a triumph of the imagination and for the first time greeted by critical acclaim throughout the national press.

For the time being the album's recording was deferred: the French director Barbet Schroeder invited them to write music for *La Vallée*. In two one-week sessions, one before and one after their tour of Japan, the band composed and recorded the entire work at the Strawberry Studios, in the Chateau d'Hérouville near Paris.[**] The album was released in June as *Obscured by Clouds* and once again the film, about a young woman's spiritual awakening in Papua New Guinea, was not a great success elsewhere but was well received in France.

As an album *Obscured by Clouds* is as striking as it is subtle, with some remarkable music that would feature on later tours. Perhaps the last true combined effort by the band, the album contains some particularly pensive lyrics by Waters. 'Free Four', for example, deals for the first time with the pressures of touring, well before the subject was taken to a conclusion on *The Dark Side of the Moon*. His father's death is also mentioned, and would fester to become the central

ABOVE: POSTER FOR THE CINEMATIC RELEASE OF *THE VALLEY* FEATURING PINK FLOYD'S MUSIC.

theme of *The Wall* but with far greater focus. Significantly, with 'Childhood's End' Gilmour made his last complete lyrical/musical composition in this line-up of Floyd. The album ends with 'Absolutely Curtains', which includes taped recordings of a religious chant performed by the Mapuga tribe of Papua New Guinea.

The album completed, and their customary August holiday period over with, Pink Floyd continued their extensive tour throughout North America and Europe, playing their largest (and generally sold-out) venues to date on both continents. At one particularly spectacular concert, at the Hollywood Bowl, eight powerful searchlights radiated beamed rays skywards from behind the domed stage of the vast amphitheatre into the night sky, and a colourful fireworks display rounded off the evening. Elsewhere impressive effects included sheets of flame shooting from cauldrons at the back of the stage during 'Careful With That Axe, Eugene', and a huge Chinese gong that burst into flames at the climax of 'Set The Controls For The Heart Of The Sun'.

However, despite the huge success of their recent North American tours, this certainly wasn't being reflected in their album sales, and fingers were being pointed at Capitol. With the *Dark Side of the Moon* also shaping up in the studio into what appeared to be a very fine album, manager Steve O'Rourke started looking at extracting themselves from their contract with EMI's counterpart. Historically their contract with EMI meant that all albums would immediately pass to licence to Capitol for North America, but that agreement was due to expire after the release of *The Dark Side of the Moon*.

So, in late 1972 a deal was struck with Clive Davis at CBS, who, like EMI in the UK, were prepared to give Pink Floyd the artistic freedom they wanted and had the financial muscle to successfully market, distribute and promote them on a much larger scale. That deal would come into effect from 1974. "We thought they would be best for us," explained Rick Wright, "largely because of their size. They're well organised....

---

* Also included on the September 2011 *Immersion* box set was an early mix of the album made by Alan Parsons on 19 December 1972, in which he experimented with a single taped recording of Commander Eugene Cernan's speech prior to departing the surface of the Moon in Apollo 17 on 14 December 1972, dubbed over the piano.

** The same studio had earlier inspired Elton John to title his critically acclaimed May 1972 album *Honky Chateau*, and here David Bowie recorded his October 1973 covers album *Pin Ups* which included a version of 'See Emily Play'.

Also, we'll be the only act of our type on CBS. When you're competing against similar acts on the same label, someone is bound to be squeezed out. We didn't want that."[8]

Although Capitol could do little to prevent Pink Floyd from moving on, their attitude changed dramatically. With the advent of *Obscured by Clouds* they suddenly gave Pink Floyd a priority in marketing, which then saw them pull out all the stops for the release of *The Dark Side of the Moon*.

1972 was also the year that Pink Floyd delved into other performing arts to enhance their work. The band had already provided incidental music for the Ballet Rambert and other stage productions in 1968 and 1969 and plans were now approaching fruition to link up with Europe's foremost contemporary ballet school, based in Marseilles and directed by Roland Petit. The band was brought to the attention of Petit by his daughter, a fan, who had suggested marrying a traditional ballet with modern music. The basic idea had already been discussed by the two parties at a meeting in Paris at the end of their autumn European tour in December 1970, when it was suggested that Proust's novel *Remembrance of Things Past* be adapted for the project. However, this idea floundered almost immediately, having failed to fire anyone's imagination sufficiently, and, after unsuccessful attempts by the band to read the monumental work, the project was abandoned. Petit even considered adapting either *A Thousand and One Nights* or *Carmen*, but again these ideas were dropped.

Further meetings obviously took place and made some concrete progress because a full page advert appeared in the US trade magazine *Cash Box* advertising a ballet performance with Pink Floyd alongside a 108-piece orchestra on 10 June 1971. This failed to materialize and attention once more turned to the production of an actual film.

A well-documented meeting was then held in London in early 1972, which Waters recalled as complete farce: "First of all it was 'Proust', then it was *Aladdin*, then it was something else. We had this great lunch one day – me, Nick [Mason] and Steve [O'Rourke]. We all went to have lunch with Nureyev, Roman Polanski, Roland Petit, some film producer or other. What a laugh. It was to talk about the projected idea for us doing the music, and Roland choreographing it, and Rudy Bryans being the star, and Roman Polanski directing the film, and making this fantastic ballet film. It was all a complete joke because nobody had any idea what they wanted to do. We all sat around this table until someone thumped the table and said, "What's the idea then?" and everyone just sat there drinking this wine and getting more and more drunk…until someone suggested *Frankenstein* and then Nureyev started getting a bit worried. And when Polanski was drunk enough he started to suggest we make the blue movie to end all blue movies, and then it all petered out into cognac and coffee and then we jumped into our cars and split. God knows what happened after we left."[9]

In what seemed like a sensible conclusion to their encounter it was agreed that the band should compose 40 minutes' worth of original material to which Petit would provide choreography. But, still pushed for time, Pink Floyd finally agreed on a 40-minute set of existing material from their current repertoire and the performance was finally staged at Marseilles, at a residency midway through the band's European tour in November 1972. Waters, for one, approached it with some trepidation: "Playing live means that we've got to be note-perfect each night, otherwise the dancers are going to get lost, and we won't be using a score, we'll be playing from memory. That might be a bit difficult."[10]

From here the production moved to Paris for a series of weekend shows in January and February of 1973. Curiously, only four of these featured Pink Floyd performing live: all of the other dates used pre-recorded music. Gilmour even mentioned plans to take the show to Canada, "but they couldn't because in the Maïakovski [Mayakovsky] ballet that goes before it, there's two pieces both written by the same man, which had something to do with the Russian Revolution and things. In one part of it there's a thing with huge red flags draped on the stage, and the Canadian government wouldn't let them use it."[11]

The conclusion of this extraordinary project illustrated yet another facet of Pink Floyd's ever-widening talents. Their shows were treated with awe and wonder by fans and critics alike. As Nick Mason said: "The thing to do is to really move people. To turn them on, to subject them to a fantastic experience, to do something to stretch their imagination."[12] But, concluded Gilmour, "The reality of all these people prancing around in tights in front of us didn't feel like what we wanted to do long term."[13]

The year 1973 was the first year in the band's career that the UK was largely ignored in favour of North America, which received the full-scale sensory assault of a much improved *Dark Side of the Moon* presentation on two extensive tours.

Additional on-stage personnel were also recruited for the very first time, including saxophonist and Cambridge associate Dick Parry, who stayed on board for the next two years.

For the two North American tours of the year Nawasa Crowder, Phylliss Lindsey and Mary Ann Lindsey, all members of the Dallas-based gospel group Black Grass, were recruited to reproduce the deep, soulful harmonies the piece now required.[*]

In October two shows in West Germany saw former Humble Pie backing vocal trio the Blackberries – comprising Billie Barnum, Venetta Fields and Clydie King – take to the stage. By the June

---

* Black Grass first came to prominence as backing vocalists for Leon Russell, performing on his albums *Carney* and *Leon Live*, the latter of which was recorded at the Long Beach Arena, Long Beach, California, on Tuesday 28 August 1972. This was followed by a tour backing Grand Funk Railroad before joining Pink Floyd for their spring tour.

ABOVE: ON STAGE AT EARLS COURT, LONDON, MAY 1973.

1974 French tour, Fields had teamed up with Carlena Williams for Pink Floyd's tour of France as a vocal duo, retaining the name the Blackberries, and remained with the band for the next two years.

The album *The Dark Side of the Moon* was finally released in March – a landmark album in every respect. However, all of Pink Floyd except Wright, boycotted the press reception at the London Planetarium because the quadraphonic mix had not been completed in time. Against the band's wishes, EMI presented a stereo playback through, what they felt was, an inferior PA system.

Waters had commented to the *NME* shortly after the release of *Meddle* that, "However long you go on working on an album I don't think you ever come out thinking, 'Bugger me, I've done it this time'. I don't think it's possible to make an album that you think is definitely all right from beginning to end." Nevertheless, the album successfully combined every element of Pink Floyd's collective ability that for the first time, was

consistent throughout, with strong dynamics, thoughtful lyrics and superb sequencing.

It also boasted enough FM radio–friendly tracks – 'Money' in particular – to make a serious dent in the hard-to-crack American market, thus exposing Pink Floyd for the very first time to a mass audience, and propelling them from underground cult band to the mainstream rock market that contemporaries such as the Who and Led Zeppelin had been enjoying for some time. But their new audience came at a price as Gilmour recalled: "It included an element that wasn't versed in Pink Floyd's ways. It started from the first show in America [Madison, Wisconsin]. People at the front shouting, 'Play "Money"! Gimme something I can shake my ass to!' We had to get used to it, but previously we'd be playing to 10,000-seaters where, in the quiet passages, you could hear a pin drop."[14]

"The thing about *Dark Side*," commented Nick Mason, "is that I think when it was finished, everyone felt it was the best thing we'd ever done to date, and everyone was very pleased

ABOVE: PERFORMING AT EARLS COURT, LONDON, MAY 1973.

with it, but there's no way that anyone felt it was five times as good as *Meddle*, or eight times as good as *Atom Heart Mother*, or the sort of figures that it has in fact sold. It was something of a phenomena, and was about not only being a good album, but also about being in the right place at the right time."[15]

No one could quite explain this meteoric success, which took the band by surprise. As Rick Wright commented: "We approached the album, I would say, in exactly the same way as any other album we've done. Except that this was a concept album. It was about madness, it was about one's fear, it was about the business – whereas none of the other albums had been about that. They may have been musically tied together, but there hadn't been a theme like that running on both sides."[16]

The album begins and ends, as did the live shows, with a heartbeat – the simple thread that pulls the whole thing together, the essence of what it is all about. As Gilmour said, "It alludes to the human condition and sets the mood for the music which describes the emotions experienced during a lifetime. Amidst the chaos there is beauty and hope for mankind. The effects are purely to help the listener understand what the whole thing is about."[17]

The album's sleeve also follows the idea through. A centre-spread gatefold repeats the central theme, showing a cardiograph blip, while the stunning front cover has an impressive, yet simple, white-light beam and a full spectrum that fans out from a central prism. The mysticism of the prism image continues in the publicity material, which used shots of the Great Pyramids at Giza in Egypt, where Storm Thorgerson and Aubrey "Po" Powell of Hipgnosis had travelled to especially to take the photographs. "It represented both the diversity and cleanliness of the sound of the music," said Thorgerson. "It was Roger's idea to turn the light into a heartbeat inside the sleeve, the sound that starts the music."[18]

The recorded material itself was significantly altered from the live originals, and many tracks featured female backing vocals for the first time, which lent a much softer edge to the overall piece. In addition, 'On The Run' was developed entirely in the studio to replace the comparatively weak guitar and keyboard jams while 'The Mortality Sequence' was changed beyond all recognition with a stunning improvised lead vocal from Clare Torry to form 'The Great Gig In The Sky'.

The vastly improved production was also largely a result of the different textures used. 'Time', for example, has a creative use of sound effects and the abstract use of total silence as a second instrument to Mason's roto-tom drumming.

It's also interesting to note how Pink Floyd was influenced at the time and how these influences contributed to the sound of the album. A quick listen to the 1971 Beaver & Krause album *Gandharva* will reveal that it is undeniably very similar in its approach. Similarly, the melody of 'Breathe' is a very close copy of the 1969 track 'Lady Magnolia' by Italian composer Piero Umiliani. Gilmour has recently confessed to stealing bit parts such as Eric Clapton's Leslie speaker sound from 'Badge' for 'Any Colour You Like', and, unlikely as it may seem, the echoey and dry sounds on 'Money' from Elton John's earlier work.

Where *Atom Heart Mother* had employed taped voices, now Roger Waters extended this idea much further by devising a system of questions that were written out on a series of cards and presented in such a way as to prevent anticipation and to elicit a definite answer. In all he interviewed about 20 people for this exercise, including Paul and Linda McCartney, who were recording *Red Rose Speedway* with Wings in an adjacent studio (although they don't appear on the album, being too well rehearsed to deliver candid responses); crew member Chris Adamson ("I've been mad for fucking years") and Peter Watts' wife, Patricia "Puddy" Watts ("That geezer was cruising for a bruising"); the Abbey Road engineers and in particular Jerry Driscoll who responded magnificently ("I've always been mad", "I'm not frightened of dying" and "There is no dark side of the moon really"). All of the questions were delivered on a one-to-one basis with very little repetition, to prevent interviewees having prior warning of what to expect from others who may have told them about their own session. The questions asked about the interviewees' thoughts on life and death, what did the dark side of the moon mean to them, had they ever been violent and, in the case of Henry McCullough (Wings guitarist), "When did you last thump someone?" According to Alan Parsons, his response was "New Year's Eve". The next question was, "Were you in the right?" and he said, "I don't know, I was drunk at the time." His wife was also asked, "When did you last thump someone?" She said "New Year's Eve too!"[19] Very noticeable on the finished album is a stream of manic laughter from one of the band's roadies known as Roger "The Hat" Manifold who also delivers the line "A short, sharp, shock", in describing a particularly memorable moment of road rage.

Despite the length of time the music had been gestating on the road, and the time the band had spent in the studio recording it, people still didn't understand its meaning. "It's amazing," said Gilmour, "At the final remixing stage we thought it was obvious what the album was about, but still a lot of people, including engineers and roadies, when we asked them, didn't know what the LP was about. I really don't know if our things get through, but you have to carry on hoping. Our music is about neuroses. We are able to see it, and discuss it. *The Dark Side of the Moon* itself is an allusion to the moon and lunacy. The dark side is generally related to what goes on inside people's heads – the subconscious and the unknown."[20]

The *Dark Side of the Moon* is also regarded as the highpoint of the band's collaborative powers, as Waters recalled with fondness: "They were very happy times. We discovered what we did, each of us, what our contributions were. We had gelled as a group, we were working very well together and we were working very hard, doing lots of gigs. We were in the springtime of Pink Floyd when it was all good fun and we had a common purpose – we wanted to be popular, we all wanted to be rich and famous and yet we weren't. And I could express myself within that context, and Dave could play his guitar, Rick could play keyboards and write and Nick could do what he did, and we were all content to be together and it was very jolly. A wonderful time."[21]

The Dark Side of the Moon was recorded and released in the stereo format, having been mixed by Chris Thomas. A short time later the album was remixed, virtually single-handedly, by Alan Parsons into quadraphonic for the expected rush in trend for the newly available quad hi-fi systems. Due to the limited interest and high cost of the new format, it is only now with the advent of the Hybrid SACD 5.1 version released in 2003 that listeners can fully appreciate the depth of sonic detail that for some had lain dormant for nigh on 30 years.

By the end of 1973 sales of *The Dark Side of the Moon* were showing little sign of tailing off on the *Billboard* US Top 100 album chart, and by now over 700,000 copies had been bought in the UK alone. From here the album would just continue to sell and sell and sell. It was calculated, some 25 years after its release, the album had sold in excess of 35 million copies worldwide, and is still in the Top Five best-selling album titles of all time. Surprisingly, it never made the UK Number One spot, being thwarted by a compilation album, *20 Flash Back Greats of the Sixties.*

Unsure of what to do next, and with no immediate label pressure to create a follow-up, the band traded creativity for experimentation and inexplicably returned briefly to the studio to develop ideas they had previously explored at the outset of *Meddle*. It is a project that has become known as 'Household Objects', which has never seen the light of day, save for one backing track, which was included on the *Wish You Were Here* expanded *Immersion* set in 2011. Despite efforts to revive the idea in late 1973 (with the tracks 'Nozee' and the appropriately titled 'The Hard Way'), Gilmour felt that it wasn't worth the time and trouble required to complete even the most basic of sequences: "We actually built a thing with a stretched rubber band this long [about two feet]. There was a g-clamp this end fixing it to a table and this end there was a cigarette lighter for a bridge. And then there was a set of matchsticks taped down this end. You stretch it and you can get a really good bass sound. Oh, and we used aerosol sprays and pulling rolls of Sellotape® out to different lengths – the further away it gets the note changes. We got three or four tracks down. It'd be very hard to make any of them really work as a piece of genuine music."[22] But contrary to popular belief, it wasn't entirely dispensed with as Gilmour later recalled: 'We did actually use some of the household objects – the wine glasses were in some of the music at the beginning of the *Wish You Were Here* album.'[23]

However, with such an exhausting period of their career behind them, Pink Floyd went into semi-retirement, not only to catch up with their families, but also to reflect on their newfound wealth and the stardom that had been thrust upon the anonymous individuals so suddenly.

1. *Zig Zag*, Issue 32, July 1973.
2. *Disc*, c.1974.
3. *Sounds*, 29 January 1972.
4. *Mojo*, March 1998.
5. *Sounds*, 19 May 1973.
6. *Sounds*, 1 June 1974.
7. *Mojo*, March 1998.
8. *Beetle*, January 1975.
9. *Zig Zag*, Issue 32, July 1973.
10. *Sounds*, 29 January 1972.
11. *Beetle*, May 1973.
12. *Beat Instrumental*, April 1971.
13–14. *Mojo*, March 1998.
15–16. *The Pink Floyd Story*, Capital Radio, 7 November 1976.
17. *Sounds*, 19 May 1973.
18–19. *Mojo*, March 1998.
20. *Sounds*, 19 May 1973.
21. *Mojo*, March 1998.
22. *Sounds*, 1 June 1974.
23. *House of Wax*, BBC Radio One, 26 November 1988.

DAY-BY-DAY 1972–73

1972

UK TOUR '72

Pink Floyd premiered a new piece of music that formed the first half of their shows which would eventually become *The Dark Side of the Moon*, and show programmes, press reports and adverts generally refer to this piece as being *Dark Side of the Moon*. However, commencing with the first North American tour on 14 April 1972, the band referred to the piece as *Eclipse* and did so right up to the end of the second North American tour ending 30 September 1972. The title reverted back to *Dark Side of the Moon* permanently thereafter. To avoid any confusion it has been listed as *The Dark Side of the Moon* in the set lists throughout the year.

PINK FLOYD ROAD CREW

Chris Adamson (Technician, Stage Crew), Seth Goldman (Technician, Stage Crew), Marek "Mick The Pole" Kluczynski (PA Technician), Arthur Max (Lighting Technician), Bobby Richardson (Technician, Stage Crew), Brian Scott (Technician, Stage Crew), Peter Watts (Head of PA, Sound Engineer).

MONDAY 3 – SATURDAY 15 JANUARY – REHEARSALS
47 Bermondsey Street, Bermondsey, London, England

A period of writing and rehearsals took place at this South London basement studio owned by the Rolling Stones.

TUESDAY 11 JANUARY – FOOTBALL MATCH
Kentish Town, London, England

Pink Floyd was challenged to a football match by the band Family. Both teams comprised band members and roadies, the game ending in a 3-3 draw. Pink Floyd's programme for their Rainbow Theatre shows even included a team photo with the caption, "Their cheerleaders braved monsoon conditions to support the team with, 'we got the shit, we got the dope, but Family's team ain't got a hope,'" followed by the cryptic message, "'Roger's title for 'Echoes' was 'We won the double.'"

ABOVE: THE PINK FLOYD FOOTBALL TEAM FEATURING VARIOUS BAND MEMBERS AND ROADIES.

MONDAY 17 – WEDNESDAY 19 JANUARY – REHEARSALS ▶
Rainbow Theatre, Finsbury, London, England

Three days of full production rehearsals were staged at the Rainbow Theatre before embarking on tour.

THURSDAY 20 JANUARY – PERFORMANCE
The Dome, Brighton, England

Set list: *The Dark Side of the Moon* (abandoned at 'Money' due to technical problems), 'Atom Heart Mother' <Intermission> 'Careful With That Axe, Eugene', 'One Of These Days', 'Echoes' <Encore> 'A Saucerful Of Secrets'.

The *NME* reported, "The Floyd opened the first set of the British tour with a new piece, tentatively titled *The Dark Side of the Moon*, and showed that their writing had taken on a new and again innovatory form. A pulsating bass beat, pre-recorded, pounded around the hall's speaker system. A voice declared Chapter Five, verses 15 to 17 from the *Book of Ephesians*. The organ built up; suddenly it soared like a jumbo jet leaving Heathrow; the lights, just behind the equipment, rose like an elevator. Floyd were on stage playing a medium paced piece. The Floyd inventiveness had returned, and it astounded the capacity house."

Pink Floyd's set was cut dramatically short at the beginning of 'Money' due to a technical breakdown. The show resumed with some more familiar numbers from their repertoire. Pink Floyd rescheduled two shows at the Dome in June to compensate their audience.

FRIDAY 21 JANUARY – PERFORMANCE
Guildhall, Portsmouth, England

Set list: *The Dark Side of the Moon* <Intermission> 'One Of These Days', 'Set The Controls For The Heart Of The Sun', 'Echoes' <Encore> 'A Saucerful Of Secrets'.

SATURDAY 22 JANUARY – PERFORMANCE
Winter Gardens, Bournemouth, England

Set list: *The Dark Side of the Moon* <Intermission> 'One Of These Days', 'Careful With That Axe, Eugene', 'Echoes' <Encore> 'A Saucerful Of Secrets'.

ABOVE: ON STAGE AT THE WINTER GARDENS, BOURNEMOUTH.

SUNDAY 23 JANUARY – PERFORMANCE
Guildhall, Southampton, England

Set list: *The Dark Side of the Moon* <Intermission> 'One Of These Days', 'Careful With That Axe, Eugene', 'Echoes' <Encore> 'A Saucerful Of Secrets'.

Frustratingly, this show was filmed in its entirety by the BBC in order to test out some new camera equipment. The film was never intended for broadcast and consequently the tapes were wiped shortly afterwards.

THURSDAY 27 JANUARY – PERFORMANCE ▶
City Hall, Newcastle-upon-Tyne, England

Set list: *The Dark Side of the Moon* <Intermission> 'One Of These Days', 'Careful With That Axe, Eugene', 'Echoes' <Encore> 'A Saucerful Of Secrets'.

N.E.M.S. ENTERPRISES LTD.
PRESENT

PINK FLOYD
in concert

CITY HALL, THURS., 27th JANUARY
at 7.30 p.m.

Tickets: £1.25, £1, 75p, 50p available from City Hall Box Office, starting Saturday 8th January at 10.30 a.m. and Mon.—Fri. 10.30 a.m.—5.30 p.m.

FRIDAY 28 JANUARY – PERFORMANCE
City Hall, Leeds, England

Set list: *The Dark Side of the Moon* <Intermission> 'One Of These Days', 'Careful With That Axe, Eugene', 'Echoes', 'Set The Controls For The Heart Of The Sun' <Encore> 'Blues'.

THURSDAY 3 FEBRUARY – PERFORMANCE ▶
Lanchester Polytechnic College Arts Festival, Locarno Ballroom, Coventry, England

Set list: *The Dark Side of the Moon* <Intermission> 'Careful With That Axe, Eugene', 'One Of These Days', 'Echoes' <Encore> 'Set The Controls For The Heart Of The Sun'.

THE LANCHESTER POLYTECHNIC COLLEGE ARTS FESTIVAL (JAN 28th–FEB 4th) PRIORY STREET, COVENTRY

PINK FLOYD
CHUCK BERRY
SLADE

VIV STANSHALL AND FRIENDS • THUNDERCLAP NEWMAN
LIGHTNIN' SLIM • J. B. HUTTO AND THE HAWKS
EDDIE 'GUITAR' BURNS • HOMESICK JAMES
ROLAND KIRK • MIKE WESTBROOK

ALSO EVENTS THROUGHOUT THE WEEK. TICKETS AND FULL PROGRAMME AVAILABLE FROM THE COLLEGE AND USUAL AGENCIES

Pink Floyd's show began at around 2.30am, instead of the advertised 10.30pm following an earlier show featuring Slade, Billy Preston and headliner Chuck Berry, who turned up over two hours late. However, it was at this show that Berry's massive worldwide hit 'My Ding-A-Ling' was recorded, and having been told by the event promoter to wrap up his show in order that Pink Floyd's could perform, he began the song with the words, "In that case we just got one more song to do…"

SATURDAY 5 FEBRUARY – PERFORMANCE
Colston Hall, Bristol, England

Set list: *The Dark Side of the Moon* <Intermission> 'One Of These Days', 'Careful With That Axe, Eugene', 'Set The Controls For The Heart Of The Sun' <Encore> 'Echoes'.

The *Bristol Evening Post* reported, "Pink Floyd, armed to the teeth with enough explosive musical gadgetry to cause a minor traffic jam of parked vans behind the Colston Hall, rose above the machinery and gave a memorable concert on Sunday [sic] night. There wasn't a single moment when their battery of tapes, multi-channel stereo systems and robot like banks of rock music technology failed to act as mere servants of the four players' talents. The group began slowly in the first half, playing the slightly less ethereal music they have been composing recently. In the second half things really began to take off as they used more and more beautifully recorded tapes through a disturbingly effective stereo system placed around the auditorium breaking down the barrier between stage and audience. All the time the band were spotlighted by their own lighting system which ran through rich, harsh contrasts of colour and brightness and reached an extraordinary climax as blinding fireworks burst into clouds of smoke. In the last 45 minutes they ran through their showstoppers, the almost theatrical 'Careful With That Axe, Eugene' and the melancholy 'Set The Controls'. Dave Gilmour's guitar and Rick Wright's keyboard work dominated the performance but the whole group's sympathy with each other has built up to one of today's most original sounds. Bassist Roger Waters and Nicky Mason on drums gave a richly textured rhythm section that was quite as important to the overall effectiveness of Pink Floyd as the guitar-keyboards front line. Tickets for this concert had been the most sought after since the Stones' shows last year. It was easy to see why."

SUNDAY 6 FEBRUARY – CANCELLED PERFORMANCE
ABC Theatre, Plymouth, England

This show was dropped from the original schedule which, according to a report in *NME*, was due to the fact "the theatre does not have the necessary licensing cover for Floyd's extensive equipment."

THURSDAY 10 FEBRUARY – PERFORMANCE
De Montfort Hall, Leicester, England

Set list: *The Dark Side of the Moon* <Intermission> 'One Of These Days', 'Careful With That Axe, Eugene', 'Set The Controls For The Heart Of The Sun', 'Echoes' <Encore> 'Blues'.

FRIDAY 11 FEBRUARY – PERFORMANCE
Free Trade Hall, Manchester, England

Set list: 'One Of These Days', 'Careful With That Axe, Eugene'.

About 25 minutes into the show, during 'Careful With That Axe, Eugene', there was a power cut and, despite cries of "Acoustic!" from the audience, the concert was abandoned.

SATURDAY 12 FEBRUARY – PERFORMANCE
City (Oval) Hall, Sheffield, England

Set list: 'One Of These Days', 'Careful With That Axe, Eugene', *The Dark Side of the Moon*, 'Set The Controls For The Heart Of The Sun' <Encore> 'Echoes'.

SUNDAY 13 FEBRUARY – PERFORMANCE
Empire Theatre, Liverpool, England

Set list: *The Dark Side of the Moon* <Intermission> 'One Of These Days', 'Careful With That Axe, Eugene', 'Echoes' <Encore> 'A Saucerful Of Secrets'.

THURSDAY 17 FEBRUARY – PERFORMANCE ▼
Rainbow Theatre, Finsbury, London, England

Set list: *The Dark Side of the Moon* <Intermission> 'One Of These Days', 'Careful With That Axe, Eugene', 'Echoes' <Encore> 'Set The Controls For The Heart Of The Sun'.

FRIDAY 18 FEBRUARY – PERFORMANCE
Rainbow Theatre, Finsbury, London, England

Set list: *The Dark Side of the Moon* <Intermission> 'One Of These Days', 'Careful With That Axe, Eugene', 'Echoes', 'A Saucerful Of Secrets', 'Blues' <Encore> 'Set The Controls For The Heart Of The Sun'.

SATURDAY 19 FEBRUARY – PERFORMANCE
Rainbow Theatre, Finsbury, London, England

Set list: *The Dark Side of the Moon* <Intermission> 'One Of These Days', 'Careful With That Axe, Eugene', 'Echoes', 'A Saucerful Of Secrets', 'Blues' <Encore> 'Set The Controls For The Heart Of The Sun'.

SUNDAY 20 FEBRUARY – PERFORMANCE
Rainbow Theatre, Finsbury, London, England

Set list: *The Dark Side of the Moon* <Intermission> 'One Of These Days', 'Careful With That Axe, Eugene', 'Echoes', 'A Saucerful Of Secrets', 'Blues' <Encore> 'Set The Controls For The Heart Of The Sun'.

WEDNESDAY 23 – TUESDAY 29 FEBRUARY
– RECORDING SESSION
Strawberry Studios,
Chateau d'Hérouville, near Paris, France

Recording for the album *Obscured by Clouds*. Unfortunately no studio records exist of these sessions.

ORTF TV broadcast a pre-recorded interview with director Barbet Schroeder and actress Bulle Ogier for the music programme *Pop 2*, including an interview with Roger Waters and David Gilmour from the recording studios, which included background music from the sessions including early versions of 'Mudmen' and 'The Gold It's In The…'. It was broadcast on ORTF2 on 4 March between 5.05pm and 5.25pm.

JAPANESE TOUR

Pink Floyd departed the UK at London Heathrow Airport on 3 March, arriving in Japan on 4 March via Japan Airlines JAL flight No. 424. The tour was promoted by Universal Orient Promotions and sponsored by Fuji T, Toshiba Music, Heibon Punch and An-An magazines (Tokyo), FM Osaka (Osaka), Kinki Broadcasting, Tokyo Music & Culture Associates and Onkyo Service Center (Kyoto).

Pink Floyd undertook a great many media interviews and press calls on this extensively publicized tour and it is very likely one or more of the concerts was recorded and broadcast on Japanese TV and radio.

The band departed Japan on 16 March from Tokyo, arriving in the UK on 17 March via Japan Airlines JAL flight No. 401.

MONDAY 6 MARCH – PERFORMANCE
Tokyo-To Taiikukan, Shibuya, Tokyo, Japan ▶

Set list: *The Dark Side of the Moon* <Intermission> 'One Of These Days', 'Careful With That Axe, Eugene', 'Echoes' <Encore> 'A Saucerful Of Secrets'.

Music Life reported, "In total 7 tons of instruments were brought to Japan, and this time the Pink Floyd show was very interesting for its effective lighting. But those who were informed it was a 'light show' might have been a bit disappointed, expecting it to be a much brighter spectacle. Their study of instruments is so impeccable and their techniques in handling them are marvellous."

TUESDAY 7 MARCH – PERFORMANCE
Tokyo-To Taiikukan, Shibuya, Tokyo, Japan

Set list: *The Dark Side of the Moon* <Intermission> 'One Of These Days', 'Careful With That Axe, Eugene', 'Echoes' <Encore> 'Set The Controls For The Heart Of The Sun'.

WEDNESDAY 8 MARCH – PERFORMANCE
Festival Hall, Osaka, Japan

Set list: *The Dark Side of the Moon* <Intermission> 'One Of These Days', 'Echoes', 'Careful With That Axe, Eugene', 'Atom Heart Mother'.

THURSDAY 9 MARCH – PERFORMANCE
Festival Hall, Osaka, Japan

Set list: *The Dark Side of the Moon* <Intermission> 'One Of These Days', 'Careful With That Axe, Eugene', 'Echoes', 'Set The Controls For The Heart Of The Sun'.

FRIDAY 10 MARCH – PERFORMANCE
Dai-Sho-Gun Furitsu Taiikukan, Kyoto, Japan

Set list: *The Dark Side of the Moon* <Intermission> 'One Of These Days', 'Careful With That Axe, Eugene', 'Echoes'.

SATURDAY 11 MARCH – CANCELLED PERFORMANCE
Kenmin Hall, Yokohama, Kanagawa, Japan

MONDAY 13 MARCH – PERFORMANCE
Nakanoshima Sports Center, Sapporo, Hokkaido, Japan

Set list: *The Dark Side of the Moon* <Intermission> 'One Of These Days', 'Careful With That Axe, Eugene', 'Echoes'.

THURSDAY 23 – MONDAY 27 MARCH – RECORDING SESSION
Strawberry Studios, Chateau d'Hérouville, near Paris, France

Pink Floyd completed recording *Obscured by Clouds*. Unfortunately no studio records exist of these sessions.

MONDAY 27 & TUESDAY 28 MARCH – RECORDING SESSION
Room 4, EMI Studios, Abbey Road, London, England

Remixing *Atom Heart Mother* for the quadraphonic album release. The session was engineered by Peter Bown and assisted by Alan Parsons. Pink Floyd was not in attendance for this session.

WEDNESDAY 29 MARCH – PERFORMANCE
Free Trade Hall, Manchester, England

Set list: *The Dark Side of the Moon* <Intermission> 'One Of These Days', 'Careful With That Axe, Eugene', 'Echoes' <Encore> 'Blues'.

This was the first of two shows staged as a replacement for the aborted show on 11 February 1972.

THURSDAY 30 MARCH – PERFORMANCE
Free Trade Hall, Manchester, England

Set list: *The Dark Side of the Moon* <Intermission> 'One Of These Days', 'Careful With That Axe, Eugene', 'Echoes' <Encore> 'Set The Controls For The Heart Of The Sun'.

THURSDAY 30 MARCH – RECORDING SESSION
Room 4, EMI Studios, Abbey Road, London, England

Remixing *Atom Heart Mother* for the quadraphonic album release. Engineered by Peter Bown and assisted by Alan Parsons. Pink Floyd was not in attendance for this session.

TUESDAY 4 & WEDNESDAY 5 APRIL – RECORDING SESSION
Room 4, EMI Studios, Abbey Road, London, England

Remixing *Atom Heart Mother* for the quadraphonic album release. The session was engineered by Alan Parsons and Peter James. Pink Floyd was not in attendance for this session.

TUESDAY 4 TO THURSDAY 6 APRIL – RECORDING SESSION
Morgan Sound Studios, Willesden, London, England

Final mixing of *Obscured by Clouds*. Unfortunately, no studio records exist of these sessions.

NORTH AMERICAN TOUR

Early drafts of Pink Floyd's tour show the band scheduled to appear at Pirates Cove, Pirates World Amusement Park, Dania, Hollywood, FL, on Saturday 15 April (rescheduled to Hollywood Sportatorium, Pembroke Pines, Hollywood); Massey Hall, Toronto, Canada, on Sunday 30 April; Mayser Center, Franklin-Marshall College, Lancaster, PA, on Saturday 6 May; and Spectrum Theater, Philadelphia, on Sunday 7 May (rescheduled to Saturday 29 April).

PINK FLOYD ROAD CREW
Chris Adamson (Technician, Stage Crew), Seth Goldman (Technician, Stage Crew), Marek "Mick The Pole" Kluczynski (PA Technician), Arthur Max (Lighting Technician), Chris Mickie (Front of House Sound Engineer), Bobby Richardson (Technician, Stage Crew), Brian Scott (Technician, Stage Crew), Peter Watts (Head of PA, Sound Engineer).

FRIDAY 14 APRIL – PERFORMANCE
Fort Homer W Hesterly Armory, Tampa, FL, USA

Set list: *The Dark Side of the Moon* <Intermission> 'One Of These Days', 'Careful With That Axe, Eugene', 'Echoes'.

SATURDAY 15 APRIL – PERFORMANCE ▶
Hollywood Sportatorium, Pembroke Pines, Hollywood, FL, USA

Set list: *The Dark Side of the Moon* <Intermission> 'One Of These Days', 'Careful With That Axe, Eugene', 'Echoes' <Encore> 'Set The Controls For The Heart Of The Sun'.

SUNDAY 16 APRIL – PERFORMANCE
Township Auditorium, Columbia, SC, USA

Set list: *The Dark Side of the Moon* <Intermission> 'One Of These Days', 'Careful With That Axe, Eugene', 'Echoes' <Encore> 'Atom Heart Mother'.

TUESDAY 18 APRIL– PERFORMANCE ▶
Symphony Hall, Atlanta Memorial Arts Center, Atlanta, GA, USA

Set list: *The Dark Side of the Moon* <Intermission> 'One Of These Days', 'Careful With That Axe, Eugene', 'Echoes' <Encore> 'A Saucerful Of Secrets'.

Great Speckled Bird reported, "Pink Floyd is one of the few bands, perhaps the only one now, to maintain the integrity of electronic and psychedelic music, principally because of their inventiveness. Their first set featured, as far as I could tell, new material. But the band seemed a bit out of synch, and their usual power and intensity was dulled. The second set was a different story. They ran through some of their best and more familiar material…with a remarkable complexity and depth, from Roger Waters eliciting pain as he thrashed the cymbals, to Dave Gilmour's spinning freaky rivulets of sound from his lead guitar as he sat on the floor and manipulated two sets of panels in addition to his amp. Nothing short of incredible."

THURSDAY 20 APRIL – PERFORMANCE ◀
KQV TV Spring Festival of Rock, Syria Mosque Theater, Oakland, Pittsburgh, PA, USA

Set list: *The Dark Side of the Moon* <Intermission> 'One Of These Days', 'Careful With That Axe, Eugene', 'Echoes'.

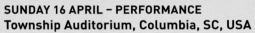

FRIDAY 21 APRIL – PERFORMANCE
The Lyric Theatre, Baltimore, MD, USA

Set list: *The Dark Side of the Moon* <Intermission> 'One Of These Days', 'Careful With That Axe, Eugene', 'Echoes' <Encore> 'Set The Controls For The Heart Of The Sun'.

SATURDAY 22 APRIL – PERFORMANCE
Civic Theatre, Akron, OH, USA

Set list: *The Dark Side of the Moon* <Intermission> 'One Of These Days', 'Careful With That Axe, Eugene', 'Echoes' <Encore> 'A Saucerful Of Secrets'.

SUNDAY 23 APRIL – PERFORMANCE
Music Hall, Cincinnati, OH, USA

Set list: *The Dark Side of the Moon* <Intermission> 'One Of These Days', 'Careful With That Axe, Eugene', 'Echoes' <Encore> 'A Saucerful Of Secrets'.

MONDAY 24 APRIL – PERFORMANCE ▶
Allen Theatre, Cleveland, OH, USA

Rescheduled from the Sports Arena, Toledo.
Set list: *The Dark Side of the Moon* <Intermission> 'One Of These Days', 'Careful With That Axe, Eugene', 'Echoes' <Encore> 'Set The Controls For The Heart Of The Sun'.

WEDNESDAY 26 & THURSDAY 27 APRIL – PERFORMANCES
Ford Auditorium, Detroit, MI, USA

Set list on 27 April: *The Dark Side of the Moon* <Intermission> 'One Of These Days', 'Careful With That Axe, Eugene', 'Echoes' <Encore> 'Set The Controls For The Heart Of The Sun', 'Blues'.

FRIDAY 28 APRIL – PERFORMANCE
Auditorium Theatre, Chicago, IL, USA

Set list: *The Dark Side of the Moon* <Intermission> 'One Of These Days', 'Careful With That Axe, Eugene', 'Echoes' <Encore> 'Set The Controls For The Heart Of The Sun'.

SATURDAY 29 APRIL – PERFORMANCE
Spectrum Theater, Philadelphia, PA, USA

Set list: *The Dark Side of the Moon* <Intermission> 'One Of These Days', 'Careful With That Axe, Eugene', 'Echoes' <Encore> 'Set The Controls For The Heart Of The Sun'.

The *Delaware County News* reported, "A sellout crowd of 5,000 at the Spectrum last night witnessed what very easily could have been one of the most freaked-out experiences of our time. Everything to do with the concert was much stranger than usual. They played for a little over three hours with only a short intermission. During the first half they did a thing entitled 'Eclipse….a piece for Assorted Lunatics'. This was a true rock 'Concert' with real, live programs for the performances being handed out. During the second half they did old favourites 'Echoes' from their latest album *Meddle* and 'Careful With That Axe, Eugene', received the warmest receptions."

MONDAY 1 MAY – PERFORMANCE
Carnegie Hall, New York, NY, USA

Set list: *The Dark Side of the Moon* <Intermission> 'One Of These Days', 'Careful With That Axe, Eugene', 'Echoes' <Encore> 'Set The Controls For The Heart Of The Sun'.

TUESDAY 2 MAY – PERFORMANCE
Carnegie Hall, New York, NY, USA

Set list: *The Dark Side of the Moon* <Intermission> 'One Of These Days', 'Careful With That Axe, Eugene', 'Echoes' <Encore> 'A Saucerful Of Secrets'.

WEDNESDAY 3 MAY – PERFORMANCE ▼
Concert Hall, John F. Kennedy Center
For Performing Arts, Washington, DC, USA

Set list: *The Dark Side of the Moon* <Intermission> 'One Of These Days', 'Careful With That Axe, Eugene', 'Echoes' <Encore> 'Set The Controls For The Heart Of The Sun'.

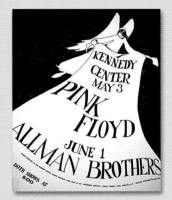

THURSDAY 4 MAY – PERFORMANCE
Music Hall, Boston, MA, USA

Rescheduled from the Orpheum Aquarius Theater, Boston due to high ticket demand.
Set list: *The Dark Side of the Moon* <Intermission> 'One Of These Days', 'Careful With That Axe, Eugene', 'Echoes' <Encore> 'Blues'.

THURSDAY 18 MAY – PERFORMANCE
Deutschlandhalle, West Berlin, West Germany

Set list: *The Dark Side of the Moon* <Intermission> 'One Of These Days', 'Careful With That Axe, Eugene', 'Echoes' <Encore> 'Set The Controls For The Heart Of The Sun'.

SUNDAY 21 MAY – PERFORMANCE
2nd British Rock Meeting, Insel Grün, Germersheim, West Germany

Set list: 'Atom Heart Mother', 'Set The Controls For The Heart Of The Sun', 'One Of These Days', 'Careful With That Axe, Eugene', 'Echoes' <Encore> 'A Saucerful Of Secrets'.

Staged between Saturday 20 and Monday 22 May, this festival was originally scheduled to take place at Friesenheimer Grün, an island on the Rhine at Mannheim, but after local authority objections another location was sought. When plans also failed for an alternative site on the nearby island of Korsika and at the Hockenheim Ring, again due to local objections, it was finally and successfully relocated to the island of Insel Grün on the Rhine located between Mannheim and Karlsruhe. It was attended by over 70,000 people, including a large contingent of US services personnel who were stationed in West Germany. It was regarded as the German Woodstock and featured a vast array of artists including Humble Pie, the Faces, the Kinks, the Doors, Family, the Incredible String Band, Atomic Rooster, Osibisa, Linda Lewis, Buddy Miles Express, Curved Air and many more. Pink Floyd performed at 3.00pm on the afternoon

ABOVE: PERFORMING AT THE AMSTERDAM ROCK CIRCUS, 22 MAY 1972.

of Sunday 21 May and reportedly received a fee of 60,000 German marks for their performance.

MONDAY 22 MAY – PERFORMANCE
The Amsterdam Rock Circus, Olympisch Stadion, Amsterdam, Netherlands

With Donovan, Gene Clark, Spencer Davis & Sneaky Pete, Dr. John the Night Tripper, Tom Paxton, Buddy Miles Band featuring Carlos Santana, Memphis Slim, New Riders of the Purple Sage, Pacific Gas & Electric, Sgt. Peppers Band, Regional Orchestra and Joe's Light's Lightshow.
Set list: 'Atom Heart Mother', 'One Of These Days', 'Careful With That Axe, Eugene', 'Echoes' <Encore> 'A Saucerful Of Secrets'.

TUESDAY 30 MAY – RECORDING SESSION
Studio 3 & Control Room 3, EMI Studios, Abbey Road, London, England

Recording commenced on Pink Floyd's eighth studio album, *The Dark Side of the Moon*.
2.30pm to 12.00midnight: Set up and test takes throughout the afternoon. In the evening 'Eclipse Part 1' ['Breathe'] was recorded (Take 1 False Start and erased, Takes 1–4 untimed and Take 5 at 2:50 and marked "best"), and Vocals, Guitar and Electric Piano overdubbed onto Take 5 of 'Eclipse Part 1'. The session was produced by Pink Floyd, engineered by Alan Parsons and assisted by Peter James.

WEDNESDAY 31 MAY – RECORDING SESSION
Studio 3 & Control Room 3, EMI Studios, Abbey Road, London, England

2.30pm to 9.15pm: Organ, Electric Piano, Volume Pedal Guitar, Harmony Vocals overdubbed onto Take 5 of 'Eclipse Part 1' ['Breathe']; "Leslie Speaker Noise" for lead into 'Eclipse Part 2' ['On The Run'] recorded; and 'Eclipse Part 2' recorded (Take 1, untimed) for *The Dark Side of the Moon*. The session was produced by Pink Floyd, engineered by Alan Parsons and assisted by Peter James.

THURSDAY 1 JUNE – RECORDING SESSION
Studio 3 & Control Room 3, EMI Studios,
Abbey Road, London, England

2.30pm to 12.30am: 'Eclipse Part 3' ['Us And Them'] recorded (Take 1 False Start, Take 2 at 8:30 and marked "best") and Guitar, Cymbals, Bass, Piano, Vocals and Harmony Vocals overdubbed onto Take 2 of 'Eclipse Part 3' for *The Dark Side of the Moon*. The session was produced by Pink Floyd, engineered by Alan Parsons and assisted by Peter James.

FRIDAY 2 JUNE – RECORD RELEASE (UK)
Obscured by Clouds

The *NME* wrote, "Despite some poor production work, this is a most satisfying, comprehensive album from Floyd. It shows that not only are they masters of their instruments, but also able song-writers."

FRIDAY 2 JUNE – RECORDING SESSION
Studio 3 & Control Room 3, EMI Studios,
Abbey Road, London, England

2.30pm to 11.15am: Piano, Vocals and Harmony Vocals re-dubbed onto Take 2 of 'Eclipse Part 3' ['Us And Them'] and 'Eclipse Part 5' ['Brain Damage'] recorded (Take 1 untimed) for *The Dark Side of the Moon*. The session was produced by Pink Floyd, engineered by Alan Parsons and assisted by Peter James.

SATURDAY 3 JUNE – RECORDING SESSION
Studio 3 & Control Room 3, EMI Studios,
Abbey Road, London, England

2.30pm to 12.30am: 'Eclipse Parts 5 & 6' ['Brain Damage' / 'Eclipse'] (Take 1 False Start, Take 2 Untimed, Takes 3 & 4 False Starts and Take 5 at 5:30 and marked "best"); and Vocals and Harmony Vocals overdubbed onto Take 5 of 'Eclipse Part 5' ['Brain Damage'] for *The Dark Side of the Moon*. The session was produced by Pink Floyd, engineered by Alan Parsons and assisted by Peter James.

TUESDAY 6 JUNE – RECORDING SESSION
Studio 2 & Control Room 2, EMI Studios,
Abbey Road, London, England

2.30pm to 1.45am: Vocals and Harmony Vocals overdubbed on the middle-eights of 'Eclipse Parts 5 & 6' ['Brain Damage' / 'Eclipse']; Tape Loops made for 'The Money Song' from various sound effects; and 'The Money Song' recorded (Take 1 untimed) for *The Dark Side of the Moon*. The session was produced by Pink Floyd, engineered by Alan Parsons and assisted by Peter James.

WEDNESDAY 7 JUNE – RECORDING SESSION
Studio 2 & Control Room 2, EMI Studios,
Abbey Road, London, England

2.30pm to 1.45am: Backing track for 'The Money Song' recorded (Take 1 also marked "best") and Guitar, Vocals, Electric Piano, Guitar Solo and Drums overdubbed onto Take 1 of 'The Money Song' for *The Dark Side of the Moon*. The session was produced by Pink Floyd, engineered by Alan Parsons and assisted by Peter James.

THURSDAY 8 JUNE – RECORDING SESSION
Studio 2 & Control Room 2, EMI Studios,
Abbey Road, London, England

2.30pm to 1.00am: Electric Piano, Piano, Drums and Trombone overdubbed onto Take 1 of 'The Money Song'; Click Track and Backing Track recorded the for 'Time Song' and 'Time Song' recorded (Take 1 also marked "best") for *The Dark Side of the Moon*. The session was produced by Pink Floyd, engineered by Alan Parsons and assisted by Peter James.

FRIDAY 9 JUNE – RECORDING SESSION
Studio 2 & Control Room 2, EMI Studios,
Abbey Road, London, England

2.30pm to 12.30am: Vocals, Harmony Vocals, Guitar, and Electric Piano overdubbed onto Take 1 of the 'Time Song'; Clocks and Chimes overdubbed onto Take 1 of 'Time Song'; and Piano and Guitar overdubbed onto the beginning of Take 1 of 'Time Song' for *The Dark Side of the Moon*. The session was produced by Pink Floyd, engineered by Alan Parsons and assisted by Peter James.

SATURDAY 10 JUNE – RECORDING SESSION
Studio 2 & Control Room 2, EMI Studios,
Abbey Road, London, England

2.30pm to 12.00midnight: Roto-Toms and Farfisa overdubbed onto Take 1 of 'Time Song'; 'Home Again' edited onto Take 1 of 'Time Song'; and Farfisa, Guitar, Vocals, Harmony Vocals and Electric Piano overdubbed onto Take 1 of 'Time Song' for *The Dark Side of the Moon*. The session was produced by Pink Floyd, engineered by Alan Parsons and assisted by Peter James.

TUESDAY 13 JUNE – RECORDING SESSION
Studio 2 & Control Room 2, EMI Studios,
Abbey Road, London, England

2.30pm to 6.00pm: 'Eclipse Part 2' re-recorded ['On The Run'] (Take 5 also marked "best"); Click-Track Tape Loop made up for Take 5 of 'Eclipse Part 2', and 7.00pm to 12.30am: Tapes of "Weird Noises" and "More Weird Noises" supplied by Pink Floyd and overdubbed onto Take 5 of 'Eclipse Part 2' for *The Dark Side of the Moon*. The session was produced by Pink Floyd, engineered by Alan Parsons and assisted by Peter James.

WEDNESDAY 14 JUNE – RECORDING SESSION
Studio 2 & Control Room 2, EMI Studios,
Abbey Road, London, England

2.30pm to 6.00pm: Bass, Drums and Guitar re-dubbed onto Take 5 of 'Eclipse Part 2' ['On The Run']; Cymbals overdubbed onto Take 5 of 'Eclipse Part 2', and 7.00pm to 12.30am: Drums overdubbed onto Take 5 of 'Eclipse Part 2' for *The Dark Side of the Moon*. The session was produced by Pink Floyd, engineered by Alan Parsons and assisted by Peter James.

THURSDAY 15 JUNE – RECORDING SESSION
Studio 2 & Control Room 2, EMI Studios,
Abbey Road, London, England

2.30pm to 7.00pm and 8.00pm to 12.00 midnight: Bass, Drums and Hi-Hat re-dubbed onto Take 5 of 'Eclipse Part 2' ['On The Run'];

OBSCURED BY CLOUDS

SIDE ONE

OBSCURED BY CLOUDS (Gilmour, Waters) 3:05
WHEN YOU'RE IN (Gilmour, Waters, Wright, Mason) 2:31
BURNING BRIDGES (Wright, Waters) 3:30
THE GOLD IT'S IN THE... (Gilmour, Waters) 3:08
WOT'S... UH THE DEAL (Gilmour, Waters) 5:09
MUDMEN (WRIGHT, GILMOUR) 4:18

SIDE TWO

CHILDHOOD'S END (Gilmour) 4:33
FREE FOUR (Waters) 4:17
STAY (Waters, Wright) 4:08
ABSOLUTELY CURTAINS (Wright) 5:53

RELEASE DATE

UK: Friday 2 June 1972.
US: Saturday 17 June 1972.

FORMAT

UK: EMI Harvest SHSP 4020 (Vinyl album).
US: Harvest ST 11078 (Vinyl album).

CHART

UK: No. 6 (*Melody Maker* 'Top 10' on Saturday 17 June 1972).
US: No. 46 (*Billboard* 'Top LPs & Tape' on Saturday 12 August 1972).

AWARDS

UK: Certified Silver on Tuesday 1 January 1974.
US: Certified Gold on Friday 11 March 1994.

ARTWORK

The deliberately out of focus cover features a figure in a tree, adapted from a still from the film.

MUSICIANS

David Gilmour (Guitars, Vocals, EMS VCS3).
Nick Mason (Drums, Percussion, Tape Effects).
Roger Waters (Bass Guitar, Vocals, EMS VCS3, Tape Effects).
Richard Wright (Hammond, Farfisa, Piano, Vocals, EMS VCS3).

RECORDING DETAILS

Pink Floyd's second feature film soundtrack for Barbet Schroeder was for his film *La Vallée* and centred around a journey of self-discovery set in New Guinea. Released as *Obscured By Clouds* it was recorded at Strawberry Studios, Chateau d'Hérouville, near Paris, France between 23–29 February and 23–27 March 1972 and produced entirely by Pink Floyd.

Typically the soundtrack contains different versions to that of the album release and the song 'Free Four' has different lyrics, and the ending of 'Absolutely Curtains' is sung by the cast. Unfortunately no studio records exist of these sessions, and few details have been revealed in contemporary or subsequent interviews.

Apparently Schroeder didn't want Pink Floyd to provide music in such a literal sense as was true of their work on *More*. Consequently the music on the DVD is sparse to say the least, and what is included is barely audible, the title track having the greatest exposure because it is played over the opening titles; the remainder are heard in the background as excerpts and, more often than not, so is the cassette player of the Land Rover in which the central characters explore the island. The tracks 'Mudmen' and 'Stay' do not appear in the film.

La Vallée was premiered at the *Venice International Film Festival* in August 1972 and once again cemented Pink Floyd's popularity in continental Europe and especially France.

Live, the band performed 'Obscured by Clouds' and 'When You're In' as part of the Ballets de Marseille season in France in November 1972 and again in Paris in January 1973. 'Childhood's End' featured as an encore on the tail end of their European tour in December 1972 and featured an extended blues jam in the middle, in some cases extending the track to over 10 minutes long, and featured some exceptional Hammond work from Richard Wright. Throughout 1973 Pink Floyd often opened the show with an extended drone leading into 'Obscured by Clouds' which segued into 'When You're In', and the set again often featured 'Childhood's End'. Gilmour has been the only solo member to perform anything from that album since that time with a rendition of 'Wot's... Uh The Deal' on his 2006 *On an Island* tour.

Hi-Hat overdubbed onto Take 5 of 'Eclipse Part 2'; Piano, White Noise and VCS3 overdubbed onto Take 5 of 'Eclipse Part 2'; and Take 5 of 'Eclipse Part 2' edited for *The Dark Side of the Moon*. The session was produced by Pink Floyd, engineered by Alan Parsons and assisted by Peter James.

FRIDAY 16 JUNE – RECORDING SESSION
Studio 2 & Control Room 2, EMI Studios, Abbey Road, London, England

2.30pm to 7.30pm and 8.30pm to 12.00midnight: 'Eclipse Part 3' ['Us And Them'] recorded (Take 1 untimed); Lead Guitar and Vocals overdubbed onto Take 1 of 'Eclipse Part 3'; and Take 1 of 'Eclipse Part 3' edited for *The Dark Side of the Moon*. The session was produced by Pink Floyd, engineered by Alan Parsons and assisted by Peter James.

SATURDAY 17 JUNE – ALBUM RELEASE (US)
Obscured by Clouds

Crawdaddy wrote, "The Floyd have discovered a sense of direction that has been lacking in their work since *Ummagumma*. If they can follow this up it may lead them back to their position as the premier space-rock band."

SATURDAY 17 JUNE – RECORDING SESSION
Studio 2 & Control Room 2, EMI Studios, Abbey Road, London, England

2.30pm to 6.30pm and 7.30pm to 11.30pm: 'Eclipse (Scat Section)' ['Any Colour You Like'] recorded (Take 1 untimed); Organ and VCS3 overdubbed onto Take 1 of 'Eclipse' for *The Dark Side of the Moon*. The session was produced by Pink Floyd, engineered by Alan Parsons and assisted by Peter James.

TUESDAY 20 JUNE – RECORDING SESSION
Studio 3 & Control Room 3, EMI Studios, Abbey Road, London, England

2.30pm to 12.00midnight: Choir on Middle Eights overdubbed onto 'Us And Them'; Choir overdubbed onto 'End Song' ['Eclipse']; 'Religious Theme' ['The Great Gig In The Sky'] recorded (Take 1 at 6:00 also marked "best"); Choir overdubbed onto verses of 'Time Song'; and Choir overdubbed onto middle-eights of 'Lunatic Song' ['Brain Damage'] for *The Dark Side of the Moon*. The session was produced by Pink Floyd, engineered by Alan Parsons and assisted by Peter James.

WEDNESDAY 21 JUNE – RECORDING SESSION
Studio 3 & Control Room 3, EMI Studios, Abbey Road, London, England

2.30pm to 7.00pm 'Religious Theme' ['The Great Gig In The Sky'] re-recorded (Take 1; also marked "best"), and 8.00pm to 12.30am: Organ and Piano overdubbed onto Take 1 of 'Religious Theme' ['The Great Gig In The Sky'] for *The Dark Side of the Moon*. The band also attended a one-hour quadraphonic demonstration in Studio 1 during the day. The session was produced by Pink Floyd, engineered by Alan Parsons and assisted by Peter James.

THURSDAY 22 JUNE – RECORDING SESSION
Studio 3 & Control Room 3, EMI Studios, Abbey Road, London, England

3.30pm to 7.00pm: Organ and Vocals overdubbed onto Take 5 of 'Breathe In The Air' and 8.00pm to 11.30pm: VCS3 and Electric Piano overdubbed onto Take 1 of 'Time Song'; 'Religious Section' ['The Great Gig In The Sky'] re-recorded (Take 2 breakdown and Take 3 untimed); and Hammond overdubbed onto Take 3 of 'Religious Section' for *The Dark Side of the Moon*. The session was produced by Pink Floyd, engineered by Alan Parsons and assisted by Peter James.

FRIDAY 23 JUNE – CANCELLED PERFORMANCE
Bièvres Festival, Bièvre, France

Pink Floyd cancelled an advertised appearance due to recording commitments at this three-day festival (Friday 23 to Sunday 25 June). It was organized by the French collective group Crium Delirium and featured performances by Soft Machine, Matching Mole, Amon Düül II, Kevin Ayers, Hawkwind, Third World War, Pink Fairies, Gong, Lard Free, Dagon, Catharis, Komintern, Moving Gelatine Plates, Opus N, Higelin, Fontaine, Areski and Catherine Ribiero with free jazz, Magic Circus and Le Cirque Bonjour.

FRIDAY 23 JUNE – RECORDING SESSION
Studio 3 & Control Room 3, EMI Studios, Abbey Road, London, England

4.30pm to 7.00pm: Harmony Vocals overdubbed onto Take 5 of 'Breathe In The Air', and 8.00pm to 12.00am: 'Intro' ['Speak To Me'], 'Breathe In The Air', 'Travel Section' ['On The Run'] and 'Rock 'n' Roll' [an extended jam that originally formed part of 'On The Run'] were transferred to a 16-track Dolby master tape for *The Dark Side of the Moon*. The session was produced by Pink Floyd, engineered by Alan Parsons and assisted by Peter James.

SATURDAY 24 JUNE – RECORDING SESSION
Studio 3 & Control Room 3, EMI Studios, Abbey Road, London, England

2.30pm to 2.00am: 'Time Song', 'Home Again' ['Breathe (Reprise)'] and 'Religious Theme' ['The Great Gig In The Sky'] transferred to a 16-track Dolby master tape and marked "to be completed in October". A rough mix of all titles was also done, and Alan Parsons' "Clock" sound effect was transferred from 4-track to 2-track stereo for *The Dark Side of the Moon*. The session was produced by Pink Floyd, engineered by Alan Parsons and assisted by Peter James.

WEDNESDAY 28 & THURSDAY 29 JUNE – PERFORMANCES
The Dome, Brighton, England

Set list at both shows: *The Dark Side of the Moon* <Intermission> 'One Of These Days', 'Careful With That Axe, Eugene', 'Echoes', 'Set The Controls For The Heart Of The Sun' <Encore> 'A Saucerful Of Secrets'.

As at Manchester, two shows were arranged as a replacement for the shows that had been abandoned in January. The show on the 29 June was filmed by Peter Clifton for inclusion in his 104-minute film *Sound of the City 1964–1973* (also known as *Rock City*). Clips of this material occasionally appear on television and compilation videos, invariably 'Careful With That Axe, Eugene', which has also appeared on the video release S*uperstars in Concert.*

WEDNESDAY 5 JULY – RECORDING SESSION
Control Room 2, EMI Studios, Abbey Road, London, England

7.00pm to 12.30am: Edited rough mixes made of 'Intro (Breathe In The Air)', 'Travel Section' and crossfades with SFX superimposed onto 'Rock 'n' Roll', 'Time Song', 'Home Again' and 'Religious Theme' for *The Dark Side of the Moon*. The session was produced by Pink Floyd, engineered by Alan Parsons and assisted by Peter James.

SATURDAY 8 JULY – RECORDING SESSION
Control Room 2, EMI Studios, Abbey Road, London, England

2.30pm to 7.00pm: Edited rough mixes made of 'Money Song', 'Us And Them', and 8.00pm to 12.30am: Edited rough mixes made of 'Scat' ['Any Colour You Like'], 'Lunatic Song' ['Brain Damage'] and 'End' ['Eclipse'], and various cross-fades done for *The Dark Side of the Moon*. The session was produced by Pink Floyd, engineered by Alan Parsons and assisted by Peter James. The band returned to the studio on 10 October to resume work on the album.

MONDAY 10 JULY – SINGLE RELEASE (US)
'Free Four'

FRIDAY 4 AUGUST – TELEVISION BROADCAST
Optische Eindrücke Der Musik Von Pink Floyd, ARD TV, West Germany

ARD regional TV (Bremen) broadcast a one-off special entitled *Optische Eindrücke der Musik von Pink Floyd* [*Optical Impressions of the Music of Pink Floyd*], the content of which is unknown. It was broadcast between 9.40pm and 10.45pm.

SATURDAY 26 AUGUST – CANCELLED PERFORMANCE
Arena Pop Festival, Arena di Verona, Verona, Italy

Pink Floyd were reported in the music press to be appearing at this event alongside America, Jefferson Airplane and many other groups, but the event never got beyond the planning stages due to strong local and press opposition. However, Pink Floyd would perform at this spectacular venue, one of the most preserved Roman arenas in the world, which is mainly devoted to classical music, some 27 years later.

SATURDAY 2 SEPTEMBER – FILM PREMIERE
Pink Floyd Live at Pompeii, 26th Edinburgh Film Festival, Cameo Cinema, Tollcross, Edinburgh, Scotland

The film was described in the festival programme as "the first live performance at Pompeii in 2,000 years", adding that, "there has not been a film made about any group to beat this for all round quality and technical presentation."

NORTH AMERICAN TOUR

Early drafts of Pink Floyd's tour show the band scheduled to appear at the Community Center Arena, Tucson, on Monday 11 September (rescheduled to Friday 15 September) and Seattle Arena, Seattle, on Friday 29 September (rescheduled to Hec Edmundson Pavilion, University of Washington, Seattle).

FRIDAY 8 SEPTEMBER – PERFORMANCE ▶
Municipal Auditorium, Austin, TX, USA

Set list included: *The Dark Side of the Moon*.

SATURDAY 9 SEPTEMBER – PERFORMANCE
Music Hall, Houston, TX, USA

Set list included: *The Dark Side of the Moon*.

SUNDAY 10 SEPTEMBER – PERFORMANCE ▶
McFarlin Auditorium, Southern Methodist University, Dallas, TX, USA

Set list: *The Dark Side of the Moon*. <Intermission> 'One Of These Days', 'Careful With That Axe, Eugene', 'Set The Controls For The Heart Of The Sun' <Encore> 'Echoes'.

MONDAY 11 SEPTEMBER – PERFORMANCE
Memorial Hall, Kansas City, MO, USA

Set list: *The Dark Side of the Moon* <Intermission> 'One Of These Days', 'Careful With That Axe, Eugene', 'Echoes'.

TUESDAY 12 SEPTEMBER – PERFORMANCE
Civic Center Music Hall, Oklahoma City, OK, USA

Set list: *The Dark Side of the Moon* <Intermission> 'One Of These Days', 'Careful With That Axe, Eugene', 'Echoes' <Encore> 'Set The Controls For The Heart Of The Sun'.

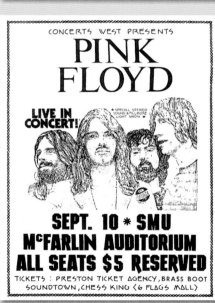

WEDNESDAY 13 SEPTEMBER – PERFORMANCE
Henry Levitt Arena, Wichita State University, Wichita, KS, USA

Set list included: *The Dark Side of the Moon*.

FRIDAY 15 SEPTEMBER – PERFORMANCE
Community Center Arena, Tucson, AZ, USA

Set list: *The Dark Side of the Moon* <Intermission> 'One Of These Days', 'Careful With That Axe, Eugene', 'Echoes' <Encore> 'Set The Controls For The Heart Of The Sun'.

SATURDAY 16 SEPTEMBER – PERFORMANCE
Golden Hall, Community Concourse, San Diego, CA, USA

Set list: *The Dark Side of the Moon* <Intermission> 'One Of These Days', 'Careful With That Axe, Eugene', 'Echoes' <Encore> 'Set The Controls For The Heart Of The Sun'.

SUNDAY 17 SEPTEMBER – PERFORMANCE
Big Surf, Tempe, AZ, USA

Set list: *The Dark Side of the Moon* <Intermission> 'One Of These Days', 'Careful With That Axe, Eugene', 'Echoes'.

The *New Times* reported, "Pink Floyd, chief explorers into the music of Space, appeared oddly in Tempe on Sunday night. A crowd entered Big Surf, looked at the speakers on their four sides, the mountain of equipment onstage surrounded by banks of coloured lights, said 'wow' and sat down. Gradually a heartbeat hit them from behind, lights begin to revolve in Mason's clear drums, a dense bank of green fog rolls onto the stage, towers of lights raise themselves high into the air and Pink Floyd begins with words from Music from the Body. Using loud effects, Pink Floyd played most of their latest album, *Obscured by Clouds* [reviewer error – this should be *The Dark Side of the Moon*], ending with the appearance of a yellow disc of light above the band. After intermission, they returned with 'One Of These Days', which was so engulfing, the audience could not help but be merged with the flashing lights. At this point we knew something was happening here in music that had needed to happen for a long time – that we couldn't criticise, analyse, evaluate or resist. After the stage exploded with light and flame during a piece from *Ummagumma* and Pink Floyd followed with 'Echoes', a long supermellow thing, it was no wonder that the wind started blowing and the rain falling. Roger Waters stopped, said rain could mean instant death to their sound stage. Pink Floyd was over."

TUESDAY 19 SEPTEMBER – PERFORMANCE
University of Denver Arena, Denver, CO, USA

Set list: *The Dark Side of the Moon* <Intermission> 'One Of These Days', 'Careful With That Axe, Eugene', 'Echoes' <Encore> 'Set The Controls For The Heart Of The Sun'.

FRIDAY 22 SEPTEMBER – PERFORMANCE ▶
Hollywood Bowl, Hollywood, Los Angeles, CA, USA

Set list: *The Dark Side of the Moon* <Intermission> 'One Of These Days', 'Careful With That Axe, Eugene', 'Echoes', 'A Saucerful Of Secrets' <Encore> 'Set The Controls For The Heart Of The Sun'.

Amusement Business reported, "Following a concert in San

Diego, 125 miles away, Floyd technicians flew to Los Angeles to prepare for the Bowl show. They required three days to set up special lighting on stage, and over the band shell. The Chester Stumph fireworks company of San Bernardino was brought in to rig up a display. Night before the show cast and crew went through a three-hour technical workout. Part of the Bowl's movable front stage was detached so fireworks could be set up in the lagoon separating stage from box seats. Quad sound was set up all around the Bowl's 18,000 seating arena, and special lights were rigged in towers alongside box seats."

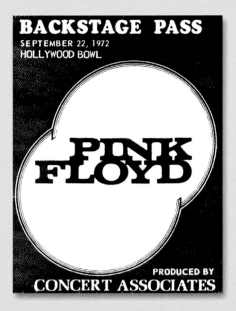

SATURDAY 23 SEPTEMBER – PERFORMANCE
Winterland Auditorium, San Francisco, CA, USA

Rescheduled from Santa Clara Fairground, San Jose.
Set list: *The Dark Side of the Moon* <Intermission> 'One Of These Days', 'Careful With That Axe, Eugene', 'Echoes' <Encore> 'A Saucerful Of Secrets'.

SUNDAY 24 SEPTEMBER – PERFORMANCE
Winterland Auditorium, San Francisco, CA, USA

Set list: *The Dark Side of the Moon* <Intermission> 'One Of These Days', 'Careful With That Axe, Eugene', 'Echoes' <Encore> 'Set The Controls For The Heart Of The Sun'.

WEDNESDAY 27 SEPTEMBER – PERFORMANCE
Garden Auditorium, Vancouver, Canada

Set list: *The Dark Side of the Moon* <Intermission> 'One Of These Days', 'Careful With That Axe, Eugene', 'Echoes' <Encore> 'Set The Controls For The Heart Of The Sun'.

Prior to the show a press conference was held at the Rembrandt hotel, attended by the Canadian media, along with crews from CBC TV, although exact broadcast details could not be found.

The *Vancouver Free Press* reported, "Pink Floyd are definitely a band whose multisensory stage performance lends them open-air performances; the confines of the Gardens Arena just don't do justice to David Gilmour's brilliant guitar playing – full of floating shadows – or the various lighting and theatric smoke and fire effects that the band have become known for. After a half-hour delay while the stage crew hassled with some of the equipment needed to run the quadraphonic sound system that is being used on this tour, the crowd was silenced by an insistent throbbing beat that passed around the four speakers (two of them situated midway back in the audience) and grew to the guitar introduction of the first number. Smoke had poured from outlets near the back of the stage during the beginning of this number and it hung in the air reflecting various coloured spotlights as the band worked into the second piece which gave the first real glimpses of Gilmour's brilliance on guitar."

THURSDAY 28 SEPTEMBER – PERFORMANCE
Memorial Coliseum, Portland, OR, USA

Set list: *The Dark Side of the Moon* <Intermission> 'One Of These Days', 'Careful With That Axe, Eugene', 'Echoes' <Encore> 'Set The Controls For The Heart Of The Sun'.

NORTHWEST RELEASING

COMING EVENTS

NORTHWEST RELEASING

PINK FLOYD

Hec Edmundson Pavilion
Friday, Sept. 29   8 p.m.

Sponsored by KOL, NW Releasing and
the ASUW.
Tickets: $3.00 for students (available in
the HUB); $4.00 for non-students in advance;
$5.00 at the door. Available at the Bon
Marche, Campus Music and all suburban
outlets.

FRIDAY 29 SEPTEMBER – PERFORMANCE ◄
Hec Edmundson Pavilion, University of Washington, Seattle, WA, USA

Set list included: *The Dark Side of the Moon* <Intermission> 'One Of These Days', 'Careful With That Axe, Eugene', 'Echoes' <Encore> 'Set The Controls For The Heart Of The Sun'.

SATURDAY 30 SEPTEMBER – PERFORMANCE
Garden Auditorium, Vancouver, Canada

Set list: *The Dark Side of the Moon* <Intermission> 'One Of These Days', 'Careful With That Axe, Eugene', 'Echoes' <Encore> 'Set The Controls For The Heart Of The Sun'.

TUESDAY 10 OCTOBER – RECORDING SESSION
Studio 2 & Control Room 2, EMI Studios, Abbey Road, London, England

2.30pm to 6.30pm: 'Intro' ['Speak To Me'], 'Breathe In The Air', 'Travel Section' ['On The Run'], 'Rock n Roll' [part of 'On The Run'], 'Time Song' transferred and edited from 16-track to 16-track Dolby, and 7.30pm to 12.30am: 'Home Again' ['Breathe (Reprise)'], 'Money Song', 'Us And Them' and 'Scat' ['Any Colour You Like'] transferred and edited from 16-track to 16-track Dolby for *The Dark Side of the Moon*. The session was produced by Pink Floyd, engineered by Alan Parsons and assisted by Peter James.

WEDNESDAY 11 OCTOBER – RECORDING SESSION
Studio 2 & Control Room 2, EMI Studios, Abbey Road, London, England

2.30pm to 1.00am: 'Scat' ['Any Colour You Like'], 'Lunatic Song' ['Brain Damage'] and 'End' ['Eclipse'] transferred and edited from 16-track to 16-track Dolby; Bass Guitar overdubbed onto

Take 5 of 'Travel Section' ['On The Run'] and Take 2 of 'Us And Them'; and Organ overdubbed onto Take 5 of 'Lunatic Song' ['Brain Damage'] and Take 5 of 'End' ['Eclipse'] for *The Dark Side of the Moon*. The session was produced by Pink Floyd, engineered by Alan Parsons and assisted by Peter James.

THURSDAY 12 OCTOBER – RECORDING SESSION
Studio 2 & Control Room 2, EMI Studios, Abbey Road, London, England

2.30pm to 11.00pm: Bass Guitar overdubbed onto Take 2 of 'Us And Them' and Take 5 of 'Lunatic Song End' ['Brain Damage']; Piano overdubbed onto Take 2 of 'Us And Them'; Synthesizer overdubbed onto Take 5 of 'Travel Section' ['On The Run']; and Synthesizer Noises recorded (Take 1 untimed and marked "best") for Take 5 of 'Travel Section' for *The Dark Side of the Moon*. The session was produced by Pink Floyd, engineered by Alan Parsons and assisted by Peter James.

SUNDAY 15 OCTOBER – RECORDING SESSION
Studio 2 & Control Room 2, EMI Studios, Abbey Road, London, England

2.30pm to 1.30am: Synthesizer Noises overdubbed onto Take 5 of 'Travel Section' ['On The Run'], Take 5 of 'Travel Section' remixed (RS1 at 5:35 and marked "best") and dubbed onto master tape for *The Dark Side of the Moon*. The session was produced by Pink Floyd, engineered by Alan Parsons and assisted by Peter James. Three hours at the start of the day are noted for the setting up of filming of what would become inserts for *Live at Pompeii*.

MONDAY 16 OCTOBER – RECORDING SESSION
Studio 2 & Control Room 2, EMI Studios, Abbey Road, London, England

2.30pm to 11.00pm: Take 5 of 'Travel Section (Synthesiser)' remixed (RS2 untimed); Saxophone (Dick Parry) overdubbed onto Take 2 of 'Us And Them'; and Drums, Guitar and Electric Piano overdubbed onto Take 5 of 'Travel Section' ['On The Run'] for *The Dark Side of the Moon*. The session was produced by Pink Floyd, engineered by Alan Parsons and assisted by Peter James. Filming took place throughout the day for inserts for *Live at Pompeii*. Interviews were also filmed in the studio canteen at lunchtime.

TUESDAY 17 OCTOBER – RECORDING SESSION
Studio 2 & Control Room 2, EMI Studios, Abbey Road, London, England

2.30pm to 6.00pm: Synthesized Electric Guitar overdubbed onto Take 1 of 'Time Song'; Piano overdubbed onto Take 2 of 'Us And Them', and 7.00pm to 11.30pm: Guitar, Piano and Bass Guitar overdubbed onto Take 5 of 'Lunatic Song' ['Brain Damage'] for *The Dark Side of the Moon*. The session was produced by Pink Floyd, engineered by Alan Parsons and assisted by Peter James. The last day of studio filming took place throughout the day for *Live at Pompeii*.

SATURDAY 21 OCTOBER – PERFORMANCE ▼
Empire Pool, Wembley, London, England

A benefit show for War on Want, the Albany Trust Deptford and
Save the Children Fund.
Set list: *The Dark Side of the Moon* (with Dick Parry on Saxophone)
<Intermission> 'One Of These Days', 'Careful With That Axe, Eugene',
'Echoes' <Encore> 'Set The Controls For The Heart Of The Sun', 'Blues'.

Sounds reported, "From the word go, they gave the packed stadium
a faultless demonstration of what psychedelic music is all about.
There wasn't a note, or a sound, out of place during the whole
evening. It's a recital more than a concert, and the Floyd don't so
much give us numbers as perform pieces of music, lasting up to
an hour each. For starters, on Saturday, we had that lengthy work
entitled 'Dark Side of the Moon', an eerie title for an equally eerie

piece of music that takes the listener
through a host of different moods,
most of which are accompanied by
unusual sounds stretching around
his head by way of the group's
quadraphonic sound system. The
effect is quite stunning. The second
half of the recital was composed
of three more major pieces, and a
couple of encores. The first – the
riveting 'Set The Controls For The
Heart Of The Sun' – was obviously rehearsed, but the second – a
bluesy jam – wasn't. It served a useful purpose to show that the
group are not confined to playing science fiction soundtrack music
all the time. The incendiary gimmicks from the stage frequently
obliterated the artists. Flash-bombs erupted here and there at well
timed places, and Roger Waters gong actually became a blazing sun
during 'Set The Controls'. All the time the group were effectively
illuminated by their imposing lighting tower at the rear of the
stage which served a dual purpose – at frequent intervals it belched
out smoke which mingled with the coloured lights and the dry ice
surface mist to effectively whisk us all away to Planet Floyd."

WEDNESDAY 25 OCTOBER – RECORDING SESSION
Studio 1 & Studio 2 & Control Room 2, EMI Studios,
Abbey Road, London, England

2.30pm to 6.00pm and 7.30pm to 12.45am: Piano and Drums
overdubbed onto Take 3 of 'Religious Section' ['The Great
Gig In The Sky'] for *The Dark Side of the Moon*. The session
was produced by Pink Floyd, engineered by Alan Parsons and
assisted by Peter James.

Although it wasn't common practice for acts to record from a
different studio to control room, Wright's piano part for 'Religious
section' ['The Great Gig In The Sky'] was recorded on a concert
Steinway Grand which was kept in Studio 1, traditionally the large
classical music recording studio at Abbey Road. Mason's drums,
however, were recorded in Studio 2.

THURSDAY 26 OCTOBER – RECORDING SESSION
Studio 2 & Control Room 2, EMI Studios,
Abbey Road, London, England

2.30pm to 6.00pm: Tape of "Rick walking away from piano"
overdubbed onto Take 3 of 'Religious Section' ['The Great Gig In
The Sky'], and 7.00pm to 12.30am Bass Guitar, Hammond Organ

and Steel Guitar overdubbed onto Take 3 of 'Religious Section'
for *The Dark Side of the Moon*. The session was produced by Pink
Floyd, engineered by Alan Parsons and assisted by Peter James.

FRIDAY 27 OCTOBER – RECORDING SESSION
Studio 2 & Control Room 2, EMI Studios,
Abbey Road, London, England

2.30pm to 7.00pm and 8.00pm to 1.00am: Saxophone (Dick
Parry) overdubbed onto Take 1 of 'Money Song' and Take 1
of 'Us And Them', and Guitar overdubbed onto Take 1 of
'Money Song' for *The Dark Side of the Moon*. The session was
produced by Pink Floyd, engineered by Alan Parsons and
assisted by Peter James.

MONDAY 30 OCTOBER – RECORDING SESSION
Studio 2 & Control Room 2, EMI Studios,
Abbey Road, London, England

2.30pm to 7.00pm and 8.00pm to 10.30pm: Electric Guitar and
Cymbals overdubbed onto Take 1 of 'Money Song' for *The Dark Side
of the Moon*. The session was produced by Pink Floyd, engineered by
Alan Parsons and assisted by Peter James.

TUESDAY 31 OCTOBER – RECORDING SESSION
Studio 2 & Control Room 2, EMI Studios,
Abbey Road, London, England

2.30pm to 11.00pm: Steel Guitar overdubbed onto Take 5 of
'Breathe In The Air' and 'Travel Section' ['On The Run'], and
'Time Song' edited for *The Dark Side of the Moon*. The session was
produced by Pink Floyd, engineered by Alan Parsons and assisted
by Peter James.

WEDNESDAY 1 NOVEMBER – RECORDING SESSION
Studio 2 & Control Room 2, EMI Studios,
Abbey Road, London, England

3.30pm to 7.00pm: Drum Heartbeat and "Silly Solo" overdubbed
onto Take 1 of 'Time Song (Intro)', and 8.00pm to 1.00am: Guitar
Solo overdubbed onto Take 1 of 'Time Song (Intro)' and VCS3
overdubbed onto Take 1 of 'Scat' ['Any Colour You Like'] for *The
Dark Side of the Moon*. The session was produced by Pink Floyd,
engineered by Alan Parsons and assisted by Peter James.

THURSDAY 2 NOVEMBER – RECORDING SESSION
Studio 2 & Control Room 2, EMI Studios,
Abbey Road, London, England

2.30pm to 7.00pm: Guitar overdubbed onto Take 1 of 'Money
Song' and Take 1 of 'Time Song', and 8.00pm to 12.30am: Guitar
overdubbed onto Take 5 of 'Lunatic Song' ['Brain Damage'] and
Vocals overdubbed onto Take 5 of 'Lunatic Song' for *The Dark Side
of the Moon*. The session was produced by Pink Floyd, engineered
by Alan Parsons and assisted by Peter James.

FRIDAY 3 NOVEMBER – RECORDING SESSION
Studio 2 & Control Room 2, EMI Studios,
Abbey Road, London, England

2.30pm to 7.00pm: Guitar and VCS3 overdubbed onto Take 5 of
'Lunatic Song' ['Brain Damage'] and a rough mix of Side One of
completed, and 8.00pm to 11.00pm: Various SFX copied for *The Dark*

Side of the Moon. The session was produced by Pink Floyd, engineered by Alan Parsons and assisted by Peter James.

EUROPEAN TOUR

FRIDAY 10 & SATURDAY 11 NOVEMBER – PERFORMANCES
KB Hallen, Copenhagen, Denmark

Set list at both shows: *The Dark Side of the Moon* <Intermission> 'One Of These Days', 'Careful With That Axe, Eugene', 'Echoes' <Encore> 'Set The Controls For The Heart Of The Sun'.

ABOVE: NICK MASON ON STAGE IN COPENHAGEN, 11 NOVEMBER 1972.

SUNDAY 12 NOVEMBER – PERFORMANCE
Ernst-Merck-Halle, Hamburg, West Germany

Set list: *The Dark Side of the Moon* <Intermission> 'One Of These Days', 'Careful With That Axe, Eugene', 'Echoes' <Encore> 'Set The Controls For The Heart Of The Sun'.

TUESDAY 14 NOVEMBER – PERFORMANCE ▼
Philipshalle, Düsseldorf, West Germany

Set list: *The Dark Side of the Moon* <Intermission> 'One Of These Days', 'Careful With That Axe, Eugene', 'Echoes' <Encore> 'Set The Controls For The Heart Of The Sun'.

WEDNESDAY 15 & THURSDAY 16 NOVEMBER –
RECORDING SESSION
Room 4, EMI Studios, Abbey Road, London, England

Remixing *Atom Heart Mother* for the quadraphonic album release. The session was engineered by Alan Parsons and assisted by Peter James. Pink Floyd was not in attendance for this session.

WEDNESDAY 15 NOVEMBER – PERFORMANCE
Sporthalle, Böblingen, West Germany

Set list: *The Dark Side of the Moon* <Intermission> 'Careful With That Axe, Eugene', 'Echoes' (announced by Roger Waters as 'Looking Through The Knotholes In Granny's Wooden Leg') / 'One Of These Days' <Encore> 'Set The Controls For The Heart Of The Sun'.

THURSDAY 16 NOVEMBER – PERFORMANCE
Festhalle, Frankfurt, West Germany

Set list: *The Dark Side of the Moon* <Intermission> 'One Of These Days', 'Careful With That Axe, Eugene', 'Echoes' (announced by Roger Waters as 'The March Of The Dambusters') <Encore> 'Set The Controls For The Heart Of The Sun'.

FRIDAY 17 NOVEMBER – PERFORMANCE
Festhalle, Frankfurt, West Germany

Set list: *The Dark Side of the Moon* <Intermission> 'One Of These Days', 'Careful With That Axe, Eugene', 'Echoes' <Encore> 'Set The Controls For The Heart Of The Sun'.

MONDAY 20 NOVEMBER – RECORDING SESSION
Room 4, EMI Studios, Abbey Road,
London, England

Remixing *Atom Heart Mother* for the quadraphonic album release. The session was engineered by Alan Parsons and assisted by Peter James. Pink Floyd was not in attendance for this session.

LES BALLETS DE MARSEILLE

Pink Floyd's extensive tour of northern Europe also incorporated a season of shows providing the musical accompaniment to the production of Les Ballets de Marseille, directed and choreographed by Roland Petit. The Ballet was presented in three parts:
1. *Allumez les Étoiles* [*Light the Stars*]. A ballet concerning Vladimir Mayakovsky (1893–1930), a poet of the Russian Revolution, with extracts of the works of Prokofiev, Chostakovitch and Moussorgski.
2. *La Rose Malade* [*The Sick Rose*]. A ballet in three movements based on the William Blake poem with extracts from Mahler's 2nd and 5th Symphonies.
3. *The Pink Floyd Ballet*. A ballet in four movements, based on the following set list: 'One Of These Days', 'Careful With That Axe, Eugene', 'Obscured by Clouds', 'When You're In' and 'Echoes'.

MONDAY 20 & TUESDAY 21 NOVEMBER – REHEARSALS
Salle Valliers, Marseille, France

Full production rehearsals for the forthcoming Ballet shows took place on these dates. The rehearsals on Tuesday 21 November were filmed by ORTF TV, including extracts of 'One Of These Days', 'Careful With That Axe, Eugene' and 'Echoes',

ABOVE: ON STAGE IN MARSEILLE, NOVEMBER 1972.

and broadcast (in colour) on the ORTF1 TV regional bulletin *Actualités* [Méditerranée] on Wednesday 22 November between 7.00pm and 7.25pm.

A further feature using different images of the same tracks also filmed in rehearsals, but with live concert audio overdubbed, was broadcast on the ORTF1 TV news bulletin *24 Heures sur la Une* in an article entitled *Pink Floyd Et Ballets Roland Petit* and broadcast (in colour) on Sunday 26 November between 7.45pm and 8.10pm.

WEDNESDAY 22, THURSDAY 23, FRIDAY 24, SATURDAY 25 & SUNDAY 26 NOVEMBER – PERFORMANCES
Salle Valliers, Marseille, France

Set list at all shows: 'One Of These Days', 'Careful With That Axe, Eugene', 'Obscured by Clouds', 'When You're In', 'Echoes'.

SATURDAY 24 NOVEMBER – CANCELLED FILM PREMIERE (UK)
Pink Floyd Live at Pompeii, Rainbow Theatre, Finsbury Park, London, England

The scheduled cinematic premiere of *Pink Floyd Live at Pompeii* was cancelled because the owners of the theatre, the Rank Organisation, gave the promoter just one day's notice of a previously ignored clause in the lease forbidding the promotion of any event that may be deemed to be competitive with its own operations. Rank further claimed that the film had not yet been given a certificate by the British Board of Film Censors, and nearly 3,000 ticket-holders who were not made aware of the problems had to be turned away at the door.

EUROPEAN TOUR CONTINUED

TUESDAY 28 NOVEMBER – PERFORMANCE
Palais des Sports, Toulouse, France

Set list: *The Dark Side of the Moon* <Intermission> 'One Of These Days', 'Careful With That Axe, Eugene', 'Echoes' <Encore> 'Set The Controls For The Heart Of The Sun'.

WEDNESDAY 29 NOVEMBER – PERFORMANCE
Les Arènas, Parc des Expositions, Poitiers, France

Set list: *The Dark Side of the Moon* <Intermission> 'One Of These Days', 'Careful With That Axe, Eugene', 'Echoes'.

Pre-show footage, intercut with a few brief live shots and interviews, were reportedly filmed by regional French TV, although broadcast details could not be found.

FRIDAY 1 DECEMBER – RECORDING SESSION
Control Room 2, EMI Studios, Abbey Road, London, England

10.00am to 6.00pm and 7.30pm to 3.30am: Rough mixes of *The Dark Side of the Moon* album completed, comprising: 'Travel Section' ['On The Run'], 'Time Song', 'Home Again' ['Breathe Reprise'], 'Religious Section' ['The Great Gig In The Sky'], 'Money Song', 'Us And Them' and 'Breathe In The Air'. The session was engineered by Alan Parsons and assisted by Peter James. Pink Floyd was not in attendance for this session.

FRIDAY 1 DECEMBER – PERFORMANCE
Centre sportif de L'Île de Vannes, St Ouen, Paris, France

Set list: *The Dark Side of the Moon* <Intermission> 'One Of These Days', 'Careful With That Axe, Eugene', 'Blues', 'Echoes' <Encore> 'Childhood's End'.

RTL radio, sponsors of the French tour, broadcast the entire show live in a three-hour presentation from 9.00pm.

SATURDAY 2 DECEMBER – PERFORMANCE
Centre Sportif de L'Île de Vannes, St Ouen, Paris, France

Set list: *The Dark Side of the Moon* <Intermission> 'One Of These Days', 'Careful With That Axe, Eugene', 'Echoes' <Encore> 'Childhood's End'.

SUNDAY 3 DECEMBER – PERFORMANCE
Parc des Expositions, Caen, France

Set list: *The Dark Side of the Moon* <Intermission> 'One Of These Days', 'Careful With That Axe, Eugene' <Encore> 'Echoes'.

TUESDAY 5 DECEMBER – PERFORMANCE
Vorst Nationaal, Brussels, Belgium

Set list: *The Dark Side of the Moon* <Intermission> 'One Of These Days', 'Careful With That Axe, Eugene', 'Echoes' <Encore> 'Childhood's End'.

VRT Radio 1 Belgium broadcast an audience recording of the show on Tuesday 1 November 2005, including excerpts of 'Time', 'Breathe (reprise)' and 'Careful With That Axe, Eugene' as part of a Pink Floyd documentary.

THURSDAY 7 DECEMBER – PERFORMANCE
Palais des Sports, Lille, France

Set list: *The Dark Side of the Moon* <Intermission> 'One Of These Days', 'Careful With That Axe, Eugene' <Encore> 'Echoes'.

This show was reportedly very nearly cancelled due to inadequate power supplies to meet Pink Floyd's demands. A compromise was reached and the show went ahead with a reduced lighting rig.

FRIDAY 8 DECEMBER – PERFORMANCE ◄
Parc des Expositions, Nancy, France

Set list: *The Dark Side of the Moon* <Intermission> 'One Of These Days', 'Careful With That Axe, Eugene' <Encore> 'Echoes'.

SATURDAY 9 DECEMBER – PERFORMANCE
Hallenstadion, Zurich, Switzerland

Set list: *The Dark Side of the Moon* <Intermission> 'One Of These Days', 'Careful With That Axe, Eugene' <Encore> 'Echoes', 'Childhood's End'.

SUNDAY 10 DECEMBER – PERFORMANCE
Palais des Sports, Lyon, France

Set list: *The Dark Side of the Moon* <Intermission> 'One Of These Days', 'Careful With That Axe, Eugene' <Encore> 'Echoes'.

The band was delayed at the border by customs authorities and took the stage two hours later than scheduled, at 8.00pm.

THURSDAY 14 DECEMBER – RECORDING SESSION
Studio 2 & Control Room 2, EMI Studios, Abbey Road, London, England

10.00am to 12.00midnight: Recording a live version of 'Careful With That Axe, Eugene' (Take 1 untimed also marked "best") and mixing Take 1 of 'Careful With That Axe, Eugene' (RS1) in preparation for the forthcoming playback concerts with the Roland Petit Ballet in Paris. The session was produced by Pink Floyd, engineered by Alan Parsons and assisted by Micheal Sheady.

FRIDAY 15 DECEMBER – RECORDING SESSION
Control Room 3, EMI Studios, Abbey Road, London, England

10.00am to 1.00pm: Various cross-fades and editing of tracks for *The Dark Side of the Moon*. The session was produced by Pink Floyd and engineered by Alan Parsons.

TUESDAY 19 DECEMBER – RECORDING SESSION
Room 4, EMI Studios, Abbey Road, London, England

7.00pm to 12.00 midnight: Various cross-fades and edits done to complete a rough remix of Side One of *The Dark Side of the Moon*. The session was produced by Pink Floyd and engineered by Alan

Parsons and Peter James. This early remix, made by Alan Parsons, appears on Disc 6 of the *Immersion* box set of *The Dark Side of the Moon* released in September 2011.

THURSDAY 21 DECEMBER – CANCELLED TELEVISION BROADCAST
***Pop Shop*, RTB TV, Belgium**

Pink Floyd was advertised to appear on the RTB–TV music show *Pop Shop*, broadcast between 6.30pm and 7.00pm, but did not appear.

1973

MONDAY 8 JANUARY – RECORDING SESSION
Studio 2 & Control Room 2, EMI Studios, Abbey Road, London, England

10.00am to 2.30am: Editing and copying 'Obscured by Clouds', 'Careful With That Axe, Eugene' (live version), 'One Of These Days'; "Rising Voices" on 'Echoes' cross-faded and edited; and recording Synthesizers in preparation for the forthcoming playback concerts with the Roland Petit Ballet in Paris. The session was produced by Pink Floyd, engineered by Alan Parsons and assisted by Peter James.

LES BALLETS DE MARSEILLE

An additional season of ballet shows was staged in Paris, following the success of those in Marseille. However, due to recording commitments Pink Floyd appeared at only eight of the 16 shows, the remainder of which featured audio playback only on Saturday 20 January (at 5.00pm and 8.45pm); Sunday 21 January (at 2.30pm and 6.00pm); Saturday 27 January (at 5.00pm and 8.45pm) and Sunday 28 January (at 2.30pm and 6.00pm). The shows followed the same programme and also featured the company of Les Ballets de Marseille with Roland Petit as choreographer and artistic director, with the participation of Maya Plisetskaya.

PINK FLOYD ROAD CREW
Chris Adamson (PA, Stage Technician), Graeme Fleming (Lighting Technician), Marek "Mick The Pole" Kluczynski (PA Technician), Arthur Max (Production Manager, Lighting), Robin Murray (Lighting Technician), Alan Parsons (Front of House Sound Engineer), Bobby Richardson (PA, Stage Technician), Robbie Williams (PA, Stage Technician), Peter Watts (Head of PA).

THURSDAY 11 & FRIDAY 12 JANUARY – REHEARSALS ►
Palais des Sports de la Porte de Versailles, Paris, France

Rehearsals on 12 January were filmed by ORTF TV for inclusion in the news bulletin *24 Heures sur la Une* and a segment of 'One Of These Days' was shown in a feature entitled *Pink Floyd Ballet* and broadcast (in black and white) on

ORTF1 TV on Friday 12 January 1973 between 7.45pm and 8.15pm.

A further feature was broadcast on the regional news bulletin *Actualités* [Paris] (in colour) on ORTF1 TV on Tuesday 16 January 1973 between 7.00pm and 7.25pm. This also included a short interview with Roland Petit and David Gilmour (spoken in French), and extracts from 'One Of These Days' and 'Echoes' filmed during the 12 January 1973 rehearsals.

SATURDAY 13 JANUARY – PERFORMANCES
Palais des Sports de la Porte de Versailles, Paris, France

Two shows at 5.00pm and 8.45pm, with the Ballet de Roland Petit. Set list at both shows: 'One Of These Days', 'Careful With That Axe, Eugene', 'Obscured by Clouds', 'When You're In', 'Echoes'.

SUNDAY 14 JANUARY – PERFORMANCES
Palais des Sports de la Porte de Versailles, Paris, France

Two shows at 2.30pm and 6.00pm, with the Ballet de Roland Petit. Set list at both shows: 'One Of These Days', 'Careful With That Axe, Eugene', 'Obscured by Clouds', 'When You're In', 'Echoes'.

THURSDAY 18 JANUARY – RECORDING SESSION
Studio 3 & Control Room 3, EMI Studios,
Abbey Road, London, England

2.30pm to 6.00pm: Recording and overdubbing "Wild Guitar" onto Take 5 of 'Travel Section' ['On The Run']; Recording Drums, Piano and Guitar for the "Big Crash" for the beginning of 'Breathe'; Recording "Wild Guitar" for "Big Crash" for 'Travel Section'; and 7.00pm to 12.00midnight: VCS3 overdubbed onto Take 5 of 'Travel Section' for *The Dark Side of the Moon*. The session was produced by Pink Floyd, engineered by Alan Parsons and assisted by Peter James.

FRIDAY 19 JANUARY – RECORDING SESSION
Studio 3 & Control Room 3, EMI Studios,
Abbey Road, London, England

2.30pm to 7.00pm: Various SFX and VCS3 overdubbed onto Take 5 of 'Travel Section' ['On The Run'], and 8.00pm to 12.00 midnight: Various speech recorded for 'Us And Them' for *The Dark Side of the Moon*. The session was produced by Pink Floyd, engineered by Alan Parsons and assisted by Peter James.

SATURDAY 20 JANUARY – RECORDING SESSION
Studio 3 & Control Room 3, EMI Studios,
Abbey Road, London, England

2.30pm to 12.30am: Piano overdubbed onto "Big Crash" of 'Travel Section'; Remixing "Big Crash" [for 'On The Run'] (RS1 and RS2, untimed); Bass Drum overdubbed onto Take 5 of 'Travel Section' ['On The Run'], and various speech recorded for *The Dark Side of the Moon*. The session was produced by Pink Floyd, engineered by Alan Parsons and assisted by Peter James.

SUNDAY 21 JANUARY – RECORDING SESSION
Studio 3 & Control Room 3, EMI Studios,
Abbey Road, London, England

2.30pm to 6.00pm: 'Time Song' remixed (RS10, untimed) and various speech recorded, and 7.00pm to 1.00am: Vocals (Clare

Torry) overdubbed onto Take 3 of 'Religious Section' ['The Great Gig In The Sky']; and Piano overdubbed onto Take 1 of 'Money Song' for *The Dark Side of the Moon*. The session was produced by Pink Floyd, engineered by Alan Parsons and assisted by Peter James.

WEDNESDAY 24 JANUARY – RECORDING SESSION
Studio 3 & Control Room 3, EMI Studios,
Abbey Road, London, England

2.30pm to 1.00am: 'Big Crash' [for 'On The Run'] remixed (RS unmarked, untimed); rough mixes made of 'Religious Section' ['The Great Gig In The Sky']; Bass Guitar overdubbed onto Take 1 of 'Money Song'; and 'Time Song Intro' remixed (RS11 untimed, RS12 False Start, RS13 to 16 untimed) for *The Dark Side of the Moon*. The session was produced by Pink Floyd, engineered by Alan Parsons and assisted by Peter James.

THURSDAY 25 JANUARY – RECORDING SESSION
Studio 3 & Control Room 3, EMI Studios,
Abbey Road, London, England

2.30pm to 6.00pm: 'Time Song' [intro] remixed (RS17 and RS18 untimed, RS19 edit piece untimed) and 7.00pm to 1.00am: Two hours spent editing speech; and Take 3 of 'Religious Section' remixed (RS10 to RS13 False Starts, RS14 untimed) for *The Dark Side of the Moon*. The session was produced by Pink Floyd, engineered by Alan Parsons and assisted by Peter James.

FRIDAY 26 JANUARY – RECORDING SESSION
Control Room 3, EMI Studios,
Abbey Road, London, England

2.30pm to 2.30am: Take 3 of 'The Great Gig In The Sky (Religious Section)' remixed (RS15 untimed, RS16 and RS17 False Starts, and RS18 marked best edited); Synthesizers on "Wild Tape" recorded for Take 5 of 'Travel Section'; Take 5 of Travel Section remixed (RS1 untimed, RS2 False Start, RS3 and RS4 untimed); and various speech recorded, including "Freaked Out Roger – The Ex-Roadie" for *The Dark Side of the Moon*. The session was produced by Pink Floyd, engineered by Alan Parsons and assisted by Peter James.

SATURDAY 27 JANUARY – RECORDING SESSION
Control Room 3, EMI Studios,
Abbey Road, London, England

2.30pm to 5.00am: Various SFX and Tape Loops brought in by Nick Mason and overdubbed onto "Big Crash" [for 'On The Run']; 'Intro' remixed (RS3 and RS4 untimed, RS5 False Start, RS6, RS7 and RS8 untimed, RS9 and RS10 False Starts, RS11 untimed and marked "best", RS12 and RS13 untimed); and Take 5 of 'Breathe In The Air' remixed (RS10 untimed, RS11, RS12 and RS13 False Starts, RS14 and RS15 untimed, RS16 Machine Breakdown and RS17 untimed) for *The Dark Side of the Moon*. The session was produced by Pink Floyd, engineered by Alan Parsons and assisted by Peter James.

MONDAY 29 JANUARY – RECORDING SESSION
Control Room 2, EMI Studios,
Abbey Road, London, England

10.00pm to 1.30am: Various loops made up from tapes brought in by Nick Mason and overdubbed onto unspecified tracks [possibly forming the origins of 'Speak To Me']; Take 1 of 'Money Song' remixed (RS10 untimed, RS11 and RS12 False Starts, RS13 untimed, RS14 False Starts, RS15 to RS19 untimed) for *The Dark Side of the Moon*. The session was produced by Pink Floyd, engineered by Alan Parsons and assisted by Peter James.

TUESDAY 30 JANUARY – RECORDING SESSION
Control Room 3, EMI Studios,
Abbey Road, London, England

2.30pm to 6.00pm: Take 5 of 'Travel Section' ['On The Run'] remixed (First Part with Roger The Roadie) (RS1 to RS9 untimed); Take 5 of 'Travel Section (Second Part)' remixed and two hours editing the above, and 7.00pm to 1.30am: Take 2 of 'Us And Them' remixed (RS10 untimed, RS11 False Start and RS12 to 15 untimed); and various SFX recorded for *The Dark Side of the Moon*. The session was produced by Pink Floyd, engineered by Alan Parsons and assisted by Peter James.

WEDNESDAY 31 JANUARY – RECORDING SESSION
Control Room 3, EMI Studios,
Abbey Road, London, England

3.00pm to 2.00am: Take 2 of 'Us And Them' edited, Take 1 of 'Scat ('Any Colour You Like') remixed (RS10 untimed, RS11 False Start, RS12 to RS16 untimed, and RS17 untimed and marked "best") for *The Dark Side of the Moon*. The session was produced by Pink Floyd, engineered by Alan Parsons and assisted by Peter James.

THURSDAY 1 FEBRUARY – RECORDING SESSION
Control Room 3, EMI Studios,
Abbey Road, London, England

2.30pm to 7.00pm: Take 5 of 'Lunatic Song' ['Brain Damage'] remixed (RS10 untimed, RS11 to RS14 False Starts, RS15 untimed and RS16 untimed and marked "best"), and 8.00pm to 4.30am: various SFX overdubbed onto mixes of various titles, and various crossfades done for *The Dark Side of the Moon*. It was also noted on paperwork that "Side One of LP Completed" on this day. The session was produced by Pink Floyd, engineered by Alan Parsons and assisted by Peter James.

FRIDAY 2 FEBRUARY – RECORDING SESSION
Control Room 3, EMI Studios,
Abbey Road, London, England

7.00am to 7.30pm: Take 2 of 'Us And Them' remixed (RS16 False Start, RS17 Breakdown, RS18 untimed, RS19 untimed and marked "best", RS20 and RS21 untimed); Piano overdubbed onto Take 2 of 'Us And Them'; and various crossfades, SFX overdubbed and edits done on Side Two of *The Dark Side of the Moon*. The session was produced by Pink Floyd, engineered by Alan Parsons and assisted by Peter James.

SATURDAY 3 FEBRUARY – PERFORMANCES
Palais des Sports de la Porte de Versailles, Paris, France

Two shows at 5.00pm and 8.45pm, with the Ballet de Roland Petit.
Set list at both shows: 'One Of These Days', 'Careful With That Axe, Eugene', 'Obscured by Clouds', 'When You're In', 'Echoes'.

SUNDAY 4 FEBRUARY – PERFORMANCES
Palais des Sports de la Porte de Versailles, Paris, France

Two shows at 2.30pm and 6.00pm, with the Ballet de Roland Petit.
Set list at both shows: 'One Of These Days', 'Careful With That Axe, Eugene', 'Obscured by Clouds', 'When You're In', 'Echoes'.

ABOVE: PINK FLOYD PERFORMING WITH THE ROLAND PETIT BALLET, PARIS, FEBRUARY 1973.

Sounds reported, "Dry ice was fuming quietly all over an apron stage and the Pink Floyd, standing above it all amongst their sound equipment and lighting towers, seemed suspended about ten feet up in the blackness. An unsteady, bright shaft of light opened up beneath them and slowly a stiff, bowed figure moved out and, gradually unbending, took command of the stage. Rudy Bryans, star soloist with the Ballets de Marseille, danced to the Pink Floyd's 'Echoes'. The audience is strange, hardly a typical crush of Floyd devotees, but a mixture of people who obviously came because it was the band, people who obviously came because it was the ballet, and people who didn't look quite sure why they'd come. The opening movement, 'One Of These Days', was fairly short, a kind of introduction with the whole troupe dancing, and it struck me at the time that that was what organised dance to rock music should look like, it was essentially rhythmic and fast. 'Obscured by Clouds' was a solo for Rudy Bryans and Daniele Jossi, beautifully lit, which had a hesitant, slightly menacing air. 'Careful With That Axe' was the troupe again, moving through various tableaux and sequences, featuring the exploding flares. 'Echoes' was the finale, a constantly changing sequence of short pieces, the most spectacular of which were Rudy's entrance from the tunnel, and a dance where he pulled Daniele right across the width of the stage with her in the splits position."

TUESDAY 6 FEBRUARY – RECORDING SESSION
Room 4, EMI Studios, Abbey Road, London, England

3.00pm to 12.00midnight: Crossfades mixed between 'Money' and 'Us And Them' (Take 1 untimed, Take 2 also marked best and Take 3 untimed); crossfades mixed between 'Us And Them' and 'Scat' ['Any Colour You Like'] for *The Dark Side of the Moon*. The Side Two master was also prepared on this day. The session was produced by Pink Floyd, engineered by Alan Parsons and assisted by Peter James.

FRIDAY 9 FEBRUARY – RECORDING SESSION
Room 4, EMI Studios, Abbey Road, England

12.00midday to 5.15pm: Various edit pieces of 'Travel Section' ['On The Run'], 'Lunatic Song' ['Brain Damage'], and 'Religious Section' ['The Great Gig In The Sky'] were recorded from the original master and edited into the new master tape, marking the completion and final session of the making of *The Dark Side of the Moon*. The session was produced by Pink Floyd, engineered by Alan Parsons and assisted by Peter James.

MONDAY 19 TO WEDNESDAY 21 FEBRUARY – REHEARSALS
Rainbow Theatre, Finsbury Park, London, England

Full production rehearsals for their upcoming US tour were staged at the Rainbow prior to their equipment being shipped.

TUESDAY 27 FEBRUARY – PRESS RECEPTION
London Planetarium, Marylebone, London, England

8.00pm to 11.00pm. EMI records held a press reception with cocktails and buffet at the Planetarium in London to preview the band's new album *The Dark Side of the Moon*. Richard Wright was the only band member in attendance, the rest having boycotted the event due to what they felt was an inferior sound system having been brought in by EMI.

SATURDAY 1 MARCH – ALBUM RELEASE (US)
The Dark Side of the Moon

Loyd Grossman, future TV personality, wrote in his review for *Rolling Stone*, "Throughout the band lays down a solid framework which they embellish with synthesizers, sound effects and spoken voice tapes. The sound is lush and multi-layered while remaining clear and well structured. *The Dark Side of the Moon* is a fine album with a textural and conceptual richness that not only invites, but demands involvement. There is a certain grandeur here that exceeds mere musical melodramatics and is rarely attempted in rock."

NORTH AMERICAN TOUR

Such was the scale of the live production that by now a small army of technicians was required to make it all possible. Additional house technicians were also needed to help deal with the equipment and run the show, which usually equated to two fork-lift drivers, six stage hands, two electricians, two soundmen, eight follow-spot operators and one house electrician. On a typical day two 40-foot articulated equipment trucks, crewed by two drivers each, would arrive at the venue for ten in the morning, usually after an overnight drive, to be met by the road crew, who would have flown with the band on the show day, to start setting up. This would take until at least four in the afternoon to complete, by which time the band would appear for their customary sound-check. After the show the equipment would take less than half the time to dismantle and, once it was loaded on the trucks, the process would start all over again. Beginning with this tour, the stage effects included a hemispherical mirror ball and two batteries of red lasers.

Early drafts of Pink Floyd's tour show the band scheduled to appear at Charlotte Park Center, Charlotte, on Wednesday 21 March (rescheduled to Friday 23 March) and Littlejohn Coliseum, Clemson Agricultural College, Clemson, North Carolina, on Friday 23 March.

ADDITIONAL TOUR PERSONNEL

For the first time Pink Floyd introduced a supporting cast of backing musicians, comprising backing singers Nawasa Crowder, Mary-Ann Lindsey and Phyllis Lindsey from Dallas-based gospel group Black Grass as well as Dick Parry on saxophone. During 'The Great Gig In The Sky' Gilmour played Hammond organ with Wright on electric piano.

SUNDAY 4 MARCH – PERFORMANCE ▼
Dane County Memorial Coliseum, Madison, WI, USA

Set list: 'Echoes', 'Obscured By Clouds', 'When You're In', 'Childhood's End', 'Careful With That Axe, Eugene' <Intermission> *The Dark Side of the Moon* <Encore> 'One Of These Days'.

In January, the *Madison Capital Times* announced the cancellation of the show, due to work permit difficulties, but by early February the show was confirmed as back on and went ahead as originally planned. The *Wisconsin State Journal* reported, "They began with a song called 'Obscured by Clouds' and before it was over the Coliseum had been obscured in a pinkish-coloured cloud emanating from the footlights and taking the audience of 9,000 completely by surprise. Pink Floyd, an English experimental rock group, kicked off their

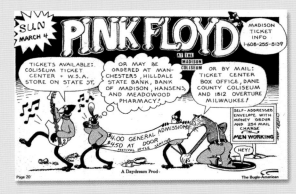

current American tour at Dane County Coliseum Sunday night showing a definite grasp of the visual and electronic potential of their music. Once referred to as psychedelic music, Pink Floyd has updated and come around into something loosely labelled space-rock, a mixture of some hard-driving sets, electronic gimmickry and quadraphonic sound. The gimmickry was Floyd's focal point Sunday and they exploited it to its fullest to add an unusual dimension to their performance. The smoke turned from green to purple as Floyd broke into one of their more recognizable hits, 'Careful With That Axe, Eugene', a song interrupted by blinding, flashing lights. The group used several special video effects ranging from the sound of cash registers in a piece called 'Money', to a soundtrack of what was apparently an Apollo flight in a song called 'Breathe'. The accompanying light show, which received a second billing and can only be described as overwhelming, tended to dwarf some of the more sensitive lyrics."

MONDAY 5 MARCH – PERFORMANCE
Cobo Arena, Detroit, MI, USA

Set list: 'Echoes', 'Obscured By Clouds', 'When You're In', 'Childhood's End', 'Careful With That Axe, Eugene' <Intermission> *The Dark Side of the Moon* <Encore> 'One Of These Days'.

During 'Careful With That Axe, Eugene' the stage pyrotechnics damaged the PA system, showering the crowd with debris. After a short break to assess the damage the second half continued without incident.

TUESDAY 6 MARCH – PERFORMANCE
Kiel Opera House, St Louis, MO, USA

Set list: 'Echoes', 'Obscured By Clouds', 'When You're In', 'Childhood's End', 'Careful With That Axe, Eugene' <Intermission> *The Dark Side of the Moon* <Encore> 'One Of These Days'.

WEDNESDAY 7 MARCH – PERFORMANCE
International Amphitheatre, Chicago, IL, USA

Set list: 'Echoes', 'Obscured By Clouds', 'When You're In', 'Childhood's End', 'Careful With That Axe, Eugene' <Intermission> *The Dark Side of the Moon* <Encore> 'One Of These Days'.

The *Chicago Sun Times* reported, "The amplifier on the bass blew late in the show, and Waters was raging around the stage while technicians frantically improvised some new connections. Meanwhile, however, Gilmour calmly continued with a solo."

THURSDAY 8 MARCH – PERFORMANCE ◄
Armory Fieldhouse, University of Cincinnati, Cincinnati, OH, USA

Set list: 'Echoes', 'Obscured By Clouds', 'When You're In', 'Childhood's End', 'Careful With That Axe, Eugene' <Intermission> *The Dark Side of the Moon* <Encore> 'One Of These Days'.

SATURDAY 10 MARCH – PERFORMANCE
Memorial Gymnasium, Kent State University, Kent, OH, USA

Set list: 'Echoes', 'Obscured By Clouds', 'When You're In', 'Childhood's End', 'Careful With That Axe, Eugene' <Intermission> *The Dark Side of the Moon* <Encore> 'One Of These Days'.

SUNDAY 11 MARCH – PERFORMANCE
Maple Leaf Gardens, Toronto, Canada

Set list: 'Echoes', 'Obscured By Clouds', 'When You're In', 'Set The Controls For The Heart Of The Sun', 'Careful With That Axe, Eugene' <Intermission> *The Dark Side of the Moon* <Encore> 'One Of These Days'.

BELOW: PINK FLOYD ON STAGE AT KENT STATE UNIVERSITY, 10 MARCH 1973.

Billboard reported, "Pink Floyd sold out Toronto's 17,000 seat Maple Leaf Gardens in 90 minutes."

MONDAY 12 MARCH – PERFORMANCE
Forum de Montréal, Montréal, Canada

Set list: 'Echoes', 'Obscured by Clouds', 'When You're In', 'Set The Controls For The Heart Of The Sun', 'Careful With That Axe, Eugene' <Intermission> *The Dark Side of the Moon* <Encore> 'One Of These Days'.
Nick Mason recalled in his book *Inside Out* that in Canada "We discovered one of our backing singers had disappeared, the reason being that she had been arrested with her boyfriend for holding up a grocery store." Unfortunately it cannot be verified which singer it was or whether the tour was completed with or without her, but reviews from this show, Boston on Wednesday 14 March, and New York on Saturday 17 March indicate three backing vocalists on stage, although the June 1973 tour did not reportedly feature Nawasa Crowder.

WEDNESDAY 14 MARCH – PERFORMANCE
Music Hall, Boston, MA, USA

Set list: 'Careful With That Axe, Eugene', 'Obscured By Clouds', 'When You're In', 'Set The Controls For The Heart Of The Sun', 'Echoes' <Intermission> *The Dark Side of the Moon* <Encore> 'One Of These Days'.

THURSDAY 15 MARCH – PERFORMANCE
Spectrum Theater, Philadelphia, PA, USA

Set list: 'Echoes', 'Obscured By Clouds', 'When You're In', 'Careful With That Axe, Eugene', 'Set The Controls For The Heart Of The Sun' <Intermission> *The Dark Side of the Moon* <Encore> 'One Of These Days'.

FRIDAY 16 MARCH – ALBUM RELEASE (UK)
The Dark Side of the Moon

Record Mirror wrote that "Pink Floyd are so good at what they do it seems almost churlish to knock it, but when you compare the effect they have now with the marvellously innovative position the Floyd enjoyed in '67, it's no wonder they're taken for granted.... *Dark Side of the Moon* has little of the awesome climax of *Atom Heart Mother*, rather less cohesion and invention than *Meddle* and considerable similarity to *Obscured by Clouds*."

SATURDAY 17 MARCH – PERFORMANCE
Radio City Music Hall, New York, NY, USA

Set list: 'Obscured By Clouds', 'When You're In', 'Set The Controls For The Heart Of The Sun', 'Careful With That Axe, Eugene', 'Echoes' <Intermission> *The Dark Side of the Moon* <Encore> 'One Of These Days'.

Sounds reported, "Pink Floyd turned out an exciting set last week with a stage half a block long, and a 6,200-seat theatre on four levels as their basic props. At one-thirty in the morning [Sunday 18 March] the lights dimmed, the audience stood, clouds of steam shot upwards from the vents in the stage, and the Floyd rose into view on one of the elevators; three light towers with a reflecting dish mounted on the centre one, created a glowing, hypnotic effect as you looked at the stage. The elevated stage section reached its full height then began to inch forward, and the crowd roared approval. Special mention

THE DARK SIDE OF THE MOON

SIDE ONE

SPEAK TO ME (Mason) **1:07**
BREATHE (Waters, Gilmour, Wright) **2:50**
ON THE RUN (Gilmour, Waters) **3:45**
TIME (Mason, Waters, Wright, Gilmour) **6:53**
THE GREAT GIG IN THE SKY (Wright) **4:44**

SIDE TWO

MONEY (Waters) **6:23**
US AND THEM (Waters, Wright) **7:49**
ANY COLOUR YOU LIKE (Gilmour, Mason, Wright) **3:26**
BRAIN DAMAGE (Waters) **3:47**
ECLIPSE (Waters) **2:13**

RELEASE DATE

US: Saturday 1 March 1973.
UK: Friday 16 March 1973.
Given the importance of this album's place in rock history a surprising amount of confusion exists as to its precise release date. The US release date was first publicized in the 24 February edition of *Billboard* as being Saturday 1 March, which tallies with many regional store ads and album reviews which began appearing the week commencing Sunday 2 March.

The accepted release date of the UK album is Friday 23 March 1973 and this is celebrated as its official worldwide anniversary date. However, press adverts, including trade paper *Music Week*, stated the album would be in stores from Friday 16 March, with album reviews having already appeared across the bulk of the UK music press the week ending Saturday 10 March 1973.

FORMAT

UK: EMI Harvest SHVL 804 (Vinyl album).
US: Harvest SMAS 11163 (Vinyl album).

HIGHEST CHART POSITION

UK: No. 2 (*Music Week* "Top Albums" on Saturday 31 March 1973), Chart re-entry No. 87 (*Music Week* "Top Albums" on Saturday 25 August 1984), Chart re-entry No. 77 (*Music Week* "Top 100 Albums" on Saturday 20 August 1988), Chart re-entry No. 4 (*Music Week* "Top 100 Albums" on Saturday 20 March 1993), Chart re-entry No. 17 (Official UK Album Chart on Saturday 12 April 2003), Chart re-entry No. 11 (Official Charts Company on Saturday 8 October 2011), Chart re-entry No. 43 (Official Charts Company on Saturday 30 March 2013).
US: No.1 (*Billboard* 'Top LPs & Tape' on Saturday 28 April 1973).

On Sunday 12 April 2013, the UK's Official Charts Company launched the Official Vinyl Charts Top 40 for both singles and albums in response to a massive resurgence of interest in what was an almost defunct format only a few years previously. Of the biggest selling vinyl albums of the decade so far, it showed *The Dark Side of the Moon* placed at No.3. The album has spent some 214 non-consecutive weeks in the UK Top 40 since its release.

Claims that the original album remained on the US *Billboard* chart for 15 consecutive years is, however, a complete myth. In fact it debuted at No. 95 on Saturday 17 March 1973 and climbed to No. 1 on Saturday 28 April 1973, staying on the chart for 84 weeks until Saturday 19 October 1974. It appeared again on Saturday 12 April 1975 and stayed on the chart for 48 weeks until Saturday 6 March 1976 and then stayed on the chart for a record 11 years until Saturday 23 April 1988, a grand total of 723 weeks. It re-entered the chart for a further 11-week run from Saturday 7 May 1988, and again on Saturday 10 September 1988 for five weeks. It dropped out again between Saturday 15 October 1988 and Saturday 25 May 1991, when it debuted at No. 24 on the *Billboard* "Top Pop Catalog Albums" list. Since then it has dropped in and out of the charts with each successive reissue but successfully climbed to No.1 again on the *Billboard* "Top Pop Catalog Albums" chart on Saturday 28 May 1994. Fuelled by the success of *The Endless River*, on Monday 8 December 2014, the album dramatically re-entered the *Billboard* "200" chart at No. 13. This was mainly thanks to cheap pricing in the Google Play store (where it was discounted to just 99 cents the week ending Sunday 7 December), moving just over 38,000 units in the US alone. This was recorded as the album's highest rank since the Saturday 15 October 2011 chart, when it re-entered at No. 12 following the new *Discovery* reissue. With 889 weeks, equating to just over 17 years, inside the *Billboard* "200" Chart, it is by far the album with the most charted weeks in history. The next closest album, in terms of longevity, is Johnny Mathis' *Johnny's Greatest Hits*, with 490 weeks.

AWARDS

UK: Certified Silver on Saturday 1 June 1974, Gold on Friday 14 June 1974, Platinum on Thursday 1 January 1976, 7 x Platinum on Saturday 1 May 1993 and 9 x Platinum on Friday 15 April 2005.

US: Certified Gold on 17 April 1973, 11 x Platinum on 16 February 1990, Platinum on 16 February 1990, 12 x Platinum on 19 September 1991, 13 x Platinum on 7 March 1994 and 15 x Platinum on 4 June 1998.

At the *16th Grammy Awards*, held at the Hollywood Palladium, Los Angeles, on 2 March 1974 *The Dark Side of the Moon* was nominated for "Best Engineered Album", losing out to *Innervisions* by Stevie Wonder.

At the *41st Grammy Awards*, held at the Shrine Auditorium, Los Angeles, on 25 February 1999 *The Dark Side of the Moon* entered the Grammy Awards Hall of Fame.

At the *2nd Annual Surround Music Awards* held during the first day of *Surround 2003*: The *5th Annual International Surround Conference and Showcase* at the Beverly Hilton Hotel, Los Angeles, on 11 December 2003 the 30th-anniversary hybrid Super Audio 5.1 CD (SACD) edition won "Best Multichannel Reissue", "*High Fidelity Review* Listeners' Choice" and "Best of Show".

SALES

The Dark Side of the Moon was, until the mid-1990s, regarded as the second-best-selling album of all time, worldwide, and the 21st best-selling album of all time in the United States.

The 2003 Hybrid SACD reissue reached No. 1 on the *Billboard* "Pop Catalog Chart" and sold over 800,000 in the US alone on release.

ARTWORK

By Hipgnosis and George Hardie. The light band emanating from the prism on the original album cover has six colours, missing indigo compared to the traditional division of the spectrum into red, orange, yellow, green, blue, indigo and violet. The reverse of the original album sleeve also depicts an incorrect refraction of light: the emerging spectrum should be divergent, not convergent.

Original vinyl editions were also issued with two posters and two stickers as inserts. The initial UK pressing has also become sought-after by collectors because it features a solid blue prism triangle on the label as opposed to a prism with a white border on black.

CREDITS

Following a high court ruling over writing credits and royalties for 'The Great Gig In The Sky', all pressings after 2005 have credited the track, "written by Richard Wright and vocal composition by Clare Torry".

In 2011, and with the re-release of *The Dark Side of the Moon* as part of the *Why? Pink Floyd* campaign, the track listing for the album was altered and the track 'Breathe' was inexplicably changed to 'Breathe (In The Air)'.

PRESSING DETAILS

On later CD pressings, many people believe a barely audible orchestral overdub of the Beatles' 'Ticket To Ride' can be heard after 'Eclipse'. This could be attributed to the use of wiped recording tapes as was a common studio practice. The bootleg album *A Tree Full of Secrets* includes an amplified, enhanced version of this oddity. More noticeable is the tape distortion at the very end of 'The Great Gig In The Sky' which has never been corrected and is even heard on the most recent reissues, including the 5.1 version.

MUSICIANS

David Gilmour (Vocals, Guitars, EMS VCS3, EMS Synthi A, Keyboards).
Nick Mason (Drums, Percussion, Tape Effects).
Roger Waters (Bass Guitar, Vocals, EMS VCS3, EMS Synthi A, Tape Effects).
Richard Wright (Grand Piano, Electric Piano, Hammond, Farfisa, EMS VCS3, EMS Synthi A, Vocals).

ADDITIONAL MUSICIANS

Lesley Duncan, Doris Troy, Barry St John, Liza Strike (Backing Vocals).
Clare Torry (Vocals on 'The Great Gig In The Sky').
Dick Parry (Saxophones on 'Us And Them' and 'Money').

RECORDING DETAILS

Recorded at EMI Studios, Abbey Road, St John's Wood, London, England and produced by Pink Floyd, engineered by Alan Parsons and Peter James and mixed by Chris Thomas.

PINK FLOYD at the PLANETARIUM.

EMI Records invite you to an evening with PINK FLOYD at the London Planetarium Marylebone Road, N.W.1. on Tuesday 27th February immediately prior to their 1973 tour of America.

The group's new album "THE DARK SIDE OF THE MOON", which has been nine months in the making, will be previewed in sound beneath the Planetarium night sky.

	PROGRAMME
8.00 – 8.40pm	Reception: Cocktails in the Arcade.
8.45 – 9.30pm	The World Premiere of "THE DARK SIDE OF THE MOON" album. (Please Note: for obvious reasons there can be no admittance to the Main Planetarium once the 'sky' has become dark and the playback has begun).
9.35 – 11pm	Dinner: Hot buffet and wine in the Restaurant; Drinks and Amusements in the Arcade.

Please bring this invitation with you.

ABOVE: EMI'S INVITATION TO THE LONDON PLANETARIUM, LONDON, TO CELEBRATE THE RELEASE OF *THE DARK SIDE OF THE MOON*, 27 FEBRUARY 1973.

THE DARK SIDE OF THE MOON

Speak To Me

(RS11).
Various SFX and Tape Loops for 'Intro (Big Crash)'
made on 27 January 1973.
Mixed on 27 January 1973 (RS11).
Further Loops and SFX overdubbed on RS11
on 29 January 1973.

Breathe

Take 5 (RS17).
Basic track recorded as 'Eclipse Part 1' on
30 May 1972 (Take 5).
Vocals, Guitar and Electric Piano overdubbed
onto Take 5 on 30 May 1972.
Organ, Electric Piano, Volume Pedal Guitar,
Harmony Vocals overdubbed onto Take 5 on
31 May 1972.
Leslie Speaker Noise leading into 'Eclipse Part 2'
recorded on 31 May 1972.
Organ overdubbed onto Take 5 on 22 June
1972.
Vocals re-dubbed onto Take 5 on 22 June 1972.
Harmony Vocals overdubbed onto Take 5 on
23 June 1972.
Steel Guitar overdubbed onto Take 5 on
31 October 1972.
Drums, Piano and Guitar recorded for Big Crash
at the beginning of 'Breathe (Speak To Me)' on
18 January 1973.
Guitar recorded wild for use on Big Crash on
18 January 1973.
Mixed on 27 January 1973 (RS17).

On The Run

Take 5 (RS1/9).
Basic track recorded as 'Eclipse Part 2' on
31 May 1972 (Take 1).
Basic track re-recorded as 'Eclipse Part 2' on
13 June 1972 (Take 5).
Click Track Tape Loop made up and overdubbed
onto Take 5 on 13 June 1972.
"Tapes of Weird Noises" and "More Weird Noises"
overdubbed onto Take 5 on 13 June 1972.
Bass, Drums and Guitar re-dubbed in second
half of Take 5 on 14 June 1972.
Cymbals and Drums overdubbed onto Take 5 on
14 June 1972.
Bass, Drums and Hi-Hat re-dubbed onto Take 5
on 15 June 1972.
Hi-Hat overdubbed onto Take 5 on
15 June 1972.
Electric Piano, White Noise and VCS3
overdubbed onto Take 5 on 15 June 1972.
Take 5 edited on 15 June 1972.
Bass Guitar overdubbed onto Take 5 on
11 October 1972.
Synthesizers overdubbed onto Take 5
on 12 October 1972.

Synthesizer Noises recorded for 'Travel Section'
on 12 October 1972 (Take 1).
Synthesizers overdubbed onto Take 5 on
15 October.
Take 5 mixed on 15 October (RS1).
Take 1 Synthesizer Noises mixed on 16 October
(RS2).
Drums, Guitar, Electric Piano overdubbed
onto Take 5 on 16 October 1972.
Take 5 edited on 31 October 1972.
"Wild Guitar" recorded and overdubbed
onto Take 5 on 18 January 1973.
Guitar overdubbed onto Take 5 on
18 January 1973.
VCS3 overdubbed onto Take 5 on
18 January 1973.
Various SFX and VCS3 overdubbed onto Take 5
on 19 January 1973.
Bass Drum overdubbed onto Take 5 on
20 January 1973.
Piano overdubbed onto "Big Crash" of 'Travel
Section' on 20 January 1973.
"Big Crash" mixed on 20 January 1973 (RS2).
"Big Crash" mixed 24 January 1973 (RS
unknown).
Synthesizers on "Wild Tape" recorded for
'Travel Section' on 26 January 1973.
Synthesizers on "Wild Tape" overdubbed onto
Take 5 on 26 January 1973.
Take 5 mixed 26 January 1973 (RS4).
"Freaked Out Roadie" recorded on
26 January 1973.
First part of Take 5 with "Roger the Roadie"
mixed on 30 January 1973 (RS9).
Second part of Take 5 mixed on 30 January 1973 (RS1).
"First Part" (RS9) and "Second Part" (RS1) of
Take 5 edited together on 30 January 1973.
Various edit pieces recorded and edited into
master tape on 9 February 1973.

Time / Breathe Reprise

Take 1 (RS19).
Click track and backing track made on
8 June 1972.
Basic track recorded as 'Time Song' on 8 June
1972 (Take 1).
Vocals and Harmony Vocals overdubbed onto
Take 1 on 9 June 1972.
Guitar, Electric Piano overdubbed onto Take 1
on 9 June 1972.
Clocks and Chimes overdubbed onto Take 1
on 9 June 1972.
Electric Piano and Guitar overdubbed on
beginning of Take 1 on 9 June 1972.
Roto Toms and Farfisa overdubbed onto Take 1
on 10 June 1972.
'Home Again' ['Breathe Reprise'] edited from
'Breathe In The Air' and edited to 'Time Song' on
10 June 1972).

Farfisa, Guitars and Vocals overdubbed onto
Take 1 on 10 June 1972.
Harmony Vocals overdubbed onto Take 1
on 10 June 1972.
Electric Piano Overdubbed onto Take 1
on 10 June 1972.
Choir overdubbed onto verses of Take 1
on 20 June 1972.
VCS3 overdubbed onto Take 1 on 22 June 1972.
Electric Piano re-dubbed onto Take 1 on
22 June 1972.
Synthesized Electric Guitar overdubbed onto
Take 1 on 17 October 1972.
Take 1 edited on 31 October 1972.
Drum Heart Beat, Silly Solo, and Guitar solo
overdubbed onto Take 1 of 'Time Song Intro' on
1 November 1972.
Guitar solo overdubbed onto Take 1 on
2 November 1972.
Take 1 mixed 21 January 1973 (RS10).
Speech recorded on 21 January 1973.
Take 1 'Intro' mixed on 24 January 1973 (RS16).
Take 1 mixed on 25 January 1973 (RS18 / RS19
edit piece).

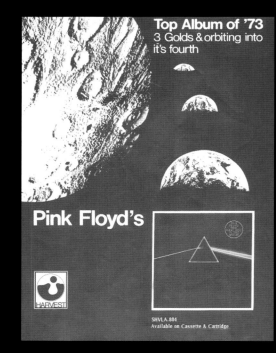

ABOVE: A HIT ALBUM ON A TRULY
GLOBAL SCALE. THIS TRADE ADVERT IS
FROM AUSTRALIA.

OPPOSITE: US TRADE PAPER
ANNOUNCEMENT FOR THE JUNE 1973 TOUR.

The Great Gig In The Sky

Take 3 (RS18).
Basic track recorded as 'Religious Theme' on
20 June 1972 (Take 1).
Basic track re-recorded as 'Religious Theme' on
21 June 1972 (Take 1).
Organ and Piano overdubbed onto Take 1 on
21 June 1972.
Basic track re-recorded as 'Religious Section' on
22 June 1972 (Take 3).
Hammond overdubbed onto 'Religious Section'
onto Take 3 on 22 June 1972.
Piano and Drums overdubbed onto 'Religious
Section' onto Take 3 on 25 October 1972.
Tape of "Rick Walking Away From Piano"
recorded and overdubbed onto Take 3 on
26 October 1972.
Bass, Hammond and Steel Guitar overdubbed
onto Take 3 on 26 October 1972.
Lead Vocal [Clare Torry] overdubbed onto Take 3
on 21 January 1973.
Take 3 mixed on 25 January 1973 (RS14).
Take 3 mixed on 26 January 1973 (RS18).
Various edit pieces recorded and edited into
master tape on 9 February 1973.

Money

Take 1 (RS19).
Basic track recorded as 'Money Song' on 6 June
1972 (Take 1).
Tape Loops made and SFX recorded and
overdubbed onto Take 1 on 6 June 1972.
Backing track recorded on 7 June 1972 (Take 1).
Guitar, Vocals, Electric Piano, Guitar Solo and
Drums overdubbed onto Take 1 on 7 June 1972.
Electric Piano, Piano, Drums overdubbed onto
Take 1 on 8 June 1972.
Piano re-dubbed and Trombone overdubbed
onto Take 1 on 8 June 1972.
Guitar and Saxophone [Dick Parry] overdubbed
onto Take 1 on 27 October 1972.
Guitar and Cymbals overdubbed onto Take 1 on
30 October 1972.
Guitar overdubbed onto Take 1 on 2 November
1972.
Piano overdubbed onto Take 1 on 21 January
1973.
Bass Guitar overdubbed onto Take 1 on
24 January 1973.
Take 1 mixed on 29 January 1973 (RS19).
Cross-fade to 'Us And Them' recorded on 6
February 1973 (Take 2).

Us And Them

Take 10 (RS19).
Basic track recorded as 'Eclipse Part 3' on
1 June 1972 (Take 2).
Guitar, Cymbals, Bass, Piano, Vocals and
Harmony Vocals overdubbed onto Take 2 on
1 June 1972.
Piano re-dubbed onto Take 2 on 2 June 1972.
Vocals and Harmony Vocals overdubbed onto
Take 2 on 2 June 1972.
Basic track re-recorded as 'Eclipse Part 3' on
16 June 1972 (Take 1).
Lead Guitar and Vocals overdubbed onto
Take 1 on 16 June 1972.
Take 1 edited on 16 June 1972.
Choir overdubbed on middle 8 of Take 1 on
20 June 1972.
Bass Guitar overdubbed onto Take 1 on 11
and 12 October 1972.
Piano overdubbed onto Take 1 on 12 October
1972.
Saxophones [Dick Parry] overdubbed onto
Take 1 on 16 October 1972.
Piano overdubbed onto Take 1 on 17 October
1972.
Saxophone [Dick Parry] re-dubbed onto Take 1
on 27 October 1972.
"Various Speech" recorded on 19 January 1973.
Take 1 mixed on 30 January 1973 (RS10).
Take 1 edited on 31 January 1973.
Take 1 / RS10 mixed on 2 February 1973 (RS19).
Piano overdubbed onto Take 1 / RS19 on 2
February 1973.
Cross-fade to 'Any Colour You Like' recorded on
6 February 1973.

Any Colour You Like

Take 1 (RS17).
Basic track recorded as 'Eclipse Scat Section' on
17 June 1972 (Take 1).
Organ and VCS3 overdubbed onto Take 1 on
17 June 1972.
VCS3 overdubbed onto Take 1 on 1 November 1972.
Take 1 mixed on 31 January 1973 (RS17).

Brain Damage / Eclipse

Take 5 (RS16).
Basic track recorded as 'Eclipse Part 5' ['Brain
Damage'] on 2 June 1972 (Take 1).
Basic track recorded as 'Eclipse Part 5 & 6' ['Brain
Damage'/'Eclipse'] on 3 June 1972 (Take 5).
Vocals overdubbed onto Take 5 of 'Eclipse Part 5
& 6' ['Brain Damage'/'Eclipse'] on 3 June 1972.
Vocals and Harmony Vocals overdubbed onto
Take 5 of 'Eclipse Part 5' ['Brain Damage'] on
3 June 1972.
Vocals and Harmony Vocals overdubbed onto
the middle 8 of Take 5 of 'Eclipse Part 5 & 6'

['Brain Damage'/ 'Eclipse'] on 6 June 1972.
Choir overdubbed onto middle-eights
of Take 5 of 'Lunatic Song' on 20 June 1972.
Organ overdubbed onto Take 5 on
11 October 1972.
Bass overdubbed onto Take 5 on
12 October 1972.
Guitar, Piano and Bass overdubbed onto
Take 5 on 17 October 1972.
Guitar and vocals overdubbed onto Take 5 on
2 November 1972.
Guitar and VCS3 overdubbed onto Take 5 on
3 November.
Take 5 mixed with 'End Song' on 1 February
1972 (RS16).
Various edit pieces recorded and edited into
master tape on 9 February 1973.

Eclipse

Take 5 (RS16).
Basic track recorded as 'Eclipse Part 5 & 6' on
3 June 1972 (Take 5).
Choir overdubbed onto Take 5 of 'End' on
20 June 1972.
Bass overdubbed onto Take 5 on
12 October 1972.
Organ overdubbed onto Take 5 of 'End Song'
11 October 1972.
Take 5 mixed with 'Lunatic Song' on
1 February 1972 (RS16).

ought to be made of the Floyd's lighting and sound crews who seemed never to miss a cue, and the 20-speaker quad system with speakers on all levels of the hall gave a close almost headphone sound. The music started with some of their well-known older pieces with 'Echoes' ending the first half. The second half was the new album *The Dark Side of the Moon* (on which they used three black singers) with an encore of 'One Of These Days'. The fifteen-foot dish hanging from the centre tower glowed and steamed in the lights, and at one point as the red spots caught it the effect was of red laser beams flashing through the dark hall. Other times when the lights caught it, it looked like one of those mirrored globes they had at 30's balls. The Floyd were at their best and the stage presentation was one of the best I've seen in a hell of a long time."

SUNDAY 18 MARCH – PERFORMANCE
Palace Theater, Waterbury, CT, USA

Set list: 'Obscured By Clouds', 'When You're In', 'Childhood's End', 'Careful With That Axe, Eugene', 'Echoes' <Intermission> *The Dark Side of the Moon* <Encore> 'One Of These Days'.

MONDAY 19 MARCH – PERFORMANCE
Providence Civic Center, Providence, RI, USA

Set list: 'Echoes', 'Obscured By Clouds', 'When You're In', 'Childhood's End', 'Careful With That Axe, Eugene' <Intermission> *The Dark Side of the Moon* <Encore> 'One Of These Days'.

THURSDAY 22 MARCH – PERFORMANCE ◄
Hampton Coliseum, Hampton, VA, USA

Set list: 'Echoes', 'Obscured By Clouds', 'When You're In', 'Childhood's End', 'Careful With That Axe, Eugene' <Intermission>*The Dark Side of the Moon* <Encore> 'One Of These Days'.

FRIDAY 23 MARCH – PERFORMANCE
Charlotte Park Center, Charlotte, NC, USA

Set list: 'Echoes', 'Obscured By Clouds', 'When You're In', 'Childhood's End', 'Careful With That Axe, Eugene' <Intermission> *The Dark Side of the Moon* <Encore> 'One Of These Days'.

SATURDAY 24 MARCH – PERFORMANCE
Municipal Auditorium, Atlanta, GA, USA

Set list: 'Obscured by Clouds', 'When You're In', 'Set The Controls For The Heart Of The Sun', 'Careful With That Axe, Eugene', 'Echoes' <Intermission> *The Dark Side of the Moon* <Encore> 'One Of These Days'.

SUNDAY 25 MARCH – CANCELLED PERFORMANCE
Bayfront Center, St Petersburg, FL, USA

Cancelled due to Santana's appearance the same night in nearby Tampa.

TUESDAY 3 APRIL – TELEVISION BROADCAST
The Old Grey Whistle Test, BBC 2 TV, London, England

Ian Emes animation film entitled *French Windows* set to the music of 'One Of These Days', was broadcast on this popular late-night music programme between 10.40pm and 11.45pm. The screening subsequently led Pink Floyd to commission Ian Emes to produce the animation sequence of 'Time' for their 1974 UK tour.

FRIDAY 5 MAY – SINGLE RELEASE (US)
'Money'

MONDAY 7 & TUESDAY 8 MAY – RECORDING SESSION
Room 4, EMI Studios, Abbey Road, London, England

Remixing *Atom Heart Mother* for the quadraphonic album release. The session was engineered by Alan Parsons and Peter James. Pink Floyd was not in attendance for this session.

FRIDAY 18 & SATURDAY 19 MAY – PERFORMANCES
Earl's Court Exhibition Hall, Earls Court, London, England

Additional musicians for the shows included Vicki Brown (Backing Vocals), Dick Parry (Saxophones) and Liza Strike (Backing Vocals). Set list at both shows: 'Obscured By Clouds', 'When You're In', 'Set The Controls For The Heart Of The Sun', 'Careful With That Axe, Eugene', 'Echoes' <Intermission> *The Dark Side of the Moon* <Encore> 'One Of These Days'.

Record Mirror reported, "This was Pink Floyd and true to their position in music their performance at Earl's Court on Saturday was a total aural experience. A quad PA brought an extra dimension to the sound. The waves streaked all over the massive hall and at times the organ and synthesiser were almost visible. Masters of mood creation, Floyd began each number slowly building to a sense shattering peak. Then they let you down gently again before the number's end. Then came the spectacular second half with rockets shooting out from the stage during 'Money', their American single. 'Breathe In The Air' followed with aeroplane sounds, spotlights scanning the roof, crashing into the stage, and exploding. After a ten minute standing ovation the band encored with 'One Of These Days'. Everyone seemed sated as we left Earl's Court to a background of spotlights searching the West London sky – truly a Floyd triumph."

RIGHT: PART OF FLOYD'S MORE ELABORATE STAGE EFFECTS: AN EXPLODING GONG PICTURED AT EARLS COURT, MAY 1973.

NORTH AMERICAN TOUR CONTINUED

ADDITIONAL TOUR PERSONNEL

Mary Ann Lindsey (Backing vocals), Phyllis Lindsey (Backing Vocals) and Dick Parry (Saxophones).

PINK FLOYD ROAD CREW

Chris Adamson (Backline Technician), Graeme Fleming (Lighting Technician), Marek "Mick the Pole" Kluczynski (Tape Operator, Drum Kit, Quad Sound), Arthur Max (Lighting, Effects), Robin Murray (Lighting Technician), Paul Padun (Lighting Technician), Alan Parsons (Front of House Sound Engineer), Bobby Richardson (PA, Stage Technician), Peter Watts (Head of PA, Tour Manager), Robbie Williams (PA, Stage Technician).

In addition to the above Pink Floyd used four drivers to haul their equipment around in two 40-foot trailers. At the show they required a local crew comprising two fork-lift drivers, six stage hands, two electricians, two soundmen, eight follow spot operators and one house electrician.

SATURDAY 16 JUNE – CANCELLED PERFORMANCE ◄ Roosevelt Stadium, Jersey City, NJ, USA

The opening night of the tour was rescheduled to a previously held "rain date" on Monday 18 June due to severe inclement weather (see Monday 18 June for further information).

SUNDAY 17 JUNE – PERFORMANCE Saratoga Performing Arts Center, Saratoga Springs, NY, USA

Set list: 'Obscured By Clouds', 'When You're In', 'Set The Controls For The Heart Of The Sun', 'Careful With That Axe, Eugene', 'Echoes' <Intermission> *The Dark Side of the Moon* <Encore> 'One Of These Days'.

Pink Floyd enjoyed a 30,000-strong sell-out attendance at this show. It was reported in the local press that venue management refused to allow Pink Floyd to use the crashing plane as part of their stage effects.

MONDAY 18 JUNE – PERFORMANCE
Roosevelt Stadium, Jersey City, NJ, USA

Set list: 'Obscured By Clouds', 'When You're In', 'Set The Controls For The Heart Of The Sun', 'Careful With That Axe, Eugene', 'Echoes' <Intermission> *The Dark Side of the Moon* <Encore> 'One Of These Days'.

Amusement Business reported, "Pink Floyd overcame a rain-out and further downpours on the rain date to set a record gross at the Roosevelt Stadium where 22,113 fans contributed to the $110,565

gross box office with tickets at $5 each. The Floyd date was initially set for June 16, but was called off at 4pm, with several thousand fans in the stands. On the rain date, the rains came down until about 2pm with a full stop about 4pm. At 8pm the group went on stage and played two one-hour and 15-minute sets until 10.45pm. All but 500 of the sold tickets sold in advance. Date had a potential of 25,000 audience. During the performance, a 7ft airplane crashed on stage from its harbor in the stands, as one of several stage effects employed by Pink Floyd."

TUESDAY 19 JUNE – PERFORMANCE
Civic Center Arena, Pittsburgh, PA, USA

Set list: 'Obscured By Clouds', 'When You're In', 'Set The Controls For The Heart Of The Sun', 'Careful With That Axe, Eugene', 'Echoes' <Intermission> *The Dark Side of the Moon* <Encore> 'One Of These Days'.

The show got off about two hours late because of a holdup with the airline bringing the band into Pittsburg. The *Pittsburg Post-Gazette* reported, "Pink Floyd last night at the Civic Arena came up with some sounds that haven't been heard outside a sound-stage at a horror film studio. The four-man British rock group played an interesting though uninspired set, which showed only spasmodic flashes of brilliance. They seemed more interested in sound effects than music, and as they performed they seemed very tired. Yet the experimental rock sound they put out was intriguing and very clean. One big factor that helped the group was their fantastic sound system – one of the best in the world."

WEDNESDAY 20 JUNE – PERFORMANCE
Merriweather Post Pavilion, Columbia, MD, USA

Set list: 'Obscured By Clouds', 'When You're In', 'Set The Controls For The Heart Of The Sun', 'Careful With That Axe, Eugene', 'Echoes' <Intermission> *The Dark Side of the Moon* <Encore> 'One Of These Days'.

The *Washington Post* reported, "The British foursome opened a two-night stand before 9,000 people at the Pavilion last night, ranging their way through an amalgam of synthesizers, echo chambers, tape units, fog machines, incendiary bombs, flaming gongs and a giant rotating mirrored ball. The effect of all this was certainly dazzling, a real show in a rock world frequently low on entertainment and performance value. The problem is to decide whether Pink Floyd creates music or merely extols advances in audio engineering."

THURSDAY 21 JUNE – PERFORMANCE
Merriweather Post Pavilion, Columbia, MD, USA

Set list: 'Echoes', 'Obscured By Clouds', 'When You're In' / 'Childhood's End', 'Careful With That Axe, Eugene', 'Echoes' <Intermission>*The Dark Side of the Moon* <Encore> 'One Of These Days'.

FRIDAY 22 JUNE – PERFORMANCE
Buffalo Memorial Auditorium, Buffalo, NY, USA

Rescheduled from Friday 15 June.
Set list: 'Obscured By Clouds', 'When You're In', 'Set The Controls For The Heart Of The Sun', 'Careful With That Axe, Eugene', 'Echoes' <Intermission> *The Dark Side of the Moon* <Encore> 'One Of These Days'.

SATURDAY 23 JUNE – PERFORMANCE
Olympia Stadium, Detroit, MI, USA

Set list: 'Obscured By Clouds', 'When You're In', 'Set The Controls For The Heart Of The Sun', 'Careful With That Axe, Eugene', 'Echoes' <Intermission> *The Dark Side of the Moon* <Encore> 'One Of These Days'.

A recording of lighting designer Arthur Max directing the local union crew was broadcast as part of the Capital Radio *Pink Floyd Story*, 'Part 4: The Dark Side of the Moon' on Friday 7 January 1977.

In June 2013, Cliff Port released an amusing short animated film based around this recording entitled *Bad Day at the Office*, which was screened in the Cinema Tent at the Glastonbury Festival on Wednesday 26 June 2013 at 11.30pm and released on YouTube shortly thereafter.

SUNDAY 24 JUNE – PERFORMANCE
Blossom Music Center, Cuyahoga Falls, OH, USA

Set list: 'Obscured By Clouds', 'When You're In', 'Set The Controls For The Heart Of The Sun', 'Careful With That Axe, Eugene', 'Echoes' <Intermission> *The Dark Side of the Moon* <Encore> 'One Of These Days'.

The *Cleveland Plain Dealer* reported that more than 18,000 fans attended the show, but post-show reports focussed on the management of the event rather than the concert itself reporting that, "Blossom Music Center officials are moving to mend fences with the Center's neighbours, some of whom were ruffled by property damage and littering…. The vast crowd for Pink Floyd's appearance on Sunday night caused a huge post-concert traffic jam and caused damage to both the Blossom grounds and private property…. The main problem was the sheer size. Blossom officials had publicized the concert as sold out and cut off the sale of tickets, but several thousand gatecrashers came anyway and got in by various means."

MONDAY 25 JUNE – PERFORMANCE
Convention Center, Louisville, KY, USA

Set list: 'Echoes', 'Obscured By Clouds', 'When You're In', 'Childhood's End', 'Careful With That Axe, Eugene' <Intermission> *The Dark Side of the Moon* <Encore> 'One Of These Days'.

TUESDAY 26 JUNE – CANCELLED PERFORMANCE
Lake Spivey Park, Jonesboro, Atlanta, GA, USA

The show was announced as cancelled on Saturday 23 June by the promoter, believed to have been due to poor ticket sales attributed to insufficient promotion for such a large-scale event.

WEDNESDAY 27 JUNE – PERFORMANCE ◄
Jacksonville Coliseum, Jacksonville, FL, USA

Set list: 'Obscured By Clouds', 'When You're In', 'Set The Controls For The Heart Of The Sun', 'Careful With That Axe, Eugene', 'Echoes' <Intermission> *The Dark Side of the Moon* <Encore> 'One Of These Days'.

THURSDAY 28 JUNE – PERFORMANCE
Hollywood Sportatorium, Pembroke Pines, Hollywood, FL, USA

Rescheduled from both Pirates Cove, Pirates World Amusement Park, Dania, Hollywood, and also Miami Baseball Stadium, Miami. Set list: 'Obscured by Clouds', 'When You're In', 'Set The Controls For The Heart Of The Sun', 'Careful With That Axe, Eugene', 'Echoes' <Intermission> *The Dark Side of the Moon* <Encore> 'One Of These Days'.

FRIDAY 29 JUNE – PERFORMANCE ►
Tampa Stadium, Tampa, FL, USA

Set list: 'Obscured By Clouds', 'When You're In', 'Set The Controls For The Heart Of The Sun', 'Careful With That Axe, Eugene', 'Echoes' <Intermission> *The Dark Side of the Moon* <Encore> 'One Of These Days'.

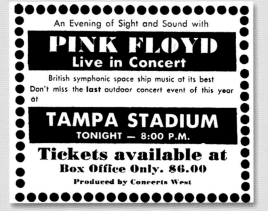

SUNDAY 23 SEPTEMBER – CANCELLED PERFORMANCE
3rd British Rock Meeting,
Sandrennbahn Altrip, Frankfurt, West Germany

Pink Floyd was heavily advertised to headline on the closing day of this huge two-day festival (Saturday 22 and Sunday 23 September), which was cancelled. Other advertised acts included Frank Zappa and the Mothers of Invention, Beck, Bogert and Appice, Chuck Berry, Wishbone Ash, Fumble, Suzy Quatro, Lou Reed, Greenslade, Jerry Lee Lewis, Rare Earth and Albert Hammond.

MONDAY 1 OCTOBER – RECORDING SESSION
Studio 2, EMI Studios, Abbey Road, London, England

2.30pm to 7.00pm: Pink Floyd commenced recording sessions for what has become known as the *Household Objects* project, with playbacks of material made in the early stages of recording *Meddle*. The session was produced by Pink Floyd, engineered by Alan Parsons and assisted by Peter James.

TUESDAY 2 OCTOBER – RECORDING SESSION
Studio 2, EMI Studios, Abbey Road, London, England

2.30pm to 5.30pm and 7.00pm to 12.00midnight: Unknown recording for the *Household Objects* project. The session was produced by Pink Floyd, engineered by Alan Parsons and assisted by Peter James.

WEDNESDAY 3 OCTOBER – RECORDING SESSION
Studio 2, EMI Studios, Abbey Road, London, England

2.30pm to 5.30pm and 7.00pm to 12.00midnight: Unknown recording for the *Household Objects* project. The session was produced by Pink Floyd, engineered by Alan Parsons and assisted by Peter James.

THURSDAY 4 OCTOBER – RECORDING SESSION
Studio 2, EMI Studios, Abbey Road, London, England

2.00pm to 6.00pm and 7.30pm to 2.00am: "Milk Bottle SFX Recorded Wild", "Various SFX recorded" and tape loops of "Milk Bottles" transferred to 16-track for the *Household Objects* project. The session was produced by Pink Floyd, engineered by Alan Parsons and assisted by Peter James.

MONDAY 8 OCTOBER – RECORDING SESSION
Studio 2, EMI Studios, Abbey Road, London, England

2.00pm to 5.30pm and 7.00pm to 1.30am: 'Nick Having A Smashing Time' recorded with overdubs (Takes 1, 2, 3 & 4 not timed); "Various SFX" and "Household Drum Kit" recorded (Take 1 at 5:00 also marked "best") for the *Household Objects* project. The session was produced by Pink Floyd, engineered by Alan Parsons and assisted by Peter James.

TUESDAY 9 OCTOBER – RECORDING SESSION
Studio 2, EMI Studios, Abbey Road, London, England

2.00pm to 4.00pm: Various SFX recorded and overdubbed onto 'Nozee, Pt. 7' [Note: The track 'Nozzee' was first recorded at Air Studios on 11 September 1971], and 9.00pm to 12.00 midnight: 'Pop Goes The Weasel' recorded and remixed to stereo for the *Household Objects* project. The session was produced by Pink Floyd, engineered by Alan Parsons and assisted by Peter James.

WEDNESDAY 10 OCTOBER – RECORDING SESSION
Studio 2, EMI Studios, Abbey Road, London, England

2.00pm to 5.30pm and 7.00pm to 11.00pm: SFX overdubbed onto 'Pop Goes The Weasel' and Various SFX overdubbed onto the track 'Papa Was A Rolling Floyd' (Take 1) for the *Household Objects* project. The session was produced by Pink Floyd, engineered by Alan Parsons and assisted by Peter James.

FRIDAY 12 OCTOBER – PERFORMANCE
Münchener Olympiahalle, Olympia Park, Munich, West Germany

Additional musicians on this and the 13 October show included Billie Barnum (Backing Vocals), Venetta Fields (Backing Vocals), Clydie King (Backing Vocals) and Dick Parry (Saxophone). Set list: 'Obscured By Clouds', 'When You're In', 'Set The Controls For The Heart Of The Sun', 'Careful With That Axe, Eugene', 'Echoes' <Intermission> *The Dark Side of the Moon* <Encore> 'One Of These Days'.

SATURDAY 13 OCTOBER – PERFORMANCE
Stadthalle, Vienna, Austria

Set list: 'Obscured By Clouds', 'When You're In', 'Set The Controls For The Heart Of The Sun', 'Careful With That Axe, Eugene', 'Echoes' <Intermission> *The Dark Side of the Moon* <Encore> One Of These Days'.

MONDAY 22 OCTOBER – RECORDING SESSION
Studio 2, EMI Studios, Abbey Road, London, England

2.00pm to 6.00pm: 'The Hard Way' click-track recorded (Take 1 marked "best"), and 7.30pm to 1.00am: Rubber Band Bass overdubbed onto 'The Hard Way' (Take 1) for the *Household Objects* project. The session was produced by Pink Floyd, engineered by Alan Parsons and assisted by Peter James.

TUESDAY 23 OCTOBER – RECORDING SESSION
Studio 2, EMI Studios, Abbey Road, London, England

2.00pm to 6.00pm: 'The Hard Way (Version 2)' recorded with overdubs (Takes 1-8 and Take 9 marked "best"), and 7.30pm to 12.00 midnight: Various SFX recorded in the studio and loops made up, and Foot Bass Drum and Hi-Hat overdubbed onto 'The Hard Way (Version 2)' for the *Household Objects* project. The session was produced by Pink Floyd, engineered by Alan Parsons and assisted by Peter James.

WEDNESDAY 24 OCTOBER – RECORDING SESSION
Studio 2, EMI Studios, Abbey Road, London, England

2.00pm to 5.30pm: 'The Hard Way (Versions 3 & 4)' recorded (Take 1 also marked "best"), and 7.00pm to 12.30am: Footsteps and other SFX recorded and loops made up; Foot Bass Drum and Rubber Band Bass overdubbed onto 'The Hard Way (Version 4)' and edited for the *Household Objects* project. The session was produced by Pink Floyd, engineered by Alan Parsons and assisted by Peter James.

THURSDAY 25 OCTOBER – RECORDING SESSION
Studio 2, EMI Studios, Abbey Road, London, England

2.00pm to 7.30pm: Copying 'The Hard Way (Version 4)' to 8-track and editing and copying back to 16-track for the *Household Objects* project. The session was produced by Pink Floyd, engineered by Alan Parsons and assisted by Peter James.

MONDAY 29 OCTOBER – RECORDING SESSION
Studio 2, EMI Studios, Abbey Road, London, England

2.00pm to 6.00pm: Transfer to 16-track of 'Wineglass Chords' for "further use" [Note: 'Wine Glass Chords' was recorded as 'Nothing Part 5' on 5 January 1971], and 7.30pm to 12.30am: "Brandy Glass, Garden Trowel, Miscellaneous Bottles and Pieces of Paper etc." overdubbed onto 'The Hard Way (Version 4)' for the *Household Objects* project. The session was produced by Pink Floyd, engineered by Alan Parsons and assisted by Peter James.

TUESDAY 30 OCTOBER – RECORDING SESSION
Studio 2, EMI Studios, Abbey Road, London, England

2.00pm to 7.00pm: "Aerosol & Knife and Chewed Carrots" and "new click track" overdubbed onto 'The Hard Way (Version 4)', and 8.30pm to 12.00midnight: "Footsteps and brush" overdubbed onto 'The Hard Way (Version 5)' (Take 1 also marked "best") and a "tape loop made up and transferred to 16-track for superimposition" for the *Household Objects* project. The session was produced by Pink Floyd, engineered by Alan Parsons and assisted by Peter James.

WEDNESDAY 31 OCTOBER – RECORDING SESSION
Studio 2, EMI Studios, Abbey Road, London, England

2.00pm to 6.00pm: "Rubber Bands" overdubbed onto 'The Hard Way (Version 5)', and 7.30pm to 12.45am: "Bass Drum (Foot)" and "Rubber Bands" overdubbed onto 'The Hard Way (Version 5)', then

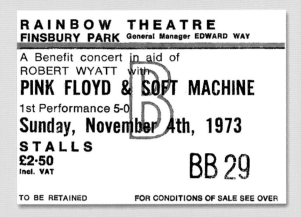

RAINBOW THEATRE
FINSBURY PARK General Manager EDWARD WAY

A Benefit concert in aid of
ROBERT WYATT with

PINK FLOYD & SOFT MACHINE

1st Performance 5-0
Sunday, November 4th, 1973

STALLS
£2·50   BB 29
Incl. VAT

TO BE RETAINED   FOR CONDITIONS OF SALE SEE OVER

transferred to 8-track and edited and transferred back to 16-track for the *Household Objects* project. The session was produced by Pink Floyd, engineered by Alan Parsons and assisted by Peter James.

FRIDAY 2 NOVEMBER – FILM PREMIERE
Pink Floyd Live at Pompeii,
Alouette Theatre, Montréal, Canada

Billboard reported that "perhaps an odd location for a premiere because 1.5 million people in Québec have already seen the core hour on television. Since then it has been expanded to feature length with the addition of music from *The Dark Side of the Moon* and some informal interviews. With the additional footage The Pink Floyd is stirring up a lot more excitement in Montréal prior to opening in other major cities across Canada."

SATURDAY 3 NOVEMBER – RECORDING SESSION
Studio 2, EMI Studios, Abbey Road, London, England

2.00pm to 6.00pm: 'Nozee' (Take 1 also marked "best") recorded and mixed down, and 7.30pm to 2.30am: 'Nozee, Pts 2 & 3' recorded (Takes 2 and 3 both marked "best") and mixed down, and 'Bottles' recorded for the *Household Objects* project. The session was produced by Pink Floyd, engineered by Alan Parsons and assisted by Peter James.

SATURDAY 3 NOVEMBER – REHEARSALS
St Augustine's Road, Camden, London, England

Pre-show rehearsals for the backing vocalists Vicki Brown and Liza Strike were arranged from 12.00pm to 2.00pm at Nick Mason's house.

SUNDAY 4 NOVEMBER – PERFORMANCES ◀
A Benefit for Robert Wyatt, Rainbow Theatre, Finsbury Park, London, England

Two shows at 5.00pm and 9.00pm, with Soft Machine. Additional musicians for both shows included Vicki Brown (Backing Vocals), Liza Strike (Backing Vocals), Clare Torry (Backing Vocals) and Dick Parry (Saxophone). Set list at both shows: *The Dark Side of the Moon* <Encore> 'Obscured By Clouds', 'When You're In'.

Melody Maker reported, "It was a splendid evening of rock co-operation, in which both groups gave their services in aid of disabled drummer Robert Wyatt, and compère[host] John Peel was pleased to announce that some 10,000 pounds was raised. Heartbeats in fact commenced proceedings, pulsating through the auditorium and stilling the more excitable elements in the crowd. Clocks ticked mysteriously and with perfect precision the Floydmen slotted their live instruments into the recorded sound, combining quadraphonic pre-recorded tapes, lights, smoke and theatrical effects into a kind of rock Son et Lumière. Overhead was suspended a huge white balloon to represent the moon, on which spotlights played, and not long after [the] performance began, searchlights began to pierce the gloom, and yellow warning lights began revolving in banks on the speaker cabinets. A choir of ladies cooed like angels of mercy and as a silver ball reflecting myriad beams of light began to revolve and belch more smoke, the audience rose to give them an ovation. They deserved a Nobel prize or at least an Oscar."

MONDAY 5 TO THURSDAY 8 AND MONDAY 12 NOVEMBER – RECORDING SESSION
Studio 2, EMI Studios, Abbey Road, London, England

2.30pm to 5.30pm and 7.00pm to 12.00am each day: Unknown recording for the *Household Objects* project. The session was produced by Pink Floyd, engineered by Alan Parsons and assisted by Peter James.

RIGHT: PINK FLOYD PERFORMING AT ONE OF THE BENEFIT CONCERTS FOR ROBERT WYATT AT THE RAINBOW THEATRE, 4 NOVEMBER 1973.

TUESDAY 13 AND WEDNESDAY 14 NOVEMBER – CANCELLED RECORDING SESSION
Studio 2, EMI Studios, Abbey Road, London, England

THURSDAY 15 NOVEMBER – RECORDING SESSION
Studio 2, EMI Studios, Abbey Road, London, England
2.30pm to 5.30pm and 7.00pm to 12.00midnight: Unknown recording for the *Household Objects* project. The session was produced by Pink Floyd, engineered by Alan Parsons and assisted by Peter James.

MONDAY 19 NOVEMBER – RECORDING SESSION
Studio 2, EMI Studios, Abbey Road, London, England
2.00pm to 5.00pm: Playback of "previous titles and work to date", and 5.00pm to 9.30pm: One rough mix of the track 'The Hard Way (Version 5)' was "put onto scrap tape and taken by group". Also copy tapes of "various SFX done and taken by group" for

the *Household Objects* project. Session produced by Pink Floyd and engineered by Alan Parsons and Peter James. This was the last of the *Household Objects*s sessions and the project was abandoned.

WEDNESDAY 5 DECEMBER – FILM PREMIERE
Crystal Voyager, **Sydney Opera House, Sydney, Australia**

SATURDAY 8 DECEMBER – ALBUM RELEASE (US)
A Nice Pair

FRIDAY 21 DECEMBER – RADIO BROADCAST
Rockspeak, **Room 605, BBC World Service, Chandos Street, London**
Roger Waters gave an interview to Michael Wale for the programme *Rockspeak* for BBC Radio One. It was broadcast between 10.00pm and 12.00am.

HOUSEHOLD OBJECTS (UNRELEASED)

Nick Having A Smashing Time
Take unknown.
Basic track recorded 8 October 1973 (Takes 1–4).

Nozee
Take 4.
Basic track recorded on 11 September 1971 (Takes 1–4).
Various SFX recorded and overdubbed onto 'Nozee, Pt. 7' on 9 October 1973.

Nozee
Take 1
Basic track re-recorded and mixed on 3 November 1973.

Nozee (Parts 2 & 3)
Takes 2 & 3.
Basic track re-recorded and mixed on 3 November 1973.

Pop Goes The Weasel
Take unknown.
Basic track recorded on 9 October 1973.
SFX overdubbed onto 'Pop Goes The Weasel' on

Papa Was A Rolling Floyd
Take 1.
Basic track recorded on 10 October 1973.
Various SFX overdubbed onto 'Papa Was A Rolling Floyd' on 10 October 1973.

The Hard Way
Take 1.
Basic track recorded on 22 October 1973.
Click-track recorded and "Rubber Band Bass" overdubbed onto 'The Hard Way' on 22 October 1973.

The Hard Way (Version 2)
Take 9.
Basic track recorded with overdubs on 23 October 1973 (Takes 1–9).
Various SFX recorded in the studio and loops made up, and Foot Bass Drum and Hi-Hat overdubbed onto 'The Hard Way (Version 2)' on 23 October 1973.

The Hard Way (Version 3)
Take unknown.

made up, and "Foot Bass Drum" and "Rubber Band Bass" overdubbed onto 'The Hard Way (Version 4)', and edited on 24 October 1973. Copying 'The Hard Way (Version 4)' to 8-track and editing and copying back to 16-track on 25 October 1973.
"Brandy Glass, Garden Trowel, Miscellaneous Bottles and Pieces of Paper etc." overdubbed onto 'The Hard Way (Version 4)' on 29 October 1973.
"Aerosol & Knife" and "Chewed Carrots" and new click track overdubbed onto 'The Hard Way (Version 4)' on 30 October 1973.

The Hard Way (Version 5)
Take 1.
Basic track recorded on 30 October 1973.
"Footsteps and Brush" overdubbed onto 'The Hard Way (Version 5)' on 30 October 1973.
Tape loop made up and transferred to 16-track for superimposition on 30 October 1973.
"Rubber Bands" overdubbed onto 'The Hard Way (Version 5)' on 31 October 1973.
Bass Drum (Foot) and "Rubber Bands" overdubbed onto 'The Hard Way (Version 5)', then transferred to 8-track and edited and transferred back to 16-track on

6 RUNNING OVER THE SAME OLD GROUND

1974—75

1974–75

Pink Floyd's break from both live performance and recording from late 1973 into early 1974 saw Gilmour and Mason, for the first time, significantly involved in projects outside the band.

Gilmour had been introduced to a talented young singer-songwriter called Kate Bush, and eventually influenced EMI's decision to sign her. He had also spotted a band called Unicorn at a friend's wedding reception the previous summer. After inviting them to test out his new home studio, he financed some recording sessions at Olympic studios in London, and produced their debut album, *Blue Pine Trees*. Steve O'Rourke became Unicorn's manager, signing them to Chrysalis, and they went on to make three albums.

Mason, meanwhile, lent his hand to producing the avant-garde performance troupe Principal Edwards Magic Theatre as well as ex-Soft Machine Robert Wyatt. With Wyatt he also performed at London's Theatre Royal, as well as appearing on BBC TV's *Top of the Pops* in September 1974 with a cover of the Monkees' 'I'm A Believer' in a pick-up band that also featured Andy Summers, later of the Police.

However, all of this was not before the UK press had picked up on the fact that on 29 April 1974 five weeks of filming was due to commence in Scotland and Northumberland on the feature film *Monty Python and the Holy Grail* (described by the Pythons as a "cheap medieval extravaganza"). After EMI pulled out of funding, and after much begging and borrowing, its chief investors were noted as being the West End theatre producer Michael White, Island Records, Charisma Records, Led Zeppelin and Pink Floyd.

Distractions aside, it wasn't long before Pink Floyd was back in the studio, finding it hard to let go of the routine of constant activity, and by spring they were already working hard on new material. They booked rehearsal time at a studio in King's Cross, London, where many of the songs for the next two albums would emerge, not least a stunning new title, 'Shine On' (later changed to 'Shine On You Crazy Diamond'), an ode to Syd Barrett.

"We started playing together and writing in the way we'd written a lot of things before. In the same way that 'Echoes' was written," Waters remembered. "'Shine On You Crazy Diamond' was written in exactly the same way, with odd little musical ideas coming out of various people. The first one, the main phrase, came from Dave, the first loud guitar phrase you can hear on the album was the starting point and we worked from there until we had the various parts of 'Shine On You Crazy Diamond'."[(1)]

A second number, entitled 'Raving And Drooling', was also worked out and both tracks were premiered in June during a tour of France – the only country outside the UK where Pink Floyd would perform this year. 'Shine On' was also notable on live dates in the period for including a few bars of 'Bike', 'The Gnome', 'Scarecrow' or 'Arnold Layne' towards the close. The finished recording would include 'See Emily Play'.

The entourage was also expanded by the hiring of many extra hands, including Phil Taylor, who remained with the band through their last tour of 1994 and continues to be Gilmour's chief technician at both his studio and on solo performances to this day.

Pink Floyd had also gone to considerable effort and expense to redesign their stage presentation to create a far greater visual impact than ever before. The show now featured, at the centre rear of the stage, a 40-foot circular screen, which was used to back-project specially prepared 35mm film and animation sequences designed by Birmingham art college student Ian Emes. The screen also served as a backdrop at the close of 'Shine On', when a huge rotating mirror-ball was raised in front of it and hit with a spotlight to produce blinding shards of white light, under cover of which the band exited. Fireworks and rockets also provided some spectacular visual effects.

A succession of cancelled and rescheduled dates for the forthcoming French tour occurred when promoters realized just how much electrical power the band's new

OPPOSITE: DAVID GILMOUR ON STAGE IN LOS ANGELES, APRIL 1975.

RIGHT: ON STAGE IN COLMAR, FRANCE, 22 JUNE, 1974. PINK FLOYD'S TOUR OF FRANCE SAW THE FIRST USE OF THEIR TRADEMARK CIRCULAR SCREEN.

equipment required and the ceiling height that was needed to accommodate the huge circular screen. However, the shows that did go ahead in the five cities in which Pink Floyd performed were well-received sell-outs, setting new attendance records at several of the venues.

Whereas problematic dates were eventually straightened out, a sponsorship campaign into which the band entered with the French soft drinks company Gini on their 1972 tour was more complicated. The agreement required a photo shoot in Morocco for press adverts and the recording of a song for TV and radio ads, which Waters penned, called 'Bitter Love'. The band was offered the princely sum of £50,000 for this, which seemed a good idea at the time, despite a disagreement with Waters having been told he wouldn't be singing on the track. However, the campaign stalled until Pink Floyd hit France in the summer of 1974 and found Gini sponsorship adorning the tour publicity. It is not clear whether the TV ad was ever aired. It is an incident that the band has chosen to put down to experience and all the monies were subsequently donated to charity.

Even so, the episode left Waters disgruntled and, after taking a short break following the tour, he started writing a new song, 'How Do You Feel', which remains unreleased, expressing his feelings about the experience. But Pink Floyd was still inviting sponsorship of sorts, and all band members were seen sporting Guinness t-shirts on stage throughout the year. Similarly an advertising campaign launched in 1973 by Avis rental vehicles also attracted the band's name, with the slogan 'Make tracks like Pink Floyd – Rent an Avis truck' and also in 1974 a bizarre US TV commercial for Dole bananas which used the track 'The Great Gig In The Sky' in a strangely psychedelic advertisement for the fruit culminating with a voiceover saying, "If you can feel it, peel it!"

A short tour of the UK spanning November and December was dubbed the *1974 British Winter Tour* and, in typical fashion, was planned to coincide with football matches in each city, in order that the band could enjoy watching an afternoon match before each show. By now 'Shine On' had become 'Shine On You Crazy Diamond' and, like 'Raving And Drooling', had been knocked into better shape. The band also added a third new song to the set, 'Gotta Be Crazy', which had been penned by Waters at home and to which Gilmour added the chord sequence at a later date. All three songs were very harsh in comparison to the softer melodies of *The Dark Side of the Moon* and the lyrics were an unforgiving tirade against society's current values. It certainly laid to rest the last traces of Floyd's psychedelic past.

Meanwhile the choice of films the band had projected on to the circular screen for *The Dark Side of the Moon* half of the show in France was now extensively refined, with whole new sequences being produced throughout the rest of the summer. In addition, a three-week rehearsal period was booked at the Elstree film studios, north of London, before

the tour to allow the band to work out the intricate timings that were required to keep the music in sync with the visual material.

Audiences in Britain were treated to a version of *The Dark Side of the Moon* with greater dimension and visual impact than ever before. The piece began with quadraphonic sound blasting out the taped maniacal laughter that appears on the album and the spoken line of "I've been mad for fucking years" repeated over and over again at high volume. A picture of the moon grew bigger and bigger until it occupied the whole screen and then, with the underlying heart beat now very audible, this gave way to a darting cardiograph blip, allowing the band to launch into 'Breathe'.

Perhaps the most outstanding feature of all was the sequence for 'On The Run' and 'Time'. A series of flashing street, car, airport and aircraft lights, in bewildering and dazzling succession, led the viewer into a tunnel with a planet at the far end. As this image seemed to rush towards the viewer, the film switched to animation, skimming across the planet's surface and then sweeping through urban landscapes to reveal scenes of utter destruction.

The 'Time' sequence, again animated, was equally remarkable: flights of clock faces were seen passing across a cloudy sky, then piling up against one another and peeling away, squadrons of them flying through the air as their hands raced around. The final scene focused on a pendulum sweeping the sky to introduce the opening line of the song.

'The Great Gig In The Sky' featured underwater shots taken from the film *Crystal Voyager* and 'Money' had a series of rapid-fire shots of banknotes, women parading in fur coats, a lyrically appropriate Learjet and even copies of *The Dark Side of the Moon* coming off the production line.

'Us And Them', the dreamy blues number from the album, featured slow-motion footage of the rush hour in the City of London in contrast with the diamond miners of South Africa. As *The Dark Side of the Moon* came to its grand finale with 'Brain Damage', film images of politicians were used to compliment the accompanying insane laughter. The eclipse of the sun by the moon concluded the epic piece.

The UK tour was a complete success, with every venue sold out. BBC Radio One even recorded a show at Wembley for a complete broadcast of *The Dark Side of the Moon*, which has since been officially released, wowing many more fans.

However, this was also the first time that a noticeable backlash against the band occurred within the national music press. Throughout the early 1970s Pink Floyd had reigned supreme, but the concerts at Wembley's Empire Pool brought disdain from a younger generation of up-and-coming critics, principally Nick Kent of the *NME*, who described their show as "a pallid excuse for creative music". Such criticisms would continue to escalate, but ultimately failed to dent their increasing popularity.

Confident they had a good starting point, Pink Floyd entered EMI's newly refitted Studio 3 at Abbey Road on Monday 13 January 1975 to start work on their seventh studio album, *Wish You Were Here*. But the reality of having to produce a new record proved to be as problematic as their late-1973 sessions. Amazingly CBS optimistically slated the new album for an April release and a West Coast tour of North America was booked to coincide with it. It became quickly apparent the album would never be ready in time but this, and a further tour of North America in June, straddled the protracted recording process.

Waters has, on many occasions, stated in print that *The Dark Side of the Moon* more or less finished the group as a creative force, since they had fulfilled at a stroke the shared ambition of fame and fortune. They were also held back by general lethargy, promoted by an alarming divorce rate within the band. Although his own marriage had hit the skids recently, Waters was able to divert his energies into song-writing. But in Mason's case his impending split "manifested itself into complete, well, rigor mortis. I didn't quite have to be carried about, but I wasn't interested. I couldn't get myself to sort out the drumming, and that of course drove everyone else even crazier."[2]

"I definitely think that at the *Wish You Were Here* recording sessions most of us didn't wish we were there at all, we wished we were somewhere else," Waters recalled. "I wasn't happy being there because I got the feeling we weren't together. The album is about none of us really being there, or being there only marginally. About our non-presence in the situation we had clung to through habit, and are still clinging to through habit – being Pink Floyd."[3] Consequently further tensions surfaced as the boredom of the process took its toll and band members became increasingly uninterested in turning up for sessions at all. "Punctuality became an issue," Mason recalled. "If two of us were on time and the others were late, we were quite capable of working ourselves up into a righteous fury. The following day the roles could easily be reversed. None of us was free from blame.'[4]

"We pressed on regardless of the general ennui for a few weeks and then things came to a bit of a head," said Waters. "I felt that the only way I could retain interest in the project was to try to make the album relate to what was going on there and then – i.e. the fact that no one was really looking each other in the eye, and that it was all very mechanical…. We all sat round and unburdened ourselves a lot, and I took notes on what everybody was saying. It was a meeting [3 March, to be precise] about what wasn't happening and why…. So I suggested we change it – that we didn't do the other two songs ['Raving And Drooling' and 'Gotta Be Crazy', which had been performed live through 1974] but tried somehow to make a bridge between the first and second halves of 'Shine On', which is how 'Welcome To The Machine', 'Wish You Were Here' and 'Have A Cigar' came in…. Dave was always clear that he wanted to do the other two songs – he never quite copped what I was talking about. But Rick did and Nicky did and he was outvoted, so we went on."[5] Gilmour

wasn't convinced: "After *Dark Side* we really were floundering around. I wanted to make the next album more musical. I always thought that Roger's emergence as a great lyric writer was such that he came to overshadow the music."[6]

Mason's inertia was but one cause for frustration in the studio. More testing was the fact that Waters' vocal sessions on 'Shine On You Crazy Diamond' were proving immensely problematic. "It was right on the edge of my range," he recalled. "I always felt very insecure about singing anyway because I'm not naturally able to sing well. I know what I wanna do but I don't have the ability to do it well. It was fantastically boring to record, 'cos I had to do it line by line, doing it over and over again just to get it sounding reasonable."[7]

The sessions through the remainder of March saw much of the same. Initial takes of 'Welcome To The Machine' were set aside in favour of recording 'Have A Cigar'. It is Waters' cynical take on the music industry and contains the immortal line: "Oh

BELOW: PERFORMING *THE DARK SIDE OF THE MOON* IN LONDON, NOVEMBER 1974.

by the way, which one's Pink?" "We did have people who would say to us: 'Which one's Pink?' and stuff like that," Gilmour recalled. "There were an awful lot of people who thought Pink Floyd was the name of the lead singer, and that was Pink himself and the band. That's how it all came about. It was quite genuine." Indeed some concert reviews of the period credit the appearance of "Pink Floyd and his band".

But Waters' singing was becoming ever more laborious and after some 55 aborted vocal takes they invited Roy Harper to have a go, who managed it in just one! "Roy was recording in the studio anyway," recalled Waters, "and was in and out all the time. I can't remember who suggested it, maybe I did, probably hoping everybody would go 'Oh no Rog, you do it', but they didn't! They all went, 'Oh yeah that's a good idea'. And he did it (as well as a vocal duet with Gilmour) and everybody went, 'Oh, terrific!' So that was that."[8] It seems to be a decision that Waters has regretted to this day, and although he was reluctantly conceded a credit on the album, there was certainly no question of payment. Tape engineer John Leckie recalled Waters saying to Harper that they must make sure he paid for his efforts. "And Roy said: 'Just get me life season ticket to Lord's [cricket ground].' He kept prompting Roger, but it never came. About 10 years later Roy wrote a letter to Roger, and decided that, due to the success of *Wish You Were Here*, £10,000 would be adequate. And heard nothing at all."[9]

Work progressed on the new album's remaining two tracks through July, starting with 'Welcome To The Machine'. Once again Waters delivered a cynical take on the treadmill

of existence. It was sung by Gilmour, whose warmer vocal delivery actually disorientates the listener. Gilmour recalled the development of the track being "very much a made-up-in-the-studio thing which was all built up from a basic throbbing made on a VCS3 [synthesizer], with a one repeat echo used so that each boom is followed by an echo repeat to give the throb. With a number like that, you don't start off with a regular concept of group structure or anything, and there's no backing track either. Really it is just a studio proposition where we're using tape for its own ends – a form of collage using sound."[10]

Ordinarily, the band would develop ideas for songs through music, but in the case of the title track it was Gilmour who built the music around an existing piece of poetry by Waters. 'Wish You Were Here'. The masterstroke of is the use of a tinny transistor radio that links the end of 'Shine On...' to Gilmour's delicate guitar work at the beginning of 'Wish You Were Here' – apparently recorded on Gilmour's car radio, with an excerpt of Tchaikovsky's *Fourth Symphony* creeping in. "It's all meant to sound like the first track getting sucked into the radio with one person sitting in the room playing guitar along to the radio,"[11] he explained.

One final incident at those sessions has since passed into Pink Floyd lore: the sudden and uncanny appearance of Syd Barrett in the studio, allegedly on 5 June; their last session before departing for their second North American tour of the year. It was all the more bizarre because none of the band recognized him at first, assuming he was a caretaker. Accounts vary considerably, as does the spectrum of so-called eyewitnesses suggesting that in some cases he was there on more than one occasion. However, one thing they all do agree on is that his appearance had changed dramatically: he had a shaven head, was extremely overweight and was wearing tatty clothes, as is evidenced from a photograph reproduced in Mason's book *Inside Out.* He hardly spoke a word and after a short time merely wandered off. It was the last time the band had any further face-to-face contact with him. "I'm very sad about Syd," Waters declared. "I wasn't for years. For years I suppose he was a threat because of all that bollocks written about him and us. Of course he was

LEFT: PERFORMING 'MONEY' AS COPIES OF THE ALBUM COME ROLLING OFF THE PRODUCTION LINE, LOS ANGELES, APRIL 1975.

very important and the band would never have fucking started without him but on the other hand it couldn't have gone on with him. He may or may not be important in rock 'n' roll anthology terms but he's certainly not nearly as important say in terms of Pink Floyd. 'Shine On' is not really about Syd, he's just a symbol for the extremes of absence some people have to indulge in because it's the only way they can cope with how fucking sad it is – modern life, to withdraw completely."[12] Listen carefully to Part 9 of 'Shine On You Crazy Diamond' and you'll hear Wright pick out the melody of 'See Emily Play' as the track fades out.

Wish You Were Here was released on 15 September and went straight to the top of the album charts on both sides of the Atlantic. By 2011 the album was estimated to have sold more than 14 million copies worldwide.

As Richard Wright fondly remembered, "I think that's my favourite album that the Floyd ever did. I feel the best material from the Floyd was definitely when two or three of us co-wrote something together. Afterwards we lost that; there wasn't that feeling of interplay of ideas between the band."[13] Ultimately *Wish You Were Here* benefits from Waters' less confrontational lyrics (these would resurface on their next album *Animals*), as well as Gilmour and Wright's classic atmospherics, to produce what is quite possibly the definitive Pink Floyd album. It is detached yet engaging.

On tour fans witnessed for the first time the full visual impact of Pink Floyd's new stage show, complete with circular film screen, giant mirror ball, crashing model aircraft and obligatory pyrotechnics, in addition to the trademark quadraphonic sound system. It was a large-scale operation in every sense: over 30 tons of equipment, much of it shipped from England, was transported around the country, and it took a full-time road crew of seventeen to make the event possible. The band also chartered a private jet to travel between shows, while the road crew moved the gear in a convoy of trucks.

The Dark Side of the Moon still formed the mainstay of the second half of the show, with 'Echoes' as an encore. The first half continued to open with 'Raving And Drooling' and 'Gotta Be Crazy' but now divided the lengthy 'Shine On You Crazy Diamond' into two halves which straddled Waters' new composition, 'Have A Cigar'.

Although the vast array of visual effects had been a spectacular feature of indoor arenas, the band had to come up with some ideas in order to deal with the larger venues booked on the East Coast leg of the tour in June. Their still primitive staging, small-scale compared to the vast structures of today's stadium concerts, looked decidedly lost in the vast expanses of the huge sports stadiums in which they were now preparing to perform.

In an attempt to boost the visual impact the band turned to Mark Fisher and Jonathan Park, two accomplished London-based architectural designers with experience of advanced inflatable and pneumatic structures. Their brief was to

construct a huge pyramid that would sail above the stage and radiate light beams in a way that was reminiscent of the cover of *The Dark Side of the Moon*.

Assembled in record time, the structure made its maiden flight at the Atlanta Stadium on 7 June, but having failed to work properly didn't resurface again until the band's show at the Three Rivers Stadium in Pittsburgh, on 20 June. The huge pyramid, its base 60-foot square, was held by guides and launched from the back of the stage at the climax of the show and rose some distance before a heavy wind blew it over, dislodging the helium balloon inside. The balloon was never seen again, nor was the pyramid which, after crashing into a number of vehicles in the stadium car park, was shredded in minutes by souvenir-hungry fans.

With the final American tour over, Pink Floyd gave a long-awaited homecoming concert at Knebworth Park in rural Hertfordshire on 5 July. But far from being a spectacular success, the concert was dogged by problems from the start, among which was the use of Pink Floyd's own PA system for the entire day's entertainment. Due to the late delivery of some new components, this was still being rigged on the morning of the show.

In addition, their stage entrance had been precisely scheduled to coincide with the fly-past of two Second World War Spitfires, but the aircraft buzzed the audience at low level while the roadies were still frantically trying to prepare the stage. Eventually when the band came on it was evident their performance was tired and was marred throughout by technical breakdowns, mainly due to power surges in the generators' output. The most noticeable result of this occurred during 'Raving And Drooling', when the stage-right PA stack failed altogether. The problem was rectified, but a further surge put Richard Wright's Hammond organ out of tune. The instrument couldn't be retuned and Wright was forced to use his Farfisa instead, which gave the rest of the show a very hard, mechanical feel.

For the audience it was an uncomfortable day. The concert was licenced only for 40,000, but by early evening the perimeter fencing was eventually removed to accommodate the audience, which had swelled to an estimated 100,000. And yet, all in all, it was not quite the return the fans had been expecting from Pink Floyd, especially as it was their first British show for seven months.

The UK music press gave mixed reviews. Some accused them of turning in a poor performance, others criticized them for playing *The Dark Side of the Moon* yet again and others for playing in their own country all too infrequently. Whereas Pink Floyd had been seen as stalwarts of the British rock underground, regular performers at festivals and smaller venues, the view now was that the industry machine had taken over and the band had distanced themselves from their roots. However, this was an inevitable outcome: those same journalists who had popularized the band had contributed to their massive success. Besides, as much as the band disliked it, they and their management couldn't ignore the fact that North America

was where the money was. Underlining this fact, the North American tour had propelled *The Dark Side of the Moon* back into the US *Billboard* Top 100 album charts, where it re-entered on 12 April 1975 remaining there until 6 March 1977.

The final mixing and overdubs for *Wish You Were Here* were completed in the immediate aftermath of the Knebworth debacle and on 7 July Gilmour married his long term partner, the American-born Virginia 'Ginger' Hasenbein. The reception was held at Abbey Road.

As on all Pink Floyd's albums the artwork was quite unique and again designed by Storm Thorgerson and friends at Hipgnosis. It acted as a very specific visual representation of the subject matter and continued the theme of alienation and absence throughout. Even the sleeve was concealed by a black shrink-wrap outer covering, which made the whole album look appropriately anonymous, much to the consternation of sales teams who insisted on an identifying sticker at the very least. On release *Wish You Were Here* went straight to the top of the album charts on both sides of the Atlantic, and became an instant platinum million seller in the US.

But the overwhelming attention and adulation the band had received on its US tour had left Roger Waters cold. He felt a distinct sense of isolation, with the back row getting further and further away. The fans' intense enthusiasm gave the impression the event was incidental to the music.

Interviews of the period are scarce; Pink Floyd actually employed a tour PR to give a negative answer to any press requests. There are also few on-stage photographs, as entry was also discouraged in a trend that continued right through their tours of 1977, and consequently stage shots from the period showing the use of pyrotechnics and inflatables are scarce in the extreme. This was seen as the beginning of Pink

Floyd's disengagement with the industry. They had never been public personalities; interviews could often be obtuse at the best of times, and reading them back in the period after they had found success with *The Dark Side of the Moon* gives the impression the band really couldn't be bothered. It was an act that would also ensure their anonymity and reinforce their cult-like status.

No doubt compounded by his personal problems, and an increasing reluctance to tour, Waters later said that, "I cast myself back into how fucking dreadful I felt on the last American tour with all those thousands and thousands and thousands of drunken kids smashing each other to pieces. I felt dreadful because it had nothing to do with us – I didn't think there was any contact between us and them."[14]

That feeling of isolation was an idea that he would nurture over the next few years, and one that would manifest itself in one of the biggest rock albums of all time.

ABOVE: ROGERS WATERS ON STAGE, DETROIT, 24 JUNE 1975.

1. *Wish You Were Here Song Book*, Music Sales America, 1975.
2. *A Saucerful of Secrets* by Nicholas Schaffner, Harmony Books, 1991.
3. *Wish You Were Here Song Book*, Music Sales America, 1975.
4. *Inside Out* by Nick Mason, Weidenfeld & Nicolson, 2004.
5. *Wish You Were Here Song Book*, Music Sales America, 1975.
6. *Mojo*, May 1994.
7. *Wish You Were Here Song Book*, Music Sales America, 1975.
8. *The Pink Floyd Story*, Capital Radio, 14 January 1977.
9. *Mojo*, May 1994.
10. *Rocking the Classics* by Edward Macan, Oxford University Press, 1996.
11. *Mojo*, May 1994.
12. *Wish You Were Here Song Book*, Music Sales America, 1975.
13. *A Saucerful of Secrets*, by Nicholas Schaffner, Harmony Books, 1991.
14. *Wish You Were Here Song Book*, Music Sales America, 1975.

1974

FRIDAY 18 JANUARY – ALBUM RELEASE (UK)
A Nice Pair

The *NME* wrote, "This tastefully wrapped double album is a repackaging of the first two Floyd albums *The Piper at the Gates Of Dawn* and *A Saucerful of Secrets*. Somewhere in between these two albums Syd Barrett left the band, ridding them temporarily of their raison d'etre and thus while *Piper* is crammed full of Syd's devastatingly original, witty humorous and incisive songs, *Saucerful* is very much a transitional album, revealing elements of both what was and what was to be."

MONDAY 4 FEBRUARY – SINGLE RELEASE (US)
'Time'

WEDNESDAY 24 APRIL – FILM PREMIERE
Pink Floyd, RKO Albee Theater, Cincinnati, OH, USA

Live at Pompeii was released to theatres in North America under the title *Pink Floyd*, with little mention of the significance of the location in the publicity. Director Adrian Maben had also taken the opportunity to further enhance the film with the inclusion of sequences shot during the recording of *The Dark Side of the Moon* sessions at Abbey Road between Sunday 15 and Tuesday 17 October 1971. This also allowed for the inclusion of 'Speak To Me' to be used as the overture for the film.

Pink Floyd was distributed by April Fool films (a company specially formed for this title by the directors of the Tri-State Theatre Service and B&R Theatres on Monday 1 April, hence the name) with screenings following in the same month in Milwaukee, Columbus, Lexington, Knoxville, and several college towns before going nationally from the last week in August.

Billboard wrote, "The film is not particularly explosive, and certainly not 'more than a movie.' It is, in fact, rather dull, unimaginative and hokey and does not do justice to the Pink Floyd vision."

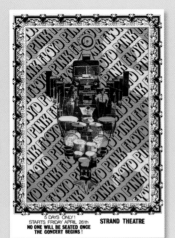

THURSDAY 6 JUNE – FILM PREMIERE (UK) ◄
Live at Pompeii, Strand Theatre, London, England

The 80-minute expanded version of *Live at Pompeii* was premiered on this date and distributed to ABC cinemas nationally from Sunday 9 June.

FRENCH TOUR ►

Many conflicting dates for shows on this tour were advertised in the French music press. This situation was caused by the additional difficulty in locating suitable venues to accommodate Pink Floyd's new stage show that used, for the first time, their trademark circular projection screen. As a result the following shows were either rescheduled or cancelled and in some cases suffered multiple cancellations following further reschedules: Palais des Sports, Cambrai on Friday 14 June (rescheduled to Tuesday 18 June, then cancelled); Palais des Sports, Lyon on Friday 14 June (rescheduled to Sunday 16 June, then Friday 21 June, then cancelled); Strasbourg on Sunday 16 June; Nancy on Sunday 16 June; Les Arènas, Parc des Expositions, Poitiers on Thursday 20 June (rescheduled to Wednesday 19 June); Parc des Expositions, Toulouse on Saturday 22 June (rescheduled to Tuesday 18 June).

ADDITIONAL TOUR PERSONNEL
Venetta Fields (Backing Vocals), Dick Parry (Saxophones), Carlena Williams (Backing Vocals).

PINK FLOYD ROAD CREW
Rufus Cartwright (Front of House Sound Engineer), Bernie Caulder (PA / Stage Technician), Alan Conway (Quad Technician), Graeme Fleming (Lighting Technician), Seth Goldman (Monitor Sound Engineer), Marek "Mick The Pole" Kluczynski (PA / Stage Technician), Mick Marshall (Lighting Technician), Arthur Max (Production Manager / Lighting), Paul Murray (Film Projection), Robin Murray (Lighting Technician), Peter Revell (Film Projection), Nick Rochford (PA / Stage Technician), Phil Taylor (Backline Technician), Robbie Williams (PA / Stage Technician).

TUESDAY 18 JUNE – PERFORMANCE
Hall 1, Parc des Expositions, Toulouse, France

Set list: 'Shine On You Crazy Diamond'*, 'Raving And Drooling', 'Echoes' <Intermission> *The Dark Side of the Moon* <Encore> 'Careful With That Axe, Eugene'.

Regional radio reportedly recorded parts of this show together with band interviews, but the content and broadcast details remain unknown.

---

*'Shine On You Crazy Diamond' is an early version of the later recorded piece 'Shine On You Crazy Diamond, Parts 1–9'.

WEDNESDAY 19 JUNE – PERFORMANCE
Les Arénas, Parc des Expositions, Poitiers, France

Set list: 'Shine On You Crazy Diamond', 'Raving And Drooling', 'Echoes' <Intermission> *The Dark Side of the Moon* <Encore> 'Careful With That Axe, Eugene'.

FRIDAY 21 JUNE – PERFORMANCE
Hall 1, Palais des Expositions, Dijon, France

Set list: 'Shine On You Crazy Diamond', 'Raving And Drooling', 'Echoes' <Intermission> *The Dark Side of the Moon* <Encore> 'Careful With That Axe, Eugene'.

SATURDAY 22 JUNE – PERFORMANCE ◄
Théâtre de Plein Air, Parc des Expositions, Colmar, France

Set list: 'Shine On You Crazy Diamond', 'Raving And Drooling', 'Echoes' <Intermission> *The Dark Side of the Moon* <Encore> 'Careful With That Axe, Eugene'.

MONDAY 24, TUESDAY 25 & WEDNESDAY 26 JUNE – PERFORMANCES
Palais des Sports, Porte de Versailles, Paris, France

Set list at all three shows: 'Shine On You Crazy Diamond', 'Raving And Drooling', 'Echoes' <Intermission> *The Dark Side of the Moon* <Encore> 'One Of These Days'.

During the afternoon of 25 June French journalists challenged Pink Floyd and their crew to a football match that was held at the University Campus, Paris. The journalists scored a 4-3 victory over Pink Floyd.

SATURDAY 24 AUGUST & SATURDAY 7 SEPTEMBER – TELEVISION BROADCAST
Point Chaud, ORTF1 TV, France

A two-part Pink Floyd special was broadcast in France following the success of their summer tour, compiling their many appearances on French TV over the years. Both programmes were broadcast between 7.00pm and 7.20pm with Part One comprising 'Atom Heart Mother' excerpt (from San Tropez, 8 August 1970), 'Set The Controls For The Heart Of The Sun' excerpt (from *Forum Musiques*, 22 January 1969), 'Let There Be More Light' (from *Samedi et Compagnie*, 6 September 1968), 'Let There Be More Light' (audio from *A Saucerful of Secrets* with images of dancers), 'Set The Controls For The Heart Of The Sun' excerpt (from *Forum Musiques*, 22 January 1969), 'Let There Be More Light' (from *Surprise Partie*, 7 September 1968) and 'Cymbaline' (from Abbaye de Royaumont, 12 June 1971); Part Two comprised 'Atom Heart Mother' excerpt (from San Tropez, 8 August 1970), *Obscured by Clouds* (from *Pop 2* broadcast 4 March 1972), 'Set The Controls For The Heart Of The Sun' (from Abbaye de Royaumont, 12 June 1971), 'One Of These Days' (from the *Pink Floyd Ballet*), 'Mademoiselle Nobs' (from *Live at Pompeii*), 'Echoes' excerpt (from Live at Pompeii), 'One Of These Days' (from *Live at Pompeii*) and 'Echoes' excerpt (*from Live at Pompeii*).

BRITISH WINTER TOUR 1974 ▼

Pink Floyd embarked on a short UK tour performing an expanded set incorporating 'Gotta Be Crazy' alongside 'Shine On You Crazy Diamond' and 'Raving And Drooling', as well as new film sequences projected on the giant circular screen.

ADDITIONAL TOUR PERSONNEL
Venetta Fields (Backing Vocals), Dick Parry (Saxophones), Carlena Williams (Backing Vocals).

PINK FLOYD ROAD CREW
Rufus Cartwright (Front of House Sound Engineer from Monday 4 to Thursday 14 November), Bernie Caulder (PA / Stage Technician), Alan Conway (Quad Technician), Paul Devine (PA / Stage Technician), Graeme Fleming (Lighting Technician), Seth Goldman (Monitor Sound Engineer), Brian Humphries (Front of House Sound Engineer from Friday 15 November to Saturday 14 December), Marek "Mick The Pole" Kluczynski (PA / Stage Technician), Mick Marshall (Lighting Technician), Arthur Max (Production Manager / Lighting from Monday 4 November to Friday 22 November), George Merriman (PA / Stage Technician), Paul Murray (Film Projection), Robin Murray (Lighting Technician), Peter Revell (Film Projection), Nick Rochford (PA / Stage Technician), Phil Taylor (Backline Technician), Jim Thompson (PA / Stage Technician), Robbie Williams (PA / Stage Technician).

MONDAY 23 SEPTEMBER – FRIDAY 18 OCTOBER – REHEARSALS
Unit Studios, Kings Cross, London, England

Band rehearsals for the forthcoming UK tour.

MONDAY 20 – WEDNESDAY 30 OCTOBER – REHEARSALS
Elstree Film Studios, Borehamwood, England

Full production rehearsals for the forthcoming UK tour were made on a sound stage at the renowned film studios, in part to work out the synching of their new backing films with animation director Ian Emes.

FRIDAY 25 OCTOBER – RADIO BROADCAST
Rockspeak, Room 605, BBC World Service, Chandos Street, London

Richard Wright gave an interview to Michael Wale for the BBC Radio One show *Rockspeak*, which was broadcast between 10.00pm and 12.00 midnight.

THURSDAY 31 OCTOBER – FILM PREMIERE
Crystal Voyager, Odeon, St Martin's Lane, London, England

Shown as a double-bill alongside *Fantastic Planet*, this unique surfing film featuring Pink Floyd's 'Echoes' enjoyed a six-month run at the Odeon. It opened across the UK from Friday 8 November.

The *Daily Express* wrote, "I've nothing against water. After all, you can use it for washing your backs, boiling an egg or as a playground for your goldfish. I don't, however, get much pleasure from watching the useful element washing over the screen for about 20 minutes as happens at the end of this film, with musical accompaniment provided by the pop group Pink Floyd. I wouldn't like it even without Pink Floyd."

MONDAY 4 & TUESDAY 5 NOVEMBER – PERFORMANCES
Usher Hall, Edinburgh, Scotland

Set list at both shows: 'Shine On You Crazy Diamond', 'Raving And Drooling', 'Gotta Be Crazy' <Intermission> *The Dark Side of the Moon* <Encore> 'Echoes'.

FRIDAY 8 & SATURDAY 9 NOVEMBER – PERFORMANCES
Odeon, Newcastle-upon-Tyne, England

Set list at both shows: 'Shine On You Crazy Diamond', 'Raving And Drooling', 'Gotta Be Crazy' <Intermission> *The Dark Side of the Moon* <Encore> 'Echoes'.

The band attended the Newcastle United vs Middlesbrough FC football match at St James Park, Newcastle-upon-Tyne on the afternoon of Saturday 9 November.

TUESDAY 12 NOVEMBER – RECORDING SESSION
Studio 2, EMI Studios, Abbey Road, London, England

Recording the sound effects track 'Jimmy Young Tape' for the introduction to the live shows and used from 14 November onwards.

THURSDAY 14 NOVEMBER – PERFORMANCE
Empire Pool, Wembley, England

Set list: 'Shine On You Crazy Diamond', 'Raving And Drooling', 'Gotta Be Crazy' <Intermission> *The Dark Side of the Moon* <Encore> 'Echoes'.

The *NME* reported, "After approximately five minutes of slightly laboured tuning up, the band start their first number of the set – a new composition entitled 'Shine On You Crazy Diamond'. It is very slow, rather low on melodic inventiveness, each note hanging in that archetypal ominous stunted fashion that tends to typify the Floyd at their most uninspired. This thoroughly unimpressive beginning is duly followed by the second of the three new numbers to be showcased in this section. 'Raving And Drooling' is motivated by a rhythm somewhat akin to that of the human heartbeat with further references gathered from numerous Floyd stylised devices. So then there was 'Gotta Be Crazy', the magnum opus of this dubious triumvirate, which features a fairly decent melody; a fetching minor chord strummed out by Gilmour who also sings over it. Unfortunately, the Floyd as always, let the song sprawl out to last twice as long as it should. The second half is, of course, taken up by the whole *Dark Side of the Moon* presentation, to be graced by the projection of a special film made as a visual complement to the music. Finally the set is completed and the

band walk off to ecstatic applause. They eventually return for an encore – no thank-yous or anything, and the band do 'Echoes'. Visuals are now relegated to luminous green orbs of circular light projected on the big screen."

FRIDAY 15 NOVEMBER – PERFORMANCE ▶
Empire Pool, Wembley, England

Set list: 'Shine On You Crazy Diamond', 'Raving And Drooling', 'Gotta Be Crazy' <Intermission> *The Dark Side of the Moon* <Encore> 'Echoes'.

SATURDAY 16 NOVEMBER – PERFORMANCE
Empire Pool, Wembley, England

Set list: 'Shine On You Crazy Diamond', 'Raving And Drooling', 'Gotta Be Crazy' <Intermission> *The Dark Side of the Moon* <Encore> 'Echoes'.

BBC Radio One recorded the show and the entire second half of *The Dark Side of the Moon* (with the spoken word expletive in 'Speak To Me' removed from the mix) was broadcast, on the *Alan Freeman Show* on Saturday 11 January 1975 between 2.00pm and 5.00pm. The complete recording was repeated on *The Friday Rock Show* on BBC Radio One on 13 April 1979 between 10.00pm and 12.00 midnight and for the third and last time, again on *The Friday Rock Show*, broadcast on BBC Radio One on Friday 23 July 1982 between 10.00pm and 12.00 midnight.

SUNDAY 17 NOVEMBER – PERFORMANCE
Empire Pool, Wembley, England

Set list: 'Shine On You Crazy Diamond', 'Raving And Drooling', 'Gotta Be Crazy' <Intermission> *The Dark Side of the Moon* <Encore> 'Echoes'.

This show was originally scheduled to commence at 3.00pm but in the event didn't start until 6.00pm, still a full two hours earlier than all of the other Wembley shows.

TUESDAY 19 NOVEMBER – PERFORMANCE
Trentham Gardens, Stoke-on-Trent, England

Set list: 'Shine On You Crazy Diamond', 'Raving And Drooling', 'Gotta Be Crazy' <Intermission> *The Dark Side of the Moon* <Encore> 'Echoes'.

An unauthorized recording of this concert found its way onto a vinyl bootleg album entitled *British Winter Tour '74*. Reports in the *NME* suggested it had been pressed in Germany or the Netherlands in upwards of 100,000 copies. In reality, very small quantities were being distributed from a record shop on London's Carnaby Street known very well to music journalists of the time.

FRIDAY 22 NOVEMBER – PERFORMANCE
Sophia Gardens Pavilion, Cardiff, Wales

Set list: 'Shine On You Crazy Diamond', 'Raving And Drooling', 'Gotta Be Crazy' <Intermission> *The Dark Side of the Moon* <Encore> 'Echoes'.

lorry and limousine, and the show had sold out within hours of the box-office opening. That eager audience was presented with a tepid mixture of well-worn material slightly spiced by a first half of new numbers. Floyd appeared uninterested, uninvolved and uninspired, and the band – who've given me more pleasure in concert than practically anyone over the years – left me cold last night. You could have stayed at home, played the albums and you would have lost nothing, because it was a note by note recreation and that's something one doesn't go to concerts for. *The Dark Side of the Moon* was accompanied by some banal movies contrasting piles of cash — of which the Floyd have plenty – with faces of elderly, clearly less affluent citizens. Big deal. It was an irritating, disappointing show, which never even looked like taking off. Rory Gallagher was playing down the road at the Colston Hall, and I wished I had been there instead."

THURSDAY 28, FRIDAY 29 & SATURDAY 30 NOVEMBER – PERFORMANCES
Empire Theatre, Liverpool, England

Set list at all three shows: 'Shine On You Crazy Diamond', 'Raving And Drooling', 'Gotta Be Crazy' <Intermission> *The Dark Side of the Moon* <Encore> 'Echoes'.

The band attended the Everton vs Bristol City football match at Goodison Park, Liverpool on the afternoon of Saturday 30 November.

TUESDAY 3, WEDNESDAY 4 & THURSDAY 5 DECEMBER – PERFORMANCES
The Hippodrome, Birmingham, England

Set list at all three shows: 'Shine On You Crazy Diamond', 'Raving And Drooling', 'Gotta Be Crazy' <Intermission> *The Dark Side of the Moon* <Encore> 'Echoes'.

MONDAY 9 & TUESDAY 10 DECEMBER – PERFORMANCES
Palace Theatre, Manchester, England

Set list at both shows: 'Shine On You Crazy Diamond', 'Raving And Drooling', 'Gotta Be Crazy' <Intermission> *The Dark Side of the Moon* <Encore> 'Echoes'.

FRIDAY 13 & SATURDAY 14 DECEMBER – PERFORMANCES
The Hippodrome, Bristol, England

Set list at both shows: 'Shine On You Crazy Diamond', 'Raving And Drooling', 'Gotta Be Crazy' <Intermission> *The Dark Side of the Moon* <Encore> 'Echoes'.

The band attended the Bristol City vs Nottingham Forest football match at Ashton Gate, Bristol on the afternoon of Saturday 14 December.

The *Bristol Evening Post* reported, "Floyd flopped in Bristol last night. The hardware and the talent had been trucked to Bristol by

1975

MONDAY 13 JANUARY – RECORDING SESSION
Studio 3 & Control Room 3, EMI Studios, Abbey Road, London, England

Recording commenced on Pink Floyd's ninth studio album, *Wish You Were Here*.

2.30pm to 12.00 midnight: Recording 'Shine On You Crazy Diamond' (Take 1 False Start, re-take of Take 1); Recording "Rick's Drone Intro" for 'Shine On You Crazy Diamond' (Take 1); and Moog overdubbed onto Take 1 of "Rick's Drone Intro" for 'Shine On You Crazy Diamond'. The session was produced by Pink Floyd, engineered by John Leckie and assisted by Peter James.

TUESDAY 14 JANUARY – RECORDING SESSION
Studio 3 & Control Room 3, EMI Studios, Abbey Road, London, England

2.30pm to 6.00pm: Click Track and Moog overdubbed onto Take 1 of "Rick's Intro" for 'Shine On You Crazy Diamond', and 7.00pm to 12.00midnight: Moog overdubbed onto Take 1 of "Rick's Intro" for 'Shine On You Crazy Diamond' for *Wish You Were Here*. The session was produced by Pink Floyd, engineered by John Leckie and assisted by Peter James and Brian Humphries.

The recording sheet shows a large exclamation mark next to Brian Humphries' name, clearly an indication that both John Leckie and Peter James were surprised by his unannounced appearance. John Leckie engineered his last session for Pink Floyd two days later, but remained at Abbey Road to produce the album *HQ* for Roy Harper, which was recorded in Studio 2 throughout March. David Gilmour appeared on Harper's 'The Game', and he in turn made a guest appearance on Pink Floyd's 'Have A Cigar'.

WEDNESDAY 15 JANUARY – RECORDING SESSION
Studio 3 & Control Room 3, EMI Studios,
Abbey Road, London, England

2.30pm to 12.45am: Recording 'Shine On You Crazy Diamond'
(Take 2, Take 3 and Take 4, with Takes 3 & 4 marked "Edit
Piece" and all marked "best to be edited") and drums
overdubbed onto Take 2, 3 and 4 of 'Shine On You Crazy
Diamond' for *Wish You Were Here*. The session was produced by
Pink Floyd, engineered by John Leckie and assisted by Peter
James and Brian Humphries.

THURSDAY 16 JANUARY – RECORDING SESSION
Studio 3 & Control Room 3, EMI Studios,
Abbey Road, London, England

2.30pm to 1.00am: Recording 'Shine On You Crazy Diamond'
(Take 5 Breakdown, Take 6 and Take 7) and Take 6 of 'Shine On
You Crazy Diamond' edited for *Wish You Were Here*. The session was
produced by Pink Floyd, engineered by John Leckie and assisted by
Peter James and Brian Humphries.

MONDAY 20 JANUARY – RECORDING SESSION
Studio 3 & Control Room 3, EMI Studios,
Abbey Road, London, England

4.00pm to 6.00pm: Guitar overdubbed onto 'Shine On You
Crazy Diamond', and 7.45pm to 12.00 midnight: Drums and Bass
overdubbed onto 'Shine On You Crazy Diamond' for *Wish You Were
Here*. The session was produced by Pink Floyd, engineered by Brian
Humphries and assisted by Peter James.

TUESDAY 21 JANUARY – RECORDING SESSION
Studio 3 & Control Room 3, EMI Studios,
Abbey Road, London, England

2.30pm to 10.45pm: Recording 'Shine On You Crazy Diamond'
"Outro Part" (Take 6, Take 7 False Start, Take 8 Breakdown);
Guitar overdubbed onto 'Shine On You Crazy Diamond' "Part 2";
"Parts 1–6" of 'Shine On You Crazy Diamond' edited together; and
Rhythm Guitar overdubbed onto 'Shine On You Crazy Diamond'
"Part 2" for *Wish You Were Here*. The session was produced by Pink
Floyd, engineered by Brian Humphries and assisted by Peter James.

WEDNESDAY 22 JANUARY – RECORDING SESSION
Studio 3 & Control Room 3, EMI Studios,
Abbey Road, London, England

2.30pm to 10.30pm: 'Shine On You Crazy Diamond' Rough Mix of
backing track completed, and Guitar and Synthesizer overdubbed
onto 'Shine On You Crazy Diamond' for *Wish You Were Here*.
The session was produced by Pink Floyd, engineered by Brian
Humphries and assisted by Peter James.

THURSDAY 23 JANUARY – RECORDING SESSION
Studio 3 & Control Room 3, EMI Studios,
Abbey Road, London, England

2.30pm to 2.00am: Recording 'Shine On You Crazy Diamond'
(Remake) Takes 1–6, and marked "Edit pieces to be edited
together" for *Wish You Were Here*. The session was produced by Pink
Floyd, engineered by Brian Humphries and assisted by Peter James.

MONDAY 27 JANUARY – RECORDING SESSION
Studio 3 & Control Room 3, EMI Studios,
Abbey Road, London, England

2.30pm to 12.30am: Recording 'Shine On You Crazy Diamond'
"Version 3" (Take 1 "Up To Arpeggio" and Take 2 "Arpeggio to
Break Section"), and a rough mix completed for *Wish You Were
Here*. The session was produced by Pink Floyd, engineered by
Brian Humphries and assisted by Peter James.

TUESDAY 28 JANUARY – RECORDING SESSION
Studio 3 & Control Room 3, EMI Studios,
Abbey Road, London, England

2.30pm to 6.30pm and 7.30pm to 8.30pm: Take 1 of 'Shine On You
Crazy Diamond' "Version 3" edited to Master Tape, and 8.30pm to
1.00am: Guitar overdubbed onto 'Shine On You Crazy Diamond'
"Version 3" and edited to Master Tape for *Wish You Were Here*.
The session was produced by Pink Floyd, engineered by Brian
Humphries and assisted by Peter James.

WEDNESDAY 29 JANUARY – RECORDING SESSION
Studio 3 & Control Room 3, EMI Studios,
Abbey Road, London, England

2.30pm to 12.00 midnight: Guitar and Harmonium overdubbed
onto 'Shine On You Crazy Diamond' for *Wish You Were Here*.
The session was produced by Pink Floyd, engineered by Brian
Humphries and assisted by Peter James.

THURSDAY 30 JANUARY – RECORDING SESSION
Studio 3 & Control Room 3, EMI Studios,
Abbey Road, London, England

2.30pm to 1.45am: Piano, Clavinet, Electric Piano and Synthesizer
overdubbed onto 'Shine On You Crazy Diamond' for *Wish You Were
Here*. The session was produced by Pink Floyd, engineered by Brian
Humphries and assisted by Peter James.

MONDAY 3 FEBRUARY – RECORDING SESSION
Studio 3 & Control Room 3, EMI Studios,
Abbey Road, London, England

2.30pm to 7.00pm: Piano, Clavinet, Electric Guitar and Moog
overdubbed onto 'Shine On You Crazy Diamond', and 8.00pm
to 12.00 midnight: Slide Guitar overdubbed onto 'Shine On You
Crazy Diamond', for *Wish You Were Here*. The session was produced
by Pink Floyd, engineered by Brian Humphries and assisted by
Peter James.

TUESDAY 4 FEBRUARY – RECORDING SESSION
Studio 3 & Control Room 3, EMI Studios,
Abbey Road, London, England

2.30pm to 12.20am: Moog, Electric Guitar, String Synthesizer,
Electric Guitar and Vocal overdubbed onto 'Shine On You Crazy
Diamond' for *Wish You Were Here*. The session was produced by Pink
Floyd, engineered by Brian Humphries and assisted by Peter James.

WEDNESDAY 5 FEBRUARY – RECORDING SESSION
Studio 3 & Control Room 3, EMI Studios,
Abbey Road, London, England

2.30pm to 6.00pm: Electric Guitar, Moog and Organ overdubbed onto 'Shine On You Crazy Diamond', and 7.00pm to 1.30am: Vocal and Backing Vocals overdubbed onto 'Shine On You Crazy Diamond' for *Wish You Were Here*. The session was produced by Pink Floyd, engineered by Brian Humphries and assisted by Peter James.

THURSDAY 6 FEBRUARY – RECORDING SESSION
Studio 3 & Control Room 3, EMI Studios,
Abbey Road, London, England

2.30pm to 1.30am: Backing vocals, Main Vocal, Moog and Guitar overdubbed onto 'Shine On You Crazy Diamond' for *Wish You Were Here*. The session was produced by Pink Floyd, engineered by Brian Humphries and assisted by Peter James.

MONDAY 10 FEBRUARY – RECORDING SESSION
Studio 3 & Control Room 3, EMI Studios,
Abbey Road, London, England

2.30pm to 7.00pm and 8.00pm to 1.00am: Backing Vocals overdubbed onto 'Shine On You Crazy Diamond' for *Wish You Were Here*. The session was produced by Pink Floyd, engineered by Brian Humphries and assisted by Peter James.

TUESDAY 11 FEBRUARY – RECORDING SESSION
Studio 3 & Control Room 3, EMI Studios,
Abbey Road, London, England

2.30pm to 2.00am: Moog, Electric Guitar and Cymbal overdubbed onto 'Shine On You Crazy Diamond' for *Wish You Were Here*. The session was produced by Pink Floyd, engineered by Brian Humphries and assisted by Peter James.

WEDNESDAY 12 FEBRUARY – RECORDING SESSION
Studio 3 & Control Room 3, EMI Studios,
Abbey Road, London, England

2.30pm to 6.30pm: Electric Guitar Solo and Rhythm Guitar overdubbed onto 'Shine On You Crazy Diamond', and 7.30pm to 2.00am: Synthesizer and Electric Guitar overdubbed onto 'Shine On You Crazy Diamond' for *Wish You Were Here*. The session was produced by Pink Floyd, engineered by Brian Humphries and assisted by Peter James.

FRIDAY 14 FEBRUARY – RECORDING SESSION
Studio 3 & Control Room 3, EMI Studios,
Abbey Road, London, England

2.30pm to 2.30am: Vocal, Synthesizer, Hammond Organ, Piano and Electric Guitar overdubbed onto 'Shine On You Crazy Diamond' for *Wish You Were Here*. The session was produced by Pink Floyd, engineered by Brian Humphries and assisted by Peter James.

MONDAY 17 FEBRUARY – RECORDING SESSION
Studio 3 & Control Room 3, EMI Studios,
Abbey Road, London, England

2.30pm to 6.30pm: "Wild Guitar" for 'Shine On You Crazy Diamond' recorded, and 7.30pm to 1.30am: "Wild Vocals" and Piano recorded for 'Shine On You Crazy Diamond'

for *Wish You Were Here*. The session was produced by Pink Floyd, engineered by Brian Humphries and assisted by Peter James.

TUESDAY 18 FEBRUARY – RECORDING SESSION
Studio 3 & Control Room 3, EMI Studios,
Abbey Road, London, England

2.30pm to 6.30pm: Electric Guitar overdubbed onto 'Shine On You Crazy Diamond', and 8.00pm to 1.45am: Moog, String Synthesizer, Electric Guitar Solo and Electric Piano overdubbed onto 'Shine On You Crazy Diamond' for *Wish You Were Here*. The session was produced by Pink Floyd, engineered by Brian Humphries and assisted by Peter James.

WEDNESDAY 19 FEBRUARY – RECORDING SESSION
Studio 3 & Control Room 3, EMI Studios,
Abbey Road, London, England

2.30pm to 12.00 midnight: Bass overdubbed onto 'Shine On You Crazy Diamond'; "Various Backwards Things" recorded; and Moog, Organ and Synthesizer overdubbed onto 'Shine On You Crazy Diamond' for *Wish You Were Here*. The session was produced by Pink Floyd, engineered by Brian Humphries and assisted by Peter James.

THURSDAY 20 FEBRUARY – RECORDING SESSION
Studio 3 & Control Room 3, EMI Studios,
Abbey Road, London, England

2.30pm to 7.00pm: Slide Guitar overdubbed onto 'Shine On You Crazy Diamond', and 8.30pm to 1.30am: Rough mix of 'Shine On You Crazy Diamond' made for *Wish You Were Here*. The session was produced by Pink Floyd, engineered by Brian Humphries and assisted by Peter James.

MONDAY 24 FEBRUARY – RECORDING SESSION
Studio 3 & Control Room 3, EMI Studios,
Abbey Road, London, England

2.30pm to 6.30pm and 7.30pm to 12.00 midnight: 'Wineglasses' ['Nothing Part 5'] recorded on 5 January 1971 overdubbed onto 'Shine On You Crazy Diamond'; and Moog overdubbed onto 'Shine On You Crazy Diamond' for *Wish You Were Here*. The session was produced by Pink Floyd, engineered by Brian Humphries and assisted by Peter James.

TUESDAY 25 FEBRUARY – RECORDING SESSION
Studio 3 & Control Room 3, EMI Studios,
Abbey Road, London, England

2.30pm to 6.00pm and 7.30pm to 1.30am: Tape reduction of 'Shine On You Crazy Diamond' for further overdubs; and recording 'The Machine' ['Welcome To The Machine'] (Take 1) for *Wish You Were Here*. The session was produced by Pink Floyd, engineered by Brian Humphries and assisted by Peter James.

WEDNESDAY 26 FEBRUARY – RECORDING SESSION
Studio 3 & Control Room 3, EMI Studios,
Abbey Road, London, England

2.30pm to 7.00pm and 7.00pm to 1.45am: Acoustic Guitar and Vocals overdubbed onto 'Shine On Extension'; and Moog overdubbed onto Take 1 of 'The Machine' ['Welcome To The Machine'] for *Wish You Were Here*. The session was produced by

Pink Floyd, engineered by Brian Humphries and assisted by Peter James.

THURSDAY 27 FEBRUARY – RECORDING SESSION
**Studio 3 & Control Room 3, EMI Studios,
Abbey Road, London, England**

2.30pm to 6.30pm and 8.45pm to 12.30am: Acoustic Guitar and Vocal overdubbed onto Take 1 of 'The Machine' ['Welcome To The Machine'] and a rough mix made for *Wish You Were Here*. The session was produced by Pink Floyd, engineered by Brian Humphries and assisted by Peter James.

MONDAY 3 MARCH – RECORDING SESSION
**Studio 3 & Control Room 3, EMI Studios,
Abbey Road, London, England**

2.30pm to 5.30pm: Playback of 'Shine On You Crazy Diamond', and 8.30pm to 10.00pm: Group meeting for *Wish You Were Here*. The session was produced by Pink Floyd, engineered by Brian Humphries and assisted by Peter James.

MONDAY 10 MARCH – RECORDING SESSION
**Studio 3 & Control Room 3, EMI Studios,
Abbey Road, London, England**

2.30pm to 12.30am: Recording 'Have A Cigar' (Takes 1 & 2 Break down, Take 3 Complete, Take 4 Break down, Take 5 False Start, Takes 6 & 7 Break down, Takes 8 & 9 False Starts, Take 10 Break down, Takes 11 & 12 Break down, Take 13 False Start and Take 14 marking the first complete take with Roger Waters on guide vocals) for *Wish You Were Here*. The session was produced by Pink Floyd, engineered by Brian Humphries and assisted by Peter James.

TUESDAY 11 MARCH – RECORDING SESSION
**Studio 3 & Control Room 3, EMI Studios,
Abbey Road, London, England**

2.30pm to 1.30am: Recording 'Have A Cigar' with Roger Waters on guide vocals (Take 18 Break down, two False Starts deleted, Take 19 & 20 Break down, Takes 21 & 22 Complete, Take 23 Break down, Take 24 False Start, Take 25 Break down, Takes 26 & 27 False Starts, Takes 28 & 29 Break down, Take 30 Complete, Take 31 False Start, Takes 32 & 33 Break down, Takes 34 to 37 False Starts, Takes 38 & 39 Break down, Take 40 False Start, Takes 41 & 42 Break down, Take 43 False Start, Take 44 Break down, Take 45 False Start, Takes 46 to 49 Break down, Take 50 Complete possibly with David Gilmour on lead vocals, Take 51 Break down, and Take 52 Complete) for *Wish You Were Here*. The session was produced by Pink Floyd, engineered by Brian Humphries and assisted by Peter James.

WEDNESDAY 12 MARCH – RECORDING SESSION
**Studio 3 & Control Room 3, EMI Studios,
Abbey Road, London, England**

2.30pm to 1.00am: Recording 'Have A Cigar' with Roger Waters on guide vocals (Take 53 Break down, Take 54 Complete, Take 55 False Start and Take 56 marked "best"); and Organ and Acoustic Guitar overdubbed onto Take 56 of 'Have A Cigar' for *Wish You Were Here*. The session was produced by Pink Floyd, engineered by Brian Humphries and assisted by Peter James.

THURSDAY 13 MARCH – RECORDING SESSION
**Studio 3 & Control Room 3, EMI Studios,
Abbey Road, London, England**

2.30pm to 6.00pm: Vocal (Roger Waters), Guitar, Piano, Clavinet and String Synths overdubbed onto Take 56 of 'Have A Cigar', and 7.30pm to 3.00am: Electric Guitar and Synths overdubbed onto Take 56 of 'Have A Cigar' for *Wish You Were Here*. The session was produced by Pink Floyd, engineered by Brian Humphries and assisted by Peter James.

MONDAY 24 MARCH – RECORDING SESSION
**Control Room 3, EMI Studios,
Abbey Road, London, England**

2.30pm to 6.00pm: Playbacks of existing tapes. The evening session was cancelled.

WEDNESDAY 26 MARCH – RECORDING SESSION
**Studio 3 & Control Room 3, EMI Studios,
Abbey Road, London, England**

2.30pm to 2.30am: Quadraphonic live effects tapes made up for the forthcoming North American tour, including the tracks 'Shine On Intro', 'Various Animal Noises (Nick)', 'Shine On Drone For End' and 'Smashing Glass' for *Wish You Were Here*. The session was produced by Pink Floyd, engineered by Brian Humphries and assisted by Peter James.

TUESDAY 27 MARCH – RECORDING SESSION
**Studio 3 & Control Room 3, EMI Studios,
Abbey Road, London, England**

2.30pm to 3.30am: Quadraphonic live effects tapes made up for the forthcoming North American tour including the tracks 'Roy and Roger's Snarling' recorded "Wild" (Takes 1–8) [This refers to Roy Harper and Roger Waters]; 'Backwards Piano Section' recorded; and Piano, Footsteps, Whistle and Various Other SFX and Voice overdubbed onto 'Backwards Piano Section' for *Wish You Were Here*. The session was produced by Pink Floyd, engineered by Brian Humphries and assisted by Peter James.

NORTH AMERICAN TOUR

Pink Floyd's April tour was announced as late as early March, primarily via a specially constructed radio simulcast to the cities where they were scheduled to appear. On the day after the broadcast all of the shows in Seattle, San Francisco, Tempe, Denver, Tucson and San Diego had all but sold out, breaking many box office records, including that of the Los Angeles Sports Arena, which in a single day sold all of its 67,000 ticket allocation for the four-night run. Even an extra fifth show sold out within hours, and indeed such was the demand for tickets that the band's residency could easily have been extended.

ADDITIONAL TOUR PERSONNEL
Venetta Fields (Backing vocals), Dick Parry (Saxophones), Carlena Williams (Backing vocals).

PINK FLOYD ROAD CREW

Bernie Caulder (PA / Stage Technician), Paul Devine (Lighting Technician), Graeme Fleming (Lighting Technician), Jed Frost (Lighting Technician), Seth Goldman (Monitor Sound Engineer), Brian Humphries (Front of House Sound Engineer), Marek 'Mick The Pole' Kluczynski (PA / Stage Technician), Mick Marshall (Film Projection), Arthur Max (Production Manager / Lighting Designer), Paul Murray (Film Projection), Robin Murray (Lighting Technician), Nick Rochford (PA / Stage Technician), Shamus (Front Man), Peter Sherriden (Lighting Technician), Phil Taylor (Backline Technician), Jim Thompson (PA / Stage Technician / Intercom), Carlos Trenidry (PA / Stage Technician), Robbie Williams (PA / Stage Technician).

TUESDAY 8 APRIL – PERFORMANCE ◄
Pacific National Exhibition Coliseum, Vancouver, Canada

Set list: 'Raving And Drooling', 'Gotta Be Crazy', 'Shine On You Crazy Diamond, Parts 1–5', 'Have A Cigar', 'Shine On You Crazy Diamond, Parts 6–9' <Intermission> *The Dark Side of the Moon* <Encore> 'Echoes'.

Reviewing the show the *Vancouver Sun* reported, "[Pink Floyd] did a live show that depends on gadgets and an excellent 360-degree sound system. This system, co-ordinated with four light towers and spotlights, transformed the sold-out Coliseum on Tuesday night into psychedelic concrete earphones. When guitarist Dave Gilmour stood in a green light and strummed a simple chord, the chord circled the Coliseum like an electronic bat. The sound effects are maximized by keeping the music simple in structure as pop art – naive, with all nuance banished. Clear melodic phrases are slow, pseudo-stately tempos are piled up like building blocks. Ideas are repeated, not developed. The four musicians stood in a row on a cluttered stage, as casual and businesslike as the technicians at the centre-ice master control board. Both Gilmour and bassist Roger Waters have undistinguished voices, much inferior to the two black women of their backing chorus. On the other hand, nothing they play or sing is actively unpleasant. The gimmicks, some of them, were slightly more impressive. The audience cheered a huge disc, shaped to suggest a cruel circular saw, as it revolved far above the stage in a spotlight. Movies were projected on to a circular screen to illustrate *The Dark Side of the Moon* suite: a flying squad of clock faces disappeared into the heavens on a song called "Time", and there were stacks of silver coins for "Money". Trusty light show clichés – rumpus room sea and sky posters, for example – tended to dominate the few good ideas, and if you have seen one close-up of the human eye, you have seen them all. A fitfully pleasing, consistently dull show, in other words. A better than average pop band lost in a lifeless farrago of tape loops and quad demo record effects."

THURSDAY 10 APRIL – PERFORMANCE
Seattle Center Coliseum, Seattle, WA, USA

Set list: 'Raving And Drooling', 'Gotta Be Crazy', 'Shine On You Crazy Diamond, Parts 1–5', 'Have A Cigar', 'Shine On You Crazy Diamond, Parts 6–9' <Intermission> *The Dark Side of the Moon* <Encore> 'Echoes'.

SATURDAY 12 & SUNDAY 13 APRIL – PERFORMANCES
Cow Palace, Daly City, San Francisco, CA, USA

Set list at both shows: 'Raving And Drooling', 'Gotta Be Crazy', 'Shine On You Crazy Diamond, Parts 1–5', 'Have A Cigar', 'Shine On You Crazy Diamond, Parts 6–9' <Intermission> *The Dark Side of the Moon* <Encore> 'Echoes'.

TUESDAY 15 APRIL – CANCELLED PERFORMANCE ►
University Activity Center, Arizona State University, Tempe, AZ, USA

The show was rescheduled to 20 April because when the band's crew first arrived at the venue they deemed the stage unsafe and the power supply inadequate to continue. The show was rescheduled to 20 April.

THURSDAY 17 APRIL – PERFORMANCE
Denver Coliseum, Denver, CO, USA

Set list: 'Raving And Drooling', 'Gotta Be Crazy', 'Shine On You Crazy Diamond, Parts 1–5', 'Have A Cigar', 'Shine On You Crazy Diamond, Parts 6–9' <Intermission> *The Dark Side of the Moon* <Encore> 'Echoes'.

SATURDAY 19 APRIL – PERFORMANCE
Tucson Community Center Arena, Tucson, AZ, USA

Set list: 'Raving And Drooling', 'Gotta Be Crazy', 'Shine On You Crazy Diamond, Parts 1–5', 'Have A Cigar', 'Shine On You Crazy Diamond, Parts 6–9' <Intermission> *The Dark Side of the Moon* <Encore> 'Echoes'.

SUNDAY 20 APRIL – PERFORMANCE
University Activity Center, Arizona State University, Tempe, AZ, USA

Set list: 'Raving And Drooling', 'Gotta Be Crazy', 'Shine On You Crazy Diamond, Parts 1-5', 'Have A Cigar', 'Shine On You Crazy Diamond, Parts 6–9' <Intermission> *The Dark Side of the Moon* <Encore> 'Echoes'.

After the concert there were allegations of ticket fraud when head counts by both the promoter and Pink Floyd's management put the attendance at 1,000 over the 9,000 capacity. Nevertheless it was regarded as a successful concert. The ASU student newspaper, *State Press*, reported, "The audience went wild when the light show began. Concertgoers were particularly impressed by a parabolic mirror, which reflected spots of light on the ceiling and walls of the Activity Center. Smoke rose from the stage. Imitation snow fell from above. A huge screen hung from the ceiling showed scenes of an operating room to accompany cuts from *Dark Side*. Hundreds of yellow clock dials were projected moving in time to the music. The crowd liked it, and that should be reason enough. But I think the crowd is wrong. A light show is a good addition to most rock shows, but when special effects are carried to the extreme they can only detract from the music and create a carnival atmosphere. The music was good enough to outweigh the gimmicks, however. And let it be said that their 32 tons of equipment was enough. My ears were ringing for hours after the show."

MONDAY 21 APRIL – PERFORMANCE
Sports Arena, San Diego, CA, USA

Set list: 'Raving And Drooling', 'Gotta Be Crazy', 'Shine On You Crazy Diamond, Parts 1–5', 'Have A Cigar', 'Shine On You Crazy Diamond, Parts 6–9' <Intermission> *The Dark Side of the Moon* <Encore> 'Echoes'.

TUESDAY 22, WEDNESDAY 23, THURSDAY 24, FRIDAY 25, SATURDAY 26 & SUNDAY 27 APRIL – PERFORMANCES
Los Angeles Memorial Sports Arena, Exposition Park, Los Angeles, CA, USA

Set list at all six shows: 'Raving And Drooling', 'Gotta Be Crazy', 'Shine On You Crazy Diamond, Parts 1–5', 'Have A Cigar', 'Shine On You Crazy Diamond, Parts 6–9' <Intermission> *The Dark Side of the Moon* <Encore> 'Echoes'.

Despite the overall success of the tour, it is also remembered for the heavy-handed actions of the Los Angeles Police Department, who arrested over 500 fans during their five-night run at the Sports Arena.

Police Chief Ed Davis, in a speech to businessmen a week before the concerts, described the forthcoming shows as an "illegal pot festival" and gave the assurance that his force was committed to bringing the full weight of the law to bear on even the most minor of offences committed at or in the grounds of the venue. Inevitably, many innocent fans were also roughed up.

BELOW: PINK FLOYD'S SIX-NIGHT RESIDENCY IN LOS ANGELES GENERATED FAR MORE PRESS FOR THE ACTIONS OF THE POLICE THAN THE CONTENT OF THE SPECTACULAR SHOWS THEMSELVES.

This confrontation had been brewing for some time; the LAPD had been waiting eagerly to deal with a big music event in the city. *Rolling Stone*, in its June 1975 edition, ran an extensive report that gave evidence that many other venues in the greater Los Angeles area had been subjected to the heavy-handed actions of Chief Davis, who was quoted as saying, "I'm the meanest chief of police in the history of the United States." The article also contained an allegation that the "bust" had been planned well in advance: "One young man arrested at the Shrine Auditorium's Robin Trower concert of 16 March claimed an officer told him, 'If you think this is something, you ought to see what we're going to do at the Sports Arena.'"

Officially only 75 police officers were deployed at the shows on each of the five nights Pink Floyd played, but venue management estimated the figure at nearer 200. Of the 511 arrests made, the majority were for possession of marijuana. The police justified their actions by claiming that there were a couple of more serious offences, including cocaine dealing and possession of a loaded gun. This fact made more headline news in the *Los Angeles Times* than the concerts themselves. Despite the tense atmosphere, the fans behaved well in the view of the Arena's management, who later praised them.

Scenes of crowd violence and police confrontation inspired by these events were depicted in the opening sequence of *The Wall* movie.

MONDAY 5 MAY – RECORDING SESSION
Studio 3 & Control Room 3, EMI Studios, Abbey Road, London, England

2.30pm to 10.00pm: Vocal overdubbed onto 'Shine On You Crazy Diamond', for *Wish You Were Here*. The session was produced by Pink Floyd, engineered by Brian Humphries and assisted by Peter James.

TUESDAY 6 MAY – RECORDING SESSION
Studio 3 & Control Room 3, EMI Studios, Abbey Road, London, England

2.30pm to 6.00pm: Take 56 of 'Have A Cigar' edited and Electric Piano overdubbed onto Take 56 of 'Have A Cigar', and 7.00pm to 1.30am: String Machine and Synths overdubbed onto Take 56 of 'Have A Cigar' for *Wish You Were Here*. The session was produced by Pink Floyd, engineered by Brian Humphries and assisted by Peter James.

WEDNESDAY 7 MAY – RECORDING SESSION
Studio 3 & Control Room 3, EMI Studios, Abbey Road, London, England

2.30pm to 6.00pm: Guitar overdubbed onto Take 56 of 'Have A Cigar', and 7.00pm to 12.30am: Playback of various live cassettes and master tape of 'Shine On' for *Wish You Were Here*. The session was produced by Pink Floyd, engineered by Brian Humphries and assisted by Peter James.

THURSDAY 8 MAY – RECORDING SESSION
Studio 3 & Control Room 3, EMI Studios,
Abbey Road, London, England

2.30pm to 6.00pm: Vocals (Roger Waters and David Gilmour) overdubbed onto 'Have A Cigar' and Synths overdubbed onto 'The Machine Song' ['Welcome To The Machine'], and 7.00pm to 2.30am: Tape Loop of Synths done for *Wish You Were Here*. The session was produced by Pink Floyd, engineered by Brian Humphries and assisted by Peter James.

FRIDAY 9 MAY – RECORDING SESSION
Studio 3 & Control Room 3, EMI Studios,
Abbey Road, London, England

2.30pm to 6.00pm: Vocals, Synths and Acoustic Guitar overdubbed onto 'The Machine Song' (remake) ['Welcome To The Machine']; Master tape of 'The Machine Song' (remake) edited and Tape Loops made up and edited, and 7.00pm to 1.00am: Vocals (Roy Harper) overdubbed onto 'Have A Cigar' for *Wish You Were Here*. The session was produced by Pink Floyd, engineered by Brian Humphries and assisted by Peter James.

MONDAY 12 MAY – RECORDING SESSION
Studio 3 & Control Room 3, EMI Studios,
Abbey Road, London, England

2.30pm to 6.30pm: Synths and Acoustic Guitar overdubbed onto 'The Machine Song' (remake) ['Welcome To The Machine'], and 7.30pm to 2.00am: Vocals and Synths overdubbed onto 'The Machine Song' (remake) for *Wish You Were Here*. The session was produced by Pink Floyd, engineered by Brian Humphries and assisted by Peter James.

TUESDAY 13 MAY – RECORDING SESSION
Studio 3 & Control Room 3, EMI Studios,
Abbey Road, London, England

2.30pm to 6.00pm: Synths, Acoustic Guitar and Vocals overdubbed onto 'The Machine Song' (remake) ['Welcome To The Machine'], and 7.00pm to 2.00am: Tympani, Electric Guitar and Vocals overdubbed onto 'The Machine Song' (remake) for *Wish You Were Here*. The session was produced by Pink Floyd, engineered byBrian Humphries and assisted by Peter James.

WEDNESDAY 14 MAY – RECORDING SESSION
Studio 3 & Control Room 3, EMI Studios,
Abbey Road, London, England

2.30pm to 6.00pm: Various Moog chords recorded and overdubbed onto 'The Machine Song' (remake) ['Welcome To The Machine'], and 7.30pm to 12.30am: Moog overdubbed onto 'The Machine Song' (remake) for *Wish You Were Here*. The session was produced by Pink Floyd, engineered by Brian Humphries and assisted by Peter James.

THURSDAY 15 MAY – RECORDING SESSION
Studio 3 & Control Room 3, EMI Studios,
Abbey Road, London, England

2.30pm to 7.00pm: Saxophones (Dick Parry) overdubbed onto 'Shine On You Crazy Diamond', and 8.00pm to 11.30pm: Moog overdubbed onto 'The Machine Song' (remake) for *Wish You*

Were Here. The session was produced by Pink Floyd, engineered by Brian Humphries and assisted by Peter James.

FRIDAY 16 MAY – RECORDING SESSION
Studio 3 & Control Room 3, EMI Studios,
Abbey Road, London, England

2.30pm to 6.00pm: 'Untitled (An Afternoon At Home With The Duke Of Roydon)' ['Wish You Were Here'] recorded (Take 1 also marked "Best For Intro") and Guitar overdubbed onto Take 1 of 'Untitled (An Afternoon At Home With The Duke Of Roydon)', and 7.30pm to 1.00am: 'Have A Cigar' Vocal (Roger Waters) overdubbed for *Wish You Were Here*. The session was produced by Pink Floyd, engineered by Brian Humphries and assisted by Peter James.

MONDAY 19 MAY – RECORDING SESSION
Studio 3 & Control Room 3, EMI Studios,
Abbey Road, London, England

2.30pm to 6.00pm: Acoustic Guitar, Drums and Bass overdubbed onto 'Untitled' ['Wish You Were Here'], and 7.30pm to 12.30am: Bass Guitar and Vocal overdubbed onto 'Shine On You Crazy Diamond' for *Wish You Were Here*. The session was produced by Pink Floyd, engineered by Brian Humphries and assisted by Peter James.

TUESDAY 20 MAY – RECORDING SESSION
Studio 3 & Control Room 3, EMI Studios,
Abbey Road, London, England

2.30pm to 6.00pm: "End Sequence" ['Shine On You Crazy Diamond Part 9'] recorded (Take 1 also marked "Best"), and Piano, Hammond Organ and Synth Chords overdubbed onto Take 1 of "End Sequence" ['Shine On You Crazy Diamond Part 9']; and 7.30pm to 2.00am: Synths, Bass and Drums overdubbed onto Take 1 of "End Sequence" of 'Shine On You Crazy Diamond' for *Wish You Were Here*. The session was produced by Pink Floyd, engineered by Brian Humphries and assisted by Peter James.

WEDNESDAY 21 MAY – RECORDING SESSION
Studio 3 & Control Room 3, EMI Studios,
Abbey Road, London, England

2.30pm to 6.00pm: Drums and Bass overdubbed onto Take 1 of "End Sequence" ['Shine On You Crazy Diamond Part 9'], and 7.30pm to 12.30am: 'Wineglass Chords' overdubbed onto Take 1 of "End Sequence" ['Shine On You Crazy Diamond Part 9'], and Vocals overdubbed onto 'The Squire Of Royden' ['Wish You Were Here'] for *Wish You Were Here*. The session was produced by Pink Floyd, engineered by Brian Humphries and assisted by Peter James.

THURSDAY 22 MAY – RECORDING SESSION
Studio 3 & Control Room 3, EMI Studios,
Abbey Road, London, England

2.30pm to 6.00pm: Bass, Guitars and Woodblock overdubbed onto 'Wish You Were Here', and 7.30pm to 2.00am: 'Wish You Were Here' re-recorded (Take 2 and Take 3 also marked "Best"), and Guitars, Vocal and Piano overdubbed onto Take 3 of 'Wish You Were Here' for *Wish You Were Here*. The session was produced by Pink Floyd, engineered by Brian Humphries and assisted by Peter James.

FRIDAY 23 MAY – RECORDING SESSION
Studio 3 & Control Room 3, EMI Studios,
Abbey Road, London, England

2.30pm to 6.00pm: Guitars, Vocals and Synths overdubbed onto Take 3 of 'Wish You Were Here', and 7.30pm to 1.00am: Vocal Harmonies and Violin (Stéphane Grappelli) overdubbed onto Take 3 of 'Wish You Were Here' for *Wish You Were Here*. The session was produced by Pink Floyd, engineered by Brian Humphries and assisted by Peter James.

TUESDAY 27 MAY – RECORDING SESSION
Studio 3 & Control Room 3, EMI Studios,
Abbey Road, London, England

2.30pm to 3.00am: VCS3 SFX for 'The Machine Song' ['Welcome To The Machine'] recorded (Takes 1–3); Rough mix of 'The Machine Song' made for reference; 'Country Montage' [wildlife sound effects] mixed (RS1 & RS2), and Bass and Synth overdubbed onto 'The Machine Song' for *Wish You Were Here*. The session was produced by Pink Floyd, engineered by Brian Humphries and assisted by Peter James.

WEDNESDAY 28 MAY – RECORDING SESSION
Studio 3 & Control Room 3, EMI Studios,
Abbey Road, London, England

2.30pm to 11.30pm: Drums, Guitar and Radio Synthesized Sound overdubbed onto Take 3 of 'Wish You Were Here'; VCS3 overdubbed onto 'The Machine Song' ['Welcome To The Machine']; and VCS3 Throb for 'The Machine Song' recorded (Takes 1–5) for *Wish You Were Here*. The session was produced by Pink Floyd, engineered by Brian Humphries and assisted by Peter James.

THURSDAY 29 MAY – RECORDING SESSION
Studio 3 & Control Room 3, EMI Studios,
Abbey Road, London, England

2.30pm to 6.30pm: Pedal Steel Guitar and Drums overdubbed onto Take 3 of 'Wish You Were Here', and 7.30pm to 1.00am: Guitar and Electric Piano and Various Edits done to 'Shine On You Crazy Diamond' for *Wish You Were Here*. The session was produced by Pink Floyd, engineered by Brian Humphries and assisted by Peter James.

FRIDAY 30 MAY – RECORDING SESSION
Studio 2 & Control Room 2, EMI Studios,
Abbey Road, London, England

3.00pm to 6.30pm and 8.00pm to 3.30am: Electric Guitar and Vocals overdubbed onto Take 3 of 'Wish You Were Here' and Clavinet overdubbed onto 'Have A Cigar' for the album *Wish You Were Here*. The session was produced by Pink Floyd, engineered by Brian Humphries and assisted by Peter James.

SATURDAY 31 MAY – RECORDING SESSION
Studio 3 & Control Room 3, EMI Studios,
Abbey Road, London, England

2.30pm to 8.30pm: Vocals overdubbed onto 'Have A Cigar' for *Wish You Were Here*. The session was produced by Pink Floyd, engineered by Brian Humphries and assisted by Peter James. This

was possibly Roger Waters' last attempt at getting the vocals nailed before conceding defeat to Roy Harper.

MONDAY 2 JUNE – RECORDING SESSION
Studio 2 & Control Room 2, EMI Studios,
Abbey Road, London, England

2.30pm to 6.30pm: Moog overdubbed onto 'Have A Cigar' and Vocals overdubbed onto 'The Machine Song' ['Welcome To The Machine'], and 8.00pm to 1.45am: Electric Piano, String Synths and Moog overdubbed onto 'Shine On You Crazy Diamond' for *Wish You Were Here*. The session was produced by Pink Floyd, engineered by Brian Humphries and assisted by Peter James.

TUESDAY 3 JUNE – RECORDING SESSION
Control Room 3, EMI Studios,
Abbey Road, London, England

2.30pm to 5.30pm: Rough mix of Side One and Side Two completed and cross-fades and edits done for Side Two of *Wish You Were Here*. The session was produced by Pink Floyd, engineered by Brian Humphries and assisted by Peter James.

THURSDAY 5 JUNE – RECORDING SESSION
Control Room 2, EMI Studios,
Abbey Road, London, England

2.30pm to 4.30pm: Tape copies made of rough mixes of the whole of *Wish You Were Here*. The session was produced by Pink Floyd, engineered by Brian Humphries and assisted by Peter James. This is the purported date of Syd Barrett's visit to Abbey Road.

NORTH AMERICAN TOUR

An East Coast tour saw the bulk of the dates hitting some of the largest stadiums they had played to date. To add to the visual spectacle, Pink Floyd commissioned the construction of a huge inflatable pyramid to be launched at the climax of *The Dark Side of the Moon*. It failed to operate on the opening night and using the next set of indoor dates to rectify the problem, the giant structure was constructed, but not launched due to high winds, at the Roosevelt Stadium in New Jersey on Saturday June 14, and launched on its maiden flight at Pittsburgh on Friday June 20, with dramatic results.

SATURDAY 7 JUNE –
PERFORMANCE ▶
Atlanta Stadium,
Atlanta, GA, USA

Set list: 'Raving And Drooling', 'Gotta Be Crazy', 'Shine On You Crazy Diamond, Parts 1–5', 'Have A Cigar', 'Shine On You Crazy Diamond, Parts 6–9' <Intermission> *The Dark Side of the Moon* <Encore> 'Echoes'.

MONDAY 9 & TUESDAY 10 JUNE – PERFORMANCE
Capital Centre, Landover, MD, USA

Set list at both shows: 'Raving And Drooling', 'Gotta Be Crazy', 'Shine On You Crazy Diamond, Parts 1–5', 'Have A Cigar', 'Shine On You Crazy Diamond, Parts 6–9' <Intermission> *The Dark Side of the Moon* <Encore> 'Echoes'.

THURSDAY 12 & FRIDAY 13 JUNE – PERFORMANCES ◄
The Spectrum, Philadelphia, PA, USA

Set list at both shows: 'Raving And Drooling', 'Gotta Be Crazy', 'Shine On You Crazy Diamond, Parts 1–5', 'Have A Cigar', 'Shine On You Crazy Diamond, Parts 6–9' <Intermission> *The Dark Side of the Moon* <Encore> 'Echoes'.

SATURDAY 14 JUNE – PERFORMANCE
Roosevelt Stadium, Jersey City, NJ, USA

Set list: 'Raving And Drooling', 'Gotta Be Crazy', 'Shine On You Crazy Diamond, Parts 1–5', 'Have A Cigar', 'Shine On You Crazy Diamond, Parts 6–9' <Intermission> *The Dark Side of the Moon* <Encore> 'Echoes'.

Reviewing the show, the *Aquarian* reported, "Roosevelt Stadium kicked off its concert season with the loud bang of M-80's and the sonic boom of Pink Floyd in middle June…. I've seen them at least six times and I was mesmerized at each show. I didn't want to be let down, but as the Christians hurl their god-forsaken bodies to the lions, all things must pass…. I wonder if anyone was seriously injured by the fireworks tossed here and there? One kid said, 'Wow, I haven't seen this much action since 'Nam'. I can see patches and tee shirts saying 'I was destroyed at Roosevelt' with a big firecracker blowing up on the silhouette of a stadium. But really, they ought to hand out medals to the ones who came home unscathed by the experience."

MONDAY 16 & TUESDAY 17 JUNE – PERFORMANCES
Nassau Veterans Memorial Coliseum, Uniondale, NY, USA

Set list at both shows: 'Raving And Drooling', 'Gotta Be Crazy', 'Shine On You Crazy Diamond, Parts 1–5', 'Have A Cigar', 'Shine On You Crazy Diamond, Parts 6–9' <Intermission> *The Dark Side of the Moon* <Encore> 'Echoes'.

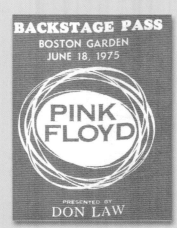

WEDNESDAY 18 JUNE – PERFORMANCE ◄
Boston Garden, Boston, MA, USA

Set list: 'Raving And Drooling', 'Gotta Be Crazy', 'Shine On You Crazy Diamond, Parts 1–5', 'Have A Cigar', 'Shine On You Crazy Diamond, Parts 6–9' <Intermission> *The Dark Side of the Moon* <Encore> 'Echoes'.

FRIDAY 20 JUNE – PERFORMANCE ▼
Three Rivers Stadium, Pittsburgh, PA, USA

Set list: 'Raving And Drooling', 'Gotta Be Crazy', 'Shine On You Crazy Diamond, Parts 1–5', 'Have A Cigar', 'Shine On You Crazy Diamond, Parts 6–9' <Intermission> *The Dark Side of the Moon* <Encore> 'Echoes'.

Reviewing the show *Pittsburgh Press* reported, "From virtually every angle, incredible was the word for Pink Floyd's Three Rivers Stadium concert last night. It was incredible how a first-place baseball team with the third best record in the majors drew only 8,200 there Thursday evening, yet a band with no hit singles to its credit attracted nearly 50,000, a stadium rock show record. Police reported no more than the usual number of underage drinkers, fist-fights and injuries from 'jumping from ramp to ramp', although one would-be gatecrasher fell a goodly distance when the rope he was using to scale a wall broke and another youth was badly cut after being slugged in the face with a bottle by an attacker who melted into the mob in the home plate area. It was still light when they started, detracting from the mood so vital to appreciating Pink Floyd's music. Call it what you will – space-rock, cerebral-rock, thinking man's rock – it needs darkness so the lights and props can raise the sound into a real sensory experience. Using the bulk of *Dark Side* as the second part of their show was the same format they employed two years ago – but what a difference this time. A huge 'tambourine' behind the band proved to be a screen on which were shown clips 'describing' each song. And to top it all off, a monstrous white pyramid that had hovered behind them all night rose slowly from its moorings as spotlights beamed off it and rose high above the crowd (on wires), riding completely out of the stadium."

ABOVE: THE GIANT PYRAMID HURTLES OUT OF CONTROL AT THE THREE RIVERS STADIUM.

SUNDAY 22 JUNE – PERFORMANCE
County Stadium, Milwaukee, WI, USA

Set list included: 'Gotta Be Crazy' <Intermission> *The Dark Side of the Moon* <Encore> 'Echoes'.

In its review of the show the *Milwaukee Sentinel* reported, "Water was like gold Sunday afternoon as a sea of shirtless, sweating

ABOVE: NICK MASON ON STAGE, DETROIT, 24 JUNE 1975.

contract with Pink Floyd, Olympia used festival-style seating for the Floyd's Monday and Tuesday concerts, and the result was sweaty thigh jammed against sweaty thigh on the main floor where fans sat cross-legged like sweltering Indians. As if the heat weren't enough, Monday's audience was denied a special film by Peter Medak, director of *Ruling Class*. The film, an interpretation of Floyd's *Dark Side of the Moon*, was on the premises, but the projector was soaked during a downpour at an outdoor date in Milwaukee on Sunday, and was out of commission. The group turned the old ballroom mirrored globe to its own use, bathing the crowd in a swirl of stars. Pink Floyd's futuristic but never garish music shows the polish over 10 years together, with only one personnel change, and the group proved Monday that its music, nothing more, is the foundation of its long success."

young persons waited for hours on blistering asphalt to fill County Stadium for a rock concert by Pink Floyd. But, shortly after Pink Floyd took to the stage at 8.30pm, there was water to spare as rain began to fall. The concert was interrupted and the crowd huddled under plastic sheets or bleachers. The concert ended at 12.30am Monday. Lightening [sic] and rain hit the Stadium just as Pink Floyd finished its third number. The group took a half-hour break as the rain cooled the crowd, and then returned to the stage, only to be washed off by another downpour. The first interruption came at about 9.15pm, when Pink Floyd's lighting was in competition with the heavens and lightening and showers stopped the show."

It was widely reported that extensive (and in some cases heavy-handed) searching of concertgoers entering the stadium grounds had resulted in 124 arrests, mainly on drug-related offences.

MONDAY 23 & TUESDAY 24 JUNE – PERFORMANCES
Olympia Stadium, Detroit, MI, USA

Set list at both shows: 'Raving And Drooling', 'Gotta Be Crazy', 'Shine On You Crazy Diamond, Parts 1–5', 'Have A Cigar', 'Shine On You Crazy Diamond, Parts 6–9' <Intermission> *The Dark Side of the Moon* <Encore> 'Echoes'.

Reviewing the show the *Detroit Free Press* reported, "Just about everything was working against Pink Floyd at its Monday night concert at Olympia Stadium. Fortunately, the one thing that was perfectly right was the music. Pink Floyd is not nearly as well known to the general public as some groups that attract legions of hard-core rock fans, but nevertheless it has been hugely successful since 1964. Monday, the four members of Floyd were put to the test. Could their music, without many of their infamous special effects, make 17,000 people forget the misery of being crammed into a building that felt like a steam bath gone mad? As part of the

THURSDAY 26 JUNE – PERFORMANCE ▶
Autostade, Montréal, Canada

Set list: 'Raving And Drooling', 'Gotta Be Crazy', 'Shine On You Crazy Diamond, Parts 1–5', 'Have A Cigar', 'Shine On You Crazy Diamond, Parts 6–9' <Intermission> *The Dark Side of the Moon* <Encore> 'Echoes'.

On a clear evening, the show is remembered for an amazing moonrise on the left side of the stage as Waters sang the lyric, "but the sun is eclipsed by the moon" at the close of 'Eclipse'.

UNE SOIRÉE ÉTOILÉE À L'AUBE DE L'ÉTÉ UN RÊVE ÉVEILLÉ
PINK FLOYD
LE 26 JUIN 1975 À 9 H. À L'AUTOSTADE DE MONTRÉAL UNE INVITATION DE KOSMOS ET DONALD K DONALD

No 12671
IVOR WYNNE STADIUM
HAMILTON, ONTARIO
Retain Stub – Good Only
SAT. **JUNE 28**
8:30 P.M.
Davis Printing Limited
C.P.I. and GARFUNKEL *present*
PINK FLOYD
PRICE — $8.50
No Refunds
CONDITION OF SALE: Upon refunding the purchase price the management may remove from the premises any person who has obtained admission by this ticket.
PINK FLOYD
8:30 P.M.
SAT. JUNE 28 1975

SATURDAY 28 JUNE – PERFORMANCE ◀
Ivor Wynne Stadium, Hamilton, Canada

Set list: 'Raving And Drooling', 'Gotta Be Crazy', 'Shine On You Crazy Diamond, Parts 1–5', 'Have A Cigar', 'Shine On You Crazy Diamond, Parts 6–9' <Intermission> *The Dark Side of the Moon* <Encore> 'Echoes'.

In a dramatic finale to the tour, Pink Floyd's crew decided to go out with a bang and used up all of their remaining pyrotechnic charges around the stadium scoreboard. The *Hamilton Spectator* reported that "the blast knocked out an eight-foot steel panel from under the scoreboard sending it out onto Balsam Avenue where it landed without hitting anyone. It blew sections out of the scoreboard causing extensive damage. Four Balsam Avenue North homes, directly behind the scoreboard, had windows broken. Two electricians dismantling high tension wires above the stage spent the night in hospital under observation for possible damage to their ears from the explosion. Promoter Jean Garofoli said, 'I haven't really got to the bottom of it. I don't know if it was accidental or whether it was a joke that backfired.' Estimated damage to the scoreboard was pegged at $20,000."

Additionally all the remaining unsold copies of the tour programme were handed out free of charge, apparently in the hundreds, most of them ending up unwanted and trodden into the grass pitch.

SATURDAY 5 JULY – PERFORMANCE ▼
Knebworth Park,
Stevenage, England

With the Steve Miller Band, Captain Beefheart and his Magic Band, Roy Harper and Trigger (featuring Chris Spedding and Bill Bruford), Linda Lewis, Graham Chapman (performing sketches between acts), and compères John Peel and Pete Drummond.

Set list: 'Raving And Drooling', 'Gotta Be Crazy', 'Shine On You Crazy Diamond, Parts 1–5', 'Have A Cigar' (with Roy Harper on Vocals), 'Shine On You Crazy Diamond, Parts 6–9' <Intermission> *The Dark Side of the Moon* <Encore> 'Echoes'.

Pink Floyd appeared with Venetta Fields and Carlena Williams (Backing Vocals) and Dick Parry (Saxophones).

Reviewing the show *Sounds* reported, "There was a long delay before the Floyd arrived while the mechanics of their production were mobilised: the giant circular screen, the lofty lighting towers, the three articulated trucks that carried their sound system and finally the brace of Spitfires that passed overhead. Their set was divided, as usual, into two halves, the first offering the newer, unrecorded material that one assumes will form the basis of their next album, and the second devoted to *The Dark Side of the Moon* in its entirety, followed again as usual,

ABOVE: PINK FLOYD'S FINAL DATE ON THEIR 1975 TOUR AT KNEBWORTH, 5 JULY 1975.

by 'Echoes' as an encore. In short, the first part was poor. *Dark Side...*hit occasional highs and 'Echoes' was pretty superb. Tuning problems hampered the early songs and Roger Waters hit many a bum note in his vocals as the group laboured along with what appeared to be little enthusiasm for the event. With the darkness falling, they appeared to gain new life and 'Crazy Diamond', the last of the three early songs, picked up as their lighting columns bathed the band in a sea of colours. At last it seemed as if an Event would happen. A model plane on a wire heralded the onset of *Dark Side...*which picked up as it went along, a majestic piece of music that the group must be over-familiar with by now. Nevertheless, 'Any Colour You Like' developed into a tremendous jam, Dave Gilmour especially shining on his Stratocaster, trading lines with Waters and Wright that moved through a spectrum of ideas not contained on the record. The closing two songs, unfortunately, suffered again through Waters' vocals and it limped, rather than romped, to its usually stunning climax.... 'Echoes' as stated, ended the day and predictably this was played flawlessly."

A short documentary film was made by French TV that followed the exploits of a large party from Paris travelling to the show and also featured an extract of the band performing 'Shine On You Crazy Diamond, Parts 6–9' at the show. It was broadcast on TF1 on 8 July 1975 between 1.00pm and 1.30pm as part of the news programme *IT1 Journal*.

One amusing incident was also reported in *Melody Maker* concerning Roy Harper who, "threw a tantrum when he discovered that his chauffeur-driven Rolls-Royce had driven away with his stage clothes in the boot. Harper wrecked one caravan and was restrained as he set about wrecking a second."

ABOVE: DAVID GILMOUR PERFORMING AT KNEBWORTH, 5 JULY 1975.

One of the two display aircraft that performed the flypast was Spitfire Mk. XIV serial no. RM689 G-ALGT owned by Rolls Royce and based at their hangar at East Midlands Airport, Castle Donington, England. Following a fatal crash at RAF Woodford airshow on Saturday 27 June 1992, it remains in storage awaiting restoration. The second aircraft was Spitfire LF Mk.Vc serial no. AR501 G-AWII based at the Shuttleworth Collection, Old Warden, England. AR501 was fitted with elliptical wings (rather than the clipped wings of an LF Vc) for its appearance in the feature film *The Battle of Britain* in 1969 and resides to this day at Old Warden, in flying condition as a Mk.Vc in 310 (Czech) Squadron RAF Colours, call sign NN-A.

MONDAY 7 JULY – RECORDING SESSION
Studio 3, EMI Studios, Abbey Road, London, England

2.30pm to 12.30am: Backing Vocals overdubbed onto 'Shine On You Crazy Diamond' and a playback of a rough mix of *Wish You Were Here*. The session was produced by Pink Floyd, engineered by Brian Humphries and assisted by Peter James. The session also coincided with the wedding reception for Gilmour's marriage to his first wife, Virginia "Ginger" Hasenbein, whom he had first met on their 1971 North American tour.

TUESDAY 8 JULY – RECORDING SESSION
Studio 3 & Control Room 3, EMI Studios, Abbey Road, London, England

2.30pm to 12.00midnight: Piano and Guitar overdubbed onto 'Shine On You Crazy Diamond'; Guitar overdubbed onto 'Have A Cigar' and Guitar overdubbed onto "End Sequence Outro" of 'Shine On You Crazy Diamond' for *Wish You Were Here*. The

session was produced by Pink Floyd, engineered by Brian Humphries and assisted by Peter James.

WEDNESDAY 9 JULY – RECORDING SESSION
Studio 3 & Control Room 3, EMI Studios, Abbey Road, London, England

2.30pm to 2.00am: Electric Guitar and Drums overdubbed onto 'Have A Cigar'; 'Have A Cigar' mixed (RS1 and RS2 also marked "Best"); and 'The Machine Song' ['Welcome To The Machine'] "Into Song" mixed (RS1 and RS2 and both marked "Best") for *Wish You Were Here*. The session was produced by Pink Floyd, engineered by Brian Humphries and assisted by Peter James.

THURSDAY 10 JULY – RECORDING SESSION
Studio 3 & Control Room 3, EMI Studios, Abbey Road, London, England

2.30pm to 6.30pm: 'Wish You Were Here' mixed (RS1), and 7.30pm to 2.00am: 'Wish You Were Here' mixed (RS2 and RS3, RS4 and RS5 both marked "Best To Be Decided") for *Wish You Were Here*. The session was produced by Pink Floyd, engineered by Brian Humphries and assisted by Peter James.

FRIDAY 11 JULY – RECORDING SESSION
Studio 3 & Control Room 3, EMI Studios, Abbey Road, London, England

2.30pm to 4.00am: 'Shine On You Crazy Diamond' "Guitar Intro" mixed (RS1); "Song Up To Moog Entry" mixed RS1 and RS2 also marked "Best"); "Moog Entry To Vocal Entry" mixed (RS1 and RS2 also marked "Best" and edited to RS2 "Song Up To Moog Entry"); and "Intro (Wineglasses)" mixed (RS1–3 marked "Best To Be Decided") for *Wish You Were Here*. The session was produced by Pink Floyd, engineered by Brian Humphries and assisted by Peter James.

MONDAY 14 JULY – RECORDING SESSION
Studio 3 & Control Room 3, EMI Studios, Abbey Road, London, England

2.30pm to 6.30pm: 'Shine On You Crazy Diamond' "1st Two Verses" mixed (RS1 and RS2 also marked "Best") and "Sax Solo" (RS1 also marked "Best" and RS2), and 7.30pm to 2.00am: "Last Verse" mixed (RS1) and Master edited for *Wish You Were Here*. The session was produced by Pink Floyd, engineered by Brian Humphries and assisted by Peter James.

TUESDAY 15 JULY – RECORDING SESSION
Studio 3 & Control Room 3, EMI Studios, Abbey Road, London, England

2.30pm to 1.30am: 'Shine On You Crazy Diamond' "Vocal Entry to Sax Solo" mixed (RS10), and various cross-fades and edits done to prepare Side One of Master for *Wish You Were Here*. The session was produced by Pink Floyd, engineered by Brian Humphries and assisted by Peter James.

WISH YOU WERE HERE

SIDE A

SHINE ON YOU CRAZY DIAMOND, PARTS I-V (Part I, Wright, Waters, Gilmour), (Part II, Gilmour, Waters, Wright), (Part III, Waters, Gilmour, Wright), (Part IV, Gilmour, Wright, Waters), (Part V, Waters, Gilmour, Wright) **13:38**
WELCOME TO THE MACHINE (Waters) **7:30**

SIDE B

HAVE A CIGAR (Waters) **5:24**
WISH YOU WERE HERE (Waters, Gilmour) **5:17**
SHINE ON YOU CRAZY DIAMOND, PARTS V-IX (Part VI, Wright, Waters, Gilmour), (Part VII, Waters, Gilmour, Wright), (Part VIII, Gilmour, Wright, Waters), (Part IX, Wright) **12:29**

RELEASE DATE

UK: Friday 12 September 1975.
US: Saturday 13 September 1975.

FORMAT

UK: EMI Harvest SHVL 814 (Vinyl album).
US: Columbia PC 33453 (Vinyl album).

HIGHEST CHART POSITION

UK: No. 1 (*Music Week* "Top Albums'" on Saturday 4 October 1975), Chart re-entry No. 97 (*Music Week* "Top 100 Albums" on Saturday 20 August 1988), Chart re-entry No. 52 (*Music Week* "Top 100 Albums" on 6 Saturday August 1994), Chart re-entry No. 43 (*Official Charts Company* on Saturday 19 November 2011).
US: No. 1 (*Billboard* "Top LPs & Tape" on Saturday 20 September 1975).

AWARDS

UK: Certified Silver and Gold on Friday 1 August 1975 and 2 x Platinum on Monday 22 July 2013.
US: Certified Gold on 17 September 1975, 3 x Multi-Platinum on 21 November 1986, Platinum on 21 November 1986, 4 x Multi-Platinum on 9 August 1989, 5 x Multi-Platinum on 2 May 1995 and 6 x multiplatinum on 16 May 1997.
At the *18th Grammy Awards*, held at the Hollywood Palladium, Los Angeles, USA on 28 February 1976, *Wish You Were Here* was nominated for 'Best Album Package' losing out to *Honey* by the Ohio Players.

SALES

Since it was first released, *Wish You Were Here* has sold in excess of 13 million copies worldwide as of 2004. In 2003 *Rolling Stone* named it No. 209 of the 500 "Greatest Albums of All Time". This happened 28 years after the magazine initially panned the recording saying that, "Passion is everything of which Pink Floyd is devoid."

ARTWORK

Artwork by Hipgnosis. Photos of the Hollywood stuntmen Ronnie Rondell and Danny Rogers who feature in the burning handshake photos were taken at Warner Brothers Studios, Los Angeles; the red veil against the trees was taken near Ely, Cambridgeshire, England; the faceless salesman was taken in the Yuma Desert, in southwestern USA; and the diver taken at Mono Lake, California, USA. The first vinyl editions had a black shrink-wrap cover obscuring the sleeve artwork with a round 'Wish You Were Here' sticker, designed by George Hardie, on the front and an inserted 'Wish You Were Here' postcard.

MUSICIANS

David Gilmour (Vocals, Guitars, Bass, EMS Synthi AKS, Tape Effects).
Nick Mason (Drums, Percussion, Tape Effects).
Roger Waters (Vocals, Bass Guitar, Acoustic Guitar, EMS VCS3, Tape Effects).
Richard Wright (Hammond, Electric Piano, Harmonium, Clavinet, ARP String Synthesizer, EMS VCS3, Moog, Backing Vocals).

ADDITIONAL MUSICIANS

Venetta Fields and Carlena Williams (Backing Vocals).
Stéphane Grappelli (Violin on 'Wish You Were Here', released 2011).
Roy Harper (Vocals on 'Have A Cigar').
Dick Parry (Saxophones on 'Shine on You Crazy Diamond').

RECORDING DETAILS

Recorded at EMI Studios, Abbey Road and produced by Pink Floyd, engineered by Brian Humphries and assisted by Peter James.

After a period of rehearsals and working on demos and having finally settled on what it was they were now going to record, Pink Floyd set about putting it all down on tape. Although both 'Raving And Drooling' and 'Gotta Be Crazy' remained a staple of their live set list through the year, they were ultimately dropped from the process as Waters developed an overall theme for the album. "Once we accepted that we were going to go off on a tangent during the sessions it did become exciting, for me anyway, because then it was a desperate fucking battle trying to make it good," Waters recalled. "Actually we expended too much energy before that point in order to be able to quite do it. By the time we were finishing it, after the second American Tour, I hadn't got an ounce of creative energy left in me anywhere, and those last couple of weeks were a real fucking struggle."[1]

'Shine On' was initially recorded as one lengthy piece. Speaking many years later Gilmour confirmed that, "We did the basic track of Shine On…' from the beginning where the first guitar solo starts, right through the sax break and on to the reprise that appears towards the end of the album. That was in all 20 minutes long and at one time it was going to be one whole side of the album. But as we worked on it and extended it and extracted things, we came to the decision that we would work on new stuff to slot in the middle of what effectively became two parts. We originally did the backing track over the course of several days."[2] But, Gilmour continued, "We came to the conclusion that it just wasn't good enough. So we did it again in one day flat and got it a lot better. Unfortunately nobody understood the desk properly and when we played it back we found that someone had switched the echo returns from monitors to tracks one and two. That affected the tom-toms and guitars and keyboards which were playing along at the time. There was no way of saving it, so we just had to do it yet again."[3]

Of particular interest was the original intention of adding violin to the title track. "Dave had made the suggestion that there ought to be a country fiddle at the end of it, or we might try it out," remembered Waters, "and Stephane Grappelli was downstairs in number one studio making an album with Yehudi Menuhin…. So they wheeled him up after much bartering about his fee…. It was wonderful to have him come in and play a bit."[4] It had long been claimed that the tapes of Grappelli's recording were lost or recorded over, but the full unreleased version formed a highlight of EMI's 2011 *Wish You Were Here Immersion* set.

1–4. *Wish You Were Here Song Book*, Music Sales America, 1975.

Shine On You Crazy Diamond (Track as a whole)

Take 1 (Various RS edited).
Basic track ['Parts 2-8'] recorded on 3 January 1975 (Take 1).
"Drone Intro" ['Part 1'] recorded on 13 January 1975 (Take 1).
Moog overdubbed onto Take 1 of "Drone Intro" ['Part 1'] on 13 January 1975.
Click-Track made for Take 1 of "Rick's Intro" ['Part 1'] on 14 January 1975.
Moog overdubbed onto Take 1 of "Rick's Intro" ("Drone Intro") on 14 January 1975.
Basic track ['Parts 2-8'] re-recorded on 15 January 1975 (Takes 2-4 all "Edit Pieces" to be edited).
Drums overdubbed onto "Edit Pieces Takes 2-4" on 15 January 1975.
Basic track ['Parts 2-8'] re-recorded on 13 January 1975 (Take 6, also edited).
Guitar, Drums and Bass overdubbed onto Take 6 on 20 January 1975.
"Outro Part" ['Part 9'] recorded on 21 January 1975 (Take 6).
Guitar overdubbed onto "Second Verse" ['Part 4'] recorded as 'Shine On You Crazy Diamond Part 2') on 21 January 1975.
Parts 1-6 edited together on 21 January 1975.

Rhythm Guitar overdubbed onto "Second Verse" ['Part 4'] on 21 January 1975.
Guitar and Synthesizer overdubbed onto "Second Verse" ['Part 4'] on 22 January 1975.
"Edit Pieces" recorded on 23 January 1975 (Takes 1–5 edited together).
Basic track re-recorded as 'Shine On You Crazy Diamond Version 3' on 27 January 1975. (Take 1 "Up To "Arpeggio" and Take 2 from "Arpeggio to Break Section") ['Part 2' to 'Part 8']
Takes 1 & 2 above edited to create "Master Take 1" on 28 January 1975.
Guitar overdubbed onto "Master Take 1" ['Part 2' to 'Part 8'] on 28 January 1975.
Guitar and Harmonium overdubbed onto "Master Take 1" ['Part 2' to 'Part 8'] on 29 January 1975.
Guitar, Clavinet, Electric Piano and Synthesizer overdubbed onto "Master Take 1" ['Part 2' to 'Part 8'] on 30 January 1975.
Piano, Clavinet, Electric Guitar, Moog and Slide Guitar overdubbed onto "Master Take 1" ['Part 2' to 'Part 8'] on 3 February 1975.
Moog, Electric Guitar, String Synthesizer and Vocal overdubbed onto "Master Take 1" ['Part 2' to 'Part 8'] on 4 February 1975.
Electric Guitar, Moog, Organ, Vocal and Backing Vocal overdubbed onto "Master Take 1" ['Part 2' to 'Part 8'] on 5 February 1975.

Backing Vocals, Main Vocal, Moog and Guitar overdubbed onto "Master Take 1" ['Part 4' and 'Part 7'] on 6 February 1975.
Backing Vocals overdubbed onto "Master Take 1" ['Part 2' and 'Part 8'] on 10 February 1975.
Moog, Electric Guitar and Cymbals overdubbed onto "Master Take 1" ['Part 6'] on 11 February 1975.
Electric Guitar Solo, Rhythm Guitar, Synthesizer and Electric Guitar overdubbed onto "Master Take 1" ['Part 6'] on 12 February 1975.
Vocal, Synthesizer, Hammond Organ, Piano and Electric Guitar overdubbed onto "Master Take 1" on 14 February 1975.
Wild Guitar, Wild Vocals and Piano recorded onto "Master Take 1" on 17 February 1975
Electric Guitar, Moog, String Synthesizer, Electric Guitar Solo and Electric Piano overdubbed onto "Master Take 1" on 18 February 1975.
Bass, Moog, Organ and Synthesizer overdubbed and "Various Backwards Things" recorded onto "Master Take 1" ['Part 2' to 'Part 8'] on 18 February 1975.
Slide Guitar overdubbed onto "Master Take 1" ['Part 2' to 'Part 8'] on 20 February 1975.
"Wineglasses" [from 'Nothing Part 5' recorded on 5 January 1971] overdubbed onto "Master Take 1" ['Part 1'] on 24 February 1975.
Acoustic Guitar and Vocals overdubbed for

WISH YOU WERE HERE

"Shine On Extension" onto "Master Take 1" ['Part 7'] on 26 February 1975.
Vocals overdubbed onto "Master Take 1" ['Part 4' and 'Part 7'] on 5 May 1975.
Saxophones [Dick Parry] overdubbed onto "Master Take 1" ['Part 5'] on 15 May 1975.
Bass Guitar and Vocal overdubbed onto "Master Take 1" ['Part 2' to 'Part 8'] on 19 May 1975.
"End Sequence" ['Part 9'] recorded on 20 May 1975 (Take 1).
Piano, Hammond Organ, Synths, Bass Guitar and Drums overdubbed onto "End Sequence" ['Part 9'] on 20 May 1975.
Chords taken from various Moog chords (originally recorded for 'Welcome To The Machine' on 14 May 1975) and overdubbed onto "End Sequence" ['Part 9'] on 20 May 1975.
Drums and Bass overdubbed onto "End Sequence" ['Part 9'] on 21 May 1975.
Guitar and Electric Piano overdubbed and various edits made to "Master Take 1" ['Part 2' to 'Part 8'] on 29 May 1975.
Electric Piano, String Synthesizer and Moog overdubbed onto "Master Take 1" ['Part 2' to 'Part 8'] on 2 June 1975.
Backing Vocals [Venetta Fields and Carlena Williams] overdubbed onto "Master Take 1" ['Part 4' and 'Part 7'] on 7 July 1975.
Piano and Guitar overdubbed onto "Master Take 1" ['Part 2' to 'Part 8'] on 8 July 1975.
Guitar overdubbed onto "End Sequence Outro" ['Part 5'] on 8 July 1975.
"Guitar Intro" ['Part 2'] Mixed on 11 July 1975 (RS1).
"Song up to Moog entry" ['Part 3'] mixed on 11 July 1975 (RS2).
"Moog entry to Vocal entry" ['Part 4'] mixed on 11 July 1975 (RS2).
RS2 of "Song up to Moog entry" and RS2 of Moog Entry to Vocal Entry edited together.
"Intro (Wineglasses)" ['Part 1'] mixed (RS1-3).
"First Two Verses" ['Part 4'] mixed on 14 July 1975 (RS2).
Sax Solo [Dick Parry] ['Part 4'] mixed on 14 July 1975 (RS1).
"Last Verse" ['Part 7'] mixed on 14 July 1975 (RS1).
"Vocal Entry" to Sax Solo ['Part 4' to 'Part 5'] mixed on 15 July 1975 (RS10).
"Beginning of Side One" ['Part 6'] cross-faded on 16 July 1975.
"End Section" ['Part 9'] edited on 16 July 1975.
"Funky Section" ['Part 8'] mixed on 16 July 1975 (RS1-3).
"Outro" ['Part 9'] mixed on 16 July 1975 (RS1).
"Slide Solo Sections" ['Part 6'] mixed on 17 July 1975 (RS5).
Bass Guitar edited onto start of "RS5 Slide Solo Sections" ['Part 6'] on 17 July 1975.
"Third Verse" ['Part 7'] mixed on 17 July 1975 (RS1-3).

"Third Verse" ['Part 7'] mixed on 18 July 1975 (RS5).
"Funky Section" ['Part 8'] mixed on 18 July 1975 (RS3).
"Outro" ['Part 9'] mixed on 18 July 1975 (RS2).
"Funky Section to Outro" ['Part 8' to 'Part 9'] cross-faded and edited on 19 July 1975.

Welcome To The Machine

Take 1 (RS2).
Basic track recorded as 'The Machine' on 25 February 1975 (Take 1).
Moog overdubbed onto Take 1 on 26 February 1975.
Acoustic Guitar and Vocal overdubbed onto Take 1 on 27 February 1975.
Synthesizeroverdubbed onto Take 1 on 8 May 1975.
"Tape Loop of Synthesizers" made on 8 May 1975.
Vocals, Synthesizer and Acoustic Guitar overdubbed onto Take 1 (remake) on 9 May 1975.
Tape loops made up and edited on 9 May 1975.
Synthesizers, Acoustic Guitar and Vocals overdubbed onto Take 1 (remake) on 12 May 1975.
Synthesizers, Acoustic Guitar, Vocals, Tympani and Electric Guitar overdubbed onto Take 1 (remake) on 13 May 1975.
Various Moog chords recorded and overdubbed onto Take 1 (remake) on 14 May 1975.
Moog overdubbed onto Take 1 (remake) on 14 May 1975.
Moog overdubbed onto Take 1 (remake) on 15 May 1975.
VCS3 Effects recorded (Takes 1-3) and overdubbed onto Take 1 (remake) on 23 May 1975.
Bass and Synth overdubbed onto Take 1 (remake) on 27 May 1975.
VCS3 overdubbed onto Take 1 (remake) on 28 May 1975.
VCS3 Throb recorded (Takes 1-5) on 28 May 1975.
Vocals overdubbed onto Take 1 (remake) on 2 June 1975.
Mixed on 9 July 1975 (RS2).
"Wild Synthesizer" recorded on 24 July 1975 (Take 1).
"Wild Synthesizers and Door Effects" recorded and "Cross-faded for end" on 28 July 1975.

Have A Cigar

Take 56 (RS3).
Basic track with vocal [Roger Waters] recorded on 10 March 1975 (Takes 1–14).

Basic track with vocal [Roger Waters] re-recorded on 11 March 1975 (Takes 18-52).
Basic track with vocal [Roger Waters] re-recorded on 12 March 1975 (Takes 53-56).
Take 56 vocal [Roger Waters] overdubbed onto Take 56 basic track and edited to make Take 56 master on 12 March 1975.
Organ and Acoustic Guitar overdubbed onto Take 56 on 12 March 1975.
Vocal [Roger Waters], Guitar, Piano, Clavinet, String Synthesizer and Electric Guitar overdubbed onto Take 56 on 13 March 1975.
Electric Piano, String Machine and Synths overdubbed onto Take 56 on 6 May 1975.
Guitar overdubbed onto Take 56 on 7 May 1975.
Vocal [David Gilmour] overdubbed onto Take 56 on 8 May 1975.
Vocal [Roy Harper] overdubbed onto Take 56 on 16 May 1975.
Clavinet overdubbed onto Take 56 on 30 May 1975.
Moog overdubbed onto Take 56 on 2 June 1975.
Guitar overdubbed onto Take 56 on 8 July 1975.
Electric Guitar and Drums overdubbed onto Take 56 on 9 July 1975.
Mixed on 9 July 1975 (RS2).
Mixed again on 19 July 1975 (RS3).
'Have A Cigar' to 'Wish You Were Here' cross-fade mixed on 24 July 1975 (RS1) and edited on 28 July 1975.

Wish You Were Here

Take 2 (RS5).
Basic track recorded as 'Untitled (An Afternoon At Home With The Duke Of Roydon)' (Take 1).
Guitar overdubbed onto Take 1 on 16 May 1975.
Acoustic Guitar, Drums and Bass overdubbed onto Take 1 on 16 May 1975.
Vocals overdubbed onto Take 1 on 21 May 1975.
Bass, Guitar and Woodblock overdubbed onto Take 1 on 22 May 1975.
Basic track re-recorded on 22 May 1975 (Take 2).
Guitars, Vocals and Piano overdubbed onto Take 2 on 22 May 1975.
Guitars, Vocals, Synths, Vocal Harmonies and Violin [Stéphane Grappelli] overdubbed onto Take 2 on 23 May 1975.
Drums, Guitar and "Radio Synthesized Sound" overdubbed onto Take 2 on 28 May 1975.
Pedal Steel Guitar and Drums overdubbed onto Take 2 on 29 May 1975.
Electric Guitar and Vocals overdubbed onto Take 2 on 30 May 1975.
Mixed on 10 July 1975 (RS5).
"Oogly-Booglies" [SFX link to 'Shine On You Crazy Diamond Part 6'] cross-faded and edited into Master on 28 July 1975.

WEDNESDAY 16 JULY – RECORDING SESSION
Studio 3 & Control Room 3, EMI Studios,
Abbey Road, London, England

2.30pm to 4.30pm: 'Shine On You Crazy Diamond' "Beginning of Side One Cross-faded"; 'Shine On You Crazy Diamond' "End Section Edited"; 'Shine On You Crazy Diamond' "Funky Section" mixed (RS1, RS2 and RS3); and 'Shine On You Crazy Diamond' "Outro" mixed (RS1 also marked "Best") for *Wish You Were Here*. The session was produced by Pink Floyd, engineered by Brian Humphries and assisted by Peter James.

THURSDAY 17 JULY – RECORDING SESSION
Studio 3 & Control Room 3, EMI Studios,
Abbey Road, London, England

2.30pm to 3.45am: 'Shine On You Crazy Diamond' "Slide Solo Section" mixed (RS1–3 marked "Rick's Mixes", and RS4 & 5 marked "Dave's Mixes"); Bass Guitar edited into start of RS5 for reference purposes; and 'Shine On You Crazy Diamond' "3rd Verse" mixed (RS1–3) for *Wish You Were Here*. The session was produced by Pink Floyd, engineered by Brian Humphries and assisted by Peter James.

FRIDAY 18 JULY – RECORDING SESSION
Studio 3 & Control Room 3, EMI Studios,
Abbey Road, London, England

2.30pm to 3.30am: 'Shine On You Crazy Diamond' "3rd Verse" mixed (RS4 and RS5 also marked "Best"), 'Shine On You Crazy Diamond' "Funky Section" re-mixed (RS1, RS2 and RS3 also marked "Best"); Various edits done to 'Shine On You Crazy Diamond'; and 'Shine On You Crazy Diamond' "Outro" mixed (RS2) for *Wish You Were Here*. The session was produced by Pink Floyd, engineered by Brian Humphries and assisted by Peter James.

SATURDAY 19 JULY – RECORDING SESSION
Studio 3 & Control Room 3, EMI Studios,
Abbey Road, London, England

2.30pm to 7.30pm: 'Have A Cigar' mixed (RS3 also marked "Best"), and "Funky Section" to "Outro" of 'Shine On You Crazy Diamond' cross-faded and edited into Master of Side 2 for *Wish You Were Here*. The session was produced by Pink Floyd, engineered by Brian Humphries and assisted by Peter James.

THURSDAY 24 JULY – RECORDING SESSION
Studio 3 & Control Room 3, EMI Studios,
Abbey Road, London, England

2.30pm to 6.30am: Various SFX recorded; Guitar Solo transferred from 2-Track Master to 24-Track for further overdubs; 'Have A Cigar' / 'Wish You Were Here' cross-fade mixed (RS1) and edited into Master; and "Wild Synthesizer" recorded (Take 1 also marked "Best") for *Wish You Were Here*. The session was produced by Pink Floyd, engineered by Brian Humphries and assisted by Peter James.

MONDAY 28 JULY – RECORDING SESSION
Studio 3 & Control Room 3, EMI Studios,
Abbey Road, London, England

2.15pm to 8.30pm: Various edits and cross-fades done to make up the final Master of Sides One and Two of album, and 12.00 midnight to 10.00am (29 July): Three hours editing Side One and Two of Masters; 'Wish You Were Here' "Oogly-Booglies" cross-faded and edited into Master; "Wild Synthesizers" recorded and cross-faded for end of 'Machine Song' ['Welcome To The Machine']; and "Door Effects" for *Wish You Were Here*. The session was produced by Pink Floyd, engineered by Brian Humphries and assisted by Peter James.

This was the last recording session for the *Wish You Were Here* album.

FRIDAY 12 SEPTEMBER – ALBUM RELEASE (UK)
Wish You Were Here

Melody Maker wrote, "I am not enthralled. I did try though to acclimatise myself to its bleak, emotionally barren landscape. I keep missing the connection somehow. From whichever direction one approaches *Wish You Were Here* it still sounds unconvincing in its ponderous sincerity and displays a critical lack of imagination in all departments. The Floyd amble somnambulantly along their star struck avenues arm in arm with some pallid ghost of creativity. *Wish You Were Here sucks*. It's as simple as that."

SATURDAY 13 SEPTEMBER – ALBUM RELEASE (US)
Wish You Were Here

Rolling Stone wrote, "'Shine On You Crazy Diamond' is initially credible because it purports to confront the subject of Syd Barrett, the long and probably forever lost guiding light of the original Floyd. But the potential of the idea goes unrealized; they give such a matter-of-fact reading of the goddamn thing that they might as well be singing about Roger Waters' brother-in-law getting a parking ticket."

MONDAY 29 SEPTEMBER – RECORDING SESSION
Control Room 3, EMI Studios,
Abbey Road, London, England

3.00pm to 1.45am: 'Have A Cigar' mixed (RQ1) and 'Wish You Were Here' mixed (RQ1) for the quadraphonic album release of *Wish You Were Here*. The session was produced by Pink Floyd, engineered by Brian Humphries and assisted by Peter Mew and Peter James. Pink Floyd was not in attendance at this session.

TUESDAY 30 SEPTEMBER – RECORDING SESSION
Control Room 3, EMI Studios,
Abbey Road, London, England

2.30pm to 3.00am: 'Wish You Were Here' mixed (RQ1 also marked "Best") and 'Welcome To The Machine' mixed (RQ1 also marked "Best") for the quadraphonic album release of *Wish You Were Here*. The session was produced by Pink Floyd, engineered by Brian Humphries and assisted by Peter Mew and Peter James. Pink Floyd was not in attendance at this session.

WEDNESDAY 1 OCTOBER – RECORDING SESSION
Control Room 3, EMI Studios,
Abbey Road, London, England

7.00pm to 3.45am: 'Shine On You Crazy Diamond' "Vocal Entry to Sax Solo" mixed (RQ1 also marked "Best") and 'Shine On You Crazy Diamond' "Sax Section to Oogly-Booglies" mixed (RQ1 also marked "Best") for the quadraphonic album release of *Wish You*

Were Here. The session was produced by Pink Floyd, engineered by Brian Humphries and assisted by Peter Mew and Peter James. Pink Floyd was not in attendance at this session.

MONDAY 6 OCTOBER – RECORDING SESSION
**Control Room 3, EMI Studios,
Abbey Road, London, England**

7.00pm to 5.45am: 'Shine On You Crazy Diamond' "Vocal Entry" mixed (RQ2 also marked "Edited Best"); 'Shine On You Crazy Diamond' "Vocal Entry to Sax Solo" mixed (RQ2 also marked "Edited Best"); 'Shine On You Crazy Diamond' "Sax Solo to Oogly-Booglies" mixed (RQ2 also marked "Edited Best"); 'Shine On You Crazy Diamond' "Oogly-Booglies to Third Verse" mixed (RQ1 also marked "Best"); 'Shine On You Crazy Diamond' "Bass Intro to Oogly-Booglies" mixed (RQ1 also marked "Best"); and 'Shine On You Crazy Diamond' "3rd Verse to Funky Section" mixed (RQ1) for the quadraphonic album release of *Wish You Were Here*. The session was produced by Pink Floyd, engineered by Brian Humphries and assisted by Peter Mew and Peter James. Pink Floyd was not in attendance at this session.

WEDNESDAY 8 OCTOBER – RECORDING SESSION
Room 4, EMI Studios, Abbey Road, London, England

3.00pm to 8.00pm: 'Wish You Were Here' "Oogly-Booglies" cross-fade recorded and VCS3 overdubbed onto cross-fade; and 'Wish You Were Here' "Oogly-Booglies" cross-fade mixed (RQ1) for the quadraphonic album release of *Wish You Were Here*. The session was produced by Pink Floyd, engineered by Brian Humphries and assisted by Peter Mew and Peter James. Pink Floyd was not in attendance at this session.

WEDNESDAY 8 OCTOBER – RECORDING SESSION
**Control Room 3, EMI Studios,
Abbey Road, London, England**

12.00 midnight to 3.45am: 'Have A Cigar' / 'Wish You Were Here' cross-fade mixed (RQ1) for the quadraphonic album release of *Wish You Were Here*. The session was produced by Pink Floyd, engineered by Brian Humphries and assisted by Peter Mew and Peter James. Pink Floyd was not in attendance at this session.

THURSDAY 9 OCTOBER – RECORDING SESSION
Room 4, EMI Studios, Abbey Road, London, England

8.00pm to 2.00am: 'Welcome To The Machine (Intro)' mixed (RQ1 also marked "Best"); "Intro" of 'Shine On You Crazy Diamond' mixed (RQ1 also marked "Best"); and "Intro" of 'Welcome To The Machine' mixed (RQ1 and RQ2 also marked "Best") for the quadraphonic album release of *Wish You Were Here*. The session was produced by Pink Floyd, engineered by Brian Humphries and assisted by Peter Mew and Peter James. Pink Floyd was not in attendance at this session.

THURSDAY 9 OCTOBER – RECORDING SESSION
**Control Room 3, EMI Studios,
Abbey Road, London, England**

2.30am to 6.00am: 'Shine On You Crazy Diamond' "Funky Section" mixed (RQ1 also marked "Best") and 'Shine On You Crazy Diamond' "Outro" mixed (RQ1 also marked "Best") for the quadraphonic album release of *Wish You Were Here*. The session was produced by Pink Floyd, engineered by Brian Humphries and assisted by Peter Mew and Peter James. Pink Floyd was not in attendance at this session.

MONDAY 13 OCTOBER – RECORDING SESSION
**Control Room 3, EMI Studios,
Abbey Road, London, England**

3.00pm to 3.45am: 'Shine On You Crazy Diamond' "Intro / Shine On" cross-fade; 'Machine Song' cross-fades, 'Shine On You Crazy Diamond' "Funky Section / Outro" cross-fades mixed to 4-Track and edited into Master; and entire album banded for the quadraphonic album release of *Wish You Were Here*. The session was produced by Pink Floyd, engineered by Brian Humphries and assisted by Peter Mew and Peter James. Pink Floyd was not in attendance at this session.

SATURDAY 25 OCTOBER – EXHIBITION
***The 1975 London Audio Fair*,
Olympia Exhibition Halls, London, England**

An early quadraphonic mix of *Wish You Were Here* was premiered to the press with a Q&A session with mixer Brian Humphries. Nick Mason attended but was not drawn into the session.

TUESDAY 28 OCTOBER – RECORDING SESSION
**Control Room 3, EMI Studios,
Abbey Road, London, England**

12.00 midday to 2.00am: 'Shine On You Crazy Diamond' "Sax Solo Start" edited for the quadraphonic album release of *Wish You Were Here*. The session was produced by Pink Floyd, engineered by Brian Humphries and assisted by Peter Mew and Peter James. Pink Floyd was not in attendance at this session.

THURSDAY 30 OCTOBER – RECORDING SESSION
**Control Room 3, EMI Studios,
Abbey Road, London, England**

10.00pm to 2.00am: 'Welcome To The Machine' mixed (RQ10) and "Start of Machine Song for Crossover" mixed (RQ1 also marked "Best") for the quadraphonic album release of *Wish You Were Here*. The session was produced by Pink Floyd, engineered by Brian Humphries and assisted by Peter Mew and Peter James. Pink Floyd was not in attendance at this session.

SATURDAY 15 NOVEMBER – SINGLE RELEASE (US)
'Have A Cigar'

7

A CERTAIN UNEASE IN THE AIR

1976–77

1976—77

Following the completion of their album *Wish You Were Here* the band acquired a three-storey block of former church halls in Britannia Row, Islington, in North London, to serve as a storage facility for an increasing amount of tour equipment which, it was felt, could be hired out to other acts between tours. "Brit Row was really started to give a reason to not fire the crew," explained the band's PA manager Robbie Williams. "So they gave Mick [Kluczynski] and I the opportunity to run Britannia Row Audio, and Graeme Fleming the responsibility of Britannia Row Lighting."[1]

"Robbie and I thought long and hard about it," adds Kluczynski. "Up until 1975, we were touring for something like nine months a year, and then it changed to six months every two years. We were on wages all that time, so for 18 months we would be doing nothing unless Dave Gilmour asked us to provide a system for a free Hyde Park gig he was doing, and it was becoming difficult to justify our existence."[2]

With their recording contract to EMI also having expired, Pink Floyd took the opportunity to build their own 24-track recording studio at the same facility. In April of 1976 with engineer Brian Humphries, and his assistant Nick Griffiths, recording commenced on their tenth studio album, *Animals*.

The core of the album was developed around reworked versions of the live tracks 'You Gotta Be Crazy' and 'Raving And Drooling', which became 'Dogs' and 'Sheep' respectively. Having had their lyrics refined the album broadly attributed animal behaviour to that of the human condition, but took a good swipe at fat-cat businessmen as much as it did the man in the street. It's almost certain that Waters was as much disaffected by his own existence as he perceived others to be with theirs.

Clearly Waters was no longer at ease within the context of the band. His outpouring of often venomous lyrics was without equal yet he excluded others from the process in order to pursue his own vision – a trend that would continue over the next two studio albums, which ultimately worked to the detriment of Pink Floyd as a functioning unit.

Wright, being less assertive than the others, was more susceptible to such divisive pressure. It was the first Pink Floyd album on which he didn't receive a writing credit. It was only many years later that he spoke of this fraught period at all. "I didn't really like a lot of the music on the album," he said. "I have to say I didn't fight very hard to put my stuff on, and I didn't have anything to put on. I played on it. I think I played well, but I didn't contribute to the writing of it but I think that also Roger was kind of not letting me do that. This was the start of the whole ego thing in the band."[3]

Waters also visualized the sleeve design as depicting a large inflatable pink pig hovering between two of the four towering chimneys of south London's Battersea power station. Hipgnosis were commissioned to realize Waters' vision but suggested that an inflatable pig could be photographed in any location and the shot then superimposed onto a separate photograph of the power station. However, Waters insisted that the shoot be done for real and so a 40-foot inflatable pig was designed by Australian artist Jeffrey Shaw of Eventstructure Research Group in Amsterdam and built in Germany by Ballon Fabrik, the same company that had constructed the original Zeppelin airships. Once it had been inflated with helium and raised on cables, it would be tethered in position.

Eleven stills photographers and an eight-man film crew (including one in a helicopter) assembled at the location to capture it for posterity on launch day, 2 December. A marksman

RIGHT: AN INFLATABLE PIG IS HOISTED BETWEEN THE CHIMNEY STACKS AT BATTERSEA POWER STATION, DECEMBER 1976, FOR THE *ANIMALS* COVER SHOOT. THE PIG WOULD GO ON TO BECOME A FEATURE OF PINK FLOYD'S STAGE SHOW FOR ALL SUBSEQUENT TOURS.

had also been hired to shoot the pig down should it break free from its moorings and escape. However, for one reason or other the creature couldn't be inflated. The following day, a bright, sunny morning, a successful launch was made, only for a gust of wind to snap the pig's mooring cables. Unfortunately, nobody had told the marksman to return that day.

It's difficult to say whether this was an intentional publicity stunt or not, but later that morning the pig, having been spotted by an astonished commercial pilot coming in to land at Heathrow airport, was tailed by a police helicopter as far as Crystal Palace, southeast London. By mid-afternoon it was seen at 5,490-metres over Chatham in Kent, by which time everybody concerned assumed it was heading for home! Eventually it deflated and crashed, rather appropriately, into a barn at East Stour Farm at Godmersham in Kent. By next morning the story was in all the national newspapers.

Fortunately the pig, nickname Algie, was recovered and patched up to enable a further launch to take place. In a final, ironic twist the picture of the power station on the last day of shooting was thought to be more interesting because of the lighting contrast (it had been dull and overcast that morning), with the image of the pig then superimposed from the second day.

Many of the photos taken during the shoot were used for the subsequent tour publicity, programme and songbook, and, much later, for the remastered CD booklet. However, the film footage has, except for the occasional documentary TV clip, only ever been seen as a backdrop film for Waters' solo tours, which incorporated material from the album.

The release of *Animals* in January 1977 revealed itself to be an extension of Waters' bleak world view, revealing a far darker edge than had been previously experienced on *Wish You Were Here*. Musically it was a complete departure: out was the warmth of the saxophone and female backing vocals, and in was the newly discovered Vocoder voice synthesizer. It was essentially Pink Floyd's heavy rock album and despite not being their best recorded effort (Mason sounds like he's hitting cardboard boxes) it contains some fine performances. But it is once again Waters' lyrics that dominate, and the shared vocal with Gilmour, coupled with the latter's searing guitar work, is what makes the album such a strong piece of work.

The more strident songs certainly caught the air of depression and gloom of the times: the mid-1970s saw a brief hiatus in a continuing breakdown between the UK trade unions and the then Labour government, which resulted in strikes, and these in turn led to a growing sense of social unrest in Britain, particularly in the industrial inner cities. Street violence was increasing, partially fuelled by gangs of punks and skinheads who had turned football into a sport of violent clashes between team supporters. Racial tensions were also on the increase, initiated by the rise of right-wing organizations such as the National Front.

RIGHT: SNOWY WHITE WAS BROUGHT ON BOARD AS A SECOND GUITARIST FOR THE *ANIMALS* TOUR. HE WENT ON TO BECOME A FUNDAMENTAL PART OF ROGER WATERS' SOLO TOURING BAND.

Given this social backdrop it's surprising how well *Animals* fared with Floyd fans, and especially some quarters of the music press considering their attempts to push rock super-groups like Pink Floyd out of favour once and for all, now that they had the likes of the Sex Pistols to fawn over.[*] Perhaps the sheer vehemence of the attack won over the more radical critics, although some reviewers thought it was simply just too much to stomach, especially given Pink Floyd's heritage. The *NME* described the album as "simple in both concept and execution…and also marks another apparent progression in Waters' obsession with paranoia. Most of the album is bleak, dark and foreboding in mood, many of its images sombre."

The album itself was released on the day of the opening show of the European tour, in Dortmund, West Germany on 23 January 1977. Each show consisted of the whole of *Animals* and, for the first time, the complete *Wish You Were Here*, as first and second half performances. While the band dispensed with backing vocalists Dick Parry remained on board and a new support guitarist, Terence "Snowy" White, was recruited.

A large part of the rehearsals had already taken place at Britannia Row in early November, with the final dress rehearsals at the Olympia Exhibition Hall in London, and for the first time Pink Floyd now truly tackled the problem of the stadium environment. Conscious of the fact that many of the larger venues would tend to isolate the audience, they attempted to make the back row feel as involved as the front – to increase the element of spectacle for everyone present.

In order to realize this ideal, and again largely conceived by Waters, the Fisher-Park design team were once more mobilized and set to work on the design and construction of various large-scale inflatable figures to symbolize the typical "nuclear-age" family. This comprised a businessman and his wife, reclining on a sofa and, as statistics would have it, 2.5 children. These characters were inflated by industrial fans and hoisted into position by hydraulic rigging halfway through 'Dogs', to be quickly deflated at the end of the song. They were first used

---

*Pistols members Paul Cook, John Lydon (aka Johnny Rotten) and Steve Jones were all at some point famously photographed wearing a Pink Floyd T-shirt with the words "I Hate" scrawled above it.

at the shows in London, but by the time the tour had reached America, a Cadillac, a fridge and a TV set, all in relative scale, had also been added.

Unusually, Pink Floyd opted out of the usual square scaffold stage for their outdoor shows, and with no permanent overhead lighting truss the stage was fitted out with a dozen or so hydraulic umbrellas that unfurled to give some shade from the summer sun and a pair of large cherry-picker cranes were fitted out with spot lamps at either side of the stage.

Appropriately, the tour motif and newly acquired mascot, the giant inflatable pig, was also used. Not as benign as the Battersea model, the helium-filled balloon sported an ugly snarl as it poked its head from out behind the stage through a massive burst of smoke during 'Pigs' and travelled the length of the audience area suspended by steel cables. At outdoor shows a second pig was floated on a cable to a position high above the stage, where the propane charge it carried was detonated to dramatic effect.

Another new element was a compressed-air "sheep-cannon" that fired small sheep made from tea-bag material deep into the audience. On stage, a transistor radio was placed on a stand and mic'd up ready for Mason to scan the airwaves randomly, often with hilarious results, for the introduction of the title track of the latter album. The encores, which depended to a great extent on the collective mood of the band, varied between 'Money' and 'Us And Them', although on occasion both were performed and always featured the familiar back-projected films of the previous tours.

But the most striking addition was the disturbing animation film designed by the English satirical cartoonist Gerald Scarfe[*], which accompanied 'Welcome To The Machine'. Scarfe's film for Pink Floyd featured a constantly changing series of environments which included a huge, lizard-like metallic creature roaming a geometric landscape; a head that is brutally severed and slowly decays; and a city enveloped by a sea

of blood whose lapping waves transform into a mass of bloody, outstretched hands worshipping a huge monolithic structure.

It was reported in *Melody Maker* that the band had allocated a budget of around £100,000 to produce the animation sequence for the concerts alone and that Scarfe had taken some six months to produce it. The result was certainly amazing when seen on the big screen.

Another piece of Scarfe animation was also used for the closing section of 'Shine On You Crazy Diamond', which ended the show. This depicted a naked, faceless and sexless body somersaulting through the air as it transformed into a falling leaf and back again[**] until the screen was slowly blanked out by a huge mirror ball, revived from the previous tour. American shows also featured a waterfall of fireworks that stretched the full width of the stage and provided a spectacular conclusion to the extravaganza.

The European tour saw Pink Floyd perform to some of its biggest audiences to date, and in the UK they performed to five sold-out nights at Wembley Empire Pool and four at the New Bingley Hall, Stafford; an unusual choice of venue but not altogether inappropriate, since it was formerly a livestock market. Similarly, the four shows in Paris were held in what was a former abattoir.

For "Snowy" White it was clearly an enjoyable experience. "With the *Animals* tour it was interesting because I played bass a lot of the time in the first half. I used to walk on stage on my own and start the show with this bass thing and then the others used to walk on. Then in the second half of the show they did 'Wish You Were Here' and various other tracks where sometimes I'd play the odd bit of harmony with Dave, sometimes I'd play rhythm, sometimes lead. Then towards the end it got a bit more freer and Dave and I would swap licks and things…. 'Shine On You Crazy Diamond', I used to be able to let fly a little bit on that. There was a certain amount of

*The band had spotted Scarfe's work as early as 1973, when he was sent to Los Angeles in 1971 by BBC TV to try out the "Dejoux" animation system, which was designed to allow sequences where one image dissolved into another. This resulted in *Long Drawn Out Trip: Sketches from Los Angeles*, an 18-minute parody that let rip at every cliché of American life and is best remembered for its depiction of a deranged Richard Nixon and a strung-out Mickey Mouse. It was broadcast on BBC TV only once and promptly withdrawn – the broadcaster having failed to obtain clearances for the music, which included songs by a variety of artists from Jimi Hendrix to Neil Diamond, but perhaps more problematic were the Disney tunes. Scarfe's first work for Pink Floyd was to draw their caricatures for the centrespread of their 1974 UK tour programme. The same design was lifted in the mid-1980s to produce fake tour posters, which bizarrely seem to attract high prices at auction, passed off as the genuine article.

**This animation sequence was re-used for *The Wall* concerts in 1980/81 as part of the "Trial" sequence.

OPPOSITE: ROGER WATERS ON STAGE AT WEMBLEY STADIUM, MARCH 1977.

RIGHT: THE GIANT MIRRORBALL RISING AS 'SHINE ON YOU CRAZY DIAMOND' REACHES ITS CLIMAX AT WEMBLEY STADIUM, MARCH 1977.

freedom and I think I managed to keep my own sound through most of it. There were times when there were echoes and fuzzes and those sorts of things: it was nice to do all that."[4]

The following month as the show, now dubbed *Pink Floyd in the Flesh?*, laboured across North America, the stadium environment began to unhinge Roger Waters. Union technicians were constantly missing lighting cues, adding to a growing frustration that their stage presentation was being compromised, as overexcited fans began yelling and screaming throughout the performances, a habit that destroyed the relatively rapt atmosphere that had existed on previous tours. This, along with the fact that firecrackers were being hurled about in abundance – especially in New York where the band were performing throughout Independence Day celebrations – contributed to a growing frustration in Waters that no one was actually listening to his songs, and eventually he came to nurse a hatred for the impersonal nature of stadium touring.[*] He was also distancing himself from his bandmates, arriving and leaving the venues alone.

The crunch came at the final show, in Montreal, where the crowd were unusually rowdy. "I was on stage and there was one guy in the front row shouting and screaming all the way through everything," Waters recalled. "In the end I called him over and, when he got close enough, spat in his face. I shocked myself with that incident enough to think: 'Hold on a minute. This is all wrong. I'm hating this.'"[5]

The whole incident struck a devastating chord in Waters' psyche. Although Gilmour recalled that neither he nor the others had been aware at the time of the effect on their bandmate, "I just thought it was a great shame to end up a six-month tour with a rotten show. In fact, I remember going back to the sound-mixing board in the middle of the audience to watch the encore while Snowy played guitar."[6]

"It was quite a long jam," White recalled. "I was enjoying myself, and then the crew started dismantling the equipment as we were playing. In the end Nick was just left with a bass drum!"[7]

Close to a nervous collapse after the tour, Waters felt that the best therapy would be to write about his own experiences. He would attempt to trace his feelings of alienation back to his childhood; his sense of solitude as a consequence of his father's death during the war; the tyranny of his schooling, and the breakup of his marriage.

Leaving Waters to his own devices, the rest of the band began recording solo albums. Gilmour's eponymous album featured his former Cambridge band mates Willie Wilson and Rick Wills, whereas Wright's *Wet Dream* featured "Snowy" White, among others. Meanwhile, Mason put his name to an album entitled *Fictitious Sports*, essentially a Carla Bley solo record, but using Mason's name as a marketing tool. Gilmour and Wright's were released in 1978, while Mason's didn't see the light of day until 1981. Only when these projects were finished did they turn their attention to Waters' proposal for a new Pink Floyd album.

---

*The assertion by Waters that it was a gruelling tour is a puzzling one. Pink Floyd's entire North American venture that year comprised of just 26 dates over two periods. By contrast, other big-hitters that year included Led Zeppelin, who performed 44 shows in North America; Fleetwood Mac 65; Lynyrd Skynyrd 42; Queen 39 and so on. Moreover, many other bands were used to travelling to far flung corners of the earth, something Pink Floyd were either averse to doing, or just not invited to do. Either way, Waters just wasn't cut out for that lifestyle. In later years this attitude to stadium touring would change dramatically.

1–2. *Sound on Stage*, April 1997.
3. *Omnibus*, BBC–TV, 15 November 1994.
4. Snowy White, *Goldtop* CD booklet, 1995.
5–6. *Musician*, December 1982.
7. Author interview, September 1996.

1976

MONDAY 24 FEBRUARY – RECORDING SESSION
Room 4, EMI Studios, Abbey Road, London, England

8.00pm to 12.30am: *Wish You Were Here* Side One remixed (RQ1 also marked "Best") and Side Two (RQ2 also marked "Best") remixed from 4-track discrete to SQ encoded for the quadraphonic album release of *Wish You Were Here*.

APRIL – DECEMBER – RECORDING SESSIONS
Britannia Row Studios, Islington, London, England

Discontinuous recording for the album *Animals* began at the band's own purpose-built studios in north London. Work here continued throughout the rest of the year and into early 1977. A bootleg recording emerged on the market in early 2014 with early versions of 'Sheep', 'Dogs' and 'Pigs (3 Different Ones)', showing works in progress and in the case of 'Sheep' a distinct similarity to its earlier live incarnation as 'Raving And Drooling'.

TUESDAY 3 AUGUST – PRESS REPORT
London, England

It was reported in the national press that former Pink Floyd road manager Peter Watts had been found dead in a house owned by the group in McGregor Road, Notting Hill, London, the previous night. A subsequent inquest found he had died from a heroin overdose.

WEDNESDAY 3 NOVEMBER – RECORDING SESSION
Room 4, EMI Studios, Abbey Road, London, England

7.00pm to 2.00am: Quadraphonic remixing of EMI masters for quad stage effects for the forthcoming tour, including 'Intro' [of 'Shine On You Crazy Diamond'], 'Machine Song Intro', 'Intro To End Section' [of 'Welcome To The Machine'] and 'Outro' [of 'Shine On You Crazy Diamond']. The session was engineered by Peter James with Nick Mason and Richard Wright in attendance.

THURSDAY 4 NOVEMBER – RECORDING SESSION
Room 4, EMI Studios, Abbey Road, London, England

7.00pm to 2.30am: Quadraphonic remixing of EMI masters for quad stage effects for the forthcoming tour, including 'Machine Song Intro' and 'Shine On Wind FX'. The session was engineered by Peter James with Nick Mason and Richard Wright in attendance.

MONDAY 8 NOVEMBER – RECORDING SESSION
Room 4, EMI Studios, Abbey Road, London, England

7.00pm to 10.30pm: Quadraphonic remixing of EMI masters for quad stage effects for the forthcoming tour, including the "Radio Section" of 'Wish You Were Here' and the "End Section" of the 'Machine Song'. The session was engineered by Peter James with Richard Wright in attendance.

THURSDAY 2, FRIDAY 3 & SATURDAY 4 DECEMBER – FILMING & PHOTOGRAPHY
Battersea Power Station, London, England

Sleeve designers Hipgnosis assembled a crew of photographers and cameramen to record the launch of a 40-foot helium-filled inflatable pig for the cover of the band's forthcoming album *Animals*. On Thursday 2 December the weather was clear and sunny but the pig failed to inflate. On Friday 3 December in similar conditions the inflatable broke its moorings and floated across the southeast of England before crashing into a barn at East Stour Farm in Godmersham in Kent. Once the pig was patched up a further flight took place against a backdrop of more dramatic skies. The final image uses the setting from Saturday 4 December and the pig from Friday 3 December. Footage from the launch on Friday 3 December has been used for various promotional purposes as well as by Roger Waters for his solo tours and Pink Floyd as part of their *Live 8* show on Saturday 2 July 2005.

ABOVE: THE INFLATABLE PIG PHOTOGRAPHED PRIOR TO ITS ESCAPE.

FRIDAY 17 DECEMBER – RADIO BROADCAST
The Pink Floyd Story, Capital Radio, Euston Tower, London, England

Capital Radio, London commenced broadcasting over the next six consecutive weeks of the first authoritative documentary on the band entitled, *The Pink Floyd Story*, between 10.00pm and 11.00pm as part of the Nicky Horne show, as follows: Part 1: 'The Early Years' broadcast Friday 17 December; Part 2: '*Piper at the Gates of Dawn* to *Atom Heart Mother*' broadcast Friday 24 December; Part 3: 'More to *Dark Side of the Moon*' broadcast 31 December; Part 4: '*The Dark Side of the Moon*' broadcast Friday 7 January 1977; Part 5: '*Wish You Were Here*' broadcast Friday 14 January 1977; Part 6: '*Animals*' broadcast Friday 21 January 1977. Each programme was at least 45 minutes long and was the most detailed study of the band to date, featuring exclusive interviews with all its current members and notable associates as well their music, including some studio out-takes and live segments.

1977

JANUARY – REHEARSALS
Olympia Exhibition Halls, Olympia, London, England

The final production rehearsals for the tour were staged at the halls prior to the production shipping to Germany for the start of the tour.

WEDNESDAY 19 JANUARY – PRESS RECEPTION ▶
Sports & Social Club, Battersea Power Station, Battersea, London, England

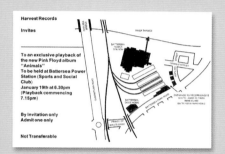

The album *Animals* was played at an evening press reception held on the site of the power station.

THURSDAY 20 JANUARY – RADIO BROADCAST
The John Peel Show, BBC Broadcasting House, London, England

John Peel played the new Pink Floyd album *Animals* in its entirety on his BBC Radio One show between 11.00pm and 12.00 midnight, beating, much to his dismay, Capital Radio's Nicky Horne, who had promised an exclusive airing at the conclusion of his epic six-part series, *The Pink Floyd Story*, on the day of release.

FRIDAY 21 JANUARY 1977 – ALBUM RELEASE (UK)
Animals

Sounds wrote, "Those in search of a new musical trend will probably criticise *Animals* for failing to provide a great leap forward. They've slammed the previous two albums for exactly the same reason but the argument is pointless. The Floyd have got a formula that appeals to millions of people around the world and I can't see any of them being disappointed with this album."

EUROPEAN TOUR, 1977

ADDITIONAL TOUR PERSONNEL THROUGH 1977

"Snowy" White (Rhythm Guitar, Bass Guitar), Dick Parry (Saxophones).
The guitar contributions for each show on the whole tour ran as follows:
'Sheep': Gilmour (Lead Guitar), Waters (Rhythm Guitar), White (Bass Guitar).
'Pigs On The Wing, Part 1': Waters (Acoustic Guitar).
'Dogs': Gilmour (Lead Guitar), Waters (Bass Guitar), White (Rhythm Guitar).
'Pigs On The Wing, Part 2': Waters (Acoustic Guitar).

'Pigs (3 Different Ones)': Gilmour (Lead Guitar), Waters (Rhythm Guitar), White (Bass Guitar).
'Shine On You Crazy Diamond, Parts 1–5': Gilmour (Lead Guitar), Waters (Bass Guitar), White (Rhythm Guitar).
'Welcome To The Machine': Gilmour (Lead Guitar), Waters (Bass Guitar), White (Acoustic Guitar).
'Have A Cigar': Gilmour (Rhythm Guitar), Waters (Bass Guitar), White (Lead Guitar).
'Wish You Were Here': Gilmour (Lead Guitar), White (Acoustic Guitar).
'Shine On You Crazy Diamond, Parts 6–9': Gilmour (Lap Steel Guitar), Waters (Bass Guitar), White (Rhythm Guitar).
'Money': Gilmour (Lead Guitar), Waters (Bass Guitar), White (Rhythm Guitar).
'Us And Them': Gilmour (Lead Guitar), Waters (Bass Guitar), White (Rhythm Guitar).
'Careful With That Axe, Eugene': Gilmour (Lead Guitar), Waters (Bass Guitar), White (Rhythm Guitar).

PINK FLOYD ROAD CREW

Bernie Caulder (PA / Stage Technician), Chris Cockram (Stage Technician), Alan Conway (Quad Technician), Graeme Fleming (Lighting Director), Seth Goldman (Monitor Sound Engineer), Brian Humphries (Front of House Sound Engineer), Marek "Mick the Pole" Kluczynski (Tour Manager), Mick Marshall (Lighting Technician), Arthur Max (Production Manager), Warwick McCredie (Tour Manager), Paul Murray (Film Projection), Robin Murray (Lighting Technician), Rocky Paulson (Rigger), Peter Revell (Film Projection), Nick Rochford (PA / Stage Technician), Shamus (Front Man), Peter Sherriden (Lighting Technician), Nigel Taylor (PA / Stage Technician), Phil Taylor (Backline Technician), Robbie Williams (Head of PA).

SUNDAY 23 JANUARY – PERFORMANCE
Westfalenhalle, Dortmund, West Germany

Set list: 'Sheep', 'Pigs On The Wing, Part 1', 'Dogs', 'Pigs On The Wing, Part 2', 'Pigs (Three Different Ones)' <Intermission> 'Shine On You Crazy Diamond, Parts 1–5', 'Welcome To The Machine', 'Have A Cigar', 'Wish You Were Here', 'Shine On You Crazy Diamond, Parts 6–9' <Encore> 'Money', 'Us And Them'.

MONDAY 24 JANUARY – PERFORMANCE ◀
Westfalenhalle, Dortmund, West Germany

Set list: 'Sheep', 'Pigs On The Wing, Part 1', 'Dogs', 'Pigs On The Wing, Part 2', 'Pigs (Three Different Ones)' <Intermission> 'Shine On You Crazy Diamond, Parts 1–5', 'Welcome To The Machine', 'Have A Cigar', 'Wish You Were Here', 'Shine On You Crazy Diamond, Parts 6–9' <Encore> 'Money'.

WEDNESDAY 26 JANUARY – PERFORMANCE
Festhalle, Frankfurt, West Germany

Set list: 'Sheep', 'Pigs On The Wing, Part 1', 'Dogs', 'Pigs On The Wing, Part 2', 'Pigs (Three Different Ones)' <Intermission> 'Shine On You Crazy Diamond, Parts 1–5', 'Welcome To The Machine', 'Have A Cigar', 'Wish You Were Here', 'Shine On You Crazy Diamond, Parts 6–9' <Encore> 'Money', 'Us And Them'.

ANIMALS

SIDE A

PIGS ON THE WING, PART 1 (Waters) **1:26**
DOGS (Waters, Gilmour) **17:05**

SIDE B

PIGS (THREE DIFFERENT ONES) (Waters) **11:26**
SHEEP (WATERS) **10:19**
PIGS ON THE WING, PART 2 (Waters) **1:29**

RELEASED

UK: Friday 21 January 1977.
US: Saturday 12 February 1977.

FORMAT

UK: EMI Harvest SHVL 815 (Vinyl album).
US: Columbia JC 34474 (Vinyl album).

HIGHEST CHART POSITION

UK: No. 2 (*Music Week* 'Top 75 Albums' on Saturday 19 February 1977),
Chart re-entry No. 88 (*Official Charts Company* on Saturday 8 October
2011).
US: No. 3 (US *Billboard* 'Top LPs & Tape' on Saturday 5 March 1977).

AWARDS

UK: Certified Silver and Gold on Thursday 21 April 1977.
US: Certified Gold on Saturday 12 February 1977, Platinum on
Thursday 10 March 1977, 2 x Platinum on Friday 26 October 1984, 3 x
Platinum on Wednesday 9 August 1989 and 4 x Platinum on Tuesday
31 January 1995.

ARTWORK

Artwork concept by Roger Waters and executed by Hipgnosis.
Photos taken at and around Battersea Power Station, Battersea,
London, England.

PROMOTION

Much of the promotion for the album centred around the theme of
farmyard animals, and advertising for the period certainly pushed the
point to varying degrees of success. In France, EMI Records came up
with a special promotional campaign for the album by manufacturing
life-size plastic display pigs, each with a capacity to hold 100 albums,
which were supplied to the major record retailers. Promotional
photographs were shot showing a farmer "herding" some of the pigs
through the French village of La Ferté-Milon, looking up the Rue du
Marché au Blé, and on the nearby open road of Route Virlet in the
forest of Retz. The village itself is located in the Aisne department of
Picardy to the north east of Paris.

MUSICIANS

David Gilmour (Vocals, Guitars, Bass).
Nick Mason (Drums, Percussion, Tape Effects).
Roger Waters (Vocals, Bass Guitar, Acoustic Guitar, Tape Effects).
Richard Wright (Hammond, Electric Piano, Backing Vocals).

ADDITIONAL MUSICIANS

Snowy White (Guitar on 'Pigs On The Wing' link for 8-track).

RECORDING DETAILS

Recorded at Britannia Row Studios, Islington and produced by
Pink Floyd and engineered by Brian Humphries[*].

[*] Britannia Row was eventually sold to Robbie Williams and Bryan Grant in 1984, and
continues to trade under that name to this day as a leading PA rental company. Mason
assumed control of the studio in the 1980's, eventually selling it on some 10 years later.

As Pink Floyd's contract with EMI terminated they could no longer afford the prospect of having to pay for studio time at Abbey Road, so they incorporated their own recording studio into the recently acquired property at Britannia Row and spent the best part of 10 months through 1976 recording their new album.

As Waters explained, "Sometime during the middle of recording it, it seemed like the right thing to tie it all together. It gave me the lead to re-write the lyrics to 'Raving And Drooling' into 'Sheep', 'cos 'Raving And Drooling' was just another shout, but it was a rather incoherent shout of abuse in a way that 'Pigs' is a kind of fairly compassionate scream of abuse. I've had the idea of *Animals* in the back of my mind for years… many years. It's a kind of old chestnut, really."[1] Comparisons have been made to the Joe Walsh track 'Turn To Stone', from his December 1974 album, *So What*.

Waters even took the step of bastardizing the 23rd Psalm in 'Sheep' and in 'Pigs (3 Different Ones)' he made a scathing attack on three household figures and in particular Mary Whitehouse, campaigner and self-appointed protector of the nation's morals.

The recording is seen by many as a turning point in Waters' exercise of an ever-increasing power over the three other members that led to a noticeable rift in the working unit, which was serving as a vehicle for his lyrical output. His dominance was perhaps buoyed by his new romantic interest, Carolyne Anne Christie, recently divorced from Grateful Dead manager Rock Scully, and to whom he dedicated the two-part solo acoustic number 'Pigs On The Wing', which bookends the album.

Newly recruited tour guitarist "Snowy" White was brought in to perform as an additional guitarist on tour. "I hadn't heard of *Dark Side of the Moon* even, "White recalled. "I must have been the only person in England that hadn't heard it, so I went down to the studio to see the boys and that was right at the end of the *Animals* album. It was funny, when I walked in the atmosphere was terrible… I thought, 'Fucking hell!' but I discovered that they'd accidentally rubbed out one of Dave Gilmour's favourite solos they were really pleased with and they'd just lost it, and that's when I walked in! Dave took me in the office and told me what the gig was all about and asked me if I fancied doing it and I said, 'Can we have a bit of a play or a jam or something?' and he said, 'Well you wouldn't be here if you couldn't play would you?' and I replied, 'Well, no not really.' So he said, 'Well, that's alright then. You start in November for [tour] rehearsals'– and that was it.'"[2]

"Oink, Oink, Woof, Woof, Baaaaa."

New sounds from Pink Floyd. "Animals" on Harvest Records and Tapes.

In the event he turned in the delicate guitar solo that was used to bridge the two parts of the track for the US eight-track cartridge release, a version of which that has only ever been re-released on his own retrospective CD *Goldtop* in 1995.

**Married in 1976, they produced two children: Harry Waters b.16 November 1976, and India Waters b.25 April 1978. They divorced in 1992. Harry Waters has been a member of his father's touring band since 2002.

1. *The Pink Floyd Story,* Capital Radio, 21 January 1977.
2. Author's interview, September 1996.

THURSDAY 27 JANUARY – PERFORMANCE
Festhalle, Frankfurt, West Germany

Set list: 'Sheep', 'Pigs On The Wing, Part 1', 'Dogs', 'Pigs On The Wing, Part 2', 'Pigs (Three Different Ones)' <Intermission> 'Shine On You Crazy Diamond, Parts 1–5', 'Welcome To The Machine', 'Have A Cigar', 'Wish You Were Here', 'Shine On You Crazy Diamond, Parts 6–9' <Encore> 'Money'.

Melody Maker reported, "It had been an evening totally without mishaps. The 12,000 natives packed into Frankfurt's Festhalle for the second successive night on Thursday were in a generally friendly mood, for the Floyd hardly attract the standard aggro crowd of people like Zep or Purple. But in an audience that size, it is a statistical certainty there are bound to be some nutters, like those who were throwing cans and bottles during the first set. An announcement in the first interval asked them to desist, *bitte*, because delicate equipment was getting damaged. I saw another bottle smash on Nick Mason's Hokusai painted drum kit – evidently a full one, for it sprayed his face with foam. In the shadow of the PA columns, a group of 'plain clothes' *polizei*, about as inconspicuous as a panzer armoured division in their uniform anoraks and regulation length haircuts, took photographs of the crowd to see if anyone was smoking dope…. The band's special effects department still hadn't got the highpoint of their contribution to the show quite right yet. In the middle of the 'Pigs' section…a gigantic inflated porker is meant to fly over the PA, emerging out of a cloud of smoke, clearing the stacks by a few inches, and making a circuit of the hall over the heads of the audience. Well, Mr Pig made it over the stack all right without toppling the driver horns on the top, but the trouble was the smoke. The first three nights of the tour they couldn't get enough product out of the rented fog-machine, so they tried a smoke bomb instead. That worked rather too well for comfort, filling the hall with billowing clouds of acrid, throat strangling murk, through which it was barely possible to see that something was happening on stage."

SATURDAY 29 & SUNDAY 30 JANUARY – PERFORMANCES
Deutschlandhalle, West Berlin, West Germany

Set list at both shows: 'Sheep', 'Pigs On The Wing, Part 1', 'Dogs', 'Pigs On The Wing, Part 2', 'Pigs (Three Different Ones)' <Intermission> 'Shine On You Crazy Diamond, Parts 1–5', 'Welcome To The Machine', 'Have A Cigar', 'Wish You Were Here', 'Shine On You Crazy Diamond, Parts 6–9' <Encore> 'Money'.

TUESDAY 1 FEBRUARY – PERFORMANCE
Halle D, Wiener Stadthalle, Vienna, Austria

Set list: 'Sheep', 'Pigs On The Wing, Part 1', 'Dogs', 'Pigs On The Wing, Part 2', 'Pigs (Three Different Ones)' <Intermission> 'Shine On You Crazy Diamond, Parts 1–5', 'Welcome To The Machine', 'Have A Cigar', 'Wish You Were Here', 'Shine On You Crazy Diamond, Parts 6–9' <Encore> 'Money', 'Us And Them'.

THURSDAY 3 & FRIDAY 4 FEBRUARY – PERFORMANCES
Hallenstadion, Zurich, Switzerland

Set list at both shows: 'Sheep', 'Pigs On The Wing, Part 1', 'Dogs', 'Pigs On The Wing, Part 2', 'Pigs (Three Different Ones)' <Intermission> 'Shine On You Crazy Diamond, Parts 1–5', 'Welcome To The Machine', 'Have A Cigar', 'Wish You Were Here', 'Shine On You Crazy Diamond, Parts 6–9' <Encore> 'Money'.

SATURDAY 12 FEBRUARY – ALBUM RELEASE (US)
Animals

Rolling Stone wrote, "The sax that warmed *Dark Side of the Moon* and *Wish You Were Here* has been replaced by a succession of David Gilmour guitar solos – thin, brittle and a sorry substitute indeed. The singing is more wooden than ever. The sound is more complex, but it lacks real depth."

ABOVE: VIEW FROM BEHIND THE SOUND AND LIGHTING DESKS AT THE SPORTSPALEIS, ROTTERDAM ON 17 FEBRUARY 1977.

THURSDAY 17, FRIDAY 18 & SATURDAY 19 FEBRUARY – PERFORMANCES
Sportpaleis Ahoy, Rotterdam, Netherlands

Set list at all three shows: 'Sheep', 'Pigs On The Wing, Part 1', 'Dogs', 'Pigs On The Wing, Part 2', 'Pigs (Three Different Ones)' <Intermission> 'Shine On You Crazy Diamond, Parts 1–5', 'Welcome To The Machine', 'Have A Cigar', 'Wish You Were Here', 'Shine On You Crazy Diamond, Parts 6–9' <Encore> 'Money'.

KOSKI / CAUCHOIS PRODUCTION PRESENTENT

PAVILLON DE PARIS / PORTE DE PANTIN
JEUDI 24 FEVRIER 1977 / 20 H
OUVERTURE DES PORTES : 19 HEURES

PINK FLOYD

35 F   N° 004843

SUNDAY 20 FEBRUARY – PERFORMANCE
Sportpaleis, Antwerp, Belguim

Set list: 'Sheep', 'Pigs On The Wing, Part 1', 'Dogs', 'Pigs On The Wing, Part 2', 'Pigs (Three Different Ones)' <Intermission> 'Shine On You Crazy Diamond, Parts 1-5', 'Welcome To The Machine', 'Have A Cigar', 'Wish You Were Here', 'Shine On You Crazy Diamond, Parts 6-9' <Encore> 'Money'.

TUESDAY 22, WEDNESDAY 23, THURSDAY 24 & FRIDAY 25 FEBRUARY – PERFORMANCES ◄
Pavillon de Paris, Porte de Pantin, Paris, France

Set list at all four shows: 'Sheep', 'Pigs On The Wing, Part 1', 'Dogs', 'Pigs On The Wing, Part 2', 'Pigs (Three Different Ones)' <Intermission> 'Shine On You Crazy Diamond, Parts 1–5', 'Welcome To The Machine', 'Have A Cigar', 'Wish You Were Here', 'Shine On You Crazy Diamond, Parts 6–9' <Encore> 'Money'.

David Gilmour and Roger Waters were interviewed for the arts programme *Journal de l'A2*, which was broadcast on ORTF2 on 21 February between 8.00pm and 8.30pm.

SUNDAY 27 & MONDAY 28 FEBRUARY & TUESDAY 1 MARCH – PERFORMANCES
Olympiahalle, Munich, West Germany

Set list at all three shows: 'Sheep', 'Pigs On The Wing, Part 1', 'Dogs', 'Pigs On The Wing, Part 2', 'Pigs (Three Different Ones)' <Intermission> 'Shine On You Crazy Diamond, Parts 1–5', 'Welcome To The Machine', 'Have A Cigar', 'Wish You Were Here', 'Shine On You Crazy Diamond, Parts 6–9' <Encore> 'Money'.

TUESDAY 15 MARCH – PERFORMANCE
Empire Pool, Wembley, England

This was the last UK show to be announced.
Set list: 'Sheep', 'Pigs On The Wing, Part 1', 'Dogs', 'Pigs On The Wing, Part 2', 'Pigs (Three Different Ones)' <Intermission> 'Shine On You Crazy Diamond, Parts 1–5', 'Welcome To The Machine', 'Have A Cigar', 'Wish You Were Here', 'Shine On You Crazy Diamond, Parts 6–9' <Encore> 'Money".

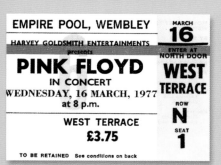

WEDNESDAY 16 MARCH – PERFORMANCE ◄
Empire Pool, Wembley, England

Rescheduled from Sunday 20 March due to a badminton tournament commencing Monday 21 March.
Set list: 'Sheep', 'Pigs On The Wing, Part 1', 'Dogs', 'Pigs On The Wing, Part 2', 'Pigs (Three Different Ones)' <Intermission> 'Shine On You Crazy Diamond, Parts 1–5', 'Welcome To The Machine', 'Have A Cigar', 'Wish You Were Here', 'Shine On You Crazy Diamond, Parts 6–9' <Encore> 'Money'.

THURSDAY 17 MARCH – PERFORMANCE
Empire Pool, Wembley, England

Set list: 'Sheep', 'Pigs On The Wing, Part 1', 'Dogs', 'Pigs On The Wing, Part 2', 'Pigs (Three Different Ones)' <Intermission> 'Shine On You Crazy Diamond, Parts 1–5', 'Welcome To The Machine', 'Have A Cigar', 'Wish You Were Here', 'Shine On You Crazy Diamond, Parts 6–9' <Encore> 'Us And Them'.

FRIDAY 18 MARCH – PERFORMANCE
Empire Pool, Wembley, England

Set list: 'Sheep', 'Pigs On The Wing, Part 1', 'Dogs', 'Pigs On The Wing, Part 2', 'Pigs (Three Different Ones)' <Intermission> 'Shine On You Crazy Diamond, Parts 1–5', 'Welcome To The Machine', 'Have A Cigar', 'Wish You Were Here', 'Shine On You Crazy Diamond, Parts 6–9' <Encore> 'Us And Them'.

SATURDAY 19 MARCH – PERFORMANCE
Empire Pool, Wembley, England

Set list: 'Sheep', 'Pigs On The Wing, Part 1', 'Dogs', 'Pigs On The Wing, Part 2', 'Pigs (Three Different Ones)' <Intermission> 'Shine On You Crazy

Diamond, Parts 1–5', 'Welcome To The Machine', 'Have A Cigar', 'Wish You Were Here', 'Shine On You Crazy Diamond, Parts 6–9' <Encore> 'Money'.

The *Financial Times* reported, "It gets easier and easier to review a Pink Floyd concert without mentioning the music. The group has always exploited theatrical effects and now, as it stands passively playing in the background, the lights swoop around the stadium; the smoke oozes along the sides; inflatable pigs and persons slide down wires suspended above the audience; images splash on to a giant screen. And all the time the expensively amplified Floyd sound of soaring guitar notes and free-flowing keyboards fills any senses not satiated with the sight…. As for the new music, the lyrics seem unnaturally aggressive for a band which is now extremely rich and mature, but then lyrics have never been important to its success. The actual sounds have changed little, still managing to stimulate one minute and bore the next. The Pink Floyd has made a serious contribution to popular music, but whether it deserves to command such devotion without developing much musically is doubtful. The fact that the Pink Floyd's appeal is to a specific audience may be commercially fortunate but musically very limiting."

MONDAY 28, TUESDAY 29, WEDNESDAY 30, & THURSDAY 31 MARCH – PERFORMANCES ▼
New Bingley Hall, Staffordshire County Showground, Stafford, England

Set list at all four shows: 'Sheep', 'Pigs On The Wing, Part 1', 'Dogs', 'Pigs On The Wing, Part 2', 'Pigs (Three Different Ones)' <Intermission> 'Shine On You Crazy Diamond, Parts 1–5', 'Welcome To The Machine', 'Have A Cigar', 'Wish You Were Here', 'Shine On You Crazy Diamond, Parts 6–9' <Encore> 'Money'.

PINK FLOYD IN THE FLESH
(NORTH AMERICA, PART 1)

FRIDAY 22 APRIL – PERFORMANCE
Miami Baseball Stadium, Miami, FL, USA

Set list: 'Sheep', 'Pigs On The Wing, Part 1', 'Dogs', 'Pigs On The Wing, Part 2', 'Pigs (Three Different Ones)' <Intermission> 'Shine On You Crazy Diamond, Parts 1–5', 'Welcome To The Machine', 'Have A Cigar', 'Wish You Were Here', 'Shine On You Crazy Diamond, Parts 6–9' <Encore> 'Money', 'Us And Them'.

High gusts of winds prevented the circular film screen from being lowered into place and the inflatable pig was blown apart by gusts as it was inflated.

SUNDAY 24 APRIL – PERFORMANCE
Tampa Stadium, Tampa, FL, USA

Set list: 'Sheep', 'Pigs On The Wing, Part 1', 'Dogs', 'Pigs On The Wing, Part 2', 'Pigs (Three Different Ones)' <Intermission> 'Shine On You Crazy Diamond, Parts 1–5', 'Welcome To The Machine', 'Have A Cigar', 'Wish You Were Here', 'Shine On You Crazy Diamond, Parts 6–9' <Encore> 'Money'.

TUESDAY 26 APRIL – PERFORMANCE
The Omni Coliseum, Atlanta, GA, USA

Set list: 'Sheep', 'Pigs On The Wing, Part 1', 'Dogs', 'Pigs On The Wing, Part 2', 'Pigs (Three Different Ones)' <Intermission> 'Shine On You Crazy Diamond, Parts 1–5', 'Welcome To The Machine', 'Have A Cigar', 'Wish You Were Here', 'Shine On You Crazy Diamond, Parts 6–9' <Encore> 'Money'.

WEDNESDAY 27 APRIL – PRESS RECEPTION
New York, NY, USA

A launch party for Pink Floyd's tour was held by CBS records commencing with a 1.00pm luncheon at Tavern on the Green, Manhattan followed by a 3.00pm gathering at Sheep Meadow in Central Park to witness the pig, retrieved from the *Animals* album sleeve shoot, inflated one last time. The inflatable pig's fate following this event is uncertain.

BELOW: PRESS LAUNCH FOR THE ANIMALS TOUR IN NYC.

ABOVE: DAVID GILMOUR AND DICK PARRY PICTURED ON STAGE IN HOUSTON, 30 APRIL 1977.

THURSDAY 28 APRIL – PERFORMANCE
Assembly Center, Louisiana State University, Baton Rouge, LA, USA

Set list: 'Sheep', 'Pigs On The Wing, Part 1', 'Dogs', 'Pigs On The Wing, Part 2', 'Pigs (Three Different Ones)' <Intermission> 'Shine On You Crazy Diamond, Parts 1–5', 'Welcome To The Machine', 'Have A Cigar', 'Wish You Were Here', 'Shine On You Crazy Diamond, Parts 6–9' <Encore> 'Money'.

SATURDAY 30 APRIL –
PERFORMANCE ▶
Jeppesen Stadium, University of Houston, Houston, TX, USA

Set list: 'Sheep', 'Pigs On The Wing, Part 1', 'Dogs', 'Pigs On The Wing, Part 2', 'Pigs (Three Different Ones)' <Intermission> 'Shine On You Crazy Diamond, Parts 1–5', 'Welcome To The Machine', 'Have A Cigar', 'Wish You Were Here', 'Shine On You Crazy Diamond, Parts 6–9' <Encore> 'Money', 'Us And Them'.

SUNDAY 1 MAY – PERFORMANCE
Tarrant County Convention Center Arena, Fort Worth, TX, USA

Set list: 'Sheep', 'Pigs On The Wing, Part 1', 'Dogs', 'Pigs On The Wing, Part 2', 'Pigs (Three Different Ones)' <Intermission> 'Shine On You Crazy Diamond, Parts 1–5', 'Welcome To The Machine', 'Have A Cigar', 'Wish You Were Here', 'Shine On You Crazy Diamond, Parts 6–9' <Encore> 'Money', 'Us And Them'.

WEDNESDAY 4 MAY – PERFORMANCE
Veterans Memorial Coliseum, Phoenix, AZ, USA

Set list: 'Sheep', 'Pigs On The Wing, Part 1', 'Dogs', 'Pigs On The Wing, Part 2', 'Pigs (Three Different Ones)' <Intermission> 'Shine On You Crazy Diamond, Parts 1–5', 'Welcome To The Machine', 'Have A Cigar', 'Wish You Were Here', 'Shine On You Crazy Diamond, Parts 6–9' <Encore> 'Money', 'Us And Them'.

PINK FLOYD IN THE FLESH

HOUSTON'S JEPPESEN STADIUM
SATURDAY, APRIL 30th 8.00 p.m.
GENERAL ADMISSION $10.00

FRIDAY 6 MAY – PERFORMANCE
Anaheim Stadium, Anaheim, CA, USA

Set list: 'Sheep', 'Pigs On The Wing, Part 1', 'Dogs', 'Pigs On The Wing, Part 2', 'Pigs (Three Different Ones)' <Intermission> 'Shine On You Crazy Diamond, Parts 1–5', 'Welcome To The Machine', 'Have A Cigar', 'Wish You Were Here', 'Shine On You Crazy Diamond, Parts 6–9' <Encore> 'Money'.

Despite intermittent downpours through the evening the show went ahead unhindered. Many witnesses to the event recall the splendour of a double rainbow over the stadium during Pink Floyd's set.

SATURDAY 7 MAY – PERFORMANCE ▼
Anaheim Stadium, Anaheim, CA, USA

Set list: 'Sheep', 'Pigs On The Wing, Part 1', 'Dogs', 'Pigs On The Wing, Part 2', 'Pigs (Three Different Ones)' <Intermission> 'Shine On You Crazy Diamond, Parts 1-5', 'Welcome To The Machine', 'Have A Cigar', 'Wish You Were Here', 'Shine On You Crazy Diamond, Parts 6-9' <Encore> 'Money'.

Rolling Stone reported, "Ultimately a Pink Floyd concert is as much an optical show as a musical one, and it is in this respect that their stance can seem coldest and most frightening. When a ghostly pig is floated over the cheering crowd and then sacrificed in a gratuitous burst of flame, the commentary couldn't be more obvious or repulsive. During a rabid Escher-like animation sequence they present a decapitation scene (the head then rots away to a grimy skull), a sea of blood spurting tentacles that turn into clawing hands, and a raw muscle twitching on a hook. One can't help but wonder why they impose such nightmares on an audience. Interestingly, while their music has become more humanistically cynical and melodious, their concerts grow more and more perfunctory and aloof, amounting to little more than a bombastic insult."

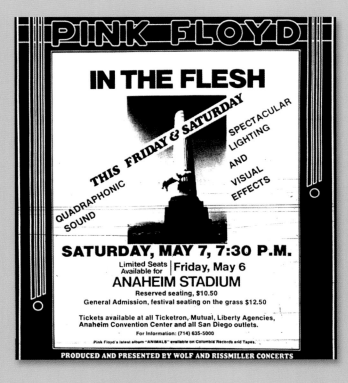

MONDAY 9 MAY – PERFORMANCE
Oakland Coliseum, Oakland, CA, USA

Set list: 'Sheep', 'Pigs On The Wing, Part 1', 'Dogs', 'Pigs On The Wing, Part 2', 'Pigs (Three Different Ones)' <Intermission> 'Shine On You Crazy Diamond, Parts 1–5', 'Welcome To The Machine', 'Have A Cigar', 'Wish You Were Here', 'Shine On You Crazy Diamond, Parts 6–9' <Encore> 'Money', 'Us And Them' <Second Encore> 'Careful With That Axe, Eugene'.

This show was noted for an impromptu performance of 'Careful With That Axe, Eugene'.

TUESDAY 10 MAY – PERFORMANCE
Oakland Coliseum, Oakland, CA, USA

Set list: 'Sheep', 'Pigs On The Wing, Part 1', 'Dogs', 'Pigs On The Wing, Part 2', 'Pigs (Three Different Ones)' <Intermission> 'Shine On You Crazy Diamond, Parts 1–5', 'Welcome To The Machine', 'Have A Cigar', 'Wish You Were Here', 'Shine On You Crazy Diamond, Parts 6–9' <Encore> 'Money'.

THURSDAY 12 MAY – PERFORMANCE
Memorial Coliseum, Portland, OR, USA

Set list: 'Sheep', 'Pigs On The Wing, Part 1', 'Dogs', 'Pigs On The Wing, Part 2', 'Pigs (Three Different Ones)' <Intermission> 'Shine On You Crazy Diamond, Parts 1–5', 'Welcome To The Machine', 'Have A Cigar', 'Wish You Were Here', 'Shine On You Crazy Diamond, Parts 6–9' <Encore> 'Money'.

PINK FLOYD IN THE FLESH (NORTH AMERICA, PART 2)

WEDNESDAY 15 JUNE – PERFORMANCE ▶
County Stadium, Milwaukee, WI, USA

Set list: 'Sheep', 'Pigs On The Wing, Part 1', 'Dogs', 'Pigs On The Wing, Part 2', 'Pigs (Three Different Ones)' <Intermission> 'Shine On You Crazy Diamond, Parts 1–5', 'Welcome To The Machine', 'Have A Cigar', 'Wish You Were Here', 'Shine On You Crazy Diamond, Parts 6–9' <Encore> 'Money'.

FRIDAY 17 JUNE – PERFORMANCE
Freedom Hall, Kentucky Fair and Exposition Center, Louisville, KY, USA

Set list: 'Sheep', 'Pigs On The Wing, Part 1', 'Dogs', 'Pigs On The Wing, Part 2', 'Pigs (Three Different Ones)' <Intermission> 'Shine On You Crazy Diamond, Parts 1–5', 'Welcome To The Machine', 'Have A Cigar', 'Wish You Were Here', 'Shine On You Crazy Diamond, Parts 6–9' <Encore> 'Money'.

The *Louisville Courier Journal* reported: "A 30x15-foot helium-filled pig with glowing amber eyes. Two human counterparts in a helium husband and wife. Billowing green smoke and fireworks. A spellbinding animation film in which a raw nerve is strung up on a meat hook only to be ripped off by a wild animal, who is then devoured himself. That and more made up the spectacular fusion of music and theatre that was the Pink Floyd concert at

Freedom Hall last night. It was an evening that not many of the 19,000 who attended the sell-out show are likely to forget, and they spared no show of appreciation for the eyes and ears that was the Pink Floyd performance. From almost every aspect, it was an unusual concert. Never once wavering in professionalism, the band began the show promptly at 8pm, launching into all of its newest album, *Animals*, and trotting out the helium props at precisely the right moment to compliment the lyrics. After the break they returned to play all of their *Wish You Were Here* album from 1975. With the helium balloons packed away, the band then began the mesmerising animation sequence that was anything but your basic, average background light show. Everyone enjoyed it last night, and part of that had to be because of the superb quad sound system (including 80, 400-watt amplifiers) around the cavernous Freedom Hall (the music drowned out the vocals for much of the first half, but that problem was cleared up by the second).… Music was not really the point of the show last night, though, and if anyone went to hear the precision musicianship Pink Floyd is known for, they found it. But they were probably too distracted by the band's trappings, which guided the audience away from the musicians themselves and into the metaphysical. And that's probably what Pink Floyd wanted."

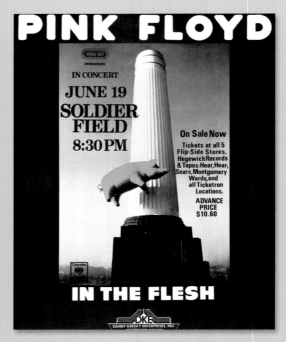

SUNDAY 19 JUNE – PERFORMANCE ▶
Super Bowl of Rock 'n' Roll, **Soldier Field, Chicago, IL, USA**

Set list: 'Sheep', 'Pigs On The Wing, Part 1', 'Dogs', 'Pigs On The Wing, Part 2', 'Pigs (Three Different Ones)' <Intermission> 'Shine On You Crazy Diamond, Parts 1–5', 'Welcome To The Machine', 'Have A Cigar', 'Wish You Were Here', 'Shine On You Crazy Diamond, Parts 6–9' <Encore> 'Money'.

Despite the success of the concert, a Federal Grand Jury investigated allegations of mail fraud, wire fraud, kickbacks and other financial irregularities connected with this concert. On the day itself, the official box-office figure showed attendance of about 67,000, but Pink Floyd, doubting its accuracy, hired a helicopter,

BELOW: PERFORMING AT SOLDIER FIELD AMID AN EXPLOSION OF SMOKE BOMBS AND FIREWORKS.

with a photographer on board, to carry out a head count. The aerial estimate was around 95,000, which meant a shortfall in the takings of several hundred thousand dollars.

TUESDAY 21 JUNE – PERFORMANCE
Kemper Arena, Kansas City, MO, USA

Set list: 'Sheep', 'Pigs On The Wing, Part 1', 'Dogs', 'Pigs On The Wing, Part 2', 'Pigs (Three Different Ones)' <Intermission> 'Shine On You Crazy Diamond, Parts 1–5', 'Welcome To The Machine', 'Have A Cigar', 'Wish You Were Here', 'Shine On You Crazy Diamond, Parts 6–9' <Encore> 'Money'.

THURSDAY 23 JUNE – PERFORMANCE
Riverfront Coliseum, Cincinnati, OH, USA

Set list: 'Sheep', 'Pigs On The Wing, Part 1', 'Dogs', 'Pigs On The Wing, Part 2', 'Pigs (Three Different Ones)' <Intermission> 'Shine On You Crazy Diamond, Parts 1–5', 'Welcome To The Machine', 'Have A Cigar', 'Wish You Were Here', 'Shine On You Crazy Diamond, Parts 6–9' <Encore> 'Money'.

SATURDAY 25 JUNE – PERFORMANCE
World Series of Rock, **Municipal Stadium, Cleveland, OH, USA**

Set list: 'Sheep', 'Pigs On The Wing, Part 1', 'Dogs', 'Pigs On The Wing, Part 2', 'Pigs (Three Different Ones)' <Intermission> 'Shine On You Crazy Diamond, Parts 1–5', 'Welcome To The Machine', 'Have A Cigar', 'Wish You Were Here', 'Shine On You Crazy Diamond, Parts 6-9' <Encore> 'Money', 'Us And Them'.

Funk-rock band Mother's Finest were initially advertised as the opening act for Pink Floyd this evening but they did not appear. Heavy downpours

forced a late start to the show, which finally commenced with the band's chartered BAC-111 jet making a low level pass over the stadium. During the show a fireworks rocket was launched at the inflatable pig, puncturing it and bringing it down into the crowd. Meanwhile, outside the stadium, up to 4,000 ticketless fans who couldn't get into the sold-out show began throwing bottles and rocks at security staff. This ended in a violent clash with the police, resulting in three officers hospitalized and 74 arrests.

MONDAY 27 JUNE – PERFORMANCE ▶
Boston Garden, Boston, MA, USA

Set list: 'Sheep', 'Pigs On The Wing, Part 1', 'Dogs', 'Pigs On The Wing, Part 2', 'Pigs (Three Different Ones)' <Intermission> 'Shine On You Crazy Diamond, Parts 1–5', 'Welcome To The Machine', 'Have A Cigar', 'Wish You Were Here', 'Shine On You Crazy Diamond, Parts 6–9' <Encore> 'Money', 'Us And Them'.

TUESDAY 28 JUNE – PERFORMANCE
The Spectrum, Philadelphia, PA, USA

Set list: 'Sheep', 'Pigs On The Wing, Part 1', 'Dogs', 'Pigs On The Wing, Part 2', 'Pigs (Three Different Ones)' <Intermission> 'Shine On You Crazy Diamond, Parts 1–5', 'Welcome To The Machine', 'Have A Cigar', 'Wish You Were Here', 'Shine On You Crazy Diamond, Parts 6–9' <Encore> 'Money', 'Us And Them'.

WEDNESDAY 29 JUNE – PERFORMANCE
The Spectrum, Philadelphia, PA, USA

Set list: 'Sheep', 'Pigs On The Wing, Part 1', 'Dogs', 'Pigs On The Wing, Part 2', 'Pigs (Three Different Ones)' <Intermission> 'Shine On You Crazy Diamond, Parts 1–5', 'Welcome To The Machine', 'Have A Cigar', 'Wish You Were Here', 'Shine On You Crazy Diamond, Parts 6–9' <Encore> 'Money', 'Us And Them' (this song performed without Roger Waters).

Prior to the show Roger Waters was diagnosed with laryngitis but despite being given a heavy dose of painkillers was forced to bow out towards the end of the show. This event was later documented by Waters in the song 'Comfortably Numb' and the

accompanying scene in the film *Pink Floyd The Wall* alludes to this concert.

FRIDAY 1 JULY – PERFORMANCE ▼
Madison Square Garden, New York, NY, USA

Set list: 'Sheep', 'Pigs On The Wing, Part 1', 'Dogs', 'Pigs On The Wing, Part 2', 'Pigs (Three Different Ones)' <Intermission> 'Shine On You Crazy Diamond, Parts 1–5', 'Welcome To The Machine', 'Have A Cigar', 'Wish You Were Here', 'Shine On You Crazy Diamond, Parts 6–9' <Encore> 'Money', 'Us And Them'.

SATURDAY 2 JULY – PERFORMANCE
Madison Square Garden, New York, NY, USA

Set list: 'Sheep', 'Pigs On The Wing, Part 1', 'Dogs', 'Pigs On The Wing, Part 2', 'Pigs (Three Different Ones)' <Intermission> 'Shine On You Crazy Diamond, Parts 1–5', 'Welcome To The Machine', 'Have A Cigar', 'Wish You Were Here', 'Shine On You Crazy Diamond, Parts 6–9' <Encore> 'Money'.

SUNDAY 3 JULY – PERFORMANCE
Madison Square Garden, New York, NY, USA

Set list: 'Sheep', 'Pigs On The Wing, Part 1', 'Dogs', 'Pigs On The Wing, Part 2', 'Pigs (Three Different Ones)' <Intermission> 'Shine On You Crazy Diamond, Parts 1–5', 'Welcome To The Machine', 'Have A Cigar', 'Wish You Were Here', 'Shine On You Crazy Diamond, Parts 6–9' <Encore> 'Money', 'Us And Them'.

The *NME* reported, "Not only was it the eve of July 4th, but also it was the week that marijuana had been decriminalised in New York State. The surprisingly young audience was thus inevitably out of it. Blitzed young men from the Bronx would periodically rise to their feet, extend their clenched fist and bellow 'Floiiiiid!' before sinking exhausted back to their seats. July 4th is, of course, the US equivalent to November 5th – it's when all the fireworks go off…. The fireworks were making the audience a bit edgy – those of them that could still feel anything – and it was a while before the Floyd were able to pull together the 20,000 sell-out crowd and get them involved. Gilmour seemed able to use the tension to put an edge on his guitar licks, but Waters was obviously not happy. Roger's lyrics came through clearer and louder than any others of the evening: 'You stupid motherfucker!' he bellowed. 'And anyone else in here with fireworks – just fuck off and let us get on with it.' Then the Floyd filled the place with smoke and brought out a huge inflatable pig which cruised about the vast space of the auditorium, the pencil beams of light from its eyes casting a malevolent gaze over the stalls. On 'Have A Cigar' a lulling repetitive riff was suddenly terminated by a quadraphonic sound sweep of the hall like being nosedived by Concorde, which must have stopped the

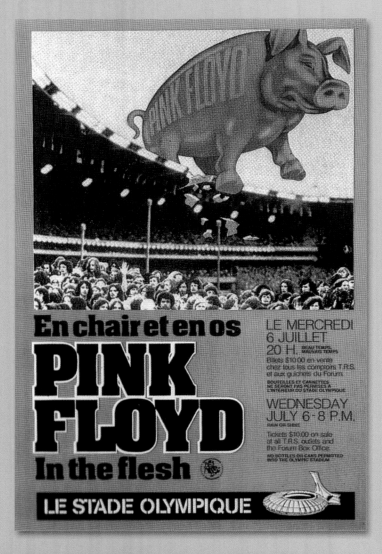

hearts of dozens of space cadets who were cruising their own contemplative mind space. Little girls screamed in shock and micro-thugs roared their approval."

MONDAY 4 JULY – PERFORMANCE
Madison Square Garden, New York, NY, USA

Set list: 'Sheep', 'Pigs On The Wing, Part 1', 'Dogs', 'Pigs On The Wing, Part 2', 'Pigs (Three Different Ones)' <Intermission> 'Shine On You Crazy Diamond, Parts 1–5', 'Welcome To The Machine', 'Have A Cigar', 'Wish You Were Here', 'Shine On You Crazy Diamond, Parts 6–9' <Encore> 'Money', 'Us And Them'.

WEDNESDAY 6 JULY – PERFORMANCE ◄
Stade du Parc Olympique, Montréal, Canada

Set list: 'Sheep', 'Pigs On The Wing, Part 1', 'Dogs', 'Pigs On The Wing, Part 2', 'Pigs (Three Different Ones)' <Intermission> 'Shine On You Crazy Diamond, Parts 1–5', 'Welcome To The Machine', 'Have A Cigar', 'Wish You Were Here', 'Shine On You Crazy Diamond, Parts 6–9' <Encore> 'Money', 'Us And Them', 'Blues' (this number performed without David Gilmour).

Vibrations magazine reported, "Anytime you get 80,000 people at a function, you've got a major happening of sorts, the terrific excitement crackling around the stadium, almost as tangible as the sweet smell of marijuana and cheap wine; the thousands of animated bodies and faces – like ants in a jar, and that somewhere, miles off, a group was playing, not very loudly. Things did improve of course, but in the first half hour, with the sun not fully set and the audience not fully settled, Pink Floyd seemed more like incidental entertainment at a be-in. With darkness came a softening sense of the senses and a heightened receptivity on the audience's part. Floyd naturally obliged, floating sheep down and other characters including the famous pig up, as they broke into material from their album *Animals*…. Pink Floyd themselves didn't care too much for the gig, admonishing some fans at one point to stop screaming. Imagine ranking out 80,000 people. You can't have your cake and eat it too."

SEPTEMBER – DECEMBER – RECORDING SESSIONS
London, England

Less than a month after the conclusion of the *Animals* tour Roger Waters retreated to his home studio to work on ideas and record demos that would later form the basis of *The Wall* album as well as his solo record, *The Pros and Cons of Hitch Hiking*.

LEFT: THE FINALE TO THE ANIMALS TOUR IN MONTREAL, 6 JULY 1977.

1978—85

1978—85

Despite massive box-office and album sales in recent years, Pink Floyd was very much in the red in the late 1970s. They reportedly signed a deal worth several millions of pounds with publishing giant Chappell in January 1980, but they had previously teamed up with financial advisors Norton-Warburg who between 1972 and 1978 had handled the band's financial affairs and invested huge sums into various high-risk capital venture schemes. The company crashed after nearly all of their investments had failed, coupled with vast sums paid out in directors' dividends and loans. The net result was that investments for some 400 clients totalling £15 million were completely wiped out.

It also meant that the exact opposite of what the scheme intended had now come to pass, leaving the band at the hands of a myriad of accountants trying frantically to reduce their now enormous tax exposure.[*]

Using this misfortune as a convenient lever, the ever-resourceful Waters proposed bailing the band out with one of two possible album projects that he had envisaged and part written in demo form since the Animals tour: *Bricks in the Wall* (later known simply as *The Wall*) and *The Pros and Cons of Hitch Hiking*, one of which he expected to complete as a solo album at a later date. Barely resembling what would later evolve into one of their most successful albums, Gilmour, at odds with Waters' later view, remembered the demos well: "Both *The Wall* and *Pros and Cons* demos were unlistenable; a shitty mess. [They] sounded exactly alike, you couldn't tell them apart. We thought of recording *Pros and Cons* at a later date, but as it turned out Roger preferred to go off and do it as a solo project."[1]

In the end it was decided that *The Wall* was the better prospect. The finished album told a desperate story of isolation and fear, far more complex than anything previously tackled by Waters. Inevitably the work is seen as partly autobiographical:

It wasn't until March 1981 that the full extent of their losses became apparent. At a creditors' meeting it was claimed that Norton-Warburg had managed to lose the band some £2.5 million and as a company had only £800,000 in remaining assets to pay off its creditors, of which Pink Floyd was only one. In short, almost everything Pink Floyd had earned from their record sales and tours over the past few years was wiped out in an instant, and on top of that they were facing a huge income tax bill.

Pink, the central character, played by Waters, is a successful rock star facing the breakup of his marriage while on tour. This leads him to review his whole life and to begin to build a protective wall around himself, each brick representing the things that have caused him to suffer: a suffocating, over-protective mother, vicious schoolteachers, a faithless wife and stupid groupies. Pink imagines himself elevated to the position of a fascist dictator, with the audience his obedient followers. Hitler-like, he wields his power to persecute. At the story's climax he faces up to his tormentors and the wall finally crumbles. However, as soon as this wall has fallen, so another slowly begins to rise, suggesting, in a bleak conclusion, a perpetual cycle of imprisonment.

Many of the scenes in the album also represented actual events in Waters' or the band's personal history. There were obvious references to Syd Barrett and Pink Floyd's hippie heyday; the loss of Waters' father in the war; and the rioting at the L.A. Sports Arena in 1975. The trashing of a motel room recalled an all too common aspect of the 1970s rock star's lifestyle. There were even a few backward messages concealed in the mix – the start of a Pink Floyd tradition.

It was an ambitious project by any stretch of the imagination. From its inception Waters envisaged a three-pronged attack: album, tour and film. Initially it was hoped that all three would be in simultaneous production, but almost at once it became evident that the sheer magnitude of effort in the recording process alone would make this plan unfeasible.

The album therefore had to come first and an initial process of selecting and reviewing the best parts of Waters demos took place at his home studio. "[We were] just sitting around and bickering, frankly," says Gilmour. "Someone would say, 'I don't like that one very much,' someone else might agree, and then Roger would look all sulky and the next day he'd come back with something brilliant. He was pretty good about that during *The Wall*. I remember 'Nobody Home' came along when we were well into the thing and he'd gone off in a sulk the night before and came back in the next day with something fantastic."[2]

From the start Waters asserted full control over the entire project. It was also true that he felt the other bandmembers

could not appreciate or contribute in any great way to his vision. Aside from the sheer complexity of the project that lay ahead, Waters needed an outside producer to collaborate on ideas, to help coordinate efforts and in many cases act as arbiter between himself and Gilmour once they had started the recording process. That job fell to Canadian-born producer Bob Ezrin.

Ezrin's task was a formidable one, but he succeeded in moulding the then-sorry story into a workable shape. Much later he said, "In an all-night session I re-wrote the record. I used all of Roger's elements, but I rearranged their order and put them in a different form. I wrote *The Wall* out in 40 pages, like a book, telling how the songs segued. It wasn't so much re-writing as re-directing."[3] That script, which incidentally, is now on display at the Rock and Roll Hall of Fame in Cleveland, undoubtedly focused the task ahead. However, even by the late stages of the recording process, significant changes were made – mainly imposed by the time constraints of the vinyl format. This explains why the album sleeve lists a different running order from that of the two discs and also why there are lyrics to tracks including the 'Empty Spaces'/'What Shall We Do Now' sequence that are not included on the records. Indeed it is often said that the recorded material would have filled three discs before it was carefully edited down.

"I could see that it was going to be a long and complex process and I needed a collaborator who I could talk to about it," said Waters. "Because there's nobody in the band that you can talk to about any of this stuff – Dave's just not interested, Rick was pretty closed down at that point, and Nick would be happy to listen because we were pretty close at that time but he's more interested in his racing cars. I needed somebody like Ezrin who was musically and intellectually in a more similar place to where I was."[4]

"There was an awful lot of confusion as to who was actually making this record when I first started," recalled Ezrin, complicated by the fact that a young producer, James Guthrie, was also drafted to act as co-producer/engineer. "So he brought me in, I think, as an ally to help him to mange this process through. As it turns out, my perception of my job was to be the advocate of the work itself and that very often meant disagreeing with Roger and other people and being a catalyst for them to get past whatever arguments might exist."[5]

The whole recording process lasted from September 1978 until just before the release of the double album in November 1979 with initial pre-recording demos beginning in earnest at Britannia Row in London. This quickly shifted to France as the band were forced to retreat into tax exile following the Norton-Warburg crash with their families in tow and all relocated to various rented accommodations in and around the city of Nice. Sessions began at Super Bear Studios in Berre-des-Alpes and Studio Miravel in Le Val; Waters vocal parts, in particular, seemingly benefitting from the clean mountain air. Curiously, the band chose to work within civilised office hours, commencing at 10 in the morning and finishing by 6 in the evening. Tensions, however, started to run high even at this early stage as Ezrin recalls: "There was tension between bandmembers, even tension between the wives of the bandmembers. Roger and I were having a particularly difficult time. During that period I went a little bit mad and really dreaded going in to face the tension. I preferred not to be there while Roger was there."[6]

"Most of the arguments came from artistic disagreements." remembers Gilmour. "It wasn't total war, though there were bad vibes – certainly towards Rick, because he didn't seem to be pulling his weight."[7]

Nevertheless the band soldiered on and after the customary August vacations production shifted to the Producers Workshop in Los Angeles, where some final recording and the entire mixing continued apace. It was here that additional session musicians were recruited by Waters to complement not just Mason, whose drum parts had already been completed in France, but also in particular, Wright's performances, considered less than able by Waters. These included the talents of Freddie Mandell (keyboards), Jeff and Joe Porcaro (drums) and even more curiously Joe DiBlasi (classical guitar) and Lee Ritenour (guitar) to supplement Gilmour. At one stage it was even hoped to include all of the Beach Boys on vocal harmonies for the tracks 'The Show Must Go On' and 'Waiting For The Worms', but this was cancelled at the last moment. Additionally Michael Kamen was also drafted in to arrange the orchestrations, which he recorded at CBS in New York.

Whereas Mason and Wright's contributions were minimal to say the least, Gilmour did at least contribute some outstanding music for three of the album's more tuneful compositions, 'Young Lust', 'Run Like Hell' and 'Comfortably Numb', (the latter derived from an unused demo from his solo album), for which he received one of only two apparently hard-fought for shared writing credits on the album. The other went to Ezrin for his contribution to 'The Trial'.

The summer break undoubtedly saved the Ezrin-Waters partnership. The same could not be said of Wright, who was, because of his increasing lack of commitment, becoming the brunt of Waters' hostility. Waters was already frustrated by Wright's belief that he should continue to be paid a quarter share of the production credits when it was clear he was in no way contributing to this element at all. The crunch finally came when Waters realized that the volume of work still required to complete the record in time for delivery could not be met. CBS were offering a bonus should the album be delivered in time for Christmas, and it was income the band could not afford to lose.

Via manager Steve O'Rourke, Waters requested that Wright join Ezrin a week ahead of the rest of the band in Los Angeles in order to catch up on the backlog of work. Ezrin reluctantly agreed but Wright refused outright, commenting that he had seen very little of his children when they were in France because he was going through a tough divorce and that he was not prepared to go.

Waters found this unacceptable. He contacted the other members and decided to communicate to Wright that he would take him to court unless he agreed to finish the album in the time frame suggested. The get-out clause for Wright, if he did not agree, was that he would be guaranteed his full share of the sales royalties but would have to leave the band quietly at the conclusion of the project.

"I did not go along with it," said Gilmour. "I went out to dinner with Rick after Roger had said this to him and said if he wanted to stay in the band I would support him in that. I did point out to Rick that he hadn't contributed anything of any value whatsoever to the album and that I was not over-happy with him myself – he did very, very little, an awful lot of the keyboard parts were done by me, Roger, Bob Ezrin, Michael Kamen, Freddie Mandell."[8]

Wright wrestled with this ultimatum, wondering if he should call Waters' bluff. In the end he resolved to leave the band but in a final, yet illogical, act of commitment agreed to stay and perform on the live shows. "It's quite simple," Wright explained. "It started because Roger and I didn't get on. There was a lot of antagonism during *The Wall* and he said either you leave or I'll scrap everything we've done and there won't be an album. Normally I would have told him to get lost, but at that point we had to earn the money to pay off the enormous back-taxes we owed. Anyway, Roger said that if I didn't leave he would re-record the material. I couldn't afford to say no, so I left."[9]

With the album barely concluded much of the final planning of the live shows was carried out in an intensive effort over the Christmas period, when Pink Floyd were enjoying a UK No.1 chart placing in the singles chart with 'Another Brick In The Wall, Part 2'.

But the US release of the single floundered, initially due to O'Rourke's reluctance to accept the role of independent PR pluggers, believing he could go to the press and radio stations directly through the label. It was a costly error of judgement: The single was released on 8 January 1980 but failed to make an impression. It wasn't even mentioned in *Billboard* and it was not until the pluggers were brought back on board that it finally charted, reaching No.1 by the middle of March.

'Another Brick' was also an unintentionally controversial release, and was immediately banned by the governments of South Africa and Korea for its anti-establishment message. It also attracted unwanted attention in the UK media, which accused the band of exploiting children from a nearby school who had been brought to Britannia Row to sing the chorus. The issue even raised its head again in early 2005 as former pupils contacted each other on the *Friends Reunited* website with a view to suing for royalties.

For now, the focus of attention was diverted to the prospect of performing the piece live and already, behind the scenes, work had begun in earnest.

On stage, *The Wall* was Pink Floyd's most overwhelming spectacle to date; presented exclusively at indoor arenas and opening in Los Angeles and New York in February 1980, it skilfully combined every aspect of the rock-theatre genre. A wall was literally constructed from hundreds of cardboard bricks before the audience's eyes, and by the close of the first half it spanned the entire width of the auditorium to a height of some 40 feet.

"The possibility of the show had been discussed ever since the end of the 1977 tour," recalled designer Mark Fisher. "In the winter of 1978–79, I made a series of drawings showing how the technical process of building the wall might work, and how the bricks might be transported and assembled. Because of the huge volume required to build the wall, it was essential that they could pack flat. Around this time, the project was heavily sidetracked by Steve O'Rourke's idea of touring the show with its own venue, which was to be a giant inflatable slug. I made a number of studies of the building, along with the show." [10]

That idea was thankfully shelved in favour of touring the production in arenas. But, as Fisher continued, "There was a lot of scepticism about the feasibility of building up a wall during the show, and then knocking it down at the end, which was what Roger's vision demanded. Roger, of course, was very keen on building the physical wall rather than relying on animation to tell the story. But plenty of other people thought it would be impossible (or impossibly expensive) and advocated a more conventional Floyd show in which the building and demolition of a metaphorical wall would be portrayed on the signature circular screen. In the early summer of '79, Graeme and I researched the practical side of building and touring a physical wall and came up with some numbers. The numbers were, of course, hopelessly unrealistic. But Graeme became a booster for the project, and in the end it was he who put his neck on the line and persuaded the band to go ahead with the project." [11]

It was also down to Fleming to test how easily the show could be moved from one venue to another. According to Jonathan Park, "[Graeme] ordered a series of load-ins and load-outs between Culver City and the Los Angeles Arena. Steve O'Rourke, who had not yet seen the set, came into the Arena where it had been set up in twenty-four hours and said, 'Cor, fuck. Is that what it's really like?' Fisher and Park decided that everything they did thereafter would have to have a 'Cor, fuck' factor.'[12]

To complicate matters further the show also incorporated a replica German WW2 Stuka dive-bomber that raced down a wire from the rear of the auditorium to crash on stage at the culmination of 'In The Flesh'; the trademark circular screen on which hideous and newly designed animations by Gerald Scarfe were projected; and three 35mm projectors, used in horizontal configuration, to throw a triptych of animated images on to the wall itself.

In addition, three giant puppets, further products of Scarfe's wild imagination, made appearances at key points, representing the villains of the piece. These were a 25-foot-high model of the Schoolteacher, a smaller one of the Wife and an inflatable Mother.

"I met with Gerald [Scarfe] and in the early summer I sculpted a maquette for an inflatable character and sewed up the full-size head," remembered Mark Fisher. "The band were recording the album at Super Bear Studios outside Nice at this time. Graeme and I stuffed the inflatable head in a hamper, gathered up the drawings, and headed to the south of France for a final sign-off meeting in September 1979."[13]

Even the familiar helium-filled pig made a mad dash around the hall during 'Run Like Hell', which Waters

ABOVE: ROGER WATERS ON STAGE AT EARLS COURT, LONDON, 7 AUGUST 1980.

regularly introduced as their "disco" number. There was even a set built into the face of the wall itself, depicting the motel room where Pink sits comatose before a TV showing an old war film. But one of the most visually striking elements was Gilmour atop the wall playing his monumental guitar solo in 'Comfortably Numb'.

As for the sound, the system was by far the band's best yet, including an unexpected feature of additional speaker cabinets under the tiered seating to accentuate the rumbling collapse of the wall, at the show's grand finale, to give the impression that the very arena itself was crumbling.

But what pleased Waters most about the whole production was that it was pleasantly removed from the stadium environment he so hated. "I went and walked all the way around the top row of seats at the back of the arena. And my heart was beating furiously and I was getting shivers right up and down my spine. And I thought it was so fantastic that people could actually see and hear something from everywhere they were seated, because after the 1977 tour I became seriously deranged, or maybe arranged, about stadium gigs. Because I do think they are awful."[14]

As his vision slowly but surely became reality the whole production called for a massive effort to meet the punishing deadlines. "We were all working furiously up until the first night," Waters recalled. "And the first time we had the wall right up across the arena with some film on it was four days before the first show!"[15]

That task alone became a living nightmare for the film editors, who now had the additional problem of transforming the animation projections from a single screen to three in order to project the film across the full width of the auditorium. Peter Hearn, who was working on this, recalled, "Just before the show he [Waters] decided it should be on three screens…. A screaming hurry to do that….we also had something go wrong with the time code and they went into rehearsal in Los Angeles and the picture and sound went out, and I tell you what happened was we were having this conversation over the phone from London with this guy in Los Angeles who was sitting in a hotel bedroom spilling film all over the floor telling him what to cut and what to look for."[16]

There were further problems during rehearsals. Graeme Fleming, it was decided, should be removed from his long-standing job as the lighting designer. That task ultimately fell to Bruce Springsteen's lighting man Marc Brickman, who was called in at 24 hours' notice before the opening night in Los Angeles. Believing the call by Steve O'Rourke to be an invitation to watch the show, he was horrified to find he'd be working the tour, which he described as being, "one of the most shocking experiences of my life".[17] Before that day he hadn't even heard the album.

With immediate sell-outs in both locations and an oversubscribed attendance, it was hardly surprising that the promoter offered to extend the band's residency in New York, but this was turned down. In addition, an offer to take the show elsewhere prompted yet another bust-up with the band, as Waters explained: "Larry Magid the promoter, a Philadelphia promoter, offered us a guaranteed million dollars a show plus expenses to go and do two dates at JFK Stadium with *The Wall*.

"To truck straight from New York to Philadelphia. And I wouldn't do it. I had to go through the whole story with the other members. I said, 'You've all read my explanation of what *The Wall* is about. It's three years since we did that last stadium and I swore then that I'd never do one again. And *The Wall* is entirely sparked off by how awful that was and how I didn't feel that the public or the band or anyone got anything out of it that was worthwhile. And that's why we've produced this show strictly for arenas where everybody does get something out of it that is worthwhile. Blah-blah-blah. And, I ain't fuckin' going!' So there was a lot of talk about whether Andy Bown could sing my part. Oh, you may laugh, and in the end, they bottled out. They didn't have the balls to go through with it."[18]

The Wall tour reached its conclusion at London's Earls Court in August 1980, delayed because the band had to postpone returning to the UK for tax reasons. An unusual period of silence followed, giving rise to the belief that it was all over. Therefore the announcement of a further string of *Wall* shows, in Dortmund, West Germany, in February 1981 and London in June 1981, came as a big surprise to fans, but ultimately it marked the end of a very limited run of shows that saw the classic four-piece Pink Floyd lineup of Waters, Gilmour, Mason and Wright perform for the very last time.

Shortly thereafter work began in earnest on the full-length movie adaptation of the third and final instalment of *The Wall*, with Waters taking the role of producer and working in close collaboration with production designer Gerald Scarfe and director Alan Parker.

As with the live shows, financing the film (allegedly all £6 million of it) fell to the band, who persuaded MGM via Alan Parker to provide funds, although it is said that this was achieved not without a little help from other sources, including a secured loan from other sources including Goldcrest and Constantin films.

LEFT: THE TEACHER MAKES A DRAMATIC ENTRANCE AT EARLS COURT, 7 AUGUST 1980.

OPPOSITE: PINK FLOYD PERFORMING AT DORTMUND, FEBRUARY 1981.

Production eventually began at Pinewood Film Studios in Buckinghamshire during September, by which time a new movie had been scripted, in which the live show sequences were removed and new animation sequences inserted, supplanting Bob Geldof, leader of the post-punk band the Boomtown Rats, in the lead role of the tormented rock star.

Parker's change of plan also meant that Scarfe would have to create an entirely new set of animation sequences, although about 20 minutes of the animation used in the shows was retained.

It is well documented that the three men were given to lengthy rows and walk-outs during the filming. Parker resolved the matter by forcing Waters to take a six-week holiday so that he could work unhindered. "In that period I was allowed to develop my vision," he said, "and I really made that film with a completely free hand. I had to have that. I couldn't be second-guessed by Roger, and he appreciated that. The difficulty came when I'd finished. I'd been shooting for 60 days, 14 hours a day – that film had become mine. And then Roger came back to it, and I had to go through the very difficult reality of having it put over to me that actually it was a collaborative effort." [19]

Waters was exceptionally pragmatic about the situation, describing it as "the most unnerving, neurotic period in my life – with the possible exception of my divorce in 1975. Parker is used to sitting at the top of his pyramid, and I'm used to sitting at the top of mine. We're both pretty much used to getting our own way. If I'd have directed it – which I'd never have done – it would have been much quieter than it is. He paints in fairly bold strokes; he is very worried about boring his audience. It suits us very well, because we did want a lot of this to be a punch in the face." [20]

The band had also re-recorded some of their works for the soundtrack, using new Michael Kamen orchestrations on 'Mother', 'Bring The Boys Back Home' (with a Welsh male choir) and an expanded 'Empty Spaces', which this time, like the stage shows, included the segue of 'What Shall We Do Now?'. In addition, Waters wrote a completely new track to act as an overture to the film: 'When The Tigers Broke Free'. It was inspired by the death of his father, a soldier of the British army, who fell in February 1944 during the ill-fated Anzio campaign in southern Italy during the Second World War.

When it opened in London, the film was generally seen as a powerful piece of celluloid rock music, but it did receive a few unfavourable reviews. Some of the more sensitive writers felt they had been subjected to a battering from start to finish. Reporting from Cannes, *Daily Express* correspondent Victor Davis wrote that, "I got no sleep for the remainder of the night because Parker's shocking images refused to go away." Even Parker admitted that, "I wasn't quite prepared for the intensity of the anger that comes off the screen." [21]

Scarfe was particularly shocked to find that a notorious gang of skinheads from Tilbury had been recruited as Pink's 'Hammer Guard' and now had his hammer logo tattooed on their skin. "I was slightly worried myself that they might be adopted by some fascist, neo-Nazi group as a symbol," confessed Gerald Scarfe. "Thank God it didn't happen." [22] A few, misreading it

completely, accused it of being neo-Nazi propaganda – a view no doubt inspired by the scenes featuring the Tilbury skinheads.

Soon after the film release, and mindful of a contractual obligation to deliver a soundtrack album, Waters began writing again, this time inspired by the British government's recent military retaliation against Argentina's invasion of the Falkland Islands in the South Atlantic. "There really wasn't enough new material in the movie to make a record that I thought was interesting," said Waters. "The project then became *Spare Bricks*, and was meant to include some of the film music, like 'When The Tigers Break Through' [the working title of 'When The Tigers Broke Free'] and the much-less ironic version of 'Outside The Wall' which finishes the movie, the sequence with the kids playing with the milk bottles, plus some music written for the movie but left on the cutting room floor. I decided not to include the new version of 'Mother' from the movie because it really is film music and it doesn't stand up. It's a very long song, and besides, I'm bored with all that now. I've become more interested in the remembrance and requiem aspects of the thing, if that doesn't sound too pretentious. Anyway, it all seemed a bit bitty then I came up with a new title for the album: *The Final Cut*." [23]

With Richard Wright now gone it seemed that Waters had successfully assumed unilateral responsibility for the direction

of the band. As a consequence it was Pink Floyd's most turbulent period, rife with arguments. "It got to the point on *The Final Cut*,' said Gilmour, "that Roger didn't want to know about anyone else submitting material."[24] It seemed that much of what the rest of the band had cherished as a democracy was fast disappearing, as Gilmour went on to explain: "There was at one time a great spirit of compromise within the group. If someone couldn't get enough of his vision on the table to convince the rest of us, it would be dropped. *The Wall* album, which started off as unlistenable and turned into a great piece, was the last album with this spirit of compromise. *With The Final Cut*, Waters became impossible to deal with."[25]

Waters himself admitted that it was a highly unpleasant time. "We were all fighting like cats and dogs. We were finally realizing – or accepting, if you like – that there was no band and had not been a band in accord for a long time. Not since 1975, when we made *Wish You Were Here*. Even then there were big disagreements about content and how to put the record together. I had to do it more or less single-handed, with Michael Kamen, my co-producer. That's one of the few things that the 'boys' and I agreed about."[26]

Mason, by his own admission, felt as if he were looking in from the outside and was becoming increasingly involved in motor sport. Gilmour refused to have anything more to do with the album's production. He was less than happy with the political content and felt so uncomfortable with the idea of criticizing the government's policy that he did not believe it could be anything other than a Waters solo piece, agreeing merely to perform, as required. "I came off the production credits because my ideas weren't the way Roger saw it. It is not personally how I would see a Pink Floyd record going."[27] Gilmour later recalled how Waters, at the end of recording, told him "the only way he'd ever consider doing another Pink Floyd album was on that basis."[28]

Even the sleeve, under Waters' artistic control, carried the subtitle "A Requiem for the Post-War Dream by Roger Waters *performed* by Pink Floyd". The obvious lack of Wright's name gave fans their first indication of his departure, confirmation of which did not emerge until three years after the album's release and the full details of which were not revealed until press interviews surrounding the release of *The Wall Live* CD set in 2000.

The Final Cut was dedicated to Waters' late father Eric Fletcher Waters and for the time being laid his ghost to rest. It was not Pink Floyd's best-selling album, which can be attributed to many factors, not least that it lacked cohesive effort from all members.

In recent years Waters has been defensive towards critics of his control in this period: "The fact is, we all had the opportunity to write as much as we wanted. There was never any question of me saying, 'Don't write. I don't want your stuff.' I was desperately keen for everybody in the band to produce as much as possible. But Nick doesn't write at all, and Dave and Rick are not prolific writers. They've written very, very little over the years. They've written some great stuff, but very little of it. So it fell to me as a more prolific writer to fill in the gaps, to actually produce the material."[29]

It's therefore hardly surprising that the album's title is seen as prophetic in marking Waters' departure and his desire to dissolve Pink Floyd.

With no intention of touring the album, the band was now considered to be on a permanent holiday, and this state of affairs, along with solo albums and extensive tours from both Waters and Gilmour during the early part of 1984, furthered the growing belief that Pink Floyd had all but split up.

1. Glenn Povey & Richard Ashton interview, 25 September 1987.
2. *Mojo*, December 1999.
3. *Circus*, 15 April 1980.
4–8. *Mojo*, December 1999.
9. *South China Sunday Morning Post*, 17 January 1988.
10–11. *Total Production Design*, website.
12. *Rock Sets: The Astonishing Art of Rock Concert Design* by Sutherland Lyall, Thames & Hudson, 1992.
13. *Total Production Design*, website.
14–15. *Q Magazine*, August 1987.
16. Author's interview with Peter

Hearn, 2 July 1986.
17. *Q Magazine*, August 1987.
18–20. *Rolling Stone*, 16 September 1982.
21–22. *The Making of Pink Floyd The Wall* by Gerald Scarfe, Weidenfeld & Nicholson, 2011.
23. Unidentified press report.
24. *Washington Post*, 19 October 1987.
25–26. *Q Magazine*, August 1987.
27. *The Sun*, 27 April 1983.
28. *Washington Post*, 19 October 1987.
29. *Uncut*, June 2004.

DAY-BY-DAY 1978–85

1978

JANUARY – JULY – RECORDING SESSIONS
London, England

Having concluded the rough ideas that would form the basis for a new project, Waters presented the band with a very rough 90-minute home-recorded demo cassette tape in July entitled *Bricks in the Wall*. Continuing to work on these demos, Waters then divided the songs into two new pieces of work, one of which would eventually become *The Wall;* the other his first solo album *The Pros and Cons of Hitch Hiking*.

The track list of Roger Waters original demo tape is noted as: 'We'll Meet Again' [the Vera Lynn song], 'Brick 1: Reminiscing' ['Another Brick In The Wall, Part 1'], 'Mother', 'Brick 2: Education' ['Another Brick In The Wall, Part 2'], 'Teacher Teacher' [which became 'The Hero's Return' on *The Final Cut*], 'Young Lust', 'Instrumental', 'Sexual Revolution' [which was used on *The Pros and Cons of Hitch Hiking*], 'Don't Leave Me Now', 'Brick 3: Drugs' ['Another Brick In The Wall, Part 3'], 'Empty Spaces', 'Backs To The Wall' ['What Shall We Do Now'], 'Goodbye Cruel World', 'Bleeding Hearts' ['Outside The Wall'], 'Follow The Worms' ['Waiting For The Worms'], 'Death Disco' [a combination of 'In The Flesh' and 'Young Lust'], 'Is There Anybody Out There?' (classical guitar version), 'Vera', 'Bring The Boys Back Home', 'Is There Anybody Out There?' (blues guitar version), 'Hey You', 'Trial By Puppet' ['The Trial'], 'Who's Sorry Now' – 'It's Never Too Late' ['The Show Must Go On'], 'Instrumental' ['The Thin Ice'].

SEPTEMBER – DECEMBER – RECORDING SESSIONS
Britannia Row Studios, Islington, London, England

Discontinuous recording of demos for *The Wall* with Roger Waters, David Gilmour and producer James Guthrie. Bob Ezrin joined the production team in December.

SATURDAY 18 NOVEMBER – PRESS REPORT
***NME*, London, England**

In an article headlined "Pink Floyd Go Camping", the *NME* reported that Pink Floyd were planning to build their own 5,000 capacity inflatable concert hall, nicknamed "The Slug" because of its shape, to take on future tours. This would supposedly avoid the problems of working around city venues, but despite being well advanced, the plans never came to fruition. Its design formed part of the overall concept that set designer Mark Fisher began working towards in this period in order to stage *The Wall* concerts.

1979

JANUARY – FEBRUARY – RECORDING SESSIONS
Britannia Row Studios, Islington, London, England

Discontinuous recording of demos for *The Wall* with Roger Waters, David Gilmour and producers James Guthrie and Bob Ezrin. Demos marked 9 January show the running order as follows: Side 1: 'We'll Meet Again' [ending with the sounds of a helicopter], 'Reminiscing' ['Another Brick In The Wall, Part 1', with different lyrics], 'Thin Ice', 'Good Bye Blue Sky', 'Teacher Teacher', 'Another Brick In The Wall' [a short version of 'Another Brick In The Wall, Part 2', also referred to as 'Education']. Side 2: 'Young Lust' [with different lyrics to the verses], 'Mother' [with the guitar solo already written], 'Don't Leave Me Now', 'Sexual Revolution', 'Another Brick In The Wall' ['Another Brick In The Wall, Part 3', also referred to as 'Drugs'], 'Backs To The Wall' [a combination of 'Empty Spaces' and 'What Shall We Do Now'], 'Goodbye Cruel World'. Side 3: 'Bleeding Hearts' ['Outside The Wall'], 'Is There Anybody Out There?', 'Vera', 'Bring The Boys Back Home', 'Is There Anybody Out There?', 'Hey You', 'Comfortably Numb' [a shorter version than the finished track and also referred to as 'The Doctor']. Side 4: 'Run Like Hell', 'Follow The Worms' ['Waiting For The Worms'] including Waters megaphone vocals and Gilmour's laugh, which were used on the final album], 'Trial By Puppet' ['The Trial'], 'Never Too Late' ['The Show Must Go On'], 'Instrumental Theme' [part two of 'The Thin Ice'].

FEBRUARY – MARCH – RECORDING SESSIONS
Britannia Row Studios, Islington, London, England

Discontinuous recording of demos for *The Wall* with Roger Waters, David Gilmour and producers James Guthrie and Bob Ezrin. Demos marked 23 March show the running order as follows: Side 1: 'The Show' [an early version of 'In The Flesh?' with accompanying sound effects], 'Thin Ice', 'Brick 1: Reminiscing' ['Another Brick In The Wall, Part 1' with an extended ending, sounds of children playing and ending with the line, "You! Yes you behind the bike-sheds. Stand still laddie!"], 'Happiest Days' ['The Happiest Days Of Our Lives'], 'Another Brick In The Wall: Education' ['Another Brick In The Wall, Part 2'], 'Mother'. Side 2: 'Goodbye Blue Sky', 'Empty Spaces', 'Young Lust', 'One Of My Turns' [with Waters saying the lines of the groupie], 'Don't Leave Me Now', 'Backs To The Wall' ['Empty Spaces' reprise followed by 'What Shall We Do Now'], 'Another Brick In The Wall: Drugs' ['Another Brick In The Wall, Part 3'], 'Goodbye Cruel World'. Side 3: 'Is There Anybody Out There?', 'Vera', 'Bring The Boys Back Home', 'Is There Anybody Out There?' [ending with a blues instrumental], 'The Doctor' ['Comfortably Numb'], 'Hey You'. Side 4: 'It's Never Too Late' ['The Show Must Go On'], 'The Show' ['In The Flesh'], 'Run Like Hell', 'Waiting For The Worms', 'Stop', 'Trial By Puppet' [a piano version of 'The Trial'], 'Outside The Wall'.

APRIL – JULY – RECORDING SESSIONS
Super Bear Studios, Berre des Alpes, France
& Miravel Studios, Le Val, France

Discontinuous recording for *The Wall* with the whole band commenced at Super Bear with Waters' vocal sessions taking place at Miravel Studios.

FRIDAY 1 JUNE – ALBUM BOX-SET RELEASE (UK)
Pink Floyd: First XI

AUGUST – RECORDING SESSIONS
CBS Studios, New York, NY, USA

Michael Kamen and John McLure under the direction of Bob Ezrin conducted and arranged the orchestral score for tracks on *The Wall*, including 'Nobody Home', 'Vera', 'Bring The Boys Back Home', 'Comfortably Numb' and 'The Trial' with members of the New York Philharmonic Orchestra, the New York Symphony Orchestra and the New York City Opera. Also recorded at this time was a 35-piece group of snare drummers for the track 'Bring The Boys Back Home'.

AUGUST – RECORDING SESSION
Nimbus Nine Soundstage Studios, Toronto, Canada

A one-day session to record actress Trudy Young for her voice-over parts for 'Young Lust' under the direction of Bob Ezrin.

AUGUST – RECORDING SESSIONS
Britannia Row Studios, Islington, London, England

With the band remaining in France on vacation during August, James Guthrie returned to London with Bob Ezrin and assembled the rough demos into a revised order. For the transition between 'The Happiest Days Of Our Lives' and 'Another Brick In The Wall, Part 2', Guthrie recorded Waters' scream over the telephone from his villa in the south of France. This was not re-recorded and is the version heard on the finished album.

Demo's marked 11–12 August from this period show the running order as: Side 1: 'The Show' ['In The Flesh?'], 'Thin Ice', 'Another Brick In The Wall, Part 1', 'The Happiest Days Of Our Lives', 'Another Brick In The Wall, Part 2', 'Mother' [with Nick Mason on drums]. Side 2: 'Goodbye Blue Sky', 'Empty Spaces', 'Young Lust', 'One Of My Turns', 'Don't Leave Me Now', 'Empty Spaces' (reprise), 'What Shall We Do Now?', 'Another Brick In The Wall, Part 3', 'Goodbye Cruel World'. Side 3: 'Is There Anybody Out There?', 'Nobody Home', 'Vera', 'Bring The Boys Back Home', 'The Doctor' ['Comfortably Numb'], 'Hey You'. Side 4: 'The Show Must Go On', 'The Show' ['In The Flesh'], 'Run Like Hell', 'Waiting For The Worms', 'Trial By Puppet' [an orchestral version of 'The Trial'], 'Outside The Wall'.

THURSDAY 6 SEPTEMBER – RECORDING SESSION
Studio 2, Cherokee Recording Studios,
Los Angeles, CA, USA

Recording Synth overdubs for 'The Show Must Go On'.

FRIDAY 7 SEPTEMBER – RECORDING SESSION
Studio 2, Cherokee Recording Studios, Los Angeles, CA, USA

Organ overdubs for 'Thin Ice'.

SATURDAY 8 SEPTEMBER – RECORDING SESSION
Studio 2, Cherokee Recording Studios, Los Angeles, CA, USA

Fender Rhodes and Synths overdubbed for 'Another Hole In The Wall, Part 1'.

WEDNESDAY 12 SEPTEMBER – RECORDING SESSION
Studios 1 & 2, Producers Workshop, Los Angeles, CA, USA

Recording overdubs in Studio 1 and remixing 'Hey You' and overdubs for 'Vera' in Studio 2.

THURSDAY 13 SEPTEMBER – RECORDING SESSION
Producers Workshop, Los Angeles, CA, USA

Recording overdubs in Studio 1 and synth for 'Vera', 'Hey You' and 'Goodbye Blue Sky' in Studio 2.

FRIDAY 14 SEPTEMBER – RECORDING SESSION
Producers Workshop, Los Angeles, CA, USA

Recording Trumpet, Flugelhorn, Conga in Studio 1 and assembling SFX master in Studio 2.

SATURDAY 15 SEPTEMBER – RECORDING SESSION
Producers Workshop, Los Angeles, CA, USA

Recording percussion on 'Young Lust' and 'Another Brick' studio 1, and recording SFX overdubs in Studio 2.

MONDAY 17 SEPTEMBER – RECORDING SESSION
Producers Workshop, Los Angeles, CA, USA

Remixing and dubbing various tracks in Studios 1 and 2.

TUESDAY 18 SEPTEMBER – RECORDING SESSION
Producers Workshop, Los Angeles, CA, USA

Recording overdubs for 'Run Like Hell' and 'Young Lust' in Studio 1, and recording "Telephone Effects" in Studio 2.

WEDNESDAY 19 SEPTEMBER – RECORDING SESSION
Producers Workshop, Los Angeles, CA, USA

Recording Bass and Guitars for 'Vera' and Vocals for 'Young Lust' in Studio 1, and remixing and dubbing various tracks in Studio 2.

THURSDAY 20 SEPTEMBER – RECORDING SESSION
Producers Workshop, Los Angeles, CA, USA

Remixing various tracks in Studios 1 and 2.

FRIDAY 21 SEPTEMBER – RECORDING SESSION
Producers Workshop, Los Angeles, CA, USA

Recording Guitar overdubs for 'Don't Leave Me Now' and 'The Show' ['In The Flesh?'] in Studio 1, and remixing 'Young Lust' and 'The Empty Spaces' in Studio 2.

SATURDAY 22 SEPTEMBER – RECORDING SESSION
Producers Workshop, Los Angeles, CA, USA

Recording overdubs for 'The Show' ['In The Flesh?'] and 'Bring The Boys Back Home' in Studio 1, and overdub remixing in Studio 2.

SUNDAY 23 SEPTEMBER – RECORDING SESSION
Producers Workshop, Los Angeles, CA, USA

Overdub remixing of various tracks in Studio 1.

MONDAY 24 SEPTEMBER – RECORDING SESSION
Producers Workshop, Los Angeles, CA, USA

Recording Vocal overdubs for 'The Show (Sides 1 & 4)' ['In The Flesh?' and 'In The Flesh'] and 'Goodbye Blue Sky' in Studio 1 and remixing in Studio 2.

TUESDAY 25 SEPTEMBER – RECORDING SESSION
Producers Workshop, Los Angeles, CA, USA

Recording Backing Vocals for 'Waiting For The Worms' and piano overdubs in Studio 1, and remixing 'What Shall We Do Now' in Studio 2.

WEDNESDAY 26 SEPTEMBER – RECORDING SESSION
Producers Workshop, Los Angeles, CA, USA

Remixing 'Is There Anybody Out There' in Studio 1 and remixing 'Goodbye Blue Sky' in Studio 2

THURSDAY 27 SEPTEMBER – RECORDING SESSION
Producers Workshop, Los Angeles, CA, USA

Remixing 'Is There Anybody Out There' and 'One Of My Turns' in Studio 1, and remixing 'Don't Leave Me Now' in Studio 2.

FRIDAY 28 SEPTEMBER – RECORDING SESSION
Producers Workshop, Los Angeles, CA, USA

Remixing overdubs in Studio 1, and dubbing 'Bring The Boys Back Home' and 'Is There Anybody Out There' and remixing 'Hey You' in Studio 2.

SATURDAY 29 SEPTEMBER – RECORDING SESSION
Producers Workshop, Los Angeles, CA, USA

Remixing 'Hey You' in Studio 1.

MONDAY 1 OCTOBER – RECORDING SESSION
Producers Workshop, Los Angeles, CA, USA

Recording overdubs for 'Mother' in Studio 1 and remixing 'The Happiest Days Of Our Lives' in Studio 2.

TUESDAY 2 OCTOBER – RECORDING SESSION
Producers Workshop, Los Angeles, CA, USA

Recording overdubs for 'Is There Anybody Out There' and 'Nobody Home' in Studio 1, and remixing 'The Happiest Days Of Our Lives' in Studio 2.

TUESDAY 2 OCTOBER – CANCELLED RECORDING SESSION
Sundance Productions Inc., Dallas, TX, USA

A recording session was booked between 2:00pm and 5:00pm to record the Beach Boys for backing vocals but was cancelled on the same day.

WEDNESDAY 3 OCTOBER – RECORDING SESSION
Producers Workshop, Los Angeles, CA, USA

Recording 'The Show (Side 4)' ['In The Flesh'] and overdubs for 'Bring The Boys Back Home' in Studio 1, and remixing 'Another Brick In The Wall, Part 1' in Studio 2.

THURSDAY 4 OCTOBER – RECORDING SESSION
Producers Workshop, Los Angeles, CA, USA

Recording Vocals, FX, Organ for 'The Show' ['In The Flesh?'], Drums and Percussion for 'Bring The Boys Back Home', and Vocal and Guitar for 'One Of My Turns' in Studio 1, and cross-fade mock-ups and remixing 'Thin Ice Part 2' in Studio 2.

FRIDAY 5 OCTOBER – RECORDING SESSION
Producers Workshop, Los Angeles, CA, USA

Recording Vocal overdubs for 'Nobody Home', Vocal overdubs for 'Bring The Boys Back Home', and Prophet Synth overdubs for the 'Doctor' ['Comfortably Numb'] in Studio 1, and remixing 'Vera' and cross-fades for 'Thin Ice, Pt. 2' in Studio 2.

SATURDAY 6 OCTOBER – RECORDING SESSION
Producers Workshop, Los Angeles, CA, USA

Recording Vocal overdubs for 'Nobody Home', bass for 'Another Brick In The Wall, Pt 2', and Vocals on 'Bring The Boys Back Home' and 'One Of My Turns' in Studio 2

SUNDAY 7 OCTOBER – RECORDING SESSION
Producers Workshop, Los Angeles, CA, USA

Remixing various tracks in Studio 2.

MONDAY 8 OCTOBER – RECORDING SESSION
Producers Workshop, Los Angeles, CA, USA

Recording Vocal, Piano and Guitar overdubs for 'Waiting For The Worms' in Studio 1, and remixing 'The Doctor' ['Comfortably Numb'], and 16-track transfer and edit of 'The Doctor' in Studio 2.

TUESDAY 9 OCTOBER – RECORDING SESSION
Producers Workshop, Los Angeles, CA, USA

Recording Vocal overdubs for 'Waiting For The Worms' and Guitar overdubs for 'The Show, Pt. 2' ['In The Flesh'] in Studio 1, and remixing the overture for 'Comfortably Numb' (both versions) in Studio 2.

WEDNESDAY 10 OCTOBER – RECORDING SESSION
Producers Workshop, Los Angeles, CA, USA

Recording overdubs for 'The Doctor' ['Comfortably Numb'], and edit SFX tape loop in Studio 1, and remixing 'The Doctor' and remixing the orchestra for 'The Doctor' in Studio 2.

THURSDAY 11 OCTOBER – RECORDING SESSION
Producers Workshop, Los Angeles, CA, USA

Recording overdub Piano for 'Stop', and Backing Vocals for 'The Show Must Go On' and 'Waiting For The Worms' in Studio 1, and recording overdubs for 'The Doctor (Comfortably Numb)' in Studio 2.

FRIDAY 12 OCTOBER – RECORDING SESSION
Producers Workshop, Los Angeles, CA, USA

Recording overdubs for 'Mother' in Studio 1, and editing 'Comfortably Numb' and remixing 'Another Brick, Education' in Studio 2.

SATURDAY 13 & SUNDAY 14 OCTOBER – CANCELLED RECORDING SESSION
Studios 1 & 2, Producers Workshop, Los Angeles, CA, USA

MONDAY 15 OCTOBER – RECORDING SESSION
Studios 1 & 2, Producers Workshop, Los Angeles, CA, USA
Recording overdubs for 'Mother' in Studio 1, and cross-fades with 'Another Brick Pt. 2' with 'Happiest Days' and 6-track transfer of 'Mother' in Studio 2.

TUESDAY 16 OCTOBER – RECORDING SESSION
Studios 1 & 2, Producers Workshop, Los Angeles, CA, USA
Recording Vocal overdub for 'The Show Must Go On' and Guitar overdub for 'Mother' in Studio 1, and remixing 'Nobody Home' and 'Run Like Hell' in Studio 2.

WEDNESDAY 17 OCTOBER – RECORDING SESSION
Studios 1 & 2, Producers Workshop, Los Angeles, CA, USA
Recording Hand Clap overdubs for 'Run Like Hell' and Guitar overdubs for 'Mother' in Studio 1, and remixing and recording Drum overdubs for 'Run Like Hell', and assembling a preview of The Wall in Studio 2.

THURSDAY 18 OCTOBER – RECORDING SESSION
Studio 2, Producers Workshop, Los Angeles, CA, USA
Recording overdub SFX for 'Waiting For The Worms' and guitar overdubs for 'Mother' in Studio 1, and showcasing The Wall and remixing 'Run Like Hell' in Studio 2.

FRIDAY 19 OCTOBER – RECORDING SESSION
Studios 1 & 2, Producers Workshop, Los Angeles, CA, USA
Recording Vocals for 'Show Must Go On' and 'Mother', and recording SFX for 'Waiting For The Worms' in Studio 1, and remixing and overdubbing in Studio 2.

SATURDAY 20 OCTOBER – RECORDING SESSION
Studio 1, Producers Workshop, Los Angeles, CA, USA
Recording Drums for 'Mother', Piano for 'Show Must Go On' and Vocal and Bass on 'Mother' in Studio 1.

SUNDAY 21 OCTOBER – RECORDING SESSION
Studio 2, Producers Workshop, Los Angeles, CA, USA
Remixing and recording overdubs in Studio 2.

MONDAY 22 OCTOBER – RECORDING SESSION
Studios 1 & 2, Producers Workshop, Los Angeles, CA, USA
Recording overdubs and SFX for 'Trial By Puppet' ['The Trial'] in Studio 1, and remixing 'Waiting For The Worms' in Studio 2.

TUESDAY 23 OCTOBER – RECORDING SESSION
Studios 1 & 2, Producers Workshop, Los Angeles, CA, USA
Recording the buskers and 'Outside The Wall', and assembling various tape loops and effects in Studio 1, and remixing 'Stop' and 'Anybody Out There' in Studio 2.

WEDNESDAY 24 OCTOBER – RECORDING SESSION
Studios 1 & 2, Producers Workshop, Los Angeles, CA, USA
Recording overdub Piano for 'Mother', SFX for 'Bring The Boys Back Home' and Vocals for 'The Trial' in Studio 1, and remixing 'Mother' in Studio 2.

THURSDAY 25 OCTOBER – RECORDING SESSION
Studios 1 & 2, Producers Workshop, Los Angeles, CA, USA
Recording cross-fades for 'Another Brick', 'Nobody Home' and 'The Thin Ice' in Studio 1, and remixing 'Mother' in Studio 2.

FRIDAY 26 OCTOBER – RECORDING SESSION
Studios 1 & 2, Producers Workshop, Los Angeles, CA, USA
Recording cross-fades for 'Another Brick In The Wall Pt 2' and 'Mother' in Studio 1, and remixing 'In The Flesh' and 'In The Flesh?' in Studio 2.

SATURDAY 27 OCTOBER – RECORDING SESSION
Studios 1 & 2, Producers Workshop, Los Angeles, CA, USA
Recording cross-fades for 'Another Brick (Drugs)', 'Goodbye Cruel World', 'Nobody Home' and 'Vera' in Studio 1, and remixing 'In The Flesh' and 'In The Flesh?' in Studio 2.

SUNDAY 28 OCTOBER – RECORDING SESSION
Studios 1 & 2, Producers Workshop, Los Angeles, CA, USA
Remixing and overdubs in Studio 1, and remixing 'In The Flesh', 'In The Flesh?' and 'Outside The Wall' in Studio 2.

MONDAY 29 OCTOBER – RECORDING SESSION
Studios 1 & 2, Producers Workshop, Los Angeles, CA, USA
Cross-fades for album in Studio 1, and remixing 'Trial By Puppets' ['The Trial'] and editing singles in Studio 2.

TUESDAY 30 OCTOBER – RECORDING SESSION
Studios 1 & 2, Producers Workshop, Los Angeles, CA, USA
Cross-fades for album in Studio 1 and remixing 'The Trial' in Studio 2.

WEDNESDAY 31 OCTOBER – RECORDING SESSION
Studios 1 & 2, Producers Workshop, Los Angeles, CA, USA
Remixing and overdubbing in Studio 1, and remixing 'Young Lust' and 'Empty Spaces' in Studio 2.

THURSDAY 1 NOVEMBER – RECORDING SESSION
Studios 1 & 2, Producers Workshop, Los Angeles, CA, USA
Cross-fades for sides 2 and 3 of The Wall made in Studio 1, and cross-fades and remixing 'Bring The Boys Back Home' in Studio 2.

FRIDAY 2 NOVEMBER – RECORDING SESSION
Studios 1 & 2, Producers Workshop, Los Angeles, CA, USA
Various SFX recorded for The Wall in Studio 1 and various cross-fades made in Studio 2.

SATURDAY 3 NOVEMBER – RECORDING SESSION
Studios 1 & 2, Producers Workshop, Los Angeles, CA, USA
Editing tracks.

SUNDAY 4 NOVEMBER – RECORDING SESSION
Studio 2, Producers Workshop, Los Angeles, CA, USA
Tape editing.

MONDAY 5 NOVEMBER – RECORDING SESSION
Studio 2, Producers Workshop, Los Angeles, CA, USA
Premixes for animation and live show.

TUESDAY 6 NOVEMBER – RECORDING SESSION
Studio 2, Producers Workshop, Los Angeles, CA, USA
TV spots copied and edited, and all four sides of the album copied in Studio 2. Also noted on this date is the finalized version passed to the Mastering Lab Inc. for urgent master pressing. This represents the last date of recording for *The Wall* album.

FRIDAY 23 NOVEMBER – SINGLE RELEASE (UK)
'Another Brick In The Wall, Part 2'
NME wrote, "It's fairly cunningly conceived, complete with easily memorable moron-chorus parts, simple enough for the thickest of terrace terrorists. Expect to hear it accompanying the sound of bladders (human or swine) being kicked around on Saturday afternoons."

FRIDAY 30 NOVEMBER – ALBUM RELEASE (UK)
The Wall
Melody Maker wrote, "Quite obviously *The Wall* is an extraordinary record. I'm not sure whether it's brilliant or terrible, but I find it utterly compelling. Despite the inevitable expensive production it can't be dismissed as comfortable easy listening, and anyone who takes ideas as challenging and uncomfortable (and pessimistic?) as Roger Waters' deep into the AOR market is worth listening to. Pink Floyd are still relevant, still important and above all, still thinking."

FRIDAY 30 NOVEMBER – RADIO BROADCAST
The Friday Rock Show, BBC Radio One, London, England
DJ Tommy Vance interviewed Roger Waters in a track-by-track commentary of *The Wall* from the Beverly Hills Hotel in Los Angeles for his *Friday Rock Show* broadcast on BBC Radio One between 10.00pm and 12.00 midnight and repeated on the *Friday Rock Show* on Friday 25 July 1980 between 10.00pm and 12.00midnight.

Much to the horror of Pink Floyd's UK concert promoter, Harvey Goldsmith, Roger Waters announced in the initial broadcast that the band would be performing in the UK at Wembley Arena between 9 and 13 June 1980. Switchboards were jammed both at the radio station and venue until a statement was issued denying this fact.

Rumours were also rife in the music press in the forthcoming year of Pink Floyd shows, including a single concert production of *The Wall* to be held at the open-air setting of Milton Keynes National Bowl, Milton Keynes, on 26 May 1980 and again at the same venue in August 1980, when it was suggested that plans were afoot to stage a single "greatest hits" concert, none of which came to fruition.

SATURDAY 1 DECEMBER – ALBUM RELEASE (US)
The Wall
Trouser Press wrote, "Pink Floyd has concocted a project so extreme even they may have trouble topping it…. Ultimately *The Wall* seems neither a daring success nor a terrible failure. By wallowing in impotent desperation and comfortable numbness, Pink Floyd exposes itself as a group of passionless facile cynics, despite their pretentions to something far greater."

PINK FLOYD, DECEMBER 1979– OCTOBER 1985

David Gilmour, Nick Mason, Roger Waters

1980

THE WALL PERFORMED LIVE (LOS ANGELES)

ADDITIONAL TOUR PERSONNEL
Richard Wright (Keyboards, Vocals), Andy Bown (Bass Guitar), "Snowy" White (Guitars), John "Willie" Wilson (Drums), Peter Wood (Keyboards), Joe Chemay (Backing Vocals), Stan Farber (Backing Vocals), Jim Haas (Backing Vocals), Jon Joyce (Backing Vocals), Cynthia Fox (MC 7, 9, 11, 12 & 13 February), Ace Young (MC 8 February), Jim Ladd (MC 10 February).

PINK FLOYD ROAD CREW – 1981
Marc Brickman (Lighting Designer), Mark Fisher (Set Design & Effects), Seth Goldman (Monitor Sound Engineer), Pat Griffiths (Wardrobe), James Guthrie (Front of House Sound Engineer), Rick Hart (PA Technician), Don Jole (Special Effects), Jonathan Park (Set Design & Effects), Rocky Paulson (Special Effects), Andy Shields (Projectionist), Nigel Taylor (PA Technician), Phil Taylor (Backline Technician), Mick Treadwell (Special Effects), Greg Walsh (PA Technician), Robbie Williams (Head of PA).

JANUARY – REHEARSALS
Leeds Rehearsal Studios, Hollywood, Los Angeles, CA, USA
At least two weeks of music rehearsals took place prior to the production rehearsals.

JANUARY – REHEARSALS
Paramount Studios, Culver City, Los Angeles, CA, USA
Running parallel to the musicians' rehearsals, construction rigging and wall building rehearsals took place inside a sound stage prior to the production rehearsals moving to the venue.

TUESDAY 8 JANUARY – SINGLE RELEASE (US)
'Another Brick In The Wall, Part 2'

THE WALL

SIDE ONE

IN THE FLESH? (Waters) 3:20
THE THIN ICE (Waters) 2:26
ANOTHER BRICK IN THE WALL, PART 1 (Waters) 3:11
THE HAPPIEST DAYS OF OUR LIVES (Waters) 1:50
ANOTHER BRICK IN THE WALL, PART 2 (Waters) 3:58
MOTHER (Waters) 5:34

SIDE TWO

GOODBYE BLUE SKY (Waters) 2:47
EMPTY SPACES (Waters) 2:07
YOUNG LUST (Waters, Gilmour) 3:29
ONE OF MY TURNS (Waters) 3:36
DON'T LEAVE ME NOW (Waters) 4:14
ANOTHER BRICK IN THE WALL, PART 3 (Waters) 1:14
GOODBYE CRUEL WORLD (Waters) 1:17

SIDE THREE

HEY YOU (Waters) 4:40
IS THERE ANYBODY OUT THERE? (Waters) 2:41
NOBODY HOME (Waters) 3:22
VERA (Waters) 1:33
BRING THE BOYS BACK HOME (Waters) 1:27
COMFORTABLY NUMB (Gilmour, Waters) 6:22

SIDE FOUR

THE SHOW MUST GO ON (Waters) 1:36
IN THE FLESH (Waters) 4:15
RUN LIKE HELL (Gilmour, Waters) 4:23
WAITING FOR THE WORMS (Waters) 3:57
STOP (Waters) 0:30
THE TRIAL (Waters, Ezrin) 5:18
OUTSIDE THE WALL (Waters) 1:46

RELEASED

UK: Friday 30 November 1979.
US: Saturday 8 December 1979.

FORMAT

UK: EMI Harvest SHVL 822 (Double vinyl album).
US: Columbia PC2 36183 (Double vinyl album).

HIGHEST CHART POSITION

UK: No. 3. (Music Week "Top 75 Albums" on Saturday 8 December 1979), Chart re-entry No. 97 (Music Week "Top 75 Albums" on Saturday 25 October 1997), Chart re-entry No.44 (Official UK Album Chart on Saturday 8 October 2011).
US: No. 1 (Billboard "Top LPs & Tape" on Saturday 19 January 1980).

AWARDS

UK: Certified Silver and Gold on Saturday 1 December 1979, Platinum on Wednesday 12 December 1979 and 2 x Platinum on Monday 22 July 2013.
US: Certified Gold and Platinum on Thursday 13 March 1980; 4 x Platinum on Friday 26 October 1984; 7 x Platinum on Wednesday 9 August 1989; 8 x Platinum on Tuesday 28 May 1991; 10 x Platinum on Tuesday 2 May 1995; 11 x Platinum on Friday 16 May 1997; 22 x Platinum on Monday 8 September 1997 and 23 x Platinum on Friday 29 January 1999.

At the 23rd Grammy Awards held at Radio City Music Hall, New York, on 25 February 1981, The Wall was nominated for "Album Of The Year" losing out to Christopher Cross by Christopher Cross and "Best Rock Vocal Group", losing out to Against the Wind by Bob Seger & The Silver Bullet Band, but won James Guthrie an award for "Best Engineered Recording, Non Classical".

ARTWORK

Artwork concept by Roger Waters and executed by Gerald Scarfe. The original album sleeve offered no credits to any musicians except the words "Written by Roger Waters". Sleeves printed from late 1980 onwards were revised to include all members of Pink Floyd.

MUSICIANS

David Gilmour, Nick Mason, Roger Waters, Richard Wright.

ADDITIONAL MUSICIANS

Joe de Blassi (Nylon String Guitar on 'Is There Anybody Out There?').
Joe Chemay (Backing Vocals).
Bob Ezrin (Additional Keyboards on 'Mother', 'One Of My Turns', 'Is There Anybody Out There?', 'Nobody Home', 'The Show Must Go On', 'In The Flesh', 'Waiting For The Worms', 'Stop' and 'The Trial').
Stan Farber (Backing Vocals).
James Guthrie (Miscellaneous Effects).
Jim Haas (Backing Vocals).
Bobbye Hall (Congas on 'Run Like Hell').

Bruce Johnson (Backing Vocals).

Jon Joyce (Backing Vocals).

Freddie Mandell (Keyboards on 'In The Flesh?' and 'In The Flesh').

Frank Marocco (Concertina on 'Outside The Wall').

Members of the New York City Opera (Backing Chorus on 'Bring The Boys Back Home').

Members of the New York Philharmonic Orchestra and New York Symphony Orchestra conducted by Michael Kamen (Orchestra on 'Nobody Home', 'Vera', 'Bring The Boys Back Home', 'Comfortably Numb' and 'The Trial').

Blue Ocean (Leading a 35-strong Snare Drum ensemble on 'Bring The Boys Back Home').

Jeff Porcaro (Drums on 'Mother').

Joe Porcaro (Lead Snare Drum on 'Bring The Boys Back Home').

Pupils of Islington Green Primary School (Backing Chorus on ' Another Brick In The Wall, Part 2').

Lee Ritenour (Additional Guitars on 'One Of My Turns' and 'Comfortably Numb').

Toni Tennille (Backing Vocals).

Trevor Veitch (Mandolin on 'Outside The Wall').

Harry Waters (Child's Voice on 'Goodbye Blue Sky').

Larry Williams (Clarinet on 'Outside The Wall').

Trudy Young (Voice of the Groupie on 'One Of My Turns').

BACKGROUND DIALOGUE

Various broadcast dialogue is heard in the background throughout the album, which Waters has attributed to being a result of either the TV or radio being on during the mixing stage of the album.

'Don't Leave Me Now' features miscellaneous US TV shows, including commentator Chick Hearn commentating on the NBA game between the LA Lakers and the Chicago Bulls broadcast on KLAC radio, Los Angeles, CA on Tuesday 16 October 1979.

'Is There Anybody Out There?' features a repeat of the CBS TV show *Gunsmoke*, and the episode 'Fandango' in which Marshall Dillon says, "…Well, only about an hour of daylight left…" It was broadcast on KHJ Channel 9 on Tuesday 2 October 1979 between 5.00pm and 6.00pm (PST).

'One Of My Turns' features an episode of the NBC–TV show *Another World*, in which Kirk Laverty brings Iris Bancroft and her maid, Vivian Gorrow, to his lodge in the Adirondacks. Dobbs is the caretaker of the lodge and is heard saying, "I'm sorry sir, I didn't mean to startle you." It was broadcast on KEYT Channel 4 on Sunday 23 September 1979 between 1.30pm and 3.00pm (PST). This section was replaced in the feature film *Pink Floyd The Wall* with an excerpt from the 1955 feature film *The Dambusters*.

'Nobody Home' features a repeat of the TV show *Gomer Pyle USMC* and the episode 'Gomer Says '"Hey" to the President', which was broadcast on KCOP Channel 13 on Thursday 25 October between 1.30pm and 2.00pm (PST). It mentions the formidable assets of character Rose Pilchek and Sgt. Carter, who is heard saying, "All right,

I'll take care of them part of the time…"

'Vera' features an excerpt from the 1969 feature film *The Battle of Britain,* in which RAF Squadron Leader "Skipper", played by Robert Shaw, calls out, "Where the hell are you, Simon?". Simon is hit by gunfire from an enemy aircraft, plunges to earth and crashes. This was also heard in the stage shows.

BACKWARD MESSAGE

There is also an intriguing backwards message located in 'Empty Spaces' that reads, "Hello punter. Congratulations. You have just discovered the secret message. Please send your answer to Old Pink, care of the Funny Farm, Chalfont."

"Old Pink" is almost certainly a reference to Syd Barrett and the "funny farm" is local colloquialism for the National Centre for Epilepsy in Chalfont St Peter, England. It is believed one or more of the band members owned property in the area, hence local knowledge. The message is interrupted by Gilmour calling out, "Roger, Carolyne on the phone."

RECORDING DETAILS

Recorded at Britannia Row Studios, London, England; Super Bear Studios, Berre des Aples, France; Miravel Studios, Le Val, France; CBS Studios, New York, USA; Cherokee Recording Studios, Los Angeles, USA and Producers Workshop, Los Angeles, USA.

Produced by Bob Ezrin, David Gilmour and Roger Waters and co-produced by James Guthrie. Engineered by James Guthrie, Nick Griffiths, Patrice Quef, Brian Christian and Rick Hart.

LEFT: UK PRESS ADVERT FOR *THE WALL*.

FRIDAY 1 FEBRUARY – PRESS REPORT
London, England

It was widely reported in the trade music press that Pink Floyd Music Publishing Limited had signed a long-term co-publishing and administration agreement with Warner-Chappell International, to include their entire back catalogue up to and including *The Wall*. The terms of the five-year deal were not made public but insiders believed it to have been worth up to £3.5 million.

MONDAY 21 JANUARY TO WEDNESDAY 6 FEBRUARY – REHEARSALS
Los Angeles Memorial Sports Arena, Exposition Park, Los Angeles, CA, USA

Three weeks of full production rehearsals were staged at the venue right up to the opening night.

MONDAY 4 & MONDAY 11 FEBRUARY – RADIO BROADCASTS
Inner-View with Jim Ladd, KMET Studios, Los Angeles, CA, USA

KMET 94.7 (Los Angeles) broadcast a pre-recorded interview between Roger Waters and presenter Jim Ladd for his *Inner-view* series in a two-part track-by-track commentary on *The Wall*. Both shows were broadcast between 10.00pm and 11.00pm (PST).

THURSDAY 7, FRIDAY 8, SATURDAY 9, SUNDAY 10, MONDAY 11, TUESDAY 12 & WEDNESDAY 13 FEBRUARY – PERFORMANCES ▼
Los Angeles Memorial Sports Arena, Exposition Park, Los Angeles, CA, USA

Set list at all shows: 'In The Flesh', 'The Thin Ice', 'Another Brick In The Wall, Part 1', 'The Happiest Days Of Our Lives', 'Another Brick In The Wall, Part 2', 'Mother', 'Goodbye Blue Sky', 'What Shall We Do Now?', 'Empty Spaces', 'Young Lust', 'One Of My Turns', 'Don't Leave Me Now', 'Another Brick In The Wall, Part 3', 'The Last Few Bricks', 'Goodbye Cruel World' <Intermission> 'Hey You', 'Is There Anybody Out There?', 'Nobody Home', 'Vera', 'Bring The Boys Back Home', 'Comfortably Numb', 'The Show Must Go On', 'In The Flesh?', 'Run Like Hell', 'Waiting For The Worms', 'Stop', 'The Trial', 'Outside The Wall'.

Note: 'The Last Few Bricks' was a title used to describe instrumental filler, usually lasting about five minutes, performed in order for the construction crews to catch up with the completion of the wall. At the first few shows this was primarily a blues instrumental with the melody of 'Another Brick' coming through.

In later shows it developed into an atmospheric synthesizer-based instrumental with elements of 'Another Brick', 'Young Lust' and 'Empty Spaces'.

The show on Thursday 7 February was temporarily halted during 'What Shall We Do Now?' in order to extinguish flames caused by pyrotechnics setting fire to the stage drapes.

THE WALL PERFORMED LIVE (LONG ISLAND, NEW YORK)

ADDITIONAL TOUR PERSONNEL
Andy Bown (Bass Guitar), Joe Chemay (Backing Vocals), Stan Farber (Backing Vocals), Jim Haas (Backing Vocals), Jon Joyce (Backing Vocals), "Snowy" White (Guitars), John "Willie" Wilson (Drums), Peter Wood (Keyboards), Richard Wright (Keyboards, Vocals), Gary Yudman (MC).

MONDAY 16 TO MONDAY 23 FEBRUARY – REHEARSALS
Nassau Veterans Memorial Coliseum, Uniondale, NY, USA

A full week of production rehearsals were staged at the venue prior to the shows.

SUNDAY 24, MONDAY 25, TUESDAY 26, WEDNESDAY 27 & THURSDAY 28 FEBRUARY – PERFORMANCES
Nassau Veterans Memorial Coliseum, Uniondale, NY, USA

Set list at all shows: 'In The Flesh', 'The Thin Ice', 'Another Brick In The Wall, Part 1', 'The Happiest Days Of Our Lives', 'Another Brick In The Wall, Part 2', 'Mother', 'Goodbye Blue Sky', 'What Shall We Do Now?', 'Empty Spaces', 'Young Lust', 'One Of My Turns', 'Don't Leave Me Now', 'Another Brick In The Wall, Part 3', 'The Last Few Bricks', 'Goodbye Cruel World' <Intermission> 'Hey You', 'Is There Anybody Out There?', 'Nobody Home', 'Vera', 'Bring The Boys Back Home', 'Comfortably Numb', 'The Show Must Go On', 'In The Flesh?', 'Run Like Hell', 'Waiting For The Worms', 'Stop', 'The Trial', 'Outside The Wall'.

TUESDAY 22 APRIL – SINGLE RELEASE (US)
'Run Like Hell'

FRIDAY 2 MAY – PRESS REPORT
London, England

A news item was published in which it was reported censors of the white minority South African government had banned the single 'Another Brick In The Wall, Part 2', after it had topped the charts there for several weeks. No specific reason was given for the banning order, which was contained in a weekly list of undesirable publications and objects published on this day, which also included Frank Zappa's album *Zappa in New York* and Marianne Faithful's *Broken English*. Some of the lyrics had been adapted by school children taking part in a two-week-old nationwide classes boycott to protest against racial discrimination in education. Also banned was the album *The Wall*. The banning order also meant that all unsold copies of the single and album had to be destroyed.

TUESDAY 24 JUNE – SINGLE RELEASE (US)
'Comfortably Numb'

THE WALL PERFORMED LIVE (LONDON)

ADDITIONAL TOUR PERSONNEL

Andy Bown (Bass Guitar), Joe Chemay (Backing Vocals), Stan Farber (Backing Vocals), Jim Haas (Backing Vocals), Jon Joyce (Backing Vocals), "Snowy" White (Guitars), John "Willie" Wilson (Drums), Peter Wood (Keyboards), Richard Wright (Keyboards, Vocals), Gary Yudman (MC).

SUNDAY 27 – THURSDAY 31 JULY – REHEARSALS
Studio J, Shepperton Film Studios, Shepperton, England
Set-up and production rehearsals prior to the Earls Court concerts.

FRIDAY 1 – MONDAY 4 AUGUST – REHEARSALS
Earls Court Exhibition Hall, Earls Court, London, England
Four days of production rehearsals were staged at the venue prior to the shows.

MONDAY 4, TUESDAY 5, WEDNESDAY 6, THURSDAY 7, FRIDAY 8 & SATURDAY 9 AUGUST – PERFORMANCES ▶
Earls Court Exhibition Hall, Earls Court, London, England

Set list at all shows: 'In The Flesh', 'The Thin Ice', 'Another Brick In The Wall, Part 1', 'The Happiest Days Of Our Lives', 'Another Brick In The Wall, Part 2', 'Mother', 'Goodbye Blue Sky', 'What Shall We Do Now?', 'Empty Spaces', 'Young Lust', 'One Of My Turns', 'Don't Leave Me Now', 'Another Brick In The Wall, Part 3', 'The Last Few Bricks', 'Goodbye Cruel World' <Intermission> 'Hey You', 'Is There Anybody Out There?', 'Nobody Home', 'Vera', 'Bring The Boys Back Home', 'Comfortably Numb', 'The Show Must Go On', 'In The Flesh?', 'Run Like Hell', 'Waiting For The Worms', 'Stop', 'The Trial', 'Outside The Wall'.

It was reported that Gerald Scarfe had 10 of his original pieces of artwork for *The Wall* stolen from their glass frames in the foyer of the Earls Court arena in the early hours of Sunday 10 August. Insurers put a price tag of more than £30,000 on the drawings and paintings, one of which was the original artwork for the cover of *The Wall* album. To date these artworks have never been recovered.

Sounds reported, "If *The Wall* turns out to be the Pink Floyd's epitaph they've bowed out with a grandiose, impressive, overblown and provocative spectacle that typified every prejudice, good or bad, that anyone could hold about them…. We knew what we'd come to hear – a presentation of their latest and massive selling album. We knew we'd get a wall too but even the expectation of it didn't prepare you for the sheer scale of the 40ft high white edifice that eventually stretched the width of the hall…. The Floyd kicked off to the accompaniment of thunder flashes and a Spitfire that sailed from one end of the hall to the other, crashing spectacularly into the half-built wall to roars from the audience… except that the band wasn't the Floyd but four clones giving an Americanised version of what the Floyd ought to look like on stage. The Floyd emerged behind them and took over after a couple of minutes. And as the wall built up so did Roger Waters' bleak tale of indoctrination and alienation, aided by huge grotesque figures of schoolteachers and judicial mothers and a series of cartoons, all

BELOW: PERFORMING 'RUN LIKE HELL' AT EARLS COURT, 7 AUGUST 1980.

the work of Gerald Scarfe who clearly shares Waters' own sense of the paranoid. The symbolism of the wall veered between the subtle and the sledgehammer but you couldn't miss the point as it closed in on the band, eventually leaving them visible through a couple of holes while the light show raged on regardless."

1981

THE WALL PERFORMED LIVE (DORTMUND)

ADDITIONAL TOUR PERSONNEL
Andy Bown (Bass Guitar), Joe Chemay (Backing Vocals), Stan Farber (Backing Vocals), Jim Haas (Backing Vocals), Jon Joyce (Backing Vocals), Andy Roberts (Guitars), Willi Thomczyk (MC), John "Willie" Wilson (Drums), Peter Wood (Keyboards), Richard Wright (Keyboards, Vocals).

TUESDAY 10 TO THURSDAY 12 FEBRUARY – REHEARSALS
Westfalenhalle, Dortmund, West Germany

Three days of production rehearsals were staged at the venue prior to the shows.

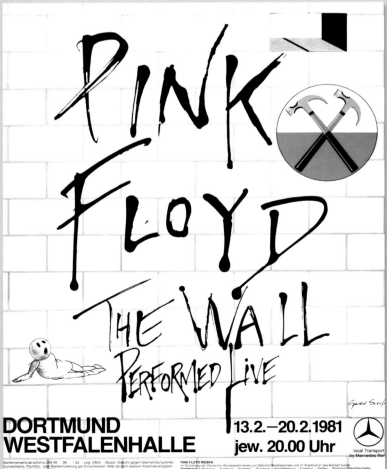

ABOVE: DAVID GILMOUR PERFORMING ATOP THE WALL AT EARLS COURT, 6 AUGUST 1980.

RIGHT: CONCERT POSTER FOR THE WALL SHOWS IN DORTMUND, FEBRUARY 1981.

FRIDAY 13, SATURDAY 14, SUNDAY 15, MONDAY 16, TUESDAY 17, WEDNESDAY 18, THURSDAY 19 & FRIDAY 20 FEBRUARY – PERFORMANCES ▶
Westfalenhalle, Dortmund, West Germany

Set list at all shows: 'In The Flesh', 'The Thin Ice', 'Another Brick In The Wall, Part 1', 'The Happiest Days Of Our Lives', 'Another Brick In The Wall, Part 2', 'Mother', 'Goodbye Blue Sky', 'What Shall We Do Now?', 'Empty Spaces', 'Young Lust', 'One Of My Turns', 'Don't Leave Me Now', 'Another Brick In The Wall, Part 3', 'The Last Few Bricks', 'Goodbye Cruel World' <Intermission> 'Hey You', 'Is There Anybody Out There?', 'Nobody Home', 'Vera', 'Bring The Boys Back Home', 'Comfortably Numb', 'The Show Must Go On', 'In The Flesh?', 'Run Like Hell', 'Waiting For The Worms', 'Stop', 'The Trial', 'Outside The Wall'.

ARD network TV, West Germany filmed part of the show of 13 February 1981 and a segment of 'The Happiest Days Of Our Lives' was featured in a news item.

MONDAY 2 MARCH – PRESS REPORT
London, England

It was widely reported in the UK national press that the investment firm Norton Warburg Group was going into liquidation, the *Daily Express* writing that, "Pink Floyd was advised on its finances by Norton Warburg Management and is believed to have invested £800,000 in venture capitalists Norton Warburg Investments between 1972 and April 1979." Six days later the same newspaper reported that Norton Warburg was being investigated by the fraud squad. Their 11 March edition revealed the full extent of their losses, which were put closer to £2.5 million. At a creditors' meeting Norton Warburg revealed to its shareholders it had assets worth only £800,000 and a deficiency in excess of £4.5m.

THE WALL PERFORMED LIVE (LONDON)

ADDITIONAL TOUR PERSONNEL
Andy Bown (Bass Guitar), Joe Chemay (Backing Vocals), Stan Farber (Backing Vocals), Jim Haas (Backing Vocals), Jon Joyce (Backing Vocals), Andy Roberts (Guitars), John "Willie" Wilson (Drums), Peter Wood (Keyboards), Richard Wright (Keyboards, Vocals), Gary Yudman (MC).

THURSDAY 11 & FRIDAY 12 JUNE – REHEARSALS
Earls Court Exhibition Hall, Earls Court, London, England

Two days of production rehearsals were staged at the venue prior to the shows.

SATURDAY 13, SUNDAY 14, MONDAY 15, TUESDAY 16 & WEDNESDAY 17 JUNE – PERFORMANCES
Earls Court Exhibition Hall, Earls Court, London, England

Set list at all shows: 'In The Flesh', 'The Thin Ice', 'Another Brick In The Wall, Part 1', 'The Happiest Days Of Our Lives', 'Another Brick In The Wall, Part 2', 'Mother', 'Goodbye Blue Sky', 'What Shall We Do Now?', 'Empty Spaces', 'Young Lust', 'One Of My Turns', 'Don't Leave Me Now', 'Another Brick In The Wall, Part 3', 'The Last Few Bricks', 'Goodbye Cruel World' <Intermission> 'Hey You', 'Is There Anybody Out There?', 'Nobody Home', 'Vera', 'Bring The Boys Back Home', 'Comfortably Numb', 'The Show Must Go On', 'In The Flesh?', 'Run Like Hell', 'Waiting For The Worms', 'Stop', 'The Trial', 'Outside The Wall'.

The show of Wednesday 17 June marked the last night of the tour and, significantly, the last time Waters would play with Pink Floyd for some 24 years. It was reported in the music press that second drummer John 'Willie' Wilson was taken ill just before the opening show. Clive Brooks, a Floyd roadie who happened to also be a former drummer of the Groundhogs, was given a crash course in the set's requirements by Nick Mason, and replaced Wilson for shows on Saturday 13 and Sunday 14 June.

TUESDAY 7 SEPTEMBER – MAY 1982 – FILMING
Pinewood Studios, Iver Heath, England ▶

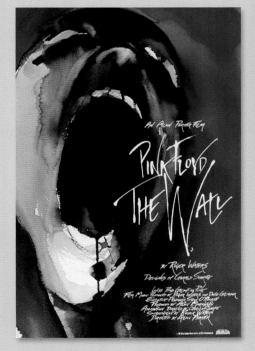

Sixty days of production filming began on *Pink Floyd The Wall* at Pinewood with Alan Parker directing. Filming continued here through to November and at various locations in England, including Wembley Empire Pool, now Wembley Arena (doubling as the LA Sports Arena), Saunton Sands, Devon (for the Anzio beach-head battlefield scenes), the Keighley & Worth Valley Railway, Yorkshire (including Mytholmes Tunnel between Haworth and Oakworth), the Royal Masonic School, Bushey (for the classroom scenes), Watford Football Club, Watford (for some scenes of crowd violence), Becton Gasworks, London (for the riot scenes), the Grand Union Canal at Kensal Green, London (where the young Pink throws a dead rat into the canal), and Muswell Hill near Alexandra Palace, London (for the 'Waiting For The Worms' march). The Royal Horticultural Society Hall, Victoria, London was used for the rally sequence and around 300 unemployed youngsters and students from the Thurrock area, including some skinheads, were recruited as extras for the film and cast as the fanatical black-shirted followers at a Nuremberg-style rally. They were recruited by Eva Samson Shaw the Warden of the Riverside Youth Centre in Tilbury. Eight double-decker buses were needed to take them to the film location and each person was paid between £50 and £100 for around two days' work on the film. Some scenes were cut from the final edit including a hotel room that is cut out of the wall, a scene of Pink's "brain" being eaten by live maggots and extended scenes of Pink in an asylum.

The animation process was largely taken care of in studios in central London and continued long after the live action filming had finished.

An end of filming party was held at the Chelsea Arts Club, London, England in May 1982 at which the Boomtown Rats performed a live set, including the songs 'Mustang Sally', 'Stir It Up', 'She Does It Right' and 'Stop! In The Name Of Love' among others. It is uncertain if any members of Pink Floyd joined the live entertainment.

SATURDAY 21 NOVEMBER – ALBUM RELEASE (US)
A Collection of Great Dance Songs

MONDAY 23 NOVEMBER – ALBUM RELEASE (UK)
A Collection of Great Dance Songs

NME wrote, "Exactly what form of body movement goes with Pink Floyd is anyone's guess. That slow, steady, rocking motion that you see in people falling asleep on buses, I should think."

1982

JANUARY – MARCH – RECORDING SESSIONS
Dubbing Theatre 2, Pinewood Studios, Iver Heath, England

Discontinuous recording of the music for the film soundtrack of *Pink Floyd The Wall*. This included the track 'When The Tigers Broke Free', which did not appear on the original album, and Bob Geldof's vocal for 'In The Flesh'.

MONDAY 1, THURSDAY 4, FRIDAY 5 & SATURDAY 6 FEBRUARY – RECORDING SESSIONS
Studio 1 & Control Room 1, Abbey Road Studios, London, England

Recording new orchestral parts for *The Wall* film soundtrack. The session on Monday 1 February was produced by John McLure, who produced the strings for *The Wall* album, and James Guthrie on the remaining dates. On the very last day of recording, Tim Renwick was invited to contribute a guitar overdub. "It was the short instrumental between 'Is There Anybody Out There?' and 'Nobody Home'", he recalled. "It is actually untitled and consists of classical guitar and orchestra. I recorded it at Abbey Road Studio 1; the orchestra was already on tape. Michael Kamen was producing and there were no members of the band present."

MAY – JUNE – RECORDING SESSIONS
The Billiard Room, Richmond, London, England

Discontinuous recording of Roger Waters' demos for *The Final Cut* were made at his home studio in south-west London. Among the first tracks written for the album were the tracks 'Your Possible Pasts', 'The Final Cut', 'The Post War Dream', 'The Hero's Return', 'The Fletcher Memorial Home' and 'Paranoid Eyes'.

SUNDAY 23 MAY – FILM PREMIERE
Pink Floyd The Wall, 35th Festival International Du Film, Palais des Festivals, Cannes, France

The world premiere of the film *Pink Floyd The Wall* was held at this prestigious annual film festival, although it was not entered into competition.

JUNE – RECORDING SESSIONS
The Billiard Room, Richmond, London, England; Hook End Studios, Hook End Manor, Checkendon, England; Mayfair Studios, Primrose Hill, London, England & Olympic Studios, Barnes, London, England

Discontinuous recording, overdubbing and remixing for the album *The Final Cut*. Mason's drum parts were predominately recorded at Olympic Studios, and Gilmour's guitar parts at Hook End, a studio which he owned at the time.

THURSDAY 17, FRIDAY 18, SATURDAY 19 & THURSDAY 24 JUNE – RECORDING SESSIONS
Mayfair Studios, Primrose Hill, London, England

Editing 'When The Tigers Broke Free' and 'Bring The Boys Back Home' (17–19 June) and remixing (24 June) for the 7-inch single.

THURSDAY 24 JUNE – FILM PREMIERE (US)
Pink Floyd The Wall, Ziegfeld Theater, New York, NY, USA

A preview of the film *Pink Floyd The Wall* was screened on this date. The event was announced via a full-page advert in the 20 June edition of the *New York Times*. The 8.00pm presentation sold out within 15 minutes and a further 10.30pm showing had to be added.

JULY – RECORDING SESSIONS
The Billiard Room, Richmond, London, England

Discontinuous recording, overdubbing and remixing for *The Final Cut*. Between July and October Waters completed the remaining songs that featured on the album, including 'The Gunner's Dream', 'Not Now John', 'Two Suns In The Sunset' and 'One Of The Few'.

WEDNESDAY 14 JULY – FILM PREMIERE (UK)
Pink Floyd The Wall, The Empire, Leicester Square, London, England

The world charity premiere of the film *Pink Floyd The Wall* in aid of the Nordoff-Robbins Music Therapy Centre was attended by Roger Waters, David Gilmour, Nick Mason, Bob Geldof and Gerald Scarfe as well as a host of celebrities including Sting, Lulu, Pete Townshend, Roger Taylor and Andy Summers. The film continued playing at the Empire cinema and opened nationally from Thursday 15 July.

MONDAY 19 JULY – SINGLE RELEASE (UK)
'When The Tigers Broke Free'

NME wrote that it was, "[o]ver inflated pomposity by the Pink Floyd Orchestra."

THURSDAY 22 & FRIDAY 23 JULY – RECORDING SESSIONS
Studio 1 & Control Room 1, Abbey Road Studios, London, England

Overdubs recorded by members of the National Philharmonic Orchestra and conducted by Michael Kamen for the tracks 'The Final

Cut', 'Paranoid Eyes', 'The Fletcher Memorial Home' and 'The Post War Dream' for *The Final Cut*.

MONDAY 26 JULY – SINGLE RELEASE (US)
'When The Tigers Broke Free'

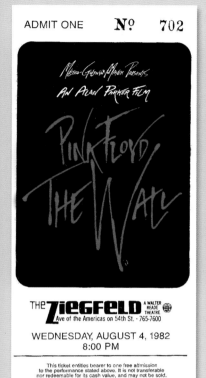

ADMIT ONE №? 702

Métso-Goldwyn-Mayer Presents
An Alan Parker Film

PINK FLOYD
THE WALL

THE ZIEGFELD A WALTER
READE
THEATRE
Ave of the Americas on 54th St. · 765-7600

WEDNESDAY, AUGUST 4, 1982
8:00 PM

This ticket entitles bearer to one free admission
to the performance stated above. It is not transferable
nor redeemable for its cash value, and may not be sold.

SUNDAY 8 AUGUST – FILM PREMIERE (US) ◄
***Pink Floyd The Wall*, Ziegfeld Theater, New York, NY, USA**

The official East Coast press premiere of the film *Pink Floyd The Wall*.

THURSDAY 12 AUGUST – FILM PREMIERE (US)
***Pink Floyd The Wall*, The Mann Village Theater, Los Angeles, CA, USA**

The official West Coast press premiere of the film *Pink Floyd The Wall*. The film opened for general release the day after.

SEPTEMBER – RECORDING SESSIONS
Olympic Studios, Barnes, London, England & Eel Pie Studios, Twickenham, England

Discontinuous recording for *The Final Cut*. One or two days were spent at Eel Pie recording Michael Kamen's piano parts.

OCTOBER – RECORDING SESSIONS
Hook End Studios, Hook End Manor, Checkendon, England; Olympic Studios, Barnes, London, England; RAK Studios, London, England & Mayfair Studios, Primrose Hill, London, England

Discontinuous recording, overdubbing and remixing for *The Final Cut*. Andy Newmark's drum parts on 'Two Suns In The Sunset' were recorded at Olympic, and Andy Bown's Hammond was recorded at RAK.

NOVEMBER – RECORDING SESSIONS
Mayfair Studios, Primrose Hill, London, England

Discontinuous recording and remixing for *The Final Cut*.

1983

WEDNESDAY 19 JANUARY – RECORDING SESSION
Mayfair Studios, Primrose Hill, London, England

Discontinuous recording and remixing for *The Final Cut*.

WEDNESDAY 26 – SUNDAY 30 JANUARY – RECORDING SESSIONS
Audio International Studios, Marylebone, London, England

Discontinuous overdubbing, remixing and sequencing for *The Final Cut*. The studio manager, Richard Millard, provided the vocal for the news broadcast as heard on 'The Post War Dream' and the forecast heard on 'Two Suns In The Sunset.'

FEBRUARY – RECORDING SESSIONS
Mayfair Studios, Primrose Hill, London, England

Discontinuous remixing and mastering for *The Final Cut*.

MONDAY 21 MARCH – ALBUM RELEASE (UK)
The Final Cut

NME wrote, "No matter how much Waters may burn and struggle over the sad, sick world he finds himself in along with the rest of us, his diagnoses sit in a stasis of unresolved, unmoving bitterness. Underneath the whimpering meditation and exasperated cries of rage it is the old, familiar rock beast: a man who is unhappy in his work."

WEDNESDAY 23 MARCH – PRESS RECEPTION
Madison Square Garden, New York, NY, USA

Columbia Records held a reception at this venue to launch *The Final Cut* to the US media.

SATURDAY 26 MARCH – ALBUM RELEASE (US)
The Final Cut

MONDAY 25 APRIL – SINGLE RELEASE (UK)
'Not Now John'

Sounds wrote, 'The dinosaur roars, part 365. More crushing misery from Roger Waters and the boys executed with all the consummate skill of Hadean craftsmen.'

MONDAY 2 MAY – SINGLE RELEASE (US)
'Not Now John'

1985

THURSDAY 12 DECEMBER – PRESS REPORT
London, England

Roger Waters was reported to have formally notified both EMI Records and CBS Records that he no longer considered himself to be a member of Pink Floyd by invoking his "leaving member" clause in his contract. Band manager Steve O'Rourke, believing that his contract with Waters had been terminated illegally, sued him for £25,000 in unpaid management commission.

PINK FLOYD, DECEMBER 1985 – JANUARY 1994

David Gilmour, Nick Mason.

THE FINAL CUT

pink
floyd
the
final
cut

SIDE ONE

THE POST WAR DREAM (Waters) **3:02**
YOUR POSSIBLE PASTS (Waters) **4:22**
ONE OF THE FEW (Waters) **1:23**
THE HERO'S RETURN (Waters) **2:56**
THE GUNNERS DREAM (Waters) **5:07**
PARANOID EYES (Waters) **3:40**

SIDE TWO

GET YOUR FILTHY HANDS OFF MY DESERT (Waters) **1:19**
THE FLETCHER MEMORIAL HOME (Waters) **4:11**
SOUTHAMPTON DOCK (Waters) **2:13**
THE FINAL CUT (Waters) **4:46**
NOT NOW JOHN (Waters) **5:01**
TWO SUNS IN THE SUNSET (Waters) **5:14**

RELEASE DATE

UK: Monday 21 March 1983.
US: Saturday 26 March 1983.

FORMAT

UK: EMI Harvest SHPF 1983 (Vinyl album).
US: Columbia QC 38243 (Vinyl album).

HIGHEST CHART POSITION

UK: No. 1 (*Music Week* "Top 100" on Saturday 2 April 1983).
US: No. 2 (*Billboard* "Top LPs & Tape" on Saturday 4 June 1983),
"Your Possible Pasts" No. 8 (*Billboard* "Album Rock Tracks"'on Saturday
9 April 1983).

AWARDS

UK: Certified Silver and Gold on Thursday 24 March 1983.
US: Certified Gold and Platinum on Monday 23 May 1983 and 2 x
Platinum on Friday 31 January 1997.

ARTWORK

In a departure from Gerald Scarfe's ubiquitous drawings of the
past four years, Waters took the credit for the design and, using
photographs taken by his brother-in-law Willie Christie, chose a more
conventional design to help illustrate his vision.

The front cover shows part of a remembrance poppy, and a
selection of British Second World War medal ribbons that would have
been awarded to a member of the Royal Air Force: the Distinguished
Flying Cross (white with diagonal purple stripes.), the 1939–45 Star
(equal stripes of dark blue, red and light blue), the Africa Star (sand
with dark blue, red and light blue stripes) and the Defence Medal
(orange with wide green edges bearing narrow black stripes). The rear
sleeve features an image of a soldier holding a film canister under his
arm with a knife in his back.

MUSICIANS

David Gilmour, Nick Mason, Roger Waters.

ADDITIONAL MUSICIANS

Andy Bown (Hammond organ).
Doreen Chanter and Irene Chanter (Backing Vocals on 'Not Now John').
Ray Cooper (Percussion).
Michael Kamen (Piano, Harmonium).
Andy Newmark (Drums on 'Two Suns In The Sunset').
Raphael Ravenscroft (Tenor Sax).
National Philharmonic Orchestra conducted and arranged by
Michael Kamen.

RECORDING DETAILS

Recorded at Mayfair Studios, London, England; Olympic Studios,
London, England; EMI Abbey Road Studios, London, England; Eel Pie
Studios, London, England; Audio International, London, England;
RAK Studios, London, England; Hookend Studios, London, England
and The Billiard Room Studios, London, England between July and
December 1982. Produced by Roger Waters, James Guthrie and
Michael Kamen and engineered by James Guthrie and Andy Jackson.

It was never going to be the most comfortable album to make,
and with Waters singular in his vision there was little room for
compromise. After an initial period of collaboration, both Waters
and Gilmour began working in isolation, Gilmour with James
Guthrie and Waters with Andy Jackson. Waters' vocals were recorded
for the most part at his home studio, the Billiard Room. During a
particularly fraught session in which Waters was having to repeat

at producer Michael Kamen
pad. Stopping to demand what
had been writing "I Must Not Fuck

our became increasingly concerned
album and its criticism of government
from his role as co-producer.
was less than enthusiastic of the
f its making aside from arranging
s.
aspect of the album is the use of
veloped by the Argentinean inventor

Hugo Zuccarelli. best appreciated throug
create a 360-degree impression of a soun
traditional two-channel stereo. Waters rep
The Pros and Cons of Hitch Hiking solo albu

PROMOTIONAL FILMS

A video EP featuring the tracks 'The Gunn
'Not Now John' and 'The Fletcher Memoria
release of the album and followed a narra
the eyes of war veteran Alex McAvoy (the
The Wall film).

pink floyd
the final cut

requiem for the post war dream
roger waters

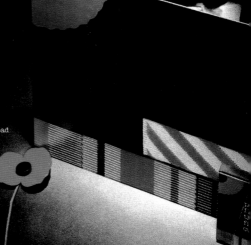

w music available on
vest records and cassettes
eased march 21

rformed by pink floyd
rid gilmour   nick mason   roger waters
h
chael kamen   piano   harmonium
dy bown   hammond organ
cooper   percussion
dy newmark   drums on "two suns"
hael ravenscroft   tenor sax
d the national philharmonic orchestra
iducted and arranged by michael kamen

e 1

e post war dream
ur possible pasts
e of the few
e hero's return
e gunner's dream
ranoid eyes

e II

your filthy hands off my desert
e fletcher memorial home
uthampton dock
e final cut
t now john
o suns in the sunset

oduced by
ger waters
nes guthrie and michael kamen

corded in england at mayfair   olympic   abbey road
pie   audio international   rak   hookend   and
e billiard room between july and december 1982

lophonics by
ccarelli labs. ltd ©

eric fletcher waters 1913-1944

vest

9 A NEW MACHINE

1986—93

1986–93

Behind the scenes, the question of Pink Floyd's future was being decided in a dramatic turn of events. In late 1985, shortly after his final *Pros and Cons of Hitch Hiking* tour, Roger Waters wrote to both EMI and CBS Records invoking his "leaving member" clause in his contract stating that he considered the band to be a "spent force" and that he wouldn't record with Gilmour and Mason ever again, or with anyone else as Pink Floyd, believing neither possessed the necessary qualities to carry on under the name.

Gilmour countered this by stating that he did not accept it could be Waters' sole decision to dissolve a band he had been a member of for some 17 years. Waters eventually had to concede: "They forced me to resign from the band because, if I hadn't, the financial repercussions would have wiped me out completely."[1]

But even then Waters could not have expected the others to carry on without him. However, a year later, at a routine board meeting of Pink Floyd Music Limited, he learnt that Gilmour and Mason were about to open a new bank account to pay out and receive money on what was being termed "the new Pink Floyd project". Outraged, and in a much-publicized chain of events, he claimed that the group was defunct and that Gilmour and Mason's pursuit, with or without his involvement, of any further projects was simply not acceptable.

As a result, Waters instigated High Court proceedings to legally determine the nature of the Pink Floyd partnership. He hoped that this would uphold his belief that, since he had written the bulk of its songs, he was entitled to prevent others' commercial exploitation of the name 'Pink Floyd'.

Within days the press was carrying misleading headlines stating that Pink Floyd had officially split up. But, Gilmour and Mason quickly countered with a statement issued by their record company, saying "Pink Floyd are alive, and well, and recording in England".

Gilmour was keen to set the record straight. Speaking to Nicky Horne on London's Capital Radio in early 1987, he said: "I think it's rather unnecessary. There's been many, many years together when we have achieved a lot together, and it's a shame when anyone wants to leave of course. But, everyone has to do what they want to do, and of course that's their decision. What is sad and unnecessary about it is trying to prevent anyone else from carrying on with their legitimate artistic and business endeavours."

Waters eventually dropped his legal action, conceding that Gilmour could continue to use the name "Pink Floyd". According to Gilmour in an interview with this author: "The situation is that Virgin wanted to release Waters' soundtrack [to *When the Wind Blows*] and in order to do so, EMI made him sign a piece of paper on the case saying, essentially, if you want to put this soundtrack out on another label, not to interfere with Pink Floyd being Pink Floyd, or pursue any activities in the name of Pink Floyd – which Roger signed and agreed to."[2] The mutual sniping continued throughout the next few years, but the two parties finally agreed to terms on their business affairs at an informal meeting held in December 1987.

Gilmour and Mason had been recording together since the autumn of 1986, having long been convinced that a new album was a better idea than just taking a greatest hits show out on the road. It was a shrewd gamble and, although over the next few months the going was tough, the result was an album that became a worldwide success. *A Momentary Lapse of Reason*, the recording of which was completed in March 1987, followed by three months' post-production in Los Angeles, was released in September of that year. The album was mainly recorded at Gilmour's River Thames houseboat studio, Astoria, with Bob Ezrin producing (much to Waters' consternation, since he had hoped Ezrin would work on his own *Radio K.A.O.S.* album). Significantly, it was the first Pink Floyd album in some fourteen years that didn't follow a conceptual path.

Not that a concept album wasn't attempted and a great deal of controversy surrounds the making of the album in an attempt to bind the project together. Eric Stewart, formerly of 10cc, had been drawn in via Nick Mason's second solo album,

Profiles, and recalled that, "Dave Gilmour and I got together around August or September 1986 to work on a concept that was definitely intended for the next Pink Floyd album. We sat around writing for a period of time, but we couldn't get the different elements to gel. The songwriting itself was acceptable in certain parts, but not as a whole, so the concept was eventually scrapped."[3]

Also drafted in was the English poet Roger McGough and Canadian songwriter Carole Pope. "The idea to contact me came from Bob Ezrin," explained Pope. "It was January 1987, and they were looking for somebody to rewrite a batch of Dave Gilmour's material, so I went over to England for a few weeks to lend assistance. Bob and David asked me if I had suggestions for concept albums in the Pink Floyd style. By the time I left England in February, they still couldn't decide what to do."[4]

Eventually, however, the idea of a concept album was abandoned in favour of a more conventional approach, with songs not linked thematically. Gilmour, who selected musicians whom he had met in recent years to help complete *A Momentary Lapse of Reason*, had become a respected session player and had performed at many charity events, including *Live Aid* (where he was the only Floyd member in attendance) and *The Secret Policeman's Ball.*

As for Rick Wright, the chance to return to the band was a welcome one, particularly since he had all but given up playing, his confidence, like Mason's, having been shattered. For legal reasons, however, Wright couldn't officially rejoin the band

and, in any case, the album was almost complete by the time he rejoined Gilmour and Mason.

When *A Momentary Lapse of Reason* appeared, much of Waters' expected criticism focused on the amount of supporting musicians they used, which infuriated Gilmour. In his opinion, "Roger never used to credit anyone. Yet he was always fussy about the credit for himself. I never had the time to worry about it, that sort of thing. On *Animals* for instance Roger took the credits for everything. Let's say that I wrote 70% of 'Sheep'. At least half of that album I played bass on and Roger was hardly in the studio during its recording. I played bass on almost all of the Pink Floyd albums, which is where Roger forgets that other people had huge, vast amounts of input, but at the time I never worried, so long as the product was completed."[5]

The album came over as a strange cross between the mechanical aspects of *Wish You Were Here* and the bleakness of *Animals*. Although it is basically a Gilmour solo album, as a first effort with a new lineup, it is an accomplished piece. At the least it offered a chance for the post-Waters band to gain self-confidence and begin the process of touring and recording again. The artwork saw Storm Thorgerson return to the fold once more. He turned Gilmour's lyric about visions of "empty beds" into reality by arranging some 800 old hospital beds on Saunton Sands beach in Devon as the basis for the cover shot. Additional artwork was also provided for the ensuing singles, tour programme, promo videos and tour backdrop films, completing the overall theme.

In order to make the comeback complete in this respect, Gilmour wanted to recreate the spectacle of the world-renowned Pink Floyd shows with a breathtaking production. With Mason (who used his valuable 1962 GTO Ferrari as security), they invested several millions of their personal wealth into the project.

Finding a promoter willing to take on an almost equal risk without knowing Pink Floyd's pulling power was likely to be a harder task than they first imagined since they had been redundant for so long. It had been over six years since the band had given a nationwide tour in either Europe or America and in addition, Waters' absence and legal threat was always going to be at the forefront of their minds. But for Michael Cohl, of the CPI Agency in Canada, who was about to have a similar success with the Rolling Stones, there was little doubt about their potential, and undaunted he took the band on.

Cohl's complete confidence was boosted on 27 April when tickets went on sale for a single show at the CNE Stadium in Toronto on 21 September. The result was that all 60,000 tickets went as fast as they could be printed, resulting in the quickest sell-out in the history of the venue. Hardly believing it, he put a second show on sale, with exactly the same result, then a third show, which also sold out, thus securing a gross income of over US$3 million.

In no time at all local promoters across North America were queuing up to take on the show, well before the album was released to radio or the public, and a massive tour was set in motion to run until the end of the year. In almost every location box-office records fell, making it the most successful US tour, by any band, that year.

To further complicate matters, Waters even went to the extent of writing to every promoter in North America threatening legal action. Gilmour and Mason played it safe by having a team of expert lawyers on hand at every city they played in, although ultimately it was a hollow threat and no actions were ever pursued.

The bankability of the name "Pink Floyd" had become increasingly apparent, and the tour simply snowballed. Tours of Australia, Japan, Europe and the UK followed, with two more tours of the US thrown in for good measure, and the band sold out at almost every venue.

For Waters, by contrast, the going was decidedly bleak. He had released *Radio K.A.O.S.* slightly ahead of *A Momentary Lapse of Reason* and decided to tour the US simultaneously. Whereas his former bandmates succeeded in selling out huge auditoria, he was struggling to pull a crowd even a third of the size. Overall, however, fans were spoilt for choice and benefited from seeing and hearing twice as much Floyd music. The side effect, of course, was that an unhealthy debate then raged between fans – fuelled by the media – over who was the rightful heir to the name. Waters further fanned the flames by having T-shirts printed for his tour with the defiant motif "Which One's Pink?" emblazoned on the front. Even the media was confused. The only certainty was that Pink Floyd's success was enduring, if baffling – a twenty-year-old rock band outstripping any other artist for sales and concert attendances the world over.

Putting Pink Floyd on the road was another matter entirely. Since they had last hit the road a great deal had happened in the world of stadium touring, from stage designs through to PA and lighting technology, and a massive investment had to be made to bring the show up to and beyond the fans' expectations. The Fisher-Park design team, hardly surprisingly, favoured working with Waters on his *Radio K.A.O.S.* tour, and for Pink Floyd the task was handed over to theatre set designer Paul Staples and lighting designer Marc Brickman. Whereas in their heyday the band had employed a handful of technicians, a crew of over a hundred strong was now required to maintain three separate stages, a massive team that leap-frogged across continents to keep the show moving.

The shows themselves incorporated many of the old trademarks: the giant circular film screen displayed much of the vintage footage, a flowering mirror ball, green-and-red lasers and over a hundred other lights. All of this was housed within a vast steel framework that measured some 80 feet high, 168 feet wide and 98 feet deep. Suspended from this were "pods" of lights and smoke machines attached to four moving units that were suspended from tracks above the stage, as well as smaller "Floyd Droids", as they became known, which rose from the stage to throw out light into the audience. Quadraphonic sound was also used, with some 240 speaker units making up the system, a crashing aeroplane during 'On The Run' (later replaced by a crashing bed, making further reference to the tour motif), an inflatable pig and a strange winged creature that launched skywards in 'Learning To Fly'.

It all made for a visually striking comeback, so much so that many reports suggested that the spectacle distracted from the music, which combined old and new. It came as a huge surprise that 'Echoes' opened the show, albeit only in the early concerts, followed by selections of the new album in the first half and a 'greatest hits' package in the second. The only frustrating aspect was that the set list remained unchanged throughout the entirety of the three-year tour, despite a rich heritage of numbers to choose from.

In November 1988, after the US tour, Pink Floyd released an album derived from recordings made at their New York concerts. *Delicate Sound of Thunder* also appeared as a video in June the following year and acted as a promotional tool for the current round of European dates.

A few days after the album's release, Gilmour and Mason accompanied President François Mitterand of France to the Baykonur Cosmodrome, in Kazakhstan, USSR, to attend the

RIGHT: ONE OF PINK FLOYD'S MORE UNUSUAL CONCERT LOCATIONS: A FLOATING STAGE MOORED NEAR THE PIAZZA SAN MARCO, VENICE, 15 JULY 1989.

BELOW: PINK FLOYD PERFORMING AT THE LONDON ARENA, JULY 1989.

launch of the Soyuz 7 space rocket, which was piloted by a Franco-Soviet crew. The cosmonauts had requested a cassette of the album to listen to when they rendezvoused with the orbiting MIR station. Pink Floyd thus made history as the first rock band to be played in space.

The comeback tour finally came to its official conclusion with a one-off show at Knebworth Park, north of London, in September 1990. It was a charity event in aid of the Nordoff Robbins Music Therapy Centre, which also saw performances by acts as diverse as Cliff Richard, Eric Clapton, Phil Collins, Tears for Fears and Status Quo, among many others and was

also televised. Unfortunately as a closing event to such a monumental tour, it was also a monumental disaster. Inclement weather – which also ripped Pink Floyd's screen rendering it useless – made it a thoroughly miserable experience for anyone unfortunate enough to attend, and rather like the Venice show of 1989 it was poorly organized.

At its conclusion, the tour had clocked up some 200 shows, attracting over 4.25 million fans and taking more than £60 million at the box office alone (merchandising revenues were separate). It certainly rammed the point home to a retreating Waters. Gilmour later summed up their return quite simply: "We wanted to leave no one in any doubt that we were still in business and meant business – and no one was going to stop us."[6]

Completing the reunion, Wright was now playing full time with the band. In this role he contributed substantially to the soundtrack for Gilmour, Mason and O'Rourke's self-produced film of their vintage motor-car racing exploits across Mexico, *La Carrera Panamericana*, which was released on video in April 1992.

1. *Uncut*, June 2004.

2. Glenn Povey & Richard Ashton interview with David Gilmour, 25 September 1987.

3–4. *Rock Lives* by Timothy White, Henry Holt 1990.

5. Glenn Povey & Richard Ashton interview with David Gilmour, 25 September 1987.

6. *Q Magazine*, September 1990.

DAY-BY-DAY 1986–93

1986

FRIDAY 31 OCTOBER – PRESS REPORT
London, England

In a late 1986 board meeting of Pink Floyd Music Limited, Roger Waters learnt that a new bank account had been opened to deal exclusively with all monies related to "the new Pink Floyd project". As he was still a shareholder in that company, he immediately began proceedings in the High Court in London in order to legally determine the nature of the Pink Floyd partnership in order to seek its dissolution, considering it to be a "spent force". Although Waters was eventually persuaded to drop the action, a bitter legal dispute continued over the next two years in order to determine the ownership of various assets, rights and intellectual property.

TUESDAY 11 NOVEMBER – PRESS REPORT
London, England

To counter Roger Waters' claims, EMI Records on behalf of the remaining members of Pink Floyd, issued a press release stating that "Pink Floyd are alive, well and recording in England", and that a new album release was anticipated during the late spring/early summer of 1987.

NOVEMBER – DECEMBER – RECORDING SESSIONS
The Astoria, Hampton, England & Britannia Row Studios, Islington, London, England

Undeterred and not wishing to cease trading under the name of Pink Floyd, David Gilmour and Nick Mason began discontinuous recording for *A Momentary Lapse of Reason*.

1987

JANUARY – FEBRUARY – RECORDING SESSIONS
The Astoria, Hampton, England & Britannia Row Studios, Islington, London England

Discontinuous recording for *A Momentary Lapse of Reason*.

FEBRUARY – RECORDING SESSIONS
Mayfair Studios, Primrose Hill, London, England & Audio International Studios, Marylebone, London, England

Discontinuous recording and mixing for *A Momentary Lapse of Reason*.

FEBRUARY – MARCH – RECORDING SESSIONS
A&M Studios, Los Angeles, CA, USA; Village Recorder, Los Angeles, USA & Can Am Studios, Los Angeles, CA, USA

Discontinuous recording and mixing for *A Momentary Lapse of Reason*.

MONDAY 6 APRIL – PRESS REPORT
London, England

Roger Waters' lawyers issued a statement to confirm that "a dispute with the other members of Pink Floyd is proceeding in the courts to resolve the question of the rights to the name and assets of Pink Floyd. Waters will not again record or perform with Dave Gilmour or Nick Mason under the name Pink Floyd or at all."

MONDAY 29 JUNE – PRESS REPORT
London, England

It was reported in the UK national press that Andrew Warburg, of investment brokers Norton Warburg (NWG), was jailed for three years for fraudulent trading and false accounting between October 1978 and March 1981.

A MOMENTARY LAPSE OF REASON WORLD TOUR (NORTH AMERICA)

ADDITIONAL TOUR PERSONNEL – 1988

Jon Carin (Keyboards, Vocals), Roberta Freeman (Backing Vocals Tuesday 3 to Thursday 5 November 1987), Rachel Fury (Backing vocals), Durga McBroom (Backing Vocals from Tuesday 3 November 1987), Scott Page (Saxophones, Guitars), Guy Pratt (Bass Guitar, Vocals), Tim Renwick (Guitars), Margret Taylor (Backing Vocals to Sunday 1 November 1987), Gary Wallis (Percussion), Richard Wright (Keyboards, Vocals).

PINK FLOYD ROAD CREW

Pink Floyd's last stadium tour of 1977 saw the band employ a core crew of around 20 persons to run the show. However, in the intervening years the touring machine had taken on a whole new dimension in logistics, sound, lighting and set design. To keep up with this demand, stadium tours now carried crews in excess of 200 personnel, including instrument technicians, sound and lighting technicians, laser technicians, pyrotechnicians, projectionists, caterers, wardrobe assistants, personal security, truck and bus drivers, site co-ordinators, scaffolders, electricians, riggers and even carpenters. A whole host of peripheral crew members were involved with the various contractors and companies providing all manner of technical equipment as well as the backroom staff developing and modifying equipment for specific use, plus managers and accountants. There's far too many to list here and if you really must know all of their names for this and all subsequent Pink Floyd tours, please consult the tour programmes!

AUGUST – REHEARSALS
Lester B. Pearson International Airport, Toronto, Canada

Pink Floyd made four weeks' use of a bonded warehouse, at a reported cost of $70,000 (Canadian), to rehearse their stage show, thus avoiding customs duty on imported sound equipment. A huge flying saucer, hovering over the audience's heads, was intended to have been a feature of the special effects for the outdoor shows, but insurance difficulties prevented its use.

A leaked video recording dated 7 August 1987, which may have been created for an unbroadcast MTV presentation, shows a well rehearsed show in which the band performed 'Echoes', 'Signs Of Life', 'Learning To Fly', 'A New Machine, Part 1', 'Terminal Frost', 'A New Machine, Part 2', 'Sorrow', 'The Dogs Of War', 'On The Turning Away', 'One Of These Days', 'Time', 'Wish You Were Here', 'Welcome To The Machine', 'Us And Them', 'Money', 'Another Brick In The Wall, Part 2', 'Comfortably Numb', 'One Slip' and 'Run Like Hell'.

MONDAY 7 SEPTEMBER – CANCELLED PERFORMANCE
Buffalo Memorial Auditorium, Buffalo, NY, USA

This show was listed on the initial tour schedule, but later withdrawn, before tickets went on sale.

MONDAY 7 SEPTEMBER – ALBUM RELEASE (UK)
A Momentary Lapse of Reason

Q Magazine wrote that "*A Momentary Lapse of Reason* is Gilmour's album to much the same degree that the previous four under Floyd's name were dominated by Waters (Mason's probably glad just to be along for the ride). Clearly it wasn't only business sense and repressed ego but repressed talent which drove the guitarist to insist on continuing under the band brand name."

MONDAY 7 SEPTEMBER – SINGLE RELEASE (UK) ▼
'Learning To Fly'

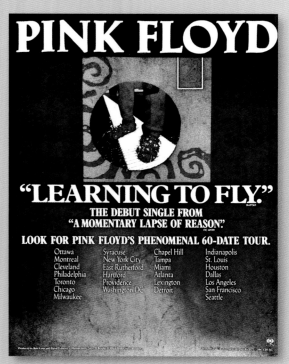

TUESDAY 8 SEPTEMBER – ALBUM RELEASE (US)
A Momentary Lapse of Reason

L.A. Times wrote, "It's hardly surprising that this album more often resembles a Gilmour solo LP than a Pink Floyd record. There's far less of the sometimes creepy verbal venom that characterizes Waters' songwriting and far more of Gilmour's fiery, piercing, almost metallic guitar lines. Indeed the lyrics are immersed in surreal sound tracks that range from shifting, billowy soundscapes to crunching, incendiary rock jams – often within the same song."

WEDNESDAY 9 SEPTEMBER – PERFORMANCE
Lansdowne Park Stadium,
Lansdowne Park, Ottawa, Canada

Set list: 'Echoes', 'Signs Of Life', 'Learning To Fly', 'Yet Another Movie', 'Round And Around', 'A New Machine, Part 1', 'Terminal Frost', 'A New Machine, Part 2', 'Sorrow', 'The Dogs Of War', 'On The Turning Away' <Intermission> 'One Of These Days', 'Time', 'On The Run', 'Wish You Were Here', 'Welcome To The Machine', 'Us And Them', 'Money', 'Another Brick In The Wall, Part 2', 'Comfortably Numb' <Encore> 'One Slip', 'Run Like Hell'.

Reviewing the show, *Canadian Press* reported, "Pink Floyd opened its world tour before about 25,000 fans Wednesday night with a multimedia extravaganza that soared during older songs, but bogged down on new material that made the absence of Roger Waters glaringly obvious…. The trio – augmented by a seven-member band – made no mention of Waters, who is on a solo tour and performing many Floyd songs. As an entertainment, it was a vintage spectacular; a comfortably numb experience enhanced by visual treats and pleasant 19-degree temperatures. For its first public performance in about five years, and first without Waters, the band trotted out many of the favourite tricks from its 1970s' shows like the giant inflated pig. And the plane. A replica flew across the football stadium on a guide wire and crashed beside the mammoth stage. Lighting modules descended from the ceiling like flying saucers. Voices and sound effects made heads turn sharply at the back of the stadium where additional speakers were set up as part of the band's quadraphonic sound system. But the band needs help. Except for Gilmour none of the musicians displayed much flash and everyone stands almost still. Many new songs are best described as droning dirges where the excitement is waiting for the monumental chord change. During the hour-long opening set, the aisles were busy with bored fans. Clearly everyone was waiting for the old stuff. It mesmerized those fans who consider a Pink Floyd concert the ultimate concert experience – especially on various recreational and industrial-strength drugs. In the end, the band delivered just what the fans wanted. Pink Floyd is no longer a leading creative entity, but as entertainment, a Floyd concert is still an aural and visual treat that any rock fan shouldn't miss."

SATURDAY 12, SUNDAY 13 & MONDAY 14 SEPTEMBER – PERFORMANCES
Forum de Montréal, Montréal, Canada

Set list: 'Echoes', 'Signs Of Life', 'Learning To Fly', 'Yet Another Movie', 'Round And Around', 'A New Machine, Part 1', 'Terminal Frost', 'A New Machine, Part 2', 'Sorrow', 'The Dogs Of War', 'On The Turning Away' <Intermission> 'One Of These Days', 'Time', 'On The Run', 'Wish You Were Here', 'Welcome To The Machine', 'Us And Them', 'Money', 'Another Brick In The Wall, Part 2', 'Comfortably Numb' <Encore> 'One Slip', 'Run Like Hell' <Second Encore> 'Shine On You Crazy Diamond'.

MONDAY 14 SEPTEMBER – SINGLE RELEASE (US)
'Learning To Fly'

WEDNESDAY 16 SEPTEMBER – PERFORMANCE
Municipal Stadium, Cleveland, OH, USA

Set list: 'Echoes', 'Signs Of Life', 'Learning To Fly', 'Yet Another Movie', 'Round And Around', 'A New Machine, Part 1', 'Terminal Frost', 'A New Machine, Part 2', 'Sorrow', 'The Dogs Of War', 'On The Turning Away' <Intermission> 'One Of These Days', 'Time', 'On The Run', 'Wish You Were Here', 'Welcome To The Machine', 'Us And Them', 'Money', 'Another Brick In The Wall, Part 2', 'Comfortably Numb' <Encore> 'One Slip', 'Run Like Hell' <Second Encore> 'Shine On You Crazy Diamond'.

THURSDAY 17 SEPTEMBER – PERFORMANCE
Municipal Stadium, Cleveland, OH, USA

Set list: 'Echoes', 'Signs Of Life', 'Learning To Fly', 'Yet Another Movie', 'Round And Around', 'A New Machine, Part 1', 'Terminal Frost', 'A New Machine, Part 2', 'Sorrow', 'The Dogs Of War', 'On The Turning Away' <Intermission> 'One Of These Days', 'Time', 'On The Run', 'Wish You Were Here', 'Welcome To The Machine', 'Us And Them', 'Money', 'Another Brick In The Wall, Part 2', 'Comfortably Numb' <Encore> 'One Slip', 'Run Like Hell'.

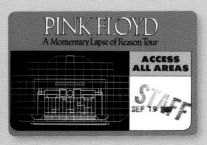

SATURDAY 19 SEPTEMBER – PERFORMANCE ◄
John F. Kennedy Stadium, Philadelphia, PA, USA

8.00pm show. Set list: 'Echoes', 'Signs Of Life', 'Learning To Fly', 'Yet Another Movie', 'Round And Around', 'A New Machine, Part 1', 'Terminal Frost', 'A New Machine, Part 2', 'Sorrow', 'The Dogs Of War', 'On The Turning Away' <Intermission> 'One Of These Days', 'Time', 'On The Run', 'Wish You Were Here', 'Welcome To The Machine', 'Us And Them', 'Money', 'Another Brick In The Wall, Part 2', 'Comfortably Numb' <Encore> 'One Slip', 'Run Like Hell' <Second Encore> 'Shine On You Crazy Diamond'.

MONDAY 21, TUESDAY 22 & WEDNESDAY 23 SEPTEMBER – PERFORMANCES ▼
Canadian National Exhibition Stadium, Toronto, Canada

Set list at all shows: 'Echoes', 'Signs Of Life', 'Learning To Fly', 'Yet Another Movie', 'Round And Around', 'A New Machine, Part 1', 'Terminal Frost', 'A New Machine, Part 2', 'Sorrow', 'The Dogs Of War', 'On The Turning Away' <Intermission> 'One Of These Days', 'Time', 'On The Run', 'Wish You Were Here', 'Welcome To The Machine', 'Us And Them', 'Money', 'Another Brick In The Wall, Part 2', 'Comfortably Numb' <Encore> 'One Slip', 'Run Like Hell' <Second Encore> 'Shine On You Crazy Diamond'.

On 27 April 1987 promoter CPI put the first show of Pink Floyd's 1987 *A Momentary Lapse of Reason* tour on sale. Within two hours all 60,052 tickets for 22 September had sold out, not only setting a record for the fastest sell-out in the history of the CNE, but

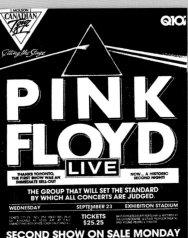

reassuring the industry that Pink Floyd's comeback would be a successful one.

FRIDAY 25 SEPTEMBER – PERFORMANCE
Rosemont Horizon, Rosemont, Chicago, IL, USA

Set list: 'Echoes', 'Signs Of Life', 'Learning To Fly', 'Yet Another Movie', 'Round And Around', 'A New Machine, Part 1', 'Terminal Frost', 'A New Machine, Part 2', 'Sorrow', 'The Dogs Of War', 'On The Turning Away' <Intermission> 'One Of These Days', 'Time', 'On The Run', 'Wish You Were Here', 'Welcome To The Machine', 'Us And Them', 'Money', 'Another Brick In The Wall, Part 2', 'Comfortably Numb' <Encore> 'One Slip', 'Run Like Hell'.

SATURDAY 26, SUNDAY 27 & MONDAY 28 SEPTEMBER – PERFORMANCES
Rosemont Horizon, Rosemont, Chicago, IL, USA

Set list at these and all remaining shows on this tour unless otherwise noted: 'Shine On You Crazy Diamond', 'Signs Of Life', 'Learning To Fly', 'Yet Another Movie', 'Round And Around', 'A New Machine, Part 1', 'Terminal Frost', 'A New Machine, Part 2', 'Sorrow', 'The Dogs Of War', 'On The Turning Away' <Intermission> 'One Of These Days', 'Time', 'On The Run', 'Wish You Were Here', 'Welcome To The Machine', 'Us And Them', 'Money', 'Another Brick In The Wall, Part 2', 'Comfortably Numb' <Encore> 'One Slip', 'Run Like Hell'.

WEDNESDAY 30 SEPTEMBER – PERFORMANCE ►
County Stadium, Milwaukee, WI, USA

The show featured, for the last time, a replica World War II German Stuka dive-bomber hurtling on a wire across the sky and crashing into the side of the stage for the culmination of 'On The Run'. Hereafter the tour motif, a large bed, replaced it. In addition, the huge scaffolding stage carried revolving radar dishes, flashing beacons and radio masts were not present at any of the later shows.

SATURDAY 3 OCTOBER – PERFORMANCE
Carrier Dome, Syracuse University, Syracuse, NY, USA

MONDAY 5, TUESDAY 6 & WEDNESDAY 7 OCTOBER – PERFORMANCES ►
Madison Square Garden, New York, NY, USA

SATURDAY 10, SUNDAY 11 & MONDAY 12 OCTOBER – PERFORMANCES ►
Brendan Byrne Arena, Meadowlands Sports Complex, East Rutherford, NJ, USA

After the show of 11 October, Gilmour, Mason, Scott Page, Rachel Fury, Margret Taylor, Guy Pratt and Tim Renwick made an impromptu

A MOMENTARY LAPSE OF REASON

A Momentary Lapse Of Reason

SIDE ONE

SIGNS OF LIFE (Gilmour, Ezrin) **4:24**
LEARNING TO FLY (Gilmour, Moore, Ezrin, Carin) **4:53**
THE DOGS OF WAR (Gilmour, Moore) **6:05**
ONE SLIP (Gilmour, Manzanera) **5:10**
ON THE TURNING AWAY (Gilmour, Moore) **5:42**

SIDE TWO

YET ANOTHER MOVIE / ROUND AND AROUND (Gilmour, Leonard / Gilmour) **7:28**
A NEW MACHINE (PART ONE) (Gilmour) **1:46**
TERMINAL FROST (Gilmour) **1:46**
A NEW MACHINE (PART TWO) (Gilmour) **0:38**
SORROW (Gilmour) **8:46**

RELEASE DATE

UK: Monday 7 September 1987.
US: Tuesday 8 September 1987.

FORMAT

UK: EMI EMD 1003 (Vinyl album) / UK: EMI CDP 7480682 (CD album).
US: Columbia OC 40599 (Vinyl album) / US: Columbia CK 40599 (CD album).

HIGHEST CHART POSITION

UK: No. 3 (*Music Week* 'Top 100 Albums' on Saturday 19 September 1987).
US: No. 1 (*Billboard* "Top Compact Discs" on Saturday 10 October 1987), No. 3 (*Billboard* 'Top Pop Albums' on Saturday 24 October 1987), "Learning To Fly" No. 1 (*Billboard* "Album Rock Tracks" on Saturday 3 October 1987), "On The Turning Away" No. 1 (*Billboard* "Album Rock Tracks" on Saturday 16 January 1988), "Dogs Of War" No. 44 (*Billboard* "Album Rock Tracks" on Saturday 7 November 1987), "One Slip" No. 5 (*Billboard* "Album Rock Tracks" on Saturday 31 October 1987), "Sorrow" No. 36 (*Billboard* "Album Rock Tracks" on Saturday 12 March 1988).

AWARDS

UK: Certified Silver and Gold on Thursday 1 October 1987.
US: Certified Gold and Platinum on 9 November 1987; 2 x Multi-Platinum on 18 January 1988; 3 x Multi-Platinum on 10 March 1992 and 4 x Multi-Platinum on 16 August 2001.

ARTWORK

Artwork by Storm Thorgerson. The front cover shot was taken at Saunton Sands, Devon, England using 800 wrought-iron hospital beds and won photographer Robert Dowling a gold award at the Association of Photographers Awards for his photo. The band portrait was by David Bailey.

PROMOTIONAL VIDEOS

A series of promo videos were shot to support the album and subsequent tour. 'Learning To Fly', the lead single from the album, had a film directed by Storm Thorgerson set against the backdrop of West Wind Ridge some 50 miles west of Calgary. It featured a native American Indian played by Lawrence Bayne who, by jumping off a cliff face, transformed from a field-worker into a soaring eagle. A further section featured a factory worker who becomes an aircraft pilot and a child who breaks free from the clutches of his mother by diving off a cliff and swimming away in the waters below. This is interspersed with concert footage, in this case taken from the track 'One Of These Days', shot at the band's tour rehearsals in Toronto. It reached No. 9 on MTV's "Video Countdown" in January 1988 and won an MTV Video Music Award for the "Best Concept Video" in 1988.

Videos for 'One Slip' and 'On The Turning Away' were screened to a lesser extent and featured mainly live footage directed by Lawrence Jordan and edited from concert footage shot at the Omni, Atlanta, USA on 3–5 November 1987.

MUSICIANS

David Gilmour, Nick Mason.

ADDITIONAL MUSICIANS

Carmine Appice (Drums on 'The Dogs Of War').
Jon Carin (Keyboards on 'Learning To Fly', 'The Dogs Of War', 'One Slip', 'Round And Around' and 'Terminal Frost'; Synthesizers on 'Signs Of Life', 'On The Turning Away' and 'Terminal Frost'; Drums on 'Round And Around').

Bob Ezrin (Sequencers, Keyboards on 'Terminal Frost', 'One Slip' and 'Sorrow'. Percussion on 'Learning To Fly' and 'Terminal Frost'; Drums on 'Round And Around').

Steve Forman (Percussion on 'Learning To Fly' and 'Yet Another Movie').

Donnie Gerrard (Backing Vocals on 'Learning To Fly', 'The Dogs Of War', 'One Slip' and 'Sorrow').

John Helliwell (Saxophone, credited as "John Halliwell", on 'Terminal Frost').

Jim Keltner (Drums on 'One Slip', 'On The Turning Away' and 'Yet Another Movie').

Darlene Koldenhoven (Backing Vocals on 'Learning To Fly', 'The Dogs Of War', 'One Slip' and 'Sorrow').

Michael Landau (Guitar on 'One Slip').

Patrick Leonard (Synthesizers on 'Yet Another Movie' and 'A New Machine, Part One').

Tony Levin (Bass guitar on 'Signs Of Life', 'Learning To Fly', 'The Dogs Of War', 'On The Turning Away', 'Yet Another Movie', 'Round And Around', 'Terminal Frost' and 'Sorrow'; Chapman Stick on 'One Slip').

Scott Page (Tenor Saxophone on 'The Dogs Of War').

Bill Payne (Hammond Organ on 'The Dogs Of War').

Phyllis St James (Backing Vocals on 'Learning To Fly', 'The Dogs Of War', 'One Slip' and 'Sorrow').

Tom Scott (Alto and Soprano Saxophone on 'The Dogs Of War' and 'Terminal Frost').

Carmen Twillie (Backing Vocals on 'Learning To Fly', 'The Dogs Of War', 'One Slip' and 'Sorrow').

Richard Wright (Backing Vocals; Keyboards on 'Learning To Fly'; Kurzweil on 'Signs Of Life', 'Terminal Frost' and 'Sorrow'; Hammond Organ on 'On The Turning Away' and 'Terminal Frost').

RECORDING DETAILS

Recorded at the Astoria, Hampton, England; Britannia Row Studios, London, England; Mayfair Studios, London, England; Audio International Studios, London, England; A&M Studios, Los Angeles, USA; Village Recorder, Los Angeles, USA; and Can Am Studios, Los Angeles, USA.

Produced by Bob Ezrin and David Gilmour and engineered and mixed by Andrew Jackson with additional re-mixing by James Guthrie.

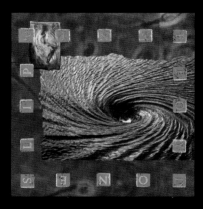

ABOVE: THE ARTWORK FOR *A MOMENTARY LAPSE OF REASON'S* THREE SINGLE RELEASES – 'LEARNING TO FLY', 'ON THE TURNING AWAY' AND 'ONE SLIP'.

A Momentary Lapse of Reason began life in the wake of the legal calamity following Roger Waters' declaration that he had left Pink Floyd. This provided David Gilmour with the catalyst to divert his attentions to what was either going to be a solo album, or indeed a new band, into a new Pink Floyd project.

Producer Bob Ezrin was hired as producer and Gilmour, never a confident lyricist, reportedly then recruited a range of collaborators, including Carole Pope, Roger McGough and Eric Stewart at various stages to assist him in creating a Pink Floyd-sounding album. According to some sources, "Dave was read the riot act at a Thames-side luncheon with Ezrin and CBS's Stephen Ralbosky, who allegedly told him, 'This music doesn't sound a fucking thing like Pink Floyd!'"[1]

Gilmour then went back to the drawing board to develop what music he did have with Bob Ezrin and the talents of Jon Carin at his side (whom he had met during his performance at *Live Aid* in Bryan Ferry's band), and then found a lyrical collaborator in Anthony Moore, who was ultimately responsible for the breakthrough track by penning the lyrics to 'Learning To Fly'. "It was a turning point", recalled Ezrin. "That memorable signal song. It was a real collaboration, but it felt like a complete Floyd work."[2]

Gilmour soon found his stride but a raft of session musicians had to be hired to help fill out the album. Mason was both out of practice and lacking confidence with his playing, and Wright came back on board far too late to make any significant contribution, although he does add his touch to a fair few tracks on the album.

By his own admission, Gilmour confessed that, "Recording *A Momentary Lapse of Reason* was a very, very difficult process. We were all sort of catatonic. Unfortunately, we didn't really work together an awful lot."[3]

For all its faults, looking back at *A Momentary Lapse of Reason* it is reasonably fair to say that it restored the balance of music versus the lyrics taking the sole centre stage during Pink Floyd's latter years, something Gilmour was keen to convey. In the same way *The Final Cut* is often perceived as a Waters solo album, so too is *A Momentary Lapse of Reason* perceived as a Gilmour solo work.

1. *A Saucerful of Secrets* by Nicholas Schaffner, Harmony Books, 1991.
2. *Q Magazine*, Pink Floyd Special Edition, September 2004.
3. *GuitarWorld*, September 1994.

appearance at the World Club, New York City, where they performed a 40-minute set of R&B standards, including 'Respect', 'Born Under A Bad Sign', 'Living In The City', 'I Heard It Through The Grapevine' and 'Kansas City'.

WEDNESDAY 14 & THURSDAY 15 OCTOBER – PERFORMANCES
Hartford Civic Center, Hartford, CT, USA

FRIDAY 16 & SATURDAY 17 OCTOBER – PERFORMANCES
Providence Civic Center, Providence, RI, USA

MONDAY 19, TUESDAY 20, WEDNESDAY 21 & THURSDAY 22 OCTOBER – PERFORMANCES
Capital Centre, Landover, MD, USA

SUNDAY 25 & MONDAY 26 OCTOBER – PERFORMANCES
Dean E. Smith Student Activities Center, University of North Carolina, Chapel Hill, NC, USA

FRIDAY 30 OCTOBER – PERFORMANCE
Tampa Stadium, Tampa, FL, USA

SUNDAY 1 NOVEMBER – PERFORMANCE
Orange Bowl, Miami, FL, USA

Heavy rainfall at the show prevented the inflatable pig from making an appearance. Backing vocalist Margret Taylor left the tour after this date to be replaced by Durga McBroom.

TUESDAY 3, WEDNESDAY 4 & THURSDAY 5 NOVEMBER – PERFORMANCES
The Omni Coliseum, Atlanta, GA, USA

All three shows were filmed using 23 Panavision cameras for promotional use, including videos for 'The Dogs Of War', 'On The Turning Away' and 'One Slip'. In addition, tracks from this concert, including 'Run Like Hell', 'The Dogs Of War' and 'On The Turning Away', were used as B-sides for a number of single releases and featured additional backing vocalists Roberta Freeman and Lorelei McBroom for these three dates. The entire concert film was due to be screened on various European networks, but was withdrawn at the last minute for unknown reasons.

SATURDAY 7 & SUNDAY 8 NOVEMBER – PERFORMANCES
Rupp Arena, Civic Center, Lexington, KY, USA

TUESDAY 10 NOVEMBER – PERFORMANCE
Pontiac Silverdome, Pontiac, Detroit, MI, USA

WEDNESDAY 11 & THURSDAY 12 NOVEMBER – PERFORMANCE
Hoosier Dome, Indianapolis, IN, USA

SUNDAY 15 & MONDAY 16 NOVEMBER – PERFORMANCES
St Louis Arena, St Louis, MO, USA

WEDNESDAY 18 NOVEMBER – PERFORMANCE
Astrodome, Houston, TX, USA

THURSDAY 19 & FRIDAY 20 NOVEMBER – PERFORMANCES
Frank Erwin Center, University of Texas, Austin, TX, USA

SATURDAY 21, SUNDAY 22 & MONDAY 23 NOVEMBER – PERFORMANCES
Reunion Arena, Reunion Park, Dallas, TX, USA

MONDAY 23 NOVEMBER – SINGLE RELEASE (US)
'On The Turning Away'

THURSDAY 26, FRIDAY 27, SATURDAY 28, MONDAY 30 NOVEMBER & TUESDAY 1 DECEMBER – PERFORMANCES ▼
Los Angeles Memorial Sports Arena, Exposition Park, Los Angeles, CA, USA

THURSDAY 3, FRIDAY 4, SATURDAY 5 & SUNDAY 6 DECEMBER – PERFORMANCES
Oakland Coliseum Arena, Oakland, CA, USA

MONDAY 7 DECEMBER – SINGLE RELEASE (UK)
'On The Turning Away'

TUESDAY 8 DECEMBER – PERFORMANCE
Kingdome, Seattle, WA, USA

THURSDAY 10 & FRIDAY 11 DECEMBER – PERFORMANCES
British Columbia Place Stadium, Vancouver, Canada

WEDNESDAY 23 DECEMBER – PRESS REPORT
London, England

Roger Waters and David Gilmour signed an agreement effectively ending their legal dispute over the rights to the Pink Floyd name. Gilmour was allowed to retain the use of the name, but one of the stipulations of the agreement was for Roger Waters to retain all rights pertaining to *The Wall*.

1988

A MOMENTARY LAPSE OF REASON WORLD TOUR (AUSTRALASIA)

FRIDAY 22 JANUARY – PERFORMANCE ◄
Western Springs Stadium, Auckland, New Zealand

A full dress rehearsal was performed at this venue on 21 January. Set list at this and all remaining shows on the tour unless otherwise noted: 'Shine On You Crazy Diamond', 'Signs Of Life', 'Learning To Fly', 'Yet Another Movie', 'Round And Around', 'A New Machine, Part 1', 'Terminal Frost', 'A New Machine, Part 2', 'Sorrow', 'The Dogs Of War', 'On The Turning Away' <Intermission> 'One Of These Days', 'Time', 'On The Run', 'Wish You Were Here', 'Welcome To The Machine', 'Us And Them', 'Money', 'Another Brick In The Wall, Part 2', 'Comfortably Numb' <Encore> 'One Slip', 'Run Like Hell'.

WEDNESDAY 27, THURSDAY 28, FRIDAY 29, SATURDAY 30 JANUARY AND MONDAY 1, TUESDAY 2, WEDNESDAY 3, THURSDAY 4 & FRIDAY 5 FEBRUARY – PERFORMANCES
Sydney Entertainment Centre, Sydney, Australia

In a PR stunt to publicize the shows on 29 January, an inflatable pig was raised above the Sydney Harbour Bridge and mysteriously slipped its moorings, in a repeat of the *Animals* cover shoot escapade in 1976.

THURSDAY 28 JANUARY – PRESS RECEPTION
Tattershall Castle, **River Thames, London, England**

A press reception to announce tickets going on sale for Pink Floyd's upcoming UK tour was held aboard the riverboat *Tattershall Castle*, which was moored at Westminster near the Houses of Parliament. The tour motif, a huge inflatable bed, was also hoisted above the boat.

SUNDAY 7 & MONDAY 8 FEBRUARY – PERFORMANCES
Entertainment Centre, Boondall, Brisbane, Australia

THURSDAY 11 FEBRUARY – PERFORMANCE
Thebarton Oval, Adelaide, Australia

SATURDAY 13, SUNDAY 14, MONDAY 15, TUESDAY 16, WEDNESDAY 17, THURSDAY 18, FRIDAY 19 & SATURDAY 20 FEBRUARY – PERFORMANCES
National Tennis Centre, Melbourne, Australia

Members of the touring party, including David Gilmour, Guy Pratt, Gary Wallis, Tim Renwick, Scott Page, Margaret Taylor,

Rachel Fury, Durga McBroom and Jon Carin performed under the name the Fishermen on 17 February and again on 19 February in after-show gigs at the Corner Hotel in Richmond, Melbourne to crowds of about 200. The first show also featured the late Roy Buchanan and 1970s Floyd backing vocalist Venetta Fields, who reportedly sang an amazing version of 'Little Red Rooster'. The second show saw the Fishermen perform a set that included 'Respect', 'I Shot The Sheriff', 'Unchain My Heart', 'Superstition', 'Reeling In The Years', 'Good Lovin' Gone Bad' and 'Pick Up The Pieces'.

WEDNESDAY 24 FEBRUARY – PERFORMANCE
East Fremantle Oval, Perth, Australia

A MOMENTARY LAPSE OF REASON WORLD TOUR (JAPAN)

WEDNESDAY 2 & THURSDAY 3 MARCH – PERFORMANCES ▼
Budokan Grand Hall, Kitanomaru Park, Tokyo, Japan

Set list at this and all remaining shows on the tour unless otherwise noted: 'Shine On You Crazy Diamond', 'Signs Of Life', 'Learning To Fly', 'Yet Another Movie', 'Round And Around', 'A New Machine, Part 1', 'Terminal Frost', 'A New Machine, Part 2', 'Sorrow', 'The Dogs Of War', 'On The Turning Away' <Intermission> 'One Of These Days', 'Time', 'The Great Gig In The Sky', 'Wish You Were

Here', 'Welcome To The Machine', 'Us And Them', 'Money' (extended version), 'Another Brick In The Wall, Part 2', 'Comfortably Numb' <Encore> 'One Slip', 'Run Like Hell'.

FRIDAY 4, SATURDAY 5 & SUNDAY 6 MARCH – PERFORMANCES
Yoyogi Olympic Pool, Shibuya, Tokyo, Japan

TUESDAY 8 & WEDNESDAY 9 MARCH – PERFORMANCES
Joh Hall, Osaka, Japan

FRIDAY 11 MARCH – PERFORMANCES
Rainbow Hall, Nagoya, Japan

A MOMENTARY LAPSE OF REASON WORLD TOUR (NORTH AMERICA)

FRIDAY 15 APRIL – PERFORMANCE
Memorial Coliseum, Los Angeles, CA, USA

A full dress rehearsal was performed at the venue on 14 April. Set list at this and all remaining shows on the tour unless otherwise noted: 'Shine On You Crazy Diamond', 'Signs Of Life', 'Learning To Fly', 'Yet Another Movie', 'Round And Around', 'A New Machine, Part 1', 'Terminal Frost', 'A New Machine, Part 2', 'Sorrow', 'The Dogs Of War', 'On The Turning Away' <Intermission> 'One Of These Days', 'Time', 'On The Run', 'The Great Gig In The Sky', 'Wish You Were Here', 'Welcome To The Machine', 'Us And Them', 'Money' (extended version), 'Another Brick In The Wall, Part 2', 'Comfortably Numb' <Encore> 'One Slip', 'Run Like Hell'.

MONDAY 18 APRIL – PERFORMANCE
Mile High Stadium, Denver, CO, USA

WEDNESDAY 20 APRIL – PERFORMANCE
Hughes Stadium, California State University at Sacramento, Sacramento, CA, USA

A 30-minute pre-show soundcheck saw the band work through various guitar and drum solos as well as vocal and guitar parts for 'Learning To Fly' and complete run-throughs of 'On The Turning Away', 'Yet Another Movie' and 'Sorrow'.

FRIDAY 22 & SATURDAY 23 APRIL – PERFORMANCES
Day on the Green, **Oakland Coliseum Stadium, Oakland, CA, USA**

MONDAY 25 & TUESDAY 26 APRIL – PERFORMANCES
Municipal Stadium, Phoenix, AZ, USA

THURSDAY 28 APRIL – PERFORMANCE
Texas Stadium, Irving, Dallas, TX, USA

SATURDAY 30 APRIL – PERFORMANCE
Citrus Bowl, Orlando, FL, USA

A shortened set was performed due to inclement weather: 'Signs Of Life', 'Learning To Fly', 'Yet Another Movie', 'Round And Around', 'A New Machine, Part 1', 'Terminal Frost', 'A New Machine, Part 2', 'Sorrow', 'The Dogs Of War', 'On The Turning Away' <Intermission> 'One Of These Days', 'Time', 'The Great Gig In The Sky', 'Wish You Were Here', 'Us And Them', 'Money' (extended version), 'Another Brick In The Wall, Part 2', 'Comfortably Numb' <Encore> 'One Slip', 'Run Like Hell'.

WEDNESDAY 4 MAY – PERFORMANCE
Carter-Finley Stadium, North Carolina State University, Raleigh, NC, USA

FRIDAY 6 & SUNDAY 8 MAY – PERFORMANCES
Foxboro Stadium, Foxborough, Boston, MA, USA

The show on 6 May saw the inflatable pig grabbed by the audience as it flew overhead, and torn down and destroyed.

WEDNESDAY 11 MAY – PERFORMANCE
Stade du Parc Olympique, Montréal, Canada

FRIDAY 13 MAY – PERFORMANCE
Canadian National Exhibition Stadium, Toronto, Canada

SATURDAY 14 & SUNDAY 15 MAY – TELEVISION BROADCAST
Pink Floyd Weekend, **MTV, USA**

MTV hosted a Pink Floyd weekend to promote the current tour. Interspersed throughout the regular programming were interviews with band and current touring musicians, clips from the 1987 tour rehearsals in Toronto, screen videos for 'Money', 'Brain Damage', 'Eclipse', 'Dogs Of War', 'Learning To Fly', 'Time' and 'Welcome To The Machine', the film *Crystal Voyager*, the inflatable pig over Battersea Power Station, 'Point Me At The Sky' and 'Another Brick In The Wall, Part 2'.

SUNDAY 15 & MONDAY 16 MAY – PERFORMANCES
Veterans Stadium, Philadelphia, PA, USA

WEDNESDAY 18 MAY – PERFORMANCE
University of Northern Iowa Dome, Cedar Falls, IA, USA

FRIDAY 20 MAY – PERFORMANCE
Camp Randall Stadium, University of Madison-Wisconsin, Madison, WI, USA

SATURDAY 21 & SUNDAY 22 MAY – PERFORMANCES
Rosemont Horizon, Rosemont, Chicago, IL, USA

TUESDAY 24 MAY – PERFORMANCE
Hubert H. Humphrey Metrodome, Minneapolis, MN, USA

THURSDAY 26 MAY – PERFORMANCE
Arrowhead Stadium, Kansas City, MO, USA

SATURDAY 28 MAY – PERFORMANCE
Ohio State University Stadium, Colombus, OH, USA

MONDAY 30 MAY – PERFORMANCE
Three Rivers Stadium, Pittsburgh, PA, USA

A power failure during 'Sorrow' forced a 10-minute break until it was restored.

WEDNESDAY 1 JUNE – PERFORMANCE
Robert F. Kennedy Stadium, Washington, DC, USA

FRIDAY 3, SATURDAY 4 & SUNDAY 5 JUNE – PERFORMANCES
Giants Stadium, East Rutherford, NJ, USA

A MOMENTARY LAPSE OF REASON WORLD TOUR (EUROPE)

THURSDAY 9 JUNE – PRESS RECEPTION
Château de Versailles, France

Pink Floyd held a press reception to launch their tour of France and specifically their upcoming historic performances at Versailles on 21 and 22 June 1988.

FRIDAY 10 JUNE – PERFORMANCE ◄
Stade de la Beaujoire, Nantes, France

Set list at this and all remaining shows on the tour unless otherwise noted: 'Shine On You Crazy Diamond', 'Signs Of Life', 'Learning To Fly', 'Yet Another Movie', 'Round And Around', 'A New Machine, Part 1', 'Terminal Frost', 'A New Machine, Part 2', 'Sorrow', 'The Dogs Of War', 'On The Turning Away' <Intermission> 'One Of These Days', 'Time', 'The Great Gig In The Sky', 'Wish You Were Here', 'Welcome To The Machine', 'Us And Them', 'Money' (extended version), 'Another Brick In The Wall, Part 2', 'Comfortably Numb' <Encore> 'One Slip', 'Run Like Hell'.

MONDAY 13 JUNE – SINGLE RELEASE (UK)
'One Slip'

MONDAY 13 & TUESDAY 14 JUNE – PERFORMANCES
Stadion Feyenoord, Rotterdam, Netherlands

'A New Machine, Part 1', 'Terminal Frost' and 'A New Machine, Part 2' were not performed at these shows.

THURSDAY 16 JUNE – PERFORMANCE
Reichstagsgelände, Platz der Republik, West Berlin, West Germany

SATURDAY 18 JUNE – PERFORMANCE
Maimarktgelände, Mannheim, West Germany

TUESDAY 21 & WEDNESDAY 22 JUNE – PERFORMANCES ►
Place d'Armee, Chateau de Versailles, France

Both shows were filmed for use on the *Delicate Sound of Thunder* concert video, but only a small segment of 'The Great Gig In The

Sky' with some audience shots was used in the finished film. As a result of the light summer evenings and unsuitability for filming the show, they were both delayed to a 10.30pm start. Pink Floyd and members of the touring band were interviewed for the UK's Channel 4 TV music programme *Wired* prior to the show. It was broadcast on 24 June 1988 between 11.05pm and 12.15am.

SATURDAY 25 JUNE – PERFORMANCE
Niedersachsenstadion, Hannover, West Germany

MONDAY 27, TUESDAY 28 & WEDNESDAY 29 JUNE – PERFORMANCES
Westfalenhalle, Dortmund, West Germany

A 45-minute pre-show soundcheck saw the band work through various tune-ups, 'Learning To Fly' (in part), various improvisations, 'Signs Of Life', various improvisations, 'Learning To Fly' and a variation of 'Young Lust'.

FRIDAY 1 JULY – PERFORMANCE
Praterstadion, Vienna, Austria

'A New Machine, Part 1', 'Terminal Frost' and 'A New Machine, Part 2' were not performed at these shows.

SUNDAY 3 JULY – PERFORMANCE
Olympiastadion, Munich, West Germany

'A New Machine, Part 1', 'Terminal Frost' and 'A New Machine, Part 2' were not performed at these shows.

WEDNESDAY 6 JULY – PERFORMANCE
Stadio Comunale, Turin, Italy

FRIDAY 8 & SATURDAY 9 JULY – PERFORMANCES
Stadio Comunale Braglia, Modena, Italy

MONDAY 11 & TUESDAY 12 JULY – PERFORMANCES
Stadio Flaminio, Rome, Italy

FRIDAY 15 JULY – PERFORMANCE
Stade du Municipal Charles Berty, Grenoble, France

Rescheduled from Stade de Gerland, Lyon.

SUNDAY 17 JULY – PERFORMANCE
Stade de l'Ouest, Nice, France

WEDNESDAY 20 JULY – PERFORMANCE
Estadi de Sarrià (RCD Espanol), Barcelona, Spain

FRIDAY 22 JULY – PERFORMANCE
Estadio Vicente Calderón, Madrid, Spain

Members of the touring party, including David Gilmour, Guy Pratt, Gary Wallis, Scott Page, Rachel Fury, Durga McBroom and Pink Floyd's security manager Barrie Knight, performed a short rhythm-and-blues set in an after-show gig at the Oh! Madrid club, Madrid, Spain.

SUNDAY 24 JULY – PERFORMANCE
Espace Richter, Montpellier, France

TUESDAY 26 JULY – PERFORMANCE
Fussballstadion St Jakob, Basel, Switzerland

THURSDAY 28 JULY – PERFORMANCE
Stadium du Nord, Villeneuve d'Ascq, Lille, France

SUNDAY 31 JULY – PERFORMANCE
Gentofte Stadion, Copenhagen, Denmark

Rescheduled from Sunday 21 August due to the addition of further North American dates. Members of the touring party, including David Gilmour, Richard Wright, Guy Pratt, Gary Wallis, Scott Page, Rachel Fury, Durga McBroom and Pink Floyd's security manager Barrie Knight, performed a short set under the name the Fishermen in an after-show gig at Annabel's Night Club, Copenhagen, Denmark. The set included 'Respect', 'Can't Get Enough Of Your Love', a blues instrumental, 'My Girl', a medley comprising 'Rock Steady', 'Rapper's Delight' and 'Le Freak', 'Rock Steady', 'Master Blaster' and 'Superstition'.

TUESDAY 2 AUGUST – PERFORMANCE
Valle Hovin Stadion, Oslo, Norway

Rescheduled from Friday 19 August due to the addition of further North American dates. 'A New Machine, Part 1', 'Terminal Frost' and 'A New Machine, Part 2' were not performed at these shows.

FRIDAY 5 &
SATURDAY 6 AUGUST
– PERFORMANCES ▶
Wembley Stadium,
Wembley, England

'A New Machine, Part 1', 'Terminal Frost' and 'A New Machine, Part 2' were not performed at these shows.

MONDAY 8 AUGUST –
PERFORMANCE
Maine Road Football
Club, Moss Side,
Manchester,
England

Rescheduled from Monday 1 and Tuesday 2 August. 'A New Machine, Part 1', 'Terminal Frost' and 'A New Machine, Part 2' were not performed at these shows.

WEDNESDAY 10 AUGUST – CANCELLED PERFORMANCE
Jumping Arena, Royal Dublin Showgrounds, Dublin,
Republic of Ireland

Show cancelled, allegedly due to poor ticket sales.

PINK FLOYD
IN CONCERT
WEMBLEY STADIUM
FRIDAY 5th AUGUST
SPECIAL ENCLOSURE
ENTRANCE 81 and 82
Special enclosure seating can only be entered through Entrance 81 or 82.
Enter by Gate F
Not valid unless accompanied by a concert ticket.
Not transferable must be stuck on.

A MOMENTARY LAPSE OF REASON WORLD TOUR (NORTH AMERICA)

FRIDAY 12, SATURDAY 13 & SUNDAY 14 AUGUST –
PERFORMANCES
The Coliseum, Richfield, Cleveland, OH, USA

Set list at this and all remaining shows on the tour unless otherwise noted: 'Shine On You Crazy Diamond', 'Signs Of Life', 'Learning To Fly', 'Yet Another Movie', 'Round And Around', 'A New Machine, Part 1', 'Terminal Frost', 'A New Machine, Part 2', 'Sorrow', 'The Dogs Of War', 'On The Turning Away' <Intermission> 'One Of These Days', 'Time', 'The Great Gig In The Sky', 'Wish You Were Here', 'Welcome To The Machine', 'Us And Them', 'Money' (extended version), 'Another Brick In The Wall, Part 2', 'Comfortably Numb' <Encore> 'One Slip', 'Run Like Hell'.

TUESDAY 16 & WEDNESDAY 17 AUGUST – PERFORMANCES
Palace of Auburn Hills, Auburn Hills, Detroit, MI, USA

On Thursday 18 August Gilmour performed at the Les Paul Tribute Concert at the Brooklyn Academy of Music, Brooklyn, USA (see David Gilmour solo appearances for further information).

FRIDAY 19, SATURDAY 20, SUNDAY 21, MONDAY 22 & TUESDAY 23 AUGUST – PERFORMANCES
Nassau Veterans Memorial Coliseum,
Uniondale, NY, USA

Saxophonist Scott Page played out the final show with a rendition of 'Auld Lang Syne'. All five New York shows were recorded and filmed for the *Delicate Sound of Thunder* concert video and live album. It has never been released on DVD and its TV debut was made on BBC4 on Friday 1 November 2013 between 10.00pm and 11.35pm as part of an evening of Pink Floyd films and documentaries.

WEDNESDAY 7 SEPTEMBER – AWARDS CEREMONY
***MTV Video Music Awards*, Universal Amphitheater,**
Los Angeles, CA, USA

'Learning To Fly' won the Best Group Video at MTV's fifth annual Video Music Awards.

TUESDAY 20 – FRIDAY 30 SEPTEMBER; SATURDAY 1 – SATURDAY 8 OCTOBER; MONDAY 10 OCTOBER – TUESDAY 1 NOVEMBER; WEDNESDAY 9 – SATURDAY 12 NOVEMBER & MONDAY 14 – SATURDAY 19 NOVEMBER – RECORDING SESSION
Control Room 2 & 3, EMI Studios,
Abbey Road, London, England

David Gilmour, Buford Jones and James Wallace edited and mixed the live album *Delicate Sound of Thunder*.

MONDAY 21 NOVEMBER – ALBUM RELEASE (UK)
Delicate Sound of Thunder

Q Magazine wrote, "The album will work best for people who were there. With no more than the mantelpiece to stir the imagination, the pomposity of the standard Floyd intro starts to grate: huge single drumbeats or bass chords left to hang in the air while you prepare your mind for blowing. 'Get on with it!' cries the voice from the armchair."

TUESDAY 22 NOVEMBER – ALBUM RELEASE (US)
Delicate Sound of Thunder

Rolling Stone wrote, "The band takes great pains to reproduce the studio versions of its classics, despite the departure of mastermind Roger Waters. But even some of the more emotional songs, such as 'Shine On You Crazy Diamond' and 'Run Like Hell', are delivered by a group of musicians who seem to be just going through the motions; none of lead guitarist Dave Gilmour's solos catch fire. No mention is made of where the tracks were recorded, although it doesn't make any difference; on this tour, one show was probably pretty much like the next. Pink Floyd is celebrating and cashing in on its past glories, playing all its hits for kids who wish they'd been around when *Ummagumma* came out."

SATURDAY 26 NOVEMBER – SPACE LAUNCH
Baikonur Cosmodrome, Kazakhstan, USSR

Gilmour and Mason attended the launch of a Soyuz TM-7 rocket bound for the Soviet space station MIR. The three-man crew took with them a cassette of the album *Delicate Sound of Thunder* (minus the cassette box, for weight reasons) and played it in orbit; this was thought to have been the first rock music recording played in space.

1989

WEDNESDAY 1 TO FRIDAY 3 MARCH; MONDAY 6 TO FRIDAY 10 MARCH & WEDNESDAY 15 TO TUESDAY 21 MARCH – RECORDING SESSION
Programme Room & Control Room 2,
EMI Studios, Abbey Road, London, England

David Gilmour and Andy Jackson edited and mixed the live video *Delicate Sound of Thunder*.

APRIL – TELEVISION BROADCAST
Nurofen Advertisement, UK

Clare Torry provided the vocal for a newly recorded version of 'The Great Gig In The Sky' for a Nurofen® headache tablet advertisement. Although Pink Floyd was not directly involved, Richard Wright gave his permission for the use of the track.

PINK FLOYD ANOTHER LAPSE (EUROPEAN TOUR)

ADDITIONAL TOUR PERSONNEL
Jon Carin (Keyboards, Vocals), Rachel Fury (Backing vocals), Durga McBroom (Backing Vocals), Lorelei McBroom (Backing Vocals), Scott Page (Saxophones, Guitars), Guy Pratt (Bass Guitar, Vocals), Tim Renwick (Guitars), Gary Wallis (Percussion), Richard Wright (Keyboards, Vocals)

TUESDAY 2 TO TUESDAY 9 MAY – REHEARSALS
London Arena, Isle of Dogs, London, England

A full week of production set up prior to the tour was staged at the same London venue they were to return to in July. On Monday 8 May full band rehearsals commenced and on Tuesday 9 May full dress rehearsals were staged. Also on Tuesday 9 May a press reception was held at the venue and the band's handprints were taken in cement for display in the venue's Hall of Fame.

SATURDAY 13 MAY – PERFORMANCE ▶
Festivalweide, Werchter, Belgium

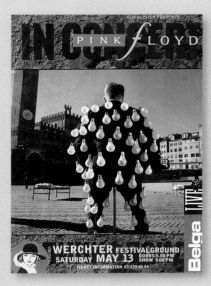

Set list at this and all remaining shows on the tour unless otherwise noted: 'Shine On You Crazy Diamond', 'Signs Of Life', 'Learning To Fly', 'Yet Another Movie', 'Round And Around', 'A New Machine, Part 1', 'Terminal Frost', 'A New Machine, Part 2', 'Sorrow', 'The Dogs Of War', 'On The Turning Away' <Intermission> 'One Of These Days', 'Time', 'The Great Gig In The Sky', 'Wish You Were Here', 'Welcome To The Machine', 'Us And Them', 'Money', 'Another Brick In The Wall, Part 2', 'Comfortably Numb' <Encore> 'One Slip', 'Run Like Hell'.

A full dress rehearsal took place at the venue on Friday 12 May heard by a considerable audience, who had camped in the surrounding roads ahead of show day.

TUESDAY 16, WEDNESDAY 17 & THURSDAY 18 MAY – PERFORMANCES
Arena di Verona, Verona, Italy

SATURDAY 20 MAY – PERFORMANCE
Arena Concerti, Autodromo Di Monza, Monza, Italy

MONDAY 22 & TUESDAY 23 MAY – PERFORMANCES
Stadio Comunale Ardenza, Livorno, Italy

TUESDAY 23 MAY – PRESS RECEPTION
CFS Conference Centre, Marylebone, London, England

EMI Records video division, PMI, held a press reception followed by a screening of the *Delicate Sound of Thunder* video. To celebrate the fact that the band was about to play in Moscow for the first time, organizers laid on complimentary Russian beer!

THURSDAY 25 & FRIDAY 26 MAY – PERFORMANCES
Stadio Simonetta Lamberti, Cava de' Tirreni, Italy

TUESDAY 30 & WEDNESDAY 31 MAY – PERFORMANCES
Olympiako Stadio Athinas [OAKA], Athens, Greece

SATURDAY 3, SUNDAY 4, TUESDAY 6, WEDNESDAY 7 & THURSDAY 8 JUNE – PERFORMANCES
Olimpiyskiy Stadium, Moscow, Russia

The show on Monday 5 June was postponed and rescheduled to Thursday 8 June after a national day of mourning was observed following a Trans-Siberian rail disaster near Ufa, Russia on Sunday 4 June.

SATURDAY 10 JUNE – PERFORMANCE
Lahden Suurhalli, Lahti, Finland

MONDAY 12 JUNE – VIDEO RELEASE (UK)
Delicate Sound of Thunder

TUESDAY 13 JUNE – VIDEO RELEASE (US)
Delicate Sound of Thunder

MONDAY 12, TUESDAY 13 & WEDNESDAY 14 JUNE – PERFORMANCES
Globe Arena, Stockholm, Sweden

FRIDAY 16 JUNE – PERFORMANCE
Festweisse Im Stadtpark, Hamburg, West Germany

SUNDAY 18 JUNE – PERFORMANCE
Mungersdorfer Stadion, Cologne, West Germany

TUESDAY 20 & WEDNESDAY 21 JUNE – PERFORMANCES ▶
Festhalle, Frankfurt, West Germany

FRIDAY 23 JUNE – PERFORMANCE
Linzer Stadion, Linz, Austria

SUNDAY 25 JUNE – PERFORMANCE
Neckarstadion, Stuttgart, West Germany

TUESDAY 27, WEDNESDAY 28, THURSDAY 29, FRIDAY 30 JUNE & SATURDAY 1 JULY – PERFORMANCES
Palais Omnisports de Paris-Bercy, Paris, France

RIGHT: DAVID GILMOUR AT THE LONDON ARENA, 8 JULY 1989.

TUESDAY 4, WEDNESDAY 5, THURSDAY 6, FRIDAY 7, SATURDAY 8 & SUNDAY 9 JULY – PERFORMANCES
London Arena, Isle of Dogs, London, England

The show on Tuesday 4 July was billed as a gala night for charity. The *Guardian* summed up the sentiments of many fans at this series of poorly received shows at the newly built London Arena: "Some middle-aged men, drained by legal confrontations with one of their number, return to the stage when the school fees become too much for compact disc sales of their back catalogue to sustain, and hide their shortcomings behind an extravaganza [of] pyrotechnics and excess hardware. If only the likeable Dave Gilmour and his team had a tenth of the energy of their acidic descendants, we might have had some fun. Instead there was smoke billowing from the ceiling, lasers cutting across the auditorium, a galaxy of spotlights picking out men hunched over keyboards playing uninspired dirges that would not have been out of place backing wildlife films. At the side of the stage three refugees from a Robert Palmer video swayed in tight dresses, occasionally moaning into the microphone in unison, unable to find a rhythm to latch their syncopated shuffle on to. This despite the fact there were two drummers on display: that two were deemed necessary for a band whose rhythmic complexities would not tax a clockwork monkey summed up the whole bloated enterprise. For the first half, Gilmour said he would like to play 'some new stuff' then 'lots of oldies after the break'. 'You play whatever you like mate,' said the chap behind me, who was clearly a veteran Floyd watcher, because that is what Gilmour appeared to be doing throughout: random guitar doodling that bore no relation to received ideas of melody. Some critics have complained that the dire evening service provided by the Dockland's Light Railway is killing the Arena at birth. I, however, owe the railway a debt of thanks. When, during the interval, it was announced that the last train left at 9.30pm, I had a genuine excuse to miss most of the second half."

MONDAY 10 JULY – PERFORMANCE
Goffertpark, Nijmegan, Netherlands

WEDNESDAY 12 JULY – PERFORMANCE
Stade Olympique de la Pontaise, Lausanne, Switzerland

SATURDAY 15 JULY – PERFORMANCE
Canale di San Marco, Piazza San Marco, Venice, Italy

Set list: 'Shine On You Crazy Diamond', 'Learning To Fly', 'Yet Another Movie', 'Sorrow', 'The Dogs Of War', 'On The Turning Away', 'Time', 'The Great Gig In The Sky', 'Wish You Were Here', 'Money', 'Another Brick In The Wall, Part 2', 'Comfortably Numb', 'One Slip', 'Run Like Hell'.

A free concert at which Pink Floyd performed an abbreviated 90-minute show from a huge barge moored off Piazza San Marco was broadcast live on TV to over 20 countries and seen by an estimated 100 million people. In the UK the show was broadcast live on BBC2 TV between 10.45pm and 12.20pm.

In 1992 two city council officers were faced with charges for allowing the concert to go ahead. A far greater number than anticipated attended the concert, and facilities were vastly inadequate. It was estimated the cleanup bill alone reached a cost in excess of £25,000 to the local authorities.

TUESDAY 18 JULY –
PERFORMANCE ▶
Stade Vélodrome,
Marseille, France

1990

SATURDAY 30 JUNE – PERFORMANCE ▼
The Silver Clef Award Winners Show,
Knebworth Park, Stevenage, England

With Tears for Fears, Status Quo, Cliff Richard, Robert Plant with Jimmy Page, Phil Collins, Genesis, Eric Clapton, Dire Straits, Elton John and Paul McCartney.

Set list: 'Shine On You Crazy Diamond, Parts 1–5', 'The Great Gig In The Sky', 'Wish You Were Here', 'Sorrow', 'Money', 'Comfortably Numb', 'Run Like Hell'.

This charity event in aid of the Nordoff–Robbins Music Therapy Centre featured 11 hours of continuous entertainment. A year on, Pink Floyd officially declared this as the final date of the *A Momentary Lapse of Reason* world tour and closed the day with a brief set in torrential rain. During a heavy storm earlier in the day, their screen had collected water and ripped while suspended above the stage.

Pink Floyd was supplemented on stage by Sam Brown (Backing Vocals), Vicki Brown (Backing Vocals), Candy Dulfer (Saxophones on 'Shine On You Crazy Diamond' and 'Money'), Michael Kamen (Keyboards on 'Comfortably Numb'), Guy Pratt (Bass Guitar), Durga McBroom (Backing Vocals) and Claire Torry (Backing Vocals on 'The Great Gig In The Sky').

Pink Floyd performed a one-hour production rehearsal between 10.00pm and 11.00pm in preparation for the show on the evening of Friday 29 June. Studio rehearsals had already taken place in London on Wednesday 27 and Thursday 28 June.

BBC Radio One broadcast the entire event live from 12.30pm through to 11.00pm, with a repeat of Pink Floyd's set broadcast on the *Christmas Concerts* broadcast on BBC Radio One on Wednesday 26 December 1990 between 7.30pm and 10.30pm. MTV broadcast highlights of the show, including Pink Floyd's performance on Saturday 14 July 1990, between 4.00pm and 9.00pm. Castle Music Pictures released a three-video set of highlights, entitled *Knebworth – The Event*, and featuring 'Shine On You Crazy Diamond' and 'Run Like Hell' in 1990. Polydor released an album of highlights featuring 'Comfortably Numb' and 'Run Like Hell', at the same time. (See Discography for further information.)

Unfortunately the event was memorable not just for Pink Floyd's closing set but for the disorganization behind it, starting with an appeal by BBC Radio 1 for people to carry plenty of water in anticipation of it being a dry hot day, only for the public to be refused entry with any form of refreshment not purchased within the arena itself. Thousands upon thousands of bottles filled containers at the entrances ready for the landfill. Once inside the arena prices for refreshments were hideously inflated and toilets were wholly inadequate.

After dark, things deteriorated further as no floodlighting had been arranged for the adjacent fields doubling as car parks and stewards abandoned the site. People spent hours searching for their vehicles in a quagmire of mud and in the ensuing chaos the last vehicles didn't leave until daylight the next day.

1991

THURSDAY 10 OCTOBER – AWARDS CEREMONY
2nd National Association of Brick Distributors'
Hall of Fame Gala, **New York, NY, USA**

Pink Floyd was inducted into the US National Association of Brick Distributors' 2nd annual Hall of Fame in recognition of their services to the brick industry for the video to their hit single 'Another Brick In The Wall, Part 2'. Other inductees included the Commodores for their 1977 hit 'Brick House' and Iggy Pop for the album *Brick by Brick*.

TUESDAY 24 DECEMBER – TELEVISION BROADCAST
La Carrera Panamericana, BBC2 TV, UK

Pink Floyd's documentary film *La Carrera Panamericana*, which captured Gilmour and Mason's participation in the 3,000-mile South American classic car race in October, was broadcast on this day on BBC2 TV between 5.00pm and 6.00pm. Both were driving replica Proteus 1952 C-type Jaguars. Mason was co-driving with Lindsay Valentine and Gilmour with manager Steve O'Rourke who, incidentally, plunged 230ft down a hillside and broke both his legs when their car veered off the road near San Luis Potosi in Mexico. Gilmour and O'Rourke were both flown to a hospital in Texas. The soundtrack featured existing and newly reworked Pink Floyd tracks and was officially released on video in 1992 (see Discography for further information). Some of the interview footage was actually filmed after the race in a bar in Notting Hill, London, England.

1992

MONDAY 13 APRIL – VIDEO RELEASE (UK)
La Carrera Panamericana

Q Magazine said, "Once a serious six-day 2,500-mile road race around Mexico, nowadays, the Panamericana is restricted to '50s grand tourers and is thus much more of a 'jolly' for well-heeled enthusiasts. Sensationally, Gilmour crashes! Alas, we never get to see him, or his ruffled ego, post prang. Meanwhile, the remaining cars roar glamorously down the road, soundtracked by Pink Floyd, with Gilmour's guitar grinding on even over the top of the mariachi bands at the victory celebrations, whose music would surely have made for a more appropriate soundtrack."

WEDNESDAY 15 APRIL – AWARDS CEREMONY
Ivor Novello Awards, Grosvenor Hotel, London, England

Pink Floyd was awarded a much coveted Ivor Novello for "Outstanding Contribution to British Music" at the annual awards ceremony.

TUESDAY 2 JUNE – VIDEO RELEASE (US)
La Carrera Panamericana

MONDAY 2 NOVEMBER – ALBUM RELEASE (UK & US)
Shine On

This was universally panned by fans. *Q Magazine* wrote, "A box of eight Pink Floyd albums lovingly inlaid in their black casket, with a 'bonus' CD of early singles along with an envelope of postcards no serious collector would ever actually send to anyone, and a cut-out cardboard shape which one is evidently meant to fold, but your reviewer has so far failed to work out how – still less what it is supposed to be when finished. There are no instructions, and that's not the only thing conspicuously absent from this recession-flouting (£100 plus) package. …Storm comes unstuck with the design of *Shine On*'s book. The text is treated as just so much grey matter, unclearly laid out and in dire need of a good edit, or even a quick proofreading. Not only is it littered with typographical errors but the odd factual howler too. Most annoyingly, the final piece of text, an unsigned music industry piece on the enduring appeal of *The Dark Side of the Moon*, actually stops mid-sentence."

1993

JANUARY – SEPTEMBER – RECORDING SESSIONS
**Britannia Row Studios, Islington, London, England
& The Astoria, Hampton, England**

Discontinuous recording for *The Division Bell*.

SEPTEMBER – DECEMBER – RECORDING SESSIONS
**Metropolis Studios, Chiswick, London, England
& The Creek Recording Studios, London, England**

Discontinuous recording and mixing for *The Division Bell*.

TUESDAY 7 SEPTEMBER – PRESS REPORT
London, England

Volkswagen AG was reported to have hired Pink Floyd to help promote its cars in European advertising. Volkswagen revealed the signing at the Frankfurt International Motor Show. Pink Floyd's 1994 *Division Bell* tour was sponsored by Volkswagen and a special limited-edition VW Golf was manufactured to tie in with the tour, which allegedly had some interior design input from Nick Mason.

**SATURDAY 18 SEPTEMBER
– PERFORMANCE ▶**
***Cowdray Ruins Concert
1993*, Cowdray Castle,
Midhurst, England**

Set list: 'Run Like Hell', 'Wish You Were Here', 'Comfortably Numb'.

COWDRAY RUINS CONCERT 1993

This was a celebrity charity event sponsored by Virgin Radio to raise £200,000 for the King Edward VII hospital in Midhurst. With a ticket price of £140 for the main arena and £80 the outer picnic zones, it was an exclusive gathering, out of the reach of the band's usual fans. The concert opened with a set from Queen, comprising on this occasion, Roger Taylor (Vocals), John Deacon (Bass), Tim Renwick (Guitar) and Gary Wallis (Drums). Also appearing were Genesis, made up of Phil Collins (Vocals), Mike Rutherford (Bass), Tony Banks (Keyboards), Tim Renwick (Guitar) and Gary Wallis and Roger Taylor (Drums). Pink Floyd headlined with a fairly standard set with the unusual addition of Mike Rutherford (Bass), Paul Young of Mike & the Mechanics (Vocals on 'Run Like Hell'), Tim Renwick (Guitar) and Gary Wallis (Drums). Nick Mason sat behind Roger Taylor's drum kit, complete with the famous Queen emblem. The last act to appear was Eric Clapton playing lead guitar on a two-song encore with Gilmour, Taylor, Young, Collins and Renwick.

TUESDAY 30 NOVEMBER – PRESS CONFERENCE
EMI Studios, Abbey Road, London, England

Pink Floyd held a press conference to announce a new album and tour for 1994 and to announce Richard Wright's reinstatement as a full member of Pink Floyd.

1994—99

1994-99

The phenomenal success of *A Momentary Lapse of Reason* and the ensuing tour provided a solid base for Gilmour to instigate the recording of a new Pink Floyd album, beginning in January 1993.

Using communication as a general theme the album was a far more personal insight into Gilmour's state of mind than *A Momentary Lapse of Reason*. However, Gilmour was less than vocal about the subject matter of the album, preferring the listener to draw their own conclusions. Instead he focused on how the album should be viewed in the context of the band's legacy: "On this album both Nick and Rick are playing all the stuff they should be playing which is why it sounds much more like a genuine Pink Floyd record to me than anything since *Wish You Were Here*. It has a sort of theme about non-communication, but we're not trying to bash anybody over the head with it. We went out last time with the intention of showing the world, 'Look we're still here,' which is why we were so loud and crash-bangy. This is a much more reflective album."[1]

Released in March 1994, *The Division Bell* took its title from the division bells that are rung to summon MPs or members of the House of Lords to vote in the UK Parliament. The title idea was suggested, almost at the last moment in the absence of a suitable alternative, to Gilmour by a friend, science-fiction writer Douglas Adams, in exchange for a £5,000 charity donation to the Environmental Investigation Agency.

Coupled with another extensive tour, *The Division Bell* went on to become one of the most successful albums in Pink Floyd's nearly 30-year history.

The inevitable tour followed and, discarding the usual format of playing the whole of the current album during one half of the show, the band chose to present a broad cross-section of their entire repertoire dating back to the very first album. Not surprisingly, although it was a disappointment to fans, nothing from *Animals* or *The Final Cut* was performed.

To compliment the core members, once again Jon Carin, Tim Renwick, Guy Pratt, Gary Wallis and Durga McBroom joined the tour. Newcomers Sam Brown and Claudia Fontaine made up the rest of the backing trio, while former Floyd saxophonist Dick Parry was rescued from retirement, in favour of the flamboyant Scott Page.

In staging the show, Pink Floyd welcomed back on board designer Mark Fisher, who, along with Marc Brickman, came up with what was inevitably seen as the band's most impressive stage show to date. (An unwritten Floyd tradition seems to demand that each tour should be more spectacular than the previous

one). A large semicircular shell now housed the production, replacing a monolithic steel frame, and this was equipped with a much larger circular projection screen. Overall the design was strongly reminiscent of the Hollywood Bowl, something Gilmour had suggested, while the lighting effects and the fantastical newly generated film sequences – both live action and computer generated – were nothing short of awe inspiring.

It was therefore hardly surprising that band manager Steve O'Rourke announced to the press that "David, Rick and Nick have put no limit on the budget. It is a matter of however much it takes to create the best show we can possibly do."[2] And it certainly showed: quadraphonic sound using some 300 speakers, a raised 40-foot circular projection screen with a 35mm back-projector, a 70mm IMAX front projector, a vast mirror ball that rose from the centre of the now giant slug-like construction that housed the front-of-house soundboard and projectors, and an array of lighting that included 400 Vari-Lites and two copper-vapour pulse lasers that were said to have been originally developed for NASA by the Hughes Corporation. The band even recalled one of their original lighting men Peter Wynne-Wilson to re-create liquid-oil patterns to illuminate the revival of the classic Barrett-era anthem 'Astronomy Domine'.

The new projection films, directed by Storm Thorgerson, were typically indulgent. The most impressive were those used for 'Shine On You Crazy Diamond', based largely on the Barrett legend; 'Money', with an untypical hilarious alien monster theme; and 'Time', a computer-generated masterpiece that seemed to suck viewers into the vast workings of a hugely intricate mechanical timing device. Reworked scenes also accompanied the classic footage used during 'Us And Them', and the renditions of *The Dark Side of the Moon* were updated with appropriate inserts of modern-day politicians for the 'Brain Damage'/'Eclipse' finale. There was the usual battery of fireworks and props, including a crashing plane for 'On The Run' and two massive comic hogs that launched out of the tops of the twin speaker columns during 'One Of These Days'. It was a total sensory bombardment.

The statistics of such a large-scale touring machine are mind-boggling, and the amount of materials and manpower required to take the band on the road simply are too fantastic to be ignored: 200 crew members, three separate touring stages (although only one set of lights was carried on tour, since it was the most expensive single element to hire), 49 container trucks, 700 tons of steel to build the set – a task which took four days – and a daily running cost of some US$500,000. Two Boeing 747 cargo planes and a chartered Russian Antonov military freight plane were used to transfer the equipment from the USA for the European tour.

Today this all seems fairly standard for stadium touring, but at the time Robbie Williams, once the band's roadie and now the production manager, looked on this complexity with a mixture of awe and disbelief. "We used to get away with a main lighting effect that consisted of four Genie towers, which came up with flashing police beacons on top and 24 par cans – and that was seen as absolutely astonishing. Now, to get the same effect on an audience you have to have 20 million dollars' worth of stuff out there. It sometimes amazes me, going back into stadiums we played in the seventies, when it was a lot more basic. Fax machines? We didn't even have telephones on some of those gigs yet we did stadium tours. Sometimes I look around and think, we're ordering 21 phone lines at every venue, and as for computers, we didn't even have calculators."[3]

At a press conference held in London on 30 November 1993 to announce the European tour, Pink Floyd said they would be performing in Greece, Turkey and Israel in addition to the shows already announced, but none of these locations was confirmed. A show in front of the Great Pyramids at Giza in Egypt was frequently touted by the press as well as additional concerts in Australia in 1995, but these plans never reached fruition.

To assist with the spiralling costs of the tour the band struck a sponsorship deal with German car manufacturer Volkswagen, who had recently sponsored a tour by rock band Genesis. The company even produced a special limited-edition 'Pink Floyd' VW Golf with interiors part-designed by Nick Mason. Although it seemed like a good idea at the time, Gilmour regretted this, "not having thought it through entirely. Meeting and greeting Volkswagen people. I was not a popular chappy with Volkswagen. I don't want them to be able to say they have a connection with Pink Floyd, that they are part of our success. We will not do it again. I didn't like it, and any money I made from it went to charity. We should remain proudly independent, that's my view, and we will in the future."[4] Little, it seems, had been learnt from the Gini episode 20 years earlier.

OPPOSITE: PINK FLOYD'S SPECTACULAR STAGE SHOW, NORTH AMERICA, APRIL 1994.

RIGHT: AS PART OF THE SPONSORSHIP PACKAGE, VW LAUNCHED A LIMITED-EDITION PINK FLOYD GOLF.

LEFT: PINK FLOYD PHOTOGRAPHED AT THE PASADENA ROSEBOWL, 16 APRIL 1994.

Pink Floyd's last two tours were now fully documented, at that time there still remained an unforgivable void between 1969's *Ummagumma* and 1988's *Delicate Sound of Thunder.*

From here on in Pink Floyd itself ceased to exist in any meaningful form, aside from lending its name to numerous reissues and marketing opportunities. Even the prospect of an anthology set, similar to the trawl of archives undertaken by the Beatles, the Who or Led Zeppelin, among many high-profile acts, seemed decidedly remote. Pink Floyd again distanced themselves from their past achievements and were as precious as ever about the non-release of archive material, which left fans feeling tired by the release of a glut of re-masters and reissues, the only saving grace of which was the mono edition of *The Piper at the Gates Of Dawn* and a superb 5.1 remix of *The Dark Side of the Moon.*

As for original material, remarkably it was Wright who made the first post–*Division Bell* move by releasing a solo album, *Broken China*, in 1996. However, his initial desire to embark on a solo tour was thwarted by relatively moderate sales, though the cancellation may be regarded as a lack of self-confidence.

It was only Roger Waters who kept the flag flying with his increasingly popular solo tours, despite a lack of any original material. This gradually secured him a solid fanbase and consequently a newfound sense of personal and professional belief. "I had a lot of negative feelings later on when the boys went off marching round the world with my songs," Waters later said. "That was problematic for me for a number of years. I'm completely over it now. I couldn't care less, and also I feel much less bullish about the notion that I was right and they were wrong. I absolutely did the right thing, difficult as it was for the first few years when I was making records on my own. It was very hard for me to carve out a niche for myself outside the context of the band."[7]

If one thing set *The Division Bell* stage show apart from all others, it was the sheer power of the delivery, and with such an audio and visual feast it was difficult to imagine Pink Floyd would ever top that achievement. Most striking was the fact that the band had captured the imagination of a new generation, with whole families attending the concerts. A huge number of teenagers who might well have been steeping themselves in rave or grunge were committing themselves to Pink Floyd. As one industry observer put it, "It's hard to tell how they attract a younger demographic. Unlike Neil Young or Aerosmith, they have no connection to nineties music. I can't even think of an act that has caught younger consumers' favour that would even lead them to Pink Floyd. This is a unique situation."[5]

At the close of Pink Floyd's 1994 world tour it was calculated that over 5.3 million tickets had been sold, grossing some $100 million. To commemorate their efforts, a live album and video, both entitled *P.U.L.S.E.*, were released. These not only gave a balanced and well-recorded picture of Pink Floyd's then current repertoire but, for the first time, contained a complete official rendition of the whole of *The Dark Side of the Moon*, which they had revived towards the close of the North American tour and performed as a complete second half at shows in Europe.

"We were bitterly disappointed that we didn't make a proper record of *The Dark Side of the Moon* at Earls Court in '73,"[6] said Mason. Inevitably, some critics would have much preferred that they had done this in the first place rather than present a rehashed latter-day version. After all, while

1. *Mojo*, May 1994.
2. *Evening Standard*, 30 November 1993.
3. *Live*, September 1994.
4. *Mojo*, July 1995.
5. *USA Today*, 16 July 1994.
6. *Mojo*, July 1995.
7. *Uncut*, June 2004.

1994

PINK FLOYD, JANUARY 1994 – SEPTEMBER 2008

David Gilmour, Nick Mason, Richard Wright.

THURSDAY 10 JANUARY – PRESS RECEPTION ▼
US Naval Air Station, Weeksville, Elizabeth City, NC, USA

A press reception was held to announce Pink Floyd's new album and world tour at this location with the launch of a specially

built Skyship 600 airship. Flown from its manufacturers in the UK to the US, it was specially painted by Burt Dodge in Elizabeth City. It then took off on a US tour and was acclaimed in the aviation industry for its performance against the jet stream in some of the worst weather for the time of year. It was sighted over many key cities over the next few weeks and even made appearances at some shows. The airship returned to Weeksville, where it was destroyed by a sudden thunderstorm on Monday 27 June 1994, and the remnants were sold off as souvenirs to fans.

TUESDAY 8 – THURSDAY 24 MARCH – REHEARSALS
Norton Air Force Base, San Bernardino, CA, USA

Pink Floyd made use of an aircraft hangar at this US military airbase for their tour rehearsals. A widely circulated unofficial recording dated Wednesday 16 March includes the band rehearsing the following tracks: 'Shine On You Crazy Diamond, 'High Hopes', 'Breathe', 'Time', 'Breathe (Reprise)', 'The Great Gig In The Sky', 'Lost For Words', 'Wish You Were Here', 'Us And Them', 'Money' and 'Comfortably Numb'.

MONDAY 21 MARCH – PRESS RECEPTION
White Waltham Airfield, Maidenhead, England

A press reception was held to announce Pink Floyd's new album and world tour aboard a specially painted A60 Airship that took off on a circular trip over central London with journalists aboard. In the run up to the European tour the airship made a promotional tour of the UK and Northern Europe. Painted to resemble a large fish, it was fabricated from a translucent material and illuminated from the inside by two large 1000 watt bulbs giving an eerie effect as it travelled the night sky.

MONDAY 28 MARCH – ALBUM RELEASE (UK)
The Division Bell

PINK FLOYD WORLD TOUR 1994 (NORTH & SOUTH AMERICA)

Additional musicians through 1994: Sam Brown (Backing Vocals), Jon Carin (Keyboards and Vocals), Claudia Fontaine (Backing Vocals), Durga McBroom (Backing Vocals), Dick Parry (Saxophones), Guy Pratt (Bass Guitar and Vocals), Tim Renwick (Guitars) and Gary Wallis (Percussion).

WEDNESDAY 30 MARCH – PERFORMANCE
Joe Robbie Stadium, Miami, FL, USA

Set list: 'Astronomy Domine', 'Learning To Fly', 'What Do You Want From Me', 'Take It Back', 'Lost For Words', 'Sorrow', 'A Great Day For Freedom', 'Keep Talking', 'One Of These Days' <Intermission> 'Shine On You Crazy Diamond', 'Breathe', 'Time', 'Breathe (Reprise)', 'High Hopes', 'Wish You Were Here', 'Another Brick In The Wall, Part 2', 'The Great Gig In The Sky', 'Us And Them', 'Money', 'Comfortably Numb' <Encore>'Hey You', 'Run Like Hell'.

A full production rehearsal for the upcoming tour was staged on Tuesday 29 March and brief clips were shown on MTV's *The Week in Rock* news programme broadcast through Friday 1 April 1994.

SUNDAY 3 APRIL – PERFORMANCE
Alamo Dome, San Antonio, TX, USA

Set list: 'Astronomy Domine', 'Learning To Fly', 'What Do You Want From Me', 'Poles Apart', 'Sorrow', 'Take It Back', 'Lost For Words', 'Keep Talking', 'On The Turning Away' <Intermission> 'Shine On You Crazy Diamond', 'Breathe', 'Time', 'Breathe (Reprise)', 'High Hopes', 'Wish You Were Here', 'One Of These Days', 'The Great Gig In The Sky', 'Us And Them', 'Money', 'Comfortably Numb' <Encore>'Hey You', 'Run Like Hell'.

TUESDAY 5 APRIL 1994 – ALBUM RELEASE (US)
The Division Bell

Teen Ink wrote, "If you are looking for another *Dark Side* or *Wish* or any of their string of hit records, you will not find it here. A band has to move on to new sounds, to a new stage in their music, or else they become redundant. However the elements are there. You can even find a bit of the old Floyd psychedelia buried in the middle of 'Poles Apart'. Overall, the album is a bittersweet memoir of friends past, and future hopes."

TUESDAY 5 APRIL – PERFORMANCE
Rice University Stadium, Houston, TX, USA

Set list: 'Astronomy Domine, 'Learning To Fly', 'What Do You Want From Me', 'Take It Back', 'Lost For Words', 'Sorrow', 'A Great Day For Freedom', 'Keep Talking', 'One Of These Days', 'Another Brick In The Wall, Part 2' <Intermission> 'Shine On You Crazy Diamond', 'Breathe', 'Time', 'Breathe (Reprise)', 'High Hopes', 'Wish You Were Here', 'The Great Gig In The Sky', 'Money' <Encore>'Run Like Hell'.

A heavy rainstorm that began during 'Another Brick In The Wall, Part 2' forced the show to stop during 'Run Like Hell' for safety reasons. Power to the entire stadium failed 15 minutes thereafter, leaving the audience to exit the stadium in complete darkness.

THE DIVISION BELL

PINK FLOYD · THE DIVISION BELL

SIDE 1

CLUSTER ONE (Wright, Gilmour) **5:29**
WHAT DO YOU WANT FROM ME (Music: Gilmour, Wright. Lyrics: Gilmour, Samson) **4:21**
POLES APART (Music: Gilmour. Lyrics: Gilmour, Samson, Laird-Clowes) **7:04**
MAROONED (Wright, Gilmour) **5:29**
A GREAT DAY FOR FREEDOM (Music: Gilmour. Lyrics: Gilmour, Samson) **4:17**
WEARING THE INSIDE OUT (Music: Wright. Lyrics: Moore) **6:49**

SIDE 2

TAKE IT BACK (Music: Gilmour, Ezrin. Lyrics: Gilmour, Samson, Laird-Clowes) **6:12**
COMING BACK TO LIFE (Gilmour) **6:19**
KEEP TALKING (Music: Gilmour, Wright. Lyrics: Gilmour, Samson) **6:11**
LOST FOR WORDS (Music: Gilmour. Lyrics: Gilmour, Samson) **5:14**
HIGH HOPES (Music: Gilmour. Lyrics: Gilmour, Samson) **8:31**

RELEASED

UK: Monday 28 March 1994.
US: Tuesday 5 April 1994.

FORMAT

UK: EMI EMD 1055 (Vinyl album).
UK: EMI CD EMD 1055 (CD album).
US: Columbia C64200 (Vinyl album and Limited edition blue vinyl album).
US: Columbia CK 64200 (CD album).
The vinyl version of the album is shorter than the CD version, with edits made to 'Poles Apart', 'Marooned', 'Wearing The Inside Out', 'Coming Back To Life', 'Lost For Words' and 'High Hopes' to allow the album to fit.

HIGHEST CHART POSITION

UK: No. 1 (*Music Week* "Top 75 Albums" on Saturday 9 April 1994), Chart re-entry No. 52 (*UK Official Chart Company* on Saturday 12 July 2014).
US: No. 1 (*Billboard* "200" on Saturday 23 April 1994), 'Keep Talking' No. 1 (*Billboard* "Album Rock Tracks" on Saturday 9 April 1994), 'What Do You Want From Me' No. 16 (*Billboard* "Album Rock Tracks" on Saturday 7 May 1994), 'Take it Back' No. 4 (*Billboard* "Album Rock Tracks" on Saturday 25 June 1994), 'High Hopes' No. 7 (*Billboard* "Album Rock Tracks" on Saturday 8 October 1994), 'Lost For Words' No. 21 (*Billboard* "Album Rock Tracks" on Saturday 7 January 1995).

AWARDS

UK: Certified Silver and Gold on Friday 1 April 1994, Platinum on Sunday 1 May 1994 and 2 x Platinum on Saturday 1 October 1994.
US: Certified Gold on 6 June 1994, 2 x Platinum on 6 June 1994, 3 x Platinum on 29 January 1999.

ARTWORK

Artwork by Storm Thorgerson.
Central to the design of the album cover were the distinctive "heads" which, facing each other, create the image of a third face. The large-scale metal heads used for the CD cover, and the stone heads used for the cassette cover, were placed in a field overlooked by the cathedral at Ely in Cambridgeshire. Variations on the design were used in the tour artwork that followed. The CD case was also praised for its moulding, which spelled out the words "Pink Floyd" in Braille on the opening edge.

PUBLICITY

An intriguing Internet marketing campaign was created for the album and tour by an anonymous individual calling themselves Publius, who began posting ambiguous messages on a Pink Floyd fan forum. It initially invited the reader to look at the new album with open minds, discuss it in the newsgroup, and solve a puzzle for which a very unique and tangible prize could be won. However, the lack of anything meaningful to work on caused inevitable questions about Publius' credentials. These were verified when readers were invited to watch for a sign at approximately 10.30pm on July 18 1994 at that evening's show in New Jersey, when the words "Publius Enigma" were flashed on the stage lights, albeit fleetingly. Many theories were entertained thereafter and a message was again displayed, this time at the Earls Court show on 20 October 1994. At the termination of the tour Publius' forum posts ceased, and while at the outset many thought this would lead to hordes of fans armed with shovels and spades combing the Cambridgeshire countryside with metal detectors for treasure, the puzzle, if there ever was one, remains unsolved and the prize unclaimed.

MUSICIANS

David Gilmour, Nick Mason, Richard Wright.

ADDITIONAL MUSICIANS

Jon Carin (Programming, Additional Keyboards).
Guy Pratt (Bass).
Gary Wallis (Played & Programmed Percussion).
Tim Renwick (Guitars).
Dick Parry (Tenor Saxophone).
Bob Ezrin (Keyboards, Percussion).
Sam Brown (Backing Vocals).
Durga McBroom (Backing Vocals).
Carol Kenyon (Backing Vocals).
Jackie Sheridan (Backing Vocals).
Rebecca Leigh-White (Backing Vocals).
Michael Kamen (Orchestra Arrangements).
Michael Kamen, Edward Shearmur (Orchestrations).

RECORDING DETAILS

Recorded at the Astoria, Hampton, England; Britannia Row Studios, Islington, London, England; Abbey Road Studios, St John's Wood, London, England; Metropolis Studios, Chiswick, London, England; the Creek Recording Studios, London, England.

Produced by Bob Ezrin and David Gilmour and engineered and mixed by Andrew Jackson.

The initial sessions for the *Division Bell* began with Gilmour, Mason and Wright in January 1993 at Britannia Row, where numerous rough sketches were recorded. Over the next few months those ideas were narrowed down with the assistance of Ezrin at Gilmour's houseboat studio, Astoria, into actual workable songs. The bulk of the album was then recorded live throughout September and October mainly at Metropolis and the Creek, where the album was also mixed.

What characterizes this album above all is not only Mason and Wright's contribution from the go, but also the contribution from Gilmour's blossoming writing partnership with his second wife, the journalist Polly Samson. Gilmour, given his admitted diffidence as a wordsmith, greatly valued her close reading of his work. "After I would write some lyrics, it just seemed natural to have her look through them", he said. "In the beginning she tried not to interfere at all, and tried to encourage me to do it on my own. But, of course, that isn't the way things stay. And as time went by, she got more and more involved with the process that was beginning to absorb me 24 hours a day. Her involvement with the lyric writing process – and, in fact, with the music – grew. Her assistance was invaluable."[1]

The reason for the regained sense of shared purpose, Gilmour suggested, was, "because we're all playing and functioning much better than we were after the trials and tribulations of the late Roger years. Recording *A Momentary Lapse of Reason* was a very, very difficult process. We were all sort of catatonic. Unfortunately, we didn't really work together an awful lot. But the success of that album and the success of the supporting tour and the enjoyment that we got out of working together meant that this one could be made in a different way."[2]

With various strands of communication/non-communication pulling the album together, the album has a broad range of styles and subject matter. 'Coming Back To Life', for instance, focuses on his recovery and new-found relationship with Polly Samson, and is juxtaposed with 'Lost For Words', which examines the collapse of his relationship with Roger Waters. This is revisited in 'Poles Apart' which also examines his relationship with Syd Barrett. The wider implications of global communication are also heard in 'A Great Day For Freedom', written following the collapse of the Eastern Bloc and the inevitable void that followed. The lead single from the album, 'Keep Talking', features a sample of the voice of the theoretical physicist and cosmologist Professor Stephen Hawking, who due to a form of motor neurone disease communicates through a speech synthesizer and it was actually lifted from a British Telecom TV advertisement. But, without doubt, the highlight is the anthemic and highly emotive 'High Hopes' – a nostalgic return by Gilmour to his Cambridge roots and the passing of the years – and the track for which Richard Wright received his first writing credit in 19 years for co-writing what is arguably the albums' stand-out song, 'Wearing The Inside Out'. The instrumental track 'Marooned' went on to be awarded a Grammy for 'Best Rock Instrumental Performance' of that year.

ABOVE: ON 6 MARCH 2010, THE ROYAL MAIL ISSUED A SET OF *DIVISION BELL* STAMPS AS PART OF THE CLASSIC ALBUM COVERS ISSUE OF STAMPS CELEBRATING THE UNIQUE ART FORM OF THE ALBUM COVER WITH 10 CULTURALLY SIGNIFICANT ALBUM COVERS OF MODERN TIMES. STORM THORGERSON WAS SAID TO HAVE BEEN A BIT 'NARKED' BY THE CHOICE OVER *THE DARK SIDE OF THE MOON*, THE ROYAL MAIL STATING THAT , 'THERE'S TOO MUCH BLACK INK IN THE DESIGN, AND THAT RENDERS INOPERATIVE THE PHOSPHOR STRIP THAT ENABLES AUTOMATIC STAMP SORTING. THE DESIGNS THEMSELVES WERE CHOSEN INDEPENDENTLY OF THE RESPECTIVE BANDS AND MANAGEMENT TEAMS.'

1–2. *Guitar World*, September 1994.

SATURDAY 9 APRIL – PERFORMANCE
Autódromo Hermanos Rodríguez, Mexico City, Mexico

Set list: 'Astronomy Domine', 'Learning To Fly', 'What Do You Want From Me', 'A Great Day For Freedom', 'Sorrow', 'Take It Back', 'Keep Talking', 'One Of These Days' <Intermission> 'Shine On You Crazy Diamond', 'Breathe', 'Time', 'Breathe (Reprise)', 'High Hopes', 'Another Brick In The Wall, Part 2', 'The Great Gig In The Sky', 'Us And Them', 'Money', 'Comfortably Numb' <Encore>'Hey You', 'Run Like Hell'.

SUNDAY 10 APRIL – PERFORMANCE
Autódromo Hermanos Rodríguez, Mexico City, Mexico

Set list: 'Astronomy Domine', 'Learning To Fly', 'What Do You Want From Me', 'A Great Day For Freedom', 'Sorrow', 'Take It Back', 'Another Brick In The Wall, Part 2', 'Keep Talking', 'On The Turning Away' <Intermission> 'Shine On You Crazy Diamond', 'Breathe', 'Time', 'Breathe (Reprise)', 'High Hopes', 'Wish You Were Here', 'One Of These Days', 'The Great Gig In The Sky', 'Us And Them', 'Money', 'Comfortably Numb' <Encore>'Hey You', 'Run Like Hell'.

THURSDAY 14 APRIL – PERFORMANCE
Jack Murphy Stadium, San Diego, CA, USA

Set list: 'Astronomy Domine', 'Learning To Fly', 'What Do You Want From Me', 'A Great Day For Freedom', 'Sorrow', 'Take It Back', 'On The Turning Away', 'Keep Talking', 'One Of These Days' <Intermission> 'Shine On You Crazy Diamond', 'Breathe', 'Time', 'Breathe (Reprise)', 'High Hopes', 'Wish You Were Here', 'Another Brick In The Wall, Part 2', 'Us And Them', 'Money', 'Comfortably Numb' <Encore>'Hey You', 'Run Like Hell'.

SATURDAY 16 APRIL – PERFORMANCE
The Rose Bowl, Pasadena, CA, USA

Set list: 'Astronomy Domine', 'Learning To Fly', 'What Do You Want From Me', 'Poles Apart', 'Sorrow', 'On The Turning Away', 'Keep Talking', 'Take It Back', 'One Of These Days' <Intermission> 'Shine On You Crazy Diamond', 'Breathe', 'Time', 'Breathe (Reprise)', 'High Hopes', 'Wish You Were Here', 'Another Brick In The Wall, Part 2', 'The Great Gig In The Sky', 'Us And Them', 'Money', 'Comfortably Numb' <Encore>'Hey You', 'Run Like Hell'.

SUNDAY 17 APRIL – PERFORMANCE
The Rose Bowl, Pasadena, CA, USA

Set list: 'Astronomy Domine', 'Learning To Fly', 'What Do You Want From Me', 'A Great Day For Freedom', 'Sorrow', 'Take It Back', 'On The Turning Away', 'Keep Talking', 'One Of These Days' <Intermission> 'Shine On You Crazy Diamond', 'Breathe', 'Time', 'Breathe (Reprise)', 'High Hopes', 'Wish You Were Here', 'Another Brick In The Wall, Part 2', 'The Great Gig In The Sky', 'Us And Them', 'Money', 'Comfortably Numb' <Encore>'Hey You', 'Run Like Hell'.

MONDAY 18 APRIL – CANCELLED PERFORMANCE
Silver Bowl, Las Vegas, NV, USA

Scheduled in early tour drafts, this show was cancelled before tickets went on sale.

WEDNESDAY 20 APRIL – PERFORMANCE
Oakland Coliseum Stadium, Oakland, CA, USA

Set list: 'Astronomy Domine', 'Learning To Fly', 'What Do You Want From Me', 'On The Turning Away', 'Poles Apart', 'Sorrow', 'Take It Back', 'Keep Talking', 'One Of These Days' <Intermission> 'Shine On You Crazy Diamond', 'Breathe', 'Time', 'Breathe (Reprise)', 'High Hopes', 'Wish You Were Here', 'Another Brick In The Wall, Part 2', 'The Great Gig In The Sky', 'Us And Them', 'Money', 'Comfortably Numb' <Encore>'Hey You', 'Run Like Hell'.

THURSDAY 21 APRIL – PERFORMANCE
Oakland Coliseum Stadium, Oakland, CA, USA

Set list: 'Astronomy Domine', 'Learning To Fly', 'What Do You Want From Me', 'On The Turning Away', 'A Great Day For Freedom', 'Sorrow', 'Take It Back', 'Keep Talking', 'One Of These Days' <Intermission> 'Shine On You Crazy Diamond', 'Breathe', 'Time', 'Breathe (Reprise)', 'High Hopes', 'Wish You Were Here', 'Another Brick In The Wall, Part 2', 'The Great Gig In The Sky', 'Us And Them', 'Money', 'Comfortably Numb' <Encore>'Hey You', 'Run Like Hell'.

FRIDAY 22 APRIL – PERFORMANCE
Oakland Coliseum Stadium, Oakland, CA, USA

Set list: 'Astronomy Domine', 'Learning To Fly', 'What Do You Want From Me', 'On The Turning Away', 'Poles Apart', 'Sorrow', 'Take It Back', 'Keep Talking', 'One Of These Days' <Intermission> 'Shine On You Crazy Diamond', 'Breathe', 'Time', 'Breathe (Reprise)', 'High Hopes', 'The Great Gig In The Sky', 'One Slip', 'Us And Them', 'Wish You Were Here', 'Money', 'Another Brick In The Wall, Part 2', 'Comfortably Numb' <Encore> 'Hey You', 'Run Like Hell'.

RIGHT: CLAUDIA FONTAINE, SAM BROWN AND DURGA MCBROOM HIT THE HIGH NOTES AT THE ROSE BOWL, PASADENA, 16 APRIL 1994.

This was the first and only time 'One Slip' was performed on the entire tour.

SUNDAY 24 APRIL – PERFORMANCE
Sun Devil Stadium, Arizona State University,
Tempe, Phoenix, AZ, USA

Set list: 'Astronomy Domine', 'Learning To Fly', 'What Do You Want From Me', 'On The Turning Away', 'Lost For Words', 'Sorrow', 'Take It Back', 'Keep Talking', 'One Of These Days' <Intermission> 'Shine On You Crazy Diamond', 'Breathe', 'Time', 'Breathe (Reprise)', 'High Hopes', 'The Great Gig In The Sky', 'Wish You Were Here', 'Us And Them', 'Money', 'Another Brick In The Wall, Part 2', 'Comfortably Numb' <Encore> 'Hey You', 'Run Like Hell'.

TUESDAY 26 APRIL – PERFORMANCE
Sun Bowl Stadium, University of Texas, El Paso, TX, USA

Set list: 'Astronomy Domine', 'Learning To Fly', 'What Do You Want From Me', 'On The Turning Away', 'Lost For Words', 'Sorrow', 'Take It Back', 'Keep Talking', 'One Of These Days' <Intermission> 'Shine On You Crazy Diamond', 'Breathe', 'Time', 'Breathe (Reprise)', 'High Hopes', 'The Great Gig In The Sky', 'Wish You Were Here', 'Us And Them', 'Money', 'Another Brick In The Wall, Part 2', 'Comfortably Numb' <Encore> 'Hey You', 'Run Like Hell'.

THURSDAY 28 APRIL – PERFORMANCE
Texas Stadium, Irving, TX, USA

Set list: 'Astronomy Domine', 'Learning To Fly', 'What Do You Want From Me', 'On The Turning Away', 'Poles Apart', 'Sorrow', 'Take It Back', 'Keep Talking', 'One Of These Days' <Intermission> 'Shine On You Crazy Diamond', 'Breathe', 'Time', 'Breathe (Reprise)', 'High Hopes', 'The Great Gig In The Sky', 'Wish You Were Here', 'Us And Them', 'Money', 'Another Brick In The Wall, Part 2', 'Comfortably Numb' <Encore> 'Hey You', 'Run Like Hell'.

FRIDAY 29 APRIL – PERFORMANCE
Texas Stadium, Irving, TX, USA

Set list: 'Astronomy Domine', 'Learning To Fly', 'What Do You Want From Me', 'On The Turning Away', 'Coming Back To Life', 'Sorrow', 'Take It Back', 'Keep Talking', 'One Of These Days' <Intermission> 'Shine On You Crazy Diamond', 'Breathe', 'Time', 'Breathe (Reprise)', 'High Hopes', 'The Great Gig In The Sky', 'Wish You Were Here', 'Us And Them', 'Money', 'Another Brick In The Wall, Part 2', 'Comfortably Numb' <Encore> 'Hey You', 'Run Like Hell'.

SUNDAY 1 MAY – PERFORMANCE
Legion Field, University of Alabama, Birmingham, AL, USA

Set list: 'Astronomy Domine', 'Learning To Fly', 'What Do You Want From Me', 'On The Turning Away', 'Take It Back', 'Lost For Words', 'Sorrow', 'Coming Back To Life', 'Keep Talking', 'One Of These Days' <Intermission> 'Shine On You Crazy Diamond', 'Breathe', 'Time', 'Breathe (Reprise)', 'High Hopes', 'The Great Gig In The Sky', 'Wish You Were Here', 'Us And Them', 'Money', 'Another Brick In The Wall, Part 2', 'Comfortably Numb' <Encore> 'Hey You', 'Run Like Hell'.

TUESDAY 3 MAY – PERFORMANCE
Bobbie Dodd Stadium,
Georgia Institute of Technology, Atlanta, GA, USA

Set list: 'Astronomy Domine', 'Learning To Fly', 'What Do You Want From Me', 'On The Turning Away', 'Take It Back', 'Lost For Words', 'Sorrow', 'Coming Back To Life', 'Keep Talking', 'One Of These Days' <Intermission> 'Shine On You Crazy Diamond', 'Breathe', 'Time', 'Breathe (Reprise)', 'High Hopes', 'The Great Gig In The Sky', 'Wish You Were Here', 'Us And Them', 'Money', 'Another Brick In The Wall, Part 2', 'Comfortably Numb' <Encore> 'Hey You', 'Run Like Hell'.

WEDNESDAY 4 MAY – PERFORMANCE
Bobbie Dodd Stadium,
Georgia Institute of Technology, Atlanta, GA, USA

Set list: 'Astronomy Domine', 'Learning To Fly', 'What Do You Want From Me', 'On The Turning Away', 'Coming Back To Life', 'Sorrow', 'Take It Back', 'Keep Talking', 'One Of These Days' <Intermission> 'Shine On You Crazy Diamond', 'Breathe', 'Time', 'Breathe (Reprise)', 'High Hopes', 'The Great Gig In The Sky', 'Wish You Were Here', 'Us And Them', 'Money', 'Another Brick In The Wall, Part 2', 'Comfortably Numb' <Encore> 'Hey You', 'Run Like Hell'.

FRIDAY 6 MAY – PERFORMANCE
Tampa Stadium, Tampa, FL, USA

Set list: 'Astronomy Domine', 'Learning To Fly', 'What Do You Want From Me', 'On The Turning Away', 'Take It Back', 'A Great Day For Freedom', 'Sorrow', 'Keep Talking', 'One Of These Days' <Intermission> 'Shine On You Crazy Diamond', 'Breathe', 'Time', 'Breathe (Reprise)', 'High Hopes', 'The Great Gig In The Sky', 'Wish You Were Here', 'Us And Them', 'Money', 'Another Brick In The Wall, Part 2', 'Comfortably Numb' <Encore> 'Hey You', 'Run Like Hell'.

The band performed an unusually lengthy soundcheck prior to the commencement of the show, including the following tracks: 'Shine On You Crazy Diamond', 'High Hopes', 'Breathe', 'Time', 'The Great Gig In The Sky', 'Lost For Words', 'Wish You Were Here', 'Money' and 'Us And Them'.

SUNDAY 8 MAY – PERFORMANCE
Vanderbilt University Stadium, Nashville, TN, USA

Set list: 'Astronomy Domine', 'Learning To Fly', 'What Do You Want From Me', 'On The Turning Away', 'Take It Back', 'A Great Day For Freedom', 'Sorrow', 'Keep Talking', 'One Of These Days' <Intermission> 'Shine On You Crazy Diamond', 'Breathe', 'Time', 'Breathe (Reprise)', 'High Hopes', 'The Great Gig In The Sky', 'Wish You Were Here', 'Us And Them', 'Money', 'Another Brick In The Wall, Part 2', 'Comfortably Numb' <Encore> 'Hey You', 'Run Like Hell'.

TUESDAY 10 MAY – PERFORMANCE
Carter-Finley Stadium, University of North Carolina, Raleigh, NC, USA

Set list: 'Astronomy Domine', 'Learning To Fly', 'What Do You Want From Me', 'A Great Day For Freedom', 'Sorrow', 'Take It Back', 'On The Turning Away', 'Keep Talking', 'One Of These Days' <Intermission> 'Shine On You Crazy Diamond', 'Breathe', 'Time', 'Breathe (Reprise)', 'High Hopes', 'Wish You Were Here', 'Another Brick In The Wall, Part 2', 'The Great Gig In The Sky', 'Us And Them', 'Money', 'Comfortably Numb' <Encore> 'Hey You', 'Run Like Hell'.

THURSDAY 12 MAY – PERFORMANCE
Clemson Memorial (Death Valley) Stadium, Clemson University, Clemson, SC, USA

Set list: 'Astronomy Domine', 'Learning To Fly', 'What Do You Want From Me', 'On The Turning Away', 'Take It Back', 'Poles Apart', 'Keep Talking', 'One Of These Days' <Intermission> 'Shine On You Crazy Diamond', 'Breathe', 'Time', 'Breathe (Reprise)', 'High Hopes', 'The Great Gig In The Sky', 'Wish You Were Here', 'Us And Them', 'Money', 'Another Brick In The Wall, Part 2', 'Comfortably Numb' <Encore>'Hey You', 'Run Like Hell'.

SATURDAY 14 MAY – PERFORMANCE
Louisiana Superdrome, New Orleans, LA, USA

Set list: 'Astronomy Domine', 'Learning To Fly', 'What Do You Want From Me', 'On The Turning Away', 'Take It Back', 'Coming Back To Life', 'Sorrow', 'Keep Talking', 'One Of These Days' <Intermission> 'Shine On You Crazy Diamond', 'Breathe', 'Time', 'Breathe (Reprise)', 'High Hopes', 'The Great Gig In The Sky', 'Wish You Were Here', 'Us And Them', 'Money', 'Another Brick In The Wall, Part 2', 'Comfortably Numb' <Encore>'Hey You', 'Run Like Hell'.

Associated Press reported that a police officer shot a man during the show. The officer pulled a gun on him while he was arresting the man's wife for failing to extinguish a marijuana cigarette. Although shot in the abdomen, the man was not seriously wounded and was later charged with aggrevated assault, illegal possession of a firearm and resisting arrest.

MONDAY 16 MAY 1994 – SINGLE RELEASE (UK)
'Take It Back'

WEDNESDAY 18 MAY – PERFORMANCE ▼
Foxboro Stadium, Foxborough, MA, USA

Set list: 'Astronomy Domine', 'Learning To Fly', 'What Do You Want From Me', 'On The Turning Away', 'Coming Back To Life', 'Sorrow', 'Take It Back', 'Keep Talking', 'One Of These Days' <Intermission> 'Shine On You Crazy Diamond', 'Breathe', 'Time', 'Breathe (Reprise)', 'High Hopes', 'The Great Gig In The Sky', 'Wish You Were Here', 'Us And Them', 'Money', 'Another Brick In The Wall, Part 2', 'Comfortably Numb' <Encore>'Hey You', 'Run Like Hell'.

THURSDAY 19 MAY – PERFORMANCE
Foxboro Stadium, Foxborough, MA, USA

Set list: 'Astronomy Domine', 'Learning To Fly', 'What Do You Want From Me', 'On The Turning Away', 'Take It Back', 'Poles Apart', 'Sorrow', 'Keep Talking', 'One Of These Days' <Intermission> 'Shine On You Crazy Diamond', 'Breathe', 'Time', 'Breathe (Reprise)', 'High Hopes', 'The Great Gig In The Sky', 'Wish You Were Here', 'Us And Them', 'Money', 'Another Brick In The Wall, Part 2', 'Comfortably Numb' <Encore>'Hey You', 'Run Like Hell'.

FRIDAY 20 MAY – PERFORMANCE
Foxboro Stadium, Foxborough, MA, USA

Set list: 'Astronomy Domine', 'Learning To Fly', 'What Do You Want From

Me', 'On The Turning Away', 'Take It Back', 'A Great Day For Freedom', 'Sorrow', 'Keep Talking', 'One Of These Days' <Intermission> 'Shine On You Crazy Diamond', 'Breathe', 'Time', 'Breathe (Reprise)', 'High Hopes', 'The Great Gig In The Sky', 'Wish You Were Here', 'Us And Them', 'Money', 'Another Brick In The Wall, Part 2', 'Comfortably Numb' <Encore>'Hey You', 'Run Like Hell'.

SUNDAY 22 MAY – PERFORMANCE
Stade du Parc Olympique, Montréal, Canada

Set list: 'Astronomy Domine', 'Learning To Fly', 'What Do You Want From Me', 'Poles Apart', 'Sorrow', 'On The Turning Away', 'Take It Back', 'Keep Talking', 'One Of These Days' <Intermission> 'Shine On You Crazy Diamond', 'Breathe', 'Time', 'Breathe (Reprise)', 'High Hopes', 'The Great Gig In The Sky', 'Wish You Were Here', 'Us And Them', 'Money', 'Another Brick In The Wall, Part 2', 'Comfortably Numb' <Encore>'Hey You', 'Run Like Hell'.

MONDAY 23 MAY – PERFORMANCE
Stade du Parc Olympique, Montréal, Canada

Set list: 'Astronomy Domine', 'Learning To Fly', 'What Do You Want From Me', 'On The Turning Away', 'A Great Day For Freedom', 'Take It Back', 'Sorrow', 'Keep Talking', 'One Of These Days' <Intermission> 'Shine On You Crazy Diamond', 'Breathe', 'Time', 'Breathe (Reprise)', 'High Hopes', 'The Great Gig In The Sky', 'Wish You Were Here', 'Us And Them', 'Money', 'Another Brick In The Wall, Part 2', 'Comfortably Numb' <Encore>'Hey You', 'Run Like Hell'.

TUESDAY 24 MAY – PERFORMANCE
Stade du Parc Olympique, Montréal, Canada

Set list: 'Astronomy Domine', 'Learning To Fly', 'What Do You Want From Me', 'On The Turning Away', 'Coming Back To Life', 'Sorrow', 'Take It Back', 'A Great Day For Freedom', 'Keep Talking', 'One Of These Days' <Intermission> 'Shine On You Crazy Diamond', 'Breathe', 'Time', 'Breathe (Reprise)', 'High Hopes', 'The Great Gig In The Sky', 'Wish You Were Here', 'Us And Them', 'Money', 'Another Brick In The Wall, Part 2', 'Comfortably Numb' <Encore>'Hey You', 'Run Like Hell'.

THURSDAY 26 MAY – PERFORMANCE
Municipal Stadium, Cleveland, OH, USA

Set list: 'Astronomy Domine', 'Learning To Fly', 'What Do You Want From Me', 'On The Turning Away', 'Take It Back', 'Poles Apart', 'Sorrow', 'Keep Talking', 'One Of These Days' <Intermission> 'Shine On You Crazy Diamond', 'Breathe', 'Time', 'Breathe (Reprise)', 'High Hopes', 'The Great Gig In The Sky', 'Wish You Were Here', 'Us And Them', 'Money', 'Another Brick In The Wall, Part 2', 'Comfortably Numb' <Encore>'Hey You', 'Run Like Hell'.

FRIDAY 27 MAY – PERFORMANCE
Municipal Stadium, Cleveland, OH, USA

Set list: 'Astronomy Domine', 'Learning To Fly', 'What Do You Want From Me', 'On The Turning Away', 'Sorrow', 'Take It Back', 'Keep Talking', 'One Of These Days' <Intermission> 'Shine On You Crazy Diamond', 'Breathe', 'Time', 'Breathe (Reprise)', 'High Hopes', 'The Great Gig In The Sky', 'Wish You Were Here', 'Us And Them', 'Money', 'Another Brick In The Wall, Part 2', 'Comfortably Numb' <Encore>'Hey You', 'Run Like Hell'.

SUNDAY 29 MAY – PERFORMANCE
Ohio State University Stadium, Columbus, OH, USA

Set list: 'Astronomy Domine', 'Learning To Fly', 'What Do You Want From Me', 'On The Turning Away', 'Coming Back To Life', 'Sorrow', 'Take It Back', 'Keep Talking', 'One Of These Days' <Intermission> 'Shine On You Crazy Diamond', 'Breathe', 'Time', 'Breathe (Reprise)', 'High Hopes', 'The Great Gig In The Sky', 'Wish You Were Here', 'Us And Them', 'Money', 'Another Brick In The Wall, Part 2', 'Comfortably Numb' <Encore>'Hey You', 'Run Like Hell'.

TUESDAY 31 MAY 1994 – SINGLE RELEASE (US)
'Take It Back'

TUESDAY 31 MAY – PERFORMANCE
Three Rivers Stadium, Pittsburgh, PA, USA

Set list: 'Astronomy Domine', 'Learning To Fly', 'What Do You Want From Me', 'On The Turning Away', 'Coming Back To Life', 'Sorrow', 'Take It Back', 'Keep Talking', 'One Of These Days' <Intermission> 'Shine On You Crazy Diamond', 'Breathe', 'Time', 'Breathe (Reprise)', 'High Hopes', 'The Great Gig In The Sky', 'Wish You Were Here', 'Us And Them', 'Money', 'Another Brick In The Wall, Part 2', 'Comfortably Numb' <Encore>'Hey You', 'Run Like Hell'.

THURSDAY 2 JUNE – PERFORMANCE
Veterans Stadium, Philadelphia, PA, USA

Set list: 'Astronomy Domine', 'Learning To Fly', 'What Do You Want From Me', 'On The Turning Away', 'Take It Back', 'Poles Apart', 'Sorrow', 'Keep Talking', 'One Of These Days' <Intermission> 'Shine On You Crazy Diamond', 'Breathe', 'Time', 'Breathe (Reprise)', 'High Hopes', 'The Great Gig In The Sky', 'Wish You Were Here', 'Us And Them', 'Money', 'Another Brick In The Wall, Part 2', 'Comfortably Numb' <Encore>'Hey You', 'Run Like Hell'.

FRIDAY 3 JUNE –
PERFORMANCE ◄
Veterans Stadium, Philadelphia, PA, USA

Set list: 'Astronomy Domine', 'Learning To Fly', 'What Do You Want From Me', 'On The Turning Away', 'Take It Back', 'A Great Day For Freedom', 'Sorrow', 'Keep Talking', 'One Of These Days' <Intermission> 'Shine On You Crazy Diamond', 'Breathe', 'Time', 'Breathe (Reprise)', 'High Hopes', 'The Great Gig In The Sky', 'Wish You Were Here', 'Us And Them', 'Money', 'Another Brick In The Wall, Part 2', 'Comfortably Numb' <Encore>'Hey You', 'Run Like Hell'.

SATURDAY 4 JUNE – PERFORMANCE ►
Veterans Stadium, Philadelphia, PA, USA

Set list: 'Astronomy Domine', 'Learning To Fly', 'What Do You Want From Me', 'On The Turning Away', 'Coming Back To Life', 'Sorrow', 'Take It Back', 'Keep Talking', 'One Of These Days' <Intermission> 'Shine On You Crazy Diamond', 'Breathe', 'Time', 'Breathe (Reprise)', 'High Hopes', 'The Great Gig In The Sky', 'Wish You Were Here', 'Us And Them', 'Money', 'Another Brick In The Wall, Part 2', 'Comfortably Numb' <Encore>'Hey You', 'Run Like Hell'.

MONDAY 6 JUNE – PERFORMANCE
Carrier Dome, Syracuse, NY, USA

Set list: 'Astronomy Domine', 'Learning To Fly', 'What Do You Want From Me', 'Take It Back', 'On The Turning Away', 'Coming Back To Life', 'Sorrow', 'Keep Talking', 'One Of These Days' <Intermission> 'Shine On You Crazy Diamond', 'Breathe', 'Time', 'Breathe (Reprise)', 'Wish You Were Here', 'Us And Them', 'High Hopes', 'Money', 'The Great Gig In The Sky', 'Another Brick In The Wall, Part 2', 'Comfortably Numb' <Encore>'Hey You', 'Run Like Hell'.

FRIDAY 10 JUNE – PERFORMANCE
Yankee Stadium, Bronx, New York, NY, USA

Set list: 'Astronomy Domine', 'Learning To Fly', 'What Do You Want From Me', 'On The Turning Away', 'Poles Apart', 'Take It Back', 'Sorrow', 'Keep Talking', 'One Of These Days' <Intermission> 'Shine On You Crazy Diamond', 'Breathe', 'Time', 'Breathe (Reprise)', 'High Hopes', 'The Great Gig In The Sky', 'Wish You Were Here', 'Us And Them', 'Money', 'Another Brick In The Wall, Part 2', 'Comfortably Numb' <Encore>'Hey You', 'Run Like Hell'.

SATURDAY 11 JUNE – PERFORMANCE
Yankee Stadium, Bronx, New York, NY, USA

Set list: 'Astronomy Domine', 'Learning To Fly', 'What Do You Want From Me', 'On The Turning Away', 'Take It Back', 'Coming Back To Life', 'Sorrow', 'Keep Talking', 'One Of These Days' <Intermission> 'Shine On You Crazy Diamond', 'Breathe', 'Time', 'Breathe (Reprise)', 'High Hopes', 'The Great Gig In The Sky', 'Wish You Were Here', 'Us And Them', 'Money', 'Another Brick In The Wall, Part 2', 'Comfortably Numb' <Encore>'Hey You', 'Run Like Hell'.

TUESDAY 14 JUNE – PERFORMANCE
Hoosier Dome, Indianapolis, IN, USA

Set list: 'Astronomy Domine', 'Learning To Fly', 'What Do You Want From Me', 'On The Turning Away', 'Take It Back', 'A Great Day For Freedom', 'Sorrow', 'Keep Talking', 'One Of These Days' <Intermission> 'Shine On You Crazy Diamond', 'Breathe', 'Time', 'Breathe (Reprise)', 'High Hopes', 'The Great Gig In The Sky', 'Wish You Were Here', 'Us And Them', 'Money', 'Another Brick In The Wall, Part 2', 'Comfortably Numb' <Encore>'Hey You', 'Run Like Hell'.

THURSDAY 16 JUNE – PERFORMANCE
Cyclone Stadium, Iowa State University, Ames, IA, USA

Set list: 'Astronomy Domine', 'Learning To Fly', 'What Do You Want From Me', 'On The Turning Away', 'Take It Back', 'A Great Day For Freedom', 'Sorrow', 'Keep Talking', 'One Of These Days' <Intermission> 'Shine On

You Crazy Diamond', 'Breathe', 'Time', 'Breathe (Reprise)', 'High Hopes', 'The Great Gig In The Sky', 'Wish You Were Here', 'Us And Them', 'Money', 'Another Brick In The Wall, Part 2', 'Comfortably Numb' <Encore>'Hey You', 'Run Like Hell'.

SATURDAY 18 JUNE – PERFORMANCE
Mile High Stadium, Denver, CO, USA

Set list: 'Astronomy Domine', 'Learning To Fly', 'What Do You Want From Me', 'On The Turning Away', 'Take It Back', 'Coming Back To Life', 'Sorrow', 'Keep Talking', 'One Of These Days' <Intermission> 'Shine On You Crazy Diamond', 'Breathe', 'Time', 'Breathe (Reprise)', 'High Hopes', 'The Great Gig In The Sky', 'Wish You Were Here', 'Us And Them', 'Money', 'Another Brick In The Wall, Part 2', 'Comfortably Numb' <Encore>'Hey You', 'Run Like Hell'.

MONDAY 20 JUNE – PERFORMANCE
Arrowhead Stadium, Kansas City, MO, USA

Set list: 'Astronomy Domine', 'Learning To Fly', 'What Do You Want From Me', 'On The Turning Away', 'Poles Apart', 'Take It Back', 'Sorrow', 'Keep Talking', 'One Of These Days' <Intermission> 'Shine On You Crazy Diamond', 'Breathe', 'Time', 'Breathe (Reprise)', 'High Hopes', 'The Great Gig In The Sky', 'Wish You Were Here', 'Us And Them', 'Money', 'Another Brick In The Wall, Part 2', 'Comfortably Numb' <Encore>'Hey You', 'Run Like Hell'.

WEDNESDAY 22 JUNE – PERFORMANCE
Hubert H. Humphrey Metrodome, Minneapolis, MN, USA

Set list: 'Astronomy Domine', 'Learning To Fly', 'What Do You Want From Me', 'On The Turning Away', 'Take It Back', 'Coming Back To Life', 'Sorrow', 'Keep Talking', 'One Of These Days' <Intermission> 'Shine On You Crazy Diamond', 'Breathe', 'Time', 'Breathe (Reprise)', 'High Hopes', 'The Great Gig In The Sky', 'Wish You Were Here', 'Us And Them', 'Money', 'Another Brick In The Wall, Part 2', 'Comfortably Numb' <Encore>'Hey You', 'Run Like Hell'.

SATURDAY 25 JUNE – PERFORMANCE
British Columbia Place Stadium, Vancouver, Canada

Set list: 'Astronomy Domine', 'Learning To Fly', 'What Do You Want From Me', 'Coming Back To Life', 'Sorrow', 'On The Turning Away', 'Take It Back', 'Keep Talking', 'One Of These Days' <Intermission> 'Shine On You Crazy Diamond', 'Breathe', 'Time', 'Breathe (Reprise)', 'High Hopes', 'Wish You Were Here', 'Another Brick In The Wall, Part 2', 'The Great Gig In The Sky', 'Us And Them', 'Money', 'Comfortably Numb' <Encore>'Hey You', 'Run Like Hell'.

SUNDAY 26 JUNE – PERFORMANCE
British Columbia Place Stadium, Vancouver, Canada

Set list: 'Astronomy Domine', 'Learning To Fly', 'What Do You Want From Me', 'A Great Day For Freedom', 'Sorrow', 'On The Turning Away', 'Take It Back', 'Keep Talking', 'One Of These Days' <Intermission> 'Shine On You Crazy Diamond', 'Breathe', 'Time', 'Breathe (Reprise)', 'High Hopes', 'Wish You Were Here', 'Another Brick In The Wall, Part 2', 'The Great Gig In The Sky', 'Us And Them', 'Money', 'Comfortably Numb' <Encore>'Hey You', 'Run Like Hell'.

TUESDAY 28 JUNE – PERFORMANCE
Commonwealth Stadium, Edmonton, Canada

Set list: 'Astronomy Domine', 'Learning To Fly', 'What Do You Want From Me', 'Sorrow', 'On The Turning Away', 'Take It Back', 'Keep Talking', 'One Of These Days' <Intermission> 'Shine On You Crazy Diamond', 'Breathe', 'Time', 'Breathe (Reprise)', 'High Hopes', 'The Great Gig In The

Sky', 'Wish You Were Here', 'Money', 'Us And Them', 'Another Brick In The Wall, Part 2', 'Comfortably Numb' <Encore>'Hey You', 'Run Like Hell'.

FRIDAY 1 JULY – PERFORMANCE
Winnipeg Stadium, Winnipeg, Canada

Set list: 'Astronomy Domine', 'Learning To Fly', 'What Do You Want From Me', 'On The Turning Away', 'Poles Apart', 'Take It Back', 'Sorrow', 'Keep Talking', 'One Of These Days' <Intermission> 'Shine On You Crazy Diamond', 'Breathe', 'Time', 'Breathe (Reprise)', 'High Hopes', 'Wish You Were Here', 'The Great Gig In The Sky', 'Us And Them', 'Money', 'Another Brick In The Wall, Part 2', 'Comfortably Numb' <Encore>'Hey You', 'Run Like Hell'.

SUNDAY 3 JULY – PERFORMANCE
Camp Randall Stadium,
University of Madison-Wisconsin, Madison, WI, USA

Set list: 'Astronomy Domine', 'Learning To Fly', 'What Do You Want From Me', 'On The Turning Away', 'Take It Back', 'A Great Day For Freedom', 'Sorrow', 'Keep Talking', 'One Of These Days' <Intermission> 'Shine On You Crazy Diamond', 'Breathe', 'Time', 'Breathe (Reprise)', 'High Hopes', 'The Great Gig In The Sky', 'Wish You Were Here', 'Us And Them', 'Money', 'Another Brick In The Wall, Part 2', 'Comfortably Numb' <Encore>'Hey You', 'Run Like Hell'.

TUESDAY 5 JULY – PERFORMANCE
Canadian National Exhibition Stadium, Toronto, Canada

Set list: 'Astronomy Domine', 'Learning To Fly', 'What Do You Want From Me', 'On The Turning Away', 'Take It Back', 'Coming Back To Life', 'Sorrow', 'Keep Talking', 'One Of These Days' <Intermission> 'Shine On You Crazy Diamond', 'Breathe', 'Time', 'Breathe (Reprise)', 'High Hopes', 'The Great Gig In The Sky', 'Wish You Were Here', 'Us And Them', 'Money', 'Another Brick In The Wall, Part 2', 'Comfortably Numb' <Encore>'Hey You', 'Run Like Hell'.

WEDNESDAY 6 JULY – PERFORMANCE
Canadian National Exhibition Stadium, Toronto, Canada

Set list: 'Astronomy Domine', 'Learning To Fly', 'What Do You Want From Me', 'On The Turning Away', 'Take It Back', 'Sorrow', 'Keep Talking', 'One Of These Days' <Intermission> 'Shine On You Crazy Diamond', 'Breathe', 'Time', 'Breathe (Reprise)', 'High Hopes', 'The Great Gig In The Sky', 'Wish You Were Here', 'Us And Them', 'Money', 'Another Brick In The Wall, Part 2', 'Comfortably Numb' <Encore>'Hey You', 'Run Like Hell'.

'Brain Damage' and 'Eclipse' were rehearsed by the band during the pre-show soundcheck.

THURSDAY 7 JULY – PERFORMANCE
Canadian National Exhibition Stadium, Toronto, Canada

Set list: 'Astronomy Domine', 'Learning To Fly', 'What Do You Want From Me', 'On The Turning Away', 'Take It Back', 'A Great Day For Freedom', 'Sorrow', 'Keep Talking', 'One Of These Days' <Intermission> 'Shine On You Crazy Diamond', 'Breathe', 'Time', 'Breathe (Reprise)', 'High Hopes', 'The Great Gig In The Sky', 'Wish You Were Here', 'Us And Them', 'Money', 'Another Brick In The Wall, Part 2', 'Comfortably Numb' <Encore>'Hey You', 'Run Like Hell'.

SATURDAY 9 JULY – PERFORMANCE
Robert F. Kennedy Stadium, Washington, DC, USA

Set list: 'Astronomy Domine', 'Learning To Fly', 'What Do You Want From Me', 'On The Turning Away', 'Poles Apart', 'Take It Back', 'Sorrow', 'Keep Talking', 'One Of These Days' <Intermission> 'Shine On You Crazy Diamond', 'Breathe', 'Time', 'Breathe (Reprise)', 'High Hopes', 'The Great Gig In The Sky', 'Wish You Were Here', 'Us And Them', 'Money', 'Another Brick In The Wall, Part 2', 'Comfortably Numb' <Encore>'Hey You', 'Run Like Hell'.

SUNDAY 10 JULY – PERFORMANCE
Robert F. Kennedy Stadium, Washington, DC, USA

Set list: 'Astronomy Domine', 'Learning To Fly', 'What Do You Want From Me', 'On The Turning Away', 'Take It Back', 'Coming Back To Life', 'Sorrow', 'Keep Talking', 'One Of These Days' <Intermission> 'Shine On You Crazy Diamond', 'Breathe', 'Time', 'Breathe (Reprise)', 'High Hopes', 'The Great Gig In The Sky', 'Wish You Were Here', 'Us And Them', 'Money', 'Another Brick In The Wall, Part 2', 'Comfortably Numb' <Encore>'Hey You', 'Run Like Hell'.

TUESDAY 12 JULY – PERFORMANCE
Soldier Field, Chicago, IL, USA

Set list: 'Astronomy Domine', 'Learning To Fly', 'What Do You Want From Me', 'On The Turning Away', 'Lost For Words', 'Sorrow', 'Take It Back', 'Keep Talking', 'One Of These Days' <Intermission> 'Shine On You Crazy Diamond', 'Breathe', 'Time', 'Breathe (Reprise)', 'High Hopes', 'The Great Gig In The Sky', 'Wish You Were Here', 'Us And Them', 'Money', 'Another Brick In The Wall, Part 2', 'Comfortably Numb' <Encore>'Hey You', 'Run Like Hell'.

THURSDAY 14 JULY – PERFORMANCE
Pontiac Silverdome, Pontiac, Detroit, MI, USA

Set list: 'Astronomy Domine', 'Learning To Fly', 'What Do You Want From Me', 'On The Turning Away', 'Poles Apart', 'Take It Back', 'Sorrow', 'Keep Talking', 'One Of These Days' <Intermission> 'Shine On You Crazy Diamond', 'Breathe', 'Time', 'Breathe (Reprise)', 'High Hopes', 'The Great Gig In The Sky', 'Wish You Were Here', 'Us And Them', 'Money', 'Another Brick In The Wall, Part 2', 'Comfortably Numb' <Encore>'Hey You', 'Run Like Hell'.

FRIDAY 15 JULY – PERFORMANCE
Pontiac Silverdome, Pontiac, Detroit, MI, USA

Set list: 'Shine On You Crazy Diamond', 'Learning To Fly', 'High Hopes', 'Coming Back To Life', 'Take It Back', 'Sorrow', 'Keep Talking', 'Another Brick In The Wall, Part 2', 'One Of These Days' <Intermission> *The Dark Side of the Moon* <Encore>'Wish You Were Here', 'Comfortably Numb', 'Run Like Hell'.

Pink Floyd performed the entire *The Dark Side of the Moon* for the first time since their show at Knebworth, England on Saturday 5 July 1975.

SUNDAY 17 JULY – PERFORMANCE
Giants Stadium, Meadowlands Sports Complex, East Rutherford, NJ, USA

Set list: 'Shine On You Crazy Diamond', 'Learning To Fly', 'High Hopes', 'Take It Back', 'Coming Back To Life', 'Sorrow', 'Keep Talking', 'Another Brick In The Wall, Part 2', 'One Of These Days' <Intermission> *The Dark Side of the Moon* <Encore>'Wish You Were Here', 'Comfortably Numb', 'Run Like Hell'.

MONDAY 18 JULY – PERFORMANCE
Giants Stadium, Meadowlands Sports Complex, East Rutherford, NJ, USA

Set list: 'Shine On You Crazy Diamond', 'Learning To Fly', 'High Hopes', 'Take It Back', 'Coming Back To Life', 'Sorrow', 'Keep Talking', 'Another Brick In The Wall, Part 2', 'One Of These Days' <Intermission> *The Dark Side of the Moon* <Encore>'Wish You Were Here', 'Comfortably Numb', 'Run Like Hell'.

Following the concert, two Boeing 747s and a massive Russian Antonov military transport were chartered to fly equipment to Europe for the next concert a mere four days later.

PINK FLOYD WORLD TOUR 1994 (EUROPE)

FRIDAY 22 JULY – PERFORMANCE
Estádio de Alvalade, Lisbon, Portugal

Set list: 'Astronomy Domine', 'Learning To Fly', 'What Do You Want From Me', 'On The Turning Away', 'Take It Back', 'Coming Back To Life', 'Lost For Words', 'Sorrow', 'Keep Talking', 'One Of These Days' <Intermission> 'Shine On You Crazy Diamond', 'Breathe', 'Time', 'Breathe (Reprise)', 'High Hopes', 'The Great Gig In The Sky', 'Wish You Were Here', 'Us And Them', 'Money', 'Another Brick In The Wall, Part 2', 'Comfortably Numb' <Encore>'Hey You', 'Run Like Hell'.

SATURDAY 23 JULY – PERFORMANCE
Estádio de Alvalade, Lisbon, Portugal

Set list: 'Shine On You Crazy Diamond', 'Learning To Fly', 'What Do You Want From Me', 'On The Turning Away', 'Poles Apart', 'Take It Back', 'Sorrow', 'Keep Talking', 'One Of These Days' <Intermission> 'Astronomy Domine, 'Breathe', 'Time', 'Breathe (Reprise)', 'High Hopes', 'The Great Gig In The Sky', 'Wish You Were Here', 'Us And Them', 'Money', 'Another Brick In The Wall, Part 2', 'Comfortably Numb' <Encore>'Hey You', 'Run Like Hell'.

Melody Maker reported, "You cannot begin to imagine. I'm taking about scene and spectacle. About time and place. About the most exorbitantly expensive and expansive stadium show since whatever the last one was…. 70,000 people were there, and another 70,000 the previous night. What is it about Pink Floyd that ensures, wherever they go, multitudes will assemble to worshipfully watch them? Do they fill Antarctic arenas with dizzy, cheering penguins? But I understand. Pink Floyd today may be trademark, a cipher, a hologram of a band who never captured the spirit of the 'Time's in the first place, but I understand. I understand because they open with 'Shine On You Crazy Diamond', which I still hold to be one of the most perfect and beautiful pieces of music ever written, and they perform it on the scale of the fall of Rome. You don't even have to watch the band. Floyd's old circular screen rises above the filament (yes, the Planetarium slides are back too), but now it's huge, 40 feet across, circled with spotlights – engorged basically, with enormous injections of cash – and an allegorical film by Storm Thorgerson plays upon it…. David Gilmour has reassembled a Pink Floyd which is more of a showband than a rock 'n' roll group. To even consider it in terms of rock 'n' roll is to miss the point. Pink Floyd belong in the same league as 'Holiday on Ice' – massive, mythic, meticulous showbiz, an orgy of stupendous and silly SFX. I have become un 'Comfortably Numb' when, at the climax, the very metaphor presents itself in the form of the world's largest revolving mirrored disco ball. It then transforms into the world largest electric palm tree. This show is no less than the exultant culmination of three decades of hi-tech kitsch."

MONDAY 25 JULY – PERFORMANCE ▼
Estadio Anoeta, San Sebastián, Spain

Set list: 'Shine On You Crazy Diamond', 'Learning To Fly', 'What Do You Want From Me', 'On The Turning Away', 'Take It Back', 'A Great Day For Freedom', 'Sorrow', 'Keep Talking', 'One Of These Days' <Intermission> 'Astronomy Domine, 'Breathe', 'Time', 'Breathe (Reprise)', 'High Hopes', 'The Great Gig In The Sky', 'Wish You Were Here', 'Us And Them', 'Money', 'Another Brick In The Wall, Part 2', 'Comfortably Numb' <Encore>'Hey You', 'Run Like Hell'.

WEDNESDAY 27 JULY – PERFORMANCE
Estadi Olímpic, Barcelona, Spain

Set list: 'Shine On You Crazy Diamond', 'Learning To Fly', 'What Do You Want From Me', 'On The Turning Away', 'Take It Back', 'Coming Back To Life', 'Sorrow', 'Keep Talking', 'One Of These Days' <Intermission> 'Astronomy Domine, 'Breathe', 'Time', 'Breathe (Reprise)', 'High Hopes', 'The Great Gig In The Sky', 'Wish You Were Here', 'Us And Them', 'Money', 'Another Brick In The Wall, Part 2', 'Comfortably Numb' <Encore>'Hey You', 'Run Like Hell'.

SATURDAY 30 JULY – PERFORMANCE ▼
Chateau de Chantilly, Chantilly, France

Set list: 'Shine On You Crazy Diamond', 'Learning To Fly', 'What Do You Want From Me', 'On The Turning Away', 'Take It Back', 'Lost For Words', 'Sorrow', 'Keep Talking', 'One Of These Days' <Intermission> 'Astronomy Domine, 'Breathe', 'Time', 'Breathe (Reprise)', 'High Hopes', 'The Great Gig In The Sky', 'Wish You Were Here', 'Us And Them', 'Money', 'Another Brick In The Wall, Part 2', 'Comfortably Numb' <Encore>'Hey You', 'Run Like Hell'. A spectacular lightening storm coincided with the finale of the show during 'Run Like Hell'.

SUNDAY 31 JULY – PERFORMANCE ▶
Chateau de Chantilly, Chantilly, France

Set list: 'Shine On You Crazy Diamond', 'Learning To Fly', 'What Do You Want From Me', 'On The Turning Away', 'Poles Apart', 'Take It Back', 'Sorrow', 'Keep Talking', 'One Of These Days' <Intermission> 'Astronomy Domine, 'Breathe', 'Time', 'Breathe (Reprise)', 'High Hopes', 'The Great Gig In The Sky', 'Wish You Were Here', 'Us And Them', 'Money', 'Another Brick In The Wall, Part 2', 'Comfortably Numb' <Encore>'Hey You', 'Run Like Hell'.

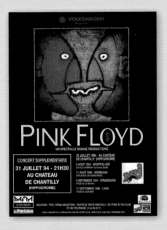

TUESDAY 2 AUGUST – PERFORMANCE ▼
Müngersdorfer Stadion, Cologne, Germany

Set list: 'Astronomy Domine', 'Learning To Fly', 'What Do You Want From Me', 'On The Turning Away', 'Take It Back', 'A Great Day For Freedom', 'Sorrow', 'Keep Talking', 'One Of These Days' <Intermission> 'Shine On You Crazy Diamond', 'Breathe', 'Time', 'Breathe (Reprise)', 'High Hopes', 'The Great Gig In The Sky', 'Wish You Were Here', 'Us And Them', 'Money', 'Another Brick In The Wall, Part 2', 'Comfortably Numb' <Encore>'Hey You', 'Run Like Hell'.

THURSDAY 4 AUGUST – PERFORMANCE
Olympiastadion, Munich, Germany

Set list: 'Astronomy Domine', 'Learning To Fly', 'What Do You Want From Me', 'On The Turning Away', 'Take It Back', 'A Great Day For Freedom', 'Keep Talking', 'Sorrow', 'One Of These Days' <Intermission> 'Shine On You Crazy Diamond', 'Breathe', 'Time', 'Breathe (Reprise)', 'High Hopes', 'The Great Gig In The Sky', 'Wish You Were Here', 'Us And Them', 'Money', 'Another Brick In The Wall, Part 2', 'Comfortably Numb' <Encore>'Hey You', 'Run Like Hell'.

SATURDAY 6 AUGUST – PERFORMANCE
Fussballstadion St Jakob, Basel, Switzerland

Set list: 'Shine On You Crazy Diamond', 'Learning To Fly', 'High Hopes', 'Take It Back', 'Coming Back To Life', 'Sorrow', 'Keep Talking', 'Another Brick In The Wall, Part 2', 'One Of These Days' <Intermission> *The Dark Side of the Moon* <Encore>'Wish You Were Here', 'Comfortably Numb', 'Run Like Hell'.

SUNDAY 7 AUGUST – PERFORMANCE
Fussballstadion St Jakob, Basel, Switzerland

Set list: 'Astronomy Domine', 'Learning To Fly', 'What Do You Want From Me', 'On The Turning Away', 'Poles Apart', 'Take It Back', 'Sorrow', 'Keep Talking', 'One Of These Days' <Intermission> 'Shine On You Crazy

Diamond', 'Breathe', 'Time', 'Breathe (Reprise)', 'High Hopes', 'The Great Gig In The Sky', 'Wish You Were Here', 'Us And Them', 'Money', 'Another Brick In The Wall, Part 2', 'Comfortably Numb' <Encore>'Hey You', 'Run Like Hell'.

TUESDAY 9 AUGUST – PERFORMANCE
Espace Grammont, Montpellier, France

Set list: 'Astronomy Domine', 'Learning To Fly', 'What Do You Want From Me', 'On The Turning Away', 'Take It Back', 'Coming Back To Life', 'Sorrow', 'Keep Talking', 'One Of These Days' <Intermission> 'Shine On You Crazy Diamond', 'Breathe', 'Time', 'Breathe (Reprise)', 'High Hopes', 'The Great Gig In The Sky', 'Wish You Were Here', 'Us And Them', 'Money', 'Another Brick In The Wall, Part 2', 'Comfortably Numb' <Encore>'Hey You', 'Run Like Hell'.

THURSDAY 11 AUGUST – PERFORMANCE ◄
Esplanade des Quinconces, Bordeaux, France

Set list: 'Astronomy Domine', 'Learning To Fly', 'What Do You Want From Me', 'On The Turning Away', 'Take It Back', 'Coming Back To Life', 'Sorrow', 'Keep Talking', 'One Of These Days' <Intermission> 'Shine On You Crazy Diamond', 'Breathe', 'Time', 'Breathe (Reprise)', 'High Hopes', 'The Great Gig In The Sky', 'Wish You Were Here', 'Us And Them', 'Money', 'Another Brick In The Wall, Part 2', 'Comfortably Numb' <Encore>'Hey You', 'Run Like Hell'.

SATURDAY 13 AUGUST – PERFORMANCE
Hockenheimring, Hockenheim, Germany

Set list: 'Astronomy Domine', 'Learning To Fly', 'What Do You Want From Me', 'On The Turning Away', 'Take It Back', 'Sorrow', 'A Great Day For Freedom', 'Keep Talking', 'One Of These Days' <Intermission> 'Shine On You Crazy Diamond', 'Breathe', 'Time', 'Breathe (Reprise)', 'High Hopes', 'The Great Gig In The Sky', 'Wish You Were Here', 'Us And Them', 'Money', 'Another Brick In The Wall, Part 2', 'Comfortably Numb' <Encore>'Hey You', 'Run Like Hell'.

TUESDAY 16 AUGUST – PERFORMANCE
Neidersachsenstadion, Hannover, Germany

Set list: 'Shine On You Crazy Diamond', 'Learning To Fly', 'Take It Back', 'Sorrow', 'High Hopes', 'Keep Talking', 'Another Brick In The Wall, Part 2', 'One Of These Days' <Intermission> *The Dark Side of the Moon* <Encore>'Wish You Were Here', 'Comfortably Numb', 'Run Like Hell'.

WEDNESDAY 17 AUGUST – PERFORMANCE
Neidersachsenstadion, Hannover, Germany

Set list: 'Astronomy Domine', 'Learning To Fly', 'What Do You Want From Me', 'On The Turning Away', 'Take It Back', 'A Great Day For Freedom', 'Sorrow', 'Keep Talking', 'One Of These Days' <Intermission> 'Shine On You Crazy Diamond', 'Breathe', 'Time', 'Breathe (Reprise)', 'High Hopes', 'The Great Gig In The Sky', 'Wish You Were Here', 'Money', 'Another Brick In The Wall, Part 2', 'Comfortably Numb' <Encore>'Hey You', 'Run Like Hell'.

'One Of These Days' was recorded at this show for the B-side of the 'High Hopes' 12-inch single release. During the day the band and some members of the crew were guests of Volkswagen at their nearby Ehra-Lessien test track-driving the new limited edition Pink Floyd Golf.

FRIDAY 19 AUGUST – PERFORMANCE
Flugfeld Wiener Neustadt, Vienna, Austria

Set list: 'Shine On You Crazy Diamond', 'Learning To Fly', 'What Do You Want From Me', 'On The Turning Away', 'Take It Back', 'Coming Back To Life', 'Sorrow', 'Keep Talking', 'One Of These Days' <Intermission> 'Astronomy Domine, 'Breathe', 'Time', 'Breathe (Reprise)', 'High Hopes', 'The Great Gig In The Sky', 'Wish You Were Here', 'Us And Them', 'Money', 'Another Brick In The Wall, Part 2', 'Comfortably Numb' <Encore>'Hey You', 'Run Like Hell'.

SUNDAY 21 AUGUST – PERFORMANCE
Maifeld am Olympiastadion, Berlin, Germany

Set list: 'Astronomy Domine', 'Learning To Fly', 'What Do You Want From Me', 'On The Turning Away', 'Take It Back', 'A Great Day For Freedom', 'Sorrow', 'Keep Talking', 'One Of These Days' <Intermission> 'Shine On You Crazy Diamond', 'Breathe', 'Time', 'Breathe (Reprise)', 'High Hopes', 'The Great Gig In The Sky', 'Wish You Were Here', 'Money', 'Another Brick In The Wall, Part 2', 'Comfortably Numb' <Encore>'Hey You', 'Run Like Hell'.

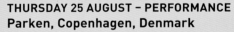

TUESDAY 23 AUGUST – PERFORMANCE ►
Parkstadion, Gelsenkirchen, Germany

Set list: 'Astronomy Domine', 'Learning To Fly', 'What Do You Want From Me', 'On The Turning Away', 'Poles Apart', 'Take It Back', 'Sorrow', 'Keep Talking', 'One Of These Days' <Intermission> 'Shine On You Crazy Diamond', 'Breathe', 'Time', 'Breathe (Reprise)', 'High Hopes', 'The Great Gig In The Sky', 'Wish You Were Here', 'Us And Them', 'Money', 'Another Brick In The Wall, Part 2', 'Comfortably Numb' <Encore>'Hey You', 'Run Like Hell'.

The number 19 was flashed on the circular backdrop screen at the end of this show. All subsequent shows displayed one number less counting down to the final date of the tour.

THURSDAY 25 AUGUST – PERFORMANCE
Parken, Copenhagen, Denmark

Set list: 'Shine On You Crazy Diamond', 'Learning To Fly', 'What Do You Want From Me', 'On The Turning Away', 'Take It Back', 'Coming Back To Life', 'Sorrow', 'Keep Talking', 'One Of These Days' <Intermission> 'Astronomy Domine, 'Breathe', 'Time', 'Breathe (Reprise)', 'High Hopes', 'The Great Gig In The Sky', 'Wish You Were Here', 'Us And Them', 'Money', 'Another Brick In The Wall, Part 2', 'Comfortably Numb' <Encore>'Hey You', 'Run Like Hell'.

SATURDAY 27 AUGUST – PERFORMANCE
Ullevi Stadion, Gothenberg, Sweden

Set list: 'Astronomy Domine', 'Learning To Fly', 'What Do You Want From Me', 'On The Turning Away', 'Take It Back', 'Sorrow', 'Keep Talking', 'One Of These Days' <Intermission> 'Shine On You Crazy Diamond', 'Breathe', 'Time', 'Breathe (Reprise)', 'High Hopes', 'The Great Gig In The Sky', 'Wish You Were Here', 'Us And Them', 'Money', 'Another Brick In The Wall, Part 2', 'Comfortably Numb' <Encore>'Hey You', 'Run Like Hell'.

Pink Floyd's sound engineer Andy Jackson was arrested by airport customs authorities for possession of marijuana in his baggage. The band threatened to cancel the concert which persuaded the authorities to release him on payment of a 10,000 Krona fine.

MONDAY 29 AUGUST – PERFORMANCE
Valle Hovin Stadion, Oslo, Norway

Set list: 'Astronomy Domine', 'Learning To Fly', 'What Do You Want From Me', 'On The Turning Away', 'Take It Back', 'Coming Back To Life', 'Sorrow', 'Keep Talking', 'One Of These Days' <Intermission> 'Shine On You Crazy Diamond', 'Breathe', 'Time', 'Breathe (Reprise)', 'High Hopes', 'The Great Gig In The Sky', 'Wish You Were Here', 'Us And Them', 'Money', 'Another Brick In The Wall, Part 2', 'Comfortably Numb' <Encore>'Marooned', 'Run Like Hell'.

Gilmour introduced a riff from the Beatles' 'Norwegian Wood' into the opening delay sequence of 'Run Like Hell' at this show and continued to do so for the rest of the tour.

TUESDAY 30 AUGUST – PERFORMANCE
Valle Hovin Stadion, Oslo, Norway

Set list: 'Astronomy Domine', 'Learning To Fly', 'What Do You Want From Me', 'On The Turning Away', 'Take It Back', 'Poles Apart', 'Sorrow', 'Keep Talking', 'One Of These Days' <Intermission> 'Shine On You Crazy Diamond', 'Breathe', 'Time', 'Breathe (Reprise)', 'High Hopes', 'The Great Gig In The Sky', 'Wish You Were Here', 'Us And Them', 'Money', 'Another Brick In The Wall, Part 2', 'Comfortably Numb' <Encore>'Marooned', 'Run Like Hell'.

The two Oslo shows were the only occasions on which 'Marooned' was performed on the whole tour. A new projection film accompanied the track that featured whales – clearly a dig at Norway's whaling policy.

WEDNESDAY 1 SEPTEMBER – CANCELLED PERFORMANCE
Olympiastadion, Helsinki, Finland

Scheduled in early tour drafts, this show was cancelled before tickets went on sale.

THURSDAY 2 SEPTEMBER – PERFORMANCE
Festivalweide, Werchter, Belgium

Set list: 'Shine On You Crazy Diamond', 'Learning To Fly', 'What Do You Want From Me', 'On The Turning Away', 'Take It Back', 'A Great Day For Freedom', 'Sorrow', 'Keep Talking', 'One Of These Days' <Intermission> 'Astronomy Domine, 'Breathe', 'Time', 'Breathe (Reprise)', 'High Hopes', 'The Great Gig In The Sky', 'Wish You Were Here', 'Money', 'Another Brick In The Wall, Part 2', 'Comfortably Numb' <Encore>'Hey You', 'Run Like Hell'.

FRIDAY 3 SEPTEMBER – PERFORMANCE
Stadion Feyenoord, Rotterdam, Netherlands

Set list: 'Astronomy Domine', 'Learning To Fly', 'What Do You Want From Me', 'On The Turning Away', 'Poles Apart', 'Take It Back', 'Sorrow', 'Keep Talking', 'One Of These Days' <Intermission> 'Shine On You Crazy Diamond', 'Breathe', 'Time', 'Breathe (Reprise)', 'High Hopes', 'The Great Gig In The Sky', 'Wish You Were Here', 'Us And Them', 'Money', 'Another Brick In The Wall, Part 2', 'Comfortably Numb' <Encore>'Hey You', 'Run Like Hell'.

SATURDAY 4 SEPTEMBER – PERFORMANCE ▶ Stadion Feyenoord, Rotterdam, Netherlands

Set list: 'Shine On You Crazy Diamond', 'Learning To Fly', 'Take It Back', 'Sorrow', 'Keep Talking', 'Wish You Were Here', 'Another Brick In The Wall, Part 2', 'One Of These Days' <Intermission> *The Dark Side of the Moon* <Encore>'High Hopes', 'Comfortably Numb', 'Run Like Hell'.

SUNDAY 5 SEPTEMBER – PERFORMANCE
Stadion Feyenoord, Rotterdam, Netherlands

Set list: 'Shine On You Crazy Diamond', 'Learning To Fly', 'Take It Back', 'Sorrow', 'High Hopes', 'Keep Talking', 'Another Brick In The Wall, Part 2', 'One Of These Days' <Intermission> *The Dark Side of the Moon* <Encore>'Comfortably Numb', 'Wish You Were Here', 'Run Like Hell'.

TUESDAY 7 SEPTEMBER – PERFORMANCE
Strahovský Stadion, Prague, Czech Republic

Set list: 'Shine On You Crazy Diamond', 'Learning To Fly', 'What Do You Want From Me', 'On The Turning Away', 'Take It Back', 'A Great Day For Freedom', 'Sorrow', 'Coming Back To Life', 'One Of These Days' <Intermission> 'Astronomy Domine', 'Breathe', 'Time', 'Breathe (Reprise)', 'High Hopes', 'The Great Gig In The Sky', 'Wish You Were Here', 'Us And Them', 'Money', 'Another Brick In The Wall, Part 2', 'Comfortably Numb' <Encore>'Hey You', 'Run Like Hell'.

Czech president Vaclav Havel was in attendance and invited the band to an after-show dinner at his residence, which by all accounts lasted well into the early hours.

THURSDAY 9 SEPTEMBER – PERFORMANCE
Stade de la Meinau, Strasbourg, France

Set list: 'Astronomy Domine', 'Learning To Fly', 'What Do You Want From Me', 'On The Turning Away', 'Take It Back', 'Coming Back To Life', 'Sorrow', 'Keep Talking', 'One Of These Days' <Intermission> 'Shine On You Crazy Diamond', 'Breathe', 'Time', 'Breathe (Reprise)', 'High Hopes', 'The Great Gig In The Sky', 'Wish You Were Here', 'Us And Them', 'Money', 'Another Brick In The Wall, Part 2', 'Comfortably Numb' <Encore>'Hey You', 'Run Like Hell'.

SATURDAY 11 SEPTEMBER – PERFORMANCE
Stade du Gerland, Lyon, France

Set list: 'Shine On You Crazy Diamond', 'Learning To Fly', 'What Do You Want From Me', 'On The Turning Away', 'Poles Apart', 'Take It Back', 'Sorrow', 'Keep Talking', 'One Of These Days' <Intermission> 'Astronomy

Domine', 'Breathe', 'Time', 'Breathe (Reprise)', 'High Hopes', 'The Great Gig In The Sky', 'Wish You Were Here', 'Us And Them', 'Money', 'Another Brick In The Wall, Part 2', 'Comfortably Numb' <Encore>'Hey You', 'Run Like Hell'.

MONDAY 13 SEPTEMBER – PERFORMANCE
Stadio Delle Alpi, Turin, Italy
Set list: 'Astronomy Domine', 'Learning To Fly', 'What Do You Want From Me', 'On The Turning Away', 'Take It Back', 'A Great Day For Freedom', 'Sorrow', 'Keep Talking', 'One Of These Days' <Intermission> 'Shine On You Crazy Diamond', 'Breathe', 'Time', 'Breathe (Reprise)', 'High Hopes', 'The Great Gig In The Sky', 'Wish You Were Here', 'Us And Them', 'Money', 'Another Brick In The Wall, Part 2', 'Comfortably Numb' <Encore>'Hey You', 'Run Like Hell'.

WEDNESDAY 15 SEPTEMBER – PERFORMANCE
Stadio Friuli, Udine, Italy
Set list: 'Shine On You Crazy Diamond', 'Learning To Fly', 'What Do You Want From Me', 'On The Turning Away', 'Coming Back To Life', 'Take It Back', 'Sorrow', 'Keep Talking', 'One Of These Days' <Intermission> 'Astronomy Domine', 'Breathe', 'Time', 'Breathe (Reprise)', 'High Hopes', 'The Great Gig In The Sky', 'Wish You Were Here', 'Us And Them', 'Money', 'Another Brick In The Wall, Part 2', 'Comfortably Numb' <Encore>'Hey You', 'Run Like Hell'.

FRIDAY 17 SEPTEMBER – PERFORMANCE
Festa Nazionale Dell' Unità, Modena, Italy
Set list: 'Shine On You Crazy Diamond', 'Learning To Fly', 'High Hopes', 'Take It Back', 'Coming Back To Life', 'Sorrow', 'Keep Talking', 'Another Brick In The Wall, Part 2', 'One Of These Days' <Intermission> *The Dark Side of the Moon* <Encore>'Wish You Were Here', 'Comfortably Numb', 'Run Like Hell'.

SUNDAY 19 SEPTEMBER – PERFORMANCE
Cinecittà Studios, Rome, Italy
Rescheduled from Ippodromo Tor Di Valle, Rome.
Set list: 'Shine On You Crazy Diamond', 'Learning To Fly', 'High Hopes', 'Take It Back', 'Coming Back To Life', 'Sorrow', 'Keep Talking', 'Another Brick In The Wall, Part 2', 'One Of These Days' <Intermission> *The Dark Side of the Moon* <Encore>'Wish You Were Here', 'Comfortably Numb', 'Run Like Hell'.

MONDAY 20 SEPTEMBER – PERFORMANCE
Cinecittà Studios, Rome, Italy
Rescheduled from Ippodromo Tor Di Valle, Rome.
Set list: 'Shine On You Crazy Diamond', 'Learning To Fly', 'High Hopes', 'Take It Back', 'Coming Back To Life', 'Sorrow', 'Keep Talking', 'Another Brick In The Wall, Part 2', 'One Of These Days' <Intermission> *The Dark Side of the Moon* <Encore>'Wish You Were Here', 'Comfortably Numb', 'Run Like Hell'.

TUESDAY 21 SEPTEMBER – PERFORMANCE
Cinecittà Studios, Rome, Italy
Rescheduled from Ippodromo Tor Di Valle, Rome.
Set list: 'Astronomy Domine', 'Learning To Fly', 'What Do You Want From Me', 'On The Turning Away', 'Take It Back', 'A Great Day For Freedom', 'Sorrow', 'Keep Talking', 'One Of These Days' <Intermission> 'Shine On You Crazy Diamond', 'Another Brick In The Wall, Part 2', 'High Hopes', 'Wish You Were Here', *The Dark Side of the Moon* <Encore>'Comfortably Numb', 'Run Like Hell'.

THURSDAY 23 SEPTEMBER – PERFORMANCE
Stade de Gerland, Lyon, France
Set list: 'Shine On You Crazy Diamond', 'Learning To Fly', 'High Hopes', 'Take It Back', 'Coming Back To Life', 'Sorrow', 'Keep Talking', 'Another Brick In The Wall, Part 2', 'One Of These Days' <Intermission> *The Dark Side of the Moon* <Encore>'Wish You Were Here', 'Comfortably Numb', 'Run Like Hell'.

SATURDAY 25 SEPTEMBER – PERFORMANCE
Stade de la Pontaise, Lausanne, Switzerland
Set list: 'Shine On You Crazy Diamond', 'Learning To Fly', 'What Do You Want From Me', 'On The Turning Away', 'Take It Back', 'Coming Back To Life', 'Sorrow', 'Keep Talking', 'One Of These Days' <Intermission> 'Astronomy Domine', 'Breathe', 'Time', 'Breathe (Reprise)', 'High Hopes', 'The Great Gig In The Sky', 'Wish You Were Here', 'Us And Them', 'Money', 'Another Brick In The Wall, Part 2', 'Comfortably Numb' <Encore>'Hey You', 'Run Like Hell'.

MONDAY 10 OCTOBER – SINGLE RELEASE (UK)
'High Hopes'

PINK FLOYD WORLD TOUR 1994 (LONDON)

WEDNESDAY 12 OCTOBER – CANCELLED PERFORMANCE
Earls Court Exhibition Hall, Earls Court, London, England
The opening night of Pink Floyd's record-breaking run at Earls Court was marred by the unfortunate collapse of a 1,200-capacity seating stand at the rear of the hall immediately after the lights went down as Pink Floyd took the stage. No one was seriously hurt, although eight people were rushed to hospital with spinal injuries, cuts, bruises and shock, some having fallen almost 20 feet to the ground.

A BBC crew was filming the show for a news item and consequently covered the accident in time for the 9.00pm news bulletin on BBC1 TV. The show was rescheduled to Monday 17 October on what was supposed to be a day off for the band. A free T-shirt and a note of apology from Pink Floyd was given to everyone who had been sitting in the collapsed stands.

THURSDAY 13 OCTOBER – PERFORMANCE
Earls Court Exhibition Hall, Earls Court, London, England
Set list: 'Astronomy Domine', 'Learning To Fly', 'What Do You Want From Me', 'On The Turning Away', 'Take It Back', 'Coming Back To Life', 'Sorrow', 'Keep Talking', 'One Of These Days' <Intermission> 'Shine On You Crazy Diamond', 'Breathe', 'Time', 'Breathe (Reprise)', 'High Hopes', 'The Great Gig In The Sky', 'Wish You Were Here', 'Us And Them', 'Money', 'Another Brick In The Wall, Part 2', 'Comfortably Numb' <Encore>'Hey You', 'Run Like Hell'.

The *Guardian* reported, "A huge circular screen sinisterly whirred up to the ceiling and Gilmour spent 10 minutes tweaking out what turned out to be the introduction to "Shine On You Crazy Diamond". Pink Floyd will never play one note where 50 will do. They also never miss a chance to lob in a special effect, such as lighting the stage a brilliant white when Gilmour sang the word "shine". Let me admit here that the "show" part of the show was spectacular. As well as the expected laser display, there were films, multi-coloured strobe lights, pyrotechnics and a row of monitors that lit up into mysterious runes. Oh, and the giant inflatable

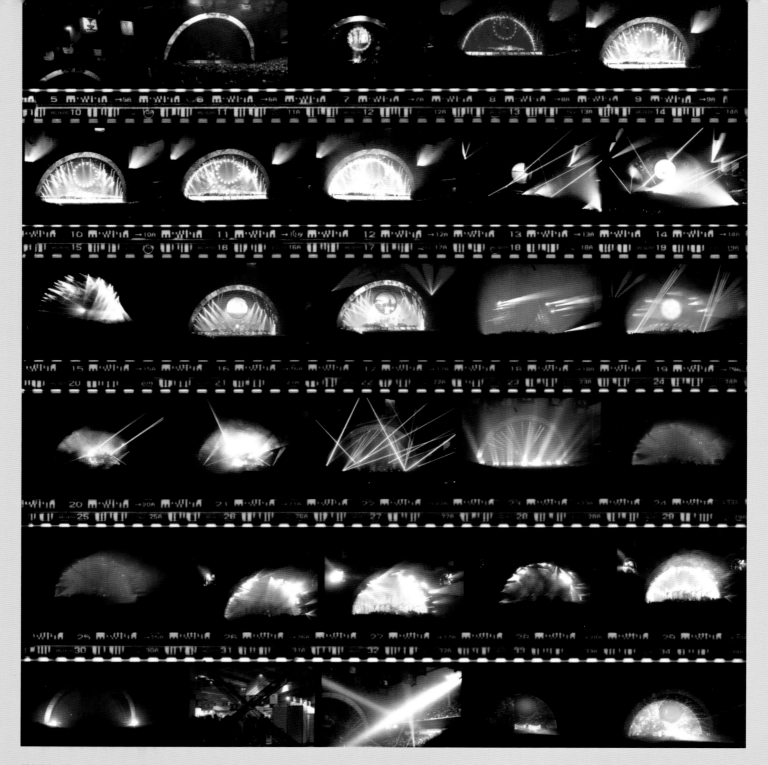

ABOVE: BATTERIES OF LIGHTS, LASERS AND FILMS MADE UP THE SPECTACULAR LIGHT SHOW
OF PINK FLOYD'S CONCERTS, PICTURED HERE FOR THE LAST TIME AT LONDON'S EARLS COURT.

pigs, which popped out of boxes at either side of the stage and shook their trotters balefully. Good thing the light show was so exciting, because the music wasn't. Floyd's brand of rockerdelia is newly back in fashion due to young bands like the Orb. But it still boils down to the same thing: portentous synth-pop dressed up with keening female vocals, saxophones and long, languid guitar passages. Apart from new songs and technical advances, this is pretty much the show they've been doing since the early Seventies…. *The Division Bell* album consumed much of the two-hour set's first half. The songs are better on record, where Gilmour's singing and the layers of sound are subtly wrought. Live, the nuances were squashed under the roar of two keyboardists, two percussionists, guitarists and three backing vocalists. To add insult to injury, each number went on for what seemed like days at a time. Half a dozen selections from *Dark Side of the Moon* were much better…. The loftiness of things like 'Breathe' and 'Time' and their co-ordinated laser accompaniment was truly impressive. But six numbers don't make a gig."

FRIDAY 14 OCTOBER – PERFORMANCE
Earls Court Exhibition Hall, Earls Court, London, England

Set list: 'Shine On You Crazy Diamond', 'Learning To Fly', 'High Hopes', 'Take It Back', 'A Great Day For Freedom', 'Sorrow', 'Keep Talking', 'Another Brick In The Wall, Part 2', 'One Of These Days' <Intermission> *The Dark Side of the Moon* <Encore>'Wish You Were Here', 'Comfortably Numb', 'Run Like Hell'.

SATURDAY 15 OCTOBER – PERFORMANCE
Earls Court Exhibition Hall, Earls Court, London, England

Set list: 'Astronomy Domine', 'Learning To Fly', 'What Do You Want From Me', 'On The Turning Away', 'Take It Back', 'Coming Back To Life', 'Sorrow', 'Keep Talking', 'One Of These Days' <Intermission> 'Shine On You Crazy Diamond', 'Breathe', 'Time', 'Breathe (Reprise)', 'High Hopes', 'The Great Gig In The Sky', 'Wish You Were Here', 'Us And Them', 'Money', 'Another Brick In The Wall, Part 2', 'Comfortably Numb' <Encore>'Hey You', 'Run Like Hell'.

SUNDAY 16 OCTOBER – PERFORMANCE
Earls Court Exhibition Hall, Earls Court, London, England

Set list: 'Shine On You Crazy Diamond', 'Learning To Fly', 'High Hopes', 'Take It Back', 'Coming Back To Life', 'Sorrow', 'Keep Talking', 'Another Brick In The Wall, Part 2', 'One Of These Days' <Intermission> *The Dark Side of the Moon* <Encore>'Wish You Were Here', 'Comfortably Numb', 'Run Like Hell'.

MONDAY 17 OCTOBER – PERFORMANCE
Earls Court Exhibition Hall, Earls Court, London, England

Rescheduled from Wednesday 12 October.
Set list: 'Astronomy Domine', 'Learning To Fly', 'What Do You Want From Me', 'On The Turning Away', 'Poles Apart', 'Take It Back', 'Sorrow', 'Keep Talking', 'One Of These Days' <Intermission> 'Shine On You Crazy Diamond', 'Breathe', 'Time', 'Breathe (Reprise)', 'High Hopes', 'The Great Gig In The Sky', 'Wish You Were Here', 'Us And Them', 'Money', 'Another Brick In The Wall, Part 2', 'Comfortably Numb' <Encore>'Hey You', 'Run Like Hell'.

WEDNESDAY 19 OCTOBER – PERFORMANCE
Earls Court Exhibition Hall, Earls Court, London, England

Set list: 'Shine On You Crazy Diamond', 'Learning To Fly', 'High Hopes', 'Lost For Words', 'A Great Day For Freedom', 'Keep Talking', 'Coming Back To Life', 'Sorrow', 'Another Brick In The Wall, Part 2', 'One Of These Days' <Intermission> *The Dark Side of the Moon* <Encore>'Wish You Were Here', 'Comfortably Numb', 'Run Like Hell'.

THURSDAY 20 OCTOBER – PERFORMANCE
Earls Court Exhibition Hall, Earls Court, London, England

Set list: 'Shine On You Crazy Diamond', 'Learning To Fly', 'High Hopes', 'Take It Back', 'Coming Back To Life', 'Sorrow', 'Keep Talking', 'Another Brick In The Wall, Part 2', 'One Of These Days' <Intermission> *The Dark Side of the Moon* <Encore>'Wish You Were Here', 'Comfortably Numb', 'Run Like Hell'.

The entire concert was filmed for the official release of the tour video, *P.U.L.S.E.*. The full *P.U.L.S.E.* version was broadcast in the UK on BBC1 TV on Tuesday 15 November 1994 between 10.55pm and 1.25am, and a repeat of *The Dark Side of the Moon* was broadcast on BBC1 TV on Friday 15 December 2006 between 11.35pm and 12.25am. An edited version of the show was broadcast as *Pink Floyd: The Dark Side of the Moon Live* in the US

on pay-per-view on Tuesday 1 November 1994 and in the UK on BBC1 TV on Friday 15 December 2006 between 11.35pm and 12.35am.

FRIDAY 21 OCTOBER – PERFORMANCE ▶
Earls Court Exhibition Hall, Earls Court, London, England

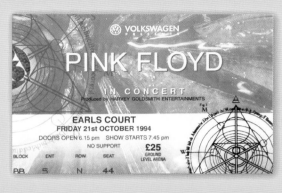

Set list: 'Astronomy Domine, 'Learning To Fly', 'What Do You Want From Me', 'On The Turning Away', 'Poles Apart', 'Take It Back', 'Sorrow', 'Keep Talking', 'One Of These Days' <Intermission> 'Shine On You Crazy Diamond', 'Breathe', 'Time', 'Breathe (Reprise)', 'High Hopes', 'The Great Gig In The Sky', 'Wish You Were Here', 'Us And Them', 'Money', 'Another Brick In The Wall, Part 2', 'Comfortably Numb' <Encore>'Hey You', 'Run Like Hell'.

SATURDAY 22 OCTOBER – PERFORMANCE
Earls Court Exhibition Hall, Earls Court, London, England

Set list: 'Astronomy Domine', 'Learning To Fly', 'What Do You Want From Me', 'On The Turning Away', 'Take It Back', 'A Great Day For Freedom', 'Sorrow', 'Keep Talking', 'One Of These Days' <Intermission> 'Shine On You Crazy Diamond', 'Breathe', 'Time', 'Breathe (Reprise)', 'High Hopes', 'The Great Gig In The Sky', 'Wish You Were Here', 'Us And Them', 'Money', 'Another Brick In The Wall, Part 2', 'Comfortably Numb' <Encore>'Hey You', 'Run Like Hell'.

SUNDAY 23 OCTOBER – PERFORMANCE
Earls Court Exhibition Hall, Earls Court, London, England

Set list: 'Shine On You Crazy Diamond', 'Learning To Fly', 'High Hopes', 'Take It Back', 'Coming Back To Life', 'Sorrow', 'Keep Talking', 'Another Brick In The Wall, Part 2', 'One Of These Days' <Intermission> *The Dark Side of the Moon* <Encore>'Wish You Were Here', 'Comfortably Numb', 'Run Like Hell'.

WEDNESDAY 26 OCTOBER – PERFORMANCE
Earls Court Exhibition Hall, Earls Court, London, England

Set list: 'Astronomy Domine', 'Learning To Fly', 'What Do You Want From Me', 'On The Turning Away', 'Take It Back', 'Coming Back To Life', 'Sorrow', 'Keep Talking', 'One Of These Days' <Intermission> 'Shine On You Crazy Diamond', 'Breathe', 'Time', 'Breathe (Reprise)', 'High Hopes', 'The Great Gig In The Sky', 'Wish You Were Here', 'Us And Them', 'Money', 'Another Brick In The Wall, Part 2', 'Comfortably Numb' <Encore>'Hey You', 'Run Like Hell'.

THURSDAY 27 OCTOBER – PERFORMANCE
Earls Court Exhibition Hall, Earls Court, London, England

Set list: 'Shine On You Crazy Diamond', 'Learning To Fly', 'What Do You Want From Me', 'On The Turning Away', 'Take It Back', 'A Great Day For Freedom', 'Sorrow', 'Keep Talking', 'One Of These Days' <Intermission> 'Astronomy Domine', 'Breathe', 'Time', 'Breathe (Reprise)', 'High Hopes', 'The Great Gig In The Sky', 'Wish You Were Here', 'Us And Them', 'Money', 'Another Brick In The Wall, Part 2', 'Comfortably Numb' <Encore>'Hey You', 'Run Like Hell'.

FRIDAY 28 OCTOBER – PERFORMANCE
Earls Court Exhibition Hall, Earls Court, London, England

Set list: 'Shine On You Crazy Diamond', 'Learning To Fly', 'High Hopes', 'Take It Back', 'Poles Apart', 'Sorrow', 'Keep Talking', 'Another Brick In The Wall, Part 2', 'One Of These Days' <Intermission> *The Dark Side Of The Moon* <Encore> 'Wish You Were Here', 'Comfortably Numb', 'Run Like Hell'.

David Gilmour's friend, the science-fiction author Douglas Adams, joined Pink Floyd on stage during 'Brain Damage' to play acoustic guitar. It was a birthday present to Adams, although his participation was unannounced and he remained in the background.

SATURDAY 29 OCTOBER – PERFORMANCE
Earls Court Exhibition Hall, Earls Court, London, England

Set list: 'Shine On You Crazy Diamond', 'Learning To Fly', 'High Hopes', 'Take It Back', 'Coming Back To Life', 'Sorrow', 'Keep Talking', 'Another Brick In The Wall, Part 2', 'One Of These Days' <Intermission> *The Dark Side of the Moon* <Encore> 'Wish You Were Here', 'Comfortably Numb', 'Run Like Hell'.

During 'Wish You Were Here' the backing singers came on dressed as cleaning ladies and began sweeping the stage, causing Gilmour to lose his train of thought. Members of the band and crew also wore wore plastic 'Groucho Marx' noses and glasses.

TUESDAY 15 NOVEMBER – TELEVISION BROADCAST
Pink Floyd The Story, BBC1 TV, London, England

BBC1 TV broadcast a 40-minute official history of Pink Floyd for its *Omnibus* series entitled *Pink Floyd The Story*. It featured previously unseen archive footage and interviews with members of the band and was aired between 10.15pm and 10.55pm. This was followed by the screening of the aforementioned Earls Court concert filmed on Thursday 20 October 1994, which was broadcast between 10.55pm and 1.25am.

1995

MONDAY 5 JUNE – ALBUM RELEASE (UK)
P.U.L.S.E.

Mojo wrote, "Far from peddling limp live renderings of the Floyd classics *Pulse* propels familiar old favourites into new dimensions. *Dark Side of the Moon* sounds more accomplished and vital now than on any bootleg from the '70's; *The Wall*'s 'Comfortably Numb' is more wildly emotive in its masturbatory guitar splendour. Forget the stoopid [sic] flashing light on the box or the predictable ageist snipes, feed the corporate rock leviathan and nourish your ears with two transcendent hours of Big Rock history."

TUESDAY 6 JUNE – ALBUM RELEASE (US)
P.U.L.S.E.

MONDAY 12 JUNE – VIDEO RELEASE (UK)
P.U.L.S.E. Earls Court London 20.10.94

The *Daily Mail* wrote, "They've got the technology, but as performers Pink Floyd come over as passionate as Thunderbirds puppets. Despite all the slick projected images and lasers a go-go filmed at Earls Court last October, the exercise is curiously one-dimensional. It includes the entire *Dark Side of the Moon* set but at two and half hours, keep your knitting close by."

WEDNESDAY 5 JULY – VIDEO RELEASE (US)
P.U.L.S.E. Earls Court London 20.10.94

1996

WEDNESDAY 17 JANUARY – AWARDS CEREMONY ▶
11th Annual Rock and Roll Hall of Fame Induction Ceremony, the Main Ballroom, Waldorf-Astoria Hotel, New York, NY, USA

Pink Floyd were inducted into the prestigious Hall of Fame at a ceremony also celebrating the induction of David Bowie, Jefferson Airplane, Little Willie John, Gladys Knight and the Pips, the Shirelles, the Velvet Underground, Pete Seeger and Tom Donahue. The band were presented with the award by Billy Corgan of the Smashing Pumpkins, after which Gilmour and Wright (Mason stood down) were joined on stage by Corgan for a rendition of 'Wish You Were Here', in 'Unplugged' fashion. Gilmour remained on stage for the presentation finale, joining Arlo Guthrie, members of Jefferson Airplane, Stevie Wonder and David Byrne for a rendition of Pete Seeger's 'Goodnight Irene'. A 29-track promotional CD (US: EMI DPRO 10467) to mark the event, which included Pink Floyd's 'Wish You Were Here', 'Money' and 'See Emily Play', was presented to attending guests.

1997

MONDAY 18 AUGUST – ALBUM RELEASE (UK)
1997 Vinyl Collection

11 WISH YOU WERE HERE

2000–15

As Waters continued to tour the world with a renewed sense of purpose, Gilmour seemed content with pursuing family life over what became a patchy solo career. But, with that came the inevitable media enquiries as to the prospect of Pink Floyd being resurrected. In reality it was as decidedly remote for the fans as it was for Gilmour. "It's a lumbering great behemoth to rouse from its torpor," he said. "*The Division Bell* was better than *A Momentary Lapse*… and it had Rick and Nick working properly together again. Maybe that's proved all I needed to prove. I don't have any hard and fast ideas about it. I haven't got myself in the mood for doing another one yet. I don't know if I want to do all that again. Certainly I'll make another record, but what it is, whether it's Pink Floyd or me, I don't know."[1]

And so this state of affairs continued. With every reissue, occasional guest appearance or solo outing, the same question reared its head and so too did the same answer. With little or no prospect of Pink Floyd reviving their recording career or touring, attentions inevitably turned to the marketing of the brand itself, with merchandise ranges working hand-in-hand with reissued product.

Pink Floyd had previously been the subject of shoddy box sets, but the March 2000 release of *Is There Anybody Out There: The Wall Live*, presented fans with a thoughtfully presented and well packaged set derived from recordings from their legendary 1980–81 concerts. Speaking of this release Mason commented that, "It's very difficult to find things from the vaults. A while back the BBC wanted to release some *Top Gear* tapes and they really weren't good enough. These tapes were almost a surprise, because I didn't realise they even existed."[2]

A year later Mason publicly renewed his friendship with Waters and even appeared as a guest at his solo shows in London the following year. In 2004, after a rewrite of an official band history due to an objection from Gilmour, he published his personal memoirs in a hugely entertaining, but not especially revealing, tome entitled *Inside Out: A Personal History of Pink Floyd*. Overall Mason has done very little in recent history as a professional musician, preferring to concentrate on his business interests.

Gilmour, meanwhile, was persuaded by his old friend Robert Wyatt to perform a solo show at London's Royal Festival Hall in June 2001, to great reviews. This was followed by four more shows the next year: two each in Paris and London with Wright as guest performer, offering a faint glimmer of hope that a full-scale tour might follow. It was not to be.

Then, in 2005, in a most surprising turn of events that began in May of that year, Bob Geldof miraculously brought together the two sparring partners to reform the classic Pink Floyd line-up for a one-off performance at his *Live 8* concert in London's Hyde Park on 2 July. Pink Floyd's participation was officially announced on 12 June and it quickly became apparent to the fans and media alike this was almost eclipsing the importance of the event itself. Tickets were free, but applications had to be submitted via a mobile phone lottery and were closing within the day, and many fans had very little chance to act on this news. Meanwhile, a fierce debate raged over unscrupulous sellers reselling tickets online at hugely inflated prices, and delays of almost a week to remove sellers from the Internet.

Gilmour was the first of the band members to issue an official statement: "Like most people I want to do everything I can to persuade the G8 leaders to make huge commitments to the relief of poverty and increased aid to the third world. It's crazy that America gives such a paltry percentage of its GNP to the starving nations. Any squabbles Roger and the band have had in the past are so petty in this context, and if re-forming for this concert will help focus attention then it's got to be worthwhile."

Waters in a later communiqué was similarly focused on the event but significantly appeared to be more excited at the prospect of the band reforming than anyone else: "It's great to be asked to help Bob raise public awareness on the issues of third world debt and poverty. The cynics will scoff, screw 'em! Also, to be given the opportunity to put the band back together, even if it's only for a few numbers, is a big bonus."

But as Nick Mason concluded, "You can't carry on World War Three forever. If we hadn't reformed for *Live 8* we'd have done it for another charity event, I suspect. It's a good reason to do it; a way of building bridges for the right reasons rather than burning them down."[3]

There was a two-hour over-run, but finally at 11.00pm, following the familiar sight of a cardiograph blip racing across the huge backdrop screens that covered the rear of the stage, David Gilmour, Roger Waters, Nick Mason and Richard Wright took to the stage for the first time together in 24 years. Arguably they turned in one of their finest ever performances to date as they wowed a 250,000-plus audience and several millions watching on TV across the globe. It was in every aspect a truly historical event.

Waters was perhaps the most vocal of the band after the event as he was actively promoting his *Ça Ira* opera immediately afterwards, giving many candid interviews. "I enjoyed playing bass [at *Live 8*]," reflected Waters. "It was more fun than I can remember having with Pink Floyd twenty-five years ago. I was there to enjoy myself. I was very happy, I definitely felt warm and cuddly toward everyone in the band. I decided that if anything came up in rehearsals – any difference of opinion – I would just roll over. And I did."[4]

Of the prospect of future appearances and tours, despite the reported $250 million pay day on offer from promoters Live Nation, Waters was hardly tempted: "I don't really need it. It would be a very hot ticket. That said, I didn't mind rolling over for one day, but I couldn't roll over for a whole fucking tour." [5] Asked what he thought David Gilmour felt: "He did send me an e-mail afterward, saying, 'Hi, Rog, I'm glad you made that phone call. It was fun, wasn't it?' So he obviously had fun." [6]

Behind the scenes however, it was a predictably awkward reunion, as guitarist Tim Renwick later testified. "Two weeks before the event, [David Gilmour] had a change of heart, and called me up to play, saying that it would be a laugh to play once more with Roger in the band. It didn't turn out to be much of a laugh! Roger appeared to want to be 'group leader' from the start of rehearsals and it made for an uncomfortable atmosphere all round. He did not seem to credit the fact that most of the musicians and crew had worked together on and off for 17 years without him being there!" [7]

Gilmour, perhaps more forcefully than the others, and in view of the success of his recent solo album and contentment with his family lifestyle, categorically stated that Pink Floyd was over and that *Live 8* was, in many ways, a convenient vehicle to achieve closure.

On 6 March 2006, to reinforce that fact, David Gilmour released his third solo album, *On an Island*. This was followed by a three-month tour of concert venues in Europe and north America, performing with a band that included Richard Wright, plus regulars Dick Parry, Jon Carin and Guy Pratt.

Later that year Syd Barrett died from pancreatic cancer on 7 July at Addenbrooke's Hospital in Cambridge, having also suffered from diabetes for some time. On 10 May 2007, Gilmour, Mason and Wright performed 'Arnold Layne' at an all-star tribute, *The Madcap's Last Laugh*, organized by Joe Boyd, and held at the Barbican Centre in London. Although Waters was there to perform in his own right, he chose not to join his former compatriots on stage.

Any further notion of a Pink Floyd reunion was sadly decided once and for all on 15 September 2008 when Richard Wright passed away following a short battle with cancer. He had performed brilliantly on Gilmour's most recent tour and in tribute Gilmour performed 'Remember A Day' live on the *Later… with Jools Holland* TV show on 23 September.

Remarkably, on 10 July 2010, David Gilmour and Roger Waters played some songs together in aid of the *Hoping Foundation* charity, at a private event held in Kiddington, Oxfordshire. Backed by a band that included Guy Pratt, Harry Waters and Andy Newmark, Gilmour and Waters performed a cover of the 1958 Teddy Bears hit single 'To Know Him Is To Love Him' and the Pink Floyd classics 'Wish You Were Here', 'Comfortably Numb' and 'Another Brick In The Wall, Part 2'. However, the event was widely criticized, not least by Nick Mason, who refused to appear, as being an exclusive event for celebrities and not the fans.

A little over a year later Roger Waters, to great fanfare, launched a hugely impressive and critically acclaimed tour recreating *The Wall*. The sold-out tour spanned three years and travelled across North and South America, Europe and Australasia. David Gilmour had also promised to perform 'Comfortably Numb' at one of Roger Waters' *Wall* concerts, and good to his word, on 12 May 2011 at the O2 Arena in London, Gilmour appeared on top of the wall to add his unique vocal and guitar styles to the choruses and solos. His appearance

LEFT: WAVING A FOND FAREWELL. THE LAST PERFORMANCE OF THE CLASSIC PINK FLOYD LINEUP AT *LIVE 8*, 2 JULY 2005.

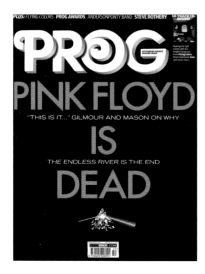

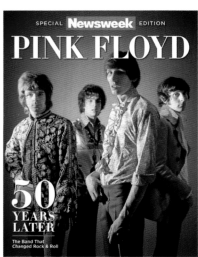

LEFT: THE WRITING'S ON THE WALL: FOLLOWING THE RELEASE OF *THE ENDLESS RIVER*, MUSIC MAGAZINES AROUND THE GLOBE PAID TRIBUTE TO PINK FLOYD AND THEIR 50-YEAR CAREER.

delighted a stunned auditorium. Nick Mason also attended the show, and both Mason and Gilmour joined Waters for the final song, 'Outside The Wall', on which Waters played trumpet, Gilmour mandolin and Mason tambourine.

Pink Floyd was then the subject of an extensive reissue campaign by EMI Records that saw their entire back catalogue re-evaluated and repackaged with the addition of previously unreleased rare and archival recordings. In a typically unique press launch and amid much fanfare, on 26 September 2011 the world's media gathered at Battersea Power station to witness the launch of the iconic inflatable pig, in a recreation of the *Animals* album cover photographed 35 years earlier.

With Roger Waters' tour concluding in the summer of 2013, fans prepared to hunker down yet again and wait out the release of his much anticipated new solo album and reworking of *The Wall* for Broadway theatre. However, it wasn't long before all indications were pointing toward David Gilmour as being the first to release an album when it was revealed by Graham Nash that both he and David Crosby were again recording with Gilmour at his home studio. This was followed up in spring 2014 by a photo appearing on a tweet by Gilmour's wife, Polly Samson, showing Gilmour along with backing singers Durga McBroom-Hudson, Sarah Brown and Louise Clare Marshal at work.

But a further tweet made by Samson on Saturday 5 July 2014, whether intentional or not, quite literally sent the Floyd community into a head-spin read, "Btw Pink Floyd album out in October is called *The Endless River*. Based on 1994 sessions is Rick Wright's swansong and very beautiful."

Surprisingly, given his previous indifference, Gilmour temporarily diverted attention away from his solo album and began reviewing material for *The Division Bell*'s 20th-anniversary release, and stumbled upon some previously unreleased instrumental recordings. Fans were naturally disappointed that the set contained no additional material, especially as rumours persisted of an ambient album that had

been recorded in parallel to the album, but were ultimately rewarded in ways they could have only dreamt of.

A statement issued by Pink Floyd's management on 7 July stated, "Pink Floyd can confirm that they are releasing a new album *The Endless River* in October 2014. It is an album of mainly ambient and instrumental music based on the 1993/4 *Division Bell* sessions which feature David Gilmour, Nick Mason and Richard Wright. The album is produced by David Gilmour with Phil Manzanera, Youth and recording engineer Andy Jackson. Work is still in progress…"

As further details began to emerge it became apparent this would be Pink Floyd's swansong and in effect a tribute to their founding keyboard player Richard Wright. Speaking to BBC 6 Music radio, Gilmour stated that Wright had been, "underestimated by the public, by the media and by us at times I hate to say. I didn't necessarily always give him his proper due. People have very different attitudes to the way they work and we can become very judgemental and think someone is not quite pulling his weight enough, without realising that theirs is a different weight to pull."[8] Mason concurred: "I think the tendency is that the most attention is paid to the songs or the guitar part or whatever, and sad old drummers and keyboard players get left behind. I think it's been a great opportunity; it is a great opportunity to recognize, remember and maybe give some credit rather late on. He was very gentle, very quiet, which doesn't help if you're in a band looking to promote yourself."[9]

For Pink Floyd fans it was a challenging listen and naturally opinions were divided. The album itself was spread over four distinct instrumental themes, which curiously worked better in the vinyl format, and closed with just one non-instrumental track, 'Louder Than Words', written by Polly Samson, as an accurate observation of Pink Floyd's collective state of mind.

Gilmour confirmed there would be no tour and there would definitely be no further original recordings released under the Pink Floyd banner, making *The Endless River* the final original album from a band who gave us one of the most fascinating, extraordinary, intriguing and tumultuous careers in rock-music history.

1–2. *Classic Rock*, January 2000.

3. *Radio Times*, 2–8 July 2005.

4. *Word*, October 2005.

5. *Rolling Stone*, October 2005.

6. *Rolling Stone*, August 2005.

7. *Gilmourish*, website, 20 May 2007.

8. BBC 6 Music, 9 October 2015.

9. *Mojo*, November 2014.

DAY-BY-DAY 2000–15

2000

THURSDAY 9 MARCH – PRESS RECEPTION
The Imperial War Museum, London, England

EMI records held a media launch for the live album *Is There Anybody Out There? The Wall Live: Pink Floyd 1980–81.* Members of the band were not in attendance.

MONDAY 27 MARCH – ALBUM RELEASE (UK)
Is There Anybody Out There?
The Wall Live: Pink Floyd 1980–81

NME wrote, "Pink Floyd were always beyond mere rock'n'roll. To the over-educated progosaurs, The Music (immaculate, impenetrable, huge) is all, with such Luddite concerns as image and – pah! – personality scornfully consigned to the evolutionary dumper. There is no place for frailty or warmth in the Floyd's stereo-perfect, genetically modified sphere. Even sprawling concept opus *The Wall* – which dealt with such everyman issues as isolation, paranoia and the general crapness of authority —was an emotionally frigid experience. Now, that album's live rendition – here culled from their stint at Earls Court between 1980 and 1981 – proves even the presence of several thousand whooping, pot-happy hippies was no obstacle to the Floyd's icy professionalism."

TUESDAY 18 APRIL – ALBUM RELEASE (US)
Is There Anybody Out There? The Wall Live: Pink Floyd 1980–81

Rolling Stone wrote, "Pink Floyd's 1980–81 stadium presentations of *The Wall* barely qualified as live rock: they were a theatrical pageant, with a wall built and demolished on stage. The sparkling clarity of this set, assembled from several London performances, only makes it obvious how slavishly the sound of the stage show followed the studio album. This is the most pointless album of its kind since Depeche Mode's *Songs of Faith and Devotion Live.*"

2001

MONDAY 5 NOVEMBER – ALBUM RELEASE (UK)
Echoes: The Best of Pink Floyd

Pop Matters wrote, "Is there a middle ground when it comes to liking the music of Pink Floyd? Can one be a 'casual' Pink Floyd fan? Personal experience would seem to dictate not, but perhaps times have changed. After all, we are talking about a 'Best Of' collection here, something that usually doesn't settle well with Floyd fans, or that does the original albums any justice whatsoever. It would seem that the undoable task of creating a successful Pink Floyd 'Best Of' has finally been taken care of.

Somehow, the Floyd have managed to keep their music going in that rare fashion that suggests they'll never go out of style, without releasing 'new' material on a regular basis. *Echoes* is ultimately a testament to that fact."

TUESDAY 6 NOVEMBER – ALBUM RELEASE (US)
Echoes: The Best of Pink Floyd

It was widely reported in the US media that the Capitol Records tower in Hollywood had a 40-foot inflatable pig moored to its roof in celebration of the release of *Echoes.* The inflatable was a replica of the pig used for the cover shoot of the *Animals* album.

2003

FRIDAY 7 NOVEMBER – MEMORIAL SERVICE
Chichester Cathedral, Chichester, England

In an extraordinary memorial to their manager Steve O'Rourke, bandmates Gilmour, Mason and Wright performed 'Fat Old Sun' at his funeral service. Additionally, Dick Parry played 'The Great Gig In The Sky' on saxophone as the gathered mourners followed the coffin into the cathedral.

2004

FRIDAY 10 OCTOBER TO SUNDAY 25 JANUARY – EXHIBITION ▶
Pink Floyd Interstellar, Cité de la Musique, Porte de Pantin, Paris, France

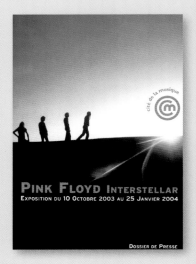

Organized by the Paris Museum of Music, this was an officially sanctioned exhibition tracing Pink Floyd's career with many display items of memorabilia, instruments and stage props loaned by band members and associates. It was officially opened by the French Minister of Culture, Jean-Jacques Aillagon, at an invitation-only preview on Thursday 9 October. Over the first three days of the exhibition there was also a programme of film screenings in the museum's theatre, including: on Friday 10 October, the BBC's Pink Floyd *Omnibus* documentary of Tuesday 15 November 1994, Peter Whitehead's film *London 1966–67* and Barbet Schroeder's film *More*; on Saturday 11 October, *Pink Floyd The Wall*, Anthony Stern's *San Francisco, Pink Floyd Live at Pompeii*, the BBC's 2001 *Omnibus* documentary *Syd Barrett, Crazy Diamond*, and the documentary film *Behind The Wall*; and on Sunday

12 October, the 1977 French TV broadcast of the Pink Floyd-Roland Petit ballet from 1973, a collection of TV clips including 'Astronomy Domine' from BBC TV's *Look of the Week* from 14 May 1967, the 'Arnold Layne' promotional film from March 1967, 'See Emily Play' from Belgian TV February 1968, 'Flaming' from ORTF's *Bouton Rouge* 1968, 'Set The Controls For The Heart Of The Sun' from BBC TV's *All My Loving* 1968, 'Let There Be More Light' from ORTF's Surprise Partie 1968, 'A Saucerful Of Secrets' from ORTF's *Forum Musiques* 1968, 'One Of These Days' from BBC TV's *Old Grey Whistle Test* and an edited screening of *P.U.L.S.E.*

SATURDAY 27 NOVEMBER – PRESS REPORT
London, England

It was widely reported in the UK press that 23 former students of the Islington Green School in London had brought a suit for what they claimed were unpaid royalties for their work on Pink Floyd's single, 'Another Brick In The Wall'. BBC News reported, "Working with royalties expert Peter Rowan, the former students appealed to the Performing Rights Society for what could amount to approximately £200 per person. 'Some of the kids have put in a claim for royalties due to session musicians for recordings played on the radio or broadcast since 1997,' says Rowan. 'We are going through the process of claiming now.' The suit hinges on the Copyright Act of 1997, which guarantees session musicians a percentage of royalties paid for broadcast rights. So far, the only compensation for the students' work has been a £1,000 payment awarded to the school at the time the recording was made in 1979, along with a platinum record of the song given to the school. The suit might be the last chapter in the unusual story of how this group of 13- and 14-year-old music students ended up singing the subversive chorus on one of Floyd's most popular songs. The group was brought to nearby Britannia Row Studios by their music teacher, Alun Renshaw, at the request of the band's management and without permission of the headmistress, Margaret Maden. 'I viewed it as an interesting sociological thing and also a wonderful opportunity for the kids to work in a live recording studio,' says Renshaw, now living in Australia. 'We had a week where we practised around the piano at school, then we recorded it at the studios. I sort of mentioned it to the headteacher, but didn't give her a piece of paper with the lyrics on it.' 'Alun Renshaw was a seriously good if somewhat anarchic music teacher,' recalls Maden. 'I was only told about it after the event, which didn't please me. But on balance it was part of a very rich musical education.' Maden refused to allow the students to appear on television singing the words that the Inner London Education Authority had termed 'scandalous."

2005

LIVE 8

Roger Waters reunited with Pink Floyd to perform at this spectacular global awareness event that saw similar concerts staged in Berlin, Paris, Philadelphia, Rome, Barrie (Toronto) and Tokyo. More than 1,000 musicians performed at the concerts, which was broadcast on 182 television networks and 2,000 radio networks worldwide. The show in London was attended by over 200,000 people, ran for almost 12 hours and featured performances by Paul McCartney, U2, Coldplay, Richard Ashcroft, Elton John, Pete Doherty, Dido, Youssou N'Dour, Stereophonics, REM, Ms Dynamite, Keane, Travis, Bob Geldof, Annie Lennox, UB40, Snoop Dogg, Razorlight, Madonna, Snow Patrol, the Killers, Joss Stone, the Scissor Sisters, Velvet Revolver, Sting, Mariah Carey, Robbie Williams and the Who alongside a whole host of other incidental guests and speakers. Pink Floyd was the penultimate act followed by Paul McCartney, who then led an all-star finale to the show.

TUESDAY 28 TO THURSDAY 30 JUNE – REHEARSALS
Black Island Studios, Acton, London, England

Pink Floyd and Roger Waters along with the supporting musicians rehearsed for just three days prior to their performance at *Live 8*, the first time the four members of this lineup had performed since the final show of *The Wall* concerts held at London's Earls Court on Wednesday 17 June 1981. Like many of the other performers, they held a final dress rehearsal on the evening prior to show day.

SATURDAY 2 JULY – PERFORMANCE
Live 8, Hyde Park, London, England

Set List: 'Breathe', 'Money', 'Wish You Were Here', 'Comfortably Numb'.

Pink Floyd and Roger Waters were supplemented on stage by Jon Carin (Keyboards), Dick Parry (Saxophones), Tim Renwick (Guitars) and Carol Kenyon (Backing Vocals).

BELOW: PINK FLOYD REUNITE AT *LIVE 8*, HYDE PARK, 2005.

Gilmour, Mason and Wright also joined in the all-star finale of 'Hey Jude', led by Paul McCartney. The entire show was transmitted live in the UK on BBC TV (BBC 2 from 1.00pm and then BBC 1 from 4.00pm) and BBC Radio One in a 12-hour presentation from 1.00pm, as well as various other TV and radio networks worldwide. The entire concert featuring all of Pink Floyd's set, plus a studio rehearsal of 'Wish You Were Here', was released in the UK as a four DVD-set entitled *Live 8* on Monday 7 November 2005 (see Discography for further details).

Brain Damage said, "With the concert overrunning two and a half hours over its extended finish, the band didn't manage to hit the stage until around 11pm, but it was worth the wait. Many reports in the media attested to the fact that the Floyd, reunited for this one, special occasion with Roger Waters, were one of the bands that stole the show at *Live 8*. Despite the late running of the show (which was to eventually finish at midnight), the band performed their complete rehearsed set of 'Breathe', 'Breathe (reprise)', 'Money', 'Wish You Were Here' and 'Comfortably Numb'. And what a performance! The band were stripped back down to a basic lineup, with only the addition of Tim Renwick on guitar, lurking in the shadows; Dick Parry on sax and Carol Kenyon on backing vocals during 'Money' and 'Comfortably Numb'; and Jon Carin, heavily to the rear of the stage, unlit, shrouded in smoke, playing keyboards during their set! To see and hear the band back chiefly to their core unit was a sheer joy, and got even the non-Floyd fans in the audience applauding for more. In one touching moment, during the introductory guitar work of 'Wish You Were Here', Roger said: 'It's actually quite emotional, standing up here with these three guys after all these years, standing to be counted with the rest of you. Anyway, we're doing this for everyone who's not here, particularly, of course for Syd.'"

MONDAY 24 OCTOBER – RADIO BROADCAST
Play it Again, BBC 6 Music Radio, UK

As part of a week-long celebration of his life under the banner of *Keeping it Peel,* the first complete rebroadcast of John Peel's debut BBC broadcast from Sunday 1 October 1967 was aired on BBC 6 Music radio between 9.00pm to 11.00pm. The *Top Gear* session which he co-hosted with Pete Drummond included Pink Floyd's session recorded on Monday 25 September 1967, which featured the tracks 'The Gnome', 'Scarecrow', 'Set The Controls For The Heart Of The Sun', 'Matilda Mother', 'Reaction In G' (used as a fade-out) and 'Flaming'.

WEDNESDAY 16 NOVEMBER – AWARDS CEREMONY ▲
UK Music Hall of Fame Induction Ceremony,
Alexandra Palace, Muswell Hill, London, England

The induction ceremony of the second annual UK Music Hall of Fame saw Pink Floyd members David Gilmour and Nick

Mason in attendance (with Roger Waters on screen via video-link from Rome, Italy) to accept their place in recognition of their contribution to popular music with an introductory speech given by Pete Townshend. The event was hosted by Dermot O'Leary and other inductees included Aretha Franklin, Bob Dylan, the Eurythmics, Joy Division/New Order, Jimi Hendrix, the Kinks, the Who, Black Sabbath and John Peel. The event was filmed and broadcast on Channel 4 TV on Thursday 17 November 2005 between 9.00pm and 11.50pm.

2006

MONDAY 3 JULY – PRESS RECEPTION
Vue Cinema, Leicester Square, London, England

EMI records held a media launch for the *P.U.L.S.E.* DVD, which was attended by David Gilmour, Nick Mason and Richard Wright and in which they participated in a Q&A session hosted by broadcaster Stuart Maconie.

FRIDAY 7 JULY – PRESS REPORT
Roger Keith "Syd" Barrett

Pink Floyd founding member, Roger Keith "Syd" Barrett, passed away on this day due to complications arising from a prolonged battle with diabetes. He was 60 years old. The current members of Pink Floyd together with Roger Waters issued a brief statement following the news, "The band are naturally very upset and sad to learn of Syd Barrett's death. Syd was the guiding light of the early band lineup up and leaves a legacy which continues to inspire." A private family service was held in Cambridge on Monday 17 July 2006.

ABOVE: WRIGHT, GILMOUR AND MASON ATTEND THE PRESS LAUNCH OF *P.U.L.S.E.*

MONDAY 7 AUGUST – DVD RELEASE (UK)
In Concert P.U.L.S.E.

Brain Damage wrote, "From various comments made over the years, the band was keen for this to be seen as one of the best music DVDs ever released. I think they've succeeded admirably. Again, Pink Floyd have raised the bar, and produced a DVD that sets new standards in the realm of music."

TUESDAY 8 AUGUST – DVD RELEASE (US)
In Concert P.U.L.S.E.

About.com wrote, "*P.U.L.S.E.* stands up well on its own merits, extraneous factors aside. Digital remastering of the audio and video makes the 1995 VHS-tape version seem like a fuzzy bootleg by comparison. The VHS version was an interesting documentation of a concert. The DVD version is an utterly captivating sensory experience. It's the closest you can get to being at a Pink Floyd performance without actually being there. It goes without saying that serious Floyd fans will want to add this to the collection. It's a completely different animal than the videotape version. For those who are relatively new to the band, *P.U.L.S.E.* offers a good education in what made this iconic band iconic."

2007

THURSDAY 10 MAY – PERFORMANCE
The Madcap's Last Laugh, Barbican Centre, London, England

Pink Floyd performed 'Arnold Layne' at this belated tribute concert to Syd Barrett, which was organized by Joe Boyd with lighting by Peter Wynne-Wilson.

BELOW: PINK FLOYD'S FINAL PERFORMANCE AT THE BARBICAN, WITH ANDY BELL AND JON CARIN.

The vast array of contributors performed the following set: 'Bike' (Sense of Sound Choir), 'Flaming' (Captain Sensible & Monty Oxymoron), 'Here I Go' (Kevin Ayers), 'Oh, What A Dream' (Kevin Ayers), 'Baby Lemonade' (Nick Laird-Clowes & Damon Albarn), 'Octopus' (the Bees), 'The Gnome' (Nick Laird-Clowes & Neulander), 'Matilda Mother' (Mike Heron), 'Golden Hair' (Martha Wainwright, Kate McGarrigle & Lily Lanken), 'See Emily Play' (Martha Wainwright, Kate McGarrigle & Lily Lanken), 'Flickering Flame' (Roger Waters & Jon Carin) <Intermission> Video presentation of vintage film featuring Barrett, 'Chapter 24' (Gordon Anderson & Sense of Sound Choir), 'Scarecrow' (Vashti Bunyan, Gareth Dickson & Nick Laird-Clowes), 'Love Song' (Vashti Bunyan, Gareth Dickson & Nick Laird-Clowes), Ian Barrett talking about his uncle Roger "Syd" Barrett, 'The Word Song' (Damon Albarn, Kate St John & David Coulter), 'Astronomy Domine' (Captain Sensible & Jon Carin), 'Terrapin' (Robyn Hitchcock), 'Gigolo Aunt' (Robyn Hitchcock, John Paul Jones & Ruby Wright), 'Dark Globe (Wouldn't You Miss Me)' (Chrissie Hynde & Adam Seymour), 'Late Night' (Chrissie Hynde & Adam Seymour), Joe Boyd talking about Roger "Syd" Barrett and organizing the show, 'Arnold Layne' (David Gilmour, Nick Mason, Richard Wright), 'Jugband Blues' from a video presentation <Encore>'Bike' (jam session with all musicians, except for Roger Waters).

WEDNESDAY 3 OCTOBER – TELEVISION BROADCAST
One Life: The Brick in The Wall Kids, BBC1 TV, UK

BBC TV's *One Life* documentary series broadcast an episode entitled *The Brick in The Wall Kids,* which brought together Alun Renshaw and several former pupils who sang on the record to recall their memories of that day, and to see what happened to their lives. It also featured an interview with Roger Waters talking about his experience of recording the single. It was broadcast on BBC1 TV between 10.40pm and 11.20pm.

MONDAY 10 DECEMBER – ALBUM RELEASE (UK)
Oh, By the Way

Uncut wrote, "Fetch the helium balloons, face paints and mobile disco. After years of rancour and torpor, Pink Floyd suddenly can't stop celebrating. First came September's 40th anniversary reissue of *The Piper at the Gates of Dawn*. Now cop a load of this mammoth, 16-CD 'instant Floyd collection' containing mini-vinyl reproductions of all their studio albums (1967–94): a deluxe, executive, gold-member, £145 crash course in Floyd."

TUESDAY 11 DECEMBER – ALBUM RELEASE (US)
Oh, By the Way

Pitchfork wrote, "Let's start with the basic facts. *Oh, By the Way* is a limited-edition 14-album, 16xCD box set containing the entirety of Pink Floyd's studio album discography, immaculately repackaged as miniature LPs with gatefold covers and the original inner sleeves, stickers and posters where applicable. Also included are a special new poster designed by longtime Floyd-affiliated cover art designer Storm Thorgerson commemorating the 40th anniversary of Pink Floyd's first LP *The Piper at the Gates of Dawn*, and a couple of 'Pink Floyd coasters' which are included as collectors' items and therefore will never see the underside of a drinking glass, ever. Depending on where you buy it, the whole thing retails for something in the neighborhood of $250-$260 – just over $15 a disc, which is a pretty fair price if you've ever wanted to own every Pink Floyd album ever in novelty faux-vinyl form. It's also one of the most superfluous pieces of collectors'-market eBay-bait I've ever heard of. There is no rarities disc, no concert material (aside from the live half of *Ummagumma*), no previously unreleased work, no interviews, no DVDs, no 5.1 audio, no historical liner notes and – most significantly – no remasters save the one you can already get on the recently-released standalone 40th Anniversary Edition of *Piper*. Assuming you're like a lot of people and already own the latest, cleanest retail-release pressings of every Pink Floyd record you'd ever want, *Oh, By the Way* will serve no purpose outside of a fan-pleasing visual novelty; it practically exists to be looked at instead of listened to."

2008

MONDAY 3 MARCH – PRESS REPORT
Norman "Hurricane" Smith

Norman "Hurricane" Smith, the Beatles' studio engineer and producer of early Pink Floyd, passed away aged 85. He was described as, "a dry-humoured old-school song and dance man" by Roger Waters. *Uncut* magazine reported, "Smith engineered all the Beatles recordings up until 1965's *Rubber Soul*, when EMI promoted him into their A&R division. Post-Beatles, one scouting trip to London's UFO Club in 1967 led to him signing Pink Floyd for a then unprecedented £5,000. Though he admitted later that 'their music did absolutely nothing for me' and that communicating with Syd Barrett was 'like talking to a brick wall', he was shrewd enough to see their potential. Smith produced

debut *The Piper at the Gates of Dawn*, along with *Ummagumma* and *A Saucerful of Secrets*, during which he even sat in for drummer Nick Mason on 'Remember A Day'. In 1968, he helmed one of the first great concept albums, the Pretty Things' rock opera *S.F. Sorrow*."

TUESDAY 26 AUGUST – AWARDS CEREMONY
2008 Polar Music Prize, Stockholm Concert Hall, Stockholm, Sweden

Sweden's King Carl XVI Gustaf presented the 2008 Polar Music Prize to American soprano Renée Fleming, and Pink Floyd band-members Nick Mason and Roger Waters, for their contributions to popular music and opera. Swedish Prime Minister Fredrik Reinfeldt said at the ceremony that the British rock band had made "a monumental contribution over the decades to the fusion of art and music in the development of popular culture. Through extensive sonic experimentation, they captured the mood and spirit of a whole generation in their reflections and attitudes. When rock 'n' roll developed, Pink Floyd was foremost in shaping the sounds that would influence artists forever."

Waters paid tribute to his 96-year-old mother. "If there is any humanity and empathy in my work, which I think there is, I would rather owe it to her," he said. Swedish artists performed Pink Floyd songs at the ceremony, ending with a sing-along to 'Another Brick In The Wall, Part 2'.

MONDAY 15 SEPTEMBER – PRESS REPORT
Richard William Wright

Pink Floyd founding member, Richard Wright, passed away on this day following a brief struggle with cancer. He was 65 years old. Gilmour said, "No one can replace Richard Wright – he was my musical partner and my friend." Writing on his website, he also added, "In the welter of arguments about who or what was Pink Floyd, Rick's enormous input was frequently forgotten."

PINK FLOYD, 16 SEPTEMBER 2008– PRESENT DAY

David Gilmour and Nick Mason.

SATURDAY 27 SEPTEMBER – PRESS REPORT
Bryan Morrison

The former manager and agent of Pink Floyd and Syd Barrett passed away aged 66, having spent over two years in a coma following a riding accident at the Royal Berkshire Polo Club, which he founded in 1985. A popular and charismatic figure in the music industry, he was already an established agent representing the Pretty Things among others when he influenced Norman Smith of EMI to sign Pink Floyd in early 1967. He represented the band through his booking agency and publishing arm, Essex Music, through the late 60s and managed Syd Barrett after his departure from Pink Floyd. He made his first fortune selling his agency to the NEMS organization in 1969 but continued to work in the music industry, guiding the early careers of the Bee Gees, the Jam and George Michael.

2010

THURSDAY 11 MARCH – PRESS REPORT
London, England

It was reported in the UK's national press that Pink Floyd were successful in their claim against record label EMI for allowing single songs to be sold as digital downloads, claiming that it had no right to sell their songs except as part of full albums. EMI were forced to pay £60,000 in costs with fines to be decided, and banned from selling Pink Floyd's music online. According to a 1999 contract, songs like 'Money' and 'Another Brick In The Wall, Part 2' cannot be unbundled from the albums on which they appear; EMI alleged this did not apply to downloads, which did not even exist at the time of signing. The *Guardian* newspaper quoted Pink Floyd's lawyer, Robert Howe QC, at the High Court hearing on 9 March, who said that "Pink Floyd [are] well-known for performing seamless pieces. Many of the songs blend into each other." To reflect this, Pink Floyd's renegotiated 1999 contract expressly prohibited EMI from selling songs out of context. And yet, Howe argued, EMI "[permit] individual tracks to be downloaded online and…[therefore allow] albums not to be sold in their original configuration. [In 1999] both parties were faced with a whole new world of potential exploitation. It was unclear whether record companies would be selling direct to the consumer or through retailers." All the same, he said, "[it] makes no commercial sense…[to say the contract] doesn't apply online." EMI's legal team dismissed this interpretation, saying the album stipulation applied only to physical releases like CDs and DVDs. "In 1999, when [the contract] was negotiated, iTunes didn't even exist," said EMI lawyer Elizabeth Jones.

2011

TUESDAY 4 JANUARY – PRESS REPORT
London, England

Ten months after taking their record label to court, Pink Floyd signed a new global partnership with EMI to allow them to continue to market and distribute their catalogue, including single track digital downloads. The new five-year contract allowed EMI to retain distribution rights to Pink Floyd's music, which included all 14 studio albums and three live albums, and put an end to all legal disputes.

MONDAY 26 SEPTEMBER – ALBUM RELEASES (UK)
Why Pink Floyd?

Pink Floyd were the subject of an extensive reissue campaign under the banner of *Why Pink Floyd?* by EMI Records, which saw their entire back catalogue re-evaluated and repackaged. All of their CDs were issued individually in card reproduction sleeves under the banner 'Discovery' and also as a 14-album CD box set of the same name. *The Dark Side of the Moon*, *Wish You Were Here* and *The Wall* were also issued as *Experience* edition double CDs containing previously unreleased live performances and archival recordings and *Immersion* edition box sets with memorabilia and photo books. *The Dark Side of the Moon*, *Wish You Were Here* and *The Wall* were also issued as 180g limited-edition vinyl albums.

Reviewing the reissue campaign *Tone Audio* said, "Why Pink Floyd? So asks the clever tagline given to EMI's exhaustive overhaul of the British legends' catalog. The statement also doubles as a straightforward query that begets two easy answers. While the group's records have seen myriad reissues, the band has never unlocked its vaults and allowed for the release of sought-after oddities. And, from a commercial standpoint, Pink Floyd and its record label realize that the open window on marketing physical media to the mainstream is quickly closing. A more apt slogan for the archival project might be 'If not now, when?'"

MONDAY 26 SEPTEMBER – PRESS RECEPTION ▼
Battersea Power Station, Battersea, London, England

In a typically unique press launch for the Pink Floyd catalogue reissues, the world's media gathered at Battersea Power station at 5.00am to witness the launch of the iconic inflatable pig, in a recreation of the *Animals* album cover photographed 35 years earlier. In the US, the top of the Capitol Records building in Los Angeles, was dressed with an inflatable pig and Pink Floyd in lettering wrapped around the top.

MONDAY 26 SEPTEMBER – PRESS RECEPTION
Rose Center for Earth and Space, American Museum of Natural History, New York, NY, USA

EMI/Capitol hosted a launch party for the *Why Pink Floyd?* reissue campaign. Nick Mason attended as a special guest and spoke briefly of the band's history adding, "I'm surprised people are still interested in us!"

MONDAY 26 SEPTEMBER – TELEVISION BROADCAST
Late Night with Jimmy Fallon, Studio 6B, NBC-TV Studios, GE Building, Rockefeller Center, New York, NY, USA

NBC's *Late Night with Jimmy Fallon* TV show commenced a week-long celebration of Pink Floyd with an interview with Nick Mason and a live performance of 'Breathe' by the Shins. Tuesday 27 September saw Roger Waters being interviewed along with a live performance of 'In The Flesh', with Waters backed by the Foo Fighters. Wednesday 28 September saw MGMT perform 'Lucifer Sam'; Thursday 29 September Dierks Bentley performed 'Wish You Were Here' and closing the show on Friday 30 September, Pearl Jam performed 'Mother'. Each show was broadcast on NBC network TV between 12.37am and 1.37am.

TUESDAY 27 SEPTEMBER – RECORD RELEASES (US)
Why Pink Floyd?

Tone Audio wrote, "Five years ago, Pink Floyd released *Oh, By the Way*, a catalog-encompassing European-made box set limited to 10,000 copies. Issued internationally in mass quantities, the new *Discovery* box set contains the same lineup of studio albums. Yet it's also worth mentioning that *Oh, By the Way* retails for close to $300, making *Discovery* a better value at $199. After spending several days listening to as many variations on the Pink Floyd catalog as imaginable, to me it's evident that the big jump in performance stems from *Oh, By the Way* as compared to the original CDs, which sound flat. Extensive A-B listening between the 2007 box and the new one reveals the slightest distinction between the two—and one that this writer strained to hear on a $60,000 dCS stack. At times, it feels as if the new box has a few more molecules of dynamic range, but overall, the sound is basically identical. There is absolutely no difference between the two sets as experienced on a $2,500 CD player, meaning, that for the mainstream listener, the box sets might as well be the same product."

MONDAY 28 NOVEMBER – PRESS REPORT
London, England

EMI Records announced the launch of the UK's first ever national Pink Floyd treasure hunt, inviting fans to find posters of all 14 Pink Floyd studio album sleeves which had been placed on advertising hoardings in 11 towns and cities across the UK, and to upload their photo alongside a poster on a dedicated website to qualify for a prize draw. The posters were situated, mainly in bus shelters, at the following locations: *The Piper at the Gates of Dawn* in St James Street, Brighton; *A Saucerful of Secrets* in Renshaw Street, Liverpool; *More* in Baldwin Street, Bristol; *Ummagumma* in Edgware Road, London; *Atom Heart Mother* in Derby Road, Nottingham; *Meddle* in Vauxhall Bridge Road, London; *Obscured by Clouds* in Aldwych Station, London; *The Dark Side of the Moon* in Holland Park Avenue, London; *Wish You Were Here* in Corporation Street, Birmingham; *Animals* in Blackett Street, Newcastle-upon-Tyne; *The Wall* in Cathedral Street, Glasgow; *The Final Cut* in New Market Street, Leeds; *A Momentary Lapse of Reason* in Princess Street, Edinburgh; and *The Division Bell* in Piccadilly, Manchester.

THURSDAY 8 DECEMBER – PRESS REPORT
Alan Styles

The former roadie for Pink Floyd, who settled in California following Pink Floyd's tour of North America in 1971, passed away aged 75. He was known to the Sausalito community where he lived as "English" Alan Styles. After school Styles joined the Merchant Navy, then taught physical fitness in the Royal Navy before his school friend David Gilmour asked him to join Pink Floyd's crew in early 1969. He is best remembered for his part on the track 'Alan's Psychedelic Breakfast' and is pictured on the rear sleeve of *Ummagumma* alongside fellow roadie Peter Watts. Gilmour was briefly reunited with Styles on his *On an Island* tour in 2006, spending several days with the touring party during its two-night stand in nearby Oakland.

2013

THURSDAY 18 APRIL – PRESS REPORT
Storm Elvin Thorgerson

Storm Thorgerson, graphic designer, best known for his work with Pink Floyd, passed away aged 69 following a battle with cancer. He attended Cambridgeshire High School for Boys with Syd Barrett and Roger Waters, and was a founding partner in the design team Hipgnosis, which was formed in 1968. It went on to design all of Pink Floyd's artwork from *A Saucerful of Secrets* in 1968 through to *Animals* in 1977. When Hipgnosis folded in 1987 he formed Storm Studios and resumed his relationship with Pink Floyd, which endured to the time of his death, despite having suffered a debilitating stroke in 2003. David Gilmour issued a brief statement: "We first met in our early teens. We would gather at Sheep's Green, a spot by the river in Cambridge and Storm would always be there holding forth, making the most noise, bursting with ideas and enthusiasm. Nothing has ever really changed. He has been a constant force in my life, both at work and in private, a shoulder to cry on and a great friend. The artworks that he created for Pink Floyd from 1968 to the present day have been an inseparable part of our work. I will miss him."

WEDNESDAY 1 MAY – PRESS REPORT
St Cloud, MN, USA

An unusual story appeared in the news on this day, which stated that a man was receiving medical treatment in a hospital in Minnesota and claiming to be David Gilmour. The report said that, "Phillip Michael Schaeffer, 53, went for treatment on April 20 and claimed he was Pink Floyd singer-guitarist David Gilmour and that he didn't have health insurance. The man was treated and released from the St Cloud Hospital, Minnesota, but not before he signed an autograph for an employee's son. He also told staff that Pink Floyd was on tour in Canada and that he stopped in St Cloud during a break to get medical treatment." His scam finally caught up with him a year later when he was arrested and charged with fraud in Utah, again for posing as David Gilmour. A staff member had recalled an earlier case where a man had claimed he was Alex Lifeson of Rush and discovered he was in fact the very same person. Fox 13 News in Salt Lake City reported that investigations showed Schaeffer had racked up $23,328.27 in medical bills under the name Lifeson and $15,067.50 posing as Gilmour. Prosecutors attempted to charge Schaeffer on two counts of communication fraud, which is a second-degree felony, but he didn't show for an initial appearance in court. Prosecutors later found out that he was incarcerated in New Mexico on unrelated charges.

WEDNESDAY 19 JUNE – PRESS REPORT
London, England

Pink Floyd's entire studio discography was made available on the popular streaming service Spotify. Although some of Pink Floyd's music had been available on Rhapsody and Rdio for some time, Spotify was the first such service to host the whole catalogue. As with individual song downloads, Pink Floyd had resisted Spotify's pull for years, previously insisting that the songs not be made available on Spotify's ad-supported free version. According to

THE ENDLESS RIVER

SIDE 1

THINGS LEFT UNSAID (Wright, Gilmour) **4:24**
IT'S WHAT WE DO (Gilmour, Wright) **6:21**
EBB AND FLOW (Gilmour, Wright) **1:50**

SIDE 2

SUM (Gilmour, Mason, Wright) **4:49**
SKINS (Gilmour, Mason, Wright) **2:37**
UNSUNG (Wright) **1:06**
ANISINA (Gilmour) **3:15**

SIDE 3

THE LOST ART OF CONVERSATION (Wright) **1:43**
ON NOODLE STREET (Gilmour, Wright) **1:42**
NIGHT LIGHT (Gilmour, Wright) **1:42**
ALLONS-Y (1) (Gilmour) **1:56**
AUTUMN '68 (Wright) **1:35**
ALLONS-Y (2) (Gilmour) **1:35**
TALKIN' HAWKIN (Gilmour, Wright) **3:25**

SIDE 4

CALLING (Gilmour, Moore) **3:38**
EYES TO PEARLS (Gilmour) **1:51**
SURFACING (Gilmour) **2:46**
LOUDER THAN WORDS (Gilmour, Samson) **6:32**

RELEASE DATE

UK: Monday 10 November 2014.
US: Tuesday 11 November 2014.

FORMAT

UK: Parlophone 825646215478 (Vinyl album).
UK: Parlophone 825646215423 (CD album).
UK: Parlophone 825646213337 (CD album & Blu-ray disc).
US: Warners 825646215478 (Vinyl album).
US: Warners 825646215423 (CD album).
US: Warners 825646213337 (CD album & Blu-ray disc).

HIGHEST CHART POSITION

UK: No. 1 (*Official Albums Chart* 'UK Top 100' on Saturday 22 November 2014).
US: No. 3 (*Billboard* 'Billboard 200' on Saturday 29 November 2104).

AWARDS

UK: Certified Gold on Friday 14 November 2014, Platinum on Friday 12 December 2014.
US: Certified Gold on Sunday 22 January 2015.

ARTWORK

Creative Director Aubrey Powell. Sleeve design by Styrolounge with artwork concept by Ahmed Emad Eldin.

Egyptian computer graphic artist Eldin was just 18 when he was discovered by Powell through the Internet website Behance.

The original piece, entitled *Beyond the Sky,* was designed in October 2013 and adapted by Powell for the album cover and promotional imagery. Overnight Eldin was fielding hundreds of interviews from around the world, reaching his Facebook "friends" limit on his personal account and taking on nearly 30,000 followers. Surprisingly, Eldin still considered his artwork a hobby and was set to begin university studies to become a doctor.

A series of art installations displaying the album cover were erected at sites across the globe to promote the launch of the album.

MUSICIANS

David Gilmour, Nick Mason, Richard Wright.

ADDITIONAL MUSICIANS

Gilad Atzmon (Tenor Saxophone and Clarinet on 'Anisina').
Sarah Brown (Backing Vocals on 'Louder Than Words').
Jon Carin (Synths on 'On Noodle Street', 'Allons-y (1)', 'Allons-y (2)'; Percussion Loop on 'Allons-y (1)' and 'Allons-y (2)').
Bob Ezrin (Bass on 'Allons-y (1)', 'Allons-y (2)', 'Louder Than Words'; Additional Keyboards on 'Things Left Unsaid').
Damon Iddins (Additional Keyboards on 'Sum' and 'Autumn '68').
Andy Jackson (Bass on 'Skins', 'Eyes to Pearls'; Effects on 'Calling').
Durga McBroom-Hudson (Backing Vocals on 'Talkin' Hawkin', 'Surfacing' and 'Louder Than Words').
Louise Marshall (Backing Vocals on 'Louder Than Words').
Anthony Moore (Keyboards on 'Calling').
Guy Pratt (Bass on 'On Noodle Street' and 'Talkin' Hawkin").
Escala on 'Louder Than Words': Chantel Leverton (Viola), Victoria Lyon (Violin), Helen Nash (Cello), Honor Watson (Violin).

RECORDING DETAILS

Recorded at the Astoria, Hampton, England; Britannia Row Studios, Islington, London, England; Abbey Road Studios, St John's Wood, London, England; Metropolis Studios, Chiswick, London, England; the Creek Recording Studios, London, England.

Produced by David Gilmour, Phil Manzanera, Youth and Andy Jackson and engineered by Andy Jackson with Damon Iddins.

Pink Floyd's 15th studio album began life as an hour-long compilation of instrumental outtakes from *The Division Bell* album compiled by studio engineer Andy Jackson, largely for his own amusement, which he dubbed *The Big Spliff*. However, during the course of compiling the 20th anniversary box-set edition of *The Division Bell* in 2012, the tapes were re-evaluated – indeed the title itself derives from a lyric in the song 'High Hopes'.

Rather than rely on Jackson's original compilation (although a small element of it survived to the finished album), some 20 hours of further excerpts from the sessions were reduced by Andy Jackson, Damon Iddins and producer Phil Manzanera, and whittled down to four, 14-minute pieces of viable music, a process that took some six weeks to accomplish. In November 2013 Gilmour temporarily suspended work on his fourth solo album, *Rattle that Lock*, to complete the project with new parts recorded by Nick Mason, Guy Pratt and Gilad Atzmon with Youth and Manzanera acting as producers.

Above all the album was designed to be a lasting tribute to the talents of keyboard player Richard Wright. Nick Mason told *Uncut* magazine, "Having lost Rick, it really brought home what a special player he was. And I think that was one of the elements that caught us up in it and made us think we ought to do something with this."

VIDEO FILM

Following in the footsteps of Storm Thorgerson, Aubrey Powell produced a typically extravagant piece to accompany the one vocal track from the album, 'Louder Than Words'. It mixed footage and stills of the band working in the studio, some of it dating back to *The Division Bell* sessions and featuring Richard Wright, and footage shot near the drought-blighted regions of the once-vast Aral Sea (once the fourth-largest saline lake in the world, having almost all but dried up in the 1960s due to the diversion of rivers) in Kazakhstan and Northern Uzbekistan. An "animated" image of the album cover of a man rowing above the scenes of desolation is central to the film.

the *Guardian* newspaper, Pink Floyd's manager Paul Loasby explained at a music industry conference in February 2012 that, "When it came to renewing our deal with EMI, we decided we did not want to go with ad-funded, but agreed to go on subscription ones. But when we went to Spotify's office in 2010, we were declined. It was all or nothing." The band announced their change of heart on Friday 14 June 2013, when it was promised that their entire catalogue would be 'unlocked' on Spotify once the song *Wish You Were Here* was streamed one million times by fans. Needless to say, the fans were able to pull off the feat and Pink Floyd is now free.

2014

FRIDAY 19 SEPTEMBER – 18 JANUARY 2015 – CANCELLED EXHIBITION
Pink Floyd: Their Mortal Remains,
La Fabbrica del Vapore, Milan, Italy

Working in conjunction with Italian tour promoter, Fran Tomasi, and designers Aubrey "Po" Powell and Peter Curzon, Pink Floyd was to have been the subject of an impressive and wide-ranging exhibition documenting their history and incorporating a vast array of stage props and memorabilia, but on Monday 11 August it was announced that the exhibition would be postponed indefinitely due to production delays. By Monday 13 October it was conceded that the exhibition had been permanently cancelled.

MONDAY 22 SEPTEMBER – PRESS REPORT
London, England

Pink Floyd formally unveiled the artwork and track listing for the upcoming release of *The Endless River* on their website and by displaying large-scale billboards in 10 cities around the world, including Berlin, Paris, Los Angeles, New York and Sydney. An eight-metre installation on London's South Bank was erected and a time-lapse video of its construction posted online.

TUESDAY 2 OCTOBER – PRESS REPORT
London, England

A remarkable number of online publications placed photos of Roger Waters alongside the breaking news of the new Pink Floyd album, which ultimately led to Waters issuing a statement, which read, "Some people have been asking Laurie, my wife, about a new album I have coming out in November. Errhh? I don't have an album coming out, they are probably confused. David Gilmour and Nick Mason have an album coming out. It's called *Endless River*. David and Nick constitute the group Pink Floyd. I, on the other hand, am not part of Pink Floyd. I left Pink Floyd in 1985, that's 29 years ago. I had nothing to do with either of the Pink Floyd studio albums, *A Momentary Lapse of Reason* and *The Division Bell*, nor the Pink Floyd tours of 1987 and 1994, and I have nothing to do with *Endless River*. Phew! This is not rocket science people, get a grip."

THURSDAY 9 OCTOBER – PRESS REPORT
London, England

Pink Floyd released an EPK (Electronic Press Kit) ahead of the release of *The Endless River* containing a pre-recorded interview with both Gilmour and Mason discussing the album, its content and reason for release. BBC Radio One played 'Louder Than Words' in an exclusive broadcast and BBC 6 Music broadcast an exclusive interview with Gilmour and Mason by Matt Everitt the same morning, which effectively confirmed this to be the last ever recorded effort from Pink Floyd.

SATURDAY 1 NOVEMBER – PRESS REPORT
Billboard, USA

The Dark Side of the Moon, Pink Floyd's most popular album, reached an historic milestone on this date. *Billboard.com* showed the album was currently sitting at No. 157 for the week ending 8 November, meaning that it had spent 884 weeks inside the "Billboard 200", equating to 17 full years on the US album chart. Its placing guaranteed the album another week on the "Billboard 200" and consequently it enjoyed its first week of its eighteenth year on the chart. On 12 December 2014 *Brain Damage* reported that the album had re-entered the *Billboard* "Top 20", at the No.13 spot. They credited this sudden jump in sales as "thanks to ultra-cheap pricing in the Google Play store (where the classic set was discounted to 99 cents in the tracking week ending 7 December). It moved just over 38,000 album equivalent units last week, comprised mostly of pure album sales (nearly 38,000; up 940 percent). That's the album's highest rank since the October 15, 2011–dated chart, when it re-entered at number 12 following a new deluxe reissue. With 889 weeks on the chart, it continues to rule as the album with most charted weeks in the history of the tally. The next-closest album, in terms of longevity, is Johnny Mathis' *Johnny's Greatest Hits*, with 490 weeks."

MONDAY 10 NOVEMBER – RECORD RELEASE (UK)
The Endless River

The Independent wrote, "What's particularly irritating is the way the album apes previous Floyd tropes in ersatz manner, with the spoken-word intro mumblings of 'Things Left Unsaid' simply reminding one that the comparable mutterings on *Dark Side of the Moon* actually served a thematic purpose: here they're just window-dressing, luring fans into a desperately disappointing experience…. It would take a Barrett-load of drugs to make this sound remotely interesting, though I wouldn't advise that. But what's blindingly clear is that, without the sparking creativity of a Syd or Roger, all that's left is ghastly faux-psychedelic dinner-party muzak. Which is fine, if you're thinking of throwing a ghastly faux-psychedelic dinner party."

TUESDAY 11 NOVEMBER – RECORD RELEASE (US)
The Endless River

Consequenceofsound.net wrote, "The redemption of this recycled music is in the hands of the fans. For everyone who looks at post-Waters Floyd as glorified Gilmour solo albums, these instrumentals could be what you've been waiting for since 1983. For fans of *Division Bell*, it's at the very least a killer bonus disc. In the tapestry of Pink Floyd, *The Endless River* doesn't end on as powerful a musical statement as *Division Bell*'s 'High Hopes', but it does end on a profoundly more personal note for a band that's taken us on 50 years of incredible sonic journeys."

THURSDAY 27 NOVEMBER – PRESS REPORT
London, England

Brain Damage reported that according to Spotify, *The Endless River* was streamed over 12 million times in its first week of release. It went on to say that, "Since joining the streaming service just over a year ago, the band's music has been added to over 3 million playlists. The largest demographic for the band appears to be the 18–22 year old users of the service." It also reported that the first week of UK sales on vinyl were the highest of any LP released since 1997, making it the fastest-selling vinyl album this century, according to official UK Charts data. The BPI, the trade body which represents the UK's record labels, has just announced that annual sales of vinyl albums have exceeded the 1 million mark for the first time since the Britpop era of the 1990s, according to Official Charts data released today. *The Endless River* is at No.2 in the current Official Vinyl Chart behind David Bowie's 'Best Of', *Nothing Has Changed*.

2015

THURSDAY 28 MAY – PRESS REPORT
London, England

Pink Floyd were the subject of a permanent memorial plaque affixed to the wall of the Westminster University building on Regent Street, London (formerly the Regent Street Polytechnic) at a brief ceremony attended by both Roger Waters and Nick Mason who, along with Richard Wright, studied there and formed the first of the precursor bands that would lead to the creation of Pink Floyd. It is only the second plaque to be unveiled as part of the Regent Street Heritage Plaque Scheme, the first being located in Haddon Street to mark the spot where David Bowie's *Ziggy Startdust* album cover was shot.

ABOVE: WATERS AND MASON, LONDON, 28 MAY 2015.

This book gives catalogue information for UK release dates first, followed by US release dates for Pink Floyd and solo pressings. It does not include every variation of re-pressed discs, variations in matrix numbers, label design, packaging or specialist collectibles such as acetates and test pressings, unless they are significantly different to that of the original releases.

However, catalogue number changes where an item has been reissued and promotional items of special interest are included. Additionally there are a vast amount of radio-show presentations, as well as various artist compilations both on vinyl and CD, that are highly collectible, but which are just too many in number to accurately catalogue, and these have been omitted from this work.

The release dates of the recordings are as accurate as can be expected, and it must be emphasized that this information is derived from contemporary press releases, media reports and music industry trade publications, which are known to contain erroneous or contradictory details. To add to the general confusion, some release dates were actually regarded as shipping dates and, depending on the efficiency of the distribution network at that time, could take several days to reach stores.

ORIGINAL RELEASES

ARNOLD LAYNE
FRIDAY 10 MARCH 1967
'Arnold Layne' / 'Candy And A Currant Bun'
UK: EMI Columbia DB 8156 (Promotional 7-inch vinyl single, with picture sleeve & 7-inch vinyl single).

MONDAY 24 APRIL 1967
'Arnold Layne' / 'Candy And A Currant Bun'
US: Capitol Tower 333 (Promotional 7-inch vinyl single, with picture sleeve & 7-inch vinyl single).

SEE EMILY PLAY
FRIDAY 16 JUNE 1967
'See Emily Play' / 'Scarecrow'
UK: Columbia EMI DB 8214 (Promotional 7-inch vinyl single, with picture sleeve & 7-inch vinyl single).
UK: EMI 5099992858473 (7-inch pink vinyl single, released for Record Store Day, came in a repro of the original West German picture sleeve [Columbia C23 574] on one side and the UK Columbia green stock sleeve and black labels [Columbia DB 8214] on the other, and a repro of the original UK promo poster, released Saturday 20 April 2013).

MONDAY 24 JULY 1967
'See Emily Play' / 'Scarecrow'
US: Tower 356 (Promotional 7-inch vinyl single, with picture sleeve & 7-inch vinyl single).
US: Tower 356 (Promotional 7-inch vinyl single, with picture sleeve, released Monday 22 July 1968).
The following text appeared on the rear sleeve: "Everything is a matter of timing. This record was released almost one year ago in England and made Top 5. Tower released it here at the same time. No action. Now is the time to release See Emily Play. That's what we have been hearing from many of the country's top PDs and DJs, as well as several music reviewers. We hope they're right. We're re-releasing the record. Will you play it?"

Unfortunately no advertising or editorial relating to the reissue could be found in any of the US trade publications including *Billboard*, *Cash Box* or *Record World* – which possibly accounts for its disappointing performance second time around.

THE PIPER AT THE GATES OF DAWN
FRIDAY 4 AUGUST 1967
The Piper at the Gates of Dawn
UK: Columbia EMI SX 6157 (Mono vinyl album) / UK: Columbia EMI SCX 6157 (Stereo vinyl album).
Reissued:
UK: EMI Fame FA 3065 (Vinyl album, released Monday 6 October 1986) / US: Capitol CDP 7463842 (CD album, released Friday 23 January 1987) / UK: EMI CDP 7463842 (CD album, released Monday 23 February 1987) / UK: EMI CD EMD 1073 (CD album, released Monday 17 October 1994) / US: Capitol CDP 077774638425 (CD album, released Tuesday 18 October 1994) / UK: EMI 5099902893525 (*Discovery* edition CD album, released Monday 26 September 2011) / US: Capitol 5099902893525 (*Discovery* edition CD album, released Tuesday 27 September 2011).

MONDAY 4 AUGUST 1997
The Piper at the Gates of Dawn: 30th Anniversary
UK: EMI CD EMD 1110 (CD album).
To mark the 30th anniversary of the album a limited edition mono CD album box set, with a selection of art prints, was released. It was issued with a limited edition CD EP *The First 3 Singles* containing 'Arnold Layne', 'Candy And A Currant Bun', 'See Emily Play', 'Scarecrow', 'Apples And Oranges' and 'Paintbox'.
UK: EMI LP EMP 1110 (Limited edition 180g vinyl album, released Monday 18 August 1997).

MONDAY 3 SEPTEMBER 2007 ►
The Piper at the Gates of Dawn: 40th Anniversary
UK: EMI 5099950392322 (40th Anniversary double CD edition of the mono and stereo albums).
US: Capitol 5099950392322 (40th Anniversary double CD edition of the mono and stereo albums, released Tuesday 4 September 2007).
UK: EMI 5099950391929 (Limited edition 40th Anniversary triple-CD bound book edition, released Monday 10 September 2007).
US: EMI 5099950391929 (Limited edition 40th Anniversary triple-CD bound book edition, released Tuesday 11 September 2007).
The bound book edition contains the mono and stereo albums plus a bonus CD containing 'Arnold Layne', 'Candy And A Currant Bun', 'See Emily Play', 'Apples And Oranges', 'Paintbox', 'Interstellar Overdrive' (French EP version), 'Apples And Oranges' (stereo version), 'Matilda Mother' (alternate version) and 'Interstellar Overdrive' (Take 6).

PINK FLOYD
SATURDAY 21 OCTOBER 1967
Pink Floyd
US: Tower T5093 (Mono vinyl album) / US: Tower ST5093 (Stereo vinyl album).

FLAMING
MONDAY 13 NOVEMBER 1967
'Flaming' / 'The Gnome'
US: Tower 378 (Promotional 7-inch vinyl single & 7-inch vinyl single).

APPLES AND ORANGES

FRIDAY 17 NOVEMBER 1967

'Apples And Oranges' / 'Paintbox'

UK: Columbia EMI DB 8310 (Promotional 7-inch vinyl single, with picture sleeve & 7-inch vinyl single).

IT WOULD BE SO NICE

FRIDAY 19 APRIL 1968

'It Would Be So Nice' / 'Julia Dream'

UK: Columbia EMI DB 8410 (Promotional 7-inch vinyl single & 7-inch vinyl single).
US: Tower 426 (Promotional 7-inch vinyl single & 7-inch vinyl single, released Monday 24 June 1968).

A SAUCERFUL OF SECRETS

FRIDAY 28 JUNE 1968

A Saucerful of Secrets

UK: Columbia EMI SCX 6258 (Stereo vinyl album) / UK: Columbia EMI SX 6258 (Mono vinyl album).
Reissued:
US: Tower ST 5131 (Stereo vinyl album, released Saturday 27 July 1968) / UK: EMI Fame FA 3163 (Vinyl stereo album, released Monday 6 October 1986) / US: Capitol CDP 7463832 (CD album, released Monday 23 January 1987) / UK: EMI CDP 7463832 (CD album, released Monday 23 February 1987) / UK: EMI CDEMD 1063 (CD album, released Monday 25 July 1994) / US: Capitol CDP 07774638326 (CD album, released Tuesday 26 July 1994) / UK: EMI 5099902893624 (*Discovery* edition CD album, released Monday 26 September 2011) / US: Capitol 5099902893624 (*Discovery* edition CD album, released Tuesday 27 September 2011).

MONDAY 26 AUGUST 1968 ◄

'Let There Be More Light' / 'Remember A Day'

US: Tower 440 (Promotional 7-inch vinyl single & 7-inch vinyl single).
Both songs were taken directly from the masters recorded for *A Saucerful of Secrets*. However, 'Let There Be More Light' has an edit during the intro, thes second verse ("Now is the time to be aware…") is missing, the beginning of the instrumental part after the last verse was cut, and there's an early fade out. Similarly 'Remember A Day' is also edited with a fade-out before the last verse.

POINT ME AT THE SKY

FRIDAY 6 DECEMBER 1968

'Point Me At The Sky' / 'Careful With That Axe, Eugene'

UK: Columbia EMI DB 8511 (Promotional 7-inch vinyl single, some issued with a postcard photo of the band depicted in flying suits & 7-inch vinyl single).

SOUNDTRACK FROM THE FILM *MORE*

FRIDAY 13 JUNE 1969

Soundtrack from the film More

UK: Columbia EMI SCX 6346 (Vinyl album).
US: Tower ST 5169 (Vinyl album, released Saturday 9 August 1969).
Reissued:
US: Harvest SW 11198 (Vinyl album, released Saturday 25 August 1973) / US: Capitol SW 11198 (Vinyl album, released Saturday 9 July 1983) / US: Capitol CDP 7463862 (CD album, released Monday 23 January 1987) / UK: EMI CDP 7463862 (CD album, released Monday 16 March 1987) / UK: EMI CDEMD 1084 (CD album, released Monday 26 February 1996) / US: Capitol 07774638623 (CD album, released Tuesday 27 February 1996) / UK: EMI 5099902893822 (*Discovery* edition CD album, released Monday 26 September 2011) / US: Capitol 5099902893822 (*Discovery* edition CD album, released Tuesday 27 September 2011).

UMMAGUMMA

FRIDAY 7 NOVEMBER 1969

Ummagumma

UK: EMI Harvest SHDW 1/2 (Double vinyl album).
US: Harvest STBB 388 (Double vinyl album, released Saturday 8 November 1969).
Reissued:
US: Capitol STBB 388 (Double vinyl album, released Saturday 8 December 1973) / US: Capitol SKBB 388 (Double vinyl album, released Saturday 9 July 1983) / UK: EMI CDP 7464048 (Double-CD album, released Monday 16 March 1987) / US: Capitol CDPB 7464048 (Double-CD album, released Tuesday 17 March 1987) / UK: EMI CDEMD 1074 (Double-CD album, released Monday 17 October 1994) / US: Capitol CDP 077774640428 (Double-CD album, released Tuesday 18 October 1994) / UK: EMI 5099902893723 (*Discovery* edition CD album, released Monday 26 September 2011) / US: Capitol 5099902893723 (*Discovery* edition CD album, released Tuesday 27 September 2011).

ATOM HEART MOTHER

FRIDAY 2 OCTOBER 1970

Atom Heart Mother

UK: EMI Harvest SHVL 781 (Vinyl album).
US: Harvest SKAO 382 (Vinyl album, released Saturday 10 October 1970).
Reissued:
UK: EMI Harvest EMI Q4 SHVL 781 (Quadraphonic vinyl album, released Friday 6 July 1973) / US: Harvest SMAS 382 (Vinyl album, Saturday 20 September 1975) / US: Capitol SMAS 382 (Vinyl album, released Saturday 9 July 1983) / US: Capitol CDP 7463812 (CD album, released Friday 5 December 1986) / UK: EMI CDP 7463812 (CD album, released Monday 23 February 1987) / UK: EMI CDP 7463812 (CD album, now with bar code, released Monday 18 July 1988) / US: Mobile Fidelity Sound Lab UDCD 595 (MFSL Original Master Recording Gold Ultra Disc II CD album, released Tuesday 4 January 1994) / US: Mobile Fidelity Sound Lab MFSL 1-202 (Half-speed Original Master Recording 200g vinyl album, limited to 5,000 copies, released Tuesday 15 February 1994) / UK: EMI CD EMD 1072 (CD album, released Monday 17 October 1994) / US: Capitol CDP 07777463818 (CD album, released Tuesday 18 October 1994) / UK: EMI LP EMP 1112 (Limited edition 180g vinyl album, released Monday 18 August 1997) / US: Quadradisc QD-002-1 (Promotional 8-track master CD album, released Tuesday 9 March 1999) / UK: EMI 5099902894027 (*Discovery* edition CD album, released Monday 26 September 2011) / US: Capitol 5099902894027 (*Discovery* edition CD album, released Tuesday 27 September 2011).

MEDDLE

FRIDAY 5 NOVEMBER 1971
Meddle
UK: EMI Harvest SHVL 795 (Vinyl album).
US: Harvest SMAS 832 (Vinyl album, released Saturday
30 October 1971).
Reissued:
US: Capitol SMAS 832 (Vinyl album, released Saturday 9 July 1983) /
UK: EMI CDP 7460342 (CD album, released Monday 30 July 1984) /
US: Capitol CDP 7460342 (CD album, released Friday 3 August 1984) /
UK: EMI Harvest SHVL 795 / ATAK 35 (Vinyl album, released Monday 7
January 1985) / UK: EMI CDP 7460342 (CD album, now with bar code,
released Monday 18 July 1988) / US: Mobile Fidelity Sound Lab UDCD
518 (MFSL Original Master Recording 24-carat gold Ultra Disc CD,
released Tuesday 11 April 1989) / US: Mobile Fidelity Sound Lab MFSL
1-190 (Half-speed Original Master Recording 118g vinyl album, released
Tuesday 4 April 1994) / UK: EMI CDEMD 1061 (CD album, released
Monday 1 August 1994) / US: Capitol CDP 7460342 (CD album, released
Tuesday 2 August 1994) / UK: EMI 0289422 (*Discovery* edition CD album,
released Monday 26 September 2011) / US: Capitol 5099902894225
(*Discovery* edition CD album, released Tuesday 27 September 2011).

MONDAY 29 NOVEMBER 1971
'One Of These Days' / 'Fearless'
US: Capitol PRO-6378 (3240) – PRO-6370 (3240) (Promotional 7-inch
vinyl single) / US: Capitol 3240 (7-inch vinyl single).
Aside from shortening the A-side to 5:50, the promo version of the single
leaves 'One Of These Days' at 3:31 and 'Fearless' at just 3:15. 'Fearless'
contains just the one verse spliced from the first verse ending "just wait a
while for the right day" and recommencing with the second verse starting
"and as you rise above the fear…" to an early fade at the end.

OBSCURED BY CLOUDS

FRIDAY 2 JUNE 1972 ▼
Obscured by Clouds
UK: EMI Harvest SHSP 4020 (Vinyl album).
US: Harvest ST 11078 (Vinyl album, released Saturday 17 June 1972).
Reissued:
US: Harvest SW 11078 (Vinyl album, released Saturday 20 September
1975) / US: Capitol SW 11078 (Vinyl album, released Saturday 9
July 1983) / US: Capitol CDP 7463852 (CD album, released Friday 5
December 1986) / UK: EMI CDP 7463852 (CD album, released Monday
6 April 1987) / UK: EMI CDP 7463852 (CD album, now with barcode, released Monday 18 July 1988) / UK: EMI CDEMD 1083 (CD album, released Monday 26 February 1996) / US: Capitol CDP 7463852 (CD album, released Tuesday 27 February 1996) / UK: EMI 0289432 (*Discovery* edition CD album, released Monday 26 September 2011) / US: Capitol 5099902894324 (*Discovery* edition CD album, released Tuesday 27 September 2011).

MONDAY 10 JULY 1972
'Free Four' / 'Stay'
US: Capitol P 3391 (Promotional 7-inch vinyl single) / US: Capitol 3391
(7-inch vinyl single).

THE DARK SIDE OF THE MOON

SATURDAY 1 MARCH 1973
The Dark Side of the Moon
US: Harvest SMAS 11163 (Vinyl album).
UK: EMI Harvest SHVL 804 (Vinyl album, released Friday 16 March 1973).
Reissued:
UK: EMI Harvest Q4 SHVL 804 (Quadraphonic vinyl album, released
Friday 12 January 1974) / US: Capitol SEAX-11902 (Picture disc vinyl
album, released Saturday 2 December 1978) / US: Mobile Fidelity Sound
Lab MFSL 1-017 (Half-speed Original Master Recording 100g vinyl
album, released Saturday 16 June 1979) / US: Mobile Fidelity Sound Lab
UHQR 1-017 (Ultra High Quality Recording 200g vinyl album box set
limited to 5,000 copies, released Saturday 10 January 1981) / UK: EMI
CDP 7460012 (CD album, released Monday 30 July 1984) / US: Capitol
CDP 7460012 (CD album, released Friday 3 August 1984).
US: Mobile Fidelity Sound Lab UDCD 517 (MFSL Ultra Disc CD album on
24-carat gold disc, released Tuesday 12 April 1988) / UK: EMI CDP 7460012
(CD album now with barcode, released Monday 18 July 1988) / UK: EMI
CD EMD 1064 (CD album, released Monday 25 July 1994) / US: Capitol
CDP 7460012 (CD album, released Tuesday 26 July 1994) / UK: EMI LP
EMD 1114 (180g vinyl album, released Monday 24 March 1997) / UK: EMI
LP CENT11 (*EMI 100 Anniversary* edition 180g virgin vinyl album, released
Monday 8 September 1997) / UK: EMI CD EMD 1064 (Limited edition
of 600 individually numbered CD albums given to employees to mark the
closure of EMI's pressing plant in Swindon with the legend on the sleeve,
"Between August 1985 and May 2002 the Company produced 662,930,600
CDs…*Dark Side of the Moon* was the first and last CD produced by EMI in
Swindon", released May 2002) / UK: EMI 5099902895529 (*Discovery* edition
CD album, released Monday 26 September 2011) / UK: EMI SHVL 804
(180g heavyweight vinyl album with MP3 download and inserts, released
Monday 26 September 2011) / US: Capitol SHVL 804 (180g heavyweight
vinyl album with MP3 download and inserts, released Tuesday 27 September
2011) / UK: EMI SHVL 804 (40th anniversary 180g heavyweight vinyl album
with MP3 download and inserts, released Monday 25 March 2013) / US:
Capitol SHVL 804 (40th anniversary 180g heavyweight vinyl album with MP3
download and inserts, released Tuesday 26 March 2013).

FRIDAY 4 MAY 1973
'Money' (Mono) / 'Money' (Stereo)
US: Harvest SPRO 3609 (Promotional 7-inch vinyl single) / Harvest
SPRO-6682 (3609) – SPRO-6669 (3609) (Promotional 7-inch vinyl single,
with an insert that reads, "Please disregard the previous Pink Floyd
promo single which you have received. This is the correct Pink Floyd
promo single with the word "Bulls—t" edited on both the mono and
stereo sides. From the LP *The Dark Side of the Moon*, a certified million
seller and #1 album in the country").

FRIDAY 4 MAY 1973
'Money' / 'Any Colour You Like'
US: Harvest 3609 (7-inch vinyl single).
Highest chart position No. 13 (*Billboard* "Hot 100" on Saturday 28 July 1973).
Reissued:
US: Capitol Starline 6256 (7-inch vinyl single, with either blue, light tan,
green or yellow labels, released Friday 6 November 1981) / US: Capitol
Starline A-6256 (7-inch vinyl single, with blue labels, released Friday 16
January 1982) / US: Capitol Starline X-6256 (7-inch vinyl single, with
blue labels, released Friday 15 July 1983) / US: Capitol Starline X-6256
(7-inch vinyl single, with black & rainbow labels, released Friday 18
September 1987) / US: Capitol Starline X-6256 (7-inch vinyl single,
with purple labels, released Friday 8 April 1988).

FRIDAY 12 OCTOBER 1973 ▶
'Time' / 'Breathe' // 'Us And Them' / 'Money'
US: Harvest PRO 6746–PRO 6747 (Promotional 7-inch vinyl EP single, issued in a picture sleeve with mono mixes for radio play. Includes an edited version of the song 'Money' with the word "bullshit" edited out).

MONDAY 4 FEBRUARY 1974
'Us And Them' (Mono) / 'Us And Them' (Stereo)
US: Harvest P-3832 (PRO-6829) (Promotional 7-inch vinyl single).
'Us And Them' / 'Time'
US: Harvest 3832 (7-inch vinyl single).
Highest chart position No. 101 (*Billboard* "Bubbling Under The Hot 100" on Saturday 9 March 1974).

MONDAY 22 MARCH 1993
The Dark Side of the Moon: XX Anniversary
UK: EMI (Promotional 20th Anniversary CD album box set with biography printed on coloured paper with postcard photos and two colour slides) / UK: EMI 7814792 (20th Anniversary CD album box set with postcards, released Monday 22 March 1993).
US: EMI Capitol C21X 81479 (20th Anniversary CD album box set with postcards, released Tuesday 23 March 1993).

THURSDAY 12 OCTOBER 2000
'Money' (Single Edit) / 'Time' (Single Edit)
US: EMI Capitol 72438-58884 (7-inch jukebox single).

TUESDAY 23 MARCH 2003
The Dark Side of the Moon: 30th Anniversary
30th anniversary hybrid Super Audio CD (SACD) with a 5.1 channel DSD surround mix mastered from the original 16-track studio tapes by James Guthrie. Alan Parsons was called in to add a small cross-fade between 'The Great Gig In The Sky' and 'Money'.
US: Capitol CDP 5821362 (30th Anniversary Hybrid SACD album).
UK: EMI 5821362 (30th Anniversary Hybrid SACD album) / UK: EMI 5821361 (30th Anniversary vinyl album with inserts, released Monday 31 March 2003).

TUESDAY 23 MARCH 2003
'Money'
US: Capitol CA 4280 (Promotional SACD).
UK: EMI CD EMDJ 620 (Promotional SACD, released Monday 31 March 2003).

MONDAY 31 MARCH 2003
The Dark Side of the Moon
UK: EMI EPK 2003 (Promotional CD with excerpts from the SACD release and interviews with David Gilmour, Nick Mason, Storm Thorgerson, Roger Waters and Richard Wright).

MONDAY 26 SEPTEMBER 2011
The Dark Side of the Moon: Experience
CD1: *The Dark Side of the Moon* original album (Digitally Remastered 2011) / CD2: *The Dark Side of the Moon* performed live at Wembley, November 1974 (2011 Mix).

> PINK FLOYD'S latest No.1 album, DARK SIDE OF THE MOON, went platinum a few months after release – with smash sales surpassing three times those of a standard gold album.
> Here are four representative selections taken from the DARK SIDE OF THE MOON LP..edited down for your airplay convenience.
>
> **TIME** (3:33)
> **BREATHE** (3:00)
> **US AND THEM** (3:15)
> **MONEY** (3:12)

UK: EMI 5099902945323 (Double-CD album).
US: Capitol 5099902945323 (Double-CD album, released Tuesday 27 September 2011).
The CD set features a live recording taken from the BBC live mix of *The Dark Side of the Moon* recorded at the Empire Pool, Wembley, England on Saturday 16 November 1974 and a previously unreleased multi-track live recording taken from Friday 15 November 1974.

MONDAY 26 SEPTEMBER 2011
The Dark Side of the Moon: Immersion
A compact box set that included a 40-page booklet designed by Storm Thorgerson; Exclusive photo book edited by Jill Furmanovsky; exclusive Storm Thorgerson art print; Roger Waters' questions card; five Collectors' Cards featuring art and comments by Storm Thorgerson; replica of *The Dark Side of the Moon* tour ticket; replica of *The Dark Side of the Moon* backstage pass; scarf; three black marbles; nine coasters (unique to this box) featuring early Storm Thorgerson design sketches; 12-page credits booklet.
CD1: *The Dark Side of the Moon* (Digitally Remastered 2011) / CD2: *The Dark Side of the Moon* performed live at Wembley, November 1974 (2011 Mix) / CD3: The Dark Side of the Moon, 1972 Early Album Mix Engineered by Alan Parsons / 'The Hard Way' (From the *Household Objects* project) / 'Us And Them' (Richard Wright Demo) / 'The Travel Sequence' (Live from Brighton, June 1972) / 'The Mortality Sequence' (Live from Brighton, June 1972) / 'Any Colour You Like' (Live from Brighton, June 1972 / 'The Travel Sequence' (Studio Recording, 1972) / 'Money' (Roger Waters' demo) / DVD1 (Audio): *The Dark Side of the Moon* (James Guthrie 2003 5.1 Surround Mix in standard resolution audio at 448 kbps) / *The Dark Side of the Moon* (James Guthrie 2003 5.1 Surround Mix in high resolution audio at 640 kbps / *The Dark Side of the Moon*, LPCM Stereo mix (as CD1) / *The Dark Side of the Moon* (Alan Parsons Quad Mix previously released only on vinyl LP/8-track tape in 1973, in standard resolution audio at 448 kbps) / *The Dark Side of the Moon* (Alan Parsons Quad Mix previously released only on vinyl LP/8-track tape in 1973, in high resolution audio at 640 kbps) / DVD2 (Audio Visual): 'Careful With That Axe, Eugene' (Live in Brighton, June 1972) / 'Set The Controls For The Heart Of The Sun' (Live in Brighton, June 1972) / *The Dark Side of the Moon* (2003 Electronic Press Kit) / Concert Screen Films (audio in stereo and 5.1 Surround Sound): British & French Tour 1974, North American Tour 1975 / BluRay Disc (Audio Visual): *The Dark Side of the Moon* (audio) (James Guthrie 2003 5.1 Surround Mix in high resolution audio at 96 kHz/24-bit) / *The Dark Side of the Moon* (Original stereo mix 1973 mastered in high resolution audio at 96 kHz/24-bit / 'Careful With That Axe, Eugene' (Live in Brighton, June 1972) / 'Set The Controls For The Heart Of The Sun' (Live in Brighton, June 1972) / *The Dark Side of the Moon* 2003 Electronic Press Kit) / Concert Screen Films (5.1 Surround Sound Mix): British & French Tour 1974, North American Tour 1975 / Concert Screen Films (High Resolution Stereo Mix): British & French Tour 1974, North American Tour 1975.
UK: EMI 5099902943121 (Box set).
US: Capitol 5099902943121 (Box set, released 27 September 2011).

MONDAY 26 SEPTEMBER 2011
The Dark Side of the Moon: Audio Visual Material
Track list: Live In Brighton 1972 ['Careful With That Axe, Eugene' and 'Set The Controls For The Heart Of The Sun'] / *The Dark Side of the Moon* 2003 Documentary / Concert Screen Films LCPM Stereo / Concert Screen Films 5.1 Surround Mix.
UK: EMI (Promotional DVD).

TUESDAY 4 JUNE 2013
'Money' (Roger Waters Demo)
An offer of a free download of the demo version of 'Money' previously only available in the Immersion box set of *The Dark Side of the Moon* was made through Pink Floyd's official website to purchasers of any version of *The Dark Side of the Moon* on CD or the 2011 remaster at iTunes or on vinyl.

WISH YOU WERE HERE

FRIDAY 12 SEPTEMBER 1975 ◄
Wish You Were Here
UK: EMI Harvest SHVL 814 (Vinyl album).
US: Columbia PC 33453 (Promotional vinyl album, banded for radio play, and issued with a pink cue sheet) / US: Columbia PC 33453 (Vinyl album, released Saturday 13 September 1975).
Reissued:
US: Columbia PCQ 33453 (Quadraphonic vinyl album, released Saturday 24 January 1976) / UK: EMI Harvest Q4 SHVL 814 (Quadraphonic vinyl album, released Friday 7 May 1976) / US: Columbia HC 33453 (Master Sound Half-Speed Master vinyl album, released Saturday 17 May 1980) / US: Columbia JC 33453 (Vinyl album, released Saturday 10 January 1981) / UK: EMI Harvest SHVL 814 (Limited edition of 1,000 vinyl albums pressed exclusively for *Hi-Fi Today* magazine and available only by mail order and a cover sticker with the following text: "Supercut – Mastered and Pressed Exclusively for Readers of *Hi Fi Today* by Nimbus Records", released Monday 30 July 1984) / UK: EMI CDP 7460352 (CD album, released Monday 30 July 1984) / US: CBS CK 33453 (CD album, released Saturday 18 August 1984) / UK: EMI CDP 7460352 (CD album, now with barcode, released Monday 18 July 1988) / US: Columbia CK 53753 (Master Sound 20 Bit Super Bit Mapping 24-carat gold CD album, released Tuesday 5 July 1994) / UK: EMI CD EMD 1062 (CD album, released Monday 25 July 1994) / US: Columbia CK 64405 (CD album, released Tuesday 26 July 1994) / UK: EMI LP EMD 1115 (180g vinyl album, released Monday 18 August 1997) / US: Columbia CK 64405 (Master Sound 20-Bit Super Bit Mapping 24-carat gold CD album, released Tuesday 16 December 1997) / US: Columbia CK 68522 (*Columbia Records 1997 Anniversary* edition CD album, released Tuesday 16 December 1997) / US: Capitol CDP 724382975021 (*Capitol Records 2000* edition CD album & Best Buy stores CD album, released Tuesday 25 April 2000) / UK: EMI 724352907120 (20th Anniversary CD album in mini album sleeve, released Monday 13 November 2000) / US: Capitol CDP 724382975021 (CD album, released Tuesday 23 March 2004) / UK: EMI 5099902894522 (Discovery edition CD album, released Monday 26 September 2011) / UK: EMI SHVL 814 (180g heavyweight vinyl album with MP3 download and inserts, released Monday 26 September 2011) / US: Capitol 5099902894522 (*Discovery* edition CD album, released Tuesday 27 September 2011) / US: Capitol SHVL 814 (180g heavyweight vinyl album with MP3 download and inserts, released Tuesday 27 September 2011).

TUESDAY 4 NOVEMBER 1975
'Have A Cigar' (Mono) / 'Have A Cigar' (Stereo)
US: Columbia 3-10248 (Promotional 7-inch vinyl single).
'Have A Cigar' / 'Welcome To The Machine'
US: Columbia 3-10248 (7-inch vinyl single).

MONDAY 16 OCTOBER 2000
'Wish You Were Here' / 'Have A Cigar'
US: EMI Capitol 72438-58885 (7-inch jukebox single).

TUESDAY 8 NOVEMBER 2011
Wish You Were Here: 35th Anniversary Edition
UK: EMI 5099952243325 (CD album).
US: Acoustic Sounds CAPP 33453 SA (CD album, Released Tuesday 8 November 2011).
In May 2012 James Guthrie posted a short documentary in the Internet entitled *The Missing Piano*. A supporting article posted on the website *A Fleeting Glimspe* picked up the story: "The title refers to a quest Guthrie undertook to preserve the integrity of the record as much as humanly possible, even with one particular piece missing from the multi-tracks for 'Shine On You Crazy Diamond, Parts 1–5'. Undeterred when his initial investigations in regards to the missing piano part provided no solid leads, Guthrie explains in the documentary how he developed a particular theory regarding its omission, discovering the supporting evidence by comparing the master reel, the multi-tracks and the quad mix of the album. After an initial 5.1 mix had been created and presented to the band in London in 2007, he then asked Richard Wright to reprise the part so it could be incorporated into the new mix, recording Wright at British Grove Studios, Chiswick, London, England on the studio's Bosendorfer concert-grand piano. Thus the 5.1 mix of the work contains an element of historical significance: one of the last-known performances of Richard Wright."

MONDAY 7 NOVEMBER 2011
Wish You Were Here: Experience
A double CD set featuring live recordings taken from the BBC live mix of the Wembley Empire Pool concert on 16 November 1974 and a previously unreleased multi-track live recording taken from 15 November 1974. The alternate version of 'Have A Cigar' is most likely a duet between Roy Harper and Roger Waters.
CD1: *Wish You Were Here* (digitally remastered by James Guthrie, 2011) / CD2: 'Shine On You Crazy Diamond, Parts 1–6' (live at Wembley, November 1974, 2011 mix) / 'Raving And Drooling' (live at Wembley, November 1974, 2011 mix) / 'You've Got To Be Crazy live at Wembley November 1974 (2011 mix and previously unreleased) / 'Wine Glasses' (from the unreleased Household Objects project) / 'Have A Cigar' (alternate version) / 'Wish You Were Here' (featuring Stéphane Grappelli).
UK: EMI 5099902894522 (Double CD)
US: Capitol 5099902894522 (Double CD, released 8 November 2011).

MONDAY 7 NOVEMBER 2011
Wish You Were Here: Immersion
A compact box set that included a 40-page booklet designed by Storm Thorgerson; exclusive photo book by Jill Furmanovsky; exclusive Storm Thorgerson Art Print; 5 x Collectors' Cards featuring art and comments by Storm Thorgerson; Replica of *Wish You Were Here* Tour Ticket; replica of *Wish You Were Here* Backstage Pass; scarf; 3 x clear marbles; 9 x coasters (unique to this box) featuring early Storm Thorgerson design sketches; 8-page credits booklet.
CD1: *Wish You Were Here* (digitally remastered by James Guthrie, 2011) / CD2: 'Shine On You Crazy Diamond, Parts 1–6' (live at Wembley, November 1974, 2011 mix) / 'Raving And Drooling' (live at Wembley, November 1974, 2011 mix) / 'You've Got To Be Crazy live at Wembley November 1974 (2011 mix and previously unreleased) / 'Wine Glasses' (from the unreleased Household Objects project) / 'Have A Cigar' (alternate version) / 'Wish You Were Here' (featuring Stéphane Grappelli) / DVD1 (Audio): *Wish You Were Here* (James Guthrie 2007 5.1 Surround Mix in standard resolution audio at 448 kbps and 640kbps) / 'Wish You Were Here' (Quad Mix previously released only on vinyl LP & 8 track tape in standard resolution audio at 448 kbps and 640 kbps) / *Wish You Were Here* (James Guthrie 2011 High Resolution Stereo Mix) / DVD2 (Audio Visual):

Concert Screen Films / 'Shine On You Crazy Diamond' Intro / 'Shine On You Crazy Diamond' / 'Welcome To The Machine' animated clip / Storm Thorgerson short film / BluRay (Audio Visual): *Wish You Were Here*, James Guthrie 2007 5.1 Surround Mix in standard resolution audio at highest resolution at 96kHz/24-bit / Concert Screen films / 'Shine On You Crazy Diamond' Intro / 'Shine On You Crazy Diamond' / 'Welcome To The Machine' animated clip / Storm Thorgerson short film.
UK: EMI 5099902943527 (Box set).
US: Capitol 5099902943527 (Box set, released Tuesday 8 November 2011).

ANIMALS
FRIDAY 21 JANUARY 1977
Animals
UK: EMI Harvest SHVL 815 (Vinyl album).
US: Columbia JC 34474 (Vinyl album, released Saturday 12 February 1977).
Reissued:
UK: EMI CDP 7461282 (CD album, released Monday 30 June 1986) / US: Columbia CK 34474 (CD album, released Saturday 12 July 1986) / UK: EMI CDP 7461282 (CD album, now with barcode, released Monday 18 July 1988) / UK: EMI CD EMD 1060 (CD album, released Monday 25 July 1994) / US: Columbia CK 34474 (CD album, released Tuesday 26 July 1994) / UK: EMI LP EMP 1116 (180g vinyl album, released Monday 18 August 1997) / US: Columbia CK 68521 (Columbia Records 1997 Anniversary edition CD album, released Tuesday 16 December 1997) / US: Capitol CDP 724382974826 (*Capitol Records 2000* edition CD album, released Tuesday 25 April 2000) / US: Capitol CDP 724382974826 (*Capitol Records 2000* edition *Best Buy* stores CD album, released Tuesday 25 April 2000) / US: Capitol CDP 724382974826 (CD album, released Tuesday 9 March 2004) / UK: EMI 5099902895123 (*Discovery* edition CD album, released Monday 26 September 2011) / US: Capitol 5099902895123 (*Discovery* edition CD album, released Tuesday 27 September 2011).

SATURDAY 12 FEBRUARY 1977
Animals: Special DJ Copy
Side 1: 'Pigs On The Wing, Part 1' / 'Dogs' (Edit, Part 1) / 'Dogs' (Edit, Part 2), 'Dogs' (Edit, Part 3) / Side 2: 'Pigs (Three Different Ones)' / 'Sheep' (Edit, Part 1) / 'Sheep' (Edit, Part 2).

US: Columbia AP-1 (Promotional vinyl album banded for radio play and issued with an orange cue sheet. 'Pigs (Three Different Ones)' is a re-recorded mix, having been changed to "you old hag" instead of "you fucked up old hag").

THE WALL
FRIDAY 23 NOVEMBER 1979
'Another Brick In The Wall, Part 2' / 'One Of My Turns'
UK: EMI Harvest HAR 5194 (7-inch vinyl single, with plain bricks label on B-side).
Highest chart position No.1 (*Music Week* 'Top 75 Singles' on Saturday 15 December 1979).
Certified Silver and Gold on Saturday 1 December 1979 and Platinum on Tuesday 1 January 1980.
The first single release from the album, 'Another Brick In The Wall, Part 2', became an unexpected overnight sensation in the UK and the initial run was pressed without a picture sleeve and without the window cartoon on its B-side label. Subsequent pressings featured a revised label design by Gerald Scarfe and a picture sleeve. A hastily produced promo video was made for inclusion on BBC TV's *Top of the Pops*, made because, following the media furore surrounding the controversial song, the Islington Green

school head teacher Margaret Maden refused permission for the children who sang on the song to appear in the video or on *Top of the Pops*, although at the time they were told it was because they didn't hold equity cards. The video used some animation that was in production for the live shows and a live-action sequence of the Teacher puppet (which was also due to be used in the live shows) was shot on location at the aforementioned school.
Reissued:
UK: EMI Harvest HAR 5194 (7-inch vinyl single, with window label on b-side, released Friday 4 January 1980) / UK: EMI Harvest HAR 5194 (7-inch vinyl single, with solid pressed silver label, released Friday 6 November 1981).

TUESDAY 8 JANUARY 1980
'Another Brick In The Wall, Part 2' / 'Another Brick In The Wall, Part 2'
US: Columbia 1-11187 (Promotional 7-inch vinyl single).
'Another Brick In The Wall, Part 2' / 'One Of My Turns'
US: Columbia 1-11187 (7-inch vinyl single).
Highest chart position No. 1 (*Billboard* "Hot 100" on Saturday 22 March 1980). Certified Gold on Monday 24 March 1980 and Platinum on Tuesday 25 September 2001.
Two versions of the US 7-inch vinyl single exist: one with the label credits reading "Co-produced and engineered by James Guthrie" and the other, "Produced by Bob Ezrin, David Gilmour and Roger Waters". At the *7th Annual American Music Awards*, broadcast from the ABC TV Center, Los Angeles, CA, USA on 18 January 1980 'Another Brick In The Wall, Part 2' was nominated for 'Favourite Single Pop/Rock' losing out to 'Another One Bites The Dust' by Queen.
Reissued:
US: Columbia 1-11187 (7-inch vinyl single, with orange labels, released Tuesday 9 June 1981) / US: Columbia 13-03118 (7-inch vinyl single, variously with grey labels, red/yellow labels, released Tuesday 3 August 1982) / US: Columbia Hall of Fame 13-03118 (7-inch vinyl single, released Tuesday 11 April 1989) / US: Columbia Hall of Fame 38K-03118 (3-inch CD single, released Tuesday 11 April 1989) / US: Columbia Collectibles 13-03118 (7-inch vinyl single, released Tuesday 9 May 2006).

FRIDAY 30 NOVEMBER 1979
The Wall
UK: EMI Harvest SHVL 822 (Double vinyl album).
US: Columbia PC2 36183 (Promotional double vinyl album, with track timing sticker on cover & double vinyl album, released Saturday 8 December 1979).
Reissued:
US: Columbia PC2 36183 (Double vinyl album, with band members names now listed on cover, released Saturday 11 October 1980) / US: Columbia H2C 46183 (Master Sound Half-Speed Master double vinyl album, released Saturday 12 March 1983) / UK: EMI CDS 7460368 (Double-CD album, released Monday 27 August 1984) / US: Columbia C2K 36183 (Double-CD album, released Saturday 19 January 1985) / UK: EMI CDS 7460368 (Double-CD album, now with barcode, released Monday 18 July 1988) / Mobile Fidelity Sound Lab UDCD 2-537 (MFSL Ultra Disc double-CD album original master recording on 24 carat gold, released Saturday 15 September 1990) / UK: EMI CD EMD 1111 (Double-CD album, released Monday 10 October 1994) / US: Capitol C2M 36183 (Double-CD album, released Tuesday 11 October 1994) / UK: EMI LP EMD 1111 (Limited edition 180g double vinyl album, released Monday 18 August 1997) / US: Columbia C2K 68519 (Columbia Records 1997 Anniversary edition double-CD album, released Tuesday 16 December 1997) / US: Capitol CDP 724383124329 (Capitol Records 2000 edition *Best Buy* stores double-CD album, released Tuesday 25 April 2000) / US: Capitol CDP 724383124329 (Capitol Records 2000 edition double-CD album, released Tuesday 25 April 2000) / US: Capitol CDP 724383124329 (Double CD, released

Tuesday 10 February 2004) / US: Capitol 5099991752338 (*Best Buy* stores double-CD album box set with XL T-Shirt released Tuesday 28 September 2010) / UK: EMI 5099902894423 (*Discovery* edition double-CD album, released Monday 26 September 2011) / US: Capitol 5099902894423 (*Discovery* edition double-CD album, released Tuesday 27 September 2011) / UK: EMI 5099902988313 (180g heavyweight vinyl album with MP3 download and inserts, released Monday 27 February 2012) / US: Capitol 5099902988313 (180g heavyweight vinyl album with MP3 download and inserts, released Tuesday 28 February 2012).

MONDAY 28 JANUARY 1980 ◄
Off the Wall
Side 1: 'Another Brick in the Wall, Part 2' /
'Goodbye Blue Sky' / 'Young Lust' /
'One of My Turns' / Side 2: 'Hey You' /
'Nobody Home' / 'Comfortably Numb' /
'Run Like Hell'.

US: Columbia AS 736 (Promotional vinyl album, banded for radio play).

FRIDAY 18 APRIL 1980
'Run Like Hell' / 'Don't Leave Me Now'
US: Columbia AS 777 (Promotional 12-inch vinyl single).

TUESDAY 22 APRIL 1980
'Run Like Hell' / 'Run Like Hell'
US: Columbia 1-11265 (Promotional 7-inch vinyl single).
'Run Like Hell' / 'Don't Leave Me Now'
US: Columbia 1-11265 (7-inch vinyl single).
Highest chart position No. 53 (*Billboard* "Hot 100" on Saturday 31 May 1980).

TUESDAY 29 APRIL 1980
'Run Like Hell' / 'Another Brick In The Wall, Part 2'
US: Columbia AS 783 (Promotional 12-inch vinyl single).

TUESDAY 9 JUNE 1981
'Run Like Hell' / 'Comfortably Numb'
US: Columbia 13-02165 (7-inch vinyl single, with grey labels).
Reissued:
US: Columbia Hall of Fame 13-02165 (7-inch vinyl single with red labels, released Tuesday 11 April 1989) / US: Columbia Hall of Fame 13K 68657 (3-inch CD single, released Tuesday 11 April 1989) / US: Columbia Collectibles 13-02165 (7-inch vinyl single with grey labels, released Tuesday 9 May 2006).

TUESDAY 24 JUNE 1980
'Comfortably Numb' (Short Version) / 'Comfortably Numb' (Long Version)
Columbia 1-11311 (Promotional 7-inch vinyl single).
'Comfortably Numb' (Short Version) / 'Hey You'
Columbia 1-11311 (7-inch vinyl single).

FRIDAY 25 NOVEMBER 2011
The Wall: Singles Collection
Single 1: 'Another Brick In The Wall, Part 2' / 'One of My Turns' /
Single 2: 'Comfortably Numb' / 'Hey You' / Single 3: 'Run Like Hell' / 'Don't Leave Me Now'.
US & US: EMI 5099902703275 (Triple 7-inch vinyl single box set released for Record Store Day 2011 in a numbered flip-top box contained the three singles in reproduction picture sleeves, complete with a fold-out poster and a specially designed 7-inch vinyl single adapter).

MONDAY 27 FEBRUARY 2012
The Wall: Experience
CD1 & CD2: *The Wall* (digitally remastered by James Guthrie, 2011) / CD3: Programme 1, band demos and Roger Waters' original demo: 'Prelude' (Roger Waters' Original Demo) / 'Another Brick In The Wall, Part 1' (Band Demo) / 'The Thin Ice (Band Demo) / 'Goodbye Blue Sky' (Band Demo) / 'Teacher, Teacher' (Band Demo) / 'Another Brick In The Wall, Part 2' (Band Demo) / 'Empty Spaces' (Band Demo) / 'Young Lust' (Band Demo) / 'Mother' (Band Demo) / 'Don't Leave Me Now' (Band Demo) / 'Sexual Revolution' (Band Demo) / 'Another Brick In The Wall, Part 3' (Band Demo) / 'Goodbye Cruel World' (Band Demo) / Programme 2, Band Demos: 'In The Flesh?' / 'The Thin Ice' / 'Another Brick In The Wall, Part 1' / 'The Happiest Days Of Our Lives' / 'Another Brick In The Wall, Part 2' / 'Mother' / Programme 3, Band Demos: 'One Of My Turns' / 'Don't Leave Me Now' / 'Empty Spaces' / 'Backs To The Wall' / 'Another Brick In The Wall, Part 3' / 'Goodbye Cruel World' / 'The Doctor' ('Comfortably Numb') / 'Run Like Hell'.
UK: EMI 5099902944623 (Triple CD album).
US: Capitol 5099902944623 (Triple CD album, released Tuesday 28 February 2012).

MONDAY 27 FEBRUARY 2012
The Wall: Immersion
A compact box set that included a 44-page booklet designed by Storm Thorgerson; exclusive photo book; exclusive Storm Thorgerson Art Print; 5 x Collectors' Cards featuring art and comments by Storm Thorgerson; replica of *The Wall* Tour Ticke; replica of *The Wall* Backstage Pass; scarf; prints of Mark Fisher's stage drawings; 3 x white marbles, 9 x Coasters (unique to this box) featuring early Storm Thorgerson design sketches, and an 8-page credits booklet.
CD1 & CD2: *The Wall* (original album, 2011 mix) / CD3 & CD4 : *Is There Anybody Out There? The Wall Live Pink Floyd 1980-81* (2011 mix) / CD5: *The Wall* Work In Progress, Part 1, 1979. Programme 1, Excerpts from Roger Waters' Original Demo: 'Prelude' ('Vera Lynn') / 'Another Brick In The Wall, Part 2' / 'Mother' / 'Young Lust' / 'Another Brick In The Wall, Part 2' / 'Mother' / 'Backs To The Wall' / 'Don't Leave Me Now' / 'Goodbye Blue Sky' / 'Don't Leave Me Now' / 'Another Brick In The Wall, Part 3' / 'Goodbye Cruel World' / 'Hey You' / 'Is There Anybody Out There?' / 'Bring The Boys Back Home' / 'The Show Must Go On' / 'Waiting For The Worms' / 'Run Like Hell' / 'Outside The Wall' / Programme 2, Excerpts from Roger Waters' Original Demo and Band Demos: 'Prelude' (Roger Waters' Original Demo) / 'Another Brick In The Wall, Part 1' (Band Demo) / 'The Thin Ice (Band Demo) / 'Goodbye Blue Sky' (Band Demo) / 'Teacher, Teacher' (Band Demo) / 'Another Brick In The Wall, Part 2' (Band Demo) / 'Empty Spaces' (Band Demo) / 'Young Lust' (Band Demo) / 'Mother' (Band Demo) / 'Don't Leave Me Now' (Band Demo) / 'Sexual Revolution' (Band Demo) / 'Another Brick In The Wall, Part 3' (Band Demo) / 'Goodbye Cruel World' (Band Demo) / Programme 3, Band Demos: 'In The Flesh?' / 'The Thin Ice' / 'Another Brick In The Wall, Part 1' / 'The Happiest Days Of Our Lives' / 'Another Brick In The Wall, Part 2' / 'Mother' / CD6: *The Wall* Work In Progress, Part 2, 1979. Programme 1, Roger Waters Original Demos and Band Demos: 'Is There Anybody Out There?' (Roger Waters Original Demo) / 'Vera' (Roger Waters Original Demo) / 'Bring The Boys Back Home' (Roger Waters Original Demo) / 'Hey You' (Band Demo) / 'The Doctor' ('Comfortably Numb') (Band Demo) / 'In The Flesh' (Band Demo) / 'Run Like Hell' (Band Demo) / 'Waiting For The Worms (Band Demo) / 'The Trial' (Band Demo) / 'The Show Must Go On' (Band Demo) / 'Outside The Wall' (Band Demo) / 'The Thin Ice (Reprise) ' (Band Demo) / Programme 2, Band Demos: 'Outside The Wall' / 'It's Never Too Late' / 'The Doctor' ('Comfortably Numb') / Programme 3, Band Demos: 'One Of My Turns' / 'Don't Leave Me Now' / 'Empty Spaces' / 'Backs To The Wall' / 'Another Brick In The Wall, Part 3' / 'Goodbye Cruel World' / Programme 4, David Gilmour Original Demos: 'Comfortably Numb' / 'Run Like Hell'

/ DVD1: 'The Happiest days Of Our Lives' (Live at Earls Court 1980) / 'Another Brick In The Wall, Part 2' (promotional video, restored in 2011) / *Behind The Wall* documentary / Gerald Scarfe Interview.

UK: EMI 5099902943923 (Box set).
US: Capitol 5099902943923 (Box set, released Tuesday 28 February 2012).

MONDAY 27 FEBRUARY 2012
The Wall: Immersion – Daytime Sampler
Track list: 'The Doctor' (*The Wall* Work In Progress Part 2 1979, Programme 1, band demo) / 'Another Brick In The Wall, Part 1' (*The Wall* Work In Progress, Part 1 1979, Programme 2, band demo) / 'Hey You' (*The Wall* Work In Progress Part 2, Programme 1 band demo) / 'Mother' (*The Wall* work in progress, Part 1 1979, Programme 2, band demo).

UK: EMI (Promotional CD).

MONDAY 27 FEBRUARY 2012
The Wall: Immersion
Track list: 'Comfortably Numb' (*The Wall* Work In Progress, Part 2, Programme 4, Dave Gilmour Original demo) / 'The Doctor' (*The Wall* Work In Progress, Part 2, Programme 1, band demo) / 'The Doctor' (*The Wall* Work In Progress, Part 2, Programme 2, band demo / 'Comfortably Numb' (2011 album remaster) / 'Comfortably Numb' (from Is There Anybody Out There? *The Wall Live 1980–81*) / 'Another Brick In The Wall, Part 2' (*The Wall* Work In Progress, Part 1, Programme 1, Excerpts from Roger Waters original demo / 'Another Brick In The Wall, Part 3' (*The Wall* Work In Progress, Part 1, Programme 1, Excerpts from Roger Waters original demo) / 'Another Brick In The Wall, Part 1' (*The Wall* Work In Progress, Part 1, Programme 1, Excerpts from Roger Waters original demo) / 'Another Brick In The Wall, Part 2' (*The Wall* Work In Progress, Part 1, Programme 1, band demo / 'Another Brick In The Wall, Part 3' (*The Wall* Work In Progress Part 1, Programme 2, band demo / 'Another Brick In The Wall, Part 1' (2011 album remaster) / 'Another Brick In The Wall, Part 2' (2011 album remaster) / 'Another Brick In The Wall, Part 3' (2011 album remaster) / 'Another Brick In The Wall, Part 1' (from Is There Anybody Out There? *The Wall Live* 1980-81) / 'Another Brick In The Wall, Part 2' (from *Is There Anybody Out There? The Wall Live 1980–81*) / 'Another Brick In The Wall, Part 3' (from *Is There Anybody Out There? The Wall Live 1980–81*).

UK: EMI (Promotional CD).

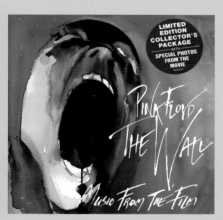

WHEN THE TIGERS BROKE FREE ◄
MONDAY 19 JULY 1982
'When The Tigers Broke Free' / 'Bring The Boys Back Home'
UK: EMI Harvest HAR 5222 (7-inch vinyl single, issued in a single and six-panel fold out picture sleeve).
Highest chart position No. 39 (*Music Week* "Top 75 Singles" on Saturday 14 August 1982).
Issued to coincide with the cinematic release of the feature film, the cover artwork featured Gerald Scarfe's distinctive screaming face design which was used for the film poster. Significantly, the rear sleeve states both tracks are taken from the forthcoming album *The Final Cut* which was originally intended to be an album of music from the film soundtrack.

TUESDAY 17 AUGUST 1982
'When The Tigers Broke Free' / 'When The Tigers Broke Free'
US: Columbia X18-03142 (Promotional 7-inch vinyl single, issued in a six-panel fold out sleeve).
'When The Tigers Broke Free' / 'Bring The Boys Back Home'
US: Columbia AS 1541 (Promotional 12-inch vinyl single).
US: Columbia X18-03142 (7-inch vinyl single, issued in a six-panel fold-out sleeve).

THE FINAL CUT
MONDAY 21 MARCH 1983
The Final Cut
UK: EMI Harvest SHPF 1983 (Vinyl album).
US: Columbia QC 38243 (Vinyl album) / US: Columbia QC 38243 (Promotional vinyl album for Record Bar stores, with two inserts and red poppy) / US: Columbia AS 1636 (Promotional vinyl album, banded for radio play, with each song separated by a gap and issued with a warning sticker on the cover that read "Lyrical content of 'Not Now John' may be objectionable in part to some", released Saturday 2 April 1983).
Reissued:
UK: EMI CDP 7461292 (CD album, released Monday 9 June 1986) / US: CBS CK 38243 (CD album, released Tuesday 10 June 1986) / UK: EMI CD EMD 1070 (CD album, released Monday 10 October 1994) / US: Columbia CK 68517 (Columbia Records 1997 Anniversary edition CD album, released Tuesday 16 December 1997) / UK: EMI 724357673426 (CD album, with the addition of 'When the Tigers Broke Free', released Monday 29 March 2004) / US: Capitol 724357673426 (CD with the addition of 'When the Tigers Broke Free', released Tuesday 4 May 2004) / UK: EMI 5099902895628 (*Discovery* edition CD album, released Monday 26 September 2011) / US: Capitol 5099902895628 (*Discovery* edition CD album, released Tuesday 27 September 2011).

MARCH 1983
Selections from The Final Cut
Side 1: 'Your Possible Pasts' / Side 2: 'The Final Cut'.
US: Columbia AS 1635 (Promotional 12-inch vinyl single).

MONDAY 25 APRIL 1983
'Not Now John' (Single Version) / 'The Hero's Return (Parts 1 & 2)'
UK: EMI Harvest HAR DJ 5224 (Promotional 7-inch vinyl single).
'Not Now John' / 'The Hero's Return (Parts 1 & 2)'
UK: EMI Harvest HAR 5224 (7-inch vinyl single).
'Not Now John' (Single Version) // 'The Hero's Return (Parts 1 & 2)' / 'Not Now John' (Album Version)
UK: EMI Harvest 12 HAR 5224 (12-inch vinyl single).
Highest chart position No. 30 (*Music Week* "Top 75 Singles" on Saturday 14 May 1983).

TUESDAY 3 MAY 1983
'Not Now John' (Obscured Version) / 'Not Now John' (Obscured Version)
US: Columbia AE7 1653 (Promotional 7-inch vinyl single with expletive edited out) / US: Columbia 38-03905 (Promotional 7-inch vinyl single with expletive edited out).
'Not Now John' / 'The Hero's Return (Parts 1 & 2)'
US: Columbia 38-03905 (7-inch vinyl single).
'Not Now John' highest chart position No. 7 (*Billboard* "Hot Mainstream Rock Tracks" on Saturday 7 May 1983).
'The Hero's Return' highest chart position No. 31 (*Billboard* "Hot Mainstream Rock Tracks" on Saturday 30 April 1983).

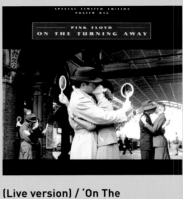

TUESDAY 4 MAY 2004
'When The Tigers Broke Free'
US: Capitol (Promotional CD)
Issued for the remastered version of *The Final Cut*. However, the
disc is marked "Excerpt 2:36 from The Wall".

A MOMENTARY LAPSE OF REASON

MONDAY 7 SEPTEMBER 1987
A Momentary Lapse of Reason
UK: EMI EMD 1003 (Vinyl album) / UK: EMI CDP 7480682 (CD album).
US: Columbia OC 40599 (Vinyl album) / US: Columbia CK 40599 (CD
album, released Tuesday 8 September 1987).
Reissued:
UK: EMI EMDS 1003 (Limited-edition poster-pack vinyl album with
a guaranteed ticket application for upcoming UK concerts, released
Monday 15 February 1988) / UK: EMI CD EMD 1003 (CD album,
released Monday 25 July 1994) / US: Columbia CK 68518 (*Columbia
Records 1997 Anniversary* edition CD album, released Tuesday 16
December 1997) / US: Columbia CK 68518 (CD album, released
Tuesday 8 February 2005) / US: Capitol 5099969515927 (CD album,
released Tuesday 2 June 2009) / UK: EMI 5099902895925 (*Discovery*
edition CD album, released Monday 26 September 2011) / US: Capitol
5099902895925 (*Discovery* edition CD album, released Tuesday 27
September 2011).

MONDAY 7 SEPTEMBER 1987
'Learning To Fly' (Edited Version) / 'Terminal Frost' (Edited Version)
UK: EMI EM26 (Promotional 7-inch vinyl single on pink vinyl, limited
to 7,500 pressings. The picture sleeve also lists a third track, 'One Slip',
which is not on the disc, and the label states 'Learning To Fly (Edited
Version)' on both sides) / UK: EMI EM26 (Promotional 7-inch vinyl
single on black vinyl, limited to 2,700 pressings. The picture sleeve also
lists a third track, 'One Slip', which is not on the disc, and the label states
'Learning To Fly (Edited Version)' on both sides).
**'Learning To Fly' (Edited Version) / 'One Slip' (Edited Version) /
'Terminal Frost' (Album Version) / 'Terminal Frost' (Do Your Own
Lead Version)**
UK: EMI CD EM 26 (CD single).

MONDAY 14 SEPTEMBER 1987
'Learning To Fly' (Edited version) / 'Learning To Fly' (Edited version)
US: Columbia 38-03905 (Promotional 7-inch vinyl single).
'Learning To Fly' (LP version) / 'Learning To Fly' (Edited version)
US: Columbia CSK 2775 (Promotional CD single) / US: Columbia CAS
2775 (Promotional 12-inch vinyl single).
'Learning To Fly' (Edited version) / 'Terminal Frost (Edited version)
US: Columbia 38-07363 (7-inch vinyl single).
Highest chart position No. 70 (*Billboard* "Hot 100 Singles" on Saturday
31 October 1987).
A promo film for the song, directed by Lawrence Jordan, and edited
from concert footage shot at the Omni, Atlanta, GA, USA on
3–5 November 1987 reached No. 9 on MTV's "Video Countdown" for
January 1988.

MONDAY 23 NOVEMBER 1987
'On The Turning Away' / 'On The Turning Away'
US: Columbia 38-07660 (Promotional 7-inch vinyl single).
**'On The Turning Away' (7-inch edit) / 'On The Turning Away'
(Live version)**
US: Columbia CAS 2878 (Promotional 12-inch vinyl single).
'On The Turning Away' / 'Run Like Hell' (Live version)
US: Columbia 38-07660 (7-inch vinyl single).

MONDAY 7 DECEMBER 1987 ▶
**'On The Turning Away' (Edit) / 'On
The Turning Away' (Album version)**
UK: EMI EMDJ 34 (Promotional
7-inch vinyl single).
**'On The Turning Away' / 'Run Like
Hell' (Live version)**
UK: EMI EM 34 (7-inch vinyl single)
/ UK: EMI EMP 34 (7-inch pink vinyl
single, limited to 2,000 pressings).
**'On The Turning Away' / 'Run Like Hell' (Live version) / 'On The
Turning Away' (Live version)**
UK: EMI 12 EM 34 (12-inch vinyl single) / UK: EMI 12 EMP 34 (Limited
edition 12-inch vinyl single, in poster sleeve).
**'On The Turning Away' / 'Run Like Hell' (Live version) / 'On The
Turning Away' (Live version)**
UK: EMI CD EM 34 (CD single).
Highest chart position No. 55 (*Music Week* "Top 75 Singles" on Saturday
26 December 1987).

MONDAY 4 APRIL 1988 ▶
*A Momentary Lapse of Reason:
Official Tour CD*
Track list: 'The Dogs Of War' (Edit) / 'The
Dogs Of War' / 'On The Turning Away'.
US: Columbia CSK 1100 (Promotional
CD).

MONDAY 13 JUNE 1988
'One Slip' / 'Terminal Frost'
UK: EMI EM 52 (7-inch vinyl single)
/ UK: EMI EMG 52 (7-inch pink vinyl
single, limited to 5,000 copies, in gatefold sleeve).
'One Slip' // 'Terminal Frost' / 'The Dogs Of War' (Live)
UK: EMI 12 EM 52 (12-inch vinyl single) / UK: EMI 12 EMP 52
(12-inch vinyl single, in poster sleeve, limited to 7,500 copies).
'One Slip' / 'Terminal Frost' / 'The Dogs Of War' (Live)
UK: EMI CD EM 52 (CD single).
Highest chart position No. 50 (*Music Week* "Top 75 Singles" on Saturday 2
July 1988).

DELICATE SOUND OF THUNDER

NOVEMBER 1988
Delicate Sound of Thunder
Side 1: 'Another Brick In The Wall, Part 2' / 'One Of These Days' / Side 2: 'Run
Like Hell'.
UK: EMI 12 PF1 (Promotional 12-inch vinyl single).
Delicate Sound of Thunder
Track list: 'Wish You Were Here' / 'Learning To Fly' / 'Run Like Hell'.
UK: EMI CD PINK 1 (Promotional CD).
Delicate Sound of Thunder
Track list: 'Comfortably Numb' / 'Learning To Fly' / 'Time' / 'Another Brick In
The Wall, Part 2'.
US: Columbia CSK 1375 (Promotional CD) / US: Columbia DISP 000031
(Promotional CD) / US: Columbia DISP 000046 (Promotional CD).

MONDAY 21 NOVEMBER 1988
Delicate Sound of Thunder
Side 1: 'Shine On You Crazy Diamond' / 'Learning To Fly' / 'Yet Another
Movie' / 'Round And Around' / Side 2: 'Sorrow' / 'The Dogs Of War' / 'On
The Turning Away' / Side 3: 'One Of These Days' / 'Time' / 'Money' / 'Another

Brick In The Wall, Part 2'/Side 4: 'Wish You Were Here'/'Comfortably Numb'/'Run Like Hell'.

UK: EMI EQ 5009 (Double vinyl album).
US: Columbia PC2 44484 (Double vinyl album, released Tuesday 22 November 1988).

MONDAY 21 NOVEMBER 1988
Delicate Sound of Thunder
CD1: 'Shine On You Crazy Diamond'/'Learning To Fly'/'Yet Another Movie'/'Round And Around'/'Sorrow'/'The Dogs Of War'/'On The Turning Away'/CD2: 'One Of These Days'/'Time'/'Wish You Were Here'/'Us And Them'/'Money'/'Another Brick In The Wall, Part 2'/'Comfortably Numb'/'Run Like Hell'.

UK: EMI CDEQ 5009 (Double CD).
Highest chart position No. 11 (*Music Week* "Top 100 Albums" on Saturday 3 December 1988).
Certified Silver and Gold on Thursday 8 December 1988.
US: Columbia C2K 44484 (Double CD, released Tuesday 22 November 1988).
Highest chart position No. 11 (*Billboard* "Top Pop Albums" on Saturday 14 January 1989).
'Comfortably Numb' (Live) highest chart position No. 24 (*Billboard* "Album Rock Tracks" on Saturday 17 December 1988).
'Another Brick In The Wall, Part 2' (Live) highest chart position No. 42 (*Billboard* "Album Rock Tracks" on Saturday 17 December 1988).
'Learning To Fly' (Live) highest chart position No. 45 (*Billboard* "Album Rock Tracks" on Saturday 17 December 1988).
'Time' (Live) highest chart position No. 34 (*Billboard* "Album Rock Tracks" on Saturday 24 December 1988).
Reissued:
UK: Parlophone 5099960919427 (Double CD, released Monday 16 December 2013) / US: Parlophone 081227961404 (Double CD, released Tuesday 13 May 2014).

THE DIVISION BELL

MONDAY 14 MARCH 1994
'Keep Talking'
UK: EMI PINK 1 (Promotional CD).
US: Columbia CSK 6007 (Promotional CD, released Tuesday 15 March 1994).

MONDAY 28 MARCH 1994
The Division Bell
UK: EMI CD EMD 1055 (CD album) / UK: EMI EMD 1055 (Vinyl album).
US: Columbia CK 64200 (CD album) / US: Columbia C64200 (Vinyl album) / US: Columbia C64200 (Limited edition blue vinyl album, released Tuesday 5 April 1994).
Reissued:
UK: EMI 5099902896120 (*Discovery* CD album, released Monday 26 September 2011) / US: Capitol 5099902896120 (*Discovery* CD album, released Tuesday 27 September 2011).

TUESDAY 5 APRIL 1994
Pink Floyd Interview
Track list: 'Keep Talking'/Interviews with David Gilmour, Nick Mason, Richard Wright/'Take It Back'.
US: Columbia CSK 6060 (38-track promotional CD album, with interviews and music for *The Division Bell*).
Printed on the inner cover is the text: "What you are hearing on this CD is music from Pink Floyd's THE DIVISION BELL and an interview done in Southern California, March 26, 1994. It took place just prior to their US tour which sold nearly three million tickets across the country. *The Division Bell*

is an album made up of songs about communication. The disc is an effort to provide you with the opportunity to have questions answered and to gain insight into Pink Floyd." (Tracks 1 and 38) 'Taken from the Columbia release: *The Division Bell*. Tracks 2–18 David Gilmour, Tracks 19–31 Nick Mason, Tracks 32–37 Richard Wright.

MONDAY 16 MAY 1994 ▶

'Take It Back'
UK: EMI CD EMDJ 309 (Promotional CD single).
'Take It Back' (Edit) / 'Astronomy Domine' (Live)
UK: EMI EM 309 (Limited edition 7-inch red vinyl single).
'Take It Back' (Album Version) / 'Astronomy Domine' (Live)
UK: EMI EM 309 (7-inch jukebox–only single).
'Take It Back' (Album Version) / 'Astronomy Domine' (Live) / 'Take It Back' (Edit)
UK: EMI CD EM 309 (CD single) / UK: EMI CD EMS 309 (Limited edition CD single, with poster).
Highest chart position No. 23 (*Music Week* "Official Singles Chart" on Saturday 4 June 1994).

TUESDAY 31 MAY 1994
'Take It Back' (Edit) / 'Take It Back' (Album Version)
US: Columbia CSK 6069 (Promotional CD single).
'Take It Back' (Edit) / 'Astronomy Domine' (Live)
US: Columbia 38-77493 (7-inch vinyl single).
'Take It Back' (Album version) / 'Astronomy Domine' (Live) / 'Take It Back' (Edit)
US: Columbia 38K 77493 (CD single).
Highest chart position No. 73 (*Billboard* "Hot 100" on Saturday 2 July 1994).

TUESDAY 7 JUNE 1994
'Lost For Words' (Clean Version) / 'Lost For Words' (Album Version)
US: Columbia CSK 6228 (Promotional CD).
The "Clean Version" has the word "fuck" bleeped out.

TUESDAY 16 AUGUST 1994
'High Hopes'
US: Columbia CSK 6440 (Promotional CD).
US: Columbia PF-HH-D2-S-031094 (Promotional VHS video).

MONDAY 10 OCTOBER 1994
'High Hopes' (Radio Edit) / 'Keep Talking' (Radio Edit)
UK: EMI CD EMDJ 342 (Promotional CD) / UK: EMI EM 342 (Limited 7-inch clear vinyl single, with poster sleeve).
'High Hopes' (Album Version) / 'Keep Talking' (Album Version) / 'One Of These Days' (Live)
UK: EMI CD EM 342 (CD single) / UK: EMI CD EMS 342 (Limited edition CD single, in digipak with postcards).
'High Hopes' (Album Version) // 'Keep Talking' (Album Version) / 'One Of These Days' (Live)
UK: EMI 12 EM 342 (12-inch one-sided etched coloured vinyl single, with postcards).
Highest chart position No. 26 (*Music Week* "Official Singles Chart" on Saturday 29 October 1994).

TUESDAY 4 APRIL 1995
'Coming Back To Life' (Edit) / 'Coming Back To Life'
US: Columbia CSK 7096 (Promotional CD).

MONDAY 30 JUNE 2014

The Division Bell: 20th Anniversary Edition

UK: Parlophone CD EMD 1055 (CD album) / UK: Parlophone 0825646293285 (180g double vinyl album).

US: Warners 0825646293285 (180g double vinyl album, released Tuesday 1 July 2014).

Pink Floyd launched the announcement of the 20th Anniversary set via an Internet teaser campaign which commenced on Wednesday 14 May 2014, revealing an image with the hashtag #TBD20. By Monday 19 May a further image was released with an accompanying link to a dedicated website on which a new video for the track 'Marooned' was shown on a loop. The film opened with images taken from the International Space Station followed by a journey through the town of Pripyat in northern Ukraine, abandoned following the Chernobyl disaster of 1986.

On Tuesday 20 May, amid much media speculation and hopes for a new album and tour, the full extent of the campaign was revealed, taking in a clutch of sets to mark the band's final album, which disappointingly didn't even contain any studio out-takes, despite indications shortly after its recording there was an album's worth of ambient remixes from the sessions. Pink Floyd had other plans, of course…

MONDAY 30 JUNE 2014 ▶

The Division Bell: 20th Anniversary Edition

Track list: 'Marooned' (2014 film, 5.1 Mix) / The Division Bell (Stereo PCM mastered by James Guthrie) / *The Division Bell* (Dolby Digital 5.1 mastered and mixed by Andy Jackson / *The Division Bell* (DTS 5.1 Mix, mastered and mixed by Andy Jackson).

UK: Parlophone 0825646262847 (DVD album).

US: Warners 0825646262847 (DVD album, released Tuesday 1 July 2014).

MONDAY 30 JUNE 2014

The Division Bell: 20th Anniversary Edition

UK: Parlophone 0825646293261 (7-Disc Collectors' Box Set).

US: Parlophone 0825646293261 (7-Disc Collectors' Box Set, released Tuesday 1 July 2014).

A deluxe box set that included seven discs, including the 180g double vinyl album, as above; the 2011 *Discovery* CD remaster of *The Division Bell*; a Blu-ray disc including the album in HD Audio; the previously unreleased 5.1 surround sound version mixed; mastered by Andy Jackson and Damon Iddins; a new video for 'Marooned' filmed in Ukraine during the first week of April 2014 and directed by Aubrey Powell; a red 7-inch vinyl replica of single 'Take It Back'; a clear 7-inch vinyl replica of 'High Hopes'; a 12-inch blue vinyl replica of 'High Hopes' with reverse laser etched design; a 24-page, 12-inch x 12-inch booklet and four 12-inch x 12-inch art prints.

TUESDAY 1 JULY 2014

The Division Bell: 20th Anniversary Edition

Track list: 'Keep Talking' (Radio Edit) / 'High Hopes' (Radio Edit) / 'Take It Back' (Radio Edit) / 'What Do You Want From Me' / 'Keep Talking' / 'High Hopes' / 'Take It Back' / 'Marooned' / 'Astonomy Domine' (Live from Miami, Florida, 30 March 1994) / 'One Of These Days' (Live from Hannover, Germany, 17 August 1994).

US: Parlophone (Promotional CD album).

P.U.L.S.E.

MONDAY 15 MAY 1995

P.U.L.S.E.

UK: EMI (Promotional PC screen-saver on floppy disc) / UK: EMI (Promotional MAC screen-saver on floppy disc).

MONDAY 15 MAY 1995

P.U.L.S.E.

Track list: 'High Hopes' / 'Breathe' / 'Wish You Were Here'.

UK: EMI (Promotional DVD for Web/TV).

MONDAY 15 MAY 1995

Floydian Snips

UK: EMI (Promotional cassette).

Contains 14:3 of segued excerpts from the album *P.U.L.S.E.*

TUESDAY 16 MAY 1995

'What Do You Want From Me' (Live)

US: Columbia CSK 7143 (Promotional CD).

Highest chart position No. 14 (*Billboard* "Album Rock Tracks" on Saturday 24 June 1995).

MONDAY 5 JUNE 1995 ▶

P.U.L.S.E.

CD1: 'Shine On You Crazy Diamond' / 'Astronomy Domine' / 'What Do You Want From Me' / 'Learning To Fly' / 'Keep Talking' / 'Coming Back To Life' / 'Hey You' / 'A Great Day For Freedom' / 'Sorrow' / 'High Hopes' / 'Another Brick In The Wall, Part 2' / CD2: 'Speak To Me' / 'Breathe' / 'On The Run' / 'Time' / 'The Great Gig In The Sky' / 'Money' / 'Us And Them' / 'Any Colour You Like' / 'Brain Damage' / 'Eclipse' / 'Wish You Were Here' / 'Comfortably Numb' / 'Run Like Hell'.

UK: EMI CD EMD 1078 (Limited edition double-CD album, with hard-back booklet and flashing LED on spine).

Highest chart position No. 1 (Music Week "Top 75 Albums" on 14 August 1995).

Certified Silver and Gold on 1 October 1995 and Platinum 22 July 2013.

US: Columbia C2K 67065 (Limited edition double CD album, with hard-back booklet and flashing LED on spine, released Tuesday 6 June 1995).

Highest chart position No. 1 (*Billboard* "Billboard 200" on Saturday 24 June 1995).

Reissued:

UK: EMI CD EMD 1078 (Double-CD album in standard case, released Monday 13 November 1995) / US: Columbia C2K 67064 (Double-CD album in standard case, released Tuesday 14 November 1995).

MONDAY 7 OCTOBER 1995

P.U.L.S.E.

LP1: 'Shine On You Crazy Diamond' / 'Astronomy Domine' / 'What Do You Want From Me' / 'Learning To Fly' / 'Keep Talking' / 'Coming Back To Life' / LP2: 'Hey You' / 'A Great Day For Freedom' / 'Sorrow' / 'High Hopes' / 'Another Brick In The Wall, Part 2' / 'One Of These Days' / LP3: 'Speak To Me' / 'Breathe' / 'On The Run' / 'Time' / 'The Great Gig In The Sky' / 'Money' / LP4: 'Us And Them' / 'Any Colour You Like' / 'Brain Damage' / 'Eclipse' / 'Wish You Were Here' / 'Comfortably Numb' / 'Run Like Hell'.

UK: EMI EMD 1078 (Four vinyl album box set, with hard-back book).

THE ENDLESS RIVER

OCTOBER 2014
Seamus Revisted
UK: Parolophone (Promotional CD album).
Designed to deter pre-release leaks, Parlophone issued this full-length CD album of *The Endless River* to the media under the assumed band name Seamus with the album title *Seamus Revisited* with the following warning, "this audio is unique and traceable", printed on the disc.

October 2014 'Louder Than Words'
UK: Parlophone (Promotional CD single).
US: Warners (Promotional CD single).

MONDAY 10 NOVEMBER 2014
The Endless River
UK: Parlophone 825646215478 (Double Vinyl album) / UK: Parlophone 825646215423 (CD album).
US: Warners 825646215478 (Double Vinyl album) / US: Warners 825646215423 (CD album, released Tuesday 11 November 2014).

MONDAY 10 NOVEMBER 2014
The Endless River
CD: *The Endless River* (full album) / Blu-ray Disc Audio Visual: 'Anisina' / 'Untitled' / 'Evrika (A)' / 'Nervana' / 'Allons-Y' / 'Evrika (B)' / Audio: 'TBS9' / 'TBS14' / 'Nervana' / Blu-ray Disc /DVD: *The Endless River* (5.1 Audio).

UK: Parlophone 825646213337 (CD album & Blu-ray Disc box set with 2 x postcards, 1 x 3D lenticular design postcard) / UK: Parlophone 825646213344 (CD & DVD album box set, as above).
US: Warners 825646213337 (CD album & Blu-ray box set with 2 x postcards, 1 x 3D lenticular design postcard) / US: Warners 825646213344 (CD & DVD album, as above, released Tuesday 11 November 2014).

COLLECTIONS

RELICS

This was the first collection of Pink Floyd tracks ever released and was an unusual compilation of single A and B sides, tracks from *Music from the film "More"* and a previously unreleased studio outtake, 'Biding My Time', recorded on Saturday 19 July 1969 (and not 9 July as noted on the original sleeve), which had featured in their live set as part of the 'Man' suite that year.

The UK original, issued on the budget Starline label, was housed in a textured sleeve and featured a line drawing and graphics by Nick Mason. The subsequent reissue on the Music for Pleasure label retained the same artwork except the sleeve was on laminated card and the name of the band was highlighted in pink lettering. The US edition on the other hand featured an unusual photograph of a clay mask. Re-releases in the 1990s saw the cover replaced by a 3D model of the strange contraption Mason had originally drawn.

FRIDAY 14 MAY 1971
Relics
Side 1: 'Arnold Layne' / 'Interstellar Overdrive' / 'See Emily Play' / 'Remember A Day' / 'Paintbox' / Side 2: 'Julia Dream' / 'Careful With That Axe, Eugene' / 'Cirrus Minor' / 'The Nile Song' / 'Biding My Time' / 'Bike'.
UK: EMI Starline SRS 5071 (Vinyl album).
Highest chart position No. 32 (*Melody Maker* "Top Twenty Albums" on Saturday 7 August 1971), Chart re-entry No. 48 (*Music Week* "Top 75

Albums"' on 9 March 1996).
Certified Silver on 22 July 2013 and Gold on 9 August 2013.
US: Capitol Harvest SW 759 (Vinyl album, released Saturday 17 July 1971).
Highest chart position No. 152 (*Billboard* "Top LPs" on Saturday 4 September 1971).
Reissued:
UK: EMI Music for Pleasure MFP 50397 (Vinyl album, released Friday 20 October 1978) / US: Capitol Harvest SN 16234 (Vinyl album, released Friday 5 December 1986) / UK: EMI CDEMD 1113 (CD album, released Monday 12 February 1996) / US: Capitol CDP 724383560325 (CD album, released Tuesday 13 February 1996) / UK: EMI LP EMP 1113 (Vinyl album, released Monday 18 August 1996).

A NICE PAIR

A double vinyl album repackage of the albums the *Piper at the Gates of Dawn* and *A Saucerful of Secrets*, also representing the first time Pink Floyd's debut album had a domestic US release.
The artwork, by Hipgnosis, featured a series of images that played on many puns – "A Fork in the Road", "A Frog in the Throat" and "A Different Kettle of Fish" to name a few. It also contained plays on words, including the dental surgery of Dr. Phang, which had to be altered on later pressings because dentists were not allowed to advertise in the UK at that time. The reprint replaced this image with that of a gargling monk.

SATURDAY 8 DECEMBER 1973 ▲
A Nice Pair
US: Capitol Harvest SABB 11257 (Double vinyl album).
Highest chart position No. 36 (*Billboard* "Top LPs & Tape" on Saturday 9 February 1974).
Certified Gold on 11 March 1994.
UK: EMI Harvest SHDW 403 (Double vinyl album, released Friday 18 January 1974).
Highest chart position No. 21 (*Music Week* "Top Albums" on Saturday 19 January 1974).
Certified Silver on 1 May 1974 and Gold on 1 February 1975.
Reissued:
US: Capitol SABB 11257 (Double vinyl album, released Friday 5 December 1986).

TOUR '75

SATURDAY 5 APRIL 1975 ▶
Tour 75
Side 1: 'The Gold It's In The…' / 'Wot's… Uh the Deal' / 'Free Four' / 'One Of These Days' / Side 2: 'Fat Old Sun' / 'Astronomy Dominé' / 'Careful With That Axe, Eugene'.
US: EMI Capitol SPRO 8116/7 (Promotional vinyl album).
A promotional vinyl album issued by Pink Floyd's former label Capitol Records in a plain white sleeve and a cover mounted stencil print showing the track listing was released to radio to coincide with the start of the band's 1975 North American tour.

FIRST XI

FRIDAY 1 JUNE 1979

First XI

UK: EMI Harvest PF11 (Vinyl album box set).

Pink Floyd's first box set was a limited edition of 1,000 sets collecting together 11 vinyl albums in their original sleeves containing the albums *The Piper at the Gates of Dawn, A Saucerful of Secrets, More, Ummagumma, Atom Heart Mother, Relics, Meddle, Obscured by Clouds, The Dark Side of the Moon, Wish You Were Here* and *Animals. The Dark Side of the Moon* and *Wish You Were Here* were issued as pictures discs.

A COLLECTION OF GREAT DANCE SONGS

An early attempt at providing fans with a rarities package was turned down in favour of a 'best of' compilation. The only unusual item this release contained was a re-recording of 'Money' produced and performed single-handedly by David Gilmour, with a new sax solo by Dick Parry, carried out for the express purpose of the album and prompted by Capitol Records' reluctance to license the track.

SATURDAY 21 NOVEMBER 1981

A Collection of Great Dance Songs

Side 1: 'One Of These Days' / 'Money' (New Version) / 'Sheep' / Side 2: 'Shine On You Crazy Diamond' (Edited) / 'Wish You Were Here' / 'Another Brick In The Wall, Part 2' (Edited).

US: Columbia TC 37680 (Vinyl album).

Highest chart position No. 31 (*Billboard* "Top LPs & Tape" on Saturday 9 January 1982).

UK: EMI Harvest SHVL 822 (Vinyl album, released Monday 23 November 1981).

Highest chart position No. 37 (*Music Week* "Top 75 Albums" on Saturday 5 December 1981).

Certified Silver and Gold on Tuesday 24 November 1981.

Reissued:

US: Columbia HC 47680 (CBS Master Sound Half-Speed Master vinyl album, released Saturday 13 February 1982) / US: Columbia FC 37680 (Vinyl album, released Saturday 8 January 1983) / UK: EMI Harvest SHVL 822/EMI ATAK31 (Vinyl album, released Monday 7 January 1985) / UK: EMI CDP 7907322 (CD album, released Monday 7 January 1985) / US: Columbia CK 37680 (CD album, released Saturday 12 January 1985) / UK: EMI Fame EMI FA 3144 (Vinyl album, released Monday 18 November 1985) / UK: EMI CDP 7907322 (CD album, with bar code, released Monday 21 November 1988) / US: Columbia CK 68520 (*Columbia Records 1997 Anniversary* edition CD album, released Tuesday 8 December 1997) / UK: EMI 7243-5262452-2 (CD album, released Monday 10 April 2000) / US: Capitol CDP 7243-5262452-2 (*Capitol Records 2000* edition CD album, released Tuesday 25 April 2000) / US: Capitol CDP 7243-5268552-3 (Capitol Records 2000 edition Best Buy stores CD album, released Tuesday 25 April 2000) / US: Capitol CDP 7243-5262452-2 (CD album, released Tuesday 20 July 2004).

SATURDAY 21 NOVEMBER 1981

'Money' (Remix) / 'Another Brick In The Wall, Part 2'

US: Columbia AS 1334 (Promotional 12-inch pink vinyl single.

MONDAY 7 DECEMBER 1981

'Money' (Edited Version)

UK: EMI Harvest HAR 5217 (One-sided promotional pink vinyl 7-inch vinyl single).

'Money' (Edited Version) / 'Let There Be More Light'

UK: EMI Harvest HAR 5217 (Promotional pink vinyl 7-inch vinyl single. The catalogue number EMI Harvest 12 HAR 5217 was allocated for the 12-inch vinyl single, but it was never pressed).

WORKS

This was Capitol Records' attempt at raising Pink Floyd's back catalogue profile in the wake of *The Final Cut*, which was released on Columbia earlier in the year. It contained an even more random selection of material than *Relics* and included the track 'Embryo', which had previously incurred the band's wrath when it had been released without approval on the UK's Harvest Records' sampler *Picnic: A Breath of Fresh Air* in 1970.

SATURDAY 18 JUNE 1983

Works

Side 1: 'One of These Days' / 'Arnold Layne' / 'Fearless' / 'Brain Damage' / 'Eclipse' / 'Set The Controls For The Heart Of The Sun' / Side 2: 'See Emily Play' / 'Several Species of Small Furry Animals Gathered Together In A Cave And Grooving With a Pict' / 'Free Four' / 'Embryo'.

US: Capitol ST 12276 (Vinyl album).
US: Capitol CDP 7464782 (CD album, released Tuesday 20 January 1987).

PINK FLOYD IN EUROPE 1988

MONDAY 6 JUNE 1988

In Europe 1988

Side 1: 'Money' / 'Shine On You Crazy Diamond, Parts 1–5' / 'Another Brick in The Wall, Part 2' / Side 2: 'One Slip' / 'On The Turning Away' / 'Learning To Fly'.

UK: EMI PSLP 1016 (Promotional 12-inch EP released to support Pink Floyd's August 1988 UK tour dates).

SHINE ON

An ill-conceived nine-CD box set that was universally panned for its high price. It was designed by Storm Thorgerson and also contained a set of postcards and a self-build prism/object along with a hardcover book that was littered with typographical errors and factual inaccuracies, much of the content lifted en-bloc from a Pink Floyd collectors' fanzine.

At the *36th Grammy Awards* held at Radio City Music Hall, New York, on Tuesday 1 March 1994, Shine On was nominated for "Best Recording Package" but lost out to *The Complete Billie Holiday on Verve 1945–1959*.

OCTOBER 1992

Selected Tracks from Shine On

Track list: 'See Emily Play' / 'Set The Controls For The Heart Of The Sun' / 'One Of These Days' / 'Money' / 'Shine On You Crazy Diamond' (radio edit) / 'Dogs' / 'Comfortably Numb' / 'Another Brick In The Wall, Part 2' / 'One Slip'.

UK: EMI SHINE 1 (Promotional CD).

OCTOBER 1992

Shine On: Selections from The Box

Track list: 'See Emily Play' / 'Set The Controls For The Heart Of The Sun' / 'One Of These Days' / 'Money' / 'Shine On You Crazy Diamond' (radio edit) / 'Dogs' / 'Comfortably Numb' / 'Another Brick In The Wall, Part 2' / 'One Slip'.

US: Columbia CSK 4848 (Promotional CD).

MONDAY 2 NOVEMBER 1992

Shine On

CD1: *A Saucerful of Secrets* (EMI CDS 78056423) / CD2: *Meddle* (EMI CDS 78056522) / CD3: *The Dark Side of the Moon* (EMI CDS 78056621 / CD4: *Wish You Were Here* (EMI CDS 78056720 / CD6: *Animals* (EMI CDS 78056829 / CD7: *The Wall* (Part 1) (EMI CDS 78056928 / CD8: *The Wall*

(Part 2) (EMI CDS 78057024) / CD9: *A Momentary Lapse Of Reason* (EMI CDS 78057123 / Bonus CD: *The Early Singles* (EMI CDS 78057222, Track List: 'Arnold Layne' / 'Candy And A Currant Bun' / 'See Emily Play' / 'Scarecrow' / 'Apples And Oranges' / 'Paintbox' / 'It Would Be So Nice' / 'Julia Dream' / 'Point Me At The Sky' / 'Careful With That Axe, Eugene').

UK: EMI PFBOX 1 (Nine-CD box set).
US: Columbia CXK 53180 S1 (Nine-CD box set, released Tuesday 30 March 1993).

A CD FULL OF SECRETS

A promotional CD issued by the Westwood One radio network. It was also issued as a limited edition of 100 in a numbered custom wooden box with the title *Pink Floyd on the Radio* printed on the box.

MONDAY 2 NOVEMBER 1992
A CD Full of Secrets
Track list: 'Candy And A Currant Bun' / 'See Emily Play' / 'Flaming' (7-inch vinyl single version) / 'Apples And Oranges' / 'Paintbox' / 'It Would Be So Nice' / 'Julia Dream' / 'Point Me At The Sky' / 'Heart Beat, Pig Meat' / 'Crumbling Land' / 'Come In Number 51, Your Time Is Up' / 'Biding My Time' / 'Money' (1981 version) / 'When The Tigers Broke Free' / 'Not Now John' (Obscured version) / 'Terminal Frost' (DYOL version) / 'Run Like Hell' (Live version from Delicate Sound of Thunder).
US: Westwood One Volume 10 (CD album).

PINK FLOYD GIFT SET

TUESDAY 6 APRIL 1993
Pink Floyd Gift Set
US: Capitol C2 91340 (Four-CD box set that included the albums *Atom Heart Mother*, *Meddle*, *Obscured by Clouds*, and *The Dark Side of the Moon*. *The Dark Side of the Moon* CD was the 1992 remastered version).

THE FIRST THREE SINGLES

A mini-CD album housed in a gatefold card sleeve was issued at the same time as the 30th anniversary edition of *Piper at the Gates of Dawn* CD and in some cases given way as a free bonus CD. It contained the original A and B side mono mixes and its front and back cover featured the sleeves of the original 7-inch vinyl singles.

MONDAY 4 AUGUST 1997
The First Three Singles ▶
Track list: 'Arnold Layne' / 'Candy And A Currant Bun' / 'See Emily Play' / 'Scarecrow' / 'Apples And Oranges' / 'Paintbox'.
UK: EMI CD EMD 1117 (CD album).

PINK FLOYD 30TH ANNIVERSARY SAMPLER

TUESDAY 5 AUGUST 1997
30th Anniversary Sampler
CD1: 'Welcome To The Machine' / 'Wish You Were Here' / 'Sheep' / 'Pigs (3 Different Ones)' / 'Another Brick In The Wall, Part 2' / 'Young Lust' / CD2: 'The Gunners Dream' / 'The Fletcher Memorial Home' / 'Learning To Fly' / 'On The Turning Away' / 'Keep Talking' / 'High Hopes' / 'Money' (live).
US: Columbia CSK 3367 (Promotional Double CD album).

1997 VINYL COLLECTION

A limited edition 30th anniversary box set containing 180g vinyl pressings of seven Pink Floyd albums: *The Piper at the Gates of Dawn* (EMI LP EMP 1110), *Atom Heart Mother* (EMI LP EMP 1112), *The Dark Side of the Moon* (EMI LP EMP 1114, issued as a picture disc), *Wish You Were Here* (EMI LP EMP 1115, issued as a picture disc), *Animals* (EMI LP EMP 1116), *The Wall* (EMI LP EMP 1111) and *Relics* (EMI LP EMP 1113). Each album had a gatefold sleeve with a sticker in the middle of the front sleeve and a catalogue insert.

MONDAY 18 AUGUST 1997
1997 Vinyl Collection
UK: EMI SIGMA 630 (Eight vinyl album box set).

IS THERE ANYBODY OUT THERE? THE WALL LIVE: PINK FLOYD 1980–81

A double-CD album set, taken from recordings of the infamous *Wall* shows at London's Earl's Court in 1980 and 1981. The packaging was designed by Storm Thorgerson and the book contained photographs from the shows with interviews and recollections from all of the band members and supporting hands.
Track list with recording sources, CD1: MC introductions (Gary Yudman) (9 August 1980) / 'In The Flesh' (7, 8 & 9 August 1980) / 'The Thin Ice' (7, 8 & 9 August 1980) / 'Another Brick In The Wall, Part 1' (7 August 1980) / 'The Happiest Days Of Our Lives' (7 August 1980) / 'Another Brick In The Wall, Part 2' (8 August 1980) / 'Mother' (16 June 1981) / 'Goodbye Blue Sky' (17 June 1981 and segue into next track 17 June 1981) / 'Empty Spaces' (14 June 1981) / 'What Shall We Do Now?' (14 June 1981) / 'Young Lust' (7, 8 & 9 August 1980) / 'One Of My Turns' (7 August 1980) / 'Don't Leave Me Now' (7 August 1980 & 17 June 1981) / 'Another Brick In The Wall, Part 3' (8 August 1980) / 'The Last Few Bricks' (8 August 1980) / 'Goodbye Cruel World' (8 & 9 August 1980) / CD2: 'Hey You' (16 June 1981) / 'Is There Anybody Out There?' (15 June 1981) / 'Nobody Home' (17 June 1981) / 'Vera' (15 June 1981) / 'Bring The Boys Back Home' (15 June 1981) / 'Comfortably Numb' (14 June 1981) / 'The Show Must Go On' (16 June 1981) / MC introductions (Gary Yudman) (9 August 1980) / 'In The Flesh' (7 August 1980) / 'Run Like Hell' (15 & 17 June 1981) / 'Waiting For The Worms' (15 June 1981) / 'Stop' (8 August 1980) / 'The Trial' (9 August 1980) / 'Outside The Wall' (8 August 1980).

MARCH 2000
Is There Anybody Out There? The Wall Live: Pink Floyd 1980–81 Radio Spots
UK: EMI (Promotional CD of seven different radio spots of 10, 15, 20 and 30 seconds).
Is There Anybody Out There? The Wall Live: Pink Floyd 1980–81 10-second Radio Teaser Advert
UK: EMI (Promotional CD, contains one 10-second radio spot).

MONDAY 27 MARCH 2000 ▶
Is There Anybody Out There? The Wall Live: Pink Floyd 1980–81
CD1: 'In The Flesh?' / 'The Thin Ice' / 'Another Brick In The Wall, Part 1' / 'The Happiest Days Of Our Lives' / 'Another Brick In The Wall, Part 2' / 'Mother' / 'Goodbye Blue Sky' / 'Empty Spaces' / 'What Shall We Do Now?' / 'Young Lust' / 'One Of My Turns' / 'Don't Leave Me Now' / 'Another Brick In The Wall,

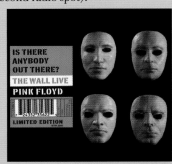

Part 3' / 'The Last Few Bricks' / 'Goodbye Cruel World' / CD2: 'Hey You' / 'Is There Anybody Out There?' / 'Nobody Home' / 'Vera' / 'Bring The Boys Back Home' / 'Comfortably Numb' / 'The Show Must Go On' / 'In The Flesh' / 'Run Like Hell' / 'Waiting For The Worms' / 'Stop' / 'The Trial' / 'Outside The Wall'.

UK: EMI 5235622 (Double CD album set in bookcase).
Highest chart position No. 15 (*Music Week* "Top 100 Albums" on Saturday 8 April 2000).
Certified Silver on Friday 7 April 2000 and Gold on Monday 22 July 2013.
US: Columbia C2K 62058 (Double-CD album set in bookcase, released Tuesday 18 April 2000).
Highest chart position No. 19 (*Billboard* "Billboard 200" on 6 May 2000) / Highest chart position No. 1 (*Billboard* "Top Internet Album Sales" on 6 May 2000).
Certified Gold and Platinum on Monday 22 May 2000.
Reissued:
UK: EMI 5235622 (Double-CD album in standard case, released Monday 24 April 2000) / US: Columbia C2K 62055 (Double-CD album in standard case, released Tuesday 25 April 2000).

TUESDAY 4 APRIL 2000
'Young Lust' (live)
US: Columbia 62055 (Promotional CD).
Highest chart position No. 15 (*Billboard* "Mainstream Rock Tracks" on Saturday 22 April 2000).

TUESDAY 4 APRIL 2000
Is There Anybody Out There? The Wall Live: Pink Floyd 1980-81
Track list: 'In The Flesh' / 'Another Brick In The Wall, Part 2' / 'Goodbye Blue Sky'.
US: Columbia CSK 12680 (Promotional CD).

TUESDAY 4 APRIL 2000
Is There Anybody Out There?
US: Columbia rt/16.09 (Promotional EPK VHS video).
Electronic press kit with separate interviews with Roger Waters and David Gilmour talking about *The Wall* shows. Also features excerpt footage from the original Earl's Court, London shows from 1981.

TUESDAY 25 APRIL 2000
'Another Brick In The Wall, Part 2' (Live) / 'Another Brick In The Wall, Part 2' (Live)
US: Columbia CS7 51388 (Promotional 7-inch white vinyl single).
Certified Gold on Thursday 8 May 2008.

ECHOES: THE BEST OF PINK FLOYD

MONDAY 22 OCTOBER 2001
Echoes: The Best of Pink Floyd – 6 Track Sampler
Track list: 'See Emily Play' / 'Money' / 'The Happiest Days Of Our Lives' / 'Another Brick In The Wall, Part 2' / 'Learning To Fly' / 'Wish You Were Here'.
UK: EMI CD LRL 054 (Promotional CD).

TUESDAY 23 OCTOBER 2001
Echoes: The Best of Pink Floyd – Pre-release Radio Spots
Track list: '60-second radio pre-release advert' / '30-second radio pre-release advert'.
US: Capitol CAP2K1-108-PFE/PFD (Promotional CD of radio spots for *Echoes*).

TUESDAY 23 OCTOBER 2001
Echoes: The Best of Pink Floyd – 8 Track Sampler
Track list: 'When The Tigers Broke Free' / 'Shine On You Crazy Diamond,

Parts 1–7' / 'Wish You Were Here' / 'Another Brick In The Wall, Part 2' / 'Echoes' (edit) / 'Hey You' / 'Comfortably Numb' / 'Money'.
US: Capitol DPRO 708761599121 (Promotional CD) / Capitol (Promotional CD, in plain card sleeve).

Echoes: The Best of Pink Floyd – 8 Track Sampler
Track list: 'Another Brick In The Wall, Part 2' / 'Astronomy Domine' / 'Comfortably Numb' / 'Breathe' / 'Hey You' / 'On The Turning Away' / 'Money' / 'One Of These Days' / 'The Great Gig In The Sky' / 'Shine On You Crazy Diamond' / 'Wish You Were Here' / 'Keep Talking'.
US: Capitol (Promotional CD).

MONDAY 5 NOVEMBER 2001
Echoes: The Best of Pink Floyd
CD1: 'Astronomy Domine' / 'See Emily Play' / 'The Happiest Days Of Our Lives' / 'Another Brick In The Wall, Part 2' / 'Echoes' / 'Hey You' / 'Marooned' / 'The Great Gig In The Sky' / 'Set The Controls For The Heart Of The Sun' / 'Money' / 'Keep Talking' / 'Sheep' / 'Sorrow' / CD2: 'Shine On You Crazy Diamond, Parts 1–7' / 'Time' / 'The Fletcher Memorial Home' / 'Comfortably Numb' / 'When The Tigers Broke Free' / 'One Of These Days' / 'Us and Them' / 'Learning To Fly' / 'Arnold Layne' / 'Wish You Were Here' / 'Jugband Blues' / 'High Hopes' / 'Bike'.

UK: EMI 5361112 (Double-CD album).
Highest chart position No. 2 (*Music Week* "Top 100 Albums" on Saturday 17 November 2001).
Certified Silver and Gold in the UK on Friday 16 November 2001, Platinum on Friday 21 December 2001, 2 x Platinum on Friday 11 January 2002 and 3 x Platinum on Monday 22 July 2013.
US: Capitol CDP 724353611125 (Double-CD album, released Tuesday 6 November 2001).
Highest chart position US No. 2 (*Billboard* "The Billboard 200" on Saturday 24 November 2001).
Certified Gold, Platinum and 2 x Platinum on Thursday 6 December 2001 and 3 x Multi-Platinum on Tuesday 8 January 2002, 4 x Platinum on Monday 10 September 2007.
Reissued:
US: Capitol 2 CD 09463745432 (Double CD, issued in a biodegradable case, released Tuesday 3 October 2006).

MONDAY 25 FEBRUARY 2002
Echoes: The Best of Pink Floyd
Side 1: 'Astronomy Domine' / 'See Emily Play' / 'The Happiest Days Of Our Lives' / 'Another Brick In The Wall, Part 2' / 'Marooned' / 'The Great Gig In The Sky' / Side 2: 'Echoes' / 'Hey You' / Side 3: 'Set The Controls For The Heart Of The Sun' / 'Money' / 'Keep Talking' / Side 4: 'Sheep' / 'Sorrow' / Side 5: 'Shine On You Crazy Diamond, Parts 1–7' / 'Time' / Side 6: 'The Fletcher Memorial Home' / 'Comfortably Numb' / 'When The Tigers Broke Free' / Side 7: 'One Of These Days' / 'Us and Them' / 'Learning To Fly' / 'Arnold Layne' / Side 8: 'Wish You Were Here' / 'Jugband Blues' / 'High Hopes' / 'Bike'.
UK: EMI LP 724353611118 (Limited edition 180g vinyl four-album box set).
US: Capitol 536111 (Limited edition 180g vinyl four-album box set, released Tuesday 26 February 2002).

OH, BY THE WAY
A lavish box set of Pink Floyd's entire catalogue to date packaged in miniature vinyl album sleeves and housed in a special box with artwork designed by Storm Thorgerson. There was no additional booklet included in the set. A DVD containing archive material to be included with the box set was allegedly shelved.

MONDAY 10 DECEMBER 2007

Oh, By the Way

CD1: *The Piper at the Gates of Dawn* (EMI 5099951122522) / CD2: *A Saucerful of Secrets* (EMI 5099951108229) / CD3: *Music from the film More* (EMI 5099951109028) / CD4: *Ummagumma* (Part 1) (EMI 5099951109325) / CD5: *Ummagumma* (Part 2) (EMI 5099951109326) / CD6: *Atom Heart Mother* (EMI 5099951110123) / CD7: *Meddle* (EMI 5099951110529) / CD8: *Obscured by Clouds* (EMI 5099951108922) / CD9: *The Dark Side of the Moon* (EMI 50999511122621) / CD10: *Wish You Were Here* (EMI 5099951 110628) / CD11: *Animals* (EMI 5099951 110727) / CD12: *The Wall* (Part 1) (EMI 5099951110925) / CD13: *The Wall* (Part 2) (EMI 5099951110926) / CD14: *The Final Cut* (EMI 5099951111120) / CD15: *A Momentary Lapse of Reason* (EMI 5099951122720) / CD16: *The Division Bell* (EMI 5099951111299).

UK: EMI 5099951126728 (16-CD box set).
US: Capitol 5099951126728 (16-CD box set, released Tuesday 11 December 2007).

WHY PINK FLOYD?

A series of promotional discs were issued to the media and radio stations in order to promote the Why Pink Floyd? campaign that encompassed the release of the *Discovery, Experience* and *Immersion* editions of Pink Floyd's catalogue.

MONDAY 26 SEPTEMBER 2011

Radio Sampler Volume 1

Track list: 'The Great Gig In The Sky' (early mix 1972) / 'Us And Them' (Richard Wright demo) / 'Us And Them' (live at Wembley 1974) / 'The Travel Sequence' (previously unreleased studio recording) / 'Money' (Roger Waters demo) / 'Money' (live at Wembley 1974).

UK: EMI (Promotional CD).

Radio Sampler Volume 2 ▲

Track list: 'Wish You Were Here' (featuring Stéphane Grappelli) / 'Have A Cigar' (Alternate Version) / 'Shine On You Crazy Diamond' (Live at Wembley).

UK: EMI (Promotional CD).

TUESDAY 27 SEPTEMBER 2011

Radio Sampler

Track list: 'Money' (2011 Remaster) / 'Wish You Were Here' (2011 Remaster) / 'Another Brick In The Wall, Part 2' (2011 Remaster) / 'Us And Them' (Live At Wembley 1974) / 'Have A Cigar' (Alternate Version) / 'Another Brick In The Wall, Part 1' (Demo).

US: EMI Capitol (Promotional CD exclusively available through Best Buy stores in North America).

In Store Sampler

Track list: 'The Great Gig In The Sky' / 'Money' / 'Shine On You Crazy Diamond, Parts 1–5' / 'Wish You Were Here' / 'Another Brick In The Wall, Part 2' / 'Comfortably Numb' / 'Run Like Hell' / 'The Fletcher Memorial Home' / 'Learning To Fly'.

US: EMI Capitol (Promotional CD).

TUESDAY 27 SEPTEMBER 2011

The Dark Side of the Moon: Why Pink Floyd?

Track list: 'Breathe' (Live At Wembley 1974) / 'Time' (Live At Wembley 1974) / 'Money' (Roger Waters Demo) / 'Us And Them' (Live At Wembley 1974) / 'Brain Damage' (Live At Wembley 1974) / 'Eclipse' (Live At Wembley 1974).

US: EMI Capitol (Promotional CD).

TUESDAY 27 SEPTEMBER 2011

Why Pink Floyd?

Track list: 'Speak To Me' (2011 Remaster) / 'Breathe (In The Air)' (2011 Remaster) / 'The Great Gig In The Sky' (Early Version 1972) / 'Money' (Live At Wembley 1974) / 'The Travel Sequence' (1972) / 'Us & Them' (Rick Wright Demo) / From *Wish You Were Here* (*Immersion* and *Experience Editions*): 'Shine On You Crazy Diamond, Parts 1–5' (2011 Remaster) / 'Raving And Drooling' (Live At Wembley 1974) / 'Wish You Were Here' (feat. Stéphane Grappelli).

US: EMI Capitol (Promotional CD).

PINK FLOYD DISCOVERY

Another lavish box set of 16 CDs packaged in miniature LP sleeves, and a 40-page booklet designed by Storm Thorgerson representing Pink Floyd's entire catalogue, was released as part of the *Why Pink Floyd?* campaign.

MONDAY 26 SEPTEMBER 2011

Discovery

CD1: *The Piper at the Gates of Dawn* (EMI 5099902893525) / CD2: *A Saucerful of Secrets* (EMI 5099902893624) / CD3: *Music from the film "More"* (EMI 5099902893822) / CD4: *Ummagumma* (Part 1) (EMI 5099902893723) / CD5: *Ummagumma* (Part 2) (EMI 5099902893724) / CD6: *Atom Heart Mother* (EMI 5099902894027) / CD7: *Meddle* (EMI 5099902894225) / CD8: *Obscured by Clouds* (EMI 5099902894324) / CD9: *The Dark Side of the Moon* (EMI 5099902895529) / CD10: *Wish You Were Here* (EMI 5099902894522) / CD11: *Animals* (EMI 5099902895123) / CD12: *The Wall* (Part 1) (EMI 5099902894423) / CD13: *The Wall* (Part 2) (EMI 5099902894423) / CD14: *The Final Cut* (EMI 5099902895628) / CD15: *A Momentary Lapse of Reason* (EMI 5099902895925) / CD16: *The Division Bell* (EMI 5099902896120).

UK: EMI 5099908261328 (16-CD box set).
US: Capitol 5099908261328 (16-CD box set, released Tuesday 27 September 2011).

A FOOT IN THE DOOR. THE BEST OF PINK FLOYD

MONDAY 7 NOVEMBER 2011

A Foot in the Door: The Best of Pink Floyd

Track list: 'Hey You' / 'See Emily Play' / 'The Happiest Days Of Our Lives' / 'Another Brick In The Wall, Part 2' / 'Have A Cigar' / 'Wish You Were Here' / 'Time' / 'The Great Gig In The Sky' / 'Money' / 'Comfortably Numb' / 'High Hopes' / 'Learning To Fly' / 'The Fletcher Memorial Home' / 'Shine On You Crazy Diamond, Parts 1–5' / 'Brain Damage' / 'Eclipse'.

UK: EMI 5099902896625 (CD album).
Highest chart position UK No. 14 (*Official UK Charts* "Top 75" on Saturday 19 November 2011).
Certified Gold on Monday 22 July 2013.
US: Capitol 5099902896625 (CD album, released Tuesday 8 November 2011).
Highest chart position US No. 50 (*Billboard* "The Billboard 200" on Saturday 26 November 2001).

FILMS & SOUNDTRACKS

TONITE LET'S ALL MAKE LOVE IN LONDON (AUDIO)

Peter Whitehead's 70-minute pop-documentary featured a variety of contemporary performers providing the soundtrack, along with the thoughts of various movers and shakers of "Swinging Sixties" London.

The original film soundtrack, which featured excerpts of 'Interstellar Overdrive', was commissioned by Whitehead in a session produced by Joe Boyd and recorded on Tuesday 10 & Wednesday 11 January 1967 at Sound Techniques studios in London. During the same session an additional instrumental track was recorded entitled 'Nick's Boogie', but this was not used in the film and was rediscovered by Peter Whitehead only when the 1990 See For Miles soundtrack reissue was being compiled. The film previewed at the *5th New York Film Festival* held at the Philharmonic Hall, Lincoln Center, New York, USA on Tuesday 26 September 1967, and opened at the Academy 2, London, England on Saturday 9 December 1967.

FRIDAY 15 NOVEMBER 1968
Tonite Let's All Make Love in London
Side 1: 'Interstellar Overdrive' (Pink Floyd) / 'Changing Of The Guard' (Marquess Of Kensington) / 'Night Time Girl' (Twice As Much) / Interview with a "Dolly Bird" / 'Out Of Time' (Chris Farlowe) / Interview with Edna O'Brien / Side 2: 'Interstellar Overdrive' (Pink Floyd) / Interview with Andrew "Loog" Oldham / 'Winter Is Blue' (Vashti) / Interview with Andrew "Loog" Oldham / 'Winter Is Blue' (Vashti) / Interview with Mick Jagger / Interview with Julie Christie / Interview with Michael Caine / 'Paint It Black' (Chris Farlowe) / Interview with Alan Aldridge / Interview with David Hockney / 'Here Comes The Nice' (the Small Faces) / Interview with Lee Marvin / 'Interstellar Overdrive' (Pink Floyd) / 'Tonite Let's All Make Love In London' (Alan Ginsberg).

UK: Instant INLP 002 (Vinyl album).

MONDAY 24 SEPTEMBER 1990 ▶
Tonite Let's All Make Love in London... Plus
Side 1: 'Interstellar Overdrive' (Full-Length Version, Pink Floyd) / Interview with Michael Caine / 'Changing Of The Guard' (Marquess Of Kensington) / 'Night Time Girl' (Twice As Much) / Interview with a "Dolly Bird" / 'Out Of Time' (Chris Farlowe) / Interview with Edna O'Brien / Side 2: 'Interstellar Overdrive' (Reprise, Pink Floyd) / Interview with Andrew "Loog" Oldham / 'Winter Is Blue' (Vashti) / Interview with Andrew "Loog" Oldham / 'Winter Is Blue' reprise (Vashti) / Interview with Mick Jagger / Interview with Julie Christie / Interview with Michael Caine / 'Paint It Black' (Chris Farlowe) / Interview with Alan Aldridge / 'Paint It Black' (Instrumental Reprise, Chris Farlowe) / Interview with David Hockney / 'Here Comes The Nice' (The Small Faces) / Interview with Lee Marvin / 'Interstellar Overdrive' (Pink Floyd) / 'Tonite Let's All Make Love In London' (Alan Ginsberg).

UK: See For Miles SEEG 258 (Vinyl album, with expanded packaging and the full version of 'Interstellar Overdrive').

MONDAY 24 SEPTEMBER 1990
Tonite Let's All Make Love in London... Plus
Track list: 'Interstellar Overdrive' (Full-Length Version, Pink Floyd) / Interview with Michael Caine / 'Changing Of The Guard' (Marquess Of Kensington) / 'Night Time Girl' (Twice As Much) / Interview with a "Dolly Bird" / 'Out Of Time' (Chris Farlowe) / Interview with Edna O'Brien / 'Interstellar Overdrive' (Reprise, Pink Floyd) / Interview with Andrew "Loog" Oldham / 'Winter Is Blue' (Vashti) / Interview with Andrew "Loog" Oldham /

'Winter Is Blue' reprise (Vashti) / Interview with Mick Jagger / Interview with Julie Christie / Interview with Michael Caine / 'Paint It Black' (Chris Farlowe) / Interview with Alan Aldridge / 'Paint It Black' (Instrumental Reprise, Chris Farlowe) / Interview with David Hockney / 'Here Comes The Nice' (The Small Faces) / Interview with Lee Marvin / 'Interstellar Overdrive' (Pink Floyd) / 'Tonite Let's All Make Love In London' (Alan Ginsberg) / 'Nick's Boogie' (Pink Floyd).

UK: See For Miles SEECD 258 (CD album, with expanded packaging and the full version of 'Interstellar Overdrive' and the previously unreleased track 'Nick's Boogie').

MONDAY 21 JANUARY 1991
Tonite Let's All Make Love in London: Mini Promotional Sampler
Side 1: 'Interstellar Overdrive' (Full-Length Version, Pink Floyd) / Side 2: 'Nick's Boogie' (Pink Floyd) / Interview with David Hockney / Interview with Lee Marvin.

UK: See For Miles SEA 4 (12-inch EP).
Track list: 'Interstellar Overdrive' full length version (Pink Floyd) / 'Nick's Boogie' (Pink Floyd) / Interview with David Hockney / Interview with Lee Marvin.

UK: See For Miles SEA CD4 (CD EP).
Contrary to popular belief this is not an industry promotional EP, but a stock item in order to carry the Pink Floyd material.
UK: See For Miles SFM 2 (CD EP, released Monday 22 November 1993).

TUESDAY 27 AUGUST 1991
Tonite Let's All Make Love in London
Track list: 'Interstellar Overdrive' (Pink Floyd) / Michael Caine Interview/ 'Changing Of The Guard' (Marquess Of Kensington) / 'Night Time Girl' (Twice As Much) / "Dolly Bird" Interview / 'Out Of Time' (Chris Farlowe)/ Edna O'Brien Interview / 'Interstellar Overdrive' (Pink Floyd) / Andrew "Loog" Oldham Interview / 'Winter Is Blue' (Vashti) / Andrew "Loog" Oldham Interview / 'Winter Is Blue' (Vashti) / 'When I Was Young' (Eric Burdon & the Animals) / Mick Jagger Interview / Julie Christie Interview / Michael Caine Interview / 'Paint It Black' (Chris Farlowe) / Alan Aldridge Interview / 'Paint It Black' (Chris Farlowe) / David Hockney Interview / 'Here Comes The Nice' (the Small Faces) / Lee Marvin Interview / 'Interstellar Overdrive' (Pink Floyd) / 'Tonite Let's All Make Love In London' (Alan Ginsberg).

US: Sony Music Special Products AK 47893 (CD album).

MONDAY 8 JUNE 1998
Pink Floyd: London '66-'67
Track list: 'Interstellar Overdrive' (full length version) / 'Nick's Boogie'.
UK: See For Miles SFMDP3 (CD).

MONDAY 13 DECEMBER 1999
Pink Floyd: In London 1966-1967
CD: 'Interstellar Overdrive' (Full Length Version) / 'Nick's Boogie' / CDROM: Interview footage with Mick Jagger, David Hockney, Michael Caine, Julie Christie, and an overview by the director, Peter Whitehead.
UK: See For Miles SFM 1966 (CD / CD Rom).

MONDAY 12 SEPTEMBER 2005
Pink Floyd: London 1966-1967
Track list: 'Interstellar Overdrive' (Full Length Version) / 'Nick's Boogie' / 'Interstellar Overdrive' (Full Length Video for Mac/PC) / Interview footage with Mick Jagger, David Hockney, Michael Caine, Julie Christie, and an overview by the director, Peter Whitehead.
UK: Pucka PUC66 (CD).

MONDAY 5 JUNE 2006
Pink Floyd: London 1966/1967
Track list: 'Interstellar Overdrive' (Full Length Version) / 'Nick's Boogie' /
'Interstellar Overdrive' (Full Length Video for Mac/PC) / Interview footage
with Mick Jagger, David Hockney, Michael Caine, Julie Christie, and an
overview by the director, Peter Whitehead.
UK: Snapper SMACD924X (Limited edition CD, in digipak sleeve).

MONDAY 5 JANUARY 2009
London 1966/1967
Side 1: 'Interstellar Overdrive' (Full Length Version) / Side 2: 'Nick's Boogie'
UK: Snapper PFLP 001 (Limited edition 12-inch vinyl EP and bonus CD
EP featuring the same tracks).

SATURDAY 16 APRIL 2011
London 1966/1967
Side 1: 'Interstellar Overdrive' (Full Length Version) / Side 2: 'Nick's Boogie'
UK: Snapper SMALP 968 (Limited edition 1500 pressings, 12-inch EP
on 180g heavyweight white coloured vinyl, for Record Store Day 2011,
although curiously still in print).

TONITE LET'S ALL MAKE LOVE IN LONDON (VIDEO)

MONDAY 24 OCTOBER 1994
Pink Floyd: London 1966/1967
UK: See For Miles PFVP1 (VHS video).
Contains footage from Pink Floyd's recording session of 'Interstellar
Overdrive' and 'Nick's Boogie', footage of their appearance at UFO on
Friday 13 January 1967, and scenes (not featuring Pink Floyd) of the
14-Hour Technicolour Dream at Alexandra Palace, London on 29 April 1967
shot by Peter Whitehead.
UK: Snapper SMADVD049 (DVD video, with bonus interviews, released
Monday 12 September 2005).
UK: Snapper SDVD540 (DVD video, with bonus interviews, released
Tuesday 6 May 2008).

TUESDAY 4 OCTOBER 2005
Pink Floyd: London 1966/1967
US: Snapper SMADVD046 (Special edition DVD video, with
bonus interviews, plus bonus audio CD of 'Interstellar Overdrive'
and 'Nick's Boogie').

MONDAY 29 OCTOBER 2007
Peter Whitehead and the Sixties
UK: BFI BFIVD 750 (DVD video).
Documentary that includes a 44-minute interview with Peter Whitehead
discussing his films *Wholly Communion, Benefit of the Doubt* and *Jeanette
Cochrane*, and includes a recording of 'Interstellar Overdrive' taken from
Tonite Let's All Make Love in London as part of the soundtrack.

DOPE

Dope tells the story of two American couples and Caroline, a beautiful
free-spirited New Zealander, living together in London at the height
of Flower Power. Caroline becomes a junkie and the story is woven
around her misadventures, which includes a visit to the *UFO* club and
includes footage of Pink Floyd's performance believed to have been shot
on Friday 30 December 1966, possibly with the music of co-headliners
Soft Machine dubbed over the images. Filmmakers Sheldon and Diane
Rochlin were forced to abandon the release of the film in 1968 due to
the bankruptcy of the distributors, but in 2007 the film was rediscovered

and made available as a privately pressed DVD (released Monday 3 March
2008) by mail order only for a brief period.

PROMENADE

Promenade was a 40-minute short based around the story of an artist living
in Brighton, England who rekindles his friendship with his former model/
mistress who is now with an older, wealthier man. The film itself is shot
in documentary style and in one particular sequence shot in a nightclub
the audio is unmistakably that of Pink Floyd, followed by a brief live shot
of the band, taken at the West Pier in Brighton on 15 April 1967. Austin
Parkinson, who worked on the whole production, recalled, "shooting on
West Pier when Pink Floyd were giving a performance and the pier was
shaking badly as we were shooting a Kinetic light show." The film was
released in 1968 although exact screening details could not be found.

A TECHNICOLOUR DREAM

This is the story of the UK underground movement and the event that
is synonymous with its existence at the *14 Hour Technicolour Dream* held
at Alexandra Palace, London on Saturday 29 April 1967. It contains
interviews with various figureheads, including Joe Boyd and Hoppy as
well as Roger Waters, Nick Mason and Pink Floyd's then manager, Peter
Jenner. The bonus features on the DVD include three well-known Pink
Floyd performances from 1967, including the Pathé newsreel footage of
'Scarecrow', the Wittering Beach 'Arnold Layne' promo, and the BBC
Look of the Week performance of 'Astronomy Domine' from Tuesday
16 May 1967.

MONDAY 13 OCTOBER 2008
A Technicolour Dream
UK: Eagle Rock Entertainment EREDV710 (DVD video).
US: Eagle Rock Entertainment EREDV710 (DVD video,
released Tuesday 28 October 2008).

THE COMMITTEE

Opening at the Cameo Poly Cinema, London, England on Thursday
26 September 1968, this renowned avant-garde film was presumed lost for
several years before being finally released on DVD in 2005. Reviewing the
release, *Jazzwise* magazine said: "This 1968 arthouse movie, written by Max
Steuer and directed by Peter Sykes, is a surreal, slightly chilling exploration
of the individual, society and alienation, that's loosely based around the
thoughts of radical sixties psychiatrist RD Laing. Atmospherically shot
in black and white, there's more than a whiff of Antonioni's early sixties
films as the central chraracter ex-Manfred Mann singer Paul Jones'
haunted presence is framed by long lingering camera pans and tracked
by an eerie improvised Pink Floyd soundtrack, that's among their most
obscure and sought-after unreleased recordings. Featuring early outlines
of 'Careful With That Axe, Eugene' and the final part of 'Saucerful Of
Secrets', among other random sonic sketches, it was recorded weeks after
guitarist David Gilmour replaced Syd Barrett and still exhibits their early
fascination with the work of AMM and John Cage. The movie also features
underground compatriots the Crazy World of Arthur Brown performing
the jazzy, jarring 'Nightmare' and a Jimmy Smith-like Hammond organ
groover filmed at a party scene in the LSE. Brilliant to some and bonkers
to others, it's a brave move for Basho and one of their most intriguing
projects to date." The DVD also includes an interview by Oscar-winning
director Jon Blair with Max Steuer (the film's writer and producer) and
Peter Sykes (director), which lasts for 50 minutes. Also included in the
package is a CD of the song 'The Committee' by Paul Jones and Max
Steuer arranged by Tim Whitehead for the Homemade Orchestra, plus
two tracks from earlier Homemade Orchestra CDs.

MONDAY 8 AUGUST 2005
The Committee
UK: Basho DVD 901 (DVD video).
US: Eclectic DVD Distribution EDD02056 (DVD video, released Tuesday 13 September 2005).

SAN FRANCISCO

This 15-minute experimental film made by Antony Stern in 1968, with funding from the British Film Institute, uses a unique take of 'Interstellar Overdrive' as its soundtrack lasting the full length of the film. According to the BFI, "Stern shot the film in the city of its namesake but returned to edit it in London, firstly at the BFI Production Board's facilities at Waterloo and then at the Arts Lab at Drury Lane." When or where the soundtrack was recorded remains a mystery and the film has never been officially released, although since its production it has been shown at various cinema events. *San Francisco* was, according to its maker, Antony Stern, "a response to hearing 'Interstellar Overdrive' by Pink Floyd. It was my desire to make permanent the Pink Floyd light shows created at the UFO club by Peter Wynne Wilson. The LSD-triggered psychedelic experience found its ultimate expression in this fusion of sight and sound, which achieved a visceral effect on the audience. San Francisco is 'painting with light' as well as a saturated archive of day to day life in the 1960s. New rhythms were created in the language of film, in using single-frame exposures and freeze-frame techniques." The film has, unfortunately, never seen a commercial video release.

ALL MY LOVING

Includes Pink Floyd's performance of 'Set The Controls For The Heart Of The Sun' for the *Omnibus* BBC TV special focusing on the socio-political context of rock music, entitled *All My Loving* (See Day-to-Day listings 28 March 1968 for further details.)

MONDAY 10 SEPTEMBER 2007
All My Loving
UK: Voiceprint TPDVD 101 (DVD video).

MORE

Barbet Schroeder's cautionary tale set largely in the idyllic island paradise of Ibiza features Pink Floyd's haunting music, with alternate versions and early mixes that don't appear on the soundtrack album. This French language film remained popular on the European cinema circuit for many years before finally receiving a home video release some 29 years later.

WEDNESDAY 5 JUNE 1991
More
US: Warner Home Video 35156 (VHS video).
US: Home Vision Entertainment MOR 070 (VHS video, released Tuesday 18 April 2000).
US: Home Vision Entertainment MOR 080 (DVD video, released Tuesday 5 April 2005).

THURSDAY 3 JULY 2003
More
UK: BFI VD587 (DVD video).
UK: BFI B1040 (Double DVD/Blu-ray Disc dual format edition. Additional extras include a *Making of "More"* documentary (2011, 17 minutes), theatrical trailers for *The Valley* (1972), *More* (1969) and *Maîtresse* (1974), and a fully illustrated booklet, released Monday 14 February 2011).

MUSIC POWER / EUROPEAN MUSIC REVOLUTION

The documentary films *Music Power* and *European Music Revolution* were produced by Gérome Laperrousaz of the *Actuel Festival* held near Mont de l'Enclus, Amougies, Belgium between Friday 24 and Tuesday 28 October 1969. The film *Music Power* focuses on the performances and features Pink Floyd performing 'Green Is The Colour' and 'Careful With That Axe, Eugene' on Saturday 25 October 1969, whereas *European Music Revolution* mixed performance and documentary and did not feature Pink Floyd, despite their name appearing on some advertising. Although parts of the festival were recorded and broadcast by various networks, including RTL radio, Europe 1 radio, ABC–TV News, Gaumont Pathé TV and RTB TV, none of them contained anything of Pink Floyd's performance. However, two one-and-a-half-minute, black and white cinema trailers were produced by Gaumont Pathé, France to advertise the film, one of which did include shots of Pink Floyd's performance. In addition a clip of 'Careful With That Axe, Eugene', taken from the film, was shown on the French music programme S*amedi et Compagnie* broadcast on ORTF1 TV on Saturday 30 May 1970 between 4.00pm and 5.50pm. *Music Power* and E*uropean Music Revolution* never saw a theatrical release in the UK or US, but both films were presented as a double bill in France, premiering at the Celtic Plaza and the Pagode, Paris on Thursday 28 May 1970. The film *Music Power* was shown in its entirety on ORTF2 TV on Sunday 24 September 1972 between 9.20pm and 10.35pm.

ZABRISKIE POINT (AUDIO)

Michaelangelo Antonioni's much anticipated follow-up to his acclaimed feature *Blow Up* centred around two disaffected students and their encounters with authority. Antonioni originally commissioned Pink Floyd to score the entire film and they produced a series of sessions at International Recording studios in Rome between Saturday 15 and Saturday 22 November 1969. As it was, much of the selected material was re-recorded at EMI Studios in London and a host of contemporary American artistes make up much of the soundtrack. *Zabriskie Point* was premiered at the Coronet Theater, New York on Wednesday 18 March 1970. It was universally panned by critics and audiences alike, although it did eventually find its place as a cult classic.

WEDNESDAY 18 MARCH 1970
Zabriskie Point: Controversy Radio Spots
Radio adverts for the movie *Zabriskie Point* containing the Pink Floyd track 'Come in Number 51, Your Time Is Up'.
Track list: 90 second advert / 60 second advert / 30 second advert
US: MGM KAL 050 (Promotional 7-inch one-sided EP single).

SATURDAY 11 APRIL 1970
Zabriskie: What's the Point?
A radio show LP distributed to colleges featuring a discussion about the film, *Zabriskie Point*, by Al Lees, WBAI film critic; John Simon, *The New Leader* film critic; Joseph Gelmis, *Newsday* film critic; Martin Last, Pacifica Stations art critic; and Harrison Starr, the film's executive producer. The cover suggests the lead-out music is Pink Floyd's 'Come In Number 51, Your Time Is Up', but this is absent from the album.
US: Erwin Frankel Productions. Sound On Film. Radio Program 5 (Vinyl album).

SATURDAY 11 APRIL 1970
Zabriskie Point: Music from the Motion Picture Soundtrack
Side 1: 'Heart Beat, Pig Meat' (Pink Floyd) / 'Brother Mary' (The Kaleidoscope) / 'Dark Star' (The Grateful Dead) / 'Crumbling Land' (Pink Floyd) / 'Tennessee Waltz' (Patti Page) / 'Sugar Babe' (The Youngbloods) /

Side 2: 'Love Scene' (Jerry Garcia) / 'I Wish I Was A Single Girl Again' (Roscoe Holcomb) / 'Mickey's Tune' (The Kaleidoscope) / 'Dance Of Death' (John Fahey) / 'Come In Number 51, Your Time Is Up' (Pink Floyd).

US: MGM SE 4668ST (Vinyl album).
UK: MGM CS 8120 (Vinyl album, released Friday 29 May 1970).
Reissued:
UK: MGM 2315 002 (Vinyl album, released Friday 26 November 1971) / UK: MGM Special 2354 040 (Vinyl album, released Friday 14 April 1978) / US: MCA Classical Soundtracks MCA 25032 (Vinyl album, released Friday 17 January 1986) / UK: CBS 70279 Hollywood Collection Vol. 6 (Vinyl album, released Monday 14 April 1986) / UK: CBS CDCBS 70279 Hollywood Collection Vol. 6 (CD album, released Monday 14 April 1986) / UK: EMI 7942171 / EMI GO 2029 (Vinyl album, released Monday 21 May 1990) / UK: EMI CDP 7942172 / EMI CZ 285 (CD album, released Monday 21 May 1990) / US: Sony Music Special Products AK 52417 (CD album, released Tuesday 17 March 1992) / US: 4 Men With Beards 4M123LP (Limited edition 180g vinyl album, released Tuesday 20 January 2004).

MONDAY 15 SEPTEMBER 1997
Zabriskie Point: Original Motion Picture Soundtrack
The original soundtrack to the Antonioni feature film reissued with four previously unreleased tracks by Pink Floyd.
CD1: 'Heart Beat, Pig Meat' (Pink Floyd) / 'Brother Mary' (The Kaleidoscope) / 'Dark Star' (The Grateful Dead) / 'Crumbling Land' (Pink Floyd) / 'Tennessee Waltz' (Patti Page) / 'Sugar Babe' (The Youngbloods) / 'Love Scene' (Jerry Garcia) / 'I Wish I Was A Single Girl Again' (Roscoe Holcomb) / 'Mickey's Tune' (The Kaleidoscope) / 'Dance Of Death' (John Fahey) / 'Come In Number 51, Your Time Is Up' (Pink Floyd) / CD2: 'Love Scene Improvisation, Version 1' (Jerry Garcia) / 'Love Scene Improvisation, Version 2' (Jerry Garcia) / 'Love Scene Improvisation, Version 3' (Jerry Garcia) / 'Country Song' (Pink Floyd) / 'Unknown Song' (Pink Floyd) / 'Love Scene, Version 6' (Pink Floyd) / 'Love Scene, Version 4' (Pink Floyd).

UK: EMI Premier Soundtracks 823364 (Double-CD album).
Reissued:
UK: Sony 88697638212 (Double-CD, released Monday 19 April 2010) / UK: Sony MOVLP 150 (Limited edition 180g triple vinyl LP, released Friday 1 October 2010).

TUESDAY 16 SEPTEMBER 1997 ◄
Zabriskie Point: Original Motion Picture Soundtrack
CD1: 'Heart Beat, Pig Meat' (Pink Floyd) / 'Brother Mary' (The Kaleidoscope) / 'Dark Star' (The Grateful Dead) / 'Crumbling Land' (Pink Floyd) / 'Tennessee Waltz' (Patti Page) / 'Sugar Babe' (The Youngbloods) / 'Love Scene' (Jerry Garcia) / 'I Wish I Was A Single Girl Again' (Roscoe Holcomb) / 'Mickey's Tune' (The Kaleidoscope) / 'Dance Of Death' (John Fahey) / 'Come In Number 51, Your Time Is Up' (Pink Floyd) / CD2: 'Love Scene Improvisation, Version 1' (Jerry Garcia) / 'Love Scene Improvisation, Version 2' (Jerry Garcia) / 'Love Scene Improvisation, Version 3' (Jerry Garcia) / 'Country Song' (Pink Floyd) / 'Unknown Song' (Pink Floyd) / 'Love Scene, Version 6' (Pink Floyd) / 'Love Scene, Version 4' (Pink Floyd) .

US: Rhino Movie Music R272462 (Double CD album).

FRIDAY 29 NOVEMBER 2013
Zabriskie Point: Original Motion Picture Soundtrack
LP1: 'Heart Beat, Pig Meat' (Pink Floyd) / 'Brother Mary' (The Kaleidoscope) / 'Dark Star' (The Grateful Dead) / 'Crumbling Land' (Pink Floyd) / 'Tennessee Waltz' (Patti Page) / 'Sugar Babe' (The Youngbloods) // 'Love Scene' (Jerry Garcia) / 'I Wish I Was A Single Girl Again' (Roscoe Holcomb) / 'Mickey's Tune' (The Kaleidoscope) / 'Dance Of Death' (John Fahey) / 'Come In Number 51, Your Time Is Up' (Pink Floyd) / LP3: 'Love Scene Improvisation, Version 1' (Jerry Garcia) / 'Love Scene Improvisation, Version 2' (Jerry Garcia) / 'Love Scene Improvisation, Version 3' (Jerry Garcia) // 'Country Song' (Pink Floyd) / 'Unknown Song' (Pink Floyd) / 'Love Scene, Version 6' (Pink Floyd) / 'Love Scene, Version 4' (Pink Floyd) .

US: Water Tower Music WTM39474 (Double 180g white vinyl album Record Store Day edition).

ZABRISKIE POINT (VIDEO)
WEDNESDAY 8 AUGUST 1984
Zabriskie Point
US: MGM/UA MV 600196 (VHS video) / MGM/UA MB 600196 (Betamax video) / MGM/UA ML 600196 (Laserdisc video).
Reissued:
US: MGM/UA ML 105730 (Laserdisc video, deluxe letter box edition, released Wednesday 25 September 1991) / US: Warner Home Video 027616019639 (VHS video, released Wednesday 27 January 1993) / US: Warner Home Video 883929039302 (DVD video, released Tuesday 26 May 2009).

MONDAY 28 SEPTEMBER 2009
Zabriskie Point
UK: Warner Home Video 5051892009553 (DVD video, initially available exclusively to HMV music stores).

STAMPING GROUND

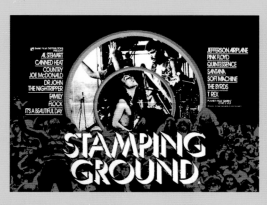

The documentary film of the *Holland Pop Festival* held on 28 June 1970 was initially released to cinema as *Stamping Ground* and premiered at the Cineac, Rotterdam, Netherlands on Wednesday 30 June 1971 and in the US at the Picwood Theatre, Westwood, Los Angeles, CA, USA on Friday 28 April 1972. It was re-released to cinema across the US on Friday 17 January 1975. The footage has since been released on video under this same title and Pink Floyd's performance has also appeared on many video compilations, including *Psychomania!*, and more recently a restored version of *Stamping Ground* entitled the *Dutch Woodstock*.

FRIDAY 28 APRIL 1972 ▲
Stamping Ground: Radio Spots
Radio spots for the 28 April 1972 opening of the film *Stamping Ground*.
Track list: 30-second advert / 10-second advert
US: Fine Films F-3 (One-sided promotional 7-inch EP single).

FRIDAY 17 JANUARY 1975
Stamping Ground: Radio Spots
Radio spots for the cinematic re-release of the film *Stamping Ground*.
Track list: 60-second advert / 30-second advert / 10-second advert
US: Atlas Films ER-7302 (One-sided promotional 7-inch EP single).

WEDNESDAY 9 MARCH 1983
Stamping Ground
Track list: 'Zero She Flies' (Al Stewart) / 'Mardi Gras Day' (Dr. John the Night Tripper) / 'Drowned In Wine' (Family) / 'Pavilions Of Sun' (T. Rex) / 'Human Condition' (Canned Heat) / 'So Sad' (Canned Heat) / 'White Rabbit' (Jefferson Airplane) / 'Saturday Afternoon' (Jefferson Airplane) / 'Ballad of You And Me & Pooneil' (Jefferson Airplane) / 'Big Bird' (Flock) / 'Open Up Your Hearts' (It's A Beautiful Day) / 'Wasted Union Blues' (It's A Beautiful Day) / 'Freedom Is A Constant Struggle' (Country Joe & The Fish) / 'Old Blue' (the Byrds) / 'Savor-Jingo–Gumbo' (Santana) / 'Set The Controls For The Heart Of The Sun' (Pink Floyd) / 'A Saucerful of Secrets' (Pink Floyd).

US: JLT Films 202 (Betamax video released as *Stamping Ground*).
Reissued:
US: Good Times 8046 (VHS video released as Stamping Ground, Tuesday 20 October 1987) / US: Substance 21928 (VHS video released as Stamping Ground, Tuesday 14 March 2000) / UK: Gonzo GZO102CD (Double DVD and CD of the soundtrack, released as *The Dutch Woodstock*, Monday 22 April 2013).

FRIDAY 1 NOVEMBER 1991
Psychomania! 20 Golden Greats
Track list: '2,000 Light Years From Home' (Rolling Stones) / 'Space Oddity' (David Bowie) / 'This Wheel's On Fire' (Julie Driscoll and the Brian Auger Trinity) / 'Space Cowboy' (Steve Miller) / 'Set The Controls For The Heart Of The Sun' (Pink Floyd) / 'Interstellar Overdrive' (Pink Floyd') / 'Fire' (Crazy World Of Arthur Brown) / 'Eight Miles High' (The Byrds) / 'White Rabbit' (Jefferson Airplane') / 'We Know What You Mean' (Soft Machine) / 'Sugar Magnolia' (Grateful Dead) / 'The Son Of Suzi Creamcheese' (the Mothers Of Invention) / 'Voodoo Chile' (Jimi Hendrix Experience) / 'It Wouldn't Last' (Soft Machine) / 'Eve of Destruction' (Barry McGuire) / 'Drowned In Wine' (Family) / 'All On A Mighty Fine Day' (Dr. John the Night Tripper) / 'Kow Kow Cowqulator' (Steve Miller Band) / 'Wasted Union Blues' (It's A Beautiful Day) / 'Upon The My Oh My (Captain Beefheart).

UK: Music World Video GEMTV-474 (VHS video).
Pink Floyd's tracks are listed on the sleeve as 'Astronomy Domine' and 'Interstellar Overdrive' respectively.

MONDAY 24 OCTOBER 1994
Psychomania! The Best of Psychedelic Rock
Track list: 'I Feel Free' (Cream) / 'Space Oddity' (David Bowie) / 'Set The Controls For The Heart Of The Sun' (Pink Floyd) / 'A Saucerful of Secrets' (Pink Floyd) / 'Fire' (Crazy World Of Arthur Brown) / 'Eight Miles High' (The Byrds) / 'White Rabbit' (Jefferson Airplane') / 'We Know What You Mean' (Soft Machine) / 'Sugar Magnolia' (Grateful Dead) / 'All On A Mighty Fine Day' (Dr. John the Night Tripper) / 'This Wheel's On Fire' (Julie Driscoll and Brian Auger Trinity) / 'Space Cowboy' (Steve Miller Band) / 'Upon The My Oh My (Captain Beefheart) / 'Sunshine Of Your Love' (Jimi Hendrix Experience) / 'I Feel Free' (Cream).

UK: Magnum Music MMGV067 (VHS video).
UK: Magnum Music MDV067 (DVD video, released Monday 29 September 2003).

LIVE AT POMPEII

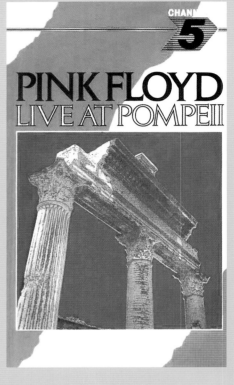

Pink Floyd's unique concert documentary directed by Adrian Maben was recorded at the Roman Arena, Pompeii in southern Italy in October 1971. Additional post-production recording and filming for the film was completed at the Studios de Boulogne and Studio Europa-Sonor in Paris, including the tracks 'Careful With That Axe, Eugene', 'Set The Controls For The Heart Of The Sun' and 'Mademoiselle Nobs', a reworking of 'Seamus'. The howling dog was a female Borzoi (Russian Wolfhound) named Nobs, which belonged to Madonna Bouglione, the daughter of circus director Joseph Bouglione. The additional studio footage and interviews were filmed at EMI Studios, Abbey Road, London, England between Sunday 15 and Tuesday 17 October 1972 as work continued on their *Dark Side of the Moon* album. *Live at Pompeii* premiered at the Cameo Cinema in Edinburgh, Scotland as part of the *26th Edinburgh Film Festival* on Saturday 2 September 1972, and in the US at the RKO Albee Theater, Cincinnati on Wednesday 24 April 1974. It was finally given a general release to UK cinemas on Sunday 21 July 1974. Some US cinemas used a "discrete" quadraphonic audio mix produced by Dan Wallin (who had received an Oscar nomination for Best Sound three years earlier for his work on *Woodstock*) at A&M Studios, Los Angeles, USA. In 2003 director Adrian Maben completed a 'Directors Cut' of the film, which incorporated some additional and unused 16mm interview footage that Maben had retained in his own collection. He also discovered that some 548 cans of 35mm negative and prints of the rushes that had been stored at the Archives du Film du Bois d'Arcy outside of Paris had only recently been destroyed to make way for storage of newer films. The video release was certified Gold in the US on Friday 12 April 1996. The 2003 video reissue was certified Platinum and 2 x Multi-Platinum in the US on Monday 5 January 2004.

WEDNESDAY 24 APRIL 1974 ▲
Live at Pompeii – Radio Spot Announcements
A promotional EP containing 12 radio spots for the cinematic release of the film *Pink Floyd Live at Pompeii*. Side 1 is labelled "Original Radio Spot Announcements" and contains four 60-second spots, and two 30-second spots. Side 2 is labelled "Revised Radio Spot Announcements" and contains five 60-second spots, and one 30-second spot. Two editions appear to have been pressed with both white and yellow labels. While the recordings are genuine, the legitimacy of the disc itself is questionable, especially as they contain both the original and revised adverts.
Side A: 60-second advert / 60-second advert / 60-second advert / 60-second advert / 30-second advert / 30-second advert / Side B: 60-second advert / 60-second advert / 60-second advert / 60-second advert / 60-second advert / 30-second advert.
US: April Fool Films AF – Floyd – 1 / AF – Floyd – 2 (Promotional 7-inch EP single).

MONDAY 14 SEPTEMBER 1981
Live at Pompeii
Track list: 'Echoes' (Part 1) / 'Careful With That Axe, Eugene' / 'A Saucerful of Secrets' / 'One Of These Days I'm Going To Cut You Into Little Pieces' / 'Set The Controls For The Heart Of The Sun' / 'Mademoiselle Nobs' / 'Echoes' (Part 2).

UK: PolyGram 7901822 (VHS video).
Reissued:
UK: PolyGram 7901821 (Laserdisc video, released Friday 23 July 1982) / UK: PolyGram 7901822 (VHS video, released Friday 23 July 1982) / UK: PolyGram 7901824 (Betamax video, released Friday 23 July 1982) / US: RCA Selecta Vision 12061 (CED Videodisc, released Saturday 18 September 1982) / UK: PolyGram CMV 1117 (VHS video, released Monday 24 January 1983) / US: Vestron Music Video MA1008 (VHS video, released Friday 20 May 1983) / US: Vestron Music Video MB1008 (Betamax video, released Friday 20 May 1983) / UK: RCA Selecta Vision 33061 (CED Videodisc, Monday 11 June 1984) / UK: Channel 5 CFV 05182 (VHS video, Monday 20 October 1986).

TUESDAY 17 NOVEMBER 1987
Live at Pompeii
Track list: 'Echoes' (Part 1) / 'Careful With That Axe, Eugene' / 'A Saucerful of Secrets' / 'Us And Them' (studio session) / 'One Of These Days I'm Going To Cut You Into Little Pieces' / 'Set The Controls For The Heart Of The Sun' / 'Brain Damage' (studio session) / 'Mademoiselle Nobs' / 'Echoes' (Part 2).

US: Vestron Music Video ID5237VE (Laserdisc video).
Reissued:
US: PolyGram Music Video ID3850PG (Laserdisc video, Saturday 15 July 1989) / UK: PolyGram Music Video 080730-3 (VHS video, released Monday 24 July 1989) / UK: PolyGram Music Video 080730-1 (Laserdisc video, released Monday 24 July 1989) / UK: PolyGram 4Front 080 730 3 (VHS video, released Monday 20 June 1994) / UK: PolyGram 4Front 080 730 1 (Laserdisc video, released Monday 20 June 1994).

MONDAY 20 OCTOBER 2003
Live at Pompeii: The Directors Cut
Track list: 'Echoes' (Part 1) / 'Careful With That Axe, Eugene' / 'A Saucerful of Secrets' / 'Us And Them' (studio session) / 'One Of These Days I'm Going To Cut You Into Little Pieces' / 'Set The Controls For The Heart Of The Sun' / 'Brain Damage' (studio session) / 'Mademoiselle Nobs' / 'Echoes' (Part 2).

UK: Universal DVD 8201310 (DVD video).
Certified Platinum 22 July 2013 and 2 x Platinum on 9 August 2013.
US: Hip-O 602498609460 (DVD video, released Tuesday 21 October 2003).
A remastered and fully repackaged edition containing the full concert film in stereo only plus a 20-minute interview with Adrian Maben along with an option to run the original concert film, a photo gallery, album graphics, lyrics, "odds 'n' sods" and a map and history of Pompeii. Unfortunately, despite the original sound masters being in the custody of Adrian Maben, the band were not supportive of this release and Universal felt that a 5.1 mix could not be satisfactorily produced. Efforts to include the original radio and TV adverts were also made, but copyright clearances could not be obtained in time for the scheduled release.

FANTASTIC ANIMATION FESTIVAL
A collection of 16 short animation films, mostly set to music, and including Pink Floyd's 'One Of These Days' set to Ian Emes 'French Windows' animation. The film had very limited cinematic distribution, opening on Friday 27 May 1977 at the Northpoint Theatre, San Francisco, USA.

TUESDAY 9 NOVEMBER 1982
Fantastic Animation Festival
US: Media Home Entertainment M301 (VHS video).

SOUND OF THE CITY 1964–1973
Sound of the City 1964–1973, sometimes known as *Rock City* and also *Heart of the Sun* was filmed as a TV documentary by Peter Clifton featuring performances by the Rolling Stones, Otis Redding, Jimi Hendrix, Donovan, Joe Cocker, the Animals, Rod Stewart and the Faces, Ike & Tina Turner, Cat Stevens and Cream. Pink Floyd was filmed at the Dome, Brighton, England on Thursday 29 June 1972 and the film features performances of 'Careful With That Axe, Eugene' and 'Set The Controls For The Heart Of The Sun'. A compilation of live footage from the above, including 'Careful With That Axe, Eugene', was released to video with additional footage in 1984 as *Superstars in Concert*. In 1979 Clifton was reviewing the original film for video release, decided to use additional inserts of the 1969 Apollo 11 mission and purchased a reel of film for $180 from the Smithsonian Institute in Washington, DC. Unbeknown to him the footage was entirely unique – the 16mm reel was in fact an original high-quality original film shot at 10 frames per second directly from the beamed back images to the Australian tracking station at the CSIRO Parkes Observatory (the footage broadcast to the world was, in fact, shot by a TV camera pointed at a monitor receiving the images from the moon). When the images reached the tracking station they were transferred onto a one-inch, 60-frame-per-second tape and sent to NASA's Goddard Space Flight Center in Maryland for safekeeping. The footage Clifton had purchased remained in his personal archive until, in 2006, he saw an appeal by NASA seeking to reclaim some 700 mislaid tapes of the mission. In total NASA had mislaid over 2,500 reels of tapes from its various Apollo missions. On Friday 24 July 1981 *Sound of the City 1964–1973* was screened at the Harold Clurman Theater, New York, but was shut down following a restraining order issued by US District Judge Charles S. Haight against Columbia Pictures, World Film Services and director Peter Clifton, which alleged that the film contained unauthorized performances of Rolling Stones material that was owned by former Rolling Stones manager Allen Klein and his company ABKCO. Klein issued the order having seen a review of the screening in the *New York Times* and Clifton's proposed expanded video release never saw the light of day. The outcome of the court order is unknown as of this writing.

FRIDAY 19 JANUARY 1989
Superstars in Concert
UK: Telstar TVE1003 (VHS video).

LA VALLÉE / OBSCURED BY CLOUDS
Pink Floyd's second feature film for Barbet Schroeder centres around a journey of self-discovery and is set in New Guinea. The soundtrack was recorded at Strawberry Studios, Chateau d'Hérouville, France between Wednesday 23 to Tuesday 29 February, and Thursday 23 to Monday 27 March 1972.

Typically the soundtrack contains different versions to that of the album release and the song 'Free Four' has different lyrics, and the ending of 'Absolutely Curtains' is sung by the cast. Apparently Schroeder didn't want Pink Floyd to provide music in such a literal sense as was their work on *More*. Consequently the music on the DVD is sparse to say the least, and what is included is barely audible, the title track having the greatest exposure as it's played over the opening titles. The remainder is heard in the background as excerpts and more often than not on the cassette player of the Land Rover in which the central characters explore the island. The tracks 'Mudmen' and 'Stay' do not appear in the film at all. *La Vallée* opened in France on Thursday 6 July 1972 and was screened at the *Venice International Film Festival* in August 1972 and once again cemented Pink Floyd's popularity in continental Europe. It received a single screening in the US at the *2nd Annual International Film Exposition* at Grauman's Chinese Theater, Hollywood, Los Angeles, on Friday 17 November as part of a panel screening discussing music in film. Thereafter it disappeared from view until it opened in the US at Cinema 3, New York, on Sunday 17 May 1981.

WEDNESDAY 26 JUNE 1991
The Valley: Obscured by Clouds
US: Warner Home Video 35149 (VHS video).
US: Home Vision Entertainment VAL020 (VHS video, released Tuesday 22 May 2001).

MONDAY 14 FEBRUARY 2011
The Valley (Obscured by Clouds)
UK: BFI B1039 (Double DVD/Blu-Ray dual format edition. Additional extras include the original un-restored ending (5 minutes, DVD only) and a series of Barbet Schroeder shorts: 'Le Cochon Aux Patates Douces' (1971, 8 minutes), 'Maquillages' (1971, 12 minutes), and 'Sing-Sing' (1971, 5 minutes), and theatrical trailers for *The Valley, More* (1969) and *Maîtresse* (1974), a fully illustrated booklet with wordy liner notes by Rob Young, who evidently wrote the booklet without having bothered to watch the film, rare on-set photographs, newly commissioned essays and director interview).

THE MAKING OF THE DARK SIDE OF THE MOON

An official release of the 40-minute BBC TV *Classic Albums* series first broadcast on BBC1 TV on Sunday 11 May 2003 and expanded to an 84-minute DVD with newly recorded interviews with Waters, Gilmour, Mason and Wright. Previously unseen and unheard material included early demos of tracks and the band performing 'On The Run' live in 1972. The set won "Best Additional Features" at the *2nd Annual Surround Music Awards* on Thursday 11 December 2003 at the Beverly Hilton Hotel, Los Angeles, during the first day of *Surround 2003: The 5th Annual International Surround Conference and Showcase*.

MONDAY 25 AUGUST 2003
Classic Albums: The Making of **The Dark Side of the Moon**
UK: Eagle Vision PFPD5 (Promotional DVD video, includes marketing information, press release, ordering information and the track 'Breathe') / UK: Eagle Vision CASAMP2005 (Promotional DVD video) / UK: Eagle Vision EREDV329 (DVD video).
Certified Platinum on Friday 29 June 2007.
US: Eagle Vision EV30042-9 (DVD video) / US: Eagle Vision EU30042-9 (PS2 video, released Tuesday 26 August 2003).
Certified Gold, Platinum and 2 x Platinum on Sunday 30 January 2005 and 3 x Platinum on Wednesday 28 February 2007.
Reissued:
UK: Eagle Vision ERUMD329 (PS2 video, released Tuesday 1 November 2005) / UK: Eagle Vision 801213099498 (Blu-ray Disc, released Monday 26 August 2013).

CRYSTAL VOYAGER

This is essentially a journey through the eyes of the American ex-pat surfer George Greenough taking, as the publicity material stated, "the camera and you on a vibrant trip into the rolling, crashing ocean". Directed by David Elfick and set to the music of Pink Floyd's 'Echoes', it is regarded as a sight and sound spectacular, which led to the footage being used by Pink Floyd for screen sequences during performances of 'The Great Gig In The Sky' on their latter day tours from 1987 onwards. A classic film in surfing circles, *Crystal Voyager* was one of Australia's most successful films, premiering at the Sydney Opera House on Wednesday 5 December 1973, and going on to achieve a six-month run

in London's West End at the Odeon Cinema, St Martins Lane commencing Thursday 31 October 1974, and also winning composer Phil Judd an award for "Best Original Music Score".

FRIDAY 16 MARCH 1980 ▶
Crystal Voyager
US: Wizard Video 012 (VHS video) / US: Wizard Video 012 (Betamax video).
UK: Video Gems R1020 (VHS video, released Wednesday 22 October 1987).
Reissued:
UK: Blue Dolphin BDV 2011 (VHS video, Monday 1 February 1999) / UK: Blue Dolphin BDVD 2003 (DVD video, released Monday 24 March 2003).

A TOTALLY UNIQUE FILM EXPERIENCE!
CRYSTAL VOYAGER
NO MAN HAS EVER BEEN ABLE OR DARED TO FILM HERE BEFORE
HEAR THE MUSIC BY **PINK FLOYD** ON HARVEST RECORDS SHVL 795
PAVILION NEWCASTLE FROM NOVEMBER 10th.

THE STORY OF WISH YOU WERE HERE

An officially endorsed documentary on the making of the album, and featuring interviews with David Gilmour, Nick Mason and Roger Waters and archive material with Richard Wright as well as Storm Thorgerson, Roy Harper, Ronnie Rondell (the burning stunt man) and engineer Brian Humphries.

It was broadcast ahead of release on VH1 on Saturday 3 March 2012 at 7.30pm. Also included on the DVD and Blu-ray releases are additional band member interviews and Gilmour and Waters performing acoustic excerpts from the album.

MONDAY 25 JUNE 2012
The Story of **Wish You Were Here**
UK: Eagle Vision EREDV932 (DVD video) / UK: Eagle Vision ERBRD5152 (Blu-ray Disc).
US: Eagle Vision EV30518 (DVD video) / US: Eagle Vision EVB334159 (Blu-ray Disc, released Tuesday 26 June 2012).

THE LOST DOCUMENTARY

A previously unreleased documentary film about *The Wall* showing the production set up at Earl's Court, London, England in August 1980, plus contemporary interviews with Mark Fisher, Seth Goldman, Harvey Goldsmith, James Guthrie, Jonathan Park, Rocky Paulson and Roger Waters.

MONDAY 5 JULY 2004
PINK FLOYD
The Lost Documentary
US: Howard Joseph Lamden (DVD video).

PINK FLOYD THE WALL

Alan Parker's vision of Pink Floyd's rock-opera *The Wall* was premiered out of competition at the *35th Festival International Du Film*, Cannes on Sunday 23 May 1982 and previewed at the Ziegfeld Theater, New York, on Thursday 24 June 1982 before receiving its official press premiere at the same venue on Sunday 8 August 1982. The official charity world premiere was held at the Empire, Leicester Square, London, England on Wednesday 14 July 1982 and opened in cinemas across the UK on Sunday 15 August 1982. Keen-eyed observers noticed that the soundtrack was available on CBS Records and Tapes, but talking to *Billboard* magazine in September 1982, Gilmour revealed that, "at one point we intended to make a soundtrack album, but we just didn't have enough new music to reasonably justify putting one out. At one point we thought more of the music in the film would be new or different, but it didn't work out that way. We re-recorded about five songs for the film, but in most cases we just remixed the original tapes."

This included the addition of the new track 'When The Tigers Broke Free' (split into two sections), 'In The Flesh?' (re-recorded with Bob Geldof lead vocals); 'The Thin Ice' (Piano overdub in second verse and baby noise removed); 'Another Brick In The Wall, Part 1' (remixed with a more prominent bass); 'Goodbye Blue Sky' (remixed), 'The Happiest Days Of Our Lives' (remixed, helicopter sounds removed and vocals added by Teacher actor Alex McAvoy); 'Another Brick In The Wall, Part 2' (remixed with additional lead guitar, children's chorus edited and vocals added by Teacher actor Alex McAvoy); 'Mother' (completely re-recorded with the lyric "Is it just a waste of time?" replaced with "Mother, am I really dying?", which is what appeared on the original album lyric sheet); 'What Shall We Do Now?' (a new track); 'Young Lust' (Screams added and phone call part removed); 'One Of My Turns' (remixed); 'Don't Leave Me Now' (remixed and shortened); 'Another Brick In The Wall, Part 3' (re-recorded with faster tempo); 'Is There Anybody Out There' / 'Nobody Home' (classical guitar bridge re-recorded by Tim Renwick); 'Bring The Boys Back Home' (re-recorded without Waters lead vocal but with the addition of the brass band and Welsh male voice choir); 'Comfortably Numb' (remixed with screams added), 'In The Flesh' (re-recorded with brass and Bob Geldof lead vocals); 'Run Like Hell' (remixed and shortened); 'Waiting For The Worms' (remixed and shortened); 'Stop' (re-recorded with Bob Geldof vocals. Just audible in the background of this scene is Gary Yudman's introduction from *The Wall Live* at Earl's Court); 'The Trial' (remixed) and 'Outside The Wall' (re-recorded with brass band and Welsh male voice choir). 'Hey You' and 'The Show Must Go On' were omitted from the film. The newly recorded material was recorded variously in London, New York and Los Angeles with Andy Bown (Bass), Bob Geldof (Vocals), Tim Renwick (Guitar), Toni Tennille (Backing Vocals) and Pontardulais Male Voice Choir led by Noel Davis (Backing Chorus).

MONDAY 28 MARCH 1983
Pink Floyd The Wall
UK: Thorn EMI TVJ 9014312 (VHS video) / UK: Thorn EMI TXA 9014314 (Betamax video).
Certified 4 x Platinum on 22 July 2013.
US: MGM/UA ML 100268 (Laserdisc video).
Reissued:
US: MGM/UA MD 100268 (CED Videodisc, released Tuesday 20 September 1983) / US: MGM/UA M 400268 (VHS video, released Monday 21 December 1987) / UK: Channel 5 CFV 08762 (VHS video, released Friday 14 July 1989) / US: MGM/UA ML 102214 (Laserdisc video, deluxe letterbox edition, released Monday 1 July 1991) / US: MGM/UA M 204694 (VHS video, deluxe letterbox edition, released Monday 1 July 1991) / UK: PolyGram 081 252-3 (VHS video, released Friday 16 April 1993) / UK: PolyGram 081 252-1 (Laserdisc video, released Friday 16 April 1993) / US: MGM/UA MV 400268 (VHS video, released Wednesday 27 April 1994) / MGM/UA MB 400268 (Betamax video, released Wednesday 27 April 1994) / UK: PolyGram 081 252-4 (Double video CD, Monday 7 November 1994) / US: MGM/UA ML 106344 (Widescreen Collector's Edition Laserdisc video, with Alan Parker commentary, theatrical trailer and photo gallery, released Wednesday 30 July 1997).

FRIDAY 7 MAY 1993
Pink Floyd The Wall / The Wall Live in Berlin
UK: PolyGram Video 0877303 (VHS video, double pack of the original feature film and Roger Waters' *The Wall Live in Berlin*).

TUESDAY 7 DECEMBER 1999
Pink Floyd The Wall: 5.1 Remaster
US: Columbia Music Video CV 501983 (VHS video).
US: Columbia Music Video CMV 501986 (DVD video) / US: Sony Music Enterprises SMV 501987 (DVD video, released Monday 7 February 2000). Remastered in 5.1 surround sound from a hi-definition film transfer with additional material including the previously unreleased 'Hey You' scene; *The Other Side of the Wall* documentary film; running commentary from Roger Waters and Gerald Scarfe; retrospective documentary featuring interviews with Roger Waters, Gerald Scarfe, Alan Parker, Peter Biziou, Alan Marshall and James Guthrie; the original film trailer and production stills; the original promo film for 'Another Brick In The Wall, Part 2'; and a reproduction film poster).

MONDAY 1 NOVEMBER 2004
Pink Floyd The Wall: 5.1 Remaster 25th Anniversary Edition
UK: Sony Music Enterprises CVD 58163 (Limited Edition 25th Anniversary DVD video).
US: Columbia Music Video CMV 58163 (Limited Edition 25th Anniversary DVD video, released Tuesday 25 January 2005).
Reissued:
UK: Sony Music Enterprises SMV 501989 (DVD video, released Monday 5 June 2006) / US: Columbia Music Video CMV 501989 (DVD video, released Tuesday 6 June 2006) / Remastered in 5.1 surround sound from a hi-definition film transfer with additional material including the previously unreleased 'Hey You' scene; *The Other Side of the Wall* documentary film; running commentary from Roger Waters and Gerald Scarfe; retrospective documentary featuring interviews with Roger Waters, Gerald Scarfe, Alan Parker, Peter Biziou, Alan Marshall and James Guthrie; the original film trailer and production stills; and the original promo film for 'Another Brick In The Wall, Part 2'.

MUSIC FROM THE FINAL CUT

A collection of promo videos which, although not officially released on video in the US, was broadcast on MTV extensively around the time of the UK release.

MONDAY 25 APRIL 1983
Music From The Final Cut
Track list: 'The Gunners Dream' / 'The Final Cut' / 'Not Now John' / 'The Fletcher Memorial Home'.
UK: Video Music Collection PM 0010 (VHS video).

DELICATE SOUND OF THUNDER

Wayne Isham's concert film of Pink Floyd's *A Momentary Lapse of Reason* tour captured the band in their full-blown glory and was recorded live at the Nassau Veterans Memorial Coliseum, New York between Friday 19 and Tuesday 23 August 1988. Although released in a variety of formats, it has never officially been released on DVD. Its TV debut was made on BBC4 on Friday 1 November 2013 between 10.00pm and 11.35pm as part of an evening of Pink Floyd films and documentaries. It was certified Gold and Platinum in the US on Monday 5 February 1990, 2 x Multi-Platinum on Monday 5 February 1990 and 2 x Multi-Platinum on Tuesday 26 March 1991. At the *32nd Grammy Awards*, held at the Shrine Auditorium in Los Angeles, on Thursday 22 February 1990, *Delicate Sound of Thunder* was nominated for "Best Longform Video" losing out to *Rhythm Nation* by Janet Jackson.

MONDAY 12 JUNE 1989 ◄
Delicate Sound of Thunder
Track list: 'Shine On You Crazy
Diamond' (Intro) / 'Signs Of Life' /
'Learning To Fly' / 'Sorrow' / 'The Dogs
Of War' / 'On The Turning Away' / 'One
Of These Days' / 'Time' / 'On The Run'
/ 'The Great Gig In The Sky' / 'Wish
You Were Here' / 'Us And Them' /
'Comfortably Numb' / 'One Slip' / 'Run
Like Hell' / 'Shine On (Reprise)' / End
Credits.

UK: PMI MVN 9911863 (VHS video) / UK: Pioneer Video PLMPB 00981
(Laserdisc video).
US: CMV Enterprises 24V 49019 (VHS video) / US: CMV Enterprises
ID6486CB (Laserdisc video, released Monday 1 July 1994).
Highest chart position No. 17 (*Billboard* "Top Music Videos" on Saturday
27 August 1994).

MONDAY 12 JUNE 1989
Delicate Sound of Thunder
CD1: Introduction / 'Shine On You Crazy Diamond' / 'Signs Of Life' /
'Learning To Fly' / 'Sorrow' / 'The Dogs Of War' / 'On The Turning Away' /
'One Of These Days' / 'Time' / 'On The Run' / 'The Great Gig In The Sky' /
'Wish You Were Here' / CD2: 'Us And Them' / 'Comfortably Numb' / 'One Slip'
/ 'Run Like Hell' / Pink Floyd Discography / End Credits.
UK: PMI PMCD 4912752/EDV 140 (Double Video CD).

KNEBWORTH (AUDIO)

Knebworth has become synonymous with Pink Floyd since their
appearance there on Saturday 5 July 1975. Their return to the venue
on Saturday 30 June 1990 to participate in the Nordoff Robbins charity
event also saw performances by acts as diverse as Cliff Richard, Eric
Clapton, Phil Collins, Tears for Fears and Status Quo among others
and was also televised. The subsequent CD and DVD releases have been
universally derided for their poor mixing and constant "drop-outs",
which may have been a result of the high winds and rain that swept
across the site throughout the day. Pink Floyd's set was represented on
the audio compilations with 'Comfortably Numb' and 'Run Like Hell'.

MONDAY 6 AUGUST 1990
Knebworth: The Event
UK: Polydor 843 921-2 (Double-CD album) / UK: Polydor 843 921-1
(Double vinyl album).
US: Polydor 847 042-2 (Double-CD album) / US: Polydor 847 042-1
(Double vinyl album, released Tuesday 7 August 1990).

MONDAY 22 MARCH 2010
Live at Knebworth
UK: Eagle Rock EDGCD410 (Double CD, digitally remastered).
US: Eagle Rock EDGCD410 (Double CD, digitally remastered,
released Tuesday 23 March 2010).

KNEBWORTH (VIDEO)

Pink Floyd's set was represented on the video compilations with 'Shine
On You Crazy Diamond' and 'Run Like Hell'.

MONDAY 6 AUGUST 1990
Knebworth: The Event – Volume 3
UK: Castle Music Pictures CMP 6008 (VHS video) / Castle Music Pictures
CMPL 6008 (Laserdisc video).

MONDAY 23 SEPTEMBER 1996
Live at Knebworth
US: Image Entertainment ID3474CA (VHS video).
US: Image Entertainment ID3475CA (Double Laserdisc video) /
US: Image Entertainment ID3950CA (DVD video, released Tuesday
16 September 1997).

TUESDAY 19 NOVEMBER 2002
Live at Knebworth: Parts 1, 2 & 3
US: Eagle Eye Media EE19015 (Double DVD video).
UK: Eagle Vision EREDV273 (Double DVD video, released Monday 25
November 2002).

TUESDAY 14 JUNE 2011
Knebworth: Deluxe Edition
UK: Eagle ERDVDCD 058 (Double DVD video and double CD set
includes a replica ticket and programme for the event).

MONDAY 16 MARCH 2015
Live at Knebworth
UK: Eagle EVSBD30984 (Blu-ray Disc).
US: Eagle EVOB251SD (Blu-ray Disc, released Tuesday 17 March 2015).

LA CARRERA PANAMERICANA

A documentary by Ian McArthur of the pan-American car rally in which
Gilmour, Mason and manager Steve O'Rourke participated. Extracts of
Pink Floyd's most recent music was used with some new instrumental
passages recorded at Astoria Studios and EMI Studios produced by
David Gilmour.

MONDAY 13 APRIL 1992 ▼
La Carrera Panmericana
Track list: 'Run Like Hell' / 'Pan Am Shuffle' / 'Yet Another Movie' / 'Sorrow' /
'Signs Of Life' / 'Country Theme' / 'Mexico '78' / 'Big Theme' / 'Run Like Hell' /
'One Slip' / 'Small Theme' / 'Pan Am Shuffle' / 'Carrera Slow Blues'.

UK: PMI MVN 9913453 (VHS video).
US: Sony Music Video 19V 49128 (VHS video) / US: Sony Music Video
MLV 49128 (Laserdisc video, released Tuesday 2 June 1992).
Highest chart position No. 9 (*Billboard* "Top Music Videos" on Saturday
1 August 1992).
Reissued:
UK: Video Collection International MC2134 (VHS video, released
Monday 9 June 1997).

P.U.L.S.E.

Pink Floyd's spectacular run of shows at London's Earls Court was captured by David Mallet on Thursday 20 October 1994 in this beautifully shot concert film. It has also been widely shown on TV across the world.

JUNE 1995

P.U.L.S.E.: Earls Court London 20.10.94 – Pink Floyd Trailer
UK: TVR (Promotional VHS video).
Promotional trailer for *P.U.L.S.E.* with running time of 3'2" and housed in a plastic case.

MONDAY 12 JUNE 1995

P.U.L.S.E.: Earls Court London 20.10.94
Track list: 'Shine On You Crazy Diamond' / 'Learning To Fly' / 'High Hopes' / 'Take It Back' / 'Coming Back To Life' / 'Sorrow' / 'Keep Talking' / 'Another Brick In The Wall, Part 2' / 'One Of These Days' / The Dark Side of the Moon / 'Wish You Were Here' / 'Comfortably Numb' / 'Run Like Hell'.

UK: PMI MVD 4914363 (VHS video) / UK: EMI PMCD 4914452 (Double video CD) / UK: Pioneer Video PLMPC 01091 (Laserdisc video).

WEDNESDAY 5 JULY 1995

P.U.L.S.E.: Earls Court London 20.10.94
Track list: 'Shine On You Crazy Diamond' / 'Learning To Fly' / 'High Hopes' / 'Take It Back' / 'Coming Back To Life' / 'Sorrow' / 'Keep Talking' / 'Another Brick In The Wall, Part 2' / 'One Of These Days' / *The Dark Side of the Moon* / 'Wish You Were Here' / 'Comfortably Numb' / 'Run Like Hell'.

US: Columbia Music Video 24V 50121 (VHS video) / US: Columbia Music Video M2V 50121 (Laserdisc video).
Highest chart position No. 1 (*Billboard* "Top Music Videos" on Saturday 1 July 1995).
Certified Gold and Platinum on Monday 14 August 1995, 2 x Multi-Platinum on Friday 1 November 1996 and 8 x Multi-Platinum on Monday 31 July 2006.

MONDAY 7 AUGUST 2006

In Concert P.U.L.S.E.
DVD1: Concert Part One: 'Shine On You Crazy Diamond' / 'Learning To Fly' / 'High Hopes' / 'Take It Back' / 'Coming Back To Life' / 'Sorrow' / 'Keep Talking' / 'Another Brick In The Wall, Part 2' / 'One Of These Days' / Screen Films: 'Shine On You Crazy Diamond' / 'High Hopes' / 'Learning To Fly' / Bootlegging The Bootleggers: 'What Do You Want From Me' / 'On The Turning Away' / 'Poles Apart' / 'Marooned' / Film: Pulse TV advert / Tour Stuff: Maps, Itinerary and Stage Plans / Videos: 'Learning To Fly' / 'Take It Back' / DVD2: Concert Part Two: *The Dark Side of the Moon* / 'Wish You Were Here' / 'Comfortably Numb' / 'Run Like Hell' / Screen Films: 'Speak To Me' (Graphic) / 'On The Run' / 'Time' (1994) / 'The Great Gig In The Sky' (Wave) / 'Money' (1987) / 'Us And Them' (1987) / 'Brain Damage' / 'Eclipse' / Alternate Screen Films: 'Time' (Ian Emes 1974) / 'Money' (1994 Alien) / 'Speak To Me' (1987 Concert) / 'The Great Gig In The Sky' (Animation) / 'Us And Them' (1994) / Behind The Scenes Footage: *Say Goodbye To Life As We Know It* / Photo Gallery / Rock And Roll Hall Of Fame Induction Ceremony, USA 1996: 'Wish You Were Here' (with Billy Corgan) / Cover Art / Additional Credits.
UK: EMI 0724349143692 (Double DVD video).
Certified Gold and Platinum on Friday 28 July 2006 and 2 x Multi-Platinum on Friday 8 September 2006.
US: Sony C2D54171 (Double DVD video, released Tuesday 8 August 2006).

TUESDAY 8 AUGUST 2006

P.U.L.S.E.: Live Audio from the DVD
Track list: 'Learning To Fly' / 'High Hopes' / 'Wish You Were Here' / 'Comfortably Numb'.
US: Columbia (Promotional CD).

THE PINK FLOYD & SYD BARRETT STORY

MONDAY 24 MARCH 2003

The Pink Floyd & Syd Barrett Story
UK: Direct Video Distribution DVDUK 009 D (DVD video) / UK: Direct Video Distribution DVDUK 010 V (VHS video).
An officially sanctioned documentary directed by John Edginton focussing on Pink Floyd's formative years and first broadcast as an edition of the BBC *Omnibus* series entitled *Syd Barrett, Crazy Diamond* on BBC2 on Saturday 24 November 2001. The video release includes interviews with Roger Waters and David Gilmour; Robyn Hitchcock performing 'Dominoes' and 'It Is Obvious'; Graham Coxon performing 'Love You'; and a biography of Syd Barrett.
UK: Slam Dunk SDMD 2016 (DVD video, released Monday 3 January 2005).

TUESDAY 4 JANUARY 2005

The Pink Floyd & Syd Barrett Story
US: Voiceprint USD473 (DVD video, track list as above).

MONDAY 6 FEBRUARY 2006

The Pink Floyd & Syd Barrett Story
UK: Direct Video Distribution DVDSD 002 D (Double DVD video).
An expanded and repackaged version of the above documentary: Disc 1 includes *The Pink Floyd & Syd Barrett Story*, as above, and a newly recorded Roger Waters interview. Disc 2 includes newly recorded interviews with David Gilmour, Richard Wright, Nick Mason and Robyn Hitchcock plus a quiz, tour of Abbey Road, biographies, discographies and a Pink Floyd time-line.

TUESDAY 9 OCTOBER 2007

The Pink Floyd & Syd Barrett Story
US: Zeit Media DVD ZM2 (Limited edition numbered double DVD video).

LIVE 8

The global multi-artist charity event held in London on Saturday 2 July 2005 saw the classic Pink Floyd line up of Waters, Gilmour, Mason and Wright reunite for the last time. This DVD set captures their entire set including 'Speak To Me', 'Breathe', 'Money', 'Wish You Were Here' and 'Comfortably Numb' and a studio rehearsal session of 'Wish You Were Here'.

The show was broadcast globally (although much to the disgust of US viewers, MTV commercials interrupteds Gilmour's guitar solo during 'Comfortably Numb'). The set also includes selections from artists performing at *Live 8 Philadelphia*, *Live 8 Rome*, *Live 8 Berlin*, *Live 8 Tokyo* and *Live 8 Scotland*.

MONDAY 7 NOVEMBER 2005

Live 8
UK: EMI ANGELDVD1 (Four DVD video).
US: Capitol C094634198295 (Four DVD video, released Tuesday 8 November 2005).

13 SOLO CAREERS

SYD BARRETT

Syd Barrett is generally regarded as the de facto founder and leader of the early Pink Floyd mainly due to his prolific songwriting, which propelled them to an initial early success with two Top 10 singles ('Arnold Layne' and 'See Emily Play'), as well as the bulk of the material on their debut album, *The Piper at the Gates of Dawn*.

Yet his tenure with the band was very short-lived, as was his solo career, extending to just two solo albums. Nevertheless his influence and impact on Pink Floyd's history has led not only to recorded tributes by his former band-mates, but a continuing fascination in his persona as much as his slim body of work. A multitude of biographies, TV documentaries and record reissue campaigns have continued to fuel a cult celebrity.

Roger Keith "Syd" Barrett was born on 6 January 1946, in Cambridge, to a family of two brothers and one sister. His father, Max, a prominent pathologist at Addenbrooke's Hospital in Cambridge, passed away when he was just 15, which had a profound effect on him.

His mother, Winifred, actively encouraged his musical and artistic interests and he won a piano-duet competition with his sister at age seven, performed in school plays and enjoyed painting. He first met his future band mate Roger Waters at Morley Memorial Junior School, where his mother taught, but it was while attending Cambridgeshire High School For Boys (commonly known as "The County") that he became successful in poetry contests and developed his musical ambition. He got a ukulele at 10, a banjo at 11, a Hofner acoustic guitar at 14 and two years later purchased a Futurama electric guitar. Along with a home-made amplifier he became guitarist with Geoff Mott and the Mottoes. Their only known appearance was in March 1962, at a church hall in support of the Cambridge Youth Campaign for Nuclear Disarmament.

It was in his very early teens, and whilst still attending the County, that he first acquired the nickname 'Sid', having been something of a mimic and a good impersonator of Sid James from the *Carry On* films. Many years later he changed the spelling to Syd after watching the Riverside Jazz Band at the YMCA in Falcon Yard. Their double-bass player went by the name of Sid Barrett and he wanted to avoid confusion.

Barrett went on to study at the Cambridgeshire College of Arts and Technology where he first met David Gilmour, with whom he often played guitar, trading licks in the common room. They even went on holiday together to the south of France in August 1965 with a group of friends, narrowly avoiding a spell in police custody in San Tropez for busking.

It was not until the summer of 1964, when in his final few months as a student, that Barrett joined his first group proper, Those Without, alternating between bass and guitar. They performed regularly in Cambridge, playing covers of chart hits and numbers by American acts such as Chuck Berry, Jimmy Reed and Bo Diddley. Even after Barrett had succeeded in gaining a scholarship to a fine art course at Camberwell School of Arts and Crafts in London in September 1964, he continued performing with the group, returning to Cambridge most weekends.

Those Without folded in Christmas 1965, at the same time Barrett was invited to join his college band the Abdabs by his friend Roger Waters. At Barrett's suggestion, and after several personnel and name changes, the band adopted the name Pink Floyd. By 1966 they had developed their own unique style of performance and by 1967 Barrett's original songwriting had superseded their staple set of R&B covers.

Unfortunately, the rigours of touring, coupled with frequent experimentation with psychedelic drugs, ensured his behaviour became ever more erratic and at the start of 1968 he was eventually replaced by his friend David Gilmour.

Barrett's solo career began in May 1968, when manager Peter Jenner booked EMI Studios at Abbey Road, London, to start work on a new album. The initial results were disappointing and recording was suspended, but when sessions resumed in April 1969 the work proved good enough to create his first solo album, and both Roger Waters and David Gilmour assisted with its production. Interviewed in *Melody Maker* in early 1970, Barrett announced he would be doing a solo tour in May of that year to promote the album, but this never materialized.

His second solo album, *Barrett* – released in November of the same year – was produced entirely by David Gilmour who also played bass, while Richard Wright contributed keyboards and Jerry Shirley from Humble Pie played drums. Sadly, this was to be Barrett's last original release. Despite Peter Jenner's efforts in the summer of 1974 to get him back in the studio, the sessions were aborted after four days when it became obvious that nothing of any value would come from them.

Barrett did little to promote either album and was rarely featured in the music press, but did record a session for John Peel's *Top Gear* BBC Radio 1 programme performing five songs (one from *Madcap*, three that later appeared on the *Barrett* album, and the song 'Two Of A Kind' written by Richard Wright) with backing from Gilmour and Shirley.

Barrett made infrequent public appearances in the following years. Gilmour and Shirley played on his one and only live concert during this period, on 6 June 1970, performing four songs at Olympia in London as part of *Extravaganza '70,* a music and fashion festival. He made one final appearance on BBC Radio, recording three songs from the album *Barrett* on 16 February 1971.

In 1972 Barrett formed a short-lived band called Stars with ex-Pink Fairies member Twink on drums and ex-Delivery member Jack Monck on bass, but after a disastrous gig supporting MC5 at the Corn Exchange in Cambridge, and a scathing review in *Melody Maker,* Barrett withdrew from the music industry completely.

A reissue package of the deleted *The Madcap Laughs* and *Barrett* was released in an effort to raise the profile of its founding member following Pink Floyd's phenomenal success with the *Dark Side of the Moon*. The artwork was designed by Storm Thorgerson, and the front cover depicts a photo taken from the original *Madcap* sessions with an orange, plum and box of matches superimposed over the top. This references items Barrett had clung to throughout an acid trip they had shared back in 1965.

On 5 June 1975 during a recording session for Pink Floyd's ninth studio album *Wish You Were Here*, Barrett inexplicably turned up at Abbey Road just as the band was listening to playbacks of 'Shine On You Crazy Diamond',

Roger Waters' tribute to his old school friend and former band mate.

Barrett eventually returned to Cambridge, initially living with his mother, where he led a reclusive life, returning to painting still lifes and abstracts. The well-intentioned Syd Barrett Appreciation Society, which was founded in the mid-1970s, did make a genuine attempt at reaching his fans. However its newsletter, *Terrapin*, folded after only a few editions, which *Sounds* accurately attributed to "a lack of anything tangible to appreciate".

Unfortunately his legacy throughout the 1980s was tainted by some of the more sensationalist elements of the national and music press, resulting in years of so-called "Syd Spotting", which did nothing to promote his music. Fortunately this was largely offset by a series of sympathetic biographies which appeared in rapid succession from the late 1990s onwards.

On 7 July 2006, following a prolonged period of illness, Barrett died of pancreatic cancer. A tribute concert, *The Madcap's Last Laugh*, was organized by Joe Boyd and held at the Barbican Centre in London on 10 May 2007 and featured performances from artists as diverse as Chrissie Hynde, Damon Albarn, Kevin Ayers and Captain Sensible. Roger Waters contributed a solo performance and David Gilmour, Richard Wright and Nick Mason performed 'Arnold Layne'.

Interest in Syd Barrett has remained unceasing and many recording artists cite him as a major inspiration. One positive aspect of this adulation was a huge public demand for EMI to release additional archive material: in response the company eventually issued a collection of rarities on a single album, *Opel*, which comprised alternate takes and previously unavailable tracks. A further archive discovery resulted in the *Best Of* collection in 2002, and in 2010 *An Introduction to Syd Barrett*, which have effectively exhausted all useable material from the vaults.

ORIGINAL RELEASES

THE MADCAP LAUGHS

FRIDAY 14 NOVEMBER 1969
'Octopus' / *'Golden Hair'*
UK: EMI Harvest HAR 5009 (7-inch vinyl single).

AT LAST THE MADCAP LAUGHS

SYD BARRETT'S NEW ALBUM on Harvest SHVL 765

OCTOPUS LATEST SINGLE Harvest 5009

E.M.I. Records (The Gramophone Co. Ltd.) E.M.I. House, 20 Manchester Square, London W1A 1ES

FRIDAY 2 JANUARY 1970 ▲
The Madcap Laughs
Side 1: 'Terrapin' / 'No Good Trying' / 'Love You' / 'No Man's Land' / 'Dark Globe' / 'Here I Go' / Side 2: 'Octopus' / 'Golden Hair' / 'Long Gone' / 'She Took A Long Cold Look' / 'Feel' / 'If It's In You' / 'Late Night'.

Produced by Syd Barrett, Malcolm Jones, Peter Jenner, David Gilmour and Roger Waters, and engineered by Jeff Jarratt, Pete Mew, Mike Sheady, Phil McDonald and Tony Clark, and featured David Gilmour (Bass, Acoustic Guitar, Drums) on 'Octopus'; Mike Ratledge (Organ, Electric Piano), Hugh Hopper (Bass Guitar) and Robert Wyatt (Drums) on 'No Good Trying' and 'Love You' and Jerry Shirley (Bass, all other tracks) and John 'Willie' Wilson (Drums, all other tracks).
UK: EMI Harvest SHVL 765 (Vinyl album, Highest chart position No. 40 *Music Week* 'Top Albums' on Saturday 7 February 1970).
Reissued:
UK: EMI CDP 7466072/CD-SHVL 765 (CD album, released Monday 17 February 1987) / UK: EMI Harvest 8289062/CDGO 2053 (CD album, as per *Crazy Diamond* box set, released Tuesday 3 May 1994) / US: Capitol CDP 7466072 (CD album, released Tuesday 7 August 1990) / US: Capitol D 102644 (CD album, manufactured for BMG Direct Marketing CD club, released Tuesday 22 January 1991) / UK: EMI Harvest 724385566318/LPCENT1 (Limited edition 180-gram vinyl album issued as part of the EMI 100 series celebrating EMI Records' centenary, released Monday 6 October 1997) / UK: EMI Simply Vinyl SVLP 289 (Limited edition vinyl album pressed on 180g virgin vinyl with original packaging, released Monday 11 December 2000) / UK: EMI 5099991755827 (CD album and bonus tracks as per *Crazy Diamond* box set edition. Noted for the Gilmour-influenced change in song title of 'She Took A Long Cold Look' to 'She Took A Long Cool Look', released Monday 11 October 2010) / US: Capitol 5099991755827 (CD album, with bonus tracks as per *Crazy Diamond* box set edition, released Tuesday 26 October 2010) / UK: Parlophone P46310791 (180g vinyl album, released Monday 30 June 2014) / US: Rhino RPLH5433151 (180g vinyl album, released Tuesday 1 July 2014).

BARRETT

FRIDAY 13 NOVEMBER 1970 ▶
Barrett
Side 1: 'Baby Lemonade' / 'Love Song' / 'Dominoes' / 'It Is Obvious' / 'Rats' / 'Masie' / Side 2: 'Gigolo Aunt' / 'Waving My Arms In The Air' / 'I Never Lied To You' / 'Wined And Dined' / 'Wolfpack' / 'Effervescing Elephant'

Additional musicians on the album included Jerry Shirley (Drums and Percussion on 'Gigolo Aunt'); David Gilmour (Bass and 12-string guitar on 'Baby Lemonade', Drums on 'Dominoes', second Organ on 'It Is Obvious', 'Gigolo Aunt' and 'Wined And Dined'); Richard Wright (Organ, Piano and Harmonium); Vic Saywell (Tuba on 'Effervescing Elephant') and John 'Willie' Wilson (Percussion on 'Gigolo Aunt').
UK: EMI Harvest SHSP 4007 (Vinyl album).
Reissued:
UK: EMI CDP 7466062/CD-SHSP 4007 (CD album, released Monday 17 February 1987) / US: Capitol CDP 7466062 (CD album, released Tuesday 3 July 1990) / UK: EMI Harvest 8289072/CDGO 2054 (CD album, with bonus tracks as per *Crazy Diamond* box-set edition, released Tuesday 3 May 1994) / UK: EMI 724382145011 (Limited edition EMI 100 Edition pressed on 180g virgin vinyl, released Monday 6 October 1997) / UK: EMI Simply Vinyl SVLP 281 (Limited edition 180g virgin vinyl album, released Monday 11 December 2000) / UK: EMI Harvest 509991755728 (CD album, with bonus tracks as per *Crazy Diamond* box-set edition, released Monday 11 October 2010) / US: Capitol 5099991755827 (CD album, with bonus tracks as per *Crazy Diamond* box-set edition, released Tuesday 26 October 2010) / UK: Parlophone P46310784 (180g vinyl album, released Monday 30 June 2014) / US: Rhino RPLH5433141 (180g vinyl album, released Tuesday 1 July 2014).

COLLECTIONS

MONDAY 8 NOVEMBER 1974 ▲
Syd Barrett
UK: EMI Harvest SHDW 404 (Double vinyl album).
US: Harvest SABB-11314 (Double vinyl album, released Saturday 20 July 1974, Highest chart position No. 163 *Billboard* 'Top LPs & Tape' on 7 September 1974) / US: Capitol SABB-11314 (Double vinyl album, released Tuesday 19 July 1983).

MONDAY 15 FEBRUARY 1988
The Peel Sessions
Side 1: 'Terrapin' / 'Gigolo Aunt' / Side 2: 'Baby Lemonade' / 'Effervescing Elephant' / 'Two Of A Kind'.
An EP release of Syd Barrett's BBC sessions from Tuesday 24 February 1970 and Tuesday 16 February 1971.
UK: Strange Fruit SFPS 043 (12-inch vinyl EP, also released in a limited-edition gold tinted sleeve) & UK: Strange Fruit SFPSCD 043 (CD EP).

MONDAY 17 OCTOBER 1988 ▶
Opel
Side 1: 'Opel' / 'Clowns And Jugglers' ('Octopus') / 'Rats' / 'Golden Hair' / 'Dolly Rocker' / 'Word Song' / 'Wined And Dined' / Side 2: 'Swan Lee' ('Silas Lang') / 'Birdie Hop' / 'Let's Split' / 'Lanky, Part 1' / 'Wouldn't You Miss Me' ('Dark Globe') / 'Milky Way' / 'Golden Hair' (Instrumental).

UK: EMI Harvest SHSP 4126 (Vinyl album) & UK: EMI Harvest CDP 7912062/CZ 144 (CD album).
US: Capitol C1-91206 (Vinyl album) & US: Capitol CDP 7912062 (CD album, released Tuesday 18 April 1989)
Reissued:
UK: EMI Harvest 8289082/CDGO 2055 (CD album, with bonus tracks as per *Crazy Diamond* box set edition, released Tuesday 3 May 1994) / UK: EMI Simply Vinyl SVLP 153 (Vinyl album, limited edition pressed on 180 gram virgin vinyl with original packaging, released Monday 11 December 2000) / UK: EMI Harvest 509991755629 (CD album, with bonus tracks as per *Crazy Diamond* box set edition, released Monday 22 November 2010) / UK: Parlophone P46310777 (180g vinyl album, released Monday 30 June 2014) / US: Capitol 077779120628 (CD album, with bonus tracks as per *Crazy Diamond* box set edition, released Tuesday 26 October 2010) / US: Rhino RPLH5433131 (180g vinyl album, released Tuesday 1 July 2014).

TUESDAY 18 APRIL 1989
'Wouldn't You Miss Me' ('Dark Globe') / 'Wouldn't You Miss Me' ('Dark Globe')
US: Capitol SPRO 79606 (Promotional 12-inch vinyl single taken from the album *Opel*).

MONDAY 16 MARCH 1992
Octopus: The Best of Syd Barrett
Track list: 'Octopus' / 'Swan Lee' ('Silas Lang') / 'Baby Lemonade' / 'Late Night' / 'Wined And Dined' / 'Golden Hair' / 'Gigolo Aunt' / 'Wolf Pack' / 'It Is Obvious' / 'Lanky, Part 1' / 'No Good Trying' / 'Clowns And Jugglers' / 'Waiving My Arms In The Air' / 'Opel'.
US: Cleopatra CLEO 57712 (Limited edition CD album of 1,500 copies packaged in a printed cloth pouch with a button badge) / US: Cleopatra CLEO 57712 (CD album without special packaging but with a new revised booklet, released Tuesday 9 June 1992).

MONDAY 26 APRIL 1993 ▶
Crazy Diamond: The Complete Syd Barrett
CD1: *The Madcap Laughs*: 'Terrapin' / 'No Good Trying' / 'Love You' / 'No Man's Land' / 'Dark Globe' / 'Here I Go' / 'Octopus' / 'Golden Hair' / 'Long Gone' / 'She Took A Long Cold Look' / 'Feel' / 'If It's In You' / 'Late Night' / 'Octopus' (Takes 1 & 2) / 'It's No Good Trying' (Take 5) / 'Love You' (Take 1) / 'Love You' (Take 3) / 'She Took A Long Cold Look At Me' (Take 4) / 'Golden Hair' (Take 5) / CD2: *Barrett*: 'Baby Lemonade' / 'Love Song' / 'Dominoes' / 'It Is Obvious' / 'Rats' / 'Maisie' / 'Gigolo Aunt' / 'Waving My Arms In The Air' / 'I Never Lied To You' / 'Wined And Dined' / 'Wolfpack' / 'Effervescing Elephant' / 'Baby Lemonade' (Take 1) / 'Waving My Arms In The Air' (Take 1) / 'I Never Lied To You' (Take 1) / 'Love Song' (Take 1) / 'Dominoes' (Take 1) / 'Dominoes' (Take 2) / 'It Is Obvious' (Take 2) / CD3: *Opel*: 'Opel' / 'Clowns & Jugglers' ('Octopus') / 'Rats' / 'Golden Hair' / 'Dolly Rocker' / 'Word Song' / 'Wined And Dined' / 'Swan Lee' ('Silas Lang') / 'Birdie Hop' / 'Let's Split' / 'Lanky, Part 1' / 'Wouldn't You Miss Me' ('Dark Globe') / 'Milky Way' / 'Golden Hair' (instrumental) / 'Gigolo Aunt' (Take 9) / 'It Is Obvious' (Take 3) / 'It Is Obvious' (Take 5) / 'Clowns And Jugglers' (Take 1) / 'Late Night' (Take 2) / 'Effervescing Elephant' (Take 2).
A box-set of *The Madcap Laughs*, *Barrett* and *Opel*, with yet more outtakes. The sleeves and 24-page booklet feature new artwork based on Barrett's lyrics.
UK: EMI Harvest SYDBOX 1 (Three CD box set) .
US: Harvest CDS 7814122 (Three CD box set, released Tuesday 4 May 1993).

TUESDAY 25 MAY 1993
Crazy Diamond
Side 1: 'Terrapin' / 'Octopus' / Side 2: 'Baby Lemonade' / 'Effervescing Elephant'.
US: Capitol NR 724385818677 (Promotional 7-inch EP single on pink vinyl).

MONDAY 15 APRIL 2001
Wouldn't You Miss Me: The Best of Syd Barrett
Track list: 'Octopus' / 'Late Nite' / 'Terrapin' / 'Swan Lee' / 'Wolfpack' / 'Golden Hair' / 'Here I Go' / 'Long Gone' / 'No Good Trying' / 'Opel' / 'Baby Lemonade' / 'Gigolo Aunt' / 'Dominoes' / 'Wouldn't You Miss Me' / 'Wined And Dined' / 'Effervescing Elephant' / 'Waving My Arms In The Air' / 'I Never Lied To You' / 'Love Song' / 'Two Of A Kind' (from the BBC sessions) / 'Bob Dylan Blues' / 'Golden Hair' (instrumental from *Opel*).
Another CD collection, this time with just one newly discovered track, 'Bob Dylan Blues', retrieved from David Gilmour's personal archive.
UK: EMI Harvest 72435323202 (CD album).
US: Capitol 53232023 (CD album, released Tuesday 11 September 2001).

MONDAY 29 MARCH 2004
The Radio One Sessions
Track list: 'Terrapin' / 'Gigolo Aunt' / 'Baby Lemonade' / 'Effervescing Elephant' / 'Two Of A Kind' / 'Baby Lemonade' / 'Dominoes' / 'Love Song'.
A CD album release collecting the BBC sessions of Tuesday 24 February 1970 and Tuesday 16 February 1971.
UK: Strange Fruit SFRSCD127 (CD album).
US: Strange Fruit SFRSCD127 (CD album, released Tuesday 11 May 2004).

MONDAY 11 OCTOBER 2010 ▼
An Introduction to Syd Barrett
Track list: 'Arnold Layne' / 'See Emily Play' / 'Apples And Oranges' (Stereo Version) / 'Matilda Mother' (2010 Mix) / 'Chapter 24' / 'Bike' / 'Terrapin' / 'Love You' / 'Dark Globe' / 'Here I Go' (2010 Remix) / 'Octopus' (2010 Mix) / 'She Took A Long Cool Look' (2010 Mix) / 'If It's In You' / 'Baby Lemonade' / 'Dominoes' (2010 Mix) / 'Gigolo Aunt' / 'Effervescing Elephant' / 'Bob Dylan Blues'.
A CD collection of Barrett-penned Floyd and solo works remastered by David Gilmour, Damon Iddins and Andy Jackson at Astoria Studios.

Five tracks were remixed, including 'Octopus', 'She Took A Long Cool Look' (The title changed by Gilmour from 'She Took A Long Cold Look'), 'Dominoes' and 'Here I Go' (on which David Gilmour also added and played bass guitar). Pink Floyd's 'Matilda Mother' also received a fresh 2010 mix and is the alternate version that first appeared on the 40th-anniversary edition of *The Piper at the Gates of Dawn*. As an additional bonus, a free download of the previously unreleased instrumental track 'Rhamadan' was also included.
UK: EMI Harvest 509990773624 (CD album).
US: Capitol 509990773624 (CD album, released Tuesday 9 November 2010).
UK: EMI Harvest 5099909850316 (Limited-edition double vinyl album, pressed on 180g vinyl, for Record Store Day, released Saturday 16 April 2011).

SATURDAY 18 APRIL 2015
'Dark Globe' (Barrett) / 'Dark Globe' (R.E.M.)
UK: Parlophone R7-547637 (7-inch vinyl single).
A double A-side single pressed on purple vinyl for Record Store Day also featured a performance of 'Dark Globe' by R.E.M. on its B-side.

GUEST APPEARANCES

JUNE 2003 – KEVIN AYERS
Joy of a Toy
Includes the previously unreleased bonus track 'Religious Experience (Singing A Song In The Morning)' on which Barrett plays guitar. Subsequent reissues have not included this track.

JUNE 2014 – THE LAST MINUTE PUT TOGETHER BOOGIE BAND
Six Hour Technicolour Dream: Cambridge 1972
A live recording of Barrett's appearance with the Last Minute Put Together Boogie Band featuring Twink (Drums), Jack Monck (Bass) and Bruce Paine (Guitar), with guest Fred Frith (Guitar), supporting Hawkwind and the Pink Fairies at the Cambridge Corn Exchange on Thursday 27 January 1972. Barrett performs on the tracks 'Drinkin' That Wine', 'Number Nine' and 'Gotta Be A Reason'.

FILMS

MONDAY 19 JULY 1993
Syd's First Trip
A limited-edition release of poor quality 8mm silent home movies. The first, shot by Nigel Lesmoir-Gordon and which lasts only a few minutes, shows a teenage Barrett with friends in the disused chalk quarry at Cherry Hinton, some clips of the Pink Floyd with co-manager Andrew King and the group's multicoloured van outside EMI Studios at Abbey Road during the recording of *The Piper at the Gates of Dawn*, and material from around the same time shot on the balcony of the infamous London flat at Cromwell Road shared by Barrett and Lesmoir-Gordon. It is said that David Gilmour purchased the rights from the producers in order to remove this exploitative film from public circulation.

MONDAY 24 MARCH 2003
The Pink Floyd & Syd Barrett Story
An officially sanctioned documentary, directed by John Edginton, focused on Pink Floyd's formative years and was first broadcast as an edition of the BBC *Omnibus* series, entitled *Syd Barrett* on BBC2 TV on Saturday 24 November 2001 between 7.25pm and 8.15pm. The video includes interviews with Roger Waters, David Gilmour, Nick Mason, Richard Wright, Jerry Shirley, Graham Coxon, Robyn Hitchcock and Bob Klose. Contains David Gilmour performing an acoustic version of 'Wish You Were Here', Robyn Hitchcock performing 'Dominoes' and 'It Is Obvious', and Graham Coxon performing 'Love You'. UK: Direct Video Distribution DVDUK 009D (DVD video) / UK: Direct Video Distribution DVDUK 010V (VHS video); US: Voiceprint USD473 (DVD video, released Tuesday 4 January 2005).

MONDAY 6 FEBRUARY 2006
The Pink Floyd & Syd Barrett Story: The Definitive Edition
An expanded and repackaged numbered limited edition version of the above documentary with artwork by Mark Wilkinson: Disc 1 includes *The Pink Floyd & Syd Barrett Story*, as above, and a newly recorded and unedited Roger Waters interview that lasts for some 55 minutes. Disc 2 includes newly recorded interviews with David Gilmour, Richard Wright, Nick Mason and Robyn Hitchcock, Graham Coxon performing 'Love You', Easter Egg of Abbey Road Tour, Biographies, Discographies, Pink Floyd time-line and a Quiz.
UK: Direct Video Distribution DVDSD002D (Double DVD video, Certified Platinum on Monday 22 July 2013); US: Zeit Media DVD ZM2 (Double DVD video, released Tuesday 9 October 2007).

MONDAY 19 MAY 2014
The Pink Floyd & Syd Barrett Story
A further repackage of the above, this time with bonus unedited interviews with David Gilmour, Nick Mason, Roger Waters and Richard Wright. UK: Eagle Rock EV306719 (Double DVD video); US: Eagle Vision EGVS306719DVD (Double DVD video, released Tuesday 20 May 2014).

LIVE PERFORMANCES

TUESDAY 24 FEBRUARY 1970 – RADIO RECORDING
Top Gear, BBC Maida Vale Studios, London, England

Two live studio recording sessions were performed on this day for *Top Gear*, hosted by John Peel for BBC Radio 1. The first was recorded between 2.30pm and 6.00pm, in which Barrett, assisted by David Gilmour (Organ, Bass, Guitar) and Jerry Shirley (Bongos, Percussion), performed, in order, 'Baby Lemonade', 'Effervescing Elephant', 'Gigolo

Aunt', 'Terrapin' and 'Two Of A Kind'. It was first broadcast on *Top Gear* on Saturday 14 March 1970 between 3.00pm and 5.00pm, except 'Two Of A Kind', which was first broadcast in the UK on *Top Gear* on Saturday 30 May 1970 between 3.00pm and 5.00pm. The complete session was officially released on vinyl and CD in February 1988 (see Discography above). The second session, logged in the BBC archives as recorded between 6.00pm and 9.00pm, appears not to have been broadcast.

SATURDAY 6 JUNE 1970 – PERFORMANCE
Extravaganza '70 Music and Fashion Festival, The Grand Hall, Olympia Exhibition Hall, Olympia, London, England

With Jackson Heights and Fairfield Parlour and headliners the Foundations and Procul Harum (Friday 29 May), the Tremeloes and Tyrannosaurus Rex (Saturday 30 May), the Fortunes and Caravan (Monday 1 June), Status Quo and Black Sabbath (Tuesday 2 June), Colosseum and Harmony Grass (Wednesday 3 June), the Move and Pretty Things (Thursday 4 June), and Steamhammer and Badfinger (Friday 5 June). Barrett's first major solo appearance was as a late addition on the last evening of this eight-day music and fashion festival (Friday 29 May to Saturday 6 June 1970). He was joined on stage by David Gilmour (Bass) and Jerry Shirley (Drums) and played a rushed set that included 'Terrapin', 'Gigolo Aunt', 'Effervescing Elephant' and 'Octopus'. His vocals were barely audible throughout and even before the last track was finished he left the stage to scattered applause.

THURSDAY 30 JULY 1970 – CANCELLED PERFORMANCE
VPRO Pik Nik Festival, Gemeendecentrum, Drijbergen, Netherlands

With Kevin Ayers and the Whole World. Barrett was advertised to appear at one of a series of VPRO-sponsored televised events, but he never appeared. Kevin Ayres' performance was nevertheless broadcast live on the programme *VPRO Picknick* on Nederlands 1 TV between 8.20pm and 10.30pm.

TUESDAY 16 FEBRUARY 1971 – RADIO RECORDING
Bob Harris Sounds of the Seventies, BBC Transcription Service Studios, Kensington House, Shepherd's Bush, London, England

Barrett's second and final radio session for BBC Radio 1, recorded between 6.00pm and 9.30pm, in which he performed 'Baby Lemonade', 'Dominoes' and 'Love Song' with David Gilmour (Bass). It was broadcast in the UK on *Bob Harris Sounds of the Seventies* on Monday 1 March 1971 between 6.00pm and 7.00pm.

THURSDAY 20 JANUARY 1972 – PERFORMANCE
Cellar Club, Cambridge Union Society, Cambridge, England

Barrett played guitar on an impromptu jam session with Twink (Drums) and Jack Monck (Bass) at this gig headlined by the Eddie Byrns Combo.

THURSDAY 27 JANUARY 1972 – PERFORMANCE ▶
Corn Exchange, Cambridge, England

Barrett performed with the Last Minute Put Together Boogie Band comprising

Twink (Drums), Jack Monck (Bass) and Bruce Paine (Guitar), with guest Fred Frith (Guitar), supporting Hawkwind and the Pink Fairies with the Blue Cube Disco and a showing of the cartoon film *Asterix the Gaul*. Last Minute Put Together Boogie Band set list: 'Sea Cruise', 'LA To London Boogie', 'Ice', 'Nadine', 'Drinkin' That Wine', 'Number Nine', 'Gotta Be A Reason', 'Let's Roll', 'Sweet Little Angel'. Barrett performed as a special guest on the tracks 'Drinkin' That Wine', 'Number Nine' and 'Gotta Be A Reason'. A poor quality recording was made of the show, which was released on CD in June 2014 (see Discography above).

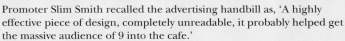

SATURDAY 5 & SATURDAY 12 FEBRUARY 1972 – PERFORMANCES ▶
The Dandelion Café, Cambridge, England

Barrett's debut with Stars featuring Twink (Drums) and Jack Monck (Bass) was at a pair of afternoon sessions at this small café in the centre of Cambridge, performing a set of blues-based numbers. Promoter Slim Smith recalled the advertising handbill as, 'A highly effective piece of design, completely unreadable, it probably helped get the massive audience of 9 into the cafe.'

THURSDAY 24 FEBRUARY 1972 – PERFORMANCE
Corn Exchange, Cambridge, England

Supporting MC5 and Skin Alley with the Blue Cube Disco.

Set list: 'Octopus', 'Dark Globe', 'Baby Lemonade', 'Waving My Arms In The Air', 'Lucifer Sam' and some improvised blues jams.

Stars' appearance, which closed the show, was reportedly a complete disaster and the situation was not improved when the house lights were accidentally switched on to reveal an audience of fewer than 30 people.

SATURDAY 26 FEBRUARY 1972 – PERFORMANCE
Corn Exchange, Cambridge, England

Supporting Nektar and Environment with the Blue Cube Disco.

This was Barrett's last advertised public appearance with Stars. Roy Hollingworth had written a fair account of the Thursday 24 February show for *Melody Maker*, but Barrett was said to have been so upset by it that he refused to perform live ever again.

MONDAY 1 MAY 1972 – PERFORMANCE
Market Square, Cambridge, England

Stars performed what was essentially an impromptu busking session in the afternoon with equipment powered from the shop *What's in a Name?*, located in Petty Cury, a side street off the Market Square.

DAVID GILMOUR

David Gilmour is best known as the voice and guitar of Pink Floyd, whose distinctive style defined the Pink Floyd sound from the late 1960s onwards.

David Jon Gilmour was born in Cambridge on Wednesday 6 March 1946. He was the second child of Douglas Gilmour, who became a senior lecturer in zoology at the University of Cambridge, and Sylvia, a teacher. The family moved around the outskirts of Cambridge over a number of years but finally settled in Grantchester.

An early enthusiast of American R&B and rock 'n' roll, he taught himself to play his chosen instrument using Bert Weedon's famous book *Play in a Day: A Guide to Modern Guitar Playing* on a borrowed guitar. By 1962 Gilmour had become an accomplished player and joined his first band, the Ramblers, in November of that year. His skills soon became very much in demand and he was able to perform concurrently with the Newcomers and other pick-up bands.

In 1963 he began studying A-Level modern languages at Cambridgeshire College of Arts and Technology and it was here that he first met art student Roger "Syd" Barrett. Despite not finishing the course, he would eventually learn to speak fluent French. After leaving college in 1964, Gilmour helped form one of the most successful semi-pro bands on the Cambridge scene, Jokers Wild. Performing primarily vocal harmony covers of everything from the Beach Boys to the Four Seasons, they enjoyed a series of residencies at the fashionable Dorothy and Victoria Ballrooms in the centre of the city.

Gilmour continued playing with Jokers Wild until he moved to London in summer 1966. With former bandmates Rick Wills and Willie Wilson they reinvented themselves as a power-trio called Bullit, influenced by the Jimi Hendrix Experience. With the advent of the 'Summer of Love' they became known as Flowers, securing residencies at clubs in Spain and France before finally calling it a day in summer 1967.

He was, among other things, a delivery driver for the clothing designers Quorum (Gilmour had already been photographed as a model for the Cambridge university newspaper *Varsity*), before accepting an invitation to join Pink Floyd in early 1968. The band initially performed as a five-piece, but as Barrett's mental health continued to deteriorate Gilmour became the lead guitarist and vocalist just a handful of gigs later.

His contribution to Pink Floyd's second album *A Saucerful of Secrets* was minimal, having joined halfway through its recording. Although he was never a particularly prolific songwriter, his vocal delivery and guitar skills quickly became a distinctive feature of Pink Floyd's sound.

Gilmour was briefly reunited with Barrett, performing on his two 1970 solo albums *The Madcap Laughs* and *Barrett*, while also co-producing the first with Roger Waters and producing the latter. Thereafter, and despite disconnecting with all those around him, Gilmour was instrumental in ensuring that Barrett's royalty payments were kept up to date. In later years he also ensured Barrett's legacy remained intact by overseeing various CD reissues.

In the mid 1970s he famously discovered Kate Bush and went on to produce and guest on many of her recordings. As a side project from Pink Floyd, he released his first solo album *David Gilmour* in 1978, reuniting with his former band mates Rick Wills and Willie Wilson. His second solo album, *About Face*, was released in 1984, and a European and

North American tour followed. Contributions from Pete Townshend on that album resulted in Gilmour performing with his 'Deep End' project the following year.

Throughout the 1980s and 1990s he became a much sought-after session guitarist and appeared on an array of albums by artists as diverse as Dream Academy, John Martyn, Paul McCartney and the Pretty Things. In July 1985 he backed Bryan Ferry as the only member of Pink Floyd to appear at *Live Aid*.

A June 2001 performance at the Robert Wyatt–curated *Meltdown* festival, and three semi-acoustic shows in January 2002 held at London's Royal Festival Hall, resulted in the live DVD, *David Gilmour in Concert*.

In 2003, Gilmour donated the £3.6 million proceeds from the sale of his London house to Crisis, the charity for the homeless, of which he was a vice-president. Two years later he was made a CBE in recognition of his work for charity and services to music, and in 2008 received a Lifetime Achievement Award from the British Academy of Composers and Songwriters. A further recognition of his contribution came in November 2009, when Gilmour was awarded an Honorary Doctorate of Arts from East Anglia's Ruskin University of Cambridge and Chelmsford.

His third solo album, *On an Island*, was released on 6 March 2006, marking his 60th birthday. A sentimental and reflective album, it showcased Gilmour's writing partnership with his wife Polly Samson, which had first blossomed during the making of Pink Floyd's *The Division Bell* in 1994. For the accompanying tour of North America and Europe he was joined on stage by Richard Wright, Phil Manzanera (of Roxy Music) and regular Floyd musicians Dick Parry, Guy Pratt and Jon Carin. The tour culminated on 26 August 2006, with 50,000 fans at Gdańsk's historic dockyards in Poland as a celebration of the 26th anniversary of the Solidarity movement, resulting in a remarkable live CD and DVD.

RIGHT: PROMOTING HIS FIRST SOLO ALBUM AT THE HOTEL PRINCE DE GALLES, PARIS, 25 MAY 1978.

Four years later a high-profile contribution to a version of Graham Nash's 'Chicago', in support of Gary MacKinnon, led in turn to a full-length album: *Metallic Spheres* by the Orb Featuring David Gilmour, released in October 2010.

Although Gilmour continued to give the impression of early retirement he has made the occasional guest appearance, as well as salvaging and reworking some outtakes from the *Division Bell* sessions to produce a brand new Pink Floyd album.

His fourth solo album, *Rattle That Lock*, was released in September 2015.

ORIGINAL RELEASES

DAVID GILMOUR

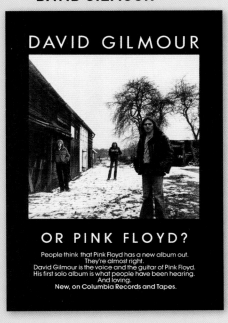

This well-received guitar-based album was the product of a regrouping of his former bandmates Rick Wills (Bass, Vocals) and John "Willie" Wilson (Drums, Percussion). Recorded at the Super Bear Studios in France, it was self-produced and engineered by John Etchells and Nick Griffiths and featured Carlena Williams, Debbie Doss and Shirley Roden (Backing Vocals), and Mick Weaver (Piano on 'So Far Away'). All of the songs were written by Gilmour, except for 'Cry From The Street' by Gilmour and Eric Stewart and 'Short And Sweet' by Gilmour and Roy Harper. 'There's No Way Out Of Here' was written by Ken Baker of Unicorn, and first appeared on that band's album *Too Many Crooks*. During the recording of the album Gilmour, Wills and Wilson were joined by their old Cambridge friends Clive Welham and Dave Parker, and they recorded a spoof version of the Four Seasons 1964 song 'Peanuts', which is currently widely available on the Internet. Six tracks from the album *David Gilmour* were filmed at the Roxy, Covent Garden in London for TV promotion, including 'So Far Away', 'There's No Way Out Of Here', 'Mihalis', 'I Can't Breathe Anymore' and 'No Way'. Gilmour was joined by his brother Mark (Rhythm Guitar) for the session, which also featured Rick Wills (Bass), John "Willie" Wilson (Drums) and Ian McLagan (Keyboards). The track 'No Way' was broadcast on BBC2 TV's contemporary rock music programme *The Old Grey Whistle Test* on Tuesday 5 December 1978 between 11.30pm and 12.00midnight.

FRIDAY 26 MAY 1978 ▲
David Gilmour
Side 1: 'Mihalis' / 'There's No Way Out Of Here' / 'Cry From The Street' / 'So Far Away' / Side 2: 'Short And Sweet' / 'Raise My Rent' / 'Deafinitely' / 'I Can't Breathe Anymore'
UK: EMI Harvest SHVL 817 (Vinyl album; Highest chart position No.17 Music Week 'Top 75 Albums' on 17 June 1978) / US: Columbia JC 35388 (Promotional vinyl album & Vinyl album, released Saturday 16 June 1978; Highest chart position No. 29 (*Billboard* "200" on Saturday 26 August 1978); Certified Gold on Friday 17 November 2000) / UK:

EMI Fame FA3071 (Vinyl album, released Monday 9 May 1983) / US: Columbia CK 35388 (CD album, released Tuesday 13 March 1984) / UK: EMI 094637084328 (CD album, released Monday 14 August 2006) / US: Columbia Legacy 828768151624 (CD album, released Tuesday 22 August 2006).

FRIDAY 28 JULY 1978
'There's No Way Out Of Here' (Edited Version) / 'Deafinately'
(UK: EMI Harvest HAR 5167, Promotional 7-inch & 7-inch single).
'There's No Way Out Of Here' (Edited Version) / 'Deafinately'
(US: Columbia 310803 (7-inch single, released Monday 21 August 1978).
'There's No Way Out Of Here' (Edited Version. Mono) / 'There's No Way Out Of Here' (Edited Version. Stereo)
US: Columbia 310803 (Promotional 7-inch single, released Monday 21 August 1978).

ABOUT FACE

Gilmour's second solo album was recorded at Pathé Marconi Studios, Paris and Abbey Road Studios, St John's Wood, London.

Many of the songs on the album lean towards middle-of-the-road adult pop rock as opposed to the guitar rock of David Gilmour, and in many respects it has not dated well. During the course of recording Gilmour asked both Roy Harper and Pete Townshend to provide lyrics for a track he was working on, but decided to shelve the idea. Harper released the track with his own lyrics as 'Hope', which appeared on the album he made with Jimmy Page, *Whatever Happened to Jugula?*, and Townshend released the track with his own lyrics as 'White City Fighting' on the album *White City: A Novel* on which Gilmour also performed. *About Face* was co-produced by Bob Ezrin and featured an array of guest musicians, including Ray Cooper (Percussion), Anne Dudley (Synthesisers), Bob Ezrin (Keyboards), Louis Jardine (Percussion), Ian Kewley (Hammond Organ and Piano), Jon Lord (Synthesizers), Pino Palladino (Bass), Jeff Porcaro (Drums and Percussion), Steve Rance (Fairlight Programming), Steve Winwood (Piano and Organ), the Kick Horns: Roddy Lorimer, Barbara Snow, Tim Sanders and Simon Clark (Brass), Vicki Brown, Sam Brown, Micky Feat and Roy Harper (Backing Vocals) and the National Philharmonic arranged by Michael Kamen and Bob Ezrin. Both Pete Townshend and Nick Laird-Clowes co-wrote many of the tracks.

MONDAY 13 FEBRUARY 1984
'Blue Light' (Extended US Remix) / 'Blue Light' (Instrumental)
UK: EMI Harvest DG1 A/B (Promotional 12-inch single).
'Blue Light' (Album Version) / 'Cruise'
UK: EMI Harvest 12 HAR 5226 (12-inch single).
'Blue Light' (Edit) / 'Cruise'
UK: EMI Harvest HAR 5226 (7-inch single).

TUESDAY 27 MARCH 1984
'Blue Light' (edit) / 'Blue Light' (Edit)
US: Columbia 38-04378 (Promotional 7-inch single).
'Blue Light' (Vocal) / 'Blue Light' (Instrumental)
US: Columbia 44-04983 (Promotional 12-inch single).
'All Lovers Are Deranged' / 'Blue Light'
US: Columbia AS 1824 (Promotional 12-inch single).
'Blue Light' (Edit) / 'Cruise'
Columbia 38-04378 (7-inch single).
'Blue Light' highest chart position No. 35 (*Billboard* "Mainstream Rock Tracks") on Saturday 31 March 1984 / No. 62 (*Billboard* "Hot 100" on Saturday 5 May 1984).

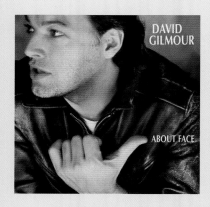

MONDAY 5 MARCH 1984 ◄
About Face
Side 1: 'Until We Sleep' / 'Murder' / 'Love On The Air' / 'Blue Light' / 'Out Of The Blue' / Side 2: 'All Lovers Are Deranged' / 'You Know I'm Right' / 'Cruise' / 'Let's Get Metaphysical' / 'Near The End'
UK: EMI Harvest SHSP 2400791 (Vinyl album, Highest chart position No. 21 Music Week "Top 75 Albums" on 17 March 1984) / US: Columbia FC 39296 (Vinyl album / US: Harvest CDP 7460312, CD album, released Tuesday 6 March 1984, Highest chart position No. 32 *Billboard* "200" on Saturday 9 June 1984; 'All Lovers Are Deranged' highest chart position No.10 *Billboard* "Mainstream Rock Tracks" on Saturday 31 March 1984; 'Murder' highest chart position No.13 *Billboard* "Mainstream Rock Tracks" on Saturday 5 May 1984; Certified Gold on Wednesday 19 April 1995) / UK: EMI Fame FA 3173 (Vinyl album, released Monday 9 May 1983) / UK: EMI Harvest CDP 7460312 (CD album, released Monday 5 March 1984) / US: Columbia CK 39296 (CD album, released Monday 6 April 1987) / UK: EMI 094637084229 (Remastered CD album, released Monday 14 August 2006) / US: Columbia Legacy 82876815172 (Remastered CD album, released Tuesday 22 August 2006).

TUESDAY 7 OCTOBER 2008
David Gilmour / About Face
US: Columbia Legacy 88697376902 (Double CD album repackage, issued in a transparent slipcase and 8-page booklet).

MONDAY 23 APRIL 1984
'Love On The Air' / 'Love On The Air'
US: Columbia 38-04490 (Promotional 7-inch single) / US: Columbia AS 1875 (Promotional 12-inch single).
'Love On The Air' / 'Near The End'
US: Columbia 38-04490 (7-inch single).

TUESDAY 24 APRIL 1984
'Love On The Air' / 'Let's Get Metaphysical'
UK: EMI Harvest HAR 5229 (7-inch single) / UK: EMI Harvest HARP 5229 (Radio-shaped picture disc single).

SATURDAY 26 MAY 1984
David Gilmour
An official document of Gilmour's Hammersmith Odeon show of Monday 30 April 1984 was released in the US. It was also broadcast on MTV on Saturday 26 May 1984 between 11.00pm and 12.00midnight (EST) and simulcast nationally on the Westwood One radio network.
Track list: 'Until We Sleep' / 'All Lovers Are Deranged' / 'There's No Way Out Of Here' / 'Short And Sweet' / 'Run Like Hell' / 'Out Of The Blue' / 'Blue Light' / 'Murder' / 'Comfortably Numb'.
US: CBS Fox Video Music 7078 (VHS video).

DAVID GILMOUR IN CONCERT

A live-concert DVD release was produced by Gilmour and culled from his critically acclaimed concerts at the Royal Festival Hall, London on Friday 22 June 2001 and Wednesday 16, Thursday 17 & Friday 18 January 2002. The release of the *In Concert* DVD as a Smartphone App on Monday 3 December 2012 was the first of its kind in the world. The DVD was previewed in a special presentation on Channel 4 TV in the UK on Tuesday 18 April 2006 between 1.40am and 1.50am.

MONDAY 21 OCTOBER 2002
David Gilmour in Concert
Track list: 'Shine On You Crazy Diamond, Parts 1–5' / 'Terrapin' / 'Fat Old Sun' / 'Coming Back To Life' / 'High Hopes' / 'Je Crois Entendre Encore' / 'Smile' / 'Wish You Were Here' / 'Comfortably Numb' (with Robert Wyatt) / 'The Dimming Of The Day' / 'Shine On You Crazy Diamond, Parts 6–9' / 'A Great Day For Freedom' / 'Hushabye Mountain' / 'Dominoes' / 'Breakthrough' (with Richard Wright) / 'Comfortably Numb' (with guest appearances by Richard Wright, Robert Wyatt and Bob Geldof). Also includes extra features: Spare Digits: 'Coming Back To Life' / 'High Hopes', 'Breakthrough' / 'Comfortably Numb' / 'Shine On You Crazy Diamond, Parts 1–5' / 'A Great Day For Freedom' (alternate live versions from the concerts) / Home Movie: 'Je Crois Entendre Encore' in rehearsals / Miscellaneous: 'I Put A Spell On You' (with Mica Paris and Jools Holland from the Channel 4 TV show *Mister Roadrunner* broadcast on Saturday 6 June 1992) / 'Don't' (from the Leiber & Stoller tribute show at the Hammersmith Apollo on Friday 29 June 2001) / 'Sonnet 18' (with Michael Kamen) / 'High Hopes' (choral from the concerts) / Lyrics for all the songs performed at the concert and a 5.1 surround sound tester.
UK: Capitol EMI 724349295896 (DVD video; Certified Gold on Friday 18 February 2005 and Platinum on Monday 22 July 2013) / US: Capitol C9724349296091 (DVD video, released Tuesday 5 November 2002).

ON AN ISLAND

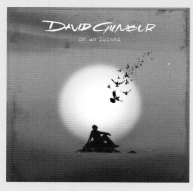

A complete departure from his previous works both as a solo artist and with Pink Floyd, Gilmour's third solo album is an introspective and very personal piece of work, with many songs co-written with his wife Polly.
    It was recorded mostly at Gilmour's Astoria studio and was co-produced with Phil Manzanera and Chris Thomas. The album features orchestral arrangements by Zbigniew Preisner conducted by Robert Ziegler and features an accomplished list of guest musicians, including: BJ Cole (Weissenborn Guitar), David Crosby and Graham Nash (Vocal Harmonies), Caroline Dale (Cello), Ilan Eshkeri (Programming), Georgie Fame (Vocals), Jools Holland (Piano), Rado "Bob" Klose (Guitar), Chris Laurence (Double Bass), Ged Lynch (Drums), Phil Manzanera (Piano), Leszek Modzer (Piano), Alasdair Molloy (Glass Harmonica), Andy Newmark (Drums), Guy Pratt (bass), Polly Samson (Piano), Chris Stainton (Hammond Organ), Chris Thomas (Keyboards), Lucy Wakeford (Harp), Willie Wilson (Drums), Richard Wright (Hammond Organ) and Robert Wyatt (Cornet).

MONDAY 30 JANUARY 2006 ▲
'On An Island'
UK: EMI CDEMDJ 688 (Promotional CD).
'On An Island' (Radio Edit) / 'On An Island' (Album Version)
UK: EMI CDEM 688 (CD single).
Highest chart position No. 72 (*Music Week* "Official Singles Chart" on Saturday 18 March 2006).
'On An Island' (Radio Edit) / 'On An Island' (Album Version)
US: Columbia 82876809762 (CD single, released Tuesday 31 January 2006).
Highest chart position No. 29 (*Billboard* "Mainstream Rock Tracks" on Saturday 11 March 2006).

FEBRUARY 2006
'Take A Breath'
US: Columbia 82876846542 (Promotional CD).

FEBRUARY 2006
'This Heaven'
US: Columbia 82876846552 (Promotional CD).

MONDAY 6 MARCH 2006
On an Island
Track list: 'Castellorizon' / 'On An Island' / 'The Blue' / 'Take A Breath' / 'Red Sky At Night' / 'This Heaven' / 'Then I Close My Eyes' / 'Smile' / 'A Pocketful Of Stones' / 'Where We Start'.

UK: EMI 0946 35569520 (CD album, housed in a 20-page clothbound booklet sleeve) / UK: EMI 0946 35569510 (Limited edition virgin vinyl album with poster insert, released Monday 5 June 2006; highest chart position No. 1 (*Official Albums Chart* "UK Top 100" on Saturday 18 March 2006; Certified Silver and Gold on Friday 17 March 2006 and Platinum on Friday 15 December 2006) / US: Columbia 828768028025 (CD album, housed in a 20-page clothbound booklet sleeve) / US: Columbia 828768143926 (CD album, 'Best Buy' edition housed in a 20-page clothbound booklet sleeve and packaged with a one track CD single 'Island Jam' (US: Columbia 82876814392) in a card sleeve, released Tuesday 7 March 2006; highest chart position No. 6 *Billboard* '200' on Saturday 23 March 2006).

At the 49th Grammy Awards, held at the Staples Center, Los Angeles, on Sunday 11 February 2007 'Castellorizon' was nominated for "Best Rock Instrumental Performance" losing out to 'The Wizard Turns On... The Giant Silver Flashlight And Puts On His Werewolf Moccasins' by the Flaming Lips.

APRIL 2006 ◄
Live Selections from On an Island
Track list: 'On An Island' / 'Take A Breath' / 'This Heaven' [taken from the *AOL Sessions*, Sony Studios, New York, USA on Friday 7 April 2006].
US: Columbia 82876875262 (Promotional CD).

APRIL 2006
Live Selections from On an Island
Track list: 'On An Island' / 'Comfortably Numb' / David Gilmour interview [taken from the *AOL Sessions*, Sony Studios, New York, USA on Friday 7 April 2006].
US: Columbia 88697037262 (Promotional CD).

MONDAY 5 JUNE 2006
'Smile'
UK: EMI CDEMDJ (Promotional CD single) / Limited edition download, packaged in a numbered CD single sleeve, and given away on the UK tour).

MONDAY 5 JUNE 2006
'Smile' / 'Island Jam'
UK: EMI CDEM 696 (CD single) / UK: EMI EM 696 (Limited edition 7-inch single on clear vinyl; Highest chart position No. 72 (*Music Week* "Official Singles Chart" on Saturday 17 June 2006).

SEPTEMBER 2006
4 Tracks Live From Abbey Road, August 2006
Track list: 'The Blue' / 'On An Island' / 'Take A Breath' / 'Smile'
US: Columbia 66897143342 (Promotional CD, issued to the PBS Network Channel recorded live at Abbey Road Studios, London, England on 29 August 2006).

MONDAY 27 NOVEMBER 2006
Live and in Session
Track list: 'Take A Breath' [from the Royal Albert Hall, London, England March 2006] / 'Astronomy Domine' [taken from the Abbey Road session filmed on Tuesday 29 August 2006] / 'On An Island' / 'This Heaven' / 'Smile' / 'Take A Breath' / 'High Hopes' / 'Comfortably Numb' [taken from the *AOL Sessions*, Sony Studios, New York, on Friday 7 April 2006].

UK: EMI 094638372394 (Limited edition DVD video) / US: Columbia Music Video CVD 91532 (Limited edition DVD video, released Tuesday 28 November 2006). Both were initially sold exclusively through the David Gilmour online shop for a few days only, with the limitation of one DVD per customer. The DVD was shipped with David Gilmour's 2006 tour programme and an insert with the following text: "Dear Fan, Please accept this complimentary tour book as a thank you for your dedication to David and his work". In the US this also came as a limited-edition double-pack sold with *On an Island*.

MONDAY 27 NOVEMBER 2006
On an Island / Live and in Session
Track list: Live And In Session: 'Take A Breath' [from the Royal Albert Hall, London, England March 2006] / 'Astronomy Domine' [taken from the Abbey Road session filmed on Tuesday 29 August 2006] / 'On An Island' / 'This Heaven' / 'Smile' / 'Take A Breath' / 'High Hopes' / 'Comfortably Numb' [taken from the AOL Sessions, Sony Studios, New York, New York, USA on Friday 7 April 2006].
UK: EMI 094637847626 (Limited-edition CD album, with bonus Live and in Session DVD video).

MONDAY 25 DECEMBER 2006 ►
'Arnold Layne' (featuring David Bowie) / 'Arnold Layne' (featuring Richard Wright) / 'Dark Globe'
UK: EMI CDEMDJ 717 (Promotional CD) UK: EMI CDEM 717 (CD single).
'Arnold Layne' (featuring David Bowie) / 'Arnold Layne' (featuring Richard Wright) / 'Dark Globe'
UK: EMI EM 701 (Limited-edition 7-inch single).
Highest chart position No. 19 (*Music Week* "Official Singles Chart" on Saturday 6 January 2007).

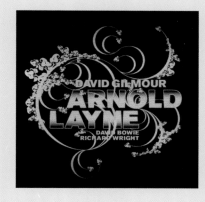

TUESDAY 26 DECEMBER 2006
'Arnold Layne' (featuring David Bowie) / 'Arnold Layne' (featuring Richard Wright) / 'Dark Globe'
US: Columbia 886970502511 (Limited-edition 10-inch single).
'Arnold Layne' (featuring David Bowie) / 'Arnold Layne' (featuring Richard Wright) / 'Dark Globe'
US: EMI CDEMDJ 717 (Promotional CD).
Both versions of 'Arnold Layne' were recorded live at the Royal Albert Hall, London, England on 29 and 30 May 2006 and 'Dark Globe' at Burg Clam, Klam, Austria on Thursday 27 July 2006.

REMEMBER THAT NIGHT

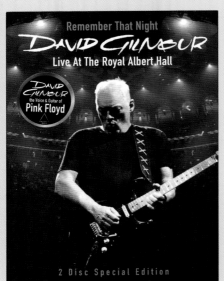

The live concert DVD recorded live at the Royal Albert Hall, London, England on Monday 29 and Tuesday 30 May 2006. Superbly filmed, if perhaps a little clinical in the sound production, it is nevertheless a superb document of Gilmour's *On an Island* tour. The DVD contains a bonus documentary with the curious inclusion of an awkward encounter between Roger Waters and David Gilmour, who were both rehearsing their tours at the same studio facility.

WEDNESDAY 18 JULY 2007 ◄
Remember That Night: Test Disc
UK: Media Motion 5043129 (Promotional double DVD video, dated 18 July 2007 on the disc). Track list the same as DVD1 of the catalogue edition.

MONDAY 6 AUGUST 2007
PAL Disc 1 & 2
UK: The Pavement (Promotional double DVD video, dated 6 August on the disc).
Track list the same as DVD1 and DVD2 of the catalogue edition of *Remember That Night*.

WEDNESDAY 8 AUGUST 2007
Remember That Night: Test Disc 1 & 2
UK: Media Motion 5043129 / 5043159 (Promotional double DVD video, dated 8 August 2007 on the disc).
Track list the same as DVD1 and DVD2 of the catalogue edition.

SEPTEMBER 2007
Remember That Night
UK: EMI (Promotional DVD video, with white labels and paper insert).
Track list the same as DVD1 of the catalogue edition.

SEPTEMBER 2007
'Fat Old Sun'
UK: EMI (Promotional DVD video, with running time 6'22" printed on disc).

SEPTEMBER 2007
Remember That Night: Wish You Were Here
Track list: 'Wish You Were Here' / 'The Blue' / 'Comfortably Numb'.
UK: EMI CDEMDJ 732 (Promotional CD recorded live at the Royal Albert Hall, London, England on Monday 29 & Tuesday 30 May 2006).

SEPTEMBER 2007
Remember That Night: 5 Live Tracks
Track list: 'Wish You Were Here' / 'On An Island' (featuring David Crosby and Graham Nash) / 'Comfortably Numb' (featuring David Bowie) / 'Shine On You Crazy Diamond, Parts 1–5' (featuring David Crosby and Graham Nash) / 'The Blue' (featuring David Crosby and Graham Nash).
US: Columbia 88697146352 (Promotional CD recorded live at the Royal Albert Hall, London, England on Monday 29 and Tuesday 30 May 2006).

MONDAY 17 SEPTEMBER 2007
Remember That Night
DVD1: Live from the Royal Albert Hall, London, England on Monday 29 & Tuesday 30 May 2006: 'Speak To Me' / 'Breathe' / 'Time' / 'Breathe (Reprise)' / 'Castellorizon' / 'On An Island' (featuring David Crosby and Graham Nash) / 'The Blue' (featuring David Crosby and Graham Nash) / 'Take A Breath' / 'Red Sky At Night' / 'This Heaven' / 'Then I Close My Eyes' (featuring Robert Wyatt) / 'Smile' / 'A Pocketful Of Stones' / 'Where We Start' / 'Shine On You Crazy Diamond, Parts 1–5' (featuring David Crosby and Graham Nash) / 'Fat Old Sun' / 'Coming Back To Life' / 'High Hopes' / 'Echoes' / 'Wish You Were Here' / 'Find The Cost Of Freedom' (featuring David Crosby and Graham Nash) / 'Arnold Layne' (featuring David Bowie) / 'Comfortably Numb' (featuring David Bowie) / DVD2: 'Wot's… Uh The Deal' / 'Dominoes' / 'Wearing The Inside Out' (featuring Richard Wright) / 'Arnold Layne' (featuring Richard Wright) / Live from Burg Clam, Klam, near Linz, Austria on Thursday 27 July 2006: 'Dark Globe' / Live from Abbey Road Studios, London, England on Tuesday 29 August 2006: 'Astronomy Domine' / Live from *AOL Sessions*, Sony Studios, New York, New York, USA on Friday 7 April 2006: 'This Heaven' / Live from the Mermaid Theatre, London, England on Tuesday 7 March 2006: 'Castellorizon' / 'On An Island' / 'The Blue', 'Take A Breath' / 'High Hopes' / Promo video's: 'On An Island' / 'Smile' / 'Island Jam' / Documentaries: 'Breaking Bread – Drinking Wine' / 'The Making of *On an Island*' / 'The West Coast' / Photo Gallery.

UK: EMI 5043119 (Double DVD video) / UK: EMI 5043099 (Blu-ray Disc; Certified Gold and Platinum on Friday 26 October 2008) / US: Columbia 88697074249 (Double DVD video) / US: Columbia 82876814392 (Double DVD video, Best Buy stores edition and packaged with a CD EP with the tracks: 'On An Island' / 'Take A Breath' / 'High Hopes' (live from the AOL Sessions)) / US: Columbia SMV BR713913 (Blu-ray Disc) released Tuesday 18 September 2007.

LIVE IN GDAŃSK

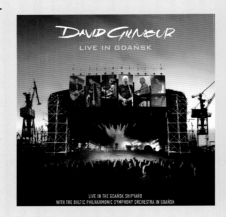

A further live concert documentary recorded from the final date of the *On an Island* tour at the Gdańsk Shipyards, Poland on Saturday 26 August 2006. *Live in Gdańsk* was released in no less than five different formats, including the audio and video recording of the concert, a 36-minute video documentary that includes Gilmour's private meeting with former president Lech Walesa, chats with the band and crew, concert rehearsals and a moving wreath-laying with Walesa at the memorial to the shipyard workers killed in the 1970 uprising. The concert film and Gdańsk Diary was directed by Gavin Elder and produced by Dione Orrom. The audio was produced by David Gilmour and Phil Manzanera, with Audio Mixing by Andy Jackson, David Gilmour, Devin Workman and Damon Iddins. The concert film was screened in 5.1 surround sound to over 160 cinemas in the US and Canada on Monday 22 September 2008, which was followed by a two-part programme beginning with *Dave Gilmour Live at Gdańsk* broadcast on BBC4 TV on Friday 26 September 2008 between 9.10pm and 10.10pm and *Dave Gilmour Gdańsk Diary* broadcast between 10.10pm and 10.40pm.

At the 51st Grammy Awards, held at the Staples Center, Los Angeles, on Sunday 8 February 2009, 'Castellorizon' was nominated for "Best Rock Instrumental Performance" losing out to 'Peaches En Regalia' by Zappa Plays Zappa featuring Steve Vai and Napoleon Murphy Brock.

JULY 2008 ▼
Live in Gdańsk: EPK
UK: EMI (Promotional DVD Electronic Press Kit, with running time 6'22" and NTSC DVD printed on disc).

JULY 2008
Live in Gdańsk: TV Spots
Track list: 1 x 30'/ 1 x 20'/ 1 x 10'TV spots).

UK: EMI (Promotional DVD TV adverts, with running time 4'10" and NTSC DVD printed on disc, timings as below and order #130151 printed on sleeve).

SEPTEMBER 2008
Live in Gdańsk
US: Columbia Creative Group (Promotional double CD and double DVD video, with source date 30 June 2008 printed on disc) / Columbia Creative Group Press 121 (Promotional double CD and DVD video, with the release date of 30 June 2008 printed on the disc and a sticker with the release date of 22 July 2008 on cover).

MONDAY 22 SEPTEMBER 2008
Live in Gdańsk
CD1: 'Speak To Me' / 'Breathe' / 'Time' / 'Breathe (Reprise)' / 'Castellorizon' / 'On An Island' / 'The Blue' / 'Red Sky At Night' / 'This Heaven' / 'Then I Close My Eyes' / 'Smile' / 'Take A Breath' / 'A Pocketful Of Stones' / 'Where We Start' / CD2: 'Shine On You Crazy Diamond' / 'Astronomy Dominé' / 'Fat Old Sun' / 'High Hopes' / 'Echoes' / 'Wish You Were Here' / 'A Great Day For Freedom' / 'Comfortably Numb'.

UK: EMI 5099923548923 (Double CD, in a fold-out card sleeve with 12-page booklet). Highest chart position No. 10 (*Official Albums Chart* "UK Top 100" on Saturday 4 October 2008). Certified Gold and Silver on Friday 14 November 2008 / US: Columbia 886973447024 (As above, released Tuesday 23 September 2008). Highest chart position No. 26 (*Billboard* "200" on Saturday 11 October 2008).

MONDAY 22 SEPTEMBER 2008
Live in Gdańsk: 3 Disc Edition
CD1 and CD2 as above. DVD track list: 'Castellorizon' / 'On An Island' / 'The Blue' / 'Red Sky At Night' / 'This Heaven' / 'Then I Close My Eyes' / 'Smile' / 'Take A Breath' / 'A Pocketful Of Stones' / 'Where We Start' / 'Astronomy Dominé' / 'High Hopes' / 'Echoes' / 'A Great Day For Freedom' / 'Comfortably Numb' / Gdańsk Diary [a 36-minute film documenting the concert].

UK: EMI 5099923548923 (Double CD and single DVD concert video, in a fold-out card sleeve and 12-page booklet) / US: Columbia 88697345462 (As above, released Tuesday 23 September 2008).

MONDAY 22 SEPTEMBER 2008
Live in Gdańsk: 4 Disc Edition
CD1, CD2 and DVD as above. DVD2 track list: Live from the Mermaid Theatre, London, 7 March 2006: 'Shine On You Crazy Diamond' / 'Wearing The Inside Out' / 'Comfortably Numb' / Live from the AOL Sessions, Sony Studios, New York, USA on 7 April 2006: 'On An Island' / 'High Hopes' / Live from Abbey Road, London, 29 August 2006: 'The Blue' / 'Take A Breath' / 'Echoes' (Acoustic) / Barn Jams 2007 (previously unreleased), recorded live in the UK, January 2007: 'Barn Jam 166' / 'Barn Jam 192' / 'Barn Jam 121' / Complete audio 5.1 surround sound version of *On an Island*.

The personnel on the 'Barn Jams' comprised David Gilmour (Guitar, Drums), Richard Wright (Keyboards), Guy Pratt (Bass, Guitar) and Steve DiStanislao (Drums, Bass).

UK: EMI 5099923549326 (Promotional Double CD and Double DVD video in a box, no booklet) / UK: EMI 5099923549326 (Double CD and double DVD video in a fold-out card sleeve and 12-page booklet) / US: Columbia 88697345472 (As above, released Tuesday 23 September 2008).

MONDAY 22 SEPTEMBER 2008
Live in Gdańsk: 5 Disc Special Edition
CD1, CD2, DVD1 and DVD2 as above. Bonus CD track list: 'Shine On You Crazy Diamond' [Vienne, Monday 31 July & Venice, Saturday 12 August] / 'Dominoes' [Paris, Wednesday 15 March] / 'The Blue' [Vienne, Monday 31 July] / 'Take A Breath' [Munich, Saturday 29 July] / 'Wish You Were Here' [Glasgow, Saturday 27 May] / 'Coming Back To Life' [Florence, Wednesday 2 August] / 'Find The Cost Of Freedom' [Manchester, Friday 26 May] / 'This Heaven' [Vienne, Monday 31 July] / 'Wearing The Inside Out' [Milan, Saturday 25 March] / 'A Pocketful Of Stones' [Vienne, Monday 31 July] / 'Where We Start' [Vienne, Monday 31 July] / 'On The Turning Away' [Venice, Thursday 31 August].

UK: EMI 5099923548428 (Double CD, double DVD and bonus CD in a deluxe box set with 24-page booklet and "collectable" memorabilia) / US: Columbia 886973454824 (As above, released Tuesday 23 September 2008).

MONDAY 22 SEPTEMBER 2008
Live in Gdańsk: 5 Vinyl Special Edition
Side 1: 'Speak To Me' / 'Breathe' / 'Time' / 'Breathe (Reprise)' / 'Castellorizon' / 'On An Island' / Side 2: 'The Blue' / 'Red Sky At Night' / 'This Heaven' / Side 3: 'Then I Close My Eyes' / 'Smile' / 'Take A Breath' / Side 4: 'A Pocketful Of Stones' / 'Where We Start' / Side 5: 'Shine On You Crazy Diamond' / 'Wot's… Uh The Deal' / Side 6: 'Astronomy Domine' / 'Fat Old Sun' / 'High Hopes' / Side 7: 'Echoes' / Side 8: 'Wish You Were Here' / 'A Great Day For Freedom' / 'Comfortably Numb' / Side 9: 'On The Turning Away' (Venice, 31 August) / Side 10: 'Barn Jam 166' / 'Barn Jam 121'.

UK: EMI 5099923548411 (Five vinyl album box set, with 20-page booklet, plus web pass to download the album) / US: Columbia 886973850923 (As above, released Tuesday 23 September 2008).

MONDAY 22 SEPTEMBER 2008
'Wot's… Uh The Deal'
US: Columbia 88697369392 (CD single, in a card sleeve given away free with *Live in Gdańsk* at selected independent record stores).

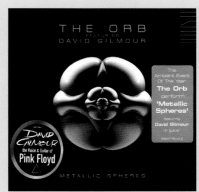

THE ORB FEATURING DAVID GILMOUR ▶

An unexpected, but not unlikely, collaboration saw Gilmour and the Orb release a double album of instrumental soundscapes. All artist royalties contributed to the support of Scottish hacker Gary McKinnon, who was diagnosed with Asperger's and accused of hacking into 97 United States military and NASA computers over a 13-month period between February 2001 and March 2002, using the name 'Solo'. For many years he faced extradition to the USA where it was felt by his supporters that he would receive an unfair hearing. The album was recorded at the Dreaming Cave, London, in June 2009 and produced by Youth and features David Gilmour (Guitars, Vocals), Alex Paterson (Sound Manipulation, Keyboards, Turntables), Youth (Bass, Keyboards, Programming), Tim Bran (Keyboards, Programming), Marcia Mello (Guitar on 'Black Graham') and Dominique Le Vac (Backing Vocals).

MONDAY 11 OCTOBER 2010
Metallic Spheres
Track list: Metallic Side: 'Metallic Spheres' / 'Hymns To The Sun' / 'Black Graham' / 'Hiding In Plain View' / 'Classified' / Sphere Side: 'Es Vedra' / 'Hymns To The Sun (Reprise)' / 'Olympic' / 'Chicago Dub' / 'Bold Knife Trophy'.
UK: Columbia 886977604423 (CD album) / UK: Columbia 886977828621 (Double CD album, in a fold out card sleeve). Highest chart position No. 12 (*Official Albums Chart* "UK Top 100" on Saturday 23 October 2010) / US: Columbia 886977604423 (As above, released Tuesday 12 October 2010; Highest chart position No. 73 *Billboard* "Billboard 200" on Saturday 30 October 2010).

MONDAY 11 OCTOBER 2010
Metallic Spheres
CD1 as above / CD2: Metallic Side 3D60 version: 'Metallic Spheres' / 'Hymns To The Sun' / 'Black Graham' / 'Hiding In Plain View' / 'Classified' / Sphere Side 3D60 version: 'Es Vedra' / 'Hymns To The Sun (Reprise)' / 'Olympic' / 'Chicago Dub' / 'Bold Knife Trophy'.
UK: Columbia 886977964527 (Double CD album, includes 3D60 Version, in a fold-out card sleeve) / US: Columbia 886977964527 (As above, released Tuesday 12 October 2010).

MONDAY 11 OCTOBER 2010
Metallic Spheres
LP1: Metallic Side: 'Metallic Spheres' / 'Hymns To The Sun' / 'Black Graham' / 'Hiding In Plain View' / 'Classified' / LP2: Sphere Side: 'Es Vedra' / 'Hymns To The Sun (Reprise)' / 'Olympic' / 'Chicago Dub' / 'Bold Knife Trophy'.
UK: Columbia 886977604416 (Double vinyl album); US: Columbia 886977604416 (Double vinyl album, released Tuesday 12 October 2010).

RATTLE THAT LOCK

David Gilmour's third solo album had just been announced at time of going to press and therefore details are incomplete:

FRIDAY 18 SEPTEMBER 2015 ◄
Rattle That Lock
Track list: '5am' / 'Rattle That Lock' / 'Faces Of Stone' / 'A Boat Lies Waiting' / 'Dancing Right In Front Of Me' / 'In Any Tongue' / 'Beauty' / 'The Girl In The Yellow Dress' / 'Today' / 'And Then…'

FRIDAY 18 SEPTEMBER 2015
Rattle That Lock
CD track list as above / DVD: 'Barn Jam 1' / 'Barn Jam 2' / 'Barn Jam 3' / 'Barn Jam 4' (Barn Jams recorded and filmed in January 2007, featuring David Gilmour (Guitar), Richard Wright (Keyboards), Guy Pratt (Bass), Steve DiStanislao (Drums) / The Animators – Alisdair + Jock (documentary on makers of the 'Rattle That Lock' video) / 'Rattle That Lock' video / The Animators – Danny Madden (documentary on maker of 'The Girl In The Yellow Dress' video) / 'The Girl In The Yellow Dress' video / Polly Samson and David Gilmour at the Borris House Festival of Words and Ideas (documentary on their creative collaboration) / The making of the 'Rattle That Lock' album (documentary) / 'Rattle That Lock' Extended Mix (Audio) / 'The Girl In The Yellow Dress' Orchestral Version (Audio) / 'Rattle That Lock' Youth Mix – 12' Extended Radio Dub (Audio) / 'Rattle That Lock' Radio Edit (Audio) / *Rattle That Lock* album in 5.1 Surround Sound.

FRIDAY 18 SEPTEMBER 2015
Rattle That Lock
CD track list as above / Blu-ray Disc as DVD track list.

FRIDAY 18 SEPTEMBER 2015
Rattle That Lock
Side 1: '5am' / 'Rattle That Lock' / 'Faces Of Stone' / 'A Boat Lies Waiting' / 'Dancing Right In Front Of Me' / Side 2: 'In Any Tongue' / 'Beauty' / 'The Girl In The Yellow Dress' / 'Today' / 'And Then…'

DOWNLOADS

THURSDAY 22 DECEMBER 2005
Island Jam
DavidGilmour.com made available for download the track 'Island Jam'.

WEDNESDAY 15 FEBRUARY – TUESDAY 11 APRIL 2006
On an Island
DavidGilmour.com made available audio clips from what appeared to be out-takes from the album *On an Island* as well as a video clip of an extended version of 'On An Island'. However, the audio clips seemed to change daily, with a new clip put up each day. Eventually the same clips were repeated, while some clips remained up for more than one day. Each clip averaged around one minute, and there were 23 pieces in total. The tracks ran as follows:
Track 1: Wednesday 15 February (1:12) / Track 2: Sunday 19 February (0.42) / Track 3: Wednesday 8 March (1:02) / Track 4: Friday 10 March (1:04) / Track 5: Saturday 11 March (1:03) / Track 6: Wednesday 15 March (1:14) / Track 7: Thursday 16 March (1:06) / Track 8: Friday 17 March (1:12) / Track 9: Saturday 18 March (1:25) / Track 10: Tuesday 21 March (1:25) / Track 11: Wednesday 22 March (1:51) / Track 12: Thursday 23 March (1:06) / Track 13: Friday 24 March (1:03) / Track 14: Saturday 25 March (1:18) / Track 15: Sunday 26 March (1:04) / Track 16: Monday 27 March (1:14) / Track 17: Tuesday 28 March (1:15) / Track 18: Wednesday 29 March (1:05) / Track 19: Thursday 30 March (1:17) / Track 20: Friday 31 March (1:11) / Track 21: Thursday 6 April (0:42) / Track 22: Saturday 8 April (1:22) / Track 23: Tuesday 11 April (0:56).

SATURDAY 20 MAY 2006
On an Island
DavidGilmour.com made available an interview with Gilmour discussing the making of the album.

WEDNESDAY 7 JUNE 2006
'Smile' / 'Island Jam' (Demo)
DavidGilmour.com made available the video of 'Smile' and iTunes made available the single 'Smile' and the track 'Island Jam' (Demo).

SATURDAY 2 DECEMBER 2006
'Arnold Layne' / 'Dark Globe'
DavidGilmour.com made available a video of 'Arnold Layne' (with David Bowie lead vocals recorded at the Royal Albert Hall, London, England on Monday 29 May 2006) and three one-minute audio clips of all three tracks on the single including the same track, plus the Richard Wright lead vocal version recorded on Tuesday 30 May 2006) and 'Dark Globe' (taken from Burg Clam, Klam, Austria on Thursday 27 July 2006).

WEDNESDAY 20 DECEMBER 2006
'Dark Globe'
DavidGilmour.com made available a video of 'Dark Globe' taken from Burg Clam, Klam, Austria on Thursday 27 July 2006.

TUESDAY 14 JULY 2009
'Chicago'
The re-recording of the Graham Nash song 'Chicago' was made available for download coinciding with Gary McKinnon's judicial review application in the hope that he could stand trial on charges of computer hacking and serve any necessary jail time in the UK

SUNDAY 23 MAY 2010
'A Pocketful of Stones'
DavidGilmour.com made available for a limited period a video of him working on the recording of this track at his Astoria studio.

SUNDAY 4 JULY 2010
'This Heaven'
DavidGilmour.com made available for a limited period a video of him working on the recording of this track at his Astoria studio.

TUESDAY 6 MARCH 2011 – WEDNESDAY 7 MARCH 2012
'A Pocketful Of Stones'
DavidGilmour.com made available a free download this track from the album *On an Island* for a 48-hour period to mark the anniversary of the release of the album and David Gilmour's 66th birthday.

SOUNDTRACKS

TUESDAY 23 OCTOBER 1984
Give My Regards to Broad Street
Gilmour played guitars on the track 'No More Lonely Nights' (Ballad) featured on the soundtrack to this ill-received film made by Paul McCartney, which featured many re-workings of familiar Beatles songs. The film premiered on Tuesday 23 October 1984 in the US and Wednesday 28 November 1984 in the UK, and was first released on video in 1985. A video game based on the film was made for Commodore Sinclair ZX Spectrum. 'No More Lonely Nights' was nominated for a Golden Globe Award and a BAFTA Film Award for "Best Original Song – Motion Picture" and featured on the album *Give My Regards to Broad Street*.

FRIDAY 13 DECEMBER 1985
Legend
Gilmour played guitars on the track 'Is Your Love Strong Enough' by Bryan Ferry as featured on the closing credits to Ridley Scott's fantasy feature film starring Tom Cruise. This otherwise featured ambient soundscapes by Tangerine Dream, although their music replaced Jerry Goldsmith's original score, which was finally restored with the advent of the DVD release. The film premiered in the UK in December 1985 and was delayed to April 1986 in the US after it was edited. The film was first released on video in October 1986, and the DVD and Blu-ray Disc re-release also included the promo video for 'Is Your Love Strong Enough'. The track also featured on the *Original Motion Picture Soundtrack* released April 1986.

FRIDAY 21 FEBRUARY 1986
9½ Weeks
The soundtrack to this feature film starring Mickey Rourke and Kim Basinger featured the Bryan Ferry song 'Slave to Love' with David Gilmour on guitar. Also available on the *Original Motion Picture Soundtrack* released March 1986.

SATURDAY 26 MAY 1990
One World, One Voice
Gilmour contributed to a musical "chain letter" devised by Kevin Godley (of 10cc) which was produced for television together with a "making

of" documentary for the finale of BBC TV's *One World Week* under the title *One World, One Voice*. It was broadcast on BBC1 TV on Saturday 26 May 1990 between 8.20pm and 10.20pm as an untitled track under the heading of 'Howard Jones' with additional musicians Hossam Ramsey, Christopher Warren-Greene, Bob Geldof, Clara Sandroni, Mari Boine Persen, Roger Ludvigsen, Venice, Terence Trent d'Arby, the Lenningrad Symphony Orchestra and the Kodo Drummers. The film was first released on VHS video in April 1993.

MONDAY 30 DECEMBER 1991
Ruby Takes a Trip
Gilmour composed and performed the soundtrack music featured on this TV programme, featuring comedienne Ruby Wax heading for California and taking a semi-serious look at the search for the meaning of life in the land of the New Age. It was broadcast in the UK on BBC2 TV on Tuesday 31 December 1991 between 8.55pm and 10.05pm.

TUESDAY 26 MAY 1992
The Last Show on Earth
Gilmour composed and performed the soundtrack music featured on this TV environmental spectacular produced to coincide with the Earth Summit, which also included music by Kate Bush, Soul II Soul, Peter Gabriel, Elton John and Seal. It was broadcast in the UK on ITV TV on Wednesday 27 May 1992 between 8.00pm and 10.00pm.

THURSDAY 11 FEBRUARY 1993
The Cement Garden
Gilmour composed and performed the song 'Me And J.C.' for the soundtrack of this acclaimed cinematic film by Andrew Birkin, which premiered at the 43rd Berlin International Film Festival between Thursday 11 to Monday 22 February 1993 and won Andrew Birkin an award for Best Director. The film was released on video in January 1998.

TUESDAY 23 FEBRUARY & TUESDAY 2 MARCH 1993
Without Walls: The Art of Tripping
Gilmour composed and performed the soundtrack music featured on a two-part edition of this TV documentary. The programme was devised by Storm Thorgerson and dealt with the relationship between drug taking and the arts. It was broadcast in the UK on Channel 4 TV on Tuesday 23 February and Tuesday 2 March 1993 between 9.00pm and 10.00pm.

SUNDAY 1 SEPTEMBER 1996
Fractals: The Colours of Infinity
Gilmour composed and performed the instrumental soundtrack music featured on this made-for-video educational film by Nigel Lesmoir-Gordon entitled *Fractals: The Colours of Infinity – The Beauty of Power and Fractals* (UK: Prism Leisure Video PLATV 956 / US: Films For Humanities & Sciences FFH 7414) based on fractal geometry and hosted by Arthur C. Clarke. It was broadcast on Channel 4 TV in the UK on Sunday 1 September 1996 between 3.00am and 3.45am. A book with an accompanying DVD was released in March 2004 featuring the original documentary plus an additional 30-minute fractal animation film *Infinit*, also by Nigel Lesmoir-Gordon and set to the music of *The Infinity Project* and *Total Eclipse*. The DVD was reissued in October 2007 with additional film shorts *Clouds Are Not Spheres* and *Is God a Number?*.

SUNDAY 7 APRIL 2002
The Triumph of Love
Gilmour played guitar on the *Original Motion Picture Soundtrack* on the tracks 'Follow That Young… Person', 'Agis And The Phocion: The Archer', 'I Am Aspasie', 'The Grotto', 'Phocion!' and 'Phocion! (Reprise)', as featured on the soundtrack to this cinematic film by Clare Peploe and scored by Jason Osborn. The film premiered at the Venice

Film Festival on Thursday 6 September 2001, in the US on Wednesday 17 April 2002, and in the UK on Friday 8 October 2004. *The Original Motion Picture Soundtrack* CD album was released in October 2001 and released on DVD on October 2002.

FRIDAY 1 AUGUST 2008
Swing Vote
The track 'Murder', taken from the album *About Face*, appeared in the feature film, starring Kevin Costner. It was released to theatres in the US on Friday 1 August 2008 and released on DVD in January 2009. The *Original Motion Picture Soundtrack* CD album was released in July 2008.

SUNDAY 31 MAY 2009
A Time Comes: The Story of the Kingsnorth Six
Gilmour co-wrote with Nick Laird-Clowes and also played guitar and sang backing vocals on the track 'Mayday', on which Guy Pratt also played bass, which featured on the 20-minute film by Nick Broomfield about Greenpeace activists who scaled a 220m chimney at the proposed site of a new coal-fired power station at Kingsnorth in Kent. The activists were arrested and charged with £30,000 worth of criminal damage, but remarkably the court case that followed drew support from leading scientists and their subsequent acquittal forced a change in government policy. Greenpeace enabled a free download of the song and accompanying film from its website from Sunday 31 May 2009 as well as a free mail-order DVD to readers of the *Observer* newspaper in its Sunday 31 May 2009 and the *Guardian* newspaper in its Monday 1 June 2009 editions.

SATURDAY 10 MARCH 2012
Bullets & Daffodils, Forum Theatre, Chester, England
Gilmour gifted the track 'There's No Way Out of Here' as the theme song of what was billed as a 'Rock Interpretation of the Timeless Tale' – a contemporary theatre piece which set the war poems of Wilfred Owen to music. The production, which premiered on this date, was directed and adapted by John Gorman (of the Scaffold) which used the track as its centrepiece. Other incidental music was composed by Sean Pugh (Flock Of Seagulls and the Triffids). The show went on to tour the North of England through 2012 before enjoying a residency in London's West End at the Tristan Bates Theatre, Covent Garden, London (Monday 1 to Saturday 6 July 2013).

PRODUCTION, COMPOSITION & GUEST APPEARANCES

JANUARY 1970 – SYD BARRETT
The Madcap Laughs
See Syd Barrett section for contribution and release details.

NOVEMBER 1970 – SYD BARRETT
Barrett
See Syd Barrett section for contribution and release details.

AUGUST 1974 – UNICORN
Blue Pine Trees
Produced by Gilmour, who played guitar on the track 'Electric Night' and pedal steel guitar on the tracks 'Ooh! Mother', 'Sleep Song', 'Autumn Wine', 'Just Wanna Hold You' and 'The Farmer' and backing vocals on 'Nightingale Crescent'. David Gilmour recalled that, "Unicorn were playing at the wedding reception of an old friend of mine, Rick Hopper. When I first saw them and while I was impressed by their vocal harmonies, their tightness and the fact that it was the drummer that sang the lead vocals, it was the songs themselves that I liked the best. Ken Baker's songs, while firmly seated in the American country rock genre,

had a very original and unusual wry English feel in the stories he told. The one that really made me notice was 'Sleep Song', about a trip to the dentist. Not a common subject for the popular song. Largely on the strength of this I invited them to my tiny home studio in Essex to record some demos. This was the start of an association that was to cover two and a half albums over the next couple of years."

MAY 1975 – ROY HARPER
HQ
Gilmour played guitars on the track 'The Game, Parts 1–5'.

MAY 1975 – UNICORN
'I'll Believe In You (The Hymn)' / 'Take It Easy'
Non-album tracks produced by Gilmour.

SEPTEMBER 1975 – SUTHERLAND BROTHERS & QUIVER
Reach for the Sky
Gilmour played pedal steel guitar on the track 'Ain't Too Proud'.

OCTOBER 1975 – DAVID COURTNEY
First Day
Gilmour played guitars on 'When Your Life Is Your Own'.

MARCH 1976 – UNICORN
Too Many Crooks
Gilmour produced the album and played pedal steel guitar on the title track. Gilmour also covered 'No Way Out Of Here' on his debut solo album as 'There's No Way Out Of Here'.

JANUARY 1977 – RACHID BAHRIRI
Rachid Bahriri
Gilmour played guitars on the tracks 'Olivier de Cromwell Road' and 'Il Survivra', the latter also featuring Nick Mason on drums. The album, including these two tracks, also featured contributions from Rick Wills, Willie Wilson and Tim Renwick.

OCTOBER 1977 – UNICORN
One More Tomorrow
Gilmour produced all but the first four tracks on this album, Side 2 of which was recorded at Britannia Row studios, and played guitar on the tracks 'The Way It Goes' and 'So Hard To Get Through' and pedal steel guitar on 'I'm Alright (When I'm With You)'.

FEBRUARY 1978 – KATE BUSH
The Kick Inside
Gilmour is credited as executive producer on 'The Saxophone Song' and 'The Man With The Child In His Eyes'.

JUNE 1979 – WINGS
Back to the Egg
Gilmour played guitars on 'Rockestra Theme' and 'So Glad To See You Here' as part of the supergroup Rockestra.

JUNE 1980 – ROY HARPER
Unknown Soldier
Gilmour co-wrote and played guitars on the tracks 'Playing Games', 'True Story', 'Old Faces', 'Short And Sweet', and 'You (The Game, Part 2)'.

SEPTEMBER 1980 – KATE BUSH
'Army Dreamers' / 'Passing Through Air'
Gilmour played guitars, produced and engineered the non-album B-side track 'Passing Through Air', which was originally recorded in 1973, and taken from the 1980 album *Never Forever*.

DECEMBER 1981 – HOLLY & THE IVY'S
'Christmas On 45'
Gilmour contributed to this spoof single co-written with Nick Laird-Clowes.

SEPTEMBER 1982 – KATE BUSH
The Dreaming
Gilmour provided backing vocals on the track 'Pull Out The Pin'.

OCTOBER 1982 – DOLL BY DOLL
Grand Passion
Gilmour played guitars on the track 'Boxers Hit Harder When Women Are Around'.

JUNE 1983 – ATOMIC ROOSTER
Headline News
Gilmour played guitars on the tracks 'Hold Your Fire', 'Metal Minds', 'Land Of Freedom' and 'Time'.

MARCH 1985 – JOHN 'RABBIT' BUNDRICK
The Rabbit Archive Vol. 5
Gilmour produced the track 'Rabbit Gets Loose'.

FEBRUARY 1985 – ROY HARPER & JIMMY PAGE
Whatever Happened to Jugula?
Gilmour co-wrote the track 'Hope' with Harper. The track originated as a tune written by Gilmour for his second solo album *About Face*. He asked Pete Townshend to supply lyrics, but then felt that he couldn't relate to them, so Townshend used the song instead, as 'White City Fighting', with Gilmour playing guitar, on his album *White City: A Novel*. Gilmour sent the same tune to Harper, whose lyrics had the same effect on Gilmour. Harper used the result, on this album, with his son Nick Harper (16 years old at the time) playing the lead guitar, and not Gilmour as is often mistakenly stated.

MAY 1985 – SUPERTRAMP
Brother Where You Bound
Gilmour played guitar solo on the title track.

JUNE 1985 – BRYAN FERRY
Boys and Girls
Gilmour played guitars on the title track, 'The Chosen One', 'Sensation', 'Slave To Love' and possibly others. 'Slave To Love' was also featured on the *Original Motion Picture Soundtrack* to the feature film *9½ Weeks* starring Mickey Rourke and Kim Basinger (see Soundtracks for film and video releases).

JULY 1985 – MASON & FENN
Profiles
Gilmour provided vocals on the track 'Lie For A Lie'. See Nick Mason section for release details.

SEPTEMBER 1985 – THE DREAM ACADEMY
The Dream Academy
Gilmour played guitars on the tracks 'Bound To Be' and 'The Party'. All tracks except one were co-produced by Gilmour.

OCTOBER 1985 – GRACE JONES
Slave to the Rhythm
Gilmour's guitar samples were used on the title track and 'The Fashion Show' but he was not credited.

NOVEMBER 1985 – ARCADIA
So Red the Rose
Gilmour played guitars on the track 'The Promise' and 'Missing'.

NOVEMBER 1985 – THE DREAM ACADEMY
'Please, Please, Please Let Me Get What I Want' / 'In Places On The Run'
Non-album single tracks co-produced by Gilmour.

DECEMBER 1985 – PETE TOWNSHEND
White City: A Novel
Gilmour played guitars on and co-wrote the track 'White City Fighting' and played guitars on 'Give Blood' and 'Magic Bus' (Live) and 'Won't Get Fooled Again' (Live) recorded at the Deep End concert at the Academy, Brixton, London, England on Sunday 3 November 1985 and later released on the album *Deep End Live!*

JUNE 1986 – ROY HARPER
In Between Every Line
Gilmour co-wrote the tracks 'Short And Sweet', 'True Story' and 'The Game' with Harper but did not appear on this live album.

AUGUST 1986 – LIONA BOYD
Persona
Gilmour played guitars on the tracks 'L'Enfant', 'Sorceress' and 'Persona'.

OCTOBER 1986 – BERLIN
Count 3 and Pray
Gilmour played guitars on the track 'Pink And Velvet'.

JANUARY 1987 – JOHN WETTON & PHIL MANZANERA
Wetton Manzanera
Gilmour co-wrote 'Talk To Me' with John Wetton, Phil Manzenera and Billy Nicolls.

APRIL 1987 – DALBELLO
She
Gilmour played guitars on the track 'Immaculate Eyes'.

NOVEMBER 1987 – BRYAN FERRY
Bête Noire
Gilmour played guitars on the tracks 'Seven Deadly Sins', 'Day For Night', 'New Town', 'Kiss And Tell', 'Limbo' and possibly 'The Right Stuff'.

OCTOBER 1987 – VARIOUS ARTISTS
The Secret Policeman's Third Ball: The Music
Gilmour played on the track 'Running Up That Hill' with Kate Bush's band on this album of highlights from the charity event of the same name, recorded at the Palladium, London, on Saturday 28 and Sunday 29 March 1987.

AUGUST 1988 – SAM BROWN
Stop!
Gilmour played guitars on the tracks 'This Feeling' and 'I'll Be In Love'. Gilmour also featured on the promo video of the same track.

AUGUST 1988 – JOHN 'RABBIT' BUNDRICK
Dream Jungle
Gilmour played guitars on 'Through The Clouds' and 'Conquest' and is credited as 'Studio Visitor'.

AUGUST 1988 – PETER CETERA
One More Story
Gilmour played guitars on the tracks 'You Never Listen To Me' and 'Body Language (There In The Dark)'.

MAY 1989 – KIRSTY MACCOLL
Kite
Gilmour played guitars on the tracks 'You And Me Baby' and 'No Victims'.

JUNE 1989 – PAUL MCCARTNEY
Flowers in the Dirt
Gilmour played guitars on the track 'We Got Married'.

JUNE 1989 – VARIOUS ARTISTS
Spirit of the Forest
Gilmour provided vocals for this double A-side multi-artist production, which also appeared on the album *Earthrise*. Gilmour was interviewed and filmed recording his contribution as part of a programme highlighting the plight of the rainforests and the making of the single for BBC2 TV's *Spirit of the Rainforest*, broadcast in the UK on Monday 5 June 1989 between 7.30pm and 8.00pm.

SEPTEMBER 1989 – VICKY BROWN
Lady of Time
Gilmour (credited as Mr. E. Guest) played guitars on the track 'Can't Let Go'.

OCTOBER 1989 – KATE BUSH
The Sensual World
Gilmour played guitars on the tracks 'Love And Anger' and 'Rocket's Tail (For Rocket)'.

OCTOBER 1989 – WARREN ZEVON
Transverse City
Gilmour played guitars on the track 'Run Straight Down'.

MONDAY 4 DECEMBER 1989 – VARIOUS ARTISTS
Smoke on the Water – The Video Collection
Gilmour played guitar on the track 'Smoke On The Water'. The bonus DVD also contains the 40-minute documentary *The Making of Smoke on the Water*, released for the first time on DVD (until now it was only available on VHS and Japanese Laserdisc with Japanese subtitles), the six-minute promo video (EPK) featuring extracts from the documentary and the full song, and a further two-minute documentary *Where the Money's Going: Rock Aid Armenia's Visit to the Octet Music School in Gyumri*.

JANUARY 1990 – VARIOUS ARTISTS
Rock Aid Armenia – The Earthquake Album
Gilmour played guitars on the track 'Smoke On The Water'. As part of the record promotion the BBC did a live broadcast to the USSR on Thursday 21 November 1989. Millions of people tuned in to hear Ian Gillan, David Gilmour and Bruce Dickinson being interviewed about their role in the *Rock Aid Armenia* project and the footage included Gilmour explaining why he hadn't asked Ian Gillan to join Pink Floyd: "We couldn't afford him." The footage was thought to have been lost but turned up in December 2013 and was posted on YouTube.

MARCH 1990 – ANDREAS ROÉ
Roé
Gilmour played guitars on the track 'Como El Agua'.

APRIL 1990 – SAM BROWN
April Moon
Gilmour provided backing vocals on the track 'Troubled Soul'.

MAY 1990 – ROY HARPER
Once
Gilmour played guitars on the tracks 'Once', 'Once In The Middle Of Nowhere' and 'Berliners (A Better World)'.

MAY 1990 – PROPAGANDA
1234
Gilmour played guitars on the track 'Only One Word'.

JUNE 1990 – VARIOUS ARTISTS
One World, One Voice
Gilmour contributed to the track 'We Will Meet Again, Everybody's Got A Hole To Fill' featuring Christopher Warren-Greene, Venice, Howard Jones, Terence Trent d'Arby and Bob Geldof. The musical "chain letter" comprised 22 tracks and was devised by Kevin Godley (of 10cc). A film of the entire album was produced for television together with a "making of" documentary for the finale of BBC TV's *One World Week* under the title *One World, One Voice*. It was broadcast on BBC1 TV on Saturday 26 May 1990 between 8.20pm and 10.20pm and released on VHS video as an untitled track under the heading of Howard Jones with additional musicians Hossam Ramsey, Christopher Warren-Greene, Bob Geldof, Clara Sandroni, Mari Boine Persen, Roger Ludvigsen, Venice, Terence Trent d'Arby, the Lenningrad Symphony Orchestra and the Kodo Drummers.

JUNE 1990 – PAUL YOUNG
Other Voices
Gilmour played guitars on the tracks 'Heaven Can Wait' and 'A Little Bit Of Love'.

AUGUST 1990 – JOHN MARTYN
The Apprentice Tour Live
Gilmour played guitar on the tracks 'The Easy Blues', 'Dealer', 'Sapphire', 'John Wayne' and 'One World' at this concert filmed on Saturday 31 March 1990 at the Shaw Theatre, London, England.

NOVEMBER 1990 – BLUE PEARL
Naked
Gilmour played guitars on the tracks 'Running Up That Hill' and 'Alive', the latter of which also featured Richard Wright on keyboards.

DECEMBER 1990 – VICKI BROWN
About Love and Life
Gilmour played guitars on the track 'I'll Always Be Waiting'.

DECEMBER 1990 – THE DREAM ACADEMY
A Different Kind of Weather
All tracks co-produced by Gilmour (except 'Love'). He also co-wrote the music for 'Twelve-Eight Angel' with Nick Laird-Clowes on which he also played guitar, bass-synth and vocals; played guitar on 'Mercy Killing'; played guitar solo, bass and vocals on 'It'll Never Happen Again'; and played guitar on 'Forest Fire'.

DECEMBER 1990 – MICHAEL KAMEN
Concerto for Saxophone
Gilmour played guitars on the track 'Sasha' which plays out the end credits to this documentary chronicling the creation of Michael Kamen's *Concerto for Saxophone*, with music videos of all three movements. Also released on DVD and Laserdisc video featuring an interview with David Gilmour.

FEBRUARY 1991 – VARIOUS ARTISTS
'The Stonk'
Gilmour played guitars on the title track of this charity record for Comic Relief by comedians Hale And Pace as a member of the backing band the Stonkers and also appeared in the promotional video film of the same title.

MARCH 1991 – THE LAW
The Law
Gilmour played guitars on the track 'Stone'.

AUGUST 1991 – ALL ABOUT EVE
Touched by Jesus
Gilmour played guitars on the tracks 'Wishing The Hours Away' and 'Are You Lonely'.

JUNE 1992 – VARIOUS ARTISTS
Earthrise: The Rainforest Album
Gilmour provided vocals on the track 'The Spirit Of The Forest' UK: Polygram TV 515 419-1 (Vinyl album). The video release also includes the Pink Floyd promo video of 'Learning To Fly'. *Earthrise* was dubbed as the 'Official United Nations Earth Summit Album'.

JUNE 1992 – ELTON JOHN
The One
Gilmour played guitars on the track 'Understanding Women' originally recorded for the four-CD box set *To Be Continued...*

JULY 1992 – JIMMY NAIL
Growing up in Public
Gilmour played guitars on the tracks 'Waiting For The Sunshine' and 'Only Love (Can Bring Us Home)'. The album was co-produced by Guy Pratt.

AUGUST 1992 – JOHN MARTYN
Couldn't Love You More
Gilmour played guitars on the tracks 'Ways To Cry', 'Could've Been Me' and 'One World'.

JULY 1993 – JOHN MARTYN
No Little Boy
Essentially a reworking of the album *Couldn't Love You More*, this release also contains the tracks 'Ways To Cry', 'Could've Been Me' and 'One World'.

JULY 1993 – PAUL RODGERS
Muddy Water Blues
Gilmour played guitars on the track 'Standing Around Crying'.

JANUARY 1994 – CHRIS JAGGER
Atcha
Gilmour played guitars on the track 'Steal The Time'.

JANUARY 1994 – SNOWY WHITE
Highway to the Sun
Gilmour played guitars on the track 'Love, Pain And Sorrow'.

JULY 1995 – JOHN MARTYN
Live
Gilmour played guitar on the tracks 'Easy Blues', 'Dealer', 'Sapphire', 'Fisherman's Dream', 'Big Muff', 'John Wayne' and 'Johnny Too Bad' at this John Martyn concert recorded at the Shaw Theatre, London, England on Saturday 31 March 1990.

OCTOBER 1995 – SNOWY WHITE
Goldtop
Gilmour played guitars on the track 'Love, Pain And Sorrow'. This retrospective collection also includes the only official release of Pink Floyd's 'Pigs On The Wing, 1 & 2', on which White played the bridge between the two parts for the 8-track version of the song.

NOVEMBER 1997 – BB KING
Deuces Wild
Gilmour played guitar on the track 'Cryin' Won't Help You Babe'.

APRIL 1997 – PAUL McCARTNEY
'Oobu Joobu'
Gilmour played guitar on the track 'I Love This House' which formed part of the 8-part track 'Oobu Joobu (Part 1)' and on the 9-part track 'Oobu Joobu (Part 2)' made up of various demos, unreleased tracks and interviews originally broadcast as part of a US radio show. Gilmour's part was probably recorded in 1984 and his contribution is not credited on the sleeve.

JULY 1998 – TOM NEWMAN (& FRIENDS)
Snow Blind
Gilmour played guitar on the track 'Nowhere To Go', recorded in 1983.

AUGUST 1998 – PEGGY SEEGER
Period Pieces: Women's Songs for Men and Women
Gilmour played guitar on the track 'Winnie And Sam'.

JANUARY 1999 – THE PRETTY THINGS
Resurrection (Died 1968 Born 1998 at Abbey Road)
Gilmour played guitars on the tracks 'She Says Good Morning', 'I See You', 'Well Of Destiny', 'Trust' and 'Old Man Going'. This was Gilmour's contribution to the live Internet broadcast of a 30th anniversary performance of the Pretty Things' album *SF Sorrow* recorded at Studio 2, EMI Abbey Road Studios, London, England on Sunday 6 September 1998.

MARCH 1999 – THE PRETTY THINGS
Rage Before Beauty
Gilmour played guitars on the track 'Love Keeps Hanging On'. Since the album was begun in 1981, it is uncertain when his part was recorded.

OCTOBER 1999 – PAUL MCCARTNEY
Run Devil Run
Gilmour played guitar on all album tracks and lap steel and backing vocals on 'Run Devil Run'.

MAY 2000 – JOHN MARTYN
Classics
Gilmour played guitar on the tracks 'Could've Been Me', 'One World', 'Ways To Cry', 'Johnny Too Bad', 'Sapphire', 'Fisherman's Dream', 'Big Muff', 'Easy Blues', 'Dealer' and 'John Wayne'.

AUGUST 2000 – UNICORN
The Best of Unicorn
Gilmour played pedal steel guitar on the tracks 'Ooh! Mother', 'Just Wanna Hold You', 'Electric Night', 'Blue Pine Trees', 'Sleep Song' and 'Too Many Crooks', a compilation from the band's two albums *Blue Pine Trees* and *Too Many Crooks*.

NOVEMBER 2001 – JOOLS HOLLAND HIS RHYTHM & BLUES ORCHESTRA AND FRIENDS
Small World Big Band
Gilmour played guitar on the track 'I Put A Spell On You' with Mica Paris.

NOVEMBER 2001 – VARIOUS ARTISTS
Il Trionfo dell' Amore (Triumph of Love) Original Motion Picture Soundtrack
Gilmour played guitar on the tracks 'Follow That Young… Person', 'Agis And The Phocion: The Archery', 'I Am Aspasie', 'The Grotto, 'Phocion!' and 'Phocion! (Reprise)' on the soundtrack to the film score by Jason Osborn.

MAY 2002 – CAROLINE DALE
Such Sweet Thunder
Gilmour co-wrote and played guitar on the track 'Babbie's Daughter'.

DECEMBER 2002 – UNICORN
Shed No Tear (The Shed Studio Sessions)
Gilmour played guitar on the track 'So Far Away', an outtake version from the sessions of *Too Many Crooks*.

2002 – DONOVAN
Celtia
Gilmour played guitar on the tracks 'Lover, O Lover', 'Everlasting Sea' and 'Rock Me' on this bootleg release of studio outtakes which was recorded in February 1990.

MARCH 2003 – RINGO STARR
Ringo Rama
Gilmour played guitar on 'Missouri Loves Company' and 'I Think, Therefore I Rock 'n' Roll' on the CD, and guitar and drums on 'Missouri Loves Company' on the DVD.

SEPTEMBER 2003 – ROBERT WYATT
Cuckooland
Gilmour played guitar on 'Forest'.

JULY 2004 – PHIL MANZANERA
6pm
Gilmour played guitar on 'Always You' and 'Sacred Days'.

AUGUST 2004 – ALAN PARSONS
A Valid Path
Gilmour played guitar on 'Return To Tunguska'.

NOVEMBER 2005 – VARIOUS ARTISTS
'Ever Fallen In Love (With Someone You Shouldn't've)'
Gilmour played guitar on this tribute single to the late DJ John Peel, which also featured Roger Daltrey, Peter Hook, Robert Plant, Elton John and its original composer Pete Shelley.

MARCH 2006 – CHRIS JAGGER'S ATCHA!
Act of Faith
Gilmour played guitar on 'It's Amazing (What People Throw Away)' and 'Junkman'.

OCTOBER 2007 – JOOLS HOLLAND
Best of Friends
Gilmour played guitar on 'I Put A Spell On You' with Mica Paris which also appears on the DVD.

OCTOBER 2009 – ROD STEWART
The Rod Stewart Sessions 1971–1998
Gilmour played guitar on 'In A Broken Dream' originally recorded in 1992, which also features John Paul Jones.

SEPTEMBER 2010 – JACKIE LEVEN
Boîte de Pandore: More Songs from the Box of Terror
Gilmour played guitar on 'Meet Me At The Top Of The World', 'Heartbeat' and 'Last Summer' taken from the unreleased Doll By Doll album *The Last Flick of the Golden Wrench* originally recorded circa 1982.

OCTOBER 2010 – BRYAN FERRY
Olympia
Gilmour played guitar on 'Me Oh My' and 'Song To The Siren'.

APRIL 2014 – BEN WATT
Hendra
Gilmour played lap steel guitar and sang backing vocals on 'The Levels'. A video of this track was also released to online media on this date.

LIVE PERFORMANCE

ABOUT FACE ON TOUR (EUROPE)

Gilmour assembled an impressive band for his first solo tour comprising Gregg Dechart (Keyboards), Mickey Feat (Bass), Jodi Linscott (Percussion), Mick Ralphs (Guitar and Vocals), Raphael "Raff" Ravenscroft (Saxophone) and Chris Slade (Drums). It was an uncomplicated presentation with a very simple stage set and lighting, which focused on the musicianship rather than the spectacle.

FRIDAY 30 MARCH 1984 – TELEVISION BROADCAST
The Tube, Tyne Tees Television Studios, Newcastle-upon-Tyne, England
Gilmour previewed his world tour on the live-music programme *The Tube*, performing two tracks, 'Until We Sleep' and 'Blue Light' with his band. It was broadcast on Channel 4 TV between 5.30pm and 7.00pm.

SATURDAY 31 MARCH 1984 – PERFORMANCE
National Stadium, Dublin, Ireland
Supported by Billy Bragg.
Set list: 'Until We Sleep', 'Run Like Hell', 'Love On The Air', 'Mihalis', 'There's No Way Out Of Here', 'All Lovers Are Deranged', 'Out Of The Blue', 'Let's Get Metaphysical', 'Cruise', 'Short And Sweet', 'You Know I'm Right', 'Murder', 'Blue Light', 'Near The End' <Encore> 'Comfortably Numb'.

MTV filmed Gilmour in pre-show rehearsal at this show along with interviews and archive footage as well as footage shot at Hammersmith Odeon, London between Saturday 28 and Monday 30 April for a documentary film entitled *Beyond the Floyd*. It was broadcast on MTV on Sunday 20 May 1984 between 11.00pm and 11.30pm (EST).

MONDAY 2 APRIL 1984 – PERFORMANCE
Whitla Hall, Belfast, Northern Ireland
Set list: 'Until We Sleep', 'Run Like Hell', 'Love On The Air', 'Mihalis', 'There's No Way Out Of Here', 'All Lovers Are Deranged', 'Out Of The Blue', 'Let's Get Metaphysical', 'Cruise', 'Short And Sweet', 'You Know I'm Right' <Encore> 'Comfortably Numb'.

THURSDAY 5 APRIL 1984 – PERFORMANCE
Grote Zaal, Muziekcentrum Vredenburg, Utrecht, Netherlands
Set list: 'Until We Sleep', 'Run Like Hell', 'Love On The Air', 'Mihalis', 'There's No Way Out Of Here', 'All Lovers Are Deranged', 'Out Of The Blue', 'Let's Get Metaphysical', 'Cruise', 'Short And Sweet', 'You Know I'm Right', 'Murder', 'Blue Light', 'Near The End' <Encore> 'Comfortably Numb', 'I Can't Breathe Anymore'.

FRIDAY 6 APRIL 1984 – PERFORMANCE
Auditorium Q, Campus Etterbeek, Vreij Universität Brussel, Brussels, Belgium

Set list: 'Until We Sleep', 'Run Like Hell', 'Love On The Air', 'Mihalis', 'There's No Way Out Of Here', 'All Lovers Are Deranged', 'Out Of The Blue', 'Let's Get Metaphysical', 'Cruise', 'Short And Sweet', 'You Know I'm Right', 'Blue Light', 'Murder' <Encore> 'Comfortably Numb', 'Near The End'.

SUNDAY 8 APRIL 1984 – PERFORMANCE
Hall A, Parc des Expositions, Nancy, France

Set list: 'Until We Sleep', 'All Lovers Are Deranged', 'Love On The Air', 'Mihalis', 'There's No Way Out Of Here', 'Run Like Hell', 'Out Of The Blue', 'Let's Get Metaphysical', 'Cruise', 'Short And Sweet', 'You Know I'm Right', 'Blue Light', 'Murder' <Encore> 'Near The End', 'Comfortably Numb'.

MONDAY 9 APRIL 1984 – PERFORMANCE
Hall Tivoli, Strasbourg, France

Set list: 'Until We Sleep', 'All Lovers Are Deranged', 'Love On The Air', 'Mihalis', 'There's No Way Out Of Here', 'Run Like Hell', 'Out Of The Blue', 'Let's Get Metaphysical', 'Cruise', 'Short And Sweet', 'You Know I'm Right', 'Blue Light', 'Murder' <Encore> 'Near The End', 'Comfortably Numb'.

TUESDAY 10 & WEDNESDAY 11 APRIL 1984 – PERFORMANCES
Le Zénith, Parc de Villette, Paris, France

Set list at both shows: 'Until We Sleep', 'All Lovers Are Deranged', 'Love On The Air', 'Mihalis', 'There's No Way Out Of Here', 'Run Like Hell', 'Out Of The Blue', 'Let's Get Metaphysical', 'Cruise', 'Short And Sweet', 'You Know I'm Right', 'Blue Light', 'Murder' <Encore> 'Near The End', 'Comfortably Numb'

The show of 10 April was recorded by RTL Radio and the following tracks were later broadcast: 'Run Like Hell', 'Out Of The Blue', 'Cruise', 'Blue Light', 'Near The End' and 'Comfortably Numb'.

THURSDAY 12 APRIL 1984 – PERFORMANCE
Salle Albert Thomas, Bourse du Travail, Lyon, France

Set list: 'Until We Sleep', 'All Lovers Are Deranged', 'Love On The Air', 'Mihalis', 'There's No Way Out Of Here', 'Run Like Hell', 'Out Of The Blue', 'Let's Get Metaphysical', 'Cruise', 'Short And Sweet', 'You Know I'm Right', 'Blue Light', 'Murder' <Encore> 'Near The End', 'Comfortably Numb'.

FRIDAY 13 APRIL 1984 – PERFORMANCE
Kongress-saal, Kongresshaus, Zurich, Switzerland

Set list: 'Until We Sleep', 'All Lovers Are Deranged', 'Love On The Air', 'Mihalis', 'There's No Way Out Of Here', 'Run Like Hell', 'Out Of The Blue', 'Let's Get Metaphysical', 'Cruise', 'Short And Sweet', 'You Know I'm Right', 'Blue Light', 'Murder' <Encore> 'Near The End', 'Comfortably Numb'.

SATURDAY 14 APRIL 1984 – PERFORMANCE
Circus Krone, Munich, West Germany

Set list: 'Until We Sleep', 'All Lovers Are Deranged', 'Love On The Air', 'Mihalis', 'Short And Sweet', 'Run Like Hell', 'Out Of The Blue', 'Let's Get Metaphysical', 'Cruise', 'There's No Way Out Of Here', 'You Know I'm Right', 'Blue Light', 'Murder' <Encore> 'Near The End', 'Comfortably Numb'.

SUNDAY 15 APRIL 1984 – PERFORMANCE
Alte Oper, Frankfurt, West Germany

Set list: 'Until We Sleep', 'All Lovers Are Deranged', 'Love On The Air', 'Mihalis', 'Short And Sweet', 'Run Like Hell', 'Out Of The Blue', 'Let's Get Metaphysical', 'Cruise', 'There's No Way Out Of Here', 'You Know I'm Right', 'Blue Light', 'Murder' <Encore> 'Near The

End', 'Comfortably Numb'.

MONDAY 16 APRIL 1984 – PERFORMANCE
Musensaal, Mannheim, West Germany

Set list: 'Until We Sleep', 'All Lovers Are Deranged', 'Love On The Air', 'Mihalis', 'Short And Sweet', 'Run Like Hell', 'Out Of The Blue', 'Let's Get Metaphysical', 'Cruise', 'There's No Way Out Of Here', 'You Know I'm Right', 'Blue Light', 'Murder' <Encore> 'Near The End', 'Comfortably Numb'.

WEDNESDAY 18 APRIL 1984 – PERFORMANCE
Saal 1, Internationales Congress Centrum, West Berlin, West Germany

Set list: 'Until We Sleep', 'All Lovers Are Deranged', 'Love On The Air', 'Mihalis', 'Short And Sweet', 'Run Like Hell', 'Out Of The Blue', 'Let's Get Metaphysical', 'Cruise', 'There's No Way Out Of Here', 'You Know I'm Right', 'Blue Light', 'Murder' <Encore> 'Near The End', 'Comfortably Numb'.

THURSDAY 19 APRIL 1984 – PERFORMANCE ▲
Saal 1, Congress Centrum Hamburg, Hamburg, West Germany

Set list: 'Until We Sleep', 'All Lovers Are Deranged', 'Love On The Air', 'Mihalis', 'Short And Sweet', 'Run Like Hell', 'Out Of The Blue', 'Let's Get Metaphysical', 'Cruise', 'There's No Way Out Of Here', 'You Know I'm Right', 'Blue Light', 'Murder' <Encore> 'Near The End', 'Comfortably Numb'.

SATURDAY 21 APRIL 1984 – PERFORMANCE
Philipshalle, Düsseldorf, West Germany

Set list: 'Until We Sleep', 'All Lovers Are Deranged', 'Love On The Air', 'Mihalis', 'Short And Sweet', 'Run Like Hell', 'Out Of The Blue', 'Let's Get Metaphysical', 'Cruise', 'There's No Way Out Of Here', 'You Know I'm Right', 'Blue Light', 'Murder' <Encore> 'Near The End', 'Comfortably Numb'.

TUESDAY 24 APRIL 1984 – PERFORMANCE
Johanneshovs Isstadion, Stockholm, Sweden

Set list: 'Until We Sleep', 'All Lovers Are Deranged', 'Love On The Air', 'Mihalis', 'Short And Sweet', 'Run Like Hell', 'Out Of The Blue', 'Let's Get Metaphysical', 'Cruise', 'There's No Way Out Of Here', 'You Know I'm Right', 'Blue Light', 'Murder' <Encore> 'Near The End', 'Comfortably Numb'.

WEDNESDAY 25 APRIL 1984 – PERFORMANCE
Falconer Teatret, Copenhagen, Denmark

Set list: 'Until We Sleep', 'All Lovers Are Deranged', 'There's No Way Out Of Here', 'Love On The Air', 'Mihalis', 'Cruise', 'Short And Sweet', 'Run Like Hell', 'Out Of The Blue', 'Let's Get Metaphysical', 'You Know I'm Right', 'Blue Light', 'Murder', 'Near The End' <Encore> 'Comfortably Numb', 'I Can't Breathe Anymore'.

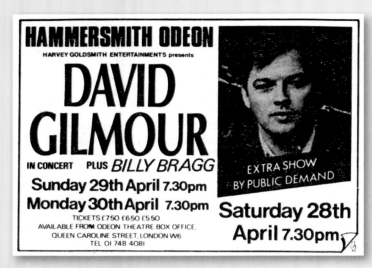

SATURDAY 28, SUNDAY 29 & MONDAY 30 APRIL 1984 – PERFORMANCES ▲
Hammersmith Odeon, Hammersmith, London, England

Supported by Billy Bragg and the Television Personalities (Saturday 28 only).
Set list at all three shows: 'Until We Sleep', 'All Lovers Are Deranged', 'Love On The Air', 'There's No Way Out Of Here', 'Mihalis', 'Cruise', 'Short And Sweet' (with Roy Harper on vocals), 'Run Like Hell', 'Out Of The Blue', 'Let's Get Metaphysical', 'You Know I'm Right', 'Blue Light', 'Murder', 'Near The End' <Encore> 'Comfortably Numb' (with Nick Mason on drums), 'I Can't Breathe Anymore' (Sunday 29 & Monday 30 April only).

The Television Personalities supported Gilmour on the first night and performed a version of 'See Emily Play' in their set before revealing Syd Barrett's home address to the audience. The band was instantly dismissed from the remaining two London dates by an infuriated Gilmour. Although Richard Wright attended the last show, he did not perform. All three London concerts were filmed for a David Gilmour special and broadcast on MTV on Saturday 26 May 1984 between 11.00pm and 12.00midnight (EST) and simulcast nationally on the Westwood One radio network. It was also released on video in the US (see Discography). Some of the footage was later combined with pre-show rehearsal footage and interviews from Dublin on 31 March and archive material for the documentary film *Beyond the Floyd* broadcast on MTV on Sunday 20 May 1984 between 11.00pm and 11.30pm (EST).

TUESDAY 1 MAY 1984 – PERFORMANCE
The Odeon, Birmingham, England

Supported by Billy Bragg.
Set list: 'Until We Sleep', 'All Lovers Are Deranged', 'There's No Way Out Of Here', 'Love On The Air', 'Mihalis', 'Cruise', 'Short And Sweet', 'Run Like Hell', 'Out Of The Blue', 'Let's Get Metaphysical', 'You Know I'm Right', 'Blue Light', 'Murder', 'Near The End' <Encore> 'Comfortably Numb'.

With poor publicity and cancellation rumours, only 200 fans attended the show. Gilmour was seen parking opposite the venue and, after signing some autographs, entered by the front doors.

ABOUT FACE ON TOUR (NORTH AMERICA)

Gilmour's band for this show and the rest of the tour were Gregg Dechart (Keyboards), Mickey Feat (Bass Guitar), Jodi Linscott (Percussion), Mick Ralphs (Guitar and Vocals), Raphael 'Raff' Ravenscroft (Saxophone) and Chris Slade (Drums). Early drafts of the tour show Gilmour scheduled to appear at Chicoutimi, Canada (Tuesday 8 May) and Rimouski, Canada (Thursday 10 May).

WEDNESDAY 9 MAY – PERFORMANCE
Colisee de Québec, Québec City, Canada

Supported by the Icicle Works.
Set list: 'Until We Sleep', 'All Lovers Are Deranged', 'There's No Way Out Of Here', 'Love On The Air', 'Mihalis', 'Cruise', 'Short And Sweet', 'Run Like Hell', 'Out Of The Blue', 'Let's Get Metaphysical', 'You Know I'm Right', 'Blue Light', 'Murder', 'Near The End' <Encore> 'Comfortably Numb'.

FRIDAY 11 MAY – PERFORMANCES
Forum de Montréal, Montréal, Canada

Supported by the Icicle Works.
Set list at both shows: 'Until We Sleep', 'All Lovers Are Deranged', 'Love On The Air', 'Mihalis', 'Cruise', 'Short And Sweet', 'Run Like Hell', 'Out Of The Blue', 'Let's Get Metaphysical', 'You Know I'm Right', 'Money', 'Blue Light', 'Murder', 'Near The End' <Encore> 'Comfortably Numb', 'I Can't Breathe Anymore'.

SATURDAY 12 MAY – PERFORMANCE
Civic Centre Theatre, Lansdowne Park, Ottawa, Canada

Supported by the Icicle Works.
Set list: 'Until We Sleep', 'All Lovers Are Deranged', 'Love On The Air', 'Mihalis', 'Cruise', 'Short And Sweet', 'Run Like Hell', 'Out Of The Blue', 'Let's Get Metaphysical', 'You Know I'm Right', 'Money', 'Blue Light', 'Murder', 'Near The End' <Encore> 'Comfortably Numb'.

MONDAY 14 MAY – PERFORMANCE
Massey Hall, Toronto, Canada

Supported by the Icicle Works.
Set list: 'Until We Sleep', 'All Lovers Are Deranged', 'Love On The Air', 'Mihalis', 'Cruise', 'Short And Sweet', 'Run Like Hell', 'Out Of The Blue', 'Let's Get Metaphysical', 'You Know I'm Right', 'Money', 'Blue Light', 'Murder', 'Near The End' <Encore> 'Comfortably Numb'.

TUESDAY 15 MAY – PERFORMANCE
Massey Hall, Toronto, Canada

Supported by the Icicle Works.
Set list: 'Until We Sleep', 'All Lovers Are Deranged', 'There's No Way Out Of Here', 'Love On The Air', 'Mihalis', 'Cruise', 'Short And Sweet', 'Run Like Hell', 'Out Of The Blue', 'Let's Get Metaphysical', 'You Know I'm Right', 'Money', 'Blue Light', 'Murder', 'Near The End' <Encore> 'Comfortably Numb'.

WEDNESDAY 16 MAY – PERFORMANCE
Shea's Buffalo Theatre, Buffalo, NY, USA

Supported by the Icicle Works.
Set list: 'Until We Sleep', 'All Lovers Are Deranged', 'Love On The Air', 'Mihalis', 'Cruise', 'Short And Sweet', 'Run Like Hell', 'Out Of The Blue', 'Let's Get Metaphysical', 'You Know I'm Right', 'Money', 'Blue Light', 'Murder', 'Near The End' <Encore> 'Comfortably Numb'.

THURSDAY 17 MAY – PERFORMANCE
Landmark Theatre, Syracuse, NY, USA

Supported by the Icicle Works.
Set list: 'Until We Sleep', 'All Lovers Are Deranged', 'Love On The Air', 'Mihalis', 'Cruise', 'Short And Sweet', 'Run Like Hell', 'Out Of The Blue', 'Let's Get Metaphysical', 'You Know I'm Right', 'Money', 'Blue Light', 'Murder', 'Near The End' <Encore> 'Comfortably Numb'.

FRIDAY 18 MAY – PERFORMANCE
Mair Hall, Mid-Hudson Civic Center, Poughkeepsie, NY, USA

Supported by the Icicle Works.
Set list: 'Until We Sleep', 'All Lovers Are Deranged', 'Love On The Air', 'Mihalis', 'Cruise', 'Short And Sweet', 'Run Like Hell', 'Out Of The Blue', 'Let's Get Metaphysical', 'You Know I'm Right', 'Money', 'Blue Light', 'Murder', 'Near The End' <Encore> 'Comfortably Numb'.

SUNDAY 20 MAY – PERFORMANCE
Bushnell Auditorium, Hartford, CT, USA

Supported by the Icicle Works.
Set list: 'Until We Sleep', 'All Lovers Are Deranged', 'Love On The Air', 'Mihalis', 'Cruise', 'Short And Sweet', 'Run Like Hell', 'Out Of The Blue', 'Let's Get Metaphysical', 'You Know I'm Right', 'Money', 'Blue Light', 'Murder', 'Near The End' <Encore> 'Comfortably Numb'.

TUESDAY 22 MAY – PERFORMANCE
Beacon Theatre, New York, NY, USA

Supported by the Icicle Works.
Set list: 'Until We Sleep', 'All Lovers Are Deranged', 'Love On The Air', 'Mihalis', 'Cruise', 'Short And Sweet', 'Run Like Hell', 'Out Of The Blue', 'Let's Get Metaphysical', 'You Know I'm Right', 'Money', 'Blue Light', 'Murder', 'Near The End' <Encore> 'Comfortably Numb'.

WEDNESDAY 23 MAY – PERFORMANCE
Beacon Theatre, New York, NY, USA

Supported by the Icicle Works.
Set list: 'Until We Sleep', 'All Lovers Are Deranged', 'Love On The Air', 'Mihalis', 'Cruise', 'Short And Sweet', 'Money', 'Out Of The Blue', 'Let's Get Metaphysical', 'You Know I'm Right', 'Run Like Hell', 'Blue Light', 'Murder', 'Near The End' <Encore> 'Comfortably Numb'.

THURSDAY 24 MAY – PERFORMANCE
Beacon Theatre, New York, NY, USA

Supported by the Icicle Works.
Set list: 'Until We Sleep', 'All Lovers Are Deranged', 'Love On The Air', 'Mihalis', 'Cruise', 'Short And Sweet', 'Money', 'Out Of The Blue', 'Let's Get Metaphysical', 'You Know I'm Right', 'Run Like Hell', 'Blue Light', 'Murder', 'Near The End' <Encore> 'Comfortably Numb'.

FRIDAY 25 MAY – PERFORMANCE
The Orpheum Theatre, Boston, MA, USA

Supported by the Icicle Works.
Set list: 'Until We Sleep', 'All Lovers Are Deranged', 'Love On The Air', 'Mihalis', 'Cruise', 'Short And Sweet', 'Money', 'Out Of The Blue', 'Let's Get Metaphysical', 'You Know I'm Right', 'Run Like Hell', 'Blue Light', 'Murder', 'Near The End' <Encore> 'Comfortably Numb', 'There's No Way Out Of Here'.

SATURDAY 26 MAY – PERFORMANCE
The Orpheum Theatre, Boston, MA, USA

Supported by the Icicle Works.
Set list: 'Until We Sleep', 'All Lovers Are Deranged', 'Love On The Air', 'Mihalis', 'Cruise', 'Short And Sweet', 'Money', 'Out Of The Blue', 'Let's Get Metaphysical', 'You Know I'm Right', 'Run Like Hell', 'Blue Light', 'Murder' <Encore> 'Comfortably Numb', 'I Can't Breathe Anymore'.

SUNDAY 27 MAY – PERFORMANCE
Veterans Memorial Coliseum, New Haven, CT, USA

Supported by the Icicle Works.
Set list: 'Until We Sleep', 'All Lovers Are Deranged', 'Love On The Air', 'Mihalis', 'Cruise', 'Short And Sweet', 'Money', 'Out Of The Blue', 'Let's Get Metaphysical', 'You Know I'm Right', 'Run Like Hell', 'Blue Light', 'Murder', 'Near The End' <Encore> 'Comfortably Numb'.

TUESDAY 29 MAY – PERFORMANCE
Tower Theatre, Upper Darby, Philadelphia, PA, USA

Supported by the Icicle Works.
Set list: 'Until We Sleep', 'All Lovers Are Deranged', 'Love On The Air', 'Mihalis', 'Cruise', 'Short And Sweet', 'Money', 'Out Of The Blue', 'Let's Get Metaphysical', 'You Know I'm Right', 'Run Like Hell', 'Blue Light', 'Murder', 'Near The End' <Encore> 'Comfortably Numb', 'I Can't Breathe Anymore'.

WEDNESDAY 30 MAY – PERFORMANCE
Tower Theatre, Philadelphia, PA, USA

Supported by the Icicle Works.
Set list: 'Until We Sleep', 'All Lovers Are Deranged', 'Love On The Air', 'Mihalis', 'Cruise', 'Short And Sweet', 'Money', 'Out Of The Blue', 'Let's Get Metaphysical', 'You Know I'm Right', 'Run Like Hell', 'Blue Light', 'Murder' <Encore> 'Comfortably Numb', 'I Can't Breathe Anymore'.

THURSDAY 31 MAY – PERFORMANCE
Tower Theatre, Philadelphia, PA, USA

Supported by the Icicle Works.
Set list: 'Until We Sleep', 'All Lovers Are Deranged', 'Love On The Air', 'Mihalis', 'Cruise', 'Short And Sweet', 'Money', 'Out Of The Blue', 'Let's Get Metaphysical', 'You Know I'm Right', 'Run Like Hell', 'Blue Light', 'Murder', 'Near The End' <Encore> 'Comfortably Numb'.

The Icicle Works withdrew from the tour after this date due to personal circumstances. Bassist Chris Layhe recalled that "touring America and North America with Dave Gilmour definitely had a huge influence on the sound. It was a chance meeting with Chrissie Hynde and the Pretenders on *The Tube* that gave us our first support dates there. You had to learn how to win over audiences in much bigger venues than we had been used to. Some we did and some…maybe not! 'Birds Fly' was, however, getting heavy rotation on the radio and MTV was a great supporter. I guess it's a dilemma that many new bands/artists face, stay at home and keep building the fan base or try to break the USA. Looking back it was a great experience and I'm glad we went there. We definitely came back a more confident rock band, especially live."

FRIDAY 1 JUNE – PERFORMANCE
Daughters of the American Revolution Constitution Hall, Washington, DC, USA

Set list: 'Until We Sleep', 'All Lovers Are Deranged', 'Love On The Air', 'Mihalis', 'Cruise', 'Short And Sweet', 'Money', 'Out Of The Blue', 'Let's Get Metaphysical', 'You Know I'm Right', 'Run Like Hell', 'Blue Light', 'Murder', 'Near The End' <Encore> 'Comfortably Numb'.

SUNDAY 3 JUNE – PERFORMANCE ▶
Public Hall, Cleveland, OH, USA

Set list: 'Until We Sleep', 'All Lovers Are Deranged', 'Love On The Air', 'Mihalis', 'Cruise', 'Short And Sweet', 'Money', 'Out Of The Blue', 'Let's Get Metaphysical', 'You Know I'm Right', 'Run Like Hell', 'Blue Light', 'Murder' <Encore> 'Comfortably Numb'.

MONDAY 4 JUNE – PERFORMANCE
Veterans Memorial Hall, Columbus, OH, USA

Set list: 'Until We Sleep', 'All Lovers Are Deranged', 'Love On The Air', 'Mihalis', 'Cruise', 'Short And Sweet', 'Money', 'Out Of The Blue', 'Let's Get Metaphysical', 'You Know I'm Right', 'Run Like Hell', 'Blue Light' <Encore> 'Comfortably Numb', 'Murder'.

WEDNESDAY 6 JUNE – PERFORMANCE
Pine Knob Music Theatre, Clarkston, MI, USA

Set list: 'Until We Sleep', 'All Lovers Are Deranged', 'Love On The Air', 'Mihalis', 'Cruise', 'Short And Sweet', 'Money', 'Out Of The Blue', 'Let's Get Metaphysical', 'You Know I'm Right', 'Run Like Hell', 'Blue Light', 'Murder' <Encore> 'Comfortably Numb'.

THURSDAY 7 JUNE – PERFORMANCE
Cincinnati Gardens, Cincinnati, OH, USA

Set list: 'Until We Sleep', 'All Lovers Are Deranged', 'Love On The Air', 'Mihalis', 'Cruise', 'Short And Sweet', 'Money', 'Out Of The Blue', 'Let's Get Metaphysical', 'You Know I'm Right', 'Run Like Hell', 'Blue Light', 'Murder' <Encore> 'Comfortably Numb'.

FRIDAY 8 JUNE – PERFORMANCE
Chicago Pavilion, University of Illinois Chicago, Chicago, IL, USA

Set list: 'Until We Sleep', 'All Lovers Are Deranged', 'Love On The Air', 'Mihalis', 'Cruise', 'Short And Sweet', 'Money', 'Out Of The Blue', 'Let's Get Metaphysical', 'You Know I'm Right', 'Run Like Hell', 'Blue Light', 'Murder', 'Near The End' <Encore> 'Comfortably Numb'.

SUNDAY 10 JUNE – PERFORMANCE
Kiel Opera House, St Louis, MO, USA

Set list: 'Until We Sleep', 'All Lovers Are Deranged', 'Love On The Air', 'Mihalis', 'Cruise', 'Short And Sweet', 'Money', 'Out Of The Blue', 'Let's Get Metaphysical', 'You Know I'm Right', 'Run Like Hell', 'Blue Light', 'Murder' <Encore> 'Comfortably Numb'.

MONDAY 11 JUNE – PERFORMANCE
Starlight Theatre, Kansas City, MO, USA

Set list: 'Until We Sleep', 'All Lovers Are Deranged', 'Love On The Air', 'Mihalis', 'Cruise', 'Short And Sweet', 'Money', 'Out Of The Blue', 'Let's Get Metaphysical', 'You Know I'm Right', 'Run Like Hell', 'Blue Light', 'Murder' <Encore> 'Comfortably Numb'.

WEDNESDAY 13 JUNE – PERFORMANCE
The Summit Sports Arena, Houston, TX, USA

Set list: 'Until We Sleep', 'All Lovers Are Deranged', 'Love On The Air', 'Mihalis', 'Cruise', 'Short And Sweet', 'Money', 'Out Of The Blue', 'Let's Get Metaphysical', 'You Know I'm Right', 'Run Like Hell', 'Blue Light', 'Murder' <Encore> 'Comfortably Numb'.

THURSDAY 14 JUNE – PERFORMANCE
Frank Erwin Center, University of Texas, Austin, TX, USA

Set list: 'Until We Sleep', 'All Lovers Are Deranged', 'Love On The Air', 'Mihalis', 'Cruise', 'Short And Sweet', 'Money', 'Out Of The Blue', 'Let's Get Metaphysical', 'You Know I'm Right', 'Run Like Hell', 'Blue Light', 'Murder', 'Near The End' <Encore> 'Comfortably Numb'.

FRIDAY 15 JUNE – PERFORMANCE
Majestic Performing Arts Center, San Antonio, TX, USA

Set list: 'Until We Sleep', 'All Lovers Are Deranged', 'Love On The Air', 'Mihalis', 'Cruise', 'Short And Sweet', 'Money', 'Out Of The Blue', 'Let's Get Metaphysical', 'You Know I'm Right', 'Run Like Hell', 'Blue Light', 'Murder' <Encore> 'Comfortably Numb', 'There's No Way Out Of Here'.

SATURDAY 16 JUNE – PERFORMANCE
Reunion Arena, Reunion Park, Dallas, TX, USA

Set list: 'Until We Sleep', 'All Lovers Are Deranged', 'Love On The Air', 'Mihalis', 'Cruise', 'Short And Sweet', 'Money', 'Out Of The Blue', 'Let's Get Metaphysical', 'You Know I'm Right', 'Run Like Hell', 'Blue Light', 'Murder' <Encore> 'Comfortably Numb'.

RIGHT: GILMOUR ON STAGE IN SACRAMENTO, 28 JUNE 1984.

TUESDAY 19 JUNE – PERFORMANCE
The Amphitheatre, Mesa, AZ, USA

Set list: 'Until We Sleep', 'All Lovers Are Deranged', 'Love On The Air', 'Mihalis', 'Cruise', 'Short And Sweet', 'Money', 'Out Of The Blue', 'Let's Get Metaphysical', 'You Know I'm Right', 'Run Like Hell', 'Blue Light', 'Murder' <Encore> 'Comfortably Numb'.

WEDNESDAY 20 JUNE – PERFORMANCE
Open Air Theatre, San Diego State University, San Diego, CA, USA

Set list: 'Until We Sleep', 'All Lovers Are Deranged', 'Love On The Air', 'Mihalis', 'Cruise', 'Short And Sweet', 'Money', 'Out Of The Blue', 'Let's Get Metaphysical', 'You Know I'm Right', 'Run Like Hell', 'Blue Light', 'Murder' <Encore> 'Comfortably Numb'.

THURSDAY 21 & FRIDAY 22 JUNE – PERFORMANCES
The New Universal Amphitheatre, Universal City, Los Angeles, CA, USA

Set list at both shows: 'Until We Sleep', 'All Lovers Are Deranged', 'Love On The Air', 'Mihalis', 'Cruise', 'Short And Sweet', 'Money', 'Out Of The Blue', 'Let's Get Metaphysical', 'You Know I'm Right', 'Run Like Hell', 'Blue Light', 'Murder', 'Near The End' <Encore> 'Comfortably Numb'.

SATURDAY 23 & SUNDAY 24 JUNE – PERFORMANCES
Irvine Meadows Amphitheater, Irvine, CA, USA

Set list at both shows: 'Until We Sleep', 'All Lovers Are Deranged', 'Love On The Air', 'Mihalis', 'Cruise', 'Short And Sweet', 'Money', 'Out Of The Blue', 'Let's Get Metaphysical', 'You Know I'm Right', 'Run Like Hell', 'Blue Light', 'Murder', 'Near The End' <Encore> 'Comfortably Numb'.

TUESDAY 26 JUNE – PERFORMANCE
Kabuki Nightclub, San Francisco, CA, USA

Set list: 'Until We Sleep', 'All Lovers Are Deranged', 'Love On The Air', 'Mihalis', 'Cruise', 'Short And Sweet', 'Money', 'Out Of The Blue', 'Let's Get Metaphysical', 'You Know I'm Right', 'Run Like Hell', 'Blue Light', 'Murder', 'Near The End' <Encore> 'Comfortably Numb'.

WEDNESDAY 27 JUNE – PERFORMANCE
Kabuki Nightclub, San Francisco, CA, USA

Set list: 'Until We Sleep', 'All Lovers Are Deranged', 'Love On The Air', 'Mihalis', 'Cruise', 'Short And Sweet', 'Money', 'Out Of The Blue', 'Let's Get Metaphysical', 'You Know I'm Right', 'Run Like Hell', 'Blue Light', 'Murder' <Encore> 'Comfortably Numb'.

THURSDAY 28 JUNE – PERFORMANCE
California Exposition Amphitheater, California Exposition Fairgrounds, Sacramento, CA, USA

Set list: 'Until We Sleep', 'All Lovers Are Deranged', 'Love On The Air', 'Mihalis', 'Cruise', 'Short And Sweet', 'Money', 'Out Of The Blue', 'Let's Get Metaphysical', 'You Know I'm Right', 'Run Like Hell', 'Blue Light', 'Murder', 'Near The End' <Encore> 'Comfortably Numb'.

Jodi Linscott broke her arm in a motorcycle accident leaving the tour without a percussionist until a replacement was found on 8 July.

FRIDAY 29 JUNE – PERFORMANCE
Greek Theatre, University of California, Berkeley, CA, USA

Set list: 'Until We Sleep', 'All Lovers Are Deranged', 'Love On The Air', 'Mihalis', 'Cruise', 'Short And Sweet', 'Money', 'Out Of The Blue', 'Let's Get Metaphysical', 'You Know I'm Right', 'Run Like Hell', 'Blue Light', 'Murder', 'Near The End' <Encore> 'Comfortably Numb'.

THURSDAY 5 JULY – PERFORMANCE
Sunrise Music Theatre, Sunrise, FL, USA

Set list: 'Until We Sleep', 'All Lovers Are Deranged', 'Love On The Air', 'Mihalis', 'Cruise', 'Short And Sweet', 'Money', 'Out Of The Blue', 'Let's Get Metaphysical', 'You Know I'm Right', 'Run Like Hell', 'Blue Light', 'Murder' <Encore> 'Comfortably Numb'.

FRIDAY 6 JULY – PERFORMANCE
Civic Centre Arena, Lakeland, FL, USA

Set list: 'Until We Sleep', 'All Lovers Are Deranged', 'Love On The Air', 'Mihalis', 'Cruise', 'Short And Sweet', 'Money', 'Out Of The Blue', 'Let's Get Metaphysical', 'You Know I'm Right', 'Run Like Hell', 'Blue Light', 'Murder', 'Near The End' <Encore> 'Comfortably Numb'.

SUNDAY 8 JULY – PERFORMANCE ▼
Garden State Arts Center, Holmdel, NJ, USA

Set list: 'Until We Sleep', 'All Lovers Are Deranged', 'Love On The Air', 'Mihalis', 'Cruise', 'Short And Sweet', 'Money', 'Out Of The Blue', 'Let's Get Metaphysical', 'You Know I'm Right', 'Run Like Hell', 'Blue Light', 'Murder', 'Near The End' <Encore> 'Comfortably Numb'.

Sue Evans replaced Jodi Linscott from this show onwards.

WEDNESDAY 11 JULY – PERFORMANCE
Syria Mosque Theater, Pittsburgh, USA

Set list: 'Until We Sleep', 'All Lovers Are Deranged', 'Love On The Air', 'Mihalis', 'Cruise', 'Short And Sweet', 'Money', 'Out Of The Blue', 'Let's Get Metaphysical', 'You Know I'm Right', 'Run Like Hell', 'Blue Light', 'Murder' <Encore> 'Comfortably Numb'.

THURSDAY 12 JULY – PERFORMANCE
Stabler Arena, Lehigh University, Allentown, PA, USA

Set list: 'Until We Sleep', 'All Lovers Are Deranged', 'Love On The Air', 'Mihalis', 'Cruise', 'Short And Sweet', 'Money', 'Out Of The Blue', 'Let's Get Metaphysical', 'You Know I'm Right', 'Run Like Hell', 'Blue Light', 'Murder' <Encore> 'Comfortably Numb'.

The show was recorded by the Westwood One radio network *In Concert* series and an edited version was broadcast in the US on 31 August 1984 with the following tracks: 'Until We Sleep', 'All Lovers Are Deranged', 'Money', 'Love On The Air', 'Short And Sweet', 'You Know I'm Right', 'Run Like Hell', 'Blue Light', 'Murder', 'Comfortably Numb'.

FRIDAY 13 JULY – PERFORMANCE
Jones Beach Theatre, Wantagh, NY, USA

Set list: 'Until We Sleep', 'All Lovers Are Deranged', 'Love On The Air', 'Mihalis', 'Cruise', 'Short And Sweet', 'Money', 'Out Of The Blue', 'Let's Get Metaphysical', 'You Know I'm Right', 'Run Like Hell', 'Blue Light', 'Murder', 'Near The End' <Encore> 'Comfortably Numb'.

SATURDAY 14 JULY – PERFORMANCE
Merriweather Post Pavilion, Columbia, MD, USA

Set list: 'Until We Sleep', 'All Lovers Are Deranged', 'Love On The Air', 'Mihalis', 'Cruise', 'Short And Sweet', 'Money', 'Out Of The Blue', 'Let's Get Metaphysical', 'You Know I'm Right', 'Run Like Hell', 'Blue Light', 'Murder', 'Near The End' <Encore> 'Comfortably Numb'.

SUNDAY 15 JULY – PERFORMANCE
Saratoga Performing Arts Center, Saratoga Springs, NY, USA

Set list: 'Until We Sleep', 'All Lovers Are Deranged', 'Love On The Air', 'Mihalis', 'Cruise', 'Short And Sweet', 'Money', 'Out Of The Blue', 'Let's Get Metaphysical', 'You Know I'm Right', 'Run Like Hell', 'Blue Light', 'Murder', 'Near The End' <Encore> 'Comfortably Numb'.

MONDAY 16 JULY – PERFORMANCE
Pier 84, New York, NY, USA

Set list: 'Until We Sleep', 'All Lovers Are Deranged', 'Love On The Air', 'Mihalis', 'Cruise', 'Short And Sweet', 'Money', 'Out Of The Blue', 'There's No Way Out Of Here', 'You Know I'm Right', 'Run Like Hell', 'Blue Light', 'Murder' <Encore> 'Comfortably Numb'.

ROBERT WYATT'S MELTDOWN

Gilmour performed a unique solo 'unplugged' style show as part of the South Bank Centre's annual *Meltdown* festival, at the invitation of that year's curator Robert Wyatt. Held over a period of a week the festival included performances by Tricky, The Residents, Baaba Maal and Elvis Costello among many others. This show as well as those at the same venue in January 2002 were filmed and recorded for the David Gilmour *In Concert* DVD.

FRIDAY 22 JUNE 2001 – PERFORMANCE
Robert Wyatt's Meltdown, Royal Festival Hall, London, England

Supported by Sparklehorse.
Set list: 'Shine On You Crazy Diamond, Parts 1-5', 'Terrapin' (by Syd Barrett), 'Fat Old Sun', 'Coming Back To Life', 'High Hopes', 'Je Crois Entendre Encore' (from the opera *Les Pecheurs de Perle* by George Bizet), 'Smile' (a new composition), 'Wish You Were Here', 'Comfortably Numb', 'The Dimming Of The Day' (by Richard Thompson), 'Shine On You Crazy Diamond, Parts 6-9' <Encore> 'A Great Day For Freedom', 'Hushabye Mountain' (from the film *Chitty Chitty Bang Bang*).

Gilmour was supplemented on stage by Dick Parry (Saxophone on 'Shine On You Crazy Diamond'), Michael Kamen (Piano, Oboe), Chucho Merchan (Bass), Neil MacColl (Guitars), Nick France (Drums, Percussion), Caroline Dale (Cello), Robert Wyatt (Additional Vocals on 'Comfortably Numb' from side of stage), and Chris Ballin, Pete Brown, Sam Brown, Margot Buchanan, Michelle Carol, Claudia Fontaine, Michelle John-Douglas, Sonia Jones, Carol Kenyon and Aitch McRobbie (Backing Vocals).

DAVID GILMOUR IN CONCERT

Following the success of his Meltdown show, Gilmour arranged a series of three more shows in London and two in Paris. His band comprised Dick Parry (Saxophone on both parts of 'Shine On You Crazy Diamond' and 'Breakthrough'); Michael Kamen (Piano, Oboe); Chucho Merchan (Bass);

Neil MacColl (Guitars); Nick France (Drums, Percussion); Caroline Dale (Cello); Richard Wright (Keyboards and Vocals on 'Breakthrough' and Piano on 'Wish You Were Here' and 'Comfortably Numb'); Robert Wyatt (Additional Vocals on 'Comfortably Numb' on Wednesday 16 January from side of stage); Sir Bob Geldof (Additional Vocals on 'Comfortably Numb' on Thursday 17 January); Kate Bush (Additional Vocals on 'Comfortably Numb' on Friday 18, Wednesday 23 and Thursday 24 January); and Chris Ballin, Pete Brown, Sam Brown, Margot Buchanan, Claudia Fontaine, Michelle John-Douglas, Sonia Jones, Carol Kenyon, David Laudat, Durga McBroom, Aitch McRobbie and Beverli Skeete (Backing Vocals).

WEDNESDAY 16, THURSDAY 17 & FRIDAY 18 JANUARY 2002 – PERFORMANCES
Royal Festival Hall, London, England

Set list for both shows: 'Shine On You Crazy Diamond, Parts 1-5', 'Fat Old Sun', 'Coming Back To Life', 'Dominoes' (by Syd Barrett), 'High Hopes' (Backing Vocals Chorus), 'Je Crois Entendre Encore' (from the opera *Les Pecheurs de Perle* by George Bizet), 'Smile', 'Breakthrough' (Richard Wright), 'Wish You Were Here', 'Comfortably Numb', 'The Dimming Of The Day' (by Richard Thompson), 'Shine On You Crazy Diamond, Parts 6-9' <Encore> 'A Great Day For Freedom', 'Hushabye Mountain' (from the film *Chitty Chitty Bang Bang*).

The shows on Wednesday 16 and Thursday 17 January were supported by Ghostland (featuring Caroline Dale on cello with the London Metropolitan Orchestra) and on Friday 18 January by Trashmonk (featuring Nick Laird-Clowes). All three shows were filmed and recorded for the David Gilmour *In Concert* DVD.

WEDNESDAY 23 & THURSDAY 24 JANUARY 2002 – PERFORMANCES
Palace de Congrès de Paris, Paris, France

Set list for both shows as above.

DAVID GILMOUR "ON AN ISLAND" WORLD TOUR

Gilmour's band for the tour comprised Jon Carin (Keyboards), Steve DiStanislao (Drums), Phil Manzanera (Guitar), Dick Parry (Saxophone), Guy Pratt (Bass) and Richard Wright (Keyboards). Rehearsals took place initially at the Ex-Serviceman's Club, Chiddingfold, England and then Black Island Studios, Acton, London, England from late February through to Sunday 5 March 2006.

Despite some inspired choices of songs in the tour set list, one could be forgiven for thinking that Gilmour had completely disowned his first two solo albums by choosing instead to perform *On an Island* in its entirety and a smattering of tracks from *The Division Bell*.

THURSDAY 2 MARCH 2006 – RADIO BROADCAST
Front Row, Broadcasting House, Portland Place, London, England

Gilmour effectively launched his tour on this date performing acoustic renditions of 'Wish You Were Here', 'Smile' and 'The Blue' as part of a live interview with John Wilson. It was broadcast on BBC Radio 4 between 7.15pm and 7.45pm.

SATURDAY 4 MARCH 2006 – RADIO BROADCAST
The Jonathan Ross Show, Broadcasting House, Portland Place, London, England

Gilmour performed 'Smile' and 'On An Island' with Phil Manzanera as part of a live interview on the *Jonathan Ross Show*. It was broadcast on BBC Radio 2 between 10.00am and 1.00pm.

MONDAY 6 MARCH 2006 – PERFORMANCE
Porchester Hall, Bayswater, London, England

Set list: 'Castellorizon', 'On An Island', 'The Blue', 'Take A Breath', 'Red Sky At Night', 'This Heaven', 'Then I Close My Eyes', 'Smile', 'A Pocketful Of Stones', 'Where We Start' <Encore> 'Wish You Were Here', 'Dominoes', 'Happy Birthday' song.

A Who's Who of celebrity guests were invited to attend David Gilmour's 60th birthday party and were treated to some musical entertainment by Gilmour and his band.

TUESDAY 7 MARCH 2006 – PERFORMANCE
Mermaid Theatre, Puddle Dock, Blackfriars, London, England

Set list: 'Castellorizon', 'On An Island', 'The Blue', 'Take A Breath', 'Smile', 'This Heaven', 'Shine On You Crazy Diamond, Parts 1-5', 'Wearing The Inside Out' <Encore> 'High Hopes', 'Comfortably Numb', 'On An Island' (Second Take), 'The Blue' (Second Take), 'Happy Birthday' song.

This show was staged by BBC Radio 2 for recording and filming purposes with an audience largely made up of competition winners and invited guests. An hour-long edit of the show comprising 'Castellorizon', 'On An Island', 'The Blue', 'Take A Breath', 'Smile', 'Shine On You Crazy Diamond, Parts 1-5', 'Wearing The Inside Out' and 'Comfortably Numb' was broadcast in the UK on BBC Radio 2 between 9.30pm and 10.30pm, and could be viewed on the BBC Radio 2 website between Saturday 11 March and Saturday 18 March 2006. Various other edits were shown and repeated on numerous broadcast channels worldwide. In what was the BBC's first ever interactive TV production, a 30-minute edit of the concert was made available via BBC Interactive TV between Saturday 11 and Tuesday 14 March 2006 featuring 'On An Island', 'Shine On You Crazy Diamond, Parts 1-5' and 'Comfortably Numb'. The complete edited show was also screened with additional footage, including 'High Hopes' live, the promo film for 'On An Island' as well as interview footage as part of a nationwide cinema presentation across 100 selected US cinemas under the banner *Big Screen Concerts* on Tuesday 16 May 2006.

FRIDAY 10 MARCH 2006 – PERFORMANCE
Konzerthaus, Dortmund, Germany

Set list: 'Castellorizon', 'On An Island', 'The Blue' , 'Red Sky At Night', 'This Heaven', 'Then I Close My Eyes', 'Smile', 'Take A Breath', 'A Pocketful Of Stones', 'Where We Start' <Intermission> 'Shine On You Crazy Diamond, Parts 1-5', 'Wot's Uh… The Deal', 'Wearing The Inside Out', 'Breathe', 'Time', 'Breathe (Reprise)', 'Dominoes', 'High Hopes', 'Echoes' <Encore> 'Wish You Were Here', 'Comfortably Numb'.

SATURDAY 11 MARCH 2006 – PERFORMANCE
Saal 1, Congress Centrum Hamburg, Hamburg, Germany

Set list: 'Castellorizon', 'On An Island', 'The Blue' , 'Red Sky At Night', 'This Heaven', 'Then I Close My Eyes', 'Smile', 'Take A Breath', 'A Pocketful Of Stones', 'Where We Start' <Intermission> 'Shine On You Crazy Diamond, Parts 1-5', 'Wot's Uh… The Deal', 'Wearing The Inside Out', 'Breathe', 'Time', 'Breathe (Reprise)', 'Dominoes', 'High Hopes', 'Echoes' <Encore> 'Wish You Were Here', 'Comfortably Numb'.

WEDNESDAY 15 MARCH 2006 – PERFORMANCE
Le Grand Rex, Paris, France

Set list: 'Castellorizon', 'On An Island', 'The Blue' , 'Red Sky At Night', 'This Heaven', 'Then I Close My Eyes', 'Smile', 'Take A Breath', 'A Pocketful Of Stones', 'Where We Start' <Intermission> 'Shine On You Crazy Diamond, Parts 1-5', 'Wot's Uh… The Deal', 'Wearing The Inside Out', 'Breathe', 'Time', 'Breathe (Reprise)', 'Dominoes', 'High Hopes', 'Echoes' <Encore> 'Wish You Were Here', 'Comfortably Numb'.

THURSDAY 16 MARCH 2006 – PERFORMANCE
L'Olympia, Paris, France

Set list: 'Castellorizon', 'On An Island', 'The Blue', 'The Great Gig In The Sky' (guest vocals Sam Brown), 'Red Sky At Night', 'This Heaven', 'Then I Close My Eyes', 'Smile', 'Take A Breath', 'A Pocketful Of Stones', 'Where We Start' <Intermission> 'Shine On You Crazy Diamond, Parts 1-5', 'Wot's Uh… The Deal', 'Wearing The Inside Out', 'Fat Old Sun', 'Breathe', 'Time', 'Breathe (Reprise)', 'High Hopes', 'Echoes' <Encore> 'Wish You Were Here', 'Comfortably Numb'.

SATURDAY 18 MARCH 2006 – PERFORMANCE
Alte Oper, Frankfurt, Germany

Set list: 'Castellorizon', 'On An Island', 'The Blue' , 'Red Sky At Night', 'This Heaven', 'Then I Close My Eyes', 'Smile', 'Take A Breath', 'A Pocketful Of Stones', 'Where We Start' <Intermission> 'Shine On You Crazy Diamond, Parts 1–5', 'Wot's Uh… The Deal', 'Wearing The Inside Out', 'Fat Old Sun', 'Breathe', 'Time', 'Breathe (Reprise)', 'High Hopes', 'Echoes' <Encore> 'Wish You Were Here', 'Comfortably Numb'.

SUNDAY 19 MARCH 2006 – PERFORMANCE
Heineken Music Hall, Amsterdam, Netherlands

Set list: 'Castellorizon', 'On An Island', 'The Blue', 'Red Sky At Night', 'This Heaven', 'Then I Close My Eyes', 'Smile', 'Take A Breath', 'A Pocketful Of Stones', 'Where We Start' <Intermission> 'Shine On You Crazy Diamond, Parts 1–5', 'Wot's Uh… The Deal', 'Wearing The Inside Out', 'Dominoes', 'Breathe', 'Time', 'Breathe (Reprise)', 'High Hopes', 'Echoes' <Encore> 'Wish You Were Here', 'Comfortably Numb'.

MONDAY 20 MARCH 2006 – PERFORMANCE
Heineken Music Hall, Amsterdam, Netherlands

Set list: 'Castellorizon', 'On An Island', 'The Blue', 'Red Sky At Night', 'This Heaven', 'Then I Close My Eyes', 'Take A Breath', 'Smile', 'A Pocketful Of Stones', 'Where We Start' <Intermission> 'Shine On You Crazy Diamond, Parts 1–5', 'Wot's Uh… The Deal', 'Fat Old Sun', 'Coming Back To Life', 'Breathe', 'Time', 'Breathe (Reprise)', 'High Hopes', 'Echoes' <Encore> 'Wish You Were Here', 'Comfortably Numb'.

FRIDAY 24 MARCH 2006 – PERFORMANCE
Teatro degli Arcimboldi, Milan, Italy

Set list: 'Castellorizon', 'On An Island', 'The Blue', 'Red Sky At Night', 'This Heaven', 'Then I Close My Eyes', 'Take A Breath', 'Smile', 'A Pocketful Of Stones', 'Where We Start' <Intermission> 'Shine On You Crazy Diamond, Parts 1–5', 'Wot's Uh… The Deal', 'Wearing The Inside Out', 'Coming Back To Life', 'Breathe', 'Time', 'Breathe (Reprise)', 'High Hopes', 'Echoes' <Encore> 'Wish You Were Here', 'Comfortably Numb'.

SATURDAY 25 MARCH 2006 – PERFORMANCE
Teatro degli Arcimboldi, Milan, Italy

Set list: 'Castellorizon', 'On An Island', 'The Blue', 'Red Sky At Night', 'This Heaven', 'Then I Close My Eyes', 'Take A Breath', 'Smile', 'A Pocketful Of Stones', 'Where We Start' <Intermission> 'Shine On You Crazy Diamond, Parts 1–5', 'Wearing The Inside Out', 'Dominoes', 'Fat Old Sun', 'Breathe', 'Time', 'Breathe (Reprise)', 'High Hopes', 'Echoes' <Encore> 'Wish You Were Here', 'Comfortably Numb'.

SUNDAY 26 MARCH 2006 – PERFORMANCE
Sala Santa Cecilia, Auditorium Parco della Musica, Rome, Italy

Set list: 'Castellorizon', 'On An Island', 'The Blue', 'Red Sky At Night', 'This Heaven', 'Then I Close My Eyes', 'Take A Breath', 'Smile', 'A Pocketful Of Stones', 'Where We Start' <Intermission> 'Shine On You Crazy Diamond, Parts 1–5', 'Wearing The Inside Out', 'Dominoes', 'Fat Old Sun', 'Breathe', 'Time', 'Breathe (Reprise)', 'High Hopes', 'Echoes' <Encore> 'Wish You Were Here', 'Comfortably Numb'.

TUESDAY 4 APRIL 2006 – PERFORMANCE
Radio City Music Hall, New York, NY, USA

Set list: 'Castellorizon', 'This Heaven', 'Smile', 'Red Sky At Night', 'Take A Breath', 'Then I Close My Eyes', 'On

RIGHT: ON STAGE AT THE SALA SANTA CECILIA, ROME, 26 MARCH 2006.

An Island' (with guest vocals David Crosby and Graham Nash), 'The Blue' (with guest vocals David Crosby and Graham Nash), 'A Pocketful Of Stones', 'Where We Start' <Intermission> 'Shine On You Crazy Diamond, Parts 1–5' (with guest vocals David Crosby and Graham Nash), 'Wearing The Inside Out', 'Dominoes', 'Fat Old Sun', 'Breathe', 'Time', 'Breathe (Reprise)', 'High Hopes', 'Echoes' <Encore> 'Wish You Were Here', 'Find The Cost Of Freedom' (with guest vocals David Crosby and Graham Nash), 'Comfortably Numb'.

WEDNESDAY 5 APRIL 2006 – PERFORMANCE
Radio City Music Hall, New York, NY, USA

Set list: 'Castellorizon', 'This Heaven', 'Smile', 'Red Sky At Night', 'Take A Breath', 'Then I Close My Eyes', 'On An Island' (with guest vocals David Crosby and Graham Nash), 'The Blue' (guest vocals David Crosby and Graham Nash), 'A Pocketful Of Stones', 'Where We Start' <Intermission> 'Shine On You Crazy Diamond, Parts 1–5' (with guest vocals David Crosby and Graham Nash), 'Wot's Uh… The Deal', 'Wearing The Inside Out' / 'Coming Back To Life', 'Breathe', 'Time', 'Breathe (Reprise)', 'High Hopes', 'Echoes' <Encore> 'Wish You Were Here', 'Find The Cost Of Freedom' (with guest vocals David Crosby and Graham Nash), 'Comfortably Numb'.

FRIDAY 7 APRIL 2006 – RADIO RECORDING
Artist Confidential, Studio Z, Sony Studios, New York, NY, USA

Gilmour and Phil Manzanera recorded an interview and performed 'Smile' and 'Where We Start' in a programme arranged by the XM Internet Radio broadcasting group and hosted by George Taylor Morris as part of their *Artist Confidential* series to an exclusive audience of no more than 30 people comprising record company executives, friends and family. It was broadcast from Monday 5 June 2006.

FRIDAY 7 APRIL 2006 – RADIO RECORDING
AOL Sessions, Studio Z, Sony Studios, New York, NY, USA

Gilmour and his touring band performed 'On An Island', 'This Heaven', 'Take A Breath', 'Smile', 'High Hopes' and 'Comfortably Numb' live

for the AOL Internet provider as part of their *AOL Sessions* series. It was available for viewing in 5.1 surround sound for a limited period from Friday 21 April 2006.

SUNDAY 9 APRIL 2006 – PERFORMANCE
Massey Hall, Toronto, Canada

Set list: 'Castellorizon', 'On An Island', 'The Blue', 'Red Sky At Night', 'This Heaven', 'Then I Close My Eyes', 'Take A Breath', 'Smile', 'A Pocketful Of Stones', 'Where We Start' <Intermission> 'Shine On You Crazy Diamond, Parts 1–5', 'Wot's Uh… The Deal', 'Wearing The Inside Out', 'Fat Old Sun', 'Breathe', 'Time', 'Breathe (Reprise)', 'High Hopes', 'Echoes' <Encore> 'Wish You Were Here', 'Comfortably Numb'.

MONDAY 10 APRIL 2006 – PERFORMANCE
Massey Hall, Toronto, Canada

Set list: 'Castellorizon', 'On An Island', 'The Blue', 'Red Sky At Night', 'This Heaven', 'Then I Close My Eyes', 'Take A Breath', 'Smile', 'A Pocketful Of Stones', 'Where We Start' <Intermission> 'Shine On You Crazy Diamond, Parts 1–5', 'Wearing The Inside Out', 'Dominoes', 'Coming Back To Life', 'Breathe', 'Time', 'Breathe (Reprise)', 'High Hopes', 'Echoes' <Encore> 'Wish You Were Here', 'Comfortably Numb'.

WEDNESDAY 12 APRIL 2006 – PERFORMANCE
Rosemont Theatre, Rosemont, Chicago, IL, USA

Set list: 'Castellorizon', 'On An Island', 'Red Sky At Night', 'The Blue' , 'Then I Close My Eyes', 'This Heaven', 'Smile', 'Take A Breath', 'A Pocketful Of Stones', 'Where We Start' <Intermission> 'Shine On You Crazy Diamond, Parts 1–5', 'Wot's Uh… The Deal', 'Wearing The Inside Out', 'Fat Old Sun', 'Breathe', 'Time', 'Breathe (Reprise)', 'High Hopes', 'Echoes' <Encore> 'Wish You Were Here', 'Comfortably Numb'.

THURSDAY 13 APRIL 2006 – PERFORMANCE
Rosemont Theatre, Rosemont, Chicago, IL, USA

Set list: 'Castellorizon', 'On An Island', 'The Blue', 'Red Sky At Night', 'This Heaven', 'Then I Close My Eyes', 'Smile', 'Take A Breath', 'A Pocketful Of Stones', 'Where We Start' <Intermission> 'Shine On You Crazy Diamond, Parts 1–5', 'Wot's Uh… The Deal', 'Dominoes', 'Coming Back To Life', 'Breathe', 'Time', 'Breathe (Reprise)', 'High Hopes', 'Echoes' <Encore> 'Wish You Were Here', 'Comfortably Numb'.

SUNDAY 16 APRIL 2006 – PERFORMANCE
Paramount Theatre of the Arts, Oakland, CA, USA

Set List: 'Breathe', 'Time', 'Breathe (Reprise)', 'Castellorizon', 'On An Island', 'The Blue', 'Red Sky At Night', 'This Heaven', 'Then I Close My Eyes', 'Smile', 'Take A Breath', 'A Pocketful Of Stones', 'Where We Start' <Intermission> 'Shine On You Crazy Diamond, Parts 1–5', 'Wot's Uh… The Deal', 'Dominoes', 'Coming Back To Life', 'High Hopes', 'Echoes' <Encore> 'Wish You Were Here', 'Comfortably Numb'.

MONDAY 17 APRIL 2006 – PERFORMANCE
Paramount Theatre Of The Arts, Oakland, CA, USA

Set list: 'Breathe', 'Time', 'Breathe (Reprise)', 'Castellorizon', 'On An Island', 'The Blue', 'Red Sky At Night', 'This Heaven', 'Then I Close My Eyes', 'Smile', 'Take A Breath', 'A Pocketful Of Stones', 'Where We Start' <Intermission> 'Shine On You Crazy Diamond, Parts 1–5', 'Wearing The Inside Out', 'Fat Old Sun', 'Arnold Layne', 'Coming Back To Life', 'High Hopes', 'Echoes' <Encore> 'Wish You Were Here', 'Comfortably Numb'.

WEDNESDAY 19 APRIL 2006 – PERFORMANCE
Kodak Theatre, Hollywood & Highland Center, Los Angeles, CA, USA

Set list: 'Breathe', 'Time', 'Breathe (Reprise)', 'Castellorizon', 'On An Island' (with guest vocals David Crosby and Graham Nash), 'The Blue', 'Red Sky At Night', 'This Heaven', 'Then I Close My Eyes', 'Smile', 'Take A Breath', 'A Pocketful Of Stones', 'Where We Start' <Intermission> 'Shine On You Crazy Diamond, Parts 1–5' (with guest vocals David Crosby and Graham Nash), 'Wearing The Inside Out', 'Fat Old Sun', 'Arnold Layne', 'Coming Back To Life', 'High Hopes', 'Echoes' <Encore> 'Wish

You Were Here', 'Find The Cost Of Freedom' (with guest vocals David Crosby and Graham Nash), 'Comfortably Numb'.

THURSDAY 20 APRIL 2006 – TELEVISION BROADCAST
The Tonight Show with Jay Leno, NBC TV studios, Los Angeles, CA, USA

Gilmour and his touring band made a live appearance on *The Tonight Show* with Jay Leno in an outdoor setting to a small audience, comprised of competition winners selected through DavidGilmour.com and performed a shortened version of 'On An Island' with David Crosby and Graham Nash. The band also performed 'Wish You Were Here' over the closing credits of the show. It was broadcast in the US on the NBC–TV network between 11.35pm and 12.35pm (PST).

THURSDAY 20 APRIL 2006 – PERFORMANCE
Gibson Amphitheater, Universal City, Los Angeles, CA, USA

Set list: 'Breathe', 'Time', 'Breathe (Reprise)', 'Castellorizon', 'On An Island' (with guest vocals David Crosby and Graham Nash), 'The Blue', 'Red Sky At Night', 'This Heaven', 'Then I Close My Eyes', 'Smile', 'Take A Breath', 'A Pocketful Of Stones', 'Where We Start' <Intermission> 'Shine On You Crazy Diamond, Parts 1–5' (with guest vocals David Crosby and Graham Nash), 'Wot's Uh… The Deal', 'Fat Old Sun', 'Arnold Layne', 'Coming Back To Life', 'High Hopes', 'Echoes' <Encore> 'Wish You Were Here', 'Find The Cost Of Freedom' (with guest vocals David Crosby and Graham Nash), 'Comfortably Numb'.

TUESDAY 23 MAY 2006 – TELEVISION BROADCAST
Later… with Jools Holland, Studio 2, BBC Television Centre, White City, London, England

Gilmour and his touring band made a live appearance on *Later…with Jools Holland* performing 'Take A Breath', 'On An Island' and 'Arnold Layne'. Also appearing on the show were David Crosby and Graham Nash who lent backing vocals to 'On An Island'. It was broadcast on BBC2 TV on 26 May 2006 between 11.35pm and 12.35pm. 'On An Island' later appeared on the DVD *Best of Later… with Jools Holland* 2000–2006 (UK: Warner Music Video 256463986-2, November 2006).

FRIDAY 26 MAY 2006 – PERFORMANCE
Bridgewater Hall, Manchester, England

Set list: 'Breathe', 'Time', 'Breathe (Reprise)', 'Castellorizon', 'On An Island' (with guest vocals David Crosby and Graham Nash), 'The Blue' (with guest vocals David Crosby and Graham Nash), 'Red Sky At Night', 'This Heaven', 'Then I Close My Eyes', 'Smile', 'Take A Breath', 'A Pocketful Of Stones', 'Where We Start' <Intermission> 'Shine On You Crazy Diamond, Parts 1–5' (with guest vocals David Crosby and Graham Nash), 'Wearing The Inside Out', 'Fat Old Sun', 'Arnold Layne', 'Coming Back To Life', 'High Hopes', 'Echoes' <Encore> 'Wish You Were Here', 'Find The Cost Of Freedom' (with guest vocals David Crosby and Graham Nash), 'Comfortably Numb'.

SATURDAY 27 MAY 2006 – PERFORMANCE
Clyde Auditorium, Scottish Exhibition & Conference Centre, Glasgow, Scotland

Set list: 'Breathe', 'Time', 'Breathe (Reprise)', 'Castellorizon', 'On An Island' (with guest vocals David Crosby), 'The Blue' (with guest vocals David Crosby), 'Red Sky At Night', 'This Heaven', 'Then I Close My Eyes', 'Smile', 'Take A Breath', 'A Pocketful Of Stones', 'Where We Start' <Intermission> 'Shine On You Crazy Diamond, Parts 1–5' (with guest vocals David Crosby), 'Wearing The Inside Out', 'Fat Old Sun', 'Coming Back To Life', 'High Hopes', 'Echoes' <Encore> 'Wish You Were Here', 'Arnold Layne', 'Comfortably Numb'.

MONDAY 29 MAY 2006 – PERFORMANCE
Royal Albert Hall, London, England

Set list: 'Breathe', 'Time', 'Breathe (Reprise)', 'Castellorizon', 'On An Island' (with guest vocals David Crosby), 'The Blue' (with guest vocals David Crosby and Graham Nash), 'Red Sky At Night', 'This Heaven', 'Then I Close My Eyes' (with

guest trumpet Robert Wyatt), 'Smile', 'Take A Breath', 'A Pocketful Of Stones', 'Where We Start' <Intermission> 'Shine On You Crazy Diamond, Parts 1–5' (with guest vocals David Crosby and Graham Nash), 'Wot's Uh… The Deal', 'Wearing The Inside Out', 'Coming Back To Life', 'High Hopes', 'Echoes' <Encore> 'Wish You Were Here', 'Find The Cost Of Freedom' (with guest vocals David Crosby and Graham Nash), 'Arnold Layne' (with guest vocals David Bowie), 'Comfortably Numb' (with guest vocals David Bowie).

All three Royal Albert Hall shows were recorded and filmed for future release, highlights of which were broadcast on BBC Radio 1 on Saturday 8 September 2007 between 11.00pm and 12.00midnight and repeated on BBC Radio 1 on Sunday 25 May 2008 between 12.00midnight and 1.00am. 'Arnold Layne' (featuring David Bowie) was shown on *Top of the Pops 2* BBC2 TV on Saturday 6 January 2007 between 5.05pm and 5.40pm.

TUESDAY 30 MAY 2006 – PERFORMANCE
Royal Albert Hall, London, England

Set list: 'Breathe', 'Time', 'Breathe (Reprise)', 'Castellorizon', 'On An Island' (with guest vocals David Crosby and Graham Nash), 'The Blue' (with guest vocals David Crosby and Graham Nash), 'Red Sky At Night', 'This Heaven', 'Then I Close My Eyes' (with guest trumpet Robert Wyatt), 'Smile', 'Take A Breath', 'A Pocketful Of Stones', 'Where We Start' <Intermission> 'Shine On You Crazy Diamond, Parts 1–5' (with guest vocals David Crosby and Graham Nash), 'Fat Old Sun', 'Arnold Layne', 'Coming Back To Life', 'High Hopes', 'The Great Gig In The Sky' (with guest vocals Mica Paris), 'Echoes' <Encore> 'Wish You Were Here', 'Find The Cost Of Freedom' (with guest vocals David Crosby and Graham Nash), 'Comfortably Numb'.

WEDNESDAY 31 MAY 2006 – PERFORMANCE
Royal Albert Hall, London, England

Set list: 'Breathe', 'Time', 'Breathe (Reprise)', 'Castellorizon', 'On An Island' (with guest vocals David Crosby and Graham Nash), 'The Blue' (with guest vocals David Crosby and Graham Nash), 'Red Sky At Night', 'This Heaven', 'Then I Close My Eyes' (with guest trumpet Robert Wyatt), 'Smile', 'Take A Breath', 'A Pocketful Of Stones', 'Where We Start' <Intermission> 'Shine On You Crazy Diamond, Parts 1–5' (with guest vocals David Crosby and Graham Nash), 'Fat Old Sun', 'Dominoes', 'Arnold Layne', 'Coming Back To Life', 'High Hopes', 'The Great Gig In The Sky' (with guest vocals Mica Paris), 'Echoes' <Encore> 'Wish You Were Here' (with guest drums Nick Mason), 'Find The Cost Of Freedom' (with guest vocals David Crosby and Graham Nash), 'Comfortably Numb' (with guest drums Nick Mason).

THURSDAY 27 JULY 2006 – PERFORMANCE
Burg Clam, Klam, near Linz, Austria

Set list: 'Breathe', 'Time', 'Breathe (Reprise)', 'Castellorizon', 'On An Island', 'The Blue', 'Red Sky At Night', 'This Heaven', 'Then I Close My Eyes', 'Smile', 'Take A Breath', 'A Pocketful Of Stones', 'Where We Start' <Intermission> 'Shine On You Crazy Diamond, Parts 1–5', 'Astronomy Dominé', 'Dark Globe', 'Fat Old Sun', 'Coming Back To Life', 'High Hopes', 'Echoes' <Encore> 'Wish You Were Here', 'Comfortably Numb'.

SATURDAY 29 JULY 2006 – PERFORMANCE
Königsplatz, Munich, Germany

Set list: 'Breathe', 'Time', 'Breathe (Reprise)', 'Castellorizon', 'On An Island', 'The Blue', 'Red Sky At Night', 'This Heaven', 'Then I Close My Eyes', 'Smile', 'Take A Breath', 'A Pocketful Of Stones', 'Where We Start' <Intermission> 'Shine On You Crazy Diamond, Parts 1–5', 'Astronomy Domine', 'Dark Globe', 'Fat Old Sun', 'Coming Back To Life', 'High Hopes', 'Echoes' <Encore> 'Wish You Were Here', 'Comfortably Numb'.

MONDAY 31 JULY 2006 – PERFORMANCE
Théâtre Antique, Vienne, France

Set list: 'Breathe', 'Time', 'Breathe (Reprise)', 'Castellorizon', 'On An Island', 'The Blue', 'Red Sky At Night', 'This Heaven', 'Then I Close My Eyes', 'Smile', 'Take A Breath', 'A Pocketful Of Stones', 'Where We Start' <Intermission> 'Shine On You Crazy Diamond, Parts 1–5', 'Wot's Uh… The Deal', 'Fat Old Sun', 'Arnold Layne', 'Coming Back To Life', 'High Hopes', 'Echoes' <Encore> 'Wish You Were Here', 'Comfortably Numb'.

WEDNESDAY 2 AUGUST 2006 – PERFORMANCE
Piazza di Santa Croce, Florence, Italy

Set list: 'Breathe', 'Time', 'Breathe (Reprise)', 'Castellorizon', 'On An Island', 'The Blue', 'Red Sky At Night', 'This Heaven', 'Then I Close My Eyes', 'Smile', 'Take A Breath', 'A Pocketful Of Stones', 'Where We Start' <Intermission> 'Shine On You Crazy Diamond, Parts 1–5', 'Wearing The Inside Out', 'Astronomy Domine', 'Fat Old Sun', 'Coming Back To Life', 'High Hopes', 'Echoes' <Encore> 'Wish You Were Here', 'Comfortably Numb'.

FRIDAY 11 AUGUST 2006 – PERFORMANCE
Piazza San Marco, Venice, Italy

Rescheduled from Thursday 3 and Friday 4 August due to a structural defect with the staging.
Set list: 'Breathe', 'Time', 'Breathe (Reprise)', 'Castellorizon', 'On An Island', 'The Blue', 'Red Sky At Night', 'This Heaven', 'Then I Close My Eyes', 'Smile', 'Take A Breath', 'A Pocketful Of Stones', 'Where We Start' <Intermission> 'Shine On You Crazy Diamond, Parts 1–5', 'Astronomy Domine', 'Wot's Uh… The Deal', 'Fat Old Sun', 'On The Turning Away', 'High Hopes', 'Echoes' <Encore> 'Wish You Were Here', 'Comfortably Numb'.

SATURDAY 12 AUGUST 2006 – PERFORMANCE
Piazza San Marco, Venice, Italy

Set list: 'Breathe', 'Time', 'Breathe (Reprise)', 'Castellorizon', 'On An Island', 'The Blue', 'Red Sky At Night', 'This Heaven', 'Then I Close My Eyes', 'Smile', 'Take A Breath', 'A Pocketful Of Stones', 'Where We Start' <Intermission> 'Shine On You Crazy Diamond, Parts 1–5', 'Wot's Uh… The Deal', 'Arnold Layne', 'Dark Globe', 'Fat Old Sun', 'On The Turning Away', 'High Hopes', 'Echoes' <Encore> 'Wish You Were Here', 'Comfortably Numb'.

SATURDAY 26 AUGUST 2006 – PERFORMANCE
Przestrzeń Wolności [Spread Freedom],
Gdańsk Shipyards, Gdańsk, Poland

Set list: 'Breathe', 'Time', 'Breathe (Reprise)', 'Castellorizon', 'On An Island', 'The Blue', 'Red Sky At Night', 'This Heaven', 'Then I Close My Eyes', 'Smile', 'Take A Breath', 'A Pocketful Of Stones', 'Where We Start' <Intermission> 'Shine On You Crazy Diamond, Parts 1–5', 'Wot's Uh… The Deal', 'Astronomy Domine', 'Fat Old Sun', 'High Hopes', 'Echoes' <Encore> 'Wish You Were Here', 'A Great Day For Freedom', 'Comfortably Numb'.

This unique concert was staged at the invitation of Polish president Lech Walesa and Pawel Adamowicz, mayor of Gdańsk. Zbigniew Preisner conducted the 40-piece Polish-Baltic Philharmonic orchestra for the show which was attended by over 50,000 people and was staged to mark the 26th anniversary of the founding of the Solidarity trade union movement. Gilmour attended a press conference the day before the show

accompanied by Pawel Adamowicz, and the chairman and vice-chairman of Fundacja Gdańska, Stanislaw Plakwicz and Ryszard Bongowski.

The entire concert was recorded and filmed and released in September 2008 on the CD and DVD package *David Gilmour Live in Gdańsk*. (See Discography for further details.) A two-part programme beginning with *Dave Gilmour Live in Gdańsk* was broadcast on BBC4 TV on Friday 26 September 2008 between 9.10pm and 10.10pm followed by *Dave Gilmour Gdańsk Diary* between 10.10pm and 10.40pm.

TUESDAY 29 AUGUST 2006 – TELEVISION BROADCAST
Live From Abbey Road, Studio 1,
Abbey Road Studios, London, England

Gilmour and his touring band performed 'On An Island', 'Take A Breath', 'Smile' and 'Astronomy Domine' live in an afternoon session with a small invited audience for the Channel 4 TV series *Live from Abbey Road*. Only the first three tracks were used for transmission. It was first broadcast in the UK on More4 TV on Friday 2 March 2007 between 11.00pm and 12.00midnight. Series highlights including 'On An Island' were released on the DVD *Live from Abbey Road Making Music History Series 1* on Monday 15 October 2007 (UK: Fremantle Home Entertainment FHED 2093), and *Live from Abbey Road Best of Series 1* on DVD on Tuesday 11 November 2008 (US: Fremantle Media 787364825097) and Blu-Ray (US: Fremantle Media 48251-9).

THURSDAY 6 SEPTEMBER 2007 – PERFORMANCE
The Odeon Cinema, Leicester Square, London, England

Gilmour performed 'Castellorizon' as a solo performance and 'Island Jam' featuring current band members Jon Carin (Guitar), Steve DiStanislao (Drums), Phil Manzanera (Guitar), Dick Parry (Saxophone), Guy Pratt (Bass Guitar) and Richard Wright (Keyboards) at the premiere screening of the live DVD *Remember That Night Live at the Royal Albert Hall*, in which an 85-minute selection of edited highlights and a tour documentary was screened as well as a Q&A session with Gilmour hosted by broadcaster Stuart Maconie. Further screenings were held nationally on the same evening.

SATURDAY 15 SEPTEMBER 2007 – PERFORMANCE
The Ritzy, Brixton, London, England

Gilmour performed 'Castellorizon' as a solo performance at a screening of the live DVD *Remember That Night Live at the Royal Albert Hall*, in which an 85-minute selection of edited highlights and a tour documentary was screened as well as a Q&A session with Gilmour hosted by Phil Manzanera. The event was also filmed and satellite broadcast in 5.1 surround sound to over 160 cinemas in North America.

TUESDAY 23 SEPTEMBER 2008 – TELEVISION BROADCAST
Later… with Jools Holland, Studio 2, BBC Television Centre,
White City, London, England

Gilmour revived his touring band to make a live appearance on the music programme *Later… with Jools Holland*, and in light of recent events dedicated a performance of 'Remember A Day' in memory of Richard Wright. It was broadcast on BBC2 TV between 10.00pm and 10.30pm. A longer version of the show which also included 'The Blue' and 'On An Island' was broadcast on BBC2 TV on Friday 26 September between 11.35pm and 12.40pm.

DAVID GILMOUR LIVE

The following dates had been announced in support of the album *Rattle That Lock* at time of going to press and therefore details are incomplete. The North American dates were heavily criticized by fans having apparently "sold out" within 15 seconds of going on sale and then immediately appearing on StubHub at hugely inflated prices of anything between $2,000 and $6,000 a seat.

SATURDAY 5 SEPTEMBER 2015
Brighton Centre, Brighton, England

SATURDAY 12 SEPTEMBER 2015 – PERFORMANCE ▼
Arena Pula, Pula, Croatia

MONDAY 14 SEPTEMBER 2015 – PERFORMANCE
Arena di Verona, Verona, Italy

TUESDAY 15 SEPTEMBER 2015 – PERFORMANCE
Ippodromo del Visarno, Florence, Italy

Rescheduled from Teatro le Mulina.

THURSDAY 17 SEPTEMBER 2015 – PERFORMANCE
Théâtre Antique d'Orange, Orange, France

SATURDAY 19 SEPTEMBER 2015 – PERFORMANCE
König-Pilsener Arena, Oberhausen, Germany

WEDNESDAY 23, THURSDAY 24, FRIDAY 25 SEPTEMBER 2015 – PERFORMANCES
Royal Albert Hall, London, England

FRIDAY 2, SATURDAY 3 OCTOBER 2015 – PERFORMANCES
Royal Albert Hall, London, England

THURSDAY 24 & FRIDAY 25 MARCH 2016 – PERFORMANCES
Hollywood Bowl, Los Angeles, CA, USA

SUNDAY 27 MARCH 2016 – PERFORMANCE
LA Forum, Los Angeles, CA, USA

THURSDAY 31 MARCH & FRIDAY 1 APRIL 2016 – PERFORMANCES
Air Canada Centre, Toronto, Canada

MONDAY 4 & FRIDAY 8 APRIL 2016 – PERFORMANCES
United Center, Chicago, IL, USA

MONDAY 11 & TUESDAY 12 APRIL 2016 – PERFORMANCES
Madison Square Garden, New York, NY, USA

SATURDAY 25 JUNE 2016 – PERFORMANCE
Rynek we Wrocławiu, Wroclaw, Poland

OTHER LIVE APPEARANCES

WEDNESDAY 28 NOVEMBER 1973 – RADIO RECORDING
Sounds of the 70s, Langham 1 Studio, BBC Broadcasting House, Portland Place, London, England

ABOVE: DAVID GILMOUR BACKING ROY HARPER AT HYDE PARK, 31 AUGUST 1974.

Gilmour played guitar with Unicorn for this live recording session for BBC Radio 1. It was broadcast on Bob Harris' *Sounds of the Seventies* on Monday 10 December 1973.

SATURDAY 31 AUGUST 1974 – PERFORMANCE
Hyde Park, London, England

Gilmour played guitar with Roy Harper, whose band was billed as "Heavy Friends" and featured John Paul Jones (Bass) and Steve Broughton (Drums). Harper's set included 'The Game' and 'I Hate The White Man'. This was one of the last Hyde Park free concerts organized by Blackhill Enterprises and featured performances by Roger McGuinn, Julie Felix, Toots & the Maytals, Chilli Willi & the Red Hot Peppers and Kokomo.

SUNDAY 10 NOVEMBER 1974 – PERFORMANCE
Ellison Building, Newcastle Polytechnic, Newcastle-upon-Tyne, England

Gilmour shared lead guitar with Tim Renwick and Richard Wright played keyboards at this Sutherland Brothers & Quiver show.

MONDAY 23 DECEMBER 1974 – PERFORMANCE
The Marquee, Wardour Street, Soho, London, England

Gilmour played guitar at this Sutherland Brothers & Quiver show, supported by Unicorn.

TUESDAY 3 OCTOBER 1978 – PERFORMANCE
Studio 2, EMI Studios, Abbey Road, London, England

Gilmour played guitar as part of a supergroup calling itself Rockestra formed by Paul McCartney for the purpose of recording the songs

'Rockestra Theme' and 'So Glad To See You Here' for his forthcoming album *Back to the Egg*. The featured musicians included: Pete Townshend, Hank Marvin, Denny Laine and Laurence Juber (Guitars); John Bonham, Kenny Jones and Steve Holly (Drums); Ray Cooper, Tony Carr, Speedy Acquaye and Maurice Pert (Percussion); Paul McCartney, Bruce Thomas and Ronnie Lane (Bass) and John Paul Jones, Gary Brooker, Tony Ashton and Linda McCartney (Keyboards); Howie Casey, Thaddeus Richard, Tony Dorsey and Steve Howard (Horns). McCartney also arranged for the session to be professionally filmed for future use and in 1980 edited the footage to produce a 40-minute programme. The film remains unreleased, save for a 15-minute excerpt that was screened at the *Back to the Egg* launch party held at Abbey Road studios on Monday 11 June 1979. The track 'Rockestra Theme' finally saw a release some 23 years later as part of the two-hour long made-for-TV documentary *Wingspan: An Intimate Portrait*, which was broadcast on ABC network TV in the US on Friday 11 May 2001 and on Channel 4 TV in the UK on Saturday 12 May 2001. It was later released on DVD in November 2001.

ABOVE: DAVID GILMOUR PERFORMING WITH BRYAN FERRY. GILMOUR WAS THE ONLY MEMBER OF PINK FLOYD TO APPEAR AT LIVE AID, 1985.

SATURDAY 3 NOVEMBER 1984 – PERFORMANCE ▼
The Guitar Greats, Capitol Theatre, Passaic, NJ, USA

As part of this all-star event sponsored by MTV, Gilmour performed 'You Know I'm Right' and 'Murder'. He also joined in the all-star finale of 'Johnny B. Goode' and 'Green Onions'. Other performers included guitarists Johnny Winter, Steve Cropper, Brian Setzer, Dickie Betts, Neal Schon, Tony Iommi, Lita Ford, Link Wray and Dave Edmunds. The house band included Kenny Aaronson (Bass), Mike Shrieve (Drums), Chuck Leavell and Jonathan Cain (Keyboards), and Stanley Harrison, Ed Manion, Mike Spengler and Steven Groppen (the Miami Horns). A one-hour edit was broadcast as part of the MTV *Rock Influences* series broadcast on Tuesday 20 November 1984.

SATURDAY 13 JULY 1985 – PERFORMANCE
Live Aid, Wembley Stadium, Wembley, England

Gilmour was the only member of Pink Floyd to appear at this

landmark event, playing guitar with Bryan Ferry's band, which consisted of Neil Hubbard (Guitar), Chester Kamen (Guitar), Jimmy Maelen (Percussion), Andy Newmark (Drums), Marcus Miller (Bass), Jon Carin (Keyboards) and Michelle Cobbs, Ednah Holt and Fonzi Thornton (Backing Vocals). The set comprised: 'Sensation', 'Boys And Girls', 'Slave To Love' and 'Jealous Guy'. Gilmour also participated in the grand finale, 'Feed The World'. The event was broadcast live on numerous global TV and radio networks, which included coverage of the sister show at the JFK Stadium in Philadelphia. 'Slave To Love' later appeared on the Bryan Ferry and Roxy Music retrospective VHS video *Total Recall: A History 1972–1982* and 'Slave To Love' and 'Jealous Guy' was released on the four-disc compilation DVD box set *Live Aid* in November 2004).

FRIDAY 10 OCTOBER 1985 – TELEVISION BROADCAST
The Tube, Tyne Tees Television Studios, Newcastle-upon-Tyne, England

Gilmour played guitar with Pete Townshend's Deep End, on the Channel 4 TV live-music programme *The Tube*, in a band that Townshend had formed to raise money for the Double O charity, in aid of victims of drug abuse. The Deep End band comprised John "Rabbit" Bundrick (Keyboards), Simon Philips (Drums), Jodi Linscott (Percussion), Pete Hope-Evans (Harmonica), Chucho Merchan (Bass), Ian Ellis, Gina Foster, Coral Gordon, Billy Nicholls and Chris Staines, (Backing Vocals) and the Kick Horns – comprising Simon Clarke, Roddy Lorimer, Dave Plews, Tim Sanders and Peter Beachill (Brass). Deep End performed 'Give Blood', 'Face The Face' and 'Second Hand Love', all from Townshend's album *White City*.

FRIDAY 1 & SATURDAY 2 NOVEMBER 1985 – PERFORMANCES
The Academy, Brixton, London, England

Gilmour played guitar with Pete Townshend's Deep End at two shows in London (a third show was booked for 3 November, but poor ticket sales forced its cancellation). The set comprised 'Mary-Anne With The Shaky Hand', 'Won't Get Fooled Again', 'A Little Is Enough', 'Second Hand Love', 'That's Alright Mama', 'Behind Blue Eyes', 'The Shout', 'Harlem Shuffle', 'Barefootin'', 'After The Fire', 'Love On The Air', 'Midnight Lover', 'Blue Light', 'I Put A Spell On You', 'I'm The One', 'Magic Bus', 'Save It For Later', 'Eyesight To The Blind', 'Walkin'', 'Stop Hurting People', 'The Sea Refuses No River', 'Boogie Stop Shuffle', 'Face The Face', 'Pinball Wizard', 'Give Blood' and 'Night Train'. (The show of 2 November also included 'Driftin' Blues' after 'I'm The One'). Film of the band's rehearsals, including a segment of 'Give Blood', was broadcast in the UK as part of an ITV *South Bank Show* documentary on Pete Townshend broadcast on Sunday 3 November 1985. A VHS video of the full 87-minute concert was later released in the US as *Pete Townshend's Deep End: The Brixton, England Concert in April 1986* and as *Pete Townshend Deep End Live in the UK* in August 1986. This footage was broadcast on the US Prism cable TV channel on Saturday 24 December 1988. A further 30-minute edited version was also released in the US as *Pete Townshend's Deep End, Mini Concert, The Brixton England Concert* and on CD and vinyl as *Deep End Live!* in October 1986, and *Pete Townshend Live Brixton Academy '85* double CD album in November 2004.

ABOVE: GILMOUR WITH PETE TOWNSHEND'S DEEP END AT CANNES, 29 JANUARY 1986.

WEDNESDAY 29 JANUARY 1986 – PERFORMANCE
Gala du MIDEM, Grand Auditorium,
Palais des Festivals, Cannes, France

Gilmour played guitar with Deep End at their final performance held to coincide with the international record industry's annual trade show, MIDEM. The set comprised 'Won't Get Fooled Again', 'Second Hand Love', 'Give Blood', 'Behind Blue Eyes', 'After The Fire', 'Slit Skirts', 'Blue Light', 'I Put A Spell On You', 'Hiding Out', 'The Sea Refuses No River', 'Face The Face', 'Pinball Wizard', 'A Little Is Enough', 'Rough Boys' and 'Night Train'. The show opened with French singer Jacques Higelin, was co-promoted by Germany's WDR TV *Rockpalast* music programme and was broadcast live across several European TV stations.

SUNDAY 9 FEBRUARY 1986 – PERFORMANCE ▶
Colombian Volcano Appeal,
**Royal Albert Hall,
London, England**

Gilmour performed 'Blue Light', 'You Know I'm Right', 'Run Like Hell', 'Out Of The Blue' and 'Comfortably Numb' at this charity fund-raising concert at the request of Deep End musician Chucho Merchan. He was backed by the 'house band' comprising Sam Brown and Paul Carrack (Vocals), Simon Philips (Drums), Mick Ralphs (Guitar), Jodi Linscott (Percussion), Chucho Merchan (Bass) and John "Rabbit" Bundrick (Keyboards). The show also featured performances by Pete Townshend with Emma Townshend and Peter Hope-Evans, Annie Lennox, Jaki Graham, Chrissie Hynde with Robbie McIntosh, the Communards, Working Week and the London School of Samba. The event was filmed for TV and 'Comfortably Numb' was broadcast in the UK on the Channel 4 TV programme *The Late Shift* on Wednesday 20 July 1988. Further highlights of the show were released on the VHS video *The Colombian Volcano Concert* in September 1992.

SUNDAY 15 FEBRUARY 1987 – PERFORMANCE
The London Jam,
Town & Country Club, London, England

Gilmour played guitar at this fund-raiser organized by *Guitar* magazine on behalf of the Childline charity alongside many other musicians including Albert Lee, James Burton, Geoff Whitehorn, Seymour Duncan, Tony Muschamp, Robbie Gladwell, Esmond Selwyn, Phil Hilborne, Andy Powell and Neil Murray.

SATURDAY 28 & SUNDAY 29 MARCH 1987 – PERFORMANCES
The Secret Policeman's Third Ball, The Palladium, London, England

Gilmour played guitar for Kate Bush in a band comprising Tony Franklin (Bass), Stuart Elliot (Drums) and Kevin McAlea (Keyboards) on renditions of 'Running Up That Hill' and 'Let It Be' for Amnesty International's occasional fund-raiser. The all-star line up for the finale of 'I Shall Be Released' included Gilmour on bass and, on the second night, Nick Mason on drums. The entire show, including 'Running Up That Hill', was given a limited UK cinematic release from Friday 25 September 1987, premiering at the Canon cinema, Shaftesbury Avenue, London. 'Running Up That Hill' was released on *The Secret Policeman's Third Ball* VHS video in September 1987 and has appeared on numerous repackages of the show since.

SUNDAY 25 OCTOBER 1987 – TELEVISION BROADCAST
Beyond The Floyd & David Gilmour: Live at the Hammersmith Odeon,
MTV, USA

MTV broadcast a 30-minute documentary, *Beyond the Floyd*, from 9.30pm (EST) featuring interviews with members of Pink Floyd and Pete Townshend as well as concert footage and scenes from the film *The Wall*, followed by a broadcast of Gilmour's Hammersmith Odeon shows of April 1984.

SATURDAY 12 DECEMBER 1987 – TELEVISION BROADCAST
Saturday Night Live, Studio 8H, NBC TV Studios, New York, NY, USA

Gilmour made a live appearance on NBC's *Saturday Night Live* performing 'Song For My Sara' with the studio house band featuring GE Smith (Guitar) and T-Bone Wilk (Bass). GE Smith later joined Roger Waters' band for his *Wall* tour in 2010.

THURSDAY 18 AUGUST 1988 – PERFORMANCE
Les Paul Tribute Concert, Majestic Theater,
Brooklyn Academy of Music, New York, NY, USA

Gilmour played guitar on 'Deep In The Blues' and the all-star finale of 'Blue Suede Shoes' at this commemoration gala for guitar guru Les Paul. Additional sets were performed by BB King, Stanley Jordan, Steve Miller, Rita Coolidge, Waylon Jennings, Stray Cats and Eddie Van Halen. Cinemax cable television network broadcast the show on Tuesday 25 October 1988. The show was first released on video as *Les Paul & Friends – He Changed the Music* in May 1991.

THURSDAY 27 APRIL 1989 – PERFORMANCE
The Red Balloon Ball, Dinosaur Room,
Natural History Museum, London, England

Gilmour played guitar on 'A Whiter Shade of Pale' alongside Mark Knopfler, Gary Brooker, Chris Rea, Gary Moore and Sam Brown at this fund-raising concert for the Lung Foundation charity. The track was recorded and broadcast the following day in the UK on BBC Radio 1's *Friday Rock Show*.

MONDAY 18 SEPTEMBER 1989 – PERFORMANCE
Hysteria 2, Sadlers Wells Theatre, Islington, London, England

Gilmour played guitar with Jools Holland (Piano) and Eddie Reader (Vocals) on 'My Girl' at this AIDS charity benefit hosted by comedian Lenny Henry. The event was released on VHS video as *Hysteria 2! – The Second Coming* in May 1990.

SATURDAY 30 SEPTEMBER 1989 – PERFORMANCE
Mitchell O'Brien's New York Deli, Soho, London, England

Gilmour played guitar at this Louise Goffin concert billed as part of the annual *Soho Jazz Festival* with Neil Conte on drums.

WEDNESDAY 11 OCTOBER 1989 – PERFORMANCE
NSPCC Benefit, Barbican Arts Centre, Barbican, London, England

Gilmour performed at this National Society for the Prevention of Cruelty to Children benefit concert.

WEDNESDAY 15 NOVEMBER 1989 – PERFORMANCE
Metropolis Studios, Chiswick, London, England

Gilmour played guitar on 'Smoke On The Water' at the media launch of the *Rock Aid Armenia* record launch (see Discography for further details). Other musicians who performed the song alongside him included Richie Blackmore, Tony Iommi, Alex Lifeson, Brian May, Bryan Adams, Bruce Dickinson, Ian Gillan, Paul Rodgers, Chris Squire, Keith Emerson, Geoff Downes and Roger Taylor.

THURSDAY 29, FRIDAY 30 AND SATURDAY 31 MARCH 1990 – PERFORMANCES
Shaw Theatre, Euston, London, England

Gilmour played guitar at this run of shows by John Martyn, playing on 'The Apprentice', 'John Wayne' and 'One World'. Gilmour and Martyn were also interviewed at this show by Nicky Horne for the Channel 4 TV music programme *Rock Steady*, in which the full band also performed 'Look At That Girl' broadcast on Tuesday 1 May 1990. (See Guest Appearances for release details.)

MONDAY 19 APRIL 1990 – TELEVISION BROADCAST
French and Saunders, BBC Television Centre, London, England

Gilmour appeared with Ralph McTell, Mark Knopfler, Lemmy, Gary Moore and Mark King in a pre-recorded edition of the comedy show featuring Dawn French and Jennifer Saunders. The sketch illustrated the pitfalls of learning to play guitar without tablature. Gilmour, pretending to be defeated by the riff from 'Another Brick In The Wall, Part 2', complained that there were no 'little pictures that show you where to put your fingers'. It was broadcast on BBC2 TV.

THURSDAY 6 DECEMBER 1990 – PERFORMANCE
The Red Balloon Ball, Alexandra Palace, London, England

Gilmour performed with Jools Holland, Ian Paice and Justin Hayward at this Lung Foundation charity concert.

FRIDAY 1 FEBRUARY 1991 – PERFORMANCE
Rock-a-Baby, Empire Theatre, Hackney, London, England

Gilmour played guitar at this charity performance as part of the all-star band on the second of a three-day event (Thursday 31 January to Saturday 2 February 1991) that also featured Paul Young and Paul Carrack (Vocals), Andy Fairweather-Low (Guitar), Guy Pratt (Bass) and Andy Newmark (Drums). The set included 'Wish You Were Here' and 'Comfortably Numb'. Support was provided by the group Five Easy Pieces.

SUNDAY 24 MARCH 1991 – PERFORMANCE
Bloomsbury Theatre, Bloomsbury, London, England

Gilmour appeared as a special guest at this Dream Academy concert.

SUNDAY 30 JUNE 1991 – PERFORMANCE
Hysteria 3, The Palladium, London, England

Gilmour played guitar with the Jools Holland Band on 'Together Again', which also featured vocals by Sam Brown at this charity fund-raiser. Highlights were broadcast on Channel 4 TV on Saturday 12 October 1991. A CD of edited highlights *The Best of Hysteria 3!* and an unedited VHS video *The Best of Hysteria 3!* were both released in November 1991. It was reissued on DVD as *Stephen Fry Presents Hysteria 3* in November 2007.

FRIDAY 13 DECEMBER 1991 – TELEVISION BROADCAST
Amnesty International's Big 3-0, Central Independent TV Studios, Nottingham, England

Gilmour and Jools Holland were installed as musical directors for the recording of Amnesty International's Big 3-0, a commemorative broadcast continuing the *Secret Policeman's Ball* series and featuring Gilmour and Holland performing 'On The Turning Away' with house band Tim Renwick (Guitar), Jon Carin (Keyboards), Pino Palladino (Bass), Jodi Linscott (Percussion), Margo Buchanan (Vocals) and Sam Brown (Vocals). Gilmour also joined Tom Jones to play on his songs 'Kiss' and 'I Can't Turn You Loose', played lead guitar on Seal's rendition of 'Hey Joe'; performed 'Hard To Handle' and 'What's Going On' with Andrew Strong of the Commitments, and played bass guitar with Spinal Tap on their song 'Big Bottom'. The entire show was broadcast on the ITV network TV on Saturday 28 December 1991. It was released on VHS video in March 1992. 'On The Turning Away' also featured on the five-DVD video compilation box set *The Secret Policeman's Ball – The Complete Edition*, released November 2004, which also included the *Amnesty International Big 3–0* show and the DVD video *The Secret Policeman Rocks!*, released September 2009.

SATURDAY 6 JUNE 1992 – TELEVISION BROADCAST
Mister Roadrunner, Channel 4 TV, UK

Gilmour appeared in a pre-recorded edition of the Jools Holland Channel 4 TV series *Mister Roadrunner* in which Holland went biking on a Vincent Rapide across Tennessee and Mississippi in search of 'The Lost Chord', stopping off at suitable locations en route, with appropriate musical interludes. One of those was provided by Mica Paris singing 'I Put A Spell On You' with a band comprising David Gilmour (Guitar), Jools Holland (Piano), Matt Irving (Keyboards), Gilson Lavis (Drums) and Pino Palladino (Bass). Other musical celebrities Holland encountered included George Harrison, Robert Palmer, Rufus Thomas and Yvonne Fair.

SATURDAY 13 JUNE 1992 – TELEVISION BROADCAST
The Right Time, ITV TV Studios, South Bank, London, England

Gilmour played guitar with Tom Jones's band comprising Tim Renwick (Guitar), Gary Wallis (Drums) and Jodi Linscott (Percussion) in a live audience edition of his six part series *Tom Jones: The Right Time*, performing 'Purple Rain'.

MONDAY 22 JUNE 1992 – PERFORMANCE
Town & Country Club, Kentish Town, London, England

Gilmour appeared as a special guest at this Tom Jones concert.

SUNDAY 11 OCTOBER 1992 – PERFORMANCE
Chelsea Arts Ball 1992, Royal Albert Hall, London, England

Gilmour joined the house band comprising Guy Pratt (Bass), Jon Carin (Keyboards), Jodi Linscott (Percussion), Tim Renwick (Guitar), Gary Wallis (Drums), Margo Buchanan (Vocals) and Sam Brown (Vocals) and guest musicians Nick Mason, Rick Wright, Tom Jones, Hugh Cornwell, Mica Paris, Elvis Costello and Sam Moore among others at this high-society AIDS fund-raiser. The set comprised 'River Deep Mountain High', 'The Sun Ain't Gonna Shine Anymore', 'Golden Brown', 'Stone Free', 'I Put A Spell On You', 'I Can't Stand Up For Falling Down', 'Another Brick In The Wall, Part 2', 'Wish You Were Here', 'Comfortably Numb', 'Superstition', 'Knock On Wood' and 'Kiss'.

SATURDAY 7 NOVEMBER 1992 – TELEVISION BROADCAST
The Happening, The Astoria, London, England

Gilmour played guitar with Jools Holland in a live audience edition of his Channel 4 TV series *The Happening*, performing 'Such A Night', 'Wide-Eyed And Legless' and 'Movin' On' with Andy Fairweather-Low (Guitar/Vocals).

FRIDAY 4 DECEMBER 1992 – PERFORMANCE
Ecomundo '92, Estadio Pascual Guerrero, Cali, Colombia

Gilmour and his band featuring Chucho Merchan (Bass) played a brief set comprising 'You Know I'm Right', 'On The Turning Away', 'Run Like Hell' and 'Comfortably Numb' at this benefit show organized as part of the Ecomundo ecology conference. Also appearing were Kool & the Gang, Roger Daltrey, Phil Manzanera, Juliet Roberts, Rata Blanca, Kronos and Dagoberto Pedraja Cepero.

SUNDAY 6 FEBRUARY 1994 – PERFORMANCE
Bop for Bosnia, Studio One, BBC Television Centre, White City, London, England

Gilmour played guitar on this invitation-only fund-raiser (the show was not recorded or broadcast, despite the location) organized by Chris Jagger that also featured a band comprising Dave Stewart (Keyboards), Leo Sayer (Vocals), Simon Kirke (Percussion), Jon Newey (Drums) and Ben Waters (Piano). As well as performing material mainly from Jagger's album *Atcha*, they performed several blues numbers.

THURSDAY 6 JULY 1995 – PERFORMANCE
Tango for Tibet, The Pagoda, Battersea Park, London, England

Gilmour performed at this dinner-dance fundraiser, which was jointly organized by the Tibet House Trust and BBC television journalist Sue-Lloyd Roberts to raise funds for Trust projects in India and Nepal. Over 420 people attended the funding raising dinner and another 100 joined in for the dance with additional music provided by Leo Sayer and the Chris Jagger Band to celebrate the 60th birthday of the Dalai Lama of Tibet.

SATURDAY 23 MARCH 1996 – PERFORMANCE
Town Hall, Fulham, London, England

A celebration for Gilmour's 50th birthday featured entertainment by the Bootleg Beatles and the Australian Pink Floyd Show, who were joined on stage by Richard Wright and Guy Pratt for a rousing rendition of 'Comfortably Numb'. The band then handed over their instruments to David Gilmour, Richard Wright, Guy Pratt, Tim Renwick, Gary Wallis and Claudia Fontaine, who treated the gathered guests to renditions of 'Money', 'What Do You Want From Me' and various other jams.

SATURDAY 29 JUNE 1996 – PERFORMANCE
The Prince's Trust Concert, Hyde Park, London, England

Gilmour played guitar on 'The Dirty Jobs' and 'Love Reign O'er Me' on the Who's reworked version of *Quadrophenia* for the Prince's Trust all-day concert, which also featured guest appearances by Phil Daniels (Narration), Trevor McDonald (Newscaster), Ade Edmundson (Bell Boy; later with shotgun and scooter), Gary Glitter (Rocker) and Stephen Fry (Hotel Manager). The event also featured sets by Bob Dylan and Ron Wood, Eric Clapton and Alanis Morissette.

SATURDAY 20 JULY 1996 – PERFORMANCE
A Day for Tibet, Alexandra Palace, Muswell Hill, London, England

Gilmour performed at a benefit for the Dalai Lama of Tibet, which also featured Sinead O'Connor, Andy Summers and the Chris Jagger Band. Gilmour performed with the latter and also gave a surprise solo acoustic rendition of Syd Barrett's 'Terrapin' followed by the more familiar 'On The Turning Away', 'Wish You Were Here' and 'Coming Back To Life' with Chucho Merchan (Bass) and other supporting musicians.

WEDNESDAY 31 DECEMBER 1997 – TELEVISION BROADCAST
Jools' 5th Annual Hootenanny, BBC Television Centre, White City, London, England

Gilmour played guitar with BB King on 'Eyesight To The Blind' as part of Jools Holland's BBC2 TV annual New Year live broadcast. The show also featured Jools Holland and his Rhythm & Blues Orchestra, 1st Battalion Welsh Guards, Shaun Ryder, Blur, Bentley Rhythm Ace and Fun Lovin' Criminals. 'Eyesight To The Blind' also featured on the DVD video *Later… with Jools Holland – Hootenanny* released in December 2003.

SATURDAY 2 MAY 1998 – PERFORMANCE
Lavender Trust Concert, Institute of Contemporary Arts, The Mall, London, England

Gilmour performed a short set at this event, for the launch of the Lavender Trust charity, which included 'The Dimming Of The Day', 'Forever Young' and 'Wish You Were Here'. The event also featured a set by former Eurythmics duo Dave Stewart and Annie Lennox, in their first public appearance together since the band split in the eighties.

SUNDAY 6 SEPTEMBER 1998 – PERFORMANCE
Studio 2, EMI Abbey Road Studios, London, England

Gilmour performed with the Pretty Things at an invitation-only reunion show to perform their album *S.F. Sorrow* with the following line-up: Phil May (Lead Vocals, Percussion), Dick Taylor (Guitar, Vocals), John Povey

(Keyboards, Vocals, Percussion, Sitar), Wally Waller (Bass, Vocals), Skip Allen (Drums, Percussion), Arthur Brown (Narration) and Gilmour on guitar on the tracks marked*: 'S.F. Sorrow Is Born', 'Bracelets Of Fingers', 'She Says Good Morning'*, 'Private Sorrow', 'Balloon Burning', 'Death', 'Baron Saturday', 'The Journey', 'I See You'*, 'Well Of Destiny'*, 'Trust'*, 'Old Man Going'*and 'Loneliest Person'. The show was also filmed and broadcast live over the Internet and released as a limited edition in January 1999. (See Guest Appearances for release details.)

SATURDAY 18 SEPTEMBER 1999 – PERFORMANCE
PETA Awards Show, Paramount Studios, Los Angeles, CA, USA

Gilmour played guitar in Paul McCartney's band, which also featured Ian Paice (Drums), Mick Green (Guitar) and Pete Wingfield (Piano) at a benefit concert for People for the Ethical Treatment of Animals (PETA), which was later broadcast in edited form on the US television channel VH1 on Saturday 16 October 1999. The performance was part of PETA's Party of the Century and Humanitarian Awards in an evening that also featured performances by the B-52s, Sarah McLachlan and Chrissie Hynde with comedy from Ellen De Generes and Margaret Cho. McCartney co-hosted the evening with Alec Baldwin, Jamie Lee Curtis and Woody Harrelson. The show was released on DVD as Paul McCartney & Friends – The PETA Concert for Party Animals in January 2002.

TUESDAY 2 NOVEMBER 1999 – TELEVISION RECORDING
Later... with Jools Holland, BBC Television Centre, White City, London, England

Gilmour played guitar in Paul McCartney's band, which also featured Ian Paice (Drums), Mick Green (Guitar) and Pete Wingfield (Piano) in an edition of the music programme Later... with Jools Holland. The set comprised of 'Honey Hush', 'Brown Eyed Handsome Man', 'There's No Other (Like My Baby)' and '(Let's Have A) Party'. It was broadcast on BBC2 TV on Saturday 6 November 1999. 'Brown Eyed Handsome Man' was also featured on the DVD Later... with Jools Holland – Giants released October 2003.

THURSDAY 2 DECEMBER 1999 – TELEVISION RECORDING
Parkinson Meets Paul McCartney, BBC Television Centre, White City, London, England

Gilmour played guitar in Paul McCartney's band, which also featured Ian Paice (Drums), Mick Green (Guitar) and Pete Wingfield (Piano) in an edition of a Michael Parkinson BBC1 TV special subtitled 'Parkinson Meets Paul McCartney' (returning a long-forgotten favour to appear on his show following Parkinson's appearance on his Band on the Run album sleeve). Although the full band did not perform on all of the songs the set list comprised 'Honey Hush', 'Twenty Flight Rock', 'Mary's Song', 'Yesterday', 'The Long And Winding Road', 'The New York Song (Chase My Blues Away)', 'The Cabaret Song', 'Suicide' and 'All Shook Up'. It was broadcast on Friday 3 December between 9.30pm and 10.30pm.

TUESDAY 14 DECEMBER 1999 – PERFORMANCE
Cavern Club, Liverpool, England

Gilmour played guitar in Paul McCartney's band, which also featured Iain Paice (Drums), Chris Hall (Accordion), Mick Green (Guitar) and Pete Wingfield (Piano). The set comprised 'Honey Hush', 'Blue Jean Bop', 'Brown Eyed Handsome Man', 'Fabulous', 'What It Is', 'Lonesome Town', 'Twenty Flight Rock', 'No Other Baby', 'Try Not To Cry', 'Shake A Hand', 'All Shook Up', 'I Saw Her Standing There' and '(Let's Have A) Party'. The show was also broadcast live over the Internet and on BBC Radio 2 as part of the Richard Allinson Show and broadcast on BBC1 TV on Wednesday 15 December as Paul McCartney at the Cavern. US radio networks and PBS TV also broadcast the show

over the weekend of Thursday 20 to Sunday 23 January 2000. An audience of some 15,000 also saw the show for free on a giant video screen in Chavasse Park, Liverpool. It was released both in the US and UK on DVD and VHS video as Paul McCartney Live at the Cavern Club! The DVDs carried bonus material that included interview footage and promo videos for 'Brown Eyed Handsome Man' and 'No Other Baby'.

FRIDAY 29 JUNE 2001 – PERFORMANCE
A Tribute to Leiber and Stoller, Hammersmith Apollo, London, England

Gilmour performed alongside a huge cast of guest musicians as part of a tribute concert to songwriters Jerry Leiber and Mike Stoller in aid of Nordoff Robbins Music Therapy. Guests featured included Ben E. King, Bob Geldof, Chris Rea, Edwin Starr, Elkie Brooks, Heather Small, Jim Capaldi, Jonathan Wilkes, Keith Emerson, Leo Sayer, Meatloaf, Michael Patto, Paul Carrack, Ruby Turner, Sam Brown, Steve Harley and Tom Jones. Gilmour's main contribution to the show was a rendition of Elvis' 'Don't', which by all accounts was one of the high spots of the show. The full show was released on DVD video in April 2002.

MONDAY 17 SEPTEMBER 2001 – PERFORMANCE
Memorial Service for Douglas Adams, St Martin-in-the-Fields Church, Trafalgar Square, London, England

Gilmour performed a rendition of 'Wish You Were Here' with Gary Brooker at the memorial service for Douglas Adams. He was a close friend of Adams, who is best remembered as the author of The Hitchhiker's Guide to the Galaxy. The service was also seen as a BBC webcast.

FRIDAY 19 OCTOBER 2001 – PERFORMANCE
Mind Your Head (A Sonic Trip on the South Bank), Royal Festival Hall, South Bank, London, England

The final concert of a season of events saw the Pretty Things performing their rock-opera S.F. Sorrow for the very first time to a public audience with a support slot from the Soft Boys. Gilmour played guitar with the Pretty Things and also played with the Soft Boys on their encore, 'Astronomy Domine'. Mind Your Head brought psychedelia and strangeness to an otherwise straight-laced auditorium and other performers over the period included Hawkwind supported by Add N To (X), Gong with the Orb supported by Acid Mothers Temple and Faust supported by Gary Lucas. The Pretty Things' set list ran as follows with Gilmour playing guitar on the tracks marked*: 'S.F. Sorrow Is Born', 'Bracelets Of Fingers', 'She Says Good Morning'*, 'Private Sorrow', 'Balloon Burning', 'Death', 'Baron Saturday', 'The Journey', 'I See You'*, 'Well Of Destiny'*, 'Trust'*, 'Old Man Going'*and 'Loneliest Person'. The encore comprised of Arthur Brown performing his hit 'Fire' (complete with flaming helmet) followed by the Pretty Things, Arthur Brown and Gilmour performing 'Rosalyn' and 'Route 66'.

WEDNESDAY 14 NOVEMBER 2001 – PERFORMANCE
The Gala Lunch, Hilton Hotel, Park Lane, London, England

Gilmour performed with other celebrity guests at this benefit event in aid of the Prince of Wales Hospice.

WEDNESDAY 21 NOVEMBER 2001 – TELEVISION RECORDING
Later... with Jools Holland, BBC Television Centre, White City, London, England

Gilmour performed 'I Put A Spell On You' with Mica Paris and Jools Holland in a pre-recorded edition of Later... with Jools Holland that also featured performances by other artists who were guests on Holland's recently released all-star album Small World Big Band. It was broadcast on BBC2 TV on Friday 23 November between 11.35pm and 12.35am. A compilation of highlights from the Jools Holland year-end shows spanning 1997 to 2003 was released on a single DVD collection as Later...

with Jools Holland – Hootenanny, which included this performance as well as his performance with BB King on Wednesday 31 December 1997.

SUNDAY 10 FEBRUARY 2002 – PERFORMANCE
When Love Speaks, The Old Vic Theatre, Lambeth, London, England

Gilmour performed a short set at this event that also featured sets by Des'Ree, Michael Kamen and Annie Lennox and Dave Stewart, in support of the launch of a fund-raising multi-artist world music album of the same title (which Gilmour did not appear on).

FRIDAY 21 JUNE 2002 – PERFORMANCE
An Evening of Beatles Music, Cowdray House, Midhurst, England

Gilmour performed 'Across The Universe', 'Revolution' and 'Long, Long, Long' as well as playing guitar with other performers' renditions of Beatles classics, including Ringo Starr, Mike Rutherford, Roger Taylor, Lulu, Bob Geldof, Paul Carrack, Donovan, Gary Brooker, Kenny Jones, Damon Hill, Mike Sanchez, and other special guests. Chris Tarrant was the host at this exclusive fundraiser for the benefit of the White Lotus School, Ladakh and the Tibet House Trust.

FRIDAY 27 SEPTEMBER 2002 – RADIO BROADCAST
The Johnnie Walker Show, BBC Broadcasting House, Portland Place, London, England

Gilmour performed 'Fat Old Sun' and 'Smile', with Melvin Duffy on slide guitar, as part of a live interview on the *Johnnie Walker Show* broadcast in the UK on BBC Radio 2 between 5.05pm and 7.00pm.

FRIDAY 11 APRIL 2003 – RADIO BROADCAST
Desert Island Discs, BBC Broadcasting House, Portland Place, London, England

Gilmour was interviewed by Sue Lawley for the long-running BBC Radio 4 radio show *Desert Island Discs*, during which he selected the following records: 'Waterloo Sunset' by the Kinks; 'Ballad In Plain D' by Bob Dylan; 'I'm Still Here' by Tom Waits; 'Dancing In The Street' by Martha and the Vandellas; 'Anthem' by Leonard Cohen; 'A Man Needs A Maid' by Neil Young; 'For Free' by Joni Mitchell; and 'Rudi With A Flashlight' by the Lemonheads. Asked what three items (record, book and luxury item) he would take on a desert island, he selected 'Dancing In The Street' by Martha and the Vandellas as his record, an English translation of the Koran as his book, and an acoustic Martin D35 guitar as his luxury.

SUNDAY 4 MAY 2003 – PERFORMANCE
Dave Douglas Freak in, Queen Elizabeth Hall, South Bank, London, England

Gilmour played guitar as part of the Dave Douglas band which comprised Dave Douglas (Trumpet), Jamie Saft (Keyboards), Ikue Mori (Electronic Percussion), Seamus Blake (Saxophone), Brad Jones (Bass) and Derrek Phillip (Drums).

SATURDAY 22 NOVEMBER 2003 – PERFORMANCE
Memorial Service for Michael Kamen, Dukes Hall, Royal Academy of Music, Marylebone Road, London, England

Gilmour performed a solo rendition of 'Wish You Were Here' at the memorial service for Michael Kamen, who had passed away on Tuesday 18 November 2003. Those able to attend included several colleagues and friends with whom Michael had worked closely over the years. Annie Lennox performed one of Michael's favourite songs, which was followed by a moving and characteristically humorous speech by Alan Rickman. Bryan Adams sang 'Everything I Do'.

THURSDAY 1 APRIL 2004 – PERFORMANCE
Teenage Cancer Trust Concert, Royal Albert Hall, London, England

Gilmour played guitar with Jools Holland's band at this show which formed part of an annual series of benefit concerts organized by the Who's Roger Daltrey. Guest performers also included Mica Paris, Jeff Beck, Ronnie Wood, Tom Jones, Solomon Burke, Chrissie Hynde, Ruby Turner and John Cale.

FRIDAY 24 SEPTEMBER 2004 – PERFORMANCE
Miller Strat Pack, Wembley Arena, Wembley, England

Gilmour performed 'Marooned', 'Coming Back To Life' and 'Sorrow' and appeared in the all-star finale of 'Stay With Me' at this Nordoff-Robins Music Therapy event to celebrate the Fender Guitar. The event included appearances by Ronnie Wood, Joe Walsh, Brian May, Hank Marvin, Phil Manzanera, Mike Rutherford, Paul Carrack, The Crickets, Gary Moore and, for some bizarre reason, Jamie Cullum and Amy Winehouse. Highlights, including Gilmour's set, entitled *The Strat Pack Live in Concert* were released on DVD video in May 2005, and Blu-Ray in November 2008. The track 'Marooned' also appeared on a free DVD issued with the June 2005 UK edition of *Guitarist* magazine.

FRIDAY 3 DECEMBER 2004 – PERFORMANCE
A Tribute to the King, Studio 2, EMI Abbey Road Studios, London, England

Gilmour performed 'Don't' with Bill Wyman & the Rhythm Kings as part of this celebration of 50 years of Elvis and the birth of rock 'n' roll. Helmed by Scotty Moore, guest performers included Eric Clapton, Mark Knopfler, Ron Wood, Ringo Starr and Keith Richards. The show, featuring Gilmour's contribution, was released on DVD video in October 2005.

THURSDAY 6 NOVEMBER 2006 – AWARDS CEREMONY
Buckingham Palace, London, England

Gilmour was honoured with the citation of CBE (Commander of the British Empire) by Queen Elizabeth II for services to music. Gilmour joked that the Queen had probably never even listened to Pink Floyd. "I suspect that if she has listened to Pink Floyd it has been one of her children or grandchildren playing it and she is more likely to be the one to say 'turn it off,'" said the guitarist. "But I do not know her taste in music." When asked what the Queen had said when he collected his honour Gilmour remarked: "She said Pink Floyd had been doing it for a very long time and I had to agree." The guitarist, who attended the investiture with his wife Polly and two of his eight children, said the CBE was a fantastic honour but he admitted he had felt nervous about meeting the Queen. "Playing to one-hundred thousand people is not so nerve wracking, playing to a few people is much harder," he said. "It was not so bad today, but I was a bit nervous." He added: "I hope that primarily it (the CBE) is for what I have done in music, but if some of my recent more publicized charity work has made a difference then I am happy about that."

TUESDAY 22 MAY 2008 – AWARDS CEREMONY
Ivor Novello Awards, Park Lane Hotel, London, England

Gilmour received a Lifetime Achievement Award from the British Academy of Composers & Songwriters. The prestigious guild of successful music creators' annual Ivor Novello Awards honoured Gilmour for all aspects of his musical life. He received a standing ovation as he collected the award from his long-time friend Robert Wyatt. The event was hosted by Paul Gambaccini.

SUNDAY 15 JUNE 2008 – PERFORMANCE
Chelsea Festival, Cadogan Hall, Chelsea, London, England

Gilmour played guitar on 'Atom Heart Mother' at the second of two Ron Geesin shows alongside the Italian four-piece band Mun Floyd, Caroline Dale on Cello and Geesin on piano, a ten-piece brass section from the Royal College of Music and the 40-strong Canticum chorus conducted by Mark Forkgen. The evening began with Geesin performing a piano piece and reciting poetry followed by a piece entitled 'Fight Or Flight' featuring Caroline Dale. The second half commenced with 'Atom 'Art Mother – The Story' in which Geesin talked about the making of the track accompanied by projected images of his original score and photographs taken in the studio. This was in turn followed by the performance of the track 'Atom Heart Mother'.

MONDAY 10 NOVEMBER 2008 – RADIO BROADCAST
Jools Holland Show, **Broadcasting House, London, England**

Gilmour performed a cover of Fleetwood Mac's 'Albatross' as part a live interview to promote *Live in Gdańsk*. It was broadcast on BBC Radio 2 between 10.30pm and 11.30pm.

SATURDAY 31 JANUARY 2009 – PERFORMANCE
Main Hall, Coldfall Primary School, Muswell Hill, London, England

Gilmour played guitar on 'Come Together' at this privately organized black-tie dinner-dance fundraiser with a scratch band of musicians under the name "Seat of Your Pants Band" featuring Suggs (Vocals), Paul "Wix" Wickens (Keyboards) and Margo Buchanan (Vocals) among others.

TUESDAY 10 FEBRUARY 2009 – PERFORMANCE
Ronnie Scott's Jazz Club, Soho, London, England

Gilmour played guitar with Phil Manzanera's band which comprised Charles Hayward (Drums), Yaron Stavi (Bass) and Leszek Mozder (Piano) on the tracks 'Autumn Leaves' and covers of Sidney Bechet's 'Petite Fleur' and Miles Davis' 'Filles de Kilimanjaro'.

MONDAY 25 MAY 2009 – PERFORMANCE
Crisis Hidden Gigs, **the Union Chapel, Islington, London, England**

Gilmour played guitar with Malian duo Amadou & Mariam at one of the Crisis charity's *Hidden Gigs* season where ticket holders are not told of the concert location until the day prior to the show. Gilmour performed throughout their 70-minute set, which also saw a rendition of 'No Way' from his first solo album, sung by Amadou & Mariam. Other performers of the evening included Catherine A.D. and Stephane Girard & Paul Webb.

THURSDAY 18 JUNE 2009 – PERFORMANCE
Hoping's Got Talent, **Café de Paris, Soho, London, England**

Gilmour played guitar at a charity karaoke fundraiser as part of an unusual duo with supermodel Kate Moss performing 'Summertime'. Other participants of the evening included Jamie Hince, Lily Allen, Suggs and Will Self.

SUNDAY 5 JULY 2009 – PERFORMANCE
Royal Albert Hall, London, England

Gilmour appeared as a special guest at this Jeff Beck concert playing guitar on the track 'Jerusalem' and 'Hi Ho Silver Lining', the latter of which also featured Imelda May.

WEDNESDAY 11 NOVEMBER 2009 – AWARDS CEREMONY
Anglia Ruskin University, Cambridge, England

Gilmour received an honorary doctorate from the Anglia Ruskin University. An extract of his citation reads: 'David Jon Gilmour CBE was born in Cambridge and attended Cambridgeshire College of Arts and Technology, a part of what is now Anglia Ruskin University. It was here that he spent many lunchtimes learning and jamming the guitar with his childhood friend Syd Barrett. Best known as a guitarist, vocalist and writer with Pink Floyd, he is also renowned for his solo work and collaborations with other artists including Kate Bush, Paul McCartney, and Pete Townshend…. David still has close ties with Anglia Ruskin University, some four decades later, supporting most recently the City Wakes project from the Cambridge School of Art. He is honoured for his outstanding contribution to music as a writer, performer and innovator.'

THURSDAY 17 JUNE 2010 – TELEVISION RECORDING
Friday Night with Jonathan Ross,
BBC Television Centre, London, England

Gilmour appeared with Al Green on BBC1 TV's *Friday Night with Jonathan Ross* show performing 'Let's Stay Together', as part of a one-off, specially recruited band to help launch Green's UK tour. Alongside Green for this performance (but not the tour) was Jools Holland (Piano), Christopher Holland (Organ), Gilson Lavis (Drums), Lisa Grahame and Phil Veacock (Saxophones), Chris Storr (Trumpet) and Barry Campbell (Bass). It was broadcast in the UK on BBC1 TV on Friday 18 June.

SATURDAY 10 JULY 2010 – PERFORMANCE
Hoping Foundation Benefit Evening,
Kidlington Hall, Woodstock, England

A surprise reunion took place between Roger Waters and David Gilmour at this high-brow charity fundraiser to 200 invited guests organized by Bella Freud and Karma Nabulsi and hosted by Jemima Khan under the banner of Hoping (Hope and Optimism for Palestinians in the Next Generation) to raise funds for the Children of Gaza. Nick Cave and Tom Jones kicked off the evening, followed by Gilmour and Waters, who performed four songs together with Guy Pratt (Bass and Acoustic Guitar), Harry Waters (keyboards), Andy Newmark (Drums), Chester Kamen (Guitar) and Jonjo Grisdale (Keyboards). Their performance was also geared to an auction for each song, which was launched with 'To Know Him Is To Love Him' (written by Phil Spector), and apparently regularly featured in Pink Floyd sound checks in the 1970s, followed by 'Wish You Were Here', 'Comfortably Numb', and the show-closer with full audience participation of 'Another Brick In The Wall, Part 2'. A "home"-quality video of the show was made available for viewing via the charity website on Monday 16 August 2010. Speaking of the event, an unimpressed Nick Mason made the point to the *Independent* that, "This particular event wasn't right for a reformation of Pink Floyd. I said I would do it, but it was a charity event for suits, and it felt wrong to turn a small thing into a big deal just because British socialite Jemima Khan was in attendance. Why play for a lot of posh totty instead of some of the other things we should save that up for – like a *Live 8* type of thing."

THURSDAY 12 MAY 2011 – PERFORMANCE
02 Arena, Greenwich Peninsula, London, England

Gilmour had promised to perform 'Comfortably Numb' at one of Roger Waters' *The Wall* concerts when he appeared at the Hoping benefit (Saturday 10 July 2010). His appearance was greeted with huge applause, but unfortunately Gilmour's nerves got the better of him and he sang the first verse of the song twice. Nick Mason also attended the show, and both Mason and Gilmour joined Waters for the final song, 'Outside The Wall', on which Waters played trumpet, Gilmour mandolin and Mason tambourine.

SUNDAY 11 MARCH 2012 – PERFORMANCE
Douglas Adams: Virtual 60th Birthday Party, Hammersmith Apollo, Hammersmith, London, England

Gilmour appeared as part of the entertainment at this celebration fundraiser event for the Environmental Investigation Agency and Save The Rhino in memory of Douglas Adams and featuring an array of guest speakers and comedians performing sketches, including appearances by Robin Ince, Helen Keen, Terry Jones, Sanjeev Bhaskar, Rory McGrath, John Lloyd, Jon Culshaw, Angus Deayton, Michael Fenton Stevens and Philip Pope among others, and hosted by Clive Anderson. To close the show a set of music was performed by a band comprising Margo Buchanan (Vocals, Guitar), Gary Brooker (Keyboards, Vocals), Paul "Wix" Wickens (Keyboards), Jodi Linscott (Percussion), Robbie McIntosh (Guitar), Dave Bronze (Bass) and Paul Beavis (Drums). The performance began with a Robbie McIntosh acoustic guitar instrumental followed by the band performing 'Dadi' (sung by Robbie McIntosh), 'Scarecrow' (sung by Robbie McIntosh – not the Pink Floyd song), 'Rockstar' (sung by Margo Buchanan), 'I Just Want To Make Love To You' (sung by Margo Buchanan), and 'A Salty Dog' (sung by Gary Brooker). Gilmour joined the band for the last three numbers: 'Wish You Were Here' (his sole lead vocal), 'Too Much Monkey Business' (sung by Gary Brooker) and 'A Whiter Shade Of Pale' (sung by Gary Brooker).

FRIDAY 27 APRIL 2012 – PERFORMANCE
20th Century Theatre, Westbourne Grove, London, England

Gilmour performed at his wife Polly Samson's 50th birthday party backed by Guy Pratt and Phil Manzanera. The set included 'Smile', 'The Blue', 'This Heaven', 'Where We Start', 'High Hopes' and an unnamed song.

THURSDAY 20 SEPTEMBER 2012 – PERFORMANCE
St Bride's Church, Fleet Street, London, England

Gilmour performed 'Smile' at a service of thanksgiving for the life of Cassandra Caroline Mary Jardine, award-winning feature writer for the *Daily Telegraph*. Gilmour was accompanied by Jardine's son Oliver Chubb on keyboards.

MONDAY 19 MAY 2015 – PERFORMANCE
Islington Assembly Rooms, Islington, London, England

Gilmour appeared as a special guest at this Ben Watts concert playing lap steel guitar on the tracks 'The Levels' and 'Spring' and guitar on 'Young Man's Game'.

SATURDAY 13 DECEMBER 2014 – PERFORMANCE
Earl's Court Exhibition Hall, Earl's Court, London, England

Gilmour joined London band Bombay Bicycle Club on stage at the last concert to be hosted at the historic venue before it was demolished. Gilmour performed on their song 'Rinse Me Down' during which he played lap steel guitar before switching to acoustic guitar to lead a performance of 'Wish You Were Here'.

SATURDAY 6 JUNE 2015 – PERFORMANCE
2015 Borris House Festival of Writing and Ideas, Borris, Ireland.

Gilmour appeared on the second day of this three-day literature festival as part of a session entitled *Louder Than Words*, which featured a discussion between David Gilmour and Polly Samson about the pair's song-writing partnership. Recordings of 'High Hopes' and 'Louder Than Words' were played as well as previews from his forthcoming album including the songs 'Whatever It Takes', 'In Any Tongue' and 'The Girl In The Yellow Dress' as well as live acoustic renditions of 'Smile' and 'The Blue'.

SUNDAY 18 OCTOBER 2015 – PERFORMANCE
Staging a Revolution – I'm With the Banned, Koko, Camden, London, England

Gilmour's participation in the above show had been announced at time of going to press as the launch event of the Belarus Free Theatre Festival, a two-week run of performances held at secret locations across London. Banned artists from Russia, Ukraine and Belarus, including the infamous Pussy Riot, as well as Brutto and Boombox also appear on the bill.

LEFT: GILMOUR AND WATERS REUNITE FOR THE HOPING FOUNDATION BENEFIT, 10 JULY 2010.

NICK MASON

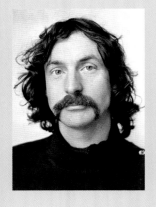

Nick Mason is the only member of Pink Floyd to have been in every lineup and played on every recorded work since its inception.

Born Nicholas Berkeley Mason in Birmingham on 27 January 1944, he grew up in Hampstead, North London, and attended Frensham Heights, a private boarding school near Farnham, Surrey. After leaving school Mason enrolled in the Regent Street Polytechnic to study architecture, and began performing in various college bands with classmates Roger Waters and Richard Wright, including Sigma 6 and the Abdabs. The addition of Syd Barrett in 1964 to the lineup ultimately led to the creation of Pink Floyd. Mason has remained the band's drummer ever since.

Throughout his career Nick Mason has produced and performed with a variety of artists, beginning with recordings made in 1969 with the female folk duo Chimera and former Manfred Mann vocalist Paul Jones. 1971's *The Asmoto Running Band,* the second album by Principal Edwards Magic Theatre, which was John Peel's first signing to his Dandelion label, encouraged Mason take a more active role as producer.

In 1974, Mason produced *Round One* by Principal Edwards and played on *Rock Bottom*, the second solo album by ex–Soft Machine drummer Robert Wyatt. This provided him with a Top 30 UK single, 'I'm A Believer', which also saw Mason playing drums on his appearance on BBC TV's *Top of the Pops* in September 1974 and a session for BBC's *Radio One Club* a month later. Mason continued his collaborations with Wyatt, occasionally performing live, and also produced his 1975 album *Ruth Is Stranger Than Richard*.

In 1976 he produced the album *Shamal* for Gong and began a long association with Michael Mantler with the album *The Hapless Child and Other Inscrutable Stories*, recorded at Pink Floyd's Britannia Row studios. Further production work followed with the Damned, and their second album *Music for Pleasure*, and a further single for Wyatt, 'Yesterday Man', in 1977. In the following year he produced *Green* by ex-Gong guitarist Steve Hillage.

Mason's own first solo album, *Fictitious Sports*, released in 1981, was actually recorded in 1979, and is essentially the work of the American free-jazz composer Carla Bley. In addition to Mason, other performers included Robert Wyatt (who sang lead vocals), Chris Spedding, Steve Swallow, Gary Windo, Michael Mantler and Terry Adams.

In 1983 Mason played on and produced Mantler's album *Something There* and in 1987 his album *Michael Mantler Live!* taken from a performance at the 1st International Art Rock Festival in Frankfurt, West Germany. Mason continued to play concerts with Mantler, performing with a modern chamber orchestra in a series of concerts, one of which was performed and recorded in Berlin in November 2007, and released as *Concertos* in November 2008.

In the early 1980s he produced the film *Life Could Be a Dream*, a semi-autobiographical account of Mason's motoring and professional career with a soundtrack featuring vocals from 10cc's Eric Stewart. Following this he formed Bamboo Music with Rick Fenn, guitarist of 10cc, to create soundtracks and music for TV commercials. Their credits include HMV, Rowenta, Rothman's and Barclay's Bank, although a great many more remain undocumented.

This eventually led to an album entitled *Profiles* (released in August 1985). The single from the album, 'Lie For A Lie' was sung by David Gilmour and Maggie Reilly.

Soundtrack production with Fenn continued through the 1980s and their credits include the Superbowl Timex® watch advertisement (1986), and scores for the films *White of the Eye* (1987), *Body Contact* (1987) and *Tank Malling* (1988), and the track 'Dance Of The Ferraris' for the Essen Motor Show 1989. In 1990 Mason produced the cast recording of the West End show *Return to the Forbidden Planet*.

Mason has since appeared infrequently both on record and on stage, but has appeared at several notable charity events, including *Rebuild the Roundhouse* (to raise funds for the restoration of the venue Pink Floyd had appeared at in the 1960s), playing drums on a performance of 'Interstellar Overdrive' with Jools Holland and Hugh Cornwell.

Rekindling his friendship with Roger Waters at the turn of the century, Mason was a guest performer on 'Set The Controls For The Heart Of The Sun' at his Wembley shows in 2002, and in 2006 appeared several times on the second half of Waters' shows performing *The Dark Side of the Moon* in its entirety. His most recent significant live performance was at the opening ceremony of the London Olympics in August 2012, backing Ed Sheeran on a rendition of 'Wish You Were Here'.

When not behind the drums, Mason's other great passion is motor racing and he owns a considerable collection of racing cars from 1901 to the present day, many of which are stored at an airfield near Cirencester. He has competed in most of them and his company Ten Tenths specialises in the supply of vintage motor vehicles to the film and television industry.

In 1985 his exploits both behind the wheel and behind the drums were the subject of a documentary *Life Could Be a Dream*. In 1991 he completed the 3,000-mile Mexican classic car race *La Carrera Panamericana*, in a replica 1952 C-type Jaguar with co-driver Lindsay Valentine, which was the subject of a 1992 documentary of the same name with soundtrack music by Pink Floyd.

In 1998 Mason wrote, with Mark Hales, the best-selling motoring book *Into the Red*, a celebration of 21 cars from his own collection complete with a CD capturing the unmistakeable sounds of the cars in action. In 2008 he even became the president of the Guild of Motoring Writers.

In 2004 Mason published a hugely entertaining memoir, *Inside Out: A Personal History of Pink Floyd*, to great critical acclaim, and has since then remained an ambassador of the band, punctuating interviews with his witty humour during each successive reissue campaign.

ORIGINAL RELEASES

NICK MASON'S FICTITIOUS SPORTS

The first album that Mason worked on outside of Pink Floyd was essentially the work of jazz artist Carla Bley, who composed and played keyboards on all the pieces with an array of guest musicians, including Robert Wyatt and Karen Kraft (Vocals), Chris Spedding (Guitar), Steve Swallow (Bass), Gary Windo (Woodwind Instruments), Gary Valente (Trombones), Michael Mantler (Trumpets), Howard Johnson (Tuba), Terry Adams (Piano), and Carlos Ward, D. Sharpe, Vincent Chancey and Earl McIntyre (Additional Vocals).

It was recorded at Grog Kill Studio, Willow, New York near Woodstock, in October 1979 by Michael Mantler and assisted by Nick Mason, and mixed at Village Recorders and the Producer's Workshop, Los Angeles, by James Guthrie in December 1979 and May 1980, and produced by Nick Mason and Carla Bley. It was not released until 1981, owing to contractual difficulties.

MONDAY 4 MAY 1981 ◄

Nick Mason's Fictitious Sports

Side 1: 'Can't Get My Motor To Start'
/ 'I Was Wrong' / 'Siam' / Side 2: 'Hot
River' / 'Boo To You Too' / 'Do Ya?' /
'Wervin' / 'I'm A Mineralist'.

UK: EMI Harvest SHSP 4116 (Vinyl
album).
US: Columbia FC 37307 (Vinyl
album, released Tuesday 23 June
1981; Highest chart position
No. 170 Billboard "Top LPs" on
Saturday 11 July 1981).
Reissued:
US: Sony Music Special Products
WK 75070 (CD album, released Tuesday 19 October 1993) / US:
Columbia PC 37307 (Vinyl album, released Tuesday 20 February
1996) / US: Sony Music Special Products A37307 (CD album, released
Tuesday 4 March 2003).

JUNE 1981

'Hot River' / 'Can't Get My Motor To Start'

US: Columbia AS 964 (Promotional 12-inch clear vinyl single).

PROFILES

Mason's second "solo" album was a joint collaboration with ex-10cc
guitarist Rick Fenn. The pair had been introduced through a mutual
friend, Eric Stewart, also of 10cc, when Mason was looking for someone
to help him with some music for a TV advert. However, Stewart was
preoccupied with other matters and suggested Fenn. The pair hit it off
and eventually formed a production company, Bamboo Music, to supply
music for films and commercials. *Profiles* was the first of their commercially
available works and was recorded at Mason's Britannia Row studios and
Fenn's Basement Studios. The album featured Mel Collins (Saxophone),
Craig Pruess (Emulator Bass on 'Malta'), Danny Peyronel (Vocals on
'Israel'), Maggie Reilly and David Gilmour (Vocals on 'Lie For A Lie')
and Aja Fenn (intro Keyboards on 'Malta'). The lyrics for 'Lie For A Lie'
and 'Israel' were written by Danny Peyronel. It was recorded at Britannia
Row Studios, Islington, London, England and Basement Studios, London,
England and produced by Nick Mason and Rick Fenn, and engineered by
Nick Griffiths (Britannia Row) and Rick Fenn (Basement).

TUESDAY 25 JUNE 1985

'Lie For A Lie' / 'Lie For A Lie'
US: Columbia 38-05456 (Promotional 7-inch vinyl single).
'Lie For A Lie' / 'Lie For A Lie'
US: Columbia CAS 2111 (Promotional 12-inch vinyl single).
'Lie For A Lie' / 'And The Address'
US: Columbia 38-05456 (7-inch vinyl single).
Highest chart position No. 21 (US *Billboard* "Mainstream Rock Tracks" on
Saturday 31 August 1985).

MONDAY 29 JULY 1985 ►

Profiles

Side 1: 'Malta' / 'Lie For A Lie' / 'Rhoda'
/ 'Profiles, Parts 1 & 2' / Side 2: 'Israel' /
'And The Address' / 'Mumbo Jumbo' /
'Zip Code' / 'Black Ice' / 'At The End Of
The Day' / 'Profiles, Part 3'.

UK: EMI Harvest MAF 1 (Vinyl album).
US: Columbia FC 40142 (Vinyl album)
& US: Columbia CK 40142 (CD album,
released Tuesday 20 August 1985)
Reissued:
US: Sony Music Special Products
A40142 (CD album, released Tuesday
22 August 1995).

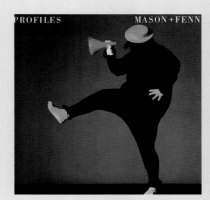

MONDAY 23 SEPTEMBER 1985

'Lie For A Lie' / 'And The Address'
UK: EMI Harvest HAR 5238 (7-inch vinyl single).
'Lie For A Lie' // 'And The Address' / 'Mumbo Jumbo'
UK: EMI Harvest 12 HAR 5238 (12-inch vinyl single).

FILMS & SOUNDTRACKS

1985

Life Could be a Dream (One of These Days)

Mason and Fenn wrote the soundtrack, including a reworking of their
'Lie For A Lie' (from *Profiles*) as well as a new recording of 'Sh-boom'
with Eric Stewart of 10cc on vocals, for *Life Could be a Dream*. Directed by
Mike Shackleton, this 26-minute film, also known as *One of These Days*, is
a semi-autobiographical account of Mason's motoring and professional
career featuring material from his home archive as well as vintage Pink
Floyd performances, including 'One Of These Days' from the film *Pink
Floyd Live at Pompeii*. It was shown as part of Britannia Airways' in-flight
film selection during the first half of 1985.

WEDNESDAY 26 DECEMBER 1984

The Cresta Run

Nick Mason and Rick Fenn composed and performed the incidental
music for this made-for-TV documentary about the St Moritz toboggan
club and their trips down the world-famous Cresta Run, in celebration
of its 100th anniversary. It was broadcast on the ITV TV network on
Wednesday 26 December 1984 between 12.00pm and 1.05pm.

SUNDAY 6 DECEMBER 1987

Body Contact

Mason and Fenn composed and performed the soundtrack to this
made-for-TV film by Bernard Rose – a rock musical set in and around a

LEFT: DAVID GILMOUR, NICK MASON AND RICK FENN
PICTURED DURING THE RECORDING OF *PROFILES*.

futuristic Tottenham and Hackney in North London. It was broadcast on BBC1 TV on Sunday 6 December 1987 between 9.20pm and 10.30pm.

FRIDAY 20 MAY 1988
White of the Eye
Mason and Fenn composed and performed the incidental music to this cinematic film by Donald Cammell. A soundtrack album was never released but the film contains some 44 separate pieces of edited music including a song called 'Slim Jenkins' Joint', written by Booker T. & the MGs, and performed by Mason and Fenn. *Supajam* wrote of the DVD reissue that "Mason's touch (aided by Rick Fenn), offers an unmistakable David Gilmour slant to the guitar licks that punctuate various scenes. Due to the time and era, there is the disappointing and hideous prevalence of electronic synths and drum machines that scatter in and out of the film elsewhere. It is an occasional audio mar to what is otherwise a sterling job."

The film was tipped for a screening at the Cannes film festival in 1987 but failed to make the list following an oversight by its distributor, and eventually opened across the US on Friday 20 May 1988. It was released on VHS video (UK: Warner Home Video PEV37208, on Friday 4 December 1987 / US: Paramount 12670, on Wednesday 7 August 1991) and reissued on dual format DVD and Blu Ray (UK: Arrow Films FCD900, on Monday 24 March 2014).

The full track list of the soundtrack runs as follows: 'Intro' / 'Jam' / 'Murder Number One' / 'Vesti La Giubba' / 'Customized Stereo' / 'In Bed at Day's End' / 'You Sexy Thing' (Hot Chocolate) / 'Slim Jenkin's Joint' (Booker T. Jones) / 'Do You Still Hunt?' / 'You Sexy Thing' (Hot Chocolate) / 'I Call That Hotel Home' / 'The Grand Tour' (David Keith) / 'Why Me?' / 'Peanut Butter' / 'A Country Boy Can Survive' (Hank Williams Jr.) / 'Murder Number Two' / 'Joanie' / 'Want Some Soup Mom?' / 'I Can't Believe You Done That' / 'Puke' / 'You Can't Kill What's Already Dead' / 'Don't You Fuckin' Move Bitch' / 'Mommy?' / 'Danielle Gets The Key' / 'Car-Chase Psycho Killer' / 'Mahler's 2nd Symphony' (Gustav Mahler) / 'Ten Years Gone'.

FRIDAY 1 DECEMBER 1989
Tank Malling
Mason and Fenn composed and performed the instrumental soundtrack to this cinematic film by James Marcus, which is sometimes called *Beyond Soho*, and starred Ray Winstone and Amanda Donohoe. The closing credits also feature the song 'See You In Paradise' written by Fenn and performed by Fenn, Mason and Maggie Reilly. *Tank Malling* was released to UK cinemas on Friday 1 December 1989 and released on DVD video on Monday 17 May 2010 (UK: Point Blank PBDVD106).

GUEST APPEARANCES & PRODUCTION

FEBRUARY 1971 – PRINCIPAL EDWARDS MAGIC THEATRE
The Asmoto Running Band
Produced by Mason.

AUGUST 1973 – PRINCIPAL EDWARDS MAGIC THEATRE
'Weekdaze' / 'The Whizzmore Kid'
Produced by Mason.

MARCH 1974 – PRINCIPAL EDWARDS MAGIC THEATRE
Round One
Produced by Mason.

JULY 1974 – ROBERT WYATT
Rock Bottom
Produced by Mason.

SEPTEMBER 1974 – ROBERT WYATT
'I'm A Believer' / 'Memories'
Produced by Mason, who also plays drums on 'I'm A Believer'.

MAY 1975 – ROBERT WYATT
Ruth Is Stranger Than Richard
The track 'Sonia' was produced by Mason for the B-side of the shelved 'Yesterday Man' single originally planned for release in October 1974, but eventually released in April 1977.

JANUARY 1976 – MICHAEL MANTLER
The Hapless Child and Other Inscrutable Stories
All tracks except 'The Hapless Child' were engineered and mixed at Britannia Row studios by Mason, between July 1975 and January 1976. Mason also appeared as an additional speaker on some tracks.

FEBRUARY 1976 – GONG
Shamal
Produced by Mason.

MARCH 1976 – BAILEY, FRITH, FITZGERALD, REICHEL
Guitar Solos 2: Bailey, Frith, Fitzgerald, Reichel
Mason is credited on the sleeve of this volume of improvised guitar solos by Derek Bailey, Fred Frith, G F Fitzgerald and Hans Reichel, indicating the album was mixed and compiled at Britannia Row Studios by him in "December 1975 or January 1976".

JANUARY 1977 – RACHID BAHRIRI
Rachid Bahri
Mason played drums on the track 'Il Survivra', which also features David Gilmour on guitars. The album also featured contributions from Rick Wills, Willie Wilson and Tim Renwick.

APRIL 1977 – ROBERT WYATT
'Yesterday Man' / 'Sonia'
Produced by Mason.

NOVEMBER 1977 – THE DAMNED
Music For Pleasure
Produced by Mason and engineered by Nick Griffiths and Brian Humphries at Britannia Row studios.

APRIL 1978 – STEVE HILLAGE
Green
Produced by Mason and Hillage. Mason also played drums on the track 'Leylines To Glassdom'.

OCTOBER 1983 – MICHAEL MANTLER
Something There
Mason played drums on this album, which was recorded in London and New York between February and June 1982.

SEPTEMBER 1987 – MICHAEL MANTLER
Michael Mantler Live
Mason played drums on this album recorded at Mantler's concert held at the *1st International Art Rock Festival*, Kongresshalle, Frankfurt, West Germany on Sunday 8 February 1987. (See Live Appearances below.)

AUGUST 1990 – VARIOUS ARTISTS
Return to the Forbidden Planet: Music from the Original Cast Recording
Produced by Mason at Britannia Row Studios.

JANUARY 1997 – GARY WINDO
His Masters Bones
Mason played drums on the tracks 'Letting Go' and 'Now Is The Time', recorded at Britannia Row on Thursday 25 March, Thursday 8 April and Thursday 15 April 1976, on this compilation of Windo material, which is sometimes referred to as *The Steam Radio Tapes*. The remainder was recorded between 1971 and 1984.

MARCH 2002 – CHIMERA
Chimera
Mason played drums on the track 'The Grail' and produced most of the tracks on this compilation album of Chimera material which also features Richard Wright. It was originally recorded between 1969 and 1970 but never released. Chimera comprised of singers Lisa Bankoff and Francesca Garnett. The CD insert gives an insight to Mason's involvement: "In May 1968 they were told by Francesca's boyfriend, Roberto, that a major pop festival to be headlined by the Pink Floyd was about to take place in the city [Rome]. With Roberto helping out with the festival's publicity, the girls were able to worm their way backstage. 'With our usual effrontery,' recalls Lisa, 'we went up to Nick Mason, drummer with the Floyd, and told him we were songwriters. We were soon chatting away with him, and found him very approachable. He took us seriously enough to give us his phone number in London, and told us to look him up when we got back, and that he would see if he could do anything to help us.'" Other musicians involved included the Smoke's Mal Luker, who played guitar and produced the earlier tracks, future Fleetwood Mac guitarist Bob Weston, and the Orange Bicycle's Wil Malone, who arranged all the songs.

OCTOBER 2005 – ROBERT WYATT
Robert Wyatt & Friends in Concert
Mason played drums on this highlights album of the Robert Wyatt concert recorded on Sunday 8 September 1974 at the Theatre Royal, Drury Lane, London, England.

MAY 2007 – PAUL JONES
Come into My Music Box: The Paul Jones Collection, Vol. 3
Mason played drums on the tracks 'My Advice To You' and 'I Don't Believe You' recorded in 1969. Although not appearing on it, there is also a previously unreleased track called 'The Committee' intended for the theme of the film of the same name recorded prior to Pink Floyd securing the soundtrack recording.

NOVEMBER 2009 – VARIOUS ARTISTS
'All You Need Is Love'
Mason played drums on the all-star track 'All You Need Is Love' featured on this charity album for the annual BBC *Children in Need* appeal. The recording and accompanying video for the single, released for download on Sunday 8 November, was filmed at Studio 2, Abbey Road Studios, London, England on Monday 7 September 2009.

JANUARY 2010 – VARIOUS ARTISTS
'Beat For Peace'
Mason played drums on an all-star video track made available for download through www.sudan365.org and entitled 'Beat For Peace'. The date marked the fifth anniversary of the Sudan Comprehensive Peace Agreement, featuring drummers and percussionists from across the world all coming together to drum for peace. Among the other performers – all filmed in a variety of locations – were Radiohead's Philip Selway, Elbow's Richard Jupp, Caroline Corr, Evelyn Glennie and Stewart Copeland.

JULY 2013 – NICKY HASLAM
Midnight Matinee
Mason played drums on the debut album of famed interior designer Nicky Haslam alongside an array of singers and musicians, many of whom were friends, including Bryan Ferry whose track 'Illusions' Mason also performs on.

NOVEMBER 2014 – KIRSTY BERTARELLI
'The Ghosts Of Christmas Past'
Mason played drums on the single by the former beauty queen and Miss UK which featured a 28-piece choir made up of members of the YMCA North Staffordshire branch and recorded at Abbey Road studios.

MAY 2015 – VARIOUS ARTISTS
'Save The Children (Look Into Your Heart)'
Mason produced a charity fundraising single recorded in response to the Nepalese earthquake that hit on 25 April 2015. It was recorded at Abbey Road studios and featured a 100-strong choir assembled by Beverley Knight and featuring Mick Jagger and Ronnie Wood.

LIVE APPEARANCES
SUNDAY 8 SEPTEMBER 1974 – PERFORMANCE
Theatre Royal, Drury Lane, London, England
Mason played drums as part of a one-off line-up comprising Robert Wyatt, Mike Oldfield, Fred Frith, Mongezi Feza, Gary Windo, Julie Tippet, Dave Stewart, Hugh Hopper, Laurie Allan and Ivor Cutler and compère John Peel. The set comprised 'Dedicated To You But You Weren't Listening', 'Opportunity Knocks', 'Memories', 'Sea Song', 'A Last Straw', 'Little Red Riding Hood Hit The Road', 'Alfie', 'Alifib', 'The God Song', 'Mind Of A Child', 'Behind Blue Eyes', 'Instant Pussy', 'Signed Curtain', 'Calyx', 'First Verse', 'Little Red Robin Hood', 'I'm A Believer' and 'The Laughing Policeman'. A CD of highlights was released in 2005 as *Robert Wyatt & Friends in Concert*.

FRIDAY 13 SEPTEMBER 1974 – TELEVISION BROADCAST
Top of the Pops, BBC Lime Grove Studios, Shepherd's Bush, London, England
Mason played drums for Robert Wyatt in a live-to-air session for *Top of the Pops* performing 'I'm A Believer'. It was broadcast on BBC1 TV between 7.00pm and 7.30pm.

FRIDAY 11 OCTOBER 1974 – RADIO RECORDING
David Hamilton Show, Studio 4, BBC Maida Vale Studios, London, England
Mason played drums for Robert Wyatt in a live recording session for BBC Radio 1 between 8.00pm and 11.30pm in which the band performed 'Alifib', 'Soup Song', 'Sea Song' and 'I'm A Believer'. It was first broadcast on BBC Radio 1 on the *David Hamilton Show* on Monday 14 October 1974 between 2.00pm and 5.00pm. 'Soup Song' was repeated on BBC Radio 1 on the *Alan Freeman Show* on Saturday 19 October 1974 between 3.00pm and 5.00pm. Repeats of 'I'm A Believer' were broadcast on BBC Radio 1 on the *David Hamilton Show* on Friday 18 October 1974 between 2.00pm and 5.00pm, and repeated again on BBC Radio 1 on the *David Hamilton Show* on Monday 21 October 1974 between 2.00pm and 5.00pm, and on BBC Radio 1 on the *Rosko Show* on Monday 21 October 1974 between 5.00pm and 7.00pm.

FRIDAY 28 NOVEMBER 1975 – PERFORMANCE
Maidstone College of Art, Maidstone, England
Mason played drums with Gary Windo's band, which featured Pam Windo (Piano), Richard Brunton (Guitars) and Bill MacCormick (Bass).

**SATURDAY 28, SUNDAY 29 & MONDAY 30 APRIL 1984 –
PERFORMANCES**
Hammersmith Odeon, Hammersmith, London, England
Mason played drums on 'Comfortably Numb' during this run of David
Gilmour solo concerts.

TUESDAY 1 MAY 1984 – PERFORMANCE
Sendesaal, Cologne, West Germany
Mason played drums in Michael Mantler and Carla Bley's *Music for Six-
Piece Orchestra* concert.

SUNDAY 8 FEBRUARY 1987 – PERFORMANCE
1st International Art Rock Festival, **Kongresshalle,
Frankfurt, West Germany**
Mason played drums on this 'Michael Mantler Projekt' concert, formed
for this one event, which also featured Rick Fenn (Guitar), Don Preston
(Keyboards), John Greaves (Bass) and Jack Bruce (Vocals). The set list
comprised: 'Alien (From Part 3)', 'Slow Orchestra Piece No.6', 'Slow
Orchestra Piece No.3', 'Slow Orchestra Piece No.8', 'Alien (From
Part 1)', 'For Instance', 'When I Run', 'The Remembered Visit', 'The
Doubtful Guest', 'The Hapless Child', 'No Answer', 'Preview' and
'Something There'. Highlights were broadcast on the German TV
channel WDR3 on Sunday 31 May 1987 and made available on CD as
Michael Mantler Live!

SUNDAY 29 MARCH 1987 – PERFORMANCES
The Secret Policeman's Third Ball, **The Palladium, London, England**
Mason made a brief appearance on drums during the all-star line-
up for the finale of 'I Shall Be Released' at this occasional Amnesty
International benefit that also featured Gilmour performing with Kate
Bush. (See David Gilmour section for further details.)

SUNDAY 11 OCTOBER 1992 – PERFORMANCE
Chelsea Arts Ball, **Royal Albert Hall, London, England**
Mason played drums at this high-society fund-raiser for the Chelsea Arts
Club and AIDS charities. Other musicians who performed included
the house band comprising David Gilmour (vocals, guitars), Guy Pratt
(bass), Jon Carin (Keyboards), Jodi Linscott (Percussion), Tim Renwick
(Guitars), Gary Wallis (Drums) and Sam Brown (Vocals), and guest
musicians Richard Wright, Tom Jones, Hugh Cornwell, Mica Paris, Elvis
Costello and Sam Moore. (See David Gilmour section for further details.)

FRIDAY 12 MARCH 1999 – TELEVISION BROADCAST
TFI: Comic Relief, **Riverside Studios, Hammersmith, London, England**
Mason played drums with a band that comprised of Jools Holland
(Piano), Elvis Costello (Lead Vocals), Damon Hill (Guitar), Dave Swift
(Bass) and All Saints (Vocals) performing 'Stand By Me' in the finale
of a special BBC edition of *TFI Friday* produced for the annual Comic
Relief fundraising night. It was broadcast in the UK on BBC1 TV between
11.30pm and 12.30pm.

SATURDAY 25 DECEMBER 1999 – RADIO BROADCAST
Aladdin: The Chinese Laundry Boy, **BBC Radio 4,
Broadcasting House, London, England**
Mason played drums and percussion with Kevin Powell on bass on the
soundtrack to *Aladdin: The Chinese Laundry Boy,* a pantomime adaptation
of the story of *Aladdin* which featured Terry Jones, Clive Anderson,
Penelope Keith and Tony Robinson. It was broadcast on BBC Radio 4
between 11.00pm and 12.00am, and repeated on Sunday 26 December
1999 between 7.15pm and 8.15pm.

WEDNESDAY 19 APRIL 2000 – PERFORMANCE
Grand Prix Anniversary Ball, **Dorchester Hotel,
Park Lane, London, England**
Mason played drums at this all-star concert hosted by Bernie Ecclestone
to celebrate the 50th anniversary of the modern Formula One
Championship and to raise money for the NSPCC. The first event in the
World Championship, won by Giuseppe Farina driving an Alfa Romeo,
took place at the British Grand Prix at Silverstone on Saturday 13 May 1950.

THURSDAY 22 JUNE 2000 – PERFORMANCE
Rebuild the Roundhouse, **The Roundhouse, London, England**
Mason played drums at this private gala to raise funds to restore the
Roundhouse as a concert venue and educational centre. The event
featured performances from Hugh Cornwell (who performed a solo
acoustic of his Stranglers' hit 'Golden Brown'), Jools Holland and his
Rhythm & Blues Band (with Cornwell on guitar with a rendition of the
Doors' 'People Are Strange') and a version of 'Interstellar Overdrive'
featuring Jools Holland, Hugh Cornwell and Nick Mason.

WEDNESDAY 26 & THURSDAY 27 JUNE 2002 – PERFORMANCES
Wembley Arena, Wembley, London, England
Mason played drums on 'Set The Controls For The Heart of The Sun' at
these Roger Waters shows. (See Roger Waters' entry for further details.)

SATURDAY 5 FEBRUARY 2005 – PERFORMANCE
Tsunami Appeal, **the Olympiad, Chippenham, England**
Mason played drums at this charity fundraiser as a member of Andy
Scott's Sweet. Other acts on the bill included Iron the Cat, the Wurzels,
the Specials, Chapter 13 and the Bersley Brothers.

SATURDAY 20 MAY 2006 – PERFORMANCE
Highclere Rocks, **Highclere Castle, Newbury, England**
Mason played drums on 'Wish You Were Here' and 'Comfortably
Numb' with Roger Waters and guests Eric Clapton (Acoustic Guitar),
Georgie Fame (Keyboards) and Andy Fairweather-Low (Guitar) in
addition to the house band, which was dubbed the Band Du Lac and
featured Gary Brooker (Electric Piano), Jodi Linscott (Percussion),
Mike Rutherford (Guitar), Geoff Whitehorn (Guitar) and Paul Carrack
(Vocals) at this benefit concert on behalf of the Countryside Alliance.
Mason continued to play drums throughout the remainder of the show,
which featured performances by Eric Clapton, Bryan Ferry, Roger
Taylor, Roger Daltrey and Georgie Fame, including a band rendition
of 'A Whiter Shade Of Pale', Clapton's rendition of 'Cocaine', Bob
Marley's 'Get Up, Stand Up' and the encore of Bob Dylan's 'Rainy Day
Women #12 & 35'.

2006 – 2008 – PERFORMANCES
Roger Waters' *The Dark Side of the Moon* **Tour**
Mason played drums in Waters' band on selected dates on his *The Dark
Side of the Moon* solo tours. (See the Roger Waters section for tour dates,
set lists and further information.)

FRIDAY 2 NOVEMBER 2007 – PERFORMANCE
Jazz Festival Berlin '07,
Haus der Berliner Festspiele, Berlin, Germany
Mason played drums in Michael Mantler's *Concertos* concert at this
multi-artist festival of events across the city alongside Michael Mantler
(Trumpet), Bjarne Roupé (Guitar), Bob Rockwell (Tenor Saxophone),
Pedro Carneiro (Marimba, Vibraphone), Majella Stockhausen-
Riegelbauer (Piano) and Roswell Rudd (Trombone). The concert was
broadcast on RBB Kulturradio, Germany on Sunday 4 November 2007.

MONDAY 12 MAY 2008 –
PERFORMANCE
Amber Rocks Party, Frankie's
Italian Bar & Grill, Knightsbridge,
London, England
Mason played drums alongside
Mike Rutherford among others at
this charity fundraiser organized
by Marco Pierre White and Eddie
Jordan for the Amber Foundation.

SATURDAY 12 JULY 2008 –
PERFORMANCE
Goodwood Festival of Speed,
Goodwood House, near
Chichester, England
Mason played drums alongside
Roger Taylor and Kenny
Jones among others at an
after-race party.

SATURDAY 2 OCTOBER 2010 –
PERFORMANCE
The Priory, Puttenham, near
Guildford, England
Mason played drums in a celebrity band that included Brian May and
Roger Daltry at the wedding reception of Queen drummer Roger Taylor.

ABOVE: NICK MASON STANDING BESIDE HIS DE HAVILLAND DOVE, 1985.

TUESDAY 22 MARCH 2011 – PERFORMANCE
The Roundhouse 5th Birthday Gala, The Roundhouse,
London, England
Mason played drums with Tres B on his song 'Best Friend' with Guy
Chambers (Keyboards), Harry B (Percussion) and others. Other
performers included the Trevor Horn-led band the Producers featuring
Alison Moyet, Gary Kemp and Tony Hadley performing the Spandau
Ballet hit 'Gold'. The spectacular finale saw Boy George join Mark
Ronson, Andrew Wyatt, Andy Burrows and the Roundhouse Choir for
the Culture Club classic, 'Do You Really Want to Hurt Me'. To round
off the evening, Ronson challenged the crowd to bid for the chance
to join him on stage for a rip-roaring rendition of his reworking of the
Zutons' song 'Valerie'. Tickets cost £500 each and included a champagne
reception, three course meal, auction and entertainment. £555,000 was
raised from donated auction lots.

THURSDAY 12 MAY 2011 – PERFORMANCE
O2 Arena, Greenwich Peninsula, London, England
Mason joined Roger Waters during one of his performances of
The Wall for the song 'Outside The Wall' on which Waters played
trumpet, David Gilmour mandolin and Mason tambourine.

SATURDAY 14 MAY 2011 – PERFORMANCE
Pancho Barn, RFC Rendcomb, near Cirencester, England
Mason played drums alongside Georgie Fame and others at
a *Help for Heroes* charity evening.

SATURDAY 30 JUNE 2012 – PERFORMANCE
Goodwood Festival of Speed, Goodwood House,
near Chichester, England
Mason played drums alongside Tony Clarke (Guitar), John Illsley (Bass),
Guy Fletcher (Keyboards) and Durga and Lorelei McBroom (Vocals) at
the after-race party. Among the many songs performed were 'One Of
These Days' and 'The Great Gig In The Sky'.

SUNDAY 12 AUGUST 2012 – PERFORMANCE
London 2012 Olympics Closing Ceremony,
Olympic Stadium, Stratford, London, England
Mason played drums alongside Ed Sheeran (Vocals, Guitar), Mike
Rutherford (Guitar) and Richard Jones (Bass) in a rendition of 'Wish
You Were Here' as part of the musical celebrations at the close of
the London 2012 Olympics. As they performed a suited man crossed
the heights of the stadium on a tightrope until he met a mannequin
double, shook hands and set it ablaze. With a cast of 4,100 performers,
including 3,880 adult volunteers and 380 schoolchildren from the six
London Olympic boroughs, and an estimated worldwide TV audience
of one billion people, the production was designed by Mark Fisher.
Other performers included the cast of *Stomp!*, Madness, Emeli Sandé,
Ray Davies, Elbow, Pet Shop Boys, Annie Lennox, Jessie J, Eric Idle,
Russell Brand, George Michael, Fatboy Slim, Beady Eye, Muse, the Kaiser
Chiefs, Queen, the Spice Girls, Take That and an explosive show closing
set by the Who. A studio recording of the track 'Wish You Were Here'
featuring the same musicians was included on a commemorative album,
*A Symphony Of British Music – Music for the Closing Ceremony of the London
2012 Olympic Games.*

20 NOVEMBER 2012 – AWARDS CEREMONY
Westminster University, Westminster, London, England
Westminster University architecture faculty awarded Mason with an
Honorary Doctor of Letters degree for his commitment to music,
influenced by his years as a student of architecture which began at
the Regent Street Polytechnic (now Westminster University) some 50
years earlier. Mason said, "Three of Pink Floyd met there, so in essence
we were formed under the roof of the Polytechnic; we rehearsed
in the common room in the basement and made some of our first
performances there. Not only did studying architecture teach us some
useful stuff, but it also gave us an opportunity to develop and put us
in touch with some fantastic mentors and industry contacts that have
helped us along the way."

ROGER WATERS

George Roger Waters was born on Monday
6 September 1943 in Great Bookham, Surrey. The family relocated to Cambridge following the death of Roger's father, Eric Fletcher Waters, a second lieutenant of the Royal Fusiliers, who perished during the Anzio campaign in Italy in 1944. Eric Waters was a devout Christian and Communist Party member who had been a conscientious objector, but his experiences driving an ambulance during the Blitz changed his opinions and he joined the British Army. He was killed when Roger was just five months old.

While attending the Morley Memorial Junior School, Roger Waters met Roger "Syd" Barrett, and a firm friendship ensued. His education continued at the Cambridgeshire High School for Boys ("The County") which, judging from the bitter resentment in his later songwriting, was not an altogether pleasant experience for him.

In 1962, Waters enrolled at the Regent Street Polytechnic where he shared classes with both Nick Mason and Richard Wright, and was instrumental in the formation of the precursor bands to Pink Floyd including Sigma 6, the Abdabs and the Tea Set.

Waters embarked on his first solo project outside of Pink Floyd as early as 1970, collaborating with the avant-garde composer Ron Geesin on a bizarre experimental documentary film *The Body,* based on the 1968 book by Anthony Smith.

He assumed the role of chief lyricist for Pink Floyd through the 1970s as he developed conceptual themes for Pink Floyd's most commercially successful albums, including *The Dark Side of the Moon, Wish You Were Here* and *The Wall.* His strong sense of the theatrical also began taking a greater role as he became the driving force in shaping the Pink Floyd concert experience as a multi-media presentation, developing the use of inflatable stage props and screen projections as a fundamental part of the show.

In May 1984, Waters released the first of his solo albums proper: *The Pros and Cons of Hitch Hiking.* A tour of Europe and North America followed, featuring Eric Clapton on guitar.

In late 1985, he formally quit Pink Floyd to pursue his solo career, and in October 1986 recorded the bulk of the soundtrack to the animated film of Raymond Briggs' 1982 graphic novel *When the Wind Blows.*

June 1987 saw the release of Waters' second full-length solo album, *Radio K.A.O.S.* It was a flawed concept piece telling the complex story of Billy, an apparent "vegetable" who accesses government defence computers to simulate a worldwide nuclear conflagration in order to convince the superpowers that they must discuss peace if global destruction is to be averted.

Following the collapse of the Eastern Bloc and the tearing down of the Berlin Wall in 1989, Waters performed *The Wall* in aid of the Memorial Fund for Disaster Relief in Berlin in July 1990. It was one of the biggest concerts ever staged, with a vast array of guest musicians. Attendance was in excess of 300,000 and a global TV audience of more than five million.

Waters' third solo album, *Amused to Death,* was released in September 1992, and was by far his most accomplished, and featured Jeff Beck on guitar. In this work he continued to vent spleen over subjects dear to his heart; foremost among these is the futility of warfare, consumerism and market forces.

To the disappointment of his fans, Waters elected not to tour the album, instead developing ideas for a classical opera entitled *Ça Ira,* released in September 2005, based around the history and politics of the French Revolution. A spectacular stage production (Waters did not perform in the piece) premiered in Rome in November 2005. Further live performances have been staged, including one in Poland in August 2006, to commemorate the fiftieth anniversary of the 1956 uprising.

In 1999, Waters returned to the live stage once more, producing a "greatest hits" collection from where he was able to develop his core audience far more effectively than before. The resultant tour, dubbed *Roger Waters: In the Flesh,* saw him perform in countries as far flung as South Africa, Latin America, Japan, Australasia, Thailand, India, UAE and the Lebanon. The European leg culminated in an appearance at the legendary Glastonbury Festival in England.

Following an invitation to perform a full live version of *The Dark Side of the Moon* at the opening of the French Grand Prix at Magny Cours in 2006, Waters decided to extend the show into a full tour, playing *The Dark Side of the Moon* as the second half of the shows, which in many cases featured Nick Mason on drums. Over the next two years his extensive touring significantly saw him perform at Latrun Monastery in Israel in June 2006, a village of Israeli-Palestinian co-existence, and at *Live Earth Day* at Giants Stadium, New Jersey, USA, in July 2007.

Prompted by the continued relevance of *The Wall* and mindful of the

limited opportunities fans had to see the shows back in the 1980s, Waters decided to revisit his 1979 masterwork with renewed energy, embracing modern technology to produce a truly spectacular show. Commencing in North America in autumn 2010, then in Europe through 2011, the tour played further dates in Australasia, and North and South America in 2012, including a record-breaking nine shows at the 80,000-capacity River Plate stadium in Buenos Aires, Argentina, concluding with a European tour in 2013.

Waters has since appeared at the occasional charity event and is reportedly working on a new rock album, although plans to tour *The Wall* once more have not been dismissed.

Waters, however, is never far from the spotlight and as a keen advocate for world peace he continues to court controversy by making thought-provoking statements, especially in regard to Middle Eastern politics.

LEFT: WATERS PERFORMING 'RADIO K.A.O.S.' AT WEMBLEY ARENA, 21 NOVEMBER 1987.

ORIGINAL RELEASES

MUSIC FROM THE BODY (ROGER WATERS & RON GEESIN)

Waters embarked on his first solo project outside of Pink Floyd in 1970, collaborating with the avant-garde performer-composer Ron Geesin on a bizarre experimental documentary film called *The Body* based on the 1968 book by Anthony Smith. Working concurrently with Pink Floyd on *Atom Heart Mother*, Waters recorded his parts between January and March 1970 at his home studio in New North Road, Islington, London while Geesin worked from his home studio at Ladbroke Grove, Notting Hill, London. The music that appears on the film soundtrack album was then re-recorded in July 1970 by Geesin at his home studio, with Waters re-recording and remixing at Island Studios, Ladbroke Grove, London with engineer Brain Humphries.

"It was intended to be a new style of making a documentary feature," recalled Geesin, "a stimulatory film. The idea in a fundamental way was to get something good with not very much, the ideal was that if you can express everything in a single melody, and variations, that would be very good. But I don't know what they replaced it with because I never actually saw it. The distributors had had an early sight and said it was too radical for their market, to tame it down, so they added some commentary. Roy Battersby, the director, was forced to get his mate Vanessa Redgrave, who was in the Workers Revolutionary Party, and they did lots of pansy, posey stuff over it, poems and things, that took the whole heat out of it."

It was not widely known until the late 1980s that the other members of Pink Floyd also appeared on the album on the final track 'Give Birth To A Smile', for which they were paid as session musicians but remain uncredited along with two female backing vocalists.

The track 'Breathe' is not the song from *The Dark Side of the Moon*, but it does begin with the song's opening lyric.

The film premiered at the Classic Cinema, Piccadilly Circus in London, Thursday 29 October 1970 with very limited nationwide cinematic distribution.

FRIDAY 27 NOVEMBER 1970
Music From The Body
Side 1: 'Our Song' / 'Sea Shell And Stone' / 'Red Stuff Writhe' / 'A Gentle Breeze Blew Through Life' / 'Lick Your Partners' / 'Bridge Passage For Three Plastic Teeth' / 'Chain Of Life' / 'The Womb Bit' / 'Embryo Thought' / 'March Past Of The Embryo's' / 'More Than Seven Dwarfs In Penis-Land' / 'Dance Of The Red Corpuscles' / Side 2: 'Body Transport' / 'Hand Dance – Full Evening Dress' / 'Breathe' / 'Old Folks Ascension' / 'Bed-Time-Dream-Clime' / 'Piddle In Perspex' / 'Embryonic Womb Walk' / 'Mrs. Throat Goes Walking' / 'Sea Shell And Soft Stone' / 'Give Birth To A Smile'.

UK: EMI Harvest SHSP 4008 (Vinyl album).
Reissued:
US: Import Records IMP 1002 (Vinyl album, released Friday 20 August 1976) / UK: EMI Harvest CDP 7925482/CZ 178 (CD album, released Monday 19 June 1989) / US: Restless Retro 772395-2 (CD album, released Tuesday 6 February 1990).

THE PROS AND CONS OF HITCH HIKING

Waters' first solo album is a concept piece with the original demos being recorded at the same time as *The Wall*. Through a series of dreams, it tells the story of a man struggling with a mid-life crisis in a motel room. Additional musicians on the album included Andy Bown (Hammond Organ and 12-string guitar), Ray Cooper (Percussion), Eric Clapton (Lead Guitar), Michael Kamen (Piano), Andy Newmark (Drums), David Sanborn (Saxophone), Raphael Ravenscroft, Kevin Flanagan and

Vic Sullivan (Horns), Madeline Bell, Doreen Chanter and Katie Kissoon (Backing Vocals), and the National Philharmonic Orchestra conducted and arranged by Michael Kamen. Voices: Madeline Bell (Hells Angel's Girlfriend), Jack Palance (Hells Angel), Cherry Vanilla (Hitch Hiker and Waitress), Roger Waters (Man), Ed Bishop and Manning Redwood (Truck Drivers), Andy Quigley (Welshman In Operating Theatre), Beth Porter (Wife).

The album was recorded at Olympic Studios, Barnes, London, England; Eel Pie Studios, Twickenham, England and the Billiard Room, Barnes, London, England between February and December 1983. It was produced by Roger Waters and Michael Kamen, and engineered by Andy Jackson and mastered by Doug Sax and Mike Reese at the Mastering Lab, Los Angeles, USA with holophonics by Zuccarelli Labs Ltd.

Gerald Scarfe's cover illustration depicting a naked female hitch-hiker was branded as sexist by many and a large number of album sleeves and advertisements were censored in some countries.

The accompanying video to the single '5.01AM (*The Pros and Cons of Hitch Hiking*)' was directed by Nicolas Roeg and filmed in London, England and Death Valley, USA, and was Roeg's first attempt at a music video.

MONDAY 9 APRIL 1984
'5:01AM (The Pros and Cons of Hitch Hiking)' / '5:01AM (The Pros and Cons of Hitch Hiking)'
US: Columbia 38-04455 (Promotional 7-inch single).
'5:01AM (The Pros and Cons of Hitch Hiking) (Extended Version)' / '5:01AM (The Pros and Cons of Hitch Hiking) (LP Version)'
US: Columbia AS 1861 (Promotional 12-inch single).
'5:01AM (The Pros and Cons of Hitch Hiking)' // '4:30AM (Apparently They Were Travelling Abroad)' / 4:33AM (Running Shoes)'
US: Columbia 44-05002 (12-inch single, released Monday 9 April 1984). Highest chart position No. 17 (*Billboard* "Mainstream Chart" on Saturday 9 June 1984).

MONDAY 16 APRIL 1984
'5:01AM (The Pros and Cons of Hitch Hiking)' / '4:30AM (Apparently They Were Travelling Abroad)'
UK: EMI Harvest HAR 5228 (7-inch single).
'5:01AM (The Pros and Cons of Hitch Hiking)' // '4:30AM (Apparently They Were Travelling Abroad)' / 4:33AM (Running Shoes)'
UK: EMI Harvest 12 HAR 5228 (12-inch single).
Highest chart position No. 76 (*Music Week* "Top 75 Singles" on Saturday 5 May 1984).

TUESDAY 8 MAY 1984
Selections from The Pros and Cons of Hitch Hiking
Side 1: '4:30am (Apparently They Were Travelling Abroad)' / '4:33am (Running Shoes)' / '4:56am (For The First Time Today, Part 1)' / Side 2: '4:41am (Sexual Revolution)' / '5:01am (The Pros and Cons of Hitch Hiking)' / '5:06am (Every Strangers Eyes)'.

US: Columbia AS 1864 (Promotional 12-inch EP)

MONDAY 7 MAY 1984 ▶
The Pros and Cons of Hitch Hiking
Side 1: '4:30am (Apparently They Were Travelling Abroad)' / '4:33am (Running Shoes)' / '4:37am (Arabs With Knives And West German Skies)' / '4:39am (For The First Time Today, Part 2)' / '4:41am (Sexual Revolution)' / '4:47am (The Remains Of Our Love)' / Side 2:

'4:50am (Go Fishing)' / '4:56am (For The First Time Today, Part 1)' / '4:58am (Dunroamin, Duncarin, Dunlivin)' / '5:01am (The Pros and Cons of Hitch Hiking, Part 10)' / '5.06am (Every Strangers Eyes)' / '5:11am (The Moment Of Clarity)'.

UK: EMI Harvest SHVL 24-0105-1 (Vinyl album; Highest chart position No. 13 *Music Week* "Top 100 Albums" on Saturday 12 May 1984) / US: Columbia FC 39290 (Vinyl album, released Tuesday 8 May 1984; Highest chart position No. 31 (*Billboard* "200" on Saturday 9 June 1984; Certified Gold on Wednesday 19 April 1995).

Reissued:
UK: EMI Harvest CDP 7460292 (CD album, released Monday 11 May 1987) / US: Columbia PC 39290 (Vinyl album, with censored sleeve) & US: Columbia CK 39290 (CD album, with censored sleeve, released Tuesday 12 May 1987).

MONDAY 11 JUNE 1984

'5:06AM (Every Strangers Eyes)' / '4:39AM (For The First Time Today, Part 2)'
UK: EMI Harvest HAR 5230 (7-inch single).

'5:06AM (Every Strangers Eyes)' / '4:39AM (For The First Time Today, Part 2)'
US: Columbia 38-04566 (Promotional 7-inch single) & Columbia 38-04566 (7-inch single, released Tuesday 21 August 1984).

WHEN THE WIND BLOWS

Waters recorded the bulk of the soundtrack to the animated film of Raymond Briggs' 1982 graphic novel, which evolved into both a radio and stage play. The animated film, made in 1986, was a runaway success. A black comedy, it focused on a retired couple living in the north of England during the Cold War era and the resultant effect on their lives with the advent of a nuclear attack on the UK.

A 30-minute 'making of' documentary: *The Wind and the Bomb* was aired in the UK on Channel 4 TV on 4 February 1987 between 11.00pm and 11.20pm, featuring an interview with Raymond Briggs. The programme featured background music from the film, including the Roger Waters tracks 'Hilda's Hair' and 'Folded Flags'.

Additional musicians on the album included Paul Carrack (Vocals and Keyboards on 'Folded Flags'), Mel Collins (Saxophone), Nick Glenny-Smith (Keyboards), John Gordon (Bass Guitar), Matt Irving (Keyboards), Freddie KRC (Drums), John Linnwood (Linn Programming), Jay Stapley (Electric Guitar) and Clare Torry (Vocals on 'Towers of Faith'). Roger Waters tracks produced by Roger Waters and Nick Griffiths, and engineered by Nick Griffiths and recorded at The Billiard Room, Barnes, London, England.

The film premiered at the Empire, Leicester Square, London, England on Saturday 31 January 1987 in support of Greenpeace and premiered in the US at the *23rd International Film Festival* at the Music Box Theater and Biograph Theater, Chicago, USA on Sunday 1 November 1987. It was cited as the festival's best animated feature, and also awarded the festival's "Oscar Getz World Peace Prize".

MONDAY 27 OCTOBER 1986 ▲

When the Wind Blows: Original Motion Picture Soundtrack
Side 1: 'When The Wind Blows' (David Bowie) / 'Facts And Figures' (Hugh Cornwell) / 'The Brazilian' (Genesis) / 'What Have They Done?' (Squeeze) / 'The Shuffle' (Paul Hardcastle) / Side 2: 'The Russian

Missile' (Roger Waters) / 'Towers Of Faith' (Roger Waters) / 'Hilda's Dream' (Roger Waters) / 'The American Bomber' (Roger Waters) / 'The Anderson Shelter' (Roger Waters) / 'The British Submarine' (Roger Waters) / 'The Attack' (Roger Waters) / 'The Fallout' (Roger Waters) / 'Hilda's Hair' (Roger Waters) / 'Folded Flags' (Roger Waters).

UK: Virgin V 2406 (Vinyl album) & Virgin CDV 2406 (CD album) / US: Virgin 90599-1 (Vinyl album, released Tuesday 25 November 1986).

MONDAY 27 OCTOBER 1986

When the Wind Blows
UK: CBS Fox 5156 (VHS video).
Reissued:
US: International Video Entertainment 68599 (VHS video, released Friday 11 March 1988) / UK: Channel 4 C4DVD 10007 (DVD video, released Monday 26 September 2005).

RADIO K.A.O.S.

Radio K.A.O.S. was another concept piece, this time telling the complex story of Billy, an apparent "vegetable", who accesses government defence computers to simulate a world-wide nuclear conflagration in order to convince the superpowers that they must discuss peace if global destruction is to be averted. Using a voice synthesizer, he communicates on air with a radio DJ, Jim Ladd, whose show becomes a vehicle for spreading his anti-war message. There is a jumbled morse code message that tops and tails the album, beginning with, "I Tuwning Syl" and ending with "Macho bullshit and mediocrity oh tike h". It is believed this was part of a missing verse that Waters occasionally shouted out on tour at the beginning of 'The Tide Is Turning'. It read, "Now the past is over but you are not alone, together we'll fight Sylvester Stallone. We will not be dragged down in his South China Sea of macho bullshit and mediocrity."

Additional musicians on the album included Andy Fairweather-Low and Jay Stapley (Guitars), Mel Collins (Saxophones), Ian Ritchie (Fairlight Programming, Drum Programming, Piano, Keyboards and Tenor Saxophone on 'Who Needs Information', 'Sunset Strip' and 'The Powers That Be'), Graham Broad (Drums and Percussion), John Linwood (Drums on 'The Powers That Be'), Nick Glenny-Smith (DX7 and Emu on 'The Powers That Be'), Matt Irving (Hammond Organ on 'The Powers That Be'), Paul Carrack (Vocal on 'The Powers That Be'), Clare Torry (vocal on 'Home' and 'Four Minutes'), Suzanne Rhatigan (Main Backing Vocals on 'Radio Waves', 'Me Or Him', 'Sunset Strip' and 'The Tide Is Turning'), Madeline Bell, Vicki Brown, Doreen Chanter, Katie Kissoon & Steve Langer (Backing Vocals on 'Who Needs Information', 'The Powers That Be' and 'Radio Waves'), John Phirkell (Trumpet on 'Who Needs Information', 'Sunset Strip' and 'The Powers That Be'), Peter Thoms (Trombone on 'Who Needs Information', 'Sunset Strip' and 'The Powers That Be'), The Pontardoulais Male Voice Choir led by Noel Davis arranged by Eric Jones, Jim Ladd (as himself), Andy Quigley (The "Forgive me, Father" speech on 'Me Or Him'), Shelley Ladd (Monkey and Dog Lady), Jack Snyder (Guppy), Ron Weldy (I Don't Like Fish), JJ Jackson (Flounder), Jim Rogers (Doesn't like fish, marine fish), John Taylor (Shellfish Shrimp Crab Lobster), Stuart the spaniel (Uncle David's Great Dane, with the help of an AKAI 900 sampler and a DX7 to make him sound bigger), BBC master computer (Billy), Harry & India Waters (Children in the garden), Horns on 'Who Needs Information' and 'The Powers That Be' arranged by Ian Ritchie, Horns on 'Sunset Strip' arranged by Roger Waters.

The album was recorded in London at the Skylight Suite (pre-production programming), the Billiard Room, Barnes, London, (October to December 1986), and Odyssey Studios, London, (February to March 1987). It was produced by Roger Waters, Ian Ritchie and Nick Griffiths and engineered by Chris Sheldon.

The cover art is based around Morse code spelling out the artist, album title and track lists, albeit with irregular separations to read:

ROGER / WATERS / RADIO / KAOS / WHONE / EDSINF / ORMA / TIONTH on the front cover, and EPOWE / RSTHAT / BEHO / METHETI / DEISTU / RNING / RADIO / WAVES on the rear.

MONDAY 11 MAY 1987
'Radio Waves' / 'Going To Live In L.A.'
UK: EMI EM6 (7-inch single)
'Radio Waves' (Extended Remix) **// 'Going To Live In L.A.' / 'Radio Waves'** (12-inch version)
UK: EMI 12EM6 (12-inch single)
'Radio Waves' (Extended Remix) **/ 'Going To Live In L.A.' / 'Radio Waves'** (7-inch single).
UK: EMI CDEM6 (CD single)
Highest chart position No. 74 (*Music Week* "Top 75 Singles" on Saturday 30 May 1987).

MONDAY 8 JUNE 1987
'Radio Waves' / 'Radio Waves'
US: Columbia 38-07180 (Promotional 7-inch single). **'Radio Waves'** (Single version)/ **'Radio Waves'** (Edit)
US: Columbia CS7 02745 (Promotional 12-inch single)
'Radio Waves' / 'Going To Live In L.A.'
US: Columbia 38-07180 (7-inch single, released).
'Radio Waves' (7-inch version) **/ 'Radio Waves'** (Album Version)
US: Columbia CAS 2723 (Promotional 12-inch single).
'Radio Waves' (Extended Remix) **// 'Going To Live In L.A.' / 'Radio Waves'** (7-inch Version)
US: Columbia 44 06816 (12-inch single).
Highest chart position No. 12 (*Billboard* "Mainstream Rock" on Saturday 4 July 1987).

MONDAY 15 JUNE 1987
Radio K.A.O.S.
Side 1: 'Radio Waves' / 'Who Needs Information' / 'Me Or Him' / 'The Powers That Be' / 'Sunset Strip' / Side 2: 'Home' / 'Four Minutes' / 'The Tide Is Turning'.
UK: EMI KAOSDJ1 (Promotional vinyl album banded for radio play with no dialogue) & UK: EMI KAOS1 (Vinyl album) & UK: EMI CDP 7468652/CD KAOS1 (CD album; Highest chart position No. 25 *Music Week* "Top 100 Albums" on Saturday 27 June 1984; Certified Silver on Monday 22 July 2013) / US: Columbia CAS 2722 (Promotional vinyl album banded for radio play with no dialogue) & US: Columbia FC 40795 (Vinyl album) & US: Columbia CK 40795 (CD album, released Tuesday 16 June 1987; Highest chart position No. 50 *Billboard* "Top 200" on Saturday 25 July 1987; 'Sunset Strip' highest chart position US No. 15 *Billboard* "Mainstream Rock" on Saturday 22 August 1987).

MONDAY 14 SEPTEMBER 1987 ▼
'Sunset Strip' / 'Money' (Live)
UK: EMI EM20 (7-inch single).
'Sunset Strip' / 'Sunset Strip'
US: Columbia 38-07364 (Promotional 7-inch single, released 11 September 1987).
'Sunset Strip' / 'Money' (Live)
US: Columbia 38-07364 (7-inch single, released 11 September 1987).
'Money' (Live) is credited on the rear sleeve and label to "Roger Waters with The Bleeding Heart Band guest vocalist Paul Carrack, recorded live at the Billiard Room, London July 14th 1987."

MONDAY 2 NOVEMBER 1987
'Who Needs Information' / 'Who Needs Information'
US: Columbia 38-07617 (Promotional 7-inch single).
'Who Needs Information' / 'Molly's Song'
US: Columbia 38-07617 (7-inch single).
MONDAY 16 NOVEMBER 1987
'The Tide Is Turning' / 'Money' (Live)
UK: EMI EM37 (7-inch single).
'The Tide Is Turning' // 'Money' (Live) **/ 'Get Back To Radio'** (Demo)
UK: EMI 12EM37 (12-inch single).
'The Tide Is Turning' / 'Money' (Live) **/ 'Get Back To Radio'** (Demo)
UK: EMI CDEM37 (CD single)
Highest chart position No. 54 (*Music Week* "Top 75 Singles" on Saturday 2 January 1988).

MONDAY 30 MAY 1988
Radio K.A.O.S.
Track list: 'Radio Waves' / 'Sunset Strip' / 'Four Minutes' / 'The Tide Is Turning'.
UK: PMI MVS KAO5 (VHS video) / US: CMV 49012 (VHS video, released Tuesday 30 May 1988).
The live sequences of this video were filmed in rehearsal at the Milwaukee Expo & Convention Centre & Arena, Milwaukee, USA on Thursday 12 November 1987.

THE WALL LIVE IN BERLIN (AUDIO)

This ambitious live project (see Live Performance section for further details) spawned a plethora of releases and promotional items documenting the concert.

The album was produced by Nick Griffiths and Roger Waters, engineered by Nigel Jopson and mixed by Nick Griffiths and Nigel Jopson. The orchestra was recorded by Steven McGlaughlin. Live recording facilities were provided by Eurosound Mobile & Manor Mobile Studios and mixed at Olympic Studios, Barnes, London, England.

SEPTEMBER 1990
The Wall Live in Berlin
UK: Mercury (Promotional Box Set with CD and VHS video of full concert, with an illustrated booklet) / US: Mercury 082730-0 (Promotional Box set, as above).

SEPTEMBER 1990
Pieces from The Wall
Track list: 'Another Brick In The Wall, Part 2' (Edit) / 'Young Lust' (Edit) / 'Run Like Hell' / 'In The Flesh?'
UK: Mercury 878147-2 (Promotional CD, housed in a 9 x 6 x 2–inch sponge 'brick').
Pieces from The Wall
Track list: 'Young Lust' / 'Another Brick In The Wall, Part 2' / 'Run Like Hell' / 'Bring The Boys Back Home'.
US: Mercury CDP 318 (Promotional CD).

MONDAY 10 SEPTEMBER 1990
'Another Brick In The Wall, Part 2' / 'Run Like Hell'
UK: Mercury MER 332 (7-inch single).
'Another Brick In The Wall, Part 2' / 'Run Like Hell' (Potsdamer Mix) **/ 'Another Brick In The Wall, Part 2'** (Full Version)
UK: Mercury MERX 332 (12-inch single).
'Another Brick In The Wall, Part 2' // 'Run Like Hell' (Potsdamer Mix) **/ 'Another Brick In The Wall, Part 2'** (Full Version)
UK: Mercury MERCD 332 (CD single).

Highest chart position No. 82 (*Music Week* "Top 75 Singles" on Saturday 22 September 1990).

'Another Brick In The Wall, Part 2'
US: Mercury CDP 342 (Promotional CD, housed in a 9 x 6 x 2–inch sponge 'brick').

MONDAY 17 SEPTEMBER 1990
The Wall Live in Berlin
CD1: 'In The Flesh' / 'The Thin Ice' / 'Another Brick In The Wall, Part 1' / 'The Happiest Days Of Our Lives' / 'Another Brick In The Wall, Part 2' / 'Mother' / 'Goodbye Blue Sky' / 'Empty Spaces' / 'Young Lust' / 'One Of My Turns' / 'Don't Leave Me Now' / 'Another Brick In The Wall, Part 3' / 'Goodbye Cruel World' / CD2: 'Hey You' / 'Is There Anybody Out There?' / 'Nobody Home' / 'Vera' / 'Bring The Boys Back Home' / 'Comfortably Numb' / 'In The Flesh' / 'Run Like Hell' / 'Waiting For The Worms' / 'Stop' / 'The Trial' / 'The Tide Is Turning'.

UK: Mercury 846611-2 (Double CD album) & UK: Mercury Phonogram 846611-1 (Double vinyl album; Highest chart position No. 27 (Music Week "Top 100 Albums" on Saturday 29 September 1990) / US: Mercury 846611-2 (Double-CD album) & US: Mercury 846611-1 (Double vinyl album, released Tuesday 18 September 1990; Highest chart position No. 56 (*Billboard* "Billboard 200" on Saturday 6 October 1990). Reissued:
UK: Mercury 038596-2 (SACD album, released Monday 19 May 2003) / US: Mercury B0000753-26 (SACD album, released Tuesday 24 June 2003).

SEPTEMBER 1990
'Hey You' (Live) / 'Another Brick In The Wall, Part 2' (Album Version)
US: Mercury CDP 349 (Promotional CD single).

SEPTEMBER 1990
The Wall Live in Berlin
Track list: 'Another Brick In The Wall, Part 2' (re-recorded with the Bleeding Hearts Band, June 1990 and unique to this CD) / 'Hey You' / 'When The Tigers Broke Free' / 'The Gunners Dream' / '5.06AM (Every Strangers Eyes)' / 'The Tide Is Turning'.
US: Mercury CSK 2126 (Promotional CD).

MONDAY 15 OCTOBER 1990
'The Tide Is Turning' (Edit) / 'Nobody Home'
UK: Mercury MER 336 (7-inch single).
'The Tide Is Turning' (LP Version) // 'Nobody Home' / 'The Tide Is Turning' (7-inch Version)
UK: Mercury MERX 336 (12-inch single).
'The Tide Is Turning' (7-inch Version) / 'Nobody Home' / 'The Tide Is Turning' (LP Version)
UK: Mercury MERCD 336 (CD single).
'The Tide Is Turning'
US: Mercury CDP 367 (Promotional CD).

THE WALL LIVE IN BERLIN (VIDEO)
To celebrate the release of the video, Channel 5 screened the film at a press reception held at the National Film Theatre, South Bank, London, England on Sunday 16 September 1990, starting at 10.30am. Waters was slated to appear in a Q&A session afterwards but didn't show, apparently due to other commitments. However, Snowy White and other musicians were spotted in the audience. Polygram held their US press conference aboard the USS *Intrepid*, New York, on Wednesday 3 October 1990.

MONDAY 24 SEPTEMBER 1990 ▶
The Wall Live in Berlin
UK: Polygram Music Video 082 648-3 (VHS video) & UK: Polygram Music Video 082 648-1 (Laserdisc video; Certified Silver on Monday 22 July 2013) / US: Polygram Music Video 082 649-3 (VHS video) & US: Polygram Music Video 082 649-1 (12-inch Laserdisc video, released Tuesday 25 September 1990; Certified Gold on Wednesday 8 January 1992).

TUESDAY 26 APRIL 2003
The Wall Live in Berlin
DVD video with digitally re-mastered visuals and DTS 5.1 surround mix produced from the original concert multi-tracks by the original recording engineer Nick Griffiths, with extras including a 30-minute documentary entitled *Behind The Wall*; a selection of Gerald Scarfe animation footage; Mark Fisher's set and character designs; unreleased footage of Rupert Everett portraying "Pink" that was never used in the concert; unreleased Ian Emes footage that was never used in the concert; digital stills from the show. UK: Universal 038 437-9 (DVD video) / US: Universal B0000369-09 (DVD video, released Tuesday 24 June 2003).

MONDAY 14 JUNE 2004
The Wall Live in Berlin: Sound & Vision Deluxe Edition
DVD video with digitally re-mastered visuals and DTS 5.1 surround mix produced from the original concert multi-tracks by the original recording engineer Nick Griffiths, with extras including a 30-minute documentary entitled *Behind The Wall*; a selection of Gerald Scarfe animation footage; Mark Fisher's set and character designs; unreleased footage of Rupert Everett portraying "Pink" that was never used in the concert; unreleased Ian Emes footage that was never used in the concert; and digital stills from the show. UK: Universal 98176054 (DVD & Double CD album) / US: Universal 98176061 (DVD & Double-CD album, released Tuesday 15 June 2004).

MONDAY 15 MAY 2006
The Wall Live in Berlin: Special Edition
DVD video in widescreen with digitally re-mastered visuals and DTS 5.1 surround mix produced from the original concert multi-tracks by the original recording engineer Nick Griffiths, with extras including a 30-minute documentary entitled *Behind The Wall*; a selection of Gerald Scarfe animation footage; Mark Fisher's set and character designs, and a multi audio option for 'Goodbye Blue Sky' and 'In The Flesh'. UK: Universal 982400-2 (DVD video) / US: Universal 982575-0 (DVD video, released Monday 14 August 2006).

MONDAY 1 OCTOBER 2007
The Wall Live in Berlin
DVD video in widescreen with digitally re-mastered visuals and DTS 5.1 surround mix produced from the original concert multi-tracks by the original recording engineer Nick Griffiths, with extras including a 30-minute documentary entitled *Behind The Wall*. UK: UMC 1144/75301144 (DVD & Double CD album, packaged in a CD digipak).

MONDAY 17 NOVEMBER 2008
The Wall Live in Berlin: Rock Legends
DVD of the full concert in DTS 5.1 surround, and no extras. UK: 5310908 (DVD).

MONDAY 28 MARCH 2011

The Wall Live in Berlin: Limited Deluxe Tour Edition

DVD video with digitally re-mastered visuals and a 5.1 surround mix produced from the original concert multi-tracks by the original recording engineer Nick Griffiths, with extras including a 30-minute documentary entitled *Behind The Wall*; a selection of Gerald Scarfe animation footage; Mark Fisher's set and character designs; unreleased footage of Rupert Everett portraying "Pink" that was never used in the concert; unreleased Ian Emes footage that was never used in the concert; digital stills from the show; and a multi audio option for 'Goodbye Blue Sky' and 'In The Flesh'. UK: Universal 0602527420592 (DVD video & Double CD album) / US: Universal 0602527420592 (DVD video & Double CD album, released Tuesday 29 March 2011).

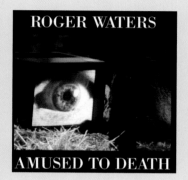

AMUSED TO DEATH

Waters' third solo album, *Amused to Death*, is by far his most accomplished. In this work he continues to vent spleen over subjects dear to his heart. Foremost among these is the futility of warfare: the piece is dedicated to Private William Hubbard, a rifleman remembered by fellow soldier Alf Razzell, who relived the horror of the First World War trenches in a TV documentary and whose words Waters samples for the album. Waters' other bugbears in this work continue to be consumerism and market forces. His main asset was to secure Jeff Beck as his lead guitarist and Patrick Leonard as his producer but, as with all of his solo albums, this concept-based work is heavy-going and best appreciated through headphones. The album was originally planned for release on EMI, but its extended production time, coupled with contractual difficulties and Waters' ongoing litigation against Pink Floyd, prompted a shift to Sony. At this time there were rumours circulating of an original sleeve design by Gerald Scarfe showing Waters' three former colleagues floating lifelessly in a cocktail glass, which Scarfe has since denied.

Additional musicians on the album included Don Henley, Rita Coolage and PP Arnold (Lead Vocals), John Joyce, Jim Haas, N'Dea Davenport, Natalie Jackson, Lynn Fiddmont-Lindsay, Katie Kissoon and Doreen Chanter (Backing Vocals), Jeff Beck, Andy Fairweather-Low, Tim Pierce, Steve Lukather, B.J. Cole, Rick DiFonzo, Bruce Gaitsch and Geoff Whitehorn (Guitars), James Johnson, John Pierce and Randy Jackson (Bass Guitars), John Patitucci (Upright and Electric Bass), Graham Broad, Denny Fongheiser and Jeff Porcaro (Drums), Luis Conte and Brian MacLeod (Percussion), Patrick Leonard (Keyboards and Piano), John "Rabbit" Bundrick (Hammond Organ), Steve Sidwell (Cornet), Guo Yi & The Peking Brothers (Dulcimer, Lute, Zhen, Oboe and Bass), The National Philharmonic Orchestra arranged and conducted by Michael Kamen and The London Welsh Chorale conducted by Kenneth Bowen.

It was produced by Patrick Leonard and Roger Waters and engineered by Hayden Bendall, Jerry Jordan and Stephen McLaughlan and recorded at the Billiard Room, Barnes; The Olympic Studios, Barnes; CTS Studios, Wembley; Angel Studios, Islington; Abbey Road Studios, St John's Wood; Compass Point Studios, Nassau, Bahamas; Devonshire Studios, Los Angeles; Ameraycan Studios, Los Angeles; Evergreen Recording, and Visual Studios, Los Angeles; mixed at Devonshire Studios, Los Angeles and Visual Studios, Los Angeles and mastered by Doug Sax & Ron Lewter at The Mastering Lab, Los Angeles.

MONDAY 24 AUGUST 1992

'What God Wants, Part 1' (Video Version) / 'What God Wants, Part 1' (Album Version)

UK: Columbia 6581390 (7-inch single).

'What God Wants, Part 1' (Video Version) / 'What God Wants, Part 1' (Album Version) / 'What God Wants, Part 3'

UK: Columbia 6581395 (CD single) / Columbia 6581399 (Limited edition CD box-set, with prints).

'What God Wants, Part 1' (Video Version) / 'What God Wants, Part 1' (Album Version) / 'What God Wants, Part 3'

UK: Columbia APCD2 (Promotional CD).
Highest chart position No. 35 (*Music Week* "Top 75 Singles" on Saturday 12 September 1992).

'What God Wants, Part 1' (Album Version) / 'What God Wants, Part 1' (Video Edit)

US: Columbia CSK 4607 (Promotional CD, released Tuesday 1 September 1992).

'What God Wants, Part 1' (Video Version) / 'What God Wants, Part 1' (Album Version)

US: Columbia 38K 74363 (7-inch single, released Tuesday 1 September 1992).
Highest chart position No. 4 (*Billboard* "Mainstream Rock" on Saturday 12 September 1992).
At the *35th Grammy Awards*, held at the Shrine Auditorium, Los Angeles, on Wednesday 24 February 1993 'What God Wants' was nominated for "Best Music Video – Short Form" losing out to 'Digging In The Dirt' by Peter Gabriel.

MONDAY 7 SEPTEMBER 1992 ◀

Amused to Death

Track list: 'The Ballad Of Bill Hubbard' / 'What God Wants, Part 1' / 'Perfect Sense, Part 1' / 'Perfect Sense, Part 2' / 'The Bravery Of Being Out Of Range' / 'Late Home Tonight, Part 1' / 'Late Home Tonight, Part 2' / 'Too Much Rope' / 'What God Wants, Part 2' / 'What God Wants, Part 3' / 'Watching TV' / 'Three Wishes' / 'It's A Miracle' / 'Amused To Death'.

UK: Columbia (Promotional box set containing the CD and cassette) / UK: Columbia 4687612 (CD album; Highest chart position No. 8 (*Music Week* "Top 100 Albums" on Saturday 19 February 1992; Certified Silver on Tuesday 1 September 1992); US: Columbia CK 47127 (CD album, released Tuesday 8 September 1992; Highest chart position No. 21 (*Billboard* "Billboard 200" on Saturday 19 September 1992); UK: Columbia COL 4687610 (Limited-edition double vinyl album set with 16-page booklet, released in response to lobbying by fans, released Monday 9 November 1992); US: Columbia CK 53196 (Limited Edition Mastersound 24-bit super bit-mapping 24-karat gold CD album, issued in a custom long box, released Tuesday 12 January 1993); US: Columbia Legacy CK 64426 (Limited Collector's Edition 24-bit super bit-mapping 24-karat gold CD album, issued in a card slipcase, released Tuesday 11 May 2004); US: Analogue Productions CAPP 468761 SA (Hybrid Stereo SACD, released Tuesday 23 September 2014) / US: Analogue Productions AAPP 468761 SA (200g double vinyl album, released Tuesday 23 September 2014); US: Sony Legacy 308378 (CD album) / US: Sony Legacy 506580 (Double vinyl picture disc album) / US: Sony Legacy

MONDAY 23 NOVEMBER 1992

Amused to Death

Track list: 'What God Wants, Part 1' / Roger Waters interview / 'What God Wants, Part 2'

Filmed at Abbey Road Studios, St John's Wood, London, England on Tuesday 12 and Wednesday 13 May 1992.
UK: Video Collection SMV 49148-2 (VHS video).

NOVEMBER 1992
'The Bravery Of Being Out Of Range'
US: Columbia CSK 4830 (Promotional CD single).

MONDAY 23 NOVEMBER 1992
'The Bravery Of Being Out Of Range' / 'What God Wants, Part 1' /
'Perfect Sense, Part 1'
UK: Columbia 6588192 (CD single).

TUESDAY 9 FEBRUARY 1993
'Three Wishes'
US: Columbia CSK 4941 (Promotional CD single).
Track list: 'Three Wishes' / 'The Bravery Of Being Out Of Range' / 'What God Wants, Part 1'
US: Columbia 6588992 (CD single).

ROGER WATERS IN THE FLESH

Following the completion of his second US tour in the summer of 2000, Waters released a document of an entire live show on a double CD taken from a selection of performances from Phoenix (Friday 16 June), Las Vegas (Saturday 17 June), Los Angeles (Saturday 24 June) and Portland (Tuesday 27 June), whilst the video was shot at just one show at Portland (Tuesday 27 June).

The album was produced and mixed by James Guthrie, who recorded the concerts on a 48-track analogue desk before mixing it down to high resolution digital. It was mastered by Doug Sax at Das Boot recording.

The cover artwork depicts a cityscape scene in the background (originally created by 4i for *The Wall Live in Berlin* show), the 'In the Flesh' tour pig logo in solid black beneath, crossed barbed wire in the foreground (similar to the graphics projected during the tour for 'Each Small Candle'), a lunar eclipse in the upper right corner and in the upper left are the words "Roger Waters" in white block lettering with blue block lettering of "in the flesh" in lower case underneath. On the back cover is the track listing above the same 4i cityscape amongst which are silhouettes of the hitchhiker, (from *The Pros and Cons of Hitch Hiking*), the monkey watching TV (from *Amused to Death*), and the radio tower (from *Radio K.A.O.S.* even though no song from that album is on the CD or was played during this leg of the tour). In the foreground is a photo of Roger standing defiantly with his bass raised in one hand. The inside 24-page booklet is filled with great photos from the tour and of course the album credits. It also contains a narrative by Roger Waters talking to Nick Sedgewick about the album, the tour and the future. The discs themselves are picture discs of a lunar eclipse with titles and track listing.

The song 'Each Small Candle' was inspired by a piece Waters read in *The Times* newspaper describing a Serbian soldier who saw an Albanian woman lying in a burned-out building. The soldier left his platoon to give aid to the woman, then rejoined his men and marched off. The image inspired Waters to adapt lyrics from the poem *Ikke Bødlen* by Danish poet Halfdan Rasmussen, which was featured as one of the best poems on Human Rights in a 1979 book published by Amnesty International.

FRIDAY 27 OCTOBER 2000
Roger Waters – In the Flesh: Disc 1 & Disc 2
US: Columbia (Promotional double CD).
Tracks as per the album, below, but with date as above and "source date 27 October 2000", printed on discs.

FRIDAY 17 NOVEMBER 2000
Roger Waters – In the Flesh: Sampler Disc for Radio
Track list: 'Mother' / 'Wish You Were Here' / 'Shine On You Crazy Diamond' / 'Each Small Candle' / 'Mother' / 'Wish You Were Here' / 'Shine On You Crazy Diamond' / 'Each Small Candle'.
US: Columbia (Promotional CD. Tracks 5 through 8 are crossfaded).

MONDAY 4 DECEMBER 2000
Roger Waters – In the Flesh
CD1: 'In The Flesh' / 'The Happiest Days Of Our Lives' / 'Another Brick In The Wall, Part 2' / 'Mother' / 'Get Your Filthy Hands Off My Desert' / 'Southampton Dock' / 'Pigs On The Wing, Part 1' / 'Dogs' / 'Welcome To The Machine' / 'Wish You Were Here' / 'Shine On You Crazy Diamond, Parts 1–8' / 'Set The Controls For The Heart Of The Sun' / CD2: 'Breathe (In The Air)' / 'Time' / 'Money' / 'The Pros and Cons of Hitch Hiking, Part 11' ['5:06 am (Every Stranger's Eyes)'] / 'Perfect Sense, Parts 1 & 2' / 'The Bravery Of Being Out Of Range' / 'It's A Miracle' / 'Amused To Death' / 'Brain Damage' / 'Eclipse' / 'Comfortably Numb' / 'Each Small Candle'.
UK: Columbia 5011372 (Double CD album) / US: Columbia C2K 85235 (Double-CD album, released Tuesday 5 December 2000; Highest chart position No. 136 US *Billboard* "Billboard 200" on Saturday 16 September 2000).
Reissued:
US: Columbia C2S 85235 (SACD double album, Tuesday 13 November 2001).

MONDAY 18 MARCH 2002
Roger Waters – In the Flesh
Track list: 'In The Flesh' / 'The Happiest Days Of Our Lives' / 'Another Brick In The Wall, Part 2' / 'Mother' / 'Get Your Filthy Hands Off My Desert' / 'Southampton Dock' / 'Pigs On The Wing, Part 1' / 'Dogs' / 'Welcome To The Machine' / 'Wish You Were Here' / 'Shine On You Crazy Diamond, Parts 1–8' / 'Set The Controls For The Heart Of The Sun' / 'Breathe (In The Air)' / 'Time' / 'Money' / 'The Pros and Cons of Hitch Hiking, Part 11' ['5:06 am (Every Stranger's Eyes)'] / 'Perfect Sense, Parts 1 & 2' / 'The Bravery Of Being Out Of Range' / 'It's A Miracle' / 'Amused To Death' / 'Brain Damage' / 'Eclipse' / 'Comfortably Numb' / 'Each Small Candle'.

The live concert video version of 'In The Flesh' features a Hi-Definition live concert video with 5.1 Dolby Digital and LPCM Stereo music mixes. Also contains additional features including a 30-minute behind-the-scenes documentary, band biographies, still photographs, projected images and lyrics. UK: Sony Music Video 54185-9 (DVD video; Certified Gold on Monday 22 July 2013) / US: Columbia Music Video CVD 54185 (DVD video) & US: Columbia Music Video CV 54185 (VHS video, released Tuesday 18 December 2001; Certified Gold on Wednesday 3 April 2002).

MONDAY 18 MARCH 2002
Roger Waters – In the Flesh
UK: Columbia 82876842682 (Limited edition double CD and single DVD video, track listing as above, housed in a thick box with slipcase and 24- page booklet).

JUNE 2002
Roger Waters – In the Flesh 2002 World Tour
UK: Columbia 5099750113721 (Promotional double CD press kit, includes standard 2CD set, 16-page press release on custom 'In The Flesh' pink pig logo headed paper with discography, world tour dates and quotes from the media from the 2001 US tour housed in a glossy black A4-sized folder).

FLICKERING FLAME: THE SOLO YEARS VOLUME 1

This "Best Of" compilation features a collection of "greatest hits", demos and soundtrack pieces that was released to coincide with the start of Waters' European 'In The Flesh' tour. The demo of 'Flickering Flame' features Jon Carin (Keyboards) and Doyle Bramall III (Guitars) and was co-produced with Nick Griffiths. It also featured as an encore track

The Solo Years Volume I
A collectors limited edition including
two rare demo recordings

roger waters

flickering flame

will not play on PC/MAC

during Waters' tours through 2002. The demo of 'Lost Boys Calling' features music by Ennio Morricone with orchestration by Rick Wentworth and was mixed by Nick Griffiths.

TUESDAY 7 MAY 2002 ◄
Flickering Flame: The Solo Years Volume 1

Track list: 'Knockin' On Heaven's Door' [From the film *The Dybbuk of the Holy Apple Field*] / 'Too Much Rope' [From *Amused To Death*] / 'The Tide Is Turning' [From *Radio K.A.O.S.*] / 'Perfect Sense, Part 1&2' (Live) [From *In the Flesh – Live*] / 'Three Wishes' [From A*mused To Death*] / '5:06am (Every Strangers Eyes)' [From *The Pros and Cons of Hitch Hiking*] / 'Who Needs Information?' [From *Radio K.A.O.S.*] / 'Each Small Candle' (Live) [From *In The Flesh – Live*] / 'Flickering Flame' (New Demo) / 'Towers Of Faith' [From *When the Wind Blows* soundtrack] / 'Radio Waves' [From *Radio K.A.O.S.*] / 'Lost Boys Calling' (Original Demo) [The finished version is featured in the film *The Legend Of 1900*].

UK: Columbia LC00162 (Promotional CD album) & UK: Columbia 5079062 (CD album).

ÇA IRA: AN OPERA IN THREE ACTS

Waters embarked on his most curious project to date: a classical opera entitled *Ça Ira* (*There is Hope*) and based around the history and politics of the French Revolution, its title taken from a popular revolutionary song of the period. The album, produced by Roger Waters and Rick Wentworth, and engineered by Simon Rhodes at Abbey Road Studios, was the result of an exhaustive 12-year process that unfortunately saw the death of Waters' three project collaborators, Philippe Constantin and Etienne and Nadine Roda-Gil who originally conceived the project.

Ça Ira features orchestration and choral arrangements by Rick Wentworth and Roger Waters. The principal characters in the opera are brought to life by the Welsh bass-baritone Bryn Terfel (as the Ringmaster, the Troublemaker and Louis Capet – the King of France); internationally acclaimed soprano Ying Huang (as Marie Marianne – the Voice of Liberty, Reason and the Republic, Marie Antoinette – the Queen of France); American tenor Paul Groves (as a Revolutionary Priest and a Military Officer); and Senegalese "one-man orchestra" Ismael Lo (as a Revolutionary Slave). Other parts were sung by Jamie Bower (as Honest Bird – the young Revolutionary Priest) and Helen Russill (as Madame Antoine – the young Marie Antoinette).

The album was produced by Roger Waters and Rick Wentworth and recorded at Air Lyndhurst, Hampstead, London; Abbey Road Studios, St John's Wood, London; Angel Studios, Islington, London; Whitfield Street Studios, Camden, London; Sony Studios, Soho, London; Sphere Studios, Battersea, London, England; Guilliaume Tell, Paris, France and Mega Studios, Paris.

MONDAY 25 JULY 2005
Selections from Roger Waters Ça Ira: An Opera in Three Acts
Track list: 'Honest Bird, Simple Bird' / 'I Want To Be King' / 'To Freeze In The Dead Of Night' / 'So To The Streets In The Pouring Rain' / 'My Dear Cousin Bourbon Of Spain' / 'To The Windward Isles' / 'The Last Night On Earth' / 'Liberty' / 'And In The Bushes Where They Survive'.

US: Sony (Promotional CD).

MONDAY 26 SEPTEMBER 2005
Ça Ira: An Opera in Three Acts
CD1: 'The Gathering Storm' / 'Overture' / 'Garden In Vienna 1765' / 'Madame Antoine' / 'Kings, Sticks And Birds' / 'Honest Bird, Simple Bird' / 'I Want To Be King' / 'Let Us Break All The Shields' / 'Grievances Of The People' / 'France In Disarray' / 'To Laugh Is To Know How To Live' / 'Slavers, Landlords, Bigots At Your Door' / 'Fall Of The Bastille' / 'To Freeze In The Dead Of Night' / 'So To The Streets In The Pouring Rain' / 'Dances And Marches' / 'Now Hear Ye' / 'Flushed With Wine' / 'The Letter' / 'My Dear Cousin Bourbon Of Spain' / 'The Ship Of State Is All At Sea' / 'Silver, Sugar And Indigo' / 'To The Windward Isles' / 'Papal Edict' / 'In Paris There's A Rumble Under The Ground' / CD2: 'The Fugitive King' / 'But The Marquis Of Boulli Has A Trump Card Up His Sleeve' / 'To Take Your Hat Off' / 'The Echoes Never Fade From That Fusillade' / 'Commune De Paris' / 'Vive La Commune De Paris' / 'The National Assembly Is Confused' / 'The Execution Of Louis Capet' / 'Adieu Louis, For You It's Over' / 'Marie Antoinette – The Last Night On Earth' / 'Adieu My Good And Tender Sister' / 'Liberty' / 'And In The Bushes Where They Survive'.

UK: Sony Classical Columbia S2H 60867 (Double CD album with an enhanced CD that includes the complete sung lyrics viewable on a CD-ROM drive) / Sony Classical Columbia S2H 60867 (Limited edition double enhanced CD album, housed in a digipak including the full opera on two SACDs, plus a bonus *Making of Ça Ira* DVD and a 60-page four-colour booklet containing the libretto, cast credits and original illustrations).

US: Sony Classical S2K 96439 (Double-CD album with an enhanced CD that includes the complete sung lyrics viewable on a CD-ROM drive) / Sony Classical S2H 60867 (Limited-edition double enhanced CD album, housed in a digipak including the full opera on two SACDs, plus a bonus *Making of Ça Ira* DVD and a 60-page four-colour booklet containing the libretto, cast credits and original illustrations, released Tuesday 27 September 2005).

THE ALBUM COLLECTION

A limited edition 8-disc box set comprising *The Pros and Cons of Hitch Hiking*, *Radio K.A.O.S.*, *Amused to Death*, *In the Flesh – Live* (Double CD & DVD) and *Ça Ira* (Double CD). It comprises all of Waters' studio and live albums housed in mini-LP replica wallets, with a 16-page booklet.

MONDAY 30 MAY 2011
The Album Collection
UK: Sony 88697763332 (Limited edition eight-CD box set).
US: Sony 88697763332 (Limited edition eight-CD box set, released Tuesday 7 June 2011).

DOWNLOADS

TUESDAY 7 SEPTEMBER 2004
'Leaving Beirut' / 'To Kill The Child'
Waters made available two new compositions for download through his official site and other approved download sites. It was released as a Japanese only, limited edition CD single on Tuesday 11 October 2005 (Sony SICP 695).

SATURDAY 8 MARCH 2008
'The Child Will Fly'
It was widely reported that Gustavo Cerati, leader of Soda Stereo, one of the biggest bands in Latin America, was in the process of recording a new track with Roger Waters at Phillip Glass's Looking Glass studio in New York on this date. It was recorded for the Fundación Alas (a foundation

created to help improve the health and education of children in Latin America) and the collaboration was engineered by the Colombian singer Shakira. The new song, which at that time had no title, was written by Cerati, who also played the lead guitar and sang on it. Further sessions saw contributions by many different international and Latin artists, including Shakira, Eric Clapton, Pedro Aznar and Gustavo Cerati, who have all worked actively with Alas. The video, which was shot during Waters' extended run of *Wall* concerts in Buenos Aires in 2010, featured the artistic supervision of Roger Waters, who took the lead role, and was directed by Argentine Diego Kaplan and became available online only on Saturday 31 May 2014, some six years after the song was first recorded.

WEDNESDAY 19 AUGUST 2009
Walled Horizons

Although containing none of his music, Waters narrated and appeared in part of this 15-minute United Nations film. It was premiered at the Al-Hakawati Theatre, East Jerusalem, Israel on this date, marking the first World Humanitarian Day and the fifth anniversary of the International Court of Justice's opinion that the West Bank wall constructed by Israel is illegal. Waters opens the film by saying, "The reason for walls is always fear, whether the personal walls that we build around ourselves or walls like this that frightened governments build around themselves. They are always expressions of a deep-seated insecurity. It fills me with horror, the thought of living in a giant prison", as the camera watches him spray-painting "We don't need no thought control" on the separation wall.

MONDAY 18 JANUARY 2010
'We Shall Overcome'

Waters recorded this infamous protest song just a few days prior to its broadcast on the Jim Ladd show on Los Angeles' KLOS 95.5 on Monday 18 January 2010. Waters has been an outspoken critic of the plight of Palestinians living in the shadow of Israel's controversial separation barrier and supported the historic Gaza Freedom March on Thursday 31 December 2009. A video of the track was released to the Internet on Friday 4 June 2010.

SATURDAY 8 MAY 2010
The Wall Tour

A promotional video was released online through AOL by promoters Live Nation to support the announcement of Roger Waters' *The Wall Live* tour, which partly used an interview with Jim Ladd, along with archive footage from the original Pink Floyd *Wall* shows, and shots of the preparations for the 2010 concerts, including brick impact testing!

FILMS & SOUNDTRACKS

MONDAY 2 APRIL 1979
L'Art et la Machine

Waters reunited with Ron Geesin to produce the soundtrack for this 1977 French-language made-for-TV film produced by Adrian Maben. It was first broadcast on Suisse-Romande TV (Switzerland) on Monday 2 April 1979. The music remains unreleased on video and the film is very rarely shown.

MONDAY 9 JULY 1979
Monsieur René Magritte

This biographical film of the surrealist artist René Magritte was made in 1978 as an Franco-German TV production, but the narration, by the director, Adrian Maben, is in English. The music is credited to a combination of Béla Bartók and Roger Waters. However, as with *L'Art et la Machine*, it is possible that the music was recorded several years beforehand: much of the passages comprise VCS3 electronica, and what appears to be an extract from 'Obscured By Clouds', all of which may

have been culled from outtakes of Maben's filming of Pink Floyd at Abbey Road for his film *Live at Pompeii*. *Monsieur René Magritte* was first broadcast on Suisse-Romande TV (Switzerland) on Monday 9 July 1979. It was released on VHS video as *Portrait of an Artist Volume 11: Monsieur René Magritte* in June 2000, and *Magritte: Monsieur René Magritte* on DVD video in September 2001.

WEDNESDAY 12 SEPTEMBER 1984
The Hit

The unreleased soundtrack to this critically acclaimed British crime thriller by Stephen Frears and starring John Hurt and Tim Roth featured a soundtrack by Paco de Lucia and Eric Clapton. Waters made a small contribution to Eric Clapton's title music. The film debuted at the *9th Toronto International Film Festival* on this date and was first released on DVD in November 2002 and re-released on DVD video in April 2009.

NOVEMBER 1986
The Samaritans

Waters remixed the Pink Floyd track 'Is There Anybody Out There?' from *The Wall* for use in an advertising campaign for the Samaritans. The *Daily Mail* reported that "Roger Waters was so keen to help with the commercial, devised by advertising agency Saatchi and Saatchi, that he personally went to great lengths to secure permission for part of the band's album *The Wall* to be used free of charge. 'We couldn't have done it without Roger's cooperation,' said Saatchi creative director Simon Dickets. 'He even mixed some extra bits for the track.'"

MONDAY 1 SEPTEMBER 1997
The Dybbuk of the Holy Apple Field

This Israeli cinematic film evolved from a 1914 play by S. Anskya entitled *The Dybbuk* – a mischievous spirit from Yiddish folklore capable of releasing repressed desires in innocent young girls. It was previewed at the *Haifa International Film Festival* in Israel in October 1997 as *Ha-Dybbuk B'sde Hatapuchim Hakdoshim* and released to cinema on Monday 1 September 1997. The soundtrack featured songs by Rick Wentworth, with whom Waters would later write the *Ça Ira* opera, and a newly recorded version of Bob Dylan's 'Knockin' On Heaven's Door' by Waters featured Simon Chamberlain (Keyboards), Clem Clempson (Guitars) and Katie Kissoon (Backing Vocals) and was produced by Nick Griffiths. This track also appeared on the Waters compilation album *Flickering Flame: The Solo Years Volume 1*. To date no soundtrack album has been officially released and the DVD has only ever been released in Israel.

WEDNESDAY 28 OCTOBER 1998
La Leggenda del Pianista Sull'Oceano [The Legend of the Pianist on the Ocean] / The Legend of 1900

Based on the fictional book *Novecento* by Alessandro Baricco published in 1994, the story was first made into a stage play making its debut during the *National Asti Theatre Festival*, Asti, Italy in July of the same year. The film interpretation by Giuseppe Tornatore and starring Tim Roth was called *La Leggeda del Pianista Sull'Oceano* and opened in Italy on Wednesday 28 October 1998. Its soundtrack was written by Ennio Morricone and featured the song 'Lost Boys Calling' over the closing titles, which was written and sung by Waters, with Edward Van Halen (Guitars), and was produced by Patrick Leonard and initially released on CD only in Italy. Exactly one year later the film was re-released as *The Legend of 1900* and featured at many film festivals across the globe. However, a different version of the same song then appeared on the *Original Motion Picture Soundtrack* CD released in October 1999. In addition, a promotional CD single was also released in October 1999 featuring 'Lost Boys Calling' and '1900 Theme'. The film was finally released on DVD in the UK some three years after its original cinematic release in December 2001 and in the United States in June 2002.

FRIDAY 23 MARCH 2007 ◄
The Last Mimzy

Waters collaborated with composer Howard Shore to record a new song 'Hello (I Love You)', which was produced by James Guthrie for use in this cinematic film by Bob Shaye based on the 1943 science-fiction story by Lewis Padgett. The film previewed at the *Sundance Film Festival*, Park City, on 23 January 2007 and opened in the States on Friday 23 March 2007 and the UK on Friday 30 March 2007. The original motion picture soundtrack featured Steve Gadd (Drums), Gerry Leonard (Guitars) and the 6-year old star of the film, Rhiannon Leigh Wryn (Vocals on chorus). It was released in the US in March 2007 and in the UK in April 2007. A promotional 7-inch single was pressed and a two-track download and CD single was made available through the Silva Screen Records' webpage featuring 'Hello (I Love You)' (Album Edit and Radio Edit). An exclusive limited edition of 1,000 audiophile 180g 12-inch singles of the Waters' tracks 'Hello (I Love You)' (Album Edit) b/w 'Hello (I Love You)' (Radio Edit) and a limited edition of 250 copies on pink vinyl of was exclusively released in the Netherlands on Monday 2 July 2007, and a limited edition 7-inch single was released in November 2008 to coincide with the publication of the Dutch discographic book P*ink Floyd on Forty-Five*. The single was re-released as a 10-inch limited edition in April 2014 as part of Record Store Day. The film itself was released on DVD in the UK and US in August 2007. In addition, a music video for the song was produced featuring images from the film as well as the recording sessions with Waters, Shore, Guthrie and Wryn.

TUESDAY 18 MARCH 2008
Body of War

Waters recorded the track 'To Kill The Child' for the soundtrack of this cinematic documentary film based around the story of Tomas Young, a US soldier who begins to question the decision by his country to go to war after he was paralyzed from a shot to the spine whilst serving in Iraq. The soundtrack was released in March 2008 as *Body of War: Songs That Inspired an Iraq War Veteran*. The film was released on DVD in October 2008.

SATURDAY 6 SEPTEMBER 2014 ►
Roger Waters The Wall

The long-awaited film of Roger Waters' reimagining of Pink Floyd's *The Wall* finally made its screen debut at the Elgin Theatre as part of the *Toronto International Film Festival* on this date. The festival, running from Thursday 4 to Sunday 14 September, held two further public screenings of the 133-minute film (Sunday 7 September at the Ryerson Theatre and Sunday 14 September at the Scotiabank Theatre) and, like the tour itself, it garnered great critical acclaim. Culled from various locations of the three-year tour, the film was interspersed with autobiographical documentary

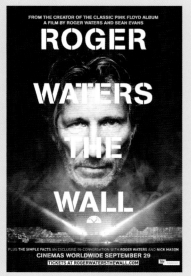

and directed by Roger Waters and the tour's creative director Sean Evans. Waters, who was also celebrating his 71st birthday, introduced the screening and, along with Evans, participated in a 30-minute after-show Q&A session. The film, which was shot in 4K and mixed on Dolby, was later released as a global cinema event on Tuesday 29 September 2015.

PRODUCTION, COMPOSITION & GUEST APPEARANCES

JANUARY 1970 – SYD BARRETT
The Madcap Laughs
See Syd Barrett section for contribution and release details.

FEBRUARY 1997 – ISMAEL LO
Jammu Africa
Includes the song 'Without Blame', a duet with Marianne Faithful, co-written by Waters, Ismael Lo and Etienne Roda-Gil.

JUNE 1999 – MARIANNE FAITHFULL
Vagabond Ways
Includes the track 'Incarceration Of A Flower Child', an unrecorded Roger Waters song from 1968, which contains the identical opening refrain of 'Your Possible Pasts' from *The Final Cut*. Waters also plays Bass Synth on this track.

NOVEMBER 2007 – VARIOUS ARTISTS
Live Earth: The Performance for a Climate In Crisis
Includes 'Another Brick In The Wall, Part 2' on DVD2, taken from Waters appearance at Giants Stadium, Brooklyn, East Rutherford, New Jersey, on Saturday 7 July 2007.

JANUARY 2013 – VARIOUS ARTISTS
12.12.12. The Concert for Sandy Relief
Includes 'Another Brick In The Wall, Part 2' (renamed 'Another Brick In The Atlantic Wall' for the purposes of this release), 'Us And Them' and 'Comfortably Numb' featuring Eddie Vedder on vocals recorded live at the show of the same name.

SEPTEMBER 2014 – MARIANNE FAITHFULL
Give My Love to London
Includes the track 'Sparrows Will Sing' written especially for this album release by Waters.

LIVE PERFORMANCE

THE PROS AND CONS OF HITCH HIKING PERFORMED LIVE (EUROPE)

For his debut solo tour Waters assembled a band that consisted of many of the key players on the album *The Pros and Cons of Hitch Hiking*, the big surprise being Eric Clapton (reportedly joining the tour against his management's advice). Also included were Mel Collins (Saxophones), Michael Kamen (Keyboards), Chris Stainton (Keyboards and Bass), Andy Newmark (Drums), Tim Renwick (Guitar and Bass), and Doreen Chanter and Katie Kissoon (Backing Vocals).

The first half of the show featured a retrospective of Waters' best-known Pink Floyd songs, complete with vintage films. The songs were performed well, but had been re-arranged and given an up-tempo feel, which in some cases didn't work at all well. Clapton, although a competent guitarist, was clearly no match for Gilmour's style on these numbers. The second half consisted of the entire *The Pros and Cons of*

Hitch Hiking album. The stage production was very similar to Pink Floyd's *The Wall* shows, using the same three-projector arrangement to project animation and film on to three screens spanning the full width of the back of the stage. To increase the visual depth, the second half of the show featured three gauze screens suspended in front of the projected images. Live-action film by Nicholas Roeg and animation by Gerald Scarfe were projected on to both the gauze and the screens behind them. One screen depicted the motel window, the second a lounge table and the third a huge TV set. The sets were designed by Mark Fisher and Jonathan Park, who had worked extensively with Pink Floyd, and quadraphonic sound was also used. However, despite its ambition, Waters had overestimated the public response to him as a solo artist and poor attendances coupled with outright cancellations marred the tour.

SATURDAY 19 MAY 1984 – TELEVISION BROADCAST
Ear Say, Channel 4 TV, UK

Roger Waters and Gerald Scarfe featured on the music programme *Ear Say*, with a look at the production behind the upcoming tour. It was broadcast on Channel 4 TV between 6.00pm and 7.00pm.

SATURDAY 16 & SUNDAY 17 JUNE 1984 – PERFORMANCES
Johanneshovs Isstadion, Stockholm, Sweden

Set list at this show and all shows on the tour unless otherwise noted: 'Set The Controls For The Heart Of The Sun', 'Money', 'If', 'Welcome To The Machine', 'Have A Cigar', 'Wish You Were Here', 'Pigs On The Wing, Part 1', 'In The Flesh', 'Nobody Home', 'Hey You', 'The Gunners Dream' <Intermission> *The Pros and Cons of Hitch Hiking* <Encore> 'Brain Damage', 'Eclipse'.

TUESDAY 19 JUNE 1984 – PERFORMANCE
Sportpaleis Ahoy, Rotterdam, Netherlands

THURSDAY 21 JUNE & FRIDAY 22 JUNE 1984 – PERFORMANCES ◄
Earls Court Exhibition Hall, Earls Court, London, England

No encore was performed on 21 June.

TUESDAY 26 & WEDNESDAY 27 JUNE 1984 – PERFORMANCES
National Exhibition Centre Arena, Birmingham, England

FRIDAY 29 JUNE 1984 – CANCELLED PERFORMANCE
Westfalenhalle, Dortmund, West Germany

Show cancelled due to poor ticket sales.

SUNDAY 1 JULY 1984 – CANCELLED PERFORMANCE
Messehalle, Frankfurt, West Germany

Show cancelled due to poor ticket sales.

SUNDAY 1 JULY 1984 – CANCELLED PERFORMANCE
Palais des Expositions, Nice, France

Show cancelled due to poor ticket sales.

TUESDAY 3 JULY 1984 – PERFORMANCE
Hallenstadion, Zurich, Switzerland

FRIDAY 6 JULY 1984 – PERFORMANCE
Palais Omnisports de Paris-Bercy, Paris, France

TUESDAY 17 & WEDNESDAY 18 JULY 1984 – PERFORMANCES
Hartford Civic Center, Hartford, CT, USA

Set list at this show and all shows on the tour unless otherwise noted: 'Set The Controls For The Heart Of The Sun', 'Money', 'If', 'Welcome To The Machine', 'Have A Cigar', 'Wish You Were Here', 'Pigs On The Wing, Part 1', 'In The Flesh', 'Nobody Home', 'Hey You', 'The Gunners Dream' <Intermission> *The Pros and Cons of Hitch Hiking* <Encore> 'Brain Damage', 'Eclipse'.

MONDAY 20, TUESDAY 21 & WEDNESDAY 22 JULY 1984 – PERFORMANCES
Brendan Byrne Arena, Meadowlands Sports Complex, East Rutherford, NJ, USA

FRIDAY 24 JULY 1984 – PERFORMANCE
The Spectrum Theater, Philadelphia, PA, USA

SUNDAY 26 JULY 1984 – PERFORMANCE
Rosemont Horizon, Rosemont, Chicago, IL, USA

TUESDAY 28 & WEDNESDAY 29 JULY 1984 – PERFORMANCES
Maple Leaf Gardens, Toronto, Canada

FRIDAY 31 JULY 1984 – PERFORMANCE
Forum de Montréal, Montréal, Canada

PROS AND CONS PLUS SOME OLD PINK FLOYD STUFF (NORTH AMERICA)

A second leg of the *Pros and Cons of Hitch Hiking* tour saw Eric Clapton (Guitar), Tim Renwick (Guitar) and Chris Stainton (Keyboards and Bass) replaced by Andy Fairweather-Low (Guitar, Bass) and Jay Stapley (Guitar).

TUESDAY 19 MARCH 1985 – PERFORMANCE
Joe Louis Arena, Detroit, MI, USA

Set list at this show and all shows on the tour unless otherwise noted: 'Set The Controls For The Heart Of The Sun', 'Money', 'If', 'Welcome To The Machine', 'Have A Cigar', 'Wish You Were Here', 'Pigs On The Wing, Part 1', 'In The Flesh', 'Nobody Home', 'Hey You', 'The Gunners Dream' <Intermission> *The Pros and Cons of Hitch Hiking* <Encore> 'Brain Damage', 'Eclipse'.

Final production rehearsals for the tour took place at this venue on Monday 18 March 1985.

WEDNESDAY 20 MARCH 1985 – PERFORMANCE
The Coliseum, Richfield, Cleveland, OH, USA

THURSDAY 21 MARCH 1985 – PERFORMANCE
Buffalo Memorial Auditorium, Buffalo, NY, USA

SATURDAY 23 MARCH 1985 – PERFORMANCE
Maple Leaf Gardens, Toronto, Canada

TUESDAY 26, WEDNESDAY 27 & THURSDAY 28 MARCH 1985 – PERFORMANCES
Radio City Music Hall, New York, NY, USA

The show on 28 March was broadcast live on the *Westwood One* radio network across the USA as a live simulcast in holophonic sound between 8.00pm and 10.00pm. It was also broadcast in the UK on BBC Radio 1 on the *Friday Rock Show* on Friday 29 November 1985 between 10.00pm and 12.00midnight.

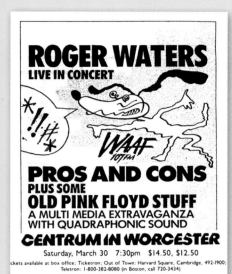

FRIDAY 29 MARCH 1985 – PERFORMANCE
The Spectrum Theater, Philadelphia, PA, USA

SATURDAY 30 MARCH 1985 – PERFORMANCE ◄
The Centrum, Worcester, MA, USA

WEDNESDAY 3 APRIL 1985 – PERFORMANCE
Oakland Coliseum Arena, Oakland, CA, USA

THURSDAY 4 APRIL 1985 – PERFORMANCE
The Forum, Inglewood, Los Angeles, CA, USA

SATURDAY 6 APRIL 1985 – PERFORMANCE
Veterans Memorial Coliseum, Phoenix, AZ, USA

MONDAY 8 APRIL 1985 – PERFORMANCE
The Summit Sports Arena, Houston, TX, USA

TUESDAY 9 APRIL 1985 – PERFORMANCE
Frank Erwin Center, University of Texas, Austin, TX, USA

THURSDAY 11 APRIL 1985 – PERFORMANCE
The Omni Coliseum, Atlanta, GA, USA

SATURDAY 13 APRIL 1985 – PERFORMANCE
Hollywood Sportatorium, Pembroke Pines, FL, USA

SUNDAY 14 APRIL 1985 – PERFORMANCE
Civic Center Arena, Lakeland, FL, USA

RADIO K.A.O.S. (NORTH AMERICA)

Waters' tour was launched at almost exactly the same time as his former band mates revived Pink Floyd. As a result, *Radio K.A.O.S.* often reached the same town within days of the Pink Floyd road show, although, as the media was at great pains to point out, Waters usually performed to considerably fewer people. For this tour the Bleeding Hearts Band comprised: Andy Fairweather-Low (Bass and Guitar), Jay Stapley (Guitar), Paul Carrack (Keyboards), Graham Broad (Drums), Mel Collins (Saxophone); and Doreen Chanter and Katie Kissoon (Backing Vocals). Jim Ladd played the part of the radio DJ. Sponsored by the Canadian beer maker Moosehead, the show was a significantly pared down production compared to *The Pros and Cons of Hitch Hiking*. Again the sets were designed by Fisher-Park, who used a backdrop with a circular mask rather than an actual screen on to which films and animation were back-projected, including some amusing adverts and sketches. A digital message board conveyed Billy's lines and a further innovation was a telephone booth in the audience with a line to the stage, allowing Waters to take fans' questions. As in Waters' previous shows, quadraphonic sound was also used.

FRIDAY 14 AUGUST 1987 – PERFORMANCE
Providence Civic Center, Providence, RI, USA

Set list at this show and all shows on the tour unless otherwise noted: Jim Ladd intro and audience telephone calls, 'Club Nowhere' (Film Sketch), Audience telephone calls to Jim Ladd / 'Tempted' (Paul Carrack solo) / 'Radio Waves',

'Welcome To The Machine' / 'Who Needs Information' / 'Money' / 'The Bimbo School' (Film Sketch) / 'In The Flesh' / 'Have A Cigar' – 'Pigs (3 Different Ones)' – 'Wish You Were Here' (Medley) / 'Mother' / 'Molly's Song' / 'Me Or Him' / 'The Powers That Be' <Intermission> Moosehead beer (tour sponsor film advert) / Audience telephone calls to Roger Waters / 'The Shredding Alternative' (Film Sketch) / 'Going To Live In LA' / 'Sunset Strip' / 'Fish Report With A Beat' (Film Sketch) / '5:01am (The Pros and Cons of Hitch Hiking)' / 'Get Your Filthy Hands Off My Desert' / 'Southampton Dock' / 'Arnold Layne' (1967 Pink Floyd Promo Film) / 'If' / '5:06am (Every Strangers Eyes)' / 'Not Now John' / 'Another Brick In The Wall, Part 1' / 'The Happiest Days Of Our Lives' / 'Another Brick In The Wall, Part 2' / 'Nobody Home' / 'Home' / 'Four Minutes' / 'The Tide Is Turning' <Encore> 'Breathe' / 'Brain Damage' / 'Eclipse'.

Final production rehearsals for the tour took place at this venue on Wednesday 12 and Thursday 13 August 1987.

SATURDAY 15 AUGUST 1987 – PERFORMANCE
Hartford Civic Center, Hartford, CT, USA

MONDAY 17 AUGUST 1987 – PERFORMANCE
Kingswood Music Theatre, Toronto, Canada

WEDNESDAY 19 AUGUST 1987 – PERFORMANCE
Blossom Music Center, Cuyahoga Falls, NY, USA

THURSDAY 20 AUGUST 1987 – PERFORMANCE
Buffalo Memorial Auditorium, Buffalo, NY, USA

SATURDAY 22 AUGUST 1987 – PERFORMANCE
Great Woods, Mansfield, Boston, MA, USA

MONDAY 24 AUGUST 1987 – PERFORMANCE
The Spectrum Theater, Philadelphia, PA, USA

WEDNESDAY 26 AUGUST 1987 – PERFORMANCE
Madison Square Garden, New York, NY, USA

FRIDAY 28 AUGUST 1987 – PERFORMANCE
Saratoga Performing Arts Center, Saratoga Springs, NY, USA

SUNDAY 30 AUGUST 1987 – PERFORMANCE
Capital Music Theatre, Landover, MD, USA

MONDAY 31 AUGUST 1987 – CANCELLED PERFORMANCE
The Coliseum, Greensboro, NC, USA

Show cancelled for unknown reasons.

WEDNESDAY 2 SEPTEMBER 1987 – PERFORMANCE
The Omni Coliseum, Atlanta, GA, USA

FRIDAY 4 SEPTEMBER 1987 – PERFORMANCE
Fox Theatre, St Louis, MO, USA

SATURDAY 5 SEPTEMBER 1987 – PERFORMANCE
Market Square Arena, Indianapolis, IN, USA

SUNDAY 6 SEPTEMBER 1987 – PERFORMANCE
Ohio Center, Columbus, OH, USA

TUESDAY 8 SEPTEMBER 1987 – PERFORMANCE
Pine Knob Music Theatre, Clarkston, MI, USA

WEDNESDAY 9 SEPTEMBER 1987 – PERFORMANCE
Poplar Creek Music Theatre, Hoffman Estates, Chicago, IL, USA

THURSDAY 10 SEPTEMBER 1987 – PERFORMANCE
Metropolitan Center, Minneapolis, MN, USA

SATURDAY 12 SEPTEMBER 1987 – PERFORMANCE
McNichols Sports Arena, Denver, CO, USA

MONDAY 14 SEPTEMBER 1987 – PERFORMANCE
Frank Erwin Center, University of Texas, Austin, TX, USA

TUESDAY 15 SEPTEMBER 1987 – PERFORMANCE
Reunion Arena, Reunion Park, Dallas, TX, USA

THURSDAY 17 SEPTEMBER 1987 – PERFORMANCE
Veterans Memorial Coliseum, Phoenix, AZ, USA

SUNDAY 20 SEPTEMBER 1987 – PERFORMANCE
The Forum, Inglewood, Los Angeles, CA, USA

'Outside The Wall' was performed as an additional encore with original *Wall* show backing vocalists John Joyce, Jim Haas and Joe Chemay.

WEDNESDAY 23 SEPTEMBER 1987 – PERFORMANCE
Sports Arena, San Diego, CA, USA

SATURDAY 26 SEPTEMBER 1987 – PERFORMANCE
Oakland Coliseum Arena, Oakland, CA, USA

MONDAY 28 SEPTEMBER 1987 – PERFORMANCE
Seattle Center Arena, Seattle, WA, USA

TUESDAY 29 SEPTEMBER 1987 – PERFORMANCE
Expo Theatre, Vancouver, Canada

RADIO K.A.O.S. (FAR EAST)

A tour of Australia and Japan was scheduled for October 1987 but was cancelled, reportedly due to poor ticket sales, including the following dates: NBC Arena, Honolulu, USA (Saturday 3 October); Festival Hall, Brisbane, Australia (Friday 9 October); Entertainment Centre, Melbourne, Australia (Thursday 15 October); Entertainment Centre, Sydney, Australia (Tuesday 20 October); Entertainment Centre, Perth, Australia (Saturday 24 October); Osaka, Japan (Tuesday 27 October); NHK Hall, Tokyo, Japan (Wednesday 28 & Thursday 29 October). Waters and his colleagues spent the time working on an as yet unreleased album at the Compass Point recording studios in the Bahamas. The tour resumed in November with the same cast.

RADIO K.A.O.S. (NORTH AMERICA)

Waters' tour resumed in November with the same band comprising Andy Fairweather-Low (Bass and Guitar), Jay Stapley (Guitar), Paul Carrack (Keyboards), Graham Broad (Drums), Mel Collins (Saxophone) and Doreen Chanter and Katie Kissoon (Backing Vocals). Jim Ladd played the part of the radio DJ.

TUESDAY 3 NOVEMBER 1987 – PERFORMANCE
Cumberland County Convention Center, Portland, USA

Set list at this show and all shows on the tour unless otherwise noted: Jim Ladd intro and audience telephone calls, 'Club Nowhere' (Film Sketch), Audience telephone calls to Jim Ladd, 'Tempted' (Paul Carrack solo), 'Radio Waves', 'Welcome To The Machine', 'Who Needs Information', 'Money', 'The Bimbo School' (Film Sketch), 'In The Flesh' – 'Have A Cigar' – 'Pigs (3 Different Ones)' – 'Wish You Were Here' (Medley), 'Mother', 'Molly's Song', 'Me Or Him', 'The Powers That Be' <Intermission> Moosehead beer (tour sponsor film advert), Audience telephone calls to Roger Waters, 'The Shredding Alternative' (Film Sketch), 'Going To Live In

LA', 'Sunset Strip', 'Fish Report With A Beat' (Film Sketch), '5:01am (The Pros and Cons of Hitch Hiking)' , 'Get Your Filthy Hands Off My Desert', 'Southampton Dock', 'Arnold Layne' (1967 Pink Floyd Promo Film), 'If', '5:06am (Every Strangers Eyes)', 'Not Now John', 'Another Brick In The Wall, Part 1', 'The Happiest Days Of Our Lives', 'Another Brick In The Wall, Part 2', 'Nobody Home', 'Home', 'Four Minutes', 'The Tide Is Turning' <Encore> 'Breathe', 'Brain Damage', 'Eclipse'.

Final production rehearsals for the tour took place at this venue on Monday 2 November 1987.

WEDNESDAY 4 NOVEMBER 1987 – PERFORMANCE
Brendan Byrne Arena, Meadowlands Sports Complex, East Rutherford, NJ, USA

FRIDAY 6 NOVEMBER 1987 – PERFORMANCE
Forum de Montréal, Montréal, Canada

SATURDAY 7 NOVEMBER 1987 – PERFORMANCE
Coliseé De Québec City, Canada

The show was recorded for the Westwood One radio network *In Concert* series and broadcast on 23 November 1987.

MONDAY 9 NOVEMBER 1987 – PERFORMANCE
Civic Center, Ottawa, Canada

TUESDAY 10 NOVEMBER 1987 – PERFORMANCE
Copps Coliseum, Hamilton, Canada

FRIDAY 13 NOVEMBER 1987 – PERFORMANCE
Milwaukee Expo & Convention Centre & Arena, Milwaukee, WI, USA

A full dress rehearsal was filmed on the 12 November at the venue for use in the *Radio KAOS* video EP.

SATURDAY 14 NOVEMBER 1987 – PERFORMANCE
Arie Crown Theater, Chicago, IL, USA

MONDAY 16 NOVEMBER 1987 – PERFORMANCE
The Centrum, Worcester, MA, USA

RADIO K.A.O.S. (UK SHOWS)

Only two shows were performed in the UK on this tour, and none at all in Europe. Clare Torry sang on 'The Great Gig In The Sky' at both Wembley Arena shows. However, Waters was unsuccessful in his efforts to get the Pontardoulais Male Voice Choir to perform on stage at this and his earlier show at New York's Madison Square Garden.

SATURDAY 21 & SUNDAY 22 NOVEMBER 1987 – PERFORMANCES ▼
Wembley Arena, Wembley, England

Set list at both shows and all shows on the tour unless otherwise noted: Jim Ladd intro and audience telephone calls, 'Club Nowhere' (Film Sketch), Audience telephone calls to Jim Ladd, 'Tempted' (Paul Carrack solo), 'Radio Waves', 'Welcome To The Machine', 'Who Needs Information', 'Money', 'The Bimbo School' (Film Sketch), 'In The Flesh' – 'Have A Cigar' – 'Pigs (3 Different Ones)' – 'Wish You Were Here' (Medley), 'Mother', 'Molly's Song', 'Me Or Him',

'The Powers That Be' <Intermission> Moosehead beer (tour sponsor film advert), Audience telephone calls to Roger Waters, 'The Shredding Alternative' (Film Sketch), 'Going To Live In LA', 'Sunset Strip', 'Fish Report With A Beat' (Film Sketch), '5:01am (The Pros and Cons of Hitch Hiking)', 'Get Your Filthy Hands Off My Desert', 'Southampton Dock', 'Arnold Layne' (1967 Pink Floyd Promo Film), 'If', '5:06am (Every Strangers Eyes)', 'Not Now John', 'Another Brick In The Wall, Part 1', 'The Happiest Days Of Our Lives', 'Another Brick In The Wall, Part 2', 'Nobody Home', 'Home', 'Four Minutes', 'The Tide Is Turning' <Encore> 'Breathe', 'The Great Gog In The Sky', 'Brain Damage', 'Eclipse'.

The show on Saturday 21 November 1987 was recorded and edited to make a 71-minute presentation for Capital Radio, London, England and broadcast on Sunday 17 April 1988 from 10.00pm comprising 'Intro Jim Ladd talks to Billy', 'Radio Waves', 'Welcome To The Machine', 'Who Needs Information', 'Me Or Him', 'The Powers That Be', 'Sunset Strip', 'If', 'Every Strangers Eyes', 'Nobody Home', 'Home', 'Four Minutes' and 'The Tide Is Turning'.

THE WALL LIVE IN BERLIN

Possibly the most ambitious outdoor concert event ever staged and at the suggestion of rock merchandiser Mick Worwood, Waters agreed to perform a one-off production of *The Wall* in order to raise money for the Memorial Fund For Disaster Relief, a charity dedicated to raising £5 (UK Sterling) for every life lost in the Second World War, for the relief of natural world catastrophes. It was founded by Leonard Cheshire VC, OM, DSO, DFC, the highly decorated Second World War airman who devoted his post-war life to charitable organizations. To get the project off the ground Waters teamed up with producer Tony Hollingsworth and Waters poured a considerable sum of his personal wealth to get the project off the ground. There was much talk of staging the concert in other prime locations, but the collapse of the Communist Bloc made the former East Berlin an appropriate location. A 25-acre site formerly occupying the no man's land between East and West was cleared, in order to stage the show. As well as harbouring a vast amount of unexploded armaments from the war, the land also contained a previously undiscovered underground bunker. In this climate of unaccustomed reconciliation, it took at least six months to establish which of the governments could give authority to stage the event. The production, designed by Fisher-Park, incorporated a wall 82 feet high by 591 feet across, with a stage wide enough and strong enough to carry a marching band, military trucks and trailers, motorbikes and limousines as well as all the necessary mechanisms and scenery. Rehearsals with the Bleeding Hearts Band began in London as early as May and in Berlin two weeks before the show and a final three days of complete production rehearsals at the venue from Wednesday 18 July.

An international array of guest musicians complemented Waters on stage, although his own Bleeding Hearts Band formed the core of his musical support: Graham Broad (Drums), Snowy White and Rick Di Fonzo (Guitars), Andy Fairweather-Low (Guitar, Bass), Nick Glennie-Smith and Peter Wood (Keyboards), Joe Chemay, Jim Haas, Jim Farber and John Joyce (Backing Vocals). Mysteriously the performance and subsequent releases omitted the track 'The Show Must Go On'. Before the beginning of the show from 5.30pm, brief performances by the Hooters, the Band and the Chieftains (with guest James Galway) were held, but none of these performances have ever been officially released. Leonard Cheshire officially opened the show with the sounding of a First World War whistle.

The estimated audience of over 250,000 (many of whom entered free after the collapse of the perimeter fence) must make it one of the biggest single concert attendances ever. It was also fortunate the last night of rehearsals was filmed, because on the night of the show so many satellite TV stations were linked to the site that power failures occurred repeatedly throughout the performance. For this reason, many scenes were re-shot for the benefit of the video after the crowds had dispersed at the end of the concert.

Despite the sale of TV rights which saw 52 countries showing the two-hour event, 20 countries showing up to five repeats of the show and 65 countries broadcasting highlights of the show, plus royalties later realized from the album and video sales, the production costs had spiralled out of control to such an extent that, by May 1992, only an estimated £100,000 had been raised for the Memorial Fund for Disaster Relief – a figure far short of the original target. Consequently the trading arm of the event suffered heavy losses and a few years later the charity was wound up and all rights reverted back to Waters.

On Friday 21 September 1990 the renowned London auction house Christie's staged a dedicated sale, in aid of the Memorial Fund for Disaster Relief, of the stage props and costumes used by the Roger Waters production of his Berlin *Wall* concert. Also on sale, and viewed with interest by Gerald Scarfe, was a large quantity of original animation cells from the original 1982 film.

SATURDAY 21 JULY 1990 – PERFORMANCE
The Wall – Live in Berlin, Potzdamer Platz, Berlin, Germany

Set list (with featured artist): 'In The Flesh' (The Scorpions), 'The Thin Ice' (Ute Lemper as the Wife), 'Another Brick In The Wall, Part 1' (Garth Hudson, Saxophone solo), 'The Happiest Days Of Our Lives' (Joe Chemay, John Joyce, Jim Farber and Jim Haas, Vocals), 'Another Brick In The Wall, Part 2' (Cyndi Lauper, Vocals; Rick Di Fonzo and Snowy White, Guitars; Peter Wood, Keyboards; Thomas Dolby as the Teacher), 'Mother' (Sinead O'Connor, Vocals with the Band), 'Goodbye Blue Sky' (Joni Mitchell, Vocals; James Galway, Flute), 'Empty Spaces' (Bryan Adams, Vocals and Guitar), 'Young Lust' (Bryan Adams, Vocals and Guitar), 'One Of My Turns' (Jerry Hall as The Groupie), 'Another Brick In The Wall, Part 3', 'Goodbye Cruel World' <Intermission> 'Hey You' (Paul Carrack, Vocals), 'Is There Anybody Out There?' (Snowy White and Rick Di Fonzo, Classical Guitar; Berliner Rundfunk Orchestra & Choir), 'Nobody Home' (Snowy White, Guitar) 'Vera' (Berliner Rundfunk Orchestra & Choir), 'Bring The Boys Back Home' (Berliner Rundfunk Orchestra & Choir), 'Comfortably Numb' (Van Morrison, Vocals; The Band; Rick Di Fonzo and Snowy White, Guitar solos), 'In The Flesh?' (Berliner Rundfunk Orchestra & Choir; Military Orchestra Of The Soviet Army – both to the end of the show), 'Run Like Hell', 'Waiting For The Worms', 'Stop', 'The Trial' (Tim Curry as the Prosecutor; Thomas Dolby as the Teacher; Ute Lemper as the Wife; Marianne Faithfull as the Mother; Albert Finney as the Judge) <Encore> 'The Tide Is Turning' (All Cast).

ROGER WATERS – IN THE FLESH (NORTH AMERICA)

Roger Waters' tour of 1999 was a far more successful venture than previous tours: he seemed at last to have found his own core audience, and indeed many of the venues had to be scaled up to larger capacities. His band for this tour comprised: Andy Fairweather-Low (Guitar), Doyle Bramhall II (Guitar, Vocals), Snowy White (Guitar), Graham Broad (Drums), Jon Carin and Andy Wallace (Keyboards), Katie Kissoon and PP Arnold (Backing Vocals).

Musicians' rehearsals were reported to have taken place at Hampton Bays High School, between Friday 2 and Sunday 11 July 1999 in Long Island, New York. Final production rehearsals for the tour took place at the former Calverton Naval Weapons Reserve in Riverhead, New York, between Monday 12 and Monday 19 July 1999, before moving to the opening venue on Wednesday 21 and Thursday 22 July 1999.

FRIDAY 23 JULY 1999 – PERFORMANCE
Bruce Hall, Milwaukee Auditorium, Milwaukee, WI, USA

Set list at this show and all shows on the tour unless otherwise noted: 'In The Flesh', 'The Thin Ice', 'Another Brick In The Wall, Part 1', 'Mother', 'Get Your Filthy Hands Off My Desert', 'Southampton Dock', 'Pigs On The Wing, Part 1', 'Dogs', 'Welcome To The Machine', 'Wish You Were Here', 'Shine On You Crazy Diamond' <Intermission> 'Breathe', 'The Great Gig In The Sky' (keyboard introduction only), 'Money', '5:06am (Every Stranger's Eyes)', 'The Powers That Be', 'What

God Wants, Part 1; 'Perfect Sense, Part 1; 'Perfect Sense, Part 2; 'It's A Miracle; 'Amused To Death; 'The Happiest Days Of Our Lives; 'Another Brick In The Wall, Part 2' <Encore> 'Brain Damage; 'Eclipse; 'Comfortably Numb'.

SATURDAY 24 JULY 1999 – PERFORMANCE
Rosemont Theatre, Rosemont, Chicago, IL, USA

SUNDAY 25 JULY 1999 – PERFORMANCE
Pine Knob Music Theatre, Clarkston, MI, USA

TUESDAY 27 JULY 1999 – PERFORMANCE
Gund Arena, Cleveland, OH, USA
Rescheduled from Nautica Stage, Cleveland, OH, USA

FRIDAY 30 JULY 1999 – PERFORMANCE
Agora du Vieux, Port de Québec, Québec, Canada

SATURDAY 31 JULY 1999 – PERFORMANCE
Molson Centre, Montréal, Canada

SUNDAY 1 AUGUST 1999 – PERFORMANCE
Molson Amphitheatre, Toronto, Canada

WEDNESDAY 4 AUGUST 1999 – PERFORMANCE
Tweeter Performing Arts Center, Mansfield, Boston, MA, USA

FRIDAY 6 AUGUST 1999 – PERFORMANCE
PNC Bank Arts Center, Holmdel, NJ, USA

SATURDAY 7 AUGUST 1999 – PERFORMANCE
Jones Beach Theatre, Wantagh, NY, USA

SUNDAY 8 AUGUST 1999 – PERFORMANCE
SNET Oakdale Theatre, Wallingford, CT, USA

TUESDAY 10 AUGUST 1999 – PERFORMANCE
Pepsi Arena, Albany, NY, USA

Rescheduled from the Landmark Theatre, Syracuse, USA on 28 July.

WEDNESDAY 11 AUGUST 1999 – PERFORMANCE
Blockbuster–Sony Music Entertainment Center,
Camden, NJ, USA

FRIDAY 13 AUGUST 1999 – PERFORMANCE
Montage Mountain Performing Arts Center,
Scranton, PA, USA

Heavy thunderstorms and rain forced a two-hour break in the show during 'Another Brick In The Wall, Part 1'. The show resumed thereafter starting with 'Another Brick In The Wall, Part 1'.

SATURDAY 14 AUGUST 1999 – PERFORMANCE
Darien Lake Performing Arts Center,
Six Flags Theme Park, Darien, NY, USA

SUNDAY 15 AUGUST 1999 – PERFORMANCE
Jerome Schottenstein Center,
Ohio State University, Columbus, OH, USA

Rescheduled from Franklin County Veterans Memorial Auditorium, Columbus, USA.

TUESDAY 17 AUGUST 1999 – PERFORMANCE
Hershey Star Pavilion, Hershey, PA, USA

WEDNESDAY 18 AUGUST 1999 – PERFORMANCE
Star Lake Amphitheatre, Burgettstown, Pittsburgh, PA, USA

Rescheduled from IC Light Amphitheatre & Tent Stadium, Pittsburgh.

FRIDAY 20 AUGUST 1999 – PERFORMANCE
Baltimore Arena, Baltimore, MD, USA

Rescheduled from Pier Six Concert Pavilion, Baltimore.

SUNDAY 22 AUGUST 1999 – PERFORMANCE
Lakewood Amphitheatre, Atlanta, GA, USA

Rescheduled from Chastain Park Amphitheatre, Atlanta. Richard Wright and members of his family reportedly attended the show.

TUESDAY 24 AUGUST 1999 – PERFORMANCE
Deer Creek Music Center, Noblesville, Indianapolis, IN, USA

WEDNESDAY 25 AUGUST 1999 – PERFORMANCE
Van Andel Arena, Grand Rapids, MI, USA

FRIDAY 27 AUGUST 1999 – PERFORMANCE
Riverport Amphitheatre, Maryland Heights, St Louis, MO, USA

SATURDAY 28 AUGUST 1999 – PERFORMANCE
Kemper Arena, Kansas City, MO, USA

ROGER WATERS IN THE FLESH (NORTH AMERICA)

Waters' band for this tour comprised: Andy Fairweather-Low (Guitar, Bass, Vocals), Doyle Bramhall II (Guitar, Vocals), Snowy White (Guitar, Vocals), Graham Broad (Drums), Jon Carin (Keyboards, Vocals), Andy Wallace (Keyboards), and Katie Kissoon and Susannah Melvoin (Backing Vocals).

In addition, a different saxophone player joined the band on stage each night as follows: Mike MacArthur (Friday 2 June); Ed Calle (Saturday 3 June); Wayne Jackson – trumpet and Andrew Love – saxophone (Tuesday 6 June); Tim Gordon (Wednesday 7 June); Shelley Carroll (Saturday 10, Sunday 11 and Tuesday 13 June); Don Menza (Friday 16, Saturday 17 & Monday 19 June); Steve Tavaglione (Wednesday 21, Thursday 22 & Friday 23 June); Norbert Stachel (Sunday 25 & Tuesday 27 June); Eric Walton (Friday 30 June & Saturday 1 July); Mark Harris (Monday 3 July); Steve Eisen (Thursday 6 July); Mel Collins (Saturday 8, Sunday 9, Tuesday 11, Thursday 13, Saturday 15 & Sunday 16 July).

The shows at Phoenix, Las Vegas, Los Angeles and Portland were filmed and recorded for the *Roger Waters – In the Flesh* live CD and DVD and veteran broadcaster Jim Ladd made appropriate introductions at each of these shows to alert the fans to this fact. A full production rehearsal took place at the opening venue on Thursday 1 June.

FRIDAY 2 JUNE 2000 – PERFORMANCE
Ice Palace Arena, Tampa, FL, USA

Set list at this show and all shows on the tour unless otherwise noted: 'In The Flesh; 'The Happiest Days Of Our Lives; 'Another Brick In The Wall, Part 2; 'Mother; 'Get Your Filthy Hands Off My Desert; 'Southampton Dock; 'Pigs On The Wing, Part 1; 'Dogs; 'Welcome To The Machine; 'Wish You Were Here; 'Shine On You Crazy Diamond' <Intermission> 'Set The Controls For The Heart Of The Sun; 'Breathe; 'Time; 'Breathe (reprise)'; 'Money; '5:06am (Every Strangers Eyes); 'What God Wants, Part 1; 'Perfect Sense, Part 1; 'Perfect Sense, Part 2; 'The Bravery Of Being Out Of Range; 'It's A Miracle; 'Amused To Death; 'Brain Damage; 'Eclipse' <Encore> 'Comfortably Numb; 'Each Small Candle'.

SATURDAY 3 JUNE 2000 – PERFORMANCE
Mars Music Amphitheatre, South Florida Fairgrounds,
West Palm Beach, FL, USA

TUESDAY 6 JUNE 2000 – PERFORMANCE
AmSouth Amphitheatre, Antioch, Nashville, TN, USA

WEDNESDAY 7 JUNE 2000 – PERFORMANCE
Blockbuster Pavilion, Charlotte, NC, USA

THURSDAY 8 JUNE 2000 – CANCELLED PERFORMANCE
New Orleans Arena, New Orleans, LA, USA

Show cancelled before tickets went on sale.

SATURDAY 10 JUNE 2000 – PERFORMANCE
Woodlands Pavilion, Houston, TX, USA

SUNDAY 11 JUNE 2000 – PERFORMANCE
Starplex Amphitheatre, Dallas, TX, USA

TUESDAY 13 JUNE 2000 – PERFORMANCE
Alamodome, San Antonio, TX, USA

FRIDAY 16 JUNE 2000 – PERFORMANCE
America West Arena, Phoenix, AZ, USA

The show was recorded for the *Roger Waters – In the Flesh* live album.

SATURDAY 17 JUNE 2000 – PERFORMANCE
MGM Grand Garden Arena, Las Vegas, NV, USA

The show was recorded for the *Roger Waters – In the Flesh* live album.

MONDAY 19 JUNE 2000 – PERFORMANCE
Coors Amphitheatre, Chula Vista, San Diego, CA, USA

WEDNESDAY 21 & THURSDAY 22 JUNE 2000 – PERFORMANCES
Universal Amphitheater, Los Angeles, CA, USA

SATURDAY 24 JUNE 2000 – PERFORMANCE
Irvine Meadows Amphitheater, Irvine, Los Angeles, CA, USA

The show was recorded for the *Roger Waters – In the Flesh* live album.

SUNDAY 25 JUNE 2000 – PERFORMANCE
Shoreline Amphitheatre, Mountain View, near San Francisco, CA, USA

TUESDAY 27 JUNE 2000 – PERFORMANCE
Rose Garden Arena, Rose Quarter, Portland, OR, USA

The show was recorded for the *Roger Waters – In the Flesh* live album.

FRIDAY 30 JUNE 2000 – PERFORMANCE
The Gorge Amphitheater, Quincy, WA, USA

The show commenced with Roger Waters' private jet buzzing the audience at about 800 feet creating a spectacular introduction to 'In The Flesh'.

SATURDAY 1 JULY 2000 – PERFORMANCE
Idaho Center Arena, Nampa, ID, USA

MONDAY 3 JULY 2000 – PERFORMANCE
Fiddlers Green Amphitheater, Englewood, Denver, CO, USA

THURSDAY 6 JULY 2000 – PERFORMANCE
Target Center, Minneapolis, MN, USA

SATURDAY 8 JULY 2000 – PERFORMANCE
New World Music Theatre, Tinley Park, Chicago, IL, USA

SUNDAY 9 JULY 2000 – PERFORMANCE
Pavilion Lawn, Riverbend Music Center, Cincinnati, OH, USA

TUESDAY 11 & THURSDAY 13 JULY 2000 – PERFORMANCES
Madison Square Garden, New York, NY, USA

SATURDAY 15 JULY 2000 – PERFORMANCE
Nissan Pavilion, Stone Ridge, Bristow, VA, USA

SUNDAY 16 JULY 2000 – PERFORMANCE
Civic Center, Providence, RI, USA

Rescheduled from Tuesday 11 July to make way for an additional New York show. This in turn forced a complete cancellation at Walnut Creek, Raleigh, USA on Sunday 16 July.

ROGER WATERS IN THE FLESH (WORLD)

Waters' most ambitious and successful tour to date saw him take his show to many new and unusual territories across the world. The tour, announced in person at a press conference at EMI Abbey Road Studios on Friday 19 October 2001, was critically acclaimed by the media and fans alike, and brought together some of his stronger solo material, some newly written, as well as vintage Pink Floyd that was performed faithfully to the original recordings. Waters' band for this tour comprised: Andy Fairweather-Low (Guitar, Bass, Vocals), Snowy White (Guitar, Vocals), Chester Kamen (Bass, Vocals), Harry Waters and Andy Wallace (Keyboards), Graham Broad (Drums), Norbert Stachel (Saxophone, Penny Whistle), Katie Kissoon, PP Arnold and Linda Lewis (Backing Vocals). Final production rehearsals for the tour took place at Bray Film Studios, Bray, England between Monday 18 and Sunday 24 February 2002.

WEDNESDAY 27 FEBRUARY 2002 – PERFORMANCE
Bellville Velodrome, Capetown, South Africa

Set list at this show and all shows on the tour unless otherwise noted: 'In The Flesh', 'The Happiest Days Of Our Lives', 'Another Brick In The Wall, Part 2', 'Mother', 'Get Your Filthy Hands Off My Desert', 'Southampton Dock', 'Pigs On The Wing, Part 1', 'Dogs', 'Shine On You Crazy Diamond, Parts 1–5', 'Welcome To The Machine', 'Wish You Were Here', 'Shine On You Crazy Diamond, Parts 6–9' <Intermission> 'Set The Controls For The Heart Of The Sun', 'Breathe', 'Time', 'Money', '5:06am (Every Strangers Eyes)' , 'Perfect Sense, Part 1', 'Perfect Sense, Part 2', 'The Bravery Of Being Out Of Range', 'It's A Miracle', 'Amused To Death', 'Brain Damage', 'Eclipse', 'Comfortably Numb' <Encore> 'Flickering Flame'

FRIDAY 1 MARCH 2002 – PERFORMANCE
MTN Sun Dome, Northgate, Johannesburg, South Africa

'Each Small Candle' was performed instead of 'Flickering Flame'.

TUESDAY 5 MARCH 2002 – PERFORMANCE
Estadio Nacional, Santiago, Chile

Rescheduled from Friday 22 February 2002. 'Each Small Candle' was performed instead of 'Flickering Flame'.

THURSDAY 7 MARCH 2002 – PERFORMANCE
Estadio Vélez Sarsfield, Buenos Aires, Argentina

SATURDAY 9 MARCH 2002 – PERFORMANCE
Sambódromo Carnaval, Praça da Apoteose, Rio de Janeiro, Brazil

'Each Small Candle' was performed instead of 'Flickering Flame'.

TUESDAY 12 MARCH 2002 – PERFORMANCE
Estádio Olímpico, Porto Alegre, Brazil

THURSDAY 14 MARCH 2002 – PERFORMANCE
Estádio do Pacaembu, São Paulo, Brazil

FRIDAY 15 MARCH 2002 – PERFORMANCE
Estádio do Pacaembu, São Paulo, Brazil

'Each Small Candle' was performed instead of 'Flickering Flame'.

SUNDAY 17 MARCH 2002 – PERFORMANCE
Caracas Pop Festival, Valle del Pop, Caracas, Venezuela

TUESDAY 19 MARCH 2002 – PERFORMANCE ◄
Foro Sol, Mexico City, Mexico

MONDAY 25 & TUESDAY 26 MARCH 2002 – PERFORMANCE
Kosei Nenkin Kaikan, Osaka, Japan

THURSDAY 28, SATURDAY 30 & SUNDAY 31 MARCH 2002 – PERFORMANCES
Hall A, Tokyo International Forum, Chiyoda-Ku, Tokyo, Japan

TUESDAY 2 APRIL 2002 – PERFORMANCE
Chamsil Sports Field, Seoul, South Korea

FRIDAY 5 & SATURDAY 6 APRIL 2002 – PERFORMANCES
Sydney Entertainment Centre, Darling Harbour, Sydney, Australia

Shows rescheduled from Newcastle Entertainment Centre, Newcastle.

MONDAY 8 APRIL 2002 – PERFORMANCE
Rod Laver Arena, Melbourne, Australia

WEDNESDAY 10 APRIL 2002 – PERFORMANCE
Impact Arena, Bangkok, Thailand

SATURDAY 13 APRIL 2002 – PERFORMANCE
Palace Grounds, Bangalore, India

Rescheduled from Sunday 14 April. This also replaced a scheduled show at New Standard Engineering Grounds, Mumbai, India on Friday 12 April.

MONDAY 15 APRIL 2002 – PERFORMANCE
Creek Golf and Yacht Club, Dubai Festival City, Dubai, United Arab Emirates

WEDNESDAY 17 APRIL 2002 – PERFORMANCE
Beirut International Exhibition and Leisure Center, Beirut, Lebanon

ROGER WATERS – IN THE FLESH (EUROPE)

Waters' band for this tour comprised: Andy Fairweather-Low (Guitar, Bass, Vocals), Snowy White (Guitar, Vocals), Chester Kamen (Bass, Vocals), Harry Waters and Andy Wallace (Keyboards), Graham Broad (Drums), Norbert Stachel (Saxophone, Penny Whistle) and Katie Kissoon, PP Arnold and Carol Kenyon (Backing Vocals).

SATURDAY 4 & SUNDAY 5 MAY 2002 – PERFORMANCES
Pavilhão Atlântico, Lisbon, Portugal

Set list at this show and all shows on the tour unless otherwise noted: 'In The Flesh', 'The Happiest Days Of Our Lives', 'Another Brick In The Wall, Part 2', 'Mother', 'Get Your Filthy Hands Off My Desert', 'Southampton Dock', 'Pigs On The Wing, Part 1', 'Dogs', 'Shine On You Crazy Diamond, Parts 1–5', 'Welcome To The Machine', 'Wish You Were Here', 'Shine On You Crazy Diamond, Parts 6–9' <Intermission> 'Set The Controls For The Heart Of The Sun', 'Breathe', 'Time', 'Money', '5:06am (Every Strangers Eyes)', 'Perfect Sense, Part 1', 'Perfect Sense, Part 2', 'The Bravery Of Being Out Of Range', 'It's A Miracle', 'Amused To Death', 'Brain Damage', 'Eclipse', 'Comfortably Numb' <Encore> 'Flickering Flame'.

WEDNESDAY 8 MAY 2002 – PERFORMANCE
Palau Sant Jordi, Parc de Montjuïc, Barcelona, Spain

FRIDAY 10 MAY 2002 – PERFORMANCE
Fila Forum, Assago, Milan, Italy

SATURDAY 11 MAY 2002 – PERFORMANCE
Hallenstadion, Zurich, Switzerland

MONDAY 13 MAY 2002 – PERFORMANCE
Sportpaleis, Antwerp, Belgium

WEDNESDAY 15 MAY 2002 – PERFORMANCE
Sportpaleis Ahoy, Rotterdam, Netherlands

FRIDAY 17 MAY 2002 – PERFORMANCE
Messe Halle, Erfurt, Germany

SATURDAY 18 MAY 2002 – PERFORMANCE
Kölnarena, Cologne, Germany

TUESDAY 20 MAY 2002 – PERFORMANCE
Arena, Oberhausen, Germany

WEDNESDAY 22 MAY 2002 – PERFORMANCE
Preussag Arena, Hannover, Germany

FRIDAY 24 MAY 2002 – PERFORMANCE
Spektrum, Oslo, Norway

SATURDAY 25 MAY 2002 – PERFORMANCE
Globen, Stockholm, Sweden

MONDAY 27 MAY 2002 – PERFORMANCE
New Arena, St Petersburg, Russia

WEDNESDAY 29 MAY 2002 – PERFORMANCE
Olimpiski Arena, Moscow, Russia

FRIDAY 31 MAY 2002 – PERFORMANCE
Hartwall Arena, Helsinki, Finland

SUNDAY 2 JUNE 2002 – PERFORMANCE
Forum København, Copenhagen, Denmark

TUESDAY 4 JUNE 2002 – PERFORMANCE
Olympiahalle, Munich, Germany

WEDNESDAY 5 JUNE 2002 – PERFORMANCE
Festhalle, Frankfurt, Germany

FRIDAY 7 JUNE 2002 – PERFORMANCE
Stadion Gwardii, Warsaw, Poland

SUNDAY 9 JUNE 2002 – PERFORMANCE
Velodrome, Berlin, Germany

MONDAY 10 JUNE 2002 – PERFORMANCE
Paegas Aréna, Prague, Czech Republic

WEDNESDAY 12 JUNE 2002 – PERFORMANCE
Stadio Flamino, Rome, Italy

Show rescheduled from Curva Olympia, Rome, Italy.

FRIDAY 14 JUNE 2002 – PERFORMANCE
Zipfer Zone, Festivalgelände, Wiesen, Austria

SATURDAY 15 JUNE 2002 – PERFORMANCE
Kisstadion, Budapest, Hungary

MONDAY 17 JUNE 2002 – PERFORMANCE
Schleyer-Halle, Stuttgart, Germany

WEDNESDAY 19 JUNE 2002 – PERFORMANCE
Palais Omnisports de Paris-Bercy, Paris, France

FRIDAY 21 JUNE 2002 – PERFORMANCE
National Exhibition Centre Arena, Birmingham, England

SATURDAY 22 JUNE 2002 – PERFORMANCE
Manchester Evening News Arena, Manchester, England

MONDAY 24 JUNE 2002 – PERFORMANCE
The Point, Dublin, Republic of Ireland

WEDNESDAY 26 & THURSDAY 27 JUNE 2002 – PERFORMANCES
Wembley Arena, Wembley, London, England

Nick Mason played drums on 'Set The Controls For The Heart Of The Sun' at both shows.

SATURDAY 30 JUNE 2002 – PERFORMANCE
Glastonbury Festival of Performing Arts,
Pyramid Stage, Worthy Farm, Pilton, England

The final date of the tour was performed in front of some 70,000 festival-goers on the second day of Europe's largest performing arts event (28–30 June). Edited highlights were broadcast in the UK on *Glastonbury 2002* on BBC2 TV on Saturday 29 June 2002 between 11.05pm and 2.00am. Set list: 'In The Flesh', 'The Happiest Days Of Our Lives', 'Another Brick In The Wall, Part 2', 'Mother', 'Pigs On The Wing, Part 1', 'Dogs', 'Shine On You Crazy Diamond, Parts 1–5', 'Wish You Were Here', 'Shine On You Crazy Diamond, Parts 6–9', 'Breathe', 'Time', 'Money', 'Perfect Sense, Part 1', 'Perfect Sense, Part 2', 'It's A Miracle', 'Amused To Death', 'Brain Damage', 'Eclipse', 'Comfortably Numb' <Encore> 'Flickering Flame'

THE DARK SIDE OF THE MOON LIVE (EUROPE)

Waters' band for his European and US tours comprised: Graham Broad (drums), Jon Carin (Keyboards), Andy Fairweather-Low (Guitar, Bass and Vocals), Dave Kilminster (Guitar, Vocals), Ian Ritchie (Saxophone), Harry Waters (Keyboards), Snowy White (Guitar, Vocals), Carol Kenyon, Katie Kissoon and PP Arnold (Backing Vocals). All shows were solo headline shows except some multi-artist festival dates, which are noted. Final production rehearsals for the tour took place at Bray Film Studios, Bray, England on Tuesday 30 and Wednesday 31 May 2006.

FRIDAY 2 JUNE 2006 – PERFORMANCE
Rock in Rio Lisboa, World Stage,
Parque da Bela Vista, Lisbon, Portugal

Waters headlined the World Stage on the first day of this three-day multi-artist festival at approximately 12.30am on 3 June. A live broadcast on AOL was cancelled at the very last minute due to a contractual dispute. Set list: 'The Happiest Days Of Our Lives', 'Another Brick In The Wall, Part 2', 'Mother', 'Shine On You Crazy Diamond, Parts 1–5', 'Have A Cigar', 'Wish You Were Here', 'Set The Controls For The Heart Of The Sun', 'The Gunners Dream', 'Southampton Dock', 'The Fletcher Memorial Home', 'Perfect Sense, Part 1', 'Perfect Sense, Part 2', 'Leaving Beirut', 'Sheep' <Intermission> *The Dark Side of the Moon* <Encore> 'In The Flesh', 'Vera', 'Bring The Boys Back Home', 'Comfortably Numb'.

SUNDAY 4 JUNE 2006 – PERFORMANCE
Verona Music Festival, Arena di Verona, Verona, Italy

Set list: 'In The Flesh', 'Mother', 'Shine On You Crazy Diamond, Parts 1–5', 'Have A Cigar', 'Wish You Were Here', 'Set The Controls For The Heart Of The Sun', 'The Gunners Dream', 'Southampton Dock', 'The Fletcher Memorial Home', 'Perfect Sense, Part 1', 'Perfect Sense, Part 2', 'Leaving Beirut', 'Sheep' <Intermission> *The Dark Side of the Moon* <Encore> 'The Happiest Days Of Our Lives', 'Another Brick In The Wall, Part 2', 'Vera', 'Bring The Boys Back Home', 'Comfortably Numb'.

MONDAY 5 JUNE 2006 – PERFORMANCE
Verona Music Festival, Arena di Verona, Verona, Italy

Set list: 'In The Flesh', 'Mother', 'Shine On You Crazy Diamond, Parts 1–5', 'Leaving Beirut', 'Have A Cigar', 'Wish You Were Here', 'Set The Controls For The Heart Of The Sun', 'The Gunners Dream', 'Southampton Dock', 'The Fletcher Memorial Home', 'Perfect Sense, Part 1', 'Perfect Sense, Part 2', 'Sheep' <Intermission> *The Dark Side of the Moon* <Encore> 'The Happiest Days Of Our Lives', 'Another Brick In The Wall, Part 2', 'Vera', 'Bring The Boys Back Home', 'Comfortably Numb'.

TUESDAY 6 JUNE 2006 – CANCELLED PERFORMANCE
Velodromo Paolo Borsellino, Palermo, Sicily, Italy

Show cancelled in April, shortly after tickets went on sale, reportedly for technical reasons.

THURSDAY 8 JUNE 2006 – PERFORMANCE
Kindl-Bühne Wuhlheide, Berlin, Germany

Set list at this show and all subsequent shows on the tour unless otherwise noted: 'In The Flesh', 'Mother', 'Set The Controls For The Heart Of The Sun', 'Shine On You Crazy Diamond, Parts 1–5', 'Have A Cigar', 'Wish You Were Here', 'Southampton Dock', 'The Fletcher Memorial Home', 'Perfect Sense, Part 1', 'Perfect Sense, Part 2', 'Leaving Beirut', 'Sheep' <Intermission> *The Dark Side of the Moon* <Encore> 'The Happiest Days Of Our Lives', 'Another Brick In The Wall, Part 2', 'Vera', 'Bring The Boys Back Home', 'Comfortably Numb'.

SATURDAY 10 JUNE 2006 – PERFORMANCE
Arrow Rock Festival, Rock Palace Stage, Lichtenvoorde, Netherlands

Waters headlined on the second day of this three-day multi-artist festival (Friday 9 to Sunday 11 June 2006).

MONDAY 12 JUNE 2006 – PERFORMANCE
Egilshöllin Arena, Reykjavík, Iceland

Nick Mason played drums on *The Dark Side of the Moon* and the encore at this show.

WEDNESDAY 14 JUNE 2006 – PERFORMANCE
Norwegian Wood Festival, Frognerbadet, Oslo, Norway

Waters appeared as part of a season of four one-day shows held at this venue. The 8,000-strong audience set an attendance record for the festival.

FRIDAY 16 JUNE 2006 – PERFORMANCE
Stadio Olympico, Rome, Italy

SUNDAY 18 JUNE 2006 – PERFORMANCE
Terra Vibe Park, Malakassa, Athens, Greece

TUESDAY 20 JUNE 2006 – PERFORMANCE
Kuruçeşme Arena, Istanbul, Turkey

THURSDAY 22 JUNE 2006 – PERFORMANCE
Latrun Monastery, Neve Shalom, Israel

Rescheduled from Ha-Yarkon Park, Tel Aviv, Israel due to protests from Palestinian pressure groups. Latrun Monastery is situated in a village of Israeli-Palestinian co-existence. The show was broadcast live on Israel's 88FM radio and Reshet Bet radio. Nevertheless Waters' performance of 'Leaving Beirut' sparked an inevitable raft of criticism from the Israeli media.

SATURDAY 24 JUNE 2006 – PERFORMANCE
Vasilyevsky Spusk, Moscow, Russia

Rescheduled from Red Square, Moscow, due to a clash with state ceremonies.

ABOVE: WATERS PERFORMING 'IN THE FLESH' AT THE VIKING STADION, NORWAY.

MONDAY 26 JUNE 2006 – PERFORMANCE
Viking Stadion, Jåttåvågen, Stavanger, Norway

THURSDAY 29 JUNE 2006 – PERFORMANCE
Live at the Marquee, The Showgrounds, Cork, Ireland

Waters appeared as part of a season of events at this venue. Nick Mason played drums on *The Dark Side of the Moon* and the encores at this show. A power cut forced an early intermission and the second half of the show began with 'Leaving Beirut' and 'Sheep'.

SATURDAY 1 JULY 2006 – PERFORMANCE
Hyde Park Calling, Hyde Park, London, England

Waters headlined on the first day of this two-day multi-artist festival (Saturday 1 to Sunday 2 July 2006). Nick Mason played drums on *The Dark Side of the Moon* and the encores at this show. Other performers on this day included Starsailor and Texas.

SUNDAY 2 JULY 2006 – PERFORMANCE
Roskilde Festival, Orange Stage, Roskilde, Denmark

Waters headlined the Orange Stage on the last day of this four-day multi-artist festival (Thursday 29 June to Sunday 2 July 2006).

FRIDAY 7 JULY 2006 – PERFORMANCE
Sportpaleis Ahoy, Rotterdam, Netherlands

SATURDAY 8 JULY 2006 – CANCELLED PERFORMANCE
Olimpiyskyi Stadium, Kiev, Ukraine

Show cancelled due to a contractual dispute.

MONDAY 10 JULY 2006 – PERFORMANCE
Loxol Car Park [formerly the Parade Grounds], Pembroke, Malta

WEDNESDAY 12 JULY 2006 – PERFORMANCE
Summer Festival, Piazza Napoleone, Lucca, Italy

Waters appeared as part of a season of events at this venue. Nick Mason played drums on *The Dark Side of the Moon* set and encores at this show. The show was broadcast live on the Italian RAI 1 radio network.

FRIDAY 14 JULY 2006 – PERFORMANCE
Circuit de Nevers-Magny Cours, Magny-Cours, France

Supported by Laurent Voulzy. Nick Mason played drums on *The Dark Side of the Moon* set and encores at this show.

SUNDAY 16 JULY 2006 – PERFORMANCE
Moon & Stars Festival '06, Piazza Grande, Locarno, Switzerland

Waters appeared as part of a season of events at this venue.

THE DARK SIDE OF THE MOON LIVE (NORTH AMERICA)

Waters' band for his North American tour comprised: Graham Broad (drums), Jon Carin (Keyboards), Andy Fairweather-Low (Guitar, Bass and Vocals), Dave Kilminster (Guitar, Vocals), Ian Ritchie (Saxophone), Harry Waters (Keyboards), Snowy White (Guitar, Vocals), and Carol Kenyon, Katie Kissoon and PP Arnold (Backing Vocals). Production rehearsals took place in East Hampton, USA between Saturday 2 and Tuesday 5 September.

WEDNESDAY 6 SEPTEMBER 2006 – PERFORMANCE
PNC Bank Arts Center, Holmdel, NJ, USA

Set list at this show and all subsequent shows on the tour unless otherwise noted: 'In The Flesh', 'Mother', 'Set The Controls For The Heart Of The Sun', 'Shine On You Crazy Diamond, Parts 1–5', 'Have A Cigar', 'Wish You Were Here', 'Southampton Dock', 'The Fletcher Memorial Home', 'Perfect Sense, Part 1', 'Perfect Sense, Part 2', 'Leaving Beirut', 'Sheep' <Intermission> *The Dark Side of the Moon* <Encore> 'The Happiest Days Of Our Lives', 'Another Brick In The Wall, Part 2', 'Vera', 'Bring The Boys Back Home', 'Comfortably Numb'

FRIDAY 8 & SATURDAY 9 SEPTEMBER 2006 – PERFORMANCES
Tweeter Center for the Performing, Mansfield, MA, USA

TUESDAY 12 & WEDNESDAY 13 SEPTEMBER 2006 – PERFORMANCES
Madison Square Garden, New York, NY, USA

Nick Mason played drums on *The Dark Side of the Moon* set and the encores at these shows.

FRIDAY 15 SEPTEMBER 2006 – PERFORMANCE
Nikon Jones Beach Theatre, Wantagh, NY, USA

SATURDAY 16 SEPTEMBER 2006 – PERFORMANCE
Tweeter Center, Camden, NJ, USA

MONDAY 18 SEPTEMBER 2006 – PERFORMANCE
Palace of Auburn Hills, Auburn Hills, Detroit, MI, USA

WEDNESDAY 20 SEPTEMBER 2006 – PERFORMANCE
Air Canada Centre, Toronto, Canada

THURSDAY 21 SEPTEMBER 2006 – PERFORMANCE
Bell Centre, Montréal, Canada

SATURDAY 23 SEPTEMBER 2006 – PERFORMANCE
Nissan Pavilion, Bristow, VA, USA

SUNDAY 24 SEPTEMBER 2006 – PERFORMANCE
Post Gazette Pavilion, Pittsburgh, PA, USA

WEDNESDAY 27 SEPTEMBER 2006 – PERFORMANCE
Quicken Loans Arena, Cleveland, OH, USA

FRIDAY 29 SEPTEMBER 2006 – PERFORMANCE
First Midwest Bank Amphitheatre, Chicago, IL, USA

SATURDAY 30 SEPTEMBER 2006 – PERFORMANCE
Verizon Wireless Music Center, Noblesville, IN, USA

TUESDAY 3 OCTOBER 2006 – PERFORMANCE
Cricket Pavilion, Phoenix, AZ, USA

THURSDAY 5, FRIDAY 6 OCTOBER & SUNDAY 8 OCTOBER 2006 – PERFORMANCES
Hollywood Bowl, Hollywood, Los Angeles, CA, USA

Nick Mason played drums on *The Dark Side of the Moon* set and the encores at these shows.

SUNDAY 8 OCTOBER 2006 – CANCELLED PERFORMANCE
Theater Under The Stars, Hard Rock Hotel, Las Vegas, NV, USA

This show was cancelled in order to accommodate an extended run of shows at the Hollywood Bowl.

TUESDAY 10 OCTOBER 2006 – PERFORMANCE
Shoreline Amphitheatre, Mountain View,
near San Francisco, CA, USA

THURSDAY 12 OCTOBER 2006 – PERFORMANCE
Key Arena, Seattle, WA, USA

THE DARK SIDE OF THE MOON LIVE 2007 (WORLD)

Despite reaching out to audiences in previously unexplored regions, many fans were left completely perplexed by Roger Waters' reversal of his long-held beliefs about the faceless nature of stadium touring, which ultimately led to the creation of *The Wall*. Perhaps even more alarming was the decision to allow a giant entertainment corporation to promote his tours and grant priority ticket to certain credit-card holders booking for his US shows. Given his supposed disdain of the corporate menace and the market forces driving globalization, which had, after all, formed the basic subject matter of his solo albums, it was not surprising that many fans labelled him a hypocrite. Production rehearsals took place at the Big Top, Luna Park, Sydney, Australia between Sunday 21 and Tuesday 23 January.

THURSDAY 25 JANUARY 2007 – PERFORMANCE
Acer Arena, Olympic Park, Sydney, Australia

Set list at this show and all subsequent shows on the tour unless otherwise noted: 'In The Flesh', 'Mother', 'Set The Controls For The Heart Of The Sun', 'Shine On You Crazy Diamond, Parts 1–5', 'Have A Cigar', 'Wish You Were Here', 'Southampton Dock', 'The Fletcher Memorial Home', 'Perfect Sense, Part 1', 'Perfect Sense, Part 2', 'Leaving Beirut', 'Sheep' <Intermission> *The Dark Side of the Moon* <Encore> 'The Happiest Days Of Our Lives', 'Another Brick In The Wall, Part 2', 'Vera', 'Bring The Boys Back Home', 'Comfortably Numb'.

SATURDAY 27 JANUARY 2007 – PERFORMANCE
Jade Stadium, Christchurch, New Zealand

MONDAY 29 JANUARY 2007 – PERFORMANCE
North Harbour Stadium, Albany, Auckland, New Zealand

THURSDAY 1 & FRIDAY 2 FEBRUARY 2007 – PERFORMANCE
Rod Laver Arena, Melbourne Park, Melbourne, Australia

ABOVE: ON STAGE IN PERTH ON WATERS' EXTENSIVE 2007 WORLD TOUR.

MONDAY 5 FEBRUARY 2007 – PERFORMANCE
Entertainment Centre, Boondall, Australia

WEDNESDAY 7 FEBRUARY 2007 – PERFORMANCE
Entertainment Centre, Hindmarsh, Adelaide, Australia

FRIDAY 9 FEBRUARY 2007 – PERFORMANCE
Members Equity Stadium, Perth, Australia

SUNDAY 11 FEBRUARY 2007 – PERFORMANCE
Grand Stage, Shanghai Gymnasium, China

THURSDAY 15 FEBRUARY 2007 – PERFORMANCE
Hall 3, Hong Kong Convention & Exhibition Center, Wancahi, Hong Kong, China

SUNDAY 18 FEBRUARY 2007 – PERFORMANCE
Mumbai Metropolitan Region Development Authority Bandra-Kurla Complex [MMRDA-BKC] Grounds, Mumbai, India

WEDNESDAY 21 FEBRUARY 2007 – PERFORMANCE
The Amphitheatre, Media City, Dubai, United Arab Emirates

Rescheduled from the Autodrome, Dubai, United Arab Emirates.

FRIDAY 2 MARCH 2007 – PERFORMANCE
Eastadio Universitario, Monterrey, Mexico

SUNDAY 4 MARCH 2007 – PERFORMANCE
Eastadio 3 de Marzo, Guadalajara, Mexico

Rescheduled from Arena VFG, Guadalajara, Mexico

TUESDAY 6 MARCH 2007 – PERFORMANCE
Foro Sol, Mexico City, Mexico

FRIDAY 9 MARCH 2007 – PERFORMANCE
Parque Metropolitano Simón Bolívar, Bogotá, Colombia

MONDAY 12 MARCH 2007 – PERFORMANCE
Explanada del Estadio Monumental, Lima, Peru

WEDNESDAY 14 MARCH 2007 – PERFORMANCE
Estadio Nacional, Santiago, Chile

SATURDAY 17 & SUNDAY 18 MARCH – PERFORMANCE
Estadio River Plate, Buenos Aires, Argentina

FRIDAY 23 MARCH 2007 – PERFORMANCE
Praça da Apoteose, Rio de Janeiro, Brazil

SATURDAY 24 MARCH 2007 – PERFORMANCE
Estádio do Morumbi, São Paulo, Brazil

THE DARK SIDE OF THE MOON LIVE (EUROPE)

WEDNESDAY 11 APRIL 2007 – PERFORMANCE
Hallenstadion, Zurich, Switzerland

FRIDAY 13 APRIL 2007 – PERFORMANCE
Sazka Arena, Prague, Czech Republic

SATURDAY 14 APRIL 2007 – PERFORMANCE
Papp László Budapest Sportaréna, Budapest, Hungary

MONDAY 16 APRIL 2007 – PERFORMANCE
Kölnarena, Cologne, Germany

WEDNESDAY 18 APRIL 2007 – PERFORMANCE
Arena Leipzig, Leipzig, Germany

THURSDAY 19 APRIL 2007 – PERFORMANCE
Color Line Arena, Hamburg, Germany

SATURDAY 21 APRIL 2007 – PERFORMANCE
Palau Sant Jordi, Parc de Montjuïc, Barcelona, Spain

MONDAY 23 APRIL 2007 – PERFORMANCE
Datch Forum, Assago, Milan, Italy

WEDNESDAY 25 APRIL 2007 – PERFORMANCE
Sportspaleis, Antwerp, Belgium

FRIDAY 27 APRIL 2007 – PERFORMANCE
Globe Arena, Stockholm, Sweden

SUNDAY 29 APRIL 2007 – PERFORMANCE
Bergenfest '07, Vestlandshallen, Bergen, Norway

TUESDAY 1 MAY 2007 – PERFORMANCE
Augustenborg Slotspark, Sønderborg, Denmark

THURSDAY 3 MAY 2007 – PERFORMANCE
Palais Omnisports de Paris-Bercy, Paris, France

SATURDAY 5 MAY 2007 – PERFORMANCE
GelreDome, Arnhem, Netherlands

MONDAY 7 MAY 2007 – PERFORMANCE
Manchester Evening News Arena, Manchester, England

TUESDAY 8 MAY 2007 – PERFORMANCE
National Exhibition Centre Arena, Birmingham, England

FRIDAY 11 & SATURDAY 12 MAY 2007 – PERFORMANCES
Earls Court Exhibition Hall, Earls Court, London, England

Nick Mason played drums on *The Dark Side of the Moon* and encores on 11 May.

MONDAY 14 MAY 2007 – PERFORMANCE
The Point, Dublin, Republic of Ireland

THE DARK SIDE OF THE MOON LIVE (NORTH AMERICA)

FRIDAY 18 MAY 2007 – PERFORMANCE
Sound Advice Amphitheater, West Palm Beach, FL, USA

SATURDAY 19 MAY 2007 – PERFORMANCE
Ford Amphitheater, FL State Fairgrounds, Tampa, FL, USA

TUESDAY 22 MAY 2007 – PERFORMANCE
Philips Arena, Atlanta, USA

THURSDAY 24 MAY 2007 – PERFORMANCE
Continental Airlines Arena, East Rutherford, NJ, USA

WEDNESDAY 30 MAY 2007 – PERFORMANCE
Madison Square Garden, New York, NY, USA

FRIDAY 1 & SATURDAY 2 JUNE 2007 – PERFORMANCES
Wachovia Center, Philadelphia, PA, USA

Prior to the first of the two shows, Waters appeared at the San Francisco Giants vs Philadelphia Phillies baseball game, and threw out the first, ceremonial pitch (making a good job of it, according to those who were there).

MONDAY 4 JUNE 2007 – PERFORMANCE
Colisée Pepsi, Québec City, Canada

Rescheduled from Scotiabank Place, Kanata, Ottawa, Canada.

WEDNESDAY 6 JUNE 2007 – PERFORMANCE
Scotiabank Place, Kanata, Ottawa, Canada

Rescheduled from Colisée Pepsi, Québec City, Canada.

THURSDAY 7 JUNE 2007 – PERFORMANCE
Bell Centre, Montréal, Canada

SATURDAY 9 JUNE 2007 – PERFORMANCE
United Center, Chicago, IL, USA

WEDNESDAY 13 JUNE 2007 – PERFORMANCE
Hollywood Bowl, Hollywood, Los Angeles, CA, USA

FRIDAY 15 JUNE 2007 – PERFORMANCE
Verizon Wireless Amphitheater, Irvine, CA, USA

SATURDAY 16 JUNE 2007 – PERFORMANCE
MGM Grand Garden Arena, Las Vegas, NV, USA

TUESDAY 19 JUNE 2007 – PERFORMANCE
Oracle Arena, Oakland, CA, USA

THURSDAY 21 JUNE 2007 – PERFORMANCE
General Motors Place Stadium, Vancouver, Canada

SATURDAY 23 JUNE 2007 – PERFORMANCE
Pengrowth Saddledome, Calgary, Canada

SUNDAY 24 JUNE 2007 – PERFORMANCE
Rexall Place, Edmonton, Canada

WEDNESDAY 27 JUNE 2007 – PERFORMANCE
MTS Centre, Winnipeg, Canada

FRIDAY 29 JUNE 2007 – PERFORMANCE
The Qwest Center, Omaha, NE, USA

SATURDAY 30 JUNE 2007 – PERFORMANCE
Xcel Energy Center, St Paul, MN, USA

MONDAY 2 JULY 2007 – PERFORMANCE
Marcus Amphitheater, Henry Maier Festival Park, Milwaukee, WI, USA

MONDAY 9 JULY 2007 – PERFORMANCE
TD Bank North Garden, Boston, MA, USA

TUESDAY 10 JULY 2007 – PERFORMANCE
New England Dodge Music Center, Hartford, CT, USA

THURSDAY 12 JULY 2007 – PERFORMANCE
Darien Lake Performing Arts Center,
Six Flags Theme Park, Darien, NY, USA

Rescheduled from Friday 13 July.

SATURDAY 14 JULY 2007 – PERFORMANCE
The Concert Hall, Rogers Centre, Toronto, Canada

THE DARK SIDE OF THE MOON LIVE 2008 (NORTH AMERICA & EUROPE)

A brief tour with exactly the same set list and band except that Andy Fairweather-Low was replaced by Chester Kamen and Katie Kasoon was replaced by Sylvia Mason-James. Production rehearsals took place at the Forum, Inglewood, Los Angeles, between Wednesday 23 and Friday 25 April.

SUNDAY 27 APRIL 2008 – PERFORMANCE
9th Annual Coachella Valley Music & Arts Festival, Coachella Stage, Empire Polo Fields, Indio, CA, USA

Waters appeared at this open-air festival with My Morning Jacket, Sean Penn, Gogol Bordello, Stars, Shout Out Louds, the Cool Kids and Austin TV, and headliners Jack Johnson (Friday 25 April) and Prince (Saturday 26 April).
Set list: 'In The Flesh', 'Mother', 'Set The Controls For The Heart Of The Sun', 'Shine On You Crazy Diamond, Parts 1–5', 'Have A Cigar', 'Wish You Were Here', 'Southampton Dock', 'The Fletcher Memorial Home', 'Perfect Sense, Part 1', 'Perfect Sense, Part 2', 'Leaving Beirut', 'Sheep' <Intermission> *The Dark Side of the Moon* <Encore> 'The Happiest Days Of Our Lives', 'Another Brick In The Wall, Part 2', 'Vera', 'Bring The Boys Back Home', 'Comfortably Numb'.

Lili Haydn appeared as special guest on violin and vocals on 'Leaving Beirut', 'Sheep' and 'Comfortably Numb'. During 'Sheep' the inflatable pig drifted off into the night sky – Waters lamenting, "That's my pig!" Organizers of the festival offered a $10,000USD reward and festival

tickets for life for its safe return, which was claimed three days later by two families in La Quinta, some 10 miles away after it had crashed onto their driveway.

WEDNESDAY 30 APRIL 2008 – PERFORMANCE
Pepsi Center, Denver, CO, USA

Set list at this show and all subsequent shows on the tour unless otherwise noted: 'In The Flesh', 'Mother', 'Set The Controls For The Heart Of The Sun', 'Shine On You Crazy Diamond, Parts 1–5', 'Have A Cigar', 'Wish You Were Here', 'Southampton Dock', 'The Fletcher Memorial Home', 'Perfect Sense, Part 1', 'Perfect Sense, Part 2', 'Leaving Beirut', 'Sheep' <Intermission> *The Dark Side of the Moon* <Encore> 'The Happiest Days Of Our Lives', 'Another Brick In The Wall, Part 2', 'Vera', 'Bring The Boys Back Home', 'Comfortably Numb'.

FRIDAY 2 MAY 2008 – PERFORMANCE
Superpages.com Center, Dallas, TX, USA

SUNDAY 4 MAY 2008 – PERFORMANCE
Cynthia Woods Mitchell Pavilion, the Woodlands, Houston, TX, USA

FRIDAY 9 MAY 2008 – PERFORMANCE
Campo de Futbol de Atarfe, Granada, Spain

SUNDAY 11 MAY 2008 – PERFORMANCE
Megaland, Landgraaf, Netherlands

TUESDAY 13 MAY 2008 – PERFORMANCE
Fionia Park, Odense, Denmark

THURSDAY 15 MAY 2008 – PERFORMANCE
Liverpool Echo Arena, Liverpool, England

SUNDAY 18 & MONDAY 19 MAY 2008 – PERFORMANCE
O2 Arena, Greenwich Peninsula, London, England

FRIDAY 6 JUNE 2008 – PERFORMANCE
Palace Square, St Petersburg, Russia

ROGER WATERS THE WALL LIVE (NORTH & SOUTH AMERICA)

Roger Waters embarked on his most ambitious tour yet, recreating *The Wall*. Prompted by the recent conflicts between nations, especially in the Middle East, he decided to revive the concept of *The Wall* as a lever for his anti-war message and that of requiem and remembrance. Waters said that, "I started to think that maybe there is something in the story of *The Wall*, which is about this one guy…that could be seen as an allegory for the way nations behave towards one another, or religions behave towards one another. In other words, could the piece be developed to describe a broader, more universal condition than we did in 1980 and I did in 1990 in Berlin?"

An impressive production by any stretch of the imagination, it featured a 240-foot-wide by 35-foot high wall constructed as the show progressed from 424 collapsible cardboard bricks, and required a 20-strong crew, using five electronic man-lifts, to build the wall each night. Digital mapping of the wall enabled the 23 video projectors to produce seamless and detailed images designed by Gerald Scarfe and based on the work of street artist Banksy. Costumes, props and pyrotechnics were an integral part of this spectacular production. Waters' band for this tour comprised: Dave Kilminster (Guitar, Vocals), G.E. Smith (Guitar), Snowy White (Guitar, Vocals), Jon Carin and Harry Waters (Keyboards), Graham Broad (Drums), Ian Ritchie (Saxophone), Robbie Wyckoff, Mark Venice, Kipp Venice and Pat Lennon (Vocals). Production rehearsals took place at Izod Center, Meadowlands Sports

Complex, East Rutherford, NJ, between Monday 6 and Saturday 11 September with a full dress rehearsal performed to invited media and guests on Sunday 12 September.

WEDNESDAY 15, THURSDAY 16 & SATURDAY 18 SEPTEMBER 2010 – PERFORMANCES
Air Canada Centre, Toronto, Canada

A full dress rehearsal was performed to invited media and guests on Tuesday 14 September.

MONDAY 20, TUESDAY 21, THURSDAY 23 & FRIDAY 24 SEPTEMBER 2010 – PERFORMANCES
United Center, Chicago, IL, USA

SUNDAY 26 SEPTEMBER 2010 – PERFORMANCE
Consol Energy Center, Pittsburgh, PA, USA

TUESDAY 28 SEPTEMBER 2010 – PERFORMANCE
Quicken Loans Arena, Cleveland, OH, USA

THURSDAY 30 SEPTEMBER, FRIDAY 1 OCTOBER 2010 – PERFORMANCE
TD Garden, Boston, MA, USA

TUESDAY 5 & WEDNESDAY 6 OCTOBER 2010 – PERFORMANCES
Madison Square Garden, New York, NY, USA

FRIDAY 8 OCTOBER 2010 – PERFORMANCE
HSBC Arena, Buffalo, NY, USA

SUNDAY 10 OCTOBER 2010 – PERFORMANCE
Verizon Center, Washington, DC, USA

TUESDAY 12 & WEDNESDAY 13 OCTOBER 2010 – PERFORMANCES
Nassau Veterans Memorial Coliseum, Uniondale, NY, USA

FRIDAY 15 OCTOBER 2010 – PERFORMANCE
XL Center, Hartford, CT, USA

SUNDAY 17 OCTOBER 2010 – PERFORMANCE
Scotiabank Place, Ottawa, Canada

TUESDAY 19 & WEDNESDAY 20 OCTOBER 2010 – PERFORMANCES
Centre Bell, Montréal, Canada

FRIDAY 22 OCTOBER 2010 – PERFORMANCE
Value City Arena, Jerome Schottenstein Center, Ohio State University, Columbus, OH, USA

SUNDAY 24 OCTOBER 2010 – PERFORMANCE
The Palace, Auburn Hills, Detroit, MI, USA

TUESDAY 26 OCTOBER 2010 – PERFORMANCE
Qwest Center, Omaha, NE, USA

WEDNESDAY 27 OCTOBER 2010 – PERFORMANCE
Xcel Energy Center, Saint Paul, MN, USA

FRIDAY 29 OCTOBER 2010 – PERFORMANCE
Scottrade Center, St Louis, MO, USA

SATURDAY 30 OCTOBER 2010 – PERFORMANCE
Sprint Center, Kansas City, MO, USA

WEDNESDAY 3 & THURSDAY 4 NOVEMBER 2010 – PERFORMANCES
Izod Center, East Rutherford, NJ, USA

SATURDAY 6 NOVEMBER 2010 – PERFORMANCE
Madison Square Garden, New York, NY, USA

MONDAY 8, TUESDAY 9 & THURSDAY 11 NOVEMBER 2010 – PERFORMANCES
Wells Fargo Center / Wachovia Center, Philadelphia, PA, USA

SATURDAY 13 & SUNDAY 14 NOVEMBER 2010 – PERFORMANCES
Bank Atlantic Center, Fort Lauderdale, FL, USA

TUESDAY 16 NOVEMBER 2010 – PERFORMANCE
St Petersburg Times Forum, Tampa, FL, USA

THURSDAY 18 NOVEMBER 2010 – PERFORMANCE
Philips Arena, Atlanta, GA, USA

SATURDAY 20 NOVEMBER 2010 – PERFORMANCE
Toyota Center, Houston, TX, USA

SUNDAY 21 NOVEMBER 2010 – PERFORMANCE
American Airlines Center, Dallas, TX, USA

TUESDAY 23 NOVEMBER 2010 – PERFORMANCE
Pepsi Center, Denver, CO, USA

FRIDAY 26 NOVEMBER 2010 – PERFORMANCE
MGM Grand Garden Arena, Las Vegas, NV, USA

SATURDAY 27 NOVEMBER 2010 – PERFORMANCE
US Airways Center, Phoenix, AZ, USA

MONDAY 29 & TUESDAY 30 NOVEMBER 2010 – PERFORMANCES
Staples Center, Los Angeles, CA, USA

FRIDAY 3 DECEMBER 2010 – PERFORMANCE
Oracle Arena, Oakland, CA, USA

SUNDAY 5 DECEMBER 2010 – PERFORMANCE
Staples Center, Los Angeles, CA, USA

TUESDAY 7 & WEDNESDAY 8 DECEMBER 2010 – PERFORMANCES
HP Pavilion, San Jose, CA, USA

The show on 7 December was rescheduled from 6 December.

FRIDAY 10 DECEMBER 2010 – PERFORMANCE
Rogers Arena, Vancouver, Canada

SATURDAY 11 DECEMBER 2010 – PERFORMANCE
Tacoma Dome, Tacoma, WA, USA

MONDAY 13 & TUESDAY 14 DECEMBER 2010 – PERFORMANCES
Honda Center, Anaheim, CA, USA

SATURDAY 18, SUNDAY 19 & TUESDAY 21 DECEMBER 2010 – PERFORMANCES
Palacio de los Deportes, Mexico City, Mexico

The traditional Mexican song 'Las Mañanitas' was performed at each of the above shows as an additional encore.

ROGER WATERS THE WALL LIVE (EUROPE)

A press conference at which Waters took questions from an assembly of journalists to announce the European tour was held at the Mandarin Oriental Hotel, Knightsbridge, London, England on Thursday 27 May 2010.

MONDAY 21 & TUESDAY 22 MARCH 2011 – PERFORMANCES
Pavilhão Atlântico, Sala Atlântico Pavilhão Multiusos de Lisboa, Lisbon, Portugal

FRIDAY 25 & SATURDAY 26 MARCH 2011 – PERFORMANCES
Palacio de Deportes Comunidad de Madrid, Madrid, Spain

TUESDAY 29 & WEDNESDAY 30 MARCH 2011 – PERFORMANCES
Palau Sant Jordi, Parc de Montjuïc, Barcelona, Spain

FRIDAY 1, SATURDAY 2, MONDAY 4 & TUESDAY 5 APRIL 2011 – PERFORMANCES
Mediolanum Forum, Assago, Milan, Italy

Sunday 3 April saw a complete technical run through of the show.

FRIDAY 8, SATURDAY 9 APRIL & MONDAY 11 APRIL 2011 – PERFORMANCES
GelreDome, Arnhem, Netherlands

WEDNESDAY 13 APRIL 2011 – PERFORMANCE
Arena Zagreb, Zagreb, Croatia

BELOW: 'THE WALL' PERFORMED LIVE IN ARNHEM, NETHERLANDS, 9 APRIL 2011.

FRIDAY 15 & SATURDAY 16 APRIL 2011 – PERFORMANCES
02 Arena, Prague, Czech Republic

MONDAY 18 & TUESDAY 19 APRIL 2011 – PERFORMANCES
Atlas Arena, Łódź, Poland

SATURDAY 23 APRIL 2011 – PERFORMANCE
Olimpiski Arena, Moscow, Russia

MONDAY 25 APRIL 2011 – PERFORMANCE
CKK Arena, St Petersberg, Russia

WEDNESDAY 27 & THURSDAY 28 APRIL 2011 – PERFORMANCES
Hartwall Areena, Helsinki, Finland

SATURDAY 30 APRIL & SUNDAY 1 MAY 2011 – PERFORMANCES
Telenor Arena, Oslo, Norway

WEDNESDAY 4 & THURSDAY 5 MAY 2011 – PERFORMANCES
Ericsson Globe, Stockholm, Sweden

SATURDAY 7 MAY 2011 – PERFORMANCE
Parken, Copenhagen, Denmark

WEDNESDAY 11, THURSDAY 12, SATURDAY 14, SUNDAY 15, TUESDAY 17 & WEDNESDAY 18 MAY 2011 – PERFORMANCES
02 Arena, Greenwich Peninsula, London, England

David Gilmour's much-anticipated appearance occurred on Thursday 12 May as he joined Waters on stage to perform 'Comfortably Numb'. Despite repeating the first verse twice, Gilmour's performance was enthusiatically received and the encore of 'Outside The Wall' also featured Gilmour (on mandolin) and Nick Mason (on tambourine). On Monday 16 May an official video, shot in black and white, was posted on the Internet documenting the pre-show on-day rehearsals for the performance and behind the scenes footage.

FRIDAY 20 & SATURDAY 21 MAY 2011 – PERFORMANCES
Manchester Evening News Arena, Manchester, England

MONDAY 23 & TUESDAY 24 MAY 2011 – PERFORMANCES
02 Arena, Dublin, Ireland

FRIDAY 27 & SATURDAY 28 MAY 2011 – PERFORMANCES
Sportpaleis, Antwerp, Belgium

MONDAY 30 & TUESDAY 31 MAY 2011 – PERFORMANCES
Palais Omnisports de Paris-Bercy, Paris, France

FRIDAY 3 & SATURDAY 4 JUNE 2011 – PERFORMANCES
SAP Arena, Mannheim, Germany

MONDAY 6 & TUESDAY 7 JUNE 2011 – PERFORMANCES
Hallenstadion, Zurich, Switzerland

FRIDAY 10 & SATURDAY 11 JUNE 2011 – PERFORMANCES
02 World, Hamburg, Germany

MONDAY 13 JUNE 2011 – PERFORMANCE
MCH Messecenter Herning, Herning, Denmark

WEDNESDAY 15 & THURSDAY 16 JUNE 2011 – PERFORMANCES
02 World, Berlin, Germany

Waters introduced an additional reprise to 'Another Brick In The Wall, Part 2' from 16 June onwards, entitled 'The Ballad Of Jean-Charles de Menezes' and in which he played solo acoustic guitar, referring to the brutal killing on the London Underground by police officers on 22 July 2005.

SATURDAY 18 JUNE 2011 – PERFORMANCE
Esprit Arena, Dusseldorf, Germany

MONDAY 20 JUNE 2011 – PERFORMANCE
Olympiahalle, Munich, Germany

WEDNESDAY 22 JUNE 2011 – PERFORMANCE
Papp László Budapest Sportaréna, Budapest, Hungary

FRIDAY 24 & SATURDAY 25 JUNE 2011 – PERFORMANCES
Hallenstadion, Zurich, Switzerland

MONDAY 27 JUNE 2011 – PERFORMANCE
National Indoor Arena, Birmingham, England

TUESDAY 28 JUNE 2011 – PERFORMANCE
Manchester Evening News Arena, Manchester, England

WEDNESDAY 29 JUNE 2011 – CANCELLED PERFORMANCE
Manchester Evening News Arena, Manchester, England

Refunds were issued against this show with the official statement being that the show was cancelled "due to filming commitments", although this cannot be verified.

THURSDAY 30 JUNE & FRIDAY 1 JULY 2011 – PERFORMANCES
Palais Omnisports de Paris-Bercy, Paris, France

SUNDAY 3 & MONDAY 4 JULY 2011 – PERFORMANCES
Mediolanum Forum, Milan, Italy

Rescheduled from Wednesday 6 and Thursday 7 July.

FRIDAY 8 & SATURDAY 9 JULY & TUESDAY 12 JULY 2011 – PERFORMANCES
Olympic Sports Hall, Athens, Greece

The show of Friday 8 July was filmed both for future release and for additional side screen footage on some of the larger outdoor stadium shows on the forthcoming 2012 tour.

ROGER WATERS THE WALL LIVE (AUSTRALASIA)

Roger Waters was nominated "Top Touring Artist" in the 2011 and 2012 *Billboard* Music Awards, losing out to U2 on both occasions. However, the *Pollstar Music Industry Awards*, as voted by the music industry, honoured Waters and *The Wall Live* with two of the highest accolades: the coveted "Major Tour of the Year" and "Most Creative Stage Production" of 2010. *The Wall Live* also won the "Most Creative Stage Production" for a second consecutive year in 2011.

FRIDAY 27 & SATURDAY 28 JANUARY 2012 – PERFORMANCES
Burswood Dome, Perth, Australia

Production rehearsals began at the venue on Friday 20 January in advance of the opening night.

WEDNESDAY 1, THURSDAY 2 & SATURDAY 4 FEBRUARY 2012 – PERFORMANCES
Brisbane Entertainment Centre, Boondall, Australia

At the final show on Saturday 4 February, an extra encore of 'Waltzing Matilda' was performed by the band.

TUESDAY 7, WEDNESDAY 8, FRIDAY 10 & SATURDAY 11 FEBRUARY 2012 – PERFORMANCES
Rod Laver Arena, Melbourne Park, Melbourne, Australia

At the final show on 11 February, an extra encore of 'Waltzing Matilda' was performed by the band.

TUESDAY 14 & WEDNESDAY 15 FEBRUARY 2012 – PERFORMANCES
Acer Arena, Olympic Park, Sydney, Australia

SATURDAY 18, MONDAY 20, WEDNESDAY 22 & THURSDAY 23 FEBRUARY 2012 – PERFORMANCES
Vector Arena, Parnell, Auckland, New Zealand

ROGER WATERS THE WALL LIVE (NORTH & SOUTH AMERICA)

FRIDAY 2 & SATURDAY 3 MARCH 2012 – PERFORMANCES
Estadio Nacional, Santiago, Chile

Construction and production rehearsals began at the venue on 23 February in advance of the opening night. Significantly it was also the first outdoor performance of *The Wall* and a specially designed cover was built over the stage area. *The Wall* was also extended a considerable distance in order span the width of a much larger setting.

WEDNESDAY 7, FRIDAY 9, SATURDAY 10, MONDAY 12, WEDNESDAY 14, THURSDAY 15, SATURDAY 17, SUNDAY 18 & TUESDAY 20 MARCH 2012 – PERFORMANCES
Estadio River Plate, Buenos Aires, Argentina

SUNDAY 25 MARCH 2012 – PERFORMANCE
Estádio Beira-Rio, Porto Alegre, Rio Grande de Sol, Brazil

Rescheduled from Saturday 17 March to accommodate additional shows in Buenos Aires.

THURSDAY 29 MARCH 2012 – PERFORMANCE
Estádio Olímpico João Havelange [Engenhão Stadium],
Rio de Janeiro, Brazil

Rescheduled from Sunday 25 March to accommodate additional shows
in Buenos Aires.

SUNDAY 1 & MONDAY 3 APRIL 2012 – PERFORMANCES
Estádio do Morumbi, São Paulo, Brazil

Rescheduled from Thursday 22 and Friday 23 March to Saturday 31 March
and Sunday 1 April to accommodate additional shows in Buenos Aires.

FRIDAY 27 & SATURDAY 28 APRIL 2012 – PERFORMANCES
Foro Sol, Mexico City, Mexico

The Niagra Index reported that, "Roger Waters' extraordinary production
of 'The Wall' has smashed attendance records in South America with
a record-breaking 15 open-air stadiums shows in Chile, Brazil and
Argentina, playing to more than 750,000 fans. This is the largest number
of stadium shows ever played in South America by an international artist
on one tour. The South American leg included a record-breaking nine
sold-out shows in Buenos Aires, River Plate Stadium, exceeding the
previous record of five nights, held by the Rolling Stones."

TUESDAY 1 MAY 2012 – PERFORMANCE
Toyota Center, Houston, TX, USA

Waters performed an additional solo acoustic verse to 'Another Brick In
The Wall, Part 2' at this show, after which he berated the local promoter
for not organizing a children's dance group to accompany the song as
is normal. He then went on to thank the proprietor of a local Meals on
Wheels programme who, on hearing about this, hurriedly organized
some children to perform with less than 24 hours' notice.

THURSDAY 3 MAY 2012 – PERFORMANCE
Frank Erwin Center, University of Texas, Austin, TX, USA

SATURDAY 5 MAY 2012 – PERFORMANCE ▼
BOK Center, Tulsa, OK, USA

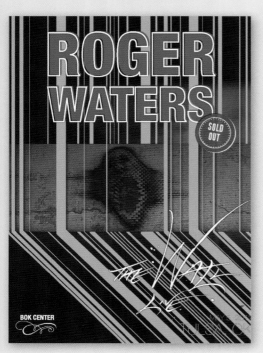

**MONDAY 7 MAY 2012 –
PERFORMANCE**
Pepsi Center,
Denver, CO, USA

**FRIDAY 11 MAY 2012 –
PERFORMANCE**
AT&T Park, San
Francisco, CA, USA

**SUNDAY 13 MAY 2012 –
PERFORMANCE**
Valley View Casino Center,
San Diego, CA, USA

**TUESDAY 15 MAY 2012
– PERFORMANCE**
US Airways Center,
Phoenix, AZ, USA

**FRIDAY 18 MAY 2012 –
PERFORMANCE**
Los Angeles
Memorial Coliseum,
Los Angeles, CA, USA

TUESDAY 22 MAY 2012 – PERFORMANCE
Rose Garden Arena, Portland, OR, USA

THURSDAY 24 MAY 2012 – PERFORMANCE
KeyArena, Seattle Center, Seattle, WA, USA

SATURDAY 26 MAY 2012 – PERFORMANCE
BC Place Stadium, Vancouver, Canada

MONDAY 28 & TUESDAY 29 MAY 2012 – PERFORMANCES
Rexall Place, Edmonton, Canada

THURSDAY 31 MAY & FRIDAY 1 JUNE 2012 – PERFORMANCES
MTS Centre, Winnipeg, Canada

SUNDAY 3 JUNE 2012 – PERFORMANCE
Xcel Energy Center, St Paul, MN, USA

TUESDAY 5 JUNE 2012 – PERFORMANCE
Joe Louis Arena, Detroit, MI, USA

WEDNESDAY 6 JUNE 2012 – PERFORMANCE
Van Andel Arena, Grand Rapids, MI, USA

FRIDAY 8 JUNE 2012 – PERFORMANCE
Wrigley Field, Chicago, IL, USA

SUNDAY 10 JUNE 2012 – PERFORMANCE
KFC Yum! Center, Louisville, KY, USA

MONDAY 11 JUNE 2012 – PERFORMANCE
Conseco [Bankers Life] Fieldhouse, Indianapolis, IN, USA

WEDNESDAY 13 JUNE 2012 – PERFORMANCE
Philips Arena, Atlanta, GA, USA

FRIDAY 15 JUNE 2012 – PERFORMANCE
BankAtlantic Center, Sunrise, FL, USA

SATURDAY 16 JUNE 2012 – PERFORMANCE
Amway Center, Orlando, FL, USA

TUESDAY 19 JUNE 2012 – PERFORMANCE
Bridgestone Arena, Nashville, TN, USA

THURSDAY 21 JUNE 2012 – PERFORMANCE
First Niagra Center, Buffalo, NY, USA

SATURDAY 23 JUNE 2012 – PERFORMANCE
Rogers Centre, Toronto, Canada

MONDAY 25 JUNE 2012 – PERFORMANCE
Scotiabank Place, Ottawa, Canada

TUESDAY 26 JUNE 2012 – PERFORMANCE
Centre Bell, Montréal, Canada

THURSDAY 28 JUNE 2012 – PERFORMANCE
Times Union Center, Albany, NY, USA

FRIDAY 29 JUNE 2012 – PERFORMANCE
XL Center, Hartford, CT, USA

SUNDAY 1 JULY 2012 – PERFORMANCE
Fenway Park, Boston, MA, USA

TUESDAY 3 JULY 2012 – PERFORMANCE
Consol Energy Center, Pittsburgh, PA, USA

FRIDAY 6 & SATURDAY 7 JULY 2012 – PERFORMANCES
Yankee Stadium, New York, NY, USA

MONDAY 9 JULY 2012 – PERFORMANCE
RBC Center, Raleigh, NC, USA

TUESDAY 10 JULY 2012 – PERFORMANCE
Time Warner Cable Arena, Charlotte, NC, USA

THURSDAY 12 JULY 2012 – PERFORMANCE
Verizon Center, Washington, DC, USA

SATURDAY 14 JULY 2012 – PERFORMANCE
Citizens Bank Park, Philadelphia, PA, USA

SATURDAY 21 JULY 2012 – PERFORMANCE
Les Plaines D'Abraham, Québec City, Canada

The *Huffington Post* said, "More than 75,000 fans attended the Saturday night mega-concert of *The Wall* on the Plains of Abraham in Quebec City. The highly visual outdoor show concluded a two-year world tour of 192 performances by the former leader of Pink Floyd. The energetic show started with 'In The Flesh?'. The crowd was delirious as fireworks exploded from the start and projections played on the wall. Accompanied by his seven musicians and four singers, Roger Waters played on an oversized stage (340 feet) surrounded by a huge white wall 728 feet long made of 750 bricks."

ROGER WATERS THE WALL LIVE (EUROPE)

A press conference at which Waters took questions from an assembly of journalists was held at the Mayfair Hotel, London, England on Wednesday 14 November 2012 to announce additional dates across Europe through the summer of 2013. At the *24th Annual Pollstar Awards* held at Club Nokia at LA Live, in Los Angeles on Thursday 7 February 2013 Waters scooped awards for "Major Tour of the Year" and "Most Creative Stage Production" for 2012.

Production rehearsals began at the opening venue on Sunday 14 July. Whether the show had played its course or not, the attendance levels at most shows were significantly lower than the previous outing, and the opening show saw only 6,000 fans in attendance at a 25,000-capacity venue, and many of the larger stadia failed to sell out by a considerable number.

THURSDAY 18 JULY 2013 – PERFORMANCE
GelreDome, Arnhem, Netherlands

SATURDAY 20 JULY 2013 – PERFORMANCE
Festivalweide, Werchter, Belgium

TUESDAY 23 JULY 2013 – PERFORMANCE
Stadion Poljud, Split, Croatia

FRIDAY 26 JULY 2013 – PERFORMANCE
Stadio Euganeo, Padova, Italy

SUNDAY 28 JULY 2013 – PERFORMANCE
Stadio Olympico, Rome, Italy

WEDNESDAY 31 JULY 2013 – PERFORMANCE
Olympiako Stadio Athinas, [OAKA], Athens, Greece

The show was set to be rescheduled to Terra Vibe Park, Malakassa, Athens on Thursday 1 August but public protest forced the show to go ahead.

SATURDAY 3 AUGUST 2013 – PERFORMANCE
İtü Stadyumu, Istanbul, Turkey

WEDNESDAY 7 AUGUST 2013 – PERFORMANCE
02 Arena, Prague, Czech Republic

Rescheduled from Eden [Synot Tip] Aréna, Prague, Czech Republic.

FRIDAY 9 AUGUST 2013 – PERFORMANCE
Commerzbank Arena, Frankfurt, Germany

SUNDAY 11 AUGUST 2013 – PERFORMANCE
Parken, Copenhagen, Denmark

WEDNESDAY 14 & THURSDAY 15 AUGUST – PERFORMANCES
Telenor Arena, Oslo, Norway

SATURDAY 17 AUGUST 2013 – PERFORMANCE
Ullevi Stadion, Gothenberg, Sweden

TUESDAY 20 AUGUST – PERFORMANCE
Stadion Narodowy, Warsaw, Poland

FRIDAY 23 AUGUST 2013 – PERFORMANCE
Ernst Happel Stadion, Vienna, Austria

SUNDAY 25 AUGUST 2013 – PERFORMANCE
Puskás Ferenc Stadion, Budapest, Hungary

WEDNESDAY 28 AUGUST 2013 – PERFORMANCE ▼
Piața Constituției [Constitution Square], Bucharest, Romania

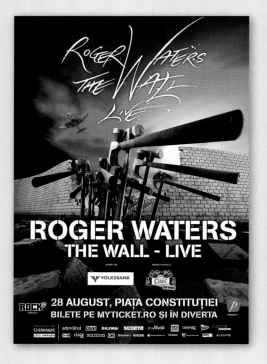

**FRIDAY 30 AUGUST 2013 –
PERFORMANCE**
Vasil Levski National
Stadium, Sofia, Bulgaria

**SUNDAY 1 SEPTEMBER 2013
– PERFORMANCE**
Kombank Arena,
Belgrade, Serbia

Rescheduled from Ušće Park,
Belgrade, Serbia.

**WEDNESDAY 4
SEPTEMBER 2013 –
PERFORMANCE**
Olympiastadion, Berlin,
Germany

**FRIDAY 6 SEPTEMBER
2013 – PERFORMANCE**
Esprit Arena,
Düsseldorf, Germany

**SUNDAY 8 SEPTEMBER
2013 – PERFORMANCE**
Amsterdam Arena,
Amsterdam, Netherlands

MONDAY 9 SEPTEMBER 2013 – PERFORMANCE
Stadion Letzigrund, Zurich, Switzerland

SATURDAY 14 SEPTEMBER 2013 – PERFORMANCE
Wembley Stadium, Wembley, England

MONDAY 16 SEPTEMBER 2013 – PERFORMANCE
Manchester Phones 4U Arena, Manchester, England

WEDNESDAY 18 SEPTEMBER 2013 – PERFORMANCE
Aviva Stadium Dublin, Ireland

SATURDAY 21 SEPTEMBER 2013 – PERFORMANCE
Stade de France, St Denis, Paris, France

Roger Waters' three-year *Wall* tour came to a close on this day. The
shows were seen by more than 1.5m in North America, 1m across Latin
and Central America, and 1m in Europe. It was the biggest worldwide
tour by a solo artist ever.

ÇA IRA (LIVE PERFORMANCES)

WEDNESDAY 16 OCTOBER 2002 – PERFORMANCE
Whip Craic, Royal Albert Hall, Kensington, London, England

A variety performance of monologue and music that saw many actors,
presenters and artists lending support to the Countryside Alliance,
including Nicholas Parsons, Robert Hardy, American rapper the
President, Jon Lord and Sir John Mortimer QC interspersed with the
Royal Philharmonic Orchestra performing pieces by Verdi, Sondheim,
and Sir Edward Elgar. The Royal Philharmonic Concert Orchestra
conducted by Rick Wentworth performed the 'Ça Ira Overture' live.
Waters then came on stage with Andy Fairweather-Low (Guitar, Bass,
Vocals), Snowy White (Guitar, Vocals), Chester Kamen (Bass, Vocals),
Graham Broad (Drums), Harry Waters and Andy Wallace (Keyboards),

Ian Ritchie (Penny Whistle), and Carol Kenyan, PP Arnold and Katie
Kissoon (Backing Vocals) to perform 'Wish You Were Here', 'Flickering
Flame' and 'Comfortably Numb'. The show finished with a rousing
performance of 'Land Of Hope And Glory'.

SATURDAY 1 MAY 2004 – PLAYBACK PERFORMANCE
Fort St Angelo, Grand Harbour, Valetta, Malta

Recorded extracts from the opera were played during the official
celebrations to mark Malta's accession to the European Union
accompanied by a huge light show and fireworks display at midnight.
Titles included 'Ça Ira Overture', 'The Taking Of Bastille' and 'Silver,
Sugar And Indigo' mixed into one continuous piece of music by Gert
Hoff. Waters was not in attendance at this show.

SATURDAY 7 AUGUST 2004 – PERFORMANCE
Bridgehampton Chamber Music Festival,
Bridgehampton Presbyterian Church, Bridgehampton, NY, USA

Concluding the evening's performances, which saw a six-piece ensemble
from the Bridgehampton Chamber Orchestra perform 'Souvenir
de Florence', Sextet for Strings, OP 70 by Tchaikovsky and Aaron
Copeland's 'Music For Movies', Waters introduced two tracks from *Ça
Ira*, 'The Letter' and 'Bastille', with music arranged for the Chamber
Ensemble by Robert Sadin at this annual classical music event.

MONDAY 25 JULY 2005 – PRESS RECEPTION
Florence Gould Hall, French Institute:
Alliance Française, New York, NY, USA

Columbia Records and Sony Classical hosted what it billed as a 'A Very
Special Evening with Roger Waters' during which a video presentation
of the forthcoming opera was shown followed by a question and answer
session. Guests were also given an 8-track promotional CD of the work in
progress (see Discography for further information).

THURSDAY 17 & FRIDAY 18 NOVEMBER 2005 – PERFORMANCES
Sala Santa Cecilia, Auditorium Parco Della Musica, Rome, Italy

This was the official live premiere of the *Ça Ira* opera, which Roger Waters introduced. Rick Wentworth conducted 100 members of the Rome Symphony Orchestra, along with an 80-strong choir that included many children. Featured performers included tenor Paul Groves, soprano Ying Huang and bass-baritone John Relyea.

FRIDAY 25 AUGUST 2006 – PERFORMANCE
Międzynarodowe Targi Poznańskie [Poznań International Fair Grounds], Poznań, Poland

The show was originally scheduled for 6 and 7 July 2006 but was moved due to Waters' solo tour commitments. This was a massive production, featuring a large cast of costumed performers, sets and props. Choirs sang on the surrounding terraces and pavilions, projectors illuminated the surrounding buildings and an abundance of pyrotechnics highlighted key moments. A further string of similar productions in other locations were to be announced at the time of writing. A special Polish edition *Ça Ira* CD was also made available for sale at the concert.

SATURDAY 16 DECEMBER 2006 – PERFORMANCE
International Expo-Congress Center, Kiev, Ukraine, Russia

Another large-scale presentation, as above, featuring an orchestra and choir conducted by Rick Wentworth.

SATURDAY 30 & SUNDAY 31 DECEMBER 2006; SUNDAY 28 JANUARY 2007; THURSDAY 8 & FRIDAY 9 MARCH 2007 – PERFORMANCES
Teatr Wielki [Opera House], Poznań, Poland

The production featured the Choir of Teatr Wielki, Chór Akademicki (Academic Choir), Chór Chłopięcy (Boys Choir) and London Community Gospel Choir with a 70-piece orchestra, a 35-strong ballet company and 120 members of the Polish Army.

TUESDAY 15, TUESDAY 22 & THURSDAY 24 APRIL 2008 – PERFORMANCES
***XII Festival Amazonas de Opera*, Teatro Amazonas, Manaus, Brazil**

The production featured the Amazonas Filarmônica, the Coral Do Amazonas and the children's chorus of the Coral Infantil Do CCCS with musical direction by Luiz Fernando Malheiro.

MONDAY 5 MAY 2008 – PERFORMANCE
World Forum Theatre, Den Haag, Netherlands

This was a special event that took place on Dutch Liberation Day, with all proceeds from the event going to the War Child charity. The show featured performances by the Dutch Concert Choir and the Tilburgs Begeleidingsorkest conducted by Rob Vermeulen. Waters was not in attendance at this show.

WEDNESDAY 17 NOVEMBER 2010 – PERFORMANCE
Nieuwe Luxor Theater in Rotterdam

With the tragic and brutal death in 2009 of the 14-year-old son of André Post, one of the soloists in *Ça Ira*, the organizer of the original show, Joke Tuinema, decided to bring *Ça Ira* back to the stage again as a benefit for the MOED campaign (which roughly translates as a word for courage – the campaign takes a stand against senseless violence). The event was also attended by Queen Beatrix, head of the Kingdom of the Netherlands. Waters was not in attendance at this show.

THURSDAY 2, SATURDAY 4, TUESDAY 7 & THURSDAY 9 MAY 2013 – PERFORMANCES
Theatro Municipal de São Paulo, São Paulo, Brazil

Waters oversaw an overhauled production with musical direction and conducting by Rick Wentworth and vocal performances from Lina Mendes, Gabriella Pace, Keila Moraes, Marcos Paulo, Giovanni Tristacci, David Marcondes, Leonardo Neiva, Eduardo Amir and Leonardo Pace. There was also a children's chorus and the Coral Lirico do Theatro provided the main chorus line. The Orquestra Sinfônica Municipal performed the score, under Wentworth and assistant conductor, Luis Gustavo Petri. For these productions, the director was Andre Heller-Lopes, with the set design by Renato Theobaldo, costume design by Rosa Magalhaes and lighting design by Fabio Retti. Waters was not in attendance at these shows.

TUESDAY 13 AUGUST 2013 – PERFORMANCE
Götaplatsen, Gothenburg, Sweden

The staging of the opera marked the grand opening event of the *Gothenburg Culture Festival*, which ran from Tuesday 13 to Sunday 18 August. The opera was performed in English, with Waters narrating, and featured the Gothenburg Symphony Orchestra.

FRIDAY 30 JANUARY 2015 – PERFORMANCE ▼
Schermerhorn Symphony Center, Nashville, TN, USA

Performed with the Nashville Symphony, Nashville Symphony Chorus and Blair Children's Chorus, Waters narrated the performance. A second show on Thursday 29 January was cancelled shortly after it was announced.

OTHER APPEARANCES

FRIDAY 13 DECEMBER 1985 – TELEVISION BROADCAST
***Did You See?*, BBC2 TV, UK**

Waters and Andy Fairweather-Low made a surprise appearance in a special tribute to John Lennon on the BBC documentary arts programme *Did You See?*, performing a pre-recorded rendition of 'Across The Universe'. It was broadcast on BBC2 TV between 10.15pm and 11.00pm.

FRIDAY 18 OCTOBER 1991 – PERFORMANCE
***Guitar Legends Expo '92*, Auditorio La Cartuja Sevilla, Seville, Spain**

Set list: 'In The Flesh', 'The Happiest Days Of Our Lives', 'Another Brick In The Wall, Part 2', 'What God Wants', 'Brain Damage', 'Eclipse', 'Comfortably Numb'.

Guitar Legends was a five-night global broadcast event which featured performances from Albert Collins, Robert Cray, Steve Cropper, Bo Diddley, Dave Edmunds and B.B. King (*Blues Night*, Tuesday 15 October); George Benson, John McLaughlin, Larry Coryell, Paco De Lucia, George Duke and Stanley Clarke (*Fusion Concert*, Wednesday 16 October); Bob Dylan, Joe Cocker, Keith Richards, Robert Cray, Phil Manzanera and Jack Bruce (*Experimental Concert*, Thursday 17 October); Brian May, Joe Satriani, Steve Vai, Joe Walsh and Paul Rodgers (*Hard Rock Concert*, Saturday 19 October). Roger Waters performed a set on the fourth night, with Roger McGuinn, Robbie Robertson, Richard Thompson and Les Paul also on the bill. It is uncertain if the all-star finale of the song 'Running And Hiding' featured Waters. This was an unusual event for Waters to take part in, since he is not chiefly known as a guitarist. However, the event was organized by Tony Hollingsworth, who had previously worked with Waters on his *Wall in Berlin* show.

Waters' backing band for his set included Snowy White and Andy Fairweather-Low (Guitars), Tony Levin (Bass), Pat Leonard and Peter Wood (Keyboards), Graham Broad (Drums), and Doreen Chanter and Katie Kissoon (Backing Vocals). Bruce Hornsby played keyboards and vocals on 'Comfortably Numb' and this was included on both the audio and video of the four-CD and one-DVD box set retrospective *Bruce Hornsby: Intersections 1985–2005* released in the US on Tuesday 25 July 2006 (RCA Legacy 78939).

Five 90-minute shows and a one-hour documentary were made and 45 countries showed at least one live show. BBC 2 TV broadcast Waters' show on Saturday 21 March 1992 between 11.00pm and 12.30am. MTV broadcast clips of 'In The Flesh' and 'Comfortably Numb' on Monday 21 October 1991, having previewed the event in a news broadcast on Tuesday 14 October 1991 that featured Waters and band rehearsing 'In The Flesh' at Nomis Studios, London, England.

WEDNESDAY 1 APRIL 1992 – PERFORMANCE
Walden Woods Benefit Concert, Universal Amphitheatre, Los Angeles, CA, USA

Waters performed 'In The Flesh', 'The Happiest Days Of Our Lives', 'Another Brick In The Wall, Part 2', 'Mother' and 'Comfortably Numb' at this benefit concert in aid of the preservation of Walden Woods in MA, at the request of Don Henley. He was joined on stage by Don Henley's band and additional sets were performed by Neil Young and John Fogerty.

THURSDAY 12 & FRIDAY 13 SEPTEMBER 2002 – PERFORMANCE
Royal Festival Hall, South Bank, London, England

Waters performed 'What God Wants, Part 1' and 'What God Wants, Part 3' as one of a number of guest performers on two of three Jeff Beck concerts held at this venue. Waters' band comprised those he had recently toured with in addition to Beck's own backing band: Andy Fairweather-Low (Guitar), Tony Hymas (Bass), Randy Hope-Taylor (Guitar), Jennifer Batten (Guitar), Steve Barney (Drums) and Carol Kenyon, PP Arnold and Katie Kissoon (Backing Vocals).

MONDAY 7 OCTOBER 2002 – PERFORMANCE
Music to My Ears, Fleet Center, Boston, MA, USA

Waters performed 'Wish You Were Here', 'Flickering Flame' and 'Comfortably Numb' (sung with Don Henley) at the above two concerts, dubbed *Music to My Ears*, which paid tribute to the rock journalist, Timothy White, who had passed away suddenly on Thursday 27 June 2002. Other guests at these events included Jimmy Buffett, Sheryl Crow, Don Henley, Billy Joel, John Mellancamp, Sting, James Taylor and Brian Wilson with the encore of 'This Train' and 'Everyday People' performed by all and sundry. Waters' backing musicians comprised the "house band" and featured Don Henley (Vocals), Steve Jordan (Drums/Music

Director), Willie Weeks (bass guitar), Danny Kortchmar and Waddy Wachtel (Guitars), Ricky Peterson (Keyboards) and Norbert Stachel (Saxophones & Horns).

TUESDAY 8 OCTOBER 2002 – PERFORMANCE
Music to My Ears, Madison Square Garden, New York, NY, USA

This was a repeat of the previous evening's performance.

SATURDAY 28 AUGUST 2004 – PERFORMANCE
Twelfth Annual Huggy Bears Invitational, Tony Forstmann's, Cobb Road Estate, Watermill, NY, USA

Waters performed 'Comfortably Numb' and 'Mother' on acoustic guitar at this Don Henley-led private fund-raising event in the Hamptons that also featured Stevie Nicks. Henley performed 'Witchy Woman' and 'Hotel California' and paired up with Nicks for a rendition of 'Leather and Lace'.

SATURDAY 15 JANUARY 2005 – TELEVISION & RADIO BROADCAST
Tsunami Aid: A Concert of Hope, USA

Waters performed 'Wish You Were Here' with Eric Clapton (both on acoustic guitars) and backing vocalists Katie Kissoon, PP Arnold and Carol Kenyon in a pre-recorded session made at BBC TV Centre, London, England on Friday 14 January 2005 as part of a two-hour joint NBC TV (New York) and Universal Studios (Los Angeles) celebrity telethon charity gala night in aid of victims of the 2004 Indian Ocean earthquake, hosted by actor George Clooney and featuring performances by Sheryl Crow, Norah Jones, Stevie Wonder and Maroon 5, among others. It was simulcast live on NBC network TV, XM Satellite Radio and all Clear Channel affiliate radio stations in the US between 8.00pm and 10.00pm (EST).

SATURDAY 20 MAY 2006 – PERFORMANCE
Highclere Rocks, Highclere Castle, Newbury, England

Waters performed 'Wish You Were Here' and 'Comfortably Numb' with guests Nick Mason (Drums), Eric Clapton (Acoustic Guitar), Georgie Fame (Keyboards) and Andy Fairweather-Low (Guitars) in addition to the house band, which was dubbed "The Band Du Lac", and featured Gary Brooker (Electric Piano), Jodi Linscott (Percussion), Mike Rutherford (Guitars), Geoff Whitehorn (Lead Guitar) and Paul Carrack (Vocals) at this benefit concert on behalf of the Countryside Alliance. Other performers included Eric Clapton, Bryan Ferry, Roger Taylor, Roger Daltrey and Georgie Fame. Waters also joined in on acoustic guitar for Clapton's rendition of 'Cocaine' and rather energetically hit a beer can with a drumstick throughout the closing song, 'Get Up, Stand Up'.

THURSDAY 10 MAY 2007 – PERFORMANCE
The Madcap's Last Laugh, Barbican Centre, London, England

Waters performed 'Flickering Flame' at this tribute concert to Syd Barrett (see the Pink Floyd section for further information).

MONDAY 11 JUNE 2007 – PERFORMANCE
Millennium Promise and Malaria No More Benefit, Cipriani's, New York, NY, USA

Waters performed 'Wish You Were Here', 'Flickering Flame' and 'Another Brick In The Wall, Part 2' with Dave Kilminster, PP Arnold, Carol Kenyon and Katie Kissoon at this exclusive charity fundraiser.

SATURDAY 7 JULY 2007 – PERFORMANCE
Live Earth, Giants Stadium, East Rutherford, NJ, USA

Waters performed an abbreviated set with his touring band at this multi-artist global awareness event that also featured performances by the

Police, Sheryl Crow, Smashing Pumpkins, Dave Matthews Band and Bon Jovi among many others. His set comprised 'In The Flesh', 'Money', 'Us And Them', 'Brain Damage', 'Eclipse', 'The Happiest Days Of Our Lives' and 'Another Brick In The Wall, Part 2' (with the youth choir of the El Bethel Baptist Church, Trenton, USA). A double compilation DVD of highlights featuring 'Another Brick In The Wall, Part 2' was released on Monday 19 November 2007 as *Live Earth: The Concerts for a Climate in Crisis* (US: Warner 245500-2).

THURSDAY 20 SEPTEMBER 2007 – PERFORMANCE
VH1 Save the Music Foundation 10th Anniversary Gala, the Tent, Lincoln Center for the Performing Arts, New York, NY, USA

Waters performed 'Another Brick In The Wall, Part 2' with Dave Kilminster, a children's choir and a gospel choir at this exclusive benefit show. Other performers included Jon Bon Jovi and John Mayer, and honourees including former president Bill Clinton and his wife Senator Hillary Clinton also appeared. The foundation is dedicated to keeping and enhancing music programs in public schools.

SUNDAY 8 JUNE 2008 – PERFORMANCE
Cries from the Heart, Theatre Royal, Haymarket, London, England

Waters performed 'Leaving Beirut' with his son, Harry Waters, as part of this charity event chiefly supported by the acting profession that also saw guest appearances by George Alagiah, Simon Callow, Julie Christie, Joanna Lumley, Ian McKellen, Antony Sher, Patti Smith, Juliet Stevenson, Patrick Stewart, Archbishop Desmond Tutu and Richard Wilson.

SUNDAY 10 AUGUST 2008 – PERFORMANCE
Bridgehampton Music Festival, Bridgehampton, NY, USA

Waters appeared as a member of the cast in an adaptation of *The Soldier's Tale* by Stravinsky, playing the part of the narrator as well as the Devil and the Soldier as part of this annual festival.

SUNDAY 7 DECEMBER 2008 – CANCELLED PERFORMANCE
Live Earth India, Andheri Sports Complex, Mumbai, India

Waters and members of his touring band were due to headline at this climate awareness and benefit concert alongside Bon Jovi and a host of Bollywood stars led by Amitaph Bachalan, but it was cancelled due to terrorist atrocities in India.

TUESDAY 27 OCTOBER 2009 – PERFORMANCE
2009 New York Rita Hayworth Gala, Grand Ballroom, Waldorf-Astoria Hotel, New York, NY, USA

Waters performed 'Wish You Were Here' with Jon Carin (Keyboards), Dave Kilminster (Guitar), GE Smith (Guitar) and the house band (comprising drums, bass and three backing vocalists) at this charity benefit for Alzheimer's Association.

SATURDAY 10 JULY 2010 – PERFORMANCE
Hoping Foundation Benefit Evening, Kidlington Hall, Woodstock, England

A surprise reunion took place between Roger Waters and David Gilmour at this high-brow charity fundraiser for 200 invited guests organized by Bella Freud and Karma Nabulsi and hosted by Jemima Khan under the banner of Hoping (Hope and Optimism for Palestinians in the Next Generation) to raise funds for the Children of Gaza. Nick Cave and Tom Jones kicked off the evening's fundraising, then Gilmour and Waters took to the stage to perform four songs together with Guy Pratt (Bass and Acoustic Guitar), Harry Waters (Keyboards), Andy Newmark (Drums), Chester Kamen (Guitar), and Jonjo Grisdale (Keyboards). The performance was geared to an auction for each song, and launched with 'To Know Him Is To Love Him' (written by Phil Spector), which was apparently regularly featured in Pink Floyd sound checks in the 1970s, followed by 'Wish You Were Here', 'Comfortably Numb' and the closer with full audience participation of 'Another Brick In The Wall, Part 2'. A "home-" quality video of the show was made available for viewing via the charity's website on Monday 16 August 2010. Speaking of the event an unimpressed Nick Mason complained, "That particular event wasn't right for a reformation of Pink Floyd. I said I would do it, but it was a charity event for suits, and it felt wrong to turn a small thing into a big deal just because British socialite Jemima Khan was in attendance. Why play for a lot of posh totty instead of some of the other things we should save that up for – like a *Live 8* type of thing."

MONDAY 15 NOVEMBER 2010 – PERFORMANCE
7th Circuit Studio, Miami, FL, USA

Waters joined in on the celebrations of Harry Waters' birthday, performing alongside Dave Kilminster (Guitar), Snowy White (Guitar), Graham Broad (Drums) and house band, the Moksha Allstars, during a break on the *Wall* tour.

SATURDAY 4 DECEMBER 2010 – PERFORMANCE
The Lennon Lounge, Santa Monica, CA, USA

Venice used a day off from their performing duties as the backing singers on Roger Waters' *The Wall* tour to stage their annual Venice Christmas Concert. After delivering a two-hour set, Venice surprised the crowd at their first encore by returning to the stage with members of Waters' band, including Robbie Wyckoff, Harry Waters, Dave Kilminster, GE Smith, Graham Broad and Jon Joyce. They proceeded to perform 'Goodbye Blue Sky', 'Comfortably Numb' and a medley consisting of Stevie Wonder's 'Superstition', David Bowie's 'Fame', Peter Gabriel's 'Sledgehammer' and the Rolling Stones' 'It's Only Rock and Roll (But I Like It)'.

FRIDAY 27 MAY 2011 – RADIO BROADCAST
Desert Island Discs, BBC Radio 4, UK

Waters was interviewed by Kirsty Young for the long-running BBC radio show *Desert Island Discs*, during which he selected the following songs: 'Helpless' by Neil Young; 'Endless Flight' by Ryuichi Sakamoto, Jaques Morelenbaum & Everton Norton; 'Bird On A Wire' by Leonard Cohen; 'My Funny Valentine' by Chet Baker; 'GA On My Mind' by Ray Charles; 'E Lucevan le Stelle – How The Stars Seemed To Shimmer' from *Tosca* by Giacomo Puccini; 'God Bless The Child' by Billie Holiday. Asked for his Castaway favourite, Waters selected 'Symphony No. 5 In C Sharp Minor – 4th Movement' by Gustav Mahler. He noted that his favourite book was *All The Pretty Horses* by Cormac McCarthy. The interview was broadcast on BBC Radio 4 between 9.00am and 9.45am.

TUESDAY 27 SEPTEMBER 2011 – TELEVISION BROADCAST
Late Night with Jimmy Fallon, NBC TV, USA

As part of the *Late Night with Jimmy Fallon* TV show, a week-long celebration of Pink Floyd was broadcast from Studio 6B, NBC TV Studios, Rockefeller Center, New York. Waters was interviewed and performed 'In The Flesh' backed by the Foo Fighters on Tuesday 27 September, broadcast on NBC network TV between 12.35am and 1.35am (EST). Further appearances in the week included Nick Mason interviewed and the Shins performing 'Breathe' (Monday 26 September), MGMT performing 'Lucifer Sam' (Wednesday 28 September), Dierks Bentley performing 'Wish You Were Here' (Thursday 29 September) and Pearl Jam performing 'Mother' (Friday 30 September).

WEDNESDAY 22 AUGUST 2012 – PERFORMANCE
The Stephen Talkhouse, Amagasnett, NY, USA

Waters was a surprise guest at *Wall* tour guitarist GE Smith's 60th birthday party. Performing a couple of blues numbers, they were accompanied by Abe Fogle on drums and Jeff Kazee on piano. Other guests the same evening included singer-songwriter Taylor Barton.

WEDNESDAY 3 OCTOBER 2012 – PERFORMANCE
Love for Levon Benefit to Save the Barn, Izod Center, Meadowlands Sports Complex, East Rutherford, NJ, USA

Waters joined an all-star lineup to help support the lasting legacy of Levon Helm following his death on Thursday 19 April 2012, by helping his estate keep ownership of his home, barn and studio, and to continue *The Midnight Ramble Sessions*. Other artists performing included John Mayer, My Morning Jacket, Dierks Bentley, Bruce Hornsby, Ray LaMontagne, Gregg Allman, Joe Walsh, John Hiatt, Mavis Staples, John Prine and Jorma Kaukonen. Waters was also at the Levon Helm Studios, Woodstock on Monday 1 October, where rehearsals for the concert were also held on Saturday 29 and Sunday 30 September. Waters appeared on stage for the last three songs, appearing in a red baseball cap and explaining it was given to him by Helm after a show, "and it's been my fishing hat ever since… and this will be with me till the day I die, because it means a lot to me." He then performed 'The Night They Drove Old Dixie Down' with My Morning Jacket and GE Smith on guitar, and 'Wide River To Cross' with GE Smith on guitar and Larry Campbell on violin with the house band Don Was (Bass), Kenny Aronoff (Drums), Amy Helm and Teresa Williams (Backing Vocals) and a five-piece horn section. The entire cast performed 'The Weight' as an encore, with Waters singing the line, "Crazy Chester followed me…"

THURSDAY 8 NOVEMBER 2012 – PERFORMANCE
Stand Up for Heroes, Beacon Theater, New York, NY, USA

Fourteen services veterans backed Waters with guitarist GE Smith at the Bob Woodruff Foundation's 6th annual *Stand Up for Heroes* benefit performing renditions of 'Wish You Were Here' and 'Knockin' On Heaven's Door'. Waters had recently met the 14 wounded soldiers at the Walter Reed Army Medical Center in Washington, DC, rehearsing with them at the hospital and for a few days prior to the show in New York. Other performers included Bruce Springsteen and John Mayer with comedians Robin Williams, Ricky Gervais, Mike Birbiglia and Patton Oswalt appearing in the second half to raise pledges for wounded troops battling the hardships of returning home from combat in Iraq and Afghanistan. An auction drew $110,000 for the guitar and harmonica Bruce Springsteen played during his acoustic set. The music half of the show was streamed live via YouTube.

TUESDAY 13 NOVEMBER 2012 – PERFORMANCE
Iraq & Afghanistan Veterans of America Sixth Annual Heroes Gala, Cipriani's, New York, NY, USA

Waters performed 'Flickering Flame' with GE Smith (Guitar) and Jon Carin (Keyboards) at this annual benefit at which Waters was also honoured as the recipient of the *IAVA 2012 Artistic Leadership Award*. On their website, IAVA noted that, "Roger Waters' achievements as a songwriter and live performer have spanned over four decades and have established him as a major force and influence in the progress and development of popular music. He was a founding member of the multi-platinum rock band Pink Floyd, serving as bassist and co-lead vocalist. Mr. Waters' *Fallen Loved Ones* project was an integral part of his recently completed record-breaking *The Wall* tour, making him an important advocate and valued friend to the veterans' community."

TUESDAY 27 NOVEMBER TO SUNDAY 2 DECEMBER 2012 – PERFORMANCES
The Exonerated, the Culture Project, New York, NY, USA

Waters made his stage-acting debut in this play about wrongfully convicted survivors of Death Row for the production's final week of seven performances (including a matinee on 2 December). *The Exonerated* follows the true stories of six people who were sentenced to death and later freed after evidence of their innocence came to light. It had its premiere in October 2002 and ran for over 600 performances, with a rotating cast of stars reading accounts by former death row inmates. The Culture Project revived the show in September 2012 to note its 10th anniversary, with several stars joining the six-person company for temporary stints, among them Stockard Channing, Brian Dennehy and Brooke Shields.

WEDNESDAY 12 DECEMBER 2012 – PERFORMANCE
12.12.12. The Concert for Sandy Relief, Madison Square Garden, New York, NY, USA

Waters performed 'Another Brick In The Wall, Part 2', 'Money', 'Us And Them' and 'Comfortably Numb' (featuring Eddie Vedder on vocals) with members of his current touring band and Ian Ritchie on saxophones, as part of a multi-artist benefit for the Robin Hood Relief Fund following the devastation caused by Hurricane Sandy on the East Coast states of the US in late October 2012. Other artists appearing included Alicia Keys, Paul McCartney (backed by Diana Krall; McCartney also appeared with former Nirvana members Dave Grohl, Krist Novoselic and Pat Smear), Billy Joel, Michael Stipe who appeared with Chris Martin, Kanye West, the Who, Rolling Stones, Bruce Springsteen and the E Street Band, Jon Bon Jovi and Adam Sandler, with Paul Schaffer and Eric Clapton among various other celebrities providing the links. The event was streamed live on various Internet channels, and 34 US TV networks, as well as television feeds to North and South America, Asia, Europe, Africa and Australia. A double CD of the same name was released in the UK on Monday 21 January 2013 (Columbia 88765448892) and in the US on Tuesday 22 January 2013 (Columbia 88765448892), featuring highlights of the show including Roger Waters' renditions of 'Another Brick In The Wall, Part 2' (renamed 'Another Brick In The Atlantic Wall' for the purposes of this release), 'Us And Them' and 'Comfortably Numb'. A DVD of the concert featuring the same tracks was released in the UK on Monday 16 September (Columbia Sony 887654596994) and in the US on Tuesday 17 September 2013 (Columbia Sony 887654596994).

WEDNESDAY 6 NOVEMBER 2013 – PERFORMANCE
Stand Up for Heroes, Madison Square Garden, New York, NY, USA

Waters performed an unusual set at the 7th annual *Stand Up for Heroes* benefit run by ABC newsman Bob Woodruff's foundation, comprising Leonard Cohen's 'Hallelujah', John Lennon's 'Imagine', Sam Cooke's 'A Change is Gonna Come' and 'Comfortably Numb'. Joining Waters on stage were GE Smith, Jon Carin and Dave Kilminster, and nearly two dozen veterans, many with limbs missing. Also appearing on the bill was Bruce Springsteen (who later auctioned off his guitar for $250,000) and comedians Jon Stewart, Bill Cosby, Jim Gaffigan and Jerry Seinfeld. Speaking at rehearsals the preceding Monday, Waters said, "I feel a great sense of empathy for the people that live on the sharp end of conflicts and the ones that actually get injured. I get so much more out of it than I put into it.… I'm not a US citizen, but I pay taxes here, and I wish a far greater per cent of my tax dollars went to look after these guys." The music half of the show was streamed live via YouTube.

TUESDAY 18 FEBRUARY 2014 – MEMORIAL SERVICE
Roselli Institute, Aprilia, Italy

Seventy years to the day after his father Eric Fletcher Waters was killed in action during a ferocious battle to the northwest of Aprilia, while fighting in the Anzio campaign of the Second World War, Roger Waters unveiled a memorial to his late father at the Roselli Institute. His remains have never been found but the previous year Harry Shindler, an Anzio veteran who also served with the Royal Fusiliers, and is head of the Italy Star Association of British veterans, read about Waters' visit to the Commonwealth Grave Cemetery at Monte Cassino on 31 March 2013 where his father's name is listed, and he became determined to find the exact details surrounding his death. Shindler scoured war diaries and military maps at the National Archives in Kew near London and came upon an intelligence report that described the desperate last few hours of Lt Waters' unit and the exact spot where he was killed. The day before the memorial service the two men paid a private visit to the exact position where it is believed Lt Waters died.

Giving a speech at the memorial Waters said that, "It is 70 years to the day since my father died here and I have finally come to the end of a journey to discover what really happened to him," after he had placed a wreath of red poppies at the foot of the monument, next to a British steel helmet peppered with shrapnel holes, retrieved from the battlefield. The monument is inscribed with the words: "In memory of 2Lt. Eric Fletcher Waters 'Z' Company, 8th Battalion Royal Fusiliers 28th December 1914 – 18th February 1944 who died here and all the other fallen who have no known grave" along with the words from the Pink Floyd track 'Two Suns in the Sunset': "Ashes and diamonds/ Foe and friend/We were all equal in the end." Afterwards, Waters met with students of the Institute and outside his fans were able to follow the event through some big screens as he was awarded an honorary citizenship of the city of Anzio by the town mayor.

Later that same day he went to the American University of Rome, where he was awarded an honorary degree and made Doctorate of Humane Letters Honoris Causa for his contribution to music and for his social activism around the globe.

SATURDAY 30 AUGUST 2014 – PERFORMANCE
Second Biennial Family Picnic & Concert, **Cindy Sherman's farmhouse, East Hampton, NY, USA**

With ticket prices starting at just $250 and escalating to $10,000, Roger Waters joined various other artists at this exclusive charity event which campaigns for toxin-free garden maintenance. The fundraiser featured performances by Suzanne Vega, Laurie Anderson, Rufus Wainright, Teddy Thompson, Jenni Muldaur and The Persuasions. GE Smith and Taylor Barton of the Persuasions appeared alongside Waters to perform 'Wish You Were Here'. Waters also performed a new song, 'If I Had Been God (Lay Down Jerusalem)'.

THURSDAY 25 SEPTEMBER 2014 – PERFORMANCE
The Bertrand Russell Tribunal on Palestine, **European Parliament, Brussels, Belgium**

The Tribunal, in effect a symbolic people's court, of which Waters is a member, concluded a session looking into the legality of Israel's recent Operation Protective Edge offensive against Palestine. The "jury" gave its findings in the morning during an international press conference held at the International Press Center, Brussels. In the afternoon, the jury was received at the European parliament. The event culminated in Waters performing 'If I Had Been God (Lay Down Jerusalem)' on acoustic guitar.

FRIDAY 24 JULY 2015 – PERFORMANCE
Newport Folk Festival, **Fort Adams State Park, Newport, RI, USA**

Waters headlined the Friday evening of this legendary three-day festival with a specially constructed show with the band My Morning Jacket, guitarist GE Smith, and backing vocalists Jess Wolfe and Holly Laessig in which he performed the tracks 'Crystal Clear Brooks' (a new song, on which Waters also played piano), 'Mother', 'The Bravery Of Being Out Of Range', Hello In There' (a cover of the John Prine song), 'Wish You Were Here' (with Sara Watkins on fiddle), 'Wide River To Cross' (a cover of the Buddy Miller song with Amy Helm guest vocals), 'Amused To Death, 'Brain Damage', 'Eclipse' and 'Forever Young' (a cover of the Bob Dylan song with Sara Watkins and Amy Helm).

FRIDAY 16 OCTOBER 2015 – PERFORMANCE
Music Heals, **Daughters of the American Revolution Constitution Hall, Washington, DC, USA**

At time of going to press Waters and the musicians of Musicorps (a programme that encourages wounded veterans to learn, re-learn and perform music as a core part of their rehabilitation) were announced as appearing at this benefit concert to aid the wounded veterans of Musicorps and their families. Also scheduled to appear is Sheryl Crow, Billy Corgan and Tom Morello.

BELOW: ROGER WATERS PERFORMING AT NEWPORT FOLK FESTIVAL, 25 JULY 2015.

RICHARD WRIGHT

Richard William Wright was born on 28 July 1943 in Hatch End, London. He was educated at the Haberdashers Aske's School in nearby Elstree, Hertfordshire and by his teens had learned trombone, saxophone, guitar and piano, inspired by an early love of jazz.

In 1962 he was persuaded to study architecture at Regent Street Polytechnic, where he met future band members Roger Waters and Nick Mason, joining them on keyboards in creating Sigma 6. The band soon evolved into the Abdabs and the lineup included vocalist Juliette Gale, whom he later went on to marry.

Concurrent with attending the Polytechnic, Wright was also taking private lessons in musical theory and composition at the Eric Gilder School of Music, and left the Poly at the end of his first year to go sailing around the Greek islands: his life-long passion. On his return he enrolled in the Royal College of Music and rejoined Mason and Waters, whose band had just added Roger "Syd" Barrett and Radovan "Bob" Klose to become the Tea Set.

Wright was also the first future member of Pink Floyd to have any of his songs published, penning 'You're The Reason Why', which appeared on the B-side of an obscure 1964 Decca single by the Liverpool trio of Adam and Mike Sedgwick and Tim Saunders.

In the early days of Pink Floyd, along with Syd Barrett, Wright was seen as the group's dominant musical force. As well as playing piano, Farfisa keyboards and Hammond organ he also sang lead vocals on several tracks, including their debut single 'Arnold Layne', as well as 'Matilda Mother' and 'Astronomy Domine' from the album *The Piper at the Gates of Dawn*.

Wright went on to compose and sing on several of his own songs, including 'Remember A Day' from *A Saucerful of Secrets* and 'Summer '68' from *Atom Heart Mother*. As the sound of the band evolved, he became focused primarily on contributing to extended instrumental compositions such as 'A Saucerful Of Secrets', 'Careful With That Axe, Eugene', and 'Echoes', all of which became mainstays of Pink Floyd's live shows throughout the early 1970s. He also made essential contributions to the soundtracks *The Committee*, *More*, *Zabriskie Point* and *Obscured by Clouds*, and Pink Floyd's most commercially recognizable tracks, including 'The Great Gig In The Sky' and 'Us And Them' from *The Dark Side of the Moon* and 'Shine On You Crazy Diamond' from *Wish You Were Here*.

He rarely performed outside of Pink Floyd but did play keyboards on Syd Barrett's second solo album, *Barrett*. He also played keyboards for the techno/house duo Blue Pearl, a project developed by Pink Floyd backing singer Durga McBroom and producer Youth. Released in 1990, their album *Naked* also featured a guest spot from David Gilmour.

Wright released his first solo album, *Wet Dream*, in September 1978. A self-produced album on which he wrote all the songs, except 'Against The Odds', which was co-written with his then-wife, Juliette. The album features Mel Collins on saxophone and Snowy White on guitar.

After Wright's relationship with Roger Waters deteriorated, he left Pink Floyd during the recording of *The Wall*. However, he was retained as a salaried session musician during the subsequent live concerts in 1980 and 1981.

During 1984, Wright formed a new musical duo with Dave Harris (from the band Fashion) called Zee and released one album, *Identity*. The album makes heavy use of the Fairlight synthesizer and by Richard's own admission was a flawed experiment.

Wright rejoined Pink Floyd following the departure of Roger Waters, contributing keyboards and vocals to the 1987 album *A Momentary Lapse of Reason*, and in 1994, he co-wrote five songs and sang lead vocals (on 'Wearing The Inside Out') for *The Division Bell* album. 'Marooned', Wright and Gilmour's instrumental from that album, won a Grammy Award in 1994 for "Best Rock Instrumental Performance", Pink Floyd's only Grammy to date.

Inspired by his successful input on *The Division Bell*, Wright released his second solo album, *Broken China*, in 1996. Essentially a four-part concept piece, it deals largely with his then wife's battle with depression. One of its stand-out tracks, 'Breakthrough', was reprised by Wright during a guest appearance at David Gilmour's concert at the Royal Festival Hall in January 2002, as released on the *David Gilmour in Concert* DVD.

Wright contributed keyboards and background vocals to David Gilmour's solo album, *On an Island*, and performed brilliantly with Gilmour's touring band on tours of North America and Europe in 2006.

After a short struggle with cancer, Richard Wright sadly died on 15 September 2008. David Gilmour performed 'Remember A Day' in tribute to Richard Wright on an appearance on the *Later... with Jools Holland* TV show on 23 September 2008.

Arguably he was an under-appreciated talent during the course of the band's heyday, and his work was celebrated on Pink Floyd's final album, *The Endless River*, released in 2014 with extracts of music taken from unused performances recorded during the *Division Bell* sessions, as well as a piece of music dating back to 1968.

LEFT: RICHARD WRIGHT PICTURED AT THE TIME OF HIS FIRST SOLO ALBUM RELEASE, 1978.

ORIGINAL RELEASES

WET DREAM

Richard Wright's first solo album was recorded at Super Bear Studios, Berre des Alpes, France between 10 January and 14 February 1978 and produced by Richard Wright and engineered by John Etchells. It featured guests Mel Collins (Saxophone), Reg Isadore (Drums, Guitars), Larry Steele (Bass) and Snowy White (Guitars).

FRIDAY 6 OCTOBER 1978 ◀

Wet Dream

Side 1: 'Mediterranean C' / 'Against The Odds' / 'Cat Cruise' / 'Summer Elegy' / 'Waves' / Side 2: 'Holiday' / 'Mad Yannis Dance' / 'Drop In From The Top' / 'Pink's Song' / 'Funky Deux'.

UK: EMI Harvest SHVL 818 (Vinyl album).
US: Columbia JC 35559 (Vinyl album, released Friday 15 September 1978).
Reissued:
US: Sony Music Special Products / One Way Records A24090 (CD album, released Tuesday 10 August 1993).

IDENTITY (ZEE)

Wright entered into a recording project with Dave Harris of the New Wave group Fashion under the name Zee, having been introduced by mutual friend Raphael Ravenscroft, the instigator of the project, who had just finished working with David Gilmour on his solo album. After several rehearsals and personnel changes, only Wright and Harris remained. They wrote all of the music together, although the lyrics were all by Harris. It was recorded at the Rectory Studio in Cambridge, overdubbed and mixed at Utopia in London and co-produced by Tim Palmer. Composed and performed almost entirely on the Fairlight CMI computer, it was regarded as too clinical by many Pink Floyd fans, who were expecting something more akin to Wright's first solo album. Wright, along with the vast majority of Pink Floyd fans, looked back on it as an experiment best forgotten.

MONDAY 12 MARCH 1984 ▶

'Confusion' (Edit) / Side B: 'Eyes Of A Gypsy'
UK: EMI Harvest HAR 5227 (7-inch vinyl single).
'Confusion' (Extended Version) // 'Eyes Of A Gypsy' (Dub Mix) / 'Confusion' (7-inch Version)
UK: EMI Harvest 12 HAR 5227 (12-inch vinyl single).

MONDAY 9 APRIL 1984

Identity

Side 1: 'Confusion' / 'Voices' / 'Private Person' / 'Strange Rhythm' / Side 2: 'Cuts Like A Diamond' / 'By Touching' / 'How Do You Do It?' / 'Seems We Were Dreaming' (The cassette release featured the additional track 'Eyes Of A Gypsy').

UK: EMI Harvest SHSP 2401018 (Vinyl album) & UK: EMI Harvest CDP 0642401012 (CD album).

BROKEN CHINA

Wright's third album, his second solo release, was in collaboration with Anthony Moore as sole lyricist and was made shortly after Pink Floyd's *Division Bell* tour. It was written and recorded variously at Studio Harmonie, Paris, France with overdubs recorded at Whitfield Street Studios, Camden, London, England; RAK Studios, St John's Wood, London, England, and Astoria Studios, Hampton, England. It was produced and engineered by Richard Wright and Anthony Moore and engineered and co-produced by Max Hayes, Jake Davies and Graeme Stewart. It was mastered by Doug Sax and Ron Lewter at the Mastering Lab, Los Angeles.

Additional musicians on the album included Sian Beli (Cello), Steve Bolton (Guitars), Manu Katche (Drums), Dominic Miller (Guitars), Sinead O'Connor (Vocals on 'Reaching For The Rail' and 'Breakthrough'), Tim Renwick (Guitars), Maz Palladino (Backing Vocals), Pino Palladino (Bass), Kate St John (Oboe). David Gilmour played guitar on 'Breakthrough' during the sessions, but his performance did not appear on the album.

While leaning towards a concept piece, it inevitably lacks the weight of a Pink Floyd album. Although Wright entertained the idea of taking the album on tour, sales were insufficient to justify the cost.

SEPTEMBER 1996

Track List: 'Night Of A Thousand Furry Toys' / 'Breakthrough' / 'Satellite' / 'Along The Shoreline'
UK: EMI CDEMDJ 1098 (Promotional CD).
Track List: 'Runaway' (R. Wright's Lemonade Mix) / 'Runaway' (Leggit Dub) / 'Night Of A Thousand Furry Toys' (Inverted Gravy Mix)

UK: EMI CDRW101 (Promotional CD).
Side A: 'Runaway' (R. Wright's Lemonade Mix) / Side B: 'Runaway' (Leggit Dub) / 'Night Of A Thousand Furry Toys' (Inverted Gravy Mix)

UK: EMI 12RW101 (Promotional 12-inch vinyl single).
Track 1 remixed by the Orb; tracks 2 and 3 remixed by William Orbit with Matt Ducasse.

SEPTEMBER 1996

Broken China

UK: EMI CDINT 105 (13-minute banded promotional interview CD – no music).

SEPTEMBER 1996

Broken China

UK: EMI (Promotional CD box set featuring the CD album *Broken China* (UK: EMI CD EMD 1098), a 13-minute banded promotional interview CD (UK: EMI CD INT 105), a 10'08" EPK video cassette in a blank white slipcase and 2-page press biography. All items were housed in a brown cardboard parcel box labelled "Glass With Care" and even contained some pieces of broken crockery.

MONDAY 7 OCTOBER 1996 ▲

Broken China

Track list: 'Breaking Water' / 'Night Of A Thousand Furry Toys' / 'Hidden Fear' / 'Runaway' / 'Unfair Ground' / 'Satellite' / 'Woman Of Custom' / 'Interlude'

/ 'Black Cloud' / 'Far From The Harbour Wall' / 'Drowning' / 'Reaching For The Rail' / 'Blue Room In Venice' / 'Sweet July' / 'Along The Shoreline' / 'Breakthrough'.

UK: EMI CD EMD 1098 (CD album; Highest chart position No. 61 *Music Week* "Top 75 Albums" on Saturday 19 October 1996).
US: Guardian Records 724385364525 (CD album, released Monday 25 March 1997).

SONGWRITING & GUEST APPEARANCES

DECEMBER 1964 – ADAM, MIKE & TIM
'Little Baby' / 'You're The Reason Why'
Wright wrote the B-side to this obscure single by Adam and Mike Sedgwick and Tim Saunders.

FEBRUARY 2006 – HELEN BOULDING
'I Don't Know What I Want But I Know What I Need' / 'Hazel Eyes'
Wright co-wrote the song 'Hazel Eyes' with Chris Difford.

NOVEMBER 1970 – SYD BARRETT
Barrett
(See Syd Barrett section for contribution and release details.)

NOVEMBER 1990 – BLUE PEARL
Naked
Wright played keyboards on the track 'Alive', which also featured David Gilmour on guitars. (See David Gilmour section for release details.)

MARCH 2002 – CHIMERA
Chimera
Wright played keyboards on 'Lady With Bullets In Her Hair'. (See Nick Mason section for release details.)

OCTOBER 2002 – DAVID GILMOUR
David Gilmour In Concert
Wright played keyboards and sang vocals on 'Breakthrough' and 'Comfortably Numb' in this live recording. (See David Gilmour section for release details.)

MARCH 2006 – DAVID GILMOUR
On An Island
Wright played Hammond on the track 'On An Island' and keyboards and vocals on 'The Blue'. (See David Gilmour section for release details.)

LIVE APPEARANCES

SUNDAY 10 NOVEMBER 1974 – PERFORMANCE
Ellison Building, Newcastle Polytechnic, Newcastle-upon-Tyne, England
Wright played keyboards and David Gilmour shared lead guitar with Tim Renwick at this Sutherland Brothers & Quiver show.

SUNDAY 11 OCTOBER 1992 – PERFORMANCE
***Chelsea Arts Ball*, Royal Albert Hall, Kensington, London, England**
Wright played keyboards at this high-society AIDS fund-raiser. Other musicians who performed included the house band comprising David Gilmour (Vocals, Guitars), Guy Pratt (Bass), Jon Carin (Keyboards), Jodi Linscott (Percussion), Tim Renwick (Guitars), Gary Wallis (Drums) and Sam Brown (Vocals) with additional guest musicians Nick Mason, Tom Jones, Hugh Cornwell, Mica Paris, Elvis Costello and Sam Moore.

ABOVE: WRIGHT PERFORMING AT THE ROYAL ALBERT HALL ON DAVID GILMOUR'S TOUR, MARCH 2006.

SATURDAY 23 MARCH 1996 – PERFORMANCE
Fulham Town Hall, Fulham, London, England
To celebrate David Gilmour's 50th birthday party entertainment was provided by the Bootleg Beatles and the Australian Pink Floyd, who were joined on stage by Richard Wright and Guy Pratt for a rousing rendition of 'Comfortably Numb'. They then handed over their instruments to David Gilmour, Tim Renwick, Gary Wallis and Claudia Fontaine, who treated the gathered guests to renditions of 'Money', 'What Do You Want From Me' and various other jams.

WEDNESDAY 16, THURSDAY 17 & FRIDAY 18 JANUARY 2002 – PERFORMANCES
Royal Festival Hall, South Bank, London, England
Wright played keyboards at this series of David Gilmour solo shows including his own song 'Breakthrough' and also piano on 'Wish You Were Here' and 'Comfortably Numb'.

WEDNESDAY 23 & THURSDAY 24 JANUARY 2002 – PERFORMANCES
Palace de Congrès de Paris, Paris, France
Wright played keyboards at this series of David Gilmour solo shows including his own song 'Breakthrough' and also piano on 'Wish You Were Here' and 'Comfortably Numb'.

2006 – 2007 – PERFORMANCES
David Gilmour *On an Island* Tour
Richard Wright played keyboards in Gilmour's band for his solo tour. (See David Gilmour section for tour dates, set lists and further information.)

SATURDAY 11 OCTOBER 2008 – RADIO BROADCAST
***Remember a Day: Richard Wright in his Own Words*, BBC Radio 2, UK**
Richard Wright was the subject of a retrospective tribute looking back at his career and told entirely in his own voice, drawing from BBC archive material and his last ever interview, conducted in September 2007 by the show producer Mark Hagen. Featured tracks broadcast which he wrote or co-wrote included 'Remember a Day', 'Sysyphus', 'Echoes', 'Us and Them', 'The Great Gig In The Sky', 'Shine On You Crazy Diamond' and 'Wearing The Inside Out'.

CREDITS

BIBLIOGRAPHY

My grateful thanks go to the authors of articles and reviews that have been reproduced from the following newspapers, magazines, trade papers, websites and periodicals:

About.com, Aquarian, Bath and Wilts Evening Chronicle, Beat Instrumental, Billboard, Bristol Evening Post, Canadian Press, Cash Box, Chatham Standard, Circus, ConsequenceofSound.net, Coventry Evening Telegraph, Crawdaddy, Croydon Advertiser, Daily Express, Daily Mail, Daily Princeton, Delware County News, Detroit Fifth Estate, Detroit Free Press, Disk And Music Echo, Eastern Evening News, Edinburgh Evening News, Financial Times, Go Set Magazine, Go!, Great Speckled Bird, Guardian, Guild Gazette, Het Laatse Nieuws, Huffington Post, Independent, International Times, Kensington Post, Kent Herald, Kentish Times, Louisville Courier Journal, Manchester Independent, Meliorist, Melody Maker, Merthyr Express, Milwaukee Sentinel, Mojo, Music Now, New Times, New York Times, Newham Express, NME, Open City, Pi, Pitchfork, Pittsburgh Press, Pop Matters, Portsmouth News, Q Magazine, Queen, Radio Times, Rave, Record Collector, Record Mirror, Redbrick, Rolling Stone, Rugby Advertiser, San Diego Union, San Diego Weekly Reader, Seattle Sabot, Seattle Times, Sound on Stage, Sounds, Spare Bricks, Sunday Times, Teen Ink, Time Out, Tone Audio, Vancouver Free Press, Vancouver Sun, Vibrations, Washington Post, West Wales Guardian, Williams Record, Wine Press, Yorkshire Evening Post and Zig Zag.

The following publications proved useful research tools for this book and, in some cases, may be of further interest to the reader.

The Music Scene of 1960s Cambridge by Warren Dosanjh, private printing, 2013
A Saucerful of Secrets: The Pink Floyd Odyssey by Nicholas Schaffner, Harmony, 1991
Crazy Diamond: Syd Barrett & the Dawn of Pink Floyd by Mike Watkinson & Pete Anderson, Omnibus, 1991
Dark Side of the Moon Revealed by Brain Southall, Clarksdale, 2013
The Flaming Cow by Ron Geesin, History Press, 2013
Inside Out: A Personal History of Pink Floyd by Nick Mason, Weidenfeld & Nicolson, 2004
Lost in the Woods: Syd Barrett and the Early Pink Floyd by Julian Palacios, Boxtree, 1998
Mind Over Matter: The Images of Pink Floyd by Storm Thorgerson, Omnibus, 2015
Random Precision: Recording the Music of Syd Barrett 1965–1974 by David Parker, Cherry Red, 2001
33 1/3: The Piper at the Gates of Dawn by David Cavanagh, Continuum, 2003